Personal Financial Planning Theory and Practice

Michael A. Dalton, Ph.D., JD, CPA, CFP™, CLU, ChFC
James F. Dalton, MBA, MS, CPA/PFS, CFA, CFP™
Randal R. Cangelosi, JD, MBA
Randall S. Guttery, Ph.D., CLU, ChFC
Scott A. Wasserman, CPA/PFS, CFP™

DALTON PUBLISHING, L.L.C.
150 James Drive East, Suite 100
St. Rose, Louisiana 70087
(504) 464-9772 • (504) 461-9860 Fax
www.daltonpfpseries.com

ISBN 1-931629-02-1   PERSONAL FINANCIAL PLANNING – THEORY AND PRACTICE

Library of Congress Card Number: 00-191690

This publication is designed to provide accurate and authoritative information in regard to the subject matter covered. It is sold with the understanding that the publisher, authors and contributors are not engaged in rendering legal, accounting, financial planning, or other professional services. If legal advice or other professional assistance is required, the services of a competent professional should be sought.

The viewpoints presented in the Professional Focus are those of the participants and not necessarily those of their affiliates or Dalton Publishing, L.L.C.

CFP™, CERTIFIED FINANCIAL PLANNER™, and CFP® (with flame logo) are certification marks owned by the CFP Board of Standards. This publication is not to be regarded as endorsed or recommended by the CFP Board.

Other texts in Dalton's Personal Financial Planning Series include:

ISBN 1-890260-04-5   Understanding Your Financial Calculator
ISBN 1-931629-00-5   Personal Financial Planning Cases and Applications

For additional information on Dalton Publishing's live instructional reviews for the CFP™ Certification Examination and CFA Examination and related study materials, please visit our website at www.daltonpfpseries.com.

Cover design by Desktop Miracles.

To Donna Delle Dalton!

Without your extraordinary leadership, dedication, and hard work, this book would have never been published. We are both so thankful to have you in our lives.

ABOUT THE AUTHORS

MICHAEL A. DALTON, PH.D., JD, CPA, CLU, CHFC, CFP™

▲ Associate professor of Accounting and Taxation at Loyola University in New Orleans, Louisiana
▲ Ph.D. in Accounting from Georgia State University
▲ J.D. from Louisiana State University in Baton Rouge, Louisiana
▲ MBA and BBA in Management and Accounting from Georgia State University
▲ Former board member of the CFP Board of Standards and Board of Governors
▲ Former chairman of the CFP Board of Examiners
▲ Member of the Financial Planning Association
▲ Member of the *Journal of Financial Planning* Editorial Advisory Board
▲ Member of the *Journal of Financial Planning* Editorial Review Board
▲ Member of the LSU Law School National Alumni Board
▲ Member of the LSU Law School Chancellors Council
▲ Author of *Dalton Review for the CFP™ Certification Examination: Volume I – Outlines and Study Guides, Volume II – Problems and Solutions, Volume III - Case Exam Book, Mock Exams A-1 and A-2*
▲ Co-author of *Dalton CFA® Study Notes Volumes I and II*
▲ Co-author of *Dalton's Personal Financial Planning Series – Cases and Applications*
▲ Co-author of *Cost Accounting: Traditions and Innovations*
▲ Co-author of the *ABCs of Managing Your Money*

JAMES F. DALTON, MBA, MS, CPA/PFS, CFA, CFP™

▲ President of Dalton Publications, L.L.C.
▲ Former Senior Manager of an international accounting firm, specializing in Personal Financial Planning, investment planning, and litigation services
▲ MBA from Loyola University in New Orleans, Louisiana
▲ Masters of Accounting in Taxation from the University of New Orleans
▲ BS in accounting from Florida State University in Tallahassee, Florida
▲ Member of the CFP Board of Standards July 1996, Comprehensive CFP™ Exam Pass Score Committee
▲ Member of the AICPA and the Louisiana Society of CPAs
▲ Member of the Financial Planning Association
▲ Member of the *Journal of Financial Planning* Editorial Review Board
▲ Member of the New Orleans Estate Planning Council
▲ Author of *Dalton's Personal Financial Planning Series –Understanding Your Financial Calculator*
▲ Author of *Dalton's Understanding Your Financial Calculator for the CFA® Exam*
▲ Co-author of *Dalton CFA® Study Notes Volumes I and II*
▲ Co-author of *Dalton's Personal Financial Planning Series – Cases and Applications*
▲ Co-author of *Dalton Review for the CFP™ Certification Examination: Volume I – Outlines and Study Guides, Volume II – Problems and Solutions, Volume III - Case Exam Book, Mock Exams A-1 and A-2, Financial Planning Flashcards*

RANDAL R. CANGELOSI, JD, MBA

- ▲ Practicing attorney in southeast Louisiana, specializing in commercial law and litigation
- ▲ J.D. from Loyola University, New Orleans
- ▲ Master of Business from Loyola University, New Orleans
- ▲ BS in Finance from Louisiana State University
- ▲ Member of the American & Federal Bar Association
- ▲ Member of the New Orleans and Baton Rouge Bar Associations
- ▲ Co-author of *Professional Ethics for CERTIFIED FINANCIAL PLANNER*™ Designees

RANDALL S. GUTTERY, PH.D., CLU, CHFC

- ▲ Associate Professor of Finance and Real Estate at the University of North Texas
- ▲ Ph.D. in Finance at the University of Connecticut
- ▲ Master of Finance from Louisiana State University
- ▲ BBA in Finance and Risk Management from the University of Texas
- ▲ Holds a Louisiana real estate brokers license
- ▲ Published several academic articles and professional journals
- ▲ Published a Real Estate Principles text for Prentice-Hall
- ▲ Research has been featured in several print media

SCOTT A. WASSERMAN, CPA/PFS, CFP™

- ▲ Senior Manager in the Personal Financial Planning practice of an international accounting firm
- ▲ Develops estate, income, and retirement planning software use by the financial planning professionals throughout the firm
- ▲ BBA from the University of Texas in Austin
- ▲ Member of AICPA, Texas Society of CPAs, and the Institute of CFPs
- ▲ Co-author of *Dalton Financial Planning Flashcards*
- ▲ Instructor of Tax, Retirement, and Estates for the Dalton Review for the CFP™ Certification Examination

CONTRIBUTORS

JOSEPH W. BELLOWS
▲ Technical Editor of Dalton Publications, L.L.C.
▲ BBA in Finance from Loyola University, New Orleans
▲ Member of the National Association of Securities Dealers, Inc.

CASSIE F. BRADLEY, PH.D.
▲ Assistant Professor and MBA Director at Mercer University in Atlanta, GA
▲ Ph.D. in Accounting from the University of Alabama
▲ BBA in Accounting from Georgia State University
▲ Member of the American Accounting Association and the American Taxation Association
▲ Former Senior Tax Manager with Federal Express Corporation
▲ Co-author of *Dalton Review for the CFP^{TM} Certification Examination: Volume I – Outlines and Study Guides*

PHYLLIS D. BRIERRE
▲ Technical Editor of Dalton Publications, L.L.C.
▲ BS in Finance from the University of New Orleans
▲ Member Beta Gamma Sigma Honor Society
▲ Member Golden Key Honor Society
▲ Former Training Specialist for an international service corporation

ALLISON DALTON
▲ BA in International Studies with a minor in Business Administration from Rhodes College in Memphis, TN
▲ Member and former Recruitment Chair of Alpha Omicron Pi fraternity
▲ Former intern for U.S. Senator Coverdell in Atlanta, GA and for U.S. Senator Frist in Memphis, TN

DONNA DELLE DALTON, MBA
▲ Vice President of Product Development for Dalton Publications, L.L.C.
▲ MBA from Loyola University, New Orleans
▲ BBA from Loyola University, New Orleans
▲ Former Marketing Director of a regional CPA firm
▲ Member of the Loyola University Alumni Board

JAN MARLBROUGH DUPONT, MBA
▲ Vice President of Reviews and Special Projects for Dalton Publications, L.L.C.
▲ MBA from University of New Orleans
▲ BBA from Loyola University, New Orleans
▲ Former Manager of Acquisitions and Logistics for an international utility company

MARGUERITE F. MERRITT, M.ED.

▲ Senior Copy Editor of Dalton Publications, L.L.C.
▲ M.Ed. from the University of New Orleans
▲ BS from the University of New Orleans
▲ Former Communications Specialist for an international utility company

KRISTI J. MINCHER, MS

▲ Senior Technical Editor of Dalton Publications, L.L.C.
▲ Pursuing a J.D. from Louisiana State University in Baton Rouge, Louisiana
▲ Masters of Accounting in Taxation from the University of New Orleans
▲ BBA in Accounting from Loyola University, New Orleans
▲ Member of the AICPA and ABA

ROBERT J. SABRIO

▲ Technical Editor of Dalton Publications, L.L.C.
▲ BBA in Finance and Economics from Loyola University, New Orleans
▲ Recipient of the *Wall Street Journal* Award for Outstanding Finance Graduate

PREFACE

We wrote *Personal Financial Planning – Theory and Practice* in response to numerous pleas from instructors and students requesting a fundamental financial planning textbook. Through this text, the authors hope to convey their knowledge of financial planning and reflect their enthusiasm for the subject.

This text is written for graduate and undergraduate students who are interested in acquiring an in-depth understanding of personal financial planning from a professional planning viewpoint. The text is also intended to serve as a reference for practicing professional financial planners.

CONTENT AND THEMES

The Financial Planner's Pyramid of Knowledge is depicted throughout this text. The base of the pyramid identifies the core knowledge that every financial planner should possess. Chapters 8 – 21 detail this foundation of knowledge upon which a successful financial planning profession can be built. The second layer of the pyramid, presented in Chapters 6 and 7, focuses on the basic financial planning tools a financial planner must be familiar with and capable of implementing. The third and fourth layers of the pyramid, presented in Chapters 1 – 5, describe the basic financial planning skills every professional financial planner must possess. Finally, the pyramid's pinnacle explores the financial planning profession and the ethical responsibilities faced by a professional financial planner. Chapters 22 and 23 cover these topics.

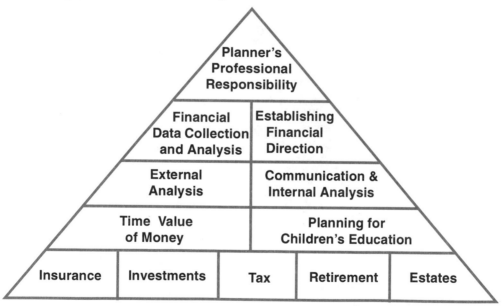

Throughout the text, we also identify two themes. The first theme of the text is that personal financial planning is about attaining financial goals and managing financial risks. There are perhaps as many goals as there are clients. Generally, the majority of clients are looking to achieve one or more of the following goals: to attain financial security for themselves, to create an accumulation of assets to fund their children's education, to save a specific lump sum to cover future expenditures, or to prepare their assets for transfer to heirs. There are many risks threatening the attainment of these goals, including disability, ill health, or untimely death. This text will identify these risks and provide ways to manage them.

The second theme emphasized throughout the text is that the professional practice of personal financial planning emphasizes data collection and analysis. For the professional financial planner, this calls for a good education in the external environmental influences and good data collection skills for interviewing and administering questionnaires. Analytical skills are invaluable when applying time-value-of-money concepts, and when preparing and analyzing personal financial statements. Excellent communication skills, including displaying empathy and using verbal and nonverbal pacing, are essential when dealing with clients. Finally, helping clients set reasonable goals that are objectively measurable in time and form, and using good follow-up and evaluation skills, are most valuable to the professional financial planner.

SPECIAL FEATURES

A variety of tools and presentation methods are used throughout this text to assist in the learning process. Some of the features presented in this text that are designed to enhance the readers' understanding and learning process include:

Section Break Features

▲ **The Financial Planner's Pyramid of Knowledge** – The financial planning pyramid is shown on every section break to focus the student's attention to the section topic. We have shaded the corresponding area on the pyramid to identify the broad knowledge topic discussed in the section. The pyramid's intricacies are discussed more fully in Chapter 1.

▲ **Knowledge Level "In Brief"** – The knowledge level "In Brief" section allows us to be more specific on the topics covered in the section. The topics are listed by difficulty, with the easier topics in the top box, medium topics in the middle, and more difficult topics in the bottom box. This was done to help the student be aware of and prepared for the difficulty of the topics. It also allowed us to give a brief "keyword" overview of the section.

▲ **Goal and Risk Identification** – Common goals and risks are identified on the section break to focus the reader's attention to the ever-present conflict between goal attainment and risk avoidance.

▲ **Data Collection and Analysis Requirements** – Data collection and data analysis requirements are identified to help the reader become adept at learning how to identify relevant information.

Chapter Features

▲ **Professional Focus** – Responses to questions posed to practicing professionals are presented throughout the text to provide real-life application scenarios.

▲ **"Where On The Web"** – Each chapter has a "Where On The Web" section that provides the reader with useful website domains.

▲ **Bolded Keywords** – Keywords appear in **boldfaced type** throughout the text to assist in the identification of important concepts and terminology. Keyword definitions appear in the margin for quick access to important concepts.

▲ **Examples** – Examples are used frequently to illustrate the concepts being discussed.

▲ **Exhibits** – The written text is enhanced and simplified by using exhibits where appropriate.

2ND EDITION CHANGES

▲ The entire text is updated to reflect the changes from the Economic Growth and Tax Relief Reconciliation Act of 2001.

▲ Recent changes to Tax, Retirement, and Social Security laws are included.

▲ Sections on Family Limited Partnerships and Registered Investment Advisors are added.

▲ Changes from the new Minimum Distribution Laws are incorporated into the text.

▲ Added sections to include new topics from the updated topic list for CFP^{TM} Certification Examinations beginning November 2001 that relate to Fundamentals of Financial Planning.

▲ The latest revisions from the CFP Board's *Standards of Professional Conduct* are reflected in the new edition.

▲ Editorial comments from instructors and students are also incorporated into the text.

ACKNOWLEDGEMENTS & SPECIAL THANKS

We are most appreciative of the tremendous support and encouragement we have received throughout this project. We are extremely grateful to the instructors and program directors of CFP Board-Registered programs who provided valuable comments concerning the first and second editions. We are fortunate to have dedicated, careful readers at several institutions who were willing to share their needs, expectations, and time with us. We also owe a debt of gratitude to all the reviewers and students who have read and commented on many drafts of *Personal Financial Planning – Theory and Practice*.

This book would not have been possible without the extraordinary dedication, skill, and knowledge of Joe Bellows, Phyllis Brierre, Donna Dalton, Jan Dupont, Ann Lopez, Marguerite Merritt, Kristi Mincher, and Rob Sabrio. To each of these individuals we extend our deepest gratitude and appreciation. Additional thanks is extended to Allison Dalton, Kathy Hartin, Pat Heckler, Sherri Knoepfler, Robin Meyer, Carolyn Rome, and Paul Tafalla for their assistance in proofreading and providing administrative support.

Developing a textbook that is aesthetically pleasing and easy to read is a difficult undertaking. We would like to thank Donna Dalton and Kristi Mincher for the overall layout design and Ann Lopez who typed and formatted the manuscript. We also extend our thanks to Barry Kerrigan and Desktop Miracles for designing the cover; David Deibel, Richard Long, Sonjie Crews, Cathy Lueck and everyone from Corley Printing Company for all their efforts in making this a reality. We would also like to thank Richard McNally for his layout advice and encouragement during the undertaking of the initial layout design.

We owe a special thanks to Peter Blackwell, Cassie Bradley, David Bergmann, Connie Brezic, James Coleman, Jack Dardis, Joe Devanny, David Durr, Jill Peetluk Feinstein, John Gisolfi, Robert Glovsky, Charlotte Hartmann-Hansen, A. Perry Hubbs II, Robert Kirby, John Ohle III, Stan Roesler, John Rossi, Gary Roques, Bradley Van Vechten, and Evan Wardner for their contribution to the "Professional Focus" feature of the text. We greatly appreciate their willingness to offer their valuable time and professional observations.

The 2nd edition is the result of thoughtful and thorough comments from many people. We feel it is only fitting to mention a few special people who went above and beyond. We would like to thank Stan Roesler, of PDP Financial Planning Group, for his valuable comments on the Introduction to Estates chapter. We owe a great debt of gratitude to Jennifer and Kevin Dalton who reviewed the text in its entirety and offered many valuable comments. Dr. Michael Dalton would like to especially thank his Loyola University students, Gregory Bordelon, Martha Gruning, David Jacobs, and Ricardo Sol, who poured over the text and offered their suggestions. Finally, we would like to thank the National Association of Securities Dealers who allowed us to use their Registered Investment Advisor materials.

We have received so much help from so many people, it is possible that we have inadvertently overlooked thanking someone. If so, it is our shortcoming, and we apologize in advance. Please let us know if you are that someone, and we will make it right in our next printing.

PROFESSIONAL FOCUS

PETER BLACKWELL, MBA, CFP™
Peter is co-owner of Aegis Financial Advisors, Inc., a registered investment advisor, and the Coordinator of the Certified Financial Planning Program at the University of Central Florida, and has been a regular presenter at the Disney Institute. Peter is also an instructor for the Dalton Review for the CFP™ Certification Examination where he teaches Investments, Insurance, Fundamentals of Financial Planning, Tax, Retirement, and Estates.

CASSIE BRADLEY, PH.D.
Cassie is the MBA Director and an Assistant Professor at Mercer University in Atlanta, GA. She is a member of the American Accounting Association and the American Taxation Association. Cassie is also a co-author to the Dalton Review for the CFP™ Certification Examination: Volume I - Outlines and Study Guides and a contributing author to the Dalton Review for the CFP™ Certification Examination: Volume II - Problems and Solutions.

DAVID R. BERGMANN, CLU, CHFC, CFP™
David is the owner and managing principal of The David R. Bergmann Group and is an instructor in UCLA's Board-Registered Program teaching both Financial Analysis and Federal Income Taxation. He was a member of the National Board of the ICFP having served as Chair of the Education Committee, Chair of the Regional Directors Committee, and Vice-President of the Board of Directors. He is currently the President-Elect of the Financial Planning Association, Los Angeles Chapter (President 2001) and a member of the editorial review board for the Journal of Financial Planning.

CONNIE BREZIK, CPA/PFS
Connie is President of Professional Asset Strategies, Inc., an investment management and financial planning firm with offices in four states. Connie has seventeen years experience with a large national accounting and consulting firm. She is a frequent speaker and authors a monthly column on financial planning and investments topics. Worth named Connie as one of the top advisors in the country for three years. Connie is currently the chair of the AICPA/PFP Technical Conference Planning Committee and is a member of the AICPA, FPA, NAPFA, and ASFG.

JAMES COLEMAN, PH.D. CPA, CFP™
James is an Assistant Professor at Mercer University Atlanta, Georgia. He previously held several management positions in the Finance, Investor Relations and Public Relations departments at Federal Express Corporation. James is also an instructor for the Dalton Review for the CFP™ Certification Examination where he teaches Investments, Insurance, and Fundamentals of Financial Planning.

JACK DARDIS, MBA, CLU, CHFC

Jack is a principal of Jack Dardis and Associates, a comprehensive financial planning firm. He received his MBA from Harvard University and his BBA from Loyola University. Jack is a member of the Board of Trustees at Loyola University, New Orleans and a former board member of the Securities Industry Automation Corporation. He is also a member of the New Orleans Estate Planning Council and is active in civic affairs throughout the Greater New Orleans Metropolitan area.

JOE DEVANNEY, MA, CLU, PFP

Joe is the President of Insurance/Investment Corporation of Mission Hills, CA, which specializes in providing consultation services in insurance and investments. He also teaches several courses in Insurance and Financial Planning at the UCLA Extension Program and serves as a member of the Board of Directors for the Western State University School of Law in Fullerton-Irvine and the Thomas Jefferson School of Law in San Diego.

DAVID DURR, PH.D., CFP™

David is the Houston Area Director of the Professional Development Institute/University of St. Thomas CFP Board-Registered Program. He is also an Assistant Professor of Finance at the University of Houston-Downtown where he teaches classes in derivative securities, international finance, and financial management. David is also an instructor for the Dalton Review for the CFP™ Certification Examination where he teaches Investments, Insurance, and Fundamentals of Financial Planning.

JILL PEETLUK FEINSTEIN, CFP™

Jill is a consultant to Chase Bank, training their employees to better educate the public on financial alternatives. She also holds adjunct faculty status with the College for Financial Planning and teaches in the CFP Board-Registered Program at the C.W. Post Campus of Long Island University. As a respected financial planner and educator, Jill was invited to serve on the Item Writing Committee of the CFP Board of Standards and Practices and serves on the Board of the Long Island Society of the Financial Planning Association.

JOHN A. GISOLFI, MS, RFC, CFP™

John is an Adjunct professor of Personal Financial Planning at Moravian College in Bethlehem, PA and an independent contractor serving as Director of Plan Design at Integrated Asset Management. He has conducted advanced educational conferences at both Muhlenberg College and Lehigh University on strategies for money management as well as other presentations on Modern Portfolio Theory. He holds NASD Series 7 and 63 general securities licenses, a Series 65 Investment Advisor license, and a Series 24 Securities Principal license.

ROBERT J. GLOVSKY, JD, LLM, CLU, CHFC, CFP^{TM}

Bob is the President of Mintz Levin Financial Advisors, LLC, providing customized financial planning and investment advisory services to individuals and families. He is also the Director of Boston University's Program for Financial Planners and served as Chair of the CFP Board of Examiners. Bob has lectured and taught extensively throughout the country on financial planning topics. *Worth* magazine selected him as one of the "Best Financial Advisors in the Country" for each of the past four years. Bob is widely renowned for his financial expertise, which was showcased for eight years in his role as co-host of "The Money Experts" on Boston radio.

CHARLOTTE HARTMANN-HANSEN, MS, CLU, CHFC, LUTCF

Charlotte, of Hartmann-Hansen Financial Services, is in private practice as a financial services consultant and insurance advisor. She is a Registered Investment Advisor (affiliate of C.J.M. Asset Management LLC) and an Independent Registered Representative (with C.J.M. Planning Corp). Charlotte is an adjunct faculty member with Moravian College Division of Continuing and Graduate Studies in the CFP Board-Registered Program, where she teaches and serves on the advisory board. She has been active in her community and profession, including presenting programs and seminars for the community, professional associations, non-profit groups, businesses, chambers of commerce and locally and regionally for Rotary International.

A. PERRY HUBBS II, MBA, CFP^{TM}

Perry's expertise is in asset allocation and pension planning. He is the President of Arden & Associates, which is a full service financial planning company, and the Program Head for the CFP Board-Registered Program with the Division of Lifelong Educations at the University of South Florida. Perry is also a member of the Board of Directors of the Chamber of Commerce in Tarpon Springs, FL, and a member of the Pinellas County Estate Planning Council.

ROBERT KIRBY, JD, CFP^{TM}

Robert has a private law practice in Winter Park, FL, specializing in Estate Planning and Probate Administration. He is an Assistant Professor at Florida Institute of Technology, serving as Director of the CFP Board-Registered Program. He is also an adjunct instructor in Trusts and Estates at the University of Central Florida. Robert is a member of the State Bar in Florida and in Texas, and is a member of the Financial Planning Association.

JOHN OHLE III, JD, MBA, CPA/PFS, CFP^{TM}

John is the Regional Director of Bank One's Innovative Strategies Group. He is also an instructor for the Dalton CFP^{TM} Examination Review where he teaches Tax, Insurance, Retirement, and Estates. John is a member of several associations including the AICPA, the American Bar Association, the American Association of Attorney-CPAs, and the National Association of Estate Planners & Councils.

STAN ROESLER, MBA, CFP™

Stan is the Principal of PDP Financial Planning Group in Vernon, CT, and the Program Coordinator for the CFP Board-Registered Program at Manchester Community College in Manchester, CT. He is a Board member of the Financial Planning Association of Connecticut, Hartford Society, and is registered with the Connecticut Department of Banking as an Investment Adviser.

JOHN D. ROSSI, III, MBA, CPA/PFS, CMA, CFM, CVA, CFP™

John is a full-time member of the Accounting Faculty at Moravian College in Bethlehem, PA. He is also the Director of Personal Financial Planning Education and Moravian College's CFP Board-Registered Program. John is a frequent presenter of workshops and continuing professional education programs on technical, tax, valuation, and business management issues. John is also president of JR3 Management Services, P.C. providing consulting services, including business valuation, financial planning, financial reporting, and taxation.

GARY ROQUES, CPA, MBA, CFP™

Gary is a Financial Advisor at Paine Webber Incorporated where he specializes in advising clients about investment strategies that are appropriate for helping them to achieve their financial goals. He provides several services to his clients, including education, and retirement planning, estate planning strategies, portfolio design and analysis, insurance planning, and IRA rollovers. Gary is a member of the Society of Louisiana Certified Public Accountants and the Association of Employee Benefit Planners of New Orleans.

BRADLEY VAN VECHTEN, CFP™

Brad is a veteran financial planner and investment advisor. He holds NASD Series 7 and 63 general securities licenses, a Series 65 Investment Advisor license, and a Series 24 Securities Principal license. He also holds a State Life Insurance and Annuities license for California and is a year 2000 candidate for the CLU and ChFC designations. Bradley is also an active member of the Financial Planning Association and the National Notary Association.

EVAN S. WARDNER, MBA, CFP™

Evan is the Program Director of Medaille College's CFP Board-Registered Program. He is a member of the Board of Directors of the Western New York Chapter of the Financial Planning Association. Evan is a licensed stockbroker and a licensed life, health, and property and casualty insurance agent and broker in private practice advising individual and business clients in Buffalo, NY.

CONTENTS IN BRIEF

INSURANCE PLANNING

Chapter 8: An Introduction to Insurance and Risk Management 233

Chapter 9: Insurance On The Person 259

INVESTMENT PLANNING

TAX AND BUSINESS PLANNING

RETIREMENT PLANNING

Chapter 18: Introduction to Retirement Planning 649

THE FINANCIAL PLANNING PROFESSION

APPENDICES

Basic Financial Planning Skills

in BRIEF →

- Personal financial planning

- The Financial Planner's Pyramid of Knowledge

- The external environment

- Communication skills of the financial planner

- Internal analysis

- Lifecycle positioning

- Financial statement preparation

- Ratio analysis and comparison to benchmarks

- Trend analysis

- Sensitivity and risk analysis

- Financial mission
- Financial goals
- Financial objectives
- Alternative strategies
- Strategy selection and financial direction

Basic Financial Planning Skills

Risks

- Inadequate data collection
- Incorrect data analysis
- Miscommunication to client
- Poor strategy
- No client buy-in

Data Collection

- Economic information
- Legal information
- Personal information
- Financial information
- Tax returns
- Mission
- Goals
- Objectives
- Strategic alternatives

Goals

- Establish appropriate mission statement
- Establish goals
- Establish objectives
- Select strategy

Data Analysis

- Economic analysis
- Personal financial analysis
- Savings analysis
- Investment analysis
- Risk tolerance of client
- Strategic alternatives

CHAPTER 1

Introduction

After learning the material in this chapter, you will be able to:

1. Define personal financial planning.

2. Discuss the benefits of personal financial planning.

3. Explain how the financial planning process promotes efficient allocation of a client's resources.

4. Explain how financial success is a relative concept.

5. Identify why people hire professional financial planners.

6. Describe the Financial Planner's Pyramid of Knowledge and explain each component's importance.

PERSONAL FINANCIAL PLANNING DEFINED

personal financial planning - the process, both artistic and scientific, of formulating, implementing, and monitoring multifunctional decisions that enable an individual or family to achieve financial goals

Comprehensive **personal financial planning** can be defined as the process, both artistic and scientific, of formulating, implementing, and monitoring multifunctional decisions that enable an individual or family to achieve financial goals. Personal financial planning involves the management of personal financial risks through cost benefit analysis. It capitalizes on personal and financial strengths while managing financial risks and weaknesses. Financial planning professionals and those studying financial planning should understand and appreciate the comprehensive nature of a competently prepared personal financial plan and what it is intended to accomplish for the person who implements it effectively.

BENEFITS OF PERSONAL FINANCIAL PLANNING

A financial plan integrates a financial mission, goals, and objectives into one cohesive plan that helps to allocate financial resources in a consistent manner. Individuals and families with no formal financial plan actually have an *informal* financial plan. This informal financial plan is their historical pattern of financial decisions and financial behavior which, when woven together, establishes their informal plan. For example, consistent late debt repayments suggest a pattern (plan), and such a pattern eventually leads to financial consequences. Conversely, consistent long-term savings and investment without any formal plan creates a pattern (plan) that also leads to financial consequences. The historical pattern of personal or family financial behavior is as difficult to change as any other personal habit. Thus, the professional financial planner must not only be strategist and planner, but may also have to serve as counselor and financial therapist to clients.

benefits of personal financial planning -
- goals identified are more likely to be achieved
- helps to clearly identify risk exposures
- is proactive rather than reactive
- creates a framework for feedback, evaluation, and control
- establishes measurable goals and expectations
- develops an improved awareness of financial choices
- provides an opportunity for an increased commitment to financial goals

Clients can derive many **benefits from the process of personal financial planning**. Perhaps the most important benefit is that goals identified and planned for are more likely to be achieved than without such planning. The planning process helps to clearly identify risk exposures that can undermine goals. Once identified, these risks can be managed using a variety of techniques. The financial planning process is one of learning, growing, and choosing wisely. The process is proactive rather than reactive, thus giving clients more control over their financial destiny. By using a more logical, systematic, and rational approach to decision-making, clients make better strategic choices about the utilization of resources. The process also creates a framework for feedback, evaluation, and control. It establishes measurable goals and expectations that can be compared to actual results.

During the financial planning process, the client develops an improved awareness of financial choices and of how the internal and external environments affect those choices. Furthermore, the process provides an opportunity for the client to increase commitment to selected goals. When clients and their families understand what they want to achieve, why they want to achieve it, and how and when it can be achieved, they often take ownership of their financial plan and become more committed to it.

A comprehensive personal financial plan helps to establish rationality and reality and purge the client of "pie in the sky" ideas and wishful thinking. For example, it is common for persons to want to retire early and maintain their preretirement lifestyle while currently spending more than 100 percent of their personal disposable income with no current or future plans or intention to save or invest. A comprehensive personal financial plan will quickly demonstrate the irrationality of such an approach and assist the client in identifying changes necessary to achieve a more realistic plan.

The financial planning process brings financial order and discipline to clients. It instills confidence that personal financial goals can be achieved. The process identifies the changes in actions and behaviors necessary to accomplish those financial goals. The process provides a forum for rationalizing the need for change and for viewing change as an opportunity rather than a threat.

Financially successful individuals (not necessarily those who are wealthy, but, rather, those who meet their financial goals) tend to do more financial planning to prepare themselves for the inevitable fluctuations in their internal and external environments. They tend to make decisions that are more informed. They also tend to better anticipate both short-run and long-run consequences. Conversely, individuals who are not as financially successful tend to underestimate the value of planning and may attribute their lack of financial success to uncontrollable factors such as a poor economy, foreign competition, government interference, or just bad luck.

There are no absolutes in financial planning any more than there are absolutes about anything in the future. Financial planning will not guarantee desired results. The ultimate outcome of a plan may vary from its prediction for a variety of reasons. The probability is, however, that the more we plan, the better we get at planning, and therefore, the less risk will be inherent in our plan.

FINANCIAL SUCCESS IS A RELATIVE CONCEPT

Financial success means different things to different people. The fisherman who lives in a poor village in a developing country and who has a slightly larger boat than most of the other local fisherman may feel financially successful. Conversely, the millionaire whose friends are all billionaires, may feel less financially successful. In a way, financial success is a comparison with the client's own benchmarks or standards. Thus, from the client's perspective, financial success is both a relative concept and a subjective one. The professional financial planner needs to keep in mind that financial success to a particular client is a relative concept, the description of which is or may be subjectively determined by the client.

financial success - for most individuals, financial success means accomplishing one's financial goals

While **subjectivity** tends to dominate the client's thinking about financial success, **objectivity** should dominate the planner's thinking about financial planning. The accomplishment of specific goals is objectively determined if objectively defined. In addition, risks that exist in the external environment are objective and real to the professional planner, while the client may have a subjective perception of the same risk. For example, the risk of untimely death can be measured actuarially, regardless of the subjective perception of the client. Another example of objectivity is recognizing the risk of permanent disability for a particular job. Consider the example of the NFL running back. The National Football League knows (and teams know, too) that the average playing life expectancy for a professional running back is approximately four years. Some players, through poor performance, are cut from the roster, and others may suffer a disabling injury on the playing field. The number of running backs who are disabled each year is a predictable percentage, League-wide. Regardless of how the players subjectively feel about their chances of suffering a disabling injury, it is mathematically objective that a certain percentage of

subjectivity - relating to the client's perception of reality

objectivity - relating to facts without distortion by personal feelings or prejudices

running backs will be injured and will be unable to play in any given year. With full knowledge of this objective risk and its catastrophic financial consequences, a professional financial planner should strongly advise his running back client to purchase long-term disability insurance that pays benefits if the player is injured while playing professional football. Most professional planners would agree with that advice even though the policy premiums will be extremely high. (The premiums are high because the insurers also understand the objective risks, and they set premiums that will both cover losses and make a profit.)

RESOURCE ALLOCATION IN FINANCIAL PLANNING

Financial planning is about making financial choices and allocating scarce resources. People make choices because scarcity exists. At any moment in time, all people want the highest level of overall satisfaction from their choices. People are aware from an early age that there are always alternative financial choices to be made, such as whether to consume today or to defer consumption until later. The internal psychological analysis that people perform when they decide among choices is a subjective evaluation and application of their own **personal utility curves** to the alternatives identified and presented to them. Personal utility curves are subjectively based and reflect our knowledge, values, and beliefs and, therefore, may be quite different for each person. Some individuals place a high value on spending time alone while some value spending time with others in social settings. If a client believes there is no tomorrow, he may as well consume today. If, however, he believes in a long "tomorrow" during which he plans not to work (some call it retirement), he may be willing to forego consumption today, so as to defer those unconsumed resources for the future.

When making choices, there are always alternatives. Each alternative has consequences and risks. Doing nothing is always included as one alternative. The highest-valued alternative not chosen is called the **opportunity cost**. Opportunity cost represents what is forgone by choosing another alternative. For example, if a client chooses to spend $2,500 on a vacation cruise as an alternative to saving for the future, the opportunity cost is the value of the $2,500 in the client's investment portfolio at a future point in time. Five years after taking the cruise, the client has fond memories and beautiful photos of the trip. Alternatively, had he skipped the cruise and invested the money in a well-structured investment portfolio for those five years, he might have doubled his investment to $5,000.

In choosing among alternatives, people have to put those alternatives into some framework for comparison. When making comparisons, human nature tends to discount anything in the future in favor of immediate gratification. In the cruise example above, the client decided to spend the $2,500 now to take the cruise, even if the client objectively knew that the money would double in five years if invested wisely. For this client, the current subjective satisfaction expected from taking the cruise is worth more today than the increased future value of the investment portfolio.

Once a financial planner presents a client with a framework of objective alternatives that identifies the opportunity cost associated with each alternative, the client can make a more informed, more rational choice among alternatives. In this way, the financial planning process promotes efficient allocation of a client's resources and avoids commitment of resources to more costly, less rational choices.

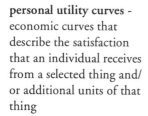

personal utility curves - economic curves that describe the satisfaction that an individual receives from a selected thing and/ or additional units of that thing

opportunity cost - the highest valued alternative not chosen

WHY DO PEOPLE HIRE PROFESSIONAL FINANCIAL PLANNERS?

Many people seek the advice of professionals, such as doctors, lawyers, and accountants, on a regular basis. Generally, professionals have a more comprehensive knowledge of their subject field than does the public. In some cases, it is simply a matter of opportunity cost. It is a lot less expensive in total satisfaction and cost to retain an "expert" than to invest the time to learn to "do it ourselves." We may lack the day-to-day cognitive references, financial benchmarks, and comparisons needed to know when a plan is competent or attainable. Even though people may have a limited knowledge of a certain subject, they may lack the confidence to make important decisions based on that limited knowledge. Essentially, people seek out and retain professional financial planners for the same reasons. People hire professional financial planners because they believe that doing so is more effective and efficient than attempting to create and implement a financial plan on their own.

The public has a reasonable expectation that a professional financial planner is knowledgeable and competent in the financial planning field. The planner should have an understanding of objective risks in the environment, such as the risks of untimely death, health problems, disability, property loss, and negligence suits and awards. The public can reasonably expect that a professional financial planner will have knowledge of life expectancies and, thus, an understanding of the average expected length of years of retirement. Planners should know that in general it takes 60-80 percent of preretirement income to maintain the preretirement lifestyle in retirement. Planners should know that for low-income workers, Social Security provides a good wage replacement, but for highly paid workers it may only replace 10-20 percent of preretirement income. Professional planners should know the risk of inflation and its historical patterns. Planners should also know the historical investment returns for various classes of assets, and which asset allocation schemes have produced the best overall investment returns for selected risk levels. Building the professional financial planner's knowledge and skill base, understanding the financial planning process, and recognizing the environment in which financial planning exists, is what this text is about.

THE FINANCIAL PLANNER'S PYRAMID OF KNOWLEDGE - APPROACH IN TEXT

The Financial Planner's Pyramid of Knowledge, as depicted in Exhibit 1.1, is presented throughout this text. The Pyramid identifies both the skills and the basic tools that the financial planner must possess, as well as the core topics of which the planner must be knowledgeable. Just as the strength of any structure depends on a strong, solid foundation, the success of any professional financial planner relies on a well-built foundation of knowledge, competency, and skill. The base of the Financial Planner's Pyramid of Knowledge identifies the core knowledge and skill sets that every financial planner should possess. Collectively, these competencies make up the financial planner's toolkit--a foundation on which a successful profession in financial planning can be built. Out of necessity, these skills, tools, and knowledge will be presented serially and compartmentally. It is important to note, however, that these are not performed sequentially or independently. Rather, they are performed simultaneously throughout the many aspects of the financial planning process.

EXHIBIT 1.1: FINANCIAL PLANNER'S PYRAMID OF KNOWLEDGE

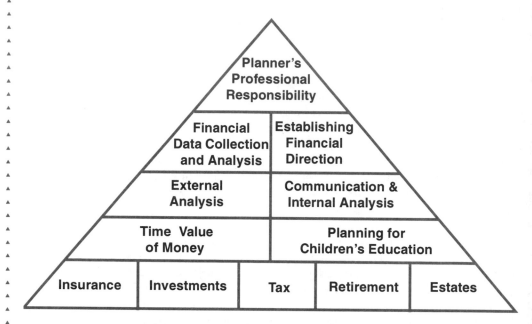

Throughout the text, we also focus on two themes. The first theme of the text is that personal financial planning is about attaining financial goals and managing financial risks. There are perhaps as many goals as there are clients. Generally, the majority of clients are looking to achieve one or more of the following goals: to attain financial security for themselves, to create an accumulation of assets to fund their children's education, to save a specific lump sum to cover future expenditures, or to prepare their assets for transfer to heirs. There are many risks threatening the attainment of these goals, including disability, ill health, or untimely death. The text will identify these risks and suggest ways for managing these risks.

The second theme that is emphasized throughout the text is that the professional practice of personal financial planning emphasizes data collection and analysis. For the professional financial planner, this requires a good education in the external environmental influences and good data collection skills for interviewing and administering questionnaires. Analytical skills are invaluable when applying time value of money concepts, and when preparing and analyzing personal financial statements. Excellent communication skills, including displaying empathy and using verbal and nonverbal pacing, are essential when gathering information and communicating with clients. Finally, helping clients set reasonable goals that are objectively measurable in time and form, and using good follow-up and evaluation skills are most valuable to the professional financial planner.

BASIC FINANCIAL PLANNING SKILLS

The first section of the text identifies that the practice of personal financial planning requires the financial planner to master good communication, data collection, and analysis skills. These skills are necessary when applying financial planning tools and when working with clients. The planner must be aware that individuals generally progress through **financial phases** during their

financial phases - accumulation, conservation/protection, and distribution/gifting lives. These phases include the asset accumulation phase, the conservation/protection phase, and the distribution/gifting phase. These phases are not mutually exclusive. A client may function in two or three phases simultaneously. If a professional planner can identify which phase or phases a client is in, the planner will have better insight into the client's financial behavior and a better understanding of the client's approach to goals and risks.

This section also identifies the process of establishing financial direction. The process begins by establishing a **financial mission**. Once the mission is identified and embraced, the planner must consider relevant internal and external environmental information and should use objective analysis and rational judgment to guide the client to effective decision-making. The client's **financial goals** and **financial objectives** are then identified and prioritized so that feasible alternative strategies can be created. After examining the alternatives, the planner aids the client in selecting the optimal alternative strategy. The last step in the process is where the plan is implemented and monitored; but by no means is the process finished. The responsible financial planner will then provide regular feedback to the client on the plan's performance.

BASIC FINANCIAL PLANNING TOOLS

The second section of the text identifies two basic financial planning tools; **time value of money** and planning for children's education.

In Chapter 6, we discuss time value of money (TVM) concepts, one of the most useful and important concepts in finance and personal financial planning. The chapter includes in-depth discussions on TVM concepts, terms, and tools such as present value, future value, amortization tables, net present value (NPV) and internal rate of return (IRR), yield to maturity, debt management, and the inflation rate.

Chapter 7 covers developing a plan for funding children's education. A primary financial goal of most parents is to provide an education for their children. Education funding is a common area of concern for those seeking financial planning advice because paying for higher education is one of the largest financial burdens a family will face. In our discussion, we cover the various issues that parents should consider when setting goals for financing their children's education, the types of financial aid information that can be gathered from a college's financial aid office, and explain the importance of the EFC (Expected Family Contribution) formula in student financial aid application. We describe the major student financial assistance programs available, and explain how time value of money concepts are used to help calculate the cost of their child's education.

CORE TOPICS

The majority of chapters, Chapters 8 through 21, provide an in-depth discussion and analysis of the topics that are core to a financial planner's knowledge base. The topics include planning for insurance, investments, tax and business, retirement, and estates.

Chapters 8 through 11 are dedicated to insurance planning. Chapter 8 discusses the legal foundation of insurance and the transference or sharing of risks using insurance contracts. Chapter 9 identifies the risks to the person, namely untimely death, catastrophic illness, disability, and the need for long-term care. Chapter 10 identifies the risks to property and liability exposures. Chapter 11 covers the types and availability of social insurance.

financial mission - a broad and enduring statement that identifies the client's purpose for wanting a financial plan

financial goals - high-level statements of financial desires that may be for the short run or the long run

financial objectives - statements of financial desire that contain time and measurement attributes making them more specific than financial goals

time value of money - the concept that money received today is worth more than the same amount of money received sometime in the future

Chapters 12 through 15 offer a discussion on investment planning. Chapter 12 introduces investment goals common to most investors, the risks that threaten those goals, and discusses modern portfolio theory and investment strategies. Chapter 13 discusses investing in lending securities, such as bonds. Chapter 14 covers equity securities, namely common and preferred stock. Chapter 15 discusses mutual funds as an investment opportunity.

Chapters 16 and 17 cover individual income tax and tax planning and the formation and taxation of business entities. Chapter 16 includes discussions on the objectives of the Federal Income Tax Law, the sources of tax-related client information, the difference between tax avoidance and tax evasion, the IRS audit selection and screening process, the various civil penalties imposed on tax law violators, and the various tax-advantaged investment options available to taxpayers. Chapter 17 identifies the several different types of business entities that a business owner may choose as a legal form of business and characterizes each type of business entity with regard to formation requirements, operation, ownership restrictions, tax treatment, legal liability risk, and management operations. The chapter goes on to discuss the basic factors that a business owner should consider when selecting a legal form of business and explains how each type of business entity differs with regard to simplicity of formation and operation, ownership restrictions, limited liability, management operations, and tax characteristics.

Chapters 18 and 19 examine retirement planning. Chapter 18 identifies and explains the major factors that affect retirement planning. Chapter 19 provides an introduction to private retirement plans, including qualified retirement plans, other tax-advantaged retirement plans, and nonqualified plans.

Chapters 20 and 21 present the goals of efficient and effective wealth transfer, during life or at death, and the risks that are associated with such transfers. Chapter 20 introduces estate planning, describes the estate planning process, discusses the objectives of and the benefits derived from planning an estate, lists the types of client information necessary to begin and complete the estate planning process, and describes the probate process and lists its advantages and disadvantages. Chapter 21 explains why a unified gift and estate tax system exists, identifies the basic strategies for transferring wealth through gifting, explains the purpose of the federal estate tax, defines the marital deduction and how it affects estate planning, and discusses the various estate tax reduction techniques available.

THE FINANCIAL PLANNING PROFESSION

Chapter 22 describes the financial planning profession today. It describes and differentiates financial institutions from individual financial professionals. The chapter outlines the methods of compensation and closes with ideas about developing and maintaining a practice. Chapter 23 on ethical responsibilities of a financial planner provides a legal framework for malpractice and civil liability and details the CFP Board's Standards of Professional Conduct, which covers its code of ethics and professional responsibility, disciplinary rules and procedures, and practice standards for CFP™ certificants.

DISCUSSION QUESTIONS

1. What is personal financial planning?
2. What does it mean to say that financial success is a "relative" concept?
3. How does the financial planning process promote efficient allocation of a client's resources?
4. Why do people hire professional financial planners?
5. What does the Financial Planner's Pyramid of Knowledge identify?
6. What benefits can a client derive from the process of personal financial planning?
7. What concepts must the professional financial planner balance in order to create a successful financial plan?
8. Through what activities is the personal financial planner expected to guide the client?

CHAPTER 2

External Environment

LEARNING OBJECTIVES:

After learning the material in this chapter, you will be able to:

1. Differentiate between the external and internal environments in which financial planning occurs.

2. Discuss how each external environmental factor links to the different areas of financial planning.

3. Give examples of how each external environmental factor might affect clients from different economic levels.

4. Give reasons why external environmental analysis is important.

5. Explain how economic factors, such as interest rates, taxes, and inflation, affect areas of financial planning.

6. Define the several phases and important extreme points that make up a business cycle and give their effect on the economy.

7. Use the formula to calculate the rate of inflation.

8. Define the consumer price index, the gross national product deflator, and the producer price index.

9. Explain how changes in monetary and fiscal policy affect the economy.

10. Identify several federal consumer protection laws and give a brief description of each.

11. List several federal programs that offer protection for workers on the jobsite.

12. Give examples of how the external environmental factors—social, technological, political, and taxation—affect a client's personal financial plan.

THE EXTERNAL ENVIRONMENT

The success of a client's financial planning is affected by both internal and external environmental factors. Internal environmental forces, which will be examined fully in subsequent chapters, include a client's current and projected financial situation, tolerance for risk, discipline regarding savings and investments, consumption patterns, and financial goals and aspirations. Exhibit 2.1 shows how the internal environment fits within the external environment.

EXHIBIT 2.1: INTERNAL AND EXTERNAL ENVIRONMENTS

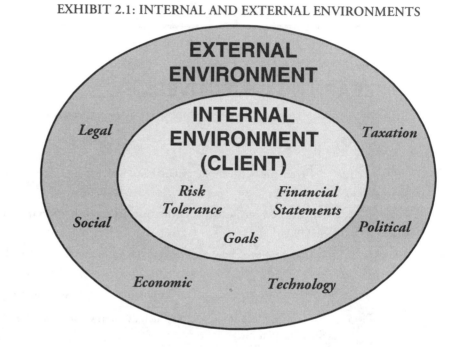

external environment - the whole complex of factors that influence the financial planning process, including economic, legal, social, technological, political, and taxation factors

The **external environment** is made up of a variety of factors, or "sub" environments, that are broad in scope but have at least some direct or indirect influence on the financial planning process. The external environment includes economic, legal, social, technological, political, and taxation factors. An abbreviated list of factors for each of the external environmental influences is presented in Exhibit 2.2.

EXHIBIT 2.2: ABBREVIATED LIST OF EXTERNAL FACTORS*

Economic Factors	Legal Factors
Gross Domestic Product (GDP)	Antitrust Acts
Inflation (CPI)	Consumer Protection Acts
Interest Rates	Securities Acts (1933-1934)
Trade Payment	Forms of Business Organization
Consumer Income/Debt/Spending	Employer/Employee Relations
Unemployment	Workers Compensation
Population Age	Continuation of Benefits (COBRA)
Index of Leading Economic Indicators	Social Security

Social Factors	Technological Factors
Age of Population – Life Expectancy	Current State of Technology
Customs and Beliefs	Creation of New Technology
Attitudes and Motivations	Human and Business Solutions
Status Symbols/Social Institutions	Advances in Service & Engineering

Political Factors	Taxation Factors
Form of Government	Income Taxes (Federal and State)
Political Ideology/Stability	Property Taxes
Foreign Trade Policy	Transfer Taxes (Gift and Estate)
Degree of Government Protectionism	Payroll Taxes
	Sales Taxes

*There are many other factors than those listed, however, a full discussion of all factors is beyond the scope of this text.

This chapter describes the external environment in which financial planning occurs. The external environment is characterized primarily by opportunities and threats. For the financial planner, the purpose of studying and monitoring the external environment is to scan for those opportunities and threats that may relate to particular clients and their particular financial goals. The financial planner may forecast external trends (or use experts to forecast trends) to help clients achieve goals and avoid external risks.

As stated previously, external environmental forces include economic, legal, social, technological, political, and taxation forces. Everyone is influenced by these environments to differing degrees as shown by the links in Exhibit 2.3 and the selected examples in Exhibit 2.4. Exhibit 2.3 summarizes the various basic external environment factors and their links to the areas of financial planning.

EXHIBIT 2.3: GENERAL LINKAGES OF EXTERNAL ENVIRONMENT TO FINANCIAL PLANNING

External Environment	Fundamentals of Financial Planning	Insurance Planning	Investments Planning	Income Taxation Planning	Retirement Planning	Estate Planning and Taxation
Economic Environment	✗		✗		✗	
Legal Environment	✗	✗	✗			✗
Social Environment	✗	✗			✗	
Technological Environment			✗	✗		
Political Environment	✗	✗	✗	✗	✗	✗
Taxation Environment		✗	✗	✗	✗	✗

Note: The ✗ indicates predominant linkages, but other linkages may exist.

Technology and scientific innovation affects everyone in society, but its benefits are usually more quickly available to those who can utilize such innovation. Because some clients are more affected by certain environmental factors than others (as illustrated in Exhibit 2.4), it is the responsibility of the professional planner to decide which influences are expected to be relevant to a particular client at a particular time and for a particular time horizon.

EXHIBIT 2.4: EXTERNAL ENVIRONMENTAL IMPACT ON FINANCIAL PLANNING
(SELECTED EXAMPLES)

Client's Economic Level	EXTERNAL ENVIRONMENTAL FORCES					
	Economic	Legal	Social	Political	Taxation	Technological
High Income Clients	• Gross Domestic Product • Interest rates	• Antitrust • Form of business organization	• Status symbols • Life expectancy	• Political • Ideology/ stability	• Income and transfer taxes • Property taxes	• Investments • Internet
Middle Income Clients	• Inflation • Interest rates	• Form of business organization • Employer/ employee relationships • Consumer protection • COBRA • Social Security	• Customs/ Beliefs • Life expectancy	• Foreign Trade Policy	• Property taxes • Income taxes • Payroll taxes	• Investments • Jobs • Electronic tax filing • Internet
Low Income Clients	• Unemployment • Inflation	• Workers compensation • Consumer protection • COBRA • Social Security	• Social institutions • Life expectancy • Customs/ beliefs	• Government protectionism	• Sales taxes • Payroll taxes	• Electronic tax filing • Internet

ANALYZING THE EXTERNAL ENVIRONMENT

External environmental analysis is the process of identifying and monitoring the environment in which a client exists and the opportunities and threats that are present. External environmental analysis is important for a variety of reasons.

▲ External trends and particular events play a significant role in affecting change in the world and in the behavior of individuals.
▲ Changes in external forces impact beliefs, economics, unemployment, inflation, and a society's well-being.
▲ The external environment shapes the way people live, work, spend, save, and think.

Professional financial planners need to have an understanding of these forces and should develop a methodology for staying abreast of the changes occurring in the environment.

In performing the external environmental analysis, the financial planner must determine the relevance of one or more external environmental factors for each particular client. The relevance of such factors may be dependent on the client's age, goals, net worth, or income. Consider the following examples:

EXAMPLE   Mr. Jones is 70 years old, married, has five adult children, seven grandchildren, and has a net worth of ten million dollars. One of his goals is to leave as much money as he can to his heirs. Since the tax environment incorporates gift taxes, estate taxes, generation-skipping transfer taxes, and in some cases, state inheritance taxes, it is highly relevant to Mr. Jones's personal financial planning, and, therefore, highly relevant to his professional financial planner.

EXAMPLE   Mr. Smith, age 36, is married, has three young children, and has debts in excess of his assets. He was injured on the job and will be unlikely to ever return to work. While the tax environment may have some relevance to Mr. Smith, it is going to be a minor influence relative to Mr. Jones. The legal environment, which addresses consumer protection, bankruptcy, workman's compensation, Medicaid, COBRA, Social Security disability benefits, and civil lawsuits, may be of utmost importance to Mr. Smith.

STUDYING THE EXTERNAL ENVIRONMENT

The regular observation and monitoring of the external environment by the financial planner is essential to providing high quality consultative services to clients. Financial planners may study the external environment formally or informally. Formal study will usually include courses in economics, taxation, political science, sociology, and the legal environment, generally studied at the university level. The external environment may also be studied informally by using a variety of sources, such as general economic periodicals, general business periodicals, books, academic and professional journals, newspapers, government statistical studies, and by obtaining environmental briefings from various information providers. Financial planners also take continuing professional education courses to stay abreast of the ever-changing external environment.

THE ECONOMIC AND LEGAL ENVIRONMENTS

The external environment—particularly the economic and legal environment—exerts far-reaching, yet often subtle influence on the accomplishment of financial goals and the occurrence of risks. For example, consider an economic environment characterized by low interest rates, modest growth, and low inflation. Such an environment is ideal for businesses to prosper and for investors to achieve excellent investment returns with relatively moderate levels of risk. Alternatively, economic periods of high interest rates and growing inflation are not as suitable for businesses, investors, or retirees who, living on fixed incomes, are losing purchasing power. The legal environment, especially consumer protection, is important because it establishes the legal rules by which consumers must abide and creates the legal rights to which consumers are entitled.

IMPORTANCE OF THE ECONOMIC ENVIRONMENT

Of all the external environments, the economic environment has the most direct influence on personal financial planning. It is the rationing system among resources, scarcity, and outputs. The economic environment includes many factors, such as gross domestic product, inflation rates, interest rates, trade payments, consumer income/debt/spending, unemployment, population age, and the index of leading economic indicators. While taxation is an economic issue, it is separated into its own category for convenience (taxes are covered in Chapters 16 and 17). Many of these factors, namely, interest rates, inflation, unemployment, and gross domestic product, play a key role in real investment returns and, therefore, in the accomplishment of financial goals.

Professional financial planners must understand the current economic environment to better forecast the economic future. By identifying the opportunities and risks that lie ahead, planners can help clients adapt to that future. The planner needs an understanding of the current economy's general condition, the current interest rate environment, the current rate of inflation, and recent changes in monetary and fiscal policy. It is essential that the planner have the ability to anticipate each element's behavior and its potential effect on a client's financial plan. Exhibit 2.5 illustrates several selected economic factors and their relationship to various areas of financial planning.

EXHIBIT 2.5: THE ECONOMIC ENVIRONMENT AND FINANCIAL PLANNING

Selected Economic Factors	Financial Planning Areas Affected	How They Are Affected
Interest rates	Investment returns	Inversely
	Purchasing power and, therefore, the costs of goods and services in the future including education, retirement funding, and health care	Inversely
Taxes	Redistribution of income through government	Directly
	Production of goods	Inversely
	Distribution of wealth	Directly
Inflation	The cost of goods, services, money, and unemployment	Inversely
Unemployment	Wage rates and other costs/expansion/contraction/consumption	Inversely
Monetary and fiscal policy	Economic expansion/contraction/expectations	Directly

Remember, these economic factors are not mutually exclusive, but, rather, are interrelated. As Exhibit 2.5 illustrates, one economic factor may influence several areas of financial planning in several different ways. It is important for professional financial planners to "read" the external economic environment accurately, so that they can adjust their clients' financial plans accordingly.

THE GENERAL ECONOMY

The economy is a resource-allocation market system that achieves its objectives through a pricing mechanism. Prices are essentially determined in the marketplace at the point where supply and demand reach equilibrium. If supply or demand is affected, prices will change.

> **In the News...**
> Consider that when the pope lifted the ban on eating meat on Friday for Catholics in 1966, the average price per pound of fish dropped 12.5%. However, with the current awareness of health issues, the price of fish has risen faster than general inflation. Thus, if demand is affected, prices will also be affected. (Frederick W. Bell "The Pope and the Price of Fish," American Economic Review 58 (December 1968): 1346-1350)

Demand

demand - the quantity of a particular good that people are willing to buy. Demand is heavily dependent on price

demand curve - the graphic depiction that illustrates the relationship between a particular good's price and the quantity demanded

The **demand** for a particular good is that quantity which people are willing to buy. Demand is heavily dependent on price. The **demand curve** (Exhibit 2.6) illustrates the general relationship between a particular good's price and the quantity demanded.

EXHIBIT 2.6: THE DEMAND CURVE

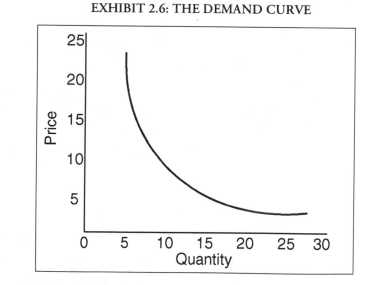

Downward sloping demand indicates that if the price is increased, the quantity demanded will fall. Conversely, when a price falls, quantity demanded increases. There are two reasons demand declines when a price increases. The first reason is consumers are ingenious about substituting other, less expensive goods when the price for a particular good rises. This phenomenon is called the substitution effect. The second reason demand declines is that consumers curb consumption when prices rise.

The average income or standard of living is also a key determinant of demand. As incomes increase, individuals demand and purchase more goods. The size of the market and the price and availability of related, substitute goods also influence the demand for a particular good.

Supply

The **supply** of a particular good is that quantity which businesses are willing to produce and sell. The **supply curve** (Exhibit 2.7) depicts the general relationship between the market price of a particular good and the quantity supplied.

EXHIBIT 2.7: THE SUPPLY CURVE

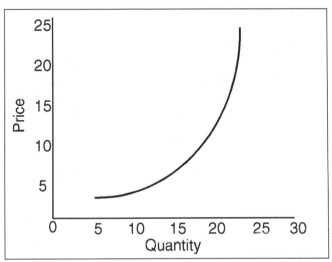

supply - the supply of a particular good is that quantity which businesses are willing to produce or sell

supply curve - the graphic depiction that shows the relationship between the market price of a particular good and the quantity supplied

The factors that affect supply include the price of the good, technological advances, input prices, prices of related goods, and special influences like price expectations.

Substitutes and Complements

Often in markets, goods are related to each other. If the price of good A changes, therefore changing the demand of good A, good B's demand will be affected as well if the goods are related. Whether this relationship is positively or negatively correlated depends on if the goods are substitutes or complements. Substitutes are products that serve similar purposes. They are related such that an increase in the price of one will cause an increase in demand for the other. For example, if the price of chicken suddenly rose sharply, the demand for pork would probably increase, even though the price of pork was initially unchanged. Conversely, complements are products that are usually consumed jointly. They are related such that a decrease in the price of one will cause an increase in demand for the other. For example, when jelly goes on sale, the supermarket can expect the demand for peanut butter to increase slightly because the two products are considered complements.

Diminishing Marginal Utility

The law of diminishing marginal utility states that as the rate of consumption increases, the marginal utility derived from consuming additional units of a good will decline. Marginal utility is the additional utility received from the consumption of an additional unit of a good. For example, if Richard's favorite food was steak, he might eat steak often. However, if Richard ate steak for "n" consecutive days for dinner, the enjoyment, or utility, that he received from the dinner would be higher the first day than on the last.

Price Elasticity

Price elasticity is the quantity demanded of a good in response to changes in that good's price. The percent change in quantity demanded divided by the percent change in price is a relative measure of price elasticity. Goods differ in their elasticity. A good is elastic when its quantity demanded responds greatly to price changes. Luxuries such as movie tickets and liquor could be considered elastic because they are, generally, highly price sensitive. A good is inelastic when its quantity demanded responds little to price changes. Milk and gasoline, considered necessities by some, will remain in demand no matter what the price. Unit elastic demand is that point at which the percent change in quantity demanded is exactly equal to the percent change in price, ignoring the direction of the change. For example, a one percent drop in price causes a one percent increase in the amount sold. Exhibit 2.8 illustrates the relative inelasticity of gasoline consumption to price for the period 1992-1997. Price elasticity is dependent on substitute goods.

EXHIBIT 2.8: GASOLINE PRICES AND CONSUMPTION

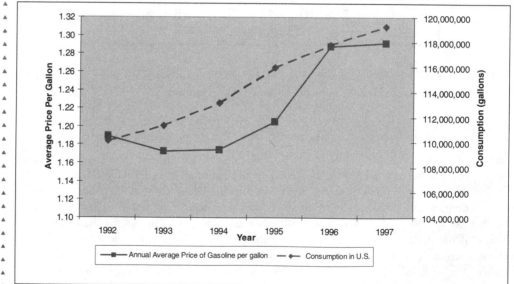

BUSINESS CYCLES

Business cycles are swings in total national output, income, and employment marked by widespread expansion or contraction in many sectors of the economy. These cycles generally occur because of shifts in aggregate demand. The financial planner should be familiar with the impact of business cycles on the economy, as different investments will perform differently during various phases of a business cycle. For example, cyclical industries (such as the automobile or housing industry) generally perform well during an economic boom (expansion) and poorly during a recession (contraction).

The business cycle (as depicted in Exhibit 2.9) consists of two general phases, expansion and contraction; and two points, peak and trough. Each phase of the business cycle passes into the next phase and is characterized by different economic conditions.

The expansion phase ends and moves into the contraction phase at the upper turning point, or peak. Similarly, the contraction phase gives way to expansion at the lower turning point, or trough. The emphasis here is not so much on high or low business activity as on the dynamic aspects of the rise and fall of business activity.

EXHIBIT 2.9: A HYPOTHETICAL BUSINESS CYCLE

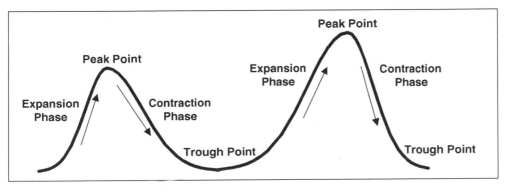

Note: The actual business cycle is not as symmetrical as drawn here. The pattern is more irregular and unpredictable. See Exhibit 2.11 for an illustration of the changes in the actual business cycle.

Business Cycle Components and Their Effect on the Economy

The **expansion phase** leads to the peak point. During the expansion phase, business sales rise, Gross Domestic Product (GDP) grows, and unemployment declines.

The **peak** point appears at the end of the expansion phase when most businesses are operating at full capacity and GDP is increasing rapidly. The peak is the point at which GDP is at its highest and exceeds the long-run average GDP. Usually employment levels also peak at this point. (See Exhibit 2.10 for a depiction of the relationship between long-run GDP and the business cycle.)

The **contraction phase** leads to the trough point. During the contraction phase, business sales fall, GDP growth falls, and unemployment increases.

The **trough** point appears at the end of the contraction phase where businesses are generally operating at their lowest capacity levels. The trough point is characterized by GDP growth being at its lowest or negative. Unemployment is rapidly increasing and finally peaks when sales fall rapidly.

expansion phase - one of the two general business cycle phases characterized by a rise in business sales, growth of Gross Domestic Product, and a decline in unemployment

peak - the point in the business cycle that appears at the end of the expansion phase when most businesses are operating at full capacity and Gross Domestic Product is increasing rapidly

contraction phase - one of the two general business cycle phases characterized by a fall in business sales, decreased growth of Gross Domestic Product, and increased unemployment

trough - the point in the business cycle that appears at the end of the contraction phase when most businesses are operating at their lowest capacity levels and Gross Domestic Product is at its lowest or is negative

recession - a decline in real Gross Domestic Product for two or more successive quarters

depression - is a persistent recession that brings a severe decline in economic activity

Recession is a decline in real GDP for two or more successive quarters characterized by:

▲ Declining consumer purchases.
▲ Expanding business inventories.
▲ Decreasing capital investment.
▲ Decreasing demand for labor.
▲ High unemployment.
▲ Falling commodity prices.
▲ Decreasing business profits.
▲ Falling interest rates due to reduced demand for money.

Depression is a persistent recession that brings a severe decline in economic activity.

EXHIBIT 2.10: THE BUSINESS CYCLE & GDP

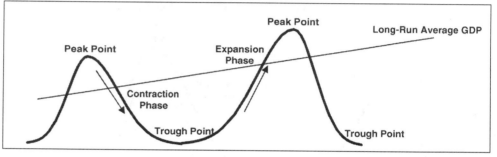

Exhibit 2.10 illustrates that in spite of the expansion/contraction cycle, the long-run average GDP trend line has had an average historical expansion of the economy at +3 percent.

capital formation - production of buildings, machinery, tools, and other equipment that will assist in the ability of economic participants to produce in the future

durable goods - products that are not consumed or quickly disposed of, and can be used for several years

consumption movements - an economic variable that fluctuates during the business cycle

While there are many economic variables that fluctuate during the business cycle, certain economic variables always show greater fluctuations than others. **Capital formation** rises and falls significantly with expansion and contraction, usually leading the trend. **Durable goods,** also a trend leader, are subject to violently erratic patterns of demand. It is the economy's durable, or capital, goods sector that by far shows the greatest cyclical fluctuations. There is good reason to believe that the movements of durable goods represent key causes in the direction of expansion or contraction. **Consumption movements,** which lag behind trends, seem to be the effect of the business cycle phase rather than its cause.

Business Cycle Theories

Two opposing theories attempt to explain the fluctuations in the business cycle. The external theories find the root of the business cycle in the fluctuations of something outside the economic system such as wars, revolutions, political events, rates of population growth and migration, discoveries of new lands and resources, scientific and technological discoveries, and innovation. The internal theories look for mechanisms within the economic system that give rise to self-generating business cycles. Thus, every expansion breeds recession and contraction. Every contraction, in turn, breeds revival and expansion in a quasi-regular, repeating, never-ending chain. Each peak and valley, however, is higher than the last, and leads to growth in the economy over the long-term, despite the business cycle.

Actual Business Cycle

The actual business cycle for the United States as depicted below has averaged growth of approximately 3.0 percent per year. Growth, as measured by gross domestic product, will exceed the average in some years while in other years growth will be less than the average. Exhibit 2.11 illustrates the actual change in the business cycle as a percentage.

EXHIBIT 2.11: ACTUAL BUSINESS CYCLE
ANNUAL CHANGE IN GDP AND CPI

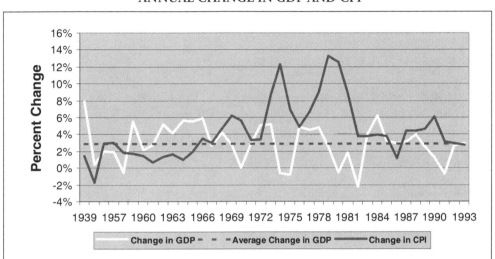

INFLATION

Inflation is another important element affecting the economic environment. Inflation is an increase in price without a simultaneous increase in productivity. Inflation increases the cost of buying a home, durable goods, and consumption goods. For retirees on fixed incomes, substantial increases in inflation can dramatically affect their financial plan. Likewise, for wage earners, the rate of inflation may sometimes be greater than the individual's wage increases, resulting in a real loss of purchasing power. Professional financial planners need to understand how the rate of inflation is calculated, how it affects the economy, and how it is measured.

The opposite of inflation is **deflation**, which occurs when the general level of prices is falling. **Disinflation** is the term used to denote a decline in the rate of inflation. **Moderate inflation** is characterized by slowly rising prices. **Galloping inflation** occurs when money loses its value very quickly and real interest rates can be minus 50 or 100 percent per year. During a period of galloping inflation, people hold only the bare minimum amount of money needed for daily transactions. Financial markets are in turmoil or disappear, and funds are generally allocated by rationing rather than by interest rates. People hoard goods, buy houses, and never lend money at the low nominal interest rate. Remember though, that during periods of inflation, all prices and wages do not increase at the same rate.

inflation - an increase in price without a simultaneous increase in productivity

deflation - the opposite of inflation, deflation occurs when the general level of prices is falling

disinflation - the term used to denote a decline in the rate of inflation

moderate inflation - inflation characterized by slowly rising prices

galloping inflation - inflation that occurs when money loses its value very quickly and when real interest rates can be minus 50 or 100 percent per year

Calculating Inflation

Inflation denotes a rise in the general level of prices. The rate of inflation is the rate of change in the general price level and is calculated as follows:

Rate of inflation (year t):

$$= \frac{\text{Price level (year t)} - \text{Price level (year t-1)}}{\text{Price level (year t-1)}} \times 100$$

The following example will help clarify the calculation of inflation.

EXAMPLE

Last year Rachel paid $20,000 for her college tuition. This year Rachel will pay $21,000 for tuition, with the increase being solely attributable to inflation. Calculate the inflation rate for Rachel's education expense.

Answer:

The inflation rate attributable to Rachel's increase in tuition is 5%. It is calculated as follows.

$$= \frac{21,000 - 20,000}{20,000} \times 100 = 5\%$$

Effects of Inflation

Inflation causes a redistribution of income and wealth among different classes of people in our economy. Changes are created in the relative prices and outputs of different goods, or sometimes in output and employment for the economy as a whole. The major redistributive impact of inflation occurs through its effect on the real value of people's wealth. In general, unanticipated inflation redistributes wealth from creditors to debtors (that is, unanticipated or unforeseen inflation helps those who have previously borrowed money and hurts those who have loaned money). An unanticipated decline in inflation has the opposite effect. If, however, inflation is anticipated, prices adjust to the expectations and there is little redistribution of wealth.

Inflation affects the real economy in two specific areas: total output and economic efficiency. There is no necessary direct relationship between prices and output. Inflation may be associated with either a higher or a lower level of output and employment. Generally, the higher the inflation rate, the greater are the changes in the relative prices of goods. Distortions occur when price changes accelerate relative to changes in costs and demand.

real interest rate adjustment - the rate of interest expressed in dollars of constant value (adjusted for inflation); and equal to the nominal interest rate less the rate of inflation

If inflation persists for a long time, markets begin to adapt, and an allowance for inflation is generally built into the market interest rate, which is known as the **real interest rate adjustment**. This phenomenon is consistent with anticipated price increases.

Measures of Inflation

A **price index** is a weighted average of the prices of numerous goods and services. The most well known price indexes are the consumer price index (CPI), the gross domestic product (GDP) deflator, the gross national product (GNP) deflator, and the producer price index (PPI).

The **Consumer Price Index (CPI)** measures the cost of a "market basket" of 364 items of consumer goods and services, including prices of food, clothing, housing, property taxes, fuels, transportation, medical care, college tuition, and other commodities purchased for day-to-day living. The CPI is constructed by weighting each price according to the economic importance of the commodity in question. Each item is assigned a fixed weight proportional to its relative importance in consumer expenditure budgets as determined by a survey of expenditures covering 1982 through 1984.

The **Gross Domestic Product (GDP)** is the market value of final goods and services produced within a country over a specific time period, usually a year. The GDP deflator is a broader price index than the CPI. In addition to consumer goods, the GDP deflator includes prices for capital goods and other goods and services purchased by businesses and government.

Exhibit 2.12 presents data for both the CPI and GDP deflator. Even though the two indexes are based on different market baskets of goods with different base years, the two measures of the annual rate of inflation are quite similar. The differences between these two measures of inflation have been small, usually only a few tenths of a percentage point per year. The closeness of the two rates is not a surprise because consumer spending makes up about two-thirds of GDP.

price index - a weighted average of the prices of numerous goods and services, for example, the consumer price index, the gross national product deflator, and the producer price index

consumer price index - a price index that measures the cost of a "market basket" of consumer goods and services purchased for day-to-day living

(GDP) - the value of all goods and services produced in the country, GDP is the broadest measure of the general state of the economy

EXHIBIT 2.12: CONSUMER PRICE INDEX AND GDP DEFLATOR

1981-1998

Year	CPI (1982-84 = 100) CPI	Inflation Rate (Percent)	Average Inflation	GDP Deflator (1992=100) GDP Deflator	Inflation Rate (Percent)	Average Inflation
1981	90.90	10.3	3.9	66.1	10.0	3.6
1982	96.50	6.2	3.9	70.2	6.2	3.6
1983	99.60	3.2	3.9	73.2	4.1	3.6
1984	103.90	4.3	3.9	75.9	3.7	3.6
1985	107.60	3.6	3.9	78.6	3.6	3.6
1986	109.60	1.9	3.9	80.6	2.5	3.6
1987	113.60	3.6	3.9	83.1	3.1	3.6
1988	118.30	4.1	3.9	86.1	3.6	3.6
1989	124.00	4.8	3.9	89.7	4.2	3.6
1990	130.70	5.4	3.9	93.6	4.3	3.6
1991	136.20	4.2	3.9	97.3	4.0	3.6
1992	140.30	3.0	3.9	100.0	2.8	3.6
1993	144.50	3.0	3.9	102.6	2.6	3.6
1994	148.20	2.6	3.9	105.1	2.4	3.6
1995	152.40	2.8	3.9	107.5	2.3	3.6
1996	156.90	3.0	3.9	109.5	1.9	3.6
1997	160.50	2.3	3.9	111.6	1.9	3.6
1998	163.00	1.5	3.9	112.7	1.0	3.6

- Price indexes are not problem free. The cost of living, as estimated by the CPI, is considered overestimated in the situation where consumers substitute relatively inexpensive goods for relatively expensive goods. The CPI does not accurately capture changes in the quality of goods. Although the CPI is modified from time to time, the CPI is not corrected for quality improvements in goods and services.

- The GNP deflator is the ratio of nominal gross national product to real gross national product and can be interpreted as the price of all components of GNP (consumption, investment, government purchases, and net exports).

producer price index (PPI) - the oldest continuous statistical series published by the Labor Department that measures the level of prices at the wholesale or producer stage

- The **Producer Price Index (PPI)** is the oldest continuous statistical series published by the Labor Department. It measures the level of prices at the wholesale or producer stage. It is based on approximately 3,400 commodity prices including prices of foods, manufactured products, and mining products.

- For professional planners, the CPI is a good proxy for overall consumer price changes. However, due to the general nature of the market basket of goods described above, it is likely that many clients' inflation experience will be different from the general CPI. Consider the fact that many people have fixed-rate mortgages rather than rent, thus the cost of the housing payment (principal and interest) associated with the mortgage payment is unaffected by inflation. The property taxes and insurance costs on the above home, however, are subject to inflation, as are any mainte-nance or repair costs. Also consider that some households will need to factor in the affect of inflation on their savings plans for their children's education, while other households are rela-tively unaffected by the costs of higher education. The planner with clients on a fixed income can review a line-item budget to determine which costs are subject to inflation and adjust their overall financial plan accordingly. Having listed some of the more dominant ways individuals are affected by inflation, it should be realized that every individual is affected in a consequential way by inflation because they pay for groceries, clothing, automobiles, fuel, and medical care.

MONETARY AND FISCAL POLICY

Monetary policy and fiscal policy exert far-reaching influence on the economic environment. Competent financial planners must identify those changes in monetary and fiscal policy that will be the most beneficial and most detrimental to their client's financial goals and objectives. Once identified, the planner should forecast the likelihood of the important policy changes and adjust the financial plan accordingly.

Monetary Policy

The **Federal Reserve** (Fed) is charged with three primary responsibilities. The first is to maintain sustainable long-term economic growth. The second is to maintain price levels that are sup-ported by that economic growth. The third is to maintain full employment. The Fed goes about its mission primarily using tools of monetary and fiscal policy. The Fed controls the supply of money, which enables it to significantly impact short-term interest rates. The Fed will follow a "loose" or *easy* monetary policy when it wants to increase the money supply, and thus, expand the level of income and employment. In times of inflation and when it wants to constrict the supply of money, the Fed will follow a *tight* monetary policy.

Federal Reserve - the banking and financial system developed under the Federal Reserve Act of 1913 which makes the basic policy decisions that regulate the country's money and banking systems

Easy monetary policy

When the Fed wants to stimulate the money supply, it lowers the cost of short-term loans to commercial banks. The supply of money increases, resulting in the circulation of more money. This leads to more funds available for banks to lend and, ultimately, to a decline in short-term interest rates.

Tight monetary policy

When the Fed wants to tighten the money supply, it raises the price of short-term borrowing for commercial banks. The supply of money is restricted, resulting in less money available for banks to lend. This leads to an increase in short-term interest rates.

reserve requirement - for a member bank of the Federal Reserve, it is the percent of deposit liabilities that must be held in reserve. As the reserve requirement is increased, less money is available to be loaned, resulting in a restriction of the money supply

The Fed has several methods for controlling the money supply, including raising the reserve requirements, raising the Federal Reserve discount rates, and using open market operations.

The **reserve requirement** for a member bank of the Federal Reserve is the percent of deposit lia-bilities that must be held in reserve. As this requirement is increased, less money is available to be loaned to customers resulting in a restriction of the money supply. Conversely, as reserve require-ments are decreased, more money is made available for loans.

Federal Reserve discount rate - the rate at which Federal Reserve member banks can borrow funds to meet reserve requirements. The Fed will lower the discount rate when it wants to increase the money supply

open market operations - the process by which the Federal Reserve purchases and sells government securities in the open market. The Fed buys government securities to cause more money to circulate, thereby, increasing lending and lowering interest rates

fiscal policy - taxation, expenditures, and debt management of the federal government

deficit spending - occurs when governmental expenditures exceed the government's tax collections

The **Federal Reserve discount rate** is the rate at which member banks can borrow funds from the Federal Reserve to meet reserve requirements. When the Fed raises the discount rate, it increases short-term borrowing cost and discourages member banks from borrowing funds. This results in the money supply contracting. The Fed will lower the discount rate when it wants to increase the money supply. Banks are able to borrow funds at lower rates and lend more money, which increases the money supply.

Note: The Federal Reserve discount rate is the borrowing rate from the Federal Reserve. The Federal Funds Rate is the overnight lending rate between member banks.

Open market operations is the process by which the Federal Reserve purchases and sells government securities in the open market. The Fed buys government securities to cause more money to circulate, thereby, increasing lending and lowering interest rates. The Fed sells government securities to restrict the money supply. As investors purchase government securities, more money leaves circulation, which decreases lending and increases interest rates.

FISCAL POLICY

Taxation, expenditures, and debt management of the federal government is called **fiscal policy**. Economic growth, price stability, and full employment are other goals that may be pursued by changes in fiscal policy.

Changes in taxation affect corporate earnings, disposable earnings, and the overall economy. As tax rates increase, corporations' after-tax income declines, which reduces their ability to pay dividends. This may cause the price for equities to decrease. Tax rate increases also reduce individuals' disposable income and limit the amount of money entering the economy. The demand for tax-free investments is also influenced by changes in taxation levels. As increases in proportional tax rates occur, the attractiveness of tax-free instruments also increases, reducing yields.

Deficit spending occurs when governmental expenditures exceed tax collections of the government. By selling debt securities to the public to finance deficits, Treasury Securities compete with other issuers of debt securities. This demand drives the value of debt down due to the increased supply of debt, causing the yields on debt instruments to rise to meet competition.

THE NATURE OF INTEREST RATES

The economic environment is greatly influenced by interest rates. Decreases in interest rates are often followed by periods of economic expansion, while increases are generally followed by economic contractions. Investment returns and purchasing power are only two areas that are affected by the rise and fall of interest rates. Simply stated, the interest rate is the price of money. The discount rate is the interest rate charged by the Fed on a loan that it makes to a member bank. The nominal interest rate measures the yield in dollars per year, per dollar invested. The return on investments in terms of real goods and services is a real interest rate measure. The return in terms of dollars is an absolute measure. The real interest rate measures the quantity of goods we receive tomorrow for goods forgone today. The real interest rate is obtained by correcting nominal or dollar interest rates for the rate of inflation.

EXPANSION AND RECESSION

As discussed earlier, the economy is in a constant state of flux. There are economic factors which tend to expand and those which tend to contract the economy. In the following section, we discuss the factors that contribute to the economy's rise and fall.

Periods of economic expansion are characterized by high employment, high resource demand, and output in excess of the historical gross domestic product average of 3 percent. As the economy expands, real wages rise, as do real interest rates. Higher interest rates decrease capital expenditures, and higher resource costs increase overall costs and reduce aggregate demand ultimately ending the expansionary period. The economy experienced such periods of expansion during the 1960's, and in 1973, 1978, 1983, and 1989.

Periods of recession are characterized by high unemployment, low resource demand, falling real wages, and decreasing real interest rates. The economy eventually pulls itself out of recession as prices for money and resources fall. The economy saw periods of recession in 1970, 1974, 1975, 1979, 1982, 1990, and 1991.

Recall Exhibit 2.9 (the drawing of the Business Cycle) with its peaks and troughs? The peaks are simply the top of the expansion, and the troughs the bottom of the recession. Each is characterized by high and low real interest rates and changes in non-farm hourly payroll, respectively. Real interest rates are at their highest at the peak and at their lowest at the trough. The rate of change in non-farm hourly labor costs is at its highest at peaks and at its lowest in troughs.

A reasonable question to ask at this point is whether the economy is self-correcting. It appears to be so, although slowly. This slowness is evidenced by a recession's prolonged high unemployment and below-capacity utilization. As a result of the belief that the economy is too slow to self-correct, there is widespread support for monetary and fiscal policy stimulation during periods of recession, and, alternatively, for monetary and fiscal restriction during periods of excessive economic expansion. Thus, monetary and fiscal policy tools are used to guide the economy to stability and long-run prosperity. The degree of policy discretion remains controversial. There are economists who believe in less discretion and more constant growth models, including the management of money supply, inflation, unemployment, and budget deficits. Then, there are economists who believe in greater discretion and aggressive monetary and fiscal management.

FORECASTING THE ECONOMY – INDEX OF LEADING ECONOMIC INDICATORS

Can anyone successfully predict the future economy? Some say that monitoring the Gross Domestic Product is useful in forecasting the economy. Others look to the Index of Leading Economic Indicators (the Index). Monitoring both GDP and the Index may be the best approach to forecasting the economy.

Gross Domestic Product (GDP) is the value of all goods and services produced in the country. It is the broadest measure of the general state of the economy. The historical growth rate is about 3 percent. Growth of GDP less than 2 percent is considered low and signals a possible recession. Growth in excess of 4 percent is robust and suggests the possibility of inflation. Monitoring GDP growth is useful in forecasting the peaks and troughs in the economy.

Another indication of future economic activity of which financial planners should be keenly aware is the Index of Leading Economic Indicators. This Index is a composite index of 11 variables. It has had a reasonable track record in predicting recessions, and has accurately predicted every recession since 1950, but has also predicted five that did not happen. When the Index declines for three months in a row, it signals a slowdown in economic growth. The eleven components listed below make up the Index.

Components of the Index of Leading Economic Indicators:

1. Length of average work week in hours
2. Initial weekly claims for unemployment
3. New orders placed with manufacturer
4. Percent of companies receiving slower deliveries from supplier
5. Contracts and orders for new plant and equipment
6. Permits for new housing starts
7. Changes in unfilled orders for durable goods
8. Changes in sensitive material prices
9. Changes in the S&P 500 Index
10. Changes in the money supply (M2)
11. Index of consumer expectations

Although the word "recession" for some investors may have a less-than-positive connotation, generally, in periods of declining economic growth, interest rates fall, making the purchases of fixed instruments prior to the decline in interest rates an attractive investment opportunity. Likewise, generally the best time to buy stocks and hold them through economic recovery may be when the economy is at its worst.

IMPORTANCE OF THE LEGAL ENVIRONMENT

The legal environment is another component of the external environment that may have far-reaching influence on the accomplishment of financial goals and the occurrence of risks. The rules of property ownership; consumer rights and protections; worker rights and protections; investor rights and protections; and the rules regarding formation of a business are established within this environment. With a high level of competence and knowledge of the legal environment, the personal financial planner can guide clients toward their financial goals while avoiding legal risks and protecting the clients' rights.

PROPERTY OWNERSHIP

Property ownership rules are generally state determined and will be discussed in Chapter 20 dealing with estate planning.

CONSUMER PROTECTION

There are arguments for and against consumer protection legislation. In general, the arguments favoring such legislation suggest a necessity to equalize economic power (that is, to protect the so-called "weak" individual from the so-called "powerful" corporation). A second reason given to support such legislation is to protect honest businesses from competition with unscrupulous businesses. The arguments against consumer protection laws question the increased costs of such protection and the inability to measure its effectiveness (no amount of laws will ever overcome consumer ignorance).

Consumer protection laws are passed at both the state and federal levels. Federal laws preempt state laws where the state law provides less protection than the federal law. However, states do have the right to grant their citizens additional protection in excess of federal laws.

Consumer protection laws accomplish their goals by primarily affecting contractual obligations. Without the right to enforce contracts, there would certainly be less private enterprise. Thus, certain consumer protection laws allow for the recission of illegal contracts and provide for monetary damages or injunctive relief for the injured party.

Federal consumer protection began with the creation of the **Federal Trade Commission (FTC)** in 1914. Its charge was to keep competition free and fair and to protect consumers. The FTC promotes competition through the enforcement of antitrust laws. It also assures consumer protection by trade practice regulation prohibiting "unfair or deceptive acts or practices in commerce."

Federal Trade Commission (FTC) - the federal organization created in 1914 to keep competition free and fair and to protect U. S. consumers

EXHIBIT 2.13: THE FTC AND FEDERAL CONSUMER PROTECTION LAWS

LAW	PURPOSE
Fair Packaging and Labeling Act	To prohibit deceptive labeling and require disclosure
Equal Credit Opportunity Act	To prohibit discrimination in granting credit
Fair Credit Reporting Act	To regulate the consumer credit reporting industry
Fair Credit Billing Act	To regulate consumer credit billing practices and rights
Truth in Lending Act	To require disclosure of terms
Magnuson-Moss Warranty Act	To regulate consumer product warranty
Fair Debt Collection Act	To prevent abusive or deceptive debt collection practices
Federal Trade Commission Act	To prohibit unfair and deceptive acts

The FTC also prohibits the unfair and deceptive advertising of prices and practices, such as "bait-and-switch" promotions. Credit and packaging also fall under FTC regulation. Federal credit regulations are a response to the magnitude of credit transactions. The laws include the regulation of credit extension and discrimination, and the collection and dissemination of credit report information. Laws also regulate consumer warranties and debt collection practices. What follows is a brief description of several FTC laws that have a direct effect on consumers.

The *Equal Credit Opportunity Act of 1975* was designed to prohibit discrimination in credit extension. The law prohibits those to whom it applies from discouraging a consumer from seeking credit based on sex, race, religion, marital status, national origin, or because of the receipt of welfare payments.

The *Fair Credit Reporting Act* applies to anyone preparing or using a credit report in connection with extending credit, selling insurance, or hiring or terminating an employee. The purpose of the law is to prevent unjust injury to an individual because of inaccurate or arbitrary information in a credit report. It is also designed to prevent undue invasion of privacy in the collection and dissemination of a person's credit record or information. The law provides consumers with the right to know the reporting agency, to require the agency to reveal the information given in a credit report, and the right to correct incorrect information or explain the consumer's version regarding disputed facts. The act is designed to cover credit-reporting agencies, not individual businesses. A consumer has 60 days to make a written request as to the nature of information received, upon which an adverse credit decision was made. If challenged, the credit agency must investigate and respond to the consumer within 30 days of such challenge.

The *Fair Credit Billing Act* (FCBA) provides a mechanism for consumers to correct credit card billing errors. The consumer provides a written billing complaint to a creditor within 60 days of receiving the alleged erroneous bill. The creditor must acknowledge the complaint within 30 days and explain the alleged error in writing or correct the error within two billing periods not to exceed 90 days.

The *Truth in Lending Act* imposes a duty on those persons regularly extending credit to private individuals to inform those individuals fully as to the cost of the credit, including financial charges and the annual percentage rate of interest (APR). The purpose of the law is to promote informed decisions about the cost and use of credit.

The *Magnuson-Moss Warranty Act* covers express consumer warranties. The terms of the warranty must be simple and in readily understandable language, and if the price of the product is greater than $10, the warranty must be labeled as "full" or "limited."

The *Fair Debt Collections Practice Act* (FDCPA) applies to agencies and individuals whose primary business is the collection of debts for others. The law regulates collectors by prohibiting the collector from physically threatening the debtor or from using obscene language. The collector cannot falsely represent himself as an attorney or threaten the debtor with arrest or garnishment unless the collector can and intends to do so. The collector must disclose that he is a collector and must limit telephone calls to after 8:00 a.m. or before 9:00 p.m. The collector cannot telephone repeatedly with the intent to annoy the debtor. The collector cannot place collect calls to the debtor or use any unfair or unconscionable means to collect the debt.

Federal Bankruptcy Laws

bankruptcy - the financial condition when a debtor is determined by the court to be unable to pay creditors

Consumers and businesses receive further protection from creditors through the federal bankruptcy laws. **Bankruptcy** proceedings are held in a separate federal bankruptcy court with the filing of a voluntary (debtor) or involuntary (creditor-forced) petition. When a debtor is determined by the court to be unable to pay creditors, the court will provide or order relief in either liquidation (also known as "Chapter 7") or adjusted debts ("Chapter 13"). Businesses and the self-employed may also enter bankruptcy under reorganization ("Chapter 11"). Debtor rehabilitation is the main objective of the bankruptcy proceeding allowing the consumer or business entity a "fresh start."

Consumer Protection at the State Level

Certain states have moved to protect citizens from unfair and deceptive acts and practices by enacting legislation that closes gaps in federal law or provides additional protection for consumers under the state law. An example of such state consumer protection is state-ordered "lemon laws" dealing with defective new automobiles. Such legislation creates public and/or private remedies for undesirable activities (illegal activities under the law). Public remedies include injunction, restitution, fines, and revocation of licenses. Private remedies include loss recovery, punitive damages, injunctions, rescission, and redhibition.

Antitrust Legislation

The purpose of **antitrust legislation** is to protect consumers from monopolistic price practices and to protect investors by promoting fair competition. Some of the most important antitrust legislation includes the Sherman Act and the Clayton Act.

antitrust legislation - laws passed to protect consumers from monopolistic price practices and to protect investors by promoting fair competition

The Sherman Act states, "Every contract, combination…or conspiracy in restraint of trade is illegal." It also states, "Every person who shall monopolize or attempt to monopolize shall be guilty of a misdemeanor."

The Clayton Act contains several sections that regulate monopolization, pricing practices, and competition. The following four sections are of particular interest to financial planners.

Section 2 prohibits sellers from discriminating in price between similarly situated buyers of goods (not services) where the effect of such discrimination may be to substantially lessen competition or create a monopoly (Robinson-Patman Act). The objective is to prevent large firms from using predatory pricing practices to drive out small competitors. *Section 3* states that persons engaged in commerce shall not contract, lease, or sell where the effect of such contract, lease, or sale may be to substantially lessen competition or tend to create a monopoly. This legislation deals with tying contracts, exclusive dealing, and requirements contracts. *Section 7* states that corporate mergers are illegal if they tend to create a monopoly in any line of business. *Section 8* prohibits persons from being directors of competing corporations. Once again, the legislation is intended to prohibit a lessening of competition.

The Federal Trade Commission Act

The Federal Trade Commission Act protects consumers through trade practice regulation. It prohibits unfair methods of competition in or affecting commerce or deceptive acts or practices in commerce. It enforces the Clayton Act provisions on price discrimination, tying and exclusive contracts, mergers and acquisitions, and interlocking directories. It is broader in scope than the Sherman Act or the Clayton Act and may be used to curtail activities that prevent fair competition but do not rise to the standard of the Sherman or Clayton Act.

WORKER PROTECTION (EMPLOYER/EMPLOYEE RELATIONS)

Worker protection is another facet of the legal environment. There are two fundamental areas of worker protection: job safety and financial security. The reasons for such protections are the same reasons as for consumer protection, except that they apply specifically to employees.

The Occupational Safety and Health Act (OSHA) ensures safe and healthy working conditions for employees. The Secretary of Labor issues federal standards for healthy and safe employment environments to safeguard employees' health.

Workers Compensation Acts are enacted both at the federal and state level and impose a form of strict liability on employers for accidental injuries occurring in the workplace. The legislation essentially removes the right of the injured employee to sue the employer for acts of ordinary negligence and replaces that right with the right to collect benefits--solely funded by employers-- from an administrative agency. Workers compensation protects against financial losses due to accidental injury, death, or disease resulting from employment. Generally, workman's compensation is the exclusive remedy to employment accidents. However, courts are now carving out exceptions to the so-called "exclusive remedy rule" recognizing that workers compensation laws may not adequately compensate those injured workers with the greatest injuries and for situations that exceed normal negligence on the employer's part.

Other federal programs that offer protection for workers are discussed below.

Unemployment compensation is a federal and state financial security program that provides for temporary payments to workers who, through no fault of their own, become unemployed. Unemployment benefits are funded with a tax on employers based on an extensive rating system.

Social Security is a federal financial security program for providing some replacement income lost due to retirement, disability, and survivorship. Additionally, Social Security provides a death benefit and Medicare benefits, all of which are more thoroughly discussed in Chapter 11.

The *Employee Retirement Income Security Act (ERISA)* was passed to protect the financial security of employees by protecting employee rights in qualified retirement plans. Chapter 19 discusses ERISA and qualified retirement plans.

The *Consolidated Omnibus Budget Reconciliation Act of 1986 (COBRA)* requires that employees and certain dependents of employees be allowed to continue their group health insurance coverage following a qualifying loss of coverage. Chapter 9 contains a discussion of COBRA.

INVESTOR PROTECTION (THE SECURITIES ACTS OF 1933 AND 1934)

The *Securities Acts of 1933 and 1934* were passed to protect investors and to regulate those providing investment services. It is important that all professional financial analysts be familiar with the Securities Acts and the related Acts that followed them.

The Securities Act of 1933 is primarily concerned with new issues of securities or issues in the primary market. It requires that all relevant information on new issues be fully disclosed, requires that new securities are registered with the SEC, requires audited financial statement information within the registration statements, and forbids fraud and deception. When sold, all securities must be accompanied by a prospectus. Small issues (under $1,500,000) and private issues are not required to comply with the Securities Act of 1933 requirements of full disclosure.

While the Securities Act of 1933 was limited to new issues, the 1934 Securities Exchange Act (SEA) extended the regulation to securities sold in the secondary markets. The Act provided the following provisions:

▲ Establishment of the SEC - The SEC's primary function is to regulate the securities markets.
▲ Disclosure requirements for Secondary Market - Annual reports and other financial reports are required to be filed with the SEC prior to listing on the organized exchanges. These reports include the annual 10K Report, which must be audited, and the quarterly 10Q Report, which is not required to be audited.
▲ Registration of organized exchanges - All organized exchanges must register with the SEC and provide copies of their rules and bylaws.
▲ Credit regulation - Congress gave the Federal Reserve Board the power to set margin requirements for credit purchases of securities. Securities dealers' indebtedness was also limited to 20 times their owners' equity capital by this act.
▲ Proxy solicitation - Specific rules governing solicitation of proxies were established.
▲ Exemptions - Securities of federal, state, and local governments, securities that are not traded across state lines, and any other securities specified by the SEC are exempt from registering with the SEC. This includes Treasury bonds and municipal bonds.
▲ Insider activities - A public report, called an insider report, must be filed with the SEC in every month that a change in the holding of a firm's securities occurs for an officer, director, or 10% or more of the shareholders. The 1934 SEA forbids insiders profiting from securities held less than 6 months and requires these profits be returned to the organization. In addition, short sales are not permitted by individuals considered to be insiders.
▲ Price manipulation - The SEA of 1934 forbids price manipulation schemes such as wash sales, pools, circulation of manipulative information, and false and misleading statements about securities.

For a complete discussion on Regulatory Requirements, see Appendix C.

FORMS OF BUSINESS ORGANIZATIONS

Each state's legal environment establishes the forms of business organizations that may be created within that state. This chapter introduces the legal forms of business. A more detailed discussion of business organizations is covered in Chapter 17 – Business Entities.

There are seven legal forms of organization that can be utilized by a business: sole proprietorship, general partnership, limited partnership, limited liability partnership, limited liability company, corporation, and S corporation. A sole proprietorship is a business owned by an individual who is personally liable for the obligations of the business. A general partnership is an association of two or more persons, who jointly control and carry on a business as co-owners for making a profit. The partners are personally liable for the obligations of the business. A limited partnership is an organization in which at least one partner is a general partner and at least one other is a limited partner with limited management participation and limited liability. A limited liability partnership (LLP) is usually a professional partnership (CPAs, attorneys) wherein the partners have limited liability to the extent of investment except where personally liable through malpractice. This form protects the individual assets of the partners who do not malpractice. A limited liability company (LLC) is an entity where the owners, or members, have limited liability for debts and claims of the business even while participating in management. The governing document is called an operating agreement. Some states prohibit single member LLCs. A corporation is a separate legal entity that is created by state law and operates under a common name through its elected management. Owners (shareholders) have limited liability. An S corporation is a corporation with 75 shareholders or less, all individuals, (excluding resident aliens, certain estates and trusts) and no more than one class of stock.

There are several other forms of business organizations:

▲ A joint venture is an association formed to carry out a single transaction or a series of similar transactions that, for tax purposes, is treated the same as a partnership (although no partnership tax return is filed).

▲ A syndicate or investment group contains a number of persons who pool their resources in order to finance a business venture.

▲ A business trust involves a number of people who turn over management and legal title to property to one or more trustees who then distribute the profits to the participants (the beneficiaries of the trust).

▲ A cooperative is an association (may be incorporated) organized in order to provide an economic service to its members (or shareholders).

IMPORTANCE OF THE SOCIAL ENVIRONMENT

A society's culture affects the way a society lives and what it values. Culture changes slowly, but it does change. How does a changing social environment affect a client's financial plan? Financial planners must accurately assess the social environment and forecast the threats and opportunities that change will bring. Some of the characteristics of a changing social environment include:

▲ Advancing population age.
▲ Increasing life expectancy.
▲ Changing customs, norms, values, folkways, and morals.
▲ Shifts in attitudes and motivations.
▲ Dedication to or alienation from traditional religious beliefs.
▲ Evolving global languages.
▲ Acceptance or rejection of traditional status symbols and social institutions.

One likely forecast for the U.S. is the flow of new cultures from around the globe into the workforce. These modern-day settlers bring new customs and cultures to be assimilated into this country. How they interpret the so-called "American Dream" may well determine the country's future social environment.

Statistics show that the U.S. population is aging. At some point in the future, retirees will outnumber active workers. The larger number of retirees will put additional pressure on the finances of the Social Security system. There will be new investment opportunities as our country is faced with the challenges of an aging population with increased life expectancies, geographical mobility, and financial freedom.

IMPORTANCE OF THE TECHNOLOGICAL ENVIRONMENT

Perhaps the most rapidly changing environment is that of technology. Technological advancement has affected our workplace, our homes, and our investment planning. Think back to when there was no Internet, no electronic income tax filing. It will not be long before the majority of tax filers file income tax returns electronically. In the not-to-distant future, the Internet, through large institutions, will provide (perhaps free of charge) basic financial planning of a discrete binary nature to anyone with access to a computer. Such assistance may include income tax preparation; credit assessment and counseling; mortgage qualification; education planning; preparation of basic personal financial statements; determination of investment selection for 401(k) plan contributions; and retirement planning. All of these services and tools will be available to many who did not have them because they could not afford to hire a financial planner. These institutions will offer better, faster, and more complete information. Why will the institutions provide these services, especially free of charge? The answer is to get more assets under management. Assets under management equals fee revenues. Such technology may displace financial planners who are currently providing the same service for persons in the same market niches.

Astute financial planners learn to recognize how the technological environment can best serve them and their clients. Success comes from keeping a constant vigil on the characteristics that make up the technological environment:

- ▲ Current state of technology.
- ▲ Information processing and communication.
- ▲ Production equipment and processes.
- ▲ Medical advances.
- ▲ Creation of new technology.
- ▲ New patents, trademarks, copyrights.
- ▲ Human and business solutions.
- ▲ Biotechnology.
- ▲ Gene identification and cloning.
- ▲ Advances in service and engineering.

IMPORTANCE OF THE POLITICAL ENVIRONMENT

The political environment is especially important to risk analysis in investments. The more stable the political environment, the less the investment risk. To evaluate the political environment of any country, the financial planner should assess a country's:

- ▲ Form of government.
- ▲ Political ideology/stability.
- ▲ Social unrest.
- ▲ Relative strength of opposing political groups and views.
- ▲ Foreign trade policy.
- ▲ Degree of government protectionism regarding foreign goods.

This analysis becomes increasingly important as the world moves to a global economy and investors try to diversify investment portfolios using worldwide investments.

IMPORTANCE OF THE TAXATION ENVIRONMENT

Taxation, in its myriad forms, leaves the taxpayer with less disposable income. In that sense, all taxes, including income taxes, estate transfer taxes, payroll taxes, property taxes, and sales taxes, have a dampening effect on consumer spending and consumption.

Many of the taxes we pay are the result of complex tax laws about which the average taxpayer has little knowledge or understanding. Enter the income tax expert, the transfer tax expert, and even the property tax expert—each offering a specialized knowledge and distinctive expertise.

Some of the taxes we pay are the result of economic choice, some from a lack of understanding of the alternatives. This is especially true in the area of transfer taxes (estate and gift taxes). If people were more keenly aware of the way to avoid transfer taxes, many would. Because of the potential burden of transfer taxes (up to 55 percent), there is a great opportunity to avoid these transfer taxes through competent tax planning.

The changing nature of taxes and tax legislation has the potential to broadly affect large segments of the financial planning community. Consider that in 2001 Congress passed a bill to eliminate death or transfer taxes (effective in 2010). Even though transfer taxes affect only 5 percent of the U.S. population (roughly 13,750,000 out of 275,000,000), those affected are the country's wealthiest. Many of these persons spend substantial amounts to avoid or mitigate the costs of transfer taxes. They spend this money with estate planners, lawyers, CPAs, and insurance professionals because it is cheaper to pay these professionals than to pay the tax. If the transfer tax were eliminated, many of the transaction costs associated with avoiding the transfer tax would also be eliminated. What would happen to the estate-planning bar? What would happen to the insurance professional that sells only multimillion-dollar second-to-die whole life policies? What would happen to the CPA who practices primarily or exclusively in the estate planning area? Perhaps many of the services, products, and devices used to avoid the transfer taxes would disappear.

The tax environment itself is constantly changing. It is common for Congress to write new tax laws as frequently as annually. If a professional financial planner is to assist clients in minimizing their legal taxes, thus giving them more disposable income for consumption, savings, and investments, the planner must have a basic education in taxation and must develop ways to remain currently competent in the field.

(Chapters 16 and 17 - Income Tax, Chapters 18 and 19 - Retirement, and Chapters 20 and 21 - Estates, introduce the environment of taxation.)

PROFESSIONAL

FOCUS

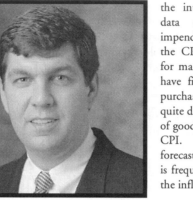

When analyzing the External Environment for a client, which economic indicators do you find most effective and why (Interest rates, the inflation rate, the unemployment rate, the Index of Leading Economic Indicators, others)?
Interest rates are very important to my clients and to myself. I regularly monitor the CPI, the T-bill rate, the treasury bond rate, and mortgage rates. I use the CPI information in educational funding and capital needs analysis. I use the treasury rates in selecting investments and as a benchmark for the riskless rate in the CAPM model. I use the mortgage rates to assist clients in making sound decisions regarding the purchasing or refinancing of personal residences.

Do your clients understand the impact of inflation on their overall financial planning goals? Explain.
Clients only have a vague understanding of the impact of inflation on their financial plans. Of course, the impact of inflation is greater with a longer time horizon. Clients have a good understanding of short term inflation as measured by the CPI. The financial planning decisions which are most affected by inflation are those in the long term such as the college education and retirement needs analysis decisions. For those decisions, we carefully plan using an inflation adjusted earnings rate concept. We further perform sensitivity analysis and quarterly or annually review, monitor, and update forecasts and plans.

What method do you use to forecast inflation and how does inflation affect your clients' financial plans?
My first step in forecasting inflation is to use a historical trend line of inflation. Next, I correlate the GDP growth trend line to the inflation trend line. In addition, I monitor

the interest rates and employment data as possible predictors of impending inflation. I believe that the CPI slightly overstates inflation for many of my clients because they have fixed rate mortgages and they purchase goods and service that are quite different from the market basket of goods and service that make up the CPI. However, it is difficult to forecast inflation. What we try to do is frequently review plans and update the inflation assumptions as necessary.

How important to your practice are Consumer Protection Laws, including credit rehabilitation and bankruptcy laws?
I am surprised how many clients have credit problems and have little or no understanding of their rights under the various federal and state consumer protection laws. We see people with errors on their credit reports who do not know how to correct them. This problem is compounded by the prevalence of credit card losses, fraud, and now internet fraud. In order to stay abreast of these issues, we participate in rigorous and thorough continuing education courses. We suspect that credit reporting is getting more and more efficient, less personal, and less forgiving while some clients still behave as if it's all right to pay a little late. "Oh I forgot" and "I'm sorry" have less influence these days then they used to with creditors.

JOHN OHLE III, JD, MBA, CPA/PFS, CFP™

DISCUSSION QUESTIONS

1. How do the external and internal environments in which financial planning occurs differ?
2. How does each external environmental factor link to the different areas of financial planning?
3. What are some examples of how each external environmental factor might affect clients from different economic levels?
4. Why is external environmental analysis so important?
5. How is the external environment analyzed?
6. Why is the economic environment so important to financial planning?
7. What is price elasticity?
8. What is unit elastic demand?
9. What is marginal utility?
10. What is diminishing marginal utility?
11. How do interest rates, taxes, and inflation affect areas of financial planning?
12. What are the components of the business cycle and how do they affect the economy?
13. What is the formula for the rate of inflation?
14. What are the Consumer Price Index, the Gross National Product deflator, and the Producer Price Index?
15. What is monetary policy?
16. What is fiscal policy?
17. What are the Federal Reserves' three economic goals?
18. What is the index of leading economic indicators?
19. What is the index of leading economic indicators used for?
20. How good is the index of leading economic indicators as a predictor?
21. What are five of the components of the index of leading economic indicators?
22. List some examples of Federal Consumer Protection Laws.
23. What are some examples of federal programs that offer protection for workers on the job-site?
24. Identify two federal securities acts that protect investors.
25. How do the external environmental factors—social, technological, political, and taxation—affect a client's financial plan?

EXERCISES

1. Define the Laws of Supply and Demand.
2. What does it mean if the demand for a product is inelastic?
3. If the Federal Reserve wanted to lower interest rates, what would it need to consider?
4. What is the adjustment process in a competitive market and how does it shift?
5. What happens in the marketplace when a decrease, or shift to the left, in the supply curve occurs?
6. Describe what has occurred when the price of a particular product decreases and consumers buy more of that product.
7. Consumer demand for sugar at 80 cents per pound results in $1,000 in company revenue. A drop in sugar price to 50 cents per pound results in $1,250 in revenue. Is the demand for sugar inelastic, elastic, or unit elastic?
8. If a substitute good is readily available for a product, is the product demand likely to be elastic or inelastic?

9. Give an example illustrating the law of downward-sloping demand.
10. An increase in the price of a product A causes a decrease in the demand for product B. What are the two products?
11. Explain the principle of diminishing marginal utility.
12. Describe reasons for a change in consumer demand.
13. Which of the following might cause an increase in supply?
    ▲ A decrease in productivity.
    ▲ Fewer sellers in the marketplace.
    ▲ More efficient technology.
    ▲ A decrease in government subsidies.
14. Identify several determinants of demand elasticity.
15. If the quantity supplied does not change significantly with a change in price, is the type of supply elastic or inelastic?
16. Define inflation.
17. How would someone living on a fixed income be affected by inflation?
18. If you have a product with an inelastic demand, which of the following is true?
    ▲ As the price increases, revenue decreases.
    ▲ As the price increases, revenue increases.
    ▲ There is no relationship between price and revenues.
19. When the economy is slowing and unemployment is increasing, what phase of the business cycle are we in?
20. Which of the following economic activities represent examples of monetary policy?
    ▲ The federal funds rate is increased.
    ▲ The Federal Reserve lowers bank reserve requirements.
    ▲ The Federal Open Market Committee sells securities.
21. What action taken by the Fed will lead to increased money supply?
22. Identify the phases and points of a typical business cycle.
23. In a typical business cycle, which phases exhibit periods of increasing employment and increasing output?

PROBLEMS

1. Identify whether each of the following involves a shift in the demand curve or a change in the quantity demanded:
    ▲ Fish prices fall after the Pope allows Catholics to eat meat on Friday.
    ▲ Auto sales decrease due to increased unemployment.
    ▲ Gasoline consumption increases as some of the taxes on gasoline are lowered.
    ▲ After a drought hits Louisiana, crawfish sales decrease.
2. If the cost of one year of college education on January 1 of 1999, 2000, and 2001 are $15,000, $16,000, and $17,500, respectively, what was the rate of education inflation for 1999 and 2000? What was the annualized education inflation rate from 1999 to year 2001?

CHAPTER 3

Communication and Internal Analysis

LEARNING OBJECTIVES:

After learning the material in this chapter, you will be able to:

1. Explain how a financial planner can successfully communicate respect, trust, and empathy to a client.

2. List several techniques that reduce the risk of misinterpretation and misunderstanding when communicating with a client.

3. List the four phases of thinking through which a client often progresses in the financial planning process.

4. Describe the Auditory Learning Style, the Visual Learning Style, and the Kinetic or Tactile Learning Style by discussing how a client with each style prefers to learn.

5. Identify the five categories that make up a client's internal environment.

6. List the factors that make up Lifecycle Positioning.

7. Name the Lifecycle Phases through which most financial planning clients eventually pass.

8. Explain how a client's tolerance for risk; savings and consumption habits; views about working, retirement, and leisure time; and attitudes on government (especially taxation) affects the setting of their financial goals.

9. Identify "special needs" that may influence the successful development of a client's financial plan.

10. Identify the financial statements and other information needed to develop an accurate assessment of a client's financial position.

11. Explain how a client's subjective perception of financial position affects the objective reality of financial position provided by a financial planner.

COMMUNICATION SKILLS

The importance of a good working relationship between the personal financial planner and the client cannot be overemphasized. The relationship requires excellent interpersonal skills, proficient communication skills, and the ability to educate. As indicated in the Planner's Pyramid of Required Knowledge, these skills are essential to achieving the pinnacle of implementing a successful financial plan. More specifically, they are required to efficiently gather accurate information from the client and to educate the client throughout the financial planning process. Without a good working relationship, the client is less willing to share information and more resistant to advice provided by the planner. A good relationship is one in which all persons involved feel as though they are treated with respect, trust, and empathy.

EXHIBIT 3.1: FINANCIAL PLANNER'S PYRAMID OF KNOWLEDGE

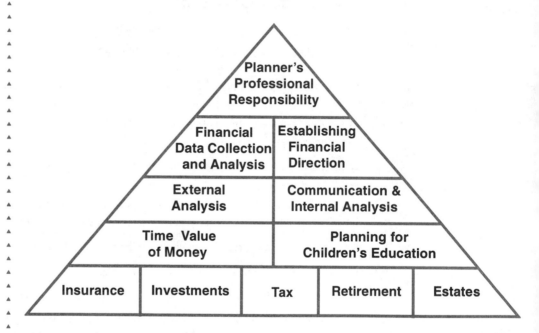

BE RESPECTFUL OF YOUR CLIENT

Respect can be conveyed in several ways. One obvious way is the manner in which the client is addressed. When first meeting a client, they should be addressed with a courteous title such as Mr., Ms., Dr., etc. If later, the client indicates a preference to be called by their first name or some other nickname, that desire should be met. Listening to the client, not talking over them, and showing value for their time also portrays respect. Always return phone calls when you say you will. Be on time for appointments. Let the client know how long a meeting is expected to last. If you are exceeding the time, ask if the meeting should continue or be rescheduled for another time. These issues may seem elementary, but being mindful of them will assist in developing a professional relationship with the client.

Trust must be developed between planner and client. Trust has to be earned, but the process is expedited by showing evidence that others deem you trustworthy. Provide prospective clients with letters of reference from previous clients, especially those that cite specific examples of how the client benefited from your skills. Care must be taken to maintain the duty of confidentiality. The client needs to know that any information they share with you will remain strictly confidential. Therefore, if specific client examples are provided, make sure the client knows that the other client's permission was received prior to any disclosure.

Respect is shown by being empathetic and viewing the client as an individual. Empathy is the identification with and understanding of another's situations, feelings, and motives. Remember, financial success is a relative concept. The client defines success subjectively. The client's definition is based on personal situations, feelings, and motives. The financial planner needs to understand the client's perspective of things and show regard for those views and values.

COMMUNICATE WITH YOUR CLIENT

A good relationship cannot be developed with the client without first mastering communication skills. Communications between the financial planner and client are difficult because of subjectivity, paradigms, and unspoken words that lead to misinterpretation and misunderstanding.

For example, suppose the client states that they want to take at least one nice vacation each year. The keen financial planner might ask them to provide an example of where they might want to go on vacation. Suppose the client states they want to vacation in the Caribbean. The planner may now believe that enough information has been gathered to include this objective into the financial plan. However, enough information has probably not been gathered. It might be assumed the client intends to vacation for one week, because that is the norm in the United States. However, the client may follow the vacation norm for Argentina and vacation for a month at a time. Additionally, it is not known how the client plans to travel. Are they going to fly? If so, do they plan to fly first class or coach? In what type of accommodations do they plan to stay? As you can see, by attributing the standards of the financial planner or by assuming the client's standards, the goal of taking one nice vacation a year is easily misinterpreted. This misinterpretation may lead to inappropriate financial planning.

Use Communication Techniques

Fortunately, there are several communication techniques that can greatly reduce the chance of misinterpretation and misunderstanding. Below are a few of the techniques that the financial planner should use when speaking with a client.

Keep the client informed. Tell the client what will happen, what is happening as it happens, and what has happened when it is completed. Although you may be very experienced in the financial planning process the client is not. Consider the client's perspective. If they do not know what to expect, they will probably be a little apprehensive. If they are not informed of the significance of particular questions, they may be resistant to answer them or only provide partial information and answers.

Clarify statements and remove ambiguity. Avoid general statements by using clarification techniques such as restating, paraphrasing, and summarizing. Apply the ideas of "Is" and "Is Not." For example, in describing the purpose of property insurance, you may state that property insurance is intended to help minimize loss in the event of a disaster. It is not intended to eliminate loss in the event of a disaster.

Seek information to understand the client's situation and goals. Use open-ended questions to draw out relevant information. Do not make assumptions. Question everything. Question the answers to the questions. When the client can no longer generate an answer, all the information the client has may be known. However, that does not mean the planner has all the relevant information necessary. It may be necessary to obtain information from other sources.

Be specific. When communicating with the client, identify the "What, Where, When, and Extent" to describe a task or a result. Avoid the use of slang and colloquialisms. Articulate goals in terms of time, place, and form. A financial plan is useless if it cannot be accurately and precisely communicated to the client.

The Engagement Letter

An **engagement letter** is a useful tool in communicating with your client. An engagement letter is written near the beginning of the client/planner relationship, usually following the first meeting. The letter should summarize and memorialize the previous meetings and conversations with the client. The letter should also contain information about any agreements or understandings that were obtained during previous meetings including, the plan of action for developing a financial plan, the expected outcome of the engagement, and the method and amounts of compensation. Exhibit 3.2 illustrates a sample engagement letter.

engagement letter - a tool of communication between client and financial planner that sets down in writing information about any agreements or understandings obtained at client/planner meetings including the plan of action for developing a financial plan, the expected outcome of the engagement, and the method of compensation

EXHIBIT 3.2: SAMPLE ENGAGEMENT LETTER

(Date)

(Name of Client)
(Address of Client)

Dear (Name of Client):

Thank you for meeting with me on *(date)*. Per our discussions, I understand your goals are as follows:
1. *(list goal)*
2. *(list goal)*
3. *(list goal)*

This letter sets forth our understanding of the terms and objectives of our engagement to provide personal financial planning services to you. The scope and nature of the services to be provided are as follows:

1. **Review and Evaluation**
    We will review and analyze all information furnished to us including:
    (list items)

2. **Written Plan**
    Based on our review and analysis, we will prepare a written analysis of your:
    (list items)

    We will also prepare, in writing, specific initial recommendations to address your concerns and issues, including goals, objectives, and risks with respect to:
    (list items)

    Our recommendations will include strategies based on our analysis of your circumstances. Where appropriate, we will include financial illustrations and financial projections to enhance your understanding of the potential outcomes of the alternatives.

    We will meet with you to discuss our analysis and will provide you with a preliminary draft copy of our recommended strategies. You will be given an opportunity to concur with the preliminary recommendations or suggest modifications. Following agreement on your personal financial goals and the strategies to be used to achieve them, we will provide you with a finalized version of the plan.

3. **Fees**
    Our fee for these services is based on our standard hourly rates and the number of hours required. We expect our fees to be no less than $_____ but not to exceed $_____. We will bill you beginning with our next regular billing cycle. The final payment will be adjusted to reflect actual time expended, not to exceed the maximum total amount quoted for the year, and will be due upon completion of the engagement.

4. **Implementation**
    We will assist you in implementing the strategies that have been agreed upon. Accordingly, we will be available on an ongoing basis, by telephone or in person, to answer questions, to assist you or your other advisors to take necessary actions, and to make recommendations regarding these matters. We will bill you for these additional services based on time expended at our standard hourly rate.

5. **Limitation on Scope of Services**

    These services are not intended to include:
    (list items)

We will bill separately for any such additional services provided, based on time expended at our standard hourly rates.

If this letter correctly sets forth your understanding of the terms and objectives of the engagement, please so indicate by signing in the space provided below.

Respectfully yours,

(Name of Planner)
(Name of Firm)

The above letter sets forth my understanding of the terms and objectives of the engagement to provide personal financial planning services.

Signed: _____   Date: _____

EDUCATE YOUR CLIENT

A significant role of a personal financial planner is to educate the client. The client may need to be taught the meaning of common financial planning terminology, such as the time value of money and opportunity costs. The professional financial planner should be an expert in the use of time value of money to be able to assist clients in putting financial choices into a logical, systematic, and quantifiable framework. For most clients, the most understandable time reference is today. The planner may project that the client will need one million dollars at age 62 to quit working (achieve financial independence) and continue to maintain the same preretirement lifestyle. If the client is currently 35 years old, the million dollars and the 27 years until the client will need the money may have little relevance. The planner can create relevance and understanding, however, by calculating the need in today's dollars. In this example, the million dollars is equal to $125,000 in invested assets or, alternatively, if the client has no investments, $731.25 will need to be saved each month. (This calculation was determined by assuming 324 months of saving $731.25 at an earnings rate of 9 percent per year to accumulate the million dollars at age 62.) The reality of the $125,000 or the $731.25 each month is much more meaningful to the client than the distant million dollars. People have a much better understanding of today's realities and values than those in the future.

Clients may need education during the development of goals and objectives or the selection and implementation of the financial strategy. Undoubtedly, clients will need to be educated on many aspects of the financial planning process throughout the relationship. Therefore, it is beneficial for the planner to understand how individuals learn. Learning is made easier, and is more effective, when people are taught in a manner conducive to their learning style. People who learn best by listening prefer the auditory learning style. Those who prefer to learn by seeing are "visual" learners. Kinetic or tactile learners learn best by "doing." Most likely, clients will not know their preferred **learning style**. Exhibit 3.3 may help you gain a better understanding of a client's learning style:

learning styles (auditory, visual, kinetic or tactile) - the conditions under which people learn best—clients whose preferred learning style is auditory, learn best by hearing information; clients who prefer a visual learning style, learn best by reading and viewing; those who prefer a kinetic or tactile style, learn best through manipulation and testing information

EXHIBIT 3.3: DETERMINING LEARNING STYLES

If your client...	Their learning style is most likely ...	They should be educated by...
Talks about situations; expresses emotions verbally; enjoys listening, but cannot wait to talk; tends to move lips or sub-vocalize when reading.	Auditory	Providing verbal instruction and repeating yourself often.
Seems to enjoy watching demonstrations; has intense concentration and ability to visually imagine information; writes things down and takes detailed notes; doodles and looks around studying the environment; often becomes impatient when extensive listening is involved.	Visual	Providing them with written information, especially with charts, graphs, and pictures. They learn best by studying alone.
Fidgets when reading; is easily distracted when not able to move; expresses emotions physically by jumping and gesturing; does not listen well and tries things out by touching, feeling, and manipulating; needs frequent breaks during meetings.	Kinetic or Tactile	Providing them with exercises or assignments to perform. They learn best by manipulating and testing information.

UNDERSTAND THE CLIENT'S THINKING PHASE

The financial planner should be aware that the financial planning process can be both comforting and confusing to a client: comforting because action is being taken to accomplish goals; confusing because this is usually when the client realizes the magnitude of the planning choices and decisions required. It is the responsibility of the planner to assist the client throughout this process and provide education and reassurance when necessary. Exhibit 3.4 depicts the common phases of thinking through which a client often progresses while establishing a financial plan. The objective is for the client to achieve the high cognitive thinking phase. The financial planner should be knowledgeable about these common phases of thinking and assist the client in progressing through them while establishing financial direction. The planner should help the client transition from the outer edge of the circle to the inner circle in Exhibit 3.4.

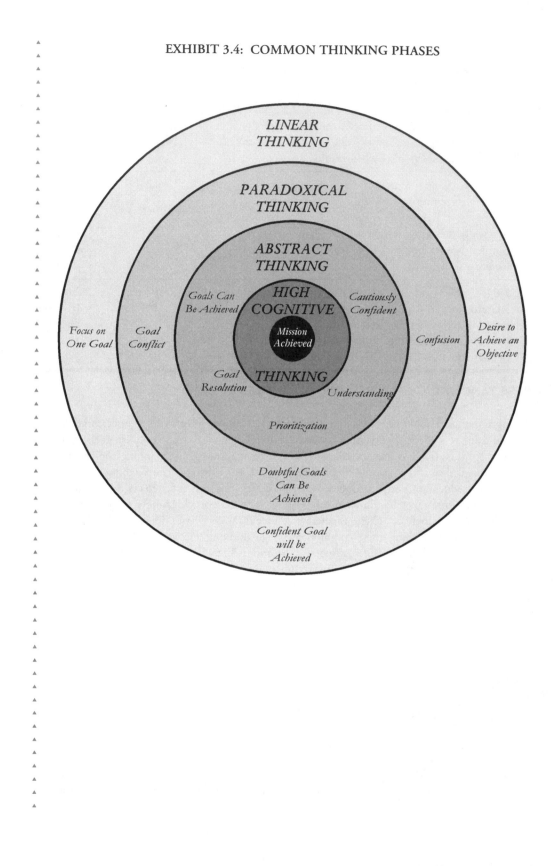

Linear Thinking

Generally, individuals who are just beginning to plan financially are in the outer phase of thinking, referred to as linear thinking. Focusing on accomplishing a particular goal or objective describes the concept of linear thinking. During this phase, an individual's financial plan is very compartmentalized and simplistic. The primary interest is in achieving one or two narrow objectives. Confidence that objectives can and will be achieved is high. However, once the individual begins to face the reality that saving for one objective means forgoing funds in another area, because funds are limited, confidence in their ability to achieve overall goals is often questioned and the person may give up. During this phase, the client may increase savings and/or set up a special savings account to save for something they desire only to find that they need to use the funds for day-to-day or unexpected expenses. Due to the frequent failure to achieve all goals, clients frequently give up the idea of developing a financial plan. However, if they are successful in the linear phase, the client's thinking usually changes from linear to paradoxical.

Paradoxical Thinking

During this phase, the client begins to focus on several simultaneous objectives. As a result, it is during this phase in particular that people become frustrated. They may become overwhelmed with the amount of financial planning required and discover that many of their objectives are in conflict with each other. They often become uncertain of their ability to financially accomplish any of their objectives. Confusion, goal conflict, and ambiguity characterize the paradoxical thinking phase. It is often during this phase of thinking when an individual seeks the advice of a financial planner. The financial planner can be of great comfort to the client during this phase by assuring them that goal conflict and confusion are common and can be overcome by good planning.

Abstract Thinking

The skilled financial planner can assist a client in advancing from paradoxical thinking to abstract thinking by providing education and encouragement. During the abstract thinking phase, clients begin to integrate elements of the financial plan into their day-to-day lives. They become aware of the consequences of their financial actions and can conceptually understand how savings and consumption decisions impact their financial plan. At this point, it is common for clients to become confident that identified goals and objectives can be achieved.

High Cognitive Thinking

The ultimate phase of development is the high cognitive thinking phase. The client becomes enlightened about financial issues as they exist in their everyday life. Once this phase is achieved, clients have a great amount of control over their financial future. They are able to successfully integrate their entire financial plan into the other aspects of their lives. During this phase, the mission of achieving financial independence and avoiding catastrophic financial occurrences and thus financial dependence is most likely achieved.

The personal financial planner greatly increases the probability of developing an appropriate financial strategy and having it properly implemented if a good relationship with the client is established, communication skills are practiced, the client's preferred learning style is identified, and the financial planner understands the client's current phase of thinking.

INTERNAL ANALYSIS

The internal environment defines the way people live, work, spend, save, and think. Internal data about the client is needed to understand the environment in which the individual exists and the strengths and weaknesses that are present. Once a good working relationship is developed with the client, and communication lines are open, it is easy to collect most of the internal data that is needed. The key is to know what information to collect and how to collect it efficiently and accurately. Internal data can be divided into five general categories, which include the client's:

▲ Lifecycle positioning.
▲ Attitudes and beliefs.
▲ Special needs.
▲ Financial position.
▲ Perception of their financial situation.

LIFECYCLE POSITIONING

lifecycle positioning - information about a client's age, marital status, dependents, income level, and net worth

Lifecycle positioning information is needed because it plays a significant role in affecting the goals and behaviors of individuals. It also suggests which financial risks currently exist. In order to identify the client's lifecycle positioning, the planner needs to have information about the client's:

▲ Age.
▲ Marital status.
▲ Dependents.
▲ Income level.
▲ Net worth.

Age

Age is one of the most important and revealing factors in financial planning. Generally, young persons give little thought or consideration to retirement goals or wealth-transfer goals. As people age, they become aware that adequate retirement income requires funding. At some time, they begin to seriously plan for this financial goal. In the recent past, it was common for persons to become conscious about their "retirement reality" as late as age 40, or even age 50. Today, it seems that clients are beginning to become more aware of this issue at a much younger age. Perhaps this phenomenon is due to the increased amount of readily available information on the cost of retirement and the necessity to plan early.

Marital Status

The second factor that affects goal determination is marital status. The desire to provide for one's dependents creates a host of goals to achieve and risks to avoid. It is common for married persons to combine their future economic resources to jointly purchase assets like a house by jointly committing to indebtedness. The purchase of a personal residence through indebtedness, which can only be afforded by combining both incomes, creates an interdependency of one spouse to the other. In the event one spouse were to suffer unemployment, untimely death, disability, or some other catastrophic event, the commitment to the repayment of the debt may not be met. Marital status is a signal to the financial planner that the client may have someone other than themselves to protect, and therefore a need to protect their income stream.

Dependents

A third factor affecting the creation of goals is dependents and their ages. Dependents may be children, grandchildren, or elderly parents. Persons with children quite commonly have goals of providing education for their children. Education can be an expensive goal that requires substantial expenditures made over a finite period. For example, the cost of a college education at some private universities in the U.S. is currently $30,000 per year. If we assume two children and four years in college, the current total cost of such an education would be $240,000. Whatever the cost, it is probably a substantial amount on a relative basis, for most 40-year-old clients to take on. Even public university education is currently about $25,000 for each student for four years. Not all persons feel obligated to provide their children with a college education. However, many parents do, and many more wish they were able to do so.

Grandchildren may also be considered as a factor of dependency. A person may have grandchildren as early as in their 30's but more commonly in their 50's or older. The significance of grandchildren as a factor is not that they are actual dependents, but rather that grandchildren may signal the initial phase of wealth transfer. Grandparents may find themselves with more assets and income than they feel necessary to sustain their lifestyle. They may then begin to provide financially for their grandchildren.

Other examples of dependencies, which affect goals, are caring for an aging parent, or providing special care to a handicapped person. It is important for the planner to realize that not only married persons with children have dependents. Single childless persons may have financial dependents by taking on the obligations of aging parents or other loved ones.

Income and Net Worth

Income and net worth are the last two factors concerning lifecycle positioning. Substantial income suggests an opportunity to achieve financial goals as long as the goals are realistic relative to the income. Lower income presents greater challenges in achieving financial security and financial independence. Persons with a low income and low net worth generally have a more difficult time overcoming financial setbacks. Whereas, a person with substantial net worth is generally less likely to suffer catastrophic consequences as a result of a single financial setback. Substantial net worth also implies a need for increased management of assets and planning. Generally, the greater the income or net worth the greater the interest in tax deferral or avoidance.

lifecycle phase - an interval in a client's lifecycle that tends to give a planner insight into the client's financial objectives and concerns—the Asset Accumulation phase, the Conservation/Protection phase, the Distribution/Gifting phase

Lifecycle Phases and Characteristics

As people progress through their lives, there is a tendency to move subtly but surely among financial objectives due to changes in personal financial circumstances. We have identified and labeled these **lifecycle phases** and characteristics as the Asset Accumulation Phase, the Conservation/Protection Phase, and the Distribution/Gifting Phase. While not all people move through these phases at the same rate, a sufficient percent of people do, so that financial planners can gain valuable insight into their client's objectives and concerns by identifying which phase or phases their client is in at a particular point in time. Exhibit 3.5 illustrates the lifecycle phases and the typical characteristics of each phase.

EXHIBIT 3.5: LIFECYCLE PHASES AND CHARACTERISTICS

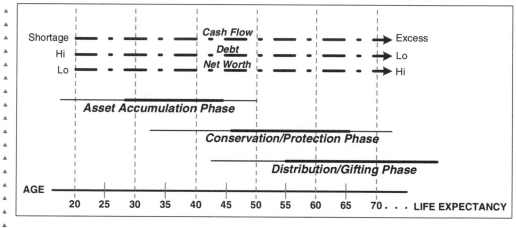

Asset Accumulation

The **Asset Accumulation Phase** is described as beginning somewhere between the ages of 20 and 25 and lasting until somewhere around age 50 for many persons. The beginning of the phase is characterized by limited excess cash flow for investing, a relatively high degree of debt to net worth, and a low net worth. At the beginning of the phase, there generally is a low appreciation for the risks that exist. As the person moves through the Asset Accumulation Phase, cash for investments generally increases, there is less use of debt as a percent of total assets, and there is an increase in net worth.

asset accumulation phase - lifecycle phase through which clients pass usually beginning somewhere between the ages of 20 and 25 and lasting until somewhere around age 50 for many persons, characterized by limited excess funds for investing, high degree of debt-to-net worth, and low net worth

Conservation/Protection

The **Conservation/Protection Phase** begins when one has acquired some assets, usually in late 30s or 40s and may last throughout the work life expectancy, and depending on the nature of the person, may last all the way to life expectancy. It is characterized by an increase in cash flow, assets, and net worth with some decrease in the proportional use of debt. People generally become more risk averse as they acquire more assets. From an investments viewpoint, they are more concerned about losing what they have acquired than acquiring more. They become aware and concerned with many of the risks they ignored at the beginning of the Asset Accumulation Phase, including an increased awareness of life's risks (untimely death, unemployment, disability, etc.). This is not to say that they have completely left the Asset Accumulation Phase. At least at

conservation/protection phase - lifecycle phase through which clients pass characterized by an increase in cash flow, assets, and net worth with some decrease in the proportional use of debt

the beginning, they are simultaneously in both phases (trying to accumulate, while trying not to lose what they have).

Making payments for children's education and saving for retirement frequently characterize the Conservation/Protection Phase. This phase is where the real struggle between current-consumption needs and deferred-consumption necessities is waged. It is also during this period when the client is most financially confused because of the conflicting goals and perceived risks. It is during this phase that one of the greatest opportunities exists for the professional financial planner to assist the client.

Distribution/Gifting

The **Distribution/Gifting Phase** begins subtly when the person realizes that they can afford to spend on things they never believed possible. The Asset Accumulation and Conservation/Protection Phases make this phase possible. It is quite common that at the beginning of this phase the person is also simultaneously in both the Asset Accumulation and Conservation/Protection Phases. (Yes, there is a period for many people when they are being influenced by all three phases simultaneously, although not necessarily to the same degree.) When parents purchase new cars for adult children, pay for a grandchild's private school tuition, or take themselves on expensive vacations relative to their tradition, they are signaling that they are likely to be in the Distribution/Gifting Phase.

The Distribution/Gifting Phase may begin as early as the late 40s and continue to life expectancy. Excess relative cash flows, low debt, and high relative net worth characterize this phase. It is at the beginning of the phase when the client begins to feel the financial pressure declining, starts to believe life is short and should be enjoyed, and material things matter less. Now clients start asking, Where did yesterday go? It is also during this period that life's risks are put into better perspective. Frequently, during this phase life insurance is dropped, deductibles are raised, and the client achieves more financial balance and confidence.

It is common for people to be in two or more lifecycle phases simultaneously, although not necessarily to the same degree. By determining where the client is in terms of these phases, we can gain some insight as to the person's financial goals, concerns, and behaviors, which will help to better serve the client.

Throughout the text, we will refer to whether the client, in a specific application, is predominately in the Asset Accumulation, Conservation/Protection, or Distribution/Gifting Phase or some combination. We do so to put the client's goals and risks into perspective and to gain insight into appropriate financial planning solutions.

Once lifecycle positioning is known, and assuming the planner has an understanding of the lifecycle phases and characteristics, the experienced financial planner can begin to develop a generic financial plan that would meet many clients' needs who have similar lifecycle positioning. Exhibit 3.6 illustrates some generalized lifecycle positions and the likely goals and risks associated with each. Remember, however, these are only generalizations. Although enough information has been obtained to provide a framework with which to begin developing a client's financial plan, much more information is required before an accurate financial plan can be developed for a particular individual.

distribution/gifting phase - lifecycle phase through which clients pass characterized by excess relative cash flows, low debt, and high relative net worth

EXHIBIT 3.6: SELECTED LIFECYCLE POSITIONS AND RELATED GOALS/RISKS

Lifecycle Positioning	Phase	Common Goals	Risks					
			L	H	D	LTC	P	LB
25–35-year-old single (S/25-35); modest income/net worth	AAP	Savings; investment; wealth accumulation; personal residence; debt management	✘	✔	✔	✘	✔	✔
25–35-year-old married with small dependent children (MWC/25-35); moderate income/net worth	AAP	Educational funding; savings; investment; wealth accumulation; personal residence; debt management	✔	✔	✔	✘	✔	✔
40-50-year-old divorced with dependent children	AAP, CPP	Retirement planning; educational funding; savings; investment; wealth accumulation; debt management	✔	✔	✔	✘	✔	✔
40-50-year-old married with dependent children	AAP, CPP	Retirement planning; educational funding; savings; investment; wealth accumulation; debt management	✔	✔	✔	✘	✔	✔
62-68-year-old retired and married with adult children and grandchildren	CPP, DGP	Estate planning	✘	✔	✘	?	?	✔

Key:
L = Life   H = Health   D = Disability   LTC = Long-Term Care   P = Property   LB = Liability
✔ = The risk is likely   ✘ = The risk is not likely   ? = The risk is possible
AAP = Asset Accumulation Phase   CPP = Conservation/Protection Phase   DGP = Distribution/Gifting Phase

Lifecycle positioning is the easiest type of internal data to collect. It is easy to collect because it is objective and therefore, not skewed by subjectivity. It is information that the client is most comfortable providing because it is not too personal and the client probably expects to be asked such questions. This information may be gathered during a face-to-face meeting, a telephone meeting, or by using a **Client Data Collection Questionnaire** similar to the one in the Appendix at the end of the chapter.

ATTITUDES AND BELIEFS

The second type of internal data identifies the client's attitudes and beliefs. Attitudes and beliefs are important because they play a significant role in affecting the goals and behaviors of individuals. Information that should be gathered includes the client's:

▲ Risk tolerance levels.
▲ Savings and consumption habits.
▲ Views about working, retirement, and leisure time.
▲ Attitude regarding government, especially taxation.

Risk Tolerance Levels

Knowledge of **risk tolerance** levels is needed to assist the financial planner in determining the types of investments and the style of risk management best suited for the client. The style of risk management refers to the issue of self-insuring reasonable risks versus over insuring in an attempt to mitigate or prevent even small losses. Risk management is the choice of balancing lower premiums with self-reliance for smaller losses, or alternatively, higher premiums with less loss exposure. However, risk tolerance levels may be misinterpreted because they are subjective. The statement, "I am not very risk tolerant," may mean something different to each client. Therefore, additional questioning is needed to ensure understanding. Implementing the communication techniques discussed earlier can assist the planner to gain an understanding of the client. The Client Data Collection Questionnaire can also assist in gathering information about the client's risk tolerance level. The concept of risk management will be emphasized throughout the text with a special emphasis in the functional chapters on insurance.

Savings and Consumption Habits

Information about a client's savings and consumption habits assists the planner in developing a successful strategic financial plan for the client. If the client does not have a history of saving money consistently, it would be wise to develop a strategy in which money is directed into savings prior to the client receiving a check from their employer. Similarly, if the client has a history of making impulsive large dollar purchases, it would be wise to encourage investments in assets with early withdrawal penalties and/or those where withdrawal is difficult. Withdrawal penalties or delays discourage clients from making such impulse purchases. Historical behavior is the best indicator of future behavior. A good way to collect information about the client's savings and consumption habits is to simply ask the client detailed questions.

Client Data Collection Questionnaire - a survey used by financial planners to gather internal data from clients, such as their tolerance for risk and their personal perception of their financial situation, as well as tax-related data, such as Social Security numbers, information relating to their dependents, and so on

risk tolerance - the choice of balancing lower premiums with self-reliance for smaller losses, or alternatively, higher premiums with less loss exposure

Views on Working, Retirement, Leisure Time

A client's view on working, retirement, and leisure time is useful information to a financial planner because it provides information about likely behavior. If a person is discontent with their job and/or places a high value on leisure time, they may be more likely to take spontaneous, or unplanned, vacations. The financial planner may want to incorporate these likely-but-unplanned expenditures into the financial strategy. Suppose a client is 55 years old, married with no dependent children, and is unsatisfied with his employment situation. Although this client may intend to work until the age of 62, the financial planner should be aware that this client might decide to retire earlier than planned, if financially able. The skilled financial planner will develop a strategy that includes contingency plans for various possibilities. Information about a client's views is best gathered through question and answer sessions with the client.

Attitude Toward Government

The last type of information about a client's attitudes and beliefs is their attitude toward government fiscal responsibility and taxation. If a client believes that government expenditures are wise and useful to the public, that client would probably be less resistant to taxation than a client who believes that government essentially wastes whatever money it receives. These attitudes toward tax and government translate into financial planning issues in numerous ways. Some clients ignore taxes and their role in financial planning. Other clients are tax conscious and view the tax environment merely as one more environment in which they live and must take into consideration. Still other clients are excessively focused on tax minimization, such that they spend extraordinary time and resources on the tax minimization objective, sometimes to the detriment of other goals.

SPECIAL NEEDS

The third type of internal data to be gathered concerns the client's special needs. Special needs may include special needs of dependent persons, business ownership, charitable planning, divorce, remarriage considerations, or a child's wedding.

Dependent Persons

When considering the special needs of a dependent, the focus is usually concentrated on the needs of a person with a handicap, physical or mental illness, or some other disabling condition. According to the National Alliance for Caregiving, in 1999, about 6.5 million people required some type of assistance, and 22 million families provided care for an older relative. Furthermore, the 85-and-older age group is expected to be seven times its present size by the year 2050 (a growth rate of 4 percent). Many persons between the age of 40 and 60 can expect to be, at least in part, financially responsible for the care of an elderly parent or relative. If financial precautions are not taken, dependent elderly persons could easily exhaust their own savings and the savings of their children.

Business Ownership

Business ownership must also be considered as a special need. The financial planner must be knowledgeable of the special considerations a business ownership adds to a financial plan. One obvious issue is the concentration of the client's assets in the business. Furthermore, the planner should be capable of advising the client as to the pros and cons of the various types of business ownership and their respective financial implications. In this text, the external environment and the second tax chapter discuss business ownership in more detail.

Charitable Donation Planning

Planning for charitable donations can be considered a special need. Persons engage in charitable planning for various reasons; some are motivated by tax reasons, others are motivated due to personal beliefs. Regardless of the reason, significant charitable donations must be considered as part of an overall financial plan.

Divorce and Remarriage

Divorce and remarriage must also be considered a special need. A certain percentage of all marriages are unfortunately destined to end in divorce, and many divorced persons remarry within a few years. Because of these statistics, a planner should tactfully inquire as to the stability of a client's marriage. The planner must use extreme caution when initiating the discussion of this topic with the client. If the client does not want to discuss the stability of his/her marriage, the planner should be sensitive not to push the issue.

Special need information may be collected using the Client Data Collection Questionnaire; however, additional special needs of the client will probably be identified with the passage of time as the planner/client relationship develops.

FINANCIAL POSITION

The fourth type of internal data needed is the client's current financial position. This information is so important Chapter 4 has been dedicated to it. We will simply introduce the highlights here. The gathering of information on financial position is the most time consuming for two reasons. First, the client often does not readily know the answers to the questions. Therefore, some information may need to be collected from third parties, such as stockbrokers, accountants, employers, and lawyers. Secondly, the financial planner may need to prepare the client's personal financial statements. Financial statements include the balance sheet, the income statement, the cash flow statement, and the statement of changes in net worth. Information that needs to be collected to develop these financial statements includes:

Assets - Assets include liquid assets, marketable and non-marketable investments, and personal assets.

Liabilities - Liabilities include current and long-term liabilities.

Income - Income includes salaries, investment income, bonuses, or profit-sharing payments.

Expenses - Expenses include living expenses, interest expense, insurance premiums, common donations, educational expenses, and taxes.

In addition to developing financial statements, the financial planner must collect information about the client's insurance policies and coverage, investments, retirement, and other employee benefits. The client's historical tax returns are useful, as is information about any wills, trusts, or other estate planning documents. The planner should be aware of any powers of attorney the client may possess or may have given to others. How to obtain each of these items and how to judge their relevance will be discussed fully in the following chapter.

CLIENT'S PERCEPTION OF THEIR FINANCIAL SITUATION

The fifth, and final type of internal data is the client's subjective evaluation of their own financial situation. This is how the client thinks they are doing. The client's perception is useful because it assesses the client's knowledge of their financial situation. It gives the financial planner an opportunity to assess the client's subjective perception compared to the objective reality of the situation. The gap between perception and reality directly influences the amount of client education necessary. The greater the gap between the subjective perception of the client and economic reality, the greater the education needed. This information may be gathered by using the Client Data Collection questionnaire in the Appendix at the end of the chapter.

It is common for the client's internal data to change over time. Therefore, it is essential to regularly revisit the data. If a good client/planner relationship has been developed, it is common for the client to notify the financial planner when a major change in life occurs. However, client notification is unreliable for many clients. A competent financial planner will contact their client with sufficient frequency (usually quarterly) to question about how the financial plan is working and to question if any significant changes have occurred that might require plan modification. Contacting clients should be made in addition to any regular face-to-face meetings.

NELSON FAMILY CASE SCENARIO

The Nelsons recently visited you, their financial planner. Upon initial discussions and completion of a client data questionnaire similar to the one presented in Appendix 3-A, you have gathered the following information. The Nelson family will be used throughout the text for various examples and explanations.

DAVID AND DANA NELSON
As of 1/1/2002

PERSONAL BACKGROUND AND INFORMATION

David Nelson (Age 37) is a bank vice president. He has been employed there for twelve years and has an annual salary of $70,000. Dana Nelson (Age 37) is a full-time housewife. David and Dana have been married for eight years. They have two children, John (Age 6) and Gabrielle (Age 3), and are expecting their third child in two weeks. They have always lived in this community and expect to remain indefinitely in their current residence.

GENERAL GOALS (not prioritized)

Save for college education.

Reduce debt.

Save for retirement.

Estate planning.

Invest wisely.

INSURANCE INFORMATION

Health Insurance: The entire family is insured under David's company plan (an indemnity plan). There is a $200 family deductible with 80/20 major medical coverage. The plan has a $500,000 lifetime limit for each family member. David's employer pays the entire health insurance premium.

Life Insurance: David has a term life insurance policy with a face amount of $25,000 provided by his employer. The policy beneficiary is Dana.

Disability Insurance: David has a private disability insurance policy covering accidental disability for "own occupation" with a 30-day elimination period. In the event that David is disabled as provided under the policy, the benefit is $2,700 per month until age 65. The annual premium is $761 and is paid by David.

Homeowners Insurance: The Nelsons have a HO3 policy with dwelling extension and replacement cost on contents. There is a $250 deductible. The annual premium is $950.

Automobile Insurance: The Nelsons have automobile liability and bodily injury coverage of $100,000/$300,000/$100,000. They have both comprehensive coverage (other than collision) and collision. The deductibles are $250 (comprehensive) and $500 (collision), respectively. The annual premium is $900.

INVESTMENT INFORMATION

The bank offers a 401(k) plan in which David is an active participant. The bank matches contributions dollar for dollar up to 3% of David's salary. David currently contributes 3% of his salary. David's maximum contribution is 16%. In the 401(k), the Nelsons have the opportunity to invest in a Money Market Fund, a Bond Fund, a Growth and Income Fund, and a Small Cap Stock Fund. The Nelsons consider themselves to have a moderate investment risk tolerance.

INCOME TAX INFORMATION

David and Dana tell you that they are barely in the 28% federal income tax bracket. They pay $820 annually in state and local income taxes.

EDUCATION INFORMATION

John is 6 years old and currently attending first grade at a private school. Gabrielle is 3 years old. She will attend private school from pre-kindergarten through high school. The current balance of the college fund is $14,000 and the rate of return is 4%. They expect to contribute $1,000 per year to this fund. They would also like to be able to send their children to school for five years instead of the traditional four years. The extra year could be used to get a graduate degree. The Nelsons will pay for grammar and high school out of their regular budget.

GIFTS, ESTATES, TRUSTS, AND WILL INFORMATION

David Nelson's will leaves everything to Dana conditioned on a six-month survivorship clause -- otherwise divided equally in separate trusts for John and Gabrielle. Dana does not have a will.

Dana and David Nelson
Balance Sheet
01/01/02

Assets

Cash/Cash Equivalents

JT	Checking Account	$1,425
JT	Savings Account	$950
	Total Cash/Cash Equiv.	$2,375

Invested Assets

W	ABC Stock	$12,500
JT	Educational Fund	$14,000
JT	401(k)	$32,197
	Total Invested Assets	$58,697

Personal Use Assets

JT	Principal Residence	$245,000
JT	Automobile	$18,000
H	Boat A	$25,000
W	Jewelry	$13,000
JT	Furniture/Household	$61,000
	Total Personal Use Assets	$362,000

Total Assets		**$423,072**

Liabilities and Net Worth

Current Liabilities

JT	Credit Cards	$4,000
JT	Mortgage on Principal Residence	$1,234
H	Boat Loan	$1,493
	Total Current Liabilities	$6,727

Long-term Liabilities

JT	Mortgage on Principal Residence	$196,654
H	Boat Loan	$12,065
	Total Long-term Liabilities	$208,719

Total Liabilities		**$215,446**

Net Worth		**$207,626**

Total Liabilities and Net Worth		**$423,072**

Notes to Financial Statements:
  JT = Jointly owned with survivorship rights
  W = Wife
  H = Husband
  All assets are stated at Fair Market Value

Do you find that your clients are educated about the financial planning process?

Generally, I find that most prospective clients are not well-informed regarding the nature of the financial planning process. Initially, they tend to think of "financial planning" rather narrowly, i.e. dealing only with the one or two issues that initially moved them to action, such as college funding, or if their 401(k) plan investments are properly allocated.

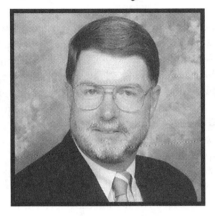

During our initial meeting, I introduce the notion that financial planning is a systematic, comprehensive process, noting out that "square one" is establishing and defining the client-planner relationship. Fortunately, the CFP Board has some excellent resources in this regard (*"What You Should Expect During the Financial Planning Process"* and *"Most Frequent Mistakes Consumers Make When Approaching the Financial Planning Process"*), which I share with prospective clients.

The general public's limited awareness regarding the nature of the financial planning process may be due, at least in part, to the popular financial media, which tends to emphasize single-issue or episodic "financial planning" i.e. "The Hottest New Fund," "3 Ways to Bet on Internet Stocks," and "10 Ways to Cut Your Taxes Now."

What techniques do you use to determine your clients attitudes and beliefs with regard to risk tolerance levels, savings, consumption, working, retirement, and the government?

I have learned that, to a considerable extent, my role is to be a good active listener. Over time, once an environment of trust, confidentiality, and confidence has been established, clients will reveal what you need to know to prepare a financial plan that is responsive to their needs. Your role as a financial planner is to properly evaluate and interpret *all* of the evidence and data, financial and otherwise, so that your recommendations are suitable and appropriate for your client.

Other techniques include using one or more of the excellent risk

profile questionnaires that are readily available from broker-dealers and mutual funds. In this regard, it is important to compare the client's risk tolerance as expressed by the risk profile instrument with the *actual* risk tolerance indicated by the client's investment portfolio. Some clients tend to overstate their risk tolerance. For example, the risk profile assessment tool may indicate a rather high risk tolerance, which is belied by a portfolio dominated by bonds, bond funds, CDs, and money market funds, or preferred stocks.

Another effective technique is to carefully review the Cash Flow Statement prepared by your client. Preparing a personal Cash Flow Statement for the first time can be an epiphany for your client, as they are confronted by their priorities and attitudes toward consumption vs. investment. The Cash Flow Statement is a road map detailing the client's economic behavior that you can use to point out in an appropriate way the consequence and impact of various resource allocation options and alternatives that are available.

Do you find that your clients have an unrealistic perception of their financial position?

Initially, they may have a sense that they need to have a trained professional "take a look at what we've done," in order to determine if their present financial position is sufficient to achieve their goals, such as early retirement or college funding. The financial position of your client may be the result of a somewhat *ad hoc*, reactive approach to personal finance matters over many years.

If, through the financial planning process, it becomes apparent that their perception is unrealistic, i.e. retiring at age 54, or sending the three children to competitive private colleges, then the task becomes one of working with the client to reframe their goals and/or examine alternative strategies.

DISCUSSION QUESTIONS

1. How does a financial planner successfully communicate respect, trust, and empathy to a client?
2. Which techniques can be used to reduce the risk of misinterpretation and misunderstanding when communicating with a client?
3. What is the purpose of an engagement letter?
4. What four thinking phases does a client progress through during the financial planning process?
5. What is the Auditory Learning Style, the Visual Learning Style, and the Kinetic or Tactile Learning Style and how does a client with each style prefer to learn?
6. What are the five categories that make up a client's internal environment?
7. Which factors make up Lifecycle Positioning?
8. What are the Lifecycle Phases through which all financial planning clients eventually pass?
9. How does a client's tolerance for risk; savings and consumption habits; views about working, retirement, and leisure time; and attitudes on government (especially taxation) affect the setting of their financial goals?
10. What are the "special needs" that may influence the successful development of a client's financial plan?
11. Which financial statements and what other information is needed to develop an accurate assessment of a client's financial position?
12. How does a client's subjective perception of financial position affect the objective reality of financial position provided by a financial planner?
13. What are the common thinking phases a client is likely to go through during the financial planning process?
14. What can the financial planner do to assist the client in progressing through the common thinking phases?
15. In which phase is it most common for a client to seek the assistance of a financial planner?
16. In which phase is the financial mission most likely to be achieved?

EXERCISES

1. Upon first meeting a client, how should you address them?
2. What are some techniques that can be used to clarify statements when speaking with a client?
3. If you noticed that your client was taking notes and occasionally doodling while you spoke with them, what would you assume their learning style to be and how would you go about educating them regarding financial planning information?
4. If your client is 30 years old, no children and has a moderate income and net worth, what risks are they most likely seeking to avoid?
5. If your clients are 73 years old, retired and have adult children and grandchildren and a high net worth, which lifecycle phase are they most likely in?
6. What might be the common goals of a client who is 24 years old and single with a modest income?
7. If your client is interested in saving for retirement, but has a history of using savings planned for the long-term on current purchases such as vacations, vehicles, etc., what type of savings plan would you recommend?

PROBLEMS

1. Write an engagement letter to conduct comprehensive personal financial planning for the Nelsons, who are introduced in this chapter.
2. Identify the internal environmental factors most likely to affect the achievement of the Nelsons' general goals.

APPENDIX 3-A: CLIENT DATA QUESTIONNAIRE

Client Name_____

Date_____

PERSONAL INFORMATION

Your Full Name _____   Social Security No. _____

U.S. Citizen?   ❏ Yes   ❏ No   Date and Place of Birth _____

Employer _____   Position _____

Work Phone _____   Years with current employer _____

Married _____   Single _____   Divorced _____

Spouse's Full Name (if married) _____   Social Security No. _____

U.S. Citizen?   ❏ Yes   ❏ No   Date and Place of Birth _____

Employer _____   Position _____

Work Phone _____   Years with current employer _____

Home Address _____

Home Phone _____   Home Fax _____

E-mail address _____

Previous Marriages

Have you been previously married?   ❏ Yes   ❏ No   Has your spouse been previously married?   ❏ Yes   ❏ No

Children

Name(s)	Date(s) of Birth	Social Security Number(s)	Tax Dependent
			❏ Yes ❏ No
			❏ Yes ❏ No
			❏ Yes ❏ No
			❏ Yes ❏ No

Grandchildren

Name(s)	Date(s) of Birth	Social Security Number(s)	Tax Dependent
			❏ Yes ❏ No
			❏ Yes ❏ No

Other Income Tax/Financial Dependents

Does anyone other than your children depend on you or your spouse for financial support?   ❏ Yes   ❏ No

If so, provide names, ages, and relationships: _____

_____

_____

Health Issues

Do you or any members of your family have serious health problems?   ❏ Yes   ❏ No

Describe: _____

Professional Advisors (include names, addresses, phone numbers, fax numbers, and e-mail addresses)

Attorney _____

Accountant (CPA) _____

Insurance Agent _____

Banker _____

Investment Advisor _____

Page 1   Initial _____   Date _____

FINANCIAL PLANNING GOALS AND OBJECTIVES

Financial Objectives (Please select and indicate degree of importance)	1	2	3	4	5
	Degree of Importance (1-high/5-low)				
Retire and maintain preretirement lifestyle					
Retire early - Indicate age _____					
Protection from risks to person/property/liability					
Provide education for children/grandchildren					
Major purchases (car, boat, second home)					
Establish an emergency fund					
Save more					
Invest for safety					
Invest for growth					
Invest for income					
Transfer of wealth					
Minimize income taxes					
Minimize transfer taxes (estates and gifts)					
Other:					

Initial _____   Date _____

71

APPENDIX 3-A: CLIENT DATA QUESTIONNAIRE (CONT.)

ASSETS

Cash Accounts (indicate current ($) dollar balance for each account)

Type of Account	Your Name	Spouse's Name	Joint w/ Spouse	Other
Cash on hand				
Checking accounts				
Savings accounts				
CDs				
Money market funds				
Treasury securities				
U.S. Savings Bonds				
Total				

Brokerage Accounts (Stocks)

Name of Security	No. of Shares	Market Value

Mutual Funds (Stocks)

Name of Institution (Fund Name)	No. of Shares	Market Value

Mutual Funds (Bonds)

Name of Institution (Fund Name)	No. of Shares	Market Value

Bonds Owned

Name of Institution	Maturity Face Value	Market Value

Page 3   Initial _____ Date _____

APPENDIX 3-A: CLIENT DATA QUESTIONNAIRE (CONT.)

Stock Options and/or Stock Purchase Plans

Do you or your spouse participate in a company stock option plan or stock purchase plan? ☐ Yes ☐ No

Receivables (owed to you and/or your spouse)

Type	Description	Interest Rate	Amount	Maturity Date
Notes Receivables				
Other Receivables				

Retirement Accounts (indicate vested values)

Type	Description	Fair Market Value You	Fair Market Value Your Spouse
IRA – Regular			
IRA – Roth			
401(k) or 403(b) plan			
Keogh plan			
Pension plan			
Profit-sharing plan			
Employee stock bonus plan			
Employee stock ownership plan			
SEP			
SIMPLE			

Real Estate (Personal Use)

Address	Type*	State Located	Original Cost	Fair Market Value	Current Mortgage Amount

* PR = Personal Residence   VH = Vacation Home

Real Estate (Held for Investment)

Address	Type*	State Located	Original Cost	Fair Market Value	Current Mortgage Amount

* R = Rental   O = Other

Page 4   Initial _____ Date _____

CHAPTER 3: COMMUNICATION AND INTERNAL ANALYSIS

73

APPENDIX 3-A: CLIENT DATA QUESTIONNAIRE (CONT.)

Closely Held Business Interest **(attach financial statement if available)**

Description	Type of Entity*	Date Acquired	Percentage Owned	Est. Fair Market Value

* P = Proprietorship   PTR = Partnership   S = S corporation   C = C corporation   LLC = Limited Liability Company

Any Other Investments

Description	Date Acquired	Est. Fair Market Value

Personal Use Property

Type	Estimated Fair Market Value
Furniture & household goods	
Jewelry & furs	
Automobiles	
Boats, aircraft	
Recreational vehicles	
Art & antiques	
Other collectibles (stamps, baseball cards)	
Other items of significant value	

Page 5

Initial _____   Date _____

74

APPENDIX 3-A: CLIENT DATA QUESTIONNAIRE (CONT.)

LIABILITIES

	Amount Owed		Monthly Payments	
	You	Spouse	You	Spouse
Bank Loans				
Student Loans				
Insurance Policy Loans				
Personal Loans				
Taxes Payable				
Installment Debt (Automobile)				
Credit Cards				
Other Unpaid Bills				
Alimony/Child Support Obligations				
Charitable Pledges				
Other (_____)				
Other (_____)				
Other (_____)				

Page 6

Initial _____ Date _____

75

APPENDIX 3-A: CLIENT DATA QUESTIONNAIRE (CONT.)

INCOME SOURCES

	You	Spouse	Joint
Employment Income			
Gross Salary			
Bonuses			
Commissions			
Other (Describe_____)			
Investment Income			
Taxable Interest			
Nontaxable Interest			
Dividends			
Net Rental Income			
Business Income			
Annuities			
Social Security Benefits			
Pension/Retirement Plan			
Other (Describe_____)			
Miscellaneous Income (Expected)			
Inheritances			
Alimony			
Child Support			
Other (Describe_____)			

Page 7

Initial _____   Date _____

APPENDIX 3-A: CLIENT DATA QUESTIONNAIRE (CONT.)

INSURANCE

Life Insurance   (Bring in policies)

Type	Policy Owner	Face Amount	Cash Value	Beneficiary	Premium Paid by Employer/You
Term – You					
Term - Your Spouse					
Permanent – You					
Permanent - Your Spouse					
Other - You (_____)					
Other - Your Spouse (_____)					

General Insurance   (Check the ones you have and bring in the policies and premium statements)

Type

Type	
Dental	
Hospital	
Short-term disability	
Long-term disability	
Automobile (Property and Liability)	
Homeowners/Renters	
Specified Personal Property	
Personal Umbrella Liability	
Other (_____)	
Other (_____)	

Page 8

Initial _____   Date _____

APPENDIX 3-A: CLIENT DATA QUESTIONNAIRE (CONT.)

RETIREMENT PLANNING AND ESTATE PLANNING

At what age do you and your spouse plan to retire?

_____ You

_____ Spouse

Describe your plans for retirement. Include a description of your retirement lifestyle.

_____

_____

_____

_____

_____

_____

_____

	You Yes	You No	Your Spouse Yes	Your Spouse No
Do you have a recent will?	☐	☐	☐	☐
Are you planning to make any changes to the will?	☐	☐	☐	☐
Do you have a medical directive?	☐	☐	☐	☐
Have you given a Power of Attorney for healthcare and property?	☐	☐	☐	☐

Page 9

Initial _____ Date _____

CHAPTER 4

Personal Financial Statements (Preparation and Analysis)

LEARNING OBJECTIVES:

After learning the material in this chapter, you will be able to:

1. Explain the need for financial statements.

2. Explain the need for financial statement preparation.

3. Identify and describe each financial statement, its information content, and its objective.

4. Be able to prepare financial statements.

5. Identify the tools of financial statement analysis.

6. Calculate ratios.

7. Perform financial statement analysis.

8. Identify which ratios are used to determine debt utilization, liquidity, and asset performance.

9. Discuss the limitations of financial statement analysis.

10. Define fair market value.

11. Define liquidity.

INTRODUCTION

Personal financial statements serve as a fundamental planning tool for the financial planner by providing important financial information to the planner and by giving the planner an opportunity to analyze such information so as to assist the client in financial decision making. Financial statements are intended to provide information about financial resources available to the client, how these resources were acquired, and what the client has accomplished financially utilizing these resources. The financial statements represent the scoring mechanism for recording and evaluating an individual's financial performance. Information obtained from financial statements can be used to analyze the financial well-being of the client and determine what factors influence the client's earnings and cash flows. Personal financial statements are different from business financial statements primarily in that business financial statements focus on future earnings, where personal statements focus on a client's current financial activities and situations in order to plan for the future.

Personal financial statements include the balance sheet, the income and expense statement, the statement of cash flows, and the statement of changes in net worth. This chapter will include a discussion of each financial statement, how it is prepared, and from where the data is obtained. The chapter provides examples illustrating the different financial statements based on the Nelson family introduced in the previous chapter. Information from the Nelsons is also used to demonstrate a thorough treatment of financial statement analysis, including ratio analysis, vertical analysis, and growth analysis.

DECISION-MAKING USES OF FINANCIAL STATEMENTS AND FINANCIAL STATEMENT ANALYSIS

Personal financial statements provide the users, planners, clients, or lenders, the necessary information to make adequate financial decisions. Clients prepare personal budgets to assist in understanding their spending patterns, to gain more control over their financial affairs, and to improve the likelihood of reaching their financial goals. As we will see in the chapter, the financial statements are used by clients to benchmark goal achievement, by planners to help clients decide financial direction, and by creditors and lenders to make decisions to extend, continue, or call indebtedness. Exhibit 4.1 presents financial actions using the different financial information that can be gathered, the most likely user of the information, and the types of decisions that can be made from the gathering and analysis of the financial information.

FINANCIAL ACTIONS	LIKELY USER	TYPE OF DECISION
Preparing personal budgets	Client/Planner	Basic planning
Evaluating spending patterns	Client/Planner	Efficiency/effectiveness
Determining the financial solvency of the client	Client/Planner/Lender	Debt management
Determining if financial goals are being achieved	Client/Planner	Redirect or steady course
Determining if the client is making adequate progress toward retirement	Client/Planner	Capital needs analysis
Evaluating the relative risk and performance of the investment portfolio	Client/Planner	Asset allocation
Evaluating the client's use and cost of debt	Client/Planner/Lender	Refinance
Determining the adequacy of income replacement insurance	Client/Planner	Insurance/estate planning
Determining the adequacy of liquidity for estate planning	Client/Planner	Liquidity at death
Evaluating net worth	Client/Planner/Lender	Lending
Financial statements required for loans	Lender	Lending

RULES REGARDING FINANCIAL STATEMENTS

The **Financial Accounting Standards Board** (FASB) is a non-governmental board that sets the standards for financial statements and generally accepted accounting principles (also known as GAAP). While these principles (GAAP) generally apply to businesses, they are also useful in the development of personal financial statements. The objectives in following such accounting conventions include consistency and comparability in the preparation and presentation of financial statements. Therefore, objective rather than subjective judgments of value should generally be used in presentation and decision-making.

Financial Accounting Standards Board (FASB) - a non-governmental board that sets the standards for financial statements and generally accepted accounting principles (GAAP)

PREPARATION OF FINANCIAL STATEMENTS

It is rare that a client is able to provide the financial planner with a complete set of competent personal financial statements. The client many times does not have the necessary documentation or a clear understanding of his or her own current financial position. With that in mind, the planner can either personally prepare the client's financial statements or have someone else prepare them, usually the client's CPA. Personally preparing and analyzing a client's financial statements provide the planner with a wealth of information and insight about the client. Because financial statement preparation and analysis are fundamental to financial planning, all competent financial planners should have a basic understanding of the terminology, evaluation and valuation methods, and the current and relevant accounting and reporting principles to develop such financial statements.

THE BALANCE SHEET

The **balance sheet** is a listing of assets, liabilities, and net worth that depicts resources and how those resources were obtained or financed. The statement is a financial snapshot of the client at a moment in time (the date of the statement). Historically, the balance sheet was the primary

balance sheet - a listing of assets, liabilities, and net worth

financial statement given to and relied upon by third parties, especially lenders. It was originally designed to meet the needs of creditors who wanted information about assets, collateral, and a person's ability (net worth) to repay debts. Currently, third parties lenders may require copies of all personal financial statements, not just the balance sheet.

BALANCE SHEET TERMS AND PRESENTATION ORDER

assets - property owned completely or partially by the client

An **asset** is property owned completely or partially by the client. Some examples of assets are cash, investments, personal residences, and automobiles. The classification of the list of assets on the balance sheet is generally based on liquidity. **Liquidity** is the length of time expected for the asset to be converted back to cash. Assets expected to be converted to cash within one year are **current assets**. Therefore, cash and cash equivalents are presented first, followed by assets held as investments, and, finally, assets held for personal use.

liquidity - the length of time expected for the asset to be converted back to cash

A **liability** is money owed by the client. Some examples of liabilities are bank loans, student loans, automobile loans, credit card debt, home mortgages, and taxes owed. On the liability side, liabilities that will or should be paid within one year are presented as current liabilities in their expected order of payoff. Liabilities extending beyond a year are presented as long-term liabilities.

current assets - assets expected to be converted to cash within one year

Net worth is the amount of wealth or equity the client has in owned assets. It is the amount of money that would remain after selling all owned assets at their estimated fair market values and paying off all liabilities. The client's net worth is therefore calculated by taking the difference between total assets and total liabilities.

liability - money owed by the client

net worth - the amount of wealth or equity the client has in owned assets

Traditionally, assets are listed on the left side of the balance sheet and liabilities on the right side. The net worth is shown below liabilities on the right side. Depending on the client and the purpose of the balance sheet, the categories may be subdivided into more or less detail. Regardless of the categorization of assets and liabilities, the statement must always balance. The basic balance sheet formula is Assets – Liabilities = Net Worth. Exhibit 4.2 shows the basic balance sheet format.

EXHIBIT 4.2: BALANCE SHEET FORMAT

ABBREVIATED BALANCE SHEET			
Cash and cash equivalents	$ xxx	Current liabilities	$ xxx
Investment assets	xxx	Long-term liabilities	xxx
Personal use assets	xxx	Total Liabilities	$ xxx
		Net Worth	xxx
Total Assets	$ xxx	Total Liabilities and Net Worth	$ xxx

CATEGORIES AND CLASSIFICATIONS OF ASSETS

Cash and Cash Equivalents

Cash and cash equivalents include cash on hand, checking accounts, savings accounts, certificates of deposit, cash value in life insurance policies (if intended for current use as cash and cash equivalents; otherwise, classify permanent insurance policies as investments), money market accounts, income tax refunds due, and accounts receivable that are expected to be collected quickly. These are assets easily converted to cash for regular or emergency expenses and assets that are expected to convert to cash within one year.

Investment Assets

Investment assets include stocks, bonds, mutual funds, real estate, collectibles (i.e., stamps and art) held for investment, cash value in life insurance policies (if not intended for use as cash and cash equivalents), and interests in closely held corporations or businesses. Generally, investment assets are held for growth or income, or both. Assets may also be distinguished in the balance sheet as tax advantaged or not tax advantaged. This distinction is useful for tax and distribution purposes.

Personal Use Assets

Personal use assets include the personal residence, personal property (furniture, clothing, etc.) jewelry, automobiles, other vehicles, and recreational boats. These assets are generally long lived and are not expected to be liquidated in the short term but rather are to be used to maintain the client's quality of life. Exhibit 4.3 lists some commonly held assets.

EXHIBIT 4.3: COMMONLY HELD ASSETS

CASH & CASH EQUIVALENTS	INVESTMENTS	PERSONAL USE ASSETS
▲ Cash on-hand	▲ Stocks and bonds	▲ Primary residence
▲ Checking accounts	▲ Certificates of Deposit (> 1 yr)	▲ Vacation home
▲ Savings accounts	▲ Mutual funds	▲ Automobiles
▲ Money market accounts	▲ Real estate	▲ Recreational equipment
▲ Certificates of Deposit (≤ 1 yr)	▲ Business ownership	▲ Household items
	▲ Cash value of life insurance (generally)	▲ Jewelry
	▲ Cash value of pensions	
	▲ Retirement accounts	
	▲ Collectibles	
	▲ Annuities	
	▲ Other investment vehicles	

CATEGORIES AND CLASSIFICATIONS OF LIABILITIES

Current Liabilities

current liability - debt owed by the client that is expected to be paid off within the year

Current liabilities include any short-term credit card debt and unpaid bills. These bills represent money the client currently owes. Unpaid credit card balances, taxes payable, bank loans, and other debts that will or should be paid off within one year are also considered current liabilities.

Long-Term Liabilities

long-term liability - debt extending beyond one year

Long-term liabilities are those debts that will not be paid off within one year, usually debts of larger assets. Generally, loans such as mortgages, automobile loans, long-term notes payable, and student loans are considered long-term liabilities. Where the debt is long term, the current portion due is listed under current liabilities.

Exhibit 4.4 gives several examples of common personal liabilities.

EXHIBIT 4.4: COMMON PERSONAL LIABILITIES

CURRENT LIABILITIES	LONG-TERM LIABILITIES
▲ Current portion of mortgages due	▲ Primary residence mortgage
▲ Utility bills due	▲ Vacation home mortgage
▲ Credit card balances due	▲ Other mortgages
▲ Insurance premiums due	▲ Automobile loans
▲ Taxes due	▲ Home improvement loans
▲ Medical bills due	▲ Student loans
▲ Repair bills due	▲ Other loans

VALUATION OF ASSETS AND LIABILITIES

For personal financial statements, assets and liabilities on the balance sheet are stated at the current fair market value. Presenting assets and liabilities at fair market value is not an easy task. There are problems with the precise determination of fair market value for many of the assets listed. Liabilities are more straight forward in terms of valuation.

fair market value - the price at which an exchange will take place between a willing buyer and a willing seller both informed and neither under duress to exchange

Fair market value is defined as the price at which an exchange will take place between a willing buyer and a willing seller, both reasonably informed and neither under duress to exchange. Fair market value for certain assets like cash, cash equivalents, some investment account balances, and most liabilities is readily available from institutional statements and/or by contacting the institution holding the asset or liability. For those assets and liabilities, such a determination should be made. However, for certain other assets, the determination of fair market value is difficult and may require an appraisal by an expert or an estimate by the client. In some cases, the cost of an appraisal is not warranted because the information gained by appraisal is not worth the cost expended. For example, a small change in the value of a personal residence from year to year may not be relevant to the financial statements, especially where the client has no intent to dispose of the personal residence. The same is true for the valuation of closely held business interests where there is no intent to dispose of such business interests.

THE NELSON FAMILY BALANCE SHEET

Exhibit 4.5 is a duplicate of the Nelsons' beginning financial statement for the year 2002 that was provided in Chapter 3. Exhibit 4.6 is an ending balance sheet for 12/31/02. Notice the changes in net worth, assets, and liabilities. Even though these changes are readily apparent by comparing the numbers, there is no explanation as to what transactions caused those changes. This is one of the weaknesses of the balance sheet.

Dana and David Nelson
Balance Sheet
01/01/02

Assets

Cash/Cash Equivalents

JT	Checking Account	$1,425
JT	Savings Account	$950
	Total Cash/Cash Equiv.	**$2,375**

Invested Assets

W	ABC Stock	$12,500
JT	Educational Fund	$14,000
JT	401(k)	$32,197
	Total Invested Assets	**$58,697**

Personal Use Assets

JT	Principal Residence	$245,000
JT	Automobile	$18,000
H	Boat A	$25,000
W	Jewelry	$13,000
JT	Furniture/Household	$61,000
	Total Personal Use Assets	**$362,000**

Total Assets — **$423,072**

Liabilities and Net Worth

Current Liabilities

JT	Credit Cards	$4,000
JT	Mortgage on Principal Residence	$1,234
H	Boat Loan	$1,493
	Total Current Liabilities	**$6,727**

Long-term Liabilities

JT	Mortgage on Principal Residence	$196,654
H	Boat Loan	$12,065
	Total Long-term Liabilities	**$208,719**

Total Liabilities — **$215,446**

Net Worth — **$207,626**

Total Liabilities and Net Worth — **$423,072**

Notes to Financial Statements:

▲ Assets are stated at fair market value.
▲ The ABC stock was inherited from Dana's aunt on November 15, 1998 who originally paid $20,000 for it on October 31, 1998. The fair market value at the aunt's death was $12,000.
▲ Liabilities are stated at principal only.
▲ H = Husband; W = Wife; JT = Joint Tenancy

Dana and David Nelson
Balance Sheet
12/31/02

Assets

Cash/Cash Equivalents

JT	Checking Account	$1,518
JT	Savings Account	$950
	Total Cash/Cash Equiv.	$2,468

Invested Assets

W	ABC Stock	$13,000
JT	Educational Fund	$15,560
JT	401(k)	$38,619
H	XYZ Stock	$10,000
	Total Invested Assets	$77,179

Personal Use Assets

JT	Principal Residence	$250,000
JT	Automobile	$15,000
H	Jet Ski	$10,000
H	Boat B	$30,000
W	Jewelry	$13,500
JT	Furniture/Household	$60,000
	Total Personal Use Assets	$378,500

Total Assets — **$458,147**

Liabilities and Net Worth

Current Liabilities

JT	Credit Cards	$3,655
JT	Mortgage on Principal Residence	$1,370
H	Boat Loan	$1,048
	Total Current Liabilities	$6,073

Long-term Liabilities

JT	Mortgage on Principal Residence	$195,284
H	Boat Loan	$16,017
	Total Long-term Liabilities	$211,301

Total Liabilities — **$217,374**

Net Worth — **$240,773**

Total Liabilities and Net Worth — **$458,147**

Notes to Financial Statements:

▲ Assets are stated at fair market value.

▲ The ABC stock was inherited from Dana's aunt on November 15, 1998 who originally paid $20,000 for it on October 31, 1998. The fair market value at the aunt's death was $12,000.

▲ Liabilities are stated at principal only.

▲ H = Husband; W = Wife; JT = Joint Tenancy

For example, in Exhibits 4.5 and 4.6, ABC stock increased from $12,500 to $13,000. Did the Nelsons buy more stock? Did the value of the stock increase? Do the Nelsons still hold the same number of shares? The two balance sheets really do not reveal the answer to these questions. A comparison only reveals an increase in the Nelsons' total assets from $423,072 to $458,147 and an increase in their net worth from $207,626 to $240,773--an increase of $33,147. Is the increase good or bad? Obviously, an increase is better than a decrease, but what was the cause? Once again, the two balance sheets do not reveal the answer. In order to answer these questions, other financial statements need to be prepared for the Nelson family, namely, the revenue and expense statement, the cash flow statement, and the statement of changes in net worth. Once all of the financial statements are prepared, they can be analyzed to gain a better understanding of the underlying financial transactions that occurred during the year. All the financial statements for the Nelsons will be presented and analyzed in this chapter. As you will see, the balance sheet does not tell the whole financial story.

VALUATION OF ASSETS AND LIABILITIES - THE NELSONS

Reviewing the 1/1/02 and the 12/31/02 balance sheets for the Nelsons, notice that the value of their personal residence has increased by $5,000 ($245,000 - $250,000). If we assume that there were no improvements to the residence, and that we did not have a real estate appraisal, where did the $250,000 number come from? Probably, the planner and client estimated inflation at 2 percent and rounded the increase in value to $5,000, assuming that real estate generally appreciates at about the inflation rate. What are the relative merits of such estimation for valuation? If you have no plans to sell an asset, but you need a valuation and no ready valuation is available, estimation is not a terrible idea. Anyone familiar with financial statements knows, or should know, that if they plan to rely on financial statements, then it is incumbent upon them to verify the valuations of important assets, and liabilities. In reality, no individual is going to have an appraisal on an annual basis for their personal residence, furnishings, automobile, or other personal use assets. Therefore, the reader of personal financial statements should be skeptical of the valuations given for personal use assets.

There is always some imprecision in valuing certain assets and liabilities. The extent to which such imprecision is acceptable to the user depends on the particular use of the financial statements. It is frequently appropriate to have the client estimate a value, particularly for a personal residence. Usually clients know what property has been selling for in their neighborhood, and have no intent to dispose of the property. Likewise, it is reasonable to have the client estimate the value of an interest in a closely held business, especially when there is no current intent to dispose of such business interest. Increased valuation precision may be necessary when the financial statements are to be used to obtain a loan from a third party and that third party cannot or will not accept estimates. For example, if the client is refinancing a home, the mortgage lender will require an appraisal.

INFORMATION SOURCES

The financial planner needs to thoroughly review the client's various assets and liabilities in order to prepare the financial statements. The planner will need to access many different documents to determine valuation, payment schedules, and applicable interest concerns. The detail desired of the financial planning engagement will determine the thoroughness of the planner's assessment of these documents. Exhibit 4.7 lists important sources of financial information and the types of information that may be obtained from the sources for the preparation of the balance sheet.

EXHIBIT 4.7: SOURCES AND TYPES OF INFORMATION FOR BALANCE SHEET

SOURCE OF INFORMATION	TYPES OF INFORMATION THAT CAN BE OBTAINED FROM SOURCE
Client	All documents and estimates of value regarding assets and liabilities
Bank statements	Bank balances and possible loan creation or repayments
Investment account statements	Investment account balance and types
Life insurance statements	Cash value of life insurance and any indebtedness
Real estate purchase agreement	Purchase price of real estate
Mortgage notes	Indebtedness of real estate and terms of indebtedness
Auto purchase agreements	Purchase price of automobile
Auto notes	Terms of indebtedness for automobile
Employer benefit statements	Vested and non-vested account balance/options/contributions by employee and employer to retirement
Credit card statements	Purchase price of use assets, balances of credit card indebtedness, payments, interest rates, late charges
Appraisals	Value of the asset appraised
Installment notes	Value of installment notes or liability and terms

In the case of the assets and liabilities other than personal use assets, there are a wide variety of sources and documents to assist the financial planner in the preparation of the balance sheet.

Exhibit 4.8 presents each account on the balance sheet and where the best source of information is to determine the correct balance sheet amount. In addition, alternative sources are presented where the cost/benefit of finding precise data does not warrant collection from the best source.

EXHIBIT 4.8: BALANCE SHEET INFORMATION BY ACCOUNT TYPE

ACCOUNTS AND ACCOUNT BALANCES	BEST SOURCE OF BALANCE SHEET INFORMATION FOR VALUATION	ALTERNATIVE SOURCE
ASSETS		
Cash and Cash Equivalents		
Checking account	Bank statements of client	Client/planner estimate
Savings account	Bank statements of client	
Certificates of Deposit	Bank statements of client	
Investment Assets		
Stocks	Brokerage or investment statements	Client/planner estimate
Bonds	Brokerage or investment statements	
Mutual funds	Account statements	
401(k) account	Account statements	
403(b) account	Account statements	
IRA/SEP	Account statements	
Personal Use Assets		
Personal residence	Appraisal if warranted	Client/planner estimate
Personal furniture & fixtures	Appraisal if warranted	
Investment real estate	Appraisal if warranted	
Closely Held Business Interests	Appraisal if warranted	Client/planner estimate
Automobiles	Blue book, Bank, credit union	Client/planner estimate
LIABILITIES		
Current Liabilities		
Credit card debt	Credit card statements	Client estimate
Bank loans	Lender	Client estimate
Long-Term Liabilities		
Mortgage loans	Amortization table/lender/Annual statements	Client/planner estimate
Auto Loans	Coupon/lender	Client/planner estimate

IDENTIFICATION OF OWNERSHIP OF ASSETS AND LIABILITIES

It is a useful idea to indicate the type of property ownership and the titling of assets and liabilities on the balance sheet when preparing financial statements for married persons. Identifying ownership is especially helpful for estate planning and where one individual has separately owned property not subject to the claims of the other spouse's creditors.

Common abbreviations for property ownership and titling on personal balance sheets are:

H = separate property of husband
W= separate property of wife
JT= property held jointly with survivorship rights by H and W (husband and wife)
CP= community property of H and W (husband and wife)

FOOTNOTES TO THE BALANCE SHEET

Generally, footnotes are used to provide additional information or to clarify the item footnoted on the financial statements. Examples of common footnotes to the balance sheet include:

▲ Assets are stated at fair market value.
▲ Property title listings.
▲ Existing contingent liabilities (guarantors/co-signed obligations).
▲ Additional notes regarding property that may be needed at a later date (i.e., basis of gifted property).

THE INCOME AND EXPENSE STATEMENT

The **income and expense statement** presents a summary of the client's income and expenses during an interval of time, usually one year. The income and expense statement may focus on realized transactions, and if so, is helpful when comparing to budgeted financial goals. The income and expense statement may also be prepared pro forma (in advance) and, therefore, can be used for budgeting and/or projections. The basic income and expense statement equation is: Income - Expenses = **Discretionary Cash Flow**.

The bottom line on a personal income and expense statement shows the amount of discretionary cash flow available to the client. As defined in the equation, discretionary cash flow represents the excess of cash flows to the individual from income, less expenses and committed savings. Such discretionary cash flow may be used for consumption, reduction of debt, additional savings, or for cash gifts, or the purchase of gifts. If such discretionary cash flows are used to reduce debt or are added to savings, balance sheet ratios are improved.

income and expense statement - summary of the client's income and expenses during an interval of time, usually one year

discretionary cash flow - money available after all expenses are accounted for

INCOME AND EXPENSE STATEMENT TERMS AND ORDER OF THEIR PRESENTATION

INCOME

income - all monies received from employment, investments or other sources

Income includes all monies received, usually on a cash basis, from employment, investments, and other sources.

▲ Employment income includes wages, salaries, bonuses, and commissions.
▲ Investment income includes interest and dividends from savings and investment accounts, proceeds from the sale of assets, income from annuities, and any other investment related activities.
▲ Other income sources may include Social Security benefits, child support, alimony, gifts, scholarships, tax refunds, pension income, and any other income that is received on a regular basis.

SAVINGS

savings - deferred consumption

Savings reduce income available for expenses. Savings, is deferred consumption and will be treated as an increase to assets on the balance sheet.

EXPENSES

expenses - recurring obligations

Expenses are recurring obligations paid, or monthly expenses paid. The three main categories of expenses are fixed, variable, and discretionary.

fixed expenses - expenses that remain constant over a period of time over which the client has little control

Fixed expenses are expenses that remain constant over a period of time over which the client has little control. Examples of fixed expenses include rent or mortgage payments, insurance premiums, tuition, and loan payments.

Variable expenses are expenses that fluctuate in amount from time to time, over which the client has some control. Examples of variable expenses include food, utilities, and transportation costs.

variable expenses - expenses that fluctuate from time to time over which the client has some control

Discretionary expenses are luxuries or expenses over which the client has complete control to incur or not. Examples of discretionary expenses are vacations, entertainment expenses, and gifts.

discretionary expenses - luxuries or expenses over which the client has complete control

INFORMATION SOURCES

The financial planner will need to thoroughly review the client's various income sources and personal expenditures in order to create the income and expense statement. Exhibit 4. 9 lists some of the more common sources of financial information that may be used in the collection of data for the preparation of the income and expense statement.

EXHIBIT 4.9: PERSONAL INCOME & EXPENDITURE SOURCES

Income Sources	Information Source
Salary	Form W-2/tax return
Interest (taxable)	Form 1099/tax return
Dividends	Form 1099

Expenditures (Savings and Expenses)	Information Source
Savings	Bank statements/401(k) statements/1099s
Food	Budget/check register/receipts
Clothing	Budget/check register/receipts
Child care	Budget/check register/receipts
Entertainment	Budget/check register/receipts
Utilities	Actual bills/check register/receipts
Auto maintenance	Budget/check register/receipts
Church	Checks and receipts
401(k) loan repayments	Participant statement
Credit card payments	Statements
Mortgage payment	Mortgage statement
Automobile/Boat loan	Loan agreement/check register
Insurance premiums	Invoice/policy/check register
Tuition and education expenses	Invoice/check stubs
Federal income tax (W/H)	Form W-2
State (and City) income tax	Form W-2
FICA	Form W-2
Property tax for real estate (principal residence)	Mortgage statement/check register

Exhibit 4.10 is the Nelsons' statement of income and expenses showing their income, savings, expenses, and discretionary cash flow for the year 2002.

EXHIBIT 4.10: STATEMENT OF INCOME AND EXPENSES

Dana and David Nelson
Statement of Income and Expenses
For the year 2002

INCOME

Salary - David		$70,000
Investment Income		
Interest Income	$900	
Dividend Income	$150	$1,050
Total Inflow		**$71,050**
Savings		
Reinvestment (Interest/dividends)	$1,050	
401(k) Deferrals	$3,803	
Educational Fund	$1,000	
Total Savings		**$5,853**
Available for Expenses		**$65,197**

EXPENSES

Ordinary Living Expenses		
Food	$6,000	
Clothing	$3,600	
Child Care	$600	
Entertainment	$1,814	
Utilities	$3,600	
Auto Maintenance	$2,000	
Church	$3,500	
Total Ordinary Living Expenses		**$21,114**
Debt Payments		
Credit Card Payments Principal	$345	
Credit Card Payments Interest	$615	
Mortgage Payment Principal	$1,234	
Mortgage Payment Interest	$20,720	
Boat Loan Principal	$1,493	
Boat Loan Interest	$1,547	
Total Debt Payments		**$25,954**
Insurance Premiums		
Automobile Insurance Premiums	$900	
Disability Insurance Premiums	$761	
Homeowners Insurance Premiums	$950	
Total Insurance Premiums		**$2,611**
Tuition and Education Expenses		**$1,000**
Taxes		
Federal Income Tax (W/H)	$7,500	
State (and City) Income Tax	$820	
FICA	$5,355	
Property Tax (Principal Residence)	$1,000	
Total Taxes		**$14,675**
Total Expenses		**$65,354**
Discretionary Cash Flow (negative)		**($157)**

COMPROMISE IN INFORMATION REPORTING

The income and expense statement is a compromise in information reporting. For an individual, the income and expense statement is almost a full cash flow statement. The exceptions, those transactions that are not considered income or expenses, but are cash flows, are generally not included in the income and expense statement. As an example, while conventional corporate accounting would only include the interest portion from any repayment of debt as an expense, it is common for personal financial statements to include both the principal and the interest in debt repayment as an expense or cash flow of the period (e.g., mortgage payments, credit card payments, bank loan repayments).

The astute planner will notice that an income and expense statement for an individual is not truly an accrual income and expense statement nor is it a full cash flow statement. Because the income statement for individuals is frequently prepared pro forma (in advance) and used as a budget, it is a presentation of recurring inflows and outflows presented in a conventional manner, and is, therefore, a compromise. If it were a full cash flow statement, it would have to consider the acquisition and disposition of all assets for and by cash.

The income statement generally does not consider the sale or purchase of assets during the period. The income statement also does not consider employer matches to qualified retirement accounts. As we will soon see, other financial statements must be prepared to present the complete financial picture of the client.

THE RELATIONSHIP OF BALANCE SHEET TO INCOME AND EXPENSE STATEMENT

The balance sheet represents the financial picture of the individual at a moment in time setting forth assets, liabilities, and net worth. The income and expense statement presents recurring revenues, savings, expenses, and discretionary cash flow over a period of time. The income statement provides a partial picture of what has happened between two balance sheet dates. As discussed previously, neither statement by itself, nor when taken together, presents the entire financial picture of the individual. This deficiency creates the need for other financial statements, such as the statement of cash flows and the statement of changes in net worth, to help further clarify the complete financial picture of the client. The purpose of the statement of cash flows is to bridge the gap between the beginning and the ending cash balance and the intervening income and expense statement.

THE STATEMENT OF CASH FLOWS

The **statement of cash flows** assists in the reconciliation of the income statement to changes between two balance sheets. For a given period, the statement of cash flows shows the inflows and outflows and the net changes in cash between two balance sheets and identifies the changes in some of the accounts from one balance sheet to the next.

statement of cash flows - summary of the client's changes to the cash account

There are numerous financial transactions involving cash flows that occur between balance sheet dates that do not show up as either a revenue (income) or expense and, therefore, are not accounted for on the income and expense statement. Such transactions include where two balance sheet accounts are affected without affecting an income or expense account.

Examples of transactions that affect cash flows but are generally not included on the personal income and expense statement include:

- ▲ Purchasing or selling a personal use asset for cash (automobile).
- ▲ Taking out a loan.
- ▲ Purchasing or selling an investment.
- ▲ Receiving a gift or inheritance in cash.
- ▲ Giving a gift of cash.

CLASSIFICATIONS

The statement of cash flows supplements the information from the income and expense statement and balance sheets to help explain the changes in account balances that have occurred between the beginning and ending balance sheets. The classification of individual items is what provides information content. The statement of cash flows has three sections: cash flows from operations, cash flows from financing activities, and cash flows from investing activities. The sum of all cash flows for the three sections is equal to the net change in cash as presented on the beginning and ending balance sheets.

Cash Flows from Operations

cash flows from operations - net cash generated or used due to normal work and living

Cash flows from operations measure the amount of net cash generated or used by the individual due to normal work and normal living. For short periods, deficits may occur but, generally, net positive discretionary cash flows are essential to produce long-term growth. Discretionary funds can then be used for (1) investments, (2) to replace use assets such as automobiles, or (3) to pay debt. Because it is a common practice to include savings, recurring investments, and recurring debt principal repayments in the income and expense statement there is a need to adjust those items out of operating cash flow and reclassify them appropriately as cash flows to investment and financing activities, respectively. This section (cash flow from operations) lists the discretionary cash flow from normal household operations on the income and expense statements and changes in the balances of current assets and liabilities (excluding cash).

Cash Flows from Investing Activities

cash flows from investing - cash receipts or expenditures for the sale or purchase of assets

Cash flows from investing are the cash outflows used to acquire assets and cash inflows from the sale of assets (investments and personal use assets) during the period. These cash flows are necessary to maintain a lifestyle and to save for future goals (i.e. education or retirement). The cash flows from investing activities section presents the acquisition and disposition of invested assets and personal use assets. Cash that is invested through savings is reclassified from operating cash flows to cash outflows from investing.

Cash Flows from Financing Activities

Cash flows from financing include cash inflows from the issuance of additional debt (notes payable) and cash outflows for the repayment of debt (principal) during the period. This section presents the cash obtained from financing sources and the cash used to repay those sources. Increases in cash flows are created by actions increasing long-term indebtedness where cash is received at the inception of the transaction (i.e. making a loan). Decreases in cash flows result from repayments of debt. For personal financial statements, it is useful to list the repayment of principal for indebtedness related to mortgages or automobiles even though they are initially accounted for in the income and expense statement. We can accomplish this with an adjustment to the operating cash flows from the income and expense statement as shown in Exhibit 4.11, the Nelsons' statement of cash flows.

OTHER CLASSIFICATION ISSUES

Several classification issues exist regarding the cash flow statement for individuals that generally do not exist for businesses. Perhaps the most common item of savings not reflected in the income and expense statement is an employer match contribution to a retirement plan. Inheritances received in cash and cash outflows of nonrecurring gifts are also among the most common for individuals but uncommon for businesses. The question is where to classify such transactions on the statement of cash flows. We have chosen, for convenience and convention, to record employer contributions under investing cash flows, and inheritances received and gifts given under investment activities. For example, an inheritance received in cash is a source of investment cash flow, and the corresponding use occurs when the cash is placed in an investment account. Conversely, gifts of property made by a donor are essentially a reduction of investments to the donor.

cash flows from financing - cash inflows from the issuance of additional debt and cash outflows for the repayment of debt

EXHIBIT 4.11: STATEMENT OF CASH FLOWS

Dana and David Nelson
Statement of Cash Flows
For the Year Ending
12/31/02

Cash from/for Operations (Income Statement)		
Discretionary Cash flow from Income Statement		**($157)**
Adjustments to operating cash flows		
Increase of Investments from savings		
Educational Fund	$1,000	
401(k)	$3,803	$4,803
Decrease in Liabilities from Principal Repayments		
Mortgage on Principal Residence	$1,234	
Boat Loan	$1,493	
Credit Card Debt	$345	$3,072
Total Cash from Operations		**$7,718**
Cash from/(for) Investment Activities		
Jet ski		($10,000)
Increases of Investments from savings		
Educational Fund	($1,000)	
401(k)	($3,803)	($4,803)
Inheritance		$10,250
Boat B		($5,000)
Total Cash from Investments		**($9,553)**
Cash from/(for) Financing Activities		
Decreases in Liabilities from Principal Repayments		
Mortgage on Principal Residence	($1,234)	
Boat Loan	($1,493)	
Credit Card Debt	($345)	($3,072)
Boat Loan		$5,000
Total Cash from Finance		**$1,928**
Net Increase (Decrease) in Cash Flows		$93
Ending Cash and Cash Equivalents		$2,468
Beginning Cash and Cash Equivalents		($2,375)
Net Increase (Decrease) in Cash Flows		$93

ADJUSTMENTS TO CASH FLOWS FROM OPERATIONS

There are a number of adjustments that need to be made to the operating cash flows of an individual to provide a clear financial picture of the client. These adjustments remove savings and debt repayments from the income statement and more properly reclassify these as cash flows to investments or to financing activities. The cash flows on the income statement used for savings are reclassified as cash flows to investing. The cash flows from principal debt repayments (included in income and expense statement), including mortgage, bank loan, auto loan, credit card and student loan payments, are reclassified as cash flows to financing activities.

RATIONALES FOR CASH FLOW CATEGORIES

The rationale for the adoption of the three categories (cash flows from operations, cash flows from investing activities, and cash flows from financing activities) on the cash flow statement is that such classification assists the reader in learning where cash comes from and where it is being used. The income and expense statement does not include borrowings, repayments, investment changes, and other items, which are not routine and recurring but still need to be accounted for. The different ways in which cash flows may be grouped can be argued and may be somewhat arbitrary; however, the statement of cash flows, when presented with two balance sheets (beginning and end), and the intervening income and expense statements, provide a wealth of financial information about the client.

THE STATEMENT OF CHANGES IN NET WORTH

Throughout the preparation of the three previously mentioned financial statements, we have tried to provide financial information useful to the client and the planner. We now need to be able to explain the changes in net worth between two balance sheets. So far, using the income statement and the statement of cash flows, we are able to explain all of the balance sheet account changes that were affected by cash. Unfortunately, there are changes in net worth that do not affect cash flows. Therefore, even when these three financial statements (balance sheet, income statement, and cash flow statement) are taken together, they cannot fully account for all the changes between the beginning and ending balance sheets. Thus, there is a need for a fourth and final statement to summarize non-cash flow changes in net worth that would not have been recorded on either the income or the cash flow statement. This fourth financial statement is called the **statement of changes in net worth**. To the extent that we have not been able to ascertain all of the exact changes in the net worth, this statement will allow us to do so. Examples of transactions or changes in account balances that would not be included in the income or cash flow statements are listed below:

statement of changes in net worth - summary of each change from one balance sheet to the next

▲ Changes in value for assets due to either appreciation or depreciation.
▲ If an asset other than cash is exchanged for some other assets (real estate for real estate).
▲ If assets other than cash are received by gift or inheritance (property).
▲ If assets other than cash are given to charities or non-charitable donees (automobiles, buildings, or investments).

Exhibit 4.12 depicts the statement of changes in net worth for the Nelson family. The Nelson's Net Worth Statement ties together the overall change in the net worth. It reflects each non-cash item that was altered during the year. Transactions that were not previously reported on any of the other statements include:

▲ An inheritance of $10,000 in XYZ Stock from David's grandmother.
▲ Appreciation in value for the jewelry, residence, ABC Stock, Educational Fund, and 401(k).
▲ Employer contribution in David's 401(k) plan ($2,100).
▲ Gift of a table to Dana's mother ($1,000 value).

EXHIBIT 4.12: STATEMENT OF CHANGES IN NET WORTH

Dana and David Nelson **Statement of Changes in Net Worth** **For the Year Ending** **12/31/02**	
Additions to Net Worth	
Add (Non Cash Flow Adjustments to Net Worth)	
Increases in Assets:	
Inheritance	
XYZ Stock	$10,000
Appreciation of Assets	
Jewelry	$500
Residence	$5,000
Adjustment from Even Exchange	
Boat B	$30,000
Purchase	
Jet Ski	$10,000
Appreciation of Investments	
ABC Stock	$500
Educational fund	$560
401(k)	$519
Increase of Investment Contributions	
Educational Fund	$1,000
401(k)-employee contribution	$3,803
401(k)-employer contribution	$2,100
Decrease in Liabilities (Debt Repayments):	
Mortgage on Principal Residence	$1,234
Boat Loan	$1,493
Credit Card Debt	$345
Total	**$67,054**
Reductions in Net Worth	
Less (Non Cash Flow Adjustments to Net Worth)	
Decrease in Assets:	
Depreciation of Assets	
Auto	($3,000)
Gifts	
Table to Mother	($1,000)
Adjustment from Even Exchange	
Boat A	($25,000)
Increase in liabilities	
Addition to Boat Loan	($5,000)
Total	**($34,000)**
Net - Non Cash Flow change in Net Worth	**$33,054**
Beginning Net Worth (Beginning Balance Sheet)	$207,626
Plus Changes from Cash Flow Statement	$93
Plus Change from Statement of Changes in Net Worth	$33,054
Ending Net Worth (Ending Balance Sheet)	**$240,773**

NELSON EXAMPLE RECAP

Recall that the initial balance sheet and the ending balance sheet do not equal. Based on this observation, we know that there were circumstances in which the overall financial status of the Nelsons changed during the year. Exhibit 4.13 illustrates a spreadsheet reconciliation of the changes for the Nelsons from one balance sheet date to the next.

EXHIBIT 4.13: SPREADSHEET RECONCILIATION OF CHANGES IN NET WORTH

Asset	1/1/02 Balance Sheet	Income Statement	Cash Flow Statement	Net Worth	12/31/02 Balance Sheet
Checking Account	$1,425		$93		$1,518
Savings Account	$950				$950
ABC Stock	$12,500			$500	$13,000
Educational Fund	$14,000			$1,560	$15,560
401(k)	$32,197			$6,422	$38,619
XYZ Stock	$0			$10,000	$10,000
Principal Residence	$245,000			$5,000	$250,000
Automobile	$18,000			($3,000)	$15,000
Jet Ski	$0			$10,000	$10,000
Boat A	$25,000			($25,000)	$0
Boat B	$0			$30,000	$30,000
Jewelry	$13,000			$500	$13,500
Furniture/Household	$61,000			($1,000)	$60,000
Credit Cards	($4,000)			$345	($3,655)
Mortgage on Residence*	($197,888)			$1,234	($196,654)
Boat Loan*	($13,558)			($3,507)	($17,065)
Net Worth	$207,626		$93	$33,054	$240,773

* Includes current and long-term liabilities

FINANCIAL ANALYSIS OF PERSONAL FINANCIAL STATEMENTS

Once the balance sheet, income and expense statement, statement of cash flows, and statement of changes in net worth have been properly prepared, financial statement analysis can be performed to gain insight into the financial strengths and weaknesses of the client. The financial planner may look upon this activity as a form of diagnosing the financial health of the client. It should be stressed that financial analysis, while somewhat comprehensive, is only one tool of the competent financial planner. Financial analysis by its very nature is limited to the past and, therefore, is not necessarily predictive of the future. Even with its inherent limitations, however, financial statement analysis is a useful and powerful tool to gain insight into the financial well-being of the client.

We begin with a traditional approach to analyzing the four financial statements, and then broaden our analysis to improve our insights. Our traditional approach utilizes ratio, vertical, and growth analysis.

Financial statement analysis (in general) and ratio analysis (in particular) can assist us in answering the following questions about a client:

▲ Can the client financially withstand a sudden negative financial disruption to income (such as, unemployment or loss of a significant asset)?
▲ Can the client meet short-term obligations?
▲ Does the client manage debt well?
▲ Does the client have an appropriate balance among various classes of expenditures relative to income?
▲ Is the client's income growing at an appropriate rate?
▲ Is the client's savings and savings rate appropriate for the given income and income growth?
▲ Is the client making a satisfactory total return on investments and savings?
▲ Is the client's net worth growing at an appropriate rate?
▲ Is the client making satisfactory progress toward funding retirement?

RATIO ANALYSIS

There are many financial ratios one might use to gain insight into the client's financial well-being. The ratios that we have selected are only suggestive. Other financial planners may have ratios that they use which we have neglected. Furthermore, some decisions require exhaustive **ratio analysis** while other decisions are quite simple and may require only the calculation of a few simple ratios. Thus, there is no one set of ratios that needs to be used all of the time, nor is there a particular ratio that is always calculated. The ratios are used to clarify and to improve the understanding of the data and are used in comparison to established benchmarks, such as those established in the mortgage lending industry, to make judgments as to their appropriateness for a particular client. We would expect, for example, that at higher income levels, there are greater amounts of savings, and larger net worths. Therefore, we must be careful to use relevant benchmarks to which we compare the financial ratios of each individual.

ratio analysis - the relationship or relative value of two characteristics used to analyze the financial and operational health of an individual and to conduct comparison and trend analysis

Financial statement analysis is both art and science. While anyone can mathematically calculate ratios, the ability to understand the implications of those ratios and to motivate the client to take actions to affect those ratios where appropriate, is truly an art. The art will only come with practice and experience.

Ratio analysis is intended to provide additional perspective to the financial statements. The selection of each numerator and denominator to calculate a particular ratio must be done with care. Not every ratio is relevant for every client. The objective of ratio analysis is twofold: to gain additional insight into the financial situation and behavior of the client, and to generate questions for the client to answer to further gain such insight.

The ratios selected for discussion in this chapter are ones that the authors have found to be particularly useful. The key to ratio analysis is, does the ratio get to the answer for the question asked, and then, is there some standard or benchmark to determine whether the result is appropriate for this particular client. Ratio analysis tends to interrelate the balance sheet and income and expense statements.

Liquidity Ratios

Liquidity ratios measure the ability of the client to meet short-term financial obligations. They compare current financial obligations such as current liabilities or financial requirements to current assets or cash flows available to meet those financial obligations. These liquidity ratios include the emergency fund ratio, the current ratio, and the cash ratio.

The Emergency Fund Ratio

The emergency fund ratio assists the planner in determining the ability of the client to withstand a sudden negative financial disruption to income. Such a financial disruption could occur as a result of a layoff, untimely death, disability, or some other event that causes the cash flows to cease or be reduced. It is calculated by comparing the amount of liquid assets to the monthly expenses of the client. The emergency fund ratio should generally be three to six months of non-discretionary cash flows to accommodate unemployment, losses of significant assets, or other unexpected major expenditures.

Reviewing Exhibit 4.6, the 12/31/2002 balance sheet, the Nelsons had $2,468 in liquid assets. In reviewing the income and expense statement, they have monthly expenses totaling $5,446 ($65,354 ÷ 12). A closer review of the monthly expenditures, however, reveals that there are certain expenses that could be reduced if necessary. Such expenditure adjustments would normally require consultation with the client, but assume that the following costs could be eliminated:

Child Care	$600
Entertainment	1,814
Federal Taxes	7,500
State and City Taxes	820
FICA	5,355
Expenses Eliminated	$16,089

Thus, the real nondiscretionary monthly expenses are $4,105 [($65,354 - $16,089) ÷ 12]. (Note that in consultation with the client, the church contribution of $3,500 was not considered discretionary.) The emergency fund ratio is calculated by dividing the liquid assets (numerator) by the nondiscretionary monthly expenses (denominator) to provide the resultant.

$$\text{Emergency Fund Ratio (EFR)} = \frac{\text{Liquid Assets}}{\text{Monthly Nondiscretionary Expenses}} = \text{Target of 3-6 Months}$$

$$\text{Nelsons' EFR} \quad \frac{\$2,468}{\$4,105} = 0.60 \text{ months}$$

The emergency fund ratio of 0.60 months is substantially below the target goal of three to six months, suggesting a substantial risk to the overall financial plan. You may observe that the Nelsons could liquidate some of their investments or borrow from their 401(k) plan in the event of an emergency. While both observations are correct, generally, it is disruptive to a long-term investment plan to have such forced liquidations. Therefore, we would place building the emergency fund as one of our current objectives with a quantitative target of initially 3 months, and over a longer time of 6 months.

The Current Ratio

The current ratio examines the relationship between current assets and current liabilities. The current ratio indicates the ability to meet short-term obligations. The ratio is calculated by dividing current assets (numerator) and by current liabilities (denominator).

$$\text{Current Ratio (CR)} = \frac{\text{Current Assets}}{\text{Current Liabilities}} = \text{Target of 1:1 - 2:1}$$

In reviewing the 12/31/2002 balance sheet of the Nelsons, we find current assets of $2,468 and current liabilities of $6,073.

$$\text{Nelsons' CR} \quad \frac{\$2,468}{\$6,073} = 0.41$$

The current ratio of 0.41 is low relative to the target of 1:1 - 2:1. It suggests insufficient current assets, or too many current liabilities, or some combination of both. Therefore, we would suggest increasing the current ratio to 1:1 over a reasonable period of time. By increasing the emergency fund ratio, the Nelsons may also increase the current ratio.

Where on the Web

Consumer Credit Counseling Service, Inc. *www.debtfree.org*

Consumer Information Center in Pueblo, Colorado *www.pueblo.gsa.gov*

Credit Union National Association *www.cuna.org*

Debt Consolidation Organization *www.debtconsolidation.com*

Myvesta.org (previously Debt Counselors of America) *www.dca.org or www.myvesta.org*

Equifax *www.equifax.com*

Debt Ratios and Debt Analysis

Debt ratios indicate how well the person manages debt. Debt is neither inherently good nor bad. All debt carries some cost, at a minimum, interest costs. Quality debt is debt that is low in cost and has a term structure that does not exceed the economic life of the asset that created the debt. When a person consistently repays debt as agreed, such repayment creates a history of good credit ratings, the borrower gains confidence in handling debt, and lenders gain confidence in extending credit to such a borrower. Excessive debt or expensive debt is a warning sign that default risk is increased. It is impossible to determine exactly how much debt a person should have, but various ratios give signals as to the person's ability to handle debt and whether or not the person may be overextended. The initial debt ratios include total debt to net worth, long-term debt to net worth, debt to total assets, and long-term debt to total assets. These debt ratios are compared from one year to the next in order to identify trends, rather than having a particular target, as with liquidity ratios.

Total Debt to Net Worth

$$\text{Total Debt to Net Worth} = \frac{\text{Total Debt}}{\text{Net Worth}}$$

The ratio indicates the portion of a person's assets derived from debt compared to net worth. Generally, we would expect that the debt to net worth ratio would decline over a person's lifetime.

Reviewing the two balance sheets for the Nelsons (1/1/2002 and 12/31/2002), we find the total debt ($6,727 + 208,719) to net worth ratio to be:

$$1/1/2002 \quad \frac{\$215,446}{\$207,626} = 1.04$$

$$12/31/2002 \quad \frac{\$217,374}{\$240,773} = 0.90$$

106

The total debt ratio has improved this year, as a lower proportion of debt indicates less financial risk.

Long-Term Debt to Net Worth

The long-term debt ratio removes short-term debt from the numerator to get a more refined look at the long-term capital structure. The ratio is calculated as follows:

$$\text{Long-Term Debt to Net Worth} = \frac{\text{Long-Term Debt}}{\text{Net Worth}}$$

Net worth should be increasing and long-term debt should be declining over time. Therefore, we should expect a decreasing ratio when comparing from one year to the next.

Again, after reviewing the two balance sheets for the Nelsons, we find the long-term debt to net worth to be:

$$1/1/2002 \qquad \frac{\$208,719}{\$207,626} = 1.01$$

$$12/31/2002 \qquad \frac{\$211,301}{\$240,773} = 0.88$$

Note that the long-term debt to net worth ratios are very close to the total debt to net worth ratios, which suggests that most of the Nelsons' debt is long-term. An examination of the long-term debt of the Nelsons reveals that the primary debt is the mortgage on the principal residence, which is generally considered high quality debt (as opposed to credit card debt).

Total Debt to Total Assets

The ratio of total debt to total assets indicates the proportion of assets furnished by creditors as a percentage of total assets.

$$\text{Total Debt to Total Assets} = \frac{\text{Total Debt}}{\text{Total Assets}}$$

Reviewing the Nelsons' two balance sheets, we find total debt to total assets to be:

$$1/1/2002 \qquad \frac{\$215,446}{\$423,072} = 0.51$$

$$12/31/2002 \qquad \frac{\$217,374}{\$458,147} = 0.47$$

Once again, the resultant ratio has modestly improved over the last year.

Long-Term Debt to Total Assets

The long-term debt to total assets ratio is a numerator refinement on the previous ratio to focus on long-term debt as a proportion of total assets.

$$\text{Long-Term Debt to Total Assets} = \frac{\text{Long-Term Debt}}{\text{Total Assets}}$$

Once again, we use the two balance sheets for the Nelsons to determine the long-term debt to total assets:

$$1/1/2002 \quad \frac{\$208,719}{\$423,072} = 0.49$$

$$12/31/2002 \quad \frac{\$211,301}{\$458,147} = 0.46$$

The ratio has modestly declined. For the Nelsons, this decline does not add very much insight due to the debt mix. However, for a client with different debt mixes, this ratio could be very revealing.

ANALYSIS OF DEBT

The proper use of debt is to match the economic benefit period of the asset purchased with the repayment period of the debt such that the economic benefit period equals or exceeds the repayment period. We expect that there is a lifecycle of indebtedness beginning at the asset accumulation phase, peaking sometime in the conservation/preservation phase, and declining rapidly during or before the gifting phase. Debt is useful for asset accumulation, but it has a cost. Once it is established that the person can manage debt well, lenders are willing to extend more debt up to the point where default risk is increased. At some point, persons who have acquired assets using debt wish to be out of debt to devote the repayment resources to other goals, frequently, saving for retirement.

Certain types of debt are often thought of as reasonable, such as student loans, mortgages, and auto loans. The underlying assets of education, housing, and transportation create long-lived economic benefits and are expensive. These assets are commonly purchased with some debt financing. Exhibit 4.14 presents the types of debts, the benefits created by those debts, the expected economic benefits period of the asset purchased, and the common repayment period. Many items may be purchased with credit cards; however, credit card debt is considered the worst kind of debt due to its high costs. Many people use credit cards to purchase consumable goods and then find themselves repaying the debt long after the period of consumption. There are some positive ways to use credit cards, such as paying off the balance monthly without increasing debt.

EXHIBIT 4.14: TYPES OF DEBT: ECONOMIC BENEFIT AND REPAYMENT PERIODS

TYPE OF DEBT	TYPE OF BENEFIT CREATED	EXPECTED BENEFIT PERIOD*	COMMON REPAYMENT PERIOD
Student loans	Education	Lifetime	10 years
Mortgage or principal residence	Shelter	40 years	15-30 years
Auto loans	Transportation	3-10 years	3-5 years
Bank loans	Various	Various	Various
Credit cards	Various[1]	Various	30 days to 1 year[2] or more

*Assumes asset held for entire economic life.

[1] Various, but many times, consumption.

[2] If credit cards are paid at the minimum payment, the interest may be high (18-21 percent), and the debt will last a very long time.

Monthly Housing Costs to Monthly Gross Income

Mortgage lenders are sophisticated lenders. They have benchmarks for loans secured with real estate used as a personal residence. The first such benchmark is:

$$\frac{\text{Monthly Housing Costs } (P+Int+T+Ins)}{\text{Gross Monthly Income}} \leq 28 \text{ \% Gross Monthly Income}$$

Where:

$$P = \text{Principal}$$
$$Int = \text{Interest}$$
$$T = \text{Taxes (Real Estate)}$$
$$Ins = \text{Insurance}$$

Housing costs include the monthly principal and interest to repay the loan, real estate taxes, and homeowners insurance. This sum is divided by monthly gross income (income before taxes and other deductions). Generally, to issue a mortgage loan at prevailing market interest rates, lenders require this ratio to be less than or equal to 28 percent.

housing costs - principal and interest to pay the mortgage loan, real estate taxes and homeowners insurance

For the Nelsons:

$$\frac{(\$20,720 + \$1,234 + \$1,000 + \$950) \div 12}{\$71,050 \div 12} = \$1,992 \div \$5,921 = 33.6\%$$

This ratio, which for the Nelsons significantly exceeds the benchmark of 28 percent, suggests that the Nelsons have taken on housing debt in excess of what is reasonable for their income.

Monthly Housing Costs and Other Debt Repayments to Monthly Gross Income

The second ratio that lenders use is to adjust the previous numerator to reflect all monthly debt repayments. This ratio should be less than or equal to 36 percent.

$$\frac{\text{Housing Costs (from above)} + \text{Other Monthly Debt Pmts. (\$)}}{\text{Gross Monthly Income (\$)}} \leq 36\% \text{ Gross Monthly Income}$$

This ratio of housing costs and all other monthly debt repayments must be less than or equal to 36 percent. A mortgage applicant must generally meet both the requirements of the 28 percent benchmark and the 36 percent benchmark to qualify for a mortgage loan at the best interest rates.

For the Nelsons:

$$\frac{\text{Housing Costs} + \text{Credit Cards} + \text{Boat}}{\text{Gross Monthly Income}} \leq 36\% \text{ Gross Monthly Income}$$

$$\frac{\$1,992 + (\$960 \div 12) + (\$3,040 \div 12)}{\$5,921} = \$2,325.33 \div \$5,921 = 39.3\%$$

The Nelsons have also exceeded the second benchmark. This should serve as a warning sign that the Nelsons have too much debt for their current income level. The second housing ratio is not grossly deficient (over the target). If the Nelsons paid off the credit cards and boat with invested assets, the second ratio would be within the established benchmark.

Because these ratios are so widely used by mortgage lenders for both initial mortgage indebtedness and for mortgage refinance, they are useful benchmark ratios to calculate for any client to determine if the client is at risk for having too much debt. The ratios indicate that monthly housing nondiscretionary costs should not exceed 28 percent of monthly gross income, and that all monthly debt repayments should not exceed 36 percent of gross monthly income. The second ratio suggests that if the full initial 28 percent of gross income is used for housing, there is only 8 percent of gross income left for auto loans, furniture loans, student loans, and monthly credit card repayments. Many clients tend to stretch beyond their means when buying a home and should be cautioned by the planner. These ratios can bring a sense of reality to a client regarding the debt picture and indebtedness decisions.

Performance Ratios - Savings

Performance ratios are designed to assess the financial flexibility of the client, as well as to assess the client's progress toward financial goal achievement. These ratios are the savings ratio and discretionary cash flow plus savings to gross income ratio.

The Savings Ratio

The savings ratio indicates the amount that is actually being saved as a percent of gross income.

$$\frac{\text{Annual Savings (Personal and Employer Related)}}{\text{Annual Gross Income \$}} = \text{Annual Rate of Savings} = \text{Target of 10\%}$$

The long-run savings rate for a client is the level of savings that has been achieved on a consistent basis and is reasonably likely to persist. The long run combined savings rate should be about 10 percent of gross income if the client begins saving by age 30 expecting to retire at normal age 62. If savings begin later, retirement must be delayed or the savings rate must be increased. For example, beginning to save at age 40 and retiring at 65 would require a 15 percent savings rate. For these savings rates to be effective, there is also an earnings rate assumption of real market returns on a growth investment portfolio. Unfortunately, many clients do not save enough to create adequate retirement capital. Some clients also do not invest wisely and, therefore, do not achieve growth investment portfolio returns.

In reviewing the Nelsons' income and expense statement, Exhibit 4.10, we have determined their savings rate to be:

$$\frac{\$5,853 + \$2,100}{\$71,050} = 11.2\%$$

The Nelsons have a good combined savings rate of 11.2 percent, which includes the 3 percent match from David's employer.

Discretionary Cash Flows Plus Savings to Gross Income

This ratio indicates the amount that could be saved as opposed to what is saved. The ratio is calculated using net discretionary cash flow from the statement of income and expense and adding scheduled savings. This sum is then divided by total gross income.

$$\frac{\text{DCF} + \text{Savings}}{\text{Annual Gross Income}} \geq 10\% \text{ Target}$$

Reviewing the Nelsons' statement of income and expenses, we determine that the ratio is:

$$\frac{(\$157) + \$5,853 + \$2,100}{\$71,050} = 11\%$$

While this ratio is unrevealing for the Nelsons, it may be useful for other clients where the savings rate is lower and or where there are significant discretionary cash flows.

Performance Ratios - Investments

Investment performance ratios are designed to assist the reader in understanding the returns on investments. They include income on investments, rate of return on investments, and investment assets to gross income.

Income on Investments

The income on investments is calculated by dividing the investment returns by the average invested assets.

$$\frac{\text{Income from Investment Returns}}{\text{Average Invested Assets}} = \text{Target depends on the client's situation}$$

Using the income and expense statement and the balance sheet for the Nelsons, we calculate their income on investments to be:

$$\frac{\$900 + \$150}{(\$58,697 + \$77,179) \div 2} = \frac{\$1,050}{\$67,938} = 0.015$$

The ratio of 0.015 indicates a low level of income from investments. However, a review of the rate of return on all investments, including any unrealized appreciation in investment assets will provide additional information that may be useful regarding investment performance.

Rate of Return on Investments (ROI)

This ratio provides us with the return on investments that we can compare to a previously established benchmark or to an appropriate investment index. The numerator is the change in investment assets from one year to the next (Ending Investments (EI) – Beginning Investments (BI)) less any savings or gifts/inheritances received that went into investments. The denominator is the average invested assets. ROI is calculated as:

$$\frac{\text{EI} - \text{BI} - \text{Savings} - \text{Gifts Received}}{\text{Average Investment}} = \text{Target of 9 - 12\%}$$

$$\frac{\text{BI} + \text{EI}}{2} = \text{Average Investment}$$

Again, using the Nelsons' income and expense statement and balance sheet, the ROI is calculated to be:

$$\frac{\$77,179 - \$58,697 - \$7,953 - \$10,000}{(\$58,697 + \$77,179) \div 2} = \frac{\$529}{\$67,938} = 0.0078$$

The rate of return on investments for the Nelsons for year 2002 was 0.78 percent. While at first glance, that may seem a poor rate of return, it will need to be compared with portfolios with similar asset allocations to determine exactly how the performance compared to a relevant benchmark. Obviously, it is a poor rate of return against the general benchmark of 9-12 percent needed annually to provide a sufficient capital base for retirement. However, it may only represent one "down" year among many "up" years that exceeded the target.

Investment Assets to Gross Income

Calculating investment assets as a percent of gross income provides a peek into the capital-needed-at-retirement issue. A simple example will help us. Assume that a person about to retire has investment assets devoted to retirement of $1,000,000; has gross income of $100,000; can invest at a rate of return of 10 percent with no inflation. The investment asset to income is 10 ($1,000,000 ÷ $100,000), and the client can produce that income in perpetuity. We expect investment assets to be equal to or greater than 10 times preretirement income at normal retirement age. This ratio calculated over time helps us to benchmark the progress toward retirement. The ratio should be about 3-4, 10 years prior to retirement, and about 1, 20 years before retirement.

$$\frac{\text{Investment Assets}}{\text{Gross Income}} = \quad \text{Target depends on the client's situation and age}$$

Using the Nelsons' income and expense statement and balance sheet, the ratio is calculated as:

$$\frac{\$77,179}{\$71,050} = 1.09$$

This investment ratio is excellent for the Nelsons at their age if all the investment assets were held for retirement. Even when the education fund is deducted from the invested assets, the ratio equals 0.84, which is good progress toward retirement for their age.

Exhibit 4.15 gives a summary of the ratio analysis for the Nelson family.

EXHIBIT 4.15: SUMMARY OF RATIO ANALYSIS
(TARGETS AND NELSONS)
YEAR END 12/31/02

Liquidity Ratios				Target	Nelsons
Emergency Fund Ratio	=	$\dfrac{\text{Liquid Assets}}{\text{Monthly Nondiscretionary Expenses}}$	=	3-6	0.60
Debt Ratios					
Current Ratio	=	$\dfrac{\text{Current Assets}}{\text{Current Liabilities}}$	=	1-2	0.41
Total Debt to Net Worth	=	$\dfrac{\text{Total Debt}}{\text{Current Liabilities}}$	=	*	0.90
Long-Term Debt to Net Worth	=	$\dfrac{\text{Long Term Debt}}{\text{Net Worth}}$	=	*	0.88
Total Debt to Total Assets	=	$\dfrac{\text{Total Debt}}{\text{Total Assets}}$	=	*	0.47
Long-Term Debt to Total Assets	=	$\dfrac{\text{Long-Term Debt}}{\text{Total Assets}}$	=	*	0.46
Monthly Housing Costs to Monthly Gross Income	=	$\dfrac{\text{Monthly Housing Costs}}{\text{Monthly Gross Income}}$	=	≤ 28%	33.6%
Monthly Housing Costs and Other Debt Repayments to Monthly Gross Income	=	$\dfrac{\text{Housing Costs and Debt Repayments}}{\text{Monthly Gross Income}}$	=	≤ 36%	39.3%
Savings Ratios					
Savings Ratio	=	$\dfrac{\text{Personal Saving \& Employer Contribution}}{\text{Annual Gross Income}}$	=	≤ 10%	11.2%
Discretionary Cash Flow plus Savings to Annual Gross Income	=	$\dfrac{\text{Discretionary Cash Flow}}{\text{Annual Gross Income}}$	=	> 10%	11%
Performance Ratios					
Income on Investments	=	$\dfrac{\text{Dividends and Interest}}{\text{Average Investments}}$	=	*	1.6%
Return on Investments	=	$\dfrac{\text{EI – BI – Savings – Gifts}}{\text{Average Investments}}$	=	9-12%	0.78%
Investment Assets to Annual Gross Income	=	$\dfrac{\text{Investment Assets}}{\text{Annual Gross Income}}$	=	*	1.09

*Target depends on the individual's age or investment objectives.

VERTICAL ANALYSIS

Vertical Analysis and Common Size Analysis

Vertical analysis of financial statements presents each statement in percentage terms. Usually, the balance sheet is presented with each item as a percentage of total assets while the income statement is prepared with each item as a percentage of total income. Percentage items allow us to compare items over time when we have multiple-year financial statements for the same client. The comparison of one statement on a percentage basis is called common size analysis because the percentages calculated ignore absolute dollars and provide information regarding stability or instability of each account in percentage terms. Exhibit 4.16 presents the two balance sheets in a vertical analysis format and Exhibit 4.17 presents the Nelsons' income statement using vertical analysis.

EXHIBIT 4.16: BALANCE SHEET – VERTICAL ANALYSIS

Dana and David Nelson
Balance Sheet-Vertical Analysis
2002

		01/01/02	12/31/02	Difference
Assets				
Cash/Cash Equivalents				
JT	Checking Account	0.34%	0.33%	-0.01%
JT	Savings Account	0.22%	0.21%	-0.02%
	Total Cash/Cash Equiv.	0.56%	0.54%	-0.02%
Invested Assets				
W	ABC Stock	2.95%	2.84%	-0.12%
JT	Educational Fund	3.31%	3.40%	0.09%
JT	401(k)	7.61%	8.43%	0.82%
H	XYZ Stock	0.00%	2.18%	2.18%
	Total Invested Assets	13.87%	16.85%	2.97%
Personal Use Assets				
JT	Principal Residence	57.91%	54.57%	-3.34%
JT	Automobile	4.25%	3.27%	-0.98%
H	Jet Ski	0.00%	2.18%	2.18%
H	Boat A	5.91%	0.00%	-5.91%
H	Boat B	0.00%	6.55%	6.55%
W	Jewelry	3.07%	2.95%	-0.13%
JT	Furniture/Household	14.42%	13.10%	-1.32%
	Total Personal Use Assets	85.56%	82.62%	-2.95%
Total Assets		100.00%	100.00%	0.00%
Liabilities and Net Worth				
Current Liabilities				
JT	Credit Cards	0.95%	0.80%	-0.15%
JT	Mortgage on Principal Residence	0.29%	0.30%	0.01%
H	Boat Loan	0.35%	0.23%	-0.12%
	Total Current Liabilities	1.59%	1.33%	-0.26%
Long-term Liabilities				
JT	Mortgage on Principal Residence	46.48%	42.62%	-3.86%
H	Boat Loan	2.85%	3.50%	0.64%
	Total Long-term Liabilities	49.33%	46.12%	-3.21%
Total Liabilities		50.92%	47.45%	-3.48%
Net Worth		49.08%	52.55%	3.48%
Total Liabilities and Net Worth		100.00%	100.00%	0.00%

Comment: Note that the primary apparent cause of the increase in net worth (3.48%) was the decrease in the mortgage (-3.86%) on the principal residence.

EXHIBIT 4.17: STATEMENT OF INCOME AND EXPENSES

Dana and David Nelson
Statement of Income and Expenses
For the year 2002

INCOME		
Salary - David		98.52%
Investment Income		
Interest Income	1.27%	
Dividend Income	0.21%	1.48%
Total Inflow		100.00%
Savings		
Reinvestment (Interest/dividends)	1.48%	
401(k) Deferrals	5.35%	
Educational Fund	1.41%	
Total Savings		8.24%
Available for Expenses		91.76%
EXPENSES		
Ordinary Living Expenses		
Food	8.44%	
Clothing	5.07%	
Child Care	0.84%	
Entertainment	2.55%	
Utilities	5.07%	
Auto Maintenance	2.81%	
Church	4.93%	
Total Ordinary Living Expenses		29.72%
Debt Payments		
Credit Card Payments Principal	0.48%	
Credit Card Payments Interest	0.87%	
Mortgage Payment Principal	1.74%	
Mortgage Payment Interest	29.16%	
Boat Loan Principal	2.10%	
Boat Loan Interest	2.18%	
Total Debt Payments		36.53%
Insurance Premiums		
Automobile Insurance Premiums	1.27%	
Disability Insurance Premiums	1.07%	
Homeowners Insurance Premiums	1.34%	
Total Insurance Premiums		3.67%
Tuition and Education Expenses		1.41%
Taxes		
Federal Income Tax (W/H)	10.56%	
State (and City) Income Tax	1.15%	
FICA	7.54%	
Property Tax (Principal Residence)	1.41%	
Total Taxes		20.65%
Total Expenses		91.98%
Discretionary Cash Flow (negative)		-0.22%

GROWTH ANALYSIS

The purpose of growth analysis is to calculate the growth rate of certain financial variables over time using time value of money tools. We expect that increases in gross income will exceed increases in the consumer price index (CPI) by greater than 1 percent. Exhibit 4.18 lists the financial variables for which growth rates should be calculated. The second column of Exhibit 4.18 presents the growth rates that indicate positive progress for the particular financial variable.

EXHIBIT 4.18: FINANCIAL VARIABLES AND GROWTH RATES

Variable		Growth Rate
Inflation	-	Should equal CPI
Gross Income	-	Should exceed CPI
Savings Increase	-	Should exceed CPI
Savings Rate	-	Should remain constant or increase
Discretionary Cash Flows (DCF)	-	Should grow somewhat
DCF + Savings	-	Should grow somewhat
Net Worth	-	Should exceed CPI
Investment Assets	-	Should grow exponentially due to combining returns and savings contributions

LIMITATIONS OF FINANCIAL STATEMENT ANALYSIS

Inflation

Because inflation exists, comparing multiple reporting periods will require adjusting certain numbers either to current dollars (inflated dollars) or to some base percentage or index. Inflation reduces the comparability of multi-period financial statements and ratios even when adjusted for such inflation. It is especially important to adjust growth rates for income and savings to real dollars. It is also useful to adjust nominal investment returns for inflation to determine real economic returns.

Use of Estimates

Whenever estimates of values are used, even if provided by expert appraisers, there is some risk that the estimated value is different from the actual fair market value. Such risks should be evaluated considering the purpose of the financial statement analysis. For example, net worth may very well be dependent on the estimated value of personal use assets (which are very difficult to value). Since net worth is used as a denominator for several ratios, an error in the denominator will affect the result of any ratio using that denominator.

Benchmarks

For corporations and industries there are published financial statements and, therefore, clear benchmarks with which to compare ratios for companies in the same industry. Unfortunately, there are few published personal financial statements and, therefore, fewer clearly established benchmarks for individuals. Recall the housing mortgage ratios where benchmarks exist at 28 percent and 36 percent of gross pay.

SENSITIVITY ANALYSIS

Some ratios are more important than others. For example, the long-term savings rate is particularly critical, while the current ratio is not. The relative size of the numerator and denominator may cause some ratios to be more sensitive to changes. Sensitivity analysis allows us to manipulate the numerators and denominators by small increments to determine the impact on the ratio.

RISK ANALYSIS

Risk analysis examines the uncertainty of cash flows to the individual. Uncertainty regarding the asset side of the balance sheet is called business or investment risk. Specifically, earnings may vary due to fluctuations in the value of investments and personal use assets. Financial risk is the risk on the liability side of the balance sheet. Indebtedness is accompanied with fixed interest and principal repayments. There is always some risk as to whether debt repayments can be made. The debt/equity ratio and other debt ratios help to measure the financial risk of the individual.

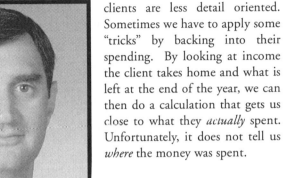

How do you gather client information?

We send out questionnaires that ask for cash flow information, asset listings, and biographical information. We ask the clients to complete them in detail and bring them to our initial meeting. These questionnaires also inquire about financial objectives and require the client to think about their risk tolerance level. Finally, we ask the client to bring all estate documents, tax returns, insurance policies, and investments statements with them to the initial meeting. Whenever possible, we use these original source materials.

Which sources of information are the most helpful?

The original source material seems to be the most helpful since we know it to be accurate. Additionally, spending just a couple of hours with the client in the initial face-to-face meeting is very valuable. This is where we define, refine, and quantify their goals and risk tolerance. Of all the sources of information we use, original source material and face-to-face meetings yield the most value.

Do you have tips on how to get all of the client information from your clients?

Having clients supply original source material is easiest for them. It motivates the client, with very little effort, to provide us with accurate data. All clients have account statements, copies of wills, tax returns, and so on. Oftentimes, though, with cash flow information,

clients are less detail oriented. Sometimes we have to apply some "tricks" by backing into their spending. By looking at income the client takes home and what is left at the end of the year, we can then do a calculation that gets us close to what they *actually* spent. Unfortunately, it does not tell us *where* the money was spent.

Do you prepare balance sheets, income statements, statements of cash flow, and/or changes in net worth for your clients?

We do prepare balance sheets, in particular, for our clients. We find balance sheets to be most useful, especially the investable assets balance sheet. This enables us to advise the client around issues such as asset allocation and investment repositioning. We do not prepare cash flow statements. Since most of our clients are high net worth individuals, cash flow is not an issue. We do provide changes in net worth on a quarter-by-quarter basis for all of our clients while we are monitoring their investments. We show them performance rates of return as well as comparative indices and change of value. Again, this is an investment valuation change, not an overall net worth change.

DISCUSSION QUESTIONS

1. What is the relationship between GAAP/FASB and personal financial statements?
2. Describe some of the uses of personal financial statements.
3. What is the purpose of the balance sheet?
4. What items are included on the balance sheet?
5. Discuss the presentation of the balance sheet (i.e., how items are listed and why).
6. What is the purpose of the income statement?
7. What items are included on the income statement?
8. Discuss the presentation of the income statement (i.e., how items are listed and why).
9. What is the purpose of the statement of cash flows?
10. What items are included on the statement of cash flows?
11. Discuss the presentation of the statement of cash flows (i.e., how items are listed and why).
12. What is the purpose of the statement of changes in net worth?
13. What items are included on the statement of net worth?
14. Discuss the presentation of the statement of net worth (i.e., how items are listed and why).
15. What are the differences between long term and current assets/liabilities?
16. Why are financial ratios important to financial planning?
17. What is the importance of keeping accurate and up-to-date financial statements?
18. What is fair market value?
19. What is liquidity?
20. Why do we prepare four financial statements?
21. Discuss the importance of vertical analysis.
22. What are some of the limitations of personal financial statements?

EXERCISES

1. What are the three balancing equations for the balance sheet?
2. What do current assets and current liabilities have in common?
3. The statement of cash flows separates cash flows into what three categories?
4. Your client purchased a new living room set for $6,500 last month. Which financial statement/s would this purchase affect and how?
5. How would each of the following items affect net worth?
   a. Repayment of a loan using funds from a savings account.
   b. Purchase of an automobile that is 75 percent financed with a 25 percent down payment.
   c. The S&P 500 increases, and the client has an S&P Indexed Mutual Fund.
   d. Interest rates increase, and the client has a substantial bond portfolio.
6. Lauren and Herb have the following assets:

Liquid assets	$6,750
Investment assets	$16,250
House	$125,000
Current liabilities	$3,100
Long-term liabilities	$86,000

   Compute the total assets, total liabilities, and net worth.
7. Compute the current ratio based on the facts given in question 6.

8. After reviewing Kenny and Jane's financial statements, the following information was determined:

Liquid assets	$ 3,976
Current assets	$10,738
Annual Nondiscretionary Expenses	$13,913
Current liabilities	$ 9,247

Compute this couple's Emergency Fund Ratio. Does it fall within the target goal?

9. After reviewing Matt and Jennifer's Annual Statement of Income and Expenses, the following information was determined:

Mortgage Principal	$ 5,467
Mortgage Interest	$21,500
Property Tax	$2,000
Homeowners Insurance Premium	$1,800

The couple has gross monthly income of $9,500. Has this couple taken on debt in excess of what is reasonable for their income, according to benchmarks set by mortgage lenders?

10. In addition to the information in Exercise 9, Matt and Jennifer had other annual debt payments of $11,600. Compute the monthly housing costs and other debt repayments to monthly gross income ratio. Do Matt and Jennifer qualify for a mortgage loan?

11. Mariska and Bryant Hahn have the following assets and liabilities:

Checking account	$2,000
House	$125,000
Savings account	$3,000
CDs	$5,000
Automobile	$13,500
Stocks	$10,000
Utilities	$500
Mortgage	$80,000
Auto loan	$5,000
Credit card bills	$1,500

Determine their net worth.

12. Use the following items to determine total assets, total liabilities, net worth, total cash inflows, total cash outflows:

Net monthly salary	$2,280
Rent	$750
Savings account balance	$2,000
Auto loan	$416
Money market investments account balance	$4,800
Clothing expense	$150
Value of home computer	$1,200
Groceries	$220
Entertainment expense	$130
Value of autos	$10,800
Student loan payment	$212
Utilities	$510
Laundry expense	$46
Insurance	$368
Balance of student loan	$8,625

13. The Coopers have a net worth of $250,000 before any of the following transactions:
   ▲   Paid off credit cards of $9,000 using a savings account.
   ▲   Transferred $5,000 from checking to their IRAs.
   ▲   Purchased $2,500 of furniture with credit.
   What is the net worth of the Coopers after these transactions?

14. What are the advantages of performing vertical analysis on financial statements?

15. Explain how inflation causes a limitation to financial statement analysis.

PROBLEMS

1. Given the following information develop a beginning of the year balance sheet.

Beginning Date	1/1/2002
End Date	12/31/2002
Client Name	Frank and Lois Fox
Year	2002

	Beginning Balance	Ending Balance	Income/Expenses Amount (Yearly)
401(k)			$750
401(k) - Frank	$0	$1,500	
403(b)			$990
403(b) - Lois	$0	$990	
Auto Loan	$15,432	$10,436	
Auto Loan Interest			$381
Auto Loan Principal			$4,996
Auto Maintenance			$600
Automobile - Frank	$20,000	$18,000	
Automobile - Lois	$5,750	$5,175	
Automobile Insurance Premiums			$2,124
Checking	$10,000	$15,570	
Child Support			$2,400
Clothing			$3,600
Credit Card	$10,870	$10,417	
Credit Card Payments Interest			$1,707
Credit Card Payments Principal			$453
Entertainment			$4,200
Federal Income Tax (W/H)			$7,018
FICA			$4,431
Food			$4,800
Furniture/Household	$36,000	$34,000	
GoCart	$0	$1,200	
Homeowners Insurance Premiums			$534
Jewelry	$6,000	$6,100	
Maid/child care			$4,800
Mortgage on Residence	$72,960	$72,164	
Mortgage Payment Interest			$5,808
Mortgage Payment Principal			$796
Personal Residence	$85,000	$89,250	
Property Tax (Principal Residence)			$850
Reinvestment in Savings Account/Trust			$5,675
Salary - Frank			$25,000
Salary - Lois			$33,000
Savings	$13,500	$14,175	
Savings Account/Trust Fund Interest			$5,675
Trust Fund	$100,000	$105,000	
Tuition and Education Expenses			$2,893
Utilities			$2,100

Additional Transactions
Gift of Bedroom set worth $2,000 to Franks little sister
401(k) match = 3% of Income
Bought a Go-Cart for Son for $1,200

2. Use the data in Problem 1 to create an income statement.

3. Use the data in Problem 1 to create a statement of cash flows.

4. Use the data in Problem 1 to create a statement of net worth.

5. Use the data in Problem 1 to create an end of the year balance sheet.

6. Compute the following ratios:
   a. Emergency Fund
   b. Current Ratio
   c. Total Debt to Net Worth
   d. Long-term Debt to Net Worth
   e. Total Debt to Total Assets
   f. Long-Term Debt To Total Assets
   g. Monthly Housing Costs To Monthly Gross Income
   h. Monthly Housing Costs And Other Debt Repayments To Monthly Gross Income
   i. Savings Ratio
   j. Discretionary Cash Flow Plus Savings To Annual Gross Income
   k. Income On Investments
   l. Return On Investments
   m. Investment Assets To Annual Gross Income

7. Prepare a vertical analysis of the ending balance sheet and the income and expense statement.

CHAPTER 5

Establishing Financial Direction

LEARNING OBJECTIVES:

After learning the material in this chapter, you will be able to:

1. Identify the 8 steps for establishing financial direction.

2. Assist clients in identifying an appropriate financial mission.

3. Identify external and internal environmental information that is relevant for a particular client.

4. Assist clients in identifying financial goals and objectives.

5. Analyze a client's internal strengths and weaknesses.

6. Analyze external environmental opportunities and threats as they apply to a client.

7. Formulate appropriate financial strategies.

8. Assist clients in analyzing and selecting the financial strategy that best meets their needs and desires.

9. Assist clients in implementing and monitoring their financial plan.

THE PROCESS

Once the financial planner has an understanding of the external environment and has gathered the client's internal and financial data, the process of establishing financial direction may begin. As depicted in Exhibit 5.1, this process has eight steps:

EXHIBIT 5.1: STEPS FOR ESTABLISHING FINANCIAL DIRECTION

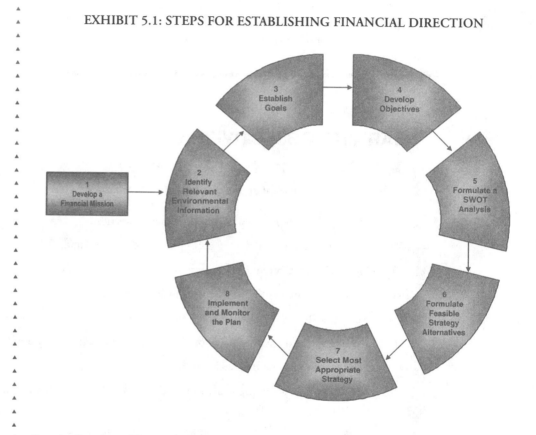

Step 1 - Develop a Financial Mission.
Step 2 - Identify Relevant Environmental Information.
Step 3 - Establish Goals.
Step 4 - Develop Objectives.
Step 5 - Formulate a SWOT Analysis.
Step 6 - Formulate Feasible Strategic Alternatives.
Step 7 - Select the Most Appropriate Strategy.
Step 8 - Implement and Monitor the Plan.

The eight steps of establishing financial direction are completed in sequential order because each step is dependent upon the previous step. The elimination of any step may result in the loss of direction and possibly result in an inappropriate financial strategy. Furthermore, the financial planner must periodically monitor the external and internal environments so that changes in the environment may be responded to appropriately. Monitoring is a continuous and ongoing process that does not end once the plan has been implemented. Modifications to the plan must be made as changes in situations and circumstances require.

In an effort to perform the process of establishing financial direction in a manner that is concise and systematic, we recommend the use of the Client/Planner Worksheet for Establishing Financial Direction illustrated in Exhibit 5.2. The application of this worksheet will be demonstrated throughout this chapter. Notice that the worksheet has a header for the client's name and date, a footer for the planner's name, a section for the financial mission, a section for financial goals and objectives, and a section where each goal/objective is identified and classified as a need or want, with the want objectives ranked from 1 (nice to have) to 5 (of great importance).

Establishing Financial Direction
Client/Planner Worksheet

Client Name_____   **Date**_____

FINANCIAL MISSION
1. Educate the client as to what a financial mission is and the importance of it being broad and enduring.
2. Working with your client, develop a financial mission that your client is willing to embrace.

_____

_____

Financial Goals & Objectives
1. Discuss and explain common financial goals with client.
2. Identify goals the client is interested in achieving.
3. Write client objective under appropriate goal classification.
4. Ensure all "need" objectives have been identified and documented.
5. Classify each objective as a want or a need; remember to remain objective.
6. For each "want" objective, the client must assign a weight between 1 and 5 (1 = objective would be nice to have, 5 = objective is of great importance).

Goal:		
Objectives:	**Need**	**Want**
	•	• _____
	•	• _____
	•	• _____

Goal		
Objectives:	**Need**	**Want**
	•	• _____
	•	• _____
	•	• _____

Goal:		
Objectives:	**Need**	**Want**
	•	• _____
	•	• _____
	•	• _____

Goal:		
Objectives:	**Need**	**Want**
	•	• _____
	•	• _____
	•	• _____

Planner's Name _____

DEVELOP THE MISSION - STEP ONE

The first step in establishing financial direction is the development of a **financial mission**. A financial mission is a broad and enduring statement that identifies the client's long-term purpose for wanting a financial plan. Since the mission statement is broad and enduring, it should not change throughout the planning process. The purpose of a financial mission is twofold. First, it ensures a common understanding between the client and the planner as to why the financial plan is being created and implemented. Second, it provides a basis for the creation of feasible alternative goals, objectives, and strategies, and for selecting among strategic alternatives. Throughout the text, we have assumed that the financial mission for most clients is to achieve financial independence and to avoid catastrophic financial occurrences and thus, financial dependence. In Chapter 1, we defined financial independence as the ability to maintain a desired lifestyle, without employment income.

Occasionally, clients may believe that their mission is to buy a house, a boat, or some other personal property. This type of thinking is common while in the **linear-thinking** phase. This misunderstanding is usually due to shortsightedness and a lack of financial planning knowledge. However, through sufficient education, the planner can assist the client in understanding the difference between a goal, an objective, and a mission. It is the responsibility of the financial planner to ensure that the client either embraces this mission or develops and embraces another, more suitable mission. To embrace a mission, the client must have a clear understanding of it and must want to achieve it.

Appropriate financial planning requires a holistic approach. All aspects of a client's past, present, and projected financial situation need to be evaluated. It is inappropriate to only focus on one or two aspects of a client's situation since all aspects are interrelated and interdependent. That is why developing an appropriate financial mission is so important. The financial planner can use the Establishing Financial Direction Worksheet to begin formalizing the financial planning process when working with the client.

Exhibit 5.3 identifies how the Nelsons, the couple introduced at the end of Chapter 3, might complete the Financial Mission section of the Establishing Financial Direction Worksheet. When completing the Financial Mission section of the Establishing Financial Direction Worksheet, the first step is for the financial planner to communicate with and educate the client so that a realistic, enduring, and broad financial mission is developed. Once the client has embraced the mission, it should be documented on the worksheet. Throughout this chapter, we will assume the Nelsons have embraced the mission, to achieve financial independence and to avoid catastrophic financial occurrences and thus, financial dependence.

financial mission - a broad and enduring statement that identifies the client's long-term purpose for wanting a financial plan

linear-thinking - the initial phase of a client's thinking process when setting financial direction, in which a client focuses on accomplishing one particular goal or narrow objective using a very compartmentalized, simplistic, self-designed financial plan

Establishing Financial Direction
Client/Planner Worksheet

Client Name___*David and Dana Nelson*___   Date___*February 16, 2002*___

FINANCIAL MISSION

1. Educate the client as to what a financial mission is and the importance of it being broad and enduring.
2. Working with your client, develop a financial mission that your client is willing to embrace.

To achieve financial independence and to avoid catastrophic financial occurrences and thus financial dependence.

IDENTIFY RELEVANT ENVIRONMENTAL INFORMATION – STEP TWO

Once the mission is established and embraced, the financial planner should identify the relevant external and internal environmental information that applies to the client. During this step, the planner should apply the skills and information discussed in Chapter 2 – The External Environment, to identify external environmental information that is current and relevant to the client. The planner must also be able to identify the relevant information that has been collected about the client. Lessons learned in Chapter 3 – Communication and Internal Environmental Analysis should also be applied during this step. It is important to keep the mission in mind to determine whether information is relevant or not. Only relevant information should be listed in order to keep the amount of information collected manageable. During this step, we will only gather and list the facts. Analysis will be conducted and conclusions will be drawn later while developing the SWOT Analysis, during step 5.

The following external and internal environmental information has been gathered and determined to be relevant to the Nelsons.

Relevant External Environmental Information

▲ Mortgage rates are 8.0 percent for 30 years and 7.5 percent for 15 years, fixed.
▲ GDP is expected to be less than 3 percent.
▲ Inflation is expected to be 3.1 percent.
▲ Expected return on investment is 10.4 percent for common stocks, 12.1 percent for small company stocks, and 3.7 percent for U.S. Treasury bills.
▲ College education costs are $15,000 per year ($15,000 for 5 years equals $75,000).

Relevant Internal Environmental Information

▲ David has been employed at the bank for twelve years and has a salary of $70,000 and a gross income of $71,050.

▲ The Nelsons are in the Asset Accumulation Phase.

▲ Relevant financial ratios, identified in Chapter 4, are as follows:

    ▲ Liquid assets to monthly non-discretionary expenses ratio is 0.60.

    ▲ Housing costs to gross income ratio is 33.6 percent.

    ▲ All debt payments to gross income ratio is 39.3 percent.

    ▲ Annual savings to annual gross income ratio is 11.2 percent.

    ▲ Investment asset ratio is 1.09 for the previous year.

▲ The family is insured under David's company indemnity plan. There is a $200 family deductible with 80/20 major medical coverage and $500,000 lifetime limit for each family member.

▲ David has a term life insurance policy provided by his employer with a face amount of $25,000.

▲ David has a private disability insurance policy covering accidental disability for "own occupation" with a 30-day elimination period. The benefit is $2,700 per month until age 65, and it has an annual premium of $761.

▲ The Nelsons have an HO3 policy with dwelling extension and replacement cost on contents. The deductible is $250 with an annual premium of $950.

▲ David currently contributes 5.43 percent of his salary into the company's 401(k) plan. The company contributes dollar for dollar up to 3 percent. David's maximum contribution is 16 percent.

▲ David and Dana are just within the 28 percent marginal federal income tax bracket.

ESTABLISH FINANCIAL GOALS – STEP THREE

The next step toward establishing financial direction is the establishment of **financial goals**. Goals are high-level statements of desires that may be for either the short or long- run. Short-run goals are those that will occur within five years. Long-run goals are those that will occur sometime beyond five years. Identifying goals requires the client to consider all aspects of a financial plan. If all goals are identified and prioritized, the client is less likely to overlook some goals while focusing on others. However, performing this process of defining and prioritizing goals often results in the client entering the second common phase of thinking--**paradoxical thinking**. Remember that advancing to the paradoxical thinking level is where the client may begin to become discouraged or frustrated with the process due to a new awareness of the extent of financial planning required to achieve multiple and often conflicting goals. During this phase, the planner should keep explanations simple and should discuss goals in present dollar value terms since future value terms are more difficult for the client to understand.

Generally, financial goals can be divided into 5 categories. Each category will be discussed fully in subsequent chapters.

▲ Insurance Planning – The goal is to mitigate the risks of catastrophic losses to persons, property, and liability by maintaining appropriate insurance coverage while paying efficient premiums.

▲ Retirement Planning –The goal is to adequately provide inflation protected retirement

financial goals - high-level statements of financial desire that may be for the short run or the long run

paradoxical thinking - the second phase of a client's thinking process when setting financial direction, in which a client tries to focus on several simultaneous objectives, causing confusion, goal conflict, and ambiguity. The paradoxical thinking phase is where a client often seeks the advice of a financial planner

income at an appropriate age for full life expectancy, conservatively estimated.

- ▲ Estate Planning – The goal is to have a proper estate plan consistent with transfer goals.
- ▲ Tax Planning – The goal is to arrange income tax affairs so as to mitigate income tax liability and take advantage of incentives in the income tax law as appropriate.
- ▲ Investment Planning – The goal is to save and invest so as to accumulate capital for retirement, wealth transfer, and other expenditure objectives such as the purchase of personal property, education, lump sum payments, and emergencies.

The financial planner can again use the Establishing Financial Direction Worksheet to assist in establishing financial goals. As the Nelson's financial planner, you should work with and educate them so that they become familiar with the common financial goals. Next you should assist them in identifying the goals they are interested in achieving. Once the Nelsons understand the importance and interdependence of all common financial goals, the goals should be documented in the Financial Goal section of the Establishing Financial Direction Worksheet. Exhibit 5.4 identifies the goals that are relevant to the Nelsons.

EXHIBIT 5.4: ESTABLISHING FINANCIAL DIRECTION - FINANCIAL GOALS

Establishing Financial Direction
Client/Planner Worksheet

Client Name_____*David and Dana Nelson*_____ Date_____*February 16, 2002*_____

FINANCIAL MISSION
1. Educate the client as to what a financial mission is and the importance of it being broad and enduring.
2. Working with your client, develop a financial mission that your client is willing to embrace.

To achieve financial independence and to avoid catastrophic financial occurrences and thus financial dependence.

Financial Goals & Objectives
1. Discuss and explain common financial goals with client.
2. Identify goals the client is interested in achieving.

Goal: *Mitigate risks of catastrophic losses by maintaining appropriate insurance coverage while paying efficient premiums.*		
Objectives:	Need	Want
	☐	☐ ____

Goal: *Provide inflation protected retirement income, assuming a life expectancy of 92 years of age.*		
Objectives:	Need	Want
	☐	☐ ____

Goal: *Develop an appropriate estate plan consistent with transfer goals.*		
Objectives:	Need	Want
	☐	☐ ____

Goal: *Arrange income tax affairs so that income tax liability is minimized and to take advantage of tax law incentives.*		
Objectives:	Need	Want
	☐	☐ ____

Goal: *Accumulate capital, through saving and investing, for the purchase of personal property, education, and emergencies.*		
Objectives:	Need	Want
	☐	☐ ____

Where on the Web

Association for Financial Consulting and Planning Education *www.afcpe.org*
Bloomberg Personal *www.bloomberg.com*
Bureau of Economic Analysis *www.bea.doc.gov*
Bureau of Labor Statistics *www.bls.gov*
CPI Home Page *stats.bls.gov/cpihome.htm*
Economy at a Glance *stats.bls.gov/eag/eag.us.htm*
Forbes Magazine *www.forbes.com*
Fortune Magazine *www.fortune.com*
National Association of Personal Financial Advisors *www.napfa.org*
Service Corps of Retired Executives *www.score.org*
Small Business Association *www.sba.gov*
Society of Financial Service Professionals *www.asclu.org*

DEVELOP FINANCIAL OBJECTIVES – STEP FOUR

financial objectives - statements of financial desire that contain time and measurement attributes making them more specific than financial goals

The fourth step in establishing financial direction is the development of **financial objectives**. Objectives are more specific than goals. Several objectives may be developed for each goal category and should include time and measurement attributes when appropriate.

Usually, clients are immersed in paradoxical thinking during this step. The client has the propensity to become confused and frustrated due to the conflicting issue of unlimited wants and limited resources. The planner can greatly assist the client, however, by presenting information in a clear, concise, systematic, and objective manner.

Once objectives have been identified for each goal category, each objective must then be classified as either a "want" or "need." Generally, the client is more focused on identifying the "want" objectives. Therefore, the planner is responsible for ensuring that all of the "need" objectives are identified. The planner should keep the mission and relevant environmental factors in mind when assisting the client in the development of financial objectives.

Distinguishing between a "want" and "need" can be difficult for clients because subjectivity and strong desires become an issue. However, asking both of the following questions of each objective can eliminate this potential difficulty.

Is this objective necessary to accomplish the financial mission?

Does the law require that this objective be implemented?

If the answer to <u>either</u> of these questions is yes, the objective is a "need." If the answer to <u>both</u> of these questions is no, the objective is a "want."

134

For example, under the goal of Protection Against Risk, the objectives of property insurance on an old car, and auto liability coverage may have been identified. If we ask the questions above in reference to auto property insurance, we find that in this case auto property insurance is a "want" objective. Implementation of this objective is not necessary to accomplish the mission of achieving financial independence and to avoid catastrophic financial occurrences nor does law require it since it is an older car and is paid for in full. However, asking the same questions with respect to liability insurance, we may find that liability insurance is a "need" objective because the state law requires all licensed automobile owners to carry liability insurance.

Objectives classified as "wants" are further analyzed by having the client attach weights to them. Assigning weights to objectives allows the planner and the client to objectively evaluate a subjective desire. A weight is a number between "1" and "5" assigned by the client to each "want" objective to express the importance or desirability of that objective relative to the others. A "5" should be assigned to a "want" objective of great importance--something the client has a strong desire to achieve. A "1" should be assigned to a "want" objective that the client would like to have but could do without, if the objective was not achieved. The weight assignment will be used during strategy selection to assist in determining which "want" objectives will be implemented. It is probable that not all of the "want" objectives will be achieved. However, all of the "need" objectives must be implemented in order to achieve the financial mission and/or comply with the law. Therefore, objectives classified as "needs" do not require weight assignment.

As the Nelson's financial planner you should continue using the Establishing Financial Direction Worksheet to document and formalize the Nelson's desired objectives. The first step is to identify all of the objectives that are relevant to the Nelsons. Next, each objective must be classified as either a "want" or a "need" objective. To assist in the classification of each objective, you should determine whether the objective is necessary to accomplish the mission, and whether the implementation of the objective is required by law. The final step is to assist the Nelsons in establishing a weight for all of the "want" objectives. The weight indicates how important implementing that objective is to the Nelsons. Exhibit 5.5 identifies a partial list of objectives that are important to the Nelsons. Throughout this chapter, we will only address a partial list of objectives in order to keep the amount of material manageable.

EXHIBIT 5.5: CLIENT/PLANNER WORKSHEET - FINANCIAL OBJECTIVES

Establishing Financial Direction
Client/Planner Worksheet

Client Name___*David and Dana Nelson*___   Date___*February 16, 2002*___

FINANCIAL MISSION
1. Educate the client as to what a financial mission is and the importance of it being broad and enduring.
2. Working with your client, develop a financial mission that your client is willing to embrace.

> *To achieve financial independence and to avoid catastrophic financial occurrences and thus financial dependence.*

Financial Goals & Objectives
1. Discuss and explain common financial goals with client.
2. Identify goals the client is interested in achieving.
3. Write client objective under appropriate goal classification.
4. Ensure all need" objectives have been identified and documented.
5. Classify each objective as a want or a need; remember to remain objective.
6. For each "want" objective, the client must assign a weight between 1 and 5. (1 = objective would be nice to have, 5 = objective is of great importance).

Goal: *Mitigate risks of catastrophic losses by maintaining appropriate insurance coverage while paying efficient premiums.*		
Objectives:	**Need**	**Want**
Within 6 months, modify Life Insurance to include $500 term, 20-year.	✔	☐ ___
Within 6 months, modify Disability Insurance to include disability by sickness.	✔	☐ ___
Within 6 months, modify Health Insurance to include major medical with $10,000 deductible due to life time limit.	✔	☐ ___

Goal: *Provide inflation protected retirement income, assuming a life expectancy of 92 years of age.*		
Objectives:	**Need**	**Want**
Retire at age 67 with an 80% wage replacement thereby, maintaining lifestyle.	✔	☐ ___
Retire at age 62 with an 80% wage replacement thereby, maintaining lifestyle.	☐	✔ _5_

Goal: *Develop an appropriate estate plan consistent with transfer goals.*		
Objectives:	**Need**	**Want**
Develop a will for David, within three months.	✔	☐ ___
Develop a will for Dana, within three months.	✔	☐ ___

Goal: *Arrange income tax affairs so that income tax liability is minimized and to take advantage of tax law incentives.*		
Objectives:	**Need**	**Want**
Reduce tax payments to the minimum amount allowable by law.	☐	✔ _5_
Within 2 months, modify contributions into 401(k) plan to ensure adequate retirement income and to reduce income tax liability.	✔	☐ ___

Goal: *Accumulate capital, through saving and investing, for the purchase of personal property, education, and emergencies.*		
Objectives:	**Need**	**Want**
Purchase a $200,000 home in Key West within 5 years.	☐	✔ _4_
Save for college tuition so that money is available when John and Gabrielle begin college.	☐	✔ _3_
Purchase a new car in two years, twelve years, and at retirement.	☐	✔ _2_
Eliminate credit card debt within six years	☐	✔ _3_

SWOT ANALYSIS – STEP FIVE

A **SWOT analysis** is a useful tool to assist the planner in converting several bits of relevant information into an understandable format. It helps the planner understand how the internal and external environments impact the client's situation-- a critical element to developing feasible and responsive strategies. The acronym, SWOT, stands for Strengths, Weaknesses, Opportunities, and Threats. A SWOT analysis is developed by analyzing the relevant environmental factors that were identified in Step 2 of the process, then listing the client's internal strengths and weaknesses and the external environment's opportunities and threats. Once the strengths, weaknesses, opportunities, and threats are identified, the planner systematically analyzes the SWOT list to assist in the generation of feasible alternative strategies.

When identifying the strengths, the planner should consider the internal and financial data collected from the client. Consider client strengths such as, appropriate consumption and savings behaviors, and positive attitudes and beliefs with regard to financial planning and financial stability. Indicate if the timing of the plan is appropriate to the client's goals and objectives, and if the client's subjective perception of their financial situation is similar to the planner's objective appraisal of the client's financial situation. Consider areas in which the client has adequate insurance coverage for life, health, disability, long-term care, property, and liability. List the financial ratios that meet or exceed recommended levels.

When identifying weaknesses, the planner should again consider the internal and financial data collected from the client. Identify client weaknesses, such as poor savings behaviors and unwise consumption habits, a poor attitude toward financial planning, special needs, and financial instability. Indicate if the timing of the plan is inappropriate for the client, and if the client's subjective perception of their financial situation is dissimilar to the objective financial situation. Consider areas in which the client has inadequate insurance coverage for life, health, disability, long-term care, property, and liability. List the financial ratios that do not meet recommended levels.

When identifying external environmental opportunities, the planner should consider monetary trends, favorable interest rates and inflation levels, technological breakthroughs, governmental controls, social attitudes towards businesses, and the emergence of new industries. List favorable trends and forecasts that may positively impact the client's financial plan.

When identifying external environmental threats, the planner should consider unfavorable interest rates and inflation forecasts, technological breakthroughs, governmental controls, public distrust of businesses, and emergence of new industries. List unfavorable trends and forecasts that may negatively impact the client's financial plan.

SWOT analysis - an analysis that helps the financial planner understand how internal and external environmental factors impact the client's financial situation. The acronym, SWOT, stands for Strengths, Weaknesses, Opportunities, and Threats

Using the Nelsons as an example, the following SWOT may be developed.

STRENGTHS	▲ David has a good job with good income. ▲ They have good net worth for their age. ▲ They have a good-investment-assets-to-income ratio for their ages.
WEAKNESSES	▲ Insufficient annual savings to drive goals. ▲ Inadequate life and disability insurance. ▲ Inappropriate investment risk. ▲ Too much debt. ▲ Unrealistic goals for current savings and investments. ▲ Deficient health insurance policy. ▲ No estate planning. ▲ Poor housing-cost-to-income ratio.
OPPORTUNITIES	▲ Mortgage rates are favorable for refinancing. ▲ Expected return on investments for stocks is high. ▲ Expected inflation rate is low. ▲ Current interest rates are low. ▲ Leading Economic Index signals expansion.
THREATS	▲ The current cost of college (room, board, and tuition) is $15,000 per year per child. ▲ Tight labor market may lead the Federal Reserve to tighten interest rates which could cause a slow down in the GDP growth and/or adversely impact investment returns and interest rates.

FORMULATE FEASIBLE STRATEGY ALTERNATIVES – STEP SIX

EXHIBIT 5.6: STRATEGY FORMULATION

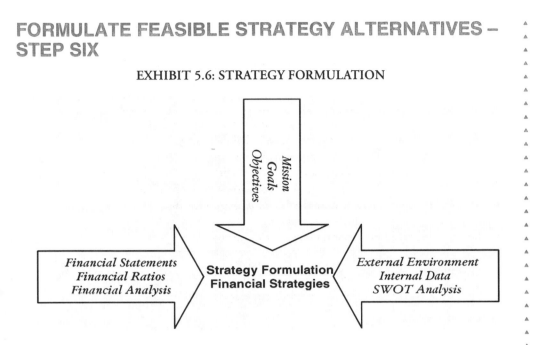

As depicted in Exhibit 5.6 several financial, environmental and internal client aspects must be considered and some analyzed before feasible strategies can be formulated for the client.

▲ The client's financial situation must be analyzed using financial data collection techniques (Chapter 4).
▲ The external environment and its affect on the client must be considered (Chapter 2).
▲ The client's internal data and lifecycle positioning must be understood (Chapter 3).
▲ The client's mission, goals, and objectives must also remain central to the development of strategies.

When formulating feasible strategies, we recommend that you begin by developing an abbreviated Income Statement to identify the client's current cash flow situation. Then, identify the costs associated with implementing the "need" objectives and add the required cash outflows necessary to meet the need requirements to the existing cash flow. This will provide an estimate of the cash flow required to implement a plan that would accomplish the "need" objectives. Do not be concerned that the addition of these costs may cause the discretionary cash flow to be negative. If a negative discretionary cash flow exists, it may help to bring the client into financial reality.

Using the Nelsons as an example and the initial income statement information gathered in Chapter 4, we can estimate the costs for implementing the "need" objectives.

EXHIBIT 5.7: ABBREVIATED INCOME STATEMENT OF CURRENT CASH FLOWS

Income	$ 71,050
Savings	(5,853)
Ordinary Living Expenses	(21,114)
Other Payments	(25,954)
Insurance Payments	(2,611)
Tuition and Education	(1,000)
Total Taxes	(14,675)
Discretionary Total Cash Flow (Deficit)	$ (157)

The estimated costs for implementing the "need" objectives for the Nelsons are as follows.

Acquire appropriate amount of insurance

▲ Life – add $500,000 term, 20-year, for an estimated cost of $500.

▲ Disability – modify coverage so that it includes disability by sickness, estimated cost of $1,400.

▲ Health – add major medical with $10,000 deductible due to life time limit at an estimated cost of $1,000.

Retire and maintain lifestyle

▲ David should save 10 percent of his salary based on his age. Since his company matches 3 percent, David should save at least 7 percent in his 401(k) plan. David is currently saving 5.43 percent (3,803/70,000). Therefore, he intends to increase his 401(k) savings by $1,099 (1.57 percent).

▲ However, by increasing his 401(k) savings, David will reduce his tax payments by $165 ($1,099 @ 15 percent = $164.85 rounded to nearest dollar). Therefore, the change in cash flow is an increased outflow of $934 ($1,099 – $165).

Reduce debt

▲ The Nelsons should increase their payments toward their credit card debt. However, no estimated amounts will be identified at this time. We will address this objective when selecting a strategy with the client.

Prepare appropriate wills

▲ David and Dana should *each* have an appropriate will created. The estimated cost of having a will drawn up is $500 each, for a total of $1,000.

The Nelsons currently have a cash flow deficit of $157; however, the implementation of all "need" objectives would increase the deficit by $4,834 ($2,900 for insurance, $934 for 401(k) savings, $1,000 for wills) for a total deficit of $4,991 ($4,834 + $157).

EXHIBIT 5.8: DISCRETIONARY CASH FLOWS AFTER IMPLEMENTATION OF "NEED" OBJECTIVES

Discretionary Cash Flow	$ (157)
Life Insurance	(500)
Disability Insurance	(1,400)
Health Insurance	(1,000)
Additional 401(k) contribution	(1,099)
Reduction of tax due to 401(k) savings	165
Will	(1000)
Discretionary cash flow after implementation of "need" objectives	$ (4,991)

Often, as in the case of the Nelsons, the analysis of the abbreviated Income Statement and the addition of costs associated with "need" objectives indicates that there is a shortage of cash. Therefore, either more cash inflow, less cash outflow, or a combination of the two, is required. There are common sources of available cash flows to increase inflows or reduce outflows including:

▲ Cutting discretionary expenses such as entertainment, vacations, utilities, charitable contributions, etc.
▲ Refinancing mortgages to reduce payment or decrease the debt term.
▲ Raising insurance deductibles to reduce premiums.
▲ Making use of tax advantaged savings.
▲ Obtaining additional income from employment.

After determining the cash flow situation, including the implementation of "need" objectives, the next step is to develop strategies that create a positive discretionary cash flow while at the same time resolving weaknesses that were identified in the SWOT analysis and accomplishing, at a minimum, the "need" objectives. Therefore, the planner should consider each of the common methods to increase cash inflow or reduce cash outflow, the opportunities identified in the SWOT analysis, and each of the objectives previously identified by the client and the planner.

While developing alternative strategies, the planner must determine how each strategy might affect cash flow and the client's objectives. Remember, all "need" objectives should be resolved first, and then the "want" objectives should be considered. These alternative strategies will be presented to the client and, with the assistance of the planner, the client will ultimately choose which strategy to implement.

Revisiting the SWOT analysis and taking advantage of the available external opportunities indicate that the Nelsons should refinance their home. Refinancing their home mortgage at 8% will reduce their annual mortgage payment by $4,529 (($1,829.48 - $1,452.03) @ 12)[1]. While analyzing the financial statements and tax returns, it was also discovered that their income taxes are currently over-withheld annually by $4,412. This type of discovery is common and an adjustment to increase receivables will be made on a future balance sheet. The combination of refinancing the home and properly adjusting their income tax withholdings will increase the Nelson's cash flow by $8,941.

1. Assume 30-year loan at 8%. N=360, I=. 6667 (8/12), PV=197,887.67 (prepaid closing costs), PMT=1,452.03.

If we now compare the total cash flow deficit of $4,991 to the newly found cash inflows of $8,941, we find that the Nelsons now have a positive net cash flow of $3,950. Some of this positive cash flow should be used to reduce credit card debt. The remainder of the cash flow may be used to achieve some of the "want" objectives or to create an emergency fund, or increase savings and investments.

Recall that there were two "want" objectives that were most important to the Nelsons (each with a 5 ranking), to minimize payment of income taxes and to retire at age 62. The next most important objective, with a 4 ranking, was to purchase a home in Key West, Florida.

The objective of minimizing the payment of income taxes was resolved while focusing on the "need" objectives. In order for David to retire at age 62 he will either need exceptional investment returns or an increase in periodic savings for retirement by $4,937[1] annually. Purchasing a $200,000 home in Key West will require annual savings of $9,619 for 5 years to create a 20 percent down payment, then monthly mortgage payments of $1,467.53 ($17,610 annually).

Since we have already taken advantage of refinancing and tax savings, we must now consider cutting discretionary expenses, raising deductibles on insurance, or obtaining additional income. Raising deductibles is usually the next option that is considered since it has little impact on the client's daily lives or overall financial plan. Clients seem to be more resistant to cutting discretionary expenses or obtaining additional income since those options can have a significant impact on the client's daily lives.

SELECT THE MOST APPROPRIATE STRATEGY-STEP SEVEN

Strategy selection is a collaborative effort between planner and client. The planner ensures that the client understands all of the aspects of the alternative strategies and educates the client on how to analyze the selection in a systematic and quantitative manner. The client, however, makes the final decision and is responsible for implementing the plan. Therefore, the client's involvement and commitment to the process and the strategy is essential to the successful implementation of the plan.

Strategy selection is made simpler when analyzed in a quantitative manner. It also helps the client move on to the **abstract thinking** level. Using the Strategy Selection Worksheet, as shown in Exhibit 5.7, can assist in this analysis. During the evaluation of each alternative, the planner should discuss the actions that the client must take and what must occur to implement the strategy and how the client might be affected by considering how the strategy might change the client's:

abstract thinking - the third phase of a client's thinking process in establishing financial direction, where a client becomes aware of the consequences of financial actions and understands how day-to-day savings and consumption decisions impact a financial plan

▲ Current consumption and savings behavior.
▲ Existing savings rate.
▲ Time horizon.
▲ Asset allocation.

1. Based on a capital needs analysis, David will need $1,664,193 at retirement. Therefore, FV=1,664,193, I=. 833 (10/12), N=300 (25*12), PV=<38,619>, Annual=10,839.94. Annual minus current: 10,839.94 - 5,903 = 4,936.94

While considering the above-mentioned issues, the client should answer the following questions with the planner's assistance:

1. How easy will it be to implement this strategy?
2. How committed am I to implementing this strategy considering the required sacrifices?

The client should respond to each of these questions using a weighting scale of 1 to 5. For the first question, a 5 would indicate the strategy is *very easy* to implement. For the second, a 5 would indicate the client is *very committed* to implementing the strategy. The answer weightings of each question are multiplied to result in a ranking for that strategy. Those strategies with the highest rankings are the ones most likely to be successful.

The ranking of the "want" objectives include one additional measure. The weight of the objective that was identified on the Establishing Financial Direction – Client/Planner Worksheet should be considered when obtaining the ranking for that strategy. Again, the strategies with the highest rankings are most likely to be successful, and therefore, should be seriously considered. Exhibit 5.9 indicates how the Nelsons may have completed the Strategy Selection Worksheet.

Strategy Selection Worksheet

Client Name _David and Dana Nelson_   **Date** _February 16, 2002_

a) List strategy options.
b) For each strategy option, indicate the objective(s) that is resolved.
c) Discuss, with the client, the impact of implementing the objective.
d) For each strategy option, the client should answer the following questions by ranking the answers 1 to 5.
  - ✓ How easy will it be to implement this strategy? (A 5 ranking indicates very easy to implement.)
  - ✓ How committed am I to implementing this strategy? (A 5 ranking indicates very committed.)
e) For "want" objectives, consider the original importance ranking that was identified when completing the **Client/Planner Worksheet**.

Strategy (Discuss how each strategy impacts relevant objectives)	Benefits of Implementing Strategy	Behavior Change Required	Ease of Implementation	Commitment Level	Ranking
Refinance Home	Increases annual cash flow by $4,529	None	5	5	25
Adjust tax withholdings	Increases annual cash flow by $4,412	None	5	5	25
Increase Savings to 401(k)	Takes advantage of tax-free savings	None since other strategies will increase current cash flow	5	5	25
Raise Insurance Deductibles	Increases cash flow by $200	Acceptance of additional risk	5	3	15
Cut discretionary expenses	Increases annual cash flow by maximum of $2,414	Do not use paid babysitters, eliminate entertainment expenses, etc.	1	2	2
Dana acquires part-time job	Increases annual cash flow	Put Gabby in daycare	2	1	2
David acquires a second job	Increases annual cash flow	Spend less time with family	2	1	2

144

After completing the Strategy Selection Worksheet, the Nelsons have decided to refinance their home, adjust their tax withholdings, and increase their contribution to the 401(k) plan. This increase in cash flow will allow them to meet all of their "need" objectives. They have also decided to reduce their credit card debt using the surplus cash flow and to begin putting money toward an emergency fund. The Nelsons now realize that purchasing a vacation home in Key West is not reasonable at this time and have decided to revisit this objective in five years. David also realizes that retiring at age 62 may not be possible; however, he has made a promise to himself to increase his 401(k) savings each time he gets a raise until he reaches the maximum allowable contribution.

David and Dana do not want to raise their insurance deductibles because they enjoy the peace of mind of having low insurance deductibles. They do not want to acquire an additional job because spending time with family is very important to both of them.

STRATEGY IMPLEMENTATION AND MONITORING - STEP EIGHT

Successful strategy implementation is primarily dependent upon the client. The client must implement and make the plan work. The financial planner can improve the probability of successful implementation by ensuring that the client has a detailed understanding of the current strategy, can measure progress toward the attainment of objectives, and, through periodic monitoring, can adjust the plan as necessary. The planner can be reasonably assured that the client has a detailed understanding of the plan if the client actively participates in the goal and objectives development and in strategy selection.

Establishing targets and measures aids in monitoring the client's progress toward attaining objectives. A minimum of one target and one measure should be established for each objective. Both the planner and the client should monitor targets and achievement. Therefore, the planner should present the client with the established targets and measures for each objective and show how they apply to each.

Periodic monitoring of the plan is critical. Internal and external circumstances change and plans do not always work as expected. Clients get married, have children, and may eventually divorce. Some remarry and begin second families. Economic forces change and technology advances. For a host of reasons, quarterly monitoring is recommended, along with annual face-to-face meetings with the client. Therefore, just as situations are expected to change over time, so is it necessary to modify the financial plan.

CHAPTER 5: ESTABLISHING FINANCIAL DIRECTION

Do you use the client/planner worksheet (i.e. a fact finder) to determine the goals and objectives of your clients?

I believe client/planner worksheets are an invaluable tool for data collection. These fact finders offer clients a structured format for assembling essential planning documents such as wills and trusts, or even a foundation for developing a rudimentary balance sheet and income statement. This preliminary data assembly most often enables our initial interview to be more productive. Probing questions attempt to highlight any potential obstacles, both financial and emotional, which may prevent a client from achieving their stated goals and objectives. These worksheets, however, can never fully replace the value of a one-on-one interview. Such interactions often produce candid conversation on sometimes delicate planning subjects. It is important to note that the human element of emotion is often lost among the sterile context of checklists, pen, and paper.

Do you find clients are aware of their financial goals and objectives or do they require more assistance from you in this area?

I find that many clients have used a fragmented approach to their own financial affairs. Most are a piecemeal assembly of mis-matched documents, haphazard investment positions, and well-intentioned yet ineffectual attempts at risk management. In short, their "comprehensive financial strategies" lack clarity of purpose and are more a result of default than design. Most lack coordination and efficiency. My role as a professional advisor is to aid clients in both identifying and prioritizing their goals and objectives. We then map out a strategy designed to achieve those goals and commit it to writing. This declaration represents an explicit linkage between a client's long-term objectives and their need to execute those actions necessary to achieve their stated goals.

How do you approach clients that have unrealistic goals?

Each of us has a finite dimension to both our capital and our time. These constraints may undermine our ability to achieve all of our stated goals and objectives. At least on some level, all clients are faced with making a choice between immediate capital consumption and long-term savings accumulations. Their decision is based, in large part, on the clients' perception for future investment performance. Sometimes overly optimistic expectations expose a client to a risk of failure. Our role is to temper this exuberance and refocus on the long-term historic normalcy of market performance. This client must be directed to review their statement of goals and objectives in light of their limited capital resources and realistic expectations for future investment performance. This client is faced with the following choices:

▲ Save more aggressively today at the expense of instant gratification.
▲ Begin investing more aggressively with the potential, but not the guarantee, of achieving greater investment performance.
▲ Or, reduce their expectations of retirement age.

When have you had the best success with the client following the financial plan you created for them?

The greatest success I have experienced as a professional planner rests squarely on my ability to help clients effectively organize their financial lives. By providing an inter-disciplinary perspective I am able to integrate structural efficiencies in both plan design and implementation. Whether it's estate or retirement planning, charitable inclinations, investment, tax or risk management, finding creative solutions to solve unique client problems affords a very fulfilling and rewarding career as a financial planner.

JOHN GISOLFI, MS, CFP™, RFC

DISCUSSION QUESTIONS

1. What are the eight steps in establishing a financial mission?
2. What is the definition of a financial mission?
3. What are the most common financial goals?
4. How do financial goals and financial objectives differ?
5. Why must a financial planner keep abreast of the external environment?
6. How does client subjectivity effect the establishment of financial objectives?
7. What is the difference between "need" and "want" objectives?
8. What questions can be asked of financial objectives to determine if the objective is a "need" or a "want" objective?
9. What does the acronym SWOT stand for?
10. How can a SWOT analysis be useful to a financial planner?
11. What must be considered when formulating strategy alternatives?
12. What are common methods to increase cash inflow or reduce cash outflow?
13. What should be considered when selecting strategies to implement?
14. How can the planner improve the probability of successful implementation of strategies?
15. How often should a financial plan be monitored?

EXERCISES

1. Suppose Wilma and Fred contacted you, a financial planner, to assist them in saving for a car, the children's education, and a boat. Which thinking phase are they probably demonstrating?
2. What would you do if a client came to you insisting that their financial mission was to buy a 1965 Mustang?
3. If you were working with a client to distinguish between a "want" and a "need" objective and the client wanted to categorize buying a vacation home as a "need" what would you do?
4. What would you say or do to assist a client in understanding the difference between a goal and an objective?
5. What should a planner and a client take into consideration when determining strategies to implement?

PROBLEMS

1. Assume that you had a client with multiple objectives requiring monthly cash flows of $400, $250, $150, $750, and $325, respectively. Also assume that the client's current discretionary cash flow per month is $380.
   ▲ What technique would you use to bring the client in #1 into economic reality?
   ▲ How would you distinguish between "need" objectives and "want" objectives?
   ▲ Where might you look for additional available cash flows to meet #1's objectives?
2. Suppose a couple hired you as their financial planner. Upon brief investigation you collect the following information. The couple has been married for 5 years. They have no children. They take expensive vacations several times a year. They both have good jobs and both save the maximum allowed in their 401(k) plans. The mortgage on the house is at a 10.3 percent rate. The current mortgage rate is 8.15 percent. Their credit cards have been maintaining a balance of about $1,500, which they never pay in full, and they have a monthly discretionary cash flow deficit of $98. What would be your recommendations to increase their monthly discretionary cash flow?

Basic Financial Planning Tools
in BRIEF →

- The power of compound interest
- Basic tools for time value of money
- Future value of an ordinary annuity
- Future value of an annuity due
- Present value of a dollar
- Present value of an ordinary annuity
- Present value of an annuity due
- Financial aid programs
- Tax advantages related to education

- Uneven cash flows
- Internal rate of return and net present value
- Yield to maturity
- Solving for terms or yield
- Serial payments

- Discount rate selection
- Amortization tables
- Rule of 72
- Education funding
- Investments for education

Basic Financial Planning Tools

CHAPTER 6   Time Value of Money
CHAPTER 7   Planning for Children's Education

Risks

- Misunderstanding the impact of inflation
- Failure to understand compounding

Data Collection

- Financial aid programs
- Financial aid information of client
- Current cost of education
- Inflation rate
- Expected earnings rate
- Tax-advantaged education programs

Goals

- Understanding the importance of time value of money to financial planning
- Adequate resources for education of children

Data Analysis

- Projected cost of education
- Education funding choices
- Educational funding analysis
- Investment selections

Time Value of Money

LEARNING OBJECTIVES:

After learning the material in this chapter, you will be able to:

1. Define the time value of money (TVM) concept and explain why it is such an important financial planning concept.

2. Define the terms present value and future value and illustrate their roles in the calculation of compound interest.

3. Calculate the future value and the present value of a dollar.

4. List and explain the tools used in TVM analysis.

5. Calculate the present and future values of an ordinary annuity and an annuity due.

6. Explain the differences between an ordinary annuity and an annuity due.

7. Calculate the reconciliation of the difference between an ordinary annuity and an annuity due.

8. Prepare an amortization table for debt repayment.

9. Explain the Rule of 72 and its uses.

10. Apply the Rule of 72.

11. Understand how unequal cash flows and serial payments affect the future value of an investment.

12. Compare and contrast the concepts of net present value (NPV) and internal rate of return (IRR).

13. Define yield to maturity and explain how it is used to determine a bond's earnings.

14. Explain how "Solving for Term Given the Other Variables" is useful in debt management.

15. Understand how the inflation rate affects the real rate of return of an investment.

16. Define perpetuities and explain how they effect financial planning.

UNDERSTANDING TIME VALUE OF MONEY

time value of money (TVM) - the concept that money received today is worth more than the same amount of money received sometime in the future

Time value of money (TVM) is one of the most useful and important concepts in finance and personal financial planning. Essentially, the concept of time value of money is that money received today is worth more than the same amount of money received sometime in the future. A dollar received today is worth more than a dollar received one year from today because the dollar received today can be invested and will be worth more in one year. Alternatively, a dollar to be received a year from now is worth less than a dollar today. Comparisons of dollars received and paid at the same point in time are necessary to solve many financial planning problems and to make sound financial decisions. Thus, time value of money calculations are fundamental to financial planning. Time value of money calculation is one of the tools that allow financial planners to properly plan for their client's goals and objectives.

present value - what a sum of money to be received in a future year is worth in today's dollars based on a specific discount rate

There are two time periods and two values for time value of money analysis: future and future value and present and present value. Future value is the future dollar amount to which a sum certain today will increase compounded at a defined interest rate and a period of time. Present value is the current dollar value of a future sum discounted at a defined interest rate and a period of time. Future value is calculated using a process called compounding. Present value is calculated using a process called discounting. Suppose, for example, that a dollar was invested in a bank savings account paying 5 percent annual interest. At the end of the year, the dollar would have grown to $1.05. The initial dollar would be referred to as the **present value**. The 5 percent represents the interest rate. The term is for one year. The $1.05 equals the **future value**. The interest earned (in this case $0.05) is compensation for delaying consumption for one year into the future. We will discuss compounding and discounting later in the chapter.

future value - the future amount to which a sum of money today will increase based on a defined interest rate and a period of time

The initial mathematical relationship between the present value and the future value is expressed as:

$$FV = PV(1+i)$$

Where: PV = Present Value

i = Interest Rate

FV = Future Value

Conversely, $PV = \dfrac{FV}{(1+i)}$

and thus, $FV = PV(1+i)$

In the above example:

FV = PV(1+i)
  = ($1)(1 + 0.05)
  = $1.05 (where 5 percent is the annual interest rate on savings)

There are numerous important questions in financial planning that can be answered using time value of money (TVM) concepts.

▲ If I have a certain dollar amount today, how much will it be worth at some time in the future, if it is invested at a certain rate of earnings (interest)?
▲ If I invested a certain dollar amount on a regular interval basis and at a constant earnings rate, how much would I accumulate at some future date?
▲ If I wanted to save for the college education of my children, how much would I need to save starting today, or some other time, on a regular interval basis to pay for that education?
▲ If I wanted to pay off my house mortgage early, how many dollars would I need to add to each monthly payment?
▲ What is the present value of my expected Social Security retirement benefits?
▲ How much investment capital will I need to retire at a particular age and still maintain my preretirement lifestyle?

All of these questions and many other financial planning questions can be answered by applying time value of money (TVM) concepts.

FUTURE VALUE AND THE POWER OF COMPOUND INTEREST

Understanding **compound interest** is essential to understanding the future value of money. Basically, compound interest is interest earned on interest. If you take the interest that you earn on an investment and reinvest it, you then earn interest on both the principal and the reinvested interest. Therefore, the interest you earn grows, or compounds. Mathematically, the growth is exponential (a power function) as opposed to linear function. An investment earns compound interest anytime the investment is held beyond one period, where interest is applied to both contributions and earnings, and where the earnings are reinvested in the investment.

compound interest -
interest earned on interest

If the entire $1.05 in the above example remained in the investment for a second year in the same bank earning 5 percent annually, the future value at the end of the second year would be $1.1025.

$$FV = PV(1+i)$$
$$FV = \$1.05(1 + 0.05)$$
$$FV = \$1.1025$$

The earnings in the second year, $0.0525, reflect the interest on the original dollar ($0.05) and the interest on the 5 cents earned in the first year ($0.0025).

The mathematical expression for compounding interest at a constant rate is:

$$FV = PV(1+i)^n$$, where

n is an exponent representing the number of periods (term) the investment is to be held. Notice that i must be expressed in the same terms as n (yearly, semiannually, quarterly, monthly, etc). If i is expressed as an annual interest or earnings rate then n must also be expressed annually.

To illustrate this compounding phenomena, assume that $2,000 is invested by a 25-year-old in an individual retirement account (IRA) and left for 5 years earning 12 percent compounded annually. What would be the future value of the investment at the end of 5 years when our investor is age 30?

$$FV = PV(1+i)^n$$
$$FV = (\$2{,}000)(1.12)^5$$
$$FV = (\$2{,}000)(1.7623) \text{ [The exact mathematical factor calculated using an HP-12C]}$$
$$FV = \$3{,}524.68$$

Future value calculations of this type can be performed a variety of different ways using the tools available for time value of money calculations. Generally the illustrated examples in this chapter have been calculated using an HP-12C calculator. Where multiple steps were required to solve a problem we did not round the intermediate steps. If the reader is attempting to calculate the problems in the chapter and is using table factors, a different calculator or if the reader rounds intermediate steps, then the reader may receive an answer slightly different from that calculated in the chapter. Where we used table factors you will notice some rounding error. Where we used mathematical exponentials you will also notice differences from calculator or table results. For example, if the problem above had been calculated with rounding the interest, then the answer would be $3,524.60 (rounding error of $0.08).

BASIC TOOLS FOR TIME VALUE OF MONEY (TVM) ANALYSIS

In addition to mathematical equations, there are a number of other tools that the financial planner can use to understand time value of money problems, to assist the client in answering time value of money questions, and to present such quantitative information to clients. Among these tools are **cash flow timelines**, time value of money tables, financial calculators, cash flow computer software, and accumulation schedules. We will illustrate the various tools of time value of money by calculating the future value for the example above ($2,000 invested for 5 years earning 12 percent compounded annually).

> **cash flow timelines** - time value of money analysis tool that graphically depicts cash inflows (future value of the investment) and cash outflows (the initial dollar investment) over a certain period of time (the term)

TIMELINES

Timelines are a useful tool to visualize cash flows--both inflows and outflows. Below is a timeline based on the previous example. Notice that the $2,000 invested in time period "0" is listed with a parenthesis indicating that it is an outflow. Respectively, the future value of $3,524.68 is presented as an inflow at time period "5."

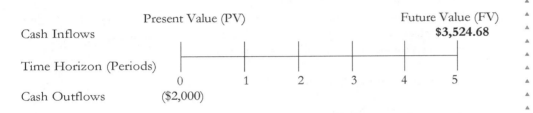

The more complex the time value of money problem, the more useful a timeline can be in illustrating the positions of the cash flows.

TIME VALUE OF MONEY TABLES

Time value of money tables represent the various values for combinations of i and n. These tables can be found in the Appendix (B-1 through B-6). The Future Value of a Dollar table is necessary to calculate the answer to our problem. The amounts given in the table represent the value of a dollar deposited today (received in the future) and compounded at a defined rate (i) for a defined period (n). The interest factor in Table 1 for 12 percent and for 5 years is 1.7623 (rounded). This number is the equivalent of $(1.12)^5$ or $(1.12)(1.12)(1.12)(1.12)(1.12) = 1.7623$. Thus, when using time value of money tables, the future value formula is also represented as FV = PV (Table 1 factor at 12 percent for 5 years). In our example: $2,000 x 1.7623 = $3,524.60.

Table 1: Future Value Factor of a Dollar
(Excerpt from Appendix B-2)

Period	2%	4%	6%	8%	10%	12%
1	1.0200	1.0400	1.0600	1.0800	1.1000	1.1200
2	1.0404	1.0816	1.1236	1.1664	1.2100	1.2544
3	1.0612	1.1249	1.1910	1.2597	1.3310	1.4049
4	1.0824	1.1699	1.2625	1.3605	1.4641	1.5735
5	1.1041	1.2167	1.3382	1.4693	1.6105	1.7623

Notice that the tables have been rounded off to four decimals for presentation convenience. The rounding in the tables will cause a slight error in calculation. The amount of the error in the above example is $0.08; $3,524.60 (1.7623 x $2,000) vs. $3,524.68 (1.762341683 x $2,000).

FINANCIAL CALCULATORS

There are a wide variety of useful hand-held financial calculators that will accurately calculate the solution to time value of money problems assuming the inputs are properly entered into the calculator. Financial calculators are fairly inexpensive and more accurate and flexible than the time value of money tables. Calculators are also useful when the financial planner is out of the office and unable to access computer time value of money software.

The following are among the most widely used financial calculators:

▲ Hewlett Packard: HP17BII.
▲ Hewlett Packard: HP12C.
▲ Hewlett Packard: HP10BII.
▲ Texas Instruments: TI BAII Plus.
▲ Sharp: EL – 733A.

Each of these has its own mathematical algorithm for solving time value of money problems, and to master each calculator requires some practice. It is strongly recommended, regardless of which calculator you select, that you review your calculator's user manual and become familiar with the various keys. Familiarity with the following keys is essential:

[PV]   = stores/calculates the present value
[FV]   = stores/calculates the future value
[PMT]   = stores/calculates the amount of each payment
[n]   = stores/calculates the total number of payments or time periods
[i]   = stores/calculates the interest or discount rate

It is also helpful to use an application based calculator text such as "Understanding Your Financial Calculator." In calculating the time value of money problems throughout this chapter and this text, we have used the HP12C.

We will illustrate the keystrokes (for the HP12C) used to solve the above future value problem.

Keystroke	Display
2,000[CHS][PV]	-2,000.0000
5[n]	5.0000
12[i]	12.0000
0[PMT]	0.0000
[FV]	3,524.6834

COMPUTER SOFTWARE

Essentially, computer software uses the same or similar mathematical algorithms as the hand-held calculators. In fact, time value of money software testers usually use a hand-held calculator to assure the computer algorithm's accuracy. Time value of money software and application software using time value of money concepts are widely available to aid both individuals and practitioners. A discussion of the available time value of money software is beyond the scope of this text.

ACCUMULATION SCHEDULES

Knowing the future value of a deposit made today is useful for investment planning for expenditures. It is also useful to know both the amount of earnings and the account balance of an investment account on a yearly or periodic basis. To determine the investment earnings and investment accumulation on a periodic basis, prepare a basic accumulation schedule similar to Exhibit 6.1.

EXHIBIT 6.1: ACCUMULATION SCHEDULE

Year (Col 1)	Beginning Balance (Col 2)	Interest (Col 3)	Ending Balance (Col 2) + (Col 3) = (Col 4)
1	$2,000.00	$ 240.00	$ 2,240.00
2	$2,240.00	$ 268.80	$ 2,508.80
3	$2,508.80	$ 301.06	$ 2,809.86
4	$2,809.86	$ 337.18	$ 3,147.04
5	$3,147.04	$ 377.64	$ 3,524.68
	$2,000.00	**$1,524.68**	**$3,524.68**
Totals	**Total Deposits**	**Total Interest**	**Final Balance**

Column 1 is the year in question, Column 2 is the account balance at the beginning of each year, Column 3 is the interest earned during the year (Column 2 x 12 percent), and Column 4 is the balance at the year-end for each year (Column 2 + Column 3). The Total row shows the original amount deposited, $2,000, interest earned over the 5 years, $1,524.68, and the final balance, $3,524.68. As we will demonstrate, this type of schedule can be expanded or modified to illustrate the extinguishments of debt and is also useful for a variety of other illustrative purposes.

157

While useful for learning, professional financial planners do not generally rely on time value of money tables and accumulation schedules. Rather, they rely on hand-held financial calculators or computer software.

FUTURE VALUE OF AN ORDINARY ANNUITY (FVOA)

Thus far we have calculated the future value of a single deposit made at the beginning of a period. Now consider, instead of a single deposit, that a series of deposits are made into an account. Instead of our previous example of the $2,000 deposited once in the IRA, our investor deposits $2,000 each year in the IRA and does so for 5 years earning an annual rate of return of 12 percent. The series of deposits of equal size is known as an annuity when deposited over a finite number of equal interval time periods. However, it will make a difference whether the deposits are made at the end of each period (known as an ordinary annuity) or deposited at the beginning of every period (known as an annuity due). The ordinary annuity is quite common in investments and in debt repayment. It is sometimes referred to as a payment made in arrears. An annuity due calculation is commonly used in educational funding and for retirement payments. We will discuss the annuity due concept in the following section.

future value of an ordinary annuity - the future amount to which a series of deposits of equal size will amount to when deposited over a finite number of equal interval time periods, at the end of those time periods, based on a defined interest rate

To demonstrate the calculation of the **future value of an ordinary annuity**, assume Davin deposits $2,000 per year at year-end for 5 years into an IRA earning 12 percent annually. For purposes of our illustration, we will present the problem in the context of the basic time value of money tools: timelines, mathematics, time value of money tables, a hand-held financial calculator, and an accumulation schedule.

FVOA TIMELINE

The ordinary annuity timeline below depicts a pattern of deposits at the end of each period (1-5).

Cash Inflows (Accumulation)   **$12,705.69**
Time Horizon (Periods)

| 0 | 1 | 2 | 3 | 4 | 5 |

Cash Outflows (Deposits)   ($2,000)   ($2,000)   ($2,000)   ($2,000)   ($2,000)

As shown on the timeline, the future value of the accumulation is equal to $12,705.69 and is shown as an inflow. The deposits of $2,000 are shown as outflows at each year-end.

FVOA USING MATHEMATICS

The mathematical calculation for the ordinary annuity is presented below.

$$FVOA = \$2,000(1.12)^0 + \$2,000(1.12)^1 + \$2,000(1.12)^2 + \$2,000(1.12)^3 + \$2,000(1.12)^4 = \$12,705.69$$

Notice that the future value of an ordinary annuity (FVOA) is calculated by multiplying each deposit of $2,000 by one plus the interest rate of 12 percent raised to the power associated with the term (e.g., the fifth deposit is raised by the zero power because it is made at the end of Year 5 and therefore earns no interest). These totals are then summed to determine the future value of the annuity.

Exhibit 6.2 below presents a tabular accumulation using the table factors for each deposit from the last (Deposit 5) to the first (Deposit 1). Notice that the summation of the factor column is equal to 6.3528 and the total future dollar equals $12,705.60.

EXHIBIT 6.2: FUTURE VALUE OF AN ORDINARY ANNUITY CALCULATION

Deposit Number	Amount		Factor	x	Deposit	=	Amount
5	$2,000 (1.12)^0$	=	1.0000	x	$2,000	=	$2,000.00
4	$2,000 (1.12)^1$	=	1.1200	x	$2,000	=	$2,240.00
3	$2,000 (1.12)^2$	=	1.2544	x	$2,000	=	$2,508.80
2	$2,000 (1.12)^3$	=	1.4049	x	$2,000	=	$2,809.80
1	$2,000 (1.12)^4$	=	1.5735	x	$2,000	=	$3,147.00
Total			6.3528				$12,705.60

($0.09 rounding error due to using table factors) Note: An amount raised to a zero power is equal to $1(1.12^0 = 1.00)$.

FVOA USING TIME VALUE OF MONEY TABLES

We can also calculate the future value of an ordinary annuity using the time value of money table for Future Value of an Ordinary Annuity (Appendix B-4). An excerpt of this table, identified as Table 2, is depicted below. The time value of money factor for an ordinary annuity of 5 periods at 12% is 6.3528, the same as the interest-compounding factor calculated above. The future value is then calculated as $12,705.60 [($2,000 x 6.3528) = $12,705.60], a difference of $0.09 from the mathematical calculation but the same as the calculation using the table factors in Exhibit 6.2.

Table 2: Future Value Factor of an Ordinary Annuity
(Excerpt from Appendix B-4)

Period	2%	4%	6%	8%	10%	12%
1	1.0000	1.0000	1.0000	1.0000	1.0000	1.0000
2	2.0200	2.0400	2.0600	2.0800	2.1000	2.1200
3	3.0604	3.1216	3.1836	3.2464	3.3100	3.3744
4	4.1216	4.2465	4.3746	4.5061	4.6410	4.7793
5	5.2040	5.4163	5.6371	5.8666	6.1051	6.3528

FVOA USING A FINANCIAL CALCULATOR

Your financial calculator will have a feature (generally a [BEGIN] or [END] key) that will allow you to switch between an ordinary annuity (use END) and an annuity due (use BEGIN). Calculate the future value of the ordinary annuity using the following keystrokes (using the HP12C):

Keystroke	Display
5[n]	5.0000
12[i]	12.0000
2,000[CHS][PMT]	-2,000.0000
0[PV]	0.0000
[FV]	12,705.6947

FVOA USING AN ACCUMULATION SCHEDULE

Exhibit 6.3 is the accumulation schedule, which shows the beginning balance, deposits, interest earned, and ending balance for each year. It also shows the total deposited, total interest earned, and the final accumulation balance of $12,705.70.

EXHIBIT 6.3: ORDINARY ANNUITY ACCUMULATION SCHEDULE

Year	Beginning Balance	Interest	Deposits	Ending Balance
1	$0.00	$0.00	$2,000.00	$2,000.00
2	$2,000.00	$240.00	$2,000.00	$4,240.00
3	$4,240.00	$508.80	$2,000.00	$6,748.80
4	$6,748.80	$809.86	$2,000.00	$9,558.66
5	$9,558.66	$1,147.04	$2,000.00	$12,705.70
Total		$2,705.70	$10,000.00	$12,705.70

($0.01 error due to rounding)

The timeline depicted above and the accumulation schedule in Exhibit 6.3 are different methods of presenting the information related to this particular problem. The timeline is best used by the planner to initially understand the position of the cash flows, while the accumulation schedule is probably the most useful exhibit to present to a client.

FUTURE VALUE OF AN ANNUITY DUE (FVAD)

The application for an annuity due is exactly the same as the ordinary annuity, except that the first depositor payment for the annuity due is made immediately. This is opposite to the ordinary annuity pattern, where the first payment is made at the end of the first term. The annuity due pattern of payments is quite common for educational funding where the educational institution demands tuition payments be made in advance rather than in arrears. Other common uses of the annuity due concept are for rents and for retirement income, which are both commonly paid in advance.

Using the previous example, we once again present the problem in the context of the basic time value of money tools: timelines, mathematics, time value of money tables, the financial calculator, and an accumulation schedule.

FVAD TIMELINE

Using the previous example, notice that the pattern of annuity due deposits shifts one period to the left from the ordinary annuity. The difference is essentially Deposit 5 of the ordinary annuity versus Deposit 1 of the annuity due. (Deposits 1, 2, 3, and 4 of the ordinary annuity correspond exactly with deposits 2, 3, 4 and 5 of the annuity due.) Notice that the annuity due timeline illustrates a pattern of deposits made at the beginning of each period instead of at the end of each period.

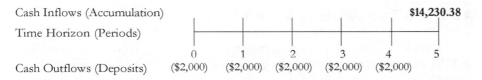

As shown in the timeline, the future value of the accumulation is equal to $14,230.38 and is shown as an inflow. The $2,000 deposits are shown as outflows at the beginning of each year.

We, therefore, have interest accumulating on all five deposits. We previously had the fifth deposit made at the end of Year 5. That deposit did not accumulate any interest. Now that we have shifted the deposit pattern to that of an annuity due, the last deposit is made at the beginning of Year 5 and therefore, earns one full year of interest. For this reason, the **future value of an annuity due** will always be greater by one period's interest than the same deposits made for an ordinary annuity of the same term and interest rate. Using the above example, you should note that $12,705.70 x (1.12) = $14,230.38.

future value of an annuity due - the future amount to which a series of deposits of equal size will amount to when deposited over a definite number of equal interval time periods, at the beginning of those time periods, based on a defined interest rate

FVAD USING MATHEMATICS

The mathematical calculation for the annuity due is presented below.

$$\text{FVAD} = \$2,000(1.12)^1 + \$2,000(1.12)^2 + \$2,000(1.12)^3 + \$2,000(1.12)^4 + \$2,000(1.12)^5 = \$14,230.38$$

Notice that the future value of an annuity due (FVAD) is calculated by raising each deposit of $2,000 by the interest rate of 12 percent and at the power associated with the term (e.g. the fifth deposit is raised by the power of one because the deposit is made at the beginning of Year 5 and receives one year of interest).

Exhibit 6.4 below presents a tabular accumulation using the table factors for each deposit from the last (Deposit 5) to the first (Deposit 1). Notice that the summation of the factor column is equal to 7.1151 (FVOA factor of 6.3528 x 1.12) and the total future dollars equals $14,230.20 (off $0.18 due to roundings in table factors).

EXHIBIT 6.4: FUTURE VALUE OF AN ANNUITY DUE CALCULATION

Deposit Number	Amount		Factor	x	Deposit	=	Amount
5	$2,000 $(1.12)^1$	=	1.1200	x	$2,000	=	$2,240.00
4	$2,000 $(1.12)^2$	=	1.2544	x	$2,000	=	$2,508.80
3	$2,000 $(1.12)^3$	=	1.4049	x	$2,000	=	$2,809.80
2	$2,000 $(1.12)^4$	=	1.5735	x	$2,000	=	$3,147.00
1	$2,000 $(1.12)^5$	=	1.7623	x	$2,000	=	$3,524.60
Total			**7.1151**				**$14,230.20**

FVAD Using Time Value of Money Tables

We can also calculate the future value of an annuity due using the time value of money table for Future Value of an Annuity Due (Appendix B-6). An excerpt of this table, identified as Table 3, is depicted below. The time value of money factor for an annuity due of 5 periods at 12% is 7.1152, 0.0001 different from the interest-compounding factor calculated above. The future value is then calculated as $14,230.40 [($2,000 x 7.1152) = $14,230.40] ($0.02 error due to table rounding and $0.20 greater than table factors which were summed to be $14,230.20).

Table 3: Future Value Factor of an Annuity Due
(Excerpt from Appendix B-6)

Period	2%	4%	6%	8%	10%	12%
1	1.0200	1.0400	1.0600	1.0800	1.1000	1.1200
2	2.0604	2.1216	2.1836	2.2464	2.3100	2.3744
3	3.1216	3.2465	3.3746	3.5061	3.6410	3.7793
4	4.2040	4.4163	4.6371	4.8666	5.1051	5.3528
5	5.3081	5.6330	5.9753	6.3359	6.7156	7.1152

FVAD Using a Financial Calculator

We can solve the problem using the HP12C. Notice that the calculator should be set to the "Begin" mode to indicate an annuity due calculation.

Keystroke	Display
[g][BEG]	0.0000 BEGIN
5[n]	5.0000
12[i]	12.0000
2,000[CHS] [PMT]	-2,000.0000
0[PV]	0.0000
[FV]	14,230.3781

FVAD Using an Accumulation Schedule

Exhibit 6.5 is the accumulation schedule, which shows the beginning balance, deposits, interest earned, and ending balance for each year. It also shows the total deposited, total interest earned, and the final accumulation balance of **$14,230.38** (notice the same as the timeline and mathematics).

EXHIBIT 6.5: ANNUITY DUE ACCUMULATION SCHEDULE

Year	Beginning Balance	Deposit	Beginning Balance After Deposit	Interest	Year Ending Balance
1	$0.00	$2,000.00	$2,000.00	$240.00	$2,240.00
2	$2,240.00	$2,000.00	$4,240.00	$508.80	$4,748.80
3	$4,748.80	$2,000.00	$6,748.80	$809.86	$7,558.66
4	$7,558.66	$2,000.00	$9,558.66	$1,147.04	$10,705.69
5	$10,705.69	$2,000.00	$12,705.69	$1,524.68	$14,230.38
Total		$10,000.00		$4,230.38	$14,230.38

(Accurate to the penny)

COMPARISON OF ORDINARY ANNUITY AND ANNUITY DUE CALCULATIONS

The annuity due has an accumulation account balance at the end of Year 5 of $14,230.38 while the ordinary annuity had an account balance of $12,705.69. The difference of $1,524.69 is equal to the total interest earned in the fifth year ($12,705.69 x 0.12 = $1,524.68). Another way to reconcile this difference is to calculate the interest on the first deposit for the annuity due and subtract the interest on the fifth deposit for the ordinary annuity.

We can prove that the difference between the annuity due and the ordinary annuity is simply the difference between the interest earned on the first deposit using the annuity due and the last deposit using the ordinary annuity. This concept is depicted in the timeline below.

Cash Inflows (FVOA)						**$12,705.70**
Cash Inflows (FVAD)						**$14,230.38**
Time Horizon (Periods)						
	0	1	2	3	4	5
Cash Outflows (FVOA)		($2,000)	($2,000)	($2,000)	($2,000)	*($2,000)*
Cash Outflows (FVAD)	*($2,000)*	($2,000)	($2,000)	($2,000)	($2,000)	

Notice that the deposits made at the end of years 1, 2, 3, and 4 are identical. We know that the future value of $2,000 deposited at the end of Year 5 for the ordinary annuity is equal to $2,000 [($2,000) x $(1.12)^0$]. The future value of Deposit 1 for the annuity due is equal to $3,524.68 [($2,000) x $(1.12)^5$].

FVAD (1)	$3,524.68
FVOA (5)	$2,000.00
Difference	$1,524.68

Proof of the reconciliation of total accumulation under the annuity due versus the ordinary annuity is depicted below:

FVAD	$14,230.38	
FVOA	$12,705.69	
Difference	$1,524.69	($0.01 rounding error)

We could also reconcile the two accounts using the time value of money table by subtracting the ordinary annuity factor by the annuity due factor and then multiplying the result by $2,000, as demonstrated below.

Annuity Due Factor	7.1152	
Ordinary Annuity Factor	(6.3528)	
	0.7624	
Multiplied By	$2,000.00	
Equals	$1,524.80	($0.12 rounding error)

There is a slight rounding error in the total of **$0.12** due to rounding the factors in the time value of money tables. All factors are rounded to the fourth decimal, which may result in a slight discrepancy.

PRESENT VALUE OF A DOLLAR (PV)

This calculation is used to determine what a sum of money to be received in a future year is worth in today's dollars based on a specific discount rate. For many financial planning decisions, such as education funding or retirement funding, it is important to determine the present value of a future amount rather than the future value of a present amount. In this section, we explain how to calculate the present value of a future investment amount. To illustrate, suppose you wanted to have $20,000 in five years, and could earn an annual return of 8 percent by investing in a certificate of deposit. How much do you need to invest today to meet your goal of $20,000 in 5 years?

We return to our basic tools and present the timeline, mathematical approach, the time value of money factor tables, the financial calculator, and the accumulation schedule to calculate the present value of a future sum certain of $20,000 in 5 years.

PV Timeline

Notice that the $20,000 is located as an inflow at Year 5. We must determine the present value dollar amount at Year 0.

Cash Inflows (Accumulation) $20,000.00

Time Horizon (Periods)

```
    0    1    2    3    4    5
```

Cash Outflows (Deposits)   **($13,611.66)**

As shown in the timeline, the present value of $20,000 five years from now is $13,611.66. In other words, $13,611.66 is the amount that should be deposited today earning 8 percent interest compounded annually to equal $20,000 in five years.

PV Using Mathematics

Mathematically, the solution to this type of problem can be derived from the original future value equation as presented below.

$$PV(1+i)^n = FV$$

$$PV = \left[\frac{FV}{(1+i)^n} \right]$$

$$PV = \left[\frac{\$20,000}{(1+0.08)^5} \right]$$

$$PV = \left[\frac{\$20,000}{1.469328} \right]$$

$$PV = \$13,611.66 \quad \text{(no rounding error)}$$

Where: PV = Present Value
       i = Interest rate for each term
       n = Term
       FV = Future Value of $20,000

Again, the amount to deposit today to have $20,000 five years from today, assuming an annual earnings rate of 8 percent, is $13,611.66.

PV Using Time Value of Money Tables

We can also calculate the present value using the time value of money table for Present Value of a Dollar (Appendix B-1). An excerpt of this table, identified as Table 4, is depicted below. The time value of money factor for the present value of a dollar of 5 periods at 8% is 0.6806. Therefore, the present value is calculated by multiplying the $20,000 future value times the time value of money table factor of 0.6806 for a present value of $13,612 (rounded) [($20,000 x 0.6806) = $13,612.00].

Table 4: Present Value Factor of a Dollar
(Excerpt from Appendix B-1)

Period	2%	4%	6%	8%
1	0.9804	0.9615	0.9434	0.9259
2	0.9612	0.9246	0.8900	0.8573
3	0.9423	0.8890	0.8396	0.7938
4	0.9238	0.8548	0.7921	0.7350
5	0.9057	0.8219	0.7473	0.6806

Another method of calculating the time value of money factor for the present value of a dollar is to take the factor in the denominator from the previous equation (1.469328) and divide it into 1. The result is 0.6806, the same factor in Table 4 as shaded at a term of 5 years and at 8% interest.

PV USING A FINANCIAL CALCULATOR

Keystroke	Display
20,000 [FV]	20,000.0000
8[i]	8.0000
5[n]	5.0000
0[PMT]	0.0000
[PV]	-13,611.6639

PV USING AN ACCUMULATION SCHEDULE

Exhibit 6.6 is the accumulation schedule to prove the results and to present a complete picture of the account accumulation for a client. In Exhibit 6.6, we have the original balance of $13,611.66, the interest for the year, the ending balance for each year, the totals for interest earned of $6,385.93, and the correct final balance of $20,000 (corrected for $0.01 rounding error).

EXHIBIT 6.6: ACCUMULATION SCHEDULE OF INVESTMENT

Year	Beginning Balance	Interest Earned	Ending Balance
1	$13,611.66	$1,088.93	$14,700.59
2	$14,700.59	$1,176.05	$15,876.64
3	$15,876.64	$1,270.13	$17,146.77
4	$17,146.77	$1,371.74	$18,518.51
5	$18,518.51	$1,481.48	$19,999.99
Total		**$6,388.33**	**$19,999.99**

PRESENT VALUE OF AN ORDINARY ANNUITY (PVOA)

It is common for persons or businesses to receive a series of equal payments for a finite period from debt repayment, from a life insurance settlement, from an annuity, or as a pension payment. The question usually asked is, what is the present value of such a series of payments? Remember that the ordinary annuity assumed that each payment is made at the end of each period (arrears). As an example, consider that you are to receive $25,000 per year for the next 5 years with each payment made at year-end. Also assume that your earnings rate is 8 percent. What is the present value in dollars of that income stream? Once again, we can apply the basic tools of time value of money to solve this problem.

PVOA TIMELINE

Cash Inflows		$25,000	$25,000	$25,000	$25,000	$25,000

Time Horizon (Periods)

0   1   2   3   4   5

Cash Outflows   **($99,817.75)**

The timeline suggests that we need to calculate the present value of $25,000 to be received annually for 5 years with each payment occurring at the end of the year and assuming an 8 percent earnings rate. As the timeline depicts, the PV equals $99,817.75.

PVOA USING MATHEMATICS

We solve this problem using a mathematical formula:

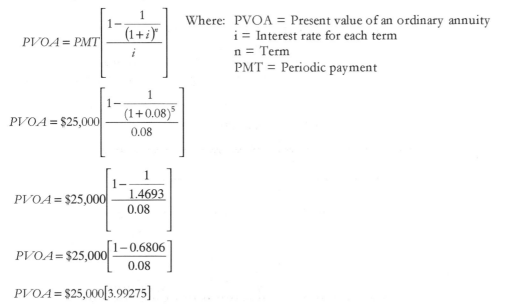

$$PVOA = PMT \left[\frac{1 - \frac{1}{(1+i)^n}}{i} \right]$$

Where: PVOA = Present value of an ordinary annuity
i = Interest rate for each term
n = Term
PMT = Periodic payment

$$PVOA = \$25,000 \left[\frac{1 - \frac{1}{(1+0.08)^5}}{0.08} \right]$$

$$PVOA = \$25,000 \left[\frac{1 - \frac{1}{1.4693}}{0.08} \right]$$

$$PVOA = \$25,000 \left[\frac{1 - 0.6806}{0.08} \right]$$

$$PVOA = \$25,000 [3.99275]$$

$PVOA = \$99,817.75$ (answer will be slightly different depending on the rounding technique used throughout the problem)

Exhibit 6.7 presents the present value calculation in tabular form for each payment and for the payments in total. Notice that the present value of five payments at $25,000 each is worth approximately $99,817.76 ($0.01 rounding error) when discounted at 8 percent.

EXHIBIT 6.7: PRESENT VALUES OF AN ORDINARY ANNUITY CALCULATION

Year	Payment				
5	$25,000 \div (1+0.08)^5$	=	$25,000 \div 1.4693$	=	$17,014.58
4	$25,000 \div (1+0.08)^4$	=	$25,000 \div 1.3605$	=	$18,375.75
3	$25,000 \div (1+0.08)^3$	=	$25,000 \div 1.2597$	=	$19,845.81
2	$25,000 \div (1+0.08)^2$	=	$25,000 \div 1.1664$	=	$21,433.47
1	$25,000 \div (1+0.08)^1$	=	$25,000 \div 1.0800$	=	$23,148.15
Total					**$99,817.76**

PVOA USING TIME VALUE OF MONEY TABLES

present value of an ordinary annuity - the value today of a series of equal payments made at the end of each period for a finite number of periods

We can also calculate the **present value of an ordinary annuity** using the time value of money table for Present Value of an Ordinary Annuity (Appendix B-3). An excerpt of this table, identified as Table 5, is depicted below. The time value of money factor for present value of an ordinary annuity of 5 periods at 8% is 3.9927. Therefore, the present value is calculated by multiplying the $25,000 payment times the time value of money table factor of 3.9927 for a present value of $99,817.50 (rounded).

$$[(\$25,000 \times 3.9927) = \$99,817.50]$$

Table 5: Present Value Factor of an Ordinary Annuity
(Excerpt from Appendix B-3)

Period	2%	4%	6%	8%
1	0.9804	0.9615	0.9434	0.9259
2	1.9416	1.8861	1.8334	1.7833
3	2.8839	2.7751	2.6730	2.5771
4	3.8077	3.6299	3.4651	3.3121
5	4.7135	4.4518	4.2124	3.9927

Another method of calculating the time value of money factor for the present value of an ordinary annuity is to take the sum of the factors for the present value of a dollar (Table 4) for each of the five years at the 8% interest rate. The total of the five individual factors will approximately equal the present value of an ordinary annuity factor (Table 5) as shown below.

Year	PV Factor (from Table 4)
1	0.9259
2	0.8573
3	0.7938
4	0.7350
5	0.6806
	3.9926 (off due to rounding)

Thus, the present value of an ordinary annuity table is constructed by taking the summation of the present value of an amount for the appropriate term at the appropriate interest rate.

PVOA USING A FINANCIAL CALCULATOR

Keystroke	Display
5[n]	5.0000
8[i]	8.0000
25,000[PMT]	25,000.0000
0[FV]	0.0000
[PV]	-99,817.7509

PVOA USING AN ACCUMULATION SCHEDULE

An accumulation schedule (Exhibit 6.8) can be presented to the client to help explain how the account should grow based on an initial deposit of $99,817.75 and an earnings rate of 8 percent.

EXHIBIT 6.8: ACCUMULATION SCHEDULE OF INVESTMENT

Year	Beginning Balance	Interest Earned	Year End Withdrawals	Ending Balance
1	$99,817.75	7,985.42	$25,000.00	$82,803.17
2	82,803.17	6,624.25	25,000.00	64,427.42
3	64,427.42	5,154.19	25,000.00	44,581.62
4	44,581.62	3,566.53	25,000.00	23,148.15
5	23,148.15	1,851.85	25,000.00	0.00

169

Notice that we placed the withdrawal column to the right of the interest column to indicate that the interest was earned on the entire beginning balance for each year and the withdrawals were made at year end each year. Also, the final withdrawal of $25,000 at the end of Year 5 depletes the account balance to zero, proving once again that the original present value calculation was correct.

PRESENT VALUE OF AN ANNUITY DUE (PVAD)

present value of an annuity due - the value today of a series of equal payments made at the beginning of each period for a finite number of periods

The difference between the **present value of an annuity due** and the present value of an ordinary annuity is that the annuity due's payments are made at the beginning of each period rather than at the end, as for an ordinary annuity. This makes the present value of an annuity due always larger than the present value of an ordinary annuity with the same payments over the same time period. The annuity due calculation is quite common in financial planning and is most often used for educational funding and for retirement capital needs analysis. Using the previous problem, and assuming that this is an educational funding problem where the parent is to pay $25,000 each year for 5 years with payments occurring at the beginning of each year and the earnings rate is 8 percent, we can calculate the present value using the basic time value of money tools. (For simplicity, we have assumed an inflation rate of zero.)

PVAD Timeline

Cash Inflows		$25,000	$25,000	$25,000	$25,000	$25,000
Time Horizon (Periods)						
		0	1	2	3	4	5
Cash Outflows		($107,803.17)				

The timeline suggests that while $107,803.17 is deposited today, $25,000 is immediately withdrawn.

PVAD Using Mathematics

The present value of an annuity due is illustrated below.

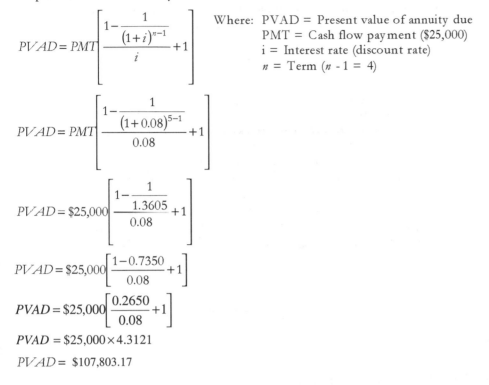

$$PVAD = PMT\left[\frac{1 - \dfrac{1}{(1+i)^{n-1}}}{i} + 1\right]$$

Where: PVAD = Present value of annuity due
PMT = Cash flow payment ($25,000)
i = Interest rate (discount rate)
n = Term (n - 1 = 4)

$$PVAD = PMT\left[\frac{1 - \dfrac{1}{(1+0.08)^{5-1}}}{0.08} + 1\right]$$

$$PVAD = \$25,000\left[\frac{1 - \dfrac{1}{1.3605}}{0.08} + 1\right]$$

$$PVAD = \$25,000\left[\frac{1 - 0.7350}{0.08} + 1\right]$$

$$PVAD = \$25,000\left[\frac{0.2650}{0.08} + 1\right]$$

$$PVAD = \$25,000 \times 4.3121$$

$$PVAD = \$107,803.17$$

The mathematical calculation of $25,000 paid as an annuity due for five payments earning 8 percent is equal to a present value of $107,803.18 ($0.01 rounding error). Exhibit 6.9 below presents the calculation by year in tabular form.

EXHIBIT 6.9: PRESENT VALUES FOR AN ANNUITY DUE (PVAD) CALCULATION

Year	PMTs	=	PMTs ÷ Factors	=	PV Amount
5	$25,000 \div (1+.08)^4$	=	25,000 ÷ 1.3605	=	$18,375.75
4	$25,000 \div (1+.08)^3$	=	25,000 ÷ 1.2597	=	$19,845.81
3	$25,000 \div (1+.08)^2$	=	25,000 ÷ 1.1664	=	$21,433.47
2	$25,000 \div (1+.08)^1$	=	25,000 ÷ 1.0800	=	$23,148.15
1	$25,000 \div (1+.08)^0$	=	25,000 ÷ 1.0000	=	$25,000.00
Total					**$107,803.18**

PVAD USING TIME VALUE OF MONEY TABLES

We can also calculate the present value of an annuity due using the time value of money tables for Present Value of an Annuity Due (Appendix B-5). An excerpt of this table, identified as Table 6, is depicted below. The time value of money factor for present value of an annuity due of 5 periods at 8% is 4.6121. Therefore, the present value is calculated by multiplying the $25,000 payment times the time value of money table factor of 4.3121 for a present value of $107,802.50 (rounded) [($25,000x4.3121) = $107,802.50].

Table 6: Present Value Factor of an Annuity Due
(Excerpt from Appendix B-5)

Period	2%	4%	6%	8%
1	1.0000	1.0000	1.0000	1.0000
2	1.9804	1.9615	1.9434	1.9259
3	2.9416	2.8861	2.8334	2.7833
4	3.8839	3.7751	3.6730	3.5771
5	4.8077	4.6299	4.4651	4.3121

PVAD USING A FINANCIAL CALCULATOR

Keystroke	Display
[g][BEG]	0.0000 BEGIN
5[n]	5.0000
8[i]	8.0000
25,000[PMT]	25,000.0000
0[FV]	0.0000
[PV]	-107,803.1710

PVAD USING AN ACCUMULATION SCHEDULE

An accumulation schedule (Exhibit 6.10) can be presented to the client by illustrating the initial deposit of $107,803.17, the annual withdrawals of $25,000 to pay the college at the beginning of each year, the interest rate earned each year, and the year end account balance. The interest is paid on the beginning balance less $25,000 each year.

EXHIBIT 6.10: ACCUMULATION SCHEDULE OF INVESTMENT

Year	Beginning Balance	Withdrawals	Interest Earned	Ending Balance
1	$107,803.17	$25,000.00	$6,624.25	$89,427.42
2	89,427.42	25,000.00	5,154.19	69,581.61
3	69,581.61	25,000.00	3,566.53	48,148.14
4	48,148.14	25,000.00	1,851.85	24,999.99
5	24,999.99	24,999.99	0.00	0.00

OTHER TIME VALUE OF MONEY CONCEPTS

Now that we have a better understanding of the concepts and basic mathematics and mechanics of time value of money, it is time to discuss some of the common time value of money applications. Included in these applications are **uneven cash flows**, combining sum certains with annuities, **net present value** (NPV), **internal rate of return** (IRR), yield to maturity (YTM), solving for term, selecting the interest rate, serial payments, perpetuities, educational funding, and capital needs analysis for retirement. In the next section of this chapter, we are going to present the basics of most of these time value of money concepts. YTM will be covered more extensively in Chapter 13 (Fixed Income Securities). We will defer coverage of education funding until Chapter 7 (Planning for Children's Education) and capital needs analysis until Chapter 18 (Introduction to Retirement Planning).

UNEVEN CASH FLOWS

Investment returns or deposits are not always single interval deposits or equal payments. For example, assume that a person deposits $400, $500, $600, and $700 into an investment account at the end of each of four years, respectively. How much would the investment be worth if the earnings rate was a constant 8 percent annually? For this situation, without a financial calculator or computer, this future value problem must be solved separately for each year since the cash flows are uneven. Once again, the cash flows can be presented in a timeline.

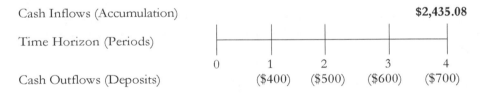

Mathematically, the future value of each cash flow can be determined using the equation $FV = PV(1+i)^n$ as follows:

$$\$400(1.08)^3 + \$500(1.08)^2 + \$600(1.08)^1 + \$700(1.08)^0$$

$$\$503.88 + \$583.20 + \$648.00 + \$700.00 = \$2,435.08$$

This problem can also be solved using an accumulation schedule as illustrated in Exhibit 6.11.

EXHIBIT 6.11: SCHEDULE OF INVESTMENT ACCUMULATION

Year	Beginning Balance	Year End Deposit	8% Interest Earned	Ending Balance
1	$0.00	$400.00	$0.00	$400.00
2	$400.00	$500.00	$32.00	$932.00
3	$932.00	$600.00	$74.56	$1,606.56
4	$1,606.56	$700.00	$128.52	$2,435.08
Total		$2,200.00	$235.08	$2,435.08

uneven cash flows - investment returns or deposits that may not be single interval deposits or equal payments

net present value (NPV) - the difference between the initial cash outflow (investment) and the present value of discounted cash inflows

internal rate of return (IRR) - a method of determining the exact discount rate to equalize cash inflows and outflows, thus allowing comparison of rates of return on alternative investments of unequal size and investment amounts

Using a financial calculator (HP12C), we can easily calculate the problem by using the uneven cash flow keys. The first step in the calculation determines the present value of the uneven deposits. The second step calculates the future value. The keystrokes for the uneven cash flow problem are below:

Step 1:

Keystroke	Display
0[g][CF$_o$]	0.0000
400 [g][CF$_j$]	400.0000
500 [g][CF$_j$]	500.0000
600 [g][CF$_j$]	600.0000
700 [g][CF$_j$]	700.0000
8[i]	8.0000
f[NPV]	1,789.8600

Step 2:

Keystroke	Display	
[CHS][PV]	-1,789.8600	(this step inputs the NPV from Step 1 as the PV for Step 2)
4[n]	4.0000	
8[i]	8.0000	
0[PMT]	0.0000	
[FV]	2,435.0848	

For problems similar to the one presented, or where the earnings rate and/or deposits fluctuate in either rate or amount, using a financial calculator or computer is far more efficient than manual methods.

COMBINING SUM CERTAINS WITH ANNUITIES

For some investments, bonds for example, the investment returns are received in the form of both an annuity and a sum certain. Assume that an investor purchased a 3-year $1,000 corporate bond paying $30 interest twice a year (semiannually) and then paying $1,000 (the maturity value) back to the holder at the end of the 3-year period. If the holder expected an 8 percent annual return, what amount should be paid for the bond at the beginning of the 3-year period? Assume that the interest is paid as an ordinary annuity (arrears).

This problem is no different than combining two different problems, one the present value of an ordinary annuity and the second the present value of a future amount. To solve the problem, complete the following steps:

Step 1 - Draw a cash flow timeline
Step 2 - Determine the PV of the ordinary annuity
Step 3 - Determine the PV of the sum certain (maturity value)
Step 4 - Add the results of Steps 2 and 3

<u>Step 1</u> – Draw a timeline

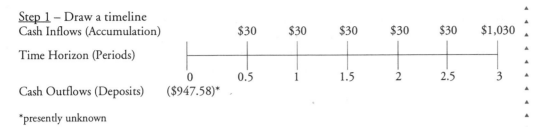

Cash Inflows (Accumulation) $30 $30 $30 $30 $30 $1,030

Time Horizon (Periods)

0   0.5   1   1.5   2   2.5   3

Cash Outflows (Deposits)   ($947.58)*

*presently unknown

<u>Step 2</u> – Determine the PV of the Annuity

PVOA $30 for 6 periods at 4 percent (double the periods and halve the rate for semiannual interest)

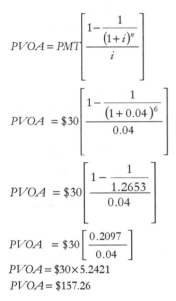

$$PVOA = PMT \left[\frac{1 - \frac{1}{(1+i)^n}}{i} \right]$$

$$PVOA = \$30 \left[\frac{1 - \frac{1}{(1+0.04)^6}}{0.04} \right]$$

$$PVOA = \$30 \left[\frac{1 - \frac{1}{1.2653}}{0.04} \right]$$

$$PVOA = \$30 \left[\frac{0.2097}{0.04} \right]$$

$$PVOA = \$30 \times 5.2421$$

$$PVOA = \$157.26$$

<u>Step 3</u> – Determine the PV of the Sum Certain

PV of $1,000 at 4 percent for 6 periods

PV = $1,000 ÷ (1+ 0.04)^6

PV = $1,000 ÷ 1.2653

PV = $790.31

<u>Step 4</u> – Add the results of Steps 2 and 3

$157.26	Present Value of Annuity Interest (ordinary)
790.31	Present Value of Final Payment
$947.57	PV of Bond (rounded)

Many investments take the form of a series of equal cash flows and then one lump sum payment (stocks with dividends, bonds). By drawing a cash flow timeline it is easier to visualize how a problem may be divided into single payments and annuities. Alternatively, the problem is easily solved using a financial calculator. The keystrokes for such a solution are :

Keystroke	Display
6[n]	6.0000
4[i]	4.0000
30[PMT]	30.0000
1000[FV]	1000.0000
[PV]	-947.5786

Obviously, the calculator greatly simplifies the amount of work necessary to solve this type of problem. We have now taken a sum certain problem and combined it with an annuity question.

NET PRESENT VALUE ANALYSIS

Net present value analysis (NPV) is a commonly used time value of money technique employed by businesses and investors to evaluate the cash flows associated with capital projects and capital expenditures. The concept is common to capital budgeting. Net present value analysis helps to answer the question of whether one should select one capital investment over another capital investment. The result of the analysis is in terms of dollars. The method discounts the future cash flows at an appropriate discount rate and allows the present value of inflows to be compared to the present value of outflows. This technique is important to financial planners in assisting clients in making decisions as to which investment projects the client should consider undertaking.

The model itself is deterministic, that is, it assumes that the information is known about the future (cash flows, life, etc.). The NPV model assumes that all reinvestments of cash flows received in unequal life assets are made at the weighted average cost of the capital of the firm or the required rate of return of the investor.

NPV equals the difference between the initial cash outflow (investment) and the present value of discounted cash inflows. For example, if the present value of a series of cash flows is $200 and the initial outflow is $150, then the NPV equals $50. As a general rule, businesses look for investments with a positive NPV.

EXAMPLE

Assume you are a financial planner debating whether to purchase a copy machine. You currently pay 12 cents a copy for reproducing materials and expect to make 3,000 copies per month. The copier you are considering purchasing costs $5,000 and is expected to last 5 years with a $1,000 salvage value. Your cost for reproducing on the new copier would be 7 cents per copy. Assuming a 12 percent discount rate, what is the net present value of the copier?

To solve this problem, first convert the relevant data to monthly figures. If you purchase a copy machine, each copy would save you $0.05 ($0.12 - $0.07 = $0.05). If you made 3,000 copies per month, you would save $150 per month ($0.05 x 3,000 = $150). We must then calculate the present value of the cash flow discounted at 12 percent (1 percent monthly). The keystrokes for this calculation (using the HP12C) are below:

Keystroke	Display
150 [PMT]	150.000
1,000 [FV]	1,000.0000
60 [n]	60.0000
1 [i]	1.0000
[PV]	-7,293.7054
5000 [+]	-2,293.7054

The present value of purchasing the copier is $7,293.71. Subtracting out the initial cash outflow of $5,000 indicates the net present value of the copier is $2,293.71. Therefore, the positive NPV indicates that you should purchase the copy machine. The purchase essentially will save you $2,293.71 in today's dollars.

INTERNAL RATE OF RETURN (IRR)

The internal rate of return (IRR) is the exact discount rate that equates the cash inflows and outflows of a specific investment or project. IRR calculations allow the financial planner to compare rates of return on alternative investments of unequal size and investment amounts. The NPV model and the IRR model make different assumptions about the reinvestment rate of cash flows received during the period of investment. Recall that NPV assumes the reinvestment rate to be the weighted average cost of capital or the required return. The IRR calculation assumes the reinvestment rate equals the IRR. The NPV is considered a superior model to IRR, when comparing investment projects of unequal lives because investing at the required return is more reasonable than at the IRR.

The formula below describes the basic present value model used for discounting cash flows.

$$P_O = \frac{Cf_1}{(1+k)^1} + \frac{Cf_2}{(1+k)^2} + \cdots + \frac{Cf_n}{(1+k)^n}$$

P_0 = The value of the security or asset today.
Cf_n = The cash flow for a particular period, n.
k = The discount rate or IRR.
n = The number of cash flows to be evaluated.

The formula states that the PV of a series of cash flows is equal to each cash flow divided by one plus the discount rate raised to a power equal to the period in which the cash flow occurs.

The internal rate of return is the exact discount rate (labeled as "k" in the above formula) that makes the discounted future cash inflows equal to the initial cash outflow or investment. One of the underlying assumptions inherent in the above equation is that the cash flows that are received during the investment period will be reinvested at the investment's internal rate of return.

EXAMPLE   Meg owns 1 share of Herring, Inc. stock.   She purchased this share of stock three years ago for $50. The current market value of the stock is $40 per share. Since buying the stock, the following dividends have been paid:

> Dividend year 1 (end)$4.80 per share
> Dividend year 2 (end)$5.90 per share
> Dividend year 3 (end)$7.25 per share

What is the IRR that Meg has earned on her investment? Because the IRR is the exact rate of discount to equalize the cash inflows and outflows, it is easiest to calculate using a financial calculator and would not be easy to calculate using tables or equations. The financial calculator keystrokes (HP12C) are below.

Keystroke	Display
50 [CHS][g][CF$_o$]	-50.0000
4.8 [g][CF$_j$]	4.8000
5.9 [g][CF$_j$]	5.9000
7.25 [ENTER]	7.2500
40 [+][g][CF$_j$]	47.2500
[f][IRR]	5.5695

The 5.5695 can be illustrated using the following schedule.

Period	Cash Flow (CF)	Divisor (x)	Factor (1/x)	Present Value (CF x Factor)
1	4.80	$1 \div (1.055695)^1$	0.9472	4.5468
2	5.90	$1 \div (1.055695)^2$	0.8973	5.2939
3	47.25	$1 \div (1.055695)^3$	0.8499	40.1593
				50.0000

YIELD TO MATURITY

Yield to maturity (YTM) is the calculation of the rate of return that will make the discounted cash flows of a bond equal to the current price of that bond. It is basically the application of the IRR model to bond investments. YTM is generally calculated based on semiannual coupon payments (even with zero-coupon bonds). Financial planners need to understand YTM to begin understanding bonds and other debt investments.

There are three adjustments that have to be made in order to calculate YTM for a bond that makes semiannual coupon payments:

▲ n – The number of periods is determined by multiplying the number of years by two so as to reflect two coupon payments per year. For example, the n for a 10-year bond would be 20 to reflect 20 coupon payments.
▲ PMT – The coupon rate is stated as a percent of the face value of the bond. Therefore, a 10 percent coupon bond will pay a total of $100 each year ($50 twice per year). The adjustment is to divide the $100 by two to reflect the two payments of $50 during the year.
▲ YTM – The YTM that will be calculated will be a semiannual YTM rate. Therefore, it is necessary to multiply the calculated YTM by two to determine the annual YTM.

Ann is considering purchasing a 5-year, $1,000 bond that is selling for $1,162.22. What is the YTM for this bond if it has a 12 percent coupon, paid semiannually? The yield to maturity is 8 percent annually or 4 percent per semiannual interest payment. The proof of this calculation is illustrated below.

EXAMPLE

Period	Cash Flow (CF)	Divisor (x)	Factor (1/x)	Present Value (CF x Factor)
1	60.0000	$1 \div (1.04)^1$	0.9615	57.6923
2	60.0000	$1 \div (1.04)^2$	0.9246	55.4734
3	60.0000	$1 \div (1.04)^3$	0.8890	53.3398
4	60.0000	$1 \div (1.04)^4$	0.8548	51.2883
5	60.0000	$1 \div (1.04)^5$	0.8219	49.3156
6	60.0000	$1 \div (1.04)^6$	0.7903	47.4189
7	60.0000	$1 \div (1.04)^7$	0.7599	45.5951
8	60.0000	$1 \div (1.04)^8$	0.7307	43.8414
9	60.0000	$1 \div (1.04)^9$	0.7026	42.1552
10	1,060.0000	$1 \div (1.04)^{10}$	0.6756	716.0980
				1,162.2179

To calculate yield to maturity using a financial calculator for the above problem:

Keystroke	Display	
10[n]	10.0000	Semiannual payment
1162.22[CHS][PV]	-1,162.2200	The current cost of the bond
60[PMT]	60	The semiannual interest payment for a 12% annual coupon
1000 [FV]	1,000	Maturity value of the bond
[i]	4.0000	(Yield to maturity – YTM)(multiply by 2 = 8 percent)

SOLVING FOR TERM GIVEN THE OTHER VARIABLES

This kind of analysis answers the question of how long (in days, months, quarters, or years) to save or pay to accomplish some goal, if you save or pay at a given rate. This type of analysis is particularly useful in debt management, such as determining the:

▲ Term to pay off student loans.
▲ Term to pay off mortgage.
▲ Term to save for college education.
▲ Term to save for a special purchase (car, home, vacation).

EXAMPLE

Margaret bought a house using a mortgage loan of $240,000 issued for 15 years at 6.25 percent per year on May 1, 2000. Her first payment was June 1, 2000. On January 1st of 2001, she has made 7 payments of $2,057.81 and has 173 payments remaining and a remaining mortgage balance of $234,256.20. Margaret wants to know how many more months she will have to pay if she increases her monthly payment by $500 to $2,557.81. Using a financial calculator (HP12C), we calculate the term using the following keystrokes:

Keystroke	Display	
234,256.20[CHS][PV]	-234,256.2000	Current balance
0 [FV]	0.0000	Future value
2,557.81 [PMT]	2,557.8100	New payment
6.25 ÷ 12 = 0.5208[i]	0.5208333	Monthly interest rate
[n]	125.0000	Number of payments remaining

Margaret is thus able to reduce her remaining payments from 173 to 125 by increasing her monthly payment by $500 to $2,557.81. Her last payment (payment 125) will be $1,982.12.

When solving for [n] on the HP12C, only integers (whole numbers) are displayed as a solution. This calculator cannot solve for non-integers (numbers with decimals). Therefore, your initial answer may be incorrect and will not match answers of other calculators. To calculate the correct term, you will have to substitute numbers for the term until you get the correct future value or present value. If the future value or present value does not match, you must adjust the term up or down and recalculate. This process must be done until the term you substitute equals the future value or present value. The first place to begin is with the term initially calculated.

SELECTING THE RATE OF INTEREST FOR ACCUMULATING OR DISCOUNTING

When utilizing time value of money analysis, the planner is frequently faced with the issue of which interest rate or earnings rate to use for which types of problems. The choices include the expected rate of earnings for a particular investment, the client's **opportunity cost**, the riskless rate, the consumer price index (CPI) for some future expenditures, the specific inflation rate for particular services (educational and medical), or the **real rate of return** which accommodates both the nominal earnings rate reduced by some measure of inflation.

Generally, when projecting the future value of an investment, either a lump sum investment or one made with annuity contributions, the appropriate compounding rate will be the expected rate of return for that particular investment. However, when discounting a future sum or series of payments back to present value, either the client's opportunity cost or the riskless rate of return will be used. The client's opportunity cost is usually the composite rate of return on the client's assets with similar risk to the assets being examined. The riskless rate is the Treasury rate for the selected period or term.

When calculating the amount of dollars that retirement will cost in the future, it is common to use the general **Consumer Price Index**, while in the case of college education, the recent and projected rate of inflation for college education should be used.

It is also useful to use an inflation adjusted earnings rate for problems like retirement capital needs or education funding. The reason for using such a rate is that the costs in the future are generally increasing at one rate (the inflation rate) and the investments are growing at a different rate (the earnings rate). Thus, the way to make the increasing cash outflows equal is to treat them as real dollars of purchasing power and use an inflation adjusted discount rate that takes into consideration the earnings rate and inflation rate. For example, if inflation is 5 percent, a product costing $1,000 today will cost $1,050 one year from now, but will only be $1,000 of real purchasing power one year from now in today's dollars. The combination of the nominal earnings rate reduced mathematically by the inflation rate is known as the real rate of return.

The loss of purchasing power is one of the risks that investors must overcome to achieve their financial goals. Real economic returns reflect the earnings from an investment that are above the inflation rate. However, simply subtracting the rate of inflation from the nominal earnings rate will not yield the real economic rate of return. Real economic returns must be calculated by using the following formula.

$$\left[\frac{1 + R_n}{1 + i} - 1\right] \times 100$$

where R_n = nominal rate of return

i = inflation rate

---

opportunity cost - when faced with investment alternatives, it is the highest-valued alternative not chosen--it represents what is forgone by choosing another alternative. When discounting a future sum or series of payments back to present value, it is the composite rate of return on the client's assets with similar risk to the assets being examined

real rate of return - the combination of the nominal earnings rate reduced mathematically by the inflation rate

Consumer Price Index (CPI) - a price index that measures the cost of a "market basket" of consumer goods and services purchased for day-to-day living

Assume that $1,000 is invested at the beginning of the year and earns 10 percent, resulting in a balance at the end of the year of $1,100. Also assume that over the same period inflation has been 4 percent. Thus, $1,040 at the end of the year is equal to the initial investment of $1,000 at the beginning of the year, in terms of real dollars or purchasing power. The real return is equal to the difference between the earnings ($100) and the increase as a result of inflation ($40), which is $60, divided by the initial investment adjusted for inflation ($1,040). This result equals a real rate of return of 5.77 percent.

▲ Conceptually, the return of 5.77 percent makes sense, in that the absolute return was 10 percent and the inflation was 4 percent, with the difference being 6 percent.

$$\left[\frac{1+0.10}{1+0.04}-1\right]\times100=5.7692$$

▲ The nominal earnings for this investment are $100. The real earnings are $57.69 in today's dollars ($60.00 ÷ 1.04 = $57.69).

SERIAL PAYMENTS

serial payment - a payment that increases at a constant rate (usually, the rate of inflation) on an annual (ordinary) basis

A **serial payment** is a payment that increases at a constant rate (usually inflation) on an annual (ordinary) basis. There are situations when investors are more comfortable increasing payments or deposits on an annual basis because the investor is expecting increases in salary or wages with which to make those increasing payments. Examples include investment deposits, life insurance premiums, educational needs, and retirement needs, or for any lump sum future expenditure.

Serial payments differ from fixed annuity payments (both ordinary annuities and annuities due) because the payments themselves are increasing at a constant rate. The result is that the initial serial payment will be less than a fixed annuity but the last deposit or payment will be greater than the fixed annuity payment.

EXAMPLE

Consider that Kathy wants to start her own business in 3 years, and she needs to accumulate $100,000 (in today's dollars) to do so. Kathy expects inflation to be 4 percent, and she expects to earn 8 percent on her investments. What serial payment should Kathy make each year to attain her goal?

The serial payment is calculated by adjusting the earnings rate for inflation to determine the real economic rate of return (nominal rate 8 percent, adjusted for inflation, 4 percent). This adjustment is accomplished using the following formula:

$$\left[\frac{1+R_n}{1+i}-1\right]\times100$$

where R_n = nominal rate of return

i = inflation rate

$$\left[\frac{1+0.08}{1+1.04}-1\right]\times100=3.8462$$

Therefore, the real rate of return used for the calculation is 3.8462.

182

The next step is to calculate the amount of an ordinary annuity payment for 3 years that would result in a $100,000 future value. This amount equals the payment needed today if made at the beginning of each year. If the payments, as in this case, are made at year end, the initial payment of $32,083.16 must be inflated by 4 percent.

$$FV = PMT (1.038462^2 + 1.038462^1 + 1.038462^0)$$

$$\$100,000 = PMT (1.0784 + 1.0385 +1)$$

$$PMT = \$100,000 \div 3.1168$$

PMT = $32,083.16 (if payments are made at the beginning of the year)

PMT = $32,083.16 x 1.04 (inflation) or $33,366.49 (if made at year end)

The second and third payments must be increased by 4 percent to reflect inflation. The $100,000 payment today grows with inflation to $112,486.40 ($100,000 x $(1.04)^3$) by the end of year 3, which is when Kathy needs it. The Schedule of Investment below proves the increasing payments are correct.

EXHIBIT 6.12: ACCUMULATION SCHEDULE OF INVESTMENT

Year	Beginning Balance Needed	Deposit (Payments)	8% Interest Earned	Accumulation Ending Balance
1	$100,000.00	$33,366.87	$0.00	$33,366.87
2	$104,000.00	$34,701.55	$2,669.35	$70,737.77
3	$108,160.00	$36,089.61	$5,659.02	$112,486.40
End of Year 3	$112,486.40	$104,158.03	$8,328.37	$112,486.40

Note: She could have saved $34,649.58 per year. An annuity of this amount would have provided her with the same future value of $112,486.40. This payment is calculated as follows:

FV = $112,486.40

N = 3

i = 8

PMT = $34,649.58

Notice that the payment of $34,649.58 is greater than the first serial payment, but less than the last one.

183

PERPETUITIES

A perpetuity is a payment cash flow stream that remains constant indefinitely. An example of a common perpetuity is preferred stock, which generally pays a set dividend each year. To determine the value of this type of payment stream, simply divide the payment (PMT) by the discount rate (i).

$$PV= \frac{PMT}{i}$$

EXAMPLE

Assume Smith Corporation always pays a $4.00 preferred stock dividend and the client's required rate of return is 10 percent. The value of the preferred stock equals $40 as illustrated below:

$$PV= \frac{PMT}{i}$$

$$PV= \frac{\$4.00}{0.10}$$

$$PV= \$40$$

A financial calculator can also be used to solve for perpetuities. Solving for the PV of the perpetuity using 1,000 as the number of periods (representing infinity) will result in the same solution as the above formula.

OTHER TIME VALUE OF MONEY TOOLS

amortization table - TVM tool used primarily to illustrate the amortization, or extinguishments of debt. The table presents the number of years of indebtedness, the beginning balance, level payments, interest amount, principal reduction, and ending balance of indebtedness

Timelines, mathematics, time value of money tables, accumulation schedules, financial calculators, and computer software are basic tools of time value of money. There are other time value of money tools, including **amortization tables** and the Rule of 72. An understanding of each of these tools will assist the financial planner in solving other complex time value of money problems.

AMORTIZATION TABLES

An amortization table is an extension of the accumulation schedules illustrated earlier in the chapter. Amortization tables are primarily used to illustrate the amortization or extinguishments of debt. Initially we create a table with the beginning balance of debt, a level payment, the portion of the payment that is interest, the portion of the payment that is used to reduce the principal indebtedness, and the ending balance of the indebtedness for each year.

184

EXHIBIT 6.13: AMORTIZATION TABLE (BLANK)

Year (Col. 1)	Beginning Balance (Col. 2)	Total Payments (Col. 3)	6.25% Interest Amortization (Col. 4) = (3)–(5)	Principal Reduction (Col. 5) = (3)–(4)	Ending Mortgage Balance (Col. 6) = (2)–(5)
-	-	-	-	-	-
-	-	-	-	-	-

The beginning balance of the indebtedness less the principal amount of reduction will equal the ending balance of the indebtedness. The remainder of the payment was interest as determined in the interest amount column. The common usage for amortization tables is for mortgages, but as a tool it can be used to illustrate any indebtedness repayment schedule.

Consider that Josh takes out a $240,000 mortgage with the first payment to be made in January and repaid over 15 years on a monthly basis at 6.25% annual interest.

EXAMPLE

EXHIBIT 6.14: MORTGAGE AMORTIZATION TABLE

Year (Col. 1)	Beginning Balance (Col. 2)	Total Payments (Col. 3)	6.25% Interest Amortization (Col. 4) = (3)–(5)	Principal Reduction (Col. 5) = (3)–(4)	Ending Mortgage Balance (Col. 6) = (2)–(5)
1	$240,000.00	12 @ $2,057.81 $24,693.78	$14,717.44	$9,976.34	$230,023.66
2	$230,023.66	$24,693.78	$14,075.74	$10,618.04	$219,405.62

PV   = $240,000   Mortgage amount

n   = 180 months   Term in months

i   = 6.25 ÷ 12   Interest per month

PMT   = $2,057.8166   Payment of an ordinary annuity

FV_{12} = $230,023.66   Balance of mortgage after 12 payments

Notice that Column 2 of Exhibit 6.14 is the beginning balance of indebtedness of $240,000. Josh then makes 12 annual payments of $2,057.81 (total $24,693.78) during Year 1 of which $14,717.44 is interest and the remainder $9,976.34 is used to reduce the mortgage balance so that at the end of Year 1, Josh owes $230,023.66 on the mortgage (Column 6).

The amortization table can be extended for the full 15 years and is useful to illustrate exactly when the balance of the mortgage will reach any certain amount, the amount of interest for a given period, and the amount of principal reduction during a given period. The table may be presented for only two years as above, or may be presented yearly or monthly for the entire indebtedness period. In the event the mortgage begins sometime other than January, the table can be modified so that the mortgage interest expense for each calendar year can be shown for use in estimating the mortgage interest income tax deduction for federal income tax.

Qualified residence interest expense is deductible for those taxpayers who itemize their expenses on their federal income tax return. The mortgage company sends the interest payer a Form 1098 (Mortgage Interest Statement) providing the payer with the amount of interest paid for the prior year. This amount may also be obtained from the amortization table, assuming payments are made as agreed. For example, Josh should have received a Form 1098 for the first year of $14,717.44 interest paid. The amortization table is a useful tool to estimate the interest deduction for future years and can be used to assist the planner in estimating future income tax liability and other income tax planning.

EXHIBIT 6.15: FORM 1098 (MORTGAGE INTEREST STATEMENT)

8181	□ VOID □ CORRECTED		
RECIPIENT'S/LENDER'S name, address, and telephone number		OMB No. 1545-0901 **2001** Form 1098	Mortgage Interest Statement
RECIPIENT'S Federal identification no. / PAYER'S social security number	1 Mortgage interest received from payer(s)/borrower(s) $		Copy A For Internal Revenue Service Center File with Form 1096.
PAYER'S/BORROWER'S name	2 Points paid on purchase of principal residence $		For Privacy Act and Paperwork Reduction Act Notice, see the 2001 General Instructions for Forms 1099, 1098, 5498, and W-2G.
Street address (including apt. no.)	3 Refund of overpaid interest $		
City, state, and ZIP code	4		
Account number (optional)			

Form 1098   Cat. No. 14402K   Department of the Treasury - Internal Revenue Service

Do Not Cut or Separate Forms on This Page — Do Not Cut or Separate Forms on This Page

THE RULE OF 72

Frequently, professionals want to approximate rates of earnings or the time needed to achieve a certain financial goal where the earnings rate or the time, but not both, is known. The professional may only need an estimate rather than a mathematically precise answer and/or does not have access to the appropriate tool to perform precise calculations.

The **Rule of 72** is such a method of approximation. Initially used by accountants, it is now used by financial planners to estimate the time that it takes to double the value of an investment where the earnings rate is known. Alternatively, the Rule of 72 will estimate the earnings rate necessary to double an investment value if the time is known. The Rule of 72 states that if you know a rate of return, you can determine the period of time that it takes to double the value of the investment by dividing 72 by the interest rate. For example, if the annual interest rate is 6 percent, then $72 \div 6 = 12$. Therefore, if a dollar is invested at 6 percent for 12 years, it should be equal to $2 at the end of the 12-year term. Conversely, if the term is known to be 12 years and you need an amount to double during that term, you can divide 72 by 12 to determine the interest rate necessary [$72 \div 12 = 6$]. Therefore, you would need an interest rate of 6 percent in order to double your investment in 12 years.

Mathematically, the rule is described by the formula below.

$$PV = \left[\frac{FV}{(1+i)^n} \right]$$

$$1 = \left[\frac{2}{(1+i)^n} \right]$$

If you know i, you can determine n by dividing 72 by i. Conversely, if you know n, you can determine i by dividing 72 by n.

EXHIBIT 6.16: RULE OF 72 EXAMPLE

Interest Rate	Period to Double (n)
4%	18.0
6%	12.0
8%	9.0
9%	8.0
10%	7.2

Consider the following question: Approximately how long does it take to double an investment that is earning 9 percent annually? Using Exhibit 6.16, we know that a 9 percent interest rate will take 8 years to double according to the Rule of 72 [$72 \div 9 = 8$ years].

Rule of 72 - a method of approximation that estimates the time that it takes to double the value of an investment where the earnings (interest) rate is known (by dividing 72 by the interest rate). Alternatively, it can also estimate the earnings (interest) rate necessary to double an investment value if the time is known (by dividing 72 by the period of investment)

CHAPTER 6: TIME VALUE OF MONEY

While an extremely helpful tool as an approximator and as a control on the reasonableness of an answer determined by a calculator or computer, the Rule of 72 has a small error in it, especially at extremely low or high rates or terms. Consider, for example, how long it would take to double $1 if the rate of interest were 72 percent annually. According to the Rule of 72, 72 ÷ 72 = 1, indicating to us that we should double our money in one year, but we know that the value at the end of one year be $1.72 not $2. Many financial planners are using the Rule of 72 without consideration of the error factor. Exhibit 6.17 is a table of the error percentage rate for the Rule of 72 at various interest rates.

EXHIBIT 6.17: ERROR RATE USING THE RULE OF 72

Interest Rate	Error %
1	2.4
2	2.0
3	1.6
4	1.3
5	1.0
6	0.6
7	0.3
8	0.05
9	<0.4>
10	<0.6>
11	<0.9>
12	<1.3>
13	<1.4>
14	<1.8>
15	<2.1>
18	<3.1>
24	<4.7>
40	<7.6>
50	<8.5>
72*	<14.0>

The error rate for a given interest rate equal to or greater than 72 percent will always be 14 percent.

The error rate is calculated above using the actual value of $2 as the numerator and the actual calculated amount as the denominator to get the error percentage. The < > signs indicate that the actual value is less than the Rule of 72 estimated by the calculated percentage. The values that are not bracketed are greater than the Rule of 72 estimated by the calculated percentage indicated. For example, at 1 percent, the actual value of $1 at 1 percent for 72 periods is $2.047 or 2.4 percent above $2.

As you can see from the Exhibit 6.17, the error rate as a percent of the future value can range from +2.4 percent to –14 percent. Therefore, while the Rule of 72 is a good approximation, especially at interest rates between 6 percent and 10 percent, it loses some of its precision when outside the 6 percent to 10 percent interest rate range.

PROFESSIONAL
FOCUS

How do you convince your younger clients to take advantage of the power of compound interest for retirement planning or saving for children's education?

I explain that $2,000 invested annually for 40 years at 12% equals $1,534,000. They are usually impressed that the invested amount is $80,000 and the earning growth is $1,454,000. I usually recommend they maximize any pre-tax savings at their companies to take advantage of any employer match. Having maximized those savings, the Roth IRA is ideal for young persons with currently low income tax rates. I also explain to the 25 to 35-year-old client that they can retire comfortably at age 55 if they will annually save 10-13% of their gross income and invest in a broadly diversified portfolio of common stocks.

How frequently do you use TVM concepts and in what ways? Do you often make use of the perpetuities model?

I use TVM concepts almost every day. Among my other activities I teach investments. Understanding investments requires a thorough understanding of TVM concepts. In making investments in fixed income securities, TVM concepts are essential to determine the price of a bond, yield to maturity, and yield to call. I also use TVM concepts for valuing common stock investments using the concepts of fundamental analysis.

When calculating TVM problems, do you usually use a nominal or real rate, and where do you get them?

When calculating the solution to an education funding situation, or when planning for retirement, I use a rate of return for discounting based on the asset allocation chosen and the expected historical return for such an allocation. The inflation rate that I use is usually the current CPI for retirement plus 1 percent for conservatism. For education funding I use an inflation rate, which is a little higher and more representative of the recent experience of tuition increases. I would only use nominal rates of return without inflation for relatively short-term investment horizons.

Are serial payments really applicable to financial planning?

Yes. In fact, serial payments are very appropriate to financial planning. Since the serial payment is to be increased by inflation each year, it is generally consistent with a client's ability to pay and save more over time.

DAVID DURR, PH.D., CFP™

DISCUSSION QUESTIONS

1. What is the Time Value of Money (TVM) concept and why is it so important in financial planning?
2. What are the important questions in financial planning that can be answered using time value of money concepts?
3. What is meant by present value and future value and how are these two concepts used in the calculation of compound interest?
4. What are the basic tools used in TVM analysis?
5. How are time value of money tables computed?
6. What is the difference between the future value of an ordinary annuity (FVOA) and the present value of an ordinary annuity (PVOA)?
7. What is the difference between the future value of an annuity due (FVAD) and the present value of an annuity due (PVAD)?
8. When would you use an ordinary annuity or an annuity due in financial planning?
9. What are the formulas for calculating the present and future values of an ordinary annuity and an annuity due?
10. What are some time value of money concepts other than annuities?
11. How do unequal cash flows affect the future value of an investment?
12. How do net present value (NPV) and internal rate of return (IRR) differ in financial planning calculations?
13. What is the yield to maturity (YTM) and how is it used to determine a bond's earnings?
14. How is the concept of "Solving for Term Given the Other Variables" useful in debt management?
15. What alternative rate choices exist when selecting the rate of interest for accumulating or discounting?
16. How is the real return of an investment affected by the inflation rate?
17. How do serial payments affect the future value of an investment?
18. What are perpetuities and how do they affect financial planning?
19. How can amortization tables and the Rule of 72 assist in solving present TVM problems?
20. Does the Rule of 72 take into account the reinvested interest? If so, at what rate is the interest reinvested at?

EXERCISES

1. Calculate the present value of $10,000 to be received in exactly 10 years, assuming an annual interest rate of 9 percent.
2. Calculate the future value of $10,000 invested for 10 years, assuming an annual interest rate of 9 percent.
3. Calculate the present value of an ordinary annuity of $5,000 received annually for 10 years, assuming a discount rate of 9 percent.
4. Calculate the present value of an annuity of $5,000 received annually that begins today and continues for 10 years, assuming a discount rate of 9 percent.
5. Calculate the future value of an ordinary annuity of $5,000 received for 10 years, assuming an earnings rate of 9 percent.
6. Calculate the future value of an annual annuity of $5,000 beginning today and continuing for 10 years, assuming an earnings rate of 9 percent.

7. Mike borrows $240,000 at 8 percent for a mortgage for 15 years. Prepare an annual amortization table assuming the first payment is due January 30, 2000 exactly 30 days after the loan.

8. Joan invested $5,000 in an interest-bearing promissory note earning an 8 percent annual rate of interest compounded monthly. How much will the note be worth at the end of 5 years, assuming all interest is reinvested at the 8 percent rate?

9. Callie expects to receive $50,000 in 2 years. Her opportunity cost is 10 percent compounded monthly. What is the sum worth to Callie today?

10. Lola purchased a zero-coupon bond 9 years ago for $600. If the bond matures today and the face value is $1,000, what is the average annual compound rate of return (calculated semiannually) that Lola realized on her investment?

11. Today Evan put all of his cash into an account earning an annual interest rate of 10 percent compounded monthly. Assuming he makes no withdrawals or additions into this account, approximately how many years must Evan wait to double his money? Use the Rule of 72 to determine the answer.

12. Anthony has been investing $1,500 at the end of each year for the past 12 years. How much has accumulated assuming he has earned 8 percent compounded annually on his investment?

13. Dennis has been dollar cost averaging in a mutual fund by investing $1,000 at the beginning of every quarter for the past 5 years. He has been earning an average annual compound return of 11 percent compounded quarterly on this investment. How much is the fund worth today?

14. Casey, injured in an automobile accident, won a judgment that provides him $2,500 at the end of each 6-month period over the next 3 years. If the escrow account that holds Casey's settlement award earns an average annual rate of 10 percent compounded semiannually, how much was the defendant initially required to pay Casey to compensate him for his injuries?

15. Stacey wants to withdraw $3,000 at the beginning of each year for the next 5 years. She expects to earn 8 percent compounded annually on her investment. What lump sum should Stacey deposit today?

16. Gary wants to purchase a beach condo in 7 years for $100,000. What periodic payment should he invest at the beginning of each quarter to attain the goal if he can earn 11 percent annual interest, compounded quarterly on investments?

17. Ann purchased a car for $25,000. She is financing the auto at a 10 percent annual interest rate, compounded monthly for 4 years. What payment is required at the end of each month to finance Ann's car?

18. Josh purchased a house for $215,000 with a down payment of 20 percent. If he finances the balance at 10 percent over 30 years, how much will his monthly payment be?

19. Chase purchased a house for $300,000. He put 20 percent down and financed the remaining amount over 30 years at 8 percent. How much interest will be paid over the life of the loan assuming he pays the loan as agreed? (Round to the nearest dollar.)

PROBLEMS

1. Lucy wants to give her son $80,000 on his wedding day in 4 years. How much should she invest today at an annual interest rate of 9.5 percent compounded annually to have $80,000 in 4 years? Alternatively, how much would she need to invest today if she could have her interest compounded monthly? Explain which interest option would be most beneficial to Lucy.

2. Rachel, who just turned 18, deposits a $15,000 gift into an interest bearing account earning a 7.5 percent annual rate of interest. How much will she have in the account when she retires at age 60 assuming all interest is reinvested at the 7.5 percent rate? If Rachel decided she only needed $300,000 at retirement, could she retire at 59? Explain.

3. Kerri won the lottery today. She has two options. She can receive $30,000 at the end of each year for the next 15 years or take a lump sum distribution of $200,000. Her opportunity cost is 12 percent compounded annually. Based on present values which option should she choose?

4. Darrin wants to donate $8,000 to his church at the beginning of each year for the next 20 years. What lump sum should Darrin deposit today if he expects to earn 11 percent compounded annually on his investment? Alternatively, how much should he deposit if he wants to have $50,000 left at the end of the 20 years?

5. James deposited $800 at the end of the last 16 years to purchase his granddaughter, Kali a car. James earned 8 percent interest compounded annually on his investment. If the car Kali chooses costs $22,999, would she have enough money in the account to purchase the vehicle? What would be the deficit or surplus?

6. Brenda has been investing $150 at the beginning of each month for the past 20 years. How much has she accumulated assuming she has earned an 11 percent annual return compounded monthly on her investment? If instead of earning 11 percent, Brenda was only able to earn 10 percent (compounded monthly), how much would her payments need to be to have the same amount accumulated?

7. Kenneth took out a loan today to purchase a boat for $160,000. He will repay the loan over a 30-year period at 9 percent interest (assume payments are ordinary annuities). What will be his remaining balance of principal at the end of the first year?

8. Cody estimates his opportunity cost on investments at 9 percent compounded annually. Which one of the following is the best investment opportunity?
   ▲ To receive $100,000 today.
   ▲ To receive $400,000 at the end of 15 years.
   ▲ To receive $1,500 at the end of each month for 10 years compounded monthly.
   ▲ To receive $75,000 in 5 years and $100,000 5 years later.
   ▲ To receive $75,000 in 5 years and $175,000 10 years later.

9. Patricia and Scott Johnson are ready to retire. They want to receive the equivalent of $30,000 in today's dollars at the beginning of each year for the next 20 years. They assume inflation will average 4 percent over the long run, and they can earn an 8 percent compound annual after-tax return on investments. What lump sum do Patricia and Scott need to invest today to attain their goal?

10. Margaret wants to retire in 9 years. She needs an additional $200,000 in today's dollars in 10 years to have sufficient funds to finance this objective. She assumes inflation will average 5.0 percent over the long run, and she can earn a 4.0 percent compound annual after-tax return on investments. What serial payment should Margaret invest at the end of the first year to attain her objective?

192

11. Determine the future value of a periodic deposit of $5,000 made at the beginning of each year for 5 years to a mutual fund expected to earn 11 percent compounded quarterly during the projection period.

12. Kristi wants to buy a house in 10 years. She estimates she will need $200,000 at that time. She currently has ten Zero-Coupon Bonds with a market value of $4,600 that she will use as part of the required amount. The Zero-Coupon Bonds have a total face value of $10,000 and will mature in 10 years. The bond has a semiannual effective interest rate of 4.323 percent. In addition to the bond, she wants to save a monthly amount to reach her goal. What is Kristi's required monthly payment made at the beginning of each month in order to accumulate the $200,000, including the Zero-Coupon Bond, at an assumed interest rate of 11 percent?

CHAPTER 7

Education Funding

LEARNING OBJECTIVES:

After learning the material in this chapter, you will be able to:

1. Discuss the various issues that parents should consider when setting goals for financing their children's education.

2. List the types of financial aid information that can be gathered from a college's financial aid office.

3. Explain the importance of the EFC (Expected Family Contribution) formula in student financial aid application.

4. Describe the major student financial assistance programs available through the U.S. Department of Education.

5. Describe the campus-based student financial aid programs available to college students.

6. Describe the several financial aid programs available to college students.

7. List the benefits of Qualified State Tuition Plans (QSTPs).

8. Describe the various financial aid vehicles created by the Economic Growth and Tax Relief Reconciliation Act of 2001 (herein referred to as TRA 2001).

9. Understand how time-value-of-money concepts are used to help calculate the cost of a child's education.

INTRODUCTION

One of the most common financial planning goals of parents is to provide an education for their children. Education funding is a common area of concern for those seeking financial planning advice because paying for higher education is one of the largest financial burdens a family will face. Even clients with high-income levels must take into account paying for their children's tuition and school-related expenses. The rate of educational costs has increased by 5 percent for 1997 and 1998, 4 percent for 1999, and 4.4 percent for 2000, according to the College Board's report, <u>Trends in College Pricing</u>. However, over the past fifteen years, tuition at colleges and universities throughout the country has increased at an annual rate of 7 percent. The Consumer Price Index (CPI) over the past fifteen years averaged 3 percent. Also, recent trends show an increasing number of years an average student remains in college and an increase in requirements for post-graduate education. Along with the expense of a home and taxes, providing for a child's education is one of the largest expenses for families, and one of the most important decisions as well.

EXHIBIT 7.1: ANNUAL TUITION INCREASE TO CPI (1985–2000)

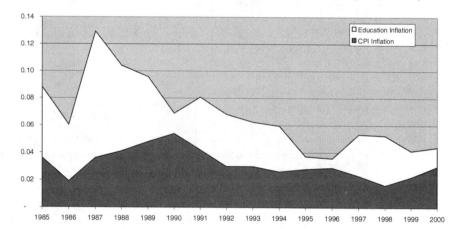

Reproduced with permission from the College Board. Copyright 2000 by College Entrance Examination Board. All Rights Reserved.

Exhibit 7.1 above illustrates that, on average, tuition costs over the last 15 years increased at a rate 2 percent to 3 percent greater than inflation. It is important for a financial planner to determine these types of economic factors when developing a client's plan to fund their children's education.

This chapter discusses how to develop a plan for funding a child's education by addressing the issues that must be raised, the information that must be gathered, and the goals that should be set taking the family's circumstances into account. Once the goals have been set, the implementation of the plan will depend on the sources of funding available, which may include a savings campaign, financial aid, and various payment options. Once the plan is designed and the strategies have been identified, action must be taken to implement and monitor the plan.

ISSUES AND GOALS

In order to formulate a plan that best meets the needs of the particular family, goals must be identified and agreed upon, so that appropriate provisions can be made to achieve those goals. The key is to set feasible, realistic goals.

When formulating a plan for the education of a child, one of the most significant considerations is how much time exists before the child enters college. There are many options available for parents of very young children who are years away from entering college. Those parents with children nearing college age or currently entering college do not have as many options and savings methods. It cannot be stressed enough that, as with most areas of planning, time is crucial in planning for a child's education. Time allows consistent and persistent contributions toward savings vehicles, allowing them to grow and, hopefully, meet or surpass the cost of tuition. Meanwhile, inflation will continue to drive tuition costs higher over the time horizon. It will clearly be less stressful and easier to manage tuition costs, however, with the benefit of ten, fifteen or more years of saving versus evaluating options, one's ability to pay, and formulating a plan during the student's junior or senior year in high school. In addition to concerns about college tuition, families should set goals as to whether they want to fund private elementary and secondary school education for their children. A family should also decide if they desire to provide some or all funding for graduate or professional school education.

One way for parents to ultimately defray the cost of education is paying for only a portion of the child's college expenses, while leaving some of the expenses to be paid by the child. Some view this method as a way of building character for the child and of "educating" the child in accepting responsibility, without forcing the child to assume all financial responsibility for college-related expenses that may burden the child with overwhelming loans and debt when beginning a career. Again, decisions such as these will depend on the preferences and desires of the parents.

During the goal-setting process, some individuals struggle with the notion of sending their children to public elementary and/or secondary school while investing resources during this time to a college education fund. This decision is often based on the quality of the public education available to the child. The parents should also consider that, while private elementary and/or secondary education will require more funds, there may be a "return" on that investment through the child obtaining a more advanced education and perhaps acceptance to prestigious colleges that may provide less stringent financial aid requirements or scholarships. Of course, these are issues that a financial planner should discuss with the parents so that they can make an informed decision based upon their own circumstances. Although there are many important issues and financial decisions to be made regarding elementary and secondary education, the majority of this chapter will deal with preparation and planning for a child's college expenses.

Parents should be reminded that families are in a better position to fund college expenses over a long time period because their income will likely increase in future years. This will motivate some parents to begin a savings regimen that does not meet all financial requirements right away, but can be increased as the years progress, and provide an incentive to increase savings as college years grow nearer.

INFORMATION GATHERING

During the goal-setting process, financial planners must forecast anticipated tuition and related expenses. This forecasting can be accomplished by first determining current tuition and related expenses for the schools in the area and for the schools that the parents believe would be appropriate for the child. This information can be found by calling the school's administrative office. Additionally, there are numerous college guides in bookstores and local libraries that provide tuition and room and board expenses at colleges and universities throughout the country. Such information is available on the Internet by using the search query "college tuition and financial aid," or by accessing *www.collegeboard.com* and its publications, including Trends in College Pricing or Trends in Financial Aid.

Once these expenses are obtained, the financial planner must adjust these expenses to account for inflation until the child enters college. The planner must assume a tuition inflation rate, probably between 5 and 8 percent per year for college and related expenses, and then calculate the anticipated expenses for each year the child will attend college.

EXAMPLE

Assumptions:

- ▲ Child's current age -- 10
- ▲ Anticipated college age -- 18-22
- ▲ Current tuition and room and board -- $13,000/year
- ▲ Tuition inflation rate -- 6 percent

Estimated costs (future value or actual cost) of tuition and room and board:

- ▲ Freshman Year -- $20,720 [$13,000 x $(1.06)^8$]
- ▲ Sophomore Year -- $21,963 [$13,000 x $(1.06)^9$]
- ▲ Junior Year -- $23,281 [$13,000 x $(1.06)^{10}$]
- ▲ Senior Year -- $24,678 [$13,000 x $(1.06)^{11}$]

Once these expenses have been identified and adjusted for inflation, one can determine the estimated 4-year cost of a college education. As will be discussed later in this chapter, depending on how much money will be available when the child enters college, a formula can be used to determine how much money must be invested now, over time, to meet the amount of savings necessary for college (i.e., the Expected Family Contribution). Other expenses that should be considered are books and school supplies, transportation, travel expenses, entertainment and the like, as shown in Exhibit 7.2.

198

EXHIBIT 7.2: COLLEGE EXPENSES CHECKLIST

These are the college expenses that most families should keep in mind when planning for payment of a child's education:

- ▲ Tuition and tuition-related expenses.
- ▲ Books, school supplies, and equipment (calculator, computer).
- ▲ Lodging.
- ▲ Meals.
- ▲ Transportation.
- ▲ Entertainment (school sporting events) and leisure (health club).
- ▲ Travel expenses.
- ▲ Tutoring (if necessary).
- ▲ Extra-curricular (fraternity/sorority dues).
- ▲ Clothing and attire.
- ▲ Other considerations particular to the student or family.

Because college is such a major investment, families should carefully evaluate potential schools. Some of the information families should obtain includes a copy of the documents describing the school's accreditation and licensing, current school tuition, and on-campus room and board. Also, families should ask about the school's loan default rate. The default rate is the percentage of students who attend the school, obtain federal student loans, and ultimately fail to repay the loan timely. This information is important because schools with high default rates may not be eligible to obtain federal aid for certain federal financial assistance programs. This may also indicate a pattern of poorly matched students with the school.

If a school advertises its job placement rates, it must also publish the most recent employment statistics, graduation statistics, and any other information that would justify its representations. Another relevant item of information is the school's refund policy. If a student enrolls but never attends classes, the student should be refunded the majority of his or her money. If a student begins attending classes but leaves prior to completing his or her coursework, the student may be able to receive a partial refund. Many state universities and certain private colleges allow for prepayment of tuition at current prices for enrollment in the future, up to even ten years prior to the child's enrollment. Over fifty private colleges currently allow for these types of prepayment programs. The individual schools can provide information on these programs and the inherent risks in participating in them. Prepaid tuition plans are discussed later in this chapter.

A prospective student can obtain the following financial aid availability information from a school:

▲ Availability of financial assistance, including information on all federal, state, local, private, and institutional financial aid programs.
▲ Procedures and deadlines for submitting financial aid program applications.
▲ The school's process for determining a financial aid applicant's eligibility.
▲ The school's method for determining a student's financial need.
▲ The school's method for determining each type and amount of assistance in a student's financial aid package.
▲ How and when the student will receive financial aid.
▲ The school's method for determining whether the student is making satisfactory academic progress, and the consequences if the student is not (whether the student continues to receive federal financial aid depends, in part, on whether the student makes satisfactory academic progress).
▲ If the student is awarded a job through the Federal Work-Study program, what type of job is involved, the amount of hours the student must work, the duties of the student in that job, the rate of pay, and how and when the student will be paid.
▲ The availability and counseling procedures of the school's financial aid office.

The client may also wish to ask the school for a copy of its "equity-in-athletics" report. Any coeducational school where a student can receive federal financial aid that has an interschool athletic program must prepare an equity-in-athletics report giving financial and statistical information for men's and women's sports. This information is designed to advise students of a school's commitment to providing equitable athletic opportunities for its men and women students.

The client should also be encouraged to consult with high school counselors, local employers, and the state higher education agency. These are invaluable sources of information for those exploring options of higher education.

DETERMINING FINANCIAL NEED

As mentioned earlier, most financial aid packages depend heavily on the financial need of the student. It is, therefore, important to evaluate whether a client may have the requisite financial need when estimating costs of tuition and availability of funds for college.

The financial aid process is initiated by filling out financial aid forms available from high schools, the United States Department of Education, or from the college the student will attend. This financial aid application form is called a "**FAFSA**," which stands for "**Free Application for Federal Student Aid**." A FAFSA must be submitted by the student applicant to become eligible for federal financial aid. The student can obtain and complete a FAFSA application in one of the following ways:

▲ Complete and mail a paper FAFSA, which can be obtained from the student's high school, potential college to attend, college where attending, or *www.ed.gov/offices/OPE/express.html.*
▲ Have the student's school submit the completed FAFSA electronically.

FAFSA - a application form that must be submitted by a college student to become eligible for federal financial aid

▲ Use "FAFSA on the Web" (*www.ed.gov/offices/OPE/express.html*) through the Internet.
▲ Use FAFSA Express software that can be obtained on-line at *www.ed.gov/offices/OPE/express.html* or by calling 1-800-801-0576.

Colleges usually appoint an agency to conduct an analysis of the financial need of the student and the student's family. The completed information on the FAFSA is sent to colleges requested by the applicant. The college where the student applies may also have the applicant complete other forms to enable the college to conduct its own needs analysis of the student. Once the student is accepted to a college, the college may inform the student at that time of any available financial aid.

When applying for student financial assistance, the information reported by the applicant is used in a formula established by Congress. The formula is called the **Expected Family Contribution** or "**EFC**" for a child's education. The EFC indicates how much of a student's family's resources ought to be available to assist in paying for the student's education. Some of the factors used in this calculation include taxable and nontaxable income, assets, retirement funds, and benefits, such as unemployment and Social Security.

Although low-income families are more likely to qualify for financial aid than higher-income families, higher-income families should not be discouraged from applying for aid because the EFC formula also takes into account various factors including the number of children in private school or college, the size of the family, the amount of years until the parents' retirement, and large financial burdens, such as medical bills. The EFC calculation is used to determine eligibility for financial aid programs, except for unsubsidized student loans and PLUS loans which are provided regardless of financial need. If the EFC is below a certain amount, the student may be eligible for financial aid, such as a Federal Pell Grant, assuming other eligibility requirements are met. Such eligibility requirements include the cost of attendance at the school (tuition, room and board, and related expenses), full-time, half-time or part-time status, and academic standing.

There is no maximum EFC because the EFC is used in a calculation depending on where the student attends school and the cost of attendance at that school. Here is how it works. When the student consults with his or her school's financial aid administrator, the financial aid administrator will calculate the student's financial need by subtracting the student's EFC from the cost of attendance at the school. The remaining figure equals the student's *financial need*. The formula is as follows:

Tuition/Cost of Attendance	$ Amount
- Expected Family Contribution (EFC)	- $ Amount
Financial Need	$ Amount

As is evident from the above calculation, a student may have financial need at one school but not another, because financial need turns on the cost of attendance, whereas the student's EFC remains constant for the year regardless of which school the student attends. Financial aid administrators, however, in their discretion, can adjust the cost of attendance or adjust data in calculating a student's EFC if circumstances so require. For more information on the EFC calculation, the *EFC Formula Book* describes how a student's EFC is calculated and can be obtained

EFC - (Expected Family Contribution) a formula that indicates how much of a student's family's resources ought to be available to assist in paying for the student's college education. Some of the factors used in this calculation include taxable and nontaxable income, assets, retirement funds, and benefits, such as unemployment and Social Security

through the Federal Student Aid Information Center, P. O. Box 84, Washington, D.C. 20044, or on the Internet at *www.ed.gov*.

It is at this point that most individuals ask how can they reduce their EFC. In other words, how can a family reduce the amount of money that it is expected to contribute to a child's education in order to receive more financial assistance? There are various methods that a family can use to reduce EFC. First, however, one must determine the dependency status of the student.

The income and assets of the student's family will only be counted if the student is considered dependent on the parents. If the student applying for financial aid is independent, then only the student's income and assets will be considered. The reasoning behind this rule is that a student who has access to parental support should not be able to reap the benefits of student financial aid programs to the exclusion of those needy, independent students who do not have access to parental support. A student is considered independent if he or she meets any one of the following criteria:

- ▲ Over the age of 23.
- ▲ Married.
- ▲ Enrolled in a graduate or professional educational program.
- ▲ Has legal dependents other than a spouse.
- ▲ Is an orphan or ward of the court.
- ▲ Is a veteran of the U.S. Armed Forces.

Another common method for reducing a family's EFC is creating a trust for the child and diminishing the family's estate through gifts. This may create problems, however, because the child's own assets will be considered in the child's financial needs analysis. A family may also reduce its EFC by providing all information surrounding the factors that tend to diminish their EFC, such as high medical bills and more than one child in the family attends college. Finally, the school's financial aid advisor may be able to adjust a family's EFC if the circumstances so require. Here, the burden is on the family or student to communicate information to the financial aid advisor that may reduce their EFC.

FINANCIAL AID PROGRAMS

The United States Department of Education has the following major student financial assistance programs:

- ▲ Federal Pell Grant.
- ▲ Stafford Loan.
- ▲ PLUS Loan.
- ▲ Consolidation Loan.
- ▲ Federal Supplemental Educational Opportunity Grant (FSEOG).
- ▲ Federal Work-Study and Federal Perkins Loans.

These federal programs are the largest sources of student aid in the United States. According to the U.S. Department of Education, available student aid topped $68 billion in 1999-2000, an increase of 4 percent over the preceding year after adjusting for inflation.

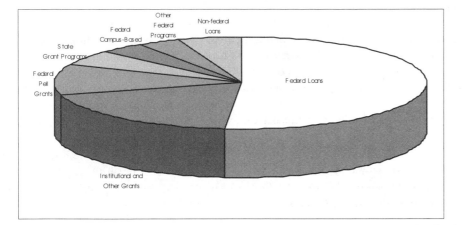

The subsections below identify and describe these federal programs, as well as some state, and other programs.

FEDERAL PELL GRANTS

A Federal Pell Grant is not a loan. It is a grant from the federal government, which does not require repayment. The EFC calculation, which is based on one's financial need, is used to determine a student's eligibility for a Pell Grant and how much is awarded to a student. Pell Grants are awarded to undergraduate students who have not earned bachelors or professional degrees. Graduate, professional, and post-graduate students are not awarded Pell Grants. Maximum awards for Pell Grants were $3,125 per student for the 1999-2000 school year. Awards for the 2000-2001 school year (July 1, 2000 to June 30, 2001) will depend on program funding and applications. The application deadline for the 2000-2001 award period was June 30, 2001. Each year's awards depend on program funding for that year. A student can receive only one Pell Grant award per year. A student can still receive a Pell Grant if enrolled part time, but will not receive as much as he or she would have received if enrolled full time.

Pell Grant - a grant from the federal government awarded to undergraduate students who have not earned bachelors or professional degrees. The EFC calculation, which is based on one's financial need, is used to determine a student's eligibility for a Pell Grant and how much is awarded to a student

DIRECT AND FFEL STAFFORD LOANS

Stafford Loan - the primary type of financial aid provided by the United States Department of Education. There are two types of Stafford Loans: Direct Stafford Loans ("Direct Loans") and Federal Family Education Stafford Loans, or "FFEL Loans"

Direct Stafford Loan - federal financial aid funds provided by the U.S. Dept. of Education directly to the student

FFEL Stafford Loans - are lent to the student through a lender (such as a bank or other approved financial institution) that participates in the FFEL program

The **Stafford Loan** is the primary type of financial aid provided by the United States Department of Education. There are two types of Stafford Loans, those being Direct Stafford Loans ("Direct Loans") and Federal Family Education Stafford Loans, or "FFEL Loans." The major differences between Direct and FFEL Stafford Loans are the sources of the loan funds and the available repayment plans. Under the **Direct Stafford Loan** system, funds are provided directly to the borrower by the United States government, whereas funds for **FFEL Stafford Loans** are lent to the student through a lender (such as a bank or other approved financial institution) that participates in the FFEL program.

Stafford Loans are either subsidized or unsubsidized. A subsidized loan means that there is no interest charged on the loan until repayment of the loan begins, which is typically six months after one of the following occurs:

▲ Graduation.
▲ Leaving school.
▲ Dropping below half-time status.

Half-time status is considered half of the minimum hours to be considered full time. For instance, if a school on a semester basis has a 12-hour minimum requirement each semester for a student to be considered full time, the student is considered half time if he or she is enrolled in at least 6 credit hours each semester. The only federal student aid programs that require at least half-time enrollment are the Stafford Direct and FFEL Loan programs. Half-time enrollment is not a requirement in the other financial aid programs, including the Federal Pell Grant, FSEOG, Federal Work Study, and Federal Perkins Loan programs.

The application process differs for each Stafford Loan program. If the school participates in the Direct Stafford Loan program, the Free Application for Federal Student Aid ("FAFSA") serves as the Stafford Loan application. If the school participates in the FFEL Stafford Loan program, the student completes a separate application in addition to the FAFSA.

A subsidized loan is based on the financial need of the student as determined by the EFC formula. An unsubsidized Stafford Loan is a loan in which the borrower is charged interest on the principal from the moment of disbursement until the loan is paid off. Those who receive unsubsidized loans have the option of allowing the interest to be capitalized (which means that the interest accumulates and is added to the principal during the life of the loan until principal reduction payments are required), or the option of paying the interest as it accrues. The process of capitalization costs more over the long-term because the interest that accumulates is added to the principal balance, and subsequent interest is charged on the entire outstanding balance. However, some students or their families may not be in a financial position to pay the interest while the student is in school, and the capitalization method provides them with the option of postponing payment. All Stafford Loans have below-market interest rates that cannot exceed 8.25 percent.

When Stafford Loans are disbursed to a student, approximately 4 percent of the loan is deducted to help defray the cost of the loan and help pay for the administrative costs of the Stafford Loan program. Thus, when determining the amount of funds through Stafford Loans required for a school term, the student must remember that the disbursement for a $7,000 Stafford Loan, for example, will only be $6,720 [$7,000 x 4 percent = $280; $7,000 - $280 = $6,720] or [$7,000 x 96 percent = $6,720]. In other words, the actual disbursement to the student will be roughly 4 percent less than the face amount of the loan, which the student must pay back.

Repayment of Stafford Loans begins after a grace period of six months following graduation, leaving school, or dropping below half-time enrollment. What is very attractive about the subsidized Stafford Loan is that no interest is charged and no principal payment is required during the six-month grace period. Essentially, the student has received a free loan during school and for six months thereafter under the subsidized loan program. Once the grace period is over, however, the subsidized loan begins to accrue interest, and principal and interest reduction payments must begin. Although interest is charged during the grace period on an unsubsidized Stafford Loan, no repayment of principal or interest is required during the grace period. By not paying the interest on an unsubsidized loan during the grace period, the interest accrues and continues to be capitalized.

Students may obtain a "deferment" of the loan, which is a temporary postponement of payments on the loan. If the student has a subsidized loan, interest will not be charged during the period of deferment. For unsubsidized loans, the interest is capitalized during deferment unless the student chooses to pay the interest as it accrues during deferment. A deferment is allowed only after proving "special circumstances" to the agency, sender, or holder of the loan. The circumstances that may give rise to a deferment of repayment on a Stafford Loan include the following:

- ▲ At least half-time enrollment at a post-secondary school.
- ▲ Enrollment in an approved fellowship program.
- ▲ Enrollment in an approved rehabilitation training program for the disabled.
- ▲ Economic hardship (for up to 3 years).
- ▲ Former student's inability to attain full-time employment (for up to 3 years).

Forbearance is a period of time when repayment of a loan is temporarily postponed upon request of a borrower and authorization by the lender. While forbearance also postpones repayment, subsidized loans accrue interest during the period of forbearance. Direct Stafford Loans can be repaid under several payment plans. Each payment plan has a different term ranging from 10 to 32 years. FFEL Stafford Loans can also be repaid under several payment plans, but cannot exceed a 10-year term.

PLUS LOANS

PLUS Loans (Parent Loans for Undergraduate Students) are loans that are available through the Direct Loan and FFEL programs. PLUS Loans allow parents with good credit histories to borrow funds for a child's educational expenses. The child must be a dependent student in at least half-time enrollment. The parents complete a PLUS Loan application and Promissory Note with the school's financial aid office. As long as the parents do not have an adverse credit history, they may be entitled to receive a loan equal to the cost of attendance less any other available financial aid.

For instance, if the cost of attendance is $7,500 and the student has $5,000 in other financial aid, then the parents could borrow up to, but no more than, $2,500. The interest rate on a PLUS

PLUS Loans - (Parent Loans for Undergraduate Students)loans available through the Direct Loan and FFEL programs that allow parents with good credit histories to borrow funds for a child's educational expenses

205

Loan is variable, but will never exceed 9 percent. Interest accrues on the loan from the moment of disbursement until the loan is paid off. As with Stafford Loans, a fee of roughly 4 percent is deducted from the funds disbursed to help defray the cost of the loan to the government. At least two disbursements of funds are made because no installment may exceed half of the loan amount.

Normally, parents must begin repaying PLUS Loans within 60 days after the final loan disbursement for the current academic year. Parents must commence repayment of both principal and interest while the student is in school. The same rules that apply to deferment or forbearance of Stafford Loans apply to PLUS Loans as well. However, because PLUS Loans are not subsidized, interest will continue to accrue and will thus be capitalized during the period of deferment or forbearance. PLUS Loans must be repaid within 10 years.

CONSOLIDATION LOANS

Consolidation Loan - a loan that provides borrowers with a way to consolidate various types of federal student loans that have separate repayment schedules into one loan

A **Consolidation Loan** provides borrowers with a vehicle to consolidate various types of federal student loans that have separate repayment schedules into one loan. The Consolidation Loan program benefits student and parent borrowers by extending the term of repayment, requiring only one payment per month, and in some cases providing a lower interest rate than on one or more of the loans. The school's financial aid advisor can explain the many combinations of Consolidation Loan options.

CAMPUS-BASED STUDENT FINANCIAL AID

There are three "campus-based" programs that are administered directly by the financial aid office at participating schools. The three programs are:

- ▲ The Federal Supplemental Education Opportunity Grant (FSEOG) Program.
- ▲ The Federal Work-Study Program.
- ▲ The Federal Perkins Loan Program.

Each program extends aid based on financial need of the student and the availability of funds at the school.

FSEOG - (Federal Supplemental Education Opportunity Grant) campus-based student financial aid grant awarded to undergraduate students with low EFCs that gives priority to students who receive Federal Pell Grants

The Federal Supplemental Education Opportunity Grant Program

A **FSEOG** is a grant, an outright gift, which need not be repaid. The FSEOG is awarded to undergraduate students with low EFCs and gives priority to students who receive Federal Pell Grants. The difference between a Federal Pell Grant and an FSEOG is that the United States Department of Education guarantees that each eligible school will receive sufficient funds to pay Federal Pell Grants to all eligible students, whereas an FSEOG is paid to eligible students if funds are available. Once all available FSEOG funds are used at the school, remaining eligible students will not receive an FSEOG grant. The FSEOG is in the range of $100 to $4,000 per academic year. The amount paid depends on the level of need, the time of application, and the school's funding level.

SECTION TWO: BASIC FINANCIAL PLANNING TOOLS

The Federal Work-Study Program

Federal Work-Study programs enable undergraduate and graduate students to earn money for education expenses through jobs that pay at least current minimum wages. Some jobs may pay higher hourly rates depending on the work done and skill required. The amount earned through the Federal Work-Study program cannot exceed the award received through the program. Federal Work-Study jobs are both on campus and off campus depending on the employer participating in the program.

The Federal Perkins Loan Program

A Federal Perkins Loan is a loan that is provided to undergraduate and graduate students that have exceptional financial need (i.e., very low EFCs). Although the loan is made with government funds, the school is the lender. The student must repay the loan, but the benefit of the Perkins Loan is that it is a low 5 percent interest loan. Unlike Stafford and PLUS Loans, there is no 4 percent charge or fee for a Perkins Loan. After graduation, leaving school, or dropping below half-time status, there is a nine-month grace period for repayment of a Perkins Loan. The Perkins Loan must be repaid within 10 years from the start of repayment. In addition to the same rules as Stafford and PLUS Loans for deferment and forbearance, the Perkins Loan can be canceled under certain conditions including:

▲ Death.
▲ Total and permanent disability.
▲ Becoming a full time special education teacher, nurse, medical technician, or certain type of teacher.
▲ Serving in the Armed Forces.

These cancellation conditions are subject to certain tests and can be explained by the school's financial aid advisor.

For more information about federal education programs and financial aid applications, visit the United States Department of Education's website at *www.ed.gov*.

STATE GOVERNMENTAL AID

Most states have programs that are very similar to the federal student financial aid programs discussed above. The state programs rely heavily on the financial need of the student as well as the student's superior academic performance. States also require that the student be a resident of the state and attend a college or university in that state. Information on a given state's financial aid programs can be obtained from the school to be attended or that state's Department of Education.

Federal Work-Study program - campus-based student financial aid program that enables undergraduate and graduate students to earn money for education expenses through jobs that pay at least current minimum wages but do not exceed the award received through the program

Federal Perkins Loan - campus-based, low-interest student loan that is provided to undergraduate and graduate students that have exceptional financial need, that is, very low EFCs

OTHER FINANCIAL AID SOURCES

Aid Directly From The Institution

Each school has its own method of providing aid through loans, scholarships, discounts, and campus jobs. The school's financial aid advisor should adequately explain to the student the school's available options and programs. Some schools will allow a student to pay tuition on a monthly installment plan, which may provide more flexibility to the student and parents. Other schools may offer discounts or scholarships for superior athletic or academic performance either prior to or after enrollment. The school has an incentive to entice superior athletes and academic students in order to increase their level of top students and to better compete with other schools, which in turn enhances the school's image.

Aid from Armed Forces

The U.S. Armed Forces have numerous programs and scholarships that may pay for tuition, fees, and books for those who enlist or enroll in the military. The student may also receive monthly payments for other expenses. Information regarding the many programs available through the U.S. Armed Forces can be obtained from the college attended or from the Administrative Office of the desired branch of military. On the Internet, try any of the following websites for Armed Forces aid:

- ▲ *www.goarmy.com/tour/educ/educ.htm*
- ▲ *www.gibill.va.gov*
- ▲ *www.usmc.mil/marinelink/websites.nsf/education*
- ▲ *www.education.airforce.com*

Other Scholarships

There are many forms of scholarships that are awarded by groups that are separate and apart from the school and state, or federal government. For instance, there are numerous civic organizations, like the American Legion, the Knights of Columbus, and the Boy Scouts of America, that award scholarships based on need, merit, and/or the student's or parents' affiliation with that civic organization. Of course, there are various types of scholarships available to students who have high grades and high standardized (entrance) test scores, including National Merit Scholarships. Also, scholarships can be provided through a particular church or religious organization. Although finding out about these scholarships will take some effort, it may prove to be time well spent.

TAX ADVANTAGES FROM EDUCATIONAL EXPENSES AND TAX ISSUES

Although much time has been spent in this chapter discussing the costs of education and the rise in educational expenses, there is some tax relief available. There are various vehicles available which allow the family or taxpayer who bear the brunt of education expenses, to realize tax savings and benefits.

In addition, TRA 2001 modified the educational incentives such that after 2001 there will be additional tax benefits to educational savings. The applicable changes are discussed within this chapter.

QUALIFIED STATE TUITION PLANS

One increasingly popular vehicle used to prepare for college tuition and related costs are **"Qualified State Tuition Plans," or QSTPs.** In 1996, Congress enacted Section 529 of the Internal Revenue Code (IRC) through the Small Business Job Protection Act of 1996. Section 529 was modified by the Taxpayer Relief Act of 1997. The Taxpayer Relief Act of 1997 also created Roth IRAs and the Educational IRA. Section 529 provides tax-exempt status to QSTPs created, sponsored, and maintained by individual states. QSTPs are also commonly referred to as "529 Plans" after IRC Section 529. The Internal Revenue Code permits the states to enact and tailor their own QSTPs within the parameters established by Section 529. More than forty states have legislation establishing 529 Plans/QSTPs, and six other states are either drafting or promoting such legislation.

The Benefits of QSTPs

The benefits of QSTPs are:

▲ Tax-deferred growth.
▲ The beneficiary/student is taxed at his or her tax bracket, not the contributor's tax bracket at the moment of withdrawal. Distributions from state sponsored qualified tuition programs are excludible from gross income if received after December 31, 2001.
▲ The contributor can remove assets from his or her taxable estate.
▲ QSTPs generally charge low commissions and have low management fees.
▲ Many states provide state tax deductions and/or tax exemptions for some contributions.
▲ The contributor/owner has full control of the asset and can change the beneficiary.

Although each state's QSTP legislation varies and has different features, all basically provide for two types of plans, Prepaid Tuition Plans and Savings Plans. QSTPs allow individuals to either participate in Prepaid Tuition Plans whereby tuition credits are purchased for a designated beneficiary for payment or waiver of higher education expenses, or participate in Savings Plans whereby contributions of money are made to an account to eventually pay for higher education expenses of a designated beneficiary.

PREPAID TUITION PLANS

Prepaid Tuition Plans are plans where prepayment of tuition is allowed at current prices for enrollment in the future. In other words, the parent can "lock in" future tuition at current rates. Participating in a school's prepayment program presupposes that the child will ultimately attend that school for college. The parents also assume the risk that the child will not meet the school's academic and admission requirements. Starting a tuition prepayment plan years in advance further prevents the student from choosing his or her own college. Other risks include the possibility that the student may be the recipient of a scholarship to that or another college. More particularly, the college chosen for tuition prepayment, although a well-respected and accredited school, could have a less than desirable curriculum in the student's major or particular area of interest. The client should weigh these risks with the benefits obtained at the particular school

QSTPs - (Qualified State Tuition Plans)also known as 529 plans, QSTPs allow individuals to either participate in prepaid tuition plans whereby tuition credits are purchased for a designated beneficiary for payment or waiver of higher education expenses, or participate in savings plans whereby contributions of money are made to an account to eventually pay for higher education expenses of a designated beneficiary

Prepaid Tuition Plans - plans where prepayment of college tuition is allowed at current prices for enrollment in the future-- in other words, a parent can "lock in" future tuition at current rates through tuition prepayment. It is, therefore, recommended that the family fully investigate the terms and conditions of the specific prepaid tuition plan so that the family will understand the consequences if the student attends a different college, fails to meet academic qualifications, or does not attend college at all. Various prepaid tuition plans treat these and other events differently.

SAVINGS PLANS

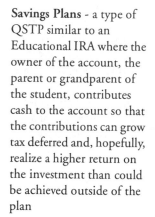

Savings Plans - a type of QSTP similar to an Educational IRA where the owner of the account, the parent or grandparent of the student, contributes cash to the account so that the contributions can grow tax deferred and, hopefully, realize a higher return on the investment than could be achieved outside of the plan

Savings Plans are similar to Educational IRAs, but have different attributes, rules, and tax ramifications, as will be seen below. In a Savings Plan, the owner of the account, the parent or grandparent, contributes money to the account so that the contributions can grow tax deferred and, hopefully, realize a higher return on the investment than could be achieved outside of the plan. Section 529 requires that all contributions to the program be made only in cash. Neither contributors nor designated beneficiaries may direct the investment of any contributions or any earnings on contributions.

QSTPs are attractive to states because they can provide incentives to residents and nonresidents (depending on the state's individual plan) to invest in higher education and into that state's educational system. These plans are inexpensive for states to run, as many states provide turn-key contracts to financial services firms or investment companies to professionally manage the state-wide plan. For instance, Merrill Lynch manages all QSTPs for Maine, Fidelity Investments manages all QSTPs for New Hampshire, and Salomon Smith Barney manages QSTPs for Colorado.

It is generally recognized that Savings Plans have distinct advantages over Prepaid Tuition Plans. First, payment to a state's Savings Plan does not prohibit the owner/contributor from withdrawing money and paying for tuition at an out-of-state school. Savings Plans allow the owner/contributor to invest his or her money into a pool and experience growth on the return on the investment. Prepaid Tuition Plans allow the owner/contributor to "lock in" on current tuition rates for college in later years, which is only attractive if the rising rate of tuition exceeds the client's after-tax rate of return. One perceived disadvantage of Savings Plans is that the owner/contributor does not have the right to choose how contributions are invested. Managers of Savings Plans generally decrease the percentage of investment in growth/equity funds as the beneficiary gets older and closer to college, while the percentage of investment into bonds and money market funds increases as the beneficiary ages. However, the income tax and estate tax advantages of QSTPs and the risks inherent in Prepaid Tuition Plans, as discussed earlier, generally make Savings Plans more advantageous for those who take time to plan their tax and saving strategies.

One of the most alluring attributes of QSTPs is that the owner/contributor controls the account, makes the withdrawals to pay for expenses, and can change beneficiaries. Do not confuse control of the account with control of the specific investments. As discussed above, the owner/contributor cannot control where the actual contributions are invested, but can control the money when it is ultimately withdrawn from the account. The owner/contributor, not the student/beneficiary, controls the withdrawal and payment of expenses. In contrast, the Uniform Gift to Minors Act, for instance (discussed later in this chapter), provides no safeguard to the contributor if the student decides not to attend college and uses the funds to go sailing to Australia!

The Mechanics of QSTPs

The mechanics of QSTPs are simple. The owner/contributor withdraws funds from the account to pay for "qualified higher education expenses." Under Section 529, qualified higher education expenses are defined as tuition, fees, books, supplies, and equipment required for attendance or enrollment at an eligible educational institution, as well as certain room and board expenses for students who attend an eligible educational institution at least half time. An eligible educational institution is an accredited post-secondary educational institution that offers credit toward a Bachelor's degree, an Associate's degree, a graduate-level or professional degree, or another recognized post-secondary credential. The institution must be eligible to participate in Department of Education student aid programs. Prior to 2002, the beneficiary/student is taxed at his or her tax rate only to the extent that the distributions exceed contributions to the account. The entire withdrawal is thus not subject to tax and the tax is based on the student's lower tax bracket.

If, however, a portion or all of the withdrawal is spent on anything other than qualified higher education expenses, the owner/contributor will be taxed at his or her own tax rate on the earnings portion of the withdrawal. A penalty is not imposed if the beneficiary dies or becomes disabled or if the beneficiary receives a scholarship. Prior to 2002, the owner/contributor will be assessed with a "more than *de minimis* penalty" on the earnings only. In other words, Section 529 was designed so that violations are not taken lightly, so something more than a nominal fee will be assessed depending on the state's individual plan.

A program must impose a "more than *de minimis* penalty" on refunds that are not used for qualified higher education expenses, not made on account of death or disability of the designated beneficiary, or not made on account of a scholarship or certain other educational allowances. A program must further provide adequate safeguards to prevent contributions in excess of those necessary to provide for the qualified higher education expenses of the beneficiary. Some states utilize the highest tuition in the state as a limit on contributions. For example, in Montana, contributions as high as $170,000 are allowed, although some states limit contributions to as low as $2,000 per year.

TRA 2001 has eliminated the "more than de minimis penalty" language of the IRC and has instead imposed a 10 percent penalty on these types of distributions after December 31, 2001. Starting in 2002, Educational IRAs permit up to $2,000 ($500 in 2001) in annual contributions, whereas QSTPs allow large contributions where some states reach as high as $100,000 and above. However, if the individual family plans to contribute only $2,000 or less annually to the student/beneficiary's college fund, then Educational IRAs might be more attractive because the owner/contributor has the power to direct the specific investments, <u>and</u> withdrawals used for qualified higher education expenses are not subject to taxation. Premature withdrawals from a traditional IRA are not subject to penalty if used for payment of higher education expenses. After 2001, if a person contributes funds to an Educational IRA, that person may also contribute funds into a QSTP in the same year for the same beneficiary.

TRA 2001 will also allow contributions (starting in 2002) by corporations, tax-exempt organizations, and others. In addition, contributions will be allowed until April 15th of the following year, rather than December 31 of the same year.

Taxes and the QSTP

As previously discussed, a student's financial aid eligibility depends on the student's and family's financial condition. The existence of a QSTP may affect the formula calculation for a student depending on the type of plan involved. For instance, a Savings Plan is deemed an asset of the parent who is the owner/contributor of the account.

Contributions to QSTPs are deemed to qualify for the annual $10,000 gift tax exclusion. A five-year averaging election for purposes of the gift tax annual exclusion may be applied to the transfer. If one's contributions exceed $10,000, the contributor is permitted to spread out one contribution over a five-year period. For example, if John (father-contributor) contributes $35,000 to a QSTP account for Matthew (beneficiary-child) in one year, then John can elect to spread this contribution over five years, that is, $7,000 per year, and avoid a gift tax (less than the $10,000 annual exclusion). The QSTP thus permits the owner/contributor to shift his or her taxable estate to the beneficiary without taxation.

As discussed, a portion of the distributions under a QSTP are includible in the gross income of the beneficiary/student if received prior to 2002. Distributions include in-kind benefits furnished to a designated beneficiary under a QSTP. Any distribution, or portion of a distribution, that is transferred within 60 days under a QSTP to the credit of a new designated beneficiary who is a member of the family of the old designated beneficiary shall not be treated as a distribution, and thus is beyond taxation and penalty. A change in the designated beneficiary of an interest in a QSTP shall not be treated as a distribution if the new beneficiary is a member of the family of the old beneficiary. If the new beneficiary is assigned to a lower generation than the old beneficiary, the transfer is a taxable gift from the old beneficiary to the new beneficiary regardless of whether the new beneficiary is a member of the family of the old beneficiary. In addition, the transfer will be subject to the generation-skipping transfer tax only if the new beneficiary is assigned to a generation which is two or more levels lower than the generation assignment of the old beneficiary.

TRA 2001 expanded the definition of "qualified tuition program" to include certain prepaid tuition programs established and maintained by one or more eligible educational institutions (which may be private institutions) that satisfy the requirements under section 529 (other than the present-law State sponsorship rule). Except to the extent provided in regulations, a tuition program maintained by a private institution is not treated as qualified unless it has received a ruling or determination from the IRS that the program satisfies applicable requirements. In addition, an exclusion from gross income is provided for distributions made in taxable years beginning after December 31, 2001, from qualified State tuition programs to the extent that the distribution is used to pay for qualified higher education expenses. This exclusion from gross income is extended to distributions from qualified tuition programs established and maintained by an entity other than a State (or agency or instrumentality thereof) for distributions made in taxable years after December 31, 2003.

TRA 2001 allows a taxpayer to claim a HOPE credit or Lifetime Learning credit for a taxable year and to exclude from gross income amounts distributed (both the principal and the earnings portions) from a qualified tuition program on behalf of the same student as long as the distribution is not used for the same expenses for which a credit was claimed.

QSTPs are extremely useful tools that provide significant tax savings, allow for substantial investments for a child's education, and provide a tool for avoidance of gift and estate taxes if used correctly. When comparing the tax savings alone from a QSTP Savings Plan versus a taxable account, the tax benefits can prove to be substantial. If a family contributes $300 per month to a taxable account earning 10 percent annually for 16 years, the accumulated value of the account would be approximately $100,000 if the assumed federal and state tax rates total 34 percent. However, if that same $300 monthly contribution is made for 16 years into a QSTP earning 10 percent annually and taxed at the child's likely rate of 15 percent when withdrawn, the account would be worth $130,000. The difference is a tax savings of approximately $30,000. This difference is further increased by the income exclusion provided by TRA 2001.

EDUCATIONAL IRAS

Educational IRAs were also authorized by the Taxpayer Relief Act of 1997. Educational IRAs are designed to offer tax benefits to those individuals who wish to save money for a child/grandchild's qualified education expenses. An Educational IRA is an investment account established with cash that is not deductible for the year contributed. The contributions are made for the benefit of children that are under 18 years of age. The contributions are allowed to grow tax-free within the account. Money withdrawn from the account is free from tax or penalty if the funds are used for qualified educational expenses. If the funds are used for anything other than higher education expenses, the earnings are subject to income tax and a 10 percent penalty.

An Educational IRA can be established for any child under the age of 18 by a parent, grandparent, other family members or friends, or even by the child, as long as the contributor who establishes the account does not have income that reaches $160,000 for 2001 ($220,000 for years after 2001) or more of modified family annual gross income (phaseout is from $150,000 to $160,000 for 2001 (or before) and $190,000 to $220,000 for years after 2001), or $110,000 (phaseout is from $95,000 to $110,000) or more if filing single. If, however, money from the Educational IRA is not used for higher educational expenses by the designated beneficiary by the time the beneficiary turns 30 years of age, then that beneficiary may not use the money without tax and penalties. However, if the beneficiary reaches 30 years, the Educational IRA may be rolled over into an Educational IRA for a family member of the original beneficiary.

No contributions can be made to the account once the beneficiary turns 18 years of age. Contributions were limited to $500 per designated beneficiary in 2001; however, starting in 2002, annual contributions can be made up to $2,000 (TRA 2001) for a particular beneficiary. Meanwhile, distributions or withdrawals from Educational IRAs are comprised of principal and earnings. The principal is always excluded from taxation, whereas earnings are excluded if used to pay for qualified educational expenses. Although a parent may establish more than one account in a given child's name, the aggregate maximum annual contribution is $500 per year for 2001, and $2,000 for years after 2001. Withdrawals are tax-free whether the student is enrolled full time, half time, or less than half time as long as the withdrawals do not exceed the child's qualified educational expenses.

TRA 2001 expands the definition of qualified education expenses (beyond undergraduate or graduate level courses) that may be paid tax-free from an education IRA to include "qualified elementary and secondary school expenses," meaning expenses for (1) tuition, fees, academic tutoring, special need services, books, supplies, and other equipment incurred in connection with the

Educational IRAs - an investment account established with cash that whose contributions are allowed to grow tax free within the account. Money withdrawn from the account remain free from tax or penalty if the funds are used for higher educational expenses. If not, the earnings are subject to income tax and a 10 percent penalty

enrollment or attendance of the beneficiary at a public, private, or religious school providing elementary or secondary education (kindergarten through grade 12) as determined under state law, (2) room and board, uniforms, transportation, and supplementary items or services (including extended day programs) required or provided by such a school in connection with such enrollment or attendance of the beneficiary, and (3) the purchase of any computer technology or equipment or Internet access and related services, if such technology, equipment, or services are to be used by the beneficiary and the beneficiary's family during any of the years the beneficiary is in school.

One of the drawbacks of Educational IRAs was that, beneficiaries taking on a tax-free distribution from an Educational IRA could not also receive either the Hope Scholarship Credit or Lifetime Learning Credit (if otherwise applicable) in the same year. The Hope Scholarship Credit and the Lifetime Learning Credit are discussed later in this section. In addition, proceeds from EE or I savings bonds that are used to pay for qualified higher education expenses reduces the amount of available tuition. However, TRA 2001 allows a taxpayer to claim a Hope credit or Lifetime Learning credit for a taxable year and to exclude from gross income amounts distributed (both the contributions and the earnings portions) from an education IRA on behalf of the same student as long as the distribution is not used for the same educational expenses for which a credit was claimed for years after 2001.

Generally speaking, if a taxpayer withdraws funds from his or her traditional IRA prior to age 59½, the taxpayer is required to pay a 10 percent early withdrawal penalty on all or part of the amount withdrawn. However, the 10 percent penalty does not apply if a taxpayer withdraws funds from a traditional IRA to pay for qualified higher educational expenses for the taxpayer, the taxpayer's spouse or the child or grandchild of the taxpayer or taxpayer's spouse. Unlike an Educational IRA, the taxpayer will owe federal income tax on the amount withdrawn. Prior to 2002, any amount contributed to an Educational IRA on behalf of a designated beneficiary in a given year where an amount is also contributed to a qualified state tuition program on behalf of the same beneficiary is treated as an excess contribution to an Educational IRA and is subject to a 6 percent excise tax each year the excess amount remains in the account. However, TRA 2001 repeals the excise tax on contributions made for years after 2001.

ROTH IRA

The Roth IRA was also created by the Taxpayer Relief Act of 1997. The Roth IRA does not provide for tax deductions for any contributions. However, contributions grow tax free within the IRA. As a result of TRA 2001, contributions are increasing to $3,000 for years 2002 through 2004; $4,000 for years 2005 through 2007; and $5,000 in 2008 and thereafter. Contributions to Roth IRAs are limited to the lesser of $2,000 or earned income in 2001. Contributions can be made as late as the due date of the individual's tax return for the previous tax year. Contributions to a Roth IRA can be made for years beyond the age of 70½, whereas traditional IRAs prevent contributions after the attainment of age 70½. Allowed contributions to Roth IRAs are phased out for joint filers with an adjusted gross income between $150,000 and $160,000, and for single taxpayers with an adjusted gross income between $95,000 and $110,000.

A distribution from a Roth IRA is not includible in the owner's gross income if it is a "qualified distribution," or to the extent that it is a return of the owner's contributions to the Roth IRA. Qualified distributions are distributions that occur after a five-year holding period and on account of one of the following four reasons:

▲ Death.
▲ Disability.
▲ Attainment of age 59½.
▲ First time house purchase (limit of $10,000).

If a distribution is not a qualified distribution and it exceeds contribution (and conversions) to Roth IRAs, then the distribution will be subject to income tax and may be subject to the 10 percent penalty. However, these excess distributions can avoid the 10 percent penalty if the proceeds are used for qualified higher education costs. The taxpayer is always able to withdraw amounts up to their total contribution without income tax or penalty.

Qualified higher educational expenses are tuition, fees, and room and board.

In short, Roth IRAs may be an even more attractive vehicle for education savings than Educational IRAs because the age of the student is irrelevant (versus the 30-year-old requirement) and because contributions are higher. In addition, funds in a Roth IRA not used for education can be used for retirement.

THE HOPE SCHOLARSHIP CREDIT

The **Hope Scholarship Credit** is another by-product of the Taxpayer Relief Act of 1997. This tax credit is available for qualified tuition and enrollment fees incurred and paid after 1997 in the first two years of post-secondary education for the taxpayer, spouse, or dependent. The Hope Scholarship Credit is comprised of 100 percent of the first $1,000 of qualified expenses paid in the tax year, plus 50 percent of the next $1,000. The maximum credit allowed in a given year is $1,500 per student. A student must be enrolled no less than half time to be eligible. The Hope Scholarship Credit is subject to a phaseout based on the taxpayer's adjusted gross income as follows:

Hope Scholarship Credit - a tax credit available for qualified tuition and enrollment fees incurred and paid after 1997 in the first two years of post-secondary education for the taxpayer, spouse, or dependent

AGI PHASEOUT FOR HOPE AND LIFETIME LEARNING CREDITS	
Married filing jointly	$80,000 - $100,000
All other taxpayers	$40,000 - $50,000

NOTE: AGI, for purposes of this chart, includes AGI and foreign earned income exclusions and United States possessions and Puerto Rico income exclusions.

Where on the Web

American Savings Education Association *www.asec.org*

College Savings Plan Network (the official website for State 529 Plans/QSTPs; affiliated with the National Association of State Treasuries; provides links on the internet to individual State plans) *www.collegesavings.org*

The College Board (a not-for-profit education association that created and controls the SAT and PSAT/NMSQT Examinations) *www.collegeboard.com*

Education Commission of the States *www.ecs.org*

Expected Family Contribution calculation, the EFCFormula Book describes how a student's EFC is calculated *www.ed.gov*

Information on Armed Forces programs and scholarships *www.goarmy.com/tour/educ/educ.htm; www.gibill.va.gov; www.usmc.mil; www.af.mil*

The National Association for College Admission Counseling *www.nacac.com*

The National Association of Student Financial Aid Administrators (partner with Peterson's College Quest) *www.collegequest.com*

The Smart Student Guide to Financial Aid (discusses financial aid eligibility and calculations; student loan analysis; scholarship availability) *www.finaid.org*

US Department of Education - College is Possible (A resource guide for parents, students, and education professionals) *www.collegeispossible.com*

THE LIFETIME LEARNING CREDIT

Lifetime Learning Credit - a tax credit available to pay for tuition and enrollment fees for undergraduate, graduate or professional degree programs paid after June 30, 1998

The **Lifetime Learning Credit** is another by-product of the Taxpayer Relief Act of 1997. This tax credit is available for tuition and enrollment fees for undergraduate, graduate or professional degree programs paid after June 30, 1998. The Lifetime Learning Credit provides annual reimbursement for college tuition and fees per family in the amount of $1,000 through the year 2002, and $2,000 per year starting in 2003. The taxpayer must spend $5,000 annually on qualified expenses through 2002 (and $10,000 annually from 2003 on) in order to qualify for the full credit. This credit is based on a 20 percent factor of the qualified expenses. In other words, to obtain the full $1,000 credit prior to 2003, there must be a qualified higher education expense of at least $5,000. Half-time enrollment or more is required. If, however, the courses taken are geared towards the acquisition or improvement of job skills, the student may be enrolled in less than half time.

The Lifetime Learning Credit can be claimed for an unlimited number of years. If two or more children in the same household incur qualified expenses in the same year, the parents may claim a Lifetime Learning Credit or Hope Scholarship Credit for both children, or a Lifetime Learning Credit for one child and a Hope Scholarship Credit for the other. However, only one credit is allowed per child per year. Also note that the maximum credit of $1,000 ($2,000 after 2002) applies to the family, not per student as with the Hope Scholarship Credit. Like the Hope

Scholarship Credit, the Lifetime Learning Credit is subject to the phaseout based on the taxpayer's adjusted gross income as shown on the chart above.

SERIES EE BONDS

Another vehicle that may be used to save for college is **Series EE United States Savings Bonds** ("**EE Bonds**"). EE Bonds are useful tools for college tuition. Face values of EE Bonds start as low as $50 and max out at $10,000. EE Bonds are purchased at one-half of their face value. EE bonds have varying interest rates, but face value must be reached within 17 years. If used to pay for qualified higher education expenses at an eligible institution or state tuition plan, EE Bonds bestow significant tax savings, that is, no federal income tax on the interest. To attain tax-free status, EE Bonds must be purchased in the name of one or both parents of the student/child. The parent(s) are considered the owners of the bond, and must be at least 24 years old before the first day of the month of the issue date of the bond. Also, the owners must redeem the bonds in the same year that the student/child's qualified higher education expenses are paid. It is worth noting that the newly issued Series I bonds (discussed in Chapter 13) have the same tax benefits as EE bonds for purposes of qualified higher education costs.

UNIFORM GIFT TO MINOR'S ACT

The **Uniform Gift to Minor's Act** ("**UGMA**") allows parents the option to put assets in a custodial account for a child. If the child is below 14 years of age, all income earned by the assets are taxed at the income tax rate of the parents. If the child is 14 years or older, the income earned by the assets is taxed at the tax rate for the child. Notably, this is considered an asset of the child and is considered in determining financial aid.

INTEREST ON EDUCATIONAL LOANS

Interest paid on student loans for undergraduate and graduate education may be deducted as an adjustment to the taxpayer's AGI. The deduction for years 2001 and beyond is $2,500. The loaned funds must have been spent on tuition and enrollment fees, books, supplies, equipment, room and board, transportation, or other necessary expenses. Prior to 2002, this deduction applies to the first 60 months of interest, and the student must be enrolled at least halftime. However, after 2001, the 60 months rule has been eliminated by TRA 2001. After 2001, there is a phaseout of this deduction for taxpayers filing jointly with an AGI from $100,000 to $130,000 and for single filers with an AGI from $50,000 to $65,000.

EMPLOYER'S EDUCATIONAL ASSISTANCE PROGRAM

Under the **Employer's Educational Assistance Program**, an employer can pay for an employee's tuition (both graduate and undergraduate), enrollment fees, books, supplies, and equipment while these employer benefits are excluded from the employee's income up to $5,250. However, the employer or employee cannot also claim an educational credit. TRA 2001 extended the exclusion to include graduate education and has made the exclusion permanent.

Series EE United States Savings Bonds ("EE Bonds") - if used to pay for qualified higher education expenses at an eligible institution or state tuition plan, EE Bonds bestow significant tax savings, that is, no federal income tax on the interest

Uniform Gift to Minor's Act ("UGMA") - allows parents the option to put assets in a custodial account for a child, for example, to pay for college tuition

Employer's Educational Assistance Program - under this program, an employer can pay for an employee's undergraduate tuition, enrollment fees, books, supplies and equipment while these employer benefits are excluded from the employee's income up to $5,250

DEDUCTION FOR QUALIFIED HIGHER EDUCATION EXPENSES

TRA 2001 permits taxpayers an above-the-line deduction for qualified higher education expenses paid by the taxpayer during a taxable year. Qualified higher education expenses are defined in the same manner as for purposes of the HOPE credit.

In 2002 and 2003, taxpayers with adjusted gross income that does not exceed $65,000 ($130,000 in the case of married couples filing joint returns) are entitled to a maximum deduction of $3,000 per year. Taxpayers with adjusted gross income above these thresholds would not be entitled to a deduction. In 2004 and 2005, taxpayers with adjusted gross income that does not exceed $65,000 ($130,000 in the case of married taxpayers filing joint returns) are entitled to a maximum deduction of $4,000 and taxpayers with adjusted gross income that does not exceed $80,000 ($160,000 in the case of married taxpayers filing joint returns) are entitled to a maximum deduction of $2,000.

Taxpayers are not eligible to claim the deduction and a HOPE or Lifetime Learning Credit in the same year with respect to the same student. A taxpayer may not claim a deduction for amounts taken into account in determining the amount excludable due to a distribution (i.e., the earnings and the contribution portion of a distribution) from an education IRA or the amount of interest excludable with respect to education savings bonds.

The provision is effective for payments made in taxable years beginning after December 31, 2001, and before January 1, 2006.

EQUITY LINES OF CREDIT

A home equity loan or line of credit is yet another vehicle that can be used to fund college related expenses. Because home equity loans are secured by a house, the interest rate on a home equity loan may be lower than rates for an unsecured student loan. Many state schools do not consider the value of the home when determining eligibility for financial aid, but numerous private colleges take equity in the home into account. If equity in the home is considered in the financial aid equation, a home equity loan could decrease home equity and possibly improve one's eligibility for financial aid. Further, the interest on home equity loans is normally deductible from the taxpayer's AGI. As a general rule, using home equity loans and lines of credit to pay for higher education expenses should be a last resort, or at least done after researching all other options, rates and conditions for alternative funding. Borrowing too much against the home could result in foreclosure or other difficult situations.

HIGHLIGHTS OF TAX BENEFITS FOR HIGHER EDUCATION

The following exhibit provides a glance at the highlights and attributes of the various vehicles covered in this section.

EXHIBIT 7.4: HIGHLIGHTS OF TAX BENEFITS FOR HIGHER EDUCATION PRIOR TO TRA 2001

	Hope credit (Education credit)	Lifetime learning credit (Education credit)	Education IRA[1]	Traditional and Roth IRAs[1]	Interest Paid on Student Loans	Qualified State Tuition Programs	Qualified U.S. Savings Bonds[1]	Employer's Educational Assistance Program[1]
What is your benefit?[2]	Tax credit (nonrefundable)		Withdrawals are tax free	No 10% additional tax on early withdrawal	Deduction to arrive at adjusted gross income	Prepay future tuition expenses	Interest is excludable from income	Employer benefits are excludable from income
What is the annual limit?	Up to $1,500 per student	Up to $1,000 per family	$500 contribution per child under 18	Amount of qualifying expenses	1999: $1,500 2000: $2,000 2001: $2,500	None	Amount of qualifying expenses	$5,250
What expenses qualify besides tuition and required enrollment fees?[2]	N/A		Books, supplies, & equipment; Room and board if at least half-time attendance; Payments to qualified state tuition program	Books, supplies, & equipment; Room & board if at least half-time attendance	Books, supplies, & equipment; Room & board; Transportation; Other necessary expenses	Books, supplies, & equipment; Room & board if at least half-time attendance	Payments to qualified state tuition programs; Payments to education IRAs	Books, supplies, & equipment
What education qualifies?	1st 2 years of undergraduate	All undergraduate and graduate levels						Under graduate level
What other conditions apply?	Can be claimed only for 2 years; Must be enrolled at least half-time in a degree program	Applies to expenses paid and for school attendance after June 30, 1998	Contributions not deductible; Cannot also contribute to qualified state tuition program or claim an education credit; Must withdraw assets at age 30	Must receive entire balance or begin receiving withdrawals by April 1 of year following year in which age 70½ is reached	Applies to the 1st 60 months' interest; Must be enrolled at least half-time in a degree program	Tax-deferred earnings are taxed to beneficiary when withdrawn	Applies only to qualified series EE bonds issued after 1989 or series I bonds	Cannot also claim an education credit; Expires for courses beginning after May 31, 2000
At what income range do benefits phase out?	$40,000–$50,000 $80,000–$100,000 for joint returns		$95,000–$110,000; $150,000–$160,000 for joint returns	N/A	$40,000–$55,000; $60,000–$75,000 for joint returns	N/A	2001: $55,750 - $70,750; $83,650 - $113,650 for joint returns	N/A

[1] Any nontaxable withdrawal is limited to the amount that does not exceed qualifying educational expenses.

[2] You must generally reduce qualifying educational expenses by any tax-free income. You generally cannot use the same educational expense for figuring more than one benefit.

Source: IRS Publication 970

EXHIBIT 7.5: HIGHLIGHTS OF TAX BENEFITS FOR HIGHER EDUCATION AFTER TRA 2001

	Hope Credit	Lifetime Learning Credit	Education IRA[1]	Traditional and Roth IRAs[1]	Student Loan Interest	State Tuition Programs[2]	Education Savings Bond Program[1]	Employer's Educational Assistance Program[1]	Qualified Higher Education Expenses
What is your benefit?	Credits can reduce the amount of tax you must pay		Earnings are not taxed	No 10% additional tax on early withdrawal	You can deduct the interest	Earnings are not taxed	Interest is not taxed	Employer benefits are not taxed	Deduction of expenses "for AGI"
What is the annual limit?	Up to $1,500 per student	Up to $1,000 per family	$2,000 contribution per beneficiary	Amount of qualifying expenses	$2,500	None	Amount of qualifying expenses	$5,250	Maximum: 2002-2003 $3,000 2004-2005 $4,000
What expenses qualify besides tuition and required enrollment fees?	None		Books Supplies Equipment / Room & board if at least a half-time student / Payments to state tuition program	Books Supplies Equipment / Room & board if at least a half-time student	Books Supplies Equipment / Room & board / Trans-portation / Other necessary expenses	Books Supplies Equipment / Room & board if at least a half-time student	Payments to education IRAs / Payments to state tuition program	Books Supplies Equipment	None
What education qualifies?	1st 2 years of under-graduate	All undergraduate and graduate[3]							Qualified higher education expenses
What are some of the other conditions that apply?	Can be claimed only for 2 years / Must be enrolled at least half-time in a degree program		Can contribute to education IRA and state tuition program in the same year / Must withdraw assets at age 30		No longer a 1st 60 months of required interest / Must have been at least half-time student in a degree program	Distribution is excluded from gross income / Hope and Lifetime Learning Credit are permitted in the same year	Applies only to qualified series EE bonds issued after 1989 or series I bonds	Does not expire after December 31, 2001	Cannot claim Hope or Lifetime Learning Credit in same year for the same student
In what income range do benefits phase out?	$40,000 - $50,000; $80,000 - $100,000 for joint returns		$95,000 - $110,000; $190,000 - $220,000 for joint returns	There is no phaseout	$50,000 – $65,000 $100,000 – $120,000 for joint returns	There is no phaseout	2001: $55,750 - $70,750; $83,650 - $113,650 for joint returns	There is no phaseout	2002-2003 Single < $65,000 MFJ < $130,000 —— 2004-2005 Single $65,000-80,000 MFJ $130,000 – 160,000

[1] Any nontaxable withdrawal is limited to the amount that does not exceed qualifying educational expenses.
[2] Exclusion is extended to distributions from Qualified Tuition programs established by an entity other than a State after December 31, 2003.
[3] For educational IRAs, qualified elementary and secondary school expenses are also permitted.

EDUCATIONAL FUNDING/SAVINGS REGIMEN EXAMPLE

Now that all sources of educational funding have been discussed and the investment vehicles and tax benefits identified, the most pressing issue is how much does the parent or family need to save now in order to pay for the child's college education. Calculating the cost of a child's college education through a savings plan is always a helpful exercise.

There are numerous ways to calculate the required funding necessary to pay for a child's college education. In the following example, John plans to pay for the college education of his daughter, Claire. As a general rule, John should establish a savings schedule for Claire's college fund. This savings schedule can be created using time-value-of-money concepts discussed in Chapter 6.

The type of information needed to conduct this analysis includes the age of the child, the age the child will attend college, the parents' after-tax earnings rate, the current cost of tuition, related costs and books, and the tuition inflation rate. John is willing to fund Claire's room and board either out of his own pocket when those expenses are incurred or by Claire working to pay them. John nonetheless is comfortable with assuming the risk of paying or funding room and board as the expense is incurred.

Claire is one day old, and John anticipates that Claire will be 18 years old when she begins college. John expects to earn an after-tax rate of return over the 18-year period of 11 percent. The current cost of tuition, tuition-related expenses, and books and equipment at Claire's projected category of schools is $25,000 per year. The rate of increase of tuition and tuition-related expenses is assumed to be 6 percent. The CPI inflation rate for this 18-year period is assumed to be 4 percent, which is less than the rate of increase of tuition. Therefore, to be conservative, the higher rate of 6 percent for tuition increases will be used instead of the CPI inflation rate. Other assumptions and necessary data for this exercise are:

▲ John's annual investment, or "savings payments," will begin at the end of each year from now until the day Claire starts college (expected to be in 18 years).
▲ John will stop making savings payments once Claire starts college, so that he can pay for Claire's monthly room and board expenses.
▲ If Claire receives any form of scholarship money or financial aid (if any), those funds will be extra.
▲ John will postpone his decision as to whether he will place any burden of education-related expenses on Claire while she is in school until a later date (i.e., work or loans).
▲ John desires to fund all college education expenses without having to borrow any funds.

This problem can be viewed in terms of a timeline (below) from year zero until year 21.

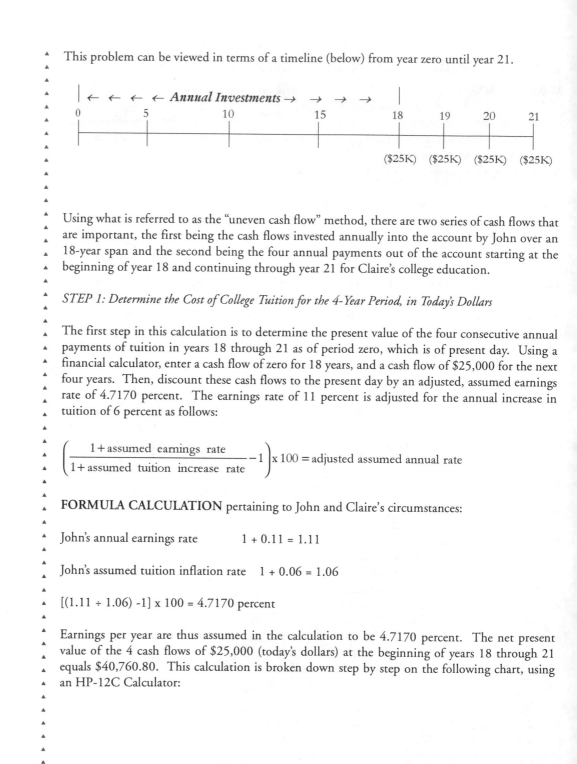

Using what is referred to as the "uneven cash flow" method, there are two series of cash flows that are important, the first being the cash flows invested annually into the account by John over an 18-year span and the second being the four annual payments out of the account starting at the beginning of year 18 and continuing through year 21 for Claire's college education.

STEP 1: Determine the Cost of College Tuition for the 4-Year Period, in Today's Dollars

The first step in this calculation is to determine the present value of the four consecutive annual payments of tuition in years 18 through 21 as of period zero, which is of present day. Using a financial calculator, enter a cash flow of zero for 18 years, and a cash flow of $25,000 for the next four years. Then, discount these cash flows to the present day by an adjusted, assumed earnings rate of 4.7170 percent. The earnings rate of 11 percent is adjusted for the annual increase in tuition of 6 percent as follows:

$$\left(\frac{1 + \text{assumed earnings rate}}{1 + \text{assumed tuition increase rate}} - 1 \right) \times 100 = \text{adjusted assumed annual rate}$$

FORMULA CALCULATION pertaining to John and Claire's circumstances:

John's annual earnings rate $\qquad$ 1 + 0.11 = 1.11

John's assumed tuition inflation rate $\quad$ 1 + 0.06 = 1.06

$[(1.11 \div 1.06) -1] \times 100 = 4.7170$ percent

Earnings per year are thus assumed in the calculation to be 4.7170 percent. The net present value of the 4 cash flows of $25,000 (today's dollars) at the beginning of years 18 through 21 equals $40,760.80. This calculation is broken down step by step on the following chart, using an HP-12C Calculator:

Keystroke	Display
[f][CLX]	0.0000
0[g][CFj]	0.0000
17[g][Nj]	17.0000
25000[g][CFj]	25,000.0000
4[g][Nj]	4.0000
1.11[enter]	1.1100
1.06[÷]	1.0472
1[-]	0.0472
100[x]	4.7170
[i]	4.7170
[f][NPV]	40,760.8045

Note: For more information on how to utilize a financial calculator or how to calculate a savings schedule for education funding, see <u>Understanding Your Financial Calculator</u>, by James F. Dalton, Dalton Publications (2nd Ed. 2001), or visit Dalton Publication's website at *www.daltonpublications.com.*

STEP 2: Determine the Annual Payments Needed to Fund College Tuition Costs

The next step is to determine the annual payments from year zero through the end of year 17 that are needed to fund the outgoing cash flows for tuition at the beginning of years 18 through 21. Using a financial calculator, the required annual investment or payment is $5,292.50. This calculation is broken down step by step on the following chart, using an HP-12C Calculator:

Keystroke	Display
40,760.80 [PV]	40,760.8000
18 [n]	18.0000
11 [i]	11.0000
0 [FV]	0.0000
[PMT]	5,292.4993

Therefore, John must save $5,292.50 per year beginning one year from now, the start of year zero, and continuing until the end of year 17 (a total of 18 payments) so that when Claire attends college at the start of year 18, John can pay for her college education.

INVESTMENT STRATEGIES TO ACCOMPLISH EDUCATION GOALS

It is important to bear in mind that the investment strategies employed by the family should rely heavily on the amount of time that exists until the child will be enrolled in school. In other words, the time horizon is probably the most important factor (besides risk tolerance) to consider in deciding what securities to invest in, how much to invest, and when to invest. The more time that exists before the child enrolls in school inevitably provides the parents or family with more options and more time for accumulation of principal and growth for a savings regimen.

Using the education funding example above, if John wants to completely pay for his one-day-old daughter, Claire's, college tuition, he has a time horizon of 18 years to invest enough money to fund 4 years of tuition. The funds invested by John will have numerous years to grow and accumulate, and John's risk tolerance for investments will be higher than those parents who start to save for their children's college expenses years after they are born. John could invest in more growth-and-equity-oriented funds with higher potential rates of return between 10 and 14 percent.

However, let's compare John's situation to that of Tad, a parent with a 10-year-old son named Ken. Tad will have only 8 years to save and invest money to pay for 4 years of college for Ken. Tad does not have the luxury of time. Further, Tad cannot tolerate as much risk as John because there is less time to recover from a bear market. Therefore, Tad would probably invest substantially more conservatively than John.

As discussed earlier in this Chapter, QSTPs follow this investment principle. QSTPs generally require a decrease in risk levels of investments the closer the child gets to the targeted year to begin college. This method is referred to as "Age-banding." Various QSTP managers will generally comply with the sequence illustrated in the exhibit below.

EXHIBIT 7.6: AGE-BANDING EXAMPLE

Student's Age	Stocks	Bonds	Money Market/Cash
0-13	70-100 percent	0-30 percent	0
14-17	25-40 percent	35-50 percent	10-40 percent
18-	0-10 percent	20-30 percent	60-80 percent

Depending upon the specifics of a state's QSTP legislation, which varies, managers of QSTPs must comply with this decrease (or a similar decrease) in the percentage of investment in growth and equity funds because, as the child ages, the risk of losing principal and earnings is too great considering that the prospect of attending school hangs in the balance.

Finally, after the analysis is complete and a savings plan has been developed and started, the contributor must monitor and reassess the plan on a consistent, periodic basis (at least annually). This review process is necessary because the parents' financial situation may change or the goals may be changed. If a family experiences a significant increase in income or finances, an increase in the savings amount may be in order to alleviate the risks of the assumptions made in the analysis, or to broaden the potential colleges and universities the child may consider. If a family experiences a decrease in income or finances, it may be more realistic to lower the expectations or assumptions in the analysis or determine if the family would qualify for financial aid or assistance, such as a Pell Grant.

Other assumptions may also change over time. For instance, in our earlier example, Claire may prove to be an extraordinary student or athlete, and the increased likelihood of her receiving a scholarship could be factored into John's plan.

In conclusion, the education funding savings plan should be developed and implemented as early as possible to take advantage of time-horizon principles. Once the plan is in place, the plan should be monitored and updated because numerous assumptions and unknowns enter into the analysis. The amount necessary to fund college must be identified, but the family can attempt to minimize the contributions it must make through identifying the issues addressed above, setting goals, gathering the necessary information regarding financial aid, school loans, scholarships and other assistance, maximizing tax benefits, choosing the best investment vehicles for themselves, and making choices that are best suited to the family's needs, expectations, and desires.

FOCUS

What do you advise clients regarding prepaid state tuition programs?

While there are positive aspects of saving through the use of prepaid state tuition programs, there can also be negative aspects. I try to advise my clients of all of the risks associated and choose the answer based on their needs. If the family has a strong tradition of all or many members attending the college at a particular place or within the state, a state tuition program may be appropriate, assuming that the state will return the amounts invested with an inflation type return. When this type of plan is used, the client benefits from a deferral of income on the earnings and a reduction in the risk of upper inflation of tuition costs. More often than not, however, I am more comfortable with the client investing in a broad portfolio of common stocks or equity mutual funds to meet the needs of educational funding. Their earnings are generally more profitable under this scenario, which will offset inflation, and the likelihood of children attending college in their home state is diminishing.

How do you feel about putting assets in the name of the child for education?

A number of issues apply to this situation. First, assets held in a child's name count more heavily against the family trying to qualify for federal financial aid than assets held in the name of the parent. Secondly, there is always the issue of control of the assets. As the child ages, it is not uncommon for the child's goals to be

different from the parents'. I always explain to clients that when children are young they can be quite cute and compliant but may not be so when they get older. In addition, the kiddie tax will apply to unearned income of a child under the age of fourteen. Of course, the kiddie tax can be avoided simply by investing in non-dividend stocks and holding the portfolio until after the child is 14.

What do you think of the Educational IRA?

Prior to 2002, the $500 limit was a very small amount per year and only accumulates to $23,000 (given 10% earnings for 18 years), which is not nearly enough to pay for a full four years at a state school, and probably not even a year at a private school. On the other hand, when a client has multiple children, some who may get scholarships or loans, and others who may decide not to go to college, the transfer feature allows some flexibility for a client who can only afford this size annual contribution. It can also be a helpful way for grandparents to assist the family by making an IRA contribution annually for each grandchild, as the amount would pass to the grandchild tax free. With the increase to $2,000 for years after 2001, the Education IRA has taken on a greater significance in educational planning.

CASSIE BRADLEY, PH.D., CFP™

DISCUSSION QUESTIONS

1. What are the issues and goals of education funding?
2. What education funding information should students and parents gather?
3. How is financial need determined?
4. What is a Federal Pell Grant?
5. What is Direct and FFEL Stafford Loans?
6. What is the difference between a subsidized student loan and an unsubsidized student loan?
7. What are PLUS Loans?
8. What is a Consolidation Loan?
9. What campus-based student financial aid is available?
10. What are the tax advantages from educational expenses and tax issues?
11. What are the benefits of Qualified State Tuition Plans and how are they taxed?
12. What are prepaid tuition plans and how do they work?
13. How do contributions affect gift taxes?
14. What is an educational IRA?
15. How can a Roth IRA be used for education funding?
16. What is the maximum credit allowed with the Hope Scholarship Credit?
17. What are the eligibility requirements to take a Lifetime Learning Credit?
18. What are Series EE bonds?
19. What is the Uniform Gift to Minor's Act?
20. What is the Employer's Educational Assistance Program?

EXERCISES

1. Compare and contrast grants, scholarships, and fellowships.
2. Compare and contrast Direct and FFEL Stafford loans.
3. Shawna, age 18, recently graduated from high school with a 3.6 GPA. Shawna currently lives at home and works part-time as an office assistant. She has been accepted to Texas State University. Her parents cannot afford to assist her. She wants to obtain a college education, but is having trouble affording tuition and other college expenses. What financial aid programs would you recommend to Shawna, and why?
4. Karen, age 20, is in her second year at the University of California. She will not be able to hold down a part-time job and complete her bachelor's degree program in four years. She will receive approximately $30,000 from a trust fund left to her by her grandmother on her 22nd birthday. What federal aid programs are available to Karen? Would you recommend that Karen borrow against the trust fund in order to support herself during the next two years? Why or why not?
5. Gordon and Rhonda want to start saving now for their two-year old daughter's college education. Tuition and fees at a four-year public school is currently $3,500 per year, and tuition has increased approximately 7 percent each year. How much should Gordon and Rhonda expect to pay for college when their daughter turns 18 years old?
6. Christian and Emily have two children, Bethany age 5 and Taylor age 7. Christian's parents would like to pay for Bethany and Taylor's college education. They are considering gifting the money to Bethany and Taylor by setting up savings accounts for them. Would you recommend this approach? Why or why not? Who should the grandparents pass the money to and why?

7. Brandon and Myra are married and have an adjusted gross income of $55,000. They have two children, Beth, age 18, and Brett, age 20. Both Beth and Brett are full-time students attending the local university. Are Brandon and Myra eligible to take advantage of any educational tax credits? If so, which ones, and what is the maximum credit they are allowed?

8. Leslie is in her third year of college and has received subsidized Stafford loans to help her pay for college. She does not have to borrow any more money before she receives her degree. She wants to start paying off her student loans now. Given the choices for repaying student loans, what would you recommend to Leslie?

9. Brad was recently awarded some financial aid through his university. Although the aid he was awarded helps, he still needs more financial aid than the school offered. What would you recommend to Brad to help him pay for college?

10. Tyra plans to attend the local university next year. Her parents make too much money to qualify for federal aid programs, but Tyra still needs help. What financial aid, if any, is available for Tyra?

11. Julie's parents would like to assist her with the cost of college tuition. Tuition and fees are estimated at $13,000 per school year. Julie's parents apply and qualify for a PLUS loan. How much can they borrow?

12. John and Sue, both age 30, have a child born today. They plan to save the maximum amount in their respective IRAs until their child goes to college in 18 years. Would you recommend a Roth IRA or an Education IRA? Explain why.

13. David intends to open a QSTP Savings Plan for his daughter, but wants to know if he can direct the specific investments himself. Can David direct where and how much of the contributions are invested? Can David direct how much of the funds are used to purchase stock or bonds? Explain.

14. In the prior exercise, David was interested in placing a percentage of the funds in the QSTP Savings Plan into stocks and a percentage into bonds. What is this principle called? Also, provide an example as to how it is used.

15. Robby plans to attend college but cannot afford tuition. He decides to apply for federal financial aid. Generally, how will Robby's financial aid eligibility be calculated?

16. Bob established a QSTP Savings Plan for his son Ricky at age 5. When Ricky turned 18 years old, Ricky decided not to attend college and begin working as a bartender in the Bahamas. Can Ricky withdraw funds from the QSTP account, which has a value of $100,000? What can Bob do (if anything) with the account?

17. Claire established a QSTP Savings Plan for Matt, her son. While Matt was attending college Matt asked Claire for money to spend on a ski boat. Claire agreed, withdrew $10,000 from the QSTP account, and purchased the boat for Matt in Matt's name. Will this $10,000 withdrawal and payment be taxed, and if so, whose tax rate will be used? Would it be important to know what portion of the $10,000 represents contributions and what portion represents earnings? Explain.

18. Let's take the prior exercise (exercise 17) one step further. Would there be any penalty assessed on the $10,000 withdrawal? Would it be important to know what portion of the $10,000 is contributed and what portion is earnings?

19. What if in the prior exercise (exercise 17), Matt had received a full scholarship for his remaining years in college, the semester before Claire gave him $10,000 for the boat?

PROBLEMS

1. Rena and Hunter Alesio have two children ages 5 and 7. The Alesios want to start saving for their children's education. Each child will spend 6 years at college and will begin at age 18. College currently costs $20,000 per year and is expected to increase at 6 percent per year. Assuming the Alesios can earn an annual compound return of 12 percent and inflation is 4 percent, how much must the Alesios deposit at the end of each year to pay for their children's educational requirements until the youngest is out of school? Assume that educational expenses are withdrawn at the beginning of each year and that the last deposit will be made at the beginning of the last year of the youngest child.

2. Chelsea was recently divorced and has two children. The divorce decree requires that she pay 1/3 of the college tuition cost for her children. Tuition cost is currently $15,000 per year and has been increasing at 7 percent per year. Her son and daughter are 12 and 16, respectively, and will attend college for four years beginning at age 18. Assume that her after-tax rate of return will be 9 percent and that general inflation has been 4 percent. How much should she save each month, beginning today for the next five years to finance both children's education?

3. Jan has a daughter, Katie, who is 14 years old. College costs are currently $12,000 per year and are expected to increase 5 percent per year, including the 4 years Katie is in college. Katie will begin college at age 18. Pursuant to a divorce decree, Jan is responsible for 1/3 of the total cost of Katie's college tuition. Jan wants to be able to have the total amount of tuition for which she is responsible by the time Katie starts college but will pay the tuition at the beginning of each school year. She estimates she can put money in a fund that earns 9 percent after tax. What amount does Jan have to deposit at the beginning of each month starting now to meet her goal?

4. Ken and Amy Charvet have two children, ages 4 and 6. The Charvets want to start saving for their children's education. Each child will spend 5 years in college and will begin at age 18. College currently costs $30,000 per year and is expected to increase at 7 percent per year. Assuming the Charvets can earn an annual compound investment return of 12 percent and inflation is 4 percent, how much must the Charvets deposit at the end of each year to pay for their children's educational requirements until the youngest goes to school? Assume that educational expenses are withdrawn at the beginning of each year and that the last deposit will be made at the beginning of the first year of the youngest child.

5. Barry and Virginia have a five-year old son, Daniel. They have plans for Daniel to attend a four-year private university at age 18. Currently, tuition at the local private university is $15,000 per year and is expected to increase at 7 percent per year. Assuming Barry and Virginia can earn an annual compound return of 10 percent and inflation is 4 percent, how much do Barry and Virginia need to start saving per year, starting today to be able to pay for Daniel's college education when Daniel turns 18?

Insurance Planning
in BRIEF →

- Risk

- Perils and hazards

- Adverse selection

- Insurable losses

- Legal principles of insurance

- Characteristics of insurance exclusions

- Risk management process

- Automobile insurance

- Homeowners insurance

- Liability insurance

- Property insurance

- Business insurance

- Long-term care insurance

- Health and disability insurance

- Life insurance ownership and benefits

- Social Security insurance and benefits

Insurance Planning

Risks

- Untimely death
- Disability
- Unemployment
- Medical illness
- Long-term health care
- Damage to property
- Tort liability

Data Collection

- Life insurance policies
- Disability policies
- Employer benefit summaries
- Health plan policies
- Long-term care policies
- Automobile policies
- Homeowners policies, riders, etc.
- Personal liability umbrella policies
- Business policies

Goals

- Appropriate insurance coverage and reasonable premiums for the risks identified to person, property and/or liabilities of the client.

Data Analysis

- Life insurance policy analysis
- Health insurance policy analysis
- Disability insurance policy analysis
- Homeowners policy analysis
- Automobile insurance analysis
- Liability insurance analysis
- Business insurance analysis

CHAPTER 8

An Introduction to Insurance and Risk Management

LEARNING OBJECTIVES:

After learning the material in this chapter, you will be able to:

1. Define insurance and explain how insurance policies operate.

2. Explain the different types of risk and understand how each risk impacts the personal financial planning process.

3. Distinguish between a peril and a hazard and understand how each relates to the need for insurance.

4. Define adverse selection and explain its impact on the insurance process.

5. Summarize the requisites for an insurable risk and understand what distinguishes insurance from gambling.

6. Explain the legal principles and distinguishing features of insurance contracts.

7. Understand the reason for, and the effect of, various contractual features in insurance contracts.

8. Understand the insurable loss exposures faced by the typical individual client.

9. Explain the steps in the risk management process.

INTRODUCTION

Proper insurance coverage, both private and social, is essential to a client's financial plan. Most people do not have the right amount of insurance coverage and therefore are either over or under-insured. Financial planners must have a basic understanding of risk and insurance in order to properly assist their clients in assessing their insurance needs and evaluating their current insurance coverage. For most clients, basic insurance needs can be covered with life insurance, health insurance, disability insurance, homeowners or renters insurance, long-term care, automobile insurance, and personal liability insurance. This section of the text is designed as an introduction to these areas of insurance. Chapter 8 discusses the legal foundation of insurance and the transference or sharing of risks using insurance contracts. Chapter 9 identifies the risks to the person, namely premature death, catastrophic illness, disability, and the need for long-term care. Chapter 10 identifies the risks to property and liability exposures. Chapter 11 covers the types and availability of social insurance.

WHAT IS INSURANCE?

insurance - pooling of fortuitous losses by transfer of risks to insurers who agree to indemnify insureds for such losses, to provide other pecuniary benefits on their occurrence, or to render services connected with the risk

Insurance allows individuals to protect themselves against certain risks of financial loss. While there are many ways to suffer a financial loss, insurance is designed specifically to deal with the financial consequences of pure risks. **Pure risks** are those that, when they occur, create a financial loss. House fires, automobile accidents, and personal illness are familiar examples.

Insurance provides that the insurer will pay for unexpected losses and, thus, provide financial security to the insured. Insurance is a valuable tool for protecting the individual against fortuitous accidental losses because it allows for the transfer of losses and for the sharing of losses with others.

pure risks - a risk that creates a financial loss when it occurs

TRANSFER OF LOSSES

Insurance transfers the risk of loss to the insurer—a financial intermediary that specializes in assuming risk. The insured pays the insurer a premium to agree that if certain events (losses) occur, money will be provided to the insured to pay for the consequences of those losses. In exchange, the insurer provides the insured with a legally binding contract—the insurance policy—that spells out, among other things, covered losses, how those losses will be valued, and what duties are owed by each party to the contract. Almost any risk can be transferred for the right price. Of course, the greater the chance that a loss will occur, the higher the price of the insurance premium and the lower the likelihood that an insurance company will agree to insure.

SHARING LOSSES WITH OTHERS

Cooperation and sharing are essential to the insurance process. Insureds facing similar risks of loss are pooled together. The insurer mathematically predicts the expected losses for the entire pool, and then divides the cost of those losses among each insured, then adds a charge for the insurer's operating expenses and profit margin.

234

Each insured person contributes a fair share of money to the pool. Those who possess a greater amount of risk contribute more to the pool, and vice versa. Actuarial science allows insurance companies to estimate losses and, thus, to estimate premiums for each person in a pool.

EXAMPLE

For example, assume First Mutual Insurance Company has a life insurance pool of 1,000 thirty-year-old males. Each insured joined the pool because he was concerned about dying during the year and wanted to leave money behind to provide for his financial obligations. Human life expectancy is quite predictable, so the actuary can determine with considerable certainty how many of those in this particular pool will die during the year. Suppose the actuary determines that two of the 1,000 men in the pool will die this year. If each man in the pool purchased $100,000 of life insurance coverage, this means that the actuary expects the insurer to pay $200,000 for the year in claims. If the $200,000 in claims (losses) is divided among the 1,000 people in the pool, each person's share is $200. The insurer will add a charge for expenses and profit, perhaps $50 per insured. Thus, the cost of insurance (premium) for each person in the pool for that year will be $250.

Each insured in the pool voluntarily pays $250 for the security of knowing that if he is one of the two insureds to die, his beneficiary will receive $100,000. At the same time, each insured hopes that he does not die, and that his $250 will be paid as someone else's death claim under the life insurance policy.

Notice that in the second year, there are only 998 insureds left in the pool if two died the preceding year. Suppose the actuary determines that, once again, only two people in the pool will die. For the $100,000 death benefit to be paid on each claim, the insurer must again collect a total of $200,000. When this amount is spread over 998 insureds, each is responsible for $200.40. When the insurer's expenses (again, assume they are $50) are added, the total premium charged is $250.40. This premium is slightly higher than for the previous year. Note that it would be even higher had the actuary determined that three or more people in the pool would likely die the following year.

Because death rates increase as people get older, life insurance premiums rise at an increasing rate. This occurs because the number of people dropping out of the pool increases each year due to death and to lapsing policies. Thus, there are fewer persons remaining in the pool to share the expense of future death claims.

UNDERSTANDING RISK

Risk can be defined as the chance of loss. The insured who owns a home knows that in most years he will not suffer a house fire. But the possibility of fire does exist, and its consequences could be financially devastating. Thus, the insured transfers the risk of fire to an insurance company and pays the insurer a premium to accept such risk.

There has to be some chance that a loss will occur for risk to exist. The person who does not own a boat has no need for boat owners insurance because there is no risk to be transferred. The person who owns a boat, however, must be concerned with the financial consequences of the boat being stolen, damaged in a fire, or being involved in an accident. While the boat owner hopes that none of these losses occurs, there is the chance that they might, so the risk must be managed in an appropriate manner.

PURE VERSUS SPECULATIVE RISK

A pure risk is one in which the results are either loss or no loss. An example of a pure risk is death. While death is a certainty, there is still risk in determining when each person will die. A speculative risk, on the other hand, is one where profit, loss, or no loss may occur. Entrepreneurs regularly encounter speculative risk when they begin a new business or sell a new product. Speculative risks are generally undertaken voluntarily and are not insurable.

Consider the risks associated with the purchase of a home. A speculative risk is the potential fluctuation in the value of the house after it is purchased. The market value of the home could remain the same as the original purchase price, decline, or even increase. There are also a variety of pure risks associated with home ownership, such as the risk of a fire, flood, or theft of property. If a fire occurs, the insured will suffer a loss; otherwise, there is no change in the condition of the house. To summarize, a pure risk has two possible outcomes, while a speculative risk has three. Only pure risks are commercially insurable.

SUBJECTIVE VERSUS OBJECTIVE RISK

Subjective risk is a particular person's perception of risk, and varies greatly among individuals. Consider two people, each having slept only two hours in the last two days, who need to drive home from work late at night. The first person drinks coffee habitually and considers an hour drive no problem, thus, reflecting a low level of subjective risk. The second person does not drink coffee and knows he is very tired. He either does not drive home at all or drives very carefully, due to the fact that he knows he has fallen asleep behind the wheel before under similar circumstances. The second person's perception is an example of high subjective risk. A perception of low subjective risk often results in less prudent conduct, whereas a perception of high subjective risk may result in more prudent conduct.

Objective risk is a concrete concept and does not depend on a particular person's perception. It is the relative variation of an actual loss from an expected loss. Suppose an auto insurer has 1,000 new cars insured each year. On average, 100 cars, or 10 percent, file collision claims each year. If in the first year 110 cars file claims, and the next year only 90 filed claims, there is a 10-car variation each year, equaling a 10 percent objective risk. Objective risk varies inversely with the number of exposures involved. As the number of exposures increases, the insurance company can predict more accurately its future loss experience based on the law of large numbers (to be discussed later in the chapter).

PROBABILITY OF LOSS

For an insurer to estimate how many losses will occur in a given year, its actuary must know the chance of loss for members of the insurance pool. The chance of loss is more commonly referred to as the probability of loss and is a measure of the long-run frequency with which an event occurs.

For example, if 700 out of 100,000 homes suffer a fire each year, then the probability of a fire can be calculated as 700 divided by 100,000 or 0.007. For each individual member of the pool, the probability of loss is a moot point. Whether the probability is 7 in 1,000 or 7 in 100, the insured's concern is that it will be his home that burns, and that such a loss will be financially devastating. Probability analysis is useful information for the insurer, however, because it allows the insurer to determine the number of insureds who will suffer losses and to estimate the aggregate claims. The expected total cost of claims can then be evenly distributed among the members of the pool.

Notice that probability is the *long-run* chance. This implies that numerous events must occur before probability can be calculated with reasonable accuracy. To illustrate, consider how one might determine the probability of a tossed coin landing with the head side up. The probability is .5 (or a 50 percent chance), but suppose one did not know this. To discover the probability of tossing a head, assume the coin is tossed ten times. With many iterations of the same test, some might obtain five out of 10 heads, but others will not. When seven heads turn up, one may erroneously conclude that the probability is .7 (7 out of 10). To calculate a true probability, one should toss the coin several thousand times, recording each of the results. Perhaps there were 5,021 heads, resulting in a better estimate of the true probability (5,021/10,000 = .5021) than tossing the coin just ten times.

How does probability relate to objective risk? Objective risk is the chance that predictions about losses will be wrong. Those predictions are based on probability. The more reliable the probability figures are, the more accurate the predictions will be and, thus, the lower the objective risk.

LAW OF LARGE NUMBERS

Probability figures must be determined over time. The previous coin toss example illustrates that the more times one repeats an experiment, the more likely it is that the true probability will reveal itself. So, the larger the number of exposure units, the more likely it is that the *ex ante* predictions will be accurate. A related conclusion is that the **law of large numbers** helps reduce objective risk, which depends on the variation in, or uncertainty of, possible outcomes.

As an illustration, consider the risk faced by an insurer that has 1,000 insureds in a life insurance pool, versus that of an insurer with 100,000 insureds. If the probability of death is 5 in 1,000, or .005, the insurer with the smaller pool estimates that 5 people in the pool will die this year. The larger insurer estimates that 500 people will die. Suppose five additional people in each pool die, above and beyond what each insurer predicted. For the smaller insurer, these extra deaths result in a 100 percent increase in claims beyond what was originally predicted. For the larger insurer, however, the five additional deaths result in an increase of only 1 percent. Because there are more observations in the larger pool, the variation in possible outcomes declines, which reduces the insurer's objective risk.

EXAMPLE

law of large numbers - concept that the greater the number of exposures, the more closely will actual results approach the probable results expected from an indefinite number of exposures

EXAMPLE

237

CAUSES OF INSURED LOSSES

PERILS

peril - the approximate or actual cause of a loss

Too often the concept of risk, or the chance of loss, is confused with the terms "peril" and "hazard." A **peril** is the proximate or actual cause of a loss. Some common perils are fire, windstorm, tornado, earthquake, burglary, and collision.

open-perils policy - a policy in which all perils or causes of loss are covered, unless they are specifically listed under the exclusions section

Insurance policies may be written in either an open-perils or named-perils format. Historically, open-perils policies were called "all-risks" policies, because they covered all risks of loss (perils) not specifically excluded. The name "all-risks" proved to be somewhat misleading to typical consumers, implying that "all" things were covered. So, the industry has moved toward the use of the term "open-perils" to describe this type of coverage agreement. An **open-perils policy** is one in which all perils or causes of loss are covered, unless they are specifically listed under the exclusions section. A named-perils policy provides protection against losses caused only by the perils specifically listed in the policy. Because there is always a chance of loss being caused by an unknown peril, an open-perils policy is preferable to a named-perils policy. Consequently, the open-perils policy premium is higher because it provides broader coverage.

HAZARDS

hazard (moral, morale, and physical) - a condition that creates or increases the likelihood of a loss occurring. Moral hazard is a character flaw or level of dishonesty an individual possesses that causes or increases the chance for loss. Morale hazard is indifference to a loss based on the existence of insurance. A physical hazard is a tangible condition or circumstance that increases the probability of a peril occurring and/or the severity of damages that result from a peril

A **hazard** is a condition that creates or increases the likelihood of a loss occurring. The three main types of hazard are:

▲ Moral hazard.
▲ Morale hazard.
▲ Physical hazard.

Moral Hazard

Moral hazard is a character flaw or level of dishonesty an individual possesses that causes or increases the chance for loss. In property insurance claims, a good example of a moral hazard is arson. Fraud in auto and health claims also occurs frequently. Dishonest insureds justify their claims by thinking, "the insurer has plenty of money, and some of it is mine, so I'm entitled to it." Unfortunately, these types of losses result in premium increases for all insureds. When an insured submits an inflated or intentionally caused claim, he is "stealing" from himself and from his fellow insureds.

Morale Hazard

Morale hazard is indifference to a loss due on the existence of insurance. Many people think that because they have insurance there is no need to be concerned about protecting their property. As a direct result, the chance of loss is increased. An individual may contend that because he is insured, there is no reason to lock his home or lock his car. This should not be confused with moral hazard, which, for example, would be burning one's own house down or purposely rear-ending another motor vehicle to collect insurance.

Physical Hazard

A **physical hazard** is a tangible condition or circumstance that increases the probability of a peril occurring and/or the severity of damages that result from a peril. Common examples of physical hazard include poor lighting, icy roads, storing gasoline in a household garage, and defective wiring.

ADVERSE SELECTION

Adverse selection is the tendency of higher-than-average risks (i.e., people who need insurance the most) to purchase or renew insurance policies. Calculating insurance premiums depends on the existence of a balance of both favorable and unfavorable risks in the pool. When higher-than-average loss levels occur among insureds, meaning a greater proportion of bad versus good risks, there may exist a problem of adverse selection.

For instance, if someone with no insurance needs surgery, lives in a flood prone area, or has recently acquired a life-threatening disease, that person is more likely to seek insurance. Adverse selection makes insurance less affordable for all insureds. It is reasonable to conclude that if all people were to purchase insurance only when they knew that they would incur a financial loss, then insurance would not exist. The premiums insurers collect would be depleted before all the claims could be accounted for, thus, causing insurance companies to go out of business.

The problem of adverse selection is primarily managed through effective underwriting, which is the process of selecting and classifying insureds according to their respective risk levels. Each level of risk can be thought of as a pool, and the insureds within that pool must all be similar in terms of expected losses, so that they can be charged a premium representative of their risk levels. While a person with a terminal illness may wish to purchase life insurance (a clear example of adverse selection), the underwriting process should detect the condition and result in the underwriter's rejection of the application for insurance. Insurers also manage adverse selection after the fact by raising premiums, by non renewal, and in the case of life insurance applying surrender charges to policies terminated.

adverse selection - the tendency of higher-than-average risks (people who need insurance the most) to purchase or renew insurance policies

INSURABLE LOSSES

INSURANCE VERSUS GAMBLING

Many people view insurance and gambling as similar activities. A commonly asked question is "Isn't insurance a gamble because the insurance company and the insured are betting if and when an unfortunate event will occur?" While it is true that in insurance there are monetary transactions that take place on the basis of chance, insurance and gambling differ in terms of their respective purposes.

Insurance allows an insured to transfer a risk to the insurer, whereas gambling creates a risk where none previously existed. In gambling, the risk of loss is created when the transaction itself occurs. For example, when a card player bets $100 on a hand against the dealer, he has immediately created a speculative risk (risk of gain or loss) for himself. Insurance takes the consequences of a pure risk (loss, no loss), and makes them manageable for the insured.

REQUISITES FOR AN INSURABLE RISK

There are several conditions that must exist before a pure risk is considered to be an insurable risk. These conditions are:

- ▲ A large number of homogeneous (similar) exposure units.
- ▲ Insured losses must be accidental from the insured's standpoint.
- ▲ Insured losses must be measurable and determinable.
- ▲ Loss must not pose a catastrophic risk for the insurer.
- ▲ Premiums must be affordable.

A Large Number of Homogeneous (Similar) Exposure Unit

The insurance process depends on the establishment of fair and accurate premiums for insureds. If accurate estimates of the probability of an occurrence are to be made, a large number of cases need to be considered. The law of large numbers states that in order to predict the average frequency and severity of a loss with accuracy, a sufficient number of homogeneous exposure units needs to be present within each class.

It is important to note the distinction between homogeneous and heterogeneous groups at this point. If dissimilar exposure units are placed in the same group to be observed, predictions on their loss experience will likely be inaccurate. Imagine a pool of homeowners that consists of people from California, Texas, Montana, and Maine. Because the natural disaster perils that each state faces are somewhat different, the resulting expected loss predictions would be imprecise. It makes more sense to estimate losses for homeowners in California as a group, and to make separate loss estimates for persons living in the other states. The exposure units must be homogeneous, or similar in nature, to obtain an accurate measure of the underlying probability for the loss experience of an insured group.

Insured Losses Must be Accidental from the Insured's Standpoint

Losses need to be unintentional and fortuitous from the insured's perspective in order to be insurable. If it were not for this requirement, moral hazards would be created and encouraged, and if intentional losses were paid, premiums would skyrocket. As a direct result, fewer people would purchase insurance. This in turn would change the ability of companies to predict probabilities based on a large number of homogeneous units.

Insured Losses Must be Measurable and Determinable

In order to prevent fraud, insurance companies' policies state whether a loss is covered and how much will be paid for that loss. A loss must be both measurable and determinable as to reason, time, location, and price before accurate loss predictions can be made. Difficult risks to predict include flood, earthquake, and nuclear contamination. Losses that are difficult to measure and determine include sentimental value of property (such as the value of a family pet) and cash losses. Although proving that a house or car existed and what each was worth is straightforward, proving how much cash one had on hand at the time a wallet is stolen is not. Thus, insurers typically provide very limited coverage for losses of cash, while they readily pay for fire damage to houses and for theft of automobiles.

Losses Must Not Pose a Catastrophic Risk for the Insurer

Logically, an insurer cannot provide coverage against some loss that could cause it to become financially insolvent. Dangerous risks for an insurer include those that are not accurately predictable and those that can cause damage to a significant portion of the insurer's pool.

Recall that insurable losses must be predictable and measurable. Otherwise, the insurer likely cannot estimate the appropriate premium for the coverage accurately. A war is an example of a risk that is simply not predictable. There is no statistical trend that can be used to determine future losses. For this reason, insurers virtually never provide coverage against war-related losses.

Another source of catastrophic risk for an insurer is any peril that could cause loss to a significant portion of the insureds in the pool. Hurricane risk is a good example of this type of loss. Imagine the loss exposure faced by an insurer that sells property coverages only in the state of Florida. With the hurricane risk faced by a large portion of that state, one such storm could damage a significant portion of the insureds' property. Compare this situation with an insurer that sells coverage in all fifty states, and does only a small portion of its business in Florida. A hurricane in Florida would not be as financially devastating in such a case.

Premiums Must be Affordable

In order for insurance to be attractive to consumers, the premiums offered must be economically feasible and related to the risk. Premiums differ in accordance with the relative frequency and severity of loss. The higher the chance for a loss, the higher the premium will be, all else held equal. Naturally, if a loss is less likely to occur or is less severe than other potential losses, the premium will be more affordable.

LEGAL PRINCIPLES OF INSURANCE CONTRACTS

A contract is valid only if the legal system enforces its terms and conditions. Our legal system has established certain principles upon which insurance contracts are based, and by which insurance contracts are interpreted when claims or disputes arise. The following sections address these various principles, but first is a discussion of what constitutes a legally binding contract.

ELEMENTS OF A VALID CONTRACT

▲ The elements of a valid contract are:
▲ Offer and acceptance.
▲ Legal competency of all parties.
▲ Legal consideration.
▲ Lawful purpose.

Offer and Acceptance

A valid contract exists only if it is based on mutual assent, or a "meeting of the minds" of the contracting parties. Mutual assent consists of a valid offer made by one party and an acceptance of that offer by the other party. In most cases, an offer is made by the prospective insured to an insurer via its agent by filling out and signing an application that is accompanied by the initial premium. Next, the insurance company must decide whether to accept, counter-offer, or reject the offer. In order for a contract to become effective, acceptance of the offer by the insurer or by the agent acting on behalf of the company is necessary.

Legal Competency of All Parties to the Contract

The law requires that both the offeror and offeree be legally competent. The vast majority of persons are considered legally competent, so it is easier to explain which persons are legally incompetent. These may include insane persons, intoxicated persons, and minors. Those under 18 are subject to special state provisions in order to provide a basis for competency.

While it is not *specifically* illegal to enter into a contract with someone who is incompetent in the eyes of the law, it is dangerous to do so. This is because the contract is generally voidable at the option of the incompetent party once he or she becomes competent, or once someone responsible for the incompetent party discovers the existence of the contract.

EXAMPLE   Suppose Joe, 16, buys a life insurance policy and pays premiums on it until he is 18 years old. If upon turning 18 Joe becomes legally competent, it is generally possible for him to void the contract on the grounds that he was not competent when he first entered into it. By voiding the contract, Joe is stating that he never wanted to be a part of it, and is thus entitled to a refund of all premiums paid. Yet, had Joe died during the two years the policy was in force, the insurer would have been legally required to pay the death claim. So, from the insurer's standpoint, entering into a contract with anyone who is not legally competent is clearly ill advised.

Legal Consideration

Each party to a contract must provide something of value known as, "consideration." Payment (or the promise of payment) of a first premium is generally consideration on the part of the insured. The insurer's consideration is its promise to pay losses covered by the policy, and uphold the terms of the policy.

Lawful Purpose

In a court of law, a contract deemed to have an illegal purpose or a purpose that is against the benefit of public interest in general is invalid. Any insurance contract that promotes actions contrary to public interest is unenforceable. For example, an insurer will not pay the beneficiary of a life insurance policy if the beneficiary murders the insured. To do so would encourage murder, which is illegal and against public policy. Recall that moral hazards are character flaws in persons who may intentionally create losses. They are willing to commit illegal acts to profit from insurance. If insurance policies did not eliminate coverage for these illegal activities, they would encourage crime and, thus, be against public policy.

LEGAL PRINCIPLES OF THE INSURANCE CONTRACT

In light of the previous discussion on what constitutes a legally enforceable contract, the following three legal principles of insurance contracts are in order.

The Principle of Indemnity

Insurance is a contract of indemnity, which means that a person is entitled to compensation only to the extent that a financial loss has been suffered. Insurance exists only to indemnify a person's losses, not to place him or her in a better financial position than before the loss occurred. If an insured could make money from the perils covered by insurance policies, she would have an incentive to make sure that those perils occurred.

In cases, an insured who finds intentionally caused perils, such as fire due to arson, will exaggerate an insurance claim. This is a violation of the **principle of indemnity**. If the insured suffers a theft of a leather jacket which was purchased at a discount store for $100, yet tells the insurance company the jacket was a designer item that cost $1,000, and the insurer pays the claim without question, the insured has actually made a profit from insurance. Making a profit from insurance is clearly a violation of the principle of indemnity, and also an inducement to moral hazard.

People fail to realize that the more money an insurance company pays for losses, the higher will be the premiums charged to everyone in the pool. Thus, even when insureds are able to violate the principle of indemnity without being caught, they are only taking money from themselves and others in their pool.

One means by which insurers enforce the principle of indemnity is by including a subrogation clause in property and liability policies. The **subrogation clause** states that the insured cannot indemnify himself or herself from both the insurance company and a negligent third party for the same claim. If the insured collects against the policy, he then relinquishes the right to collect damages from the negligent party.

The Principle of Insurable Interest

An insured must be subject to emotional or financial hardship resulting from damage, loss, or destruction in order to have an insurable interest. The **principle of insurable interest** as a legal principle is clearly congruent with the principle of indemnity. For example, if Susan is allowed to insure a building she does not own and has no financial interest in, she has every incentive to destroy the building. Similarly, if she were allowed to insure the life of someone with whom she had no financial or emotional attachment, she would have an incentive to, at least, use insurance as a gambling device, and, at worst, kill the insured.

In property and liability insurance, an insurable interest must be present both at the time of policy inception and at the time of loss. In the case of life insurance, however, an insurable interest is necessary only when the policy is issued. These rules exist in part because life insurance is a long-term investment, whereas property and liability contracts are short-term contracts, usually renewed at six-month or one-year intervals. To require a property owner to give up insurance on property he no longer owns does not impose a financial burden on him. On the other hand, the policyowner who insures her spouse for 20 years and then gets divorced might suffer a severe

principle of indemnity - states that a person is entitled to compensation only to the extent that financial loss has been suffered

subrogation clause - states that the insured cannot indemnify himself or herself from both the insurance company and a negligent third party for the same claim

principle of insurable interest - to have an insurable interest, an insured must be subject to emotional or financial hardship resulting from damage, loss, or destruction

financial penalty and loss of investment if the policy were automatically terminated due to the loss of insurable interest.

The Principle of Utmost Good Faith

principle of utmost good faith - also known as the principle of fair dealing, the principle of utmost good faith requires that the insured and the insurer both be forthcoming with all relevant facts about the insured risk and the coverage provided for that risk

Also known as the principle of fair dealing, the **principle of utmost good faith** requires that both the insured and the insurer be forthcoming with all relevant facts about the insured risk and the coverage provided for that risk. Recall that to have a binding contract, there must be both a valid offer and a valid acceptance, which together constitute mutual assent. Unless all pertinent facts are revealed by the insured in the application process, the insurer does not have a valid offer on which to base its acceptance. The same is true of any counteroffer the insurer might make to the insured before binding coverage.

Throughout the life of the insurance policy, it is presumed that both parties will tell each other the truth about all matters relevant to the contract. If this standard of honesty is not upheld, then the insured could legally commit insurance fraud (thus violating the principle of indemnity). Similarly, the insurer could refuse to pay claims for which the insured is legally entitled to receive compensation. The insurer is expected to comply with all terms of the contract and all provisions of the insurance law in the state(s) where it operates. The legal system recognizes three different areas of enforcement that apply to the insured:

▲   Warranty.
▲   Representation.
▲   Concealment.

Warranty

A warranty is merely a promise made by the insured to the insurer. The promise can be that something is true when coverage is applied for (also called an affirmative warranty), or it can be a promise that the insured will or will not do something during the life of the policy (promissory warranty). Historically, any violation of warranty was grounds for contract avoidance; however, most U.S. jurisdictions have determined that statements made on an application for insurance coverage are not affirmative warranties, but are instead representations. The legal effects of representations are covered below.

The effect of a breach of a promissory warranty is much clearer and more severe. For example, consider a homeowner who promises to purchase and maintain a security system for his home as part of the insurance contract. He decides that he needs to save money, so he disconnects his security service. If he is burglarized three months later, the insurer likely will not have to pay the claim because a breach of warranty is grounds for voiding a policy.

Representation

Representations are statements made by the insured to the insurer in the application process. Material (relevant) misrepresentations give the insurer the right to void the policy once they are discovered. Why? Once again, mutual assent is a necessary element to any contract. If the insured lies to the insurer in the application (offer) process, then the insurer has not received a valid offer, so mutual assent is never reached.

The misrepresentation must be *material* before the insurer may void the policy and ultimately deny payment of a claim. The test of materiality is a simple one--if the insurer had known the truth, would it have affected the insurer's underwriting decision to such an extent that the policy would not have been issued? For example, if Carmen states on her application for life insurance that she does not smoke when in fact she does, it definitely would have affected the insurer's underwriting decision. While coverage might have still been sold to Carmen, she would have been placed into a different underwriting class and, thus, charged a higher premium.

Now, suppose on Carmen's life insurance application the insurer asked if she had ever been seen by a doctor for any medical condition over the past five years (which is a very vague question), and she said "no." In reality, she had been seen once a year for an annual check-up and was treated for the flu two years ago. If the insurer discovered the misrepresentation and wanted to void the policy, it would have to prove that knowing she had annual check-ups plus one case of the flu would have changed its underwriting decision. In reality, this type of routine medical treatment probably would not affect the underwriting decision, so the insurer would be barred from voiding the policy.

Concealment

Concealment occurs when the insured is silent about a fact that is material to the risk. If an insured does not reveal material information that she knows and that she is not specifically asked about, then she has concealed that information. Contrast the notion of concealment with that of misrepresentation—a misrepresentation is an untruthful answer to a question, whereas concealment is not revealing a fact that is of importance to the insurer.

In practice, most insurers do not void coverage on the grounds of concealment because it is very difficult to prove. U.S. law requires the insurer to prove the concealed information was important to the underwriting process, and that the insured knew that it was important but intentionally kept it a secret. This is a very difficult standard of proof because the typical consumer has no way of knowing precisely what is relevant to an underwriter's decision.

DISTINGUISHING CHARACTERISTICS OF INSURANCE CONTRACTS

Insurance is a contract of adhesion. It is also aleatory, unilateral, and conditional.

Adhesion (A take it or leave it contract)

In most cases, two parties form a contract through the bargaining process. In insurance, however, this is not the case because insurance is a contract of **adhesion**. Adhesion means the insured must accept the contract as written, without any bargaining over its terms and conditions. Most insurance companies today use standardized policy forms that may be modified by the insurer to

representations - statements made by the insured to the insurer in the application process

concealment - occurs when the insured is silent about a fact that is material to the risk

adhesion - a characteristic of insurance which means that insurance is "a take it or leave it" contract. The insured must accept (or adhere to) the contract as written, without any bargaining over its terms and conditions

meet individual needs, and in the vast majority of cases the insured cannot bargain over the specific terms and conditions contained in the contract.

If the drafter of the contract, (in this case, the insurer) leaves the contract ambiguous in any way, such ambiguities will be interpreted in favor of the person who was not allowed to bargain over the terms of the contract (in this case, the insured). This legal doctrine imposes a stringent burden on the insurer to use very precise wording in its contractual products. The test of ambiguity is, "How would a reasonable layperson (not an insurance expert) interpret this contract?" If a court determines that a contractual provision is ambiguous to the average person, it will require the insurer to interpret the provision in a manner that is most favorable to the insured.

Aleatory (money exchange may be unequal)

Monetary values exchanged by each party in an insurance agreement are unequal. This is known as the **aleatory** feature of insurance contracts. While the insured pays a small premium, the insurer might ultimately pay a large dollar amount as the result of a claim. There have been cases, for example, where the insured died within a few days of the life insurance policy's issuance. Perhaps one $80 premium payment was made, yet the insurer had to pay a $250,000 death claim.

Unilateral (Only one promise, made by insurer)

Insurance policies are unilateral contracts because only one party, the insurer, agrees to a legally enforceable promise to provide the coverages shown in the policy and to abide by all terms and conditions of the policy. On the other hand, the insured is not legally obligated to uphold his or her agreement to pay premiums. Although the insured must continue to pay premiums if he wants to keep his insurance protection, the insurer cannot legally force him to remain in the contract and to continue paying premiums.

Conditional (Conditioned on paying the premium)

Every contract lists provisions or conditions that outline the duties of each party involved. An insurance policy is conditional in the fact that the insurer is obligated only to compensate the insured if certain conditions are met. Due to this characteristic, it is the duty of every insured to carefully read and understand the conditions listed in a policy before it is signed.

IMPORTANT FEATURES OF INSURANCE CONTRACTS

EXCLUSIONS

Exclusions are a necessary part of every insurance contract, because not every peril or property can be covered in every policy. Moreover, some items are simply uninsurable because they do not meet the requisites of an insurable risk.

The exclusions in an insurance contract outline what specifically will not be covered. The doctrine of concurrent causation makes it necessary for even named-perils policies to include numerous exclusions. Concurrent causation exists when a loss can be attributed to more than one peril.

aleatory - a characteristic of insurance which means that monetary values exchanged by each party in an insurance agreement are unequal

The law states that if at least one of the contributing perils is covered, then the insurer must pay the entire loss. So, even though a named-perils policy might agree to cover fire, the insurer may not wish to cover fires that result from an earthquake. If the insurer does not specifically state that fires caused by earthquake are excluded from coverage, then when an earthquake occurs, and even a small fire results, the entire loss will have to be paid.

Insurers may exclude coverage for perils (such as war and flood), losses (the cost of a private hospital room when a semiprivate room will do), or specific items of property (valuable papers and money are typically excluded from homeowners coverage).

RIDERS AND ENDORSEMENTS

Riders and endorsements are two terms used interchangeably by the insurance industry. They are written additions to an insurance contract that modify its original provisions. They make it possible to customize an insurance contract to fit an individual's needs. These attachments to the contract may extend coverage, change premiums, or make corrections to the policy that take precedence over any conflicting terms in the preprinted policy form.

VALUATION OF INSURED LOSSES

Insurance policies must not only specify what is covered and what is excluded, they must also explain how losses will be paid. Without valuation provisions in the policy, the insured and the insurer could have numerous disputes over how much a particular claim is worth.

Most insurance policies value losses in one of three ways:

- ▲ Replacement cost.
- ▲ Actual cash value.
- ▲ Agreed-upon value.

Replacement Cost

Replacement cost is the current cost of replacing property with new materials of like kind and quality. If, for example, a house were damaged by fire, the damaged carpet would be replaced with new carpet, even though the old carpet was somewhat worn and soiled. Replacement cost is often found by comparing what was once owned with what is currently on the market. Many homeowners policies have replacement cost provisions.

Actual Cash Value (ACV)

Actual cash value is equal to replacement cost minus functional depreciation. For example, if the functional life of a roof is 20 years, and it is destroyed after five years, the roof is assumed to be 25 percent depreciated at the time of the loss. The insurer would thus pay 75 percent of the roof's replacement cost if the policy valued losses on an ACV basis.

From the standpoint of a homeowner, ACV coverage can impose a serious financial burden if a severe loss occurs on older property. Replacement cost coverage is therefore suggested, even though it is more expensive. Virtually all automobile policies use ACV, rather than replacement

actual cash value - one of three ways in which losses are valued in most insurance policies. Actual cash value (ACV) is calculated as replacement cost minus functional depreciation cost, because automobiles depreciate so rapidly. The cost of providing replacement cost coverage on autos would be too high for most consumers to purchase it.

Agreed-upon Value

Due to the difficulty of valuing certain losses, amounts paid for a loss are agreed upon by the insurer and the insured at the time a policy is issued. In writing a contract of this type, there is no violation of the principle of indemnity because the insurer will generally agree to a value that is reflective of the property's fair market value. Fine arts are often insured under the valued policy principle, as are antiques. Life insurance is a valued policy because it is impossible to determine the precise value of a person's life objectively, and there really is no such thing as the replacement cost of a person.

Deductibles and Co-payments

deductible - a stated amount of money the insured is required to pay on a loss before the insurer will make any payments under the policy conditions

A **deductible** is a stated amount of money the insured is required to pay on a loss before the insurer will make any payments under the policy conditions. Deductibles help to eliminate small claims, reduce premiums, and decrease morale hazard. Deductibles are used mainly in property, health, and automobile insurance contracts. They are not used in life insurance contracts, however, because death is a complete loss (there is never a partial claim under a life insurance policy). Disability policies use an elimination period, which essentially provides a deductible.

co-payments - a loss-sharing arrangement whereby the insured pays a percentage of the loss in excess of the deductible

Co-payments are in addition to deductibles and are commonly used in health insurance policies. **Co-payments** are loss-sharing arrangements whereby the insured pays a percentage of the loss in excess of the deductible. One example of a co-payment is when a person must pay the first $500 of medical expenses each year, and then 20 percent of all expenses over that amount. The insurer pays 80 percent of covered medical expenses that exceed the $500 deductible.

COINSURANCE

coinsurance - the percentage of financial responsibility that the insured and the insurer must uphold in order to achieve equity in rating

Coinsurance defines the percentage of financial responsibility that the insured and the insurer must uphold in order to achieve equity in rating. Coinsurance exists primarily in property insurance and encourages all insureds to cover their property to at least a stated percentage of the property's value, or else suffer a financial penalty. Because the vast majority of property losses are partial, without coinsurance clauses many insureds would attempt to save money on insurance by purchasing less insurance than the full value of their property. While underinsuring is not an illegal practice, it presents a problem for the underwriter and actuary who based expected loss estimates, and thus premiums, on the full value of the properties in the pool.

INDIVIDUAL LOSS EXPOSURES AND INSURANCE COVERAGES

PERILS THAT CAN REDUCE AND/OR ELIMINATE THE ABILITY TO EARN INCOME

There are three main types of pure risk that can interrupt one's earned income stream: dying too soon, living too long, and accidents and illnesses.

Dying Too Soon

The risk of a person dying before reaching full life expectancy is known as premature death. In most cases, the person who dies prematurely has a number of financial obligations, including a family to support, a mortgage to pay, and children to send through college. To prevent a great economic struggle for surviving dependents, proper financial and estate planning using life insurance will provide for those dependents in the event of the premature death of a breadwinner.

Living Too Long

While it may sound ridiculous to say that someone lived "too long," there is the risk of outliving one's financial resources (called superannuation). Medical and technological advances have led to substantial increases in human life expectancy. Currently, the average person retiring at age 65 may be expected to live another 20 years. Approximately fifty percent of all retirees will live beyond the normal life expectancy of 20 years. How does one make certain that savings and other assets will last until death? Various financial planning products make it possible to assure that one does not outlive his assets.

Accidents and Illness

An unexpected accident or illness may result not only in high medical costs, but also in the inability to work and earn income. The cost of medical treatment continues to rise at a rate that exceeds general inflation. The cost of providing a lifetime of medical care, while simultaneously being unable to earn an income, can be astronomical. Long-term disability insurance can be used to mitigate this risk.

PERILS THAT CAN DESTROY OR DEPLETE EXISTING ASSETS

With the income earned in one's lifetime, various assets such as cash, real estate, and automobiles are acquired. Even if the individual's ability to earn an income is never hindered, financial loss could result if existing assets are destroyed or lost by theft. There are two main exposures that exist in this category: damage to property and legal liability for injuries inflicted upon others.

Damage to Property

A host of perils threaten the individual's property, including natural disasters, crimes, and careless accidents. The financial consequences of these perils and their resulting damage can be severe.

Damage to property can result in one of two types of financial losses: direct and indirect. A direct loss is an immediate result of an insured peril. The cost of repairing fire damage to one's house is a direct loss. An indirect loss occurs as a result of a direct property loss. The types of expenses that are incurred as indirect losses are numerous. If a section of the fire-damaged house mentioned above is being rented out, the lost rent due to the property being uninhabitable is an example of an indirect loss. Because the fire damage leaves the house untenable, the family also has to pay for the cost of hotel accommodations until the house can be repaired, which is another indirect loss resulting from the fire damage. If the hotel does not accept pets, the family will have to pay a kennel or other boarding facility to keep the pets until the home is repaired. All of these expenses add up quickly and can easily exceed the cost of the direct property loss.

Legal Liability for Injuries Inflicted upon Others

Under the U.S. legal system, one is held legally liable if he causes bodily injury or property damage to another. Personal savings and other assets can be seized to pay for this liability.

Liability risk is especially dangerous from a financial standpoint, due to the fact that there is no upper limit on the amount of loss one can suffer. Consider the physician who treats 20 to 40 patients each day. If one of those patients is injured as a result of the doctor's malpractice, she might be willing to accept a small settlement of $10,000 for her pain and suffering, whereas another patient suffering the exact same injury might demand $10 million. Assuming a court of law finds the doctor did commit malpractice, the injured patient might very well be awarded $10 million (or even more). In addition to the damages claimed by the injured party, the insured also suffers another loss--the cost of settling and/or defending lawsuits. With professional legal fees starting at about $150 per hour, even a person who is ultimately found not to be responsible for injuring someone else could still have enormous legal bills to pay.

RISK MANAGEMENT

Risk management is a systematic process for identifying, evaluating, and managing pure risk exposures faced by a firm or individual. The three steps in the risk management process are:

- ▲ Identifying and evaluating pure risks.
- ▲ Selecting the best risk management technique.
- ▲ Implementing a risk management plan.

Most medium and large-size businesses have some type of formal risk management program, and many have at least one full-time risk manager. As individuals, we each act as personal risk managers for ourselves, and can thus use the three-step process described below.

IDENTIFYING AND EVALUATING PURE RISKS

The first step in risk management is to identify all possible pure risk exposures. Though it is difficult to generalize risks that companies face due to differences in structure and conditions, potential exposures again mirror those described for individuals. Businesses of course are concerned with damage to existing assets, and any perils that might interrupt their ability to generate income. As most businesses generate income through the efforts of their personnel, risk managers are also concerned with the recruitment, selection, hiring, training, health, and welfare of personnel.

In order for a corporate risk manager to become aware of the risks that his company faces, he must delve into the operations of the firm. Some common methods of research are physical inspection, risk analysis questionnaires, flow process charts, and reviewing financial statements and reports on past losses.

For the individual consumer, identifying risks is a somewhat simpler process. Analyzing and valuing the properties owned or leased, recognizing activities that could result in injuries to others, and determining how to protect one's ability to generate an income are all reasonably straightforward activities.

The next logical step in the risk management process is to evaluate the potential frequency and severity of losses. Loss frequency is the expected number of losses that will occur within a given period of time. Loss severity refers to the potential size or damage of a loss. By identifying loss frequency and severity, a risk manager can prioritize the urgency of dealing with each specific risk.

Recall that probability is useful when applied to large numbers. However, relying solely on probability-based predictions for an individual is not recommended. Of greater concern to the individual is the potential severity of the losses that occur. The person who owns a $200,000 home has a maximum possible severity of loss on that asset equal to $200,000. This would be, for the vast majority of consumers, a high-severity loss. On the other hand, the person who owns a car worth $1,500 has a fairly low severity-loss potential. The $1,500 loss to a particular person might be severe and could even adversely affect income generation if they could no longer drive to work.

SELECTING AN APPROPRIATE RISK MANAGEMENT TOOL

Insurance is not necessary, nor is it even available, for each and every risk of loss an individual faces. Choosing the appropriate risk management tool depends largely on the potential severity and frequency of the loss exposures faced. Where more than one tool is deemed appropriate, the costs and benefits of each should be examined to determine which is most economical and beneficial. Before explaining how to choose the proper method for handling each risk, consider the various risk management tools that are available for handling pure risk exposures:

▲ Risk avoidance.
▲ Loss control.
▲ Risk retention or assumption.
▲ Risk transfer.

Risk Avoidance

Risk avoidance is simply the avoidance of any chance of loss. If the probability of loss becomes zero, then there is no need to worry about future losses. How does one eliminate the possibility of dying in an airplane crash? Don't get into an airplane!

Avoidance works for some loss exposures, but it is impossible to avoid all possible loss exposures. For example, the person who wishes to avoid dying in a plane crash can certainly avoid flying, but then how does he get from one distant place to another? Perhaps using a car, but many people would also prefer to avoid dying in an automobile accident. So, those persons would have to walk. In today's society, it is not feasible for many persons to avoid driving or flying.

If one risk is avoided, another risk likely will replace it. However, certain risks can be avoided when their potential frequency and severity are too high to justify *not* avoiding them. As an example, some doctors have left private practice because of the fear of medical malpractice suits. They find other ways to earn a living (teaching or research, for example), thus, avoiding the risk of a malpractice suit completely.

Loss Control

loss control - activities that reduce the frequency or severity of losses

Loss control consists of activities that reduce the frequency or severity of losses. Loss prevention efforts focus specifically on reducing the potential frequency of losses, while loss reduction techniques are aimed at reducing the severity of losses that do occur. A person who cannot avoid driving faces the risk of an auto accident, but has several loss control devices at her disposal. Taking a defensive driving class and practicing defensive driving techniques are means of preventing accidents. In the same way, wearing a seatbelt minimizes injuries sustained in an automobile accident.

Loss control measures are undertaken only when they are cost-feasible. To minimize the severity of injuries sustained in a car accident, one might decide to purchase the safest automobile on the market; however, if that automobile costs $50,000, it may be cost prohibitive.

252

Certain loss control features that reduce the severity of losses, such as seat belts, may give some drivers a false sense of security and, thus, those drivers might increase undesirable behavior, such as speeding, which may increase the frequency of losses, thus mitigating the loss control advantage.

Risk Retention or Assumption

When a person or firm is exposed to risk and decides to bear all or part of the financial burden if a loss occurs, this is known as risk retention or risk assumption. It may occur in one of two forms, active or passive. Active risk retention means that one is fully aware of the chance for loss and consciously plans to retain all or part of the risk. The person who has a $100,000 home may choose to retain the first $500 of any loss through a deductible clause, whereas the person with a $1,500 automobile may choose to retain the whole risk of property damage by not carrying comprehensive and collision because the severity of loss is low.

Passive risk retention is being unaware of a risk and, thus, taking no steps to manage it. When another method is not actively chosen, retention is selected by default.

Risk Transfer

As discussed earlier, the purchase of insurance is a way to transfer a pure risk. Three other techniques for handling the transfer of risk include contracts, hedging, and incorporation. Contractual agreements may often include guarantees at the time of sale, often known as warranties. Hedging is a means of trying to match profit on one transaction to the expected loss of another. In stock market transactions, a speculator can hedge unfavorable price fluctuations by buying and selling futures contracts. Incorporation results in limited liability for a business' owners. In situations where a business is operated as a sole proprietorship or a partnership, liability is unlimited for the owners; however, if a business is incorporated, stockholder liability is limited and the risk of insufficient funds or assets to meet the demands of business expenses rests with the corporation or is shifted to creditors.

How does one know whether to avoid, reduce, retain, or transfer a risk? Exhibit 8.1, based on the frequency and severity of expected losses, can be used as a general guideline for selecting an appropriate tool.

EXHIBIT 8.1: RISK MANAGEMENT GUIDELINES

	HIGH FREQUENCY	LOW FREQUENCY
HIGH SEVERITY	Avoidance	Insurance
LOW SEVERITY	Retention/Reduction	Retention

The first type of loss exposure is a combination of high severity and high frequency. This is perhaps the most serious type of exposure and is often handled by avoidance. Assume John applies for the position of chauffeur for Divine Limousine Company. He has previously been arrested for miscellaneous misdemeanors and convicted twice for driving while intoxicated. He is clearly an unsafe driver and hiring him as an employee creates potential liability for Divine. It makes sense for Divine Limousine to avoid this exposure by not hiring John.

Exposures that are low in frequency yet high in potential severity are best handled by insurance. The high severity losses can leave a person in a dire financial position, yet the low frequency makes sharing the cost of losses with others economically feasible. Examples of high severity/low frequency loss exposures include fire damage to a house and losses due to automobile collisions.

The remaining types of losses are both low severity in nature. Transferring low severity losses to an insurer is not economically feasible because the insurer will have substantial expenses associated with processing numerous small claims. Low severity losses should generally be retained. However, when low severity losses occur with high frequency, their aggregate impact can have financially devastating effects. So, it is suggested that high frequency, low severity losses not only be retained, but also controlled in an effort to reduce frequency. For an individual, low severity losses include dings on cars, road-damaged tires, sustaining minor injuries and illnesses, and small kitchen grease fires in the home.

IMPLEMENTING AND REVIEWING THE RISK MANAGEMENT PLAN

After selecting the most appropriate risk management tool for each risk, the risk management plan must be implemented. For example, deciding that insurance is the right method for handling the risk of a house fire is not enough. The insurance must be applied for and purchased, and then renewed at regular intervals. Because risk management is an ongoing process, the plan must be reviewed to identify new exposures as property is acquired or sold and life situations change.

Do you feel that many of your clients underestimate their need for insurance?

Clients often misjudge their need for insurance to manage their risk exposure. There is a tendency to focus on protection of ownership interests in real and other tangible property, while underestimating the need to insure liability exposure. An uncovered loss of a piece of property such as an automobile or a home can have a major financial impact, but the liability exposure related to the ownership and operation of that automobile or home can be much more significant. An uncovered adverse lawsuit decision can have a devastating effect on a client's current and future financial prospects. One big liability claim can literally wipe out years of financial planning and wealth accumulation.

What have you found to be the best way to evaluate an individual's insurance risks?

There is no substitute for good old fashioned roll up you sleeves work to accomplish a comprehensive evaluation of a client's risk exposures. This is one area where the "know your customer" rule is of critical importance. An in-depth investigation of a client's lifestyle will often uncover exposures that had never occurred to the client.

A careful inspection of the client's insurance policies is certainly a necessary element of a comprehensive review of his risk management program, but this step should arguably be delayed until after the identification of all risk exposure. Focusing on in-force policies from the start can skew the perspective of the planner, possibly causing neglect of exposures that are not covered by a policy.

How do you approach situations where you have found a misrepresentation or concealment in the insurance contract by the client?

When misrepresentation or concealment, or other fraudulent activity may exist, it is important to clearly explain the potential ramifications of such acts, without being judgmental or accusatory. Clients can thereby make informed decisions to rectify situations that could void essential coverage. Certainly, in cases where the planner is also acting as the agent or broker providing the coverage a higher standard of diligence is required.

Do you believe that your clients read their insurance policies and are fully aware of the specifics of the contract? Explain.

The vast majority of clients either do not read the policy at all, or do not read it carefully enough to understand the coverage provided under the contract. In fact, a reading of the contracts alone may not provide a precise understanding of coverage, as many words and phrases used in the contract have specific meanings, which often do not mirror common everyday language. For a complete understanding, a client should read his policies and then confirm his understanding of his policies with his planner or insurance professional. Frankly, many financial planners have insufficient knowledge of the various forms and coverage applicable, and therefore should defer the provision of advice to a competent insurance professional.

In general, are clients more eager to purchase insurance or accept the personal responsibility the risk of loss? Explain.

Generally clients will purchase insurance or self-insure based on common practice. For example, many people will carry property coverage on a low value automobile just because they have always done so. Yet at the same time they will choose to self-insure an expensive recreational vehicle because they have traditionally gone without coverage even though these might be more substantial exposures.

DISCUSSION QUESTIONS

1. What is insurance and how does the insurance mechanism operate?
2. What are the different types of risk and how does each impact the personal financial planning process?
3. What is the difference between subjective and objective risk?
4. How does a peril differ from a hazard and how does each relate to the need for insurance?
5. What is adverse selection and how does it affect the insurance mechanism?
6. What are the requisites for an insurable risk and what distinguishes insurance from gambling?
7. What are the legal principles and distinguishing features of insurance contracts?
8. What is the reason for, and the effect of, various contractual features in insurance contracts?
9. What is the principle of indemnity?
10. What is the principle of insurable interest?
11. What is adhesion?
12. What does it mean that an insurance contract is aleatory?
13. What are the insurable-loss exposures faced by the typical individual consumer?
14. What are the steps in the risk management process?
15. What does frequency of loss and severity of loss have to do with risk management?

EXERCISES

1. Briefly explain the difference between pure and speculative risk. Give an example.
2. Name three perils that could cause a loss around your home or apartment. What are the hazards that may increase the probability of such perils?
3. Explain the difference between moral hazard and morale hazard. Give two examples of each.
4. Differentiate between gambling and insurance.
5. How would you reduce the risk of or manage the risk of adverse selection in a group dental insurance program?
6. John has an insurance policy for $150,000 on a building located at 175 Pine Street. The policy expires December 31, 2002. John sold the property to Bill on October 31, 2002, for $150,000. That very night, the building burned to the ground. Can John collect on the policy? If so, how much? If not, what legal characteristics would prevent him from collecting? Will John get any money from the insurer?
7. Which of the following people have an insurable interest in Mike's life?
   - ▲ Angel, Mike's 25-year-old daughter
   - ▲ James, Mike's 30-year-old son
   - ▲ Cassie, Mike's former wife and mother of Angel
   - ▲ John, Mike's former business partner
   - ▲ Donna, Mike's daughter-in-law
   - ▲ Scott, Mike's current business partner
   - ▲ Rita, Mike's new girlfriend

8. Leon is the risk manager for ABC, Inc. He has evaluated the following risks in terms of frequency and severity and asks your opinion as to which risk management tool to use.

		Probability/ Frequency	Severity per Occurrence
A	Fire destroys plant	0.0001	$10,000,000
B	Loss of property through employee theft	0.1	$1,000
C	On the job employee disability	0.01	$1,500,000
D	Loss due to misplaced inventory (computer)	0.1	$2,000
E	Loss due to failure to reduce energy bill (lights off, air conditioner off on weekends)	0.02	$400
F	Air conditioning unit goes out (compressor)	0.01	$2,000

CHAPTER 9

Insurance On The Person

LEARNING OBJECTIVES:

After learning the material in this chapter, you will be able to:

1. Identify and explain the various needs for life insurance.

2. Distinguish between term and whole life insurance, and explain the advantages/disadvantages of each.

3. List and define the various types of term life insurance.

4. List and define the various types of whole life insurance.

5. Explain the differences between annuities and life insurance contract.

6. List and define the various types of annuities.

7. Explain the tax implications of life insurance and annuities.

8. Understand the various contractual provisions and options that pertain to life and annuity contracts. Understand the need for health and disability insurance.

9. List and describe the major types of individual health and disability coverages.

10. Be familiar with important policy provisions and major contractual features of individual health and disability coverages.

11. List and describe the major types of employer-provided group health coverages.

12. Be familiar with important policy provisions and major contractual features of group health and disability coverages.

13. Determine how much the insured must pay out of his/her own funds, and how much the insured will collect from the insurer, given information about particular health coverage.

14. Understand the purpose of disability income insurance, and be able to define and discuss the various definitions of disability.

15. Be able to describe the tax treatment of health and disability coverages.

16. Distinguish between indemnity plans and managed care plans.

INTRODUCTION

Risks to the person, namely premature death, catastrophic illness, disability, and the need for long-term care, can be detrimental to a client's financial objectives. While low in frequency, they are potentially catastrophic in severity. Thus, the financial planner must assist the client in mitigating the impact of such risks by selecting and implementing appropriate insurance coverage. This chapter examines each of the above catastrophic risks and describes the proper insurance device, particularly life insurance and health insurance, to mitigate such risk.

Life insurance is a fundamental element in a comprehensive financial plan for most clients, particularly those with dependents. The financial planner should be familiar with each type of life insurance in order to satisfy client needs.

Health insurance is crucial for each member of the family, since an uninsured illness can disrupt income security and reduce personal wealth. The financial planner must be familiar with not only major medical insurance but also disability and long-term care insurance.

WHY PURCHASE LIFE INSURANCE?

While it may be impossible to predict the timing of a person's death, it is possible to plan against the financial distress that survivors can suffer from the loss of an income provider. The purchase of life insurance is one of the most effective methods of protecting against the financial consequences of untimely death. Financial planners recognize two fundamental needs for the monies generated by a life insurance policy: replacing income and preserving assets.

INCOME REPLACEMENT

Life insurance policy proceeds can replace the income lost when a breadwinner dies. There are several different needs that can be addressed using life insurance proceeds.

Income for the Readjustment Period

The loss of a breadwinner may have a significant financial impact on surviving dependent family members, at least in the short run. Family income will diminish, and the risk that family members may experience a lower standard of living is great. Ultimately, the family may adjust its standard of living to fit its new income level, or other members of the family may be able to work to replace the lost income of the deceased. However, after a family suffers the loss of a loved one, it usually encounters an unsettling and emotionally stressful readjustment period. It will take time for the surviving spouse or other dependents to reconcile grief and resume their lives. In more serious cases, the surviving spouse may have to be educated and trained to enter the workforce for the first time. Life insurance made payable directly to the family members or heirs of one's estate can provide for the family's financial support during such a period of readjustment.

Financial Support of Dependents

Where a breadwinner has dependents, the concern for their financial well-being exists. The mother who is the sole support of two children concerns herself with how their financial needs will be met if she dies prematurely. A life insurance policy guarantees that when the insured dies, a certain amount of money will be available to support those dependents.

When considering how much money is needed for this particular life insurance need, two important points need to be considered. First, who actually qualifies as a "dependent"? For tax purposes, most people are able to claim only persons who are children as their dependents. However, many other people may be financially dependent upon the insured. Perhaps the insured's parents, who are older and on a fixed income, rely on the insured for a certain amount of support. There may be a spouse who either does not work outside the home or does not earn enough income to survive without the insured's wages. Responsible financial planning considers the needs of all dependents, not just underage children.

Second, how much financial support should be given to various dependents? Should dependent children be supported until they are 18 years old, or should they be supported until they complete college? What standard of living does the insured wish to guarantee for survivors? These questions must be answered before the insured may accurately determine her life insurance needs.

Other Personal Financial Plans

In addition to the fundamental notion of providing survivors with income, insureds may also wish to provide survivors with funds to achieve a specific goal. Such goals might include redeeming a mortgage so the surviving spouse no longer has to make a mortgage payment or paying for college tuition for each child.

ESTATE PRESERVATION

People work throughout their lives to accumulate wealth in the form of various assets. A common fear of most consumers is that after they die, those assets will be lost. The following types of posthumous expenses that are imposed on dependents make it clear why this is a reasonable fear.

Medical Expenses Prior to Death

Even when death is sudden and swift, final medical expenses are typically incurred. In more extreme situations, one can incur exorbitant medical bills fighting to live, yet still not prevail in the fight. In many cases, a loss of life occurs after months or even years of treatment and hospital stays. Unless adequate health insurance exists to cover the bulk of such expenses, the survivors must worry about paying those final medical expenses. Even when health insurance has been purchased, many policies have a lifetime maximum benefit of $1 million or $2 million. A serious illness could easily exhaust those coverage limits, leaving many unpaid medical bills.

Disposal and Ceremonial Expenses

Each person has specific preferences about how their body should be handled after death. Some people prefer cremation, while others prefer burial. Still, there are others who wish to be placed in a mausoleum and even those who wish to have their bodies donated to medical science. Some of these procedures can be very expensive. The final ceremonies or services held for a person, whether they include a simple memorial service or an elaborate funeral, must also be paid. The amount of money that should be available to survivors to pay for these types of expenses will vary depending upon personal preferences, but one thing to remember is that they often are much more expensive than one might imagine. Adequate life insurance proceeds prevent survivors from having to liquidate other assets to pay disposal and ceremonial expenses.

Probate Expenses

After death, a person's estate may go through the probate court for final settlement of all financial matters. The probate process provides for the distribution of the deceased's assets which are under the will and for payment of debts. Life insurance proceeds may be used to expedite the prompt settlement of a person's probate estate, including the payment of court costs, taxes, and miscellaneous outstanding debts.

Taxes. During the probate process, federal and state inheritance taxes, accrued property taxes, and federal and state income taxes for the current year, as well as any back taxes due, will be collected by the appropriate agencies. If cash is not available to survivors to pay such taxes, then assets may have to be liquidated to satisfy the debts. Life insurance can provide the liquidity to satisfy the tax liabilities.

Debt Retirement. Most people die with miscellaneous outstanding debts, including credit card charges, accrued taxes, unpaid bills, student loans, automobile loans, and other miscellaneous consumer loans. An executor fund may be set up to retire some/all of a person's debts after death in order to avoid saddling survivors with such obligations. An executor fund also usually includes funds to provide for burial and funeral expenses. Naturally, the executor fund can be funded with life insurance proceeds.

TAX BENEFITS

An often-overlooked feature of life insurance is tax benefits. Most people pay a variety of taxes ranging from sales, property, and gift taxes to state and federal estate taxes. The impact of these taxes on a family depends on its level of income. The more money that is earned or vested within a family, the more taxes that eventually will be paid. For this reason, financial planning helps to utilize non-taxable investments for the benefit of the family whenever possible.

Life insurance policies are generally purchased to protect one's survivors in the event of an unexpected death, not to save on taxes. However, certain tax advantages make the purchase of life insurance attractive:

▲ Life insurance death proceeds are not taxable as income to the recipient.
▲ The interest accumulated on a cash value life insurance policy is tax deferred until the **cash value** is withdrawn. If the insured dies without surrendering the policy and withdrawing the cash value, the cash value accumulations are never taxed.

cash value - amount payable to the owner of a life insurance policy should he or she decide it is no longer wanted

APPROACHES TO PROVIDING ADEQUATE PROTECTION

Determining the amount of life insurance to purchase can be difficult because many factors affect a person's future financial goals and resulting need for life insurance. There are three recognized methods currently used to determine the amount of life insurance appropriate for a particular client:

▲ The Needs Approach.
▲ The Human Life Value Approach.
▲ The Capital Retention Approach.

NEEDS APPROACH

The **needs approach** to determining the adequate amount of life insurance evaluates the income replacement needs of one's survivors in the event of untimely death. Monetary values in present value terms are then placed on these needs and summed. Some common needs of a family in the event of death include:

▲ Income during the readjustment period.
▲ Estate clearance fund or a comparable means to liquidate assets.
▲ Life income to widow(er).
▲ Educational funds for dependents.
▲ Emergency funds.
▲ Retirement funds.

After summing the present values of income replacement for all of the financial needs of dependents, existing assets plus the face amount of current life insurance in force can be subtracted to determine the amount of life insurance needed.

The needs approach is merely a "snapshot" that is accurate at one point in time. The needs approach analysis should be reevaluated on a regular basis as financial status changes.

HUMAN LIFE VALUE APPROACH

What is the value of a human life? For purposes of financial planning, the value of a human life is determined by estimating the present value of income generated over the client's work life expectancy, adjusted for the expected consumption of the client. The death of a father who brings home $100,000 a year to a wife and three children has a significant impact on the welfare of his family. In such a scenario, the father's human life value in the event of death is equal to the present value of his family's share of his income.

To determine **human life value**, perform the following steps:

1. Calculate the expected amount of money available to the family each year of the worker's life. Average Annual Earnings - Taxes and Self-maintenance Fees = Family's Share of Earnings (FSE).

needs approach - one of three recognized methods used to determine the amount of insurance one should purchase. The needs approach evaluates the income replacement needs of one's survivors in the event of untimely death

human life value approach - one of three recognized methods used to determine the amount of insurance one should purchase. The human life value approach determines the value of a human life as his or her monetary contribution to dependents

2. Determine the number of years the worker is expected to generate income. Expected age of Retirement - Present Age = Work Life Expectancy (WLE).
3. Determine the present value of the worker's stream of expected earnings: (FSE) x (Present Value of An Annuity Factor, using a reasonable discount rate for the WLE) = HUMAN LIFE VALUE.

CAPITAL RETENTION APPROACH

capital retention approach - one of three recognized methods used to determine the amount of life insurance one should purchase. The capital retention approach first determines what level of annual income the insured wishes to provide for the family. The insured then determines what amount of life insurance is needed in addition to existing income-producing assets to provide the desired level of income

The **capital retention approach** determines the amount of life insurance needed by first determining what level of annual income the insured wishes to provide for the family. The insured then determines what amount of life insurance is needed *in addition to existing income-producing assets* to provide the desired level of income.

Suppose Bob wants to provide his family with $50,000 of annual income. He will first prepare a personal balance sheet that states all existing assets and liabilities. From total assets, he will subtract all liabilities, plus the value of all non-income-producing assets (such as home equity, automobiles, and other personal property). The result is the total amount of capital available for income (CAI). Assuming a CAI of $100,000, and that the family can earn income of 7 percent on that amount, Bob knows that his CAI will generate $7,000 of income for his family. The next step in the process requires Bob to determine where the remaining annual income of $43,000 can be obtained. Other sources of income, such as Social Security survivor benefits, are included in the analysis.

To continue this example, suppose Bob determines that his family will receive $15,000 in annual Social Security benefits. This leaves $28,000 of income needed. According to the capital retention approach, the amount of life insurance Bob should purchase equals the amount of capital needed to produce $28,000 of annual income. Again, assuming an interest rate of 7 percent, the amount of capital needed is $28,000 divided by 7 percent, or $400,000. The interest rate selected for the calculations should, in practice, be adjusted to reflect expected inflation.

INDIVIDUAL LIFE INSURANCE POLICIES

There are many different life insurance products. Yet they are all based upon one or two basic product models: term insurance and permanent life insurance. In this section, each of these major types is discussed.

TERM INSURANCE

term insurance - type of life insurance that provides temporary protection for a specified number of years

Term insurance represents over 38 percent of life insurance sold in the United States today. Term is an inexpensive and efficient method of meeting temporary insurance needs. A key feature of a term life policy is that it is payable only if the insured dies within the designated number of years, or term, of the contract. Term life policy's benefits are not payable in the event that the insured outlives the policy period.

264

Characteristics

Affordability. Term life, because it is temporary pure death protection, tends to be very affordable in the early years of the policy. However, price and risk are directly related. Premium rates on term insurance policies remain less expensive than rates on others in the market, but only because it provides few guarantees, ends after a certain time, and does not generate any type of savings element or cash value accumulation.

Maximum Coverage per Premium Dollar. Given a choice between a life insurance policy that provides death protection only and a policy that provides death protection plus a cash value accumulation, the one that provides only death protection should be less expensive. The greatest coverage per premium dollar is usually available through term insurance, where each dollar goes toward only death protection (and, of course, administrative expenses and a reasonable profit).

Fulfills Temporary Need. Insurance protection under term insurance is temporary. The amount of time the policy remains in effect depends upon the contract purchased. Available in today's marketplace are one-year, five-year, ten-year, and twenty-year policies. An insured may also declare a certain age that he wishes his policy to terminate, such as age 65 or 70. In any case, a temporary need is fulfilled under the term limits.

Ensures Insurability. Suppose that a person recognizes the needs to provide his family of four with a large amount of permanent insurance, but can presently afford only the premiums on term insurance. The vast majority of term policies are issued with a convertible feature, meaning they can be converted to permanent insurance at a later date without proof of insurability. As long as premiums are maintained, the purchase of basic term coverage can guarantee the future availability of permanent insurance. The convertibility feature is not offered in permanent policies; otherwise, terminally ill insureds would convert to less expensive term coverage.

Purposes

Term life insurance exists to *temporarily* indemnify against the loss of a valued person who provides income or financial security to dependents or others. Term insurance is appropriate for a person who has a temporary need for insurance, such as funding mortgage redemption or a child's college education. Because of its affordability, term is also useful for persons who have little disposable income to spend on life insurance, yet who need the most coverage available to fund their family obligations if they were to die early.

Various Types

Yearly Renewable Term. A yearly renewable term policy is purchased one year at a time; it is the least expensive term policy. If at the end of the contract year the policyowner wishes to continue coverage, he/she may do so by renewing the policy for as many successive one-year periods as desired (within the limits set forth in the contract).

An advantage of yearly renewable term is that no evidence of insurability is required at the time of renewal. One disadvantage is that premiums are reevaluated at the end of each annual term and will increase as the death rate increases. Because the rate of death increases at an increasing rate with age, the premiums for this type of policy may become prohibitively expensive as the insured ages. Exhibit 9.1 illustrates the comparison of level term insurance premiums with yearly renewable term premiums. Notice the exponential nature of the yearly renewable term premium reflecting the increased probability of mortality as people age.

EXHIBIT 9.1: RENEWABLE TERM PREMIUM AND PREMIUM FOR ORDINARY LIFE (ISSUED 25)

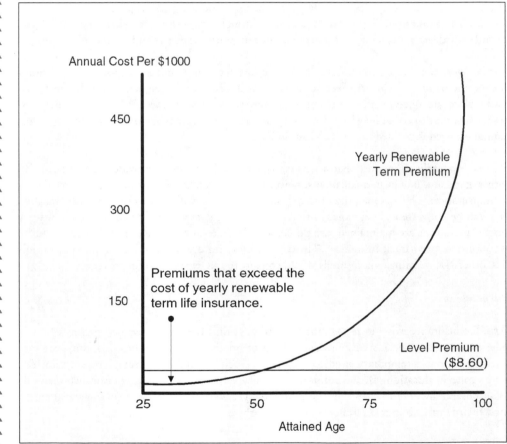

5-Year, 10-Year, 15-Year, and 20-Year Term (Level Premium). As human mortality is quite predictable, so is the calculation of insurance premiums representing mortality. An actuary can calculate the annual (or monthly) rate that should be charged for a five-year policy, ten-year policy, or any other policy of a particular length. The price for this coverage is level over the term of the contract. In earlier years, the premium is higher than it would be for a yearly-renewable term policy. This "overpayment" in early years funds the coverage for later ages when the price has risen to a level that would be prohibitively expensive had the insured purchased yearly-renewable term. Most of these policies are renewable for the same length of term, without proving insurability, until the insured reaches a particular age (typically 65 or 70).

Term-to-65/70. Term policies may also be purchased to last until the insured reaches a particular age. The age to which these policies remain in force is typically 65 to 70 years old. The older the insured is when the policy is purchased, the higher the premium will be, but it will then remain level until the insured reaches the contract expiration age. The premiums for this type of policy are again funded through overpayments in early years that offset an underpayment in later years.

Decreasing and Increasing Term. While most term policies have static face amounts, there are certain situations in which a variable face amount may be desirable. A decreasing term policy involves a gradual reduction in the face value of the contract while the premiums paid by the insured remain the same. Decreasing term policies are most commonly used to pay off a mortgage because the payoff will decline over time. An increasing term policy's face value increases as premiums remain level. Insureds often purchase such policies to hedge against inflation. Significant increases in insurance generally require meeting some insurability standard.

Reentry Term. Many insurers now offer a reentry feature on their term insurance. The insured is given a preferred rate at the beginning of the policy term. At regular intervals, the insured must pass medical examinations to continue paying the reduced rates. If the insured does not pass the medical exam, the policy remains in force, but the insured must then pay a different price for the policy. The rate schedules are provided in the policy, and there is a "guaranteed maximum" rate that the insured must pay if he no longer qualified for the preferred rates. These policies reward insureds that remain in good health, while maintaining the insurance coverage of those who, for whatever reason, no longer qualify as "preferred risks."

Optional Features

Renewability. Term policies can be renewed without proof of insurability if the insured has purchased a **guaranteed insurability option**. Relatively inexpensive, this option protects the insured in cases where disease or illness has left the insured uninsurable. At the expiration of the term policy, the insured may choose to renew the coverage without being subjected to the underwriting process.

guaranteed insurability option - if the insured has purchased this relatively inexpensive option, term policies can be renewed without proof of insurability

At each renewal, premiums increase in accordance with the insured's age. Of course, as age increases, so do the renewal premiums. Adverse selection results when older insureds know they are in poor health, so insurers generally allow renewals only until the insured reaches age 65. Older insureds who are in good health may decide to lapse term insurance, thereby leaving the insurer with a less desirable risk pool.

Convertibility. Most term policies provide a convertibility option, which gives the policyholder the right to exchange her current policy for a permanent policy without providing proof of insurability. To minimize adverse selection, many companies place time restrictions on when a policy may be converted.

There are two ways in which an insured may convert a term policy. Under the *attained age method,* the insured will date the permanent policy at the time of conversion and base the premium on the insured's age at that time. The *retroactive method* bases the new policy's premiums on the insured's age when the term policy was first issued. The premiums will be lower than those using the attained age method; however, to compensate for this, companies usually require a lump sum payment at the time of conversion.

Limitations

Cost Prohibitive at Older Ages. Perhaps the most notable limitation of term insurance is the increasing premiums on the basis of age. This makes term insurance impractical for many older people. Term insurance should never be viewed as a form of lifetime protection, because it generally may not be renewed after age 65 or 70.

No Savings Feature. A term insurance policy does not possess a tax-deferred cash value buildup or savings feature. Its primary function is to provide pure death protection. If one's goal is to accumulate wealth for retirement through an insurance policy, term life is inappropriate. Many financial plans include buying term insurance and investing the difference between permanent life insurance premiums and the term insurance premiums. The term insurance provides the immediate need for death protection, while the outside investments can build savings. It should be pointed out that most term insurance is lapsed due to living beyond the term or for failure to pay premiums. However, the same can be said for most property and liability insurance.

WHOLE LIFE INSURANCE

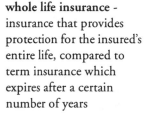

whole life insurance - insurance that provides protection for the insured's entire life, compared to term insurance which expires after a certain number of years

Whole life insurance provides protection for the insured's *entire life*, while term insurance expires after a certain number of years. In addition, whole life insurance generates a cash value that can be used for many things during the insured's lifetime.

Purposes

Provide Permanent Protection. Whole life insurance provides protection over the entire lifetime of the insured, regardless of the number of years premiums are paid. As long as the premiums are paid as agreed, the face value of a whole life policy will be paid upon the insured's death, no matter when it occurs. Life insurance mortality tables assume that everyone dies by age 100. Premiums are thus calculated in such a manner that the cash value of the policy will equal the face value of the policy when the insured reaches age 100. For this reason, insurers pay the face amount of the policy when the insured reaches 100. Thus, whole life is referred to as permanent insurance because as long as premiums are paid, the policy remains in force.

Cash Value Build-up. Unlike term insurance, which exists solely for the purpose of providing death protection, whole life policies may be purchased as a low-risk investment. In addition to providing death protection, they accumulate savings through cash value build-up. Cash values in whole life policies increase slowly during the first few years of most policies and then grow at an increasing rate throughout the life of the insured. Note, however, that there is no FDIC-type government insurance for the cash value build-up.

Traditional whole life insurance policies pay a very low rate of interest on the cash value accumulation. Typically, the most an insurer might pay is four to five percent. This rate of return is unattractive to many consumers, so traditional whole life should not be purchased solely for investment purposes. However, permanent insurance can be used as part of an overall investment asset allocation plan combined with a risk management plan. The insurance component will provide a death benefit and a low risk investment component of an overall plan.

Exhibit 9.2 illustrates the savings element of permanent life insurance. Notice that the original per thousand premium of $13.50 is substantially greater than the $1.95 per thousand mortality cost at the inception of the policy.

EXHIBIT 9.2: THE SAVINGS ELEMENT OF A LEVEL-PREMIUM, WHOLE LIFE INSURANCE POLICY

```
- - - Mortality Cost

─── Level Premium
    Whole Life

$13.50 ─────────────────────────

$1.95

        0        25
        Years Policy Is In Force

        30       55
        Age of the Insured
```

Characteristics

Level Premium. Unlike term life in which premiums increase with age, whole life policies are based on a level premium throughout the duration of the payment period. Whole life policies build money in the early years by prepaying premiums in the early years and investing the excess to pay premiums in the later years of the policies. The excess premiums in the beginning are kept in a fund called a legal reserve. Legal reserves cover the costs of providing lifetime protection to insureds.

Mortality Charge. All whole life policies include a **mortality charge**, which is the cost of paying death claims for those persons who die during the year. Few people die at younger ages, so the mortality charge is fairly low. As the insureds age, however, mortality increases and so does the mortality charge. Term insurance premiums also have a mortality charge, which represents the bulk of each term premium payment.

mortality charge - the cost of paying death claims for those persons who die during the year

Administrative Costs and Insurer Profit. As with all types of insurance, whole life (and term life) premiums must include compensation for the insurer. This compensation covers the insurer's operating expenses and profit.

Saving (cash value). Cash value is usually accumulated by periodic dividend or interest payments made towards the policy after it has been in force for a certain length of time. This premium component is not included in term life insurance premiums. At any time during the policy, the policyowner may withdraw the cash surrender value (which is less than or equal to the cash value, due to exit charge for adverse selection) and forfeit the death protection. In addition, policyowners may borrow out the cash value at a low interest rate, yet maintain their death protection. The option to withdraw the cash value makes whole life insurance a useful tool for both saving *and* protecting against dying too soon.

Various Types

Single Premium. When one lump sum payment is made at policy inception and no future premiums are due, the whole life policy is referred to as a single premium policy. For most people, single premium policies are usually not affordable or feasible. However, in the case that one needs to offset death taxes and estate settlement costs, the purchase of a single premium policy could prove beneficial. Or, when an unexpected windfall leaves a consumer with a large sum of cash to invest, the single premium policy is one investment option. Single premium life insurance is also used as a means to provide gifts to children.

Continuous Premium (Ordinary Life). In a continuous premium policy, premiums are paid regularly until either the date of death or age 100. The insured may choose whether to pay premiums monthly, quarterly, semiannually, or annually. Premiums are naturally higher when paid on a more frequent basis to offset the insurer's higher administrative costs. The continuous premium policy provides the maximum permanent death protection for the lowest possible premium, but consumers should be aware that those premiums must be paid continuously, even past retirement, until death.

Limited-Pay Policy. Limited-pay policy premiums are higher than continuous premiums, but lower than a single premium. The policyowner can specify that he only wants to pay premiums until age 65 or for a specific number of years. The insurer then calculates an actuarially fair rate that gives the insurer enough money over the payment period to fund coverage for the insured's entire life.

Those who anticipate a limited number of high-income years, during which they can best afford life insurance premium payments, often desire limited-pay policies. For example, a singer or an athlete may anticipate that they have only five to ten more years of a career left. They may wish to purchase a limited-pay policy of five or ten years so that at the end of the payment period, they have fully-funded their death protection.

universal life - insurance that allows the insured to buy death protection similar to that provided by term insurance, and then invest an additional amount with the insurer, similar to the savings element in whole life coverage

Universal Life. **Universal life** insurance allows the insured to buy death protection similar to that provided by term insurance and invest an additional amount with the insurer, similar to the savings element in whole life coverage. Additionally, the interest rate paid on universal life is generally variable and more competitive, especially in times of high interest rates, than that paid on traditional whole life policies.

The insurer sets a minimum initial premium payment that must be paid to cover mortality costs, administrative expenses, and insurer profit. After this premium payment is made, the insured is free to pay in an additional amount of money for investment in the cash value. At any given time, as long as there is enough money in the cash value account to fund the cost of the pure death protection, the insured does not have to pay any further premiums. If the cash value account builds to a high level in relation to the face amount of the policy, then the death benefit will increase accordingly. Universal life policies offer many variations and policy options in terms of death benefit arrangements and premium payments.

270

Variable Life. **Variable life** insurance is a form of whole life in which cash values are invested in the policyowner's choice of investments. Some common investment options include common stock funds, money market funds, bond funds, and mutual funds. The insurer charges a fixed premium in most cases and guarantees a minimum death benefit. Premiums minus expenses and mortality charges are deposited into the selected investment vehicles, and the policyowner bears all of the investment risk. If the investments provide favorable returns, the cash value will grow. If, however, the investments fail, the policyowner suffers the loss of cash value. The cash value of a variable life insurance policy is not guaranteed; all investment risk rests solely with the policyowner. The death benefit, however, is guaranteed, provided the policyowner pays the required premiums.

Variable Universal Life. A **variable universal life policy** is a combination of variable life and universal life. Its features include increasing or decreasing death benefits and flexibility of premium payments that mirror the universal life policy options. The cash value of a variable universal life policy is not guaranteed, but a minimum death benefit is guaranteed, and the policyowner chooses where the cash values will be invested, so in these respects it is similar to a variable life policy.

To sell life insurance requires a license from the state for the sale of life insurance products. Variable insurance and universal variable are both insurance and investments products. Therefore, to sell variable insurance products, the representative must be licensed in insurance and investments. Exhibit 9.3 compares the features of these permanent policies.

variable life - a form of whole life insurance in which cash values are invested in the policyowner's choice of investments

variable universal life - a combination of variable life and universal life whose features include increasing or decreasing death benefits and flexibility of premium payments that mirror the universal life policy options, and a guaranteed minimum death benefit and policyowner chosen investments, similar to a variable life policy

EXHIBIT 9.3: MATRIX COMPARISON OF LIFE INSURANCE FEATURES

	Whole Life	Universal Life	Variable Life	Variable Universal Life
Premium Amount	Fixed	Variable, subject to a required minimum	Fixed	Variable, subject to a required minimum
Death Benefit	Fixed	May increase above initial face amount, depending on cash value accumulation	Has a guaranteed minimum, but can increase if investment experience on cash value is good	Has a guaranteed minimum, but can increase if investment experience on cash value is good
Policyowner's Control Over Cash Value Investments	None	None	Complete	Complete
Rate of Return on Cash Value Investment	Fixed rate	Minimum guaranteed rate, but may be higher depending on interest rates	No minimum guarantee, but positive investment experience can yield very high returns	No minimum guarantee, but positive investment experience can yield very high returns

Interest-Sensitive. Often referred to as current assumption whole life insurance (CAWL), interest-sensitive whole life is somewhat similar to universal life. The insurer agrees to share its investment experience and profits with the policyowner. The interest rate paid on the cash values fluctuates with the experience of the insurer, but is always at least a guaranteed minimum of 4 percent or 5 percent.

Modified Life. Under modified whole life insurance, premiums are lower for the first few years after policy inception, typically three to five years. The difference between what would have been the normal premium and the lowered premium is then redistributed throughout the rest of the premium payments after the three to five year term ends. Modified life is merely traditional whole life insurance with a unique premium payment arrangement offered to the policyowner who currently has a problem paying for the desired amount of insurance, but who expects later to be able to afford a higher premium.

Limitations to Permanent Insurance

Inadequate Coverage. The major limitation of ordinary life insurance is that some people will remain underinsured after a policy is purchased because of the large premiums that make it unaffordable. Because of the savings feature attached to whole life, many consumers are more attracted to it than term life. However, the problem of inadequate coverage exists when people can afford only a certain amount of whole life when they really need to purchase more to cover their families needs. In this case, purchasing the least expensive option, term life, with the greater amount of coverage, may be the better option.

Slow Cash Value Growth. Cash values are small in the early years of a whole life policy. They gradually increase over the duration of the policy; however, the process is slow. This is especially true if the interest rate paid on the cash value is 4 percent or less.

Surrender Charges. Most insurers heavily penalize the policyowner for not renewing the whole life policy, especially during the first few years of the policy. This penalty is administered through surrender charges, which are deductions from the cash value. As the insurer's major expenses associated with policy issuance (including underwriting costs and agent commissions) are incurred up front, the insurer imposes surrender charges so that it can recoup some of its costs if the policy lapses.

GROUP LIFE INSURANCE

About 44 percent of all life insurance in the United States today is sold on a group basis under an employee benefit plan. Group life insurance consists of a large group of insureds covered by a single master contract. The employer holds the master contract and is responsible for making premium payments to the insurer. The employer can fund premium payments in whole or in part and, in many cases, the employee pays no portion of the premium at all. Where employees are expected to pay some or all of the cost of the life insurance, the employer generally collects the employee contributions through payroll deduction.

Group insurance is typically cheaper than individual policy insurance because of the savings the insurer realizes in terms of lower administrative expenses and underwriting costs. Individual underwriting is not required of group insurance participants, so no evidence of insurability is required and no medical examinations are necessary. The employer may set up its requirements for eligibility. Eligibility requirements for a typical plan might include that participating employees be full-time workers and satisfy a minimum probationary period.

GROUP TERM

Group term insurance is the most common form of group insurance selected by employers. Group term offers the same benefits as an individual term insurance policy. Group term premiums, like those of individual term policies, increase at an increasing rate with age. If the employer provides the group term insurance, the insured may receive up to $50,000 of group term without having taxable income on the contributions by the employer. Premiums paid by the employee in a contributory plan typically come from after-tax dollars because life insurance is not considered a tax-deductible expense for individuals. The actual premiums paid by the employer for group term insurance are tax-deductible to the employer as a business expense.

The amount of coverage provided by an employer through a group term plan must be determined by some formula that precludes adverse selection on the part of employees. So, most employers provide employees with either a flat amount of coverage, such as $25,000, or they provide coverage equal to one or more times the employee's annual salary. In some cases employees are then allowed to purchase additional amounts of coverage in pre-specified multiple amounts. The insurer may require proof of insurability for these optional higher coverage amounts.

GROUP WHOLE LIFE INSURANCE

Group whole life insurance allows the insured to gain coverage for basic death benefits through term insurance, as well as to accumulate a level of savings for retirement through a cash value fund. Group whole life insurance is not a frequently chosen employee benefit because it does not have the tax advantages that group term life insurance offers. Generally, the employee must report the premiums paid by the employer for a group whole life policy as taxable income.

Some employers are now offering group universal life plans that serve as optional supplements to the more traditional group term plans. Employees pay the entire cost of the coverage, but the premiums are paid through payroll deductions, so there is a slight saving in administrative expenses for the insurer. These savings are then passed on to employees in the form of lower premiums. Most plans allow the employee to purchase coverage (up to a specified maximum face value) without proving insurability.

CONVERSION

A covered employee typically has the right to convert a group term policy, upon termination from the company, to a regular cash value policy at a rate that is commensurate with his attained age. The insurer grants a 31-day **grace period** after an employee withdraws from the group in which basic death benefits remain in effect. The conversion privilege is advantageous to the insured because no evidence of insurability is necessary upon conversion.

grace period - period of time during which a policyowner may convert a group term policy, upon termination from a company, to a regular cash value policy at a rate that is commensurate with his or her attained age without losing coverage

COVERAGE FOR RETIREES

Many employers make group term life insurance benefits available to their employees after retirement. There are three main forms of coverage provided:

1. Continuation of a portion of the policy.
2. Retired lives reserves.
3. Conversion to cash value life insurance.

The employer may choose to offer the retiree a flat dollar amount of coverage for basic final medical bills, funeral, and burial expenses. The amount offered represents a small portion of the pre-retirement benefits offered. This portion generally ranges anywhere from 25 percent to 50 percent of original coverage.

A retired lives reserve can be set up to provide for the continuance of life insurance beyond retirement. The retired lives reserve is a combination of annually renewable term insurance and an accumulated reserves fund used to pay the premiums on the term insurance policy. This form of post-retirement coverage allows the insured to enjoy the same amount of coverage as he/she previously held, and the employer may still reap tax benefits for the cost of the coverage.

As discussed earlier, cash value life insurance allows for the insured to pre-fund the higher rate of mortality costs in retirement years. The retiring employee simply converts the term insurance to a permanent form of coverage, as would be done with an individual term policy. The cost of conversion, however, may be prohibitively expensive.

LIFE ANNUITY CONTRACTS

WHAT IS AN ANNUITY?

annuity - periodic payment to an individual that continues for a fixed period or for the duration of a designated life or lives

A life annuity is not life insurance, but is sold by life insurance companies. The **annuity** contract provides protection against outliving assets by providing a series of periodic payments, known as "rent," to the annuitant. Payments will be made as long as the annuitant lives. Annuities are commonly used to fund retirement benefits. For example, a retiree might retire with $1 million in retirement funds. Instead of trying to budget the money over the retirement years, the retiree can purchase a life annuity that will guarantee a steady income until death.

Similar to life insurance benefits, annuity payments are based on the pooling of the risk and life expectancy of a group. As some annuitants live to be 85 or 90, others die at much younger ages. Thus, some persons draw out more money than others do, and the risk of living "too long" is thus shared among the group members. The remaining principal from those who die at younger ages is applied to a fund, which is used by the group to pay those who survive beyond their life expectancies. Annuity payments are comprised of the combination of premium payments, interest earnings, and unliquidated principal of annuitants who die early.

TYPES OF ANNUITIES

Immediate vs. Deferred

The insured has the option of having annuity payments made monthly, quarterly, semiannually, or annually. In addition, the insured may also specify whether he would like his payments to be immediate or deferred. An immediate annuity is one whose first payment is due one payment interval from its purchase date. Immediate annuities are purchased with one single lump sum premium.

A deferred annuity provides income at some date in the future. The most popular form of a deferred annuity is a retirement annuity in which monetary value accumulates for a number of years and is paid in installments when the insured reaches retirement. Deferred annuities are purchased with either a single premium or periodic level premiums.

Flexible-Premium vs. Single-Premium

A flexible premium annuity allows the insured the option to vary premium deposits. The amount of retirement income will relate directly to the accumulated sum in the annuity when it becomes due. Under a flexible-premium plan, the insured spreads payments out over a designated period of time by paying periodic premiums.

An annuity purchased with a single lump sum is known as a single premium annuity. Proceeds from life insurance policies can be used easily to purchase single premium annuities at special rates under life income settlement options.

TIMING OF ANNUITY PAYMENTS

Pure Life Annuity

Often referred to as a straight-life annuity, a pure life annuity provides a lifetime income to the annuitant, whether he lives 6 months or 60 years after payments begin. After the annuitant dies, no further payments are made. For a given purchase price, the highest amount of lifetime income per dollar spent is earned through the pure life annuity.

For many people, this form of annuity is objectionable because it is possible to purchase a pure life annuity, receive one rent payment, and then die. As there is no guaranteed minimum number of payments the insurer must make, the dependents of the annuitant receive nothing from the contract once the annuitant has died. For this reason, the pure life annuity is ideal for the person who needs maximum income spread out over his lifetime and has no living dependents to whom he wishes to leave assets.

Life Annuity with Guaranteed Minimum Payments

A life annuity with guaranteed minimum payments ensures that the annuitant either receives a minimum number of payments or will have lifetime income, whichever is greater. Two common guarantee options are the ten-year period certain and the twenty-year period certain. If the annuitant dies before the guarantee period, the named beneficiary receives the remaining guaranteed payments. If the annuitant outlives the guarantee period, payments continue until death.

Installment Refund Annuity

This annuity is similar to the one described previously, except the insurer promises to continue periodic payments after the annuitant has died until the sum of all annuity rent payments equals the purchase price of the annuity.

Joint and Survivor Annuity

A **joint and survivor annuity** is based on the lives of two or more annuitants, usually husband and wife. Annuity payments are made until the last annuitant dies. A true joint and survivor annuity pays the full amount of monthly rent to both parties together and continues the same rent payment for the survivor. Some persons, however, choose a joint and survivor annuity that pays the survivor only a portion of the rent that was paid on both lives. A common amount might be 75 percent, in which case the annuity would be called a joint and 75 percent survivor annuity. Joint and last survivor is the most popular form of the multi-life annuity today. Premiums are higher than those charged for single life annuities, because the insurer guarantees payment for what is almost always a longer time period.

SELECTING A LIFE INSURANCE COMPANY

Since life insurance contracts are expected to last for many years, plus provide financial security for their owners, selecting a reliable life insurance company is essential. Of critical importance is the long-term financial stability of an insurance company. The policyowner needs to be concerned with financial stability for obvious investment reasons, and the financial planner should be concerned as a professional. Recommending a life insurance product that is ultimately useless because of insurer insolvency could result in an errors-and-omissions lawsuit filed by an injured policyholder.

Presently there are five private rating agencies that evaluate the financial condition of insurers and make their ratings available to the public. These agencies are A.M. Best's, Fitch, Moody's, Standard & Poor, and Weiss. Each agency has its own scale for evaluating insurers. Exhibit 9.4 provides the highest three ratings and the lowest three ratings for each agency.

When purchasing life insurance and annuity products, the consumer ideally will use a company that has received a top-tier rating from all five of the agencies, but at a minimum it is critical that the insurer have top-tier ratings from *at least two* agencies. For safety's sake, any company that has received a low-tier rating from any of the agencies probably should be avoided.

joint and survivor annuity - an annuity based on the lives of two or more annuitants, usually husband and wife. Annuity payments are made until the last annuitant dies

EXHIBIT 9.4: INSURER RATING AGENCIES' TOP AND BOTTOM-TIER FINANCIAL RATINGS

	A.M. Best's	Fitch	Moody's	Standard & Poor	Weiss
Highest Three Ratings	A++	AAA	Aaa	AAA	A+
	A+	AA+	Aa1	AA+	A
	A	AA	Aa2	AA	A-
Lowest Three Ratings	D	B	B3	B	E
	E	B-	Caa	B-	E-
	F	CCC	Ca	CCC	F

WHY PURCHASE HEALTH INSURANCE?

Prudent financial planning includes preparation for the financial impact of a serious injury or illness. Not only may medical bills be incurred, but there might also be a loss of income if the ill or injured person is unable to continue working. Various forms of health insurance can compensate for these losses.

TO PAY MEDICAL BILLS

Persons not covered under a social insurance program, such as Medicare or Medicaid, or who do not have some form of privately funded health insurance, should consider purchasing at least some minimum level of medical expense coverage. The probability of needing medical attention during one's life is very high. However, the severity of the illness and the ultimate cost of treatment are unknown. While treating the flu is generally affordable for most people, obtaining a heart or liver transplant is not.

TO REPLACE LOST INCOME

Many workers have some type of paid sick leave benefit offered by their employers. In the majority of cases, this benefit may prevent an ill worker from suffering a financial hardship. There are, however, very severe injuries and illness that can leave a worker unable to work for months, years, or at all. Many employee benefit plans do not provide paid sick leave for such long absences. An often-overlooked exposure in this area is the self-employed professional such as a doctor or an attorney. When such professionals are unable to work, they may have no employer-provided benefits to replace lost income. Disability income insurance is a form of health coverage that replaces a portion of a disabled person's regular income while they are unable to work.

INDIVIDUAL HEALTH INSURANCE COVERAGES

PURPOSE

Individual health insurance coverages allow the individual to customize his or her own insurance package. Provided the insured has no health problems that limit insurability, health insurers typically allow insureds to choose from a wide array of coverages to meet individual needs. At the same time, there exists a direct relationship between the amount of coverage desired and the price of the premium. Naturally, the more coverages one chooses, the higher the premium.

COST CONCERNS

Most people who have health insurance coverages today obtain them through either a group plan or a social insurance program. Individual health coverages are not as popular as group coverages, because the insured must pay the full cost of the coverage with *after-tax* dollars and individual health coverages are typically not as generous as those offered through group plans.

ELIGIBILITY

To obtain individual health insurance coverage, proof of insurability must be provided to the insurer. Proof of insurability is not required for group plans. The completion of a fairly lengthy application is required and the insured must usually submit to some form of medical examination. The underwriter may also wish to see copies of previous medical records before making a coverage decision.

MEDICAL EXPENSE INSURANCE

Basic Medical Insurance Coverages

There are three coverages an insured can purchase to cover a variety of medical expenses: hospital expense insurance, surgical expense insurance, and physician's expense insurance.

Hospital Expense Insurance. Hospital expense insurance provides payment for expenses incurred by the insured while in the hospital. Coverage under hospital expense insurance includes a daily hospital benefit and a miscellaneous expense benefit. The daily hospital benefit pays a specified amount for room and board charges incurred during each day the insured is hospitalized. This benefit may be paid on a reimbursement basis, subject to a maximum daily limit, or it may be a flat amount per day. These plans also have a maximum number of days covered, such as 90 or 180.

A lump sum benefit may be paid if the patient incurs miscellaneous expenses for items such as X-rays, medications, surgical supplies, and use of the operating room. The miscellaneous expense benefit will, of course, be subject to a maximum dollar amount.

Caution must be exercised in purchasing this type of coverage because many expensive procedures are now performed outside of a hospital. Also, physician and surgeon's fees are billed separately from hospital services, so hospital expense coverage does not provide for payment of those

278

fees. Purchasing only hospital expense coverage is not sufficient to meet the needs of most individuals.

Surgical Expense Insurance. Surgical expense insurance may be added to a hospital expense insurance policy to provide for the payment of the surgeon's fees, even when surgery is not performed in a hospital. Insurers typically base maximum benefits payable on a generic list of surgical procedures and their estimated costs, but some other benefit determination formula may be used.

Physician's Expense Insurance. This coverage pays for fees charged by physicians who provide the insured with nonsurgical care. Treatment can be administered in the doctor's office, the patient's home, or the hospital. Again, maximum coverage limits will be specified.

Limitations. Basic medical coverages set rigid limits on the amount payable for any one event. The maximum benefit provided for a single illness or injury may not be enough to pay the actual expenses incurred. While having these coverages is better than having no coverage at all, insureds must be aware that benefit levels are restricted.

MAJOR MEDICAL INSURANCE

Characteristics

Major medical insurance is designed to provide broad coverage of all reasonable and necessary expenses associated with an illness or injury, whether incurred at a doctor's office, a hospital, or the insured's home. Some major medical policies are "stand-alone" coverages that pay for a wide range of medical services; others are written in conjunction with a basic medical plan to provide coverage in excess of that provided by the basic coverages. Many consumers are attracted to major medical insurance because it generally covers a wide range of expenses including hospitalization charges, physician and surgeon's fees, nursing care, prescription drugs, wheelchairs and other medical supplies. High limits of coverage are usually provided, such as a $1 million lifetime maximum.

Major medical policies have few exclusions. Routine eye exams and dental care typically are not covered, nor are self-inflicted injuries, injuries sustained in war, and elective cosmetic procedures.

Most major medical policies have a deductible of $500 or less. The deductible may apply per illness, per person per year, or per family per year. After the deductible has been met, the insurer typically pays some percentage of all remaining expenses that are usual and customary. Coinsurance is the division of expenses between the insured and the insurer in health insurance, with a common amount being 80 percent/20 percent. This clause requires the insurer to pay 80 percent of medical bills above the deductible and the insured to pay the remaining 20 percent.

After a deductible is met, the insured usually has a maximum time in which to incur expenses associated with one illness or injury. The period of time major medical benefits will be paid after the deductible is fulfilled is referred to as the benefit period. When the benefit period expires, the insured must then satisfy another deductible to be eligible for benefits again.

Limitations. In addition to a lifetime maximum benefit limit, many policies contain internal coverage limits, such as a maximum allowable daily charge for hospitalization, or perhaps a

major medical insurance - health insurance that provides broad coverage of all reasonable and necessary expenses associated with an illness or injury, whether incurred at a doctor's office, a hospital, or the insured's home

$25,000 lifetime maximum on mental health benefits. While these limits may satisfy the needs of most insureds, some may find them too prohibitive.

Another problem with major medical insurance is the insurer's agreement to pay only 80 percent (or whatever the designated coinsurance percentage is) of *usual and customary* medical expenses. If the insurer determines that a particular surgical procedure should cost $10,000, it will pay only $8,000 of that amount, even if the surgeon's charges are $13,000 or $14,000.

Finally, unless the policy provides for some maximum out-of-pocket limit on the insured's portion of the coinsurance, a serious illness can still be financially devastating to the insured. Considering that all treatment associated with a heart transplant can easily cost $1 million, it is easy to see that most insureds could not afford their 20 percent (or even 10 percent) of that amount.

EXAMPLE Assume that Brenda has a major medical insurance policy with a $500 annual aggregate deductible, a 90 percent/10 percent cost sharing provision, and a $2,000 out-of-pocket cap (also referred to as a "stop loss provision.") If Brenda has surgery that costs $8,000, her plan will require her to pay $500, and then 10 percent of the remaining $7,500 in expenses, or $750. So, Brenda's total out-of-pocket expense for the surgery will be $1,250. If later the same year, she has another illness that results in $10,000 of covered medical expenses, she will have to pay $750 (and not $1,000) because once she has spent $2,000 of her own money during the year, the insurer will pay 100 percent of all remaining covered expenses.

DISABILITY INCOME INSURANCE

Purpose

disability income insurance - a type of insurance that provides a regular income while the insured is unable to work because of illness or injury

Disability income insurance provides replacement income while the insured is unable to work because of illness or injury. Premiums for this coverage are a function of the insured's health, occupation, gender, age, and the level of income benefits provided by the policy. Most insureds purchase either a flat dollar amount of coverage, such as $2,000 per month, or coverage that replaces some portion of pre-disability earnings (such as 60 to 80 percent).

To qualify for disability income, one must become totally disabled while the policy is in force and remain so until the elimination (exclusion) period has ended. Once these qualifications are met, monthly indemnity will be made payable at the end of each month of disability.

Definitions of Disability

A key feature of disability income insurance is that it specifies what constitutes a "disability" for the purposes of receiving policy benefits. Unless the insured person's condition complies with the disability definition in the policy, the insurer does not pay income benefits. Different types of disability definitions exist. The most common ones are "any occupation," "own occupation," and a combination of the two.

It is important to realize that Social Security may also provide disability benefits to a disabled person; however, the Social Security definition of disability is much more restrictive than most definitions used in private disability income insurance. The Social Security program requires the disabled person to wait five months before receiving benefits. The disabled person also must prove that he cannot engage in any occupation, and that the disability is expected to last at least twelve months, or end in death.

When purchasing individual disability income coverages, the client should determine if coverage "integrates" with Social Security disability coverages. A policy that integrates with Social Security will reduce payable benefits by the amount of Social Security the disabled person is eligible to receive. This type of coverage will be cheaper than a similar policy that does not integrate with Social Security, because the insurer expects to pay out lower benefits if the insured is disabled for a lengthy period of time.

"Any Occupation." A person insured under the any occupation clause is considered totally disabled if he or she cannot perform the duties of *any* occupation. The courts have interpreted this clause to mean any occupation for which the insured is suited for by education, experience and training. Thus, a disabled brain surgeon can draw benefits from the policy even if he is still able to work at a fast food restaurant. But, if the surgeon is able to teach, lecture, or do research related to his field of expertise, then the insurer would likely not consider him disabled.

"Own Occupation." The own occupation definition is much more liberal than the any occupation definition. It states that the insured must be able to perform each and every duty of his *own* occupation. This means that a surgeon who cannot perform surgery due to a broken hand is considered totally disabled even if he moves to a hospital administration position. Because he cannot perform all of the duties of his chosen profession, he is considered totally disabled.

Split Definition. Many disability income insurance policies today include a combination of the any and own occupation clauses. Typically, the own occupation definition of disability will apply only during the first one-to-five years after an illness or injury. After that, the any occupation definition applies.

Characteristics

Elimination Period. To reduce unnecessary small claims and moral hazards, an elimination or waiting period of one month to one year from the date of disability is included in a disability income policy. During this waiting period, disability income benefits are not being paid.

Partial Disability. Many policies include coverage for partial disability, defined as the inability to perform at least one important duty of the insured's normal occupation. The partial disability provision provides payments that are less than those paid for total disability, but these benefits usually last for only a short time (such as six months). By covering partial disability in this manner, the insurer gives the insured some incentive to return to work sooner than she otherwise might.

Waiver of Premium. Premiums are waived under a disability income policy during the period of total disability that is the shorter of 90 days or the elimination period. As soon as the insured recovers from his disability, he is once again held responsible for premium payments. However, as long as the insured remains disabled, his premiums are waived.

Cost of Living Rider. The cost of living rider preserves the purchasing power of the insured's disability income benefits. Disability insurance claims often result in benefit payments that last for a number of years. This rider protects benefits from the effects of inflation. A cost of living adjustment is made for each year of benefits paid to the insured. Adjustments are computed by using the same rate of change as, say, the Consumer Price Index. The rate of change is limited to a specific rate of inflation, usually between 5 percent-10 percent compounded annually.

Taxation of Benefits

Individual disability income insurance premiums are generally not tax deductible by the insured and, as a result, benefit payments received during a period of disability are not subject to income taxation. If before-tax dollars fund the premium, benefits will be subject to income taxation. If the premiums are paid by an employer (group plan), the benefits are includible in the taxable income as "in lieu of wages."

Integration of Benefits

Some policies integrate benefits with Social Security or other sources of disability income. The insured may have a $2,000 monthly disability benefit provided by the policy, but if she is also eligible for a $1,200 monthly Social Security disability benefit, the individual policy might pay only $800 per month. When shopping for an individual disability income policy, the insured should be aware that some policies contain such integration provisions.

Termination of Benefits

Benefit payments cease at either the end of the benefit period or the date one is no longer disabled whichever occurs first.

Residual Benefits

A disability policy can provide for residual benefits. The residual benefits provision will supplement the income, assuming the insured has returned to work at a lesser income.

PORTABILITY OF GROUP PLANS

In 1997, President Clinton signed into law the *Health Insurance Portability and Accountability Act (HIPAA)*. This law eliminates the previously detrimental effects of changing jobs and starting a new health plan with a new pre-existing exclusions clause. For example, suppose John Dear worked at BigGuy Industries for 10 years and was covered under their group health plan. John then took a job at LittleGuy Consolidated. Prior to the passage of HIPAA, John would have to satisfy a new pre-existing conditions exclusion period (usually at least 6 months and sometimes as long as 18 or 24 months) before benefits would be payable under LittleGuy's health plan. So, if John had some type of serious medical condition, he would probably be unable to change jobs.

The HIPAA guarantees that persons who change jobs do not suffer such penalties. The HIPAA requires that employers give departing employees a certificate of creditable coverage to take to their next employer. This certificate shows how many months the employee was covered by the employer's group plan. When the employee enrolls in a new group plan, both of the following rules apply:

▲ Pre-existing conditions can be excluded for a maximum of 12 months.
▲ The 12-month pre-existing conditions exclusion under the new plan must be reduced for every month of coverage the employee had under a previous plan.

A pre-existing condition is defined as any medical condition that was treated or diagnosed within six months prior to enrolling in the new group plan.

The HIPAA would thus require that LittleGuy ignore the pre-existing conditions exclusion in John's case, since he already has creditable coverage of 10 years in a previous employer's plan. Had John only worked for BigGuy for 8 months, and been a participant in the BigGuy plan for 7 months, LittleGuy would have to give him 7 months of credit on its pre-existing conditions exclusion. So, John's illness would be excluded, but only for five months.

LONG-TERM CARE INSURANCE

An elderly person might be able to live alone, but may need assistance once each day with dressing and bathing. Medical expense policies (including Medicare coverage provided through the federal government) do not cover these types of expenses, nor do they pay for stays in extended care facilities such as nursing homes. **Long-term care insurance** provides coverage for nursing home stays and other types of routine care that are not covered by health insurance.

The premiums charged for long-term care coverage depend on the extent of benefits provided. There are five levels of coverage: skilled nursing care, intermediate nursing care, custodial care, home health care, and adult day care.

long-term care insurance - provides coverage for nursing home stays and other types of routine care that are not covered by health insurance. There are five levels of coverage: skilled nursing care, intermediate nursing care, custodial care, home health care, and adult day care

Skilled nursing care is the highest level of medical care and is what traditional nursing homes provide. Daily nursing care is provided, along with rehabilitation services, and the patient's care is ordered and monitored by a physician. Intermediate nursing care is similar to skilled nursing care, except care is provided occasionally rather than on a daily basis. Again, a physician must order this type of treatment.

Custodial care provides assistance with regular tasks of daily life, such as, eating, dressing, bathing, and taking medications. These services can normally be provided by non-medical personnel and do not have to be ordered or supervised by a physician.

Home health care allows the patient to remain at home and receive part-time skilled nursing care, rehabilitative therapy, and other necessary assistance. Depending upon the level of treatment needed, these services may be provided by a skilled professional or a homemaker.

Finally, adult day care is provided for persons who need assistance and supervision during the day, but whose spouse or other family members must work. The purpose of adult day care is quite similar to that of infant and child day care--to allow family members living with a person who cannot take care of herself to maintain their careers.

Most long-term care policies provide at least skilled and intermediate nursing care, plus custodial care. Some policies also cover home health care and adult day care. Most of the same features that apply to health insurance policies are found in a long-term care policy, including waiver of premium, elimination periods, and benefit periods.

The need for long-term care insurance is often overlooked in the financial planning process. When an individual requires long-term care that health insurance will not pay for, assets may be quickly depleted paying for such care. In extreme cases, some people ultimately liquidate all assets so they can qualify for long-term care benefits through the Medicaid (welfare) insurance program. As many long-term care facilities are not Medicaid providers, the insured's choice of care facilities may be severely restricted under these impoverished circumstances.

GROUP HEALTH INSURANCE

Over 90 percent of all medical expense insurance coverage sold today is in the form of a group policy. By pooling together of a large number of employees, the administrative costs of providing coverage are lowered and adverse selection is usually reduced. As a result, more features and benefits are usually provided through a group health insurance plan.

ELIGIBILITY

To be eligible for group health care coverage, one must be a member of a group that has come together for some purpose other than to purchase insurance. Some examples of eligible groups are: debtor-creditor groups, labor union groups, multiple-employer trusts, trade and professional associations, and any single employer group. Most eligible groups require that their participants:

▲ Be a full time employee (or a qualifying member) of the group.
▲ Satisfy a probationary period.
▲ Be actively at work the day coverage begins.

CHARACTERISTICS

Group underwriting procedures are different from those for individual health coverages. Instead of looking at each insured on an individual basis, the underwriter looks at the overall composition of the insured group. All employees in the group are automatically eligible for coverage under the group contract. The insurer clearly saves a great deal of money by not performing medical examinations and not underwriting each covered individual.

The employer holds the master contract and employees are given individual coverage certificates. The employer generally pays most, or all, of the premium, which further prevents adverse selection. The employer is responsible for enrolling new employees and collecting any premiums due from employees. The insurer thus saves a great deal on administrative expenses and those savings are passed on to the employer and/or employees in the form of lower premiums.

VARIOUS TYPES

Basic and Major Medical

Group basic medical insurance provides coverage for hospital, surgical, and physician's visits expense benefits that are very similar to those discussed previously under Individual Health Coverages. Basic medical plans have low maximum limits on coverage and are often used in conjunction with major medical plans.

Group major medical expense coverage is also very similar to individual major medical coverage. The two main types of group major medical plan are supplemental and comprehensive. Group supplemental plans are often attached to basic medical expense coverages. This allows the employer to use more than one provider for coverage, offer first dollar coverage, or use different contribution rates for basic and supplemental coverages.

Comprehensive major medical is a stand-alone coverage that provides for a broad range of medical services and has high limits of coverage. Deductibles are usually low and employees pay some percentage of all medical expenses above the deductible, subject to some maximum out-of-pocket dollar limit. As with individual plans, these group major medical plans cover all necessary medical expenses unless they are specifically excluded in the contract. Recently, coverages under these plans have expanded to pay for items such as extended care facilities, home health care centers, hospice care, ambulatory care, birthing centers, diagnostic x-ray and laboratory services, radiation therapy, supplemental accident benefits, prescription drugs, and vision care.

EXAMPLE

As an illustration of a typical group plan, assume that Jerry's employer offers him comprehensive group major medical coverage. The policy might have a $250 per person annual deductible and after that pay 80 percent of all covered charges. The policy might further limit Jerry's out-of-pocket expenses to $1,000 per year (including the deductible). After Jerry has spent $1,000 of his own money, the insurer will then pay 100 percent of covered medical expenses up to the maximum benefit stated in the contract, frequently $1,000,000 or more.

If Jerry is involved in a boating accident and incurs $1,250 of medical expenses, he must pay the first $250 of these covered expenses. Then, the insurer will pay 80 percent of the remaining $1,000, or $800, and Jerry will pay $200. If two months later, Jerry suffers another injury, he does not have to pay the $250 deductible again because he has a "per person per year" deductible. He only has to pay 20 percent of his medical expenses. Once he has paid $1,000 out of his pocket for the entire year (including the deductible), his insurer will begin paying 100 percent of all covered expenses.

Dental and Vision

Typical medical health insurance plans do not provide coverage for dental or optical care. However, most companies today offer supplemental plans for vision and dental coverage. Preventive care is usually encouraged under these plans, so routine check-ups are often covered. Employee benefit consultants see these types of coverages as positive benefits, meaning there is no need to experience death or illness to take advantage of them. They are thus quite popular with employees, even when the employees must pay 100 percent of the cost of coverage. These are the types of coverage where the risk of adverse selection is so high that benefits are quite limited and premiums frequently adjusted.

Disability Income

Group disability income insurance is structured in much the same fashion as individual disability income coverage. Under a group disability income plan, however, payments are based on the disability being either long-term or short-term. Generally, short-term disability payments are made from either the first day of injury resulting from an accident or the eighth day of disability resulting from sickness. Benefits are payable on a weekly basis for up to 13, 26, or 52 weeks. Long-term disability coverage will pay when short-term benefits expire or when the insured has satisfied the required long- term elimination period. Long-term disability benefits under a group plan are usually paid until the disability ends or until the insured reaches age 65, whichever occurs first. It is always advisable, however, to check the term of benefits, since they may not be as long as the remaining work life expectancy.

Managed Care

The goal of managed care techniques is to reduce the overall costs of providing health coverage, while simultaneously ensuring the quality of medical services delivered. Much variation exists among managed care plans, but most plans will, at a minimum, arrange for the delivery of medical and health services, review the quality and appropriateness of services rendered, and reimburse the providers who deliver services to plan participants.

The consumer must join a plan and agree to its contractual terms. The consumer is then able to obtain health care with a small co-payment or other deductible. The managed care plan assembles a network of doctors and other health care providers who agree to provide services to plan participants. The health care providers are under contract with the plan and must agree to abide by the plan's terms and conditions, plus agree to accept whatever compensation the plan allows without penalizing the patient.

When the need for care arises, the consumer will access the plan through a primary care physician who either provides treatment or refers the patient to a medical specialist. Each doctor col-

286

SECTION THREE: INSURANCE PLANNING

lects the required co-payment from the patient and then bills the managed care plan for other charges allowed by the plan.

EXAMPLE

Assume that Blue Hope Managed Care Plan provides coverage to Bob. Bob goes to his primary care physician (PCP) and asks her to look at a cyst on his arm. The PCP determines that the cyst is severe enough to use the services of a surgeon, so she refers Bob to one of the plan's surgeons. When the surgeon removes the cyst, he charges Bob the plan's required co-pay of $20. His usual fee for that type of surgery is $1,000, so he bills Blue Hope for the remaining $980. If Blue Hope allows the surgeon only $500 for the procedure (it will pay $480, because Bob has already paid $20), the surgeon may not then go back to Bob and ask him to pay the remaining $500.

It is important to clarify the major differences between a managed care plan and an indemnity plan. The major medical coverages discussed previously are examples of indemnity plans. An indemnity plan agrees to pay a certain percentage of covered medical expenses the insured person incurs, while a managed care plan agrees to provide needed medical services. There is no contractual arrangement between the major medical insurer and the doctor (or other service provider). A managed care plan, however, contracts with doctors and hospitals and other health care providers *and* it contracts with persons who wish to receive health care services.

HMOs. As a direct result of the HMO Act of 1973, **Health Maintenance Organizations (HMOs)** have flourished in the United States. All HMOs share common goals of comprehensive care, delivery of services, and cost control. An HMO assumes the responsibility and risk of providing a broad range of services to its members, including preventive medical services such as check-ups and mammograms, in exchange for a fixed monthly or annual enrollment fee. HMOs usually allow their members very little choice of service providers. The patient must generally use a contract provider or no benefits are paid. A $10 to $15 co-payment must usually be paid by the insured for each office visit.

health maintenance organization (HMO) - organized system of health care that provides comprehensive health services to its members for a fixed prepaid fee

Primary care doctors are either salaried employees of the HMO, or they are in private practice and receive a monthly fee ("capitation payment") for each patient they agree to treat, whether the patient receives care or not. Specialists may also be salaried employees or they may be in private practice and receive fees for only the services they provide.

PPOs. A **Preferred Provider Organization (PPO)** is merely a contractual arrangement between the insured, the insurer, and the health care provider that allows the insurer to receive discounted rates from service providers. PPOs are structured in much the same way as HMOs with two main exceptions: members are allowed to use non-PPO providers, although they will be required to pay higher deductibles and coinsurance than required when they use PPO doctors, and primary care doctors (as well as specialists) are paid on a fee-for-service basis, rather than as employees under the usual HMO.

preferred provider organization (PPO) - a contractual arrangement between the insured, the insurer, and the health care provider that allows the insurer to receive discounted rates from service providers

PPOs offer insureds a greater choice of health care providers than most HMOs. Many find the HMO concept objectionable because benefits are not provided if the covered (in other than an emergency) person uses a doctor outside of the HMO's network of providers. Although the insured pays more out of her pocket by going outside the network of preferred providers offered by a PPO, medical benefits are still payable.

Advantages and Disadvantages. Managed health care companies are highly competitive and often improve services and/or reduce costs to gain market share. Most managed health care plans are service-oriented and focus on assisting the patient to receive the most appropriate care for the money. To maintain quality of care, managed care plans provide coordination and continuity in the process of delivering care that is deemed medically necessary.

The primary disadvantage of managed care is reduced choice for the patient. While many managed care plans allow the insured to go outside the network of preferred providers, the vast majority of plans do not allow physicians to perform certain procedures without prior approval from the plan. This in turn reduces the patient's options for care. Furthermore, some managed care organizations put "gag clauses" in their contracts with providers. These clauses require the provider to remain silent about treatment options for the patient if the managed care plan excludes coverage for those procedures, such as experimental bone marrow transplants.

Coordination of Benefits

Due to the rising number of dual-income families across America today, measures have been taken by insurers to prevent insureds from making a profit by receiving benefits twice for the same ailment. One such measure is known as the Coordination of Benefits (COB) clause. COB is used in all group health insurance plans to prevent the insured who is covered by both her own employer's plan and her spouse's plan from receiving more than 100 percent of the actual cost of health care received.

Termination of Benefits

Upon permanent termination of employment with a company, one may still maintain group health insurance benefits for 31 days. This opportunity is extended to the former employee so that he or she will have adequate time to replace the group insurance with individual insurance. If new employment provides health insurance for the terminated employee, the previous employer's coverage automatically expires even if the 31-day period has not ended.

Consolidated Omnibus Budget Reconciliation Act (COBRA)

Employees and dependents previously covered under a group health insurance may have that group coverage extended under a federal law is known as the *Consolidated Omnibus Budget Reconciliation Act (COBRA)*. COBRA requires certain employers to provide the previously covered persons (including dependents and spouses) with the same coverage he or she received prior to unemployment. The benefit recipient must pay the full cost of the coverage, however, which may be prohibitively expensive if the recipient is unemployed. The employer is also allowed to charge up to 2 percent of the premium to cover administrative expenses, but under no circumstances may the employee be charged more than 102 percent of the total cost of the plan during the period of coverage.

To continue health insurance coverage through COBRA, the group coverage must terminate because of a qualifying event, including:

▲ Death of the covered employee.
▲ Voluntary or involuntary termination of the employee (except for gross misconduct).
▲ Reduction of employee's hours from full-time to part-time.
▲ Separation of covered employee from spouse.
▲ Employee becomes eligible for Medicare.
▲ A dependent child is no longer eligible for coverage under the employee's plan, as would be the case when the child left school, reached a certain age, or married.

Coverage for Elderly Employees

Employees who are 65 and older, and who are also eligible for Medicare benefits, must still be covered by the employer's group health coverage. The group plan is the primary payor of benefits and Medicare is the secondary payor.

Coverage for Retirees

Historically, many companies continued group health insurance coverage on their retired employees, although Medicare was the primary payor of benefits and the group plan served to fill coverage gaps in the Medicare program. The employer would pay some or all of the premiums on the retiree's coverage. In 1993, however, the Federal Accounting Standards Board (FASB) began requiring employers to recognize (on the balance sheet) the present value of the cost of providing retiree coverage *during the employee's active working years.* This ruling had a very negative effect on the earnings of most employers; so many employers have stopped offering paid benefits to retirees.

Another problem employers face in offering paid health benefits to retirees is the tendency of U.S. courts to prohibit a reduction in benefits after retirement. If an employer offers a retiree benefits, it may have to continue those benefits as long as the retiree desires them. This is a rather lengthy commitment for the employer that could prove financially burdensome during periods of reduced sales or profits.

Taxation of Group Health Benefits

Currently, employer-provided medical expense coverages are not taxable as income to the employee and the premiums paid by the employer are tax deductible as a business expense. Employer-paid premiums for disability income coverage are not taxed as current income to the employee, but if a disability occurs the benefits paid by the plan are taxable as income to the employee. If the employee pays the entire cost of disability income coverage, the premiums are not tax deductible for the employee. However, any disability benefits received from an employee-paid policy are not subject to income tax. If the employer and employee share the cost of disability income coverage, then disability benefits that are attributable to employer contributions are taxable as income to the employee.

PROFESSIONAL FOCUS

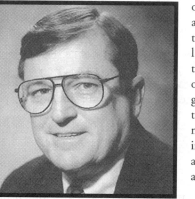

How do you determine the amount of life insurance to recommend that a client carry? Do you use the needs approach or the human value approach, why or why not?

First I review the entire financial and family situation with the client. What I am looking for is how the client expects to provide for his or her family in the event of death, interrupting the source of income. I have models including the needs approach to life insurance and the human value or capitalized income approach. I use both of these to band the actual amount of insurance that is needed. The needs approach is generally my floor and the income capitalization model is my ceiling. I then consult with the client regarding whether the policy is to be term or permanent before he or she decides on the amount of insurance. Another aspect to take into consideration is we are going to get unit price discounts. For example, there are significant discounts per $1000 of coverage for larger policies, particularly in term insurance.

How do you help clients choose between term and permanent life insurance?

Usually affordability is the biggest factor that drives the term insurance decision. Many clients simply have a need for insurance that is large, but temporary, and that risk is best served with term insurance. Permanent insurance is more suitable for clients who are a little older and have more discretionary cash flow. Usually these older, wealthier clients have estate transfer objectives and estate liquidity objectives, which significantly influence the type and amount of permanent insurance that is purchased. My perspective is that it takes 10 to 15 years

of holding variable policies to adequately and efficiently spread the costs of such policies. However, life insurance policies under which the insured has no incidence of ownership pass outside the insured's gross estate under our current transfer tax scheme. Therefore, I might also suggest that permanent insurance is best owned directly by a competent beneficiary or held in an irrevocable life insurance trust.

When recommending term life insurance, what are the issues for clients regarding yearly renewable versus fixed premiums for the term? What do clients tend to prefer and why?

The reality is that 90-95% of term policies are lapsed or do not pay benefits due to the term expiring. My experience is that clients are much more likely to continue coverage of a term policy where the premiums are fixed, even though I believe that annual renewable term may be the least expensive. The fixed premium payment is increasingly more palatable as the client's income rises. Therefore, the client is less likely to lapse the policy. I regularly review the insurance coverage for clients and consider replacing old policies with newer, more efficient policies when appropriate and when the insured is insurable.

JACK DARDIS, MBA, CLU, ChFC

DISCUSSION QUESTIONS

1. What are the various needs for life insurance?
2. What are the three recognized methods used to determine the amount of life insurance one should purchase?
3. What are component needs that make up the needs approach to the amount of life insurance needed?
4. How do term and whole life insurance differ, and what are the advantages/disadvantages of each?
5. What are the various types of term life insurance?
6. What are the various types of whole life insurance?
7. What differentiates variable life insurance from universal variable life insurance?
8. At what threshold is an employee taxed on group term life insurance provided by an employer?
9. How do annuities differ from life insurance contracts?
10. What are the various types of annuities?
11. What are the tax implications of life insurance and annuities?
12. What are the various contractual provisions and options that pertain to life and annuity contracts?
13. What are the major types of individual health and disability coverages?
14. What are the important policy provisions and major contractual features of individual health and disability coverages?
15. What are the major types of employer-provided group health coverages?
16. What are the important policy provisions and major contractual features of group health and disability coverages?
17. What is the purpose of disability income insurance, and what are some of the various definitions of disability?
18. What is the tax treatment of health and disability coverages?
19. How do indemnity plans and managed care plans differ?
20. How can group health coverage be continued or transferred when employment terminates?

EXERCISES

1. Comment on each of the following statements concerning the methods of providing life insurance protection:
   ▲ An insurance company can use two approaches to provide life insurance protection; term insurance, which is temporary, or cash value insurance, which is permanent protection that builds up a reserve or savings component.
   ▲ Term insurance is a form of life insurance in which the death proceeds are payable in the event of the insured's death during a specified period and nothing is paid if the insured survives to the end of that period.
   ▲ The net premium for term insurance is determined by the mortality rate for the attained age of the individual involved.
   ▲ Because death rates rise at an increasing rate as ages increase, the net premium for term insurance also rises at an increasing rate.
   ▲ Because many individuals need insurance that can be continued until death, at whatever age it might occur, cash value or permanent life insurance was developed.

2. Comment on the following statements:
   ▲ The face amount of a term policy is payable only if the insured dies during the specified period, and nothing is paid if the insured survives.
   ▲ The premium for term insurance is initially relatively low because most term contracts do not cover the period of old age when death is most likely to occur and when the cost of insurance is high.

3. Briefly explain the difference between life insurance and annuities?

4. Identify and briefly describe the features of a major medical plan.

5. Identify and briefly describe the features of a long-term disability insurance policy.

6. Comment on the need for long-term care insurance.

7. Briefly explain the differences between term life and permanent life insurance policies.

8. Marty, age 45, who is married to Michelle, makes $120,000 per year. He has 2 children, ages 9 and 10. He pays income taxes of $26,000 per year and FICA taxes of $5,000 per year. He plans to retire at age 65 and he has an opportunity cost of 9 percent. Calculate the amount of life insurance needed using the human life approach.

9. Describe the distinguishing features of whole life, universal life, variable life, and variable universal life in terms of premium amount, death benefit, the policy owner's control over investment, and the expected rate of return form the cost value invested.

10. Which is the higher rated insurance company?

	AM Best Rating	Moody's
XYZ	A+	
ABC		Aaa

11. Explain and differentiate a D or below insurance rating.

12. Calculate the amount of money an insurance will pay if:
    ▲ The surgeon's charge is $12,500
    ▲ There is a 80/20 coinsurance clause
    ▲ The deductible is $500
    ▲ The usual and customary charge for this surgery is $10,000

13. Briefly explain the purpose of an elimination period in a long-term disability policy.

14. Differentiate between an HMO and a PPO.

15. What are the qualifying events that allow for COBRA benefits?

PROBLEMS

Problem 1

Chris Jones, age 27, has two children, ages 4 and 3, from his first marriage. He is now married to Faith. The children live with their mother, Alice. They each make $26,000 per year and have recently bought a house for $100,000, using a mortgage of $95,000. Chris and Faith have the following life, health, and disability coverage:

Life Insurance:

	Policy A	Policy B	Policy C
Insured	Chris	Chris	Faith
Face Amount	$250,000	$78,000[2]	$20,000
Type	Whole Life	Group Term	Group Term
Cash Value	$2,000	$0	$0
Annual Premium	$2,100	$156	$50
Who pays premium	Trustee	Employer	Employer
Beneficiary	Trustee[1]	Alice	Chris
Policy Owner	Trust	Chris	Faith
Settlement options clause selected	None	None	None

[1] Children are beneficiaries of the trust required by divorce decree.
[2] This was increased from $50,000 to $78,000 January 1, 2002.

Health Insurance:

Chris and Faith are covered under Chris' employer plan which is an indemnity plan with a $200 deductible per person per year, an 80/20 major medical co-insurance clause with a family annual stop loss of $1,500, and lifetime benefit maximum of $500,000.

Long-Term Disability Insurance:

Chris is covered by an "own occupation" policy with premiums paid by his employer. The benefits equal 60 percent of his gross pay after a 180-day elimination period. The policy covers both sickness and accidents. The term of benefits is five full years (60 months). Faith is not covered by disability insurance.

1. Assume that Chris dies. Who would receive the proceeds of the insurance policies?
2. Does Chris have adequate life insurance?
3. Is Chris' health and disability adequate? If not, why not?
4. Should Faith have disability insurance? Why?
5. Are any of the premiums or benefits received from the life, health, or disability insurance taxable to the Jones?

Problem 2

Sanchez Richard graduated from State University with a Bachelor of Science degree in accounting. He has been employed at Knoth & Cartez, a small local accounting firm (50 employees) for almost 7 years. He makes $31,000 per year. Sanchez has been married to Marianne for 6 years. She graduated from Private University with a Bachelor of Science degree in elementary education. She is employed as a fourth grade teacher at Riverside Preparatory private school. She makes $22,000 per year. Sanchez and Marianne have three children: Carlos, age four; and twin girls, Maria and Anna, ages two.

The Richards have the following insurance:

Health Insurance:

Health insurance is provided for the entire family by Knoth & Cartez. The Richards are covered by an HMO. Doctor's visits are $10 per visit, while prescriptions are $5 for generic brands and $10 for other brands. There is no co-payment for hospitalization in semi-private accommodations. Private rooms are provided when medically necessary. For emergency treatment, a $50 co-payment is required.

Life Insurance:

Sanchez has a $50,000 group term life insurance policy through Knoth & Cartez. Marianne has a $20,000 group term policy through Riverside Preparatory School. The owners of the policies are Sanchez and Marianne, respectively, with each other as the respective beneficiary.

Disability Insurance:

Sanchez has disability insurance through the accounting firm. Short-term disability benefits begin for any absence due to accident or illness over 6 days and will continue for up to 6 months at 80 percent of his salary. Long-term disability benefits are available if disability continues over 6 months. If Sanchez is unable to perform the duties of his own current position, the benefits provide him with 60 percent of his gross salary while disabled until recovery, death, retirement, or age 65 (whichever occurs first). All disability premiums are paid by Knoth & Cartez.

Marianne currently has no disability insurance.

1. What happens to the Richard's health insurance if Sanchez is terminated from his job? What are the alternatives?
2. Does Sanchez have adequate life insurance?
3. How much life insurance does Sanchez need?
4. Do either of the group term policies cause taxable income to the Richards?
5. Should Marianne have disability insurance?

CHAPTER 9 SUPPLEMENT

LIFE INSURANCE POLICY PROVISIONS

Grace Period

Life insurance policies allow for a grace period (typically 31 days) after the premium due date. During this grace period, the policy remains in force. If the policy owner decides at any time during that period to make the overdue premium payment, the insurer will accept it and continue the policy, although interest may be charged on the overdue premium. If the insured dies within the grace period, the insurer assumes that the overdue premium would have been paid and simply deducts it (plus interest) from the death proceeds due the beneficiary.

Incontestability

Normal contract law states that any contract involving fraud is voidable at any time within the statue of limitations. However, in a life insurance contract there exists an incontestability clause, which states that the policy becomes incontestable (not arguable or rejectable) after a designated period of time (the "contestable" period). Most states have adopted a one to two year period of contestability. After the contestable period, the insurer may not void a policy or avoid payment of a death claim on the basis of misrepresentation or concealment made by the insured at the time at which coverage was applied.

Misstatement of Sex or Age

All other things being equal, younger persons pay less for life insurance than older persons do, and women pay less than men do. For this reason, the applicant for life insurance might be tempted to misstate age or sex, so as to pay a lower premium. If upon death, the insurer discovers that the insured misstated age or gender, the policy will be re-rated to reflect the true age or sex of the insured. In other words, the death benefit will be adjusted to reflect the underpayment of premium the insured made while the policy was in force. The policy will not be voided, however.

Suppose Mrs. Robinson is age 45, but looks much younger. She lies about her age on a life insurance application by saying she is 32 years old. Suppose the face value of her policy is $100,000 and Mrs. Robinson is charged a monthly premium of $100. The insurer would have charged Mrs. Robinson $200 per month had it known she was 45. When she dies and the insurer discovers the misstatement of age, it will recalculate her death benefit based on the premium amount she *should* have paid. Because she paid only half as much as she should have ($100 instead of $200), the insurer will pay only half the death benefit, or $50,000.

Assignment

Assignment is the process of transferring all or part of the policy's ownership rights. A policyholder might wish to assign his interest in a life insurance contract to a bank as collateral for a loan, with or without the insurance company's consent. Two main types of assignments exist in today's insurance industry: absolute and collateral. An absolute assignment gives the entity that has received the assignment all policy ownership rights, subject to any limitations set forth in the assignment. A collateral assignment is used to serve as security for debt and gives the lender or "assignee" limited ownership rights under the policy. The assignment automatically terminates when the debt is paid and policy ownership rights are usually exercisable only if the borrower defaults on the loan.

Suicide

To mitigate against the risk that a person will purchase a life insurance policy in contemplation of suicide, life insurance policies include a suicide exclusion clause. The suicide clause excludes coverage for suicide if the insured takes her own life within a certain time period (usually one or two years, depending upon state law). If a suicide occurs within this time frame, the insurance company is then liable only to return the amount of premiums paid to date without interest, which will be paid to the policy beneficiary. Where suicide is suspected within the exclusion period, the burden of proof falls on the insurance company in a court of law. Most courts require clear and convincing proof of suicide before the insurer will be allowed to deny payment of the death claim. In fact, some states require that there be a suicide note before the death can be declared a suicide.

Reinstatement

A life insurance policy will lapse if the premium payments made by the insured are not kept current. Reinstatement simply places a lapsed policy back into effect; it does not create a new policy. The reinstatement provision was designed so that policyholders would not have to forfeit their interests completely, after having made payments for several years.

If a policy is reinstated within 31 days of the grace period, there is no need for evidence of insurability. However, a policy that has been lapsed for several months may require a medical examination. There is also a maximum time limit beyond which reinstatement will not be allowed (typically three years).

Policy Loan Provision

Some policies include a provision for an automatic premium loan, which states that if the policyholder does not make a premium payment upon its due date, it will be paid for out of the policy's cash value and then deemed a loan to the policyholder. The policy owner must specifically request this automatic premium loan provision either on the initial coverage application or in writing at a later date.

Additionally, all permanent policies allow the policy owner to borrow some or all of the cash value in the policy. The interest rate on such loans is generally quite low and there is no legal requirement that the loan ever be repaid. However, any loans and interest payments outstanding at the time of the insured's death will be deducted from the death proceeds, which could be detrimental to the beneficiary.

Beneficiary Designations

A beneficiary is the person designated by the policy owner to receive the policy proceeds in the event of the insured's death. The owner of the policy reserves the right to choose as many beneficiaries as he wishes. It is strongly encouraged to choose a primary, secondary, and perhaps even a tertiary (third) beneficiary. If the primary beneficiary is deceased at the time the insured dies, then the secondary beneficiary will receive the death proceeds. If the secondary beneficiary is also deceased, the tertiary beneficiary will receive payment. What should be avoided is having the death proceeds revert to the insured's estate, which is what happens when there is no valid beneficiary to receive payment of the policy proceeds. If the proceeds are paid to the insured's estate, they will be included in the probate estate and, therefore, subject to costs and delays. This could cause a liquidity problem for the survivors.

If a policy beneficiary clause reserves the policy owner's right to change the designated beneficiary at any time during the policy's life, the beneficiary is referred to as a revocable beneficiary. Changes must of course be made in writing and submitted to the insurer. An irrevocable beneficiary is one who cannot be removed as beneficiary without granting prior consent. Irrevocable beneficiary designations are often used in divorce cases, where valuable life insurance policies are divided along with other assets of the divorcing couple. The irrevocable beneficiary does not have other ownership rights under the policy, but he or she must give consent before the owner can name someone else as beneficiary. Policy owners can use a survivorship clause as to beneficiaries in which the beneficiary must survive the insured by 60 days. Use of the survivorship clause supercedes a simultaneous death provision and may create liquidity problems at death.

Aviation Exclusion

Though no longer a common exclusion in policies issued today, the aviation exclusion denies coverage for those who die in noncommercial flights, such as private pilots and their passengers, and military pilots. Premiums are usually returned to the beneficiary, however, the death benefit is not paid.

War Exclusion

This exclusion allows the insurer to deny the death claim if the insured dies while in the military or as the result of a military action. Premiums are usually returned to the beneficiary with interest and the death benefit is not paid.

Simultaneous Death Provisions

A situation may arise in which the insured and the beneficiary both die in the same accident and it is not determinable who died first. The Uniform Simultaneous Death Act has been adopted by some states to handle this situation. It states that the proceeds of the life insurance policy will be distributed as though the insured died last. If more than one beneficiary has been named on the policy, the next in the line of succession shall receive the proceeds. However, in the case that there are no other beneficiaries listed, the proceeds will be included in the insured's probate estate and subject to the expenses of probate.

POLICY OPTIONS

Non-Forfeiture Options

Non-forfeiture options protect the cash values of a policy owner who chooses to discontinue coverage under a whole life policy. This provision states that the insured, by lapsing or surrendering the policy, does not automatically forfeit the cash value accumulation. The non-forfeiture options give the policy owner some choice in how to receive the cash value of the policy. The most common non-forfeiture options include:

- ▲ Cash Surrender Value.
- ▲ Reduced Paid-Up Insurance.
- ▲ Extended Term Insurance.

Cash Surrender Value

This option gives the owner immediate access to a certain amount of cash specified in the policy, in exchange for termination of the policy. This option should be exercised with care because the same amount of cash may be obtained through one of the other options, which provide for a continuing amount of coverage. Where an insured is retired or elderly with no surviving dependents, the need for a large amount of life insurance is reduced, so the cash surrender option could be a suitable choice. In any other situation where the need for death protection has ceased or where alternative death protection has been purchased, this is a viable option. Consumers who surrender policies may incur an income tax liability on part of the cash value accumulation, so a complete policy surrender should be thoroughly evaluated from a tax perspective. Note that surrender value is usually less than cash value for the first 10-15 years of the policy.

Reduced Paid-Up Insurance

This option allows the policy owner to purchase a fully paid-up whole life insurance policy using the cash value of the policy. The face amount of the policy will be dependent upon the amount of cash value accumulation, less surrender charges. Extended term insurance can be thought of as the option to purchase a single premium whole life insurance policy. It is suitable for someone who wants to maintain some level of permanent death protection, but does not want to pay any future premiums.

Extended Term Insurance

Extended term insurance uses net cash surrender value as a net single premium to purchase a paid-up term insurance policy equal to the original face amount for a limited period of time, usually a certain number of years and days. The length of the term protection is dependent upon the insured's age at the time he or she chooses to exercise the option. The net single premium will also be determined by the company's current premium rates. This option is most suitable for someone who wants to preserve, for only a limited time, death protection equal to the forfeited policy's face value.

Dividend Options

Insurance companies often conservatively estimate premiums charged to customers and, in such cases, the excess premiums are refunded to the policy owners. These refunds are called policy dividends. Note that dividends in this context differ from dividends paid on shares of stock. Policyholders are entitled to receive policy dividends declared by the insurer if the contract is a participating policy. Under a non-participating policy, no such dividends are paid.

Participating policies allow the insured to receive dividends in a number of different ways.

Cash Option

A cash dividend may be paid out by the insurance company in the form of a check on the policy's anniversary date. Cash dividends are usually payable only after the policy has been in force for a certain period of time (designated in the policy).

Paid-Up Additions Option

Cash dividends may be used to purchase additional paid-up insurance at a reduced amount. The advantage of choosing this option is a purchase of additional insurance at net rates with no loading fees or expenses attached. It should be noted that some companies tend to overprice paid-up increments of insurance. In addition, reduced paid-up insurance is a form of a single premium whole life policy, which may not be sufficient to meet an insured's short-term coverage needs.

Interest Accumulation Option

Dividend payments may be retained by the insurance company and accumulated at a guaranteed interest rate. Most companies pay 4-5% minimum interest on accumulated dividends. The interest accumulation is available for withdrawal at any time therein. If the policy owner does not exercise her option to withdraw the interest accumulation while living, the insurer will add all accumulated dividends and interest to the face amount of the policy and pay them as death proceeds when the insured dies.

Reduction of Premiums Option

Regular dividends may be applied towards the premium payment due to the company by the insured. Thus, the insured is then responsible only for making a premium payment equal to the difference between the original premium payment and dividends received.

Fifth Dividend Option (Term Insurance)

A dividend may be used to purchase as much one-year term insurance as possible, given the insured's age and the insurer's current rate schedule. Another option allows the dividend to purchase a one-year term policy equal to the face value of the original policy. Any remaining dividend is then used to purchase increments of paid-up life insurance or is accumulated at interest.

Settlement Options

Advantages and Disadvantages

Settlement options allow the policy owner or beneficiary to specify how death proceeds are to be paid to the beneficiary. If the policy owner fails to designate which option should be exercised in the event of death in the contract, the very reasons for which the policy was purchased ultimately may not be achieved. Settlement options may protect the beneficiary who is incapable of managing a lump sum of cash; and they make it possible for the policy owner to provide for both primary and secondary beneficiaries.

Interest-Only Option

The interest option requires the insurance company to retain the death benefit of the policy and pay interest on that sum to the primary beneficiary. The interest payments are made to the beneficiary on a regular basis. A minimum interest rate is guaranteed, but the insurer usually pays a higher rate of interest. Following the death of the primary beneficiary, the insurer pays the policy death proceeds to the secondary beneficiary.

Fixed-Amount Option

The fixed-amount settlement option specifies that a designated amount of income will be provided to the beneficiary on a regular basis until the proceeds and accumulated interest are depleted. Under this option, the beneficiary has the right to select another settlement option for the remainder of unpaid proceeds or to vary withdrawal patterns. The fixed-amount option provides the greatest amount of flexibility to the beneficiary, as compared to the other settlement options.

Fixed-Period Option

This option divides a certain number of periods into the total available proceeds (plus interest) to derive a regular payment amount. The payment is then dispersed every period for some fixed amount of time. Whether payments are made monthly, quarterly, semiannually, or annually, they continue until the policy face amount plus interest are depleted.

The fixed period option is quite inflexible for the beneficiary. Once a payment period is established, there may be no substantial withdrawals or changing of options. If the beneficiary dies within the payment period, the balance of payments is forwarded to the succeeding beneficiary or included in the deceased beneficiary's estate.

Life Income Options

The life income options allow the policy owner to leave the beneficiary (or beneficiaries) an income payment for their entire life (lives). This option is, essentially, the purchase of an annuity for the beneficiary. Annuities are discussed later in this chapter. While this section is geared toward those who may not be familiar with annuities, the reader might find it helpful to review this section again after a thorough reading of the annuity material.

Life income options available to the policy owner:

▲   Pure Life Income.
▲   Life Income with Period Certain.
▲   Refund Life Income.
▲   Joint and Last Survivor Income.

Pure Life Income. Under the pure life income option, installment payments are made until the beneficiary dies. Once the beneficiary dies, no further payments are made. This is similar to purchasing a straight-life annuity on the beneficiary (discussed below). Pure life income provides the highest amount of life income per $1000 of proceeds; however, there is the risk of forfeiting a large part of the proceeds should the beneficiary die within a short period after the insured's death.

Life Income with Period Certain. This option guarantees that the beneficiary will receive a life income. It also guarantees that payments will be made for a minimum period of time, even if the beneficiary dies. If the primary beneficiary dies within the guarantee period, the insurer then makes payments to the secondary beneficiary. If the primary beneficiary outlives the guarantee period, the insurer continues to make regular payments until the primary beneficiary dies. The period certain option is the most popular form of life income and is usually contracted on a 10- or 20-year basis.

Refund Life Income. With this option, if the beneficiary should die before receiving payments equal to the face value of the insurance policy, the remaining amount will be dispersed either in installment payments or a lump sum to the contingent beneficiary.

Joint and Last Survivor Income. The joint and survivor income option provides income payments to two people during their lifetimes. This is often a popular settlement option when the beneficiaries of the policy proceeds are a married couple. When one spouse dies, settlement payments continue to the survivor. The payments may either remain the same or be reduced to suit the needs of the survivor.

LIFE INSURANCE POLICY RIDERS

Guaranteed Insurability Option (GIR)

Also known as the additional purchase option, the guaranteed insurability option guarantees insureds that they will be able to purchase additional life insurance without providing evidence of insurability. Most young people just graduating college and beginning their careers purchase only a minimal amount of coverage, due to their limited incomes. The GIR allows, at selected periodic intervals, the policy owner to purchase specific additional amounts of insurance without proving insurability.

Waiver of Premium

The waiver of premium rider was designed to protect the insured that suffers severe bodily injury or disease and, thus, could not earn adequate income to pay insurance premiums. Under this policy option, if the insured becomes disabled from bodily injury or disease before some stated age in the insurance contract (usually 65), he or she will not be held responsible for any premiums due during the period of disability. This does not negatively affect the remaining terms of the policy, including cash values, accumulating interest, or death benefits.

To meet the waiver of premium qualification, the insured must be able to prove all of the following to the insurance company:

▲ There exists a disability that began before some age specified in the policy.
▲ The disability lasted for a minimum of six months.
▲ The disability was one defined in the policy (either cannot work in any occupation reasonably fitted by experience and training or cannot perform duties of his or her own regular occupation).
▲ Medical proof of disability.

Double Indemnity

The double indemnity rider is attached to the life insurance contract to provide for accidental death. In the event that the death of an insured is caused by an accident, the face value of the policy will either double or triple. The probability that death will occur as a result of an accident is very low; therefore, double indemnity premiums are inexpensive relative to other coverages (sometimes only $1-$2 per $1000 benefit).

For a double indemnity benefit to be paid, the following requirements must be met:

▲ Death must occur within 90 days of accident.
▲ Death must occur before age 65 or 70.
▲ Death must be the result of an "accident," as defined within the policy.

Accelerated Death Benefit

Also referred to as living insurance, accelerated death benefits pay a designated amount of the life insurance policy's face value before the insured's death. Accelerated death benefit is utilized in cases where the insured suffers from a severe medical condition. The accelerated death benefit may be provided in one of the following three forms:

▲ Terminal Illness Coverage.
▲ Catastrophic Illness Coverage.
▲ Long-Term Care Coverage.

Terminal illness coverage pays some percentage of the death benefit in the case where the insured is diagnosed as terminally ill. Policies generally require medical certification that the insured will die within six months or a year, and then the requested lump sum will be discounted for time value of money. The policy face amount is reduced accordingly. To illustrate, suppose Jonita

302

has a $200,000 term life insurance policy with a terminal illness rider attached. After discovering that she is terminally ill, she asks the insurer to give her $75,000 in a lump sum. The insurer will reduce the requested sum for interest, and the resulting amount that Jonita receives might hypothetically be $67,238. The face value of her policy is then reduced by the full $75,000. If she takes no more accelerated benefits under the policy, then at her death the beneficiary will receive $125,000.

At this juncture, it is important to distinguish between terminal illness accelerated benefits and viatical settlements. A viatical settlement is the private sale of a terminally ill policyowner's ownership of a policy. A viatical settlement company brings together investors and terminally ill persons who need to access a portion of the face value of their policies. The terminally ill insured, also called the viator, receives some portion of the face value of her policy while she is still alive, and the investor receives the right to be the sole beneficiary of the policy's death benefit. In theory, this arrangement should be beneficial for all parties involved. The viator receives much-needed cash to pay medical and living expenses, the investor earns a profit, and the settlement company receives a fee or commission for its services.

Suppose Susan has AIDS and has a life expectancy of 24 months. She can approach a viatical settlement company and ask that her $100,000 life insurance policy be purchased. The company will verify that her illness is indeed terminal and that her policy ownership is transferable. Prudent viatical settlement companies will also verify the financial stability of the insurer that issued the life insurance policy. An investor will then purchase the policy for some amount that is less than the face value of the policy, say, $60,000. Susan receives the $60,000, and, in return, the investor is named as the irrevocable beneficiary of the policy. From that point on, Susan's ownership of policy benefits effectively ceases; when she dies, the investor receives $100,000. Investors offer such a deep discount because they assume the risk of the viator living beyond his or her life expectancy. The longer he or she lives, the lower the investors' return will be.

Catastrophic Illness Coverage operates in the same fashion as a terminal illness. However, the diagnosis that triggers payment of a portion of the face value must be one that is specified in the policy, such as stroke, heart attack, or lung cancer.

Long-Term Care Coverage provides monthly payments to the insured in the case of a confining sickness. For example, if a person must be placed in a custodial care facility such as a nursing home, payments may be made against death benefits while the insured is still alive. Long-term care coverage may be attached to the standard life insurance policy through a rider or be purchased as a separate policy. To be covered under long-term care, one must be able to prove that he or she is confined to a qualified facility and that it is medically necessary to reside there.

Disability Income Rider

Assuming that the insured is totally disabled, the disability income rider to the insurance policy pays monthly disability income benefits in the amount of $10 for every $1000 of insurance. The insured's disability must occur before some stated age (usually 65). If the disability persists beyond this stated age, the face amount of the policy will be paid out as an endowment. A four to six month waiting period is normally required before disability benefits will be paid, so this rider does not fulfill the need for total disability income.

HEALTH INSURANCE POLICY PROVISIONS

Pre-existing Conditions

The pre-existing conditions exclusion clause helps control adverse selection. A pre-existing condition generally is defined as one the insured person was treated for during the six-month or one-year period prior to the policy's inception date. Pre-existing conditions are not covered under health insurance policies, although this exclusion usually lasts for only one or two years, after which treatment for the pre-existing condition will be covered, as it would be for any other medical condition.

Grace Period

A grace period of 31 days is granted to the insured in the event that he or she is late making a premium payment. During the grace period, a policy may not be canceled by the insurer. However, if payment of the overdue premium is not received by the last date of the grace period, the coverage automatically lapses.

Reinstatement

Included in every health insurance policy is a procedure for policy reinstatement, should coverage lapse due to nonpayment of premium. Certain policies specify a time limit within which the insured may reinstate the policy without proof of insurability. Other policies require the insured to again submit to the underwriting process before coverage is reinstated. Reinstated policies usually exclude coverage for illnesses incurred during the first ten days after reinstatement (again to control adverse selection problems).

Time Limit Clause

The time limit clause is attached to the policy so that an insurer may void a policy on the grounds of misrepresentation made by the insured on the application for coverage. The insurer must usually discover and contest the misstatement during the first two years the contract is in force. After that time, the policy is incontestable and misstatements may not be used against the insured to void a policy or deny a claim. This is similar to the incontestability clause in a life insurance contract.

Renewal Clauses

Renewal clauses in the individual health insurance policy specify the length of time that an insurance policy can remain in force. This can have a serious effect on the duration of coverage. In the case of group insurance policies, as long as the insured is employed by the group, then he or she may retain coverage.

Guaranteed Renewable

Under a guaranteed renewable clause, the company promises to renew the policy to a stated age, usually 65. The insurance company cannot cancel the insured at any time during the benefit period, regardless of bad health or the number of claims filed by the insured. The renewal of the policy is at the sole discretion of the insured. However, the insurance company reserves the right to increase premiums as deemed necessary, as long as such premium increases are for the entire group covered.

Noncancellable

A health insurance policy with a noncancellable renewal clause provides the greatest amount of security for the insured. The insurer guarantees the renewal of the policy until age 65 and the premiums may not be increased. Noncancellable premiums are about 25 percent higher than they are for a similar guaranteed renewable policy because the insured is afforded much more protection.

Renewable at Insurer's Option

With this renewal clause, the insurer may not cancel the policy during its term (usually one year), but it may refuse to renew the policy for a subsequent term. Clearly, this provision is not safe for the insured. One should carefully consider the purchase of a policy with this provision.

Conditionally Renewable

A conditionally renewable contract cannot be canceled by the insurer during the policy term (again, usually one year), but it may refuse to renew the contract for another term if certain conditions exist. For example, if full-time employment ceases, the insurer reserves the right to cancel the policy at the end of the last month of employment. Also, renewal may be denied on the basis of unpaid premiums or the insured reaching age 65 and becoming eligible for Medicare coverage. This renewal clause gives the insured more protection than the one discussed previously, but still is not as safe as the guaranteed renewable and noncancellable options.

CHAPTER 10

Personal Property and Liability Insurance

LEARNING OBJECTIVES:

After learning the material in this chapter, you will be able to:

1. Identify the need for homeowners, auto, and umbrella insurance coverages.

2. List and define the basic coverages provided by a homeowners policy.

3. Be aware of the various homeowners forms that are available.

4. Understand and explain the various contractual options and provisions in homeowners insurance.

5. List and define the basic coverages provided by a personal automobile insurance policy.

6. Understand and explain the various contractual options and provisions in personal automobile insurance.

7. Identify the need for a personal umbrella policy and explain the umbrella's distinguishing characteristics.

8. Identify the coverages available to businesses and business owners.

INTRODUCTION

The professional planner should be just as knowledgeable about the risk of liability to a client's property as with life and health insurance. While property insurance protects the assets the client already owns, liability insurance protects the client against financial loss from legal action. Therefore, both property and liability insurance coverages are essential parts of a client's financial plan.

Property insurance includes homeowners, renter's insurance and automobile insurance. The home is considered one of the largest single purchases that a person makes. Although the frequency of perils causing financial losses to the home is small, the severity of loss is potentially large. The automobile policy is a device used to mitigate against the risk of loss to the automobile and those involved in an automobile accident. It may be among the most expensive aspects of owning a car for the client. The personal liability umbrella policy provides coverage in excess of the liability coverage provided in the homeowners and automobile policies.

Various types of insurance coverages, such as the commercial package policy, the business owner's policy, and professional insurance, provide protection for business owners and self-employed professionals.

This chapter introduces each of these types of insurance to help the planner adequately evaluate his client's property and liability needs and recommend appropriate coverage.

PERSONAL PROPERTY AND LIABILITY INSURANCE

Many individuals in society either own or rent a dwelling. Within that dwelling are various personal possessions, most of which are owned. Many individuals own at least one automobile. The home and automobile can represent a substantial portion of a person's assets. Thus, insurance on each is a critical concern in financial planning.

The United States' legal environment makes individuals responsible for bodily injuries and/or property damage they cause to others. When one is legally liable for injuries to another, the law requires that payment be made for those injuries. Where money is not available to make the necessary restitution, other assets can be seized, thus jeopardizing the wealth of the individual. Liability insurance provides the insured with financial protection against lawsuits and other claims for damages that result from the insured's actions.

In this chapter, the three policies used most commonly to protect against personal property and liability risks are discussed: homeowners insurance, automobile insurance, and personal umbrella liability insurance. Homeowners and automobile insurance are package policies that provide both property and liability coverage in one contract. The personal umbrella policy provides a layer of personal liability protection above the coverages provided in the homeowners and automobile policies, in the unfortunate event that those policies do not provide adequate compensation to injured parties.

308

Each of the following discussions is based on the standard policy forms issued by the Insurance Services Office (ISO). Since insurance is regulated at the state level, each state may require certain modifications to the standard ISO form. Thus, the ensuing discussions are general in nature. Absolute statements cannot be made about a particular policy without reading that particular policy thoroughly.

HOMEOWNERS (HO) INSURANCE: BASIC COVERAGES

Each **homeowners insurance** form consists of two sections: Section I provides property coverage, and Section II provides liability coverage. Exhibit 10.1 gives an overview of the basic coverages and the different HO forms available. Later in the chapter, the HO forms and their contractual provisions will be discussed in detail.

homeowners insurance - a package insurance policy that provides both property and liability coverage for the insured's dwelling, other structures, personal property, and loss of use

EXHIBIT 10.1: LIST OF COVERED PERILS

BASIC NAMED PERILS	
1. Fire	2. Vehicles
3. Lightning	4. Smoke
5. Windstorm	6. Vandalism or malicious mischief
7. Hail	8. Explosion
9. Riot or civil commotion	10. Theft
11. Aircraft	12. Volcanic eruption

BROAD NAMED PERILS

Basic **Named Perils** 1-12, plus 13-18:

13. Falling objects.

14. Weight of ice, snow, sleet.

15. Accidental discharge or overflow of water or steam.

16. Sudden and accidental tearing apart, cracking, burning, or bulging of a steam, hot water, air conditioning, or automatic fire protective sprinkler system, or from within a household appliance.

17. Freezing of a plumbing, heating, air conditioning, or automatic fire sprinkler system, or of a household appliance.

18. Sudden and accidental damage from artificially generated electrical current.

named perils - perils specifically listed in an insurance policy

	HO1	HO2	HO3	HO4	HO6	HO8
Coverage A Dwelling	Basic	Broad	All Risk	N/A	Broad	Basic
Coverage B Other Structures	Basic	Broad	All Risk	N/A	N/A	Basic
Coverage C Personal Property	Basic	Broad	Broad	Broad	Broad	Basic
Coverage D Loss of Use	Basic	Broad	All Risk/ Broad	Broad	Broad	Basic

SUMMARY OF SECTION I COVERAGES

Section I provides the four coverages: dwelling, other structures, personal property, and loss of use.

It consists of 5 sections identified as A through D and Additional Coverage.

- ▲ Section A—Dwelling
- ▲ Section B—Other structures
- ▲ Section C—Personal property
- ▲ Section D—Loss of use
- ▲ Additional coverage—Debris removal, damage to trees, credit card loss, etc.

Coverage A: Dwelling

dwelling - residential structure covered under a homeowners insurance policy

This coverage pays for repair and/or replacement of damage to the house itself. The homeowner typically buys an amount of coverage equal to the replacement cost of the **dwelling**, and in some cases, will be required to carry even more if the property is mortgaged. A mortgage lender usually demands an amount of coverage on the dwelling at least equal to the total amount owed on the mortgage.

replacement cost - the amount necessary to purchase, repair, or replace the dwelling with materials of the same or similar quality at current prices

Covered losses to the dwelling and other structures are paid on the basis of replacement cost with no deduction for depreciation. **Replacement cost** is the amount necessary to purchase, repair, or replace the dwelling with materials of the same or similar quality at current prices. The insured must carry insurance of at least 80 percent of the replacement cost at the time of the loss or the insured will receive the larger of the following:

- ▲ Actual cash value of the part of the dwelling that is damaged.
- ▲ [(amount of insurance carried)/(80 percent of replacement cost)] x replacement cost loss. (This is called the coinsurance clause and is discussed later in this chapter.)

Certain properties attached to the dwelling or considered an integral part of the dwelling are covered only on an actual cash value basis. These properties include awnings, household appliances, outdoor antennas, outdoor appliances, and non-building structures. Building glass is replaced with safety-glazing materials, if required by local building codes.

Coverage B: Other Structures

In addition to the main house, some homeowners have small, detached structures on their property. These include detached garages, small greenhouses, or storage buildings. Coverage B pays for damage to these structures. The limit of insurance in Coverage B is typically 10 percent of the Coverage A (Dwelling) limit. This coverage also pays on a replacement cost basis (just as it pays for the dwelling).

Other structures may not be eligible for coverage if they are used for business purposes. If another structure is rented to someone who is not also a tenant of the dwelling, no coverage applies (unless the structure is rented for use solely as private garage space). If a part of the dwelling is rented out to another person not considered the tenant, there is no coverage for the other structure in the event of a loss.

other structures - small detached structures on insured's property in addition to the main house, such as garages, greenhouses, or storage buildings

Coverage C: Personal Property

The value of a homeowner's **personal property** should not be underestimated. Imagine what it would cost just to replace the typical family room's furniture, entertainment equipment, music collection, videos, tables, paintings, lamps, and books. The HO forms provide coverage on the personal property of the insured (and resident family members), irrespective of where the property is located at the time of loss. The limit of insurance for Coverage C is typically equal to 50 percent of the Coverage A (Dwelling) limit.

personal property - valuable items owned by the insured that are covered under homeowners insurance

Note that the standard HO form provides only actual cash value (ACV) coverage on personal property. An optional endorsement is available to add replacement cost coverage to personal property, and this option is strongly recommended for most homeowners. Actual cash value is the depreciated value of personal property. Since the contents of a home depreciate rapidly, a homeowner could suffer a serious financial loss if replacement cost coverage were not provided.

Consider the price of a gentleman's suit. The typical suit starts at $300. As soon as the consumer buys that suit, however, it likely cannot be resold for even half of its original price. The insurer will only pay what the suit is worth at the time of loss under the ACV option. Assuming a homeowner has five suits, it will cost at least $1,500 to replace all of them, yet the insurer will probably pay $600 or $700, at most, on an ACV basis.

EXAMPLE

Only 10 percent of coverage on personal property can be applied to property off of the insured's premises. Coverage to plants, trees, and shrubs is limited to $250, versus the $500 limit on other homeowners policies.

Certain kinds of personal property have maximum dollar limits on the amount that will be paid for any loss. A typical HO policy contains the following limits of liability:

▲ $200—money, bullion, coin collections, and bank notes.
▲ $1,000—securities, bills, evidence of debt, airline tickets, and manuscripts.
▲ $1,000—theft of jewelry, watches, gems, precious metals, and real furs.
▲ $1,000—watercraft, including trailers (not boat affiliated) and equipment.
▲ $2,000—theft of firearms.

- ▲ $2,500—theft of silverware, goldware, pewterware, and similar property.
- ▲ $250—loss of business use property not on premises.
- ▲ $2,500—loss of business use property on premises.
- ▲ $1,000—loss of electronic apparatus.

If the insured owns many valuable personal items, it may be necessary to purchase additional amounts of insurance beyond the special limits listed above. The additional increments of insurance purchased are listed in what is referred to as a schedule. A schedule is a list of dollar limits or amounts of insurance provided for specified personal items attached to the homeowners policy. Note, however, that scheduled assets are no longer covered under the general HO.

Certain items of personal property are excluded from coverage because they are either uninsurable or outside the "normal" range of properties owned by the typical homeowner. Homeowners having these unusual properties and, thus, unusual risk exposures, must request special coverage in addition to that provided by their HO form. The following personal property items are specifically excluded from coverage:

- ▲ Animals, birds, and fish.
- ▲ Articles separately described and specifically insured.
- ▲ Motorized land vehicles used off premises.
- ▲ Property of roomers or boarders not related to the insured.
- ▲ Aircraft and parts.
- ▲ Furnishings on property rented out to others.
- ▲ Property held as samples, held for sale, or sold but not delivered.
- ▲ Business data, credit cards, and funds transfer cards.
- ▲ Business property held away from the residence premises.

Coverage D: Loss of Use

loss of use - under homeowners insurance coverage, loss of use is a combination of additional living expenses and loss of rental income

Loss of use is defined as a combination of additional living expenses and loss of rental income. Coverage is limited to a maximum of 20 percent of the Coverage A (Dwelling) limit.

A direct property loss can result in a family having to live in a hotel or apartment for days, weeks, or even months. The incremental difference between the cost of living in these temporary arrangements and normal costs that would have been incurred had there been no loss is known as additional living expense. The increase in housing costs, food, transportation, laundry, and so on, are all examples of additional living expenses. Benefits are provided only for the additional (incremental) costs required to maintain the homeowner's normal standard of living.

Under loss of use, a lessor may recover the loss of fair rental value on property held for rental purposes by the insured lessor. Benefits are paid on the basis of rental value less charges and expenses that do not continue during the period in which the property is uninhabitable.

EXAMPLE

Suppose Clyde (lessor) owns a house in which he rents a section to a university student (lessee) for $250 per month. If the house is deemed uninhabitable for two months after a fire, Clyde can recover $500 for loss of rent.

If a civil authority prevents an insured from using his or her premises due to damage by a covered peril to a neighborhood, loss of use coverage will be provided for up to two weeks. This is a unique feature of the HO form, considering that the insured need not suffer any damage to his property to collect from the policy. The value of this coverage should not be underestimated. Consider the various forest fire episodes in California. If a civil authority orders a homeowner to vacate the premises due to the spread of fire in the area, the cost of putting a family of four in a hotel room, plus paying for restaurant meals, laundry service, pet boarding, and so on, can amount to several thousand dollars in a very short period of time.

SUMMARY OF PERILS COVERED

Each HO form specifies which causes of loss it covers and which it excludes. Later in this chapter, the different HO forms and the perils covered by each are presented. Listed below are the general exclusions:

- ▲ Movement of the ground.
- ▲ Ordinance or law.
- ▲ Damage from water.
- ▲ War.
- ▲ Nuclear hazards.
- ▲ Power failure.
- ▲ Intentional act.
- ▲ Neglect.

Movement of the Ground

Property damage arising from earth movement is excluded. This includes damage from an earthquake, volcanic eruption, or landslide.

Ordinance or Law

A loss due to an ordinance or law that regulates the construction, repair, or demolition of a building or structure is excluded.

Damage from Water

Property damage from the following are specifically excluded from coverage under the homeowners policy:

- ▲ Floods, surface water, waves, tidal water, and overflow or spray of a body of water.
- ▲ Water below the surface of the ground that exerts pressure on or seeps through a building, sidewalk, driveway, foundation, swimming pool, or other structure.
- ▲ Water backing through sewers or drains.

Coverage for naturally occurring floods is available through the National Flood Insurance Program offered by the federal government. Coverage for sewer backup is available in some areas as an endorsement to the HO policy.

War or Nuclear Hazards

Property damage from war or nuclear hazard, including radiation, or radioactive contamination is excluded. If a radiation leak from a nuclear power plant near an insured's home contaminates his or her property, there is no coverage for the loss.

Power Failure

Losses due to power failure caused by an uninsured peril, such as a freezer thawing out and its contents spoiling because of local power plant malfunctions, are not covered. If, however, a covered peril such as fire or lightning on the premises causes the power failure, then the resulting damage is covered.

Intentional Acts

If a loss is discovered to be an intentional act on the part of any insured, it is not covered. For example, one cannot intentionally burn his house down and recover insurance benefits.

Neglect

If an insured fails to use all reasonable and necessary means to save and preserve his property during or after the loss, or when the property is endangered by an insured peril, the loss is not covered.

SUMMARY OF SECTION II COVERAGES

Coverage E: Personal Liability

Coverage E protects the named insured and all resident family members against liability for bodily injuries and property damage they or their resident premises cause others to suffer. The minimum limit of coverage is $100,000 per occurrence, although many homeowners carry a $200,000 or $300,000 limit. In addition to the coverage, the insurer pays all defense and settlement costs associated with a claim for damages made by an injured party.

This coverage provides liability coverage for *personal* (that is, non-business) activities. The insuring agreement is quite broad, and simply agrees to protect against claims or suits for bodily injury or property damage. The coverage is then narrowed to exclude most non-personal liability situations and other uninsurable exposures.

EXHIBIT 10.2: LIABILITY EXCLUSIONS APPLICABLE TO COVERAGES E & F

EXCLUSION	COVERAGE E: PERSONAL LIABILITY	COVERAGE F: MEDICAL PAYMENTS
Intentional Injury	✔	✔
Business & Professional Activities	✔	✔
Rental of Property	✔	✔
Professional Liability	✔	✔
Uninsured Premises	✔	✔
Motor Vehicles	✔	✔
Watercraft	✔	✔
Aircraft	✔	✔
War	✔	✔
Communicable Disease	✔	✔
Sexual Molestation or Abuse	✔	✔
Nuclear Exclusion	✔	✔
Workers Compensation	✔	✔
Controlled Substance	✔	✔
Contractual Liability	✔	-
Property owned by or in custody of Insured	✔	-
Injuries of Insured Person	✔	-
Residence Employee Away from Premises	-	✔
Persons Residing on Premises	-	✔

Coverage F: Medical Payments to Others

This coverage pays necessary medical expenses of others that result from bodily injury. The bodily injuries must arise out of the insured's activities, premises, or animal(s). Medical expenses must be incurred within three years of the accident, and it is important to note that this coverage will *not* pay for medical expenses incurred by the insured or any regular resident of the household, except a residence employee (such as a maid or butler).

On the surface, this coverage may seem to duplicate the coverage provided in Coverage E; however, there is an important difference between the two. Coverage F is a "no-fault" coverage that will automatically pay for bodily injuries, while Coverage E pays for both bodily injuries and property damage *for which the insured is legally liable.*

EXAMPLE

Suppose Jennifer has a party at her house and invites Randy. While dancing on the coffee table, Randy slips, falls, and is injured. Jennifer rushes Randy to the hospital. Coverage F will pay for his medical expenses incurred by the incident, even though his injuries are his own fault, because they occurred on Jennifer's premises. If on the following day Randy files a lawsuit against Jennifer, asking her for $1 million for pain and suffering damages, her homeowners policy will defend her, but if a court determines that Randy's injuries were his own fault, it may deny payment to him under a theory that Jennifer is not legally liable.

In summary, Coverage F pays regardless of fault, while Coverage E pays only when the insured is legally liable. A typical amount of coverage purchased under this policy is $5,000 per person per occurrence. So, if ten guests at Bill's party get sick from eating bad dip, each one of them may receive up to $5,000 to cover necessary medical expenses that result.

The policy contains three different types of exclusions: those that apply to Coverages E and F, those that apply only to Coverage E, and those that apply only to Coverage F.

Medical Payment Exclusions to Coverages E and F

Neither Coverage E nor Coverage F will pay for injuries or damages:

- ▲ That are *expected or intended* by the insured.
- ▲ Resulting from the *insured's business or professional activities.*
- ▲ Resulting from the *rental of premises* (however, coverage will be provided when 1) Part of an insured location is rented either on an occasional basis, or when part of an insured location is rented out solely as a residence to no more than two roomers or boarders, and 2) Part of an insured location is rented out as an office, school, studio, or private garage).
- ▲ Arising out of premises the insured owns, rents, or leases to others that have not been declared an insured location.
- ▲ Arising out of the *ownership or use of watercraft, motorized vehicles, and aircraft* (however, certain vehicles and watercraft are covered for liability):
  - ❑ Trailers that are not connected to a motorized land conveyance.
  - ❑ A vehicle designed primarily for use off public roads that the insured does not own or that the insured does own but that is on an insured location.
  - ❑ Motorized golf carts while being used on a golf course.
  - ❑ Vehicles not subject to motor vehicle registration that include lawnmowers, motorized wheelchairs, and vehicles in dead storage on the insured location.
  - ❑ Non-motorized watercraft (canoes and rowboats, for example).
  - ❑ Low-powered boats the insured owns or rents, and small (under 26 feet long) sailboats.
  - ❑ Model and hobby aircraft that are not designed to carry people or cargo.
  - ❑ Note that the exclusions of watercraft liability are very detailed. Any time the insured plans to purchase, rent, or use a watercraft, the HO policy should be consulted to determine whether or not coverage exists.
- ▲ Caused by *war or nuclear weapons* of any kind.
- ▲ Caused by the *transmission of a communicable disease.*
- ▲ Arising out of *sexual molestation, corporal punishment, or physical or mental abuse.*
- ▲ Arising out of the *use, sale, manufacture, delivery, transfer, or possession of a controlled substance* (other than legally obtained prescription drugs).

One final exception to all of these exclusions: liability for injuries to a residence employee (maid, butler, nanny, and so on) is generally covered. This type of liability coverage is provided to protect the homeowner who needs to hire domestic help, but who is not required to purchase workers compensation coverage for such employees.

Exclusions to Coverage E Only

Certain exclusions pertain only to Coverage E of the policy. They are:

- Damage to *property of any insured* (should be covered under Section I).
- Damage to *premises the insured is renting* or has control of, unless caused by fire, smoke or explosion.
- *Contractual liability*; (however, two types of contractual liability are covered). First, where the insured has entered into a contract that directly relates to the ownership, maintenance, or use of an insured location, coverage is provided. Second, where the liability of others is assumed by the insured in a contract prior to an occurrence, coverage is provided.
- Liability for *loss assessments charged against the insured* as a member of an association or organization of property owners (one example is a condominium association, which may charge individual unit owners for damage to community property).
- Liability for injuries to employees that falls under a *workers compensation or other disability law.*
- Liability for bodily injury or property damage for which the insured is also covered by a *nuclear energy liability policy.*
- Bodily injury to any insured.

Exclusions to Coverage F Only

Coverage F will not provide coverage for bodily injuries:

- Sustained by the *insured* or any *family member.*
- Sustained by a *regular resident* of an insured location.
- Sustained by a *residence employee* of the insured that occur outside of the scope of employment.
- Sustained by anyone eligible to receive benefits for their injuries under a *workers compensation or similar disability law.*
- Resulting from *nuclear reaction radiation*, etc., regardless of how caused.

HOMEOWNERS (HO) INSURANCE: BASIC FORMS AVAILABLE

The basic homeowners (HO) insurance forms available are:

- HO-1: Basic Form.
- HO-2: Broad Form.
- HO-3: Special Form.
- HO-4: Contents Broad Form (designed for tenants).
- HO-6: Unit Owners Form (for condominium owners).
- HO-8: Modified Form.

HO-1: BASIC FORM

The HO-1 provides all of the coverages mentioned previously (Coverage A through F). The distinguishing characteristic of the HO-1 is the perils it covers. As the name indicates, this policy provides only "basic" perils coverage for the dwelling and personal property. The basic covered perils are: fire, lightning, windstorm, hail, riot, civil commotion, aircraft, vehicles, explosion, smoke, vandalism, malicious mischief, theft, and volcanic eruption. The limited coverage provided by this form makes it quite unattractive to both homeowners and mortgage lenders; thus, it is not available in some markets.

HO-2: BROAD FORM

The HO-2 is virtually identical to the HO-1, except it adds coverage for seven additional perils: falling objects, weight of frozen precipitation, collapse, accidental discharge of water, bursting of steam appliances or hot water systems, freezing, and accidental damage caused by artificially generated electrical current.

HO-3: SPECIAL FORM

The HO-3 provides all of Coverages A through F, but offers greater protection for the dwelling by providing coverage on an "open-perils" (formerly called "all-risks") basis. Specifically, the HO-3 covers physical damage to the dwelling and other structures on an open-perils basis and personal property on a named-perils basis.

"Open-perils" means that unless a peril is specifically excluded in the policy, it will be covered. All of the perils in the HO-2 are covered, and all of the exclusions mentioned previously (war, nuclear, etc.) are included in the policy. The value of the HO-3 is that it will cover certain unusual losses not specifically named as perils in the HO-2. For example, suppose the insured under a HO-2 has his house trampled by a herd of cattle. As none of the named perils addresses this particular situation, the loss would not be covered. With the HO-3, however, there is no such exclusion, so the damage would be covered.

HO-4: CONTENTS BROAD FORM (DESIGNED FOR TENANTS)

The Contents form is designed for tenants who do not own their rented dwelling premises. In such cases, what the tenant really needs are personal liability coverages, plus coverage for contents and loss of use. Therefore, the HO-4 policy does not provide coverages A or B. The Contents Broad Form provides coverage for the losses caused by the perils noted under HO-2.

The minimum amount of coverage sold under the HO-4 is $6,000 of personal property coverage (Coverage C). The Coverage D (Loss of Use) limit is then equal to 20 percent of the Coverage C limit.

HO-6: UNIT OWNERS FORM (FOR CONDOMINIUM OWNERS)

The condominium association insures most condominium buildings; however, certain components of real property, such as additions, improvements and betterments, carpeting, etc., may be the responsibility of the unit owner to insure. The HO-6 provides the unique coverage needed for these special exposures. This form covers the same perils as the HO-2 and HO-4, but does not provide building coverage (other than for additions and alterations). The minimum amount of insurance that must be purchased for Coverage C (personal property) under HO-6 is $6000. Loss of use coverage is limited to 40 percent of Coverage C.

HO-8: Modified Form

The HO-8 policy provides repair cost coverage instead of replacement cost coverage for damage to property by a covered peril. The HO-8 form makes homeowners insurance affordable for persons who live in older homes that can be quite expensive to repair with original construction materials. Therefore, the functional replacement cost of the home might be much less than the actual replacement cost. The HO-8 is identical to the HO-2, except that it provides "functional replacement cost" coverage. The insured's damaged dwelling and other structures will be repaired or replaced in the event of a covered loss, but the insurer pays only for currently accepted building materials.

HOMEOWNERS (HO) INSURANCE: ADDITIONAL COVERAGES

In addition to providing Coverages A through D, Section I provides supplementary coverages as follows:

- ▲ All-risk coverage is provided for *property while it is being moved from one place to another* and for an additional thirty days thereafter.
- ▲ The cost of *removing debris of covered property* damaged by an insured peril is paid for.
- ▲ A *fire department service charge* is covered up to $250 for loss by an insured peril; however, a fire department call for rescuing a cat from a tree or people in a home being threatened by a flood is not covered.
- ▲ The additional coverages under the homeowners policy also pays for *reasonable repairs to protect the property from further damage* after a covered loss occurs.
- ▲ An additional amount of insurance is provided to *cover damage to trees, shrubs, plants, and lawns* from all covered perils except for wind (limited to five percent of the dwelling coverage, but not more than $500 for any one tree or plant).
- ▲ Up to $1,000 per loss for *assessments against an insured* by a group of property owners arising from loss or damage to property jointly owned by all of the members collectively (for example, condominium owners or cooperative apartment projects).
- ▲ Coverage may exist for damage to property arising from *the collapse of a building* caused by an insured peril in addition to several circumstances per the insurance contract.
- ▲ Damage caused by *breakage of glass or safety glazing material* that is part of the building, storm doors, or storm windows is covered (limited to $100).
- ▲ Up to $2,500 may be paid for *damage to landlord's furnishings* in an apartment on the insured's dwelling premises.
- ▲ Up to $500 of coverage for loss due to *unauthorized use of credit cards*, fund transfer cards, forgery of checks, acceptance of counterfeit money, and any incurred court costs or attorney fees may be available.

HOMEOWNERS (HO) INSURANCE: AVAILABLE ENDORSEMENTS

REPLACEMENT COST FOR PERSONAL PROPERTY

All of the forms previously discussed provide only Actual Cash Value (ACV) coverage for personal property. This endorsement adds replacement cost coverage on the personal property of the insured. Since the ACV of household contents is typically only about 25 cents of the replacement cost dollar, the replacement cost coverage option is strongly recommended. (This may not be available in all states.)

ALL-RISKS COVERAGE FOR PERSONAL PROPERTY (OPEN PERILS)

open-perils - all-risk coverage for personal property that provides for a much broader and comprehensive protection program than named-perils coverage

All-risk coverage, also known as "**open-perils**" coverage, provides for a much broader and comprehensive protection program than named-perils coverage. Under an all-risk policy, an insurance company must provide evidence that the loss is not covered under the policy before it can deny payment. The burden of proof lies with the insurer. Depending on the policy form purchased, some amount of all-risk coverage may be included on certain types of property. However, if it is not included, its purchase is recommended on both homeowners and personal property.

INFLATION PROTECTION

To avoid a coinsurance penalty, or an "under-insurance" situation, one should add an inflation-guard endorsement to the homeowners policy. This endorsement increases the face value of insurance on both the dwelling and other coverages by a specified percentage every three months, such as 1, 1½, or 2 percent.

It is rare that insurance amounts will increase at precisely the same rate as inflation in property values. Although an inflation-guard endorsement is a worthwhile purchase, it is not a complete form of protection against inflation and should not be a substitute for regular and careful review of adequate insurance coverage. As expected, the insured's premiums rise as coverage increases.

EARTHQUAKE INSURANCE

An earthquake endorsement can be added to any homeowners policy to provide coverage for earthquakes, landslides, volcanic eruption, and earth movement. A minimum deductible of $250 applies to any one loss, and there is a 2 to 5 percent deductible of the total amount of applicable insurance that applies to the loss.

SEWER BACKUP COVERAGE

This endorsement will provide coverage under Section I for property damage caused by sewer backup problems.

PERSONAL INJURY

Section II of the standard HO policy protects the insured only against liability for bodily injury and property damage. An insured may be liable for personal injury or damage to someone's reputation, as well. The HO policies can be endorsed to provide limited personal injury protection to the insured. This endorsement adds coverage for the following *unintentional* offenses (remember that if the loss is intentionally caused, the policy will not provide coverage):

▲ False arrest, detention or imprisonment, or malicious prosecution.
▲ Libel, slander, defamation of character, or violation of the right of privacy.
▲ Invasion of right of private occupation, wrongful eviction, or wrongful entry.

BUSINESS PURSUITS

This endorsement will provide the insured with liability for business activities, as long as the insured does not have an ownership or controlling interest in the business. This endorsement is designed to protect the insured as an employee of someone else who may or may not provide liability protection for the insured.

WATERCRAFT

Certain types of watercraft can be added back to the policy for coverage; however, a boat owner's policy is typically the wisest choice for any insured who owns watercraft. The boat owner's policy is quite similar in format and coverages to the Personal Auto Policy, which will be discussed later.

HOMEOWNERS INSURANCE CONTRACTUAL CONDITIONS

SECTION I CONDITIONS

Duties after a Loss

If there is a loss to an insured's property, the insured is required to fulfill a number of obligations before the loss can be settled. Immediately following the loss the insured must:

1. Give notice immediately to the insurance company or agent.
2. Protect the property from any further damage.
3. Prepare an inventory of loss to the building and personal property.
4. File written proof of the loss with the insurance company, given the company's time constraints. The insurer must provide a state-promulgated form for the proof of loss.

LOSS SETTLEMENT

This condition specifies how certain property items will be valued (whether on an ACV basis or a Replacement Cost basis, etc.). The coinsurance provision of the policy is also contained in this clause.

Loss to a Pair or a Set

When there has been a loss to pair or set (such as a partial loss of a set of china, or the theft of only one earring), the insurer may either repair or replace the damaged/lost items, or pay the difference between the value of the property as a set (before the loss) and the value after the loss.

Appraisal

This clause gives the insured the right to dispute the amount of settlement offered by the insurer. If either the insured or the insurer disagrees on the amount of loss, either person may demand an appraisal by a competent appraiser. Then, both the insurer and the insured hire their own appraisers. If the two appraisers cannot reach an agreement on the loss amount, an umpire may be chosen to mediate their differences. Each party pays for its own appraiser, and both the insured and the insurer equally share the expense of hiring the umpire.

Other Insurance

When a loss covered under this policy is also covered by some other policy, the insured cannot collect from each policy in full. To do so would violate the principle of indemnity. The Other Insurance clause states that when another policy also covers a loss, the insurer will only pay a proportion of the loss based on the limits of coverage provided by each policy.

Suppose Mary has two HO policies. One provides a limit of $50,000 and one provides a limit of $100,000. Her house is worth only $100,000; and after a fire destroys it, she will collect a proportion of the loss from each insurer. Because the first insurer provides 1/3 of all coverage provided ($50,000 / $150,000), it will pay 1/3 of the loss, or $33,333. The second insurer will pay 2/3 of the loss, or $66,667.

Suit Against Us

This clause gives the insured the right to sue the insurer *only after* all the policy provisions have been complied with. It also requires that the suit be brought within one year of the date of the loss.

Settlement at Insurer's Option

The insurer retains the right to repair or replace any part of damaged property with similar property, as long as it notifies the insured of this right within 30 days after receiving the insured's sworn proof of loss.

Loss Payment

The insurer has 60 days *after* an agreement is reached regarding the amount of loss to provide payment to the insured. Most insurers will of course pay sooner, but the standard HO policy does give the insurer 60 days to actually make payment.

SECTION THREE: INSURANCE PLANNING

Abandonment of Property

The insurer does not have to accept property abandoned by an insured. A homeowner who suffers fire damage, for example, might try to force the insurer to take control of the house and be responsible for cleanup and repairs, and even mortgage payments.

Mortgage Clause

Because many homes are mortgaged, the insurer includes this clause to protect the mortgagee's (lender's) interest in the insured home. This clause gives the mortgagee important rights. The mortgagee has the right to receive payment for valid claims on the property, even if the insurer has denied the insured's claim (which would happen in the case of misrepresentation by the insured or an intentionally caused loss). Next, the mortgagee has the right to receive notice of policy cancellation or nonrenewal at least 10 days before the coverage on the property ends.

This clause also imposes certain obligations on the mortgagee. The mortgagee is responsible for notifying the insurer if there is a change in ownership or occupancy of the mortgaged property. The mortgagee must also pay any homeowner premiums that are due but that the insured has neglected to pay, and file proof of loss statements if the insured fails to do so.

No Benefit to Bailee

If the insured has left property with a bailee, such as a moving company or dry cleaner, the insurer will not pay for loss or damaged property on behalf of the bailee. This clause does not say that claims by the insured will not be paid; it merely states that the coverage will not protect or benefit the bailee. If, for example, a fire on the premises of a dry cleaner destroyed the insured's personal property, the insurer would pay the insured's claim; however, it would then subrogate against the dry cleaner.

Recovered Property

When the insured or the insurer recovers property for which the insurer has already paid a claim (as might be the case following a theft), each must notify the other party of the recovery. The insured then has the option either to return the recovered property to the insurer or to keep the recovered property. If the insured keeps the property, the loss payment must be adjusted accordingly.

Volcanic Eruption Period

All volcanic eruptions occurring within a 72-hour period are considered one occurrence. Because volcanoes tend to erupt gradually over a period of days, this clause protects the insured from having to pay a new deductible for each eruption.

SECTION II CONDITIONS

Limit of Liability

The insurer will not pay more than the policy's coverage limit for each occurrence, regardless of the number of suits or claims filed against the insured for any one event.

Duties after a Loss

The insured is expected to give notice of any accident or occurrence to the insurer or its agent. The insured must also promptly forward to the insurer all summons and demand letters. The insured must cooperate and assist the insurer in the investigation and settlement of any claims. Finally, the insured must not voluntarily make payments for anything other than first aid at the time a bodily injury is sustained.

Duties of an Injured Person - Coverage F

An injured person or a representative must give the insurer written proof of a claim as soon as practical after a loss, and give the insurer permission to obtain medical records of the injured person. The injured person must also submit to a physical exam by the insurer's doctor, if instructed to do so by the insurer.

Payment of Claim - Coverage F

This clause states that paying any claim under Coverage F is in no way an admission of liability by the insurer or the insured.

Bankruptcy of an Insured

The bankruptcy or insolvency of any insured does not terminate coverage or relieve the insurer of its obligations under the policy.

SECTIONS I AND II CONDITIONS

Concealment or Fraud

Dishonesty either before or after a loss may void the policy. Examples of dishonesty that will void the policy include intentionally concealing or misrepresenting material facts, and intentionally causing losses to occur.

Cancellation and Nonrenewal

Every state imposes its own restrictions on the insurer's right of cancellation and nonrenewal, so it is important to examine the specific policy to understand what is allowed. Generally, however, the insured may cancel the policy at any time by notifying the insurer, while the insurer may cancel the policy only for certain reasons: nonpayment of premium, material misrepresentation of fact, or a substantial change in the risk. In most cases, the insurer must only provide a 10-day notice of cancellation when it is canceling a newly issued policy, or when it is canceling for non-payment of premium. Other cancellations and nonrenewals usually require a 30-day notice. Cancellations generally result in a pro-rata refund of unused premium.

Assignment

The insured may not assign rights under the policy without the insurer's written consent.

Subrogation

The insurer may require the insured to assign rights of recovery for payments made by the insurer. This allows the insurer to take over the insured's subrogation rights against negligent third parties. The insurer does not, however, subrogate for claims made under Coverage F of the policy.

EXHIBIT 10.3: SUMMARY OF HOMEOWNERS INSURANCE POLICIES

	HO1 (Basic Form)	HO2 (Broad Form)	HO3 (Special Form)	HO8 (For Older Homes)	HO4 (Renter's Contents Broad Form)	HO6 (For Condominium Owners)
Perils covered (descriptions are given below)	Perils 1 - 12	Perils 1 - 18	All perils except those specifically excluded from buildings; perils 1-18 on personal property.	Perils 1 - 12	Perils 1 - 18	Perils 1 - 18
Section 1: Property coverages/limits						
House and any other attached buildings	Amount based on replacement cost, minimum $15,000	Amount based on replacement cost, minimum $15,000	Amount based on replacement cost, minimum $20,000	Amount based on actual cash value of the home	10% of personal property insurance on additions and alterations to the apartment	$1,000 on owner's additions and alterations to the unit
Detached buildings	10% of insurance on the home	10 % of insurance on the home	10% of insurance on the home	10% of insurance on the home	Not covered	Not covered
Trees, shrubs, plants, etc.	5% of insurance on the home, $500 maximum per item	5% of insurance on the home, $500 maximum per item	5% of insurance on the home, $500 maximum per item	5% of insurance on the home, $500 maximum per item	10% of personal property insurance, $500 maximum per item	10% of personal property insurance, $500 maximum per item
Personal Property (Contents)	50% of insurance on the home	50% of insurance on the home	50% of insurance on the home Covers same as Broad Form	50% of insurance on the home	Chosen by the tenant to reflect the value of the items, minimum $6,000	Chosen by home owner to reflect the value of the items, minimum $6,000
Loss of use and/or add'l living expense	10% of insurance on the home	20% of insurance on the home	20% of insurance on the home	20% of insurance on the home	20% of personal property insurance	40% of personal property insurance
Credit card, forgery, counterfeit money	$500	$500	$500	$500	$500	$500
Section 2: Liability						
Comprehensive personal liability	$25,000 - $100,000	$25,000 - $100,000	$25,000 - $100,000	$25,000 - $100,000	$25,000 - $100,000	$25,000 - $100,000
Damage to property of others	$250 - $500	$250 - $500	$250 - $500	$250 - $500	$250 - $500	$250 - $500
Medical payments	$500 - $1,000	$500 - $1,000	$500 - $1,000	$500 - $1,000	$500 - $1,000	$500 - $1,000
Special limits of liability*	*Special limits apply on a per-occurrence basis (e.g. per fire or theft): money, coins, bank notes, precious metals (gold, silver, etc.), $100 to $200; securities, deeds, stocks, bonds, tickets, stamps, $500-$1,000; watercraft and trailers, including furnishings, equipment, and outboard motors, $500-$1,000; trailers other than for watercraft, $500-$1,000; jewelry, watches, furs, $500-$1,000; silverware, goldware, etc., $1,000-$2,500; guns, $1,000-$2,000.*					

326

AUTOMOBILE INSURANCE

Automobile insurance is required in virtually every state, either expressly or implicitly. Mandatory automobile insurance laws exist in many states, and they expressly require the purchase of liability insurance before owning or operating a motor vehicle. Some states further require the purchase of "no-fault" coverages that pay for bodily injuries on a first-party basis. Other states implicitly require automobile insurance by requiring motorists to be "financially responsible" for a minimum amount of bodily injury and property damage. Purchasing automobile insurance generally proves financial responsibility, although some opt to post a bond or other proof of responsibility.

In addition to these statutory requirements, many people purchase automobile insurance because their automobile is financed, and the lender requires the borrower to carry coverage for direct physical damage on the auto. Finally, many people purchase automobile insurance because they recognize that the financial burden associated with an automobile accident could be devastating. One at-fault accident could injure or kill one person or many people, and the insured would be responsible for those damages. In addition, with most new cars costing over $20,000, the damage to the insured's owned vehicle could cost thousands to repair.

To simplify, the owner and operator of an automobile should be concerned about the following losses:

▲ Liability for injuries and damages to persons outside the vehicle.
▲ Liability for injuries and damages to persons inside the vehicle.
▲ The cost to repair or replace a damaged or stolen vehicle.

In the next section of the chapter, the personal auto policy is presented. This policy can provide protection against the three major losses listed above.

PERSONAL AUTO POLICY (PAP) COVERAGES

The ISO **personal automobile policy** is the policy that is sold in almost every state; however, various state laws may result in different policy provisions and coverages. It is always important to read each policy carefully. The following discussion focuses merely on the basic ISO PAP.

ELIGIBLE AUTOS

The PAP may be used to insure four wheel passenger automobiles, pickup trucks, and vans that are owned by individuals or leased for at least six months. Pickups and vans must have a gross vehicle weight of less than 10,000 pounds and not be used primarily for business purposes (other than farming or ranching). The policy may be used to insure one vehicle or all the vehicles owned in a household (usually subject to a maximum of four vehicles on one policy). It is generally cheaper to insure all the vehicles in one household on the same policy than to insure each vehicle with a separate policy.

The PAP may be used to insure vehicles that are used for pleasure and recreation, driving to and from work, farming and ranching, and even for business use by a sole proprietor.

personal auto policy - insurance policy that covers liability for injuries and damages to persons inside and outside the vehicle and covers the cost to repair/replace a damaged or stolen vehicle

IMPORTANT POLICY DEFINITIONS

The PAP contains a section of definitions that are important for reference purposes when reading the policy. Each defined word is put in quotation marks whenever it is used in the policy. While many of the definitions are straightforward, one deserves explanation before the various coverages are discussed.

"Your covered auto" is defined as any of the following:

▲ Any vehicle shown in the policy declarations.

▲ Any new vehicle *in addition to* those shown in the declarations, but only for 30 days or until the new vehicle is reported to the insurer. The insurer will charge a premium from the date the vehicle was acquired. The new vehicle will have the broadest coverage provided on any declared vehicle for the 30-day period.

▲ Any new vehicle *that replaces* a vehicle shown in the declarations. The new vehicle will have the same coverage as the vehicle it replaced. The insured must report the new vehicle within 30 days *only if* coverage for damage to your auto is desired.

▲ Any trailer the insured owns.

▲ Any auto or trailer that the insured does not own, but that is used as a temporary substitute while a covered vehicle is unavailable due to loss, breakdown, repair, service, or destruction.

The reason this definition is so important is that sometimes coverages are provided for *any* auto, while others are provided only for "your covered auto." Thus, this distinction is important to remember when determining which losses the PAP covers.

Throughout the policy, "you" and "your" refer to the named insured. These terms will not be put in quotation marks, however, in the subsequent discussions throughout this chapter.

▲ Part A--Liability coverage.

▲ Part B--Medical payments.

▲ Part C--Uninsured motorists.

▲ Part D--Damage to your auto.

▲ Part E--Duties after an accident or loss.

▲ Part F--General provisions.

PART A: LIABILITY COVERAGE

Part A agrees to provide liability protection for bodily injuries and property damages caused by an auto accident for which any insured becomes legally liable. The insurer retains the right to defend or settle any claim or suit, and settlement and defense costs are paid in addition to the policy limits.

Covered Persons and Autos

Who is an insured under Part A? The policy clearly defines an insured as one of four parties:

▲ You or any family member for the ownership, maintenance, or use of any auto or trailer (this includes the use of borrowed autos, and even rental cars).
▲ Any person using "your covered auto."
▲ Any organization that is responsible for the conduct of someone driving "your covered auto," (such as an employer or charitable organization).
▲ Any organization that is responsible for your conduct or the conduct of a family member, while you are driving a non-owned automobile (such as an employer that might be responsible for your actions when you are using a co-worker's car for business purposes).

Exclusions

The PAP liability coverage is quite broad in nature. It excludes coverage only for the following persons and situations.

▲ *Vehicle used by auto dealer*--No coverage is provided for any auto dealer or other person in the auto business who is driving your car (the person in the auto business should have their own liability coverage).
▲ *Bodily injury to an employee*--No coverage is provided for injuries to an employee, because those should be covered by workers compensation benefits. One exception is that the insured will be covered for liability for injuries to a domestic employee.
▲ *Insured's owned property*--Liability insurance is designed to pay for damages to third parties that are caused by the insured. By definition, liability insurance cannot pay for damages to the insured's owned property. Therefore, in an auto accident, damages to the insured's car and its contents are not paid by the liability coverage. Damage to the car would have to be covered by Part D, and damage to contents of the vehicle would have to be paid by the homeowners coverage.
▲ *Property in the insured's care, custody, and control*--Along the same lines as the previous exclusion, this one prohibits the insured from recovering under his/her own liability insurance for items that are not true liability losses. When property such as a rental car is damaged in an automobile accident, the PAP treats it as if it were the insured's owned auto. The insured may not use the liability coverage to pay for damages to the rental car.
▲ *Intentional acts*--Any person who intentionally causes an auto accident is not covered for liability by the policy.
▲ *Public livery*--Coverage is not provided for any person or vehicle while transporting people or property for a fee. A share-the-expense car pool is not considered a for-fee activity, and is thus covered.

- ▲ *Commercial vehicles used in business*--This exclusion eliminates coverage for business use of automobiles, but then gives back coverage for business use of any private passenger auto, or any owned pickup or van, or any temporary or substitute pickup or van. The intent is to limit business coverage on autos to either private passenger autos, or owned pickups and vans.
- ▲ *Using auto without permission*--No coverage is provided for any person who uses an automobile without having a reasonable belief that he or she has permission to do so.
- ▲ *Regular use of non-owned auto*--When the insured has the regular use of an automobile that is not shown on the declarations page, either because the employer provides a company car or because the insured owns a non-declared vehicle, coverage is not provided. If the insured has a company vehicle, the employer should provide coverage or the insured should declare the vehicle as a non-owned vehicle and purchase coverage for it. Recall that the named insured is covered while using "any" auto. If this exclusion were not in the policy, the insured could own ten vehicles, buy coverage on only one, but have coverage on all ten. This exclusion makes it clear that the insurer will only cover those owned vehicles that have been declared, and for which a premium has been paid.
- ▲ *Autos with less than four wheels*--Motorcycles and recreational vehicles having fewer than four wheels must be specifically insured under a different policy. No coverage is provided for these types of vehicles, regardless of whether they are owned or borrowed.

Coverage Limits

The limits of coverage for Part A are shown on the declarations page, and in most cases there are actually three separate liability coverage limits--two for bodily injury, and one for property damage. All limits are on a per occurrence basis. The first bodily injury limit is the per person limit. A per person limit of $50,000 indicates that any one injured person may not receive more than $50,000 for bodily injuries. The second bodily injury limit is the per occurrence limit for all bodily injuries. If this limit were $100,000, the insurer would pay up to $100,000 for all the bodily injuries sustained in one accident, regardless of the number of persons injured. The property damage limit is also a per occurrence limit, and specifies the most the insurer will pay for all property damages caused by one accident.

These "**split limits**" are often written as follows: 50/100/25. The first number is the per person bodily injury limit, the second number is the per occurrence bodily injury limit, and the third number is the property damage liability per occurrence limit. Of course, these numbers are expressed in thousands.

EXAMPLE

split limits - three separate liability coverage limits covering bodily injury (per person and per occurrence) and property damage

Assume that the insured carried such limits and had a major accident that is deemed to be her fault, imagine the following claims filed by injured parties in the other vehicle: Arnie sustains $75,000 in bodily injuries, Betty sustains $22,000 in bodily injuries, and Carl sustains $53,000 in bodily injuries. Arnie, the driver, also incurs $17,000 in automobile repair and rental car costs. Deborah, a nearby homeowner on whose lawn the two cars ultimately landed, sustained $9,000 in lawn and shrubbery damage. Assume that all claims are settled in the order they are mentioned above.

First, address the bodily injury claims. Arnie is allowed to collect only $50,000, because that is the per person limit. Note that Arnie likely will sue for the $25,000 deficiency. Betty may collect the full $22,000. Carl will collect only $28,000 because at that point, the $100,000 per

330

occurrence limit has been reached. Claims are paid in the order that they are settled, not on a pro rata basis, so it is important that claimants begin the settlement process as soon as possible.

Next, consider the property damage claims. The policy provides a total of $25,000 of coverage, yet there is a total of $26,000 in property damage claims. Nevertheless, the insurer will pay Arnie's damages of $17,000 under the comprehensive/collision part of the policy, and Deborah's $9,000 claim will be paid in full.

Increased Limits in Another State

As mentioned previously, all states require some minimum level of financial responsibility or automobile liability insurance. When the insured in one state drives to another state and has an accident, the insured must generally have sufficient limits to meet the requirements of the state in which the accident was held.

A driver from Arizona who has only the minimum required limits of 15/30/10 who drives to Texas, where the minimum limits are 20/40/15, would be expected to have those coverage limits if an accident occurred in Texas. The PAP automatically provides the increased limits required by state law. Therefore, the Arizona driver's policy would pay up to 20/40/15 if an accident occurred while in Texas.

EXAMPLE

It is important to note that this policy provision never reduces the limits of liability the insured has purchased. If a Texas driver having the 20/40/15 coverage limits drives to Arizona, her policy will pay up to those limits for any accident. The policy will not reduce the amount of coverage provided to 15/30/10.

Loss Sharing with Other Coverage

When more than one auto policy covers a loss, the general rule is that insurance on the automobile is primary, while insurance on the driver is excess.

If Albert borrows Sue's car and has an accident while driving it, Sue's PAP coverage will pay first. When Sue's limits of coverage have been exhausted, then Albert's policy will pay on an excess basis. If more than one policy is primary (for example, if an automobile is declared and covered by two separate policies), then the primary policies share losses on a proportionate basis (as discussed under homeowners insurance).

EXAMPLE

PART B: MEDICAL PAYMENTS

Medical payments are a no-fault, first-party coverage designed to pay for bodily injuries sustained in an auto accident. Expenses must be incurred within three years of the auto accident. Limits of insurance are provided on a per person, per occurrence basis. A typical limit of coverage is $5,000/person/occurrence. This means that if four covered persons are injured in an auto accident, each may collect up to $5,000 for reasonable and necessary medical and funeral expenses.

medical payments - a no-fault, first-party insurance coverage designed to pay for bodily injuries sustained in an auto accident

Who is Covered?

An insured in this coverage is defined as any of the following:

▲ You or any family member while occupying a motor vehicle.
▲ You or any family member as a pedestrian when struck by a motor vehicle.
▲ Any other person while occupying "your covered auto."

Exclusions

Medical payment coverages exclude the following:

▲ *Public livery*--Again, no coverage is provided while the vehicle is used to carry persons or property for a fee.
▲ *Auto used as a residence*--Although trailers are included as covered autos, this exclusion prevents someone from having medical payments coverage on a house trailer. This type of nonstandard risk must be specifically insured.
▲ *Injury while working*--Any benefits that are payable under workers compensation or other disability benefit laws preclude coverage under this policy.
▲ *Using auto without permission*--No coverage is provided for any person who uses an automobile without having a reasonable belief that he or she has permission to do so.
▲ *Regular use of non-owned or non-declared auto*--Once again, when the insured has the regular use of an automobile that is not shown on the declarations page, either because the employer provides a company car or because the insured owns a non-declared vehicle, coverage is not provided.
▲ *Autos with less than four wheels*--Motorcycles and recreational vehicles having fewer than four wheels must be specifically insured under a different policy. No coverage is provided for these types of vehicles, regardless of whether they are owned or borrowed.
▲ *Auto used in insured's business*--The same exclusion that was discussed in Part A applies here. Coverage is again provided for private passenger autos used in business and for owned pickups and vans used in business.
▲ *War and nuclear hazard injuries*--Consistent with other policies, this coverage does not apply to any injuries sustained because of acts of war or because of nuclear contamination or radioactive hazards.
▲ *Racing*--No coverage is provided when the vehicle is located inside a racing facility, when the vehicle is practicing for, preparing for, or competing in any type of racing or speed contest.

PART C: UNINSURED MOTORISTS

Purpose

Because so many drivers do not obey financial responsibility and compulsory automobile insurance laws, the PAP offers insureds the option of purchasing uninsured motorist coverage that acts as the liability insurance for an uninsured or underinsured motorist.

What is Covered?

Part C will pay for bodily injuries and, in many states, property damages that are sustained by an insured because of an uninsured or underinsured motorist. In simpler terms, this coverage will pay what the uninsured, at-fault motorist's liability insurance *should* have paid, had it existed.

Who is Covered?

An insured for this coverage is defined as follows:

▲ You or any family member.
▲ Any other person occupying "your covered auto."
▲ Any person who might also be entitled to damages (such as a spouse or child) for the injuries sustained by a person described above.

Definitions of an Uninsured/Underinsured Auto

An uninsured or underinsured motorist is defined as one who has no liability coverage, one who has limits of liability coverage less than those required by the insured's home state law, one who is an unidentified hit-and-run driver, or one who has liability insurance, but whose insurer cannot or will not pay the claim. Once again, it is important to emphasize that for the insured to collect from this coverage, the uninsured or underinsured driver *must be at fault* in the accident.

Exclusions and Limitations

Many of the exclusions contained in Part B are repeated in this coverage:

▲ Public livery.
▲ Regular use of non-owned auto.
▲ Injury while working.
▲ Regular use of non-declared auto.
▲ Using auto without permission.
▲ Auto used in insured's business.

In addition, the insurer will not pay for any bodily injuries when the insured or their legal representatives settle a bodily injury claim without the insurer's consent. Furthermore, this coverage will not pay for punitive or exemplary damages.

PART D: COVERAGE FOR DAMAGE TO YOUR AUTO

Coverage D provides direct damage coverage on "your covered auto," plus any "non-owned auto." "Your covered auto" was defined previously, so it is only necessary to define "non-owned auto." A "non-owned" auto is any private passenger, auto, pickup, van or trailer not owned by or furnished for the use of a family member that is in your (or a family member's) custody. This would include a borrowed car, a rental car, and a temporary substitute auto.

Two Coverages Available

Part D provides the insured with two different direct damage coverages: collision and other-than-collision. The insured may purchase one or both of these coverages (automobile lenders will generally require the insured to carry both coverages).

Collision coverage protects the insured against upset and collision damages, such as those sustained in an accident involving other vehicles, or those sustained when an auto runs off the road and into a lake. These types of accidents are generally viewed to be the insured's fault because if there were another party to blame for the accident, the insured could ask that party's liability insurance to pay for the damages.

Other-than-Collision coverage protects the insured against the following perils: missiles or falling objects, fire, theft, explosion, earthquake, windstorm, hail, water or flood, malicious mischief or vandalism, riot or civil commotion, contact with bird or animal, and breakage of glass. These perils are typically viewed as accidental and out of the insured's control. Thus, the premium for this coverage is lower than that for collision coverage.

Dispute Resolution (Appraisal Clause)

If the insured and the insurer do not agree on the amount of a loss, the insured may demand an appraisal process similar to that provided for in the homeowners policy.

Loss Payment

The insurer retains the sole option either to pay for repairs or to declare the vehicle a "total loss" and pay the actual cash value of the vehicle, less any deductible. The collision coverage deductible is typically twice as high as the other-than-collision deductible. In most cases, insureds should carry a minimum $250 other-than-collision deductible and $500 collision deductible. Higher (and lower) deductibles are available, however. Higher deductibles generally reduce premiums.

Loss Sharing with Other Policies

When more than one auto policy covers a loss, insurance on the automobile is primary, while insurance on the driver is excess. Therefore, if Joe borrows Fred's car and has an accident while driving it, Fred's collision damage coverage will pay first. Joe's policy will pay on an excess basis, but will not pay more than the loss, and will still require Joe to pay his own deductible.

If more than one policy is primary (for example, if an automobile is declared and covered by two separate policies), then the primary policies share losses on a proportionate basis (as discussed under homeowners insurance).

---

collision - auto insurance coverage that protects the insured against upset and collision damages, such as those sustained in an accident involving other vehicles, or those sustained when an auto runs off the road and into a lake

other-than-collision - auto insurance coverage that protects the insured's auto against perils out of the insured's control, such as missiles or falling objects, fire, theft, earthquake, hail, flood, and vandalism

Exclusions

Many of the exclusions described in other coverages apply here:

- ▲ Public livery.
- ▲ Custom furnishings on a pickup or van.
- ▲ Using auto without permission.
- ▲ Radar detectors.
- ▲ Racing.
- ▲ Most electronic equipment (except permanently-installed sound reproducing equipment).
- ▲ War.
- ▲ Nuclear damages.

As with most direct property coverages, the PAP excludes coverage for normal wear and tear, and ordinary maintenance losses such as road damage to tires. Loss caused by destruction or confiscation of governmental authorities is also excluded, as could occur if the insured vehicle were involved in a crime. Losses to non-owned autos are not covered when the auto is used or maintained by anyone in the automobile business.

Finally, no coverage is provided for a rental vehicle if the insured has purchased a loss damage waiver from the rental car company. Loss damage waivers relieve the insured of liability for damage to the rented vehicle, so the insurer will not provide coverage.

PART E: DUTIES AFTER AN ACCIDENT OR LOSS

Most of the duties required of the insured are common sense: notify the insurer, file proof of loss, and cooperate with the insurer in the investigation and settlement of any claim. In addition, the insured must file a police report to have theft coverage for a stolen vehicle, or to have uninsured motorist coverage for a hit-and-run incident.

PART F: GENERAL PROVISIONS

There are several general provisions and conditions of the auto policy that are similar to those contained in the HO policies. One, however, deserves special attention: the PAP coverage territory.

The PAP provides coverage *only in* the United States, its territories and possessions, Puerto Rico, and Canada. When the insured travels to Mexico (where auto accidents are automatically criminal offenses), or to any other country outside the coverage territory, it is important to realize that the PAP is NOT effective. If the insured intends to drive in such a locale, the appropriate local coverages must be arranged.

PERSONAL LIABILITY UMBRELLA POLICY

PURPOSE

personal umbrella policy - coverage designed to provide a catastrophic layer of liability coverage on top of the individual's homeowners and automobile insurance policies

The **personal umbrella policy** (PUP) is designed to provide a catastrophic layer of liability coverage on top of the individual's homeowners and automobile insurance policies. A standard amount of coverage is $1 million, although higher limits may be purchased. The need for the PUP is largely dictated by the insured's personal wealth. The more the insured stands to lose, the more likely it is that a PUP is a suitable purchase.

CHARACTERISTICS

Most PUP insurers will require the insured to maintain certain underlying limits of coverage through an HO and a PAP; and, if the insured also has other liability exposures to insure, such as watercraft liability, minimum limits of coverage will be required for those policies as well.

self-insured retention - a payment similar to a deductible that an insured is usually required to pay for each loss under a personal umbrella policy

The PUP provides the insured with a large amount of coverage at an affordable price. A $1 million PUP limit might cost as little as $250 or $300 per year. The coverage provided is generally quite broad, and may even provide coverages in addition to those provided by the underlying policies. For example, the PUP might provide personal injury coverage (for defamation of character, false arrest, etc.) even though the underlying HO policy does not. Where these additional coverages are provided, the insured is usually required to pay a **self-insured retention** (SIR) for each loss. This SIR is similar to a deductible.

Where both the umbrella and an underlying policy cover a loss, the umbrella does not pay any claims until the underlying coverage has exhausted its limits. From there, the umbrella picks up with no SIR imposed on the insured.

EXAMPLE

If Bob has an HO policy with a Coverage E limit of $200,000, and a $1 million PUP, and is held liable for bodily injuries totaling $700,000, his HO policy will pay the first $200,000 of the claims, then the PUP will pay the remaining $500,000.

EXCLUSIONS

PUP forms are nonstandard, so it is hard to generalize about what exclusions will be included in each policy. Certain exclusions almost universally found in PUPs include: damage to the insured's property; injuries sustained by the insured or a family member; injuries that were intentionally inflicted or caused by the insured; injuries to another party that should be paid under a workers compensation law; and business and professional liability incidents.

BUSINESS AND PROFESSIONAL USE OF PROPERTY AND LIABILITY INSURANCE

Similar to individuals, businesses also have insurance needs. Some of the policies used by businesses to cover property and liability include the commercial package policy, inland marine policies, the business owners policy, business liability insurance, workers compensation, business automobile, business liability umbrella policies, professional insurance, and errors and omissions.

The Insurance Services Office (ISO) has developed a commercial insurance program including a package policy (two or more coverages).

THE COMMERCIAL PACKAGE POLICY (CPP)

The commercial package policy (CPP) is both a property and a liability coverage combined into a single policy. The advantages of such a policy include lower premiums and fewer gaps in overall coverage. Workers compensation coverage and surety coverages are not part of a CPP. A CPP policy format includes: (1) a declarations page, (2) a policy conditions page, and (3) two or more coverage parts or forms (property, general liability, crime, boiler and machinery, inland marine, commercial auto, farm). Each part or form of the CPP will specify covered property, additional coverages, extension of coverages, other provisions, deductibles, coinsurance, valuation provisions, optional coverages, and a cause of loss form. Coverages for causes of loss are basic, broad, special, or earthquake form. These forms are similar to the parallel homeowners forms. Business interruption insurance may be added. Also, a builders risk coverage form can be added to the CPP for buildings under construction.

INLAND MARINE POLICIES

Inland marine policies cover domestic goods in transit, property held by bailees, mobile equipment and property, property of certain dealers and means of transportation and communication.

THE BUSINESS OWNER'S POLICY (BOP)

The business owner's policy is specifically designed for the needs of small to medium size businesses and covers buildings, business personal property (two forms: basic and special). Basic covers listed perils, as distinguished from special, which covers all perils not excluded. The policy has a standard $250 deductible and covers business liability for bodily injury and property damage.

BUSINESS LIABILITY INSURANCE

General liability is the legal liability arising out of business activities excepting autos, motorized vehicles, aircraft, and employee (workers compensation) injuries. Liability issues, not including exceptions mentioned, are covered by commercial general liability policies (CGL). CGL can be written either as a stand-alone policy or as a part of a commercial package policy (CPP). The usual coverage, Coverage A, is for bodily injury, property damage and legal defense, but it has significant exclusions. Coverage B is for personal and advertising injury liability. Part C covers medical payments.

WORKERS COMPENSATION

Most businesses are required to carry workers compensation insurance providing the following coverages: workers compensation insurance, employer liability insurance, and other state insurance. The workers compensation insurance covers benefits provided by the insurer (state). Part two covers lawsuits by employees injured in the course of employment, but not covered by state workers compensation law. Part three covers for other states listed (business trips, etc.).

BUSINESS AUTO

Businesses also use commercial automobile insurance policies covering both physical damage to property and liability insurance.

BUSINESS LIABILITY UMBRELLA

Businesses may make use of commercial liability umbrella policies for excess coverage on liability, beyond the coverage provided by the firm's basic liability policy.

PROFESSIONAL INSURANCE

The professional liability policy provides coverage for malpractice causing harm or injury to the professional's client. The usual types of coverage included are broad coverage, liability not restricted to accidental acts, and negligent acts. There is a maximum per incident limit and an aggregate limit. The practitioner professional also needs general liability insurance.

ERRORS AND OMISSIONS

Errors and omissions coverage provides protection against loss from negligent acts, errors, or omissions by the insured. Many professionals (real estate agents, insurance agents, accountants, stockbrokers, attorneys, engineers) need errors and omissions coverage for negligent acts, or omissions, or failure to act within their own profession causing legal liability. Policies usually have large deductibles ($1,000).

EXHIBIT 10.4: INSURANCE CONCEPT SUMMARY FOR BUSINESSES AND PROFESSIONALS

	BUSINESSES	PROFESSIONALS
Property Insurance - Buildings	CPP	CPP
Property Insurance - Personalty	CPP	CPP
General Liability Insurance	As needed	As needed
Inland Marine Coverage	If transporting goods	If transporting goods
Business Interruption Coverage	As needed	As needed
Build on Risk Insurance	If construction	If construction
Workers Compensation	If employees	If employees
Commercial Auto Insurance	If autos	If autos
Commercial Umbrella Policy	Excess liability coverage	Excess liability coverage
Malpractice	N/A	Yes
Errors and Omissions	N/A	Yes

PROFESSIONAL FOCUS

Do your clients really understand the difference between a listed peril homeowners policy HO2 and an open peril policy? Do your clients understand the difference between an actual cash value policy and a replacement value policy on contents? Explain.

Unfortunately, many clients have very little understanding of even basic homeowners insurance policies. We regularly recommend open perils policies as opposed to listed perils policies. We also recommend endorsing the homeowners policies for open perils on contents and for replacement value on contents. Most clients who have actual cash value coverage on contents do not realize that in the event of a loss they may not receive a sufficient settlement to provide them with adequate funds to replace the lost items.

What information collection procedures do you use to determine if a client has an item that they mistakenly believe is insured, when in fact it is not?

We regularly use questionnaires to determine if property has been acquired (such as boats, motorcycles, airplanes, second homes, and rental property) which may not be sufficiently insured from both a property loss point of view and from a liability perspective. We try to help clients understand that boats, motorcycles, and airplanes need their own separate policies from any personal automobile policy. We also see clients who erroneously think that rental property or vacation homes with mixed use are sufficiently covered for renter liability exposure under their homeowners policy. We also like to list all serious liability exposures with the excess liability provider of the personal liability policy. We also recommend that they periodically review the actual property casualty with the agent involved.

How do you determine what advice to give to clients about how much personal liability umbrella coverage to purchase? Do you review quantitative studies or consider the net worth? Do you find resistance from insurers in issuing large personal umbrella policies, such as 5 and 10 million?

We generally look for one to three million dollars in personal liability umbrella excess coverage. We are less concerned with the size of the client's net worth than the risk exposures and their loss potential to the client. We find great resistance in purchasing umbrella excess liability coverage in the five to ten million dollar range due to the severity of the underwriting and the possible need for reinsurance at that level. We find that one million is adequate for most clients and three million is appropriate for our high net worth clients.

JAMES COLEMAN, PH.D., CPA, CFP™

DISCUSSION QUESTIONS

1. Identify the need for homeowners, auto, and umbrella insurance coverages.
2. List and define the basic coverages provided by a homeowners policy.
3. What are the various homeowners forms that are available?
4. Explain the various contractual options and provisions in homeowners insurance.
5. List and define the basic coverages provided by a personal automobile insurance policy.
6. Explain the various contractual options and provisions in personal automobile insurance.
7. Identify the need for a personal umbrella policy, and explain the umbrella's distinguishing characteristics.
8. What does Section 1 of a homeowners policy provide for?
9. What does Section 2 of a homeowners policy provide for?
10. Are intentional acts usually covered by insurance?

EXERCISES

1. What are the three types of property and liability loss exposures facing families and business?
2. If a driver loses control of a car and has an accident that causes a property loss to the car, and if the driver must rent a substitute vehicle while the car is being repaired, what is that additional loss called?
3. What are the two broad categories of property insurance with respect to covered perils?
4. What is a named-perils policy?
5. Why is it that property insurance policies only pay for the policy owner's insurable interest in a loss?
6. What are the ways that property insurance policies determine how losses will be valued?
7. List some examples of types of property with limited coverage under a typical homeowners policy.
8. List two major exclusions in almost all homeowners insurance policies that cover real property?
9. List the 12 perils identified as basic.
10. What additional 6 perils constitute broad coverage?
11. Identify personal property that has maximum dollar limits if covered by a homeowners policy.
12. If Joe is injured in an automobile wreck, will his own auto policy pay for his medical injuries?
13. Differentiate between the HO2 and HO3 form of homeowners insurance.
14. Jan rents an apartment and has $40,000 content coverage. If she is unable to occupy her apartment due to a negligent fire could she recover if, temporarily, her rent went from $600 per month to $700 per month? If so, for how many months?
15. Patrice lives in Nebraska where she carries the state-mandated minimum liability insurance on her car (10/25/10) through her personal automobile policy (PAP). She is driving through Texas and has a wreck. Texas requires minimum liability insurance of 25/50/20. She injures Sherri in an amount equal to $30,000 and Sherri's vehicle in an amount of $15,000. How much will Sherri collect from Patrice's PAP?

16. Pat and Matt are fraternity brothers who frequently drive each other's cars. Their automobiles are insured as follows:

Insured	Insurance Company	Amount
Pat	State Farm	25/50/10
Matt	All Auto	100/300/25

Pat is negligent while driving Matt's car and has an accident and the bodily injury loss is $30,000. Which insurer will pay, and how much?

PROBLEMS

1. Jimmy and Mary Sue North are married, age 28 and 27, respectively and have net worth of $100,000. They both work and Jimmy has a 1980 Chevy truck and Mary Sue has a 1994 Toyota Corolla. They also own a 1964 Indian motorcycle. They rent an apartment and have the following automobile and renter's insurance policies:

Renters Insurance:
   ▲ The Norths have a HO4 renter's policy without endorsements.
   ▲ Content Coverage - $25,000; Liability - $100,000.

Automobile Insurance:
   ▲ Both Car and Truck

Type	PAP
Bodily Injury	$25,000/$50,000
Property Damage	$10,000
Medical Payments	$5,000 per person
Physical Damage	Actual Cash Value
Uninsured Motorist	$25,000/$50,000
Comprehensive Deductible	$200
Collision Deductible	$500
Premium (annual)	$3,300

   ▲ What risk exposures are not covered by the HO4 policy?
   ▲ Comment on the efficiency and effectiveness of the PAP.
   ▲ Is the motorcycle covered under the PAP?
   ▲ Do they have adequate liability coverage? If not, what would you suggest?

2. The Nicholsons recently purchased a fabulous stereo system (FMV $10,000). They asked and received permission to alter the apartment to build speakers into every room. The agreement with the landlord requires them to leave the speakers if they move, as they are permanently installed and affixed to the property. The replacement value of the installed speakers is $4,500, and the non-installed components are valued at $5,500. The cost of the entire system was $10,000.

The Nicholsons have an HO4 policy with $25,000 content coverage and $100,000 of liability coverage.

- ▲ If the Nicholsons were burglarized and had their movable stereo system components stolen, would the burglary be covered under the HO4 policy, and, if so, for what value?
- ▲ If there were a fire in the Nicholsons' apartment building and their in-wall speaker system was destroyed, would they be covered under the HO4 policy, and if so, to what extent?
- ▲ If a fire caused them to have to move out of their apartment for a month and rent elsewhere at a higher cost, would the HO4 policy provide any coverage?

3. Ken and Mary Claire Powell are married, both age 40. They own their own home, with the land valued at $80,000 and the dwelling valued at $150,000. They have a total net worth of $550,000. They have the following property/liability insurance coverages:

Homeowners Insurance:
The Powells currently have an HO3 policy with a replacement value endorsement on contents. The policy is an open perils coverage. The deductible is $250 and the premium is $533.60 per year.

The building coverage is $100,000, contents $50,000, and liability $100,000.

Automobile Insurance:
The Powells have full coverage on both cars, including:
    $100,000 bodily injury for one person
    $300,000 bodily injury for all persons
    $50,000 property damage
    $100,000 uninsured motorist

Deductibles are:
    $500 comprehensive
    $1,000 collision

This insurance includes medical payments, car rentals, and towing.

The cost of the auto insurance is $2,123.50 per year because of the number of speeding tickets Mary Claire has received.

- ▲ The Powells suffer a burglary and lose content items that had cost them $20,000 and they have a replacement value of $27,000. How much will the insurance company pay?
- ▲ If a fire destroys 2/3 of their house and the loss is $100,000, how much will the insurance company pay?
- ▲ Do the Powells have adequate liability coverage?
- ▲ What would you recommend regarding liability coverage?
- ▲ While Mary Claire's car was parked in a parking lot next to a playground, a young student missed a ball being thrown and it dented the hood of Mary Claire's car. The damage was estimated to cost $1,840 to repair. How much will the insurer pay?

CASE

Derek Bannister, age 26, is employed at a computer store as a salesperson and trainer. He has been employed with this company for 5 years. He earns $30,000 per year. His wife, Olga Bannister, age 26, is a German citizen and is employed as a floral designer for a local florist. She earns $28,000 per year. Derek and Olga have been married for 2 years and have 1 child, Prissy, age 1.

While on a vacation in Colorado, the Bannisters had several unfortunate incidents.

▲ A deer collided into their car causing $800 worth of damage to the front of their car.
▲ Derek rented a motorcycle. While riding the motorcycle, his wallet was stolen, but he thought he had lost the wallet on the mountain during a fall, so he did not report the loss to the credit card company until he returned home.
▲ Derek, not experienced driving in the mountains, drove the motorcycle into another motorcycle on the road causing damage to both motorcycles and to Derek. The driver of the other motorcycle, Oscar Applebaum, had minor medical injuries.
▲ Upon returning home, they discovered that their apartment building had been destroyed by fire.

Insurance Information:

Life Insurance

Insured	Derek
Owner	Derek
Beneficiary	Olga
Face Amount	$50,000
Cash Value	0
Type of Policy	Term
Settlement Options	Lump Sum
Premium	Employer provided

Health Insurance

Premium	Employer provided for Derek; Olga and Prissy are dependents under Derek's policy
Coverage	Major medical with a $500,000 lifetime limit on a 80/20 basis. Maternity coverage also has 80/20 coinsurance
	Dental coverage is <u>not</u> provided
Deductible	$250 per person (3 person maximum)
Family out-of-pocket limit	$2,500

Disability Insurance

Neither Derek nor Olga has disability insurance.

Automobile Insurance

Premium	$1,000 total annual premium for both vehicles
Bodily Injury and Property Damage	$10,000/$25,000/$5,000 for each vehicle
Comprehensive	$250 deductible
Collision	$500 deductible

Renter's Insurance

Type	HO4
Contents Coverage	$35,000
Premium	$600 annually
Deductible	$250
Liability	$100,000
Medical Payments	$1,000 per person

HOMEOWNERS 04 POLICY DECLARATION PAGE

Policy Number: **H04-123-ZA-996**
Policy Period: **12:01 a.m. Central Time at the residence premises**
From: **January 1, 2002**   To: **December 31, 2002**

Name insured and mailing address:
Derek and Olga Bannister
123 Raleigh Way, Apartment 8
Anytown, State 00001

The residence premises covered by this policy is located at the above address unless otherwise indicated.
Same as above.

Coverage is provided where a premium or limit of liability is shown for the coverage.

SECTION I COVERAGES	Limit of Liability	Premium
A. Dwelling	N/A	N/A
B. Other Structures	N/A	N/A
C. Personal property	$35,000	$475
D. Loss of use	N/A	N/A
SECTION II COVERAGES		
A. Personal liability: each occurrence	$100,000	$100
B. Medical payments to others: each occurrence	$1,000	$ 25
Total premium for endorsements listed below		
	Policy Total	$600

Forms and endorsements made part of this policy:

Number	Edition Date	Title	Premium
Not applicable.			

DEDUCTIBLE - Section I: **$250**
In case of a loss under Section I, we cover only that part of the loss over the deductible stated.
Section II: Other insured locations: **Not applicable.**

[Mortgagee/Lienholder (Name and address)]
Not applicable.

Countersignature of agent/date   Signature/title - company officer

1. How much will the insurance company pay to have the front of the car repaired from the collision with the deer?

2. The fire that destroyed the apartment building also destroyed all of their personal property. While the depreciated or actual cash value of all their property is $8,000, it would cost the Bannisters about $37,000 to replace all of their lost items. How much will the insurance company pay for this loss?

3. Derek's collision with the motorcycle caused $2,000 of damage to the motorcycle owned by Mr. Oscar Applebaum. Will the HO4 liability policy cover this loss?

4. Mr. Applebaum, the motorcycle owner, suffered $350 in emergency medical expense to reset his broken arm caused by the incident. Will the HO4 cover this loss?

5. In the motorcycle accident, Derek suffered medical expenses of $1,850. Is Derek covered by the HO4 for this loss? Any other coverage?

6. What deficiencies do you think are in the Bannisters' overall insurance program?

CHAPTER 11

Social Security and Social Security Benefits

LEARNING OBJECTIVES:

After learning the material in this chapter, you will be able to:

1. Identify the six major categories of benefits administered by the Social Security Administration.

2. Understand how the Social Security program works.

3. Explain the structure of the Social Security system of trust funds.

4. List the eligibility requirements that must be satisfied for a person to qualify as a Social Security beneficiary.

5. Describe how the Social Security eligibility system works.

6. Calculate a worker's average indexed monthly earnings (AIME) and primary insurance amount (PIA).

7. Discuss how "bend points" affect a worker's Social Security benefit.

8. Understand how early and late retirement options affect a worker's Social Security benefit.

9. List the ways that a worker's Social Security benefit might be reduced.

10. Explain how "combined income" affects the taxation of Social Security benefit.

11. Understand how Medicare is structured and the benefits it offers.

12. Discuss the pros and cons of privatization of Social Security.

OVERVIEW OF THE U.S. SOCIAL SECURITY SYSTEM

Social Security benefits were never intended to provide total financial support upon retirement. Social Security was created to supplement one's pension, savings, investments and assets. A benchmark of financial planning is that, typically, individuals who retire need seventy to eighty percent of their preretirement income to maintain their same preretirement standard of living.

Through Social Security, low wage earners receive benefits of roughly sixty percent of preretirement income. However, average wage earners receive only forty-two percent of their preretirement income from Social Security benefits, while high wage earners receive only twenty-six percent of their preretirement income.

EXHIBIT 11.1: SOCIAL SECURITY BENEFITS AS A PERCENTAGE OF PRERETIREMENT INCOME

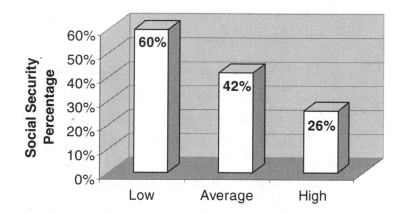

It is thus important from a financial planning standpoint to understand Social Security and the various benefits that are available. This chapter provides a basic overview of the Social Security system and its benefits. There are six major categories of benefits administered by the Social Security Administration: (1) Retirement Benefits, (2) Disability Benefits, (3) Family Benefits, (4) Survivors' Benefits, (5) Medicare, and (6) Supplemental Security Income (SSI) Benefits. Remember, however, that SSI benefits are not funded by Social Security taxes, but are funded by the general Treasury.

The **retirement benefit** is the benefit of which most people are aware. Full retirement benefits are payable at "full retirement age," with reduced benefits as early as age 62, to anyone who has obtained at least a minimum amount of Social Security credits. Based on a change in Social Security law in 1983, the age where full retirement benefits are paid begins to rise from age 65 in the year 2000 and increases to age 67 by the year 2027. Those workers who delay retirement beyond the full retirement age will receive a special increase in their retirement benefits when they ultimately retire.

retirement benefits - the most familiar Social Security benefit, full retirement benefits are payable at full retirement age with reduced benefits as early as age 62, to anyone who has obtained at least a minimum amount of Social Security credits

The **disability benefit** is payable at any age to workers who have sufficient credits under the Social Security system. Recipients must have a severe physical or mental impairment that is expected to either prevent them from performing "substantial" work for at least a year, or result in death. Earnings of $500 or more monthly is considered substantial. The disability insurance program has built-in incentives to smooth the transition back to the workforce including continuation of benefits and health care coverage while a person tries to work.

The **family benefit** is provided to certain family members of workers eligible for retirement or disability benefits. Such family members include spouses age 62 or older, or spouses under age 62 but caring for a child under age 16, and unmarried children under 18, or those under 19 but still in school, or those who are 18 years or older but disabled. **Survivors benefits** apply to certain members of the worker's family if the worker earned sufficient Social Security credits. Family members entitled to survivors benefits include those listed for family benefits, and may also include the worker's parents if the worker was their primary means of support. A special one-time payment of $255 may be made to the spouse or minor children upon the death of a Social Security covered worker.

The next benefit, **Medicare**, provides hospital and medical insurance. Those who have attained the full retirement age or those who receive disability benefits for at least 2 years automatically qualify for Medicare. Others must file an application to become qualified.

Finally, **Supplemental Security Income (SSI)** (although funded by general tax revenues and not by Social Security taxes) is another benefit of monthly payments to those 65 or older or disabled who have a low income and few assets. Generally, those who receive SSI also qualify for Medicaid, food stamps and other assistance. These major areas of benefits are discussed more fully throughout this chapter.

THE HISTORY OF SOCIAL SECURITY BENEFITS

Ever-changing social and economic conditions have dictated the social welfare structure of the United States. During its infancy, the country's economy was predominantly agricultural. As late as 1870, over half of the nation's adult workers were farmers. The country then began to transform. With the advent of the Industrial Revolution, the country began to specialize. One of the consequences of this industrialization and specialization was that more individuals became dependent on wages and income to maintain and provide for the family.

Federal, state and local governmental bodies throughout the country recognized the inherent risks in an industrialized and ever-specializing economy. It was perceived that such risks could best be handled through an approach dominated by a philosophy of social insurance. Social insurance is the act of contributing financing over time to social programs to provide protection as a matter of right to everyone without regard to need. Social insurance has its roots in workers' compensation laws dating back to as early as 1908. Various social and other retirement programs developed gradually and were implemented in piecemeal fashion. The federal government began programs to provide benefits to those who served in the Armed Forces.

disability benefit - Social Security benefit available to recipients who have a severe physical or mental impairment that is expected to either prevent them from performing "substantial" work for at least a year, or result in death and who have the sufficient amount of Social Security

family benefit - Social Security benefit available to certain family members of workers eligible for retirement or disability benefits

survivors benefit - Social Security benefit available to surviving family members of a deceased, eligible worker

Medicare - a federal health insurance plan for people who are 65 and older, whether retired or still working

SSI (Supplemental Security Income) - program administered by the Social Security Administration and funded by the general Treasury that is available to those age 65 or older or disabled who have a low income and few assets

The Depression of the 1930s necessitated action by the federal government. State and local governmental entities could not shoulder the immense needs of so many Americans. The federal government extended loans and grants to the states to provide relief and created special programs. However, by 1935, President Franklin D. Roosevelt proposed that Congress enact economic security legislation, resulting in the passage of the Social Security Act signed into law August 14, 1935.

The Social Security Act established two national social insurance programs: old-age benefits and unemployment benefits. The old-age benefits were intended for retired workers employed in industry and commerce, while unemployment benefits were for breadwinners faced with limited employment opportunities. Congress added benefits to dependents of retired and deceased workers to the program in 1939.

COLA - cost-of-living adjustments provided for Social Security benefits

By 1950, the Social Security program was expanded to cover a substantial amount of jobs that previously had been excluded. The range of the program was further broadened by the inclusion, in 1956, of disability insurance for severely disabled workers aged 50 or older and for adult disabled children of deceased or retired workers. The requirement of attaining age 50 was removed in 1960, and disability benefits were available to widows and widowers by 1967. Annual cost-of-living adjustments ("COLA") based on the Consumer Price Index were implemented through legislation in 1972, as was the delayed retirement credit that increased benefits for workers who retire after the full retirement age.

Medicaid - provides medical assistance for persons with low incomes and resources

The Medicare program was established through the 1965 amendments to the Social Security Act. The program provided for medical coverage for those aged 65 or older, regardless of income. Legislation passed in 1965 also created **Medicaid**, which provides medical assistance for persons with low incomes and resources. Medicare and Medicaid have been subject to numerous legislative changes since 1965. In 1972, the state-administered assistance programs for the aged, blind, and disabled were replaced by the essentially federally administered SSI program.

The 1983 amendments made coverage compulsory for federal civilian employees and for employees of nonprofit organizations, and state and local governments were prohibited from opting out of the system. Gradual increases in the age of eligibility for full retirement benefits from age 65 to age 67 were implemented to begin with persons attaining the age 62 in the year 2000 and ending in 2027. Benefits also became subject to income tax for those with higher earnings.

SOCIAL SECURITY TAXES AND CONTRIBUTIONS

Although the Social Security retirement benefits program is thought by many to be one of the most complicated and confusing programs ever created, the basic concept is actually quite simple. The basic concept or theory is that employees, employers, and self-employed individuals pay Social Security taxes, that is, FICA taxes, during their working years. These payments or receipts are pooled in special trust funds. Contributing workers become "covered" workers, meaning that they will fall under the Social Security umbrella of benefits, after contributing for approximately 10 years, and will receive retirement benefits based on those contributions.

FICA (Federal Insurance Contributions Act) - the law allowing Social Security taxes, including Medicare, to be deducted from paychecks

FICA stands for the **Federal Insurance Contributions Act**, the law allowing Social Security taxes, including Medicare, to be deducted from paychecks. These deductions are called Social Security taxes, which are used to pay for Social Security benefits. A portion of these FICA taxes pays part of the Medicare coverage. Separate and apart from Social Security taxes, general tax revenues are used to finance Supplemental Security Income, commonly referred to as "SSI." SSI is a program administered by the Social Security Administration that pays benefits to persons who have limited income and assets.

Employers and employees pay the taxes for Social Security and Medicare. For the year 2001, an employer and employee each pay 7.65 percent (6.2 percent for **OASDI (Old Age and Survivor Disability Insurance)** and 1.45 percent for Medicare) of the employee's gross salary up to a limit of $80,400. The salary limit rises annually based on annual increases in average wages. Self-employed workers pay 15.3 percent (7.65 percent x 2) of their taxable income up to the same salary limit. Workers who earn over the salary limit continue to pay for the Medicare portion of the Social Security tax on all earnings. The Medicare portion of the Social Security tax is 1.45 percent for employers and employees each and is 2.9 percent for self-employed workers. For example, if an employee earns a salary of $100,000 in 2001, the first $80,400 of the employee's salary will receive a tax of 7.65 percent, while the remaining $19,600 will be subject to a tax of only 1.45 percent. The employer pays the same amount as the employee.

OASDI - Old Age and Survivor Disability Insurance

THE SOCIAL SECURITY TRUST FUNDS AND THEIR RELATIVE SOLVENCY

The United States Social Security system operates on a "pay-as-you-go" basis. Social Security taxes are collected and divided among several trust funds. The federal Old-Age and Survivors Insurance ("OASI") Trust Fund pays retirement and survivors' benefits. The OASI Trust Fund receives 5.30 percent of the FICA tax. The federal Disability Insurance ("DI") Trust Fund pays benefits to workers with disabilities and their families. The DI Trust Fund receives 0.90 percent of the FICA tax. OASI and DI are the two trust funds used for payment of Social Security benefits.

The two Medicare trust funds are the federal Hospital Insurance ("HI") Trust Fund, which pays for services covered under the hospital insurance provisions of Medicare (Part A) and the federal Supplementary Medical Insurance ("SMI") Trust Fund which pays for services covered under the medical insurance provisions of Medicare, known as Part B. The SMI Trust Fund is partially funded by the general fund of the Treasury, with the remainder funding coming from monthly premiums paid by the individuals enrolled in Part B.

EXHIBIT 11.2: SOURCES OF FUNDING TO SOCIAL SECURITY TRUST FUNDS

OASI Trust Fund	5.30 percent (limited to the maximum taxable earnings)
DI Trust Fund	0.90 percent (limited to the maximum taxable earnings)
HI Trust Fund	1.45 percent (all earnings are taxed)(In 1993, the Omnibus Budget Reconciliation Act of 1993 abolished the ceiling on taxable earnings for Medicare)
SMI Trust Fund	-0- (no FICA taxes used; funded by general federal tax revenues and monthly premiums paid by enrollees)

As a general rule, for every dollar of Social Security taxes that is spent, 68 cents goes to retirement and survivor benefits, 19 cents goes to Medicare benefits, 12 cents goes to disability benefits, and 1 cent goes to administrative costs.

EXHIBIT 11.3: BREAKDOWN OF HOW $1.00 OF SOCIAL SECURITY TAX IS SPENT

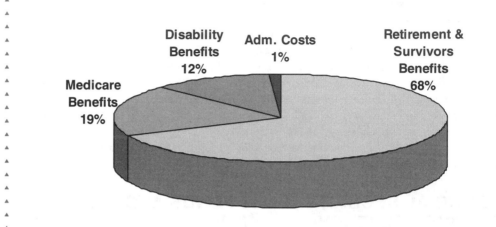

Contrary to public perception, less than one cent of every Social Security tax dollar is used to pay for administrative costs. One percent of $800 billion, however, is a large amount of money.

Tax revenues are deposited into the trust funds daily. Social Security benefits are paid from these funds. Money that is not needed to pay benefits is invested daily in Unites States government bonds. This method of investing leftover funds into U.S. government bonds is called the "partial reserve" method of funding, which has been utilized since 1983. In 2000, the Social Security Trust Funds earned over $64.5 billion in interest, representing an effective annual interest rate of roughly 6.9 percent. The goal is to receive more revenue than that which is paid out so as to accumulate large reserve funds to aid in paying benefits to the increasing number of retired workers. The increase in retired workers represents a society that is living longer due to medical improvements, better health information, and wiser lifestyles. The number of retired workers will continue to rise within the next ten years because of the baby boom generation (born from 1946 to 1964) that will begin retirement around 2010.

The trust funds are governed by The Board of Trustees of the Social Security and Medicare Trust Funds. Members of the Board of Trustees are the Secretary of the Treasury, Secretary of Labor, Secretary of Health and Human Services, the Commissioner of Social Security, and two public trustees with 4-year terms. By law, the trust funds can only be used to pay Social Security benefits and pay for administrative costs of the program. However, recent legislation has been adopted to help control future HI program costs and to extend the retirement age to receive retirement benefits. These and other measures may help extend the useful life of the trust funds. A recent report from the Board of Trustees released in March 2001 estimated that in 2038, the OASI and DI Trust Funds would become exhausted, while the HI Trust Fund will be able to pay benefits for only 25 more years. Nonetheless, for purposes of financial planning, it must be recognized that the Social Security system and benefits as they exist today are likely subject to significant change.

Based on the Board of Trustees 2001 Summary Annual Report, by the end of 2000 approximately 38.7 million individuals were receiving OASI benefits, 6.7 million individuals were receiving DI benefits and over 39 million individuals were covered by Medicare. The operations of the trust funds for the year 2000 are summarized in Exhibit 11.4:

EXHIBIT 11.4: TRUST FUNDS OPERATIONS, 2000 (DOLLARS IN BILLIONS)

Trust Fund	OASI	DI	HI	SMI
Assets (end of 1999)	$798.0	$ 97.0	$141.0	$44.8
Income during 2000	$490.0	$ 77.9	$167.2	$89.9
Outgo during 2000	$358.0	$ 56.8	$131.1	$90.7
Net increase in assets	$132.0	$ 21.1	$ 36.1	-$0.8
Assets (end of 2000)	$931.0	$118.0	$177.5	$44.0

Source: 2001 Annual Report by the Board of Trustees

SOCIAL SECURITY BENEFITS – ELIGIBILITY AND CALCULATIONS

COVERED WORKERS AND INSURED STATUS

To qualify for retirement benefits, a worker must be "fully insured," which means that a worker has earned a certain number of quarters of coverage under the Social Security system. Since 1978, quarters of coverage have been determined based on annual earnings. In other words, earning a designated amount of money, regardless of when it was earned during the year, will credit the worker with a quarter of coverage for that year. In 2000, the designated amount for a quarter of coverage was $780, while it is $830 for 2001. Thus, workers who earned at least $3,120 are credited with 4 quarters of coverage for 2000, and workers who earned at least $3,320 are credited with 4 quarters of coverage for 2001. The following is a list of the designated amounts for a quarter of coverage dating back to 1978:

EXHIBIT 11.5: DESIGNATED AMOUNTS FOR A QUARTER OF SOCIAL SECURITY COVERAGE

Year	Amount Needed to Receive a Credit for One Quarter	Year	Amount Needed to Receive a Credit for One Quarter
1978	$250	1990	$520
1979	$260	1991	$540
1980	$290	1992	$570
1981	$310	1993	$590
1982	$340	1994	$620
1983	$370	1995	$630
1984	$390	1996	$640
1985	$410	1997	$670
1986	$440	1998	$700
1987	$460	1999	$740
1988	$470	2000	$780
1989	$500	2001	$830

For most persons, 40 quarters of coverage, that is, 10 years of work in employment covered by Social Security, will fully insure a worker for life. Fully insured workers are entitled to the benefits under the Social Security system, although some benefits, like survivor's benefits, are available to "currently" (although not necessarily fully) insured individuals. "Currently" insured workers are those individuals that have at least 6 quarters of coverage out of the previous 13 quarters.

SOCIAL SECURITY BENEFICIARIES

As we discussed, Social Security benefits are paid upon retirement, disability, or death, if the eligibility requirements are satisfied. The worker's spouse and children may also be eligible to receive benefits when the worker satisfies eligibility requirements. Generally, monthly Social Security benefits can be paid to:

- ▲ A disabled insured worker under age 65.
- ▲ A retired insured worker at age 62 or over.
- ▲ The spouse of a retired or disabled worker entitled to benefits who:
  - ☐ is at least 62 years old, or
  - ☐ has in care a child under age 16, or over age 16 and disabled who is entitled to benefits on the worker's Social Security record.
- ▲ The divorced spouse of a retired or disabled worker entitled to benefits if age 62 or over and married to the worker for at least 10 years.
- ▲ The divorced spouse of a fully insured worker who has not yet filed a claim for benefits if both are age 62 or over, were married for at least 10 years, and have been finally divorced for at least 2 continuous years.
- ▲ The dependent, unmarried child of a retired or disabled worker entitled to benefits, or of a deceased insured worker if the child is:
  - ☐ under age 18, or
  - ☐ under age 19 and a full-time elementary or secondary school student; or
  - ☐ age 18 or over but under a disability that began before age 22.
- ▲ The surviving spouse (including a surviving divorced spouse) of a deceased insured worker if the widow(er) is age 60 or over.
- ▲ The disabled surviving spouse (including a surviving divorced spouse in some cases) of a deceased insured worker if the widow(er) is age 50-59.
- ▲ The surviving spouse (including a surviving divorced spouse) of a deceased insured worker, regardless of age, if caring for an entitled child of the deceased who is either under age 16 or disabled before age 22.
- ▲ The dependent parents of a deceased insured worker at age 62 or over.

In addition to monthly survivors benefits, a lump-sum death payment of $255 is payable upon the death of an insured worker. Exhibit 11.6 provides a summary of those eligible for OASDI benefits and the percentages of the worker's primary insurance amount ("PIA") that each beneficiary will receive. The PIA is the retirement benefit that the worker would receive if he or she retires at full retirement age. The full explanation of the PIA calculation and how to determine one's retirement benefit is discussed later in this chapter.

EXHIBIT 11.6: SUMMARY OF SOCIAL SECURITY OASDI BENEFITS

Assuming Normal Retirement Age of 65 and 2 Months

	Retirement	Survivorship		Disability
	Fully Insured (2)	Fully Insured (2)	Currently Insured (3)	(4)
Participant	100% @ 65	Deceased	Deceased	100%
Child Under 18	50%	75%	75%	50%
Spouse with child under 16	50%	75%	75%	50%
Spouse - Age 65 (1)	50%	100%	0%	50%
Spouse - Age 62 (1)	40%	83%	0%	40%
Spouse - Age 60 (1)	N/A	71.5%	0%	N/A
Dependent Parent	0%	75/82.5 (5)	0%	0%

(1) Includes divorced spouse who has been married 10 years (unless they have remarried).

(2) Fully insured is 40 quarters of coverage.

(3) Currently insured is at least six quarters of coverage in the last 13 quarters.

(4) Disability insured is based on age as follows:

  Before age 24 - Must have 6 quarters of coverage in the last 12 quarters.

  Age 24 through 30 - Must be covered for half of the available quarters after age 21.

  Age 31 or older - Must be fully insured and have 20 quarters of coverage in the last 40 quarters.

(5) Parent benefit is 82.5% for one parent, and 75% for each parent if two parents.

SOCIAL SECURITY RETIREMENT BENEFITS – A CLOSER LOOK

The most commonly known Social Security benefit is the Retirement Benefit. Until 2000, full retirement age, the age where full retirement benefits are available to the retiree, was 65 years. The age at which full benefits are paid began to rise in the year 2000. Exhibit 11.7 shows the phase-out, which raises full retirement age with full benefits to age 67:

EXHIBIT 11.7: AGE FULL RETIREMENT BENEFITS BEGIN

Full Retirement Age With Full Benefits	Year Born
65 years	Before 1938
65 years, 2 months	1938
65 years, 4 months	1939
65 years, 6 months	1940
65 years, 8 months	1941
65 years, 10 months	1942
66 years	1943-1954
66 years, 2 months	1955
66 years, 4 months	1956
66 years, 6 months	1957
66 years, 8 months	1958
66 years, 10 months	1959
67 years	1960-present

People who delay retirement beyond full retirement age receive a special increase in their benefit when they do retire, while people who take early retirement, currently as early as age 62, receive an actuarially reduced monthly benefit, which is a 5/9th of one percent reduction, 1/180th, for each month of early retirement. Early and late retirement options are discussed in the next section.

When engaging in financial planning for an individual, it may be appropriate to compute the individual's expected Social Security retirement benefit and consider the benefit in that individual's retirement plan. However, some financial planners choose not to consider the estimated retirement benefit in order to be conservative in developing a financial plan, while others justify exclusion of Social Security retirement benefit from financial planning based on fear of drastic changes to the Social Security system through legislative action or through economically driven forces.

THE SOCIAL SECURITY STATEMENT

Social Security Statement, Form SSA-7005 - a written report mailed by the Social Security Administration to all workers age 25 and over who are not yet receiving Social Security benefits that provides an estimate of the worker's eventual Social Security benefits and instructions on how to qualify for those benefits

As of October 1999, the Social Security Administration began automatically mailing a **Social Security Statement--Form SSA-7005,** to all workers age 25 and over who are not yet receiving Social Security benefits. The Social Security Statement should prove to be a valuable tool in the process of personal financial planning for the worker and his or her family. The statement, formerly known as the Social Security Personal Earnings and Benefits Estimate Statement ("PEBES") is a written report that provides an estimate of the worker's eventual Social Security benefits and instructions on how to qualify for those benefits.

Specifically, the new Social Security Statement includes the worker's complete lifetime earnings history that has been reported to the Social Security Administration, an estimate of the amount of Social Security taxes (FICA) and Medicare taxes (FICA-Med) that the worker and employer (if applicable) have paid, and forecasts the ultimate benefits to be paid to the worker and family through retirement, disability and/or survivorship.

The all-encompassing mail out campaign is designed to keep the worker informed as to his or her earnings history and to ensure the accuracy and completeness of the Social Security Administration's records. If any earnings are incorrect or incomplete, the worker can notify the Social Security Administration of the problem well in advance of the time of the worker's retirement age when records are not as easily verifiable or available. The statement also serves as a quick and reliable reference to the worker for use in financial planning and forecasting, whether done by the individual worker or by a financial planner. The statement will be mailed to the individual worker roughly three months prior to his or her birthday and will continue to be mailed at or near that time every year until the worker begins to receive Social Security benefits. An example of the Social Security Statement is provided at the end of this chapter (Chapter Appendix 11.1).

Beyond the automatic statement mail-out, workers can request a Social Security Statement at any time from the Social Security Administration. A statement can be requested by the worker from the Social Security Administration by filling out and mailing a Request for a Social Security Statement, SSA Form 7004 (Chapter Appendix 11.2), or by requesting it online at *www.ssa.gov.* Applicants can also obtain the request form by calling Social Security at 1-800-772-1213 and asking for the Form SSA-7004. The Social Security Administration will also answer questions and set up appointments with local Social Security offices through the toll-free number. Even with an estimate, financial planners may still want to explain to their clients exactly how the clients' benefit is determined.

THE RETIREMENT BENEFIT CALCULATION

Determining a worker's retirement benefit requires specific, detailed information pertaining to age, earnings history and the worker's retirement date. Social Security benefits are based on earnings averaged over most of a worker's lifetime. Actual earnings are first adjusted or "indexed" to current dollars to account for changes in average wages since the year the earnings were received. Then, the Social Security Administration calculates **average indexed monthly earnings** ("AIME") during the 35 years in which the applicant earned the most. The Social Security Administration applies a formula to these earnings and arrives at a basic benefit, which is referred to as the **primary insurance amount** or **PIA**. The Social Security retirement benefit is based on the worker's PIA. The PIA determines the amount the applicant will receive at his or her full retirement age, but the amount of the benefit depends on the year in which the retiree turns age 62. The PIA is indexed to the consumer price index (CPI) annually.

Figuring the Worker's Average Indexed Monthly Earnings (AIME)

To determine a worker's AIME, the worker's annual earnings from age 22 to 62 must be converted into current dollars by multiplying the worker's total annual earnings for each year by an indexing factor. The indexing factor is the result of dividing the national average wage for the year in which the worker attains age 60 by the national average wage for the actual prior year being indexed. For instance, for a worker age 63 in 2001, the indexing factor for the year 1970 is determined by dividing the national average wage for 1998 (when the worker attained age 60), which was $28,861.44, by the national average wage for 1970 (the year being indexed), which was $6,186.23, which yields a factor of 4.66543. Exhibit 11.8 provides national average wages from 1952 to 1999.

AIME (average indexed monthly earnings) - calculation that adjusts, or indexes, a worker's actual earnings to current dollars to account for changes in average wages since the year the earnings were received during the 35 years in which the worker earned the most

PIA (primary insurance amount) - calculation on which a worker's retirement benefit is based, the PIA determines the amount the applicant will receive at his or her full retirement age, but the amount of the benefit depends on the year in which the retiree turns age 62. The PIA is indexed to the consumer price index (CPI) annually

EXHIBIT 11.8: NATIONAL AVERAGE WAGE INDEXING SERIES, 1952-1999

Year	Amount	Year	Amount	Year	Amount
1952	2,973.32	1968	5,571.76	1984	16,135.07
1953	3,139.44	1969	5,893.76	1985	16,822.51
1954	3,155.64	1970	6,186.24	1986	17,321.82
1955	3,301.44	1971	6,497.08	1987	18,426.51
1956	3,532.36	1972	7,133.80	1988	19,334.04
1957	3,641.72	1973	7,580.16	1989	20,099.55
1958	3,673.80	1974	8,030.76	1990	21,027.98
1959	3,855.80	1975	8,630.92	1991	21,811.60
1960	4,007.12	1976	9,226.48	1992	22,935.42
1961	4,086.76	1977	9,779.44	1993	23,132.67
1962	4,291.40	1978	10,556.03	1994	23,753.53
1963	4,396.64	1979	11,479.46	1995	24,705.66
1964	4,576.32	1980	12,513.46	1996	25,913.90
1965	4,658.72	1981	13,773.10	1997	27,426.00
1966	4,938.36	1982	14,531.34	1998	28,861.44
1967	$5,213.44	1983	$15,239.24	1999	30,469.84

Source: Social Security Administration (www.ssa.gov)

Next, each year's annual earnings must be multiplied by its indexing factor to arrive at the indexed earnings for the years from age 22 to 60. Note that the indexing factor will always equal one for the year in which the worker attains age 60 and later years. After all annual earnings are indexed or converted to current dollar amounts, the highest 35 years of indexed earnings are added together for a sum total. The sum of the highest 35 years is then divided by 420 (which represents 35 years multiplied by 12 months per year), which yields the average amount of monthly earnings for all indexed years, hence the name average indexed monthly earnings, or AIME. Once the worker's AIME is determined, the next step in determining the worker's retirement benefit is to calculate the primary insurance amount, or PIA, for the worker.

Figuring the Worker's Primary Insurance Amount (PIA)

Generally, the PIA is the actual Social Security retirement benefit for the retiree who retires at full retirement age. For those who retire early or late and for family or surviving beneficiaries, the PIA is not the actual amount of the benefit, but the PIA is used to determine their actual benefit.

The PIA is a figure derived from the worker's AIME. The PIA is calculated by applying a "benefit formula" to AIME. This benefit formula changes from year to year and depends on the worker's first year of eligibility, that is, when the worker turns 62, becomes disabled before age 62, or dies before attaining age 62.

bend points - the three separate percentages of portions of the AIME that are summed to arrive at the PIA

The PIA is the sum of three separate percentages of portions of the AIME. These portions are also known as "**bend points**." For the year 2001, these portions are the first $561 of AIME, the amount of AIME between $561 and $3,381, and the AIME over $3,381. The bend points for 2001 are thus $561 and $3,381. Accordingly, for individuals who first become eligible for retirement benefits or disability insurance benefits in 2001 or who die in 2001 before becoming eligible for benefits, their PIA will be the sum of:

> 90 percent of the first $561 of their AIME, *plus*
> 32 percent of their AIME over $561 up to $3,381, *plus*
> 15 percent of their AIME that exceeds $3,381.

The sum of these three calculations is rounded down to the next lower multiple of $0.10 (if it is not already a multiple of $0.10). For calculations in subsequent years, it is useful to know how to determine a given year's bend points. Exhibit 11.9 shows the established bend points from 1979 through 2001.

EXHIBIT 11.9: BEND POINT TABLE

	Dollar Amounts (bend points) in PIA Formula	
Year	First	Second
1979	$180	$1,085
1980	194	1,171
1981	211	1,274
1982	230	1,388
1983	254	1,528
1984	267	1,612
1985	280	1,691
1986	297	1,790
1987	310	1,866
1988	319	1,922
1989	339	2,044
1990	356	2,145
1991	370	2,230
1992	387	2,333
1993	401	2,420
1994	422	2,545
1995	426	2,567
1996	437	2,635
1997	455	2,741
1998	477	2,875
1999	505	3,043
2000	531	3,202
2001	561	3,381

Source: Social Security Administration (www.ssa.gov)

In order to determine future years' bend points, the 1979 bend points are converted into dollars for that year. The bend points for 2001 were determined by multiplying the 1979 bend points ($180 and $1,085) by the ratio between the national average wage for 1999, which was $30,469.84, and the national average wage for 1977, which was $9,779.44, rounded to the nearest dollar. $30,469.84 divided by $9,779.44 is 3.1157040. When multiplying the 1979 bend points of $180 and $1,085 by 3.1157040, the rounded results are $561 and $3,381, the bend points for 2001. For subsequent years, the 1979 bend points should be indexed by multiplying them by the ratio for the national average wage for the year the worker attains age 60 over the national average wage for 1977.

EXAMPLE

In this example, we use the retirement benefit calculation to estimating the Social Security retirement benefit for John, a covered worker born in 1938. John was born in January 1938, began working at age 22 and plans on retiring at his full retirement age of 65 years and 2 months in March 2003. Below is a listing of John's actual earnings from 1960 through 1998, which John obtained by requesting a Form SSA-7004. The chart below also lists the maximum amount of creditable earnings for the specific calendar year, and the national average wage for the specific calendar year. John wants to know what his retirement benefit will be when he gets his first Social Security retirement benefits check.

Step 1: Calculate the Indexing Factor for all years from 1960 to 2001. For 1960, this is done by dividing the national average wage for 1998 (the year John reached age 60) by the national average wage for 1960. $28,861.44 (1998 national average wage) divided by $4,007.12 (1960 national average wage) equals 7.202539. For 1961, divide the national average wage for 1998 (the year John reached age 60) by the national average wage for 1961. $28,861.44 (1998 national average wage) divided by $4,086.76 (1961 national average wage) equals 7.062181. Continue the calculation for every year until 1998. The indexing factor for 1998 and all subsequent years will equal 1. The chart below lists the indexing factors for 1960 through 1998. To avoid manually making this calculation when determining one's retirement benefit, the Social Security Administration's website provides the indexing factors for the current year at *www.ssa.gov/pubs/10070.html*

Year	A Maximum Creditable Earnings	B John's Actual Earnings by Year	C National Average Wage	D Indexing Factor
1960	4,800	$4,000	$4,007.12	7.202539
1961	4,800	$4,200	$4,086.76	7.062181
1962	4,800	$4,400	$4,291.40	6.725414
1963	4,800	$4,700	$4,396.64	6.564431
1964	4,800	$5,000	$4,576.32	6.306692
1965	4,800	$5,100	$4,658.72	6.195144
1966	6,600	$4,000	$4,938.36	5.844337
1967	6,600	$4,100	$5,213.44	5.535969
1968	7,800	$4,200	$5,571.76	5.179950
1969	7,800	$4,900	$5,893.76	4.896949
1970	7,800	$8,200	$6,186.24	4.665425
1971	7,800	$8,900	$6,497.08	4.442217
1972	9,000	$7,200	$7,133.80	4.045732
1973	10,800	$8,500	$7,580.16	3.807497
1974	13,200	$11,500	$8,030.76	3.593862
1975	14,100	$12,000	$8,630.92	3.343959
1976	15,300	$14,800	$9,226.48	3.128110
1977	16,500	$12,000	$9,779.44	2.951236
1978	17,700	$11,000	$10,556.03	2.734119
1979	22,900	$13,000	$11,479.46	2.514181
1980	25,900	$14,000	$12,513.46	2.306432
1981	29,700	$18,500	$13,773.10	2.095493
1982	32,400	$22,000	$14,531.34	1.986151
1983	35,700	$22,500	$15,239.24	1.893890
1984	37,800	$24,500	$16,135.07	1.788740
1985	39,600	$35,000	$16,822.51	1.715644
1986	42,000	$35,500	$17,321.82	1.666190
1987	43,800	$36,000	$18,426.51	1.566300
1988	45,000	$42,200	$19,334.04	1.492779
1989	48,000	$47,000	$20,099.55	1.435925
1990	51,300	$54,500	$21,027.98	1.372526
1991	53,400	$55,500	$21,811.60	1.323215
1992	55,500	$58,000	$22,935.42	1.258379
1993	57,600	$59,000	$23,132.67	1.247648

	A	B	C	D
Year	Maximum Creditable Earnings	John's Actual Earnings by Year	National Average Wage	Indexing Factor
1994	60,600	$60,000	$23,753.53	1.215038
1995	61,200	$51,000	$24,705.66	1.168212
1996	62,700	$42,000	$25,913.90	1.113744
1997	65,400	$43,500	$27,426.00	1.052339
1998	68,400	$46,000	$28,861.44	1.000000
1999	72,600	$30,000	$30,469.84	1.000000
2000	76,200	$35,000	Unavailable	1.000000
2001	80,400	$38,000	Unavailable	1.000000

Step 2: Index John's annual earnings from 1960 to 2001 by multiplying John's annual earnings (remember, do not exceed the maximum creditable earnings) by the indexing factor for that year. The result is John's earnings for each year, converted to current dollars. The chart below shows John's indexed earnings from 1960 to 2001.

	A.	B.	C.	D.
Year	Maximum Creditable Earnings	John's Actual Earnings by Year	Indexing Factor	Indexed Earnings (indexing factor x actual earnings not more than maximum creditable earnings)
1960	4,800	$4,000	7.202539	$28,810.56*
1961	4,800	$4,200	7.062181	$29,661.16
1962	4,800	$4,400	6.725414	$29,591.82
1963	4,800	$4,700	6.564431	$30,852.83
1964	4,800	$4,800	6.306692	$30,272.12
1965	4,800	$4,800	6.195144	$29,736.69
1966	6,600	$4,000	5.844337	$23,377.35*
1967	6,600	$4,100	5.535969	$22,697.47*
1968	7,800	$4,200	5.179950	$21,755.79*
1969	7,800	$4,900	4.896949	$23,995.05*
1970	7,800	$7,800	4.665425	$38,256.49
1971	7,800	$7,800	4.442217	$34,649.29
1972	9,000	$7,200	4.045732	$29,129.27*
1973	10,800	$8,500	3.807497	$32,363.72
1974	13,200	$11,500	3.593862	$41,329.41
1975	14,100	$12,000	3.343959	$40,127.51
1976	15,300	$14,800	3.128110	$46,296.03
1977	16,500	$12,000	2.951236	$35,414.83
1978	17,700	$11,000	2.734119	$30,075.31
1979	22,900	$13,000	2.514181	$34,684.35
1980	25,900	$14,000	2.306432	$32,290.05
1981	29,700	$18,500	2.095493	$38,766.62
1982	32,400	$22,000	1.986151	$43,695.32
1983	35,700	$22,500	1.893890	$42,612.52
1984	37,800	$24,500	1.788740	$43,824.13
1985	39,600	$35,000	1.715644	$60,047.54

	A.	B.	C.	D.
Year	Maximum Creditable Earnings	John's Actual Earnings by Year	Indexing Factor	Indexed Earnings (indexing factor x actual earnings not more than maximum creditable earnings)
1986	42,000	$35,500	1.666190	$59,149.75
1987	43,800	$36,000	1.566300	$56,386.80
1988	45,000	$42,200	1.492779	$62,995.27
1989	48,000	$47,000	1.435925	$67,488.48
1990	51,300	$51,300	1.372526	$70,410.58
1991	53,400	$53,400	1.323215	$70,659.68
1992	55,500	$55,500	1.258379	$69,840.03
1993	57,600	$57,600	1.247648	$71,864.52
1994	60,600	$60,000	1.215038	$72,902.28
1995	61,200	$51,000	1.168212	$71,260.93
1996	62,700	$42,000	1.113744	$46,777.25
1997	65,400	$43,500	1.052339	$45,776.75
1998	68,400	$46,000	1.000000	$46,000.00
1999	72,600	$30,000	1.000000	$30,000.00
2000	76,200	$35,000	1.000000	$35,000.00

*denotes that the indexed earnings for the given year is not one of the 35 highest amounts.

Step 3: Take the highest 35 amounts of yearly indexed earnings and add them together. The result is $1,616,062.06.

Step 4: Divide the sum total of the 35 highest amounts of indexed earnings by 420, the number of months in 35 years, and round that number to the nearest dollar. The result is $3,848, which is John's AIME, or average indexed monthly earnings ($1,615,189.33 ÷ 420).

Step 5: Calculate John's PIA by adding the sum of 3 separate percentages of the bend points for 2000 as follows:

    (a) Multiply the first $531 of John's AIME by 90 percent
           $561 x 0.90 = $504.90;
    (b) Multiply any amount over $561 and less than $3,381 by 32 percent
           $2,820 x 0.32 = $902.40; and
    (c) Multiply any amount over $3,381 by 15 percent
           $467 x 0.15 = $70.05.

Step 6: Add the multiplication results from (a), (b), and (c) from Step 5 together. Round down to the next lowest $.10. The result is $1,477.30. This is John's PIA, or estimated monthly retirement benefit at his full retirement age, 65 and 2 months.

Note, in Step #5 above, the AIME is converted to the "Primary Insurance Amount." As shown below, there are different dollar amounts that are used in the PIA formula for workers born before 1936:

EXHIBIT 11.10: DOLLAR AMOUNTS FOR THE PIA FORMULA

YEAR OF BIRTH	90% FACTOR*	32% FACTOR*	15% FACTOR*
1928	First $356	Next $1,789	Over $2,145
1929	$370	$1,860	$2,230
1930	$387	$1.946	$2,333
1931	$401	$2,109	$2,420
1932	$422	$2,123	$2,545
1933	$426	$2,141	$2,567
1934	$437	$2,198	$2,635
1935	$455	$2,286	$2,741
1936	$477	$2,398	$2,875

Indexed to CPI

These figures for the PIA rise each year based on a cost-of-living adjustment ("COLA") that is applied to reflect changes in the cost of living. Recent COLAs, which are based on inflation, are shown in Exhibit 11.11.

EXHIBIT 11.11: COST OF LIVING ADJUSTMENT (COLA) PER YEAR

COLA	YEAR
5.4%	1990
3.7%	1991
3.0%	1992
2.6%	1993
2.8%	1994
2.6%	1995
2.9%	1996
2.1%	1997
1.3%	1998
2.4%	1999
3.5%	2000

Annual COLA increases are determined by October of each year and go into effect in time so that they first appear on monthly benefit checks received in January. In 2001, the maximum monthly retirement benefit for retirees at full retirement age is $1,536, compared to $1,433 in 2000.

Early and Late Retirement Options

Workers entitled to retirement benefits can currently take early retirement benefits as early as age 62. The worker will receive a reduced benefit because he or she will receive more monthly benefit payments, as payments commence earlier than if the worker had waited and retired at full retirement age. The reduction to one's monthly benefit for early retirement is permanent.

Whether the worker who takes early retirement will ultimately receive more or less in value from retirement benefits depends on how long the worker lives. Conversely, a delayed or postponed retirement will increase the monthly retirement benefit for a worker as late as age 70.

For each month of early retirement, a worker will receive a reduction in his or her monthly retirement benefit by 0.555 percent, or 1/180, for each month of early retirement taken up to the first 36 months. For subsequent months of early retirement, the permanent reduction percentage is 0.416 percent, or 1/240, per month.

EXAMPLE   Korie, a fully insured worker born in 1938, takes retirement benefits at age 64 years and 1 month in 2001. Korie will receive her retirement benefit, less 11/180ths, because Korie retired 11 months before her full retirement age. If Korie's monthly retirement benefit would have been $1,000 had she retired at age 65, Korie would receive $938 per month instead, for the remainder of her life, subject of course to COLA adjustments.

Although the full retirement age will be phased out to age 67, workers will still have the option of taking early retirement at age 62. However, the reduction percentage that is applied to the monthly retirement benefit will increase until 2027. Before 2000, those who retired at age 62 received 80 percent of their retirement benefit, but the increase in full retirement age has increased the number of months from 62 until full retirement age. For instance, in the year 2009, covered workers who retire at age 62 will receive 75 percent of their monthly retirement benefit, that is, 25 percent less than his or her full retirement benefit. By 2027, a covered worker retiring at age 62 (full retirement age would be 67) will receive only 70 percent of his or her monthly retirement benefit, versus the previous 80 percent for 62-year-old retirees before 2000. Exhibit 11.12, which was compiled by the Social Security Administration, shows the phase-in of the Social Security full retirement age and accompanying reductions for early retirement at age 62.

EXHIBIT 11.12: SOCIAL SECURITY FULL RETIREMENT AND REDUCTIONS* BY AGE

Year of Birth	Full Retirement Age	Age 62 Reduction Months	Monthly Percent Reduction	Total Percent Reduction
1937 or earlier	65	36	.555	20.00
1938	65 & 2 months	38	.548	20.83
1939	65 & 4 months	40	.541	21.67
1940	65 & 6 months	42	.535	22.50
1941	65 & 8 months	44	.530	23.33
1942	65 & 10 months	46	.525	24.17
1943-1954	66	48	.520	25.00
1955	66 & 2 months	50	.516	25.84
1956	66 & 4 months	52	.512	26.66
1957	66 & 6 months	54	.509	27.50
1958	66 & 8 months	56	.505	28.33
1959	66 & 10 months	58	.502	29.17
1960 and later	67	60	.500	30.00

Percentage monthly and total reductions are approximate due to rounding. The actual reductions are .555 or 5/9 of 1 percent per month for the first 36 months and .416 or 5/12 of 1 percent for subsequent months.
Source: Social Security Administration (www.ssa.gov)

No matter what your full retirement age is, you may start receiving benefits as early as age 62. You can also retire at any time between age 62 and full retirement age; however, if you start at one of these early ages, your benefits are reduced a fraction of a percent for each month before your full retirement age.

EXAMPLE

Let's assume that Josephine, a worker born in 1939, decided to retire on her 62nd birthday. Assume that her full retirement benefit would have been $1,429.20 at age 65 and 4 months, her full retirement age. If she retires at age 62, what will her monthly retirement benefit be?

The answer is $1,119. Josephine is retiring 38 months early. The monthly retirement benefit reduction percentage is 1/180 for the first 36 months (1/180 x 36 = 20 percent) and 1/240 for the 4 subsequent months of early retirement (1/240 x 4 = 1.6668 percent), yielding a total permanent reduction to Josephine's monthly retirement benefit of 21.6667 percent. 21.6667 percent x $1,429.20 = $309.66. $1,429.20 - $309.66 = $1,119.50 (rounded off).

EXAMPLE

What if Josephine retires at age 64 and 6 months? What will her permanent monthly retirement benefit be? (subject to COLA increases)

The answer is $1,349. 1/180 x 10 = 5.5556 percent. 5.5556 percent x $1,429.20 = $79.40. $1,429.20 - $79.40 = $1,349.80 (rounded off).

For those covered individuals who postpone retirement, that is, take late retirement, or when benefits are lost due to the earnings limitation, the monthly retirement benefit and the benefit paid to the surviving spouse will increase each year (until age 70) as follows:

EXHIBIT 11.13: PERCENTAGE INCREASES FOR DELAYED RETIREMENT

Increase For Year Born	Annual Percentage Each Year Of Late Retirement	After Age
1917-1924	3.0%	65
1925-1926	3.5%	65
1927-1928	4.0%	65
1929-1930	4.5%	65
1931-1932	5.0%	65
1933-1934	5.5%	65
1935-1936	6.0%	65
1937	6.5%	65
1938	6.5%	65 and 2 months
1939	7.0%	65 and 4 months
1940	7.0%	65 and 6 months
1941	7.5%	65 and 8 months
1942	7.5%	65 and 10 months
1943	8.0%	66

Those taking delayed retirement receive a permanent increase to their monthly retirement benefit.

Although the calculations explained above can provide estimates of what benefits a retiring worker may receive, a financial planning advisor should have the client obtain his or her entire earnings history up to the moment of retirement from the Social Security Administration to get the most accurate benefit estimate.

Reduction of Social Security Benefits

Besides early retirement, there are two other manners in which beneficiaries can have their benefits reduced. The first method is through reduction of benefits based on exceeding earnings limitations, referred to as the **retirement earnings limitations test**. The other method is through taxation of Social Security benefits. Both of these measures ultimately reduce one's net benefits.

First, a person generally can continue to work even though he or she is considered "retired" under Social Security. Those earnings obtained by the beneficiary must not exceed certain limitations. Beneficiaries can work and earn up to the limitation and still receive all of their benefits, but if those earnings exceed the designated limit for the calendar year, then some or all benefits will be withheld. For 1999, the earnings limitation for beneficiaries under the age of 65 was $9,600 and at age 65 to 69 was $15,500. The law provided for earnings limitations of $10,080 for those under age 65 for 2000, whereby the Social Security Administration deducted $1 in benefits for each $2 earned by those beneficiaries above $10,080. For 2001, these beneficiaries under age 65 have an earnings limitation of $10,680. However, in April 2000, Social Security law was changed, effective January 1, 2000, to delete the retirement earnings limitation for retirees at age 65, not up to age 70 as before. In the year that the retiree reaches age 65, $1 in benefits will be deducted for each $3 earned above the given year's limit, but only for earnings before the month the retiree reaches his or her 65th birthday. In 2000, the limit for earnings in the year the retiree reaches age 65 was $17,000. For 2001, the limit for earnings in the year the retiree reaches age 65 is $25,000. The earnings limitation increases every year as median earnings nationwide increase.

In the event that a beneficiary's earnings exceed the limitation, that beneficiary's benefits will be reduced depending on his or her age. The beneficiary must file an annual report of his or her earnings to the Social Security Administration by April 15 of the year following the year worked and must provide the exact earnings for that year and an estimate for the current year. The filing of a federal tax return with the IRS does not satisfy the filing requirement with the Social Security Administration. Also, the wages count toward the earnings limitation when they are earned, not when paid, whereas income for the self-employed normally counts when paid, not earned. If other family members receive benefits based on the beneficiary's Social Security record, then the total family benefits may be affected by the beneficiary's earnings that exceed the earnings limitation. In such a case, the Social Security Administration will withhold not only the worker's benefits, but will withhold those benefits payable to family members as well. However, if an individual receives benefits as a family member, that individual's earnings will affect only his or her own benefits.

EXAMPLE

Matthew is 64 years old and, despite being retired from his occupation as an attorney, earned $30,000 in 2001 while working as a golf instructor at a local golf course. Matthew's monthly retirement benefit from Social Security is normally $1,200, which totals $14,400 for the entire

retirement earnings limitations test - one of the ways in which Social Security benefit recipients can have their benefits reduced based on exceeding earnings limitations

year. Because Matthew exceeded the retirement earnings limitation, how much money will be deducted from Matthew's retirement benefit for 2001?

Matthew's total earnings in 2001	$30,000
Earnings Limitation	
	(10,680)
Remainder Excess	$19,320
One-half deduction	÷ 2
	$ 9,660

The Social Security Administration will thus deduct $9,660 from Matthew's benefits for the year. Matthew will receive $4,740 in retirement benefits ($14,400 annual retirement benefit less $9,660 reduction). Matthew's total income for 2001 would be $34,740, instead of $44,400.

Another commonly asked question is what income counts toward the retirement earnings limitation. Generally, only wages and net self-employment income count, whereas income from savings, investments, or insurance does not. The following is a nonexclusive list of those sources of income that DO NOT count toward the earnings limitation:

▲ Pension or retirement pay.
▲ 401(k) and IRA withdrawals.
▲ Dividends and interest from investments.
▲ Capital gains.
▲ Rental income.
▲ Workers' compensation benefits.
▲ Unemployment benefits.
▲ Court-awarded judgments, less components of award that include lost wages.
▲ Contest winnings.

TAXATION OF SOCIAL SECURITY BENEFITS

Separate and apart from the earnings limitation scenario, some beneficiaries may be required to pay taxes on their Social Security benefits. For persons with substantial income in addition to Social Security benefits, up to 85 percent of their annual benefits may be subject to federal income tax. The Social Security Administration is concerned with beneficiaries' **combined income**. On the 1040 federal tax return, combined income is the sum of adjusted gross income, plus nontaxable interest, plus one-half of Social Security benefits.

Generally, 50 percent of Social Security benefits are subject to federal income taxes for beneficiaries who file a federal tax return as an "individual" and have a combined income between $25,000 and $34,000. For those with a combined income over $34,000, 85 percent of their Social Security benefits will be subject to federal income taxation. For those beneficiaries that file a joint federal tax return and have a combined income with their spouse between $32,000 and $44,000, 50 percent of their Social Security benefits will be subject to federal income taxes. Finally, if beneficiaries filing a joint tax return have a combined income that exceeds $44,000, 85 percent of their Social Security benefits will be subject to federal income taxation.

combined income - on the 1040 federal tax return, combined income is the sum of adjusted gross income, plus nontaxable interest, plus one-half of Social Security benefits

In sum, for persons with substantial income in addition to their Social Security benefits, up to 85 percent of their annual benefits may be subject to federal income tax. The amount of benefits subject to federal income tax is the smaller of:

▲ One-half of their benefits.
▲ One-half of the amount by which their adjusted gross income, plus tax-exempt interest, plus one-half of their Social Security exceeds:
  ❑ $25,000 if single.
  ❑ $25,000 if married and not filing a joint return and did not live with a spouse at any time during the year.
  ❑ $32,000 if married and filing a joint return.
  ❑ $0 if married and not filing a joint return and did live with a spouse at any time during the year.

OTHER SOCIAL SECURITY BENEFITS

DISABILITY BENEFITS AND DISABILITY INSURED

Benefits are payable at any age to people who have enough Social Security credits and who have a severe physical or mental impairment that is expected to prevent them from doing "substantial" work for a year or more or who have a condition that is expected to result in death. Workers are insured for disability if they are fully insured and, except for persons who are blind or disabled before age 31, have a total of at least 20 quarters of coverage during the 40-quarter period ending with the quarter in which the worker became disabled. Workers who are disabled before age 31 must have total quarters of coverage equal to half the calendar quarters which have elapsed since the worker reached age 21, ending in the quarter in which the worker became disabled. However, a minimum of 6 quarters is required.

Generally, earnings of $500 or more per month are considered substantial. The disability program includes incentives to smooth the transition back into the workforce, including continuation of benefits and health care coverage while a person attempts to work. Disability under the Social Security system is defined as an inability to engage in substantial gainful activity by reason of a physical or mental impairment expected to last at least 12 months or to result in death. The impairment must be of such severity that the applicant is not only unable to do his or her previous work but cannot, considering age, education, and work experience, engage in any other kind of substantial gainful work which exists in the national economy.

FAMILY BENEFITS

If an individual is eligible for retirement or disability benefits, other members of the individual's family might receive benefits as well. Family members who may receive benefits include the following:

▲ A spouse, if the spouse is at least 62 years old or under 62 but caring for a child under age 16.
▲ A child, if the child is unmarried and under age 18, under age 19 but still in school, or age 18 or older but disabled.

For those workers who are entitled to retirement or disability benefits, an ex-spouse could also be eligible for benefits on the worker's record.

A child's benefit stops the month before the child reaches 18, unless the child is unmarried and is either disabled or is a full-time elementary or secondary school student. Approximately five months before the child's 18th birthday, the person receiving the child's benefits will get a form explaining how benefits can continue. A child whose benefits stop at 18 can have them started again if the child becomes disabled before reaching 22 or becomes a full-time elementary or secondary school student before reaching 19. If the child continues to receive benefits after age 18 due to a disability, the child also may qualify for SSI disability benefits. When a student's 19th birthday occurs during a school term, benefits can be continued up to two months to allow completion of the school term.

SURVIVORS' BENEFITS

If a worker earned enough Social Security credits during his or her lifetime, certain members of the worker's family may be eligible for benefits when the worker dies. The family members of the deceased worker who may be entitled to survivors' benefits include:

▲ A widow or widower age 60 or older, age 50 or older if disabled, or any age if caring for a child under age 16.
▲ A child of the deceased worker, if the child is unmarried and under age 18, under age 19 but still in school, or age 18 or older but disabled.
▲ A parent or parents of the deceased worker, if the deceased worker was the parent or parents primary means of support.

Family members may be eligible for Social Security survivors' benefits when a retired worker dies. A special one-time payment of $255 may be made to a deceased worker's spouse or minor children upon death. If a spouse was living with the beneficiary at the time of death, the spouse will receive a one-time payment of $255. The payment may be made to a spouse who was not living with the beneficiary at the time of death or an ex-spouse if the spouse or ex-spouse was receiving Social Security benefits based on the deceased's earnings record. If there is no surviving spouse, a child (or children) who is eligible for benefits on the deceased's work record in the month of death may claim the payment.

THE MAXIMUM FAMILY BENEFIT

When a person dies, his or her survivors receive a percentage of the worker's Social Security benefits ranging from 75 percent to 100 percent each. There is a limit on the amount of monthly Social Security benefits that may be paid to a family. This limit is called the **maximum family benefit**, which is determined through a formula based on the worker's PIA. While the limit varies, it is equal to roughly 150 percent to 180 percent of the deceased worker's PIA. If the sum of the family members' benefits exceeds the limit, the family members' benefits are proportionately reduced. For old-age and survivor family benefits, the formula computes the sum of four separate percentages of portions of the worker's PIA. For 2001, these portions are the first $717 of PIA, the amount between $717 and $1,034, the amount between $1,034 and $1,349, and the

maximum family benefit - the limit on the amount of monthly Social Security benefits that may be paid to a family

amount over $1,349. These are the bend points for the maximum family benefit formula for the year 2001, with the following percentage calculations:

150 percent of the first $717 of the worker's PIA, *plus*
272 percent of the worker's PIA over $717 through $1,034, *plus*
134 percent of the worker's PIA over $1,034 through $1,349, *plus*
175 percent of the worker's PIA over $1,349.

This number is rounded to the next lower $0.10. See the table of bend points below concerning the maximum family benefit formula.

EXHIBIT 11.14: HISTORICAL BEND POINT TABLE FOR FAMILY MAXIMUM BENEFITS

Dollar amounts in maximum family benefit formula			
Year	First	Second	Third
1979	$230	$332	$433
1980	248	358	467
1981	270	390	508
1982	294	425	554
1983	324	468	610
1984	342	493	643
1985	358	517	675
1986	379	548	714
1987	396	571	745
1988	407	588	767
1989	433	626	816
1990	455	656	856
1991	473	682	890
1992	495	714	931
1993	513	740	966
1994	539	779	1,016
1995	544	785	1,024
1996	559	806	1,052
1997	581	839	1,094
1998	609	880	1,147
1999	645	931	1,214
2000	679	980	1,278
2001	717	1,034	1,349

Source: Social Security Administration (www.ssa.gov)

MEDICARE BENEFITS

Medicare is a federal health insurance plan for people who are 65 and older, whether retired or still working. People who are disabled or have permanent kidney failure can get Medicare at any age. The Health Care Financing Administration, part of the United States Department of Health and Human Services, administers Medicare. Medicare is the nation's largest health insurance program, covering over 39 million individuals. There are two parts to Medicare: Hospital Insurance (sometimes called Part A) and Medical Insurance (sometimes called Part B).

Generally, individuals who are over the age of 65 and receive Social Security benefits automatically qualify for Medicare. Also, individuals who have received Social Security disability benefits for at least two years automatically qualify for Medicare. All other individuals must file an application for Medicare.

Part A, Hospital Insurance, is paid for by a portion of the Social Security tax. Part A helps pay for necessary medical care and services furnished by Medicare-certified hospitals, inpatient hospital care, skilled nursing care, home health care, hospice care and other services. The number of days that Medicare covers care in hospitals and skilled nursing facilities is measured in what is termed **benefit periods**. A benefit period begins on the first day a patient receives services as a patient in a hospital or skilled nursing facility and ends after 60 consecutive days of no further skilled care. There is no limit to the number of benefit periods a beneficiary may have. Benefit periods are identified because various rules pertain to deductibles, co-insurance and premiums. For instance, for coverage of Medicare under Part A, a deductible of $792 applies per benefit period. For the 61st through the 90th day of each benefit period, the insured individual must pay $198 a day in the form of co-insurance, and $396 a day for the 91st through 150th day. Any days over 90 days for a benefit period are considered lifetime reserve days that are nonrenewable once used. It is therefore important to determine the amount of each benefit period.

benefit periods - the number of days that Medicare covers care in hospitals and skilled nursing facilities

EXHIBIT 11.15: MEDICARE DEDUCTIBLE, COINSURANCE AND PREMIUM AMOUNTS FOR 2001

Hospital Insurance (Part A)

- ▲ **Deductible** - $792 per each Benefit Period
- ▲ **Coinsurance**
  - ▲ $198 a day for the 61st through the 90th day, per Benefit period;
  - ▲ $396 a day for the 91st through the 150th day for each lifetime reserve day (total of 60 lifetime reserve days – non-renewable).
- ▲ **Skilled Nursing Facility coinsurance** - $99.00 a day for the 21st through the 100th day per Benefit Period;
- ▲ **Hospital Insurance Premium** - $300 per month (Note: This premium is paid only by individuals who are not otherwise eligible for premium-free hospital insurance.)
- ▲ **Premium surcharge for late enrollment** - $331.10
- ▲ **Reduced Hospital Insurance Premium** - $165 (Note: For individuals having 30 or more quarters of coverage. These individuals must pay a premium plus surcharge total of $182.60 for late enrollment.)

Medical Insurance (Part B)

- ▲ **Deductible** - $100 per year
- ▲ **Monthly Premium** - $50.00

Source: Social Security Administration (www.ssa.gov)

Medicare Part A helps pay for up to 90 days of inpatient hospital care during each benefit period. Covered services for inpatient hospital care include: semiprivate room and meal, operating and recovery room cost, intensive care, drugs, laboratory tests, x-rays, general nursing services, and any other necessary medical services and supplies. Convenience items such as television and telephones provided by hospitals in private rooms (unless medically necessary) are generally not covered. Medicare does not pay for custodial services for daily living activities such as eating, bathing, and getting dressed. Medicare does, however, pay for skilled nursing facility care for rehabilitation, like recovery time after a hospital discharge from one benefit period. Part A may help pay for up to 100 days in a participating skilled nursing facility in each benefit period. Medicare pays all approved charges for the first 20 days relating to skilled nursing facility care, and the patient pays a co-insurance amount for days 21-100. As discussed earlier, Medicare may also pay the full, approved cost of covered home health care services, which includes part-time or intermittent skilled nursing services prescribed by a physician for treatment or rehabilitation of homebound patients. Normally, the only instance where the insured is required to pay for home health care is through a 20 percent co-insurance charge for medical equipment, like wheelchairs or walkers.

Medicare Part B, Medical Insurance, is optional, and a premium is charged. Part B is paid for by monthly premiums of those who are enrolled and paid for out of the general revenues from the general Treasury. Medicare Part B is used to pay for doctor's services, ambulance transportation, diagnostic tests, outpatient therapy services, outpatient hospital services including emergency room visits, X-rays and laboratory services, some preventative care, home health care services not covered by Part A, durable medical equipment and supplies, and a variety of other health services. Part B may also pay for home health care services that are not paid for by Part A.

Medicare Part B pays for 80 percent of approved charges for most covered services. Unless an individual declines Part B medical insurance protection, the premium will be automatically deducted from their benefits. The 1999 and 2000 premium amount was $45.50 a month, whereas it is $50.00 for 2001. The deductible for Part B is $100 per year. The insured is responsible for paying a $100 deductible per calendar year and the remaining 20 percent of the Medicare-approved charge. Medicare Part B usually does not cover charges for most prescription drugs, routine physical examinations, or services unrelated to treatment of injury or illness. Dental care, dentures, cosmetic surgery, hearing aids and eye examinations are not covered by Part B.

Various plans under Medicare are available to insureds. The original Medicare Plan is the way most individuals get their Medicare Part A and Part B benefits. This is the traditional payment-per-service arrangement where the individual insured may go to any doctor, specialist, or hospital that accepts Medicare, and Medicare pays its share after services are rendered. Medicare carriers and fiscal intermediaries are private insurance organizations that handle claims under the original Medicare Plan. Carriers handle Part B claims, while fiscal intermediaries handle Part A plans. The Social Security Administration does not handle claims for Medicare payments.

Many private insurance companies sell Medicare supplemental insurance policies, Medigap, and Medicare SELECT. These supplemental policies help bridge the coverage gaps in the original Medicare Plan. These supplemental policies also help pay Medicare's co-insurance amounts and deductibles, as well as other out of pocket expenses for health care.

When a worker is first enrolled in Part B at age 65 or older, there is a six-month open enrollment period in Medigap. During that time of open enrollment, the health status of the applicant cannot be used as a reason to refuse a Medigap policy or to charge more than other open enrollment applicants. The insurer may require a six-month waiting period for coverage of pre-existing conditions. If, however, the open enrollment period has expired, the applicant may be denied a policy based on health status, or may be charged higher rates. At age 65, open enrollment in Medigap is available to beneficiaries who are enrolled in Part B.

OTHER MEDICARE HEALTH PLAN CHOICES

Medicare offers alternative methods of obtaining Medicare benefits through other health plan choices. Choices that vary by area include coordinated-care or Medicare managed care plans, such as Health Maintenance Organizations (HMOs), HMOs with a point of service option, Provider Sponsored Organizations (PSOs), and Preferred Provider Organizations (PPOs). These plans involve specific groups of doctors, hospitals and other providers who provide care to the insured as a member of the plan, like many employer-sponsored plans throughout the country. Medicare-managed care plans not only provide the same services that are covered by Part A and Part B, but most Medicare managed plans offer a variety of additional benefits like preventative care, prescription drugs, dental care, eyeglasses and other items not covered by the original Medicare Plan. Of course, the cost of these extra benefits varies among the plans.

Other Medicare health plan choices beyond the original Medicare Plan and Medicare managed care plans include: Private Fee for Service Plans, Medicare Medical Savings Account Plans (MSAs), or religious fraternal benefits plans. These plans provide all services covered by both Part A and Part B, as well as a variety of additional benefits. MSAs are funded through a lump sum payment from traditional Medicare to obtain a high deductible insurance policy. Any remaining balance can be used by the beneficiary for payment of medical expenses not covered by traditional Medicare or for other use. This amount could be subject to taxation if not used for medically related purposes. For information about these various health plan choices, the official Internet site of Medicare at *www.medicare.gov* is very helpful and provides many links to other informative sources.

APPLYING FOR MEDICARE BENEFITS AND COVERAGE

If a worker applies for retirement or survivors' benefits before his or her 65th birthday, there is no need to file a separate application for Medicare. The worker will receive information in the mail before he or she turns 65, explaining what needs to be done. Coverage starts automatically at age 65, even without receiving a Medicare card in the mail.

For those who are not already receiving Social Security benefits, they must file an application for Medicare benefits. Spouses can qualify for Medicare Part A at age 65 based on the other spouse's work record if the other spouse is eligible for monthly Social Security benefits or if the other spouse is receiving Social Security disability benefits. Applications should be submitted three months before the applicant's 65th birthday. If the worker does not enroll and delays taking Part B for one year, that worker's monthly premiums for Part B will increase. For each 12 months the worker could have used Part B, but does not take it, the monthly premium increases by 10 percent. If the worker decides to delay opting into Part B because of the worker's current group health plan coverage (if applicable), the worker may be able to avoid the increased monthly premium by applying for Part B (i) while participating in the group coverage or (ii) within eight months after the employment ends or group health coverage ends, whichever occurs first.

Even if an individual continues to work after turning 65, he or she should sign up for Part A of Medicare. Part A may help defray some costs not otherwise covered by group health plans. Applying for Part B may or may not be advantageous if the worker has health insurance through an employer. The worker would be required to pay the monthly Part B premium, yet the Part B benefits may be of limited value because the employer plan is the primary source of payment of medical bills.

For those who receive Medicare and have low income and few resources, states may pay Medicare premiums, and, in some cases, other "out-of-pocket" Medicare expenses such as deductibles and coinsurance. Only the state can decide if individuals qualify. For more general information about Medicare, the Social Security Administration's leaflet *Medicare Savings for Qualified Beneficiaries* (HCFA Publication No. 02184) is helpful, as are the websites *www.ssa.gov* and *www.medicare.gov.*

SUPPLEMENTAL SECURITY INCOME BENEFITS

SSI makes monthly payments to individuals having a low income and few assets. In order to obtain SSI benefits, an individual must be age 65 or older or must be disabled. The definition of disability is that the individual is unable to engage in any substantial gainful activity due to a physical or mental problem expected to last at least a year or expected to result in death. Children as well as adults qualify for SSI disability payments. As its name implies, Supplemental Security Income supplements the beneficiary's income up to various levels, depending on where the beneficiary lives. If an otherwise eligible SSI applicant lives in another's household and receives support from that person, the federal SSI benefit is reduced by one-third.

The federal government pays a basic rate. For 2000, the basic monthly SSI check was the same in all states, $512 for one person and $769 for married couples. In 2001, it is $530 per month for one person and $796 per month for married couples. Some states add money to that amount. To ascertain the SSI benefit rates in a certain state, those interested can contact a local Social Security office in that state, or visit the Social Security Administration's website. Generally, individuals who receive SSI benefits also qualify for Medicaid, food stamps, and other assistance.

To get the monthly SSI benefit, the beneficiary must not have assets that exceed $2,000 for one person or $3,000 for married couples. This asset determination does not include the value of the home and some personal belongings, such as a first car. If the potential beneficiary does not work, he or she may be eligible for SSI benefits if monthly income is less than $520 for one person and $771 for a couple. If the potential beneficiary works, more monthly income is allowed -- $1,085 a month for one person and $1,587 for a couple. In short, SSI benefits are not paid from Social Security trust funds and are not based on past earnings of the beneficiary. Rather, SSI benefits are financed by general tax revenues and assure a minimum monthly income for needy, elderly, and disabled persons.

FILING FOR SOCIAL SECURITY CLAIMS

The Social Security Administration has reported that too many people make the mistake of failing to file claims with the Social Security Administration or failing to do so in a timely fashion. Individuals should file for Social Security or SSI disability benefits as soon they become too disabled to work or should file for survivors benefits when a family breadwinner dies. Social Security benefits do not start automatically. Social Security will not begin payment of benefits until the beneficiary files an application. When filing for benefits, applicants must submit documents that show eligibility, such as a birth certificate for each family member applying for benefits, a marriage certificate if a spouse is applying and most recent W-2 forms or tax returns.

To file for benefits, obtain information, or to speak to a Social Security representative, interested individuals must call the Social Security Administration's toll-free number, 800-772-1213, or visit the Social Security Administration's website. The toll-free number can be used to schedule an appointment to visit local Social Security offices. The Social Security Administration treats all calls confidentially. Periodically, a second Social Security representative will monitor incoming and outgoing telephone calls to ensure accurate and courteous service.

SOCIAL SECURITY CHANGES FOR 2001

The Social Security Commissioner, Larry G. Massanari, issues each year a Fact Sheet summarizing the changes in Social Security. The following is the Commissioner's Fact Sheet for 2001.

EXHIBIT 11.16: SOCIAL SECURITY CHANGES FOR 2001

Cost-of-Living Adjustment (COLA):
Based on the increase in the Consumer Price Index (CPI-W) from the third quarter of 1999 through the third quarter of 2000, Social Security beneficiaries and Supplemental Security Income (SSI) recipients received a 3.5 percent COLA for 2001. Other important 2001 Social Security information is as follows:

Tax Rate:	**2000**	**2001**
Employee	7.65%	7.65%
Self-Employed	15.30%	15.30%

NOTE: The 7.65% tax rate is the combined rate for Social Security and Medicare. The Social Security portion (OASDI) is 6.20% on earnings up to the applicable maximum taxable amount (see below). The Medicare portion (HI) is 1.45% on all earnings.

Maximum Earnings Taxable:	**2000**	**2001**
Social Security (OASDI only)	$76,200	$80,400
Medicare (HI only)	No Limit	No Limit

Quarter of Coverage:	$ 780	$ 830

Retirement Earnings Test Exempt Amounts:
As of January 2000, the Retirement Earnings Test has been eliminated for individuals age 65-69. It remains in effect for those ages 62 through 64. A modified test applies for the year an individual reaches age 65. (The Senior Citizens' Freedom To Work Act of 2000, signed into law by President Clinton on April 7, 2000.)

2000
Year individual reaches 65 - $17,000/yr. ($1,417/mo.)
--Applies only to earnings for months prior to attaining age 65. One dollar in benefits will be withheld for every $3 in earnings above the limit. There is no limit on earnings beginning the month an individual attains age 65.
Under age 65 - $10,080/yr. ($ 840/mo.)
--One dollar in benefits will be withheld for every $2 in earnings above the limit.

2001
Year individual reaches 65 - $25,000/yr. ($2,084/mo.)
--Applies only to earnings for months prior to attaining age 65. One dollar in benefits will be withheld for every $3 in earnings above the limit. There is no limit on earnings beginning the month an individual attains age 65.
Under age 65 - $10,680/yr. ($ 890/mo.)
--One dollar in benefits will be withheld for every $2 in earnings above the limit.

SSI Federal Payment Standard:	**2000**	**2001**
Individual	$512/mo.	$530/mo.
Couple	$769/mo.	$796/mo.
SSI Resources Limits:		
Individual	$2,000	$2,000
Couple	$3,000	$3,000

**Estimated Average Monthly Social Security Benefits
Before and After the December 2000 COLA:**

	Before 3.5% COLA	**After 3.5% COLA**
All Retired Workers	$ 816	$ 845
Aged Couple, Both Receiving Benefits	$1,363	$1,410
Widowed Mother and Two Children	$1,639	$1,696
Aged Widow(er) Alone	$ 783	$ 811
Disabled Worker, Spouse and One or More Children	$1,266	$1,310
All Disabled Workers	$ 759	$ 786

OTHER ISSUES

EFFECT OF MARRIAGE OR DIVORCE ON BENEFITS

Marriage or divorce may affect one's Social Security benefits, depending on the kind of benefits received. If a worker receives retirement benefits based on his or her own earnings record, the worker's retirement benefits will continue whether married or divorced. If an individual receives benefits based on his or her spouse's record, the individual's benefits will cease upon divorce unless the individual is age 62 or older and was married at least 10 years. Widows and widowers, whether divorced or not, will continue to receive survivors' benefits upon remarriage if the widow or widower is age 60 or older. Disabled widows and widowers, whether divorced or not, will continue to receive survivors' benefits upon remarriage if the disabled widow or widower is age 50 or older.

For all other forms of Social Security benefits, benefits will cease upon remarriage, except in special circumstances. The reasoning behind this rule is that when a person marries, it is presumed that at least one person in the marriage can provide adequate support. Likewise, Social Security benefits may recommence if the marriage ends.

CHANGE OF NAME

If an individual changes his or her name due to marriage, divorce or a court order, that individual must notify the Social Security Administration of the name change so the Social Security Administration will be able to show the new name in their records and properly credit that individual for earnings. This will also ensure that the individual's work history will be accurately recorded and maintained.

LEAVING THE UNITED STATES

Beneficiaries who are United States citizens may travel or live in most foreign countries without affecting their eligibility for Social Security benefits. However, there are a few countries where Social Security checks cannot be sent. These countries currently include Cuba, Cambodia, North Korea, Vietnam, and the republics that were formerly in the U.S.S.R. (except Estonia, Latvia, and Lithuania).

Beneficiaries should inform the Social Security Administration of their plans to go outside the United States for a trip that lasts 30 days or more. By providing the name of the country or countries to be visited and the expected departure and return dates, the Social Security Administration will send special reporting instructions to the beneficiaries and arrange for delivery of checks while abroad.

THE FUTURE OF SOCIAL SECURITY AND THE PRIVATIZATION ALTERNATIVE

In the last few decades, much debate has raged over whether the current United States Social Security system will survive in the not-to-distant future. Numerous reports using a 75-year outlook typically spell doom for the current system. Numerous forecasts and predictions about Social Security have been made—some negative, some positive, some neutral--all unanimously point out that the current system will fail if left unchanged. The question then becomes, how much must be changed, and if so, when?

Congress established the Board of Trustees for the Social Security and Medicare Trust Funds to specifically address and bring to the forefront, without political bipartisanship, the crucial issues facing Social Security. The Board of Trustees' reports provide forecasts concerning the future solvency of the trust funds. One of the members of the Board of Trustees is the Commissioner of Social Security. Yet, even the Board of Trustees' 2000 Summary Annual Report acknowledges that, if nothing significant is changed, the Social Security Trust Funds, the lifeblood of Social Security, will become exhausted by 2037, while the HI Trust Fund will be unable to pay all benefits as early as 2025. The point is that even the supporters of the current system and its utility to national social welfare agree that there is a real and strong chance that the Social Security system will soon find itself in a perilous situation and that significant changes must occur to avoid collapse.

As discussed earlier in this chapter, the Social Security Trust Funds had a positive value of roughly $800 billion by the start of 2000. Social Security taxes currently exceed the benefits being paid out, and the surpluses are used to earn interest and grow. Estimates are that these surpluses will grow to over $4 trillion before being used to pay benefits. However, factual reports compiled by the Social Security Administration reveal that by 2015, benefit payments will begin to exceed all FICA taxes received, and the Social Security Administration will be forced to use these surpluses until they are exhausted. The main reason for this unavoidable operating deficit is that the approximate 75 million baby-boomers will begin taking retirement in 2010, and fewer workers will be paying for more beneficiaries. In 1999, Americans age 65 and older comprised 13 percent of the total population of the country, but by 2030, the percentage will be 20 percent. The Social Security Administration reports that the covered worker to Social Security beneficiary ratio is 3.3 to 1, but by 2030, that ratio will drop to 2 to 1. Also, life expectancy in 1935 was 77.5 years, but that figure has now grown to 82.5 years, and should continue to rise.

Federal Reserve Chairman Alan Greenspan testified before the Special Committee of the United States Senate on Aging in March 2000, where he stressed the necessity of Social Security reform. Greenspan indicated, "Social Security and Medicare will have to undergo reform. The goal of this reform must be to increase the real resources available to meet the needs and expectations of retirees, without blunting the growth in living standards among our working population.... From this perspective, it becomes clear that increasing our national saving is essential to any successful reform of Social Security and Medicare."

In recent years, Greenspan has made favorable comments concerning the privatization of Social Security. In 1997 before the Senate's Task Force on Social Security, Greenspan testified that "perhaps the strongest argument for privatization is that replacing the current under-funded system with a fully funded one could boost domestic saving" and further noted that Social Security reform incorporating personal retirement accounts (versus the current pay-as-you-go system) would have a positive correlative relationship to increased saving rates.

Many privatization proponents argue that increasing "savings," that is, taxes into the Social Security system as a solution to imminent problems of funding benefits fails to address the severe shortcomings of the Social Security system as a whole. The focus instead, according to many privatization proponents, should be on the best retirement system possible, which in today's society and financial world would most likely be in federally mandated, individually owned privately invested accounts. A system dominated by privately invested accounts would allow workers to accumulate real family wealth, and avoid poverty, through higher rates of return on investments and higher retirement benefits while under the workers' control, not the control of Congress.

Based on what we have learned in this chapter, let's take a closer look at the alternative of Social Security privatization. Privatization would reform the current system to allow workers to deposit payroll taxes into personally owned and invested accounts, similar to IRAs and 401(k) Plans. These contributions would be mandatory through deduction from paychecks so that the worker would not have the option to spend that contribution elsewhere as in the current system. The major distinction is that the money would not be pooled in the Social Security Trust Funds, but invested into a specific account designated for that specific worker. In other words, there would be a single trust fund for that specific worker, resulting in millions of trust funds rather than the OASI and DI Trust Funds. Employers and the worker would have the discretion to choose a company to invest and manage the worker's personal account.

Currently, workers are taxed under FICA 12.4 percent of their earnings, 6.2 percent from the employee and 6.2 percent from the employer, or 12.4 percent for self-employed individuals. The 12.4 percent contribution would be invested in the worker's personal trust fund account. The other 2.9 percent for Medicare (1.45 percent for the employee and 1.45 percent for the employer; 2.9 percent for self-employed individuals) would still go to the federal Medicare system under many privatization models. Rather than Congress setting the retirement benefit, which currently has a maximum retirement benefit of $1,433 per month for high wage earners, the worker's account would grow in value without limitation and likely far exceed the current system's eventual benefit. Funds in the individual account could also be used to purchase and pay for premiums on life insurance and disability insurance, replacing the disability and death benefit portions of the current system. Upon retirement, death or disability, the wealth accumulated in the worker's personal account could be used to acquire a lifetime annuity whereby the annuity would pay monthly installments to a retiree and/or the retiree's family members.

Those opposed to privatization stress that privatization has serious pitfalls, which include (i) investment into the "risky" stock market, rather than the current system's guaranteed payments, (ii) loss of previous contributions by current workers upon transition to privatization, (iii) potential mishandling of the contributions through intentional acts or ignorance, and (iv) low wage earners would receive less benefits than under the current system's retirement benefit. Privatization proponents discard these claimed pitfalls as being unfounded.

First, although the stock market has no guaranteed rates of return and is volatile, history proves that despite volatility, over any 20 to 40-year period (which are the time horizons that should be considered in retirement analyses), the stock market has easily and resoundingly outperformed the rate of return of the Social Security Trust Funds. According to studies from the Cato Project on Social Security Privatization, the Social Security Trust Funds have over time earned only a 2 percent real rate of return. Further, with individual accounts, funds contributed during the worker's early years will have the opportunity to grow and compound over 20 to 40 years, whereas under the current pay-as-you-go system, funds contributed are paid out much faster, mostly to fund today's retirees, without the luxury of compounding over time. Under a pay-as-you-go financing protocol, the maximum rate of return payable to future beneficiaries is determined by the real rate of growth of taxable wages, generally assumed to be 2 percent over the long term, whereas the real rate of return to private capital investment is estimated to be 9 percent. In addition, workers and employers who are uncomfortable with the perceived risk of the stock market over the long-term could have the option under a privatized system to invest conservatively in federally backed government bonds which generally yield a 3 percent to 5 percent rate of return.

Second, privatization could be phased in through steps allowing workers to recoup the taxes they have already paid under the current system through government refunds based on the present value of the workers' total contribution. The source of this governmental refund has been the subject of sharp debate because it would not only need to come from the present Social Security Trust Funds, but also from the general fund of the Treasury. However, even if previous contributions to the current system were forfeited in favor of individual accounts, privatization proponents estimate that workers age 45 or younger would likely have a higher retirement benefit under the privatization model than under the current system.

Third, mishandling of individual funds is unlikely, according to privatization proponents, because a privatized system would still mandate automatic investment into the worker's designated personal account, prohibiting the worker from spending the funds. Moreover, many workers are obviously not experts in investing, capital management or finances, but experienced account managers, fiduciaries and/or trustees would manage, or help to manage, the private personal account. Scam artists and risky investment vehicles would be diffused under privatization similar to IRAs and 401(k) plans.

Fourth, low wage earners would probably fare better under a privatized system. Low wage earners on average have little or no money to save for retirement, as they are more challenged by provision of necessities and other living expenses. As a result, low wage earners depend more, (sometimes solely) on Social Security retirement benefits. However, monthly benefits for retired low wage earners under a privatized system would still exceed the current system's retirement benefits, according to various studies and calculations of privatization proponents. Also, Social Security actuaries state that low wage earners have lower life expectancy in comparison to higher wage earners. The current system stops payment to the retiree upon death, and thus low wage earners who do not live as long realize less benefits. However, under privatization, any funds remaining from all workers' personal accounts would be passed on to their family and survivors because the worker owns the personal account. Finally, as a safety net to privatization for low wage earners, modifications (if any) to the SSI program could be made to accommodate low wage earners, if necessary.

With regard to the overall benefits of privatization, numerous studies claim that privatization would provide a significant boon to the economy, since it would place an additional $10 to $20 trillion into the United States economy, increase savings rates, add almost 5 percent to Gross National Product and boost family wealth. Privatization proponents also point to the successful privatized retirement system in Chile where its once governmentally controlled pay-as-you-go retirement system was changed to a privatized retirement system in 1981. Chilean pension fund assets have soared in value, and the system as a whole has flourished and outperformed Chile's old pay-as-you-go system. By 1994, Chilean workers' pensions were over 50 percent higher than under its old system. Although successful, there have been many critics of the Chilean system who emphasize its high administrative costs and high transition costs. Growing pains notwithstanding, the success and sheer growth of the Chilean privatized system cannot be ignored.

In short, the current system of Social Security is operating under annual surpluses fueled by a strong economy and the taxable earnings of the baby boomers. However, those same baby boomers will soon begin retiring around 2010 and will begin receiving benefits rather than paying for them. By paying out more in benefits than they collect through FICA taxes, the trust funds will operate at an annual deficit starting in the year 2015. Inevitably by 2037, the Social Security Trust Funds, $800 billion in value at the start of 2000, will reach a value of zero and be unable to fully fund the required benefit payments. Shortfalls from FICA tax receipts would need to be funded by the general Treasury and would reek havoc with the federal budget. Privatization is an alternative to this catastrophic scenario. There are other alternatives that have been addressed and will obviously continue to be addressed. Such alternatives include raising the FICA tax rate from 12.4 percent to somewhere in the neighborhood of 18 to 22 percent, reducing Social Security benefits by significant amounts ranging from 25 percent to 33 percent, a combination of tax increases and cuts in benefits, or a governmental stock market investment campaign. Governmental investing, according to privatization proponents, would be improperly motivated by political considerations and would encroach on American ideals of a free economy by making the federal government the largest shareholder in American corporations. These alternative measures are too drastic and would undermine the intent of Social Security and its underlying theory and principles of social welfare.

Despite the continuing debate for and against privatization and the other alternatives, the one thing about which privatization supporters and opponents do agree is that the current system must change to survive the inevitable crisis it faces. For an excellent source of more information on privatization and other alternatives to the current Social Security system, see the website for the Cato Project on Social Security Privatization at *www.socialsecurity.org/pubs/ssps*, or see the Social Security Administration's website at *www.ssa.gov.*

For more information about Social Security programs, any of the following publications can be ordered by calling the Social Security Administration at 1-800-772-1213. These publications can be ordered at night, on weekends and on holidays, 365 days a year:

- ▲ *Understanding Social Security* (Publication No. 05-10024)
- ▲ *Retirement* (Publication No. 05-10035)
- ▲ *Survivors* (Publication No. 05-10084)
- ▲ *Disability* (Publication No. 05-10029)
- ▲ *Medicare* (Publication No. 05-10043)
- ▲ *Social Security...What Every Woman Should Know* (Publication No. 05-10127)
- ▲ *Your Social Security Taxes...What They're Paying For...Where The Money Goes* (Publication No. 05-10010)
- ▲ *Your Social Security Number* (Publication No. 05-10002)

PROFESSIONAL

FOCUS

Do you find clients are aware of the limitations of Social Security (i.e. that it may run out, that it may not provide enough income to higher income workers)?

Yes, my clients are concerned that Social Security benefits may run out. These clients generally fall into two categories: (1) Those in 50+ age bracket who are really concerned because they have included Social Security benefits as a major component of their retirement plan and (2) those clients in the 30-50 age bracket who are of the strong opinion that the Social Security benefits may no longer exist by the time they reach retirement age. As a planner what I try to do with the first group is get them to voluntarily spend a little less and save small amounts in a growth portfolio to offset the risk that Social Security benefits will be reduced or eliminated. For the second group we plan without Social Security benefits and we are fairly certain that for the older members of this group there will be some benefits which we plan to invest in growth securities because we never counted on them anyway. My expectation is that while Social Security benefits will change the legislated changes are unlikely to adversely affect those persons who are 50 and are registered to vote.

Do you find clients are aware of the benefits they should receive from Social Security? Are they surprised by the amount (i.e. they find it lower than they expected)?

Until recently, clients were totally unaware how much they would receive in Social Security benefits from retirement. They still have little knowledge when we are speaking of early (before normal age) retirement and families who receive survivor or disability benefits. The ability to file the SSA 7004 and receive the SSA 7005 has helped both planners and clients to estimate realistic Social Security benefits. Social Security for a covered worker with a non-working same age spouse may reface from 20% to 57% of pre-retirement income. Social Security retirement benefits in spite of the issues regarding soundness of the system continue to represent a major source of retirement income for many especially the lower and middle class.

What steps do you take to ensure your client is aware of the need to file for Social Security benefits?

We create retirement projections and plans as early as the client allows us. We regularly monitor and review our retirement projections as we meet with clients quarterly and annually. We begin serious discussions of Social Security benefits and other retirement sources of income around age 55. We also discuss early retirement, the reduction in Social Security benefits from early retirement. For some of our very early retirees (age 55) we use Social Security as a predictable boost in cash inflows that will enter the picture at age 62. If such a client has sufficient assets and income to maintain their pre-retirement lifestyle for the 7 or so years Social Security benefits give them a boost in lifestyle at age 62. We regularly review all income, assets, and investment performance on a quarterly or annual basis for each client regardless of age. We do, however, pay particular attention to our seniors.

Do you believe Medicare is an adequate source of health insurance for the aged. If not, what types of products do you recommend to supplement Medicare.

We find that Medicare is not an adequate source of health insurance for seniors except those in very good health. We review supplemental plan (A-J), Medigap plans and we explore the need for Long Term Care Insurance policies which have become much more affordable and now provide better benefits for less cost. As always the purchase of long term care policies require a cost/risk/benefits analysis.

We are increasingly alarmed with the number of HMOs that are dropping Medicare enrollees. We expect that Congress will have to address this issue by either raising the fees paid to providers or the HMO Medicare enrollees will have to turn back to regular indemnity Medicare plans.

JOE DEVANNEY, MA, CLU, PFP

DISCUSSION QUESTIONS

1. For purposes of Social Security and disability benefits, what is the meaning of "substantial" work?
2. When was Social Security legislation passed?
3. When was Social Security cost of living adjusted?
4. How are Social Security benefits financed?
5. Is there a maximum payroll amount to which Social Security taxes apply?
6. In order to qualify for OASDI disability benefits, what definition of disability must be met?
7. Describe the major benefits under the Social Security program.
8. Identify and describe the benefits available to those covered under OASDI.
9. When can a person who is entitled to social security benefits become ineligible for benefits?
10. What are the coverages that comprise the Medicare program?
11. Define and explain the meaning of fully insured, currently insured, and disability insured under the OASDI program.
12. What are the requirements to be "fully insured" under OASDI?
13. What Social Security benefits are available to the dependents of a deceased worker who was only currently insured?
14. What Social Security benefits would a "fully insured" worker have that a "currently insured" worker would not have?
15. What requirements must a person satisfy to collect social security (OASDI) disability income benefits?
16. How is Social Security funded?
17. To qualify for Social Security OASDI benefits, how many credits does one need? How is a credit determined?
18. What percentage of income does Social Security typically replace?
19. How is an OASDI insured status determined, and why is it important?
20. How are monthly payments under OASDI determined?
21. What is normal age retirement in year 2001 for OASDI benefits?
22. Are Social Security benefits means tested?
23. For a recipient of Social Security benefits, is there a risk of loss from purchasing power declines?
24. What are the four benefits payable under the OASDI program?
25. If a taxpayer's income exceeds specified base amount, as much as one-half of Social Security retirement benefits must be included in gross income. How much is the taxable amount of Social Security benefits?

EXERCISES

1. Michael was divorced after 15 years of marriage. He had 2 dependent children ages 4 and 6 who are cared for by their mother. He was currently, but not fully, insured under Social Security at the time of his death. What are the benefits that his survivors are entitled to under Social Security?
2. In 2001, James earned $4,000 from employment subject to Social Security between January 1 and March 31. He was then unemployed for the remainder of the year. How many quarters of coverage does he earn for Social Security for 2001?
3. Charles, age 38, has just died. He has been credited with the last 30 consecutive quarters of social security coverage since he left school. He had never worked before leaving school.

Which of the following persons are eligible to receive Social Security survivor benefits as a result of Charles' death?

- ▲ Bill, Charles' 16-year-old son.
- ▲ Dawn, Charles' 18-year-old daughter.
- ▲ Margaret, Charles' 38-year-old widow.
- ▲ Betty, Charles' 60-year-old dependent mother.

4. Under Social Security (OASDI), what benefits are available to the survivors of a deceased but currently insured worker?

5. Which of the follower persons are eligible to receive immediate survivor income benefits based on a deceased worker's Primary Insurance Amount (PIA), under OASDI (Social Security)?

- ▲ A surviving spouse age 55 or older caring for an under 16-year-old child.
- ▲ Unmarried children under age 18 who are dependents.
- ▲ Unmarried disabled children who became disabled before age 22.
- ▲ Any surviving divorced spouse over 50, with no children who was married to decedent for over 10 years and who is disabled.

6. How is a worker's insured status determined under Social Security?

7. Philip began his professional corporation single practitioner CPA firm 38 years ago at age 27. He worked profitably as a sole practitioner for the full 38 years and is now age 65 and 2 months. He retired December 31st. On January 1st of this year he sold his practice for $400,000 to be received in 4 equal annual annuity due payments to be made on January 1st of each of the next four years beginning January 1st, this year. Is Philip eligible for social security retirement benefits during this year? Why or why not?

8. Rob earned $62,000 last year. Calculate his FICA contribution for the year. How much did his employer pay toward FICA?

9. Last year Michelle, filing single, received $10,400 in Social Security benefits. For the entire year, she had adjusted gross income of $28,000. How much, if any, of her Social Security benefit is taxable?

10. Mike is 66 years old. He has a full-time job working as a masseur. This year he anticipates earning $22,000 from his job. How much, in dollars, will Mike's Social Security benefits be reduced?

11. A married couple with adjusted gross income of $40,000, no tax-exempt interest, and $11,000 of Social Security benefits who file jointly must include how much of their Social Security benefits in gross income?

PROBLEMS

1. Larry was married at the following ages and to the following wives. Larry is now 62 and married to Dawn.

	Wife	Current Age	Larry's Age at Marriage	Current Marital Status	Length of Marriage
1	Alice	62	20	Single	10 years, 1 month
2	Betty	63	31	Single	10 years, 1 month
3	Claire	64	42	Single	9 years
4	Dawn	65	53	Married	9 years

Who, among the wives, may be eligible to receive Social Security retirement benefits based upon Larry's earnings if Larry is retired or not retired?

2. George White is single and files Form 1040 for 2001. He received the following income in 2001:

Fully taxable pension	$18,600
Wages from part-time job	9,400
Interest income	990
Total	$28,990

George also received Social Security benefits during 2001. The Form SSA-1099 he received in January 2002 shows $7,200 in box 3, $1,220 in box 4, and $5,980 in box 5. How much of George's Social Security benefits are taxable?

Your Social Security Statement

Prepared especially for Wanda Worker

April 10, 2000

WANDA WORKER
456 ANYWHERE AVENUE
MAINTOWN, USA 11111-1111

See inside for your personal information ➡

▼ What Social Security Means to You

We are pleased to send you this *Social Security Statement* to help you understand what Social Security means to you and your family. We encourage you to use it in planning your financial future. As the law requires, we will send you a new *Statement* showing your updated earnings record and your potential benefits each year. You should receive it about three months before your birthday.

Be sure to read this *Statement* carefully. If you think there might be a mistake, please let us know. That's important because your benefits will be based on our record of your lifetime earnings. Remember, the future's in your hands when you read your *Social Security Statement*.

Social Security is for people of all ages...
Social Security is more than a retirement program. It can help you whether you're young or old, male or female, single or with a family. It can provide benefits if you become severely disabled and help support your family when you die. And it's there for you when you retire.

Work to build a secure future...
Social Security is the largest source of income for most elderly Americans and plays a major role in keeping them out of poverty. But Social Security can't do it all. Social Security benefits were not intended to be the only source of income for you and your family when you retire. You'll need to supplement your benefits from a pension, savings or investments. Think of Social Security as a foundation on which to build your financial future.

About Social Security's future...
Will Social Security be there when you retire? Of course it will. But changes will be needed to meet the demands of the times. We're living longer, healthier lives; 76 million "baby boomers" will start retiring in about 2010; and, in about 30 years, there will be nearly twice as many older Americans as there are today.

Social Security now takes in more in taxes than it pays out in benefits. The excess funds are credited to Social Security's trust funds, which are expected to grow to over $4 trillion before we need to use them to pay benefits. In 2015, we will begin to pay out more in benefits than we collect in taxes. By 2037, the trust funds will be exhausted and the payroll taxes collected will be enough to pay only about 72 percent of benefits owed. We're working to resolve these issues. For more information about the present and what may lie ahead, call us to ask for a copy of the booklet, *The Future of Social Security*.

Kenneth S. Apfel
Kenneth S. Apfel
Commissioner of Social Security

What's inside...

▼ Your Estimated Benefits

To qualify for benefits, you earn "credits" through your work—up to four each year. This year, for example, you earn one credit for each $780 of wages or self-employment income. When you've earned $3,120, you've earned your four credits for the year. Most people need 40 credits, earned over their working lifetime, to receive retirement benefits. For disability and survivors benefits, young people need fewer credits to be eligible.

We checked your records to see whether you have earned enough credits to qualify for benefits. If you haven't earned enough yet to qualify for any type of benefits, we can't give you an estimate now. If you continue to work, we'll give you an estimate when you do qualify.

What we assumed — If you already have enough work credits, we then estimated the amount of your benefits, using your average earnings over your working lifetime. For your credits through 2000 and your earnings up to retirement, we assumed you'll continue to work and make about the same as the latest earnings shown on your record for 1998 or 1999.

We can't provide your actual benefit amount until you apply for benefits. **And that amount may differ from the estimates stated below because —**

(1) Your earnings may increase or decrease over the years.

(2) Your benefit figures shown here are only estimates based on those for current law, and the laws governing benefit amounts may change because, by 2037, the payroll taxes collected will be enough to pay only about 72 percent of benefits owed.

(3) Other factors, such as receiving a pension for government work not covered by Social Security, may affect your benefit amount.

Generally, estimates for older workers are more accurate than those for younger workers because they're based on a longer earnings history with fewer uncertainties, such as earnings fluctuations and future law changes.

These estimates are in current dollars. As you receive benefits, they will be adjusted for cost-of-living increases.

▼ Retirement
You have earned enough credits to qualify for benefits. At your current earnings rate if you stop working...

At age 62, your payment would be about...	$746 a month
At your full retirement age (67 years), your payment would be about...	$1,096 a month
At age 70, your payment would be about...	$1,365 a month

Note: When you continue working beyond your full retirement age, your benefit amount increases because of your additional earnings and the special credits you will receive for delaying your retirement. This increased benefit can be important to you later in your life. It also can increase the future benefit amounts your family and survivors could receive.

▼ Disability
You have earned enough credits to qualify for benefits. If you became severely disabled right now,

Your payment would be about...	$950 a month

▼ Family
If you get retirement or disability benefits, your spouse and children also may qualify for benefits.

▼ Survivors
You have earned enough credits for your family to receive the following benefits if you die this year.

Total family benefits cannot be more than...	$1,835 a month
Your child...	$750 a month
Your spouse who is caring for your child...	$750 a month
Your spouse who reaches full retirement age...	$1,000 a month

Your spouse or minor child may be eligible for a special one-time death benefit of $255.

▼ Medicare
You have enough credits to qualify for Medicare at age 65. Even if you do not retire at age 65, be sure to contact Social Security three months before your 65th birthday to enroll in Medicare.

We based your benefit estimates on these facts

Your name...	Wanda Worker
Your date of birth...	May 16, 1960
Your estimated taxable earnings per year after 1999...	$30,364
Your Social Security number...	999-99-9999

2

Help Us Keep Your Earnings Record Accurate

You, your employer and Social Security share responsibility for the accuracy of your earnings record. From the first year you began working, we recorded your reported earnings under your name and Social Security number. Since then, we have updated your record each time your employer (or you, if you're self-employed) reported your earnings.

Remember, it's your earnings — not the amount of taxes you paid or the number of credits you have — that determine your benefit amount. When we figure that amount, we base it on your average earnings over your lifetime. If our records are wrong, you may not receive all the benefits to which you are entitled.

▼ Review this chart carefully using your own documents (pay stubs, W-2 forms and tax returns) to make sure our information is correct.

▼ Make sure we have recorded every year you worked.

▼ Check the earnings to see if they are correct. You are the only person who can look at the earnings chart and know whether it is complete. If you worked for more than one employer during the year, or if you had both earnings and self-employment income, we combined your earnings for that year.

▼ Remember, **there is a limit on the amount of earnings on which you pay Social Security taxes each year.** This limit usually increases yearly. Only the maximum amount that was taxable will appear on the chart. (For Medicare taxes, the maximum earnings amount began rising in 1991. Since 1994, *all* of your earnings are taxed for Medicare.)

▼ **Act right away** if any of your earnings are shown incorrectly. **Call us at 1-800-772-1213.** If possible, have your W-2 or tax return for those years available. (If you live outside the U.S., follow the directions at the bottom of page 4.)

Your Earnings Record at a Glance

Years You Worked	Your Taxed Social Security Earnings	Your Taxed Medicare Earnings
1976	742	742
1977	1,023	1,023
1978	3,896	3,896
1979	6,711	6,711
1980	8,951	8,951
1981	9,381	9,381
1982	9,146	9,146
1983	9,756	9,756
1984	10,097	10,097
1985	11,458	11,458
1986	12,531	12,531
1987	12,949	12,949
1988	11,568	11,568
1989	14,067	14,067
1990	15,738	15,738
1991	18,919	18,919
1992	21,308	21,308
1993	24,441	24,441
1994	26,069	26,069
1995	27,350	27,350
1996	28,302	28,302
1997	29,384	29,384
1998	30,364	30,364
1999	not yet recorded	

Did you know... Social Security is more than just a retirement program? It's here to help you when you need it most.

For instance, Social Security helps you if you become disabled — even at an early age. It is possible for a young person who has worked and paid Social Security taxes for as few as 18 months to become eligible for disability benefits. If you become disabled, you could receive valuable benefits to help you for as long as you're completely disabled.

Social Security has another important feature. It is portable and moves with you from job to job throughout your career.

Totals over your working career:

Estimated taxes paid for Social Security:		Estimated taxes paid for Medicare:	
You paid:	$20,563	You paid:	$4,831
Your employers paid:	$20,563	Your employers paid:	$4,831

Note: If you are self-employed, you pay the total tax on your net earnings.

3

Some Facts About Social Security

About Social Security and Medicare...

Social Security pays retirement, disability, family and survivors benefits. Medicare, a separate program run by the Health Care Financing Administration, helps pay for inpatient hospital care, nursing care, doctors' fees, and other medical services and supplies to people over 65 or to people who have received Social Security disability benefits for two years. Your Social Security covered earnings qualify you for both programs.

Here are some facts about Social Security's benefits:

▼ **Retirement** — If you were born before 1938, your full retirement age is 65. Because of a 1983 change in the law, the full retirement age will increase gradually to 67 for people born in 1960 and later.

  Some people retire before their full retirement age. They can retire as early as age 62 and take their benefits at a reduced rate. Others continue working after their full retirement age. They receive higher benefits because of additional earnings and special credits for delayed retirement.

▼ **Disability** — If you become severely disabled before full retirement age, you can receive disability benefits after six months if you have:

  — enough Social Security credits, and

  — a physical or mental impairment that's expected to prevent you from doing "substantial" work for a year or more, *or* a condition that's expected to result in death.

▼ **Family** — If you're eligible for disability or retirement benefits, your current or divorced spouse, minor children, or adult children disabled before age 22 also may receive benefits. Each may qualify for up to 50 percent of your benefit amount. The total amount depends on how many family members qualify.

▼ **Survivors** — When you die, certain members of your family may be eligible for benefits:

  — your spouse age 60 or older (50 or older if disabled, or any age if caring for your children under age 16); and

  — your children if unmarried and under age 18, still in school and under age 19, or adult children disabled before age 22.

  If you are divorced, your ex-spouse could be eligible for a widow's or widower's benefit on your record when you die.

Receive retirement benefits and still work

You can continue to work and still get retirement benefits. If you're under your full retirement age, there are limits on how much you can earn without losing some or all of your retirement benefits. These limits change each year. When you apply for benefits, we'll tell you what the limits are at that time and whether work would affect your monthly benefits. When you reach your full retirement age, the earnings limits no longer apply.

Before you decide to retire, think about your benefits for the long term. Everyone's situation is different. For example, be sure to consider the advantages and disadvantages of early retirement. If you choose to receive benefits before you reach full retirement age, your benefits will be permanently reduced. However, you'll receive benefits for a longer period of time.

  To help you decide when is the best time for you to retire, we offer a free booklet, *Social Security — Retirement Benefits* (Publication No. 05-10035), that provides specific information about retirement.

  There are other free publications that you may find helpful, including:

▼ *The Future Of Social Security* (Publication No. 05-10055) — a discussion of the present and what may lie ahead;

▼ *Understanding The Benefits* (Publication No. 05-10024) — a general explanation of all Social Security benefits;

▼ *How Your Retirement Benefit Is Figured* (Publication No. 05-10070) — an explanation of how you can calculate your benefit;

▼ *A Pension From Work Not Covered By Social Security* (Publication No. 05-10045) — how it affects your Social Security retirement or disability benefits; and

▼ *Government Pension Offset* (Publication No. 05-10007) — a law that affects spouse's or widow(er)'s benefits.

  We also have leaflets and factsheets with information about specific topics such as military service, self-employment or foreign employment. You can request Social Security publications by following the instructions in the **If you need more information...** section below.

If you need more information...

If you have questions or want to request this Statement in Spanish (*Para solicitar Su Declaración en español*), call 1-800-772-1213, contact your local Social Security office or reach us at *www.ssa.gov/mystatement* on the Internet. If you're deaf or hard of hearing, call TTY 1-800-325-0778. If your address is incorrect on this *Statement*, ask the IRS to send you an IRS Form 8822. We don't keep addresses for persons not receiving Social Security benefits.

SECTION THREE: INSURANCE PLANNING

CHAPTER APPENDIX 11.2: FORM 7004

Request for Social Security Statement

Form Approved
OMB No 0960-0466

[ ] SP

☐ Please check this box if you want to get your statement in Spanish instead of English.

Please print or type your answers. When you have completed the form, fold it and mail it to us. (If you prefer to send your request using the internet, contact us at http://www.ssa.gov)

1. Name shown on your Social Security card:

First Name _____ Middle Initial _____

Last Name Only _____

2. Your Social Security number as shown on your card:

[ ][ ][ ] - [ ][ ] - [ ][ ][ ][ ]

3. Your Date of Birth (Mo.-Day-Yr.)

[ ][ ] - [ ][ ] - [ ][ ]

4. Other Social Security numbers you have used:

[ ][ ][ ] - [ ][ ] - [ ][ ][ ][ ]
[ ][ ][ ] - [ ][ ] - [ ][ ][ ][ ]

5. Your Sex: ☐ Male ☐ Female

For items 6 and 8 show only earnings covered by Social Security. Do NOT include wages from State, local or Federal Government employment that are NOT covered for Social Security or that are covered ONLY by Medicare.

6 Show your actual earnings (wages and/or net self-employment income) for last year and your estimated earnings for this year.

A. Last year's actual earnings: (Dollars Only)

$ [ ][ ][ ] , [ ][ ][ ] . 0 0

B. This year's estimated earnings:(Dollars Only)

$ [ ][ ][ ] , [ ][ ][ ] . 0 0

7. Show the age at which you plan to stop working.

[ ][ ] (Show only one age)

8. Below, show the average yearly amount (not your total future lifetime earnings) that you think you will earn between now and when you plan to stop working. Include performance or scheduled pay increases or bonuses, but not cost-of-living increases.

If you expect to earn significantly more or less in the future due to promotions, job changes, part-time work, or an absence from the work force, enter the amount that most closely reflects your future yearly earnings.

If you don't expect any significant changes, show the same amount you are earning now (the amount in 6B).

Future average yearly earnings (Dollars Only)

$ [ ][ ][ ] , [ ][ ][ ] . 0 0

9. Do you want us to send the statement:
• To you? Enter your name and mailing address.
• To someone else (your accountant, pension plan etc.)? Enter your name with "c/o' and the name and address of that person or organization.

Name _____

Street Address (Include Apt. No, PO Box, or Rural Route) _____

City _____ State _____ Zip Code _____

NOTICE

I am asking for information about my own Social Security record or the record of a person I am authorized to represent. I understand that if I deliberately request information under false pretenses, I may be guilty of a Federal crime and could be fined and/or imprisoned. I authorize you to use a contractor to send the statement of earnings and benefit estimates to the person named in item 9.

⇧

Please sign your name(Do Not Print)

_____

Date _____ (Area Code) Daytime Telephone No. _____

Mail to: Social Security Administration, Wilkes Barre Data Operations Center, P.O. Box 7004, Wilkes Barre, PA 18767-7004

Form SSA-7004-SM (6-98)

- Risk and return of asset classes

- Tradeoff between risk and return

- Risks of investment vehicles

- Efficient frontier

- Types of investment vehicles

- Types of mutual funds

- Correlation between asset classes

- Efficient market hypothesis

- Calculation of difficult return measures

- Valuing fixed income securities

- Capital asset pricing model

- Blending asset classes together to build a portfolio
- Calculating standard deviation of a portfolio
- Calculating duration of fixed income securities
- Immunizing bond portfolios
- Valuing equity securities
- Mutual fund selection for inclusion in portfolios

Investment Planning

Risks

- Unrealized financial planning goals
- Investment losses
- Purchasing power risk
- Reinvestment rate risk
- Interest rate risk
- Market risk
- Exchange rate risk
- Business risk
- Financial risk
- Default risk
- Country risk

Data Collection

- Investment history
- Risk tolerance of clients
- Tax returns
- Current investments
- Current asset allocation

Goals

- Preservation of capital
- Capital accumulation
- Sufficient investment returns to meet other financial planning goals
- Minimizing risks

Data Analysis

- Asset class risks and returns
- Correlations between asset classes
- Portfolio risks and returns
- Benchmark comparison
- Tax efficiency of portfolio

CHAPTER 12

Introduction to Investment Concepts

LEARNING OBJECTIVES:

After learning the material in this chapter, you will be able to:

1. List the investment goals common to most investors and how to achieve them.

2. Differentiate between systematic risk and unsystematic risk, giving examples of each.

3. Define lending investments and ownership investments and discuss the differences between these two categories.

4. Explain the difference between direct investing and indirect investing.

5. Describe the two common measures of risk—beta and standard deviation.

6. Discuss several measures of return—holding period return, arithmetic mean, geometric mean, internal rate of return, and real rate of return.

7. Define the "Efficient Frontier" and explain its role in modern portfolio theory.

8. Describe the "Efficient Market Hypothesis" and compare it to other investment strategies and theories.

INTRODUCTION TO INVESTING

As this text's opening chapters point out, the professional financial planner's purpose is to assist clients in accomplishing their financial goals and objectives, while helping them reduce certain personal and financial risks. Investment planning and portfolio evaluation are key elements in accomplishing many financial planning goals, such as saving for retirement, saving for children's education, and the accumulation and preservation of wealth. This chapter should provide the financial planner with the background and reference information necessary to develop a solid foundation of investment planning—an essential ingredient in the financial planning process.

Investing is based on the concept that forgoing immediate consumption provides for greater future consumption. Investing provides an opportunity for discretionary funds to grow and to accumulate over time to facilitate future consumption. Therefore, the first step in investing is to save assets instead of consuming them. This current sacrifice is in hopes that funds saved today will allow for greater expenditures in the future.

Without the ability to invest and grow through savings, interest income, dividend payments, rental income, and capital appreciation, investors would find it very difficult to achieve their financial goals. However, financial growth is only one element to consider in achieving financial goals. Taxes, inflation, and other investment risks stand in the way. The starting point in the investment planning process is to establish financial goals.

ESTABLISHING FINANCIAL GOALS

Goals establish the financial target. Strategies establish the path to reach the target. The more specific and measurable the goals are, the more useful they become. In general, goals should be **SMART**.

- ▲ **S**pecific
- ▲ **M**easurable
- ▲ **A**ttainable
- ▲ **R**ealistic
- ▲ **T**imely

The time horizon for goals can be short, intermediate, or long-term. Short-term goals are those accomplished within two years, such as saving for small purchases or for a down payment for an automobile. We think of intermediate goals as those that can be accomplished within two to ten years, such as funding for a child's college education or saving for a down payment on a home. Long-term goals are those that generally take over ten years to accomplish, such as saving for retirement. A discussion of the different approaches to investing for goals with different time horizons appears later in this chapter.

TYPICAL FINANCIAL PLANNING GOALS

Although clients may have financial planning goals that are unique to them, most individuals share a certain number of specific goals with other people. These typical goals include saving for a home (or down payment), funding children's education, and planning for retirement.

Purchasing a home will likely be one of the largest financial commitments someone makes, and most people begin the process by saving for a few years to accumulate a down payment. If the price of an average home is $100,000, many people attempt to make a down payment of approximately $20,000 or 20 percent. The average time it takes for someone to save for a down payment is generally between two and five years. This short time period leaves little room for growth and even less opportunity to tolerate a significant amount of risk. Therefore, the appropriate types of securities for this type of investment situation should be relatively conservative.

One typical goal for most parents is funding their children's college tuition. The cost of higher education can be as low as a few thousand dollars a year to over thirty thousand dollars annually. In some cases, parents will pay the entire cost of education from their current budget. However, with tuition costs increasing at an inflation rate of approximately five to seven percent per year, it is becoming increasingly difficult to pay for college education. As a result, many parents are beginning to plan and save for college as soon as their child is born, giving themselves an investment time horizon of approximately eighteen years. Other parents with young children may not have the resources to begin planning for college until the child is beginning high school. In their case, the time horizon for saving and investing is closer to four or five years. Clearly, the eighteen-year horizon allows a longer compounding period of growth and a greater amount of risk tolerance than does the shorter time horizon.

Even individuals and couples without children, or those whose children choose not to attend college, still need to plan for retirement. Today's Social Security system will not provide enough income for most individuals to maintain their lifestyle during retirement. Today, the burden of funding one's retirement income falls mainly upon the individual. As people become more knowledgeable about financial planning, they are beginning to save for retirement earlier. Someone who is 25 years old has forty years to save for retirement, assuming that normal retirement age is 65. Others will not begin to save until much later, but will still have a long-term investment time horizon since the average person will spend ten to twenty years in retirement.

In each of these cases, accomplishing the specific financial planning goal requires that the individual save and invest funds for a certain period. However, since the time horizon of each goal is different, the ability to tolerate fluctuation in the value of the invested assets is also different. Obviously, there is more tolerance for fluctuation when planning for retirement than when saving for a down payment on a home. Although each of these financial planning goals may be different and have a different time horizon, in most cases, investors will have basic, common investment goals.

COMMON INVESTMENT GOALS

In addition to the financial planning goals mentioned above, it is probably fair to say that all investors, both individuals and institutions, are concerned about the more fundamental investment goals of capital accumulation, capital preservation, maximizing returns, and minimizing risk. While these goals seem and are contradictory in nature, they are fundamental elements that must be addressed by every investor.

Capital Accumulation

Accumulation of capital is the reason for investment. Without a need to accumulate capital, there would be no reason to invest.

Preservation of Capital

Preservation of capital is one of the most basic investment objectives. Investors are always willing to take some degree of risk, but with the idea that they will be increasing their wealth as opposed to risking it to the market.

Maximizing Returns

Maximizing returns is another goal for which investors strive. However, since risk and return are related, it is unlikely that returns can maximize while simultaneously attempting to preserve capital and reduce risk.

Minimizing Risk

Minimizing risk is the fourth basic objective of most investors. Investors are often willing to accept risk, but complain in the event of the first downturn in the market value of their investments. Therefore, the planner must be able to assist the investor in balancing these four somewhat contradictory goals and help the investor obtain his specific goals.

BUDGETING

Unless a client is already financially secure, a key element in achieving his financial goals will be the ability to save money from the current budget. Those who cannot live within their current budget will be hard pressed to achieve their financial goals. Many people spend more money than they earn. Oftentimes their credit cards have large balances and worse, they are paying interest rates as high as 21 percent. Purchases with short-term credit, such as with credit cards, should generally be limited to an amount that can be easily paid off each month.

The purpose of budgeting is to manage the amount of income and expenses on a monthly basis. Income for most people is reasonably fixed in the short-term. That is, most people have a salary with which they can anticipate a certain fixed amount of income each month. Expenses may vary widely throughout the year. For example, some items are paid monthly, such as utilities, mortgage payments, and phone bills, while other items are paid semiannually, such as automobile insurance. In addition, certain expenses are necessities, such as mortgage payments, groceries, and utilities, while other expenses are discretionary, such as dining out or purchasing new clothes. Having determined which expenses are necessary every month and which expenses are discretionary, one can then begin to find ways to reduce expenses and increase savings. For those who live on a relatively fixed salary, the only way to increase savings is to ultimately reduce expenditures.

398

METHODS OF INCREASING SAVINGS

Reducing expenditures, especially discretionary expenditures, is an excellent way to increase savings for investment. One way to accomplish this is a savings method called "pay yourself first." Paying yourself first means that the first bill paid every pay period is what the investor owes to his or her savings. With savings set aside, the investor must then live within the reduced budget. This method of savings is very effective for those people without much savings discipline because it can be accomplished automatically. For instance, mutual funds accounts can be set up to automatically draft a certain amount of savings from the primary checking account every month or each pay period. Paying yourself first assures saving on a regular basis and promotes living within budget.

Exhibit 12.1 below illustrates the calculation by the Bureau of Economic Analysis for personal savings as a percentage of disposable personal income for the years 1929 – 2000. Notice the dramatic decrease in the savings rate over the last decade.

EXHIBIT 12.1: NATIONAL SAVINGS RATE

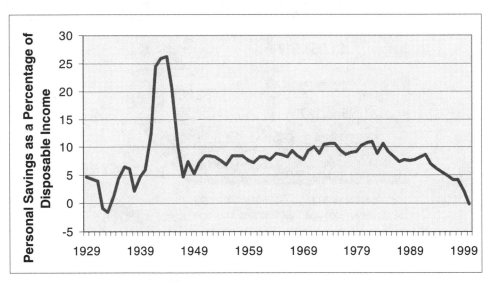

Another method to increase savings over time is to allocate a portion of future raises to savings. As increases in salary occur, increases in savings should also occur. If an investor was able to live on $4,000 per month last month and received a ten percent raise, the investor should be able to live on less than $4,400 next month and can allocate up to $400 of the raise to savings.

Elective savings programs, such as 401(k) plans (cash or deferred arrangements) are another excellent method of increasing savings and net worth. These plans not only facilitate automatic savings in the form of payroll deduction, they also increase the current budget by saving on a pretax basis instead of on an after-tax basis. Most of the time, salary deferrals are accompanied by employer-matching contributions. These employer contributions are like "free money," and individuals should take full advantage of these contributions. A 401(k) plan can facilitate both the "paying yourself first" and the "allocating raises" methods of increasing savings.

Dividend reinvestment plans (DRIPs) allow individuals to accumulate wealth over time by reinvesting dividends back into their equity holdings. DRIPs have traditionally been programs established by corporations to allow their shareholders to purchase additional shares without the need of a broker and to automatically reinvest dividend payments. These programs can provide cost efficient investing for the average investor.

EXAMPLE

Probably the most important step in achieving financial goals is to begin today. Time is a great asset in achieving financial planning objectives. In the area of investing, time is crucial to success. For example, a 25-year-old saving $2,000 per year for ten years will accumulate more by age 65 than a 35-year-old saving $2,000 for 30 years. Although the younger investor invested only one-third of the amount of the older investor, the younger investor has more assets at age 65. How can this be? The simple answer is time. The 25-year-old investor had time working for him. Exhibit 12.2 demonstrates this concept at three earnings rates.

EXHIBIT 12.2: TIME/SAVINGS EXAMPLE (ACCUMULATION AT AGE 65)

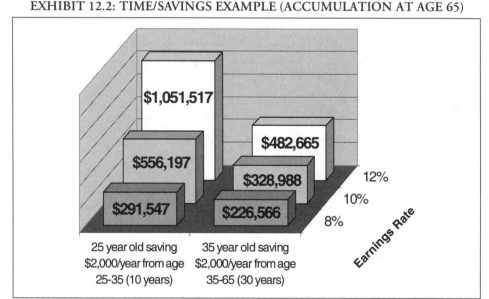

Each of these methods can be an effective way to accumulate wealth over time. However, all investors are subject to factors outside their control that may negatively affect the accomplishment of their financial goals. These factors, known as investment risks, are discussed below.

INVESTMENT RISKS

Individuals, corporations, and institutions all invest to grow wealth. The investor's returns, however, are indeterminable at the inception of the investment due to uncertainty. This uncertainty is risk, and it can mean different things to different investors. Risk can be thought of as the uncertainty of future outcomes, or risk might be defined as the probability of an adverse result. In either case, investors expect higher returns when they accept higher levels of uncertainty or risk. This concept is fundamental to the topic of investments.

Investors must choose to accept a certain level of risk. Some investors think that they can completely avoid all risk; however, certain risks influence all securities, such as the risk of inflation and fluctuations in interest rates. Even the most conservative investors, who invest in the least risky fixed-income securities, are subject to purchasing power risk (inflation) and interest rate risk (changes in interest rates). Other types of risk may only affect a single security, industry, or country. Based on these differences, there are two broad categories of risk: systematic risks and unsystematic risks. Exhibit 12.3 summarizes the types of risks under each category.

EXHIBIT 12.3: SYSTEMATIC AND UNSYSTEMATIC RISKS

SYSTEMATIC RISKS	UNSYSTEMATIC RISKS
• Market Risk	• Business Risk
• Interest Rate Risk	• Financial Risk
• Purchasing Power Risk	• Default Risk
• Foreign Currency Risk	• Country Risk
• Reinvestment Rate Risk	• Regulation Risk

SYSTEMATIC RISKS

Systematic risks are those risks impacted by broad macroeconomic factors, which influence all securities. These risks include market risk, interest rate risk, purchasing power risk, foreign currency risk, and reinvestment risk. Diversification cannot eliminate systematic risk because these factors affect all securities.

Market Risk

The tendency for stocks to move with the market is **market risk.** When the market is increasing, most stocks have a tendency to increase in value. Conversely, most stocks tend to fall with declines in the market. Often, a move in the market is prefaced by some change in the economic environment. (About 85 percent of stocks are positively correlated to some degree with the market).

Interest Rate Risk

The risk that changes in interest rates will affect the value of securities is known as **interest rate risk.** There is a tendency for an inverse relationship to exist between the value of fixed investments and changes in interest rates—as interest rates increase, the value of bonds decline. Rising interest rates generally have a negative effect on stocks as well. Reasons for this negative pressure include the increased discount rate utilized for valuation of cash flows, increased borrowing costs for corporations (thus, an expectancy of lower earnings), and increased yields on alternative investments, such as bonds.

systematic risks - investment risks impacted by broad macroeconomic factors that influence all securities

market risk - a systematic risk where stocks tend to move with the market

interest rate risk - a systematic risk where changes in interest rates will affect the value of securities

purchasing power risk - a systematic risk where inflation will erode the real value of the investor's assets

foreign currency risk - a systematic risk where a change in the relationship between the value of the dollar (or investor's currency) and the value of the foreign currency will occur where the investment is made

EXAMPLE

EXAMPLE

reinvestment risk - a systematic risk where earnings (cash flows) distributed from current investments will be unable to be reinvested to yield a rate of return equal to the yields of the current investments

Purchasing Power Risk

The risk that inflation will erode the real value of the investor's assets is **purchasing power risk**. As the price of goods increases, the purchasing power of assets decreases. The objective of investment planning is to generate returns in excess of inflation so that the real value of assets does not erode. Inflation is the main cause of purchasing power risk. Bonds held to maturity are likely to suffer from purchasing power risk because maturity value remains constant regardless of price changes.

Foreign Currency Risk (or Exchange Rate Risk)

Foreign currency risk is the risk that a change in the relationship between the value of the dollar (or investor's currency) and the value of the foreign currency will occur during the period the investment is held.

John invests $1,000,000 in the Orval Corporation based in Mexico. If the conversion rate for pesos to dollars were ten to one, John would have to invest 10 million pesos in Orval Corporation. Orval Corporation does extremely well, and John is able to sell his interest for 15 million pesos. If John attempts to convert the pesos into dollars when the exchange rate has changed to 12 to 1, he will receive $1,250,000 (15,000,000 ÷ 12).

This gain is comprised of a 50 percent (5,000,000 pesos) gain on the investment and a loss of 16.67 percent ($250,000 ÷ $1,500,000) or $250,000 from the change in the currency rate. The net result is a 25 percent gain on the original investment; however, it is only half of the gain generated from the appreciation of Orval Corporation.

Assume the same facts as in the previous example except that the exchange rate is now 8 to 1 instead of 12 to 1. In this case, John liquidates his interest in Orval Corporation and converts the pesos to $1,875,000. This $875,000 gain consists of $500,000 from the appreciation of Orval Corporation and $375,000 from the devaluation of the dollar relative to the pesos.

In the first example, John's gain decreases by 50 percent, and in the second example, John's gain increases by 75 percent. Money managers often attempt to avoid such drastic changes in gains and losses by hedging against currency fluctuations. Forward or futures contracts are often used as hedging devices against currency risk.

Reinvestment Risk

Reinvestment risk is the risk that earnings (cash flows) distributed from current investments will be unable to be reinvested to yield a rate of return equal to the yields of the current investments. For example, if a bond is purchased today to yield 8 percent and the market interest rate subsequently declines, interest payments from the bond will be unable to be reinvested at 8 percent; thus, the overall yield to maturity will decline. Zero-coupon bonds are not subject to reinvestment rate risk during the term of the bond because payments are not made to the investor until maturity.

UNSYSTEMATIC RISKS

Unsystematic risks are those risks that are unique to a single security, company, industry, or country. These risks include default risk, business risk, financial risk, and country risk. Unlike systematic risk, these risks can be eliminated through diversification. Several studies have found that unsystematic risk declines significantly with a portfolio consisting of as few as ten to fifteen randomly chosen stocks. As more stocks are added to a portfolio, the less impact the losses of one company in the portfolio will have on the total performance of the portfolio of securities. This concept is illustrated in the example below.

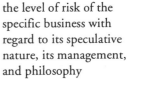

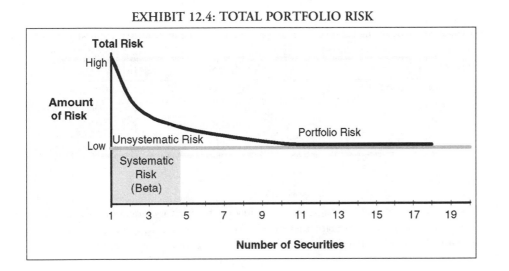

EXHIBIT 12.4: TOTAL PORTFOLIO RISK

The figure above illustrates the concept of diversification. As more securities are added to the portfolio, the overall risk of the portfolio declines. There are several other points of interest. First, unsystematic risk can be reduced and effectively eliminated. This is not the case for systematic risk. Systematic risk cannot be eliminated because it represents the risk to all securities. Systematic risk is generally measured by beta, whereas total risk is measured by standard deviation. For portfolios that have significantly reduced unsystematic risk, beta is a good measure of total risk. However, when unsystematic risk is not reduced, beta does a poor job of estimating total risk.

Business Risk

Business risk, or the level of risk of the specific business, includes the speculative nature of the business, the management of the business, the philosophy of the business, and so on. Different types of businesses will have different levels of risk. For instance, searching for gold would generally be riskier than operating a grocery store. However, each has unique risks associated with that type of business. Business risk can also be thought of as the certainty or uncertainty of income. Utility companies have relatively stable and predictable income streams and, therefore, have lower business risk. Since cyclical companies, such as auto manufacturers, have unsteady or fluctuating income levels, they are classified as having higher business risk. Business risk relates to the activities of the company and is associated with the asset side of the balance sheet.

unsystematic risks - types of investment risks unique to a single company, industry, or country that can be eliminated by portfolio diversification

business risk - an unsystematic risk based on the level of risk of the specific business with regard to its speculative nature, its management, and philosophy

financial risk - an unsystematic risk based on the capital structure of a firm which affects the return on equity (ROE) for a company

EXAMPLE

default risk - an unsystematic risk where a business will be unable to service its debt to creditors

country (or regulation) risk - an unsystematic risk where changes in a country's laws or political situation will have an adverse effect on an investment

Financial Risk

Financial risk is based on the capital structure of a firm, which affects the return on equity (ROE) for a company. The use of debt magnifies ROE and makes gains and losses more volatile.

For example, a firm that has 75 percent debt (25 percent equity) will have a ROE four times larger than a similar firm with the same net income and 100 percent equity. This financial leverage occurs because the return is based on a smaller amount of equity. In this example, the equity of the leveraged company is one-fourth that of the non-leveraged firm, so that returns and losses for the leveraged firm will be four times larger on a percentage basis. Financial risk is associated with the liability side of the balance sheet since it relates to the debt ratio a company maintains.

	COMPANY A	COMPANY B
Net Income	$50,000	$50,000
Debt	$0	$300,000
Equity	$400,000	$100,000
ROE (Return on Equity)	12.5%	50%

Default Risk

The risk that a business will be unable to service its debt to creditors is **default risk**. Bonds issued by both corporations and municipalities are subject to default risk. Rating agencies, such as Moody's and Standard & Poor's, rate bonds issued from corporations and municipalities from the highest grade to default. Generally, obligations of the U.S. Government (Treasuries and Ginnie Maes) are free from default risk. In addition, equity investments are not subject to default risk.

Country (or Regulation) Risk

International investments are subject to **country risk**, which is the unique risk within each country. These risks include political and economic risks. The United States is generally thought to have the lowest country risk, since its political and economic systems are the most stable. An investor is able to minimize country risk by investing in several countries instead of just a few.

RISK AND RETURN

There is a direct relationship between risk and return. As the level of risk increases, the expected return increases. Meanwhile, as the level of risk declines, the expected return declines. Thus, to receive higher returns, an investor must accept the trade-off of greater risk and typically more volatile returns. As mentioned above, this concept of risk and return is essential to the theories within investments and is essential when planning for the financial well-being of clients.

LIQUIDITY AND MARKETABILITY

Liquidity is the ability to sell an investment quickly and at a competitive price, with no loss of principal and little price concession. Liquidity is a risk that investors must face. If the security markets do not have sufficient liquidity to absorb a trade, then the trader may find that there is a price concession to execute the trade. **Marketability** refers to the ability of an investor to find a ready market where the investor may sell his or her investment. There is a subtle difference between liquidity and marketability. For instance, real estate is marketable but may not be liquid. Treasury bills are both liquid and marketable. Liquidity and marketability should be thought of as a spectrum with cash being the most liquid and the most marketable.

INVESTMENT CHOICES

The level of risk and the specific risks an investor must face greatly influence the investor's choice of investments. Investors today have a wide variety of investment options, ranging from interest-bearing checking accounts to sophisticated derivatives. Although investments can be extremely complicated and risky, as in the case of derivatives, investments generally fall within one of two categories: lending investments or ownership investments.

LENDING INVESTMENTS

Savings accounts and bonds are both examples of lending investments. When cash is deposited into a savings account, it is as if the owner has loaned money to the bank. The bank, which will lend money to others in the form of a mortgage or some other loan, will in return pay the owner interest, which is the payment for the use of the money. Interest can be paid based on a fixed rate, or it can vary based on some agreed upon variable-rate benchmark, such as the 91-day Treasury bill rate.

Bonds are more structured investments than savings accounts. For example, bonds have specific maturity dates, specified face values, and defined interest (coupon) payments. While a savings account is, in effect, an indefinite loan, bonds have a specific maturity date. This date is the time at which the borrower (bond issuer) must repay the loan. The maturity of a bond can range from a few months, as with a 91-day Treasury bill, to thirty years or more.

Bonds generally have a standard or par value (face value) of $1,000. Therefore, to invest $10,000, a purchase of ten bonds trading at par would be made. Bond issuers compensate the lender (bondholder) by making specified interest payments. These interest payments, generally paid semiannually (twice per year), are based on a rate of interest called the coupon rate. For example, a bond with a stated coupon rate of 10 percent will pay interest of $50 ($1,000 x 10 percent x ½) twice each year for a total of $100 per year. These coupon payments, which are really the payment by the lender for the use of the money, continue over the life of the bond. Therefore, a thirty-year bond will generally make sixty coupon payments. At the time the bond matures, the investor will also receive the par (face) value of the bond (generally $1,000). This payment is the repayment of the original loan proceeds.

Bonds provide investors with a certain level of security since they generally make regular, specified payments to the bondholders. Many investors, especially retired individuals, rely on these

liquidity - the ability to sell an investment quickly and at a competitive price, with no loss of principal and little price concession. The length of time expected for the asset to be converted back to cash

marketability - the ability of an investor to find a ready market where the investor may sell his or her investment

coupon payments as a source of income. Although bonds provide some certainty, there are risks inherent in investing in bonds. Two of the more important risks are default risk and interest rate risk.

Default Risk

Because bonds are essentially loans to an organization or corporation, bond investors must be concerned with the ability of the organization to repay the proceeds from the loan. The risk that an institution or government will fail to repay its loan is called credit risk or default risk. Default risk is an unsystematic risk that can be either diversified or eliminated. Diversifying default risk is accomplished by investing in several bond issues instead of a single issue. This strategy reduces the potential exposure to any one of the borrowers (issuers). Default risk can be eliminated by purchasing bonds that are direct obligations of the United States government. U.S. Treasuries are default risk-free and are, therefore, a good choice for those investors concerned about default risk. However, the basic principle of risk and return still holds: as default risk is reduced for a bond, so is the related return. Investors will require higher investment returns from investments that have higher default risk.

Interest Rate Risk

Even if credit risk were eliminated, as in the case of U.S. Treasuries, bonds are still impacted in several ways by fluctuations in interest rates. Changes in interest rates influence both the current market price of the bond, and the value of the reinvested coupon payments. As interest rates increase, the current value and price of outstanding bonds should decline. This decline results because bonds, which are a series of cash flows, must be reevaluated or re-priced in accordance with the new market rate of interest. Any bond that is paying a coupon rate lower than the current market rate of interest will decrease in value (sell at a discount).

If an increase in interest rates results in a decline in the value of a bond, how would the reinvested coupon payments be impacted? If an investor was reinvesting the cash flow from the coupon payments that were received from the bond, then these coupon payments could be reinvested to earn higher rates of return. Thus, when interest rates increase, there is a decline in the value of a bond, but an increase in the value of the reinvested cash flows from the coupon payments. These offsetting values are an important aspect of immunizing bond portfolios, discussed in the following chapter.

OWNERSHIP INVESTMENTS IN BUSINESS (COMMON AND PREFERRED STOCK)

Ownership investments take the form of common or preferred stock. Common stockholders accept the risks inherent in owning a company. While bondholders have a right to be repaid funds that were loaned, common stockholders have invested in the potential future profitability of the business. If the company is successful, then the value of the common stock will increase. If the company is unsuccessful, then the value of the common stock will decline. Investors in common stock are rewarded for accepting risk in two ways. The first is through appreciation in the value of the stock. The second is from earnings that are paid to the shareholders in the form of dividends. A dividend is a payment made by the corporation to the shareholders as a return of the profits of the corporation.

406

There is more risk for common stockholders than for bondholders since, in the event of bankruptcy, bondholders are paid before stockholders. Investors require higher returns for common stock to compensate them for the increased risks associated with owning equity securities. In addition, equities tend to have more price volatility than bonds.

Preferred stock has characteristics of both bonds and common stock. Like bonds, preferred stock generally pays a fixed payment, called a preferred stock dividend, which is determined as a percentage of the par value of the preferred stock. Preferred stock is valued similarly to bonds and is subject to many of the same risks as bonds. However, preferred stock does not have a finite maturity date. Instead, like common stock, preferred stock continues for as long as the company continues or until it is retired.

OWNERSHIP INVESTMENTS IN REAL ESTATE

Real estate is another type of ownership asset. It differs from common stock because rather than being an intangible asset, real estate is a tangible asset that has unique characteristics. Real estate is clearly a valuable asset to investors. In fact, oftentimes the largest asset owned by an individual is his personal residence. Stocks, bonds, money markets, and derivatives are all intangible financial assets while real estate is a tangible asset. Real estate differs from financial assets due to the following attributes:

▲ Each parcel of land or real estate is unique in its location and composition.
▲ Real estate is immovable.
▲ Real estate is virtually indestructible.
▲ There is a limited supply of real estate.

There is a variety of real estate investments an investor can purchase, including residential real estate, commercial real estate, partnerships and limited partnerships, developed land, undeveloped land, and real estate investment trusts (REITs). Most real estate investments have the following advantages:

Cash Flow

Generally, real estate investments generate a generous amount of cash flow through rents. Some real estate investments, however, like undeveloped land, may not have this advantage.

Depreciation Deductions

Many real estate investments have deductions for depreciation that can offset taxable income from the investment and from other sources. In many cases, real estate investments can generate positive cash flow without having taxable income. In some cases, taxable losses are generated along with positive cash flow. These taxable losses are due to the deductibility of depreciation. However, the Tax Reform Act of 1986 limited this advantage with the creation of the passive activity loss rules.

Low Correlation to Other Asset Classes

As will be discussed in the portfolio theory section, it is often advantageous to add asset classes that have a low correlation to equities and fixed income securities to portfolios to reduce the overall risk of the portfolio. Real estate has a low correlation of returns to common stock, preferred stock, and bonds.

DERIVATIVES

Investors have become increasingly aware of the concept of derivatives in recent years. Much of this awareness is due to the devastating financial results that derivatives have had on certain organizations. These disastrous outcomes have generally been due to mismanagement of derivatives within the organizations. However, when derivatives are used properly, they can provide investors with an investment tool that can create many benefits, including the reduction of risk.

Derivatives are securities whose value is based on the value of some other security or proxy. For example, an IBM option contract will derive its value from the value of IBM stock. Changes in the value of IBM stock will cause the associated option contract to also change in value. This text's discussion of derivatives will be limited to options contracts and futures contracts.

Options Contracts

Options are derivatives that give the holder or buyer the right to do something. **Call options** give the holder the right to purchase the underlying security, generally stock, at a specified price within a specified period.

For example, assume Brooke wants to purchase ABC Company stock, which is currently trading at $50 per share. She expects the company to greatly increase in value over the next couple of months. However, she does not have enough cash to purchase the security today, but will have the funds in three months when she receives her partnership distribution. Brooke could purchase a call option on ABC stock that would give her the right to purchase the stock in three months for $50 per share.

Put options give the holder the right to sell the underlying security, generally stock, at a specified price within a specified period. Options can either be purchased or sold (also referred to as written). Therefore, there are four unique positions that an investor could take with an option: to purchase a call option, to sell (write) a call option, to purchase a put option, or to sell (write) a put option. However, investors will often combine multiple options positions or combine an option position with a stock position to create different risk return characteristics.

The **exercise price** of an option contract is the price at which the underlying stock will either be sold (put) or purchased (call) by the holder of the option. The **premium** for any option is simply the cost of the option contract. The premium is generally impacted by the following factors: price of the underlying security, the exercise price of the underlying security, the time until the option expires, the volatility of the underlying security, and the risk free rate.

---

derivatives - securities whose value is based on the value of some other security or proxy

options - derivatives that give the holder or buyer the right to do something

call options - a derivative that gives the holder the right to purchase the underlying security, generally stock, at a specified price within a specified period of time

EXAMPLE

put option - a derivative that gives the holder the right to sell the underlying security, generally stock, at a specified price within a specified period

exercise price - the price at which an underlying stock will either be sold (put) or purchased (call) by the holder of an option

premium - the cost of an option contract

What are the reasons that an investor might enter into an option contract? As with most derivatives, options can be used for specific purposes or simply as a leveraged investment. Investors who believe that the underlying security is going to appreciate may purchase call options. Investors will generally sell (write) call options when they believe that the underlying security is going to either remain flat or decline in value. Often, when an investor is holding a long position in a stock that has appreciated rapidly within a short period, the investor will sell (write) a call option to generate the premium for additional income. As long as the stock does not continue to appreciate, the investor will have enhanced his return by the amount of the call option premium.

Put options are generally purchased to establish a floor or protect against a decline in the value of a long position in stock. For example, an investor might own Microsoft and be concerned that the stock is overvalued. In such a case, the investor might purchase a put option at a level slightly below the current market price. In the event that the stock decreased in value, the investor could sell the stock at the put exercise price. In other words, the put provides downside protection because it establishes the minimum price at which the investor will be able to sell the Microsoft stock.

Put options can be sold (written) by an investor to generate an option premium for a stock that the investor believes will increase in price and that he may own or wish to own. If the investor is correct and the stock does increase, then the investor will receive the option premium as income. In the event that the stock should go down and someone "puts" the stock to the investor (forces the investor to purchase the stock), the investor probably would still believe that the stock was a good purchase and a good stock to own.

Futures Contracts

Unlike options, which give the holder a *right* to purchase or sell a specific security, a **futures contract** is an agreement to do something in the future. Generally, purchasing (selling) a futures contract obligates the buyer (seller) to take delivery (make delivery) of a specific commodity at a specific time in the future. Since a futures contract is an agreement to make or take delivery in the future, the investor will be required to put up a good faith deposit until the agreement is fulfilled, known as an initial margin.

futures contract - an agreement to do something in the future--generally, purchasing (selling) a futures contract obligates the buyer to take delivery (make delivery) of a specific commodity at a specific time in the future

Over time, the futures contract, which is required to be marked-to-market on a daily basis, will generate gains and losses. Each of these daily gains and losses will either add to or reduce the initial margin. If the initial amount put up is reduced to a level below the maintenance margin, the investor will be required to restore the initial margin or put up enough funds to restore the initial margin. Both the initial margin percentage and the maintenance margin amount are set at the inception of the contract.

Speculators and hedgers use futures contracts for different reasons. Speculators use futures contracts as a leveraged investment. Government studies have suggested that approximately 90 percent of individual investors who speculate in futures lose money. The majority of these investors only invest in futures contracts once. Unlike speculators, hedgers use futures contracts to reduce or offset certain risks.

For example, farmers who sell commodities, such as cotton, are concerned about decreasing commodity prices. To offset this risk, farmers can sell futures contracts to insure that the cotton produced sells at a specific price. This type of hedge, referred to as a short hedge, protects against decreasing prices.

Other investors who hedge using futures contracts include manufacturers who use commodities as raw material. For example, if a furniture manufacturer was concerned about rising lumber prices, the manufacturer might purchase lumber futures contracts to lock in the price at which to buy lumber in the future. This type of hedge, referred to as a long hedge, protects against rising prices. The following table summarizes the two types of hedge positions.

Hedger	Cash Position	Hedge Needed	Action
Grower	Long	Short	Sell futures contracts
Manufacturer	Short	Long	Buy futures contracts

In general, derivatives provide investors with a variety of speculative and hedging strategies that would not be available using traditional investment alternatives and allows for a more complete market.

DIRECT VS. INDIRECT INVESTING

direct investing - a process of investing where investors purchase actual securities

Investing in bonds or stocks can be accomplished by purchasing the actual securities or by investing in companies that purchase actual securities. **Direct investing** occurs when investors purchase actual securities. For example, an investor who purchased an IBM corporate bond or the common stock of Microsoft would be investing directly. Direct investing can be accomplished by investing through a brokerage account or some other source, such as a Dividend Reinvestment Plan (DRIP).

indirect investing - a process of investing where investors invest in companies that invest directly

Indirect investing is a process of investing in securities that invest directly. For example, mutual funds are companies that invest in stocks, bonds, and other securities.

Over the last 20 years, indirect investing has gained extensive popularity. In fact, there are currently more investment companies (mutual funds) than there are listed securities. Investment companies or mutual funds provide a variety of benefits to shareholders, including ease of access, diversification, professional management, and investor services. These issues will be discussed further in Chapter 15.

HISTORICAL PERFORMANCE

All assets do not have the same historical investment returns. Exhibit 12.5 provides the historical investment returns, inflation adjusted returns, and the standard deviation of various asset classes:

EXHIBIT 12.5: HISTORICAL RETURNS, INFLATION ADJUSTED RETURNS, AND STANDARD DEVIATION OF ASSET CLASSES

ASSET CLASS	HISTORICAL RETURNS	INFLATION ADJUSTED RETURNS	STANDARD DEVIATION
Small Capitalization Stocks	13	10	30
Large Capitalization Stocks	11	8	20
Fixed Income Securities	6	3	8
Consumer Price Index (CPI)	3	N/A	4

Exhibit 12.5 illustrates how risk and return are closely related. Small capitalization stocks have had the highest returns among the asset classes, but have also been the most volatile. After adjusting for inflation, returns on fixed income securities have been extremely low. Once the effects of taxation are considered, these returns are further reduced. Therefore, it is important to include equity investments in portfolios to provide for real after-tax growth, instead of relying solely on fixed income securities.

MEASURES OF RISK

We defined risk earlier in the chapter as the probability of a negative outcome. In the field of investments and financial planning, risk is generally measured in terms of volatility. Clients are very concerned about fluctuations in their portfolio. As was the case in the year 2000, the markets can be extremely volatile. These market moves cause investors' portfolios to significantly change in value without significant changes in the economy. As previously discussed, the two common measures of risk, from the standpoint of volatility, are beta and standard deviation. Semi variance is a third measure of risk that is gaining popularity.

BETA

Beta is a commonly used measure of risk derived from regression analysis. It is a measure of systematic risk and provides an indication of the volatility of a portfolio compared to the market. The market is defined as having a beta of 1.0. Portfolios with a beta greater than 1.0 are more volatile than the market, while portfolios with a beta less than 1.0 are less volatile than the market. A portfolio with a beta of 1.5 is considered to be 50 percent more volatile than the market. Similarly, a portfolio with a beta of 0.7 is considered to be 30 percent less volatile than the market.

beta - a commonly used measure of systematic risk that is derived from regression analysis

Since beta measures systematic risk, it is a good measure of risk for fully diversified portfolios. Diversified portfolios have minimal unsystematic risk, which means that beta is capturing the majority of the risk of the portfolio. However, when the diversification of the portfolio is low and the portfolio has a substantial amount of unsystematic risk, then beta does not capture all of the volatility within the portfolio. Therefore, beta is more appropriate for portfolios and mutual funds that are well diversified and highly correlated to the market.

STANDARD DEVIATION

Unlike the limitation of beta, **standard deviation** measures total volatility of the portfolio and total risk (that is systematic and unsystematic risk) of the portfolio. Standard deviation is a statistical measure of how far actual returns deviate from the mean return. The formula for calculating standard deviation is as follows:

$$\sigma = \sqrt{\frac{\sum\limits_{t-1}^{n}(R_t - \bar{R})^2}{n-1}}, \text{ where}$$

$\sigma =$ Standard deviation of the security or portfolio

$\bar{R} =$ Mean return, calculated as an average

$R_t =$ Historical return for period t

$n =$ Number of observations

Although there have been many articles on the limitations and usefulness of standard deviation, it remains one of the most prominent and vital measures of risk used by investment practitioners.

SEMI VARIANCE

Semi variance is another statistical measure of risk. However, it differs from variance in that semi variance only considers the downside volatility of an investment. Specifically, semi variance measures the variability of returns below the average or expected return.

Critics of variance and standard deviation state that investors do not complain, nor are concerned about volatility above the average return. Rather, investors are only concerned about volatility below the average return. Therefore, a portfolio manager with a large variance may be punished for having superior positive returns. Semi variance attempts to correct for this perceived flaw by only considering returns and volatility below the expected or average return.

MEASURES OF RETURN

There are a variety of measures of return, including holding period return, arithmetic mean, geometric mean, internal rate of return, and real rate of return. Each of these calculations of return has certain advantages and disadvantages. Each measure of return is discussed below:

HOLDING PERIOD RETURN

The **holding period return** (HPR) measures the total return an investor receives over the life of the investment. It is written as:

$$\text{HPR} = \frac{\text{Ending Value of Investment} - \text{Beginning Value of Investment} + / - \text{Cashflows}}{\text{Beginning Value of Investment}}$$

Assuming Glen purchases a stock for $50 per share and sells it for $75 and the stock paid dividends of $10, then the holding period return equals 70 percent as follows:

EXAMPLE

$$HPR = \frac{\$75 - \$50 + \$10}{\$50} = 70\%$$

Is a 70 percent return a good return? At first, you might think that a 70 percent return is great. However, we have no idea how long the investment was held. Therefore, there is no way to compare a HPR to other alternative investments, such as the risk-free rate of return. Because the HPR does not address the time value of money, it is not commonly used as a return measure.

ARITHMETIC MEAN

The arithmetic mean is the result of averaging periodic returns. The formula for the **arithmetic mean** is written as follows:

arithmetic mean - a measure of investment return that is the result of averaging period returns

$$AM = \frac{\sum_{t=1} HPR_t}{n}, \text{ where}$$

R_t = Return for period t

n = Number of periods in the analysis

Assume a client had the following returns for years 1999 through 2002:

EXAMPLE

YEAR	RETURN
1999	12%
2000	3%
2001	10%
2002	15%

The arithmetic mean equals 10 percent, calculated as follows:

$$AM = \frac{12\% + 3\% + 10\% + 15\%}{4} = 10\%$$

GEOMETRIC MEAN

The **geometric mean** is a method of calculating the internal rate of return based on periodic rates of return. The formula for the geometric mean is written as follows:

geometric mean - a method of calculating the internal rate of return based on periodic rates of return

$$GM = \sqrt[n]{(1 + R_1)(1 + R_2)\dots(1 + R_n)} - 1, \text{ where}$$

R_n = Return for period n

n = Number of periods in the analysis

Assume a client had the following returns for years 1999 through 2002 (same example as above):

YEAR	RETURN
1999	12%
2000	3%
2001	10%
2002	15%

The geometric mean equals 9.91 percent, calculated as follows:

$$GM = \sqrt[4]{(1+.12)(1+.03)(1+.10)(1+.15)} - 1$$

$$GM = \sqrt[4]{1.4593} - 1$$

$$GM = 1.0991 - 1$$

$$GM = .0991 \text{ or } 9.91\%$$

Using the same example has resulted in a different outcome for the arithmetic mean and the geometric mean. This difference is a result of the geometric mean taking into consideration the compounding of the investment returns over time, whereas the arithmetic mean does not.

In this case, the geometric mean is less than the arithmetic mean. Will this always be the case? The answer to this question is that it depends. The two measures will be the same if the returns for each year are equal, such as 10 percent for every year. Otherwise, the geometric mean will be less than the arithmetic mean. The geometric mean cannot be greater the arithmetic mean.

The difference between the two measures will increase as the volatility in returns increases. The following example illustrates this increase.

John invests $100 at the beginning of the year. At the end of the year, his investment is worth $200. At the end of the following year, the investment is worth $100. The returns for the two years are as follows:

YEAR	BEGINNING OF THE YEAR	END OF THE YEAR	RATE OF RETURN
1	$100	$200	100%
2	$200	$100	(50%)

The arithmetic mean equals 25 percent, calculated as follows:

$$AM = \frac{100\% + (50\%)}{2} = 25\%$$

The geometric mean equals 0.00 percent, calculated as follows:

$$GM = \sqrt[2]{(1 + 1.00)(1 + .50)} - 1$$

$$GM = \sqrt[2]{1.00} - 1$$

$$GM = 1.00 - 1$$

$$GM = 0.00 \text{ or } 0.00\%$$

Obviously, there is a big difference between a 25 percent return and a 0 percent return. In addition, it should be clear that if you began with $100 and ended up with $100 that your return is zero. Therefore, the arithmetic mean is not as accurate as the geometric mean, and the difference becomes greater as the returns are more volatile.

INTERNAL RATE OF RETURN

The **internal rate of return** (IRR) is one of the most common measures of return. It equates the future cash flows to the present value. Consider the basic present value model:

$$PV = \frac{CF_1}{(1+k)^1} + \frac{CF_2}{(1+k)^2} + \dots + \frac{CF_n}{(1+k)^n} \text{ , where}$$

PV = Present value of future cash flows

CF_n = Cash flows for period n

n = Number of cash flows in the analysis

k = Internal rate of return

An important assumption of this model is that any cash flows that occur before the end of the investment will be reinvested at the IRR. If these cash flows are not reinvested at the IRR, then the actual return received by the investor will be different than expected.

A bond that is selling for par ($1,000) and has an annual coupon rate of 10 percent (coupon payments of $100) will have an IRR of 10 percent. If the annual coupon payments of $100 are reinvested at a rate of return of 10 percent, then the actual return received by the investor will be 10 percent. However, if the coupon payments are invested at a rate of return less (or greater) than 10 percent, then the actual return the investor receives will be less (or greater) than 10 percent.

internal rate of return - a measure of return that equates the discounted future cash flows to present value

EXAMPLE

REAL RATE OF RETURN

nominal return - the
stated return from an
investment

As discussed earlier in the chapter, inflation erodes the purchasing power of assets and returns. Therefore, it is important to understand both nominal returns as well as real returns. The **nominal return** is the stated return from the investment. The **real rate of return** is the nominal return adjusted for inflation. The formula for the real return is as follows:

real rate of return - the
nominal return adjusted
for inflation

$$\text{Real return} = \frac{(1 + R_n)}{(1 + I)} - 1 \text{, where}$$

R_n = Nominal rate of return

I = Rate of inflation

Assume that the nominal return equals 10 percent and the rate of inflation equals 3 percent. Based on these assumptions, the real rate of return equals 6.8 percent, as follows:

$$\text{Real return} = \frac{(1 + 0.10)}{(1 + 0.03)} - 1 = 0.068 \text{ or } 6.8\%$$

The calculation for the real rate of return can be used in determining retirement funding requirements and educational funding requirements.

MODERN PORTFOLIO THEORY

Just about everyone is familiar with the saying, "Don't put all your eggs in one basket." The interpretation of this saying is that it is safer to spread your risk around than to concentrate it in one area. The same concept applies to investing. Investors diversify risk by investing in more than one security or more than one asset class. Through diversification, investors are able to reduce the risk to their investment portfolios.

The reason that diversification works is that the unsystematic risks that a security is subject to can be minimized by adding additional securities to the portfolio. Similarly, adding additional asset classes to a portfolio can minimize or reduce the unique risks to which an asset class is subject.

Modern portfolio theory (MPT) is the concept that describes this diversification process among asset classes. Harry Markowitz, considered the father of modern portfolio theory, was responsible for the development of MPT and received the Nobel Prize in economics in 1990 for his work.

efficient frontier - consists
of investment portfolios
with the highest expected
return for a given level of
risk

Markowitz found that by combining different asset classes and varying the weightings of each asset class, he could create portfolios that had higher returns with less portfolio volatility (risk). The portfolios that had the highest expected return for the given level of risk he called "efficient portfolios." By combining these efficient portfolios, he created the **Efficient Frontier**. The following figure is a graphical representation of the Efficient Frontier.

EXHIBIT 12.6: THE EFFICIENT FRONTIER

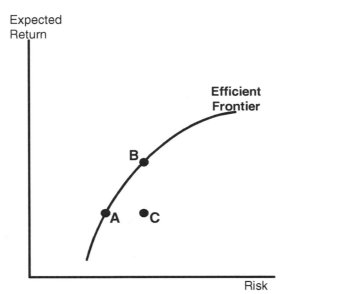

The Efficient Frontier consists of portfolios with the highest expected return for a given level of risk. Notice in Exhibit 12.6 above that portfolios A and B are efficient portfolios. Portfolio C is not. Portfolio A is more efficient than Portfolio C because it has the same expected return with less risk. Portfolio B is more efficient than Portfolio C because it has a much higher expected return for the same level of risk. Markowitz came up with the following three rules for choosing efficient portfolios:

▲ For any two risky portfolios with the same expected return, choose the one with the lowest risk.
▲ For any two portfolios with the same risk, choose the one with the highest expected return.
▲ Choose any portfolio that has a higher expected return and lower risk.

Portfolios, such as Portfolio C above, are considered inefficient, since they have not maximized the return for a given level of risk. Portfolios may not exist above the efficient frontier since the efficient frontier consists of the most efficient portfolios (portfolios of assets with the _highest_ expected return for a given level of risk).

Markowitz illustrated that a model can be developed to estimate the efficient frontier by using security standard deviations, correlation coefficients, and expected returns in the following two formulas:

STANDARD DEVIATION OF A MULTI-ASSET PORTFOLIO

$$\sigma_p = \sqrt{\sum_{i=1}^{n} W_i^2 \sigma_i^2 + \sum_{i=1}^{n} \sum_{\substack{j=1 \\ i \neq j}}^{n} W_i W_j \sigma_i \sigma_j R_{ij}}$$

W_i = Percentage of the portfolio invested in asset i

σ_p = Standard deviation of the portfolio

σ_i = Standard deviation of asset i

R_{ij} = Correlation between asset i and asset j

EXPECTED RETURN OF THE PORTFOLIO

$$E(R_p) = \sum_{i=1}^{n} W_i E(R_i) \text{ , where}$$

$$\sum_{i=1}^{n} W_i = 1.0$$

These formulas are the foundation for most of the asset allocation (mean-variance optimization) software packages used by financial planners. The purpose of these software packages is to build an investment portfolio capable of accomplishing the goals of the client, while matching the level of risk in the portfolio to the investor's tolerance for risk. Most financial planners who provide investment counseling use some type of mean-variance optimization software to determine an optimum portfolio or asset allocation based on a client's goals, risk tolerance, time horizon, tax situation, and economic forecasts.

The goal in using these software packages is to build an efficient portfolio for the client. Remember that an efficient portfolio is one that has the highest-level return (in practice, the return should be an after-tax return) for the given level of risk.

SOFTWARE INPUTS

These software packages generally make use of the following inputs:

ECONOMIC VARIABLES	CLIENT VARIABLES
Asset classes	Risk tolerance
Expected returns for each asset class	Time horizon of goals
Standard deviation of each asset class	Tax bracket
Correlation coefficient of each asset class to every other asset class	

Asset Classes

The asset classes to be included in the analysis are an important starting point for the economic variables. Since there are numerous asset classes to consider, and practitioners often have limited access to all asset classes, these must be chosen for the analysis. Exhibit 12.7 is a sample of some of the asset classes that might be included in an analysis.

EXHIBIT 12.7: ASSET CLASSES

Large cap value	Small/mid cap core	U.S. Treasury fixed income
Large cap core	Small/mid cap value	U.S. Corporate fixed income
Large cap growth	International equity	U.S. Municipal fixed income
Small/mid cap growth	Emerging market equity	International fixed income

Another common reason to limit asset class inclusion is the investment restrictions on certain types of asset pools, such as government funds, retirement plans, and trust assets. Oftentimes, these entities are not permitted to invest in certain asset classes, or they may have limitations on the amount of certain securities that are included in the portfolio. As a result, it may be appropriate to exclude these asset classes from the analysis.

Expected Returns

The expected returns for each asset class must be included in the analysis to determine which combinations of investments produces the highest level of return for the appropriate level of risk for the client. Expected returns can be based on historical data or can be an estimate of what future returns will be. As with most of these variables, different methods of calculating the variable result in a different input. It is the financial planner's responsibility to determine the most appropriate method for determining these variables.

Standard Deviation

The standard deviation for each asset class must be included in the analysis to help determine which combinations of investments produce lower portfolio risk. Standard deviation is a measure of dispersion around a mean and is really a method of quantifying the volatility of investments. As with expected return, standard deviation is forecast based on expectation or calculated based on historical data. The calculation of standard deviation using historical returns is as follows:

$$\sigma = \sqrt{\frac{\sum_{t=1} (R_t - \bar{R})^2}{n-1}}, \text{ where}$$

σ = Standard deviation of the security or portfolio

$\bar{R}$ = Mean return, calculated as an average

R_t = Historical return for period t

n = Number of observations

Assume that an investor had earned annual returns of 15 percent, 25 percent, and 20 percent over the last three years. The historical standard deviation equals 5 percent, as calculated below:

ANNUAL RETURN	MEAN RETURN	DIFFERENCE	DIFFERENCE SQUARED
0.15	0.20	(0.05)	0.0025
0.25	0.20	0.05	0.0025
0.20	0.20	0.00	0.0000

Sum of the differences squared equals	0.0050
0.0050 divided by 2 (n-1) equals	0.0025
The square root of 0.0025 equals	0.0500

Correlation Coefficient

The correlation coefficient, generally denoted with the symbol "R," is a statistical measure generated from a regression analysis that provides insight into the relationship between two securities, two portfolios, or two indexes. The correlation coefficient indicates the direction of the relationship between the two indexes or securities and the strength between the two items. The correlation coefficient ranges between positive one and negative one. At positive one, there is perfect positive correlation between the two items. In other words, the two items will move together over time. At negative one, there is perfect negative correlation between the two items. In other words, the two items will move in opposite directions over time. At a correlation of zero, there is no relationship between the two items and they will move independent of each other. Exhibit 12.8 depicts these relationships.

EXHIBIT 12.8: CORRELATION COEFFICIENTS

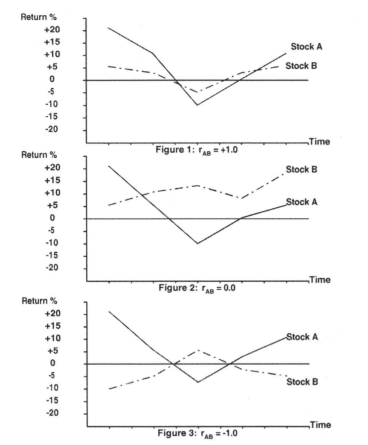

The correlation coefficient is the key to the concept of asset allocation. When the correlation coefficient between two asset classes is less than 1.0, then combining the asset classes will reduce the overall risk of the investment portfolio. The lower the correlation, the lower the standard deviation of the combined portfolio.

Risk Tolerance

The **risk tolerance** of an investor is an estimate of the level of risk that he is willing to accept in his portfolio. There are clearly those investors who are unwilling to accept any risk, while there are others who invest in only the most risky securities. There are two common ways a planner estimates a client's tolerance for risk. The first method is a clear understanding of the client and the client's history with investment securities. This information provides a basis for determining how comfortable a client is with investments in equities, fixed income securities, and other risky securities. The second method is to use a questionnaire designed to solicit feelings about risky assets and the comfort level of the client given certain changes in the portfolio. These methods combined can guide the planner in assessing a client's risk tolerance.

risk tolerance - an estimate of the level of risk an investor is willing to accept in his or her portfolio

Time Horizon

Along with risk tolerance, the time horizon of an investor's goal is vital in determining an appropriate investment decision. Specific investments are simply not conducive to short-term investment time horizons. For example, it is a common understanding that equities will earn higher returns than fixed income investments, but have more risk of principal. Therefore, it is important to expect to invest in equities for a period of at least ten years. Exhibit 12.9 illustrates that the volatility of asset classes is reduced over time.

Very often people saving money towards a down payment for a house will ask about appropriate investment vehicles. In most cases, the purchase of a house will be within a couple of years and thus, eliminate most of the long-term investment choices.

EXHIBIT 12.9: TIME DIVERSIFICATION

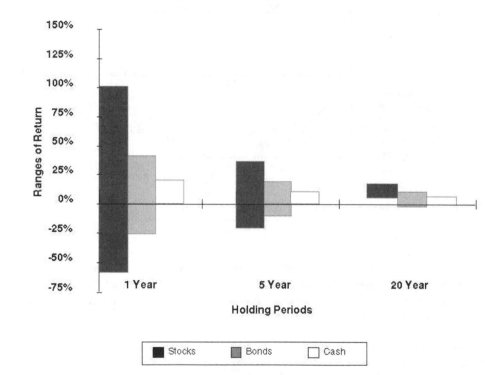

Investor Tax Bracket

Tax issues are another important consideration in the investment planning process. The most apparent issue impacted by an investor's tax bracket is whether to invest in taxable or tax-free municipal fixed income securities. For high net worth investors, municipal bonds generally provide a higher after-tax return, while for taxpayers in lower tax brackets, taxable bonds will generally provide higher after-tax returns. However, assets in qualified plans or other tax-deferred accounts should generally not be invested in municipal bonds, since returns for these securities are traditionally lower than the returns for taxable fixed-income securities.

The tax bracket of the investor also affects the type and style of equity investments. For investors in higher tax brackets, equities that do not pay dividends are preferred for tax purposes since they do not generate current taxable income. In the same regard, high turnover investment styles are not as conducive to tax efficiency as lower turnover styles. In other words, when portfolio managers buy and sell at high turnover rates during the year, it can often generate more taxable income with short-term rather than long-term capital gains. A strategy that emphasizes more of a buy-and-hold strategy will reduce the recognition of current taxable income and minimize transaction costs.

SOFTWARE OUTPUTS

Mean variance optimization software packages provide advisors with a useful tool in assisting clients with the achievement of their investment goals and other financial planning goals. Among the outputs to these types of packages are asset allocations, expected returns (both before tax and after tax), expected standard deviation of the portfolio, and projections on the future value of the portfolio.

Asset Allocation

The primary purpose of a mean-variance optimization model is to determine an efficient allocation for an investor's portfolio based on the goals of the client and his tolerance for risk. An **asset allocation** provides an investor with a guide to how much of his portfolio should be invested in each asset class. Exhibit 12.10 illustrates three possible asset allocations: one for a conservative investor, one for a moderate investor, and one for an aggressive investor.

asset allocation - provides an investor with a guide to how much of his portfolio should be invested in each asset class

EXHIBIT 12.10: SAMPLE ASSET ALLOCATIONS

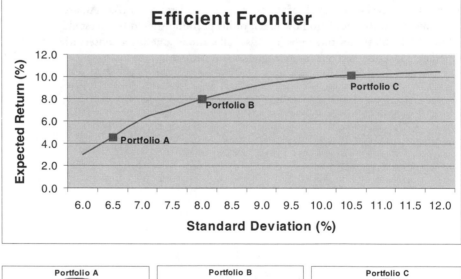

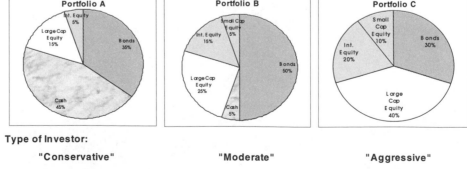

Type of Investor:

"Conservative"   "Moderate"   "Aggressive"

Expected Return

Investors are clearly interested in the expected return they can anticipate from their portfolios. In many cases, a financial planner can calculate the rate of return necessary to achieve some financial planning goal. Generally, these software packages provide for both pre-tax and after-tax rates of return.

Expected Volatility (Standard Deviation)

Investors are certainly wary about large fluctuations in the value of their invested assets. Therefore, understanding the expected volatility of their portfolio is an important factor to consider when choosing a final asset allocation.

Projected Portfolio Values

Based on the expected returns and the expected volatility, these packages can project the future value of an investor's portfolio. This process is useful in estimating whether or not a goal will be within reach, or if the goal needs to be revised. This projection should be updated at least annually to determine whether the client is on track to meet his objectives. If the portfolio is not doing as well as anticipated, the investor should evaluate why and make any necessary changes.

INVESTMENT STRATEGIES & THEORIES

ASSET ALLOCATION

It is widely accepted that asset allocation accounts for the majority of variation in a portfolio's returns. In fact, studies indicate that the percentage change in a portfolio that is attributable to asset allocation is between 90 percent and 95 percent! Therefore, 90 percent to 95 percent of the variation in returns of a portfolio is attributable to the choice in asset allocation. As we have discussed, asset allocation is the process of distributing an investor's portfolio over various asset classes. Two of the more common methods of asset allocation include strategic asset allocation and tactical asset allocation.

Strategic asset allocation is a method of allocating portions of a portfolio to various asset classes based on long-term capital market expectations. This type of strategy is often referred to as a constant mix approach since the allocations to each asset class remain the same until the next allocation process. This strategy is, therefore, not a buy-and-hold strategy, since rebalancing will become necessary as the portfolio allocation differs from the strategic allocation over time. Investors who want to establish a long-term asset allocation strategy will often use this type of approach based on their risk tolerance.

Tactical asset allocation is a more dynamic approach than strategic asset allocation. It involves the continual change between asset classes based on perceived investment opportunities in certain asset classes. In effect, it is a form of timing the market, but within the setting of a portfolio.

LIFECYCLE AND ASSET ALLOCATION

As discussed throughout the text, individuals move through distinct phases during their lifetime. The appropriate asset allocation will generally become less aggressive as investors age and move through the later stages of the lifecycle. Obviously, each client will have unique circumstances that will contribute to the appropriate allocation, but planners cannot ignore the client's current stage of the lifecycle.

TIMING THE MARKET

Market-timing has classically been a strategy whereby investors attempt to be fully invested in periods of upward movements in the market and to be out of the market when it is declining. This type of strategy can be applied to equities, fixed income securities, or portfolios. Knowing when to buy and when to sell is the inherent difficulty with this type of strategy. Although there are a tremendous number of methods to time the market, many of which are on the Internet, the majority of academic studies indicate that it is not possible to outperform the market by attempting to time its rise and fall. According to The Hulbert Financial Digest, a publication that rates market-timing newsletters, only 25 out of 201 market-timing newsletters in 1999 were able to beat the Wilshire 5000 index. Exhibit 12.11 illustrates the ineffectiveness of market-timing newsletters over 1-year, 5-year, 10-year, and 15-year periods.

EXHIBIT 12.11: MARKET-TIMING NEWSLETTERS THAT BEAT THE WILSHIRE 5000

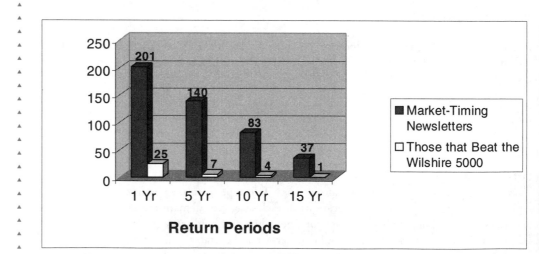

EFFICIENT MARKET HYPOTHESIS

efficient market hypothesis - a theory that suggests that securities are priced fairly and efficiently by the market and that investors are unable to outperform the market on a consistent basis without accepting additional risk

The **Efficient Market Hypothesis** (EMH) is a theory that suggests that the market prices securities fairly and efficiently and investors are unable to outperform the market on a consistent basis without accepting additional risk. In fact, the EMH states that securities prices reflect all historical information. Therefore, analyzing historical information using technical or fundamental analysis will not provide an advantage and the only information that will affect the price of a security will be new, unknown information. As new information that affects a security is released, the price of the security will increase if the information is positive and decrease if the information is negative. Since new information is by its very nature unknown, it is random or unpredictable. Thus, security prices should follow a **random walk**, or an unpredictable pattern.

The Efficient Market Hypothesis is often evaluated under three forms. These three forms of the EMH are the weak form, semi-strong form, and the strong form. Each of these differs as to the level of information that is efficiently incorporated into a securities price.

The weak form asserts that securities prices reflect information related to the security's trading data, including price information, volume information, and short interest information. Under this form, analyzing trends in the price of securities, such as done in **technical analysis**, is irrelevant since the price of the security should already reflect this information.

The semi-strong form asserts that securities prices not only reflect a security's trading data, but also all publicly available information related to the security. This public information includes analysis of the company's products, management, fixed and variable cost structure, earnings and cash flow, and analysis of the industry in which the company is included. This type of analysis of publicly available information is referred to as **fundamental analysis** and is commonly used in attempts of determining the intrinsic value of a security. For those who believe in the semi-strong form, there is no benefit to using fundamental analysis.

The strong form goes even farther than the other forms. It asserts that all public and private information is included in the price of a security. Therefore, even inside information will not allow investors to outperform the market on a consistent basis.

Is the Efficient Market Hypothesis correct? Are the markets so efficient that investors are unable to outperform on a consistent basis without accepting additional risk? These questions have been plaguing the investment community for decades without a definitive answer. For our purposes, it is fair to say many of the aspects of the EMH are correct. Stock prices will generally move because of new information. It is difficult for investors to outperform the market on a consistent basis, as evidenced by the thousands of mutual funds that do not outperform the market each year (even after adjusting for transaction costs and expenses).

However, there are certainly counter-arguments to the validity of the EMH. The most obvious of these includes **anomalies**. Anomalies are occurrences in the stock market that are not supported by the concept of an efficient market. For example, if a method of trading results in superior returns, then the trading method implies that the market is not perfectly efficient. There are numerous anomalies that have been studied at great length. Some of these anomalies end up supporting the EMH based on the extended research, while others are still unexplained in accordance with the EMH.

The October 1987 crash of the stock market is an example that the markets may not be as efficient as explained in the EMH. According to the research, there was no change in expectations that could account for the 23 percent decline in the market. This type of volatility is not based on new information received by the market. Therefore, there are arguments that may imply that the EMH is not entirely correct.

random walk - the unpredictable pattern that security prices should follow as new information about the security becomes known. As new information that affects a security is released, the price of the security will increase if the information is positive and decrease if the information is negative

technical analysis - the search for identifiable and recurring stock price patterns

fundamental analysis - the analysis of a stock's value using basic, publicly available data such as the stock's earnings, sales, risk, and industry analysis

anomalies - occurrences in the stock market that are not supported by the concept of the Efficient Market Hypothesis

Finally, it is fair to say that the markets are efficient, without defining the level of efficiency, and that it is certainly difficult for professional portfolio managers to outperform the market on a consistent basis without accepting additional risk. In addition, certain markets are more efficient than other markets. For example, the U.S. large cap equity market is clearly more efficient than the international emerging equity market. The degree to which you believe in the efficiency of the market will impact your choice as to active or passive management.

ACTIVE VS. PASSIVE INVESTING

Active and passive strategies are commonly used approaches to investing. Active management is an attempt to outperform the returns that are available to those investors using a passive approach. It is through the process of finding undervalued or mispriced securities that active managers attempt to earn these higher returns. Active management generally requires more research and support than passive strategies. Therefore, the expenses associated with active management are generally higher than for passively managed approaches.

A passive approach to investment management does not attempt to find undervalued securities. Instead, this approach assumes, as does the Efficient Market Hypothesis, that investors will be unable to consistently outperform the market over the long-term. As a result, managers will not employ active strategies and will generally hold a well-diversified portfolio, often based on an asset allocation strategy. Over time, the portfolio may have to be rebalanced, due to different rates of return for different asset classes within the portfolio. However, a passive approach will have lower costs, both transaction fees and management fees. One method of passive investing is the use of index funds.

INDEXING

An obvious and natural question that investors ask about their investment performance is, "How did my portfolio perform compared to the market?" The market is generally represented by an index, such as the Standard & Poor's 500 Index. These indexes provide investors with a representation of the performance of different segments of the market.

Indexing is the concept of investing in the same securities and in the same proportions represented by an index. For instance, an investor might purchase the same securities that make up the S&P 500 Index. However, purchasing 500 stocks and purchasing them in the correct proportions requires a substantial investment. Therefore, investors will often invest in index mutual funds. These funds provide an inexpensive method for investors to receive the performance of an index without the hassle of having to mimic the structure of the index.

Indexing has actually been an effective strategy. It turns out that the majority of active managers do not produce returns in excess of returns earned by indexes or index mutual funds.

PROFESSIONAL

FOCUS

How difficult is it to come up with goals and objectives for clients, and what do you do to minimize the difficulty?

The job of setting goals and objectives becomes easier when a client is willing to inventory their assets, which includes financial, personal, business, and family, and then review their obligations. I offer all prospects the opportunity to meet with me for a no-cost consultation where we determine what our expectations are of each other before deciding to work together. In some cases, I refer prospects to other professionals (tax accountants, estate lawyers, and so on) to put their affairs in order either prior to or while planning and prioritizing objectives with me.

When a client is not willing to "see where they are" financially or to plan for specific things they want to have in their lives, this person is not a good prospect for the services of a financial adviser. They may require a reality check before they realize that playing the lottery is not the way to build a sound financial foundation.

Under what circumstances do you have your best success convincing your clients to follow the investment plan that you set up?

There are various programs and processes I use to lead the clients through the planning of protection needs, savings approaches, and wealth creation. I emphasize current and future tax savings, retirement programs, and employee benefits that can be incorporated into their plan. After working closely with clients to prioritize what they want to accomplish and when they want it accomplished, the clients are usually motivated to follow their plan.

How do you convey the concepts and benefits of asset allocation to your clients?

The risk profiles that are now available with many products and programs make it very easy to educate clients in marketplace idiosyncrasies and prepare them for the asset mixes that match their risk tolerance and expectations. The dream of high returns with no risk comes into focus as we review historical performance of securities and funds in different mixes, leading the clients to more realistic planning.

Which do you think is better for the client: to pay loads and commissions or fixed fees for professional investment advice?

This question is a challenge because of the style of each client. If a do-it-myself person needs occasional support or some resource and direction, a fee for the service based on time or a retainer may work. Plans developed for fee-for-service cases have frequently produced fancy documents, but have not resulted in the client taking action in a timely fashion: the result of procrastination.

Commission products are appropriate in many cases, especially when a client worries over each mailing they receive. A fee appearing on each statement can cause them more concern, even though it may equal or be less than what a commission product pays. The agent/representative has more resources from fund families and insurance companies on the load products where the managers can be objective with more access to information than the small investor has open to them.

The bottom line is not whether a fee is charged or a commission paid, but whether the clients are taking action and getting reasonable returns that match their goals. Advice has a cost along with rewards. The choices of where and how the costs are covered depend on each situation and the participants' comfort zone.

Charlotte Hartmann-Hansen, CLU, ChFC, is an Independent Registered Representative affiliated with C.J.M. Planning Corp., & a Registered Investment Advisor with C.J.M. Asset Management LLC, 223 Wanaque Ave, Pompton Lakes, NJ 07442. The viewpoint presented is that of Charlotte Hartmann-Hansen and not necessarily that of C.J.M. Planning Corp.

CHARLOTTE HARTMANN-HANSEN, MS, CLU, CHFC, LUTCF

DISCUSSION QUESTIONS

1. How does investment planning fit into the overall framework of financial planning?
2. What are the investment goals common to most investors and how are these goals achieved?
3. What are two methods of increasing savings for an investor?
4. How do systematic risk and unsystematic risk differ?
5. What are lending investments and ownership investments and how to they differ?
6. What are the benefits of owning real estate in an investment portfolio?
7. What are the two types of derivatives discussed in the chapter?
8. What are the differences in the obligations and rights with regard to option contracts and futures contracts?
9. What is the difference between direct investing and indirect investing?
10. How does the historical performance, in terms of returns and standard deviation, differ among small capitalization stocks, large capitalization stocks, and fixed income securities?
11. How do the two common measures of risk—beta and standard deviation—differ?
12. What are the differences between the arithmetic average rate of return and the geometric average return?
13. How are the nominal rate of return and real rate of return different?
14. What is the Efficient Frontier and what is its role in modern portfolio theory?
15. What two factors are identified with the correlation coefficient?
16. What is the Efficient Market Hypothesis?
17. What makes timing the market such a difficult process?
18. What are anomalies and how do they provide a counter argument to the validity of the EMH?
19. What is indexing and how is it used?
20. What is the difference between active and passive portfolio management?

EXERCISES

1. List five systematic risks and explain each.
2. List four unsystematic risks and explain each.
3. Michael invests $10,000 in Bonsai Inc., which is based in Japan. The conversion rate at the time of the investment is 100 yen to 1 dollar. Michael sells his interest six months later for 1,750,000 yen. However, the exchange rate now is 125 yen to 1 dollar. What is Michael's gain on the investment (before yen to dollars), loss due to exchange rate risk, and net result on the original investment?
4. Compare and contrast common and preferred stock.
5. Hewkard stock has recently had a market correction. If Bill likes the long-term potential of the stock, what option positions might be feasible and why?
6. Harry bought XYZ Company fifteen years ago. The stock has greatly appreciated recently and Harry is concerned about a correction. List three alternatives that he could implement to minimize losses in the event of a correction.
7. Kyle purchases one lot (100 shares) of Microsoft for $6,500. One year later, he sells the lot when the stock is trading for $79 per share. Microsoft does not pay dividends. What is Kyle's holding period return?
8. Eric had the following returns on his portfolio from 1995 through 1999: 10%, 8%, 13%, 15%, 11%. What is the arithmetic mean for Eric's portfolio?

9. Tyler had the following returns on his high-risk portfolio over a five-year period: 35 percent, -10 percent, 25 percent, 65 percent, -5 percent. What is the geometric mean for Tyler's portfolio?

10. Sandra expects to earn an after tax rate of return over a long period of time of 10 percent. If inflation is expected to continue at 3 percent, what is Sandra's real rate of return?

11. Alfred is a very conservative investor and expects to earn 5 percent before tax. If Alfred is in the 40 percent tax bracket and inflation equals 4 percent, then what real rate of return is he earning?

12. Danny had earned annual returns of 13 percent, 11 percent, and 18 percent over the last three years. Calculate the historical standard deviation over the time period.

13. The Efficient Market Hypothesis is often evaluated under three forms. List and explain how each of these forms differs as to the level of information that is efficiently incorporated into a securities price.

14. If portfolio A has a correlation with the market of 0.80, then what portion of the risk of the portfolio is considered unsystematic risk?

15. If Portfolio B has a correlation with the market of 0.70, then what portion of the risk of the portfolio can be eliminated through diversification?

PROBLEMS

1. Use the chart to answer the following questions:

YEAR	RETURN
1	10%
2	-5%
3	18%
4	6%
5	1%

   ▲ Calculate the standard deviation of returns for the five-year period.
   ▲ Calculate the holding period return for the five-year period.
   ▲ Calculate the arithmetic mean for the five-year period.
   ▲ Calculate the geometric mean for the five-year period.

2. Janet has a portfolio that has a correlation with the market of 0.8 and a standard deviation of 20 percent. Determine how much unsystematic risk is within Janet's portfolio.

3. What is the implication of the historical performance of various asset classes on the investment choices made by investors in different stages of the life cycle?

CHAPTER 13

Fixed Income Securities

LEARNING OBJECTIVES:

After learning the material in this chapter, you will be able to:

1. Explain how the value of a bond is calculated.

2. Define a zero-coupon bond and explain its advantages and disadvantages as an investment.

3. Describe the various measures of return—current yield, yield to maturity, and yield to call.

4. Compare corporate returns and municipal returns.

5. List the various types of fixed income securities.

6. Describe the types of risks to which investors in fixed income securities are subject.

7. Explain how changes in interest rates affect fixed income securities.

8. Describe a yield curve and explain its importance in examining bond interest rates.

9. Discuss the concepts of duration and immunization and explain their relationship to each other.

BASIC CONCEPTS OF LENDING SECURITIES

fixed income securities -
securities with specified
payment dates and
amounts, primarily bonds

As described in the last chapter, **fixed income securities**, including bonds, are known as **lending securities** or instruments. An investor of bonds lends funds to the issuer in exchange for a promise to a stream of periodic interest payments and a repayment of the loaned principal at the maturity of the bond. Generally, these interest payments are called coupon payments and are often paid on a semiannual basis, or twice per year. **Coupon payments** are based on a percentage of the face value or par value of the bond, which is typically $1,000. For example, a bond that contains a 10 percent coupon will pay $100 per year (generally, $50 twice per year) for the life of the bond. Coupon payments can vary widely and can be as low as zero in the case of zero-coupon bonds.

lending securities -
securities where an investor
of bonds lends funds to the
issuer in exchange for a
promise to a stream of
periodic interest payments
and a repayment of the
loaned principal at the
maturity of the bond

Bonds provide investors with an excellent alternative to other types of securities and can be used for the purpose of diversifying portfolios or providing income to those individuals who are in need of a stream of cash flows. Although bonds generally have lower returns than equity investments, they are generally less risky than equities and provide higher returns than bank certificates of deposit, savings accounts, and other lending alternatives.

coupon payments -
interest payments paid to
the bondholder on a
semiannual basis and based
on a percentage of the face
value or par value of the
bond

There are a variety of issuers of bonds including domestic and foreign governments and domestic and foreign companies; however, the U.S. federal government, its agencies, municipalities, and domestic corporations issue the majority of the fixed income securities. The bonds of each of the issuers may be issued in public or private markets and generally have different characteristics. Each of the differences in the characteristics of bonds will impact the perceived value of the bond, and as a result, impact the required returns.

maturity - the period of
time through which the
issuer has control over the
bond proceeds and the
period of time it must
continue to pay coupon
payments

One of the key features of a bond is the length of its term, or **maturity**. The maturity of the bond indicates the period of time through which the issuer has control over the bond proceeds and the period of time it must continue to pay coupon payments. The maturity of a bond also impacts the yield that is received by the investor. Generally, the yield that is received by the investor will be higher for longer maturity bonds. However, as we will see later, this depends on the shape of the yield curve. The maturity also impacts the volatility of the bond and can impact other types of risk associated with the bond.

Although most bonds are issued with maturities ranging from one to thirty years, bonds are sometimes issued with maturities as long as 100 years. In addition, some issuers will include features in the bond agreement that allows the issuer to call the bond from the holder. A call feature allows the issuer to redeem the bond issue prior to its scheduled maturity, which may be beneficial to the issuer if interest rates have declined. In such a case, the bond issuer may call the bonds from the holder and issue new bonds at a lower coupon rate, thereby reducing the cost of its debt. Call features will be discussed later in this chapter.

VALUATION OF FIXED INCOME SECURITIES

As with most financial securities, the value of a bond is equal to the present value of the expected future cash flows. Conceptually, the cash flows of a bond are generally straightforward: fixed coupon payments on a periodic basis and a return of principal at maturity. To determine the present value of a bond, these expected cash flows are discounted at an appropriate discount rate,

434

which depends on the market yields being offered on comparable fixed income securities. The value of a bond is determined in the same manner as the value of an annuity using the time-value-of-money concepts.

BASIC CALCULATION EXAMPLE

EXAMPLE

Assume a three-year bond (face value of $1,000) is issued by XYZ Company that pays an 8 percent coupon semiannually ($40 twice each year). What is the value of the bond if comparable bonds are yielding 10 percent?

$$P_0 = \frac{Cf_1}{(1+k)^1} + \frac{Cf_2}{(1+k)^2} + \frac{Cf_3}{(1+k)^3} + \frac{Cf_4}{(1+k)^4} + \frac{Cf_5}{(1+k)^5} + \frac{Cf_6}{(1+k)^6}$$

$$P_0 = \frac{40}{(1.05)^1} + \frac{40}{(1.05)^2} + \frac{40}{(1.05)^3} + \frac{40}{(1.05)^4} + \frac{40}{(1.05)^5} + \frac{1,040}{(1.05)^6}$$

$$P_0 = 38.10 + 36.28 + 34.55 + 32.91 + 31.34 + 776.06$$

$$P_0 = \$949.24 \quad \text{(The bond should sell for \$949.24)}$$

Each cash flow is discounted by first raising the sum of 1 plus the periodic discount rate to the power in which the cash flow occurs and then dividing the cash flow by this amount. For example, the present value of the first cash flow is equal to $40 divided by (1 plus 0.05)^1 resulting in a discounted value of $38.10. We used 5 percent since it is half of the 10 percent yield to reflect the semiannual payments.

The method for valuing a bond can be summarized by the following formula:

$$PV = \sum_{t=1}^{2n} \frac{C/2}{(1+i/2)^t} + \frac{P_P}{(1+i/2)^{2n}} \text{, where}$$

PV = Present value of the future cash flows (price of the bond)

n = Number of years to maturity

C = Annual coupon interest payment

i = Current yield to maturity for the bond

P_p = Par value of the bond

The value of a bond can also be calculated using a financial calculator. Using the example above, a bond's value would be calculated using the following method:

Present Value of a Bond			
n	=	6 (3 years x 2)	Term
i	=	5 (10 ÷ 2)	Discount Rate or YTM
PMT_{OA}	=	$40 ($80 ÷ 2)	Semiannual coupon
FV	=	$1,000	Maturity Value
PV	=	($949.24)	Present Value

CALCULATION INPUTS

In the above examples, all of the inputs to the calculation were provided. However, in practice, this is not always the case. Therefore, the following section discusses two of the most important inputs, including the cash flows from the security and the appropriate discount rate to use in the valuation.

Cash Flows

As we said before, the cash flows for the bond will consist of periodic coupon payments and the par value or maturity value of the bond. The coupon payments can be made over any period, but are more often paid on a semiannual or annual basis. Although the examples above illustrate the first coupon payment occurring exactly six months from the valuation point, in practice, this is not always the case. If the first coupon payment does not occur exactly six months from the valuation point, then it will occur earlier and will require an adjustment to be made to the calculation to account for this short period. The par value or maturity value of the bond will generally be the face value of $1,000. However, if the bond contains a call feature, then the term of the bond to be used for purposes of valuation will likely change, as will the expected maturity value of the bond.

asset-backed securities - securities issued against some type of asset-linked debts bundled together, such as credit card receivables or mortgages

Asset-backed securities, such as mortgage-backed securities and collateralized mortgage obligations, contain more uncertainty with regard to their cash flows. First, coupon payments and repayment of principal are based on payments made by the mortgagors who often have the right to prepay principal. Prepayments cause the schedule of cash flows to change, which adjusts the value of the bond. The second issue related to asset-backed securities concerns the potential for defaults. Clearly, in a large pool of mortgages, it is likely that some of the mortgages will result in default. In such a case, the cash flows are impacted, causing the value of the bond to change. Each of these issues can be incorporated into the projection of the expected cash flows and, therefore, incorporated into the valuation of the asset-backed securities.

Discount Rate

The other important factor in determining the value of the bond is the discount rate, or the rate at which the cash flows are discounted. The yield that an investor will earn from a bond is determined by evaluating yields being offered in the market on similar instruments. Similar instruments are those that have the same maturity and credit quality. The yield that is used in the valuation of a fixed income security is generally stated in the form of an annual rate of return.

This annual return is simply divided by two to adjust for semiannual payments. In the above example, the annual yield of 10 percent was divided by 2 resulting in a periodic rate of 5 percent.

Zero-Coupon Bonds

A **zero-coupon bond** is a bond that does not pay periodic coupon or interest payments; therefore, these bonds always sell at a discount from (less than) par. As a result, the only cash flow that occurs and that needs to be considered in the valuation of a zero-coupon bond is the maturity value or principal value. Although coupon payments are not actually paid, the number of periods that are used when valuing zeros is the same as if the coupon payments were being paid. In other words, the number of periods will equal the number of years until maturity of the bond multiplied by two. Therefore, the valuation methodology of a zero-coupon bond will be consistent with and comparable to the valuation methodology of a bond that makes coupon payments.

MEASURES OF RETURN

One of the important issues relating to bonds is the determination of various measures of return. Investors of fixed income securities will be rewarded with interest or coupon payments, capital appreciation (or loss), and the reinvestment of coupon payments. Each of the following types of return takes into consideration some or all of these factors.

CURRENT YIELD

The **current yield** of a bond is an indication of the income or cash flow an investor will receive based on the coupon payment and the current price. The current yield measure is calculated by dividing the annual coupon payment by the current price of the security. The formula for calculating the current yield is:

$$\text{Current yield} = \frac{\text{Annual coupon payment in dollars}}{\text{Current market price}}$$

For example, a ten-year bond that has a 10 percent coupon and is currently selling for $850 will have a current yield of 11.76 percent calculated as follows:

$$\text{Current yield} = \frac{\$1,000 \times 10\%}{\$850}$$

$$\text{Current yield} = \frac{\$100}{\$850}$$

$$\text{Current yield} = 11.76\%$$

This type of measure is useful for determining the income or cash flow that can be earned on the purchase of a bond. For example, a person living on a fixed income might choose to invest in fixed income securities if the yield is sufficiently high enough to cover living and other expenses. Notice that the calculation does not consider appreciation of the bond or reinvestment of the coupon payments. Therefore, it is not as complete a measure as other measures, such as yield to maturity.

YIELD TO MATURITY

yield to maturity (YTM) - the promised compounded rate of return on a bond purchased at the current market price and held to maturity

In the previous section, we illustrated the method for determining the price of a bond, which is based on the cash flows from the bond and the discount rate. The discount rate that is used in the calculation is generally the **yield to maturity (YTM)** and is determined by solving for the earnings rate that equates the current market price of the bond to the cash flows from the bond. In calculating the yield to maturity, you would solve for the "k" that equates the present value of the bond to the cash flows from the bond.

$$P_o = \frac{Cf_1}{(1+k)^1} + \frac{Cf_2}{(1+k)^2} + \frac{Cf_3}{(1+k)^3} + \frac{Cf_4}{(1+k)^4} + \frac{Cf_5}{(1+k)^5} + ...+ \frac{Cf_n}{(1+k)^n}$$

Where

P = Present value

Cf_n = Cash flow for period n

k = Yield to maturity

EXAMPLE

Calculating yield to maturity using the above formula is a long and arduous process. Instead, we will generally use a financial calculator to calculate the yield to maturity using the present value of the bond, term of the bond, yield to maturity for the bond, and the par value of the bond. For example, a 30-year bond that pays a coupon of 9 percent semiannually and is selling for $1,249.45 has a yield to maturity of 7 percent, calculated as follows:

Present Value of a Bond			
PV	=	($1,249.45)	Current Bond Price
n	=	60 (30 years x 2)	Semiannual periods
PMT$_{OA}$	=	$45 ($90 ÷ 2)	Semiannual cash flow
FV	=	$1,000	Maturity value
i	=	3.5 x 2 = 7%	Yield to maturity

If you were to check the answer, you would find that the present value equals $1,249.45 by using 7 percent as the annualized discount rate. The present value is reflected as a negative number to illustrate that the purchase of the bond requires a cash outflow being paid from the investor, whereas the coupon payments and the future value are positive to reflect the payments made to the investor.

The calculation of the yield to maturity is based on certain important assumptions. It assumes that the investor will hold the bond until it matures and the calculation accounts for the timing of the cash flows. This calculation also assumes that any cash flows that occur during the life of the bond will be reinvested at the calculated yield to maturity rate of return. This is an important limitation of the model. If the reinvestment rate differs from the yield to maturity, then the actual yield received on the bond will be different from the yield calculated at inception. Specifically, if the reinvestment rate is less than the yield to maturity, then the actual yield earned on the bond will be less than the calculated yield to maturity. If the reinvestment rate is greater than the yield to maturity, then the actual yield earned on the bond will be greater than the calculated yield to maturity.

As stated above, the calculation assumes that the bond is held until it matures. If the investor sells the bond prior to maturity and the bond is sold at either a premium or discount, then the actual yield will differ from the calculated yield to maturity, because of the capital gain or loss. A premium occurs when the bond sells for a price in excess of par, while a discount occurs when the price of a bond is less than par. Note the following relationships between the price of a bond, the coupon rate, the current yield and the yield to maturity:

Bond Selling At:	Relationship:					
Par	Coupon Rate	=	Current Yield	=	Yield to Maturity
Discount	Coupon Rate	<	Current Yield	<	Yield to Maturity
Premium	Coupon Rate	>	Current Yield	>	Yield to Maturity

YIELD TO MATURITY FOR A ZERO-COUPON BOND

Calculating the yield to maturity for a zero-coupon bond can be done using the same method described above. The only difference is that the periodic payments are equal to zero. Since there are no coupon payments to consider, however, you can use a simplified method to calculate the YTM. The formula for this simplified method is as follows:

$$\text{Yield to Maturity} = (\text{FV Factor})^{\frac{1}{n}} - 1, \text{ where}$$

$$\text{FV Factor} = \frac{\text{Maturity value of bond}}{\text{Purchase price of a bond}}$$

For example, the yield to maturity for a twenty-year zero-coupon bond that is selling for $156.26 equals 9.5 percent, calculated as follows:

$$\text{FV Factor} = \frac{\$1,000}{\$156.26} = 6.3996$$

$$\text{Yield to Maturity} = \left[(6.3996)^{\frac{1}{40}} - 1 \right] \times 2 = 0.0950 = 9.5\%$$

Two adjustments must be made to account for semiannual compounding. First, 40 payments or periods are used instead of 20. Second, the YTM that results from the equation must be multiplied by 2 to reflect an annual rate instead of a semiannual rate. Solving the same example using the time-value-of-money keys on a financial calculator results in the same answer, as illustrated below:

Present Value of a Bond			
PV	=	($156.26)	Current price
n	=	40 (20 years x 2)	Semiannual periods
PMT_{OA}	=	$0	Coupon payment
FV	=	$1,000	Maturity value
i	=	4.75 x 2 = 9.5%	Yield to maturity

YIELD TO CALL (YTC)

yield to call (YTC) - the promised return on a bond from the present to the date that the bond may be called

Yield to call (YTC) is the rate of return that equates the present value of the bond (purchase price) to the expected cash flows, adjusted for the call feature. Calculating yield to call is performed using the same methodology as calculating yield to maturity, with two adjustments. A bond containing a call feature generally allows the issuer the right to call the bond prior to the standard maturity, but usually at a premium above par value. Therefore, in the calculation of yield to call, the number of periods will need to be adjusted to reflect the shorter term of the bond resulting from the call feature, and the future value must be adjusted to reflect the premium paid by the issuer. In a sense, this is a worst-case scenario for an investor who would otherwise plan to hold the security to the full term of maturity.

EXAMPLE

For example, assume a 30-year bond ($1,000) that pays a coupon of 9 percent semiannually is selling for $1,249.45, has a yield to maturity of 7 percent, and has a call provision. If the call provision provides that the bond may be called in 5 years at 104 (meaning 104 percent of the par value), then the yield to call equals 4.15 percent, calculated as follows:

Present Value of a Bond			
PV	=	($1,249.45)	Present value
n	=	10 (5 years x 2)	Semiannual periods
PMT_{OA}	=	$45 ($90 ÷ 2)	Semiannual coupon payments
FV	=	$1,040 (104% x $1,000)	Par value plus premium
i	=	2.076 x 2 = 4.152%	Yield to call

Note that the yield to call is different from the yield to maturity. It is important for investors who are considering the purchase of a callable bond to calculate both the YTM and the YTC in case the issuer decides to call the bond. The lesser of the YTM or YTC is the more conservative estimate of what the actual yield may be.

COMPARING CORPORATE RETURNS AND MUNICIPALS RETURNS

The taxable bond market and the tax-exempt bond market make up the United States bond market. The **taxable bond market** consists of U.S. Treasury bonds, U.S. government agency bonds, and corporate bonds. The **tax-exempt bond market** consists of bonds issued by municipalities, which includes states, counties, cities, and parishes. The exemption from federal income tax is why municipal bonds are referred to as tax exempt. Interest from bonds issued by these municipalities is exempt from federal income tax, and in some cases, exempt from state income tax. Interest from U.S. Treasury securities is subject to federal income tax, but is not subject to state income tax. Corporate bond interest and interest derived from U.S. agency bonds are subject to federal and state income tax. Since the various types of bonds have different tax treatment, it is essential to compare yields for different bonds on a consistent basis. This comparison can be performed on an after-tax basis or a pre-tax basis.

An investor can convert a municipal bond yield to an equivalent taxable yield using the following formula:

$$\text{Pre-tax yield} = \frac{\text{Tax-exempt yield}}{1 - \text{marginal tax rate}}$$

For example, Tom, who is in the 45 percent tax bracket, is considering the purchase of a Big State municipal bond that is offering a 5 percent yield, while comparable credit-worthy corporate bonds are offering a yield of 7.5 percent. To determine which bond is preferred, based on yield, Tom could determine the pre-tax yield for the municipal bond, as illustrated:

$$\text{Pre-tax yield} = \frac{0.05}{1 - 0.45} = 0.0901 = 9.01\%$$

Since the pre-tax equivalent yield equals 9.01 percent, it seems obvious that the municipal bond yield of 5 percent is preferable to the corporate bond yield of 7.5 percent. The comparison can also be made on an after-tax basis by multiplying the taxable yield of the corporate bond by the difference between 1 and the marginal tax rate, as follows:

$$\text{After-tax yield} = 0.075 \times (1 - 0.45) = 0.04125 = 4.125\%$$

Since the 5 percent tax-free municipal yield is greater than the 4.125 percent after-tax corporate bond yield, the municipal bond appears to be the better choice, based on yield. A third method of comparison is to determine the equilibrium tax rate. This rate is the marginal tax rate at which the yields of the taxable bonds are equal to the yields of the municipal bonds. Using the example above, the equilibrium tax rate equals 33 percent:

$$\text{Pre-tax yield} = \frac{\text{Tax-exempt yield}}{1 - \text{marginal tax rate}}$$

$$(1 - \text{marginal tax rate}) = \frac{\text{Tax-exempt yield}}{\text{Taxable yield}}$$

taxable bond market - one of two markets that make up the United States bond market, and that consists of U.S. Treasury bonds, U.S. government agency bonds, and corporate bonds

tax-exempt bond market - one of the two markets that make up the United States bond market, and that consists of municipal bonds

EXAMPLE

$$(1 - \text{marginal tax rate}) = \frac{0.050}{0.075}$$

$$(1 - \text{marginal tax rate}) = 0.6667$$

$$\text{marginal tax rate} = 0.3333$$

Since the equilibrium tax rate is 33 percent, investors in a marginal tax bracket that exceeds 33 percent, such as Tom, will want to invest in municipal bonds, while those investors in a tax bracket below 33 percent will be better off with taxable bonds.

For tax-exempt entities, there is almost never a reason to purchase a municipal bond over a taxable bond because pre-tax yields on taxable instruments are generally higher than yields for tax-exempt securities of similar risk. Similarly, municipal bonds should not be used in tax-deferred accounts, such as IRAs and 401(k) plans. The yields on municipals will usually be lower than yields on taxable bonds.

TYPES OF FIXED INCOME SECURITIES

THE MONEY MARKET

The **money market** consists of securities that have the following characteristics: short-term maturity, low credit risk, and high liquidity. These securities include Treasury bills, commercial paper, certificates of deposit, banker's acceptances, and repurchase agreements.

Treasury Bills

The U.S. Treasury issues 13, 26, and 52-week bills in denominations of $1,000. The Treasury auctions 13-week and 26-week bills on a weekly basis, while 52-week bills are auctioned on a monthly basis. In addition to being purchased directly from the Treasury, these securities can be purchased and sold in the **secondary market**. The secondary market allows investors to freely buy and sell securities with other investors. The **primary market** is the place where securities are first offered to the public.

money market - consists of securities that have the following characteristics: short-term maturity, low credit risk, and high liquidity

secondary market - the market where investors can freely buy and sell securities with other investors

primary market - the market where new issues of securities are first offered to the public

EXHIBIT 13.1: RECENT TREASURY BILL AUCTION RESULTS

Term	Issue Date	Maturity Date	Discount Rate %	Investment Rate %	Price Per $100	CUSIP
91-DAY	01-20-2000	04-20-2000	5.350	5.512	98.648	912795DS7
182-DAY	01-20-2000	07-20-2000	5.535	5.789	97.202	912795ED9
91-DAY	01-13-2000	04-13-2000	5.235	5.392	98.677	912795DR9
182-DAY	01-13-2000	07-13-2000	5.420	5.665	97.260	912795ET4
91-DAY	01-06-2000	04-06-2000	5.360	5.525	98.645	912795DQ1
182-DAY	01-06-2000	07-06-2000	5.585	5.844	97.176	912795ER8
364-DAY	01-06-2000	01-04-2001	5.645	5.997	94.292	912795ES6
91-DAY	12-30-1999	03-30-2000	5.300	5.463	98.660	912795DP3
182-DAY	12-30-1999	06-29-2000	5.505	5.757	97.217	912795EC1

Note: the CUSIP number is a unique number identifying each security.

Source: http://www.publicdebt.treas.gov/servlet/OFBills

EXAMPLE

Treasury bills are issued at a discount or percentage of face value. For example, the 91-day bills (first line in table above) issued on 1-20-2000 were issued at a price of $98.648 per $100. An investor would have paid $986.48 for a $1,000 bill. The bill will mature at its face of $1,000, providing the investor with income of $13.52.

The discount rate, price, and investment yield are determined in each auction. Bidding is in terms of the discount rate. Competitive and noncompetitive bids are awarded at the highest rate of bids accepted in the auction. The single-price auction technique became effective for all sales of Treasury marketable securities beginning on November 2, 1998.

Commercial Paper

Commercial paper consists of a private sector company's issue of short-term, unsecured promissory notes. This type of debt is issued in denominations of $100,000 or more and serves as a substitute for short-term bank financing. Maturities for commercial paper are 270 days or less (costly SEC registration procedures are required for securities issued with maturities over 270 days) and are often backed by lines of credit from banks. In comparison to Treasury bills, these instruments have a slightly higher default risk and are slightly less liquid. Therefore, commercial paper has slightly higher yields than T-bills of similar term structures.

Certificates of Deposit

Negotiable certificates of deposit (also known as Jumbo CDs) are deposits of $100,000 or more placed with commercial banks at a specific stated rate of interest. These short-term securities can be bought and sold in the open market. These instruments usually yield slightly higher returns than T-bills because they have more default risk and less marketability. CDs with smaller denominations (as low as $500) are sold by some banks; however, these smaller CDs are not negotiable certificates of deposit and, thus, are not traded on the open market.

Banker's Acceptances

Bankers' acceptances are securities that act as a line of credit issued from a bank. Usually, the bank acts as an intermediary between a U.S. company and a foreign company. Companies that are too small to issue commercial paper will use banker's acceptances to fund short-term debt needs. These securities usually have slightly higher interest rates than commercial paper, reflecting greater default risk and less liquidity.

Repurchase Agreements

Securities dealers use repurchase agreements (known as "repos") to finance large inventories of marketable securities from one to a few days. The issuer or seller both sells and agrees to repurchase the underlying security at a specific price and specific date. The repurchase price is higher than the selling price, creating the required return to compensate the holder participating in the repurchase agreement.

TREASURY NOTES AND BONDS

Treasury Notes and Bonds

U.S. Treasury notes and bonds have virtually the same characteristics with the exception of maturity. U.S. Treasury notes are issued with maturities of at least one year, but not exceeding ten years. U.S. Treasury bonds are sold with maturities of 30 years. The minimum purchase amount for both types of securities is $1,000 with additional amounts purchased in $1,000 increments. Treasury notes and bonds are coupon securities that pay interest on a semiannual basis. Like Treasury bills, pricing for notes and bonds is done through the auction process.

Inflation Indexed Treasury Notes and Bonds

In 1997, the Treasury began issuing notes and bonds that are indexed with the consumer price index. These securities have the same basic characteristics as non-inflation adjusted Treasury notes and bonds, except for the inflation adjustment feature.

The interest rate paid on these securities is determined through the auction process, just as the other Treasury obligations; however, the principal value of the bond is adjusted for changes in the consumer price index. Thus, the semiannual interest payments received by the investor are determined by multiplying the inflation-adjusted principal value by one-half of the stated coupon payment.

One of the primary risks that fixed-income securities are subject to is change in interest rates, both from devaluation in principal and from loss of purchasing power. The indexed Treasuries provide protection from both of these risks making them an attractive security for those investors concerned about rising inflation and devaluation due to loss of purchasing power.

Like the non-indexed Treasury notes and bonds, indexed Treasury securities are eligible for the STRIPS program discussed below.

Treasury STRIPS

The Treasury STRIPS program was introduced in February 1985. **STRIPS** is the acronym for Separate Trading of Registered Interest and Principal of Securities. The STRIPS program permits investors to hold and trade the individual interest and principal components of eligible Treasury notes and bonds as separate securities. The Treasury does not issue or sell STRIPS directly to investors. STRIPS can be purchased and held only through financial institutions and government securities brokers and dealers who are the parties that separate the original security into its component parts.

When a Treasury-fixed principal or inflation-indexed note or bond is stripped, each interest payment and the principal payment becomes a separate zero-coupon security. Each component has its own identifying number and can be held or traded separately. For example, a Treasury note with 10 years remaining to maturity consists of a single principal payment at maturity and 20 interest payments, one every six months for 10 years. When this note is converted to STRIPS form, each of the 20 interest (coupon) payments and the principal payment become a separate (zero-coupon) security. STRIPS are also called zero-coupon securities because the only time an investor receives a payment during the life of a STRIP is when it matures.

How is a Treasury Security Stripped?

A financial institution, government securities broker, or government securities dealer can convert an eligible Treasury security into interest and principal components through the commercial book-entry system. Generally, an eligible security can be stripped at any time from its issue date until its call or maturity date.

Securities are assigned a standard identification code known as a CUSIP number. CUSIP is the acronym for Committee on Uniform Security Identification Procedures. Just as a fully constituted security has a unique CUSIP number, each STRIPS component has a unique CUSIP number. All interest STRIPS that are payable on the same day, even when stripped from different securities, have the same generic CUSIP number. The principal STRIPS from each note or bond, however, have a unique CUSIP number.

For example, if several fixed-principal notes and bonds that pay interest on May 15 and November 15 are stripped, the interest STRIPS that are payable on the same day (for example, May 15, 2005) have the same CUSIP number. The principal STRIPS of each fixed-principal note and bond have a unique CUSIP number, however, and principal STRIPS with different CUSIP numbers that pay on the same day are not interchangeable (or "fungible").

In the case of inflation-indexed notes and bonds, the semiannual interest STRIPS that are payable on the same day (for example, April 15, 2005) have the same CUSIP number. The principal STRIPS also have a unique CUSIP number. The CUSIP numbers for STRIPS from inflation-indexed securities are different from those for STRIPS from fixed-principal securities.

Source: http://www.publicdebt.treas.gov/of/ofstrips.htm

STRIPS - acronym for Separate Trading of Registered Interest and Principal of Securities—a program that permits investors to hold and trade the individual interest and principal components of eligible Treasury notes and bonds as separate securities

Generally, an investor must report as income, for federal income tax purposes, the interest earned on STRIPS in the year in which it is earned. Inflation adjustments to principal on inflation-indexed securities must also be reported in the year earned. Income must be reported even though it is not received until maturity or the STRIPS are sold. Every investor in STRIPS receives a report each year displaying the amount of STRIPS interest income from the financial institution, government securities broker, or government securities dealer that maintains the account in which the STRIPS are held. This statement is known as IRS Form 1099-OID, the acronym for original issue discount. The income-reporting requirement has meant that STRIPS are attractive investments for tax-deferred accounts, such as individual retirement accounts and 401(k) plans, and for non-taxable accounts, which include pension funds.

UNITED STATES SAVINGS BONDS

Series EE Savings Bonds

The series E bond was designed to encourage more people to save money. It was sold in denominations of $25, $100, $500, and up to $10,000. Series E bonds were sold at a discount and paid no annual interest, similar to zero-coupon bonds. The Treasury issued the new series EE savings bond beginning July 1, 1980 in order to replace the older series E bond. The rate of interest changed from a fixed rate, as with the series EE savings bonds, to a variable rate now equal to 90 percent of the average of prevailing market yields on 5-year Treasury marketable securities. A new earnings rate is announced each May and November. Since the interest rate for Series EE bonds is a market-based, variable rate, there is no way to predict with certainty when a bond will reach face value.

Series EE bonds are accrual bonds, whose price on original issue is half of the face amount. Series EE bonds are issued in face amounts of $50, $75, $100, $200, $500, $1,000, $5,000, and $10,000. Series EE bonds issued on or after May 1, 1997, reach original maturity at 17 years after the date of issue and reach final maturity at 30 years after the date of issue. Bonds cease to earn interest at final maturity.

One of the attractions of series EE bonds is the special tax treatment of the income attributable to these securities. Interest earned from bonds that are issued at a discount, such as zero-coupon bonds and STRIPS, is required to be reported as taxable income on an annual basis even though cash may not be received during the year. Because of the special tax treatment afforded series EE bonds, however, the interest accrued on these securities is generally not taxed on an annual basis, but rather is taxed upon redemption. However, taxpayers are permitted to make an election to include for tax purposes the income from these securities on an annual basis. This elected tax treatment can be beneficial under certain circumstances, such as for a child with income under the standard deduction. In such a case, basis can be established without incurring tax.

Another tax benefit of series EE bonds is that the interest earned on these securities can be completely excluded from taxable income if the proceeds from the bonds are used for qualified higher education costs of the taxpayer, spouse, or dependents. These costs include books, tuition, and fees for these family members.

Series EE bonds can be exchanged for series HH bonds at any time after six months. If EE bonds are exchanged for HH bonds, then the interest accrued on series EE bonds will continue to be deferred until the HH bonds are redeemed.

Series HH Savings Bonds

Unlike series EE bonds that are sold for cash, series HH savings bonds can only be acquired through an exchange of series E or EE bonds (and savings notes issued prior to 1970). Series HH bonds are issued at 100 percent of the face amount in denominations of $500, $1,000, $5,000, and $10,000. Series HH bonds pay interest semiannually at a rate of 4 percent, beginning six months after issuance. The interest payments are required to be included in income for federal income tax purposes.

Series HH bonds have an original maturity period of 10 years and have been granted one 10-year extension of maturity with interest, bringing their final maturity to 20 years. Like EE bonds, HH bonds are issued only in registered physical form and are not transferable. In other words, EE and HH bonds are not marketable securities.

Like Treasury securities, neither EE nor HH bonds are subject to state or local income tax. The tax treatment of these savings bonds can be quite beneficial in those states and cities with an income tax.

Series I Savings Bonds

The Treasury began selling series I savings bonds on September 1, 1998 in an attempt to offer individuals a way to accrue income and to protect the purchasing power of their investment. Series I bonds are issued at 100 percent of the face amount in denominations of $50, $75, $100, $200, $500, $1,000, $5,000, and $10,000. Series I bonds have a maturity period of 30 years, consisting of an original maturity period of 20 years and an automatic extension period of 10 years. The bonds have an interest-paying life of 30 years after the date of issue and cease to increase in value on that date. Like EE and HH bonds, series I bonds are not transferable or marketable.

The series I bond earnings rate is a combination of two separate rates: a fixed rate of return and a semiannual inflation rate. Each May and November, the Treasury announces a fixed rate of return that applies to all series I bonds issued during the six-month period beginning with the effective date of the announcement, May 1 or November 1. The fixed rate for any given series I bond remains the same for the life of the bond.

In addition, every May and November, the Treasury announces a semiannual inflation rate based on changes in the Consumer Price Index for all Urban consumers (CPI-U). The semiannual inflation rate announced in May is a measure of inflation from the previous October through March; the rate announced in November is a measure of inflation from the previous April through September. The CPI-U is published monthly by the Department of Labor's Bureau of Labor Statistics. The semiannual inflation rate is then combined with the fixed rate of the series I bond to determine the bond's earnings rate for the next six months.

Eight Americans are honored on the I Bonds, representing the diversity that built this country. Portraits of the following prominent Americans appear on the eight I Bond denominations:

- ▲ **$50 - Helen Keller** - Noted author and advocate for people with disabilities; responsible for Braille becoming the standard for printed communications with the blind.

- ▲ **$75 - Dr. Hector P. Garcia** - Physician; leading advocate for Mexican-American veterans' rights; activist in Latino civil rights movement and founder of the American G.I. Forum.

- ▲ **$100 - Dr. Martin Luther King, Jr.** - Prominent civil rights leader; minister; Nobel Peace Prize recipient.

- ▲ **$200 - Chief Joseph** - Nez Perce Chief; a great Native American leader.

- ▲ **$500 - General George C. Marshall** - U.S. Army Chief of Staff during World War II; Secretary of State; Secretary of Defense; Nobel Peace Prize recipient.

- ▲ **$1,000 - Albert Einstein** - Physicist; author of the Theory of Relativity; Nobel Prize recipient for Physics.

- ▲ **$5,000 - Marian Anderson** - World-renowned vocalist (contralto); first African-American to sing with the Metropolitan Opera.

- ▲ **$10,000 - Spark Matsunaga** - U.S. Senator and Congressman; World War II hero; obtained redress for survivors of World War II internment camps.

Source: U.S. Treasury at www.publicdebt.treas.gov/sav/sbiwho.htm

Series I bonds are U.S. Treasury securities backed by the U.S. Government. Series I bonds even protect investors from the effects of deflation. In the rare event that the CPI-U is negative during a period of deflation and the decline in the CPI-U is greater than the fixed rate, the redemption value of the I bonds remains the same until the earnings rate becomes greater than zero.

Like EE bonds, I bonds receive special income tax treatment. The interest from I bonds is not subject to state and local income tax. Interest is accrued for I bonds and is not taxable until redeemed. In addition, the interest can be completely excluded from taxable income if the proceeds are used for qualified higher education expenses of the taxpayer, spouse, or dependents.

Series I bonds can be redeemed anytime six months after the issue date to get the original investment plus the earnings. However, I bonds are meant to be longer-term investments. So, if an I bond is redeemed within the first five years, there is a 3-month earnings penalty. For example, if an I bond is redeemed after 18-months, only 15 months of earnings will be awarded.

The following exhibit illustrates the primary differences between the three types of savings bonds.

EXHIBIT 13.2: SUMMARY OF U.S. SAVINGS BONDS

	Series EE	Series HH	Series I
Denominations	$50, $75, $100, $200, $500, $1,000, $5,000, $10,000	$500, $1,000, $5,000, $10,000	$50, $75, $100, $200, $500, $1,000, $5,000, $10,000
Purchased	With cash	By exchanging E or EE bonds	With cash
Issued at	50% of face value	100% face value	100% face value
Maturity	30 years	20 years	30 years
Interest Rate	90% of average 5 year Treasury	4% fixed rate	Combination of fixed and variable rates
Interest	Accrues	Paid semiannually	Accrues
Taxation of Interest	Deferred	Taxable annually	Deferred
Interest Can be Completely Excluded for Qualified Higher Education Costs	Yes	No	Yes

FEDERAL AGENCY SECURITIES

Governmental agencies, such as the Federal Home Loan Bank and the Resolution Trust Corporation, issue public debt as a means of raising funds for operations of the respective agency. Although not issued by the Treasury, **federal agency securities** are extremely safe and have minimal credit risk as a group. These securities have slightly higher yields than Treasuries due to the minimal increase in credit risk.

federal agency securities - public debt issued by agencies of the U.S. government as a means of raising funds for operations of the respective agency

MUNICIPAL BONDS

Municipalities include states, counties, parishes, cities, and towns. These governmental agencies issue debt instruments, referred to as **municipal bonds**. The unique characteristic of municipal bonds is their income tax treatment. The interest from municipal bonds is not subject to federal income tax, and in some cases, not subject to state income tax. Although the yields on municipals are generally lower than that of Treasuries, their special tax treatment makes them the choice for higher income investors because of their higher after-tax yields. The two common types of municipal bonds include general obligation bonds and revenue bonds.

municipal bonds - debt instruments issued by municipalities (states, counties, parishes, cities, towns) as general obligation bonds or revenue bonds

General obligation bonds are backed by the full faith and credit of the government issuing the debt and are repaid through taxes collected by the government body. These bonds are backed by the taxing authority of the municipality and, therefore, have minimal default risk.

Revenue bonds are issued by governmental bodies in order to raise funds to finance specific revenue producing projects. Examples of revenue bonds include airport revenue bonds, college and university revenue bonds, hospital revenue bonds, sewer revenue bonds, toll road revenue bonds, and water revenue bonds. These bonds are not backed by the full faith and credit of the issuing body. Instead, the interest and principal are repaid from revenue generated from the project that was financed with the bond proceeds. Because the revenue generated from the project may differ from what is expected, these bonds are more risky than general obligation bonds and, thus, require higher yields for similar maturities.

Municipal bonds may have other differences. For example, municipal bonds may be either term bonds or serial bonds. The principal for term bonds is repaid in full upon maturity, whereas, serial bonds require that the municipality retire a certain amount of the bond issue each year.

Another important difference is that interest from municipal bonds that are considered private activity bonds is taxable for alternative minimum tax purposes. Investors with large amounts of private activity bonds could be required to pay alternative minimum tax.

Generally, a private activity bond is part of a state or local government bond issue for which the proceeds are to be used for a private business use, such as a sports stadium.

Although relatively safe, municipal bonds are often insured by third party insurance companies to further reduce credit risk. Three of the more common insurance companies that insure municipal bonds include: AMBAC Financial Group (American Municipal Bond Assurance Corporation), MBIA Insurance Corporation (a subsidiary of MBIA, Inc., formally known as Municipal Bond Insurance Association and Municipal Bond Investors Assurance), and Financial Guaranty Insurance Company (FGIC). Since insured municipal bonds have lower risk, they will have lower returns.

CORPORATE BONDS

Corporations raise funds by issuing both equity and debt obligations. A discussion on equity obligations appears in Chapter 14. Debt obligations provide corporations with a method of raising needed capital funds without diluting the ownership of the entity; however, excessive amounts of debt can cause strain on the financial health of the company by using precious resources for debt service. In general, debt increases the leverage of a company and specifically, its return on equity. Excessive use of debt can cause increased fluctuations in the share price of the common stock, producing both positive and negative volatility.

The corporate bond market is very broad and is typically classified by the type of issuer. The five broad categories of corporate bonds are banks and finance companies, industrials, public utilities, transportations, and international (Yankee). Each of these categories can be further subdivided. For example, transportation can be divided into airlines, railroads, and trucking. These subcategory classifications can assist investors in analyzing and comparing various debt issues.

bond indenture agreement - the legal document that sets forth the repayment schedules, restrictions, and promises between the issuer of a corporate bond and the borrower

The **bond indenture agreement** is the legal document that sets forth the repayment schedules, restrictions, and promises between the issuer and the borrower. Some of the information that may be found in the indenture agreement includes call provisions, sinking fund provisions, collateral provisions, and conversion options.

450

Call Provisions

A call provision provides the issuer of the debt instrument the right to redeem the bond issue prior to maturity. Generally, a call provision will require the issuer to pay a premium if the bond issue is redeemed prior to maturity. When interest rates decline, call provisions allow the issuer to redeem the outstanding debt and reissue it at a lower interest rate. By refinancing the debt, companies can save significant amounts of interest payments that would have been paid to the creditors.

From the investor's point of view, the worst time for a company to redeem a bond issue is when interest rates have declined. Such a redemption requires investors to reinvest the proceeds in an interest rate environment that is unfavorable to the investor. Since the potential for a call provision is disadvantageous, investors require that bonds with call provisions have higher yields than bonds without call provisions. Call provisions also create risk because they introduce uncertainty with regard to the stream of cash flows from the bond.

Sinking Fund Provisions

Sinking funds may be established and funded by the bond issuer each year and may accumulate to pay off debt upon maturity. These funds are usually held by a trustee to ensure the repayment of the borrowed principal.

Collateral Provisions

Bonds may be unsecured or secured. If a bond is secured then it has a claim on specific assets of the issuing company in the event of liquidation. A mortgage bond is secured by real property or buildings. Generally, a mortgage bond will have a lien on the specified property, but could have a lien on all assets of the firm. Mortgage bonds may be open-ended, limited open-ended, or closed-ended, which indicates the degree to which additional debt may be issued against the same property.

Collateral trust bonds are usually secured by stocks and bonds of other companies held in trust. For companies that have insufficient real property, providing a lien on securities held by the company is a method of providing security to its creditors. The investments that are pledged act as collateral for the loan.

Companies are willing to provide security for bond issues to reduce and minimize interest payments and expense. The market interest rate required for secured bonds will be less than that of unsecured bonds.

Unsecured bonds are called **debentures**. Investors who hold debentures do not have a claim to specific assets of the corporation. Instead, debenture holders are general creditors of the issuing corporation and will be paid in liquidation only after secured creditors have been repaid. Subordinated debentures have an even lower claim on assets than general creditors, such as debenture holders.

debentures - unsecured corporate bonds whose holders have no claim to specific assets of the issuing corporation

CONVERTIBLE BONDS

convertible securities - hybrid securities that permit the holder to acquire shares of common stock from the issuing company by exchanging the currently held debt security under a specific formula

Corporate bonds may contain provisions permitting the conversion of the fixed income security into equity securities. **Convertible securities** are hybrid securities that permit the holder to acquire shares of common stock from the issuing company by exchanging the currently held debt security under a specific formula. Similar to an option contract, the holder's ability to convert the current security into common stock is a right that the holder has, not an obligation. The conversion decision hinges on the value of the stock upon conversion. If the value of the stock after conversion were less than the value of the bond, then the investor would be wise to hold on to the fixed income security.

Convertible securities allow the issuer to reduce the cost of interest for a bond issue by paying a lower yield. The lower yield is a result of the buyer purchasing not only a steady stream of cash flows, but also an option to convert the bond to common stock.

Convertible securities provide investors with several advantages over non-convertible securities. They provide the holder with a steady stream of cash flows and the ability to participate in the growth of the underlying company, assuming that it is prospering. Convertible securities have a relatively low correlation with bonds and only a moderate correlation to stocks, thus providing the opportunity to diversify within a portfolio. Convertible securities are senior securities in terms of liquidation when compared to common stock and are generally very marketable.

MORTGAGE-BACKED SECURITIES & COLLATERALIZED MORTGAGE OBLIGATIONS

securitization - the process of transforming mortgages into securities that can be sold to the public

Although relatively new, the market for mortgage-backed securities has seen tremendous growth since its inception in the 1970s. Mortgage-backed securities are ownership claims on a pool of mortgages. The originating mortgage lender will sell loans to investors in the secondary market. These investors pool mortgages together and sell interests in the pool to other investors. This process of transforming mortgages into securities that can be sold to the public is known as **securitization**.

Mortgage-Backed Securities

mortgage-backed securities (MBSs) - ownership claims on a pool of mortgages

Mortgage-backed securities (MBSs) are often referred to as "pass-through" securities because the monthly mortgage payments are passed along to the holders of the MBSs, less a small servicing fee. These monthly mortgage payments consist of scheduled interest and principal payments, as well as unscheduled principal prepayments. These unscheduled principal prepayments result from borrowers making additional principal payments on their loans or from paying off loans, such as in the case of refinancing.

Because MBSs are backed by mortgages, many of which are backed by the government and all of which are secured by real property, they have little credit risk. However, MBSs are subject to other risks. Just like other fixed income obligations, these securities are subject to the fluctuation in interest rates. As interest rates increase, the value of the MBS decreases and as interest rates decrease, the value of the MBS increases.

Since MBSs pass through payments on a monthly basis, the investor must reinvest these cash flows into some other investment. This reinvestment rate risk impacts MBSs in the same manner as other fixed income securities that have cash flows occurring during the life of the security.

Unlike other fixed income obligations, MBSs are subject to **prepayment risk**, which is the risk that homeowners will pay off their loans before the scheduled loan maturity date. Since the value of these securities is based on the schedule of cash flows, any mortgage prepayments will impact the return an investor receives on a mortgage backed security. In addition to creating uncertainty as to the timing of the cash flows, these prepayments create a situation in which the investor must reinvest the additional principal payments perhaps at a lower interest rate, furthering the reinvestment risk.

prepayment risk - the risk that homeowners will pay off their loans before the scheduled loan maturity date

EXHIBIT 13.3: HISTORICAL LANDMARKS OF THE SECONDARY MORTGAGE MARKET

1934	Congress established FHA under the National Housing Act of 1934.
1938	Congress established Fannie Mae to serve as refinance facility for FHA-insured mortgages.
1944	VA given authority to guarantee mortgages for U.S. veterans under the Servicemen's Readjustment Act of 1944.
1968	Fannie Mae rechartered as a private corporation. Ginnie Mae established by the Housing and Urban Development Act as a government corporation to serve as a secondary mortgage market institution for FHA/VA/RHS loans.
1970	Under the Emergency Home Finance Act, the Federal Home Loan Mortgage Corporation (Freddie Mac) was chartered as a government-sponsored private corporation to purchase conventional mortgages.
1970	Ginnie Mae issued the first mortgage-backed security (MBS).
1983	The first collateralized mortgage obligation (CMO) was issued using Ginnie Mae MBS pools as collateral, spawning market innovations in multiple class securities. It was issued by an investment bank called Lehman Brothers Kuhn Loeb.
1986	The Tax Reform Act of 1986 propelled CMOs by creating REMICs, a vehicle that minimizes tax liability for multiple class MBSs.
1988	The Basle Agreement was issued by the Basle Committee on Banking Supervision, establishing risk-based capital guidelines. It affected the treatment of mortgage products on institution's balance sheets.

Source: GNMA

The majority of the mortgage-backed securities have been issued by three government agencies. These include the Federal National Mortgage Association (FNMA or "Fannie Mae"), the Government National Mortgage Association (GNMA or "Ginnie Mae"), and the Federal Home Loan Mortgage Corporation (FHLMC or "Freddie Mac"). In 1938, the federal government established Fannie Mae to expand the flow of mortgage money by creating a secondary market. Fannie Mae became a private shareholder-company in 1968 and was listed on the New York and Pacific stock exchanges two years later. Ginnie Mae was created in 1968 and remains a government agency within the Department of Housing and Urban Development (HUD). Freddie

Mac is a stockholder-owned corporation chartered by Congress in 1970 to create a continuous flow of funds to mortgage lenders in support of home ownership and rental housing. Freddie Mac became a private corporation in 1989. With the exception of minor differences, the pass-through securities of each of the three organizations are virtually the same.

Collateralized Mortgage Obligations (CMOs)

Due to the popularity of the mortgage-backed securities, private investment firms have created their own pass-through securities, which are referred to as collateralized mortgage obligations (CMOs). Collateralized mortgage obligations are similar to MBSs in that they are backed by mortgages. They differ from MBSs, however, in that the cash flows associated with a pool of mortgages are divided into repayment periods called tranches. In the traditional MBS, each investor will receive a pro-rata share of principal and interest each month. In effect, the note is being paid off every month.

The principal repayment method is different for collateralized mortgage obligations than for MBSs. As described above, tranches or repayment periods are established which dictate when an investor will receive principal repayments. Each of the tranches will receive regular interest payments with the investors of the first tranche receiving all principal payments until they are completely repaid their principal. Once the obligations of the first tranche are satisfied, all principal payments are made to the second tranche, and so on until all of the tranches are repaid. The holders of the CMOs of the first tranche have less interest rate risk than the holders of the CMOs for the last tranche since the maturity is longer for the securities of the last tranche.

RATING AGENCIES

Rating agencies are responsible for assisting investors in evaluating the default risk of fixed income securities. Bond rating agencies analyze the financial information of thousands of companies attempting to determine a credit rating for the various debt issues in the market. The two largest and most popular rating agencies are Standard & Poor's and Moody's. Their credit rating system is listed in exhibit 13.4.

EXHIBIT 13.4: STANDARD CREDIT RATING SYSTEM

Bonds	Standard & Poor's	Moody's
Investment Grade:		
▲ High Grade	AAA - AA	Aaa - Aa
▲ Medium Grade	A - BBB	A - Baa
Non-Investment Grade:		
▲ Speculative	BB - B	Ba - B
▲ Default	CCC - D	Caa - C
Overall Range	AAA - D	Aaa - C

Investment grade bonds have a high probability of timely payment of both interest and repayment of principal, while non-investment grade bonds are those where a significant risk exists to either interest or principal payments or both. The definition of each rating follows:

EXHIBIT 13.5: DEFINITION OF CREDIT RATINGS

AAA/Aaa	The highest rating and indicates very high ability to service debt.
AA/Aa	Only slightly lower than AAA/Aaa, this rating indicates a very high rating but not as much protection as AAA/Aaa.
A/A	These companies are strong and possess favorable characteristics, but may not be able to sustain adverse economic conditions.
BBB/Baa	These issuers currently have the capacity to service debt, but do not possess the financial strength to withstand weakened economic conditions.
BB	This rating and the ratings below are considered junk bonds. There is little protection for payment of principal and interest.
B	There is little assurance that principal and interest will be paid for these bonds.
CCC/Caa	These issues are in default or may soon be in default.
CC/Ca	Very poor quality issue that is likely in default or extremely close to default.
C/C	No interest is being paid on these bonds. This is Moody's lowest rating, indicating that the company may be in bankruptcy soon.
D	These bonds are in default and interest and principal payments are in arrears.

Besides Standard & Poor's and Moody's, there are two other large rating agencies: Duff and Phelps, and Fitch. In general, all rating agencies rate bonds the same. In some cases, there may be a slight difference between the ratings of a specific issue by the different agencies. In such a case, this difference is referred to as a split rating.

The first four ratings are considered investment grade bonds. Anything below BBB or Baa should be considered junk bonds.

RISKS OF FIXED INCOME SECURITIES

Fixed income securities can provide substantial returns to investors; however, there are a variety of risks that investors of fixed income securities are subject to, including interest rate risk, default risk, reinvestment rate risk, purchasing power risk, call risk, exchange rate risk, and liquidity risk. These risks are discussed below.

SYSTEMATIC RISKS	UNSYSTEMATIC RISKS
▲ Interest Rate Risk	▲ Default (Credit) Risk
▲ Reinvestment Rate Risk	▲ Call Risk
▲ Purchasing Power Risk	▲ Liquidity Risk
▲ Exchange Rate Risk	

INTEREST RATE RISK

Interest rate risk is the risk that fluctuations in interest rates will adversely impact the value of a security. This risk is generally the greatest risk for an investor of bonds. There is an inverse relationship between changes in interest rates and bond prices. As interest rates fall, bond prices increase. Conversely, as interest rates increase, the value of bonds decline.

A 10-year $1,000 bond (that pays interest semiannually) yields 10 percent and sells at par or 100 percent of face value ($1,000). If prevailing interest rates increase to 12 percent, buyers will pay less than par value for the bond so that the yield equals 12 percent (that is, the prevailing market interest rate). Because of the increase in market interest rates, investors will only be willing to pay $885.30 (a $114.70 discount) for the bond, which sold for $1,000 when the prevailing interest rates were 10 percent. Thus, this bond will sell for a discount due to the coupon rate of the bond being less than the prevailing rate of interest for bonds of similar risk and maturity.

EXAMPLE

Prior to Interest Rate Changes 10%		After Interest Rates Change to 12%		After Interest Rates Change to 8%	
(Bond Sells at Par)		(Bond Sells at a Discount)		(Bond Sells at a Premium)	
n	= 20 (10 x 2)	n	= 20 (10 x 2)	n	= 20 (10 x 2)
i	= 5 (10 ÷ 2)	i	= 6 (12 ÷ 2)	i	= 4 (8 ÷ 2)
PMT_{OA}	= $50 (100 ÷ 2)	PMT_{OA}	= $50 (100 ÷ 2)	PMT_{OA}	= $50 (100 ÷ 2)
FV	= $1,000	FV	= $1,000	FV	= $1,000
PV	= ($1,000)	PV	= ($885.30)	PV	= ($1,135.90)

Similarly, as interest rates decline, bond prices will increase. Considering the bond above, if prevailing interest rates drop from 10 percent to 8 percent, then the price of the bond will increase to $1,135.90 (a $135.90 premium). The inverse relationship between interest rates and bond prices is not a linear relationship. Instead, as the following chart indicates, the relationship between bond prices and interest rates is curvilinear:

EXHIBIT 13.6: RELATIONSHIP BETWEEN PRICE AND YTM

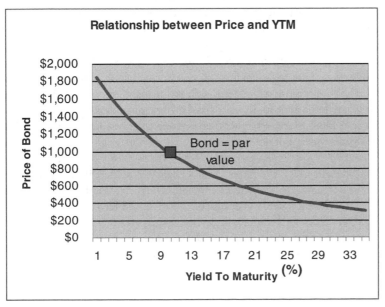

Notice that as the yield to maturity increases, the bond price decreases.

It is important to understand that a decline in the value of a bond, which is attributable to an increase in interest rates, is of little relevance to an investor holding until maturity. In such a case, the decline in value of the bond is simply a reflection of the change in market interest rates. The investor will still receive the scheduled coupon payments and will still receive the par value (usually $1,000) upon maturity. For an investor who sells prior to maturity, an increase in interest rates means that the investor will incur a capital loss. Interest rate risk impacts bonds, bond portfolios, and bond mutual funds.

DEFAULT (OR CREDIT) RISK

As discussed earlier, investing in a fixed income obligation is a process of lending money. The bond issuer is effectively borrowing money from the investor in return for a promise to make periodic interest (coupon) payments and to repay the principal at the maturity of the bond. However, since bonds are often issued with maturities exceeding ten, twenty, and thirty years, there is a risk that the financial well-being of the bond issuer will change over this long period of time. In some cases, the financial health of a company will be in such turmoil that the company cannot uphold its promise to repay the borrowed proceeds. The risk that this might occur is referred to as credit risk or default risk. Rating agencies, such as Moody's, Standard & Poor's, and Duff & Phelps, provide investors with analysis of the financial stability of companies and their ability to service their debt.

Fortunately, default risk is an unsystematic risk that can be eliminated (or at least minimized) through choice of investment and through diversification. Investors who are overly concerned about default risk can eliminate it by investing exclusively in U.S. Treasury fixed income securities. These securities are considered default risk free since they are backed by the full faith and credit of the United States government. In addition to Treasuries, fixed income securities of the Government National Mortgage Association (GNMAs) are also backed by the full faith and credit of the U.S. government and considered default risk free.

Municipal bonds provide a sufficient level of protection against default risk, especially ones that are insured; however, there still remains some level of default risk, even with these insured municipal bonds. To minimize default risk with municipals, corporates, and other fixed income obligations, it is very important to diversify fixed income portfolios. Purchasing a variety of fixed income obligations minimizes the impact that any single security has on the overall bond portfolio. This is the basic concept of diversification.

Another issue of default risk is the impact that a change in a company's financial well-being will have on the value of a bond issue. When a company's financial health diminishes, it increases the likelihood or probability of default. Because of this increased likelihood of default, as small as it may be, the market value of the bond will decline relative to other bonds with similar characteristics. Therefore, it is not simply a matter of default, but also how changes in the general financial health of the bond issuer impact the price of a fixed income security.

REINVESTMENT RATE RISK

Simply put, reinvestment rate risk is the risk that cash flows occurring during the holding of an investment will not be able to be invested at a rate that is at least as great as the rate of return being earned by the investment. As we discussed in calculating the yield to maturity for a bond, there is an implicit assumption that cash flows are reinvested at the YTM rate. If cash flows are reinvested at a rate that is less than the YTM rate, then the actual earnings will be less than the YTM rate calculated at inception. Likewise, if the cash flows are reinvested at a rate that is greater than the YTM rate, then the actual earnings will be greater than the YTM rate calculated at inception.

EXAMPLE

A 10-year $1,000 bond making coupon payments (semiannually) of 10 percent ($50 twice per year) and selling for par or 100 percent of face value ($1,000) must have a YTM of 10 percent. The YTM is calculated assuming the $50 coupon payments will be reinvested to earn 10 percent. What happens if the coupon payments are invested in a savings account earning 5 percent? If the coupon payments are invested to earn 5 percent for the 10 years, the final future value (the amount of money at the maturity of the bond) will be $2,277.23. The future value consists of the reinvested coupon payments and the return of principle. Using a present value of $1,000 (the current value of the bond) and a future value of $2,277 will result in an actual yield of 8.4 percent instead of the expected yield of 10 percent.

Calculation of YTM Prior to Interest Rate Changes			Calculation of FV of Coupon Payments Earning 5%			Calculation of Actual Yield after adjusting for Coupons earning 5%		
n	=	20 (10 x 2)	PMT_{OA}	=	$50 (100 ÷ 2)	PV	=	($1,000)
PMT_{OA}	=	$50 (100 ÷ 2)	i	=	2.5 (5 ÷ 2)	n	=	20 (10 x 2)
FV	=	$1,000	n	=	20 (10 x 2)	PMT_{OA}	=	0
PV	=	($1,000)				FV	=	$2,277.23 ($1,000 + $1,277.23)
i	=	5% x 2 = 10%	FV	=	($1,277.23)	i	=	4.2% x 2 = 8.4%

PURCHASING POWER RISK

As a type of systematic risk, purchasing power risk cannot be eliminated. Purchasing power risk is the risk that inflation will erode the purchasing power of investor's assets. Bondholders can especially be impacted by purchasing power risk. For example, if an investor owns a bond with a coupon of 5 percent when inflation is 6 percent, then he is losing purchasing power at a rate of 1 percent per year. As discussed above, there are certain inflation-adjusted bonds, such as the ones issued by the U.S. Treasury, that can minimize the adverse impact of inflation.

CALL RISK

For bonds that have a call feature, there is a risk that the bond will be called from the investor. Bond issuers will generally call a bond when interest rates decline, which means that the investor will have to reinvest the proceeds in an environment of lower interest rates. One of the characteristics that appeal to bondholders is the scheduled and known cash flow of a bond. Call features increase the uncertainty of the scheduled cash flows of a callable bond.

EXCHANGE RATE RISK

Bonds issued by foreign governments or foreign companies are subject to the fluctuations in currency rates. Investors may either be compensated or hurt when currency rates change. In addition to currency risk, foreign bonds are subject to other risks such as political risk and country risk.

LIQUIDITY RISK

The primary measure of liquidity is the spread between the bid price and the ask price for a fixed income security. The level of risk is directly related to the spread. The larger the spread, the greater the liquidity risk. Typically, the greater the volume of transactions in a bond market, the smaller the spread will be for the security. For example, because the Treasury market is very large, spreads are very small.

VOLATILITY OF FIXED INCOME SECURITIES

As we discussed, bond prices fluctuate with changes in interest rates. However, different bonds will vary by different amounts. The two key factors that influence volatility are coupon rate and maturity.

COUPON RATE

The volatility in price for a bond is inversely related to the bond's coupon payment when interest rates change. Bonds with higher coupon rates are more stable to interest rate changes than bonds with lower coupon rates. A zero-coupon bond will have a tendency to be more volatile in value than a bond with a 10 percent coupon.

MATURITY

Bonds with longer terms are subject to more volatility with changing interest rates than bonds with shorter terms. A 30-year Treasury bond will be more volatile than a 5-year Treasury note when interest rates change. This can be illustrated with the following example:

EXAMPLE   Bond A is a 5-year bond with a 10 percent coupon rate. Bond B is a 30-year bond also with a 10 percent coupon rate. Since Bond B has a longer maturity, it should be more volatile when interest rates change.

EXHIBIT 13.7: IMPACT OF MATURITY ON BOND VOLATILITY

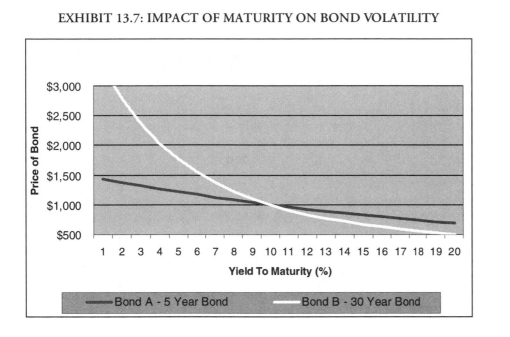

Notice that Bond B does in fact change more than Bond A when interest rates change. At a YTM of 10 percent, the price of the bonds is equal at $1,000. When interest rates decrease, the price of Bond B increases more than Bond A. When interest rates increase, the price of Bond B decreases more than Bond A.

TERM STRUCTURE OF INTEREST RATES

YIELD CURVES

Traditionally, interest rates for bonds have been reflected in graphical representations called **yield curves**. These yield curves reflect current market interest rates for various bond maturities. The most popular of these yield curves is the Treasury yield curve, which depicts current yields for Treasury securities. The yield curve is generally upward sloping indicating that yields on longer-term bonds are higher than yields on shorter-term bonds. However, there have been times when the structure of interest rates has caused the yield curve to be shaped differently. Although there have been other shapes, the three yield curves that are generally thought of include the upward sloping, flat, and downward or inverted shaped yield curves as shown in Exhibit 13.8.

yield curves - graphical representations that reflect current market interest rates for various bond maturities

EXHIBIT 13.8: YIELD CURVES

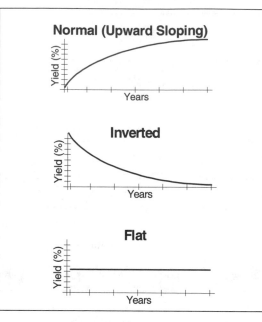

The Treasury yield curve is often used as a benchmark for other fixed income securities. The Treasury yield curve is an effective benchmark for pricing bonds and determining yields of bonds in other sectors since it is not impacted by credit risk or liquidity risk. Treasuries are backed by the full faith and credit of the U.S. government and are therefore not subject to credit risk. The Treasury market is extremely liquid, since it is the largest and most actively traded bond market.

The traditional method for valuing or pricing non-Treasury bonds has been to use the yield on the Treasury yield curve for the appropriate maturity, plus a premium for additional risk. There are arguments, however, that this method has certain inherent problems.

EXAMPLE   Assume that two 10-year Treasury bonds, Bond A and Bond B, have coupon rates of 10 percent and 0 percent, respectively. These bonds would theoretically have the same yield since they have the same maturity; however, their cash flow characteristics are completely different. Bond A pays $50 for nineteen periods with $1,050 paid at the twentieth period, while Bond B simply pays $1,000 at the twentieth period.

An alternative way to consider the valuation of bonds is to consider them as a series of individual cash flows with each cash flow being viewed as an independent zero-coupon bond. For example, Bond A (from above) could be viewed as 20 separate and distinct zero-coupon bonds and Bond B could be viewed as a single zero-coupon bond. These individual cash flows should then be valued based on market yields for zero-coupon Treasuries with similar maturities.

YIELD CURVE THEORIES

There are several theories that attempt to explain the reason for the shape of the yield curve. These include the pure expectations theory, the liquidity theory, the preferred habitat theory, and the market segmentation theory.

The Pure Expectations Theory

The expectations theory is based on the concept that longer-term rates, or forward rates, are based on expected future short-term rates. In other words, forward rates should indicate the market's perception of which direction rates will be moving. For example, an upward sloping yield curve would indicate that future short-term rates would be increasing; a flat yield curve indicates that future short-term rates will remain constant; and a downward or inverted yield curve represents the expectation that short-term rates will be declining. This concept can be illustrated with the following example.

Assume that the 1-year rate equals 6 percent and the 2-year rate equals 8 percent. Under this assumption, an investor who was willing to invest for a period of two years could receive a return of 8 percent for each of the two years, whereas the investor who was only willing to invest one year would receive 6 percent. There is a 2-percentage point difference in the returns that the 2-year investor will receive in the first year compared to the return for the 1-year investor. Under the expectations theory, the reason that an investor could receive 8 percent over two years and only 6 percent for one year is that the market expects short-term rates to increase in one year. In other words, the 8 percent rate for two years actually consists of the 1 year rate of 6 percent and the 1-year rate one year from today. This future 1-year rate turns out to be 10.04 percent, as follows:

Future Value of 2-Year Bond	= 1.08 x 1.08	= 1.1664	The investor should have 16.64% more than the initial investment at the end of 2 years.
Future 1-Year Rate	= 1.1664 ÷ 1.06	= 1.1004 − 1.00 = 10.04%	Since the 1-year rate equals 6%, the future 1-year rate must equal 10.04%.
Proof	= 1.06 x 1.1004	= 1.1664	A rate of 6% for the first year plus a rate of 10.04% for the second year is equal to a 2-year rate of 8%.

One shortcoming of this theory is that it does not reflect the inherent increased risk or uncertainty in longer-term bonds. There is clearly more uncertainty with a 2-year bond than with a 1-year bond. In the above example, the theory explains that the 2-year return of 8 percent results from a 6 percent return the first year and a 10.04 percent return the second year. Based on this theory, it seems reasonable that an investor with a 1-year time horizon would purchase the 2-year bond to earn 8 percent for the first year and then sell it at the end of one year. However, there is no guarantee that the bond could be sold at a specific price at the end of one year, which introduces the element of risk into the decision. As a result, an investor with a 1-year time horizon might choose the 1-year bond instead of the 2-year bond, even though the return for the 1-year bond is lower. Therefore, it seems as though the forward rate, in our example 10.04 percent, may consist of a risk premium as well as expectations of higher future rates.

The Liquidity Preference Theory

According to the liquidity preference theory, investors prefer certainty and expect to be rewarded or compensated for uncertainty. This theory is based on the expectations theory, but goes on to incorporate a liquidity premium into the model. Under this theory, forward rates incorporate both expectations about future rates as well as a premium for the increased risk of longer-term bonds. Longer-term bonds should have higher premiums than shorter-term bonds. Based on this theory, yield curves will generally be upward sloping, reflecting higher premiums for longer-term bonds.

The Preferred Habitat Theory

Like the liquidity preference theory, the preferred habitat theory explains forward rates based on expectations of future rates plus a risk premium. However, the risk premium is not simply based on the length of maturity of the bond in question. Rather, the preferred habitat theory, similar to the market segmentation theory (described below), states that institutions (generally financial institutions) have certain preferences as to the maturity of their assets, for matching to their liabilities. In other words, institutions generally try to match the maturity or duration of their assets and liabilities. However, this theory states that these institutions will sometimes shift their maturities or duration if the premiums for the switch are significant enough. Therefore, it is possible to have any shape yield curve under this theory.

Market Segmentation Theory

According to the market segmentation theory, interest rates for varying maturities are determined by supply and demand. Institutions may have liabilities that are short-term, intermediate-term, or long-term and will generally want to match the maturity of their assets with the maturity of their liabilities. As a result, there are certain types of institutions that lend and borrow at the different categories of maturities. This results in a separate market for short-term borrowings, intermediate-term borrowings, and long-term borrowings. Each market has its own balance between supply and demand. Therefore, based on the supply and demand in each maturity market, the yield curve can be any shape.

DURATION & IMMUNIZATION

duration - a concept developed by Fred Macaulay in 1938, that provides a time-weighted measure of a security's cash flows in terms of payback

The concept of **duration**, developed by Frederick Macaulay in 1938, provides a time-weighted measure of a security's cash flows in terms of payback. There are three important uses for duration, which include:

1. Providing a measure of a bond's volatility;
2. Estimating the change in the price of a bond based on changes in interest rates; and
3. Immunizing a bond or bond portfolio against interest rate risk.

As described above, it is not enough to evaluate a bond based on yield alone. The bond should also be evaluated based on its cash flows. The calculation of duration allows us to evaluate not only a bond's yield, but also its cash flows.

CALCULATING DURATION

There are several methods for calculating duration. The following formula is one method for calculating Macaulay duration:

$$D = \frac{\sum_{t=1}^{n} \frac{Cf_t(t)}{(1+k)^t}}{\sum_{t=1}^{n} \frac{Cf_t}{(1+k)^t}}$$

where: n = Number of periods until maturity

         Cf_t = Cash flow that occurs in period t

         k = Yield to maturity

         t = Time period

The denominator is the market price of the bond, defined as the present value of future cash flows beginning in period 1. The numerator is the sum of each discounted cash flow adjusted for the period in which it occurs.

For example, the duration for a 10-year bond that pays a 10 percent coupon annually and is yielding 10 percent can be calculated as follows:

EXAMPLE

(A) Period	(B) Cash Flow	(C) PV Factor	(D) PV @ 10%	(E) PV x Period
1	$100.00	0.9091	$90.91	$90.91
2	$100.00	0.8264	$82.64	$165.29
3	$100.00	0.7513	$75.13	$225.39
4	$100.00	0.6830	$68.30	$273.21
5	$100.00	0.6209	$62.09	$310.46
6	$100.00	0.5645	$56.45	$338.68
7	$100.00	0.5132	$51.32	$359.21
8	$100.00	0.4665	$46.65	$373.21
9	$100.00	0.4241	$42.41	$381.69
10	$1,100.00	0.3855	$424.10	$4,240.98
			$1,000.00	$6,759.02

$$(F) \quad \text{Duration} = \frac{\$6,759.02}{\$1,000.00} = 6.76 \text{ years}$$

The calculation of duration requires five broad steps. The first step is to list the periods relevant to the bond (**A**). In the above example, there are ten periods associated with the bond. The second step is to list the cash flow for each period (**B**). The cash flows will consist of coupon payments and/or principal payments. The third step is to calculate the present value of each of the cash flows (which can be done by multiplying column two (**B**) by column three (**C**)) at the yield to maturity for the number of periods that matches the period in which the cash flow occurs (**D**). The fourth step is to multiply column one (**A**) by column four (**D**). For example, period 3 is multiplied by $75.13, which equals $225.39. The final step is to divide the sum of column five (**E**) by the sum of column four (**D**). The result of this fifth step is the duration in years (**F**).

Duration can be calculated on a periodic basis to accurately account for semiannual coupon payments by listing each semiannual period and cash flow. This adjustment will result in an answer in terms of period, which can be converted into years simply by dividing by two (for semiannual payments).

Another method of calculating duration is using the following closed-end formula:

$$\text{Dur} = \frac{1+k}{k} - \frac{(1+k)+T(C-k)}{C\left[(1+k)^T - 1\right]+k}, \text{ where}$$

k = Yield to maturity, as a decimal

T = Time until maturity, in periods

C = Coupon rate, as a decimal

This calculation of this formula can be illustrated using the above example:

$$\text{Dur} = \frac{1+0.10}{0.10} - \frac{(1+0.10)+10(0.10-0.10)}{0.10[(1+0.10)^{10} - 1]+0.10}$$

$$\text{Dur} = 11 - \frac{1.10}{0.25937}$$

$$\text{Dur} = 11 - 4.24$$

$$\text{Dur} = 6.76 \text{ years}$$

This formula is a more efficient method of calculating duration than the previous method for longer-term bonds. In addition, it can be used easily in spreadsheets when building economic models involving duration.

DURATION AS A MEASURE OF A BOND'S VOLATILITY

Duration provides investors with a method of easily comparing a bond's volatility to the volatility of other bonds. Very simply, bonds with higher durations are more volatile when interest rates change, than bonds with lower durations. Therefore, the volatility of bonds increases as the duration increases. The three main factors that impact a bond's duration are coupon rate, maturity, and yield to maturity.

Coupon Rate

There is an inverse relationship between a bond's coupon rate and its duration. As a rule, the duration of a bond cannot exceed the maturity of a bond. Therefore, the maximum duration equals its term to maturity. A bond's duration will only equal its maturity if the bond is a zero-coupon bond. The only adjustment that can be made to the coupon rate for a zero-coupon bond is to increase it. If this happens, then the duration must decline, since it cannot exceed its maturity.

Another way to think of this concept is that when the coupon rate is increased, the investor is receiving cash flows faster, decreasing the time the investor must wait to be paid back the initial investment. A quicker payback means a smaller duration, in years.

Maturity

There is a direct relationship between a bond's maturity and its duration. As a rule, the duration of a bond increases as its maturity increases. However, the increase in duration is at a diminishing rate. The figure below illustrates this point. It is a graph of the duration for a bond with a 10 percent coupon and a 10 percent YTM, calculated for maturities ranging between 1 year and 30 years.

EXHIBIT 13.9: DURATION AT VARIOUS MATURITIES FOR A 10% COUPON BOND WITH YTM OF 10%

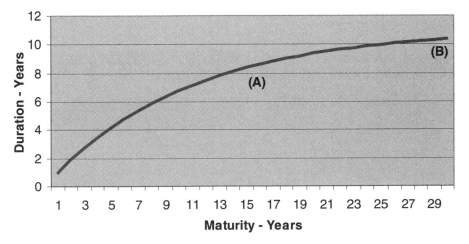

As illustrated in Exhibit 13.9, duration is directly impacted by maturity, however, at a decreasing rate. In this example, the duration for a maturity of 15 years is approximately 8.4 years (**A**), while the duration for a maturity of 30 years is only 10.4 years (**B**). Although the actual maturity doubled, the duration of the bond increased by only 2 years. It should also be noted that the coupon rate will impact the degree to which the duration changes, as will the YTM.

Yield to Maturity

Generally, yield to maturity is inversely related to duration. When the YTM is increased for a coupon bond, the duration will decline. As stated above, the duration of a zero-coupon bond is its term to maturity, therefore, its duration is unaffected by changes in the YTM.

ESTIMATING THE CHANGE IN THE PRICE OF A BOND BASED ON CHANGES IN INTEREST RATES

Another important application of duration is its use in determining the price change in a bond or bond portfolio based on changes in interest rates. It should be clear that as interest rates change, bond prices are impacted. However, what is important to a fixed income investor is his exposure to interest rate risk. What is the percent change in the bond or bond portfolio given a specific change in interest rates? The answer to this question can be determined by understanding the relationship between a bond's price and its duration. As we discussed, coupon, maturity, and YTM all impact duration. If you recall, these same factors also determine the price of a bond. Therefore, duration can assist us in determining the estimated change in the price of a bond based on changes in interest rates. The following formula is an estimate of the percentage change in the price of a bond based on the duration and the change in market interest rates:

$$\frac{\Delta P}{P} = \frac{-D}{1 + YTM} \times \Delta YTM \text{ , where}$$

$\Delta P/P$ = Percentage change in the price of a bond

D = Duration of the bond

YTM = Yield to maturity for the bond

ΔYTM = Change in YTM as a decimal

As the formula above describes, the change in the price of a bond equals the duration of a bond divided by one plus the YTM and multiplied by the change in interest rates.

For example, the duration for a ten-year bond that pays a 10 percent coupon, annually, and is yielding 10 percent was determined earlier to be 6.76 years. How much will the price of the bond change in value if interest rates decrease by 1 percent or 100 basis points to 9 percent?

$$\frac{\Delta P}{P} = \frac{-D}{1 + YTM} \times \Delta YTM$$

$$\frac{\Delta P}{P} = \frac{-6.76}{1 + 0.10} \times (0.09 - 0.10)$$

$$\frac{\Delta P}{P} = -6.1455 \times -0.01$$

$$\frac{\Delta P}{P} = 0.06145 = 6.145\%$$

Based on the above formula, the price of the bond should increase by approximately 6.15 percent. This estimation of the price change of a bond is very useful in analyzing the exposure that a bond portfolio has to interest rate risk. Based on this estimate, we would expect the new price of the bond to be $1,061.45 ($1,000 x 1.06145). This estimate can be verified by calculating the price of the bond using time-value-of-money concepts.

FV	=	$1,000
n	=	10
i	=	9%
PMT	=	$100
PV	=	($1,064.18)

Based on this calculation, our estimate is off by $2.73 or 0.25 percent. The estimation model is very effective for small changes in interest rates; and in the market, we rarely find large changes in interest rates.

USING DURATION TO IMMUNIZE BOND PORTFOLIOS

As we have emphasized, interest rate risk is one of the major concerns of fixed income investors, as well as managers of fixed income portfolios. As interest rates increase, the price of bonds will decline. However, there is an offsetting position that must be considered. When interest rates increase, the reinvested coupon payments should be invested at higher rates, thus, offsetting the decline in the value of the bond. This offsetting of price and reinvested coupon payments is illustrated below:

Interest Rates Move	Value of Bond (Inverse to interest rates)	Value of Reinvested Coupon Payments (Move is direct to interest rates)
↑	↓	↑
↓	↑	↓

As you can see, when interest rates increase, the value of bonds decline, but the value of reinvested coupon payments increase. Similarly, as interest rates decline, bond prices increase and the value of reinvested coupon payments decreases. This offsetting is the basis for immunizing a bond or bond portfolio against interest rate risk.

immunization - the concept of minimizing the impact of changes in interest rates on the value of investments

Immunization is the concept of minimizing the impact of changes in interest rates on the value of investments. The goal of immunization is to protect the bond portfolio from interest rate fluctuations and reinvestment rate risk. Immunization should provide a stable compound rate of return that equals the calculated YTM at the purchase of the bond, despite interest rate fluctuations. The portfolio is considered immunized if the realized rate of return is at least as great as the computed YTM calculated at inception. Another way to think of immunization is that a bond portfolio is immunized when the actual future value is at least as great as it had been expected at inception. For example, the expected future value of a zero-coupon bond at maturity will be $1,000.

A bond portfolio is defined as being initially immunized at the point of duration. Therefore, if an investor were to match the duration of a bond portfolio to the time horizon of his goal, then his portfolio is initially immunized. This can be easily accomplished with a zero-coupon bond. An investor who had a cash need in ten years could simply purchase a ten-year, zero-coupon bond and eliminate all reinvestment rate risk. However, zero-coupon bonds are not always feasible. Therefore, although not as ideal as zeros, ordinary coupon bonds can be effectively immunized. Consider the following example.

EXAMPLE

Assumptions:
- ▲ Coupon rate of 8 percent, paid annually.
- ▲ Term of bond is 10 years.
- ▲ The yield on the bond equals 10 percent.
- ▲ The duration of the bond is approximately 7 years.
- ▲ Time horizon of client's cash needs is 7 years.

IMMUNIZATION EXAMPLE					
Assuming Interest Rates Remain at:		Interest Rates Change to the Following:			
	10%	8%	9%	11%	12%
Coupon Payment Reinvested					
PMT	$ 80.00	$ 80.00	$ 80.00	$ 80.00	$ 80.00
i	10.00%	8.00%	9.00%	11.00%	12.00%
n	7.000	7.000	7.000	7.000	7.000
FV@7years	$758.97	$ 713.82	$ 736.03	$ 782.66	$ 807.12
Proceeds of Bond Sales @ Year 7					
FV	$ 1,000.00	$ 1,000.00	$ 1,000.00	$ 1,000.00	$ 1,000.00
PMT	$ 80.00	$ 80.00	$ 80.00	$ 80.00	$ 80.00
i	10.00%	8.00%	9.00%	11.00%	12.00%
n	3.000	3.000	3.000	3.000	3.000
PV@7years	$950.26	$1,000.00	$ 974.69	$ 926.69	$ 903.93
Reinvested Coupon Pmts.	$758.97	$ 713.82	$ 736.03	$ 782.66	$ 807.12
Bond Sale Proceeds	$950.26	$1,000.00	$ 974.69	$ 926.69	$ 903.93
Total@7years	$1,709.24	$1,713.82	$1,710.72	$1,709.35	$1,711.05

The example above illustrates the concept of immunization. The investor should have $1,709.24 at the end of seven years, assuming yields remain steady at 10 percent. The $1,709.24 consists of the reinvested coupon payments ($758.97) plus the sales proceeds of the bond ($950.26) at year seven. Thus, $1,709.24 is the future value that we are expecting assuming no change in interest rates at seven years (duration). This bond will be considered immunized if the future value at other rates of return is at least as great as $1,709.24. As the chart illustrates, although the interest rate changes from 10 percent, the future value at the point of duration (7 years) for these other points is at least as great as the future value if the interest rates had remained at 10 percent. (This is the definition of immunization.) Therefore, an investor who had a cash need in seven years could use this bond as a method of minimizing the exposure to interest rate risk.

It should be noted that matching the duration to the investor's cash need immunizes the portfolio against initial changes in interest rates. As time passes, however, the bond portfolio will need to be rebalanced so that the duration and remaining time continue to match. Rebalancing should be done once or twice per year. If rebalancing is performed more frequently than twice per year, then the transaction costs will minimize any benefit derived through rebalancing.

TRADITIONAL METHODS OF IMMUNIZING BOND PORTFOLIOS

The three traditional strategies for immunizing bond portfolios from interest rate risk include the ladder strategy, the barbell strategy, and the bullet strategy. Each strategy has certain unique advantages and disadvantages.

The ladder strategy is accomplished by establishing a portfolio of bonds with staggered maturities. For example, $20,000 of bonds could be purchased with maturities ranging from one to ten years for a total portfolio of $200,000. The shorter maturity bonds would be less subject to price fluctuation and, therefore, would reduce the overall portfolio interest rate risk. This approach provides two advantages. First, since there is a combination of long-term and short-term bonds in the portfolio, the laddered portfolio will provide higher yields than a portfolio consisting entirely of short-term bonds. Second, because one bond matures each year, cash is available to the investor. Furthermore, the funds may be used to purchase another bond with a 10-year maturity that will maintain the original structure of the bond portfolio and minimize the risk of increasing interest rates. One important disadvantage of the laddered approach is that it reduces flexibility of the portfolio because all bonds may need to be liquidated in the event that the investor wishes to restructure the portfolio.

Under the barbell strategy, one-half of the portfolio is invested shorter-term, while the other half of the portfolio is invested longer-term. This approach creates a structure that has the appearance of a barbell. For example, a $200,000 fixed income portfolio might be invested with $100,000 in 5-year bonds and $100,000 in 15-year bonds. The barbell strategy provides the advantage of only selling one group of bonds in the event that the structure of the portfolio needs to be changed due to changing interest rates. This strategy will not maintain its original structure because each year the maturity of the two groups of bonds will decline by one. Under this strategy, it is costly to maintain the original structure of the bond portfolio since the entire portfolio must be liquidated.

When investors purchase a series of bonds with similar maturities that are focused around one point in time, it is considered a bullet strategy. The bullet strategy is one in which the average maturity declines by one each year and may be effective in matching duration to the cash needs of an investor. Like the barbell strategy, to maintain the original structure, the entire portfolio must be liquidated, resulting in significant transaction costs.

When using fixed income securities in a portfolio, when do you prefer to use actual fixed income securities versus mutual funds?

I often use short-term, very low-cost bond funds to reduce overall volatility of a portfolio and to complete the fixed income portion of an asset allocation plan.

I like using individual securities to generate a known source of cash flow. We use highly rated securities when buying individual securities with the intent of holding them to maturity.

I prefer individual securities for clients that are new to investing or have a fear of the markets. It is easier to explain how an individual fixed income security works and get them comfortable with investing.

How do you make decisions with regard to allocating among short, medium and long-term fixed income securities?

I almost always use short-term (no greater than 5 year maturity) securities. Research has shown that the risk of owning fixed income securities significantly increases after 2 to 5 years while the returns do not. Why take increased risks with the fixed income portion of a client's portfolio?

We use fixed income securities to reduce volatility and/or produce cash flow while using stocks or stock funds to produce growth. If a client is willing to take higher risks, invest in stocks where you have the potential for long-term growth.

Bond values will fluctuate from changes in interest rates,

however, shorter-term bonds will have less fluctuation than long-term bonds.

When do you use individual fixed income securities for your client's portfolio and why?

I prefer to use individual securities to generate known cash flow. I often build bond ladders to generate a steady stream of cash flow over a number of years. The cash generated from the bonds maturing in addition to the regular interest payments provide a source of spending funds for many retired clients.

This works well for clients that also need growth in their portfolio, but are more risk averse. Once you can show them they will have steady cash flow, they are more comfortable having the remainder of their portfolio invested in equities for long-term growth.

When using municipal bonds for clients in high federal and state income tax brackets, I prefer individual bonds as opposed to municipal bond mutual funds. Depending on the state, inventories of highly rated municipals may be low at times, however. It may take some time to build a bond ladder of municipal bonds for this reason.

CONNIE BREZIC, CPA/PFS

DISCUSSION QUESTIONS

1. How do fixed income securities differ from equity investments?
2. How is the value of a bond calculated?
3. What two types of payments make up the cash flows of a bond?
4. How do asset-backed securities differ from other fixed-income securities?
5. What is a zero-coupon bond and what are its advantages and disadvantages as an investment?
6. What is the current yield of a bond and how is it useful in measuring a bond's return?
7. What is the yield to maturity of a bond and what assumptions is the calculation based on?
8. What adjustments to the calculation of yield to maturity must be made when computing yield to call?
9. How does a corporate return and a municipal return differ?
10. What is the STRIPS program?
11. What are the different types of U.S. Savings Bonds and how do they differ?
12. What are the advantages of the I Savings Bond over the EE and HH Savings Bonds?
13. What types of provisions are found in the bond indenture agreement of corporate bonds?
14. What are the differences between MBS and CMOs?
15. What types of risks are investors in fixed income securities subject to?
16. How do changes in interest rates impact bonds?
17. How does credit risk impact the yield on bonds?
18. What is a yield curve and why is it important when examining bond interest rates?
19. What are the uses of duration?
20. How do coupon rate, maturity, and yield to maturity impact the calculation of duration?
21. What is immunization and how it is achieved?
22. What are the three methods of structuring bond portfolios?

EXERCISES

1. Stephen buys a two-year bond with a $1,000 face value that pays a 9 percent coupon semi-annually ($45 twice each year). What is the value of the bond if comparable bonds are yielding 10 percent?
2. What is Elizabeth's current yield on a ten-year bond that has a 10 percent coupon and is currently selling for $920?
3. David is considering purchasing a 10-year bond that is selling for $1,213.10. What is the yield to maturity for this bond if it has a 10 percent coupon, paid semi-annually?
4. Susan wants to purchase a zero-coupon bond. What is the yield to maturity for a five-year bond selling for $643.92? (Hint: assume semi-annual payments, if they existed)
5. Discuss why each of the following statements is incorrect and change them to correct statements.

   ▲ To calculate yield to call, you use a different formula than with yield to maturity.

   ▲ Yield to maturity is the promised return from a bond over its maturity.
6. Katy is considering purchasing a 20-year bond ($1,000) that pays a coupon of 12 percent semiannually, is selling for $945.50, and has a yield to maturity of 12.76 percent. The bond is callable in three years at 103. What is the yield to call for the bond?

7. Discuss why each of the following statements is incorrect and change them to correct statements.
   ▲ Current yield is a bond's annual coupon multiplied by the current market price.
   ▲ Yield to maturity (YTM) is the promised compounded rate of return an investor will receive from a bond purchased at the current market price and sold before maturity.

8. Rob, who is in the 40 percent tax bracket, is looking to buy a state municipal bond that offers a 5.5 percent yield, while comparable credit-worthy corporate bonds are offering a yield of 9 percent. Which bond will offer the greatest after-tax yield?

9. Discuss why each of the following statements is incorrect and change them to correct statements.
   ▲ Money markets include short-term, highly liquid, relatively high-risk debt instruments sold by governments, financial institutions, and corporations to investors with temporary excess funds to invest.
   ▲ Investors may invest indirectly in some of the money market securities, but more often they invest directly through money market mutual funds.
   ▲ Treasury bills are an example of an equity security and are used as a benchmark asset because of their risk-free nature.

10. If Jeff had bought a 182-day treasury bill on January 13, 2000, what income will the bill provide when it matures at its face value of $1,000? (Refer to Exhibit 13.1)

11. Determine whether each of the following is a bond issued in the United States. If not, state why.
    ▲ Federal government securities.
    ▲ Treasury bills.
    ▲ Government agency securities.
    ▲ Municipal securities.
    ▲ Corporate bonds.

12. Randy buys a 2-year bond that is yielding 7 percent. Using ONLY the pure expectations theory of interest rates, what is the expected 1-year rate one year from today if the current yield on one-year bonds is 6 percent?

13. Discuss why each of the following statements is incorrect and change them to correct statements.
    ▲ Bonds are valued using a future value process. The cash flows for a bond--interest payments and principal repayments--are inflated at the bond's required yield.
    ▲ Without regard to other factors, the price of a bond will generally remain constant over time because it is worth face value (typically, $1,000) on the maturity date.

14. Discuss why each of the following statements is incorrect and change them to correct statements.
    ▲ The term structure of interest rates refers to the relationship between time to maturity and yields for a particular category of bonds at any point in time.
    ▲ The term structure is usually plotted in the form of a yield curve, which is a graphical depiction of the relationship between yields and time for bonds that are identical including for maturity.

15. Discuss why each of the following statements is incorrect and change them to correct statements.
    ▲ Duration, stated in years, is the weighted average time to recovery of all interest payments minus principal repayment.
    ▲ Duration gets smaller with time to maturity but at a decreasing rate, and it is inversely related to coupon and yield to maturity.

PROBLEMS

1. Mindy's bond portfolio is currently yielding 8 percent. If the duration of her portfolio is 5 years and interest rates increase by 75 basis points, then by what percent will the portfolio change and in what direction?

2. Marleen has a ten-year bond that is yielding 7.65 percent. If it pays an annual coupon of ten percent, then what is the duration of Marleen's bond?

3. Illustrate that a bond with the following characteristics is immunized at the point of duration when interest rates initially increase by 200 basis points or decrease by 200 basis points.

   ▲ Ten-year maturity.
   ▲ Coupon rate equals ten percent (paid annually).
   ▲ Yield to maturity equals 7.65 percent.

CHAPTER 14

Equity Securities

LEARNING OBJECTIVES:

After learning the material in this chapter, you will be able to:

1. Understand how dividends, capital appreciation, voting rights, maintaining ownership percentage, and liability contribute to the meaning of "ownership" investments.

2. Identify the phases of the industry life cycle and describe each phase.

3. Describe the types of equity securities.

4. Define common stock and preferred stock and explain how they are alike and how they differ.

5. List the types of foreign securities available to investors and the characteristics of each type.

6. Discuss the systematic and unsystematic risks that are inherent to equity securities.

7. Identify the markets on which equity securities are traded and compare each to the other.

8. List the market indexes and averages that provide information to investors on the overall movement and performance of the securities markets.

9. Explain the primary characteristics of a good benchmark as a measure of a security's performance.

10. Describe the ways in which an investor can measure the return of a security.

11. Differentiate between taking a long position and a short position when purchasing equity securities.

12. List the types of orders used to purchase shares of common stock.

13. Compare and contrast technical analysis and fundamental analysis.

14. Compare and contrast the several models used to determine a security's value.

INTRODUCTION

Equity securities play a vital role in the investment strategies of many investors. As mentioned in Chapter 12, their returns have been significantly better than the returns for other asset classes. These high returns are a key aspect in making equity investments attractive. This chapter will explain the basic concepts of equity type investments, the risks of equity investments, how equity securities are traded, and how equity securities are valued.

BASIC CONCEPTS OF OWNERSHIP TYPE INVESTMENTS

WHAT OWNERSHIP MEANS

In Chapter 12, we discussed the two general types of securities, lending securities and ownership securities. Lending securities, which are investments with interest payments made to the investor (lender) for the use of the loaned funds, were discussed in the previous chapter (Chapter 13). By ownership securities, we mean securities that represent some form of ownership interest in a corporation. Corporations are artificial, legal entities, whose creation and operation are controlled by state statutes. To become a corporation, a business must incorporate within a state. As part of the incorporation process and as one method of raising additional capital, a corporation issues shares of common stock. These shares have certain rights and benefits, including the right to receive dividends, the right to vote on corporate issues, the right to limited liability, and finally, the right to ultimate distribution of assets in the event of liquidation.

Numerous risks are inherent in owning common stock. The primary reason that investors are willing to accept these risks is that equities have earned significantly higher returns than other types of investments over long periods. These returns consist of two primary sources – dividends and capital appreciation.

Dividends

Companies have positive net income when their earnings are greater than their expenses. A company has two choices with regard to the additional earnings or cash flow. This additional cash can be reinvested into the business in the form of new or existing projects or it can be paid to the shareholders of the corporation. These payments to shareholders are referred to as cash dividends.

From a theoretical standpoint, the company should reinvest the additional income if it is able to earn returns that are higher than shareholders could earn on their own. If this is not the case, then companies should pay the additional cash to the shareholders in the form of **dividends**.

Four dates are important related to the payment of a dividend. These dates include the **date of declaration**, the **date of record**, the **date of x-dividend**, and the **date of payment**. The board of directors declares a dividend payment, which creates an obligation on the company to make a dividend payment to shareholders. The date of record represents the date at which an owner of the common stock is entitled to receive the dividend payment. If a shareholder owns the stock as of the date of record, he is entitled to receive the dividend.

---

dividends - positive net income that is paid to the shareholders of a corporation

date of declaration - date a corporation's board of directors declares a dividend payment which creates an obligation on the company to make a dividend payment to shareholders

date of record - the date at which an owner of the common stock of a corporation is entitled to receive the dividend payment

date of x-dividend - the date at which the market reflects the dividend payment

date of payment - the date that the dividend will actually be paid

---

The x-dividend date is the date at which the market reflects the dividend payment.

If a stock is currently valued at $100 and the company declares a $5 dividend, then the stock should decline in value by $5 to $95 on the x-dividend date. From an economic standpoint, the shareholder is in the same position after the x-dividend date as before. Prior to the dividend, the shareholders owned a stock worth $100. After the dividend payment, the shareholders own a stock worth $95 and have $5 in cash.

EXAMPLE

Finally, the date of payment is simply that date that the dividend will actually be paid. Remember that the dividend will be paid to those who owned shares as of the date of record. Therefore, someone who sells his or her shares after the date of record, but before the date of payment will receive the dividend payment.

Capital Appreciation

A company has choices with the income it generates. Even if the company is highly profitable, it may choose to retain the earnings to invest in additional projects. In such a case, the owner or investor receives his return in the form of appreciation of the stock, which is referred to as **capital appreciation**. Microsoft is a good example of a company that does not pay dividends, but has generated significant stock appreciation (Exhibit 14.1).

capital appreciation - when a company chooses to retain the earnings to invest in additional projects, the investor receives his return in the form of appreciation of the stock

EXHIBIT 14.1: MICROSOFT'S STOCK PRICE 1986-2000

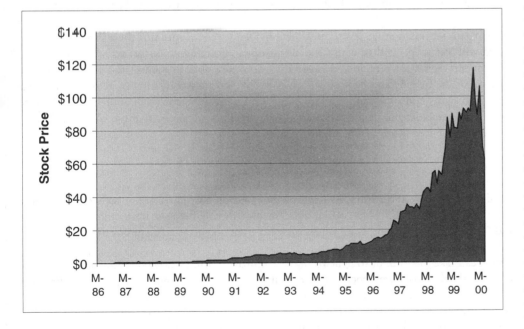

Exhibit 14.1 shows that investors who purchased Microsoft stock during the 1980's have received huge gains from the appreciation of the stock. The company was able to earn returns higher than most investors could have earned on their own or through other investments.

479

Dividends or Capital Appreciation: Which is better?

There are two primary differences between dividend income and capital appreciation that need to be considered before answering the question, "Which is better?" These two differences include the tax treatment and the perceived risk between the two types of income.

Dividends are taxed as ordinary income in the year in which the dividend payment is received. The tax rates for ordinary income range from 10 (after 1/1/01) percent to 38.6 percent for 2001. (The tax rates were decreased per TRA 2001. See Chapter 16 for more information). Appreciation in the price of a stock is taxed as a capital gain and is taxed only when the stock has been sold. Long-term (defined as a period of one year plus one day) capital gains for securities are taxed at rates ranging between 8 percent and 20 percent in 2001. Therefore, from a tax standpoint, capital gains are preferred over dividend income due to the beneficial tax treatment.

If capital gain income is preferred over dividend income from a tax standpoint, then why do individual investors often prefer dividend income? To answer this question, we have to understand the nature of dividend income versus capital gain income.

Generally, a company's dividend policy will remain relatively constant over a period of time. In other words, if a company paid a $2.00 dividend last year, then it is reasonable to expect the company to pay $2.00 or a little more this year and next year. Companies do not generally change their dividend payments drastically from one year to the next, thus allowing investors to have confidence in the amount of dividend income they will receive from their investment.

Capital gain income is much less reliable than dividend income, meaning there is more risk associated with capital gains than with dividend income. Therefore, investors with long time horizons prefer capital appreciation, because they are more able to control the recognition and taxation of the income and because with higher risk generally comes higher returns. Investors who need current income cannot afford the risk of whether a stock will appreciate enough to cover living expenses during a given year. These investors are generally more comfortable with dividend income or income from lending securities.

Voting

In addition to the returns from dividend income and capital appreciation, owners of common stock have voting rights. These voting rights include the right to vote for the board of directors and the right to vote on corporate issues, such as certain mergers and acquisitions.

Voting can take the form of straight voting or cumulative voting. Straight voting authorizes one vote per share of common stock, while cumulative voting allows one vote per share times the number of seats on the board of directors. Cumulative voting is used to protect minority shareholder interests. In addition, voting can be done in person or by proxy. Proxy voting involves sending a written authorization to an agent to cast the vote for the shareholder.

Maintaining Ownership Percentage

Some companies permit owners to maintain their ownership percentage in the event of any new offering of their stock. For example, an investor who owned 10 percent of a company might be given the opportunity to purchase 10 percent of any new stock offering. This right allows him to maintain his ownership percentage. This type of right is known as a preemptive right.

Liability

Because corporations are separate legal entities, they are generally responsible for all debts and claims arising from all sources. As a result, shareholders are protected from personal liability. One of the distinctions that will be discussed in detail in the business organizations chapter is the liability exposure owners may have for different types of entities.

INDUSTRY LIFE CYCLE

As we have discussed throughout the text, individual investors move through phases of the life cycle and understanding these phases will assist the planner in developing a financial plan for their client. Similar to the life cycle of an individual is the **industry life cycle**. Industries move through certain phases including start up, rapid growth, growth, maturity, and finally decline. The characteristics of each phase are illustrated in Exhibit 14.2 and discussed below.

industry life cycle - phases through which an industry moves—start up, rapid growth, growth, maturity, and decline

EXHIBIT 14.2: INDUSTRY LIFE CYCLE

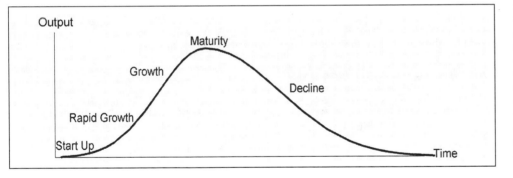

Start Up

During this initial stage, the first stages of a product are being created. For example, the personal computer began in the early 1980's. There is significant research and development being done with high costs. Sales revenue is generally low to moderate and income is generally negative. The potential for growth is enormous.

Rapid Growth

The second phase of the life cycle is an exciting time. Demand for the product or service is large and growing at a substantial rate. Companies are increasing sales at tremendous rates. However, the large increases in demand often cause backlogs due to limited capacity. Competitors are often attracted to enter the market due to the high growth rates of the market and due to the capacity problems firms are experiencing.

Growth/Consolidation

During this phase, market leaders begin to emerge. These companies have been able to establish dominance in the industry. The industry is still growing at rates higher than the economy in this stage; however, the tremendous growth of the previous phase is gone, and the bigger market leaders often buy out less competitive companies. This phase of the life cycle is also a time where forecasts become easier due to the steady growth and consolidation of competitors.

Maturity

At this phase, the industry growth has slowed and only moderate growth will continue. Market leaders will compete based on differentiation and price. Earnings are greatly influenced through cost management, since growth is now relatively stable.

Decline

The industry sales growth declines and total sales may begin to decline. This phase may be caused by obsolescence or competition from substitute products.

Which Phase is the Best Time to Invest?

Each phase has its unique characteristics. These characteristics include risk and return expectations for investors. Exhibit 14.3 summarizes some of the issues inherent in each phase.

EXHIBIT 14.3: CHARACTERISTICS OF LIFE CYCLE PHASES

Industry Phase	Returns	Risk	Description
Start Up	Very High	Very High	Many of the companies that begin in the industry go out of business.
Rapid Growth	Very High	High	Less risky than the start-up phase, but still considerable risk as to which companies will be market leaders and prosper.
Growth/Consolidation	High	Moderate	Identifying and investing in market leaders will provide substantial growth and high returns.
Maturity	Moderate	Low	Returns shift from growth in stock price to higher dividends. These companies typically have excess cash. Risk is consistent with equity market.
Decline	Low/Moderate	Low/Moderate	Companies in the decline phase may have opportunities for a turnaround or may continue to grow in a declining market.

As depicted by the above chart, investments in companies in the different phases carries different return expectations, including the form of returns (growth versus dividends), and different risk expectations. Each of the phases is appropriate to different investors, depending on their risk tolerances.

A recent example of an industry that saw tremendous growth was the Internet and technology sector expansion during 1999. The NASDAQ, heavily weighted toward technology, saw unprecedented gains with no end in sight. However, the following year the market tumbled as investors lost confidence in the markets. The NASDAQ dropped more than 60 percent of its value from its high. This example illustrates the risky nature of industries in the early phases of the life cycle.

TYPES OF EQUITY SECURITIES

COMMON STOCK

Common stock represents an ownership interest in a firm. If the company succeeds then the investor will have good returns from his investment. However, if the company does not perform well, then the value of the stock will decline. With thousands of companies, there needs to be a classification system to categorize equity securities. One classification system is based on the type of stock. This classification system includes defensive stocks, cyclical stocks, blue chip stocks, growth stocks, income stocks, interest-sensitive stocks, value stocks, and new economy stocks.

common stock - ownership interest in a company

Defensive Stocks

defensive stocks - a type of stock that is relatively unaffected by general fluctuations in the economy

Stocks that are relatively unaffected by general fluctuations in the economy are considered to be **defensive stocks**. These companies tend to have steady (although slow) growth and become more popular during economic recessions and less popular during economic booms. Many of these companies provide products that are necessary for everyday life. Thus, the demand for the products will not be adversely affected by changing economic cycles. Since the demand for these products does not change, the demand for these products is considered inelastic. Defensive stocks are usually found in the following industries:

▲ Utilities.
▲ Soft drinks.
▲ Groceries.
▲ Candy.
▲ Drug/Pharmaceuticals.
▲ Tobacco.

Another way to think of defensive stocks is that they have low systematic risk, since they are not greatly affected by changes in the economy and the market. Therefore, these securities will typically have low betas relative to the overall market.

Cyclical Stocks

cyclical stocks - a type of stock that tends to prosper in expanding economies and do poorly during down business cycles

Cyclical stocks tend to prosper in expanding economies and tend to do poorly during down business cycles. When the economy is growing, demand strengthens and these companies are able to make large profits. When the economy is in a downturn, these companies are hurt by declines in demand and are less profitable. In recessions, they begin cost cutting measures to improve the bottom line (earnings) and as a result, these companies end up in a healthy financial position for the next economic upturn. The companies, regarded as cyclicals, usually have large investments in plant and equipment and, therefore, have high fixed costs. These stocks come from industries that include the following:

▲ Automobiles.
▲ Cement.
▲ Paper.
▲ Airlines.
▲ Railroads.
▲ Machinery.
▲ Steel.

Because these stocks typically perform well when the economy is booming and perform poorly when the economy is in recession, cyclical stocks are highly correlated with the overall stock market. In addition, these stocks will typically have higher betas than the overall market.

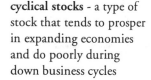

Blue Chip Stocks

Stocks issued by highly regarded investment quality companies are called **blue chip stocks**. These companies tend to be older, well established companies that maintain the ability to pay dividends both in years the company has income and in years the company has losses. These companies are generally leaders in their respective industries. They tend to offer investors quality investments with both steady dividend streams and relatively consistent growth. Examples of blue chip stocks include:

▲ General Electric.
▲ General Motors.
▲ ExxonMobil.
▲ Wal-Mart.
▲ IBM.

Although blue chip companies are by definition high quality, sound financial companies, are they good investments? The answer to this question depends on a variety of issues related to the company. However, it is certainly the case that not all good companies make good investments. This distinction occurs because the price for quality companies may be bid up so high that it makes the investment a poor decision.

Growth Stocks

Growth stocks are stocks issued by companies that have sales, earnings, and market share growing at higher rates than average companies or the general economy. Many blue chip stocks can also be classified as growth stocks. Because these companies are growing and expanding, they do not typically pay large dividends. Most of the earnings generated from these companies are reinvested back into the company to support future growth. An example of this type of stock is Microsoft, which has never paid dividends, but whose stock has appreciated substantially over the last twenty-five years. Therefore, these companies are expected to grow and appreciate more rapidly than ordinary companies.

Price appreciation is appealing to investors because it remains untaxed until the appreciation is recognized (that is, there is no taxable gain until the stock is sold and the gain is recognized for tax purposes). This growth acts as an income tax deferral and allows for higher compounding returns. Since investors trying to accumulate wealth do not usually need current income, these stocks match their financial needs better than other investments due to smaller dividends and tax deferred appreciation.

Long-term (held for a year and a day) capital gains currently receive favorable tax treatment. These gains are ordinarily taxed at a maximum rate of 20 percent (some long-term capital gains are taxed at an intermediate rate of 28 percent, such as collectibles), whereas ordinary income can be taxed at marginal rates of 38.6 percent (for 2001). This large difference in tax rates causes investors to adjust their asset allocations to maximize after-tax returns at their level of risk tolerance.

blue chip stocks - a type of stock issued by older, well established companies that maintain the ability to pay dividends both in years the company has income and in years the company has losses

growth stocks - a type of stock issued by companies whose sales, earnings, and market share are growing at higher rates than average companies or the general economy

In addition to growth stocks, there are also emerging growth stocks that are typically smaller and younger growth companies. These companies have survived the early years and are just beginning to grow and expand. Emerging growth stocks have great potential for investment, but are also subject to tremendous risk.

Income Stocks

income stock - a type of stock issued by companies in the maturity phase of the industry life cycle and payout the majority of their earnings in the form of dividends

As we discussed, dividends are one of the two ways investors benefit from investing in common stock. Some stocks are attractive because they make large divided payments relative to other firms in the economy. Often times, these companies are in the maturity phase of the industry life cycle and payout the majority of their earnings in the form of dividends. These companies will generally appreciate moderately, but will continue to be profitable and grow over time. Utilities are a good example of an **income stock.**

Interest Sensitive Stocks

interest sensitive stock - a type of stock issued by companies whose performance is largely affected by changes in interest rates

Because the performance of some companies is largely affected by changes in interest rates, their stock is considered **interest sensitive stock**. For example, the housing industry is more productive and has more demand when interest rates are low since it is cheaper for consumers to purchase homes. When interest rates increase, the cost of purchasing homes goes up, causing the demand for new homes typically to decline. These trends also affect lumber, plumbing, furnishing, and household equipment companies. Rising interest rates cause the cost of debt to increase; therefore, companies that have large amounts of debt will have increasing interest expense. These companies, like consumers, have the opportunity to refinance their debt during low interest rate periods.

Some companies that are affected by interest rates are:

▲ Insurance companies.
▲ Savings and loans.
▲ Commercial banks.
▲ Telephone companies.
▲ Utility companies.

Value Stocks

value stocks - a type of stock trading at prices that are low given the stock's historical earnings and current asset value

Stocks trading at prices that are low given their historical earnings and current asset value are referred to as **value stocks**. These securities tend to have low price to earnings ratios and tend to be out of favor in the market. Value managers attempt to find these high quality companies that are temporarily undervalued by the market in hopes that the market will recognize the true value of the companies resulting in stock appreciation.

New Economy Stocks

new economy stocks - a type of stock within the technology industry that is expected to benefit greatly from the popularity and mainstreaming of the Internet

During the early part of the year 2000, the term "**new economy stocks**" became popular. This new term was used to describe the stocks within the technology industry that were expected to benefit greatly from the popularity and mainstreaming of the Internet. These companies included companies selling products to consumers directly over the Internet, such as Amazon, E-Bay, Yahoo, and numerous others. In addition, companies providing access to the Internet, such as cable companies and telephone companies, were benefiting from the new economy. Providers of hardware, such as Cisco Systems, were seeing tremendous growth and prosperity due to the demand for Internet systems.

Within a short period, these companies and many more had benefited from the Internet. The media hype on Internet and technology stocks led many to believe that we had entered into a new era and that traditional methods of valuation were somehow outdated and not in touch with the new economy. During the latter part of 2000 and in 2001, the euphoria of the Internet and technology stocks dissipated and the markets took a nosedive, losing more than 60 percent of the market capitalization. Investors found that despite the hype, traditional valuation models do hold.

Equities can also be classified in other ways. For example, equities might be segregated into sectors of the economy or classified by size (large-cap, mid-cap, and small-cap).

PREFERRED STOCK

Preferred Stock has characteristics of both fixed income investments and of common stock. Shareholders of preferred stock generally receive dividends each year equal to a stated percentage of the par value of the stock if the corporation declares them. For instance, a $100 par, 5.5 percent issue of preferred stock pays a dividend of $5.50 each year for each share owned. The corporation must satisfy these dividend payments each year before paying a dividend to the common shareholders. If the corporation is required to pay any unpaid preferred dividends from prior years before paying a dividend to the common stockholders, the preferred stock is referred to as cumulative.

Preferred stock may also be participating, meaning that preferred shareholders share in the profits of the corporation. Usually, the preferred shareholders receive dividend payments. Then, holders of common stock will receive their dividends equal to the amount paid to the preferred shareholders. If the preferred stock is participating, additional funds for dividends will then be allocated between the preferred and common shareholders according to stock agreements.

Preferred stock has a preferential right over common shareholders to the assets of the corporation equal to the par value of the stock. This right must be satisfied before the common shareholders receive any assets upon liquidation. However, secured and unsecured creditors will be compensated before preferred shareholders receive any assets of the corporation.

Convertible preferred stock has a conversion right that allows holders to redeem or trade in the preferred stock for a specified number of common shares. Convertible preferred stock provides the safety of a fixed income security with the growth potential of a stock.

preferred stock - a type of stock that has characteristics of both fixed income investments and of common stock in that dividend payments must be paid each year prior to paying a dividend to the common shareholders

FOREIGN SECURITIES

foreign securities - securities from developed countries or emerging markets

Although the United States is the largest financial market in the world, as measured by market capitalization, it only represents approximately 35 to 40 percent of the world financial market capitalization. This means that between 60 and 65 percent of companies are outside the United States. Thus, **foreign securities** may provide significant benefits to United States investors.

First, securities outside the U.S. have substantial return potential. Many of the countries outside the U.S. are less developed and, therefore, provide opportunities for significant growth. Second, foreign markets are generally not as efficient as the U.S. market and, therefore, provide opportunities to find undervalued securities. Third, foreign securities provide benefits of diversification. The returns and movements in the equity markets of most foreign countries are not highly correlated with that of the U.S. market. Therefore, adding foreign asset classes to a portfolio may increase the efficiency of the portfolio.

Foreign securities are generally classified as being from developed countries or emerging markets. Developed countries include countries such as the U.S., Canada, Japan, England, and France. Emerging markets include those countries with significant growth potential, but that are currently underdeveloped. Examples of emerging markets include Argentina, Brazil, Chile, Taiwan, and Venezuela. The returns from emerging market countries are generally less correlated to the returns of the U.S. market than that of developed countries. However, the returns of emerging markets can be extremely volatile.

There are currently several methods for U.S. investors to invest in foreign securities. These include purchasing American Depositary Receipts, investing in international or foreign mutual funds, investing in international or foreign closed-end funds, purchasing foreign shares on foreign stock exchanges, and purchasing international iShares.

American Depositary Receipts (ADRs)

American Depositary Receipts (ADRs) - certificates of ownership issued by U.S. banks representing ownership in shares of stock of a foreign company that are held on deposit in a bank in the firm's home country

American Depositary Receipts (ADRs) are one of the easiest methods of acquiring individual foreign securities. They are certificates of ownership issued by U.S. banks representing ownership in shares of stock of a foreign company that are held on deposit in a bank in the firm's home country. These ADRs are denominated in U.S. dollars and pay dividends in U.S. dollars. Although they are denominated in U.S. currency, they do not protect holders from exchange rate risk. Changes in currency rates between the firm's currency and the U.S. dollar will be reflected by a change in the value of the ADR.

ADRs are considered "cross listed" since the foreign shares are listed both on the U.S. stock exchange as well as the foreign exchange. One of the benefits of ADRs is that the foreign company is generally required to comply with the requirements of U.S. exchanges including compliance with U.S. GAAP (Generally Accepted Accounting Principles) and certain disclosure and reporting requirements.

Foreign Mutual Funds

Today, numerous mutual funds have the objective of investing internationally. These **foreign mutual funds** provide investors with the easiest method of investing in foreign markets in the context of a diversified portfolio. These foreign funds have a variety of objectives, ranging from different regions of the world to different sized markets. International funds generally invest in securities throughout the world, while foreign funds strictly invest outside the U.S. Mutual funds are discussed in detail in Chapter 15.

Foreign Closed-end Funds

Foreign closed-end funds provide the same basic benefits as foreign mutual funds. However, because closed-end funds trade on exchanges, they do not have the cash inflow and outflow that mutual funds frequently experience. This fixed capitalization allows managers of closed-end funds to invest in less liquid securities without fear that investors will wish to liquidate their positions, forcing the manager to liquidate the illiquid securities in the portfolio.

Purchasing Foreign Shares on Foreign Stock Exchanges

Direct purchasing of foreign securities on foreign exchanges is more difficult than the other methods. However, with the benefits of technology, the process has become more simplified. Establishing a brokerage account in a foreign country or using a foreign branch of a U.S. broker can accomplish the purchase of foreign shares on foreign exchanges. The foreign transactions require completion in the local currency. Monitoring direct foreign investments is certainly more difficult than with the use of a mutual fund.

International iShares

In 1996, Morgan Stanley introduced World Equity Benchmark Shares (commonly referred to as WEBS) as an alternative method of investing in foreign markets. WEBS are investment companies that are designed and structured to mimic the Morgan Stanley Capital International (MSCI) stock market indexes for single foreign countries. Effectively, WEBS are passively managed index funds that invest in a single foreign country. WEBS have been subsequently renamed as **iShares**.

International iShares are designed after Standard & Poor's Depositary Receipts (SPDRs), which track the S&P 500 index. They are similar to open-end investment companies (mutual funds) in that they are open-ended and the shares trade at or near net asset value (NAV). However, like closed-end funds, iShares trade in the secondary market.

Although relatively new, there are already iShares for twenty-four various international indexes. These represent indexes in Europe, Asia, North and South America, as well as one global index.

International iShares, along with the other methods of foreign investing, provide investors with numerous advantages over investing strictly in domestic equities. These advantages include higher potential returns, lower levels of risk, and portfolios that are more efficient.

foreign mutual funds - securities that provide investors with the easiest method of investing in foreign markets in the context of a diversified portfolio

foreign closed-end funds - securities that provide the same basic benefits as foreign mutual funds, except that since closed-end funds trade on exchanges, they do not have the cash inflow and outflow that mutual funds frequently experience

iShares - passively managed index funds

RISKS OF EQUITY SECURITIES

As with all securities and investments, there are certain inherent risks (both systematic and unsystematic) associated with equity investments that must be considered. The most important systematic risks that we will discuss include market risk, interest rate risk, and exchange rate risk. The key unsystematic risks that we will discuss include business risk, financial risk, and country risk.

SYSTEMATIC RISKS

Systematic risks are those that affect all securities. In other words, these risks cannot be diversified away. Systematic risks include market risk, interest rate risk, and exchange rate risk.

Market Risk

Market risk represents the tendency for changes in the market to influence the prices of equities. When the market is increasing, most stocks have a tendency to increase in value. Conversely, stocks tend to fall with declines in the market. Often, a move in the market is prefaced by some change in the economic environment.

The equity market is quite volatile and may change in value significantly within short periods of time. This occurs without there necessarily being any direct cause. When the change occurs, especially on the downside, all equities have a tendency to decline in value. The volatility of the U.S. equity market, as represented by the S&P 500 index, is illustrated in Exhibit 14.4 below.

systematic risk - investment risk impacted by broad macroeconomic factors that influence all securities

market risk - a systematic risk where stocks tend to move with the market

EXHIBIT 14.4: S&P 500 INDEX

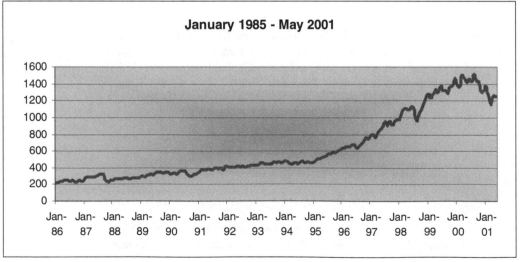

Notice that when the market changes direction, it often does so rapidly and the changes are often extremely significant. These ups and downs in the market cause the value of investor's portfolios to change dramatically within short periods of time.

Interest Rate Risk

Interest rate risk is one of the major risks affecting fixed income securities and bond portfolios. Similarly, equity securities are impacted by changes in interest rates. When interest rates increase, there is negative pressure on the value of common stocks and when interest rates decrease, stocks tend to increase in value. There are three primary reasons for this relationship. These three reasons are increased borrowing costs, attractiveness of alternative investments, and valuation of securities.

Increased Borrowing Costs

Most companies use debt as a means of financing capital expansion and acquisition of assets. The cost of debt is in the form of interest payments. When interest rates increase, the cost of future borrowing increases. This increased borrowing cost can cause earnings to decline. When earnings decrease, the value of the company is reduced. Therefore, changes in interest rates have a direct impact on the cost of borrowing and, thus, on the earnings of a firm.

Attractiveness of Alternative Investments

When interest rates increase, so do the corresponding yields on fixed income securities. As yields increase, bonds become more attractive. Investors become unwilling to assume the inherent risks in equities when the spread between the expected return on bonds and stocks is decreasing (due to the increasing yields on bonds). Therefore, as investors decrease investments in equities so that they can take advantage of the fixed income yields, there is downward pressure created on the equity market causing it to decline.

Valuation of Securities

The method of valuing securities involves discounting future cash flows to today. As interest rates increase, the discount rate used to value a security must also increase. Because an increase in the discount rate results in a lower valuation, stocks generally decline when interest rates increase.

Each of these three interest rate issues cause downward pressure on equity prices when interest rates increase. However, there are times when interest rates increase and stock prices also increase. In these cases, there are other factors working on the positive side, such as increased corporate earnings.

Exchange Rate Risk

The uncertainty of returns in foreign investments due to changes in the value of a foreign currency relative to the valuation of the investor's domestic currency is referred to as **exchange rate risk**. A foreign investment is subject to not only the inherent risk of the investment, but also the risk that the foreign currency weakens relative to the domestic currency, decreasing the gains (or increasing the losses) from the investment.

Matthew invests $1,000,000 in the Eiffel Corporation based in France. If the conversion rate for francs to dollars is 8 to 1, Matthew would have to invest 8 million francs in Eiffel Corporation. Eiffel Corporation does extremely well, and Matthew is able to sell his interest for 12 million francs. If Matthew attempts to convert the francs into dollars when the exchange rate has

interest rate risk - a systematic risk where changes in interest rates will affect the value of securities

exchange rate risk - a systematic risk where a change in the relationship between the value of the dollar (or investor's currency) and the value of the foreign currency will occur where the investment is made

EXAMPLE

changed to 10 to 1 (the dollar strengthened relative to the franc), he will receive $1,200,000 (12,000,000 ÷ 10). This gain is comprised of a 50 percent (4,000,000 francs) gain on the investment and a loss of 20 percent ($300,000 ÷ $1,500,000) or $300,000 from the change in the currency rate. The net result is a 20 percent gain on the original investment; however, it is only 40% of the gain generated from the appreciation of Eiffel Corporation.

Assume the same facts as in the previous example except that the exchange rate is now 6 to 1 instead of 10 to 1. In this case, Matthew liquidates his interest in Eiffel Corporation and converts the francs to $2,000,000 (12,000,000 ÷ 6). This $1,000,000 gain is attributable to the appreciation of Eiffel Corporation and from the devaluation of the dollar relative to the franc.

International equity managers often attempt to avoid such drastic results from changes in currency rates by hedging against currency fluctuations. Forward or futures contracts tend to be used as hedging devices against currency risk. However, academic studies have shown that over long periods of time, hedged and unhedged portfolios will generally perform comparably.

UNSYSTEMATIC RISKS

unsystematic risks - types of investment risks unique to a single company, industry, or country that can be eliminated by portfolio diversification

Unsystematic risks are those risks that are unique to individual securities, industries, or countries. These risks include business risk, financial risk, and country risk.

Business Risk

business risk - an unsystematic risk based on the riskiness of the specific business with regard to its speculative nature, its management, and philosophy

Business risk is the riskiness of a specific business, which includes the speculative nature of the business, the management of the business, and the philosophy of the business. Different types of businesses will have different levels of risk. For instance, technology securities are generally considered to have more risk than defensive stocks. However, both will have unique risk associated with their specific type of business.

Business risk can also be thought of as the certainty or uncertainty of income. Utilities companies have relatively stable and steady income streams and, therefore, have lower business risk. Since they have unsteady or fluctuating income levels, cyclical companies (such as auto manufacturers) are classified as having higher business risk.

From the perspective of a firm's financial position, business risk relates to the asset side of the balance sheet.

Financial Risk

financial risk - an unsystematic risk based on the capital structure of a firm which affects the return on equity (ROE) for a company

The method by which a firm acquires its assets is directly related to **financial risk** or financial leverage. Companies have two choices with regard to capital structure: firms may use debt through the issuance of bonds or other means of borrowing or through the issuance of equity securities. When a company chooses to use debt as the method to finance the purchase of additional assets, it is increasing the financial risk of the firm. This increased leverage is the same result that individuals find when using margin to purchase securities.

492

Consider two firms that each earn $50,000 of net income. Both firms are in the same business and each has $400,000 of assets. However, Company A has issued no debt and instead financed all of its assets with the use of equity. Company B has issued $300,000 of debt with the remaining $100,000 of equity.

EXAMPLE

	Company A	Company B
Net Income	$50,000	$50,000
Debt	$0	$300,000
Equity	$400,000	$100,000
ROE (Return on Equity)	12.5%	50%

Notice that while each company's earnings are the same, as are the assets, the return on equity is quite different. This difference results from the different capital structures of the firms. Because Company B has chosen to use debt as a method of financing, it has increased the leverage of the firm. Therefore, Company B's returns will be more volatile over time than Company A's returns. Financial risk is directly related to the capital structure of the firm and is therefore, related to the liability side of the balance sheet.

Country Risk

International investments are subject to **country risk**, which is the unique risk within each country. These risks include political and economic risks. The United States is generally thought to have the lowest country risk, since its political and economic systems are the most stable.

country (or regulation) risk - an unsystematic risk where changes in a country's laws or political situation will have an adverse effect on an investment

It is important to remember that unsystematic risks are unique to an individual security, industry, or country. Therefore, these risks can be diversified away, unlike systematic risks.

EQUITY MARKETS AND BENCHMARKS

PRIMARY MARKET

The **primary market** is the place where securities are initially offered to the public. These security offerings are in the form of initial public offerings, commonly referred to as IPOs. IPOs allow businesses and entrepreneurs access to the capital markets. These business owners issue additional shares to the public for raising capital to expand and grow their business. While an IPO will dilute the ownership of the existing shareholders, it provides for the capital and resources to dramatically expand the business.

primary market - the market where new issues of securities are first offered to the public

Underwriting

To issue shares to the public, companies enlist the assistance of investment bankers to underwrite the stock issue. In the process of **underwriting** an IPO, the investment banker may assume some of the risk associated with selling the securities to the public. For example, an investment banker might agree to purchase an issue for $12 per share and then resell the issue to the public for $13 per share. This $1 profit is referred to as an underwriter's spread. In addition, underwriters often help the issuing firm determine its financial needs and the best investment vehicle to

underwriting - the process by which investment bankers purchase an issue of securities from a firm and resell it to the public

achieve the needed funds. Underwriting can take one of four forms. These include firm commitment, stand-by underwriting, best efforts, and private placements.

Firm Commitment

The underwriter purchases the entire issue of securities at a specific price then sells at a higher price. This arrangement shifts all risk to the underwriter. If the issue cannot be resold at a price above the purchase price, the underwriter will lose money on the transaction. Often, a syndicate of underwriters will be setup to spread the potential risk.

Stand-By Underwriting

The underwriter purchases the remaining securities left after an initial offering (usually to existing shareholders/owners) at a predetermined price.

Best-Efforts

The underwriter sells as much of the issue as possible, and the remainder of the stock issue is returned to the issuing company. No risk is shifted to the underwriter. This arrangement occurs when the issuing company is confident that the issue will be sold or the underwriter is concerned about the risk because of the financial stability and risk of the company.

Private Placement

The attraction of a private placement is that it does not have the registration requirements of an IPO and is therefore less expensive and less time consuming. Generally, the issue can be placed in the market quickly and at a low cost. Underwriters help find investors and receive a finder's fee or commission of 0.25 percent to 1.5 percent. Bonds have been the most common of the privately placed issues. A private placement must be sold to no more than 35 unaccredited investors. An unaccredited investor is anyone who does not fit into one of the following categories:

▲ Net worth of $1,000,000, or
▲ Gross Income of $200,000 for each of the past two years, with the anticipation of the same level of income.

In addition to cost, private placements avoid all the registration requirements of the SEC and avoid the public access to information that occurs when conforming to SEC requirements. Although private placements are limited to 35 unaccredited investors, there is no limit as to the number of accredited investors that may purchase shares from the issuance of shares in a private placement.

SECONDARY MARKET

secondary market - the market where investors can freely buy and sell securities with other investors

The **secondary market** is where investors buy and sell securities that have previously been issued in the primary markets. The secondary market provides liquidity to the capital markets and allows for the free trade of public securities.

The secondary markets consist of exchanges, such as the New York Stock Exchange and the American Stock Exchange, and Over the Counter (OTC) Trading. These exchanges house the buying and selling of securities that are listed on the particular exchange. This buying and selling represents the primary function of the secondary market.

THIRD AND FOURTH MARKETS

The **third market** consists of over-the-counter trading of equity shares that are listed on an exchange. This market is important especially when the exchanges are not trading a security or before the opening of the exchange or after the close of the exchange.

third market - over-the-counter trading of equity shares that are listed on an exchange

fourth market - comprised of institutional traders that trade without the help of brokers

The **fourth market** is comprised of traders who trade without the help of brokers. They trade directly with other interested parties. These traders can make use of the communication systems such as Instinet to allow them to find other interested parties. Most of these traders are institutional type investors, with very large volumes.

EXHIBIT 14.5: THIRD AND FOURTH MARKETS

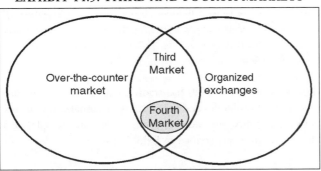

MARKET INDEXES AND AVERAGES

The purpose of a market index or average is to provide information to investors and advisors concerning the overall movement and performance of the securities markets. Since most securities are positively correlated with their respective index, these securities tend to increase when their index is increasing and decrease when their index is decreasing.

Dow Jones Industrial Average

The **Dow Jones Industrial Average (DJIA)** is probably the best-known financial index in the United States. It is a price weighted average of thirty leading industrial stocks used to measure the status of the equity market. The thirty stocks currently included in the DJIA are identified in Exhibit 14.6.

Dow Jones Industrial Average (DJIA) - a financial index that is a price weighted average of thirty leading industrial stocks used to measure the status of the equity market

EXHIBIT 14.6: DJIA STOCKS
(As of July 2001)

AT & T	Eastman Kodak	Intel	Philip Morris
Alcoa	ExxonMobil	International Paper	Proctor & Gamble
American Express	General Electric	J P Morgan	SBC Communications
Boeing	General Motors	Johnson & Johnson	United Technologies
Caterpillar	Hewlett-Packard	McDonalds	Wal-Mart
Citigroup	Home Depot	Merck	Walt Disney
Coca Cola	Honeywell	Microsoft	
Du Pont	IBM	Minnesota Mining & Mfr.	

The DJIA consists of stocks that are generally considered to be blue-chip stocks. Although these companies are often some of the leaders in their industry, the composition of the average does change over time.

Standard & Poor's 500 Index

Standard & Poor's Index (S&P 500) - a financial index of 500 U.S. equities based on market size, liquidity, and industry group representation

The **Standard & Poor's Index (S&P 500)** has traditionally been the measure of the U.S. large capitalization market used by academics and financial professionals. It consists of 500 U.S. equities based on market size, liquidity, and industry group representation. These 500 stocks are currently represented by the industries described in Exhibit 14.7.

EXHIBIT 14.7: S&P 500 INDUSTRY GROUP REPRESENTATION
(As of May 31, 2001)

Industry	# of Companies	# of Companies As % of 500
Consumer Discretionary	85	17.0%
Consumer Staples	37	7.4%
Energy	26	5.2%
Financials	70	14.0%
Health Care	41	8.2%
Industrials	70	14.0%
Information Technology	77	15.4%
Materials	41	8.2%
Telecommunication Services	13	2.6%
Utilities	40	8.0%
	500	100%

Of the 500 securities, 426 are listed on the New York Stock Exchange (NYSE), while the remaining stocks are listed on the NASDAQ and the American Stock Exchange (AMEX). The 500 securities that make up the index have a market value of over $11 trillion.

The S&P 500 index is a market value weighted index. This means that a company's market capitalization (outstanding shares times the current stock price) is represented in the index. Market value indexes typically provide a better measure of the market than averages, such as the DJIA (however, the DJIA is highly correlated to the S&P 500 index).

In addition to the S&P 500 index, Standard & Poor's maintains numerous other U.S. indexes, including:

▲ S&P MidCap 400 Index
▲ S&P SmallCap 600 Index
▲ S&P SuperComposite 1500
▲ S&P 100 Index
▲ S&P/BARRA Growth and Value Indexes

Each of these indexes provides a different view of the U.S. market.

NASDAQ

The **NASDAQ** system began in 1971 and was the first electronic trading system. The NASDAQ is one of the fastest growing indexes in the world. Many of today's leading technology and Internet related companies are listed on NASDAQ. Exhibit 14.8 describes the history of this index.

NASDAQ - the first electronic trading system made up of leading technology and Internet-related companies

EXHIBIT 14.8: HISTORY OF THE NASDAQ INDEX

1961	In an effort to improve overall regulation of the securities industry, Congress asks the U.S. Securities and Exchange Commission (SEC) to conduct a special study of all securities markets.
1963	The SEC releases the completed study, in which it characterizes the over-the-counter (OTC) securities market as fragmented and obscure. The SEC proposes a solution—automation—and charges The National Association of Securities Dealers, Inc. (NASD) with its implementation.
1968	Construction begins on the automated over-the-counter securities system—then known as the National Association of Securities Dealers Automated Quotation—or "NASDAQ"—System.
1971	Nasdaq celebrates its first official trading day on February 8th—the first day of operation for the completed NASDAQ automated system, which displays median quotes for more than 2500 over-the-counter securities.
1975	Nasdaq establishes new listing standards—which it requires all listed companies to meet—effectively separating Nasdaq-listed securities from other OTC securities.
1980	Nasdaq begins to display inside quotations—the market's best bid and offer prices—on-screen. As a result, both displayed and published spreads decline on more than 85 percent of Nasdaq stocks.
1982	The top Nasdaq companies split off to form the Nasdaq National Market®, which requires higher listing standards. The Nasdaq National Market also offers real-time trade reporting, which provides investors with broader access to market information.
1984	Nasdaq introduces the Small Order Execution System (SOES SM). Designed to automatically execute small orders against the best quotations, SOES enhances Nasdaq' trading capacity and efficiency.
1986	The Federal Reserve Board grants Nasdaq National Market stocks marginability, meaning that customers can purchase these securities on credit extended by a broker/dealer.
1990	Nasdaq formally changes its name to "The Nasdaq Stock Market."Creation of the OTC Bulletin Board SM (OTCBB) gives investors information on and access to securities not listed on Nasdaq.
1991	Nasdaq National Market securities attain virtual parity with the NYSE and AMEX on blue-sky laws—applicable state laws concerning the registration and sale of new securities. (*Note: The National Securities Market Improvement Act of 1996 mandated that all states must exempt Nasdaq National Market securities from state blue-sky regulations*).
1992	Nasdaq International SM Service begins operation, allowing Nasdaq National Market securities to be traded during early morning hours, when the London financial markets are open. Real-time trade reporting is initiated for The Nasdaq SmallCap Market SM.
1994	A landmark year: The Nasdaq Stock Market surpasses the New York Stock Exchange in annual share volume.
1997	The SEC approves Nasdaq' request to begin quoting in 1/16ths of a dollar for stocks trading above $10. Nasdaq implements new order handling rules. In combination with Nasdaq' move to quoting in 1/16ths, these rules produce better prices and an average spread reduction of 40%.
1998	Merger between the NASD and the AMEX creates The Nasdaq-Amex Market Group.

Nasdaq Highlights: 1998
The Nasdaq Stock Market closed 1998 with the Nasdaq CompositeSM Index gaining over 20 percent for a fourth consecutive year, closing up 39.6%.
In 1998, Nasdaq® had nine days with more than one-billion shares trading hands.
For the year, share volume reached 202.0 billion, up 23 percent from 163.9 billion in 1997.
The market value of the 5,126 companies listed on Nasdaq stood at $2.6 trillion, up over 44 percent from year-end 1997.
This year saw 273 initial public offerings that raised just under $14 billion.
The market's best index performers were the Nasdaq Computer and Telecommunications, up 83.3 percent and 63.4 percent, respectively.
The Nasdaq-100 Index® was up 85.3 percent over 1997. The Nasdaq Composite at year end stood at 2192.69, up 39.6 percent from 1570.35 in 1997.
The dollar value of trading on Nasdaq in 1998 surpassed the previous record of $4.5 trillion in 1997 by 28 percent; 1998 trading was valued at $5.8 trillion.
Average daily share volume on Nasdaq reached over 802 million shares in 1998, up from 648 million shares in 1997.
Twelve non-U.S. companies listed on Nasdaq in the fourth quarter of 1998, bringing the total number of foreign companies listed to 440, more than on any other U.S. market.

Russell Indexes

The Frank Russell Company maintains over 21 U.S. stock indexes, as well as foreign indexes in Australia, Canada, Japan, and the United Kingdom. All of the **Russell Indexes** are market capitalization weighted and the 21 U.S. indexes are subsets of the Russell 3000 Index, which represents the majority of U.S. equities. The Russell 2000 Index is a well-known index that is used to benchmark small capitalization companies. The Russell 1000 Index represents the thousand largest companies in the Russell 3000 Index. Russell also maintains numerous value and growth indexes that allow for comparisons with various portfolio manager styles.

Wilshire 5000 Index

The **Wilshire 5000 Index** is another well-known index that is used as a measure of the U.S. broad market. It consists of over 7000 U.S. based companies and is often used as a measure of the overall market within the United States.

EAFE Index

In 1969, the Europe, Australia, and Far East (**EAFE**) **index** was created as a measure of the international securities markets. It provides an indication of how a portfolio consisting of companies outside the United States might perform over time. It is probably the most well known measure of international markets.

BENCHMARKS

The indexes discussed above can all be used as a comparison with a portfolio manager's performance to determine whether the manager is performing well or not. Although many investors use comparisons to other managers as a measure of performance, benchmarks should contain certain characteristics. The primary characteristics of a good benchmark include the following:

- ▲ Unambiguous. The composition and weighting of the components of the benchmark must be clearly delineated.
- ▲ Investable. The option to invest in the benchmark is available.
- ▲ Measurable. It should be possible to calculate the benchmark's return on a relatively frequent basis.
- ▲ Appropriate. The benchmark must be consistent with the manager's investment philosophy and style.
- ▲ Reflective of current investment opinions. The manager has current investment knowledge of the securities that make up the benchmark.
- ▲ Specified in advance. The benchmark should be constructed before the beginning of the evaluation period.

These six properties improve the usefulness of a benchmark as an investment management tool and allow for a better measure of a portfolio manager's performance.

Russell Indexes - a collection of financial indexes made up of over 21 U.S. stock indexes, as well as foreign indexes in Australia, Canada, Japan, and the United Kingdom, maintained by the Frank Russell Company

Wilshire 5000 Index - a financial index consisting of over 7,000 U.S. based companies that is often used as a measure of the overall market within the U.S.

EAFE Index - the Europe, Australia, and Far East (EAFE) index created as a measure of the international securities markets

MEASURES OF RETURN

As we have discussed, the primary purpose of investing is to earn returns. Investors seek out investments that are consistent with their risk and return preferences in attempts of achieving their financial goals. Therefore, it is important to be able to understand and calculate the returns from equity securities. There are several methods of calculating returns from equity securities, each with their advantages and disadvantages. We will examine holding period return, arithmetic mean, geometric mean, time weighted return, dollar weighted return, and dividend yield.

HOLDING PERIOD RETURN

holding period return - measures the total return an investor receives over the life of an investment

The **holding period return** is a basic measure of an investment's rate of return over the lifetime of the investment. It is sometimes referred to as the single period rate of return. The holding period return measures the change in value of an investment over the holding period and is calculated as follows:

$$HPR = \frac{Ending\ Value\ of\ Investment - Beginning\ Value\ of\ Investment +/- Cashflows}{Beginning\ Value\ of\ Investment}$$

EXAMPLE

Morgan buys one share of ABC stock for $25 and sells it for $35. During the holding period, the stock pays total dividends of $5. The holding period return for this investment is calculated as follows:

$$HPR = \frac{\$35 - \$25 + \$5}{\$25} = 0.60\ or\ 60\%$$

Therefore, the holding period return for Morgan is 60 percent. However, knowing this return does not indicate how well the investment performed because there is no indication of the time over which the investment was held. If the investment was held for a week, the 60 percent return is probably very good. However, if the investment was held for ten years, it may not be very good. The holding period return is often used as a measure of return for a single period, such as a year or a month.

ARITHMETIC MEAN

arithmetic mean - also called the arithmetic average rate of return; a measure of investment return that is the result of averaging period returns

Investors often evaluate holding period returns of an investment for a certain length of time. One easy method of evaluating these periodic returns is to determine the **arithmetic mean**. The arithmetic mean is calculated by dividing the sum of the returns for each period by the total number of periods (*n*) being evaluated. The formula is written as follows:

$$AM = \frac{\sum_{t=1}^{n} HPR_t}{n}$$

Assume ABC stock earned the following returns over the last five years:

Year	Return
1	10%
2	5%
3	20%
4	0%
5	-12%

The arithmetic return is calculated as follows:

$$AM = \frac{10\% + 5\% + 20\% + 0\% + -12\%}{5} = 4.6\%$$

Therefore, ABC stock has earned an average return over the five-year period of 4.6 percent per year.

GEOMETRIC MEAN

Although the arithmetic mean is an extremely common measure that is used by many, the **geometric mean** is considered a better and truer measure of the return from a security over time. The geometric mean is calculated using the following formula:

$$GM = \sqrt[n]{(1+R_1)(1+R_2)\cdots(1+R_n)} - 1$$, where

geometric mean - also known as geometric average return; a method of calculating the internal rate of return based on periodic rates of return

R_n = Return for period n

n = Number of periods in the analysis

Using the historical data for ABC stock from above, the GM is calculated as follows:

$$GM = \sqrt[5]{(1+.10)(1+.05)(1+.20)(1+0)(1+-.12)} - 1$$

$$GM = \sqrt[5]{1.21968} - 1$$

$$GM = 4.05\%$$

Notice that the return for the geometric mean is less than the arithmetic mean. As we discussed in Chapter 12, the geometric mean will always be less than the arithmetic mean, except when the returns for each period are the same. The difference between the arithmetic mean and the geometric mean will be exaggerated as the volatility of returns increases. The calculation of the geometric mean is one method of calculating the time-weighted rate of return.

Another way to calculate the geometric mean is to use the present value keys of a financial calculator. Assume that $100 is invested into an account that earns 10 percent the first year, 5 percent the second year, 20 percent the third year, zero in the fourth year, and loses 12 percent in the fifth year. How much is in the account at the end of the fifth year? The answer is $121.97, which can be calculated by multiplying the $100 times the sum of one plus each years return (just as we did in the GM calculation). Once the future value is determined, it is simple to determine the GM.

Keystroke	Display
100 [CHS][PV]	-100.0000
5[n]	5.0000
121.97[FV]	121.9700
[i]	4.0520

Therefore, over the five-year period, the investment earned an annualized return of 4.05 percent per year.

TIME WEIGHTED AND DOLLAR WEIGHTED RETURNS

Although time weighted returns and dollar weighted returns are both methods of determining an internal rate of return, they have very different purposes. **Time weighted returns** are used as a method of evaluating the performance of portfolio managers without the influence of cash inflows or outflows to or from the portfolio. **Dollar weighted returns** are used to determine the rate of return an individual investor earned based on the investor's particular cash flows into and out of the portfolio. The following example illustrates the difference between dollar-weighted returns and time weighted returns.

Assume we are comparing two portfolio managers, A and B. Over a four-year period, they each earn exactly the same return per period. However, each portfolio manager has different sets of cash inflows and outflows from their portfolios.

PORTFOLIO MANAGER A				
Period	Cash Inflow or Outflow	Beginning of Period Value	End of Period Value	Periodic Rate of Return
0	1000	1000	1200	20.00%
1	(400)	800	700	-12.50%
2	300	1000	1400	40.00%
3	(200)	1200	1000	-16.67%
4	(1000)	-	-	-
DWR =	8.2311%		TWR =	5.2044%

time weighted returns - a method of determining an internal rate of return by evaluating the performance of portfolio managers without the influence of cash inflows or outflows to or from the portfolio

dollar weighted returns - a method of determining an internal rate of return an individual investor earned based on the investor's particular cash flow into and out of the portfolio

	PORTFOLIO MANAGER B			
Period	Cash Inflow or Outflow	Beginning of Period Value	End of Period Value	Periodic Rate of Return
0	1000	1000	1200	20.00%
1	400	1600	1400	-12.50%
2	(400)	1000	1400	40.00%
3	400	1800	1500	-16.67%
4	(1500)	-	-	-
DWR =	2.0245%		TWR =	5.2044%

Using the uneven cash flow keys of a financial calculator, we have calculated the dollar weighted return (DWR) for Portfolio Manager A to be 8.23 percent, while the DWR for Portfolio Manager B equals 2.02 percent. Is it reasonable to use a methodology that results in drastically different returns when each manager produced the same periodic rates of return? The simple answer is no. The dollar weighted return should not be used to evaluate managers for this very reason.

Time Weighted Return

The time weighted return is used to compare returns from portfolio managers without the influence of cash inflows and outflows. The above example is a clear indication of what can happen when dollar weighted returns are used to evaluate portfolio manager performance. The cash flows of Portfolio Manager A helped his overall performance while the cash flows of Portfolio Manager B hurt his performance.

To compare these two managers, we can use the geometric mean calculation to determine the time weighted return for each manager:

$$TWR = \sqrt[4]{(1+.20)(1+-.1250)(1+.40)(1+-.1667)} - 1$$

$$TWR = \sqrt[4]{1.225} - 1$$

$$TWR = 5.2044\%$$

Since each manager had the same periodic returns over the four periods, their time weighted returns both equal 5.20 percent.

Dollar Weighted Return

Although we illustrated how the dollar weighted return can erroneously influence our decision about the performance of a portfolio manager, the dollar weighted return has its usefulness. The dollar weighted return is most appropriately used for determining a client's return over time when the client is either investing additional money into the account or removing money from the account, or some combination of both. For example, assume the above charts actually represent different clients with their unique cash flows. Although each client had the same periodic returns, their overall dollar weighted returns would be quite different and quite relevant to each client.

The dollar weighted return is calculated using the cash flows for each period. The above DWRs are calculated as follows:

Portfolio Manager A

Keystroke	Display
[f][CLX]	0.0000
1000[CHS]	-1,000
[g] [CF$_o$]	-1,000.0000
400[g][CF$_j$]	400.0000
300[CHS]	-300
[g][CF$_j$]	-300.0000
200[g][CF$_j$]	200.0000
1000[g][CF$_j$]	1,000.0000
[f][IRR]	8.2311

Portfolio Manager B

Keystroke	Display
[f][CLX]	0.0000
1000[CHS]	-1,000
[g] [CF$_o$]	-1,000.0000
400[CHS]	-400
[g][CF$_j$]	-400.0000
400 [g][CF$_j$]	400.0000
400[CHS]	-400
[g][CF$_j$]	-400.0000
1500[g][CF$_j$]	1,500.0000
[f][IRR]	2.0245

The primary reason that the DWR for each client is so different is that in the case of client A, the cash inflows were in periods of positive performance and the cash outflows were in periods of negative performance. For client B, just the opposite is true. Cash inflows were in periods of negative performance, while cash outflows were in periods of positive performance.

DIVIDEND YIELD

We defined income stocks as those with high dividend payments compared to other stocks. The measure used to compare the dividend payments from one company to another is called the **dividend yield** and is calculated as follows:

$$DY = \frac{\text{Dividend per share}}{\text{Market Price of the Stock}}$$

If XYZ Company is paying a dividend of $4 per share and the current market price of the stock is $50, then the dividend yield of XYZ equals 8 percent ($4 ÷ $50).

The dividend yield measure is useful for selecting stocks to be included in a portfolio for an investor who needs the income derived from the portfolio. Stocks that have high dividend yields are included, while those that have low dividend yields are excluded.

PURCHASING EQUITY SECURITIES

LONG POSITIONS

The most prevalent type of position investors take is referred to as a long position. A **long position** is simply where an investor will purchase a stock in hopes that it will appreciate over time. If a stock is purchased for $45 and is sold for $100, then the stock has increased, resulting in a gain of $55.

SHORT POSITIONS

Investors may also benefit in the market when they find securities that are overvalued. A short sale allows the investor to benefit from the decline in the value of the security. A short sale is the process of selling shares that are not owned by the investor. This transaction is accomplished by borrowing shares of stock from a broker. Once the shares are sold in the market, the investor is credited with the proceeds. However, the investor must, at some point, replace the borrowed shares. This is known as covering the **short position** and is accomplished by purchasing the shares in the market and replacing the shares that were borrowed.

The short seller will be profitable if the shares can be purchased at a price less than the price at which the shares were sold. If the stock appreciates after the shares are sold short, then the investor will lose money.

Three technical issues must be discussed regarding short selling. First, a short sale must occur on an uptick or zero plus tick. A zero plus tick is a zero tick which has been proceeded by a plus tick or uptick. The uptick rule requires that the security trade up in price before the short sale can be executed.

dividend yield - the measure of a securities dividend payment as a percent of the current market price

EXAMPLE

long position - the most prevalent type of position investors take when purchasing equity securities where an investor will purchase a stock in hopes that it will appreciate over time

short position - a type of position investors take by selling borrowed shares in hopes that the stock price will decline over time

If ABC stock trades at the following prices: $45.00, $44.50, $44.50, $41.00, $41.50, $41.50, $42.00, then a short sale could not occur until the stock price moved from $41.00 to $41.50. The price of $41.50 represents the first uptick in the series. The second trade at $41.50 represents a zero tick or zero plus tick.

The second issue concerning short sales is that of dividend payments that occur before closing the short position. A short sale involves borrowing stock and selling it in the market. At the time of a short sale, two investors believe that they own the stock and are entitled to receive any dividend payment that is declared and paid. However, the company declaring the dividend will only recognize one owner (the third party who purchased the shares in the market) and will only make one dividend payment. Therefore, it is the responsibility and requirement of the short seller to make up the other dividend payment to the party from whom the stock was originally borrowed. From an economic standpoint, paying this dividend is irrelevant since the price of the security should decline by the same amount as the dividend payment.

The third issue is that short sellers are required to have a margin account and post margin just as if an investor was acquiring stock. If the stock increases, then the short seller may be required to restore his margin. This issue is discussed below from the standpoint of an investor acquiring stock.

MARGIN ACCOUNTS

cash accounts - a type of brokerage account that requires that all securities purchased by the investor be paid for in full without any indebtedness

When an investor opens a brokerage account, it is either a cash account or a margin account. **Cash accounts** require that all securities purchased by the investor be paid for in full without any indebtedness. If a cash account is fully invested in securities, then the only way to purchase additional securities is to add cash to the account or sell some of the current securities to generate cash. In contrast, **margin accounts** allow the investor to borrow funds from the broker to purchase additional securities without adding additional cash to the account. Margin accounts allows investors flexibility and the ability to leverage the account.

margin accounts - a type of brokerage account that allows the investor to borrow funds from the broker to purchase additional securities without adding additional cash to the account

Margin accounts require that the account owner pay for a certain percentage of the cost of an investment. The margin percentage that must be established for the purchase of a security is referred to as the initial margin. The Federal Reserve sets the initial margin percentage, which is currently 50 percent. Therefore, the initial purchase of a security requires that the investor put up at least 50 percent of the initial purchase.

In addition to the amount that must be initially put up by the investor, the investor must maintain an equity position in the account that equals or exceeds the maintenance margin. The maintenance margin is typically 35 percent, which means that the equity in the account must equal or exceed 35 percent. If the equity in the account drops below the maintenance margin, then the account holder receives a margin call from the broker. A margin call is a request for funds to restore the account equity to the maintenance margin.

Determining the Price for a Margin Call

The account equity is defined as the market value of the securities in the account less the outstanding debt. The equity percentage equals the account equity divided by the market value of the securities. The price at which a margin call is received occurs at the point that the equity percentage drops below the maintenance margin. Therefore, we can solve for the price (or account value) when a margin call will be received by setting the equity percentage equal to the maintenance margin, as follows:

$$\frac{\text{Account Value} - \text{Debt}}{\text{Account Value}} = \text{Maintenance Margin}$$

$$\text{Account Value} - \text{Debt} = \text{Maintenance Margin} \times \text{Account Value}$$

$$\text{Account Value} - (\text{Maintenance Margin} \times \text{Account Value}) = \text{Debt}$$

$$\text{Account Value} \times (1 - \text{Maintenance Margin}) = \text{Debt}$$

$$\text{Account Value} = \frac{\text{Debt}}{1 - \text{Maintenance Margin}}$$

Hardy purchases one share of Solvent Company for $104. Hardy uses a margin account with a 50 percent initial margin for the purchase and is concerned about receiving a margin call. If the maintenance margin equals 35 percent, then Hardy will receive a margin call if the stock declines below $80, as illustrated below:

EXAMPLE

$$\text{Account Value} = \frac{\text{Debt}}{1 - \text{Maintenance Margin}}$$

$$\text{Account Value} = \frac{\$52}{1 - 0.35} = \$80$$

Determining How Much to Put Up to Restore the Account Equity

If the stock or account drops below the price at which there is a margin call, then the account owner must deposit sufficient funds to restore the account equity to the maintenance margin. Determining this amount can be accomplished by asking two questions. How much equity does the broker require? And, how much equity does the investor currently have?

Using the above example, assume that the stock drops in value to $70. In such a case, Hardy would be required to put up $6.50 per share ($24.50 - $18.00).

Required Equity		Current Equity Position	
Current Value of Stock	$70.00	Current Value of Stock	$70.00
Equity %	35%	Loan Amount	(52.00)
Required Equity	$24.50	Equity	$18.00

Regardless of the price of the security (or account), the investor must maintain an equity position of 35 percent, which is the given maintenance margin. Therefore, because the price of the stock is currently $70, Hardy must have $24.50 ($70 x 35%) of equity in his account. To determine Hardy's current equity position, subtract the outstanding debt from the value of the stock. Since his current equity position equals $18 and he must have $24.50 of equity, Hardy must fund the account with the difference of $6.50.

TYPES OF ORDERS

When purchasing equity investments it is important to understand the different types of orders that can be used to acquire shares of common stock. The four standard types of orders include market orders, limit orders, stop loss orders, and stop limit orders. All orders are considered day orders unless otherwise specified. If an order is not filled within the trading day, it will expire. Orders can be good for a specific length of time, or they can be "good-til-cancel." Time limits are often used with limit and stop orders because they are not as likely to be filled during the day, as are market orders.

Market Order

The majority of orders are market orders. In fact, 75 percent to 80 percent of all orders have traditionally been market orders, and these orders have the highest priority. A market order is an order to buy or sell a security at the best current market price. These orders must be filled prior to other types of orders being considered. However, while these are the fastest orders, they do not have limits or a specific price and, therefore, are subject to the fluctuations and timeliness of the market.

It is possible that an investor puts in a market order to buy when the stock is trading at $22 per share, and his order is filled at $23. This might occur because there are more buy orders than sell orders, which causes the market price to increase.

Limit Order

The objective of a limit order is to acquire or sell a security at a specific price; one that is better than the market at the time the order is placed. The price acts as a ceiling for purchases and a floor for sales, and the order will be held until filled or canceled. Limit orders are maintained in chronological order. Higher priced purchase limit orders take priority over lower priced purchase limit orders. Even if the price for the stock is below (or above) the limit order, there is no guarantee that it will be filled.

EXAMPLE

David, a shrewd investor, has analyzed all the relevant financial information and has determined that the Ashbey Corporation is worth $45 per share. While the stock is trading between $48 and $50, he places a limit order at $45. This will assure that if the order is filled to purchase shares of Ashbey Corporation, David's price will be no higher than $45. If Ashbey continues to trade above $45, David's order will not be filled.

Stop Loss Order

Stop loss orders are used to protect investors from large losses. If the market price reaches a certain point, the stop order will turn into a market order. For instance, an investor who is long in a security might place a stop order at 10 points below the current market price to protect the appreciation of the stock against serious declines in market price. Likewise, these orders can be used to limit losses in connection with short sales.

Steve purchased Roland, Inc. for $29 per share. It is now trading at $73 per share. He has an unrealized gain of $44. If Steve is concerned about the price of the stock declining, he can place a stop order at $70. If the stock price drops to $70, a market order is placed immediately. However, it may be filled at $69 or $68. The stop order protects his profit position.

EXAMPLE

Stop Limit Order

Stop limit orders are similar to stop loss orders except they turn into limit orders when triggered. The stop order price and the limit order price are both specified. Stop limit orders are the least often used types of orders.

If Dina owns 5,000 shares of Prez's Pretzels, which is selling at $35 per share, and she is concerned about the price dropping, she may want to place a stop limit order. If she places the order "sell 5,000 shares at $32 stop, $30 limit," and the price drops to $32, the broker will attempt to sell the stock for $32 but will not sell below the $30 limit order.

EXAMPLE

Online Trading

With access to the Internet increasing, online trading of securities is increasingly popular. **Online trading** is a method of buying and selling securities over the Internet without the use of a broker. While Schwab was the first brokerage house to allow account holders to trade over the Internet, most brokerage houses now have the ability to accept trades over the Internet. Trading over the Internet has become so popular that there are brokerage houses that are almost exclusively tailoring themselves to online traders.

online trading - a method of buying and selling securities over the Internet without the use of a broker

Exhibit 14.9 is a sample of TD Waterhouse's webBroker that allows customers to buy and sell securities over the Internet. The form allows for trades of stocks, options, mutual funds, and bonds. The form also allows for market orders, limit orders, and stop loss orders.

509

TD WATERHOUSE webBroker

Help | Customer Service | Log Off

Welcome | Trading | Account | Quotes | Research | Tools | IPO Center | webBanking

Order Status | Stocks | Options | Mutual Funds | Extended Hours | Bonds

Stocks

Account: XXXXXXXX

Order to:	Select Action ▾	webBroker Trading Limitations Bottom of Form
Number of Shares:	☐ **All or none**	Trading in volatile markets
Symbol:		
Order Type:	Select an Order Type ▾	*Please note that "stop-limit" orders cannot be placed via TD Waterhouse webBroker.*
Limit or Stop Price:		*Please contact an Account Officer to place a "stop-limit" order.*
Time Limit:	Good for the Day ▾	
Account Type:	Please Select Account ▾	
Telephone #:	**Ext.**	

In addition to enhancing the trading of securities over the Internet, these online brokers allow customers to research securities directly from their personal computers. Although trading over the Internet is relatively new, it seems to be the trend that will continue for some time.

VALUATION METHODS

There are two primary methods of valuing and analyzing equity securities. These methods are technical analysis and fundamental analysis. Each method is discussed below.

TECHNICAL ANALYSIS

technical analysis - the search for identifiable and recurring stock price patterns

Technical analysis is an attempt to determine the demand side of the supply/demand equation for a particular stock or set of stocks. This methodology is based on the belief that studying the history of security trades will help predict movements in the future. These technical analysts or chartists, referring to the reliance on charts, believe that the history of the stock price will tell the whole story of the security and that there is no need to be concerned with earnings, financial leverage, product mix, and management philosophy. Recall that technical analysis is in direct contradiction to the efficient market hypothesis which, at all levels, states that the current price already reflects all historical price data. Technical analysts believe there are basic economic assumptions that support the theories of technical analysis. These assumptions include the following:

- ▲ The interaction between supply and demand is the foundation for the value of any good or service.
- ▲ Both rational and irrational factors control supply and demand. The market weighs each of these factors.
- ▲ Generally, both the market and individual securities tend to move in similar trends that endure for substantial lengths of time.
- ▲ Variations in the relationship between supply and demand cause changes in the prevailing trends.
- ▲ Shifts or variations in supply and demand can always be detected in the movement of the market.

Technical analysts use a variety of techniques to predict the trend of the market, such as moving averages, relative strength analysis, contrary opinion rules, and breadth of the market indicators. One of the most significant stock price and volume techniques is referred to as the Dow theory.

The Dow theory was developed initially by Charles H. Dow and later expanded by William Hamilton. It is the basis for many of the theories of technical analysis. The Dow theory suggests three types of price movements. Primary moves are the first type of movement and represent large trends that last anywhere from one to four years. These moves are considered bull or bear markets for up or down moves, respectively. The second type of movement is called an intermediate move that is a temporary change in movement called a technical correction. The time frame for these corrections is generally less than two months. The final type of movement is referred to as a ripple that occurs during both primary and secondary movements and represents a small change in comparison to the first two movements. It is believed that all three of these movements are occurring at the same time.

The Dow Theory uses the Dow Jones Industrial Average (DJIA) and the Dow Jones Transportation Average (DJTA) as indicators of the market. This theory is based on the concept that measures of stock prices, such as averages and indexes, should move coincidentally. Thus, if the DJIA is moving upwards, the DJTA should also be increasing. Support from both market indicators would suggest a strong bull market. Likewise, if both averages are declining, there is considerable support for a strong bear market. When the averages are moving in opposite directions, then the future direction of stock prices is unclear.

FUNDAMENTAL ANALYSIS

Fundamental analysis is the process of determining the true value of a security. This true value is referred to as the intrinsic value and it is generally thought of as the present value of the future cash flows (often times the dividend stream of an equity security). Through fundamental analysis, investors attempt to determine what the company is worth. Once the value is determined, it is compared to the market value of the security. If the market value of the security is less than the intrinsic value, then the investor will purchase the security. If the market value of the security is greater than the intrinsic value, then the investor should sell the shares currently held or at least not buy additional shares of the security.

fundamental analysis - the analysis of a stock's value using basic, publicly available data such as the stock's earnings, sales, risk, and industry analysis

The process of determining the value of a security encompasses many aspects. The fundamental analyst incorporates broad macroeconomic trends, industry analysis, and company analysis into his estimate of the value of a security. The analysis of broad economic trends includes analyzing growth of the economy, analyzing monetary and fiscal policy, interest rates, unemployment, consumer spending, and inflation. Analysts look at industry data to determine market competitiveness, strengths and weaknesses, and other factors that impact on the value of a security within the context of its industry. At the company level, fundamental analysts use financial statement analysis, valuation models, and ratio analysis to assist in determining a company's worth. Once forecasts about future cash flows are developed, a fundamental analyst uses the valuation models to determine the value of the company.

VALUATION MODELS

One of the keys to selecting a stock to invest in is to determine its value. The value of a common stock is equal to the present value of its future cash flows. Conceptually, we use the same model to value all securities, whether bonds, preferred stock, or common stock. However, each case has its unique issues that must be accounted for.

The basic model for valuing any security or project is as follows:

$$PV = \frac{Cf_1}{(1+k)^1} + \frac{Cf_2}{(1+k)^2} + \cdots + \frac{Cf_n}{(1+k)^n} \quad \text{or} \quad PV = \sum_{t=1}^{n} \frac{Cf_t}{(1+k)^t}$$

In this model, Cf_n represents the cash flow for period n and k represents the internal rate of return or the required rate of return. This model is the same basic model that we used to value bonds. The series of cash flows are discounted at an appropriate discount rate to determine the value of the security.

VALUING PREFERRED STOCK

Because preferred stock generally pays a fixed dividend, it is considered a perpetuity. In other words, the dividend continues indefinitely. Therefore, we can use a simplified version of the above model to determine the value of preferred stock. The model used to value preferred stock is as follows:

$$V = \frac{D}{k}$$

The value of preferred stock equals the dividend (D) divided by the required rate of return of the investor (k). For example, if a preferred stock is paying a dividend of $6 and the investor's required rate of return equals 12 percent, then the value of the preferred stock should equal $50:

$$V = \frac{\$6}{0.12} = \$50$$

If the current market price of the security was greater than $50, then the investor should not purchase the preferred stock as an investment. However, if the stock were trading at a price of $50 or less, then the purchase of the security would be a wise decision.

DIVIDEND DISCOUNT MODEL

Common stock dividends do not typically remain steady over time. Generally, the dividend from common stock grows over time. Assuming a constant rate of growth for the dividend, we can expand the above model to accommodate the growth component of the dividend stream. The following formula is used to value common stock with a constant growing dividend:

$$V_0 = \frac{D_1}{k - g}$$

The value of common stock equals the dividend one period from today (D_1) divided by the difference between the investor's required rate of return (k) and the growth of the dividend (g).

A common stock is paying a dividend that is currently $6 and is growing at a constant rate of 6 percent per year. If the investor's required rate of return equals 12 percent, then the value of the common stock equals $106:

$$V = \frac{\$6(1.06)}{0.12 - 0.06} = \$106$$

EXAMPLE

D_1 must be determined by multiplying the current dividend (D_0) by one plus the growth rate $(1+ g)$. The model is based on a constant growing dividend and on the required return of the investor. Notice that the model will not work if the growth rate (g) equals or exceeds the required rate of return of the investor (k).

Both the preferred stock and the common stock are currently paying a dividend of $6 per share. However, the value of the common stock is $56 more than the value of the preferred stock. The reason for this difference is the growth of the future dividends. Therefore, the growth of the future dividends can be valued at $56.

PRICE TO EARNINGS (P/E) RATIO

The price to earnings (P/E) ratio is a measure of how much the market is willing to pay for each dollar of earnings of a company. The **P/E ratio** is determined by dividing the current market price of the security by the earnings per share (EPS) for the company:

$$\text{Price to Earnings Ratio} = \frac{\text{Market Price per Share}}{\text{Earnings per Share}}$$

P/E ratio - a measure of how much the market is willing to pay for each dollar of earnings of a company; the price per earnings ratio

EXAMPLE   If XYZ stock is trading at $50 per share and it has earnings per share of $4, then its P/E ratio equals 12.5.

The P/E ratio can be viewed differently by using the constant growth dividend model as the price and dividing both sides of the equation by earnings (*E*). This is illustrated below:

$$V = P = \frac{D_1}{k - g}$$

$$P/E = \frac{D_1/E}{k - g}$$

Based on this model, the P/E ratio is dependant on three components. The first component is referred to as the payout ratio (D_1/E). The payout ratio represents the portion of earnings that a company pays to the shareholders in the form of dividend payments. The second component is the required return for the security, and the third is the growth of the dividend payment.

The P/E ratio is used to measure how expensive a stock is priced. Better quality companies generally have higher P/E ratios than lower quality companies. Investors are willing to pay more for each dollar of earnings from a high quality company.

The P/E ratio is also used for comparing companies within the same industry. Generally, an industry will consist of companies that have similar P/E ratios. This allows investors to compare companies within the same industry based on how expensive the market prices of the companies are within the industry.

VALUING THE COMPANY VERSUS VALUING THE STOCK

Up to this point, we have confined our valuation methodology to those stocks that pay dividends. With preferred stock, we use the valuation of perpetuity to determine its price. Similarly, we valued common stock with a constant growing dividend. However, what about those companies that do not pay dividends, such as Microsoft. Since these companies do not pay dividends, our valuation models do not seem to work. However, our focus simply needs to shift from the valuation of the stock to the valuation of the company. Instead of looking at the cash flows from the security, we need to address the cash flows that are generated by the company.

By using the same models developed for finding the present value of any stream of cash flows, the value of the company can be obtained. The obvious inputs in the model are the relevant cash flows and the discount rate.

514

The term **"free cash flow to equity"** describes the available cash after meeting all of the firms operating and financial needs. It is generally calculated as follows:

	Revenue
-	Operating expenses
=	**Earnings before interest, taxes and depreciation (EBITDA)**
-	Depreciation
-	Amortization
=	**Earnings before interest and taxes (EBIT)**
-	Interest
-	Taxes
=	Net Income
+	Depreciation
+	Amortization
=	*Cash flows from operations*
-	Preferred dividends
-	Capital expenditures
-	Working capital needs
-	Principal repayments (loan)
+	Proceeds from new debt issues
=	*Free cash flow to equity*

Once the cash flow is forecasted, then it can be used to value the company. The discount rate that is used can be derived from reviewing comparable companies in the market or by using models such as the Capital Asset Pricing Model, which is discussed below.

Once the value of the company is established, then the value of the stock can be derived from the company's valuation. However, valuing the share price of the stock is not as simple as dividing the value of the company by the outstanding shares of common stock. The value of the company reflects an inherent control premium. This premium reflects the ability to change the board of directors, change the dividend policy, and influence the business opportunities that are undertaken. The concept of the control premium can be seen in the market anytime a company acquires another company. The acquiring company is willing to pay more than the current market price of the stock because it is acquiring control. Therefore, the value of a share of stock as listed on an exchange has been discounted from the proportionate value of the company because of the stock being a minority interest.

CAPITAL ASSET PRICING MODEL

The **Capital Asset Pricing Model (CAPM)** is an asset pricing model that developed from the Markowitz efficient frontier (discussed in Chapter 12) and the introduction of a risk-free asset. As you recall from the discussion of Markowitz, any portfolio that lies on the efficient frontier is considered an efficient portfolio and thus, it has the highest level of return for the given level of risk. However, by introducing a risk free asset (R_f), there is a new set of portfolios created that is more efficient than the ones lying on the efficient frontier. Exhibit 14.10 illustrates this concept.

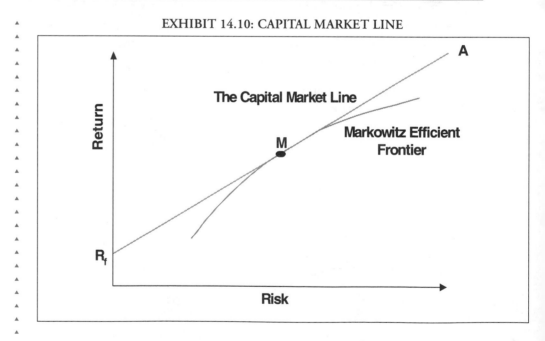
EXHIBIT 14.10: CAPITAL MARKET LINE

The capital market line (CML) is the new efficient frontier. However, instead of providing a maximum return, as did the efficient frontier of Markowitz, the CML provides an expected return based on the level of risk. The equation for the CML is written as follows:

$$E(R_p) = R_f + \left(\frac{[R_m - R_f]}{\sigma_m}\right) \times \sigma_p, \text{ where}$$

$E(R_p)$ = Expected return of the portfolio

R_f = Risk free rate

R_m = Return on the market

σ_m = Standard deviation of the market

σ_p = Standard deviation of the portfolio

The CML provides an expected return for a portfolio based on the expected return of the market, the risk free rate of return and the standard deviation of the portfolio in relation to the standard deviation of the market. The CML is generally used with efficient portfolios. It is not appropriate to be used as an estimate of the expected return for individual securities. However, the securities market line (SML), which is derived from the CML, does allow us to evaluate individual securities.

The SML is written as follows:

$$E(R_i) = R_f + B_i(R_m - R_f), \text{ where}$$

$E(R_i)$ = Expected return for asset i

R_f = Risk free rate

R_m = Return on the market

B_i = Beta of asset i

The securities market line determines the expected return for a security (i) based on its beta and the expectations about the market and the risk-free rate.

EXAMPLE

If the beta of ABC Company is 1.2 and the market return is expected to be 13 percent with a risk free return of 3 percent, then the expected return of ABC is 15 percent, as follows:

$$E(R_i) = R_f + B_i(R_m - R_f)$$
$$E(R_i) = 0.03 + 1.2(0.13 - 0.03) = 0.15 \text{ or } 15\%$$

Therefore, based on the level of systematic risk of ABC Company, it should earn a return of 15 percent. The SML helps to identify how the characteristics of a portfolio will be impacted when a security is added to the portfolio.

Do you prefer using actual equity securities or mutual funds in your client's portfolio and why?

"It depends" on many factors. First, how much money are we talking about investing? If we were talking about investing $25,000, my inclination would be to invest all of the money in a diversified portfolio of mutual funds. Why? Because we do not have enough money to take a meaningful position in any individual equities. If we were talking about investing $100,000, my response would be to invest some portion in individual equities some portion in mutual funds. My reasoning is that depending on my client's age, risk tolerance, investment experience, etc, their recommended asset allocation may require some exposure to International, Small Cap, Mid Cap, Venture Capital, REITS, and so on. I feel I am just as capable of picking the Ciscos, GEs, IBMs, Intels, and Citigroups of this world as the 40 analysts who follow these large, industry-dominant companies. So I would be inclined to invest in mutual funds in the areas that require special research, or that are highly volatile, such as small cap and international. If we were to invest $500,000, I would be inclined to place portions, (subject to asset allocation) with various money managers who specialize within asset categories. My experience has been that they tend to have less style drift, (or they are least accountable for style drift), and they can be sensitive to issues such as capital gain exposure.

Do you believe that the equity markets are efficient or that active management can indeed add value?

In spite of recent evidence that only a limited number of mutual fund managers consistently beat the indices they are measured against, there is no question in my mind that actively managed portfolios add value. The concern I have with index funds is that consumers are of the mistaken impression that they are getting a diversified portfolio of stocks, when because of capitalization weighting, they are not. When the top 25 (5%) companies of the 500 that comprise the S&P Index represent 40% of the entire value of the index, the client is exposed to a far greater degree of risk than they may be aware. Index funds tend to look great when the market is up, but when the market is down, I believe that a manager who has the ability to get out of a troubled holding in a hurry is of great value.

What do you think about the recent valuation of the "new economy" stock such as the "internet" and "dot com" stocks?

My opinion of the majority of these "new economy" stocks is that they are purely speculative in nature, and that the client had better be prepared for a bumpy ride at best, and a total loss at worst. My feeling is that unless these companies can show some evidence of profitability in the recent past or immediate future, that an investor would get just as much satisfaction out of going to Las Vegas. Investing in most of these as-yet unproven companies is not investing, it is gambling.

What is the process that you use to select individual equities for clients' portfolios?

When I propose portfolio allocations to my clients, I always include both growth and value investment styles, particularly in the large cap asset category. The breakdown is generally weighted in favor of whatever investment style is in favor at that particular time, but at least the other style is represented to a significant degree. I feel this is important because we never know when the markets will rotate out of one buying style to the other.

DISCUSSION QUESTIONS

1. What is the difference between dividend income and capital appreciation?
2. How does the industry life cycle of companies compare to the life cycle of the individual?
3. What is the difference between defensive stocks and cyclical stocks?
4. What are the characteristics of growth stocks?
5. What is preferred stock and how does it differ from common stock?
6. What are the types of foreign securities available to investors and what are the characteristics of each type?
7. What are the systematic risks that affect equity securities?
8. What are the three reasons that common stocks generally decline in value when interest rates rise?
9. What are the unsystematic risks that impact equity securities?
10. What are the differences between the primary market, secondary market, third market, and fourth market?
11. What are the primary characteristics of a good benchmark, and what indexes are used as benchmarks by portfolio managers in the U.S.?
12. What is the difference between the arithmetic mean and the geometric mean?
13. What are the different purposes of dollar weighted returns and time weighted returns?
14. What is the concept of selling short?
15. What are margin accounts and how do they differ from cash accounts?
16. What are market orders, limit orders, stop loss orders, and stop limit orders?
17. What are the advantages and disadvantages of using margin to purchase securities?
18. What are the two methods of valuing equity securities and how are they used?
19. How can the P/E ratio be used to forecast future stock prices of equities?
20. What is the Capital Asset Pricing Model?

EXERCISES

1. Ajax Company had $15,200 of net income and $200,000 in assets (40% of which was equity) for the current year. Comet Company had $19,950 of net income and $175,000 in assets (60% of which was equity) for the current year. Compute and compare the return on equity for each company for the current year.
2. Rob buys 1,000 shares of ABC stock for $75 per share. He sells the stock for $200 per share. If he receives $20 of dividend income per share, what is Rob's holding period return?

Use the following chart to answer exercises #3 and #4:

Period	Cash Inflow or Outflow	Beginning of Period Value	End of Period Value
0	2000	2000	2300
1	(300)	2000	2200
2	(200)	2000	2500
3	600	3100	3600
4	(3600)	-	-

3. Compute the time weighted return over the four-year period.
4. Compute the dollar weighted return over the four-year period.
5. Cybertech stock is currently paying a dividend of $2 per share. If its market value is $50 per share, then what is its dividend yield?
6. Holly buys Volatile stock for $200 on margin. If the initial margin is 60 percent and the maintenance margin is 40 percent, then what price will Holly receive a margin call?
7. Molly buys Growth stock for $150 on margin. If the initial margin is 50 percent and the maintenance margin is 35 percent, then what price will Molly receive a margin call?
8. Holly buys Volatile stock for $200 on margin. The initial margin is 60 percent and the maintenance margin is 40 percent. If the stock drops to $100, then how much must Holly put up to restore the margin in her account?
9. Molly buys Growth stock for $150 on margin. The initial margin is 50 percent and the maintenance margin is 35 percent. If the stock drops to $100, then how much must Molly put up to restore the margin in her account?
10. XYZ preferred stock pays a dividend of $8 per share. What is the value of XYZ preferred stock if the investor's required rate of return equals 14 percent?
11. XYZ common stock pays a current dividend of $8 per share. What is the value of XYZ common stock if the investor's required rate of return equals 14 percent and the dividend is growing at a constant rate of 3 percent?
12. Based on the answers to the two previous questions, what is the value of the future growth of the common stock dividend payments?
13. Greg is considering investing in a security that has a beta of 1.5. If the market is expected to return an average rate of return of 13 percent and the risk-free rate of return equals 3 percent, then what is the expected return for this security?
14. A well-diversified portfolio had a standard deviation of 30 percent in the current year. Compute the expected return of the portfolio if the risk free rate is 6 percent, the return on the market was 15 percent and the standard deviation of the market was 20 percent.
15. Dalts stock increased from $27 to $35 during the year. The market earned a return of 15 percent over the same period. If Dalts has a beta of 1.2 and the risk free rate equals 3 percent, then how has the stock performed compared to the expected return (based on the Capital Asset Pricing Model)?

PROBLEMS

1. Use the table below and answer the following questions:

Period	Beginning of Year Value	End of Year Value	Dividend Payment	Holding Period Return
1	$50	$54	$2	?
2	$54	$60	$2	?
3	$60	$58	$2	?
4	$58	$52	$3	?
5	$52	$63	$3	?
6	$63	$68	$3	?

▲ Calculate the holding period return for each of the six periods above.
▲ Calculate the arithmetic mean for the six periods above.
▲ Calculate the geometric mean for the six periods above.

2. John purchases 1,000 shares of stock at $80 per share on margin, with an initial margin of 55 percent and a maintenance margin of 35 percent.
   ▲ At what price will John receive a margin call?
   ▲ If the stock dropped to $50 per share, how much would he have to put up to restore the equity in his account?
   ▲ If the stock dropped to $50 per share and John does not have enough cash to restore the equity in the account, then how much stock must be sold to restore the equity?

3. SG stock is currently paying a dividend of $6. The dividend has been growing at a constant rate over the last nine years and is expected to continue growing at the same rate. If SG was paying a dividend of $3 nine years ago, and the required return is 12 percent, then what is the most the investor should pay for the stock?

CHAPTER 15

Mutual Funds

LEARNING OBJECTIVES:

After learning the material in this chapter, you will be able to:

1. Explain why mutual funds have become the increasingly predominant method for small investors to gain access to equity and fixed income investments.

2. List the three types of investment companies and describe how they function.

3. Discuss the various fees charged by mutual fund companies.

4. Describe the three classes of load fund shares.

5. Explain how fund expenses impact fund performance.

6. Discuss the advantages and disadvantages of mutual funds.

7. List and discuss the types of mutual funds.

8. Explain how professional investment advisers select mutual funds for inclusion in a portfolio.

9. Discuss how the information in a mutual fund's prospectus can help in evaluating that fund.

10. Describe the ways modern portfolio theory statistics provide insight into a mutual fund's risk-return characteristics.

11. Describe the issues to look for when managing portfolios of mutual funds.

INTRODUCTION TO MUTUAL FUNDS

mutual funds - an open-end investment company that sells shares of stock to the public and uses the proceeds to invest in a portfolio of securities on behalf of their shareholders

Mutual funds are investment vehicles that provide individual investors and institutional investors with easy access to capital markets. They are a type of investment company that sells shares of stock to the public and use the proceeds to invest in a portfolio of securities on behalf of its shareholders. The many benefits to investing in mutual funds will be discussed in this chapter.

Within the last twenty years or so, mutual funds have become the predominant method for small investors to gain access to equity and fixed income investments. The increased popularity of mutual funds is evidenced by the increasing number of mutual funds available to investors as well as the amount of assets invested in mutual funds. There are now almost eight thousand mutual funds, meaning that there are more mutual funds than there are listed equity securities.

EXHIBIT 15.1: MUTUAL FUND ASSETS
(TRILLIONS OF DOLLARS)

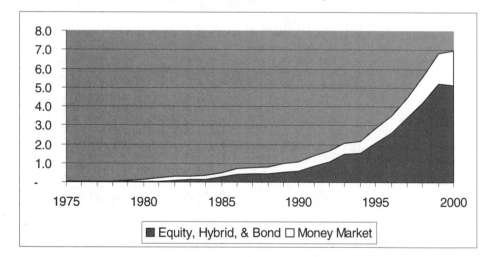

Source: 2001 Mutual Fund Fact Book, Investment Company Institute, Washington, DC

As illustrated in Exhibit 15.1, assets invested in mutual funds have increased to $6.97 trillion by year-end 2000. This increase in mutual fund assets has grown at a tremendous rate and is attributable to several important changes that have occurred in the recent decades.

The work place environment has changed significantly in the last twenty to thirty years. Gone are the days when employees would stay with a company for their entire work career. In the past, employers and employees had a great deal of mutual loyalty and, as a result, companies generally provided significant retirement benefits to employees. These benefits, along with Social Security, traditionally provided sufficient income during retirement to maintain preretirement life styles. Today, such mutual loyalty is rare. Employees change employers frequently, and employers are quick to terminate employees in an attempt to become more competitive. Employers today are also reducing the retirement benefits that were once provided. Instead of employer funded retirement plans, companies are establishing an increasing number of 401(k) plans, which allow individuals to save for retirement on a pre-tax basis. These changes have caused individuals to become self-reliant in an attempt to sufficiently save for their own retirement. In most cases, these retirement plan savings are invested in mutual funds.

In addition to changes occurring in the work place, the public is becoming more aware of the need for financial planning and the potential investment returns that are available in the securities markets. The public, being more educated about investments, is more willing to accept the additional risk of equities and fixed income securities. Mutual funds are allowing these individuals easy access to investment securities and markets.

Another cause for increased savings in 401(k) plans and increased self-reliance is the public awareness of increasing life expectancies. At the time Social Security was created, the remaining life expectancy for someone entitled to receive full retirement benefits was at most ten or fifteen years. Today, the remaining life expectancy for someone retiring at 65 may be twenty to thirty years. The increased time spent in retirement increases the amount of money needed for retirement and increases the amount that must be saved prior to retirement.

Mutual funds are considered an indirect method of investing and are an alternative to investing directly in equities and other securities. Mutual funds provide numerous benefits to investors, many of which are unavailable from other methods of investing. Investors need to be cautious, however, when investing in mutual funds because of certain disadvantages and complexities that are presented later in this chapter.

TYPES OF INVESTMENT COMPANIES

Mutual funds are actually a subcategory of what is referred to as regulated investment companies. **Investment companies** are financial services companies that sell shares of stock to the public and use the proceeds to invest in a portfolio of securities. Although each investor or shareholder may have a relatively small investment in total, the funds of all shareholders pooled together allow the investment company to create a widely diversified portfolio with certain economies of scale.

Investment companies are generally non-taxable entities. These companies do not pay federal or state income tax. Instead, investment companies act as flow-through entities or conduits whereby interest income, dividends, and capital gains all flow through from the investment company to the shareholders and are reported on the investor's individual tax returns. The income that flows through retains its character as to ordinary income or capital gain and is allocated to each shareholder based on the number of shares owned. The tax treatment of investment companies is similar in concept to the tax treatment of partnerships and S-corporations.

investment companies - financial services companies that sell shares of stock to the public and use the proceeds to invest in a portfolio of securities

To qualify for non-taxable treatment, investment companies, under Internal Revenue Code Section 851, must meet the following criteria:

▲ The investment company must earn at least 90 percent of its income from interest, dividends, and capital gains derived from investing in stocks, bonds, currencies, or other securities.

▲ At least 90 percent of the investment company's taxable income must be distributed to its shareholders.

▲ For 50 percent of the portfolio, an investment in any one issuer is limited to an amount not greater than 5 percent of the total assets of the fund, and no more than 10 percent of the outstanding voting securities of such issuer.

▲ No more than 25 percent of the value of a fund's total assets can be invested in the securities of one issuer.

In addition to meeting specific requirements of the Internal Revenue Code, investment companies are also regulated by the Securities Exchange Commission (SEC) under the Investment Company Act of 1940. Investment companies are also regulated under the Securities Act of 1933, the Securities Exchange Act of 1934, and the Investment Advisors Act of 1940. For more information on these Acts, see Appendix C at the end of the text.

As indicated above, mutual funds are only one type of investment company. The three types of investment companies are unit investment trusts, closed-end funds, and open-end investment companies (mutual funds).

UNIT INVESTMENT TRUSTS

unit investment trust (UIT) - a registered investment company that is passively managed and may invest in stocks, bonds, or other securities

A **unit investment trust (UIT)** is a registered investment company that is passively managed and may invest in stocks, bonds or other securities. Investors generally purchase units, which are sold at net asset value plus a commission, with the idea that they will hold the units until they mature. As income is earned and securities mature, investors will receive both income (interest and/or dividends) and principal from the trust.

In the case of UITs that invest in stocks, the trust will have a defined maturity date at which time the investor will have the option of rolling over the proceeds, receiving a pro rata distribution of the UIT's underlying securities, or receiving cash from the investment.

UITs are known as unmanaged or passively managed funds because professional managers initially select securities to be included in the portfolio and those securities are generally held until they mature. For example, a UIT investing in municipal bond securities may have a portfolio of municipal bonds with staggered maturities. These bonds will generally be held until they mature. As coupon payments are received from the bond issuer, they are passed along to the unit holders. When a bond matures, the face value will be passed through to the unit holders. Although the holdings of UITs are monitored, the securities within the fund generally remain the same throughout the life of the fund.

The traditional UIT invested in fixed income securities. Today, however, there are a variety of UITs available to meet the objectives and risk tolerances of investors. UITs invest in a wide array of securities, including municipal bonds, corporate bonds, U.S. government bonds, international bonds, and mortgage backed securities.

The intent of most investors is to hold these UITs until maturity. However, for investors who wish to divest themselves of the units, trusts are required to redeem units at net asset value.

CLOSED-END INVESTMENT COMPANIES

A **closed-end fund** is a type of investment company whose shares trade in the same manner that other publicly traded stocks trade in the secondary market. Shares of closed-end funds are listed on a stock exchange or trade in the over-the-counter market. Because shares trade in the same manner as other stocks, their prices are subject to the fluctuations in the supply and demand for the shares in the market. Although it is relatively easy to determine the value of securities held within the fund, the share price for the fund will rarely be directly equal to the value of the underlying securities. Since the shares for closed-end funds are subject to supply and demand, the shares will generally sell at a premium or discount relative to the net asset value of the fund.

After the initial public offering, a closed-end fund will generally not issue additional shares in the market. Unlike an open-end fund, a closed-end fund's capitalization is considered to be fixed since it does not generally add assets to the fund after initial capitalization.

Since the pool of assets to be invested for a closed-end fund is fixed and shares are not redeemed, the manager of a closed-end fund has a great deal of flexibility in managing the assets within the fund. He does not have to worry about or plan for cash redemptions like a mutual fund (open-end investment company). This one characteristic of closed-end funds allows the manager to invest in less liquid securities that may have higher expected returns than more liquid securities.

Closed-end funds invest in a wide array of securities, including municipal bonds, corporate bonds, U.S. government bonds, international bonds, mortgage-backed securities, convertible securities, domestic equities, and foreign equities. A particularly interesting closed-end fund is what is known as an equity dual-purpose fund. This type of fund invests primarily in securities of U.S. companies but has two classes of shares. The first class of shares consists of income shares that receive all dividend income, but no capital appreciation. The second class of shares consists of capital shares that receive all capital appreciation, but no dividend income. An investor interested in income only, such as a retiree, might purchase the first class of shares. This class of shares would provide a steady stream of income. Alternatively, an investor who had a long-term time horizon and did not have any need for current income would most likely be interested in long-term growth securities. The second class of shares would provide this long-term growth with little or no current income tax cost. In addition, returns would be taxed at the current capital gains tax rate, which is significantly less than the current ordinary income tax rates.

Although closed-end investment companies have been around since before the economic depression of the 1930s, the growth of these funds has paled in comparison to the growth of open-end investment companies (mutual funds).

closed-end fund - a type of investment company whose shares trade in the same manner that other publicly traded stocks trade in the secondary market

EXHIBIT 15.2: GROWTH OF CLOSED-END FUNDS VS. OPEN-END FUNDS

Closed-end Funds

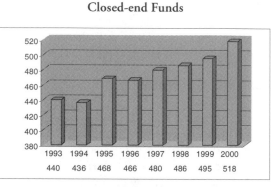

	1993	1994	1995	1996	1997	1998	1999	2000
	440	436	468	466	480	486	495	518

Open-end Funds

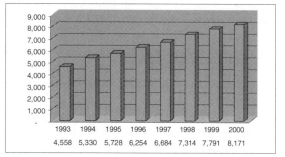

	1993	1994	1995	1996	1997	1998	1999	2000
	4,558	5,330	5,728	6,254	6,684	7,314	7,791	8,171

Source: A Guide to Closed-End Funds, Investment Company Institute, Washington, DC.

One likely reason that closed-end funds have not been as popular as open-end funds is that the fees that can be generated by the fund managers and operators are not as high as those with open-ended funds. Good performance in an open-end fund attracts significant increases in fund assets resulting in a larger base of assets upon which to charge the management fee. A closed-end fund that has great performance may have shares selling at a premium, but additional funds are generally not forthcoming. Therefore, it is easier to increase the management fees through an open-end mutual fund than a closed-end fund.

Another reason that closed-end funds may not have been as popular as open-end funds is the requirement of a broker to buy or sell shares for a closed-end fund. With an open-end fund, an investor must simply call the fund to request the shares be redeemed. The process of purchasing mutual fund shares directly from a fund family is easier than setting up a brokerage account and purchasing closed-end fund shares. In addition, open-end funds are easier for investors to comprehend since their share price is solely based on the price of the underlying securities. Remember, closed-end fund shares may sell at a premium or discount to net asset value.

528

OPEN-END INVESTMENT COMPANIES (MUTUAL FUNDS)

Open-end investment companies are referred to as open-end because they are not limited in the number of shares that are sold. The total capitalization of these funds is constantly changing. Some investors are purchasing shares, while others are selling their shares. All shares are sold by the mutual fund family and redeemed by the mutual fund family.

The price at which shares are sold is referred to as **net asset value (NAV)**. Subtracting total liabilities from total assets of the fund and dividing the difference by the outstanding shares determines the net asset value of the fund. Each day, as the prices of the underlying securities change in value, so will the NAV for the fund. All shares will be purchased for and sold at NAV. However, commissions and other sales charges may be charged against the purchase or sale of shares.

Mutual fund shares are either purchased directly from the fund family or they are purchased through a broker. Purchases made directly with the fund family are done so either by mail, telephone, Internet, or by visiting office locations. Shares purchased through a broker or other financial services person will generally be charged a commission or a sales charge. These fees serve to compensate the broker as an investment adviser.

Exhibit 15.3 depicts the basic structure of a mutual fund.

open-end investment companies - an investment company whose capitalization constantly changes as new shares are sold and outstanding shares are redeemed

net asset value (NAV) - the price at which shares of an open-end investment company are sold. The NAV of a fund is determined by subtracting total liabilities from total assets of the fund and dividing the difference by the outstanding shares

EXHIBIT 15.3: MUTUAL FUND STRUCTURE

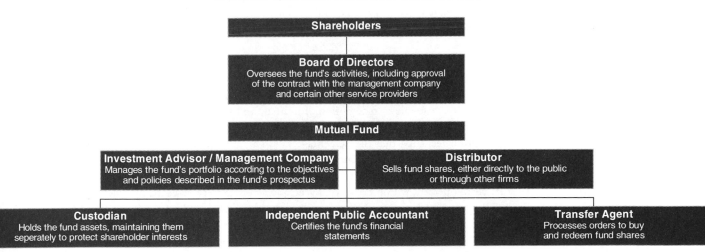

Source *2001 Mutual Fund Fact Book, Investment Company Institute, Washington, DC.*

MUTUAL FUND FEES

Just like any other service, investment professionals charge fees for the management of an investor's assets. Fees are charged by the mutual fund company and by investment professionals who sell mutual funds to their clients. Fees are generally categorized into loads or sales charges and operating expenses. All mutual funds will have annual operating expenses, and many also have one or more sales charges.

LOADS OR SALES CHARGES

Front-End Load

front-end load - a sales charge based on the initial investment into a mutual fund

A **front-end load** is simply a term to describe a sales charge based on the value of the initial investment into the mutual fund. This load is incurred when an investor purchases shares of a mutual fund from a commission-based financial adviser and is used to compensate the investment professional (usually someone unrelated to the fund itself) for advice related to the selection of the mutual funds. Although most funds that charge a front-end load will charge less than 6 percent, there are some funds that impose sales charges as high as 8.5 percent.

The front-end load works to offset the initial, or any subsequent, investment into the fund. For example, if ABC Mutual Fund had a 6 percent front-end load, then an investment of $1,000 would result in a sales charge of $60 and a net investment into the mutual fund of $940. Once the sales charge is paid, the fund will operate similar to a no-load fund. However, any subsequent investments will generally be subject to the same sales charge.

Back-End Load or Redemption Fee

back-end load - a sales charge incurred upon the ultimate sale or redemption of mutual fund shares rather than at the time of purchase

Back-end load is also a term used to describe a sales charge. However, the sales charge is incurred upon the ultimate sale or redemption of mutual fund shares rather than at the time of purchase. Today, many of the back-end loads found in mutual funds are in the form of a declining redemption fee, such that the percentage sales charge declines each year that the fund is held. For example, a fund might charge a five percent declining redemption fee. In such a case, an investor would pay 5 percent of the amount invested into the fund for redemption within the first year, 4 percent within the second year, and so on. After five years, no redemption fee would be charged in such a case. A back-end load is typically assessed on the lesser of the redemption value or the initial investment value.

OTHER MUTUAL FUND FEES

12b-1 Fees

12b-1 fee - a fee that pays for the services of brokers who sell mutual funds and who maintain the client relationship

Under the Investment Company Act of 1940, Section 12b-1, fees are permitted to pay for marketing and distribution expenses directly from a fund's asset base. The so-called **12b-1 fee** charged by the mutual fund company is used to pay for the services of brokers who sell the mutual funds and who maintain the client relationships. This fee is often paid in the form of trailing commissions, where commissions are paid to the broker over a period of years. The trailing commissions are based on the size of the investment in the mutual fund. Brokers will receive larger commissions for larger investments. As the investment in the mutual fund grows over time, so does the trailing commission that the broker receives.

The maximum 12b-1 fee that can be charged is 75 basis points per year. However, another 25 basis points can be charged as a "service fee," which effectively raises the annual potential 12b-1 charge to 100 basis points or 1 percent of assets per year.

Management Fees

The **management fee** is the fee that is charged by the investment adviser for the management of the fund assets. This fee is generally the single largest expense of a mutual fund and is included in the expense ratio.

Expense Ratio

The **expense ratio** is disclosed by all mutual funds in the fund prospectus and is an indication of the annual fund expenses and is stated as a percentage of total assets. Included in this figure are the management fees, the 12b-1 fees, and other operating expenses related to running and operating the fund (e.g., rent, computer). The expense ratio does not include sales charges.

It is important for an investor to realize that reducing the expense ratio by one percent is essentially the same as increasing the rate of return by 1 percent. Therefore, managing the expenses paid for the management of mutual fund assets is an important element of the investment planning process.

MUTUAL FUND CLASSIFICATION

There are no-load funds and load funds. No-load funds are sold directly by the fund to the investor and do not charge front or back-end loads as described below. An investment of $100 goes directly into the fund at the NAV. Load funds are discussed below.

Load versus No-Load Funds

Mutual funds that charge either a front-end load or a back-end load are considered **load funds**. As stated above, sales charges are used to compensate the brokers or sales force for the fund. In addition, funds without a front-end load or a back-end load that have a 12b-1 fee that exceeds 25 basis points (0.25 percent or 0.0025) are also considered to be load funds. Only if the 12b-1 fee is 25 basis points or less can the fund be called a no-load fund. Generally, **no-load funds** are purchased directly through the mutual fund family without the assistance of a broker. These funds do not charge annual sales charges, but will have operating expenses, as do all other mutual funds.

Classes of Load Fund Shares

Many of the fund families that offer load funds have different classes of shares that contain different sets of loads and expenses. Although there are no legal requirements as to the classification of shares of a load fund, most of the industry follows a similar classification system. Shares are generally classified into three classes, known as class A shares, class B shares, and class C shares:

▲ *Class A shares* – These shares usually charge a front-end load with a smaller 12b-1 fee.
▲ *Class B shares* – These shares usually charge a deferred redemption fee plus the maximum 1 percent 12b-1 fee. In addition, many of the class B shares will have a conversion feature that automatically converts the class B shares to class A shares after a period of years. The advantage of the conversion feature is that the investor will save expenses because the 12b-1 fee is lower for class A shares than for class B shares.
▲ *Class C shares* – These shares will often have a level deferred sales charge (often 1 percent), plus the maximum 1 percent 12b-1 fee. However, these shares do not convert to class A shares.

Many fund families have additional classes of shares that have a variety of meanings. As a result, investors should carefully review the prospectus of each fund to determine the actual fees that are being charged to shareholders for each class of shares of a particular fund.

HOW DO FUND EXPENSES IMPACT PERFORMANCE?

High quality funds may have high or low expense ratios. However, as a general rule, the higher the expenses of the mutual fund, the more the fund manager will have to overcome to achieve strong return performance. Consider the following example:

EXAMPLE

Assume an investment of $10,000 into two funds, each with an annual return of 10 percent, before expenses. Fund A has an expense ratio of 1 percent while Fund B has an expense ratio of 1.6 percent. The investment in the Fund B will grow to $112,429 after 30 years. The investment in Fund A will grow to $132,677 after 30 years. The $20,248 (18 percent) difference is attributable to the higher expenses of Fund B.

EXHIBIT 15.4: GROWTH OF $10,000 AFTER EXPENSES

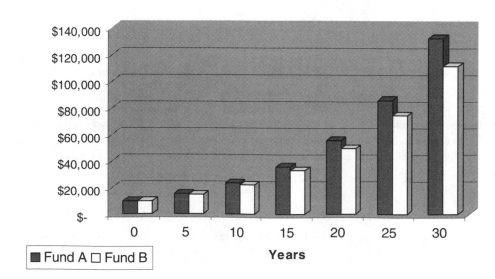

As illustrated by Exhibit 15.4, mutual fund expenses can make a significant difference in an investor's wealth over a period of years. It is important to realize the impact of expenses on overall performance of a potential mutual fund. However, it is also important to realize that the returns reported by the various mutual funds are net of annual fees. This makes it easier for investors to compare returns of one fund with other funds.

EXPENSE RATIOS FOR DIFFERENT TYPES OF FUNDS

What expense ratio is appropriate for a mutual fund? The answer to this question depends on the objectives of the mutual fund. For example, actively managed funds (those that frequently buy and sell securities) require more research and support than passively managed index funds. Therefore, most actively managed funds will have higher expense ratios than passively managed funds. Similarly, it is more costly to manage international equities than domestic equities because there are many more companies internationally than within the United States. In addition, the availability of accounting and financial information outside the U.S. is not as sufficient as within, thus making research more difficult and more costly. Therefore, it is quite common for international equity funds to have higher expense ratios relative to domestic equity funds.

ADVANTAGES OF MUTUAL FUNDS

Mutual funds provide many benefits to investors including easy access to a diversified portfolio with professional management, as well as other benefits that are not found in typical securities, such as low initial investment amounts, easy access, tax efficiency, liquidity, transaction cost efficiency, and services.

LOW INITIAL INVESTMENT

The majority of mutual funds have very low minimum investment requirements, allowing smaller investors access to many choices of mutual funds. In fact, approximately 61 percent of mutual funds have minimums of $1,000 or under, and 82 percent have minimums of $5,000 or under (see Exhibit 15.5). These low minimum investment requirements allow individuals, who would otherwise be precluded from such investments, access to the equity and fixed income markets.

EXHIBIT 15.5: MUTUAL FUND MINIMUM INVESTMENT REQUIREMENTS, 2000

Percent distribution of funds by minimum investment requirement*

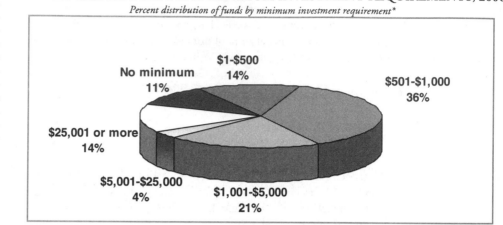

No minimum 11%

$1-$500 14%

$501-$1,000 36%

$25,001 or more 14%

$5,001-$25,000 4%

$1,001-$5,000 21%

*Many mutual funds offer lower investment minimums for Individual Retirement Accounts (IRAs) and automatic investment plans.
Source 2001 Mutual Fund Fact Book, Investment Company Institute, Washington, DC.

DIVERSIFICATION

Mutual funds provide an easy way to diversify a portfolio at a low cost. Some mutual funds have as many as 2,000 different securities in a single portfolio (CREF-Stock). Many mutual funds have 100 to 1,000 different securities in one portfolio. Such broad diversification, coupled with a minimum investment requirement, achieves diversification at a very low cost. Minimum initial investments for mutual funds are usually between $1,000 and $5,000 allowing investors to achieve broad diversification without requiring them to invest large sums of money into individual stocks and bonds. There is really no other way to achieve the same level of diversification with such a small investment.

Trying to achieve the same level of diversification that a mutual fund can offer would require a substantially greater investment than the usual minimum fund requirement. In addition, the transaction costs in acquiring a diversified portfolio would be high. For example, buying 40 equity securities in round lots (100 shares) at an average price of $25 per share would require an investment of $100,000. This investment is far more than an initial investment in most mutual funds. In addition, the transaction cost of purchasing 40 issues could range from $500 to $1,600.

EASE OF ACCESS

Investors can purchase mutual funds easily. Mutual funds can be purchased directly from the mutual fund family or through a broker, bank, or other financial institution. To invest in a mutual fund directly through the fund family, an investor must call the fund family for an account application and prospectus, complete the application, and return the application to the fund family with a check for the amount of the initial investment. Investing in a mutual fund through a broker is as easy as calling the broker and requesting the purchase of the mutual fund. Usually, a brokerage account must be established before the purchase of the mutual fund can be made.

PROFESSIONAL MANAGEMENT

Individuals and institutions that manage money usually charge a fee that is in the form of a percent of the assets managed. For example, a manager might charge 1 percent of assets annually to manage a portfolio. For an account with a value of $1 million, the fee at 1 percent of assets equals $10,000 annually. However, most professional money managers have minimum account size requirements. These minimum account sizes can be $1 million, $5 million, $50 million, or more for institutional managers. Institutional managers only manage very large pools of assets. Since most managers have specific account minimums, it is difficult to achieve professional management for small investors without access to mutual funds.

The same benefits that institutional investors find with professional portfolio managers can be found in mutual funds. The manager is constantly evaluating the holdings of the funds and alternative investment choices. Managers either have research departments or access to research that assists them in achieving above average returns. It is quite difficult for individual investors to match the performance of professional managers over time and through different markets. Therefore, mutual funds provide access to professional management without subjecting investors to the same restrictions on minimum account size.

TAX EFFICIENCY OF MANAGEMENT FEES

Mutual funds have a tax benefit compared to separately managed accounts. Separately managed accounts are pools of assets that are separately managed by an investment adviser. These funds are not commingled with assets of other investors, as in the case of a mutual fund. Advisers managing separately managed accounts typically charge a management fee based on a percent of assets under management.

The fee that is charged for the management of investments is deductible for income tax purposes as an itemized deduction, subject to 2 percent. If an investor pays $20,000 for an investment advisor to manage his assets, then the investor can deduct the $20,000 as an itemized deduction (subject to the 2 percent limit). However, since the fee can only be deducted as an itemized deduction, it is a deduction after adjusted gross income (AGI) and may be limited by the 2 percent floor or the phase out of itemized deductions.

Management fees for mutual funds are deducted from the returns of the fund and, therefore, are not reported for tax purposes by the investor. The returns that investors receive from mutual funds are after the charge for the management of the assets. Since the returns are after the management fee, AGI is automatically reduced, which lowers the threshold for various other tax limits. Therefore, mutual funds provide a tax benefit that is not available to separately managed accounts.

LIQUIDITY

Investors of mutual funds are always able to redeem their shares and know the price at which their shares will be redeemed. Mutual funds are required to redeem shares when requested by investors. These shares will be redeemed at net asset value, which is the price of the mutual fund shares based on the underlying assets.

TRANSACTION COST EFFICIENCY

Since mutual funds generally have hundreds of millions, and some have billions, of dollars under management, they have economies of scale with regard to transaction costs. Many of their investment trades can be executed for pennies per share, or less. These transaction costs are significantly less on a per share and dollar basis than most individuals could achieve on their own. However, with the increased online securities trading over the Internet, investor's direct transaction costs are also being reduced. In fact, shares of common stock can be traded at less than $0.01 per share with online trading.

VARIETY OF MUTUAL FUNDS

With approximately 8,200 mutual funds, an investor has a plethora of choices of how to invest in mutual funds. There are mutual funds that can meet almost any investor's objectives, whether a growth fund, sector fund, or a "green" fund.

SERVICES

Mutual funds provide investors with a variety of services that they would not have with an individual portfolio of securities. Basic services such as reporting may include monthly or quarterly statements that provide the investor with a variety of information about their investments. This information generally includes number of shares owned, net asset value of shares, and value of the mutual fund investment. In addition, statements will often provide information on the investor's rate of return that has been earned and an investor's tax basis in the fund.

Other services that are extremely helpful in accomplishing certain goals include automatic investing (purchasing) into the fund. Investors can set up a mutual fund account such that an automatic electronic transfer of a certain dollar amount from the investor's checking or savings account is invested into the fund on a certain day(s) of each month. This allows an investor to automatically invest on a periodic basis, similar to payroll reduction with a 401(k) plan.

Similar to automatic investing is automatic withdrawals or sales. Individuals who need a certain sum of money every month can set up a directive to the mutual fund so that it automatically sells a certain number of shares to provide for this need. The proceeds from the sale are then transferred into the investor's checking or savings account.

Other services that are common to mutual funds include automatic reinvestment of dividends and capital gain distributions, check writing privileges, maintaining the shareholder adjusted taxable basis, and telephone and wire redemptions. All of these services provide convenience and flexibility to investors that would not be provided by a single individual portfolio.

DISADVANTAGES OF MUTUAL FUNDS

Although mutual funds provide tremendous advantages to investors, there are certain disadvantages that investors should be aware of including poor performance and unreasonable expenses of mutual funds.

PERFORMANCE

Many, if not most, mutual funds do not outperform their appropriate investment benchmarks. For example, consider large-cap equity funds reported by Morningstar (period ended September 30, 1999). The average large-cap equity fund underperformed the S&P 500 index for both the ten and fifteen-year periods by more than 300 basis points (3 percent). For the three and five-year periods, the average large-cap equity fund underperformed the S&P 500 index by more than 600 basis points (6 percent). Such performance should give the investor sufficient notice to be cautious when selecting a particular mutual fund.

Exhibit 15.6 illustrates this same point (for the period ended September 30, 1999).

EXHIBIT 15.6: HOW MUTUAL FUNDS COMPARE TO THE S&P 500 INDEX

	3 Years	5 Years	10 Years	15 Years
Annualized S&P 500 Index Return for period	25%	25%	17%	18%
Approx. Number of Equity Funds Reporting for Each Period	4,324	2,677	941	486
Approx. Number of Equity Funds Outperforming Index	278	119	98	45
Percentage of funds outperforming the S&P 500 index	6.4%	4.4%	10.4%	9.3%

Only a small percentage of mutual funds outperform the appropriate index over time. One explanation for this underperformance is that mutual funds have expenses that must be incurred for the operation of the fund. Performance for indexes does not include expenses or transaction costs. Although many of the funds underperform, they provide good returns when compared to returns achieved by unsophisticated investors.

FEES, LOADS, AND EXPENSES

Investors should be conscious of fees, loads, and expenses of mutual funds. While all funds will have operating and management expenses, some funds have sales charges (loads) that can be as high as 8.5 percent (Yes, even in the 21st century!). It should be obvious that the higher the summation of all fund costs, the more difficult it will be to outperform the appropriate benchmark.

THE ABUNDANCE OF CHOICES

With approximately 8,200 (and the number is growing), it may be difficult for an investor to choose only one, or a few, mutual funds. There are now more mutual funds than listed equities. Mutual fund selection will be discussed later in this chapter.

LIQUIDITY

While liquidity is one of the primary advantages of mutual funds, it is also a disadvantage. To accommodate cash flowing into and out of the fund on a regular basis, fund managers must maintain a certain amount of cash on hand at all times. This cash reserve may cause funds to not be fully invested, thus leading to lower returns than otherwise possible were the fund fully invested at all times.

EXECUTION

Recall that one of the advantages of mutual funds is that they trade in large volumes, resulting in low transaction costs. Unfortunately, however, since the volume of trades made by mutual funds is high, there is some risk that such buying and selling may cause the market price of securities to increase or decrease. This potential effect of flooding the market can result in purchasing shares at a higher price than expected and selling shares at a lower price than expected. The effect of flooding may result in lower returns on mutual fund assets than otherwise could have been achieved.

CLASSIFICATION SYSTEM FOR MUTUAL FUNDS

A mutual fund classification system can assist investors in choosing funds that are consistent with their goals and objectives. Using an objective-based classification system, an investor can compare mutual funds under consideration with the other funds within the classification category. Once a comparison is made, the investor can make a more informed choice about which funds are suitable for that particular investor. Mutual fund investors should be aware, however, that funds have a tendency to be misclassified. One reason for such misclassification is that there is not a specific classification system that defines each category. Although the SEC regulates investment companies, it does not provide a system for differentiating between types of mutual funds. Since there are mutual funds that are misclassified, it is more difficult for investors to select appropriate funds relative to their objectives.

BUILT-IN GAINS

Mutual funds will generally have appreciated securities within their portfolio. This appreciation is considered a built-in gain inside the mutual fund. Selling these appreciated securities by the mutual fund causes income to be recognized for income tax purposes by the fund and then passed through to the investor. Taxable investors who purchase shares of mutual funds having these built-in gains subject themselves to potential taxable income without any associated economic gain. The built-in gain on mutual funds can range widely and depends on past performance of the fund. Investors should be cautious when purchasing mutual funds with large amounts of unrealized appreciation.

Overall, the dramatic growth of mutual funds has provided a great service to the small investor. This growth has allowed more and more individuals to have access to professional money managers, in both 401(k) plans and taxable investment accounts. When calculating mutual fund investments, however, investors must be careful to consider the risks that are inherent in investing in the underlying securities and in selecting a particular mutual fund.

TYPES AND OBJECTIVES OF MUTUAL FUNDS

While the classification system for mutual funds is not completely standardized or precise, there are certainly specific types and objectives of mutual funds that can be discussed. Mutual funds can be categorized into equity funds, bond funds, balanced (hybrid) funds, or money market funds. As Exhibit 15.7 shows, by the end of 2000, there were 4,395 equity funds, 2,210 bond funds, 525 hybrid funds, and 1,041 money market funds.

EXHIBIT 15.7: NUMBER OF MUTUAL FUNDS (2000)

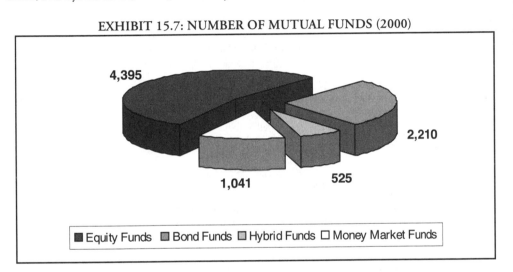

EXHIBIT 15.8: TYPES OF MUTUAL FUNDS

Equity Funds

- **Aggressive growth funds** invest primarily in common stock of small, growth companies with potential for capital appreciation.
- **Emerging market equity funds** invest primarily in equity securities of companies based in less-developed regions of the world.
- **Global equity funds** invest primarily in worldwide equity securities, including those of U.S. companies.
- **Growth and income funds** attempt to combine long-term capital growth with steady income dividends. These funds pursue this goal by investing primarily in common stocks of established companies with the potential for both growth and good dividends.
- **Growth funds** invest primarily in common stocks of well-established companies with the potential for capital appreciation. These funds' primary aim is to increase the value of their investments (capital gain) rather than generate a flow of dividends.
- **Income equity funds** seek income by investing primarily in equity securities of companies with good dividends. Capital appreciation is not an objective.
- **International equity funds** invest at least two-thirds of their portfolios in equity securities of companies located outside the United States.
- **Regional equity funds** invest in equity securities of companies based in specific world regions, such as Europe, Latin America, the Pacific Region or individual countries.
- **Sector equity funds** seek capital appreciation by investing in companies in related fields or specific industries, such as financial services, health care, natural resources, technology or utilities.

Bond Funds

- **Corporate bond—general funds** seek a high level of income by investing two-thirds or more of their portfolios in corporate bonds and have no explicit restrictions on average maturity.
- **Corporate bond—intermediate term funds** seek a high level of income with two-thirds or more of their portfolios invested at all times in corporate bonds. Their average maturity is five to ten years.
- **Corporate bond—short term funds** seek a high level of current income with two-thirds or more of their portfolios invested at all times in corporate bonds. Their average maturity is one to five years.
- **Global bond—general funds** invest in worldwide debt securities and have no stated average maturity or an average maturity of more than five years. Up to 25 percent of their portfolios' securities (not including cash) may be invested in companies located in the United States.
- **Global bond—short term funds** invest in worldwide debt securities and have an average maturity of one to five years. Up to 25 percent of their portfolios' securities (not including cash) may be invested in companies located in the United States.
- **Government bond—general funds** invest at least two-thirds of their portfolios in U.S. government securities and have no stated average maturity.
- **Government bond—intermediate term funds** invest at least two-thirds of their portfolios in U.S. government securities and have an average maturity of five to 10 years.
- **Government bond—short term funds** invest at least two-thirds of their portfolios in U.S. government securities and have an average maturity of one to five years.
- **High yield funds** seek a high level of current income by investing at least two-thirds of their portfolios in lower-rated corporate bonds (Baa or lower by Moody's and BBB or lower by Standard and Poor's rating services).
- **Mortgage-backed funds** invest at least two-thirds of their portfolios in pooled mortgage-backed securities.
- **National municipal bond—general funds** invest predominantly in municipal bonds and have an average maturity of more than five years or no stated average maturity. The funds' bonds are usually exempt from federal income tax but may be taxed under state and local laws.
- **National municipal bond—short term funds** invest predominantly in municipal bonds and have an average maturity of one to five years. The funds' bonds are usually exempt from federal income tax but may be taxed under state and local laws.
- **Other world bond funds** invest at least two-thirds of their portfolios in a combination of foreign government and corporate debt. Some funds in this category invest primarily in debt securities of emerging markets.
- **State municipal bond—general funds** invest primarily in municipal bonds of a single state and have an average maturity of more than five years or no stated average maturity. The funds' bonds are exempt from federal and state income taxes for residents of that state.
- **State municipal bond—short term funds** invest predominantly in municipal bonds of a single state and have an average maturity of one to five years. The funds' bonds are exempt from federal and state income taxes for residents of that state.
- **Strategic income funds** invest in a combination of domestic fixed-income securities to provide high current income.

Hybrid Funds

- **Asset allocation funds** seek high total return by investing in a mix of equities, fixed-income securities and money market instruments. Unlike Flexible Portfolio funds (defined below), these funds are required to strictly maintain a precise weighting in asset classes.
- **Balanced funds** invest in a specific mix of equity securities and bonds with the three-part objective of conserving principal, providing income and achieving long-term growth of both principal and income.
- **Flexible portfolio funds** seek high total return by investing in common stock, bonds and other debt securities, and money market securities. Portfolios may hold up to 100 percent of any one of these types of securities and may easily change, depending on market conditions.
- **Income mixed funds** seek a high level of current income by investing in a variety of income-producing securities, including equities and fixed-income securities. Capital appreciation is not a primary objective.

Money Market Funds

- **National tax-exempt money market funds** seek income not taxed by the federal government by investing in municipal securities with relatively short maturities.
- **State tax-exempt money market funds** invest predominantly in short-term municipal obligations of a single state, which are exempt from federal and state income taxes for residents of that state.
- **Taxable money market government funds** invest principally in short-term U.S. Treasury obligations and other short-term financial instruments issued or guaranteed by the U.S. government, its agencies or instrumentalities.
- **Taxable money market non-government funds** invest in a variety of money market instruments, including certificates of deposit of large banks, commercial paper and banker's acceptances.

Source: Investment Company Institute: "A Guide to Mutual Funds"

MONEY MARKET MUTUAL FUNDS

money market mutual funds - a mutual fund that invests in money market instruments, such as Treasury bills and negotiable CDs

Although not created until 1974, **money market mutual funds** had tremendous growth in the late '70s and early '80s due to the extremely high short-term interest rates during the period. Money market mutual funds provided investors with an easy method of investing in short-term fixed income securities during this period of high interest rates without buying the actual securities. Although short-term interest rates have decreased significantly since the early '80s, money market mutual funds still provide investors an easy and effective method of investing in money market instruments and provide a good alternative to the returns that can be earned on bank certificates of deposit and bank savings accounts.

Money market mutual funds provide investors the opportunity to earn competitive money market returns with the added benefits of ease of access and liquidity. Investors that have a portion of their portfolio invested in cash, or those who create cash by selling other long-term securities can use money market mutual funds as an appropriate, competitive money market investment or as a temporary holding place for cash. In addition, investors can choose to invest in either taxable or tax-exempt money market mutual funds, depending on the investor's tax situation. Many high net worth clients use tax-exempt funds due to their income tax bracket, while qualified retirement assets (tax-advantaged funds, such as funds in a 401(k) plan or IRA) should always use taxable funds because the rate of return for taxable funds is always higher than the rate of return for municipal funds.

Money market instruments include securities such as Treasury bills, commercial paper, negotiable certificates of deposit, repurchase agreements, and short-term municipal debt. Taxable money market mutual funds will often invest in a variety of these short-term securities or they may only invest in Treasury bills. Tax-exempt funds will generally invest exclusively in short-term municipal debt resulting in earnings that are exempt from federal tax and may be fully or partially excluded from state and local income tax. As mentioned above, these tax-exempt funds are popular with taxpayers in the higher marginal tax brackets.

The majority of money market mutual funds have securities with maturities of less than two months. The Securities Exchange Commission regulations prohibit the average maturity of money market mutual funds from exceeding 90 days.

With such short maturities, these funds have minimal interest rate risk, and because of the quality and diversity of the investments, these funds have little or no credit risk. Although these funds have minimal interest rate risk and credit risk, they are subject to reinvestment risk and purchasing power risk.

Money market mutual funds have net asset values of one dollar. Interest for these funds is earned and credited on a daily basis. Most of these funds allow investors check-writing privileges as long as a minimum balance is maintained. This check-writing feature allows competitive short-term returns with the flexibility of a checking account.

Unlike some fixed income and equity mutual funds, money market mutual funds do not charge front-end loads or redemption fees. However, a fee is charged for the management of the assets within the fund.

FIXED INCOME MUTUAL FUNDS

Fixed income or bond mutual funds invest primarily in fixed income securities ranging in maturity from several months to thirty years or longer. Just like money market mutual funds, bond funds invest in numerous bond issues to diversify the investment portfolio from default risk. Fixed income funds provide investors with current income making them ideal for inclusion in portfolios of retired investors who need continuing income generated by their investments for retirement expenditures. In addition, bond funds are appropriate for other investors wishing to allocate a certain portion of their portfolio to fixed income securities.

The risks that investors accept when making investments in bond funds are the same risks that any investor faces with fixed income securities. Since the mutual fund portfolio is well diversified, there is minimum default risk with bond mutual funds. As with other fixed income securities, purchasing power risk is a relevant factor to consider when investing in bond mutual funds. However, the most significant risk associated with bond mutual funds is interest rate risk. Recall that interest rate risk is the risk that fluctuations in interest rates will have a negative impact of the value of investments. Just as the value of an individual bond will decline when interest rates increase, so will the value of a bond mutual fund. Conversely, as interest rates decrease, the value of bond mutual funds will increase. During the '80s and '90s, we witnessed a continual decline in interest rates making bond mutual funds' performance excellent (Exhibit 15.9).

fixed income (or bond) mutual funds - a mutual fund that invests in fixed income securities ranging in maturity of several months to thirty years or longer. Bond funds invest in numerous bond issues to diversify the investment portfolio from default risk

EXHIBIT 15.9: CONSTANT MATURITY RATES OF U.S. TREASURY SECURITIES

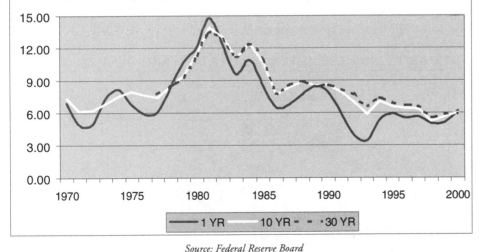

Source: Federal Reserve Board

The overall net worth of an individual with bond mutual funds in his investment portfolio will decline when interest rates increase. However, is the income that he receives on a monthly basis impacted? The answer to the question is a difficult one. If the bond fund portfolio remains the same (no trading of the underlying securities), then theoretically, the income should also remain constant, since the interest coupon payments from the bonds within the portfolio will remain the same. As time elapses, however, other issues become relevant. If the fund manager were to purchase new bonds in the market with the proceeds from principal repayments, bond maturities, or bond sales, then the proceeds would be invested at a higher yield, producing more income, thereby reflecting the increase in interest rates. Therefore, as interest rates increase, the net asset value of the bond mutual fund may decline, but the yield on the fund should begin to increase to reflect higher interest rates (and the lower NAV). If the investor were not living off the monthly income distributions, but rather, was reinvesting them back into the bond fund, then the reinvested dividends would be purchasing shares of the fund at a lower NAV, resulting in a higher number of shares. When interest rates decline, the value of the bond fund will increase, offsetting previous losses by the investor. Thus, bond mutual funds are very similar to other fixed income securities with regard to interest rate risk.

Bond mutual funds may have a variety of fees, costs, and expenses, including management fees, sales charges (both front-end and deferred), and 12b-1 fees. As is indicated in Exhibit 15.8, "Types of Mutual Funds," there are a variety of objectives of bond funds. With regard to the management fee, some of the objectives will require higher management fees than others. For example, a fund that matches the Lehman Brothers index will require less cost and time than a fund that is actively managed because no research is required to determine which securities to select when a manager is trying to perfectly emulate an index. Most bond funds have an expense ratio of 1 percent or under, with higher expenses for actively managed and international bond funds.

EQUITY MUTUAL FUNDS

equity mutual funds - a mutual fund that invests primarily in equity securities, such as preferred stock and common stock

Equity mutual funds invest primarily in equity securities and have a variety of objectives (Exhibit 15.8: Types of Mutual Funds). These funds have become tremendously popular over the last few decades and in fact, have the highest percentage of the total assets invested in mutual funds (Exhibit 15.10: How Mutual Fund Assets are Invested).

EXHIBIT 15.10: HOW MUTUAL FUND ASSETS ARE INVESTED (2000)

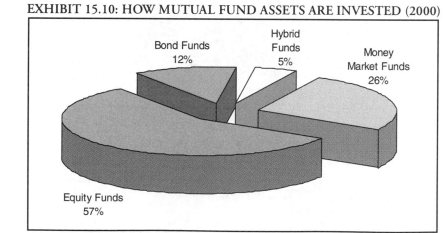

Source 2001 Mutual Fund Fact Book, Investment Company Institute, Washington, DC.

As we previously discussed, equities have had significantly higher performance returns than fixed income securities and equity mutual funds provide investors easy access to common stock securities in an efficient method. The public's increased awareness of higher returns is a major contributing factor to the popularity of the equity mutual funds. Another contributing factor is the increase in the number of 401(k) plans that employers are establishing. With the increase in 401(k) plans, there is an increase in assets invested in mutual funds, and especially equity funds.

Just as bond mutual funds have a variety of risks, so do equity mutual funds. One of the most important risks that an equity mutual fund investor must consider is market risk. Recall that market risk is the risk that movements in the equity market will have a detrimental effect on the value of an investment. There is a strong tendency for equities and equity mutual funds to fluctuate in the same direction and at a similar rate as the entire equity market. If the market has a sudden decline, it is likely that most equity funds will also decline in value.

For those investors who invest similar amounts on a monthly basis into an equity mutual fund, temporary declines in the market and equity funds provide the opportunity to invest at lower prices. Equity funds are, however, generally more volatile than bond funds, but historically have earned higher returns over a long-term horizon.

HYBRID OR BALANCED FUNDS

Hybrid mutual funds are those mutual funds that cannot be categorized into any of the three types of fund classifications discussed above (money market, bond, or equity). These funds generally have an objective of investing in a balanced fashion, such that a portion of the portfolio is invested in cash, fixed income securities, and/or equity securities.

Investors can build appropriate asset allocated portfolios by investing in a combination of selected money market funds, bond funds, and equity funds. Alternatively, investors can simply select a hybrid fund, such as an asset allocation fund, that meets their asset allocation objective and use it as their only or primary investment vehicle.

EXCHANGE TRADED FUNDS (ETFs)

Exchange traded funds (ETFs) are portfolios or baskets of stocks that are traded on an exchange (offerings are generally traded on the American Stock Exchange). ETFs are index-based equity instruments that represent ownership in either a fund or a unit investment trust and give investors the opportunity to buy and sell shares of an entire stock portfolio as a single security. Common examples include QQQ (Nasdaq-100) and SPDRs (Standard & Poor's Depository Receipts, tracking the S&P 500 index, or sectors of the index).

Unlike mutual funds, ETFs can be purchased and sold throughout the day. In addition, they can be bought on margin and can be sold short (and are not subject to the uptick rule). These ETFs typically have lower annual expenses compared to mutual funds. However, since ETFs are traded on exchanges, it is possible that in a market correction, investors may be unable to sell their shares. Recall that mutual funds must redeem investors' shares upon request.

ETFs are passively managed. They generally track a specific index, sector, or region. Although ETFs are traded on exchanges, investors may be able to buy or redeem shares from the fund family, generally in 50,000 share blocks. However, redemptions generally require the delivery of the underlying shares of stock. Generally, investors will buy and sell ETFs in the secondary market by using a broker. The price of ETF shares is certainly based on the value of the underlying securities; however, it may not be equal to NAV due to supply and demand for the shares. Although

hybrid (or balanced) mutual funds - a mutual fund that invests in a combination of cash, fixed income securities, and/or equity securities, such as an asset allocation fund

exchange traded funds (ETFs) - a type of investment company whose investment objective is to achieve the same return as a particular market index

the price of ETF shares may trade at a discount or premium, the difference should be minimal. If the shares were selling at a discount, then a large financial institution could purchase a large quantity (in blocks of 50,000 shares) of ETF shares and then redeem the shares for the underlying securities. These securities could then be sold in the market for a profit. Arbitrageurs can employ a similar strategy in the event that shares are trading at a premium. Generally, however, the gap from NAV is small to non-existent in free markets where arbitrageurs can operate.

Generally, the annual expense ratio for ETF shares is lower than for the majority of index mutual funds. For example, the annual expense ratio is 12 basis points (0.12%) for SPDRs, while Vanguard's 500 Index Fund charges 18 basis points (0.18%). However, ETF shares that are purchased using a broker will require a commission to be paid. Depending on the commission and the size of the investment, either alternative may be better. ETFs have low turnover and, therefore, lower taxable distributions than most mutual funds. When there is a substantial amount of selling of mutual fund shares, the manager is forced to sell some of the underlying securities to generate enough cash for redemptions. This does not occur in an ETF. Shares are either sold, or redeemed in-kind.

Most mutual funds have cash that is not invested, which is a result of either investments into the fund or cash that is maintained for redemptions. ETFs do not have this cash management problem and may have better performance than similar mutual funds.

HOLDRs (Holding Company Depositary Receipts) have many of the same characteristics as ETFs except that HOLDRs are depositary receipts that represent an investor's ownership in the common stock or ADRs (American depositary receipts) of specified companies in a particular industry, sector, or group. The following table compares various types of ETFs, the index they track, and the annual expenses associated with each exchange traded fund.

EXHIBIT 15.11: EXCHANGE TRADED FUNDS (ETF)

Exchange Traded Funds	Index	Annual Expenses
DIAMONDS	DJIA	18 bp
HOLDRs (Holding Company Depositary Receipts) Merrill Lynch	Various sectors	$2 per 100 shares
Ishares*	Numerous sectors and regions	9 to 99 bp
SPDRs (Standard & Poor's Depository Receipts)	S&P 500	12 bp
Midcap SPDRs	S&P 400	25 bp
NASDAQ-100 Index Tracking Stock (QQQ)	Nasdaq-100	18 bp
Select Sector SPDRs	Sectors of S&P 500	28 bp
streetTRACKS	Various Dow Jones and MS indexes	20-50 bp

* iShares MSCI Series were formerly known as WEBS; bp = basis points

ASSET ALLOCATION USING MUTUAL FUNDS

Research has shown that asset allocation is the most important factor in determining long-term variation (risk) in portfolio returns. Asset allocation may actually account for more than 90 percent of such variation. Based on these studies, it is clear that asset allocation is an important facet of the investment planning process that should be considered by investors and financial professionals. How then, can mutual funds be used in implementing such an asset allocation strategy?

Early in the investment planning process, an investment planner together with the client, identifies the client's goals and objectives, as well as the client's risk tolerance. Once these have been determined, the planner will often help the client select an appropriate asset allocation. In other words, the planner assists the client in determining what portion of the client's assets should be invested in cash, fixed income investments, equity investments, real estate, international investments, and so on. The asset allocation decision usually involves a narrowing process where the allocation to fixed income investments is separated into municipal (tax free) versus taxable, and an appropriate average duration is chosen. Similarly, the equity portion of the portfolio will be subdivided into core, value, and growth investment styles and then separated into large, mid, and small capitalization equities. International investments are generally separated into large capitalization or emerging markets and could be divided into different regions or countries around the world.

EXAMPLE

James and Stacey, who are age 40 and 37, respectively, would like to develop an investment plan for their retirement. Assume that after evaluating the timing of their goal and through discussions with them, James and Stacey are classified as moderately aggressive investors. Also, assume that an appropriate asset allocation for them is a portfolio that is 80 percent equity (60 percent domestic equities and 20 percent foreign equities) and 20 percent fixed income investments, with no allocation to cash or money markets. The allocation might be further divided as shown in the following table:

Equities		Fixed Income	
Large-cap value	10%	Taxable fixed income	8%
Large cap core	20%	Municipal fixed income	8%
Large cap growth	10%	Foreign fixed income	4%
Mid cap growth	10%		
Small cap growth	10%		
Large cap foreign	20%		
Total equity allocation	80%	Total fixed income allocation	20%

The above asset allocation provides James and Stacey with an investment portfolio that is heavily weighted toward equity investments. This equity allocation is divided between domestic and foreign and between large, mid, and small capitalization securities. The fixed income allocation is also divided between domestic and foreign, as well as taxable and municipal.

Once the asset allocation decision has been made, mutual funds can be used as the vehicle to implement the investment plan. It is important to select mutual funds that are consistent with the concepts and underlying assumptions of the asset allocation process. Specifically, an asset

mean-variance optimization model - used to determine the highest level of return (based on combinations of asset classes and different weightings of asset classes) for a specified level of risk tolerance

allocation for a client's portfolio is derived through a **mean-variance optimization model**. This type of model is used to determine the highest level of return (based on combinations of asset classes and different weightings of asset classes) for a specified level of risk. This level of risk is generally the client's risk level or risk tolerance. A mean-optimization model generally uses all of the following inputs for each asset class represented in the model:

▲ Historical return or expected return for each asset class.
▲ Standard deviation of each asset class (historical or expected).
▲ Correlation coefficients (historical or expected) for each asset class compared to all other asset classes.

Most of the time, these inputs for the asset classes are derived from indexes that represent the asset class. For example, the large cap equity asset class is usually represented by the S&P 500 index. Small cap equities are often represented by the Russell 2000 index, and fixed income securities may be represented by one of the Lehman Brothers indexes.

Since the assumptions that are used in the model are derived from indexes, funds to be used for implementation should have characteristics consistent with the index they are representing. This means that if there is an allocation to the large-cap, growth-asset class, then the fund that is chosen to represent this asset class should have consistent risk and return characteristics to that index. This does not mean, however, that index funds are the only choice for implementing an asset allocation strategy. It simply means that the funds that are chosen should be highly correlated with the index that is being represented.

As with all facets of financial planning, the investment planning process is not complete at implementation. The portfolio selections and allocations must be monitored on a continual basis to ensure that the quality of the investments has not changed and that the allocations and risk tolerances of the client have not significantly changed. This monitoring process generally includes quarterly, semiannual, or annual performance measurement reports and meetings with the client.

An investment performance report should include sufficient information to determine whether the investment portfolio has performed as intended and what, if any, changes should be made to the investment portfolio. The report should indicate the return for the overall portfolio, as well as the return for each asset class. These returns should be reported for the recent quarter, as well as the past year, 3-year, and 5-year periods (if available). Each of these returns should be compared to an appropriate benchmark to determine the performance of the fund or investment.

In addition to return information, performance reports should provide the investor with information about the risk characteristics of the overall portfolio. This includes measures for standard deviation, and possibly beta.

HOW DO PROFESSIONAL INVESTMENT ADVISERS SELECT MUTUAL FUNDS?

With the thousands of mutual funds available to investors, how does an investor or a professional adviser select and choose a mutual fund for inclusion in a portfolio? In other words, what distinguishes a good mutual fund from a not-so-good mutual fund? The first step is to identify the goals of the investor. Once the goals and objectives of the investor have been established, then the next step is to find funds that meet those objectives. In general, a good fund is one that meets the client's objectives and has had good risk-adjusted historical performance.

Professionals use databases of mutual fund information, such as Morningstar or Wiesenberger, to help narrow the thousands of mutual funds down to a few that meet the objectives of the investor. These databases contain a substantial amount of information about each mutual fund and allow advisors to search through voluminous information quickly to select appropriate funds for clients. Much of this information comes from the mutual fund prospectus; the remainder comes from the database company's analysis of the funds. Information that can be found in the prospectus includes the mutual fund objective, the investment policy and strategy, the fund manager's background and tenure with the fund, the fund's historical performance, the portfolio turnover for the fund, the fees and expenses, how to purchase and sell shares, the minimal initial investments, and the investor services available from the fund.

EXAMINE THE PROSPECTUS

Mutual Fund Objective

The goals for a mutual fund are broadly defined in the prospectus objective. Generally, the objective indicates two things: the type of securities that the fund invests in, and whether the fund is trying to achieve income, capital appreciation, or some combination of both. If the fund invests in fixed income securities, the prospectus objective will often specify the type of fixed income securities and the duration or maturity of those securities (that is, whether the securities are short-term, intermediate, or long-term). Fixed income securities can be domestic corporates, Treasuries, municipals, municipals confined to a single state, high-yield, or international. If the fund invests in equity securities, the predominant capitalization will often be indicated, as well as the investment style. Equities are generally classified as large-cap, mid-cap, or small-cap, and the investment style will either be growth, value, or a blend (core) strategy.

It is important to know the fund's objective in order to match the appropriate investments to the goals of the investor (or for inclusion in an asset allocation strategy). Younger, more aggressive investors will often want equities with substantial growth potential and minimal income. When returns consist of capital appreciation instead of income, the investor's after-tax returns will generally be higher. The reason for the higher returns is twofold. First, long-term capital gains are taxed at lower rates than ordinary income, such as interest or dividend payments. Second, capital appreciation is only taxed when the capital gain is recognized (security is sold).

Although it is important to match the stated objectives of the fund to the needs of the investor, in many cases, the fund does not invest in the same exact manner as their stated objective. This inconsistency may occur because of manager turnover, changes in market condition or other reasons. However, in building a portfolio of mutual funds, or including a mutual fund in a portfolio, one of the primary concerns of the investment advisor should be the consistency of the fund to its stated objectives. This type of information is generally not found in the fund prospectus, but can be found in the databases of information discussed above.

Investment Policy and Strategy

The investment strategy more clearly defines the investment approach of the mutual fund. For example, most funds will provide limits on the portion of the fund that is normally invested in the types of securities listed in the "objectives" section. Ranges will often be provided for the portion of the portfolio that will normally be invested in cash, fixed income securities, and equities. In addition, whether the company invests in foreign securities and to what extent is often found in this section. This type of information is especially important for pools of investable assets that have restrictions on the types of securities that can be included in the portfolio, and restrictions on the amount or percentage of certain securities that are included in a mutual fund.

Manager Tenure

The fund manager is listed in the fund prospectus with a description of his or her background and tenure with the fund. If you are selecting a fund based on "good" historical performance, it is important that the manager responsible for the "good" performance is still in charge of the fund. Unfortunately, some funds operate using a team approach, which makes it more difficult for shareholders and potential investors to monitor changes in the management structure.

Historical Performance

Funds generally provide total annual return information for the most recent 1-year, 5-year, and 10-year periods, as available. Total returns from the inception of the fund are also provided for most funds. In many cases, the fund will provide index performance for the given time periods so that a comparison can be made between the fund's performance and an appropriate benchmark. These comparisons are easy to make when the information is included in some type of database.

Portfolio Turnover

The fund will generally have a specific investment style that leads to low, medium, or high portfolio turnover. Higher turnover involves buying and selling securities more often throughout the year resulting in higher transaction costs. Higher turnover can result in more short-term capital gains and can accelerate other taxable income. Such short-term capital gains that flow through from mutual funds are generally taxed as ordinary income, instead of the lower long-term capital gains tax rate. Funds that have higher turnover will often cause the recognition of more frequent taxable gains through the selling of securities. Since the recognition of capital gains by the mutual fund requires shareholders to report these gains as income for federal income tax purposes, higher turnover funds accelerate the tax payments of the investor.

Since combined federal and state tax rates can range from 10 percent to 15 percent on the low side to over 50 percent on the high side, it is clear that taxes are the highest expense attributable to an investment. For example, management fees average about 1 percent, significantly lower than the tax rates just mentioned. Therefore, it is extremely important to manage the taxation of mutual funds and be aware of the fund's portfolio turnover. This being said, turnover is of minimal concern for tax-deferred accounts, such as pension plans, 401(k) plans, and IRAs since the gains are not taxed until distributed by such plan, usually at or during retirement.

Fees and Expenses

The costs that an investor is subject to are described in the Fees and Expenses section of the prospectus, including loads, management fees, other operating costs, and 12b-1 fees. There will often be an example of the fees a shareholder will pay over a period of years based on certain rate of return assumptions.

Buying and Selling Shares

The prospectus explains how potential investors can purchase shares and how shareholders can sell or redeem shares. Oftentimes, investors can redeem shares by mail, phone, fax, or via the Internet.

Minimum Initial Investment

All mutual funds have minimum initial investments. As described earlier in the chapter, most of these minimums are low. When selecting mutual funds, it is important to establish what the minimum investment is, so as to exclude funds that are not economically feasible due to the minimum requirement. In most cases, this information is found in the prospectus and on the mutual fund account application.

Investor Services

Mutual funds provide a variety of services to shareholders, including automatic investments, automatic redemptions, telephone representatives to answer questions, reports to shareholders, and so on. All of this information will be found within the prospectus.

Although all of the above information can be helpful in determining whether or not a fund is appropriate for an investor, the above is certainly not an exhaustive list of what a professional should review before recommending a fund. In addition to the above information, funds should be evaluated based on risk-adjusted returns, load adjusted returns, tax adjusted returns, relative performance compared with similar funds, capital gain exposure, risk characteristics, sector weightings, price earnings ratios, etc. These additional characteristics of mutual funds are not generally found in fund prospectuses, but can be found in the Morningstar and Wiesenberger databases. In addition to the above, most planners consider modern portfolio theory statistics when choosing funds for a portfolio.

EXHIBIT 15.12: SAMPLE MORNINGSTAR ANALYSIS

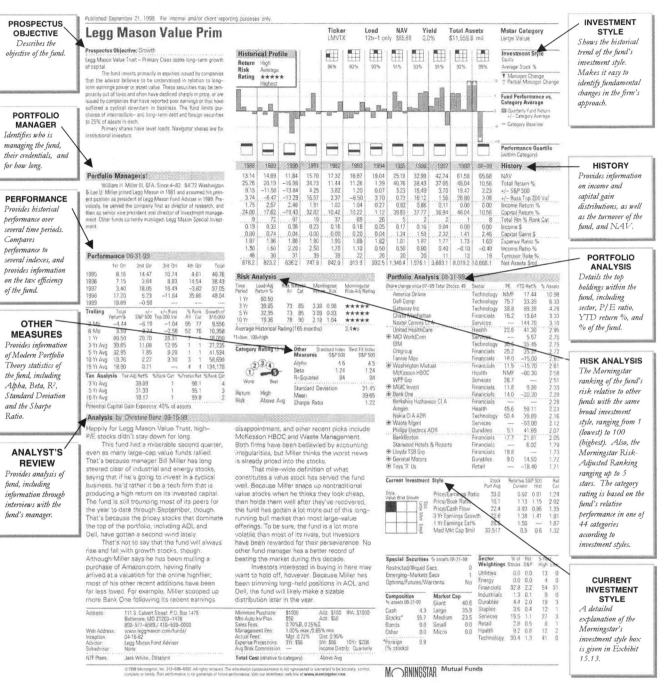

Source: Morningstar Mutual Funds, 2000. Morningstar, Inc., Chicago, IL

EXHIBIT 15.13: MORNINGSTAR'S INVESTMENT STYLE BOXES

Equity Style Box:

Risk	Value	Blend	Growth	Median Market Capitalization
Low	Large-Cap Value	Large-Cap Blend	Large-Cap Growth	Large
Moderate	Mid-Cap Value	Mid-Cap Blend	Mid-Cap Growth	Medium
High	Small-Cap Value	Small-Cap Blend	Small-Cap Growth	Small

Fixed-Income Style Box:

Risk	Value	Blend	Growth	Quality
Low	Short-Term High Quality	Interm-Term High Quality	Long-Term High Quality	High
Moderate	Short-Term Medium Quality	Interm-Term Medium Quality	Long-Term Medium Quality	Medium
High	Short-Term Low Quality	Interm-Term Low Quality	Long-Term Low Quality	Low

The equity style box contains nine possible combinations, ranging from large-cap value to small-cap growth.

The fixed-income style box contains nine possible combinations, ranging from short maturity, high quality for the safest funds to long maturity, low quality for the riskiest.

Source: Morningstar Mutual Funds, 2000. Morningstar, Inc., Chicago, IL

MODERN PORTFOLIO THEORY (MPT) STATISTICS & PERFORMANCE MEASURES

As described in Chapter 12, the concepts of modern portfolio theory have been widely accepted among financial practitioners. These MPT statistics provide insight into the fund's risk-return characteristics. Some of the more common statistics that are considered include R^2, beta, Jensen's alpha, Sharpe ratio, and Treynor ratio.

R^2 (Coefficient of Determination)

(R^2) coefficient of determination - a modern portfolio theory statistic that indicates the percent change in a portfolio or mutual fund that can be explained by changes in the market (generally defined by an index)

The **coefficient of determination**, which is generally referred to as R^2, is found by squaring the correlation coefficient. The correlation coefficient, generally denoted with the symbol "R", is a statistical measure generated from a regression analysis that provides insight into the relationship between two securities or two indexes. The correlation coefficient indicates the direction of the relationship between the two indexes or securities and the strength of the relationship between the two items.

The result of squaring the correlation coefficient is the coefficient of determination. R^2 is an indication of the percentage change in a dependant variable that can be explained by changes in an independent variable. In the context of portfolios, it is an indication of percent change in a portfolio or mutual fund that can be explained by changes in the market (generally defined by an index). R^2 ranges from 0 to 100. When R^2 equals 100 (such as with an index fund), it indicates that 100 percent of the change in the portfolio or mutual fund is attributable to changes in the market. When R^2 equals 50, it indicates that 50 percent of the change in the portfolio or mutual fund is attributable to changes in the market.

Since R^2 provides insight into the changes in a portfolio that are attributable to a market or index, it actually provides insight into the percentage of systematic risk included in the portfolio. For example, a mutual fund that has an R^2 of 85 indicates that 85 percent of the change in the portfolio results from changes in the market. The remaining 15 percent (100 percent - 85 percent) of the change in the portfolio is from some other source than changes in the market. This other source, since it is not systematic risk, must be unsystematic risk. Therefore, 15 percent of the change in the portfolio must be attributable to business risk, financial risk or one of the other unsystematic risks.

When using an asset allocation strategy, it is important to select funds that are highly correlated to the asset classes included in the portfolio. Funds or portfolios that have a high R^2 are funds that are highly correlated to the market.

Beta

Beta is a commonly used measure of risk that is also derived from regression analysis. It is a measure of systematic risk and provides an indication of the volatility of a portfolio compared to the market. The market is defined as having a beta of 1.0. Portfolio betas greater than 1.0 are more volatile than the market, while portfolios with betas less than 1.0 are said to be less volatile than the market. A portfolio with a beta of 1.5 is considered to be 50 percent more volatile than the market. Similarly, a portfolio with a beta of 0.7 is considered to be 30 percent less volatile than the market.

Since beta measures systematic risk, it is a good measure of risk if the portfolio is sufficiently diversified. Diversified portfolios have minimal unsystematic risk, which means that beta is capturing the majority of the risk of the portfolio. However, when the R^2 of the portfolio is low, then the portfolio has a substantial amount of unsystematic risk and beta does not capture all of the relevant risk. Therefore, beta is more appropriate for portfolios and mutual funds that are highly correlated to the market and sufficiently diversified.

Measures of Performance

Three performance measures commonly used with mutual funds include Jensen's Alpha, Sharpe ratio, and Treynor ratio. As with all investments, investors are concerned about both returns and risk. These performance measures provide a method of quantifying the risk-adjusted performance of investments, including mutual funds.

Jensen's Alpha

Jensen's Alpha is an absolute measure of performance. It indicates how the actual performance of the investment compares with the expected performance. The expected performance is calculated using the Capital Asset Pricing Model (discussed in Chapter 14), which uses beta as its measure of risk.

beta - a commonly used measure of systematic risk that provides an indication of the volatility of a portfolio compared to the market

Jensen's Alpha - an absolute measure of performance - it indicates how the actual performance of an investment compares with the expected performance

The formula for alpha is often written as follows:

$$\alpha = R_p - [R_f + \beta(R_m - R_f)], \text{ where}$$

α = Alpha

R_p = Actual return of the portfolio

R_f = Risk-free rate of return

β = Beta of the portfolio

R_m = Expected return of the market

Notice that alpha is equal to the difference between the actual return (R_p) and the expected return, which is found by using the Capital Asset Pricing Model (security market line): $R_f + \beta(R_m - R_f)$. A higher alpha indicates that the actual return of the investment is better than what was expected, based on the level of risk of the investment. For instance, if the actual return of a portfolio is 25 percent and the expected return was 20 percent, then the alpha equals 5 percent. In other words, the portfolio performed five percentage points better than expected on a risk-adjusted basis. Similarly, a negative alpha implies that the return of the investment was less than expected based on the level of risk. An alpha of zero means that the investment performed as expected.

It is worth mentioning that since alpha uses beta as its measure of risk, it is important to understand the limitations of beta. As we said, beta is less reliable when R^2 is low. Therefore, if beta is unreliable, then the output, alpha, is also unreliable.

Sharpe Ratio

Sharpe ratio - a measure of risk-adjusted portfolio performance that uses standard deviation as the risk measure

The **Sharpe ratio** is also a measure of risk-adjusted performance. However, like the Treynor model, it is a relative measure of performance, meaning that the ratio by itself has little or no meaning. The ratio is only meaningful when compared to other alternative investments. The formula for the Sharpe ratio is written as follows:

$$S_p = \frac{R_p - R_f}{\sigma_p}, \text{ where}$$

S_p = Sharpe ratio

R_p = Actual return of the portfolio

R_f = Risk-free rate of return

σ_p = Standard deviation of the portfolio

The Sharpe ratio is calculated by dividing the incremental return that the portfolio has generated above the risk-free rate of return by the standard deviation of the portfolio. For example, if ABC growth mutual fund returned 12 percent, while the risk-free rate was 3 percent and the standard deviation was 20 percent, then the Sharpe ratio would equal 0.50. The ratio of 0.50 has no meaning in and of itself. However, when compared to alternative investments, it becomes meaningful. For instance, the Sharpe ratio for the following mutual funds is provided:

Fund Name	Sharpe Ratio
High Growth Mutual Fund	1.20
S&P 500 Index Mutual Fund	0.95
ABC Growth Mutual Fund	0.50
XYZ Growth Mutual Fund	0.30

In the above table, it now seems clear that on a risk-adjusted basis, XYZ Growth Mutual Fund (0.30 Sharpe Ratio) and ABC Growth Mutual Fund (0.50 Sharpe Ratio) are mediocre performing funds. Two better alternatives appear to be the High Growth Mutual Fund (1.20 Sharpe Ratio) and the S&P 500 Index Mutual Fund (1.00 Sharpe Ratio).

Since the Sharpe ratio uses standard deviation as the measure of risk, it incorporates total risk (both systematic and unsystematic risk) into the calculation. Therefore, Sharpe ratio does not have the same limitations as alpha with regards to R^2.

Treynor Ratio

The **Treynor ratio** is a similar relative performance measure to the Sharpe ratio except for its measure of risk. Treynor uses beta as its measure of risk. Therefore, the same issues with regard to the use of beta in the calculation of alpha also apply to the calculation of the Treynor ratio. The formula for the Treynor ratio is generally depicted as:

$$T_p = \frac{R_p - R_f}{\beta_p}, \text{where}$$

T_p = Treynor ratio

R_p = Actual return of the portfolio

R_f = Risk-free rate of return

β_p = Beta of the portfolio

Treynor ratio - a measure of risk adjusted portfolio performance that uses beta as the risk measure

The formulas for Treynor and Sharpe are very similar, except for the measure of risk. The Treynor ratio also evaluates the incremental return above the risk-free rate of return. Similar to Sharpe, alternative investments should be ranked in order from the highest to the lowest ratio. The investment with the highest Treynor ratio is the one that has the highest risk-adjusted return.

If all of the performance measures provide a quantification of the risk-adjusted return of investments, should the rankings, from highest to lowest, for each of the three measures be the same? The answer to this question is that "it depends." Specifically, it depends on the value of R^2. If R^2 is high, then the three performance measures will provide similar rankings. However, if R^2 is not high, then the three performance measures may not provide similar rankings. This inconsistency occurs because of the use of beta instead of standard deviation as the measure of risk in two of the performance measures.

ISSUES TO LOOK FOR WHEN MANAGING PORTFOLIOS OF MUTUAL FUNDS

Once an investment strategy, including one that involves mutual funds, has been implemented, the portfolio must be monitored to be certain that it is performing in the way expected. There are certain aspects of mutual funds that should be monitored to be certain that the fund is performing as anticipated. These characteristics include changing asset size, style shift, manager changes, and capital gain exposure.

CHANGING ASSET SIZE

When mutual funds have good performance for several years in a row, new assets flow to these funds making them bigger. This changing asset size can result in a change in the basic dynamics of the fund. This is especially true for funds that invest in small-cap and mid-cap asset classes. There are only a limited number of small and mid-sized companies to invest in and, as we discussed above, mutual funds have restrictions on the amount that can be invested in any one particular company. Therefore, when a small-cap mutual fund dramatically increases its asset base, the fund may no longer be able to invest the additional assets as efficiently or effectively as it had in the past. If this occurs, returns suffer and assets may begin to leave the fund. To prevent this problem, some funds will close temporarily to new investors, thus limiting the asset base of the fund to protect the dynamics of the fund. Therefore, it is important to monitor the asset size of small-cap and mid-cap equity funds to be sure they are not growing too fast.

STYLE SHIFT

As part of the asset allocation process, the large cap equity allocation is often segregated into value, growth, and core styles. The purpose of this segregation is to have one growth fund, one value fund, and one core fund, for example. What happens, though, if the value fund begins using more of a growth style? All of a sudden, the diversified portfolio is now more heavily weighted toward growth. It may be that the portfolio is performing well at this time, but it is also likely that when the growth style goes out of favor the portfolio may decline significantly. Therefore, it is important to monitor that the fund's style remains consistent with the fund's stated objective.

MANAGER CHANGES

The reason managers of mutual funds are well compensated is that they are the ones making the buy-and-sell decisions, which causes the fund to have good or poor performance. Since the manager is responsible for the performance of the fund, it is important to watch for changes in the management structure of the fund. In most cases, one person manages the fund while in other cases a team manages the fund. A change in investment management means that there is increased risk that the fund will not be managed as before and, therefore, historical returns may have less significance to predicting future returns.

CAPITAL GAIN EXPOSURE

All equity funds have some amount of unrecognized built-in capital gains within the portfolio. This results from the unrealized appreciation of securities within the portfolio. This capital gain exposure is important to monitor for a fund in an existing portfolio, but is critical to consider when initially evaluating whether to purchase a particular fund.

When you are using Mutual Funds as the investment vehicle for a client's portfolio how many funds do you generally use?

A client's financial situation will dictate the number of funds I utilize in a portfolio. The number of funds is determined by the amount of assets to be invested and the best way to achieve a diversified asset allocation. This allocation will usually include investments in large cap growth and value, small cap growth and value, mid-cap growth and value, international securities, domestic fixed income, and cash.

The amount of assets we have to invest will drive fund selection. If possible, I will recommend funds in each of these asset classes but sometimes there are not enough dollars to go around. In that case, I will select funds that incorporate more than one investment class, i.e. global funds, balanced funds, etc.

What are the key investment issues that you consider when selecting among fixed income mutual funds?

When selecting fixed income mutual funds, I first determine whether a taxable or tax-exempt fund is appropriate. Once the universe has been narrowed down to taxable or tax-exempt, I evaluate the average credit quality of the fund. Whether I select a fund with investment grade or non-investment grade issues is determined by the risk tolerance and goals of my client.

Evaluating the average duration is very important in minimizing interest rate risk. I match the average duration of the funds I choose to my client's time horizon and I try to incorporate a range of durations into the portfolio.

What are the key investment issues that you consider when selecting among equity mutual funds?

My goal in the selection of equity funds is to include five funds, at a minimum: a small cap growth fund, a small cap value fund, a large cap growth fund, a large cap value fund and an international equity fund. If the client has enough assets, I will also include a mid-cap growth fund and a mid-cap value fund. Therefore, the manager's

investment style will be my first consideration. The weighting in each of these classes will be determined by the client's risk tolerance and time horizon. The more aggressive we can be, the heavier the weighting in small cap and foreign stocks.

I usually choose funds with at least a five year track record, 10 years is preferable, although there are some exceptions to that. Once I have narrowed the universe of equity funds based on asset class and track record, I then evaluate the critical risk measures of like funds. I will compare the standard deviation, beta, Sharpe ratio and alpha on each of the funds I am considering in order to select the fund that, historically, has had the best risk-adjusted returns over the long-haul. Although this is no guarantee of future performance, it's a starting point.

When building a portfolio based on Asset Allocation how important is the coefficient of determination (r^2) in your selection of funds?

When I am building a portfolio based on asset allocation, my investment class selection is driven by correlation. I want to incorporate assets in the portfolio that have little correlation, no correlation or negative correlation with one another in order to achieve maximum diversification and minimize risk.

For your taxable clients how important is your funds turnover rate?

Consideration of the turnover rate is important in fund selection but not a driving force. High turnover rate will increase fund expenses, which will cut into return. In addition, the net return will be reduced after taxes are paid on the distributions generated by turnover. In this regard, I am cognizant of historic after-tax returns for funds with high turnover rates. If a fund has managed to consistently perform well on a risk-adjusted basis in spite of its high turnover rate, I will consider it for the portfolio. The best solution to this dilemma is to put a high turnover fund in a nontaxable account where taxable distributions are irrelevant.

JILL PEETLUCK FEINSTEIN, CFP™

DISCUSSION QUESTIONS

1. Why have mutual funds become the increasingly predominant method for small investors to gain access to equity and fixed income investments?
2. What are the qualifications that investment companies must meet to receive non-taxable treatment?
3. What are the three types of investment companies and how does each function?
4. What are the various fees that mutual fund companies charge?
5. What are the three classes of mutual fund shares?
6. How do fund expenses impact fund performance?
7. What are expense ratios and how do they differ among mutual funds?
8. What are the advantages of mutual funds?
9. What are the disadvantages of mutual funds?
10. What are the types of mutual funds?
11. How are the objectives of money market mutual funds and fixed income mutual funds similar?
12. What are the contributing factors that make equity mutual funds so popular?
13. What is the most important factor in determining long-term variation (risk) in portfolio returns?
14. What is the mean-variance optimization model?
15. How do professional investment advisers select mutual funds for inclusion in a portfolio?
16. How does the information in a mutual fund's prospectus help an investor evaluate a fund?
17. How is the coefficient of determination useful in measuring the performance of a portfolio?
18. What is beta and what are its limitations?
19. What makes Jensen's Alpha an absolute measure of performance?
20. What are the issues to be aware of when managing mutual fund portfolios?

EXERCISES

1. List the characteristics of unit investment trusts.
2. List the characteristics of closed-end investment companies.
3. List the characteristics of open-ended investment companies.
4. List the differences between a front-end load and a back-end load.
5. Compare and contrast load and no-load funds.
6. Compare and contrast the Sharpe Ratio and the Treynor Ratio as measures of portfolio performance.
7. Sandra has a portfolio with a beta of 1.2 and an actual return of 15%. Given a risk-free rate of 6% and an expected market return of 12%, compute Jensen's alpha.
8. The Performance Fund had returns of 21 percent over the evaluation period and the benchmark portfolio yielded a return of 19 percent over the same period. Over the evaluation period, the standard deviation of returns from the Fund was 20 percent and the standard deviation of returns from the benchmark portfolio was 15 percent. Assuming a risk free rate of return of 5 percent, use the Sharpe index to find the performance of the fund and the benchmark portfolio over the evaluation period.
9. Rebecca Williams has a portfolio with a beta of 1.5 that earned 12 percent during the current year. The market (S&P 500) earned 10 percent over the same period. The risk free rate of return was 5 percent. Using the Treynor Index, did Rebecca's portfolio outperform the market on a risk-adjusted basis?

10. Barbara invests $50,000 into a mutual fund that has a 5 percent front-end load. How much is actually invested in the fund?

11. Barbara invests $50,000 into a mutual fund that has a 5 percent front-end load. What rate of return does she have to earn to restore her investment back to $50,000?

12. Constance invested in a fund that had a declining redemption fee. The fee for withdrawing her investment is 5 percent within the first year, 4 percent within the second year, 3 percent within the third year, 2 percent within the fourth year, and 1 percent within the fifth year. If Constance redeemed her investment for $100,000 in the third year, how much is her redemption fee?

13. Compare and contrast, in terms of objectives, a growth fund and a growth-and-income fund.

14. Compare and contrast, in terms of objectives, an equity-income fund and a high-grade corporate bond fund.

15. Compare and contrast, in terms of objectives, an international fund and a balanced fund.

PROBLEMS

1. Damian is considering investing in the Growth mutual fund. He has a choice of investing in A, B, or C shares. Each class has an annual rate of return of 10% after operating expenses. However, each class of shares has a combination of loads and 12b-1 fees that must be considered. The loads and fees for the A, B, and C shares are described below:

CLASS	LOAD	12b-1 FEE	CONVERSION
A Shares	5% front load	25 basis points	N/A
B Shares	5% declining redemption fee*	100 basis points	Converts to A Shares after 5 years
C Shares	1% redemption fee	100 basis points	No conversion

*5% fee for redemption within the first year, 4% fee within the second year, 3% fee within the third year, 2% fee within the fourth year, and 1% fee within the fifth year.

▲ Determine which class of shares is the best choice if the fund is held for 1 year.
▲ Determine which class of shares is the best choice if the fund is held for 3 years.
▲ Determine which class of shares is the best choice if the fund is held for 7 years.
▲ Determine which class of shares is the best choice if the fund is held for 10 years.
▲ Determine which class of shares is the best choice if the fund is held for 20 years.

Tax and Business Planning

in **BRIEF** →

- Collecting tax returns and other client information
- Income tax rates
- Tax advoidance vs. tax evasion
- The Internal Revenue Service and Administration
- Audits
- Interest and penalties
- Payroll taxes
- Tax-advantaged investments

- Proprietorships
- Partnerships
- Limited liability partnerships
- Family limited partnerships
- Corporations
- S corporations
- Limited liability companies

- Calculating tax liability
- Selecting tax-advantaged investments
- Matching entity goal with entity type
- Selecting proper business form

Tax and Business Planning

Risks

- Overpayment of income tax liability
- Audit
- Interest and penalties
- Improper entity selection
- Excessive taxation
- Excessive tax liability

Data Collection

- Client questionnaire
- Prior income tax returns
- Information forms (W-2, 1099)
- Details of taxable transactions
- Entity characteristics
- Formation and operation of entity
- Ownership and transfer issues
- Limited liability tax characteristics
- Goals for entity

Goals

- Legally minimize the income tax liability
- Select the business form that best fits entity goals

Data Analysis

- Calculation of tax liability
- Alternative tax strategies for tax savings
- Taxable transactions
- Entity type selection

CHAPTER 16

Individual Income Tax and Tax Planning

LEARNING OBJECTIVES:

After learning the material in this chapter, you will be able to:

1. List the objectives of the Federal Income Tax Law and give examples of each.

2. Identify the sources of tax-related client information and explain how each affects tax planning.

3. Name three different tax rate structures under which income can be taxed and discuss how those rate structures differ.

4. Perform the calculation to determine a client's income tax liability.

5. Discuss the difference between tax avoidance and tax evasion.

6. Describe the IRS organization's new structure and give examples of the types of rulings issued as guidance to taxpayers.

7. Understand the IRS audit selection and screening process.

8. List the various civil penalties imposed on taxpayers who violate the tax law.

9. Identify the various payroll taxes imposed on individuals through the Federal Insurance Contributions Act (FICA) and the Federal Unemployment Tax Act (FUTA).

10. Discuss the various tax-advantaged investment options available to taxpayers.

INCOME TAX PLANNING

One of the most important areas of financial planning is income tax planning. Income taxes have an impact on almost every business and investment decision as well as many personal decisions. The objective of tax planning is to pay the lowest tax legally permissible consistent with overall financial planning objectives. The financial planner must not only consider the tax ramifications of a proposed action or transaction, but must also develop an appropriate tax planning strategy consistent with the client's goals and objectives.

Effective tax planning has been complicated over the years by the constant changes to the tax law. The federal income tax system in the United States is among the most complex tax systems in the world. The 1980s and 1990s witnessed frequent tinkering with the Internal Revenue Code in an attempt to raise revenues for the federal government. This tinkering has resulted in Title 26 (the Income Tax Section) containing over two thousand code sections. This complexity alone has caused many individuals to seek the advice of CPAs and attorneys regarding tax matters of planning and compliance.

HISTORY

Under the United States Constitution, any direct tax imposed by Congress was required to be apportioned among the individual states based on that state's relative population. In 1909, Congress passed the Sixteenth Amendment to the U.S. Constitution, which allowed Congress to levy a tax on all income without apportionment among the states.

The Sixteenth Amendment, ratified in 1913, stated that:

"The Congress shall have the power to lay and collect taxes on incomes, from whatever source derived, without apportionment among the several states, and without regard to any census or enumeration."

After 1913, Congress further exercised its taxing authority with the passage of several revenue acts, further adding to the complexity of the income tax system. In an attempt to resolve confusion, Congress combined the separate sources of the tax law in 1939. This legislation, named the Internal Revenue Code of 1939, systematically arranged all previous legislation and provided the basis for a standardized income tax law.

The 1939 Code was revised in 1954 and again in 1986. The governing federal income tax law today is the Internal Revenue Code of 1986 (the Code), as amended.

2001 TAX REFORM

The Economic Growth and Tax Relief Reconciliation Act of 2001 (herein referred to as TRA 2001) was signed by President George W. Bush in June of 2001 providing a $1.35 trillion tax cut. While some changes are effective for 2001, many changes are phased in over the next several years. This chapter presents the applicable provisions prior to TRA 2001 as well as after.

OBJECTIVES OF THE FEDERAL INCOME TAX LAW

There are several objectives of the federal income tax law. These objectives can be classified as revenue raising, economic, and/or social in nature.

The revenue-raising objective is the most important of these objectives. The primary goal of taxation is to provide the resources necessary to fund governmental expenditures. Individual income taxes provide almost 50 percent of the annual revenues of the federal government.

EXHIBIT 16.1: INTERNAL REVENUE COLLECTIONS BY PRINCIPAL SOURCES (1997)

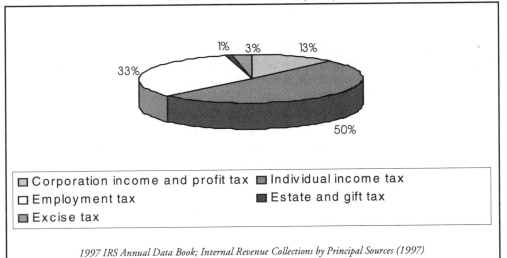

1997 IRS Annual Data Book; Internal Revenue Collections by Principal Sources (1997)

The federal income tax system is also used as a means to address certain economic goals. Taxation is a major tool used by the government to achieve the goals of economic growth and full employment. During periods of recession, taxes can be lowered, thereby increasing the disposable income in the hands of taxpayers. This allows individuals to spend more money, thus increasing demand, resulting in economic growth.

Social objectives are also accomplished through effective income tax legislation. The Internal Revenue Code (the Code) contains many economic incentives designed to encourage social objectives. For example, it is socially desirable to contribute to charitable organizations. Therefore, to encourage such contributions, the Code permits limited deductions for contributions of money or property to qualified charitable organizations. In addition, the Code provides various beneficial treatments for homeowners and those saving for retirement.

Other socially motivated provisions include the targeted jobs credit, which helps certain citizens find employment, and larger standard deductions for older and/or blind taxpayers.

DATA COLLECTION AND RISK ANALYSIS

Before a financial planner can provide tax advice or prepare tax estimates for a client, sufficient data must be gathered from the client. The data gathered would help the planner understand a client's economic situation, his or her tolerance for risk, and the role income taxes play in the client's overall financial plan.

Tax data can be gathered from many sources. Three major sources of data include the client questionnaire, prior income tax returns, and information forms sent to the client by various individuals, corporations, and partnerships. Each of these sources of data is discussed below.

CLIENT QUESTIONNAIRE

The client questionnaire is frequently the starting point of comprehensive financial planning engagements. The questionnaire, which is completed by the client, contains information about the client, the client's financial position, and the client's family. The planner can use several elements of the questionnaire to devise a tax projection and develop tax-planning strategies. See the Appendix in Chapter 3 for a sample Client Data Collection Questionnaire.

Although questionnaires can be prepared and presented to clients in many ways, several items of information should always be requested from a client in the questionnaire. Many of these items can assist the planner in the tax planning process.

The following is an overview of the tax-related information items that should appear in a client questionnaire:

- ▲ Client and spouse name, address, age, and Social Security numbers.
- ▲ Family information, including the names of children and parents and their Social Security numbers.
- ▲ Detail of investment assets and retirement plans.
- ▲ Detail of personal residence and rental property.
- ▲ Salaries, bonuses, and other sources of income.
- ▲ Detail of expenses and other deductions for budgeting and income tax.

Each of the items listed above may provide the planner with information necessary to provide a comprehensive tax projection. For example, the family information section of the questionnaire may allow the planner to determine if the client's parents can be claimed as dependents by the taxpayer.

PRIOR INCOME TAX RETURNS

Prior income tax returns are generally a major source of information to the planner. The returns should be carefully analyzed to ascertain key client financial information, as well as to determine the client's general tolerance for risk. This can be determined by the investment return sources (for example, money markets, aggressive mutual funds, etc.) When reviewing prior tax returns, the planner should ask the following questions:

▲ Do the tax returns indicate the taking of aggressive tax positions?
▲ Is the client's tax return risk taking consistent with other client risk taking, such as investment risk?
▲ How does the client feel regarding a potential IRS audit?
▲ What is the client's lifestyle and personality?

The financial planner can also determine whether to accept the individual as a client based on the positions taken on prior tax returns. If the client has taken positions on prior returns that are contrary to tax law, the planner may not want to become involved with such an individual.

INFORMATION FORMS

When a taxpayer provides goods or performs services during the year, the taxpayer will receive compensation in the form of income. This **earned income** (as well as any **unearned income** such as interest or dividends) must be reported on the individual's tax return. The payer of this earned or unearned income usually must provide the recipient with a written statement detailing the amount paid. These written statements, known as **information returns**, provide the taxpayer with a significant portion of the information needed to prepare the federal income tax return.

A large number of information returns exist, each serving a different purpose. The most common information returns are the Form W-2, Form 1098, and the Form 1099 series. These forms are discussed below.

If the taxpayer is an employee, he or she will receive a Form W-2 from the employer on or before January 31 following the tax year. The form discloses the amount of taxable wages and other compensation paid to the employee, as well as income taxes withheld and Social Security (FICA) taxes withheld. In addition, this form details employee contributions to 401(k) plans, distributions received from deferred-compensation plans, taxable fringe benefits, taxable group term life insurance coverage, and state wages and withholding.

earned income - income from personal services as distinguished from income generated by property

unearned income - also referred to as investment income, it includes such income as interest, dividends, capital gains, rents, royalties, and pension and annuity income

information returns - a written statement provided to the taxpayer after the end of each tax year detailing the amount of income (as well as unearned income such as interest or dividends) earned by the taxpayer. The most common information return is the Form W-2

a Control number	22222	Void ☐	For Official Use Only ▶ OMB No. 1545-0008		
b Employer identification number			1 Wages, tips, other compensation $		2 Federal income tax withheld $
c Employer's name, address, and ZIP code			3 Social security wages $		4 Social security tax withheld $
			5 Medicare wages and tips $		6 Medicare tax withheld $
			7 Social security tips $		8 Allocated tips $
d Employee's social security number			9 Advance EIC payment $		10 Dependent care benefits $
e Employee's first name and initial Last name			11 Nonqualified plans $		12a See instructions for box 12 $
			13 Statutory employee ☐ Retirement plan ☐ Third-party sick pay ☐		12b $
			14 Other		12c $
					12d $
f Employee's address and ZIP code					

15 State Employer's state ID number	16 State wages, tips, etc. $	17 State income tax $	18 Local wages, tips, etc. $	19 Local income tax $	20 Locality name
	$	$	$	$	

Form **W-2** Wage and Tax Statement

2001

Department of the Treasury—Internal Revenue Service

Copy A For Social Security Administration— Send this entire page with Form W-3 to the Social Security Administration; photocopies are not acceptable.

For Privacy Act and Paperwork Reduction Act Notice, see separate instructions.

Cat. No. 10134D

Do Not Cut, Fold, or Staple Forms on This Page — Do Not Cut, Fold, or Staple Forms on This Page

---

If income other than salary is received during the tax year, the taxpayer may receive one or more of the Form 1099 series. The payer of the income is required to furnish the appropriate Form 1099 to the recipient of the income. In addition, the payer must also file the form with the IRS.

Form 1099 INT is the form used to report interest income paid to any individual. Reportable interest includes interest on deposits with banks, brokers, or investment companies.

Form 1099 DIV is the form used to report dividend income paid to any individual. Reportable dividends include corporate dividends paid to shareholders.

Form 1099 G is the form used to report certain government payments made to an individual. For example, a state income tax refund would be reported on this form.

Form 1099 R is the form used to report distributions from retirement plans. Retirement plans include pension plans, profit-sharing plans, and IRAs.

Form 1099 MISC is the form used to report other income, such as income from rental property, royalties, and self-employment income.

Form 1098 is the form used to report payments of mortgage interest by a taxpayer. The form must also include any points paid by the buyer of a residence.

INDIVIDUAL INCOME TAX RATES

Tax rates are applied to an individual's taxable income to determine the amount of tax due. Currently, income can be taxed under three different rate structures: ordinary tax rates, capital gain tax rates, and alternative minimum tax (AMT) rates.

ORDINARY RATES

Once taxable income has been calculated, the income must be separately classified as ordinary or capital, since different tax rates may apply to capital gains.

Ordinary income includes any income that arises from services, or from property that is not classified as a capital asset. Salaries, interest, dividends, rents, and income earned from a sole proprietorship, partnership, S corporation, or LLC/LLP are all considered ordinary income.

> **ordinary income** - any income that arises from services, or from property that is not classified as a capital asset

If the taxpayer's income is classified as ordinary income, the tax on this income is calculated based upon one of four rate tables. The appropriate tax rate table is chosen based upon the individual's filing status, which is one of the following:

▲ Married individuals filing joint returns (includes qualifying widow/widower).
▲ Married individuals filing separate returns.
▲ **Head of household**.
▲ Single.

> **head of household** - the filing status that identifies a taxpayer as an unmarried individual who maintains a household for another and satisfies certain conditions set forth in the Internal Revenue Code

The income tax rate tables are graduated, meaning that the rates increase as taxable income increases. The ordinary income tax rates are the same for each filing status; however, the taxable income thresholds for which these rates apply vary between the tables. For the 2001 tax year, ordinary income tax rates are 10%, 15%, 27.5%, 30.5%, 35.5%, and 39.1%. These rates and the rates in Exhibit 16.3 are a blended annual rate that takes into consideration the decrease in the tax rates beginning July 1, 2001. For example, the 39.1% bracket is found by taking the average of the old rate of 39.6% and the new top rate of 38.6%.

573

EXHIBIT 16.3: 2001 TAX RATES AND BRACKETS

Single – Schedule X

If taxable income is: Over --	But not over --	The tax is:	Of the amount over --
$0	$6,000	-------------- 10.0% *	$0
6,000	27,050	$600 + 15.0%	6,000
27,050	65,550	3,757.50 + 27.5%	27,050
65,550	136,750	14,345.00 + 30.5%	65,550
136,750	297,350	36,061.00 + 35.5%	136,750
297,350	----------	93,074.00 + 39.1%	297,350

Head of Household – Schedule Z

If taxable income is: Over --	But not over --	The tax is:	Of the amount over --
$0	$10,000	-------------- 10.0% *	$0
10,000	36,250	$1,000.00 + 15.0%	10,000
36,250	93,650	4,937.50 + 27.5%	36,250
93,650	151,650	20,722.50 + 30.5%	93,650
151,650	297,350	38,412.50 + 35.5%	151,650
297,350	----------	90,136.00 + 39.1%	297,350

Married Filing Jointly or Qualifying Widow(er) – Schedule Y-1

If taxable income is: Over --	But not over --	The tax is:	Of the amount over --
$0	$12,000	-------------- 10.0% *	$0
12,000	45,200	$1,200.00 + 15.0%	12,000
45,200	109,250	6,180.00 + 27.5%	45,200
109,250	166,500	23,793.75 + 30.5%	109,250
166,500	297,350	41,255.00 + 35.5%	166,500
297,350	----------	87,706.75 + 39.1%	297,350

Married Filing Separately – Schedule Y-2

If taxable income is: Over --	But not over --	The tax is:	Of the amount over --
$0	$6,000	-------------- 10.0% *	$0
6,000	22,600	$600.00 + 15.0%	6,000
22,600	54,625	3,090.00 + 27.5%	22,600
54,625	83,250	11,896.88 + 30.5%	54,625
83,250	148,675	20,627.50 + 35.5%	83,250
148,675	----------	43,853.38 + 39.1%	148,675

New income rate bracket established by TRA 2001

The ordinary income tax rates will be gradually lowered in future years based on the provisions of TRA 2001. The following table details the future ordinary tax rates.

EXHIBIT 16.4: ORDINARY TAX RATES (2002 AND LATER)

Calendar Year:	27.5% Rate Reduced to:	30.5% Rate Reduced to:	35.5% Rate Reduced to:	39.1% Rate Reduced to:
2002 - 2003*	27%	30%	35%	38.6%
2004 - 2005	26%	29%	34%	37.6%
2006 and later	25%	28%	33%	35.0%

These rates are also effective for the period July 1, 2001 through December 31, 2001

CAPITAL GAIN RATES

Taxpayers may be eligible to use lower tax rates when they incur a gain upon the disposition of certain types of assets, known as capital assets. Several factors must be present for a gain to be afforded preferential treatment. In general, the asset must be:

▲ A capital asset.
▲ Sold or exchanged.
▲ Held for a long-term period.

Capital Asset

The Internal Revenue Code defines a **capital asset** by listing the types of assets that are <u>not</u> considered capital. All other assets disposed of are presumably capital assets. The following types of assets are <u>not</u> considered capital assets:

▲ Inventory or property held for sale to customers in the ordinary course of the taxpayer's trade or business.
▲ Accounts or notes receivable arising in the ordinary course of a trade or business.
▲ Depreciable real or personal property used in a trade or business.
▲ Copyrights or creative works held by the creator.
▲ A United States Government publication held by a taxpayer who received it other than by purchase.

Therefore, property held for personal use is a capital asset, as is property used for the production of income. Examples of capital assets include securities held for investment, a personal residence, and a personal automobile.

capital asset - broadly speaking, all assets are capital except those specifically excluded by the Internal Revenue Code, including property held for resale in the normal course of business (inventory), trade accounts and notes receivable, and depreciable property and real estate used in a trade or business

Sale or Exchange

Gains or losses from the disposition of property will not qualify as a capital gain or loss unless the property is disposed of by a sale or exchange. A sale is a transfer of property for an amount of money or money equivalent that is fixed or determinable. An exchange is a transfer of property for property other than money.

It is generally not difficult to determine whether a sale or exchange has occurred. However, the Internal Revenue Code has provided for several situations in which capital gain treatment is afforded even though a sale or exchange has not occurred. For example, capital loss treatment is allowed for a security that becomes worthless during the year, even though no sale or exchange has occurred.

In addition, there are situations when capital gain treatment is not available. **Like-kind exchanges** are generally not taxable transactions. For example, if a company trades in a used automobile as part of the down payment on a new automobile, there will be no gain or loss on the old automobile.

Long-Term Holding Period

Once it has been determined that the asset is a capital asset that has been sold or exchanged, the taxpayer may qualify for the lower capital gain tax rates if the property is held long-term. In general, a capital asset is held long-term if the taxpayer owned the asset for more than one year (that is, a year and one day). The date the asset is disposed of is part of the holding period. For example, if property is acquired on March 3, 2000, the property would need to be sold on or after March 4, 2001, to be considered long-term.

Tax Treatment of Long-Term Capital Gains

If the taxpayer recognizes a **long-term capital gain**, the gain may be taxed at a lower rate than the individual's ordinary income tax rate. In general, long-term capital gains are taxed at a maximum rate of 20 percent (18 percent if the asset was held more than five years) unless the individual is in the 10 percent or 15 percent ordinary income tax bracket, in which case the capital gain is taxed at a maximum rate of 10 percent (8 percent of the asset was held more than five years).

If the asset is a collectible, such as a work of art, or if the asset is small business stock (as defined in Section 1202), the maximum capital gain rate is 28 percent. In addition, capital gains on sales of depreciable real estate are taxed at a rate of 25 percent, to the extent of any unrecaptured straight-line depreciation on the property. The following table summarizes the different capital gain rates:

like-kind exchanges - an exchange of property held for productive use in a trade or business or for investment (except inventory, stocks and bonds, and partnership interests) for other investment or trade or business property

long-term capital gain - a gain from a sale or exchange of a capital asset that has been held for more than one year

EXHIBIT 16.5: CAPITAL GAIN RATES

Type of Capital Asset	Minimum Holding Period	Maximum Rate
Collectibles (antiques, etc.)	Greater than 1 year	28%
Depreciable real estate	Greater than 1 year	25%
Other capital assets (taxpayer is not in 10% or 15% ordinary income tax bracket)	Greater than 1 year	20%
Other capital assets (taxpayer is not in 10% or 15% ordinary income tax bracket)	Greater than 5 years and asset was acquired after year 2000	18%
Other capital assets (taxpayer is in 10% or 15% ordinary income tax bracket)	Greater than 1 year	10%
Other capital assets (taxpayer is not in 10% or 15% ordinary income tax bracket)	Greater than 5 years	8%

Tax Treatment of Short-Term Capital Gains

A **short-term capital gain** receives no special treatment, and is taxed as ordinary income.

short-term capital gain - a gain from a sale or exchange of a capital asset that has been held for less than one year

Tax Treatment of Capital Losses

An individual taxpayer may deduct **capital losses** only to the extent of capital gains plus the lesser of $3,000 or the net capital loss. The net capital loss is the excess of capital losses for the year over capital gains for the year.

capital losses - a loss from the sale or exchange of a capital asset

For example, if an individual has a short-term capital loss of $200 and a long-term capital loss of $3,700, the taxpayer is permitted a deduction from ordinary income of $3,000. The remaining loss of $900 ($200 + $3,700 - $3,000) can be carried forward to later years indefinitely until it is absorbed. The short-term loss is utilized first, so the carryover is $900 of long-term capital loss.

Alternative Minimum Tax Rates

The Alternative Minimum Tax (AMT) is a separate tax system that runs parallel to the regular tax system. The AMT system was designed to ensure individuals with large deductions and other tax benefits pay at least a minimum amount of tax.

The AMT calculation begins with the individual's taxable income, which is adjusted to arrive at alternative minimum taxable income (AMTI). AMT tax rates are then applied to AMTI, resulting in the tentative minimum tax. If the tentative minimum tax exceeds the individual's regular tax liability, the excess amount is the alternative minimum tax. The AMT calculation is summarized in the table below.

EXHIBIT 16.6: ALTERNATIVE MINIMUM TAX CALCULATION

	Taxable Income
+	Positive AMT adjustments
-	Negative AMT adjustments
=	**Taxable income after AMT adjustments**
+	Tax preferences
=	**Alternative Minimum Taxable Income (AMTI)**
-	AMT exemption
=	**Minimum tax base**
x	AMT rate
=	**Tentative AMT**
-	Regular income tax on taxable income
=	**AMT**

A taxpayer may incur an AMT liability if he or she has one or more of the following items of deduction or income:

▲ State and local income taxes.
▲ Real property taxes.
▲ Accelerated depreciation.
▲ Interest income on certain private activity bonds.
▲ Exercise of incentive stock options.
▲ Gain on sale of small business stock (as defined in Section 1202).

The tentative minimum tax is applied at a rate of 26 percent of AMTI up to $175,000. AMTI exceeding $175,000 is taxed at a 28 percent rate.

DETERMINING INCOME TAX LIABILITY

Of all the sources providing revenues to the federal government, the individual income tax is the largest. Computing an individual's income tax liability can be very complicated. The tax liability itself is a product of the taxpayer's taxable income, which is summarized in the following formula:

EXHIBIT 16.7: TAXABLE INCOME

Total Income (From Whatever Source Derived)	$xx,xxx
Less: Exclusions From Gross Income	(x,xxx)
Gross Income	$xx,xxx
Less: Deductions for Adjusted Gross Income	(x,xxx)
Adjusted Gross Income (AGI)	$xx,xxx
Less: The Larger of:	
Standard Deduction or Itemized Deductions	(x,xxx)
Less: Personal and Dependency Exemptions	(x,xxx)
Taxable Income	$xx,xxx

TOTAL INCOME AND GROSS INCOME

The tax computation begins with the determination of the taxpayer's total income, from whatever source derived. In general, all income is taxable unless Congress has specifically exempted the income from taxation. In tax terminology, income exempt from tax and not included in a taxpayer's **gross income** is referred to as an "**exclusion**."

gross income - income subject to the federal income tax. Gross income does not include income for which the IRC permits exclusion treatment

exclusion - income exempt from tax and not included in a taxpayer's gross income

In determining gross income, the taxpayer may exclude many different types of income received. A list of the more common types of income that may be excluded appears below:

▲ 401(k) salary deferrals.
▲ 403(b) salary deferrals.
▲ Accident insurance proceeds.
▲ Bequests.
▲ Child support payments received.
▲ Certain employee fringe benefits.
▲ Gifts received.
▲ Group term life insurance premiums (limited).
▲ Inheritances.
▲ Interest received from municipal bonds.
▲ Life insurance proceeds received.
▲ Meals and lodging (furnished for the convenience of the employer on the employer's premises).
▲ Scholarship grants (for tuition and books of a degree candidate).
▲ Veteran's benefits.
▲ Workers compensation.

The amount of income remaining after removing the exclusions is termed the taxpayer's gross income. Gross income is generally the starting point for the federal individual income tax return (Form 1040).

During 2001, Joe received salary of $60,000, dividends of $2,000, tax-exempt interest of $500, and a gift of $20,000 from his parents. Joe has total income for 2001 of $82,500, since total income is based on income from all sources. However, Joe's gross income reported on his tax return is $62,000, the sum of the $60,000 salary and the $2,000 taxable dividend income. The remaining $500 of tax-exempt interest income and $20,000 gift is excluded from gross income.

ADJUSTED GROSS INCOME (AGI)

The gross income can further be reduced by allowed deductions. Deductions that reduce gross income directly are referred to as "deductions for AGI" or "**above-the-line**" **deductions**. The "line" referred to in this phrase is **Adjusted Gross Income**, commonly referred to as AGI.

AGI is a very important concept for individual income taxation. It represents the basis for computing percentage limitations on certain itemized deductions such as the charitable, medical, and miscellaneous itemized deductions. AGI also serves as a benchmark for percentage limitations of total itemized deductions, personal and dependency exemptions, and passive rental real estate losses.

In determining adjusted gross income, the taxpayer may reduce gross income by the following:

▲ Ordinary and necessary expenses incurred in a trade or business.
▲ Net capital losses (limited).
▲ One-half of self-employment tax paid.
▲ Alimony paid to an ex-spouse.

"above-the-line" deductions - an above-the-line deduction (also known as a deduction for AGI) is one that reduces gross income directly

adjusted gross income - a determination peculiar to individual taxpayers that represents gross income less business expenses, expenses attributable to the production of rent or royalty income, the allowed capital loss deduction, and certain personal expenses (deductions for AGI)

- ▲ Certain payments to a Keogh or SEP retirement plan.
- ▲ Contributions to a traditional IRA (limited).
- ▲ Qualifying moving expenses.
- ▲ Forfeited interest penalty for premature withdrawal of time deposits.
- ▲ Self-employed health insurance premiums (limited).
- ▲ Interest paid on qualifying education loans.
- ▲ Qualified higher education expenses (allowed as a deduction for tax years after 2001).

Deductions for AGI are more favorable than itemized deductions because they are generally subject to fewer limits than itemized deductions, and they do not require the taxpayer to itemize to receive a benefit from the deduction. They also reduce AGI, which reduces calculated hurdles for itemized deductions, and can reduce phased-out items.

ITEMIZED DEDUCTIONS AND THE STANDARD DEDUCTION

"below-the-line" - (also known as a deduction from AGI) is one that is subtracted from AGI in arriving at taxable income

Several deductions are allowed to reduce adjusted gross income. These deductions are often referred to as "deductions from AGI" or **"below-the-line" deductions**.

basic standard deduction - the amount allowed all taxpayers who do not itemize their deductions

The **basic standard deduction** is the amount allowed all taxpayers who do not itemize their deductions. It represents the government's estimate of tax-deductible expenses a taxpayer might have. The allowed standard deduction is based on the tax year and the taxpayer's filing status. The allowed basic standard deduction for 2001 is summarized in the table below:

EXHIBIT 16.8: 2001 ALLOWED BASIC STANDARD DEDUCTION

Filing Status	2001 Basic Standard Deduction
Single	$4,550
Married, Filing Jointly	$7,600
Qualifying Widow(er)	$7,600
Head of Household	$6,650
Married, Filing Separately	$3,800

itemized deductions - itemized deductions are ones that are in excess of the standard deduction and are used in lieu of the standard deduction

Taxpayers who have deductible expenses in excess of the standard deduction may choose to itemize and deduct these itemized expenses instead of taking the standard deduction. These expenses, referred to as **itemized deductions**, are generally expenses that are personal in nature. In addition, some of the itemized deductions have separate AGI limitations that may reduce their deductibility.

For example, medical expenses are only deductible if they exceed 7.5 percent of the taxpayer's AGI. If an itemizing taxpayer's AGI is $100,000, and he incurs unreimbursed medical expenses during the year of $8,000, only $500 ($8,000 – ($100,000 x 7.5%)) of the medical expenses is deductible.

The following is a brief list of some of the more common itemized deductions. It should be noted that some of the deductions listed below are subject to AGI or income limitations.

▲ Medical expenses. *
▲ State and local income taxes.
▲ Real estate taxes.
▲ Personal property taxes.
▲ Mortgage interest. *
▲ Investment interest. *
▲ Charitable contributions. *
▲ Casualty and theft losses. *
▲ Miscellaneous expenses (such as tax return preparation fees, etc.). *

* AGI or Income Limited

EXAMPLE

Mary is a single taxpayer. In the year 2001, she paid mortgage interest of $3,500, real estate taxes of $1,500, state income taxes of $2,000, and incurred medical expenses of $600. Assuming Mary's AGI is $50,000, her itemized deductions would total $7,000 ($3,500 + $1,500 + $2,000). The medical expenses are not deductible as itemized deductions, since they do not exceed 7.5 percent of Mary's AGI. Since Mary is a single taxpayer, her standard deduction would only be $4,550 for 2001, and therefore it would be beneficial for Mary to itemize her deductions. If Mary were married, she and her husband should take the standard deduction, which is $7,600 for 2001.

Not all individuals are entitled to the standard deduction. No standard deduction is allowed for the following individuals:

▲ A married person filing a separate return if his or her spouse itemizes deductions.
▲ A nonresident alien.
▲ An individual filing a tax return for a period of less than 12 months.

The basic standard deduction is reduced under IRC Section 63(c)(5) for an individual who may be claimed under Section 151 as a dependent of another taxpayer for a taxable year beginning in the calendar year in which the individual's taxable year begins. The basic standard deduction is limited to the greater of $750, or the sum of $250 and such individual's earned income.

In addition to the basic standard deduction, a taxpayer will be entitled to an additional standard deduction if he or she is blind or had attained the age of 65 by the end of the tax year.

EXHIBIT 16.9: 2001 ADDITIONAL STANDARD DEDUCTION

Filing Status	2001 Additional Standard Deduction
Single	$1,100
Married, Filing Jointly	$ 900
Qualifying Widow(er)	$ 900
Head of Household	$1,100
Married, Filing Separately	$ 900

PERSONAL AND DEPENDENCY EXEMPTIONS

dependent - an individual who can be claimed by a taxpayer for an exemption on an income tax return

exemptions - a basic deduction to which a taxpayer is entitled for self support (personal exemption) or for the support of a spouse and/or dependent (dependency exemption)

Every taxpayer is entitled to a basic deduction to support himself or herself, the spouse, and any **dependents**. The deduction allowed for the taxpayer is called the **personal exemption**, while the deduction allowed for the spouse and dependents is called the **dependency exemption**. For 2001, the personal and dependency exemption amount is $2,900. Therefore, a married taxpayer with three dependent children will be entitled to a personal and dependency exemption in the amount of $14,500 ($2,900 x 5). The allowed exemption amount is phased out for higher income taxpayers.

In order to claim an individual as a dependent, five tests must be met:

Support test – the taxpayer must provide over half the support to the dependent (unless a multiple support agreement exists).

Relationship test – the dependent must be a relative of the taxpayer, or a member of the taxpayer's household.

Gross income test – the dependent's income must be less than $2,900 for 2001 (unless an exception is met – child of taxpayer).

Joint return test – the dependent cannot file a joint income tax return, except to receive a refund of income tax withheld.

Citizenship test – the dependent must be a citizen or resident of the United States (or a resident of Canada or Mexico).

TAXABLE INCOME AND TAX RATES

Taxable income is calculated by reducing the adjusted gross income by the standard or itemized deduction, and further reducing this amount by the personal and dependency exemption. Taxable income is the tax base upon which the tax rates are applied to determine the taxpayer's tax liability before credits.

The tax rate schedule is based on the current tax year and the individual's filing status. The 2001 tax rates for all filing statuses are listed in Exhibit 16.3.

TAX CREDITS

Once the individual's tax liability is determined, it may further be reduced by any allowable tax credits. Tax credits result in a direct, dollar-for-dollar reduction in tax liability. A credit may be either refundable or nonrefundable. Most credits are nonrefundable, meaning that the credit can reduce an individual's tax liability to zero, but not below zero. Common tax credits include the Foreign Tax Credit, the Child and Dependent Care Credit, the Child Tax Credit, the Hope Credit, and the Lifetime Learning Credit.

TAX AVOIDANCE VS. TAX EVASION

The goal of most income tax planning is the reduction and minimization of the amount of tax that a person must pay to the government. **Tax avoidance** is the legal minimization of taxes. This avoidance is accomplished by applying knowledge of the Internal Revenue Code and the Treasury regulations to an individual's income tax situation. Every individual has the right to reduce his or her tax burden within the scope of the law.

The taxpayers' legal right to minimize or reduce personal income taxes has been upheld by the courts. In the case of Commissioner vs. Newman, Judge Learned Hand wrote:

"Over and over again courts have said that there is nothing sinister in so arranging one's affairs so as to keep taxes as low as possible. Everybody does so, rich or poor, and all do right, for nobody owes any public duty to pay more than the law demands; taxes are enforced extractions, not voluntary contributions. To demand more in the name of morals is mere cant."

Tax planning and tax avoidance involve only legal actions. Tax planning is the process of arranging one's actions in light of their tax consequences. In many cases, tax planning can be accomplished simply by changing the form of a transaction. For example, if an individual is invested in tax-exempt bonds, the individual would not be required to pay tax on the interest income earned by the bonds, and therefore his or her tax liability would be less than if he or she invested in taxable bonds.

While tax avoidance is the term applied to the legal interpretation of the tax laws to minimize tax liabilities, **tax evasion** is the term generally applied to any of the various fraudulent methods by which a taxpayer may pay less than his or her proper tax liability.

For example, if an individual works part-time at home babysitting the neighbors' children, the income received must be reported as income on the individual's income tax return. Since the babysitting income may not be reported to the government by the individual's neighbors, the individual may decide illegally to exclude the income from the tax return.

This example of tax evasion may lead to additional tax liability, as well as interest and penalties if the tax return is audited. The amount of interest and penalties depends on the amount of understatement. Tax evasion can even lead to fines and an occasional jail sentence.

THE MARRIAGE PENALTY

Before 1969, the opportunity to file a joint tax return was intended to be a benefit to married couples. Under the old law, the joint filing rates were designed to tax one-half of the married income at the single rates. This tax was then doubled to arrive at the tax due for married couples. This calculation of tax for married couples was inequitable for unmarried taxpayers, who would usually wind up paying more tax on the same amount of income.

In 1969, Congress attempted to alleviate this "singles penalty" by reducing the tax rates for unmarried taxpayers. This action did result in lower taxes for unmarried individuals, but it created an inequity in our current progressive income tax system. This inequity is often referred to

tax avoidance - the legal minimization of taxes, which is accomplished by applying knowledge of the IRC and the Treasury regulations to an individual's income tax situation

tax evasion - any of the various fraudulent methods by which a taxpayer may pay less than his or her proper tax liability

as the marriage penalty. The marriage penalty may occur when the incomes of both spouses are combined and taxed at the married filing joint (or separate) rates. The couple may wind up paying more in income taxes than they would if they were single, if their combined income pushes the couple into a higher tax bracket. Today, two-income couples are more common than in past years, and the marriage penalty is receiving more attention.

EXAMPLE

If a husband and wife each earn $25,000 in 2001, the income tax due (assuming the couple did not itemize) would be $4,890. However, if two single individuals each earned $25,000, the tax at single rates would be $2,332.50 each, for a grand total of $4,665. In this example, the marriage penalty is $225 ($4,890 – $4,665).

	MARRIED FILING JOINTLY	SINGLE
Adjusted Gross Income	$50,000.00	$25,000.00
Standard Deduction	(7,600.00)	(4,550.00)
	42,400.00	20,450.00
Personal Exemption	(5,800.00)	(2,900.00)
Taxable Income	36,600.00	17,550.00
Tax at 10%	1,200.00	600.00
Tax at 15%	3,690.00	1,732.50
Total tax	4,890.00	2,332.50
		x 2
		4,665.00
Total Tax MFJ		$4,890.00
Total Tax Two Singles		$4,665.00
Marriage Penalty		$ 225.00

In an attempt to reduce or eliminate the marriage penalty, legislation was passed that will increase the basic standard deduction for married taxpayers filing jointly (TRA 2001) to twice the standard deduction allowed for single filers. The standard deduction will be increased over a period of several years, beginning in 2005.

EXHIBIT 16.10: INCREASE OF STANDARD DEDUCTION FOR MARRIED FILING JOINTLY

Calendar Year	Standard Deduction for Joint Filers as % of Standard Deduction for Single Filers
2005	174%
2006	184%
2007	187%
2008	190%
2009 and later	200%

Filing status is determined as of the last day of the tax year, which is generally December 31st for individual taxpayers. Therefore, if a couple is contemplating a divorce, they could avoid the marriage penalty and save tax dollars by obtaining the divorce prior to year-end. Alternatively, a couple contemplating marriage in December should consider postponing the wedding until after the New Year to avoid the marriage penalty. (This does presuppose that the couple is tax conscious and does not find such planning to be unromantic).

THE INTERNAL REVENUE SERVICE AND ADMINISTRATIVE ISSUES

The Internal Revenue Service (IRS) is part of the Treasury Department. The IRS is responsible for administering and enforcing federal tax laws. To help satisfy this responsibility, the IRS issues Revenue Rulings and Revenue Procedures, which are official interpretations of the law.

ORGANIZATION OF THE IRS

The IRS structure, as of September 1, 1998, was built around districts and service centers, the basic organizational units were established many years ago and have evolved over decades. Each of these 43 units is charged with administering the entire tax law for every kind of taxpayer, large and small, in a defined geographical area. Consequently, both a service center and a district office serve every taxpayer with responsibility shifting depending on whether the work is done by phone, mail, or in person.

In the Collection division, three kinds of organizations use four computer systems to collect taxes. Each of these units and systems collect taxes from every kind of taxpayer, from individuals to large businesses.

This complicated structure was not enabling the IRS to achieve its strategic goals. Therefore, the IRS adopted a new mission statement in October 1998:

To provide America's taxpayers top quality service by helping them understand and meet their tax responsibilities and by applying the tax law with integrity and fairness to all.

Achieving the new mission statement has required the IRS to implement fundamental changes in many aspects of the institution. The modernized IRS will be organized around the needs of specific groups of taxpayers.

Under the new IRS structure, four operating divisions will be responsible for serving specific groups of taxpayers. Four functional organizations will be responsible for specific issues and cases. Two support organizations will be responsible for providing common services across the entire agency. Finally, a much smaller National Office will provide high-level strategy and policy setting.

Operating Divisions

The key operational units of the redesigned IRS will be four operating divisions, each charged with full, end-to-end responsibility for serving a set of taxpayers with similar needs. These divisions are summarized below.

Wage and Investment Division – will focus on individual taxpayers with wage and investment income only. Most of these taxpayers interact with the IRS once a year to file a return, and most receive refunds. This operating division will have a structure focused on meeting the pre-filing, filing, and post-filing needs of these individuals.

Small Business and Self-Employed Division – will focus on taxpayers that are fully or partially self-employed individuals, as well as small businesses. These taxpayers deal more frequently with the IRS on more complex issues and pay the IRS nearly 40% of the total cash collected each year. This operating division will also have a structure that focuses on meeting the pre-filing, filing, and post-filing needs of these taxpayers.

Large and Mid-Size Business Division – will focus on the largest filers, with assets over $5 million. While collection issues are rare, many complex issues arise, such as tax law interpretations, accounting, and regulation.

Tax Exempt and Government Entities Division – will focus on pension plans, exempt organizations, and governmental entities, representing a large economic sector with unique needs. This operating division will be organized around the distinct groups of taxpayers it serves--exempt organizations, pension plans, and governmental entities--with common supporting elements.

Functional Organizations

Four functional organizations will be nationwide organizations that address specific issues and cases. These organizations are summarized below.

Counsel – will provide the correct legal interpretation of the internal revenue laws consistently and uniformly for all taxpayers and all operating divisions. Counsel will establish a senior legal executive as the Division Counsel for each operating division to participate fully in the plans and activities of the operating division management and to provide high-quality legal advice and representation.

Appeals – will remain an independent channel for taxpayers having a dispute over a recommended enforcement action.

Taxpayer Advocate – has been centralized under the National Taxpayer Advocate to establish an independent channel for taxpayers who are having problems with a specific case. Taxpayer Advocate employees will be geographically distributed to provide local contact with taxpayers.

Criminal Investigation – will include approximately 3,000 IRS employees who provide a necessary element of law enforcement.

IRS GUIDANCE

Due to the complexity of the federal tax law, the IRS often issues guidance as to how it will treat certain transactions for tax purposes. This guidance is often given using letter rulings, determination letters, revenue rulings, revenue procedures, and technical advice memoranda.

A **letter ruling** is essentially a statement by the IRS of the way it will treat a prospective or contemplated transaction for tax purposes. In response to a written request from a taxpayer, the National Office prepares the letter ruling. A ruling will generally be honored only with respect to the specific taxpayer to whom the ruling was issued. Other taxpayers cannot assume that the IRS will apply the letter ruling to them, even if they engage in the same transaction set out in the letter ruling. It does, however, provide other taxpayers with an idea of the IRS's application of the law.

A **determination letter** is a written statement issued by a District Director of the IRS. The letter applies the principles and precedents announced by the National Office to a given set of facts. Determination letters are issued only if the issue can be resolved based on clearly established rules. They are typically used when establishing a qualified retirement plan, such as a pension or profit-sharing plan.

The National Office of the IRS issues **revenue rulings**, and they provide an official interpretation on how the law should be applied to a specific set of facts. They are typically issued because of many requests for **private letter rulings** with respect to an area of the tax law. Taxpayers may rely on revenue rulings in determining the tax consequences of their transactions; however, taxpayers must determine if their facts closely resemble the facts presented in the ruling.

Revenue procedures are statements reflecting the internal management practices of the IRS that affect the rights and duties of taxpayers.

Technical advice memoranda give advice or guidance in memorandum form and are furnished by the National Office of the IRS. An IRS agent typically requests the memorandum during an audit. The purpose of technical advice is to help IRS personnel close cases and to help establish and maintain consistent holdings throughout the IRS.

AUDIT PROCESS/PENALTIES AND INTEREST

A goal of the IRS is to promote the highest degree of compliance with the Internal Revenue Code. Tax compliance is a voluntary process. Without some sort of audit process, the IRS would have no means by which to ensure compliance with the law. Before conducting an audit, the IRS must use a screening process to determine which taxpayers will be subject to audit, and must determine who will perform the audit and what type of audit will be conducted.

The percentage of returns audited each year varies depending on the IRS's available staff. Returns on which all or most of the income was subject to withholding and where taxpayers did not itemize their deductions are the returns least likely to be audited.

letter ruling - a written statement issued by the National Office of the IRS that giving guidance on the way the IRS will treat a prospective or contemplated transaction for tax purposes

determination letter - a written statement issued by an IRS district director that applies the principles and precedents announced by the National Office to a given set of facts

revenue rulings - official pronouncements of the National Office of the IRS

private letter rulings - statements issued for a fee upon a taxpayer's request that describe how the IRS will treat a proposed transaction for tax purposes

revenue procedures - official pronouncements of the National Office of the IRS

technical advice memoranda - advice or guidance in memorandum form furnished by the National Office of the IRS to IRS agents who request such advice or guidance during an audit. Technical Advice Memoranda help to close cases and establish and maintain consistent holdings throughout the IRS

Where on the Web

Certified Financial Planner Board of Standards *www.CFP-Board.org*

Society of Financial Service Professionals (formerly known as the American Society of CLU & ChFC) *www.asclu.org*

American Institute of Certified Public Accountants (CPA/PFS) *www.aicpa.org*

Financial Planning Association *www.fpanet.org*

National Association of Insurance Commissioners *www.naic.org/splash.htm*

National Association of State Boards of Accountancy *www.nasba.org*

North American Securities Administrators Association *www.nasaa.org*

American Bar Association *www.abanet.org*

National Association of Personal Financial Advisors *www.napfa.org*

Association for Investment Management and Research (CFA designation) *www.aimr.org*

Securities and Exchange Commission *www.sec.gov*

National Association of Securities Dealers, Inc. *www.nasd.com*

The American College *www.amercoll.edu*

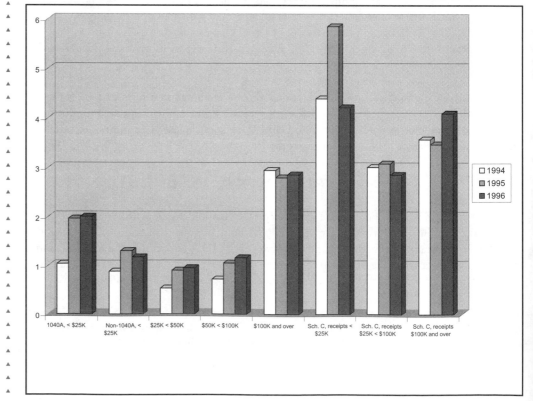

EXHIBIT 16.11: INDIVIDUAL INCOME TAX RETURNS EXAMINED

SELECTION AND SCREENING PROCESS

The IRS employs various methods and procedures for identifying and selecting individual returns for examination.

One selection method employed by the IRS is the **Discriminant Index Function System (DIF)**. The DIF system is a mathematical technique used to classify tax returns as to their examination potential. Under this system, returns are divided into different audit classes. Weights are then assigned to certain return characteristics in accordance with a formula that varies with each audit class. These weights are added together to arrive at the total DIF score for the return. DIF returns with the highest scores are made available to the examination division of the IRS for manual screening.

Although DIF scores indicate examination potential, tax examiners must manually screen returns to identify issues in need of examination and to eliminate those returns where an audit is not warranted. Either revenue agents or tax auditors, depending on the complexity of the issues involved and the degree of auditing skills required to perform the examination, manually screen individual returns.

If an audit examination is to be conducted, a classification check sheet is prepared and attached to the return. The check sheet lists significant items to be considered and identifies whether a correspondence audit, an office audit, or a field audit will be performed. The determination of which type of audit to conduct is made based on the complexity of the return and which type of audit is most conducive to effective and efficient tax administration.

TYPES OF AUDITS

A **correspondence audit** is conducted almost entirely by written correspondence and telephone contact with the taxpayer. These audits typically involve simple issues, such as itemized deductions, IRA contribution limits, and self-employment tax.

Office audits usually involve issues too complicated to be resolved by mail, such as travel and entertainment expenses, income from rents, and large itemized deductions. In most cases, the audit is conducted at the IRS office located near the taxpayer's home. The taxpayer is informed that his or her tax return is being audited and is usually requested to furnish certain information.

Field audits are conducted for complex individual returns with business or other financial activities. IRS revenue agents handle field audits, as opposed to office audits, which are conducted by less-skilled tax auditors. These audits are typically conducted at the taxpayer's business location or at the location where the taxpayer's books are maintained. Before the field audit begins, the examiner makes a pre-contact analysis of the return to determine which items should be examined.

discriminant index function system (DIF) - a mathematical technique used to classify tax returns as to their examination potential

audits - correspondence, office, field- inspection and verification of a taxpayer's return or other transactions possessing tax consequences. Correspondence audits are conducted by mail; office audits are conducted in the tax agent's office; field audits are conducted on the business premises of the taxpayer or in the office of the tax practitioner representing the taxpayer

OUTCOMES OF AUDITS

Once the audit is complete, there are four possible outcomes to determinations made by the examiner.

No Change to the Return– the examiner proposes no change in the taxpayer's tax liability.

Taxpayer Agrees with Examiner's Findings – if the taxpayer agrees with the examiner's proposed changes, the taxpayer signs an agreement form and pays any additional taxes and interest owed. The taxpayer may even receive a refund because of the audit.

Taxpayer Does Not Agree with Examiner's Findings – if the taxpayer does not agree with the examiner's proposed changes, the taxpayer has the right to appeal. The IRS will send the taxpayer a "30-day letter" notifying the taxpayer of his or her right to appeal the proposed changes within 30 days. If the taxpayer does not respond within 30 days, the IRS will send a "90-day letter," which is a notice of deficiency.

The notice of deficiency officially informs the taxpayer that the IRS has determined that a tax deficiency exists, and details both the basis for and the amount of the deficiency. Once an individual has received a "90-day letter," he or she may pay the deficiency, file a Tax Court petition, or take no action.

Taxpayer Partially Agrees with Examiner's Findings – the taxpayer agrees with some, but not all, of the examiner's proposed changes.

If a taxpayer has exhausted all of his or her administrative remedies, he or she may litigate a case in court. The following chart details the court system as it applies to tax litigation.

EXHIBIT 16.12: INCOME TAX APPEAL PROCEDURE

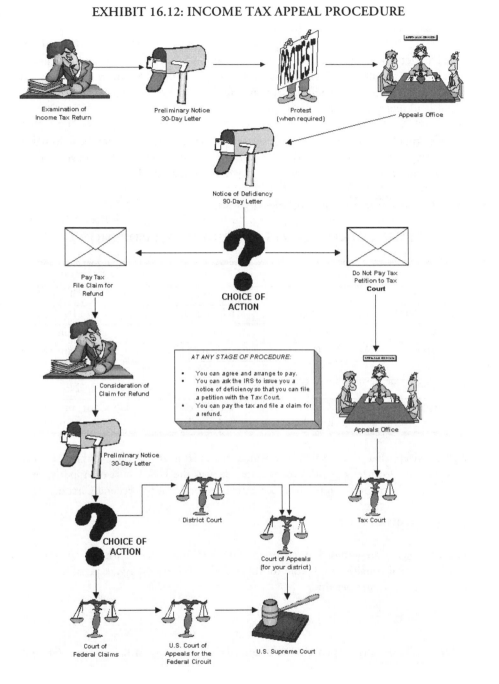

The litigation begins in a court of original jurisdiction, or trial court. The U.S. Tax Court, U.S. District Court, and U.S. Court of Federal Claims are all trial courts that may hear tax cases.

The U.S. Tax Court tries only tax cases. The taxpayer does not pay the alleged deficiency, but files suit against the IRS Commissioner to stop the collection of tax. The court consists of 19 judges and a jury trial is not available. The Small Claims Division may try the case if the deficiency is equal to or less than ($50,000).

The U.S. District Court tries tax cases, as well as many other types of civil and criminal cases. The taxpayer pays the alleged deficiency and files suit against the U.S. government for a refund. There are 95 district courts and a jury trial is available. If the taxpayer has filed for bankruptcy, the Federal Bankruptcy Division may try the case.

The U.S. Court of Federal Claims tries tax cases, as well as other cases against the federal government. The taxpayer pays the alleged deficiency and files suit against the U.S. government for a refund. The court consists of 16 judges and a jury trial is not available.

Exhibit 16.13 summarizes the courts of original jurisdiction.

EXHIBIT 16.13: COURTS OF ORIGINAL JURISDICTION

	U.S. Tax Court	U.S. District Court	U.S. Claims Court
Number of Courts	1	95	1
Number of Judges	19	1 (per court)	16
Jurisdiction	National	District	National
Subject Matter	Tax Only	Criminal & Civil	Claims Against Govt.
Pay Deficiency?	No	Yes	Yes
Jury Available?	No	Yes	No
Where to Appeal?	US Court of Appeals	US Court of Appeals	US Court of Appeals - Fed Circuit

The appropriate appellate court depends on which trial court hears the case. If the case is tried in the Tax Court or District Court, the appeals are taken to the U.S. Court of Appeals. Appeals from the Claims Court are taken to the U.S. Court of Appeals for the Federal Circuit.

PENALTIES AND INTEREST

Various civil penalties are imposed on taxpayers and tax return preparers who violate the tax law. Included in the civil penalties are failure-to-file penalties, failure-to-pay-tax penalties, accuracy-related penalties, and fraud penalties.

Failure-to-File-Tax-Return Penalty

The **failure-to-file penalty** was enacted to ensure the timely filing of tax returns. Generally, a return is considered filed on the date it is delivered to the IRS.

The penalty is 5 percent of the amount of tax required to be shown on the return for each month or fraction of a month that the failure continues, up to a maximum penalty of 25 percent. The penalty period runs from the due date of the tax return, including extensions, to the date the IRS actually receives the return.

failure-to-file penalty - a civil penalty imposed on taxpayers and tax return preparers who fail to file tax returns according to the requirements of tax law

The failure-to-file penalty is reduced by any failure-to-pay penalty.

Failure-to-Pay-Tax Penalty

The **failure-to-pay-tax penalty** is imposed on taxpayers who, without reasonable cause, fail to pay the tax shown on a return. The penalty is one-half of one percent of the tax shown for each month that it is not paid, up to a maximum penalty of 25 percent.

Jim files his tax return 40 days after the due date. He remits a check for $7,000 that represents the balance of the tax due. Jim's failure-to-file and failure-to-pay penalties total $700, calculated as follows:

Failure to Pay ($7,000 x .5% x 2 months)		$70
Failure to File ($7,000 x 5% x 2 months)	$700	
Less: Failure-to-Pay Penalty	(70)	$630
Total Penalty		$700

Interest is generally payable whenever any tax or civil penalty is not paid when due, even if the taxpayer has been granted an extension of time to pay the tax. Interest on unpaid tax liabilities runs from the last day prescribed by the Code for payment to the date paid.

Accuracy-Related Penalties

The **accuracy-related penalty** is a penalty of 20 percent of the portion of the tax underpayment attributable to negligence, substantial understatement of tax, or substantial valuation misstatement.

Negligence includes any failure to make a reasonable attempt to comply with the tax laws, exercise reasonable care in return preparation, and keep proper books and records or properly substantiate items. If the IRS has evidence that the taxpayer was negligent, the taxpayer must establish that he or she was not negligent by a preponderance of the evidence.

A Substantial Understatement of Income Tax occurs when an individual fails to report on his or her income tax return the appropriate amount of tax that should be imposed, and this understatement exceeds the larger of (a) 10 percent of the correct tax, or (b) $5,000.

Substantial Valuation Misstatement occurs when a taxpayer undervalues or overvalues property or services, resulting in the understatement of income tax liability. The valuation misstatement is considered substantial if the value claimed on the return is 200 percent or more of the correct value. However, the penalty does not apply unless the understatement of tax liability exceeds $5,000.

Scott, who has a 30.5% marginal tax rate, contributes artwork to a charitable organization and claims a deduction of $40,000. Assuming the actual fair market value of the art is $18,000, Scott would be subject to the 20 percent accuracy-related penalty since the overstatement of the asset's value was more than 200 percent of the correct value, and the understatement of tax liability is more than $5,000.

---

failure-to-pay-tax penalty - a civil penalty imposed on taxpayers who, without reasonable cause, fail to pay the tax shown on their return

EXAMPLE

accuracy-related penalty - a penalty of 20% of the portion of the tax underpayment attributable to negligence, substantial understatement of tax, or substantial valuation misstatement without intent to defraud

EXAMPLE

The accuracy-related penalty does not apply with respect to any portion of an underpayment if the taxpayer has a reasonable cause for the position taken on the return. The determination of whether a taxpayer acted with reasonable cause and in good faith is made on a case-by-case basis, taking into account all pertinent facts and circumstances.

Fraud Penalties

The fraud penalty is a penalty of 75 percent of the portion of the tax underpayment attributable to the fraud. With respect to this penalty, the IRS must prove that there was an underpayment and that the underpayment was attributable to fraud.

For the **fraud penalty** to apply, there must be a willful attempt to evade tax. The taxpayer must have intended to mislead the IRS or conceal information to prevent the collection of taxes. Civil fraud has not been clearly defined, but courts have inferred fraudulent intent from factors such as understatement of income, failure to file tax returns, and failure to cooperate with tax authorities.

The fraud penalty does not apply with respect to any portion of an underpayment if the taxpayer has a reasonable cause for the position taken on the return. In addition, the imposition of the fraud penalty precludes the imposition of the accuracy-related penalty on the same underpayment.

PAYROLL TAXES

The federal government, through the Federal Insurance Contributions Act (FICA), imposes employment taxes on employers, employees, and self-employed individuals. These taxes provide for a federal system of old age, survivors, disability, and hospital insurance.

The Federal Unemployment Tax Act (FUTA) provides for payments of unemployment compensation to workers who have lost their jobs.

FICA TAXES FOR EMPLOYERS AND EMPLOYEES

The Federal Insurance Contributions Act (FICA) created several different programs designed to prevent people from becoming poverty stricken. The two most important and well-recognized programs created by FICA are the Old Age, Survivor, and Disability benefits program (OASDI), better known as Social Security, and the Hospital Insurance (HI) program, better known as Medicare. These taxes have different tax rates and only OASDI tax has a wage base limit.

Contributions to these programs are made by salary reductions for employees and by direct payments to the government by employers and self-employed individuals. FICA taxes are imposed on employees at a combined rate of 7.65 percent. This rate represents the total of the 6.2 percent rate for the Social Security (OASDI) portion, and the 1.45 percent rate for the Medicare (HI) portion. These rates are applied to the employee's total wages for the year, up to a maximum of $80,400 for the year 2001 for the Social Security portion of the tax. The employer is required to make a matching contribution for each employee.

fraud penalty - a penalty levied against a taxpayer by the IRS after it has proven an underpayment of tax by the taxpayer and proven that the underpayment was attributable to a willful attempt to evade tax

For example, if Tom earns a salary of $100,000 for ABC Company, he will have $6,434.80 withheld from his paycheck for FICA taxes, computed as follows:

EXAMPLE

Social Security Portion (6.2% x $80,400)	$4,984.80
Medicare Portion (1.45% x $100,000)	$1,450.00
Total FICA Taxes	$6,434.80

ABC Company will be required to pay the amount withheld from Tom's paycheck, plus their own equal matching contribution. ABC Company will also receive a deduction for their share of the FICA taxes paid.

SELF-EMPLOYMENT TAX

Self-employed individuals must bear the burden of both the employer and employee portion of FICA taxes. Therefore, the **self-employment tax** rate is 15.3 percent, double the employee's rate of 7.65 percent. This tax is calculated on Schedule SE, which is attached to the individual's Form 1040.

Self-employment tax is calculated in the same fashion as FICA tax; however, the tax is based on net earnings from self-employment, not on the individual's wages. The net earnings from self-employment is the gross income from the trade or business, less any allowable deductions. Before applying the income tax rates, net earnings may be reduced by 7.65 percent, which is one-half of the self-employment tax rate.

For example, if Andrea owns her own business, and during the year her income after allowed deductions is $200,000, she would incur $15,325.90 in self-employment tax, calculated as follows:

Net earnings from self-employment	$200,000
Less: 7.65% of net earnings	($15,300)
Amount subject to self-employment tax	$184,700
Social Security portion (12.4% x $80,400)	$9,969.60
Medicare portion (2.9% x $184,700)	$5,356.30
Total self-employment taxes	$15,325.90

Andrea will report the self-employment tax on her income tax return, and will receive a deduction of $7,662.95, one-half of the self-employment tax. This amount will be deducted in arriving at Adjusted Gross Income (above-the-line deduction).

self-employment tax - tax paid by self-employed individuals which is based on net earnings, not on the individual's wages. Since the self-employed must bear the burden of both the employer and employee portion of FICA, the self-employment tax rate is 15.3%--double the employee's rate of 7.65%

EXAMPLE

EXHIBIT 16.14: FORM 1040 - ADJUSTMENTS TO INCOME

Income	7	Wages, salaries, tips, etc. Attach Form(s) W-2		**7**	
	8a	**Taxable** interest. Attach Schedule B if required		**8a**	
Attach	b	**Tax-exempt** interest. DO NOT include on line 8a . . .	**8b**		
Copy B of your	9	Ordinary dividends. Attach Schedule B if required		**9**	
Forms W-2 and	10	Taxable refunds, credits, or offsets of state and local income taxes (see page 21) . .		**10**	
W-2G here.	11	Alimony received		**11**	
Also attach	12	Business income or (loss). Attach Schedule C or C-EZ		**12**	
Form(s) 1099-R	13	Capital gain or (loss). Attach Schedule D if required. If not required, check here ▶ ☐		**13**	
if tax was	14	Other gains or (losses). Attach Form 4797		**14**	
withheld.	15a	Total IRA distributions . **15a**	b Taxable amount (see page 22)	**15b**	
If you did not	16a	Total pensions and annuities **16a**	b Taxable amount (see page 22)	**16b**	
get a W-2,	17	Rental real estate, royalties, partnerships, S corporations, trusts, etc. Attach Schedule E		**17**	
see page 20.	18	Farm income or (loss). Attach Schedule F		**18**	
	19	Unemployment compensation		**19**	
Enclose, but do	20a	Social security benefits . **20a**	b Taxable amount (see page 24)	**20b**	
not staple, any	21	Other income. List type and amount (see page 24) --------------		**21**	
payment. Also,	22	Add the amounts in the far right column for lines 7 through 21. This is your **total income** ▶		**22**	
please use					
Form 1040-V.					
Adjusted	23	IRA deduction (see page 26)	**23**		
Gross	24	Student loan interest deduction (see page 26)	**24**		
Income	25	Medical savings account deduction. Attach Form 8853 .	**25**		
	26	Moving expenses. Attach Form 3903	**26**		
	27	One-half of self-employment tax. Attach Schedule SE .	**27**		
	28	Self-employed health insurance deduction (see page 28)	**28**		
	29	Keogh and self-employed SEP and SIMPLE plans . .	**29**		
	30	Penalty on early withdrawal of savings	**30**		
	31a	Alimony paid b Recipient's SSN ▶ _____	**31a**		
	32	Add lines 23 through 31a		**32**	
	33	Subtract line 32 from line 22. This is your **adjusted gross income** . . . . . . ▶		**33**	

For Disclosure, Privacy Act, and Paperwork Reduction Act Notice, see page 54.   Cat. No. 11320B   Form **1040** (1999)

FEDERAL UNEMPLOYMENT TAX ACT

The Federal Unemployment Tax Act (FUTA) provides for payments of unemployment compensation to workers who have lost their jobs. Most employers pay both a federal and state unemployment tax. The employee is not responsible for the payment of unemployment tax.

Federal unemployment taxes are imposed on employers who pay wages of $1,500 or more during any calendar quarter during the year, or who employ at least one individual on each of 20 days during the current or previous year. The FUTA tax rate is 6.2 percent, and it is applied to the first $7,000 the employer pays each employee as wages during the year. Therefore, the maximum FUTA payment required for a covered employee is $434 ($7,000 x 6.2%).

TAX-ADVANTAGED INVESTMENTS

One goal shared by most financial planners and their clients is the minimization of all current and future taxes. Since taxes are often an individual's highest expenditure each year, effective reduction of taxes is of extreme importance.

Although Congress has significantly reduced the opportunities available to minimize income taxes, there are still a few opportunities available for investors interested in or already involved in tax-advantaged investments. Included in these opportunities are investments in tax-exempt securities, investment in tax shelters and vacation homes, use of tax-advantaged employee benefits, use of acceleration/deferral techniques, and awareness of exemption opportunities.

INVESTMENT IN TAX-EXEMPT SECURITIES

As a rule, interest income is taxable regardless of its source. However, interest income from certain state and local bonds and interest on educational savings bonds is excluded from income for federal income tax purposes.

Interest on obligations of a state, territory, U.S. possession (such as Puerto Rico), or any of their political subdivisions is nontaxable. If an individual has money to invest, he or she may wish to invest in state bonds if income tax reduction is an important goal. It should be noted, however, that state governments typically offer lower interest rates on these bonds than the rate offered on taxable investments. Therefore, to determine if an investment in a tax-exempt security is a wise choice, one can calculate an interest rate that a tax-exempt investment must earn to "break even" with the higher rate offered by a taxable investment. The formula to determine the break-even interest rate is:

Taxable Interest Rate x (1 – Marginal Tax Rate) = Tax-free Rate

EXAMPLE

Joe has a 35.5 percent marginal income tax rate, and he would like to invest in state of Kentucky bonds. If similar taxable investments yield 10 percent, Joe must earn a rate of return on the state of Kentucky bonds of at least 6.45% (10% x (1 – 35.5%)) to make this a worthwhile investment.

In addition to state bonds, interest on U.S. savings bonds such as Series EE bonds may be either tax deferred or tax exempt. The interest earned on the bond is tax deferred until the year the bond matures or is redeemed by the individual. Upon maturity, the individual may choose to exchange the Series EE bond for a Series HH bond to continue the tax deferral of interest. The interest income from a Series EE bond is completely tax free if the bond was issued after 1989, and if the accrued interest and principal amount of the bond is used to pay for qualified educational expenses of the taxpayer, spouse, or dependents.

TAX SHELTERS

Under prior law, an individual could reduce or eliminate his or her tax liability by investing in "tax shelters" that produced losses that could be used to offset other income. These shelters often created paper losses in excess of the amount of capital the investor provided, causing the tax shelter business to grow into a thriving industry.

Typically, tax shelters took the form of limited partnerships, thus allowing losses to flow through to the individual partners. In the first few years of the partnerships' operation, losses were generally high due to low revenues and high expenses, such as interest, taxes, and accelerated depreciation.

The Tax Reform Act of 1986 significantly curtailed the benefits available to investors in tax shelters by the introduction of the passive activity loss limits. Passive activities include all rental operations and all other businesses in which the taxpayer does not materially participate. An individual meets the material participation test only if he or she is involved in the operation of the activity on a regular, continuous, and substantial basis.

Although there are many exceptions, a taxpayer will be considered a material participant if he or she spends more than 500 hours in the activity during the year, or if he or she spends more than 100 hours in the activity and no other individual spends more time on the activity. If the investor is not a material participant, the activity is considered passive. Investors may not use passive activity losses to offset ordinary taxable income, such as salary, interest, and dividends. Passive losses can only be used to offset income from passive investments. If a loss is disallowed (suspended), it can subsequently be utilized when the taxpayer disposes of the activity.

Even though deductions for passive losses are generally disallowed, there are situations in which a taxpayer would benefit by investing in a tax shelter. For example, if the taxpayer has an investment in a passive activity that is generating income, any passive losses could be used to offset the passive income. In addition, a taxpayer may deduct a limited amount of loss against active income when the taxpayer invests in rental real estate.

A taxpayer who actively participates in a rental real estate activity may deduct up to $25,000 of losses annually. A taxpayer is considered an active participant if he or she participates in management decisions such as approving new tenants, and owns at least a 10 percent interest in the activity. The $25,000 allowance is reduced by 50 percent of the excess of the individual's AGI over $100,000, and is therefore completely phased out when the taxpayer's AGI reaches $150,000.

EMPLOYEE BENEFITS

Employee benefits can take several forms, including deferral of compensation and fringe benefits. Deferral of compensation can be accomplished under a variety of methods, including qualified and nonqualified plans. Both of these plans offer tax-advantaged benefits to employees, provided the employer satisfies various tests.

When an employer contributes to a qualified retirement plan on behalf of an employee, the employee is not required to include the employer's contribution in gross income, and the employer receives a current tax deduction in the amount of the contribution. In addition, earnings generated by investments in the qualified plan are nontaxable until the employee receives distributions from the plan, which usually occurs at retirement. Qualified plans fall into two basic categories, defined-benefit plans and defined-contribution plans.

A defined-benefit plan is designed to provide the employee with a specific benefit for a period of years or for life. The benefit is usually based on the employee's average or final compensation and length of service with the company. In order to provide the employee with the appropriate benefit at retirement, the company must employ an actuary to determine the required contribution to the plan each year. Defined-benefit plans can take the form of either a Defined-Benefit plan or a Cash Balance plan.

Defined-contribution plans provide for annual contributions to an employee's retirement account, but do not guarantee a specific benefit to the employee upon retirement. The employer may have discretion as to the annual contribution made to the plan, but such contributions must be recurring and substantial for the plan to qualify. These plans generally constitute profit-sharing plans, but may take the form of a Stock Bonus plan, or an Employee Stock Ownership Plan (ESOP), or a Money Purchase Pension plan.

A Stock Bonus plan is a qualified defined-contribution plan in which the company contributes shares of company stock. This plan is subject to the same requirements as a profit sharing plan, however, plan benefits are generally paid in the form of company stock, and the distribution may receive special tax treatment.

A Money Purchase plan is a defined-contribution plan in which the employer is required to make annual contributions, determined as either a percentage of employee compensation or a flat dollar amount. Although the employer is required to contribute to the plan each year, the employee has no guarantee as to his or her benefit at retirement. The retirement benefit from a money-purchase plan, as with any defined-contribution plan, is based on the employee's account balance when distributions begin.

Nonqualified plans allow employers to provide additional benefits to certain employees without the constraints imposed by the nondiscrimination rules of the Code. These plans lack the tax-favored treatment of qualified plans, but they do allow for tax-deferred growth of earnings within the plan.

Nonqualified plans often take the form of deferred compensation arrangements. With this arrangement, the employee agrees to give up a specified portion of current compensation in exchange for an employer promise to pay a benefit in the future. The future benefit is generally equal to the deferred amount plus a predetermined earnings rate. This plan enables employees to defer taxation on a portion of their earned income during high-tax-bracket years.

ACCELERATION OF DEDUCTIONS

In addition to pursuing tax-advantaged investments, the taxpayer may take advantage of opportunities to accelerate income tax deductions or defer income tax gains.

The Internal Revenue Code allows individual taxpayers to claim deductions for various personal, investment, and business expenses. The deduction can generally be claimed in the year in which the expenses are paid; therefore, individuals have some flexibility with respect to the timing of deductions. A taxpayer wishing to reduce or eliminate a potential tax liability can accelerate deductions by prepaying the expense. For example, state income taxes can be paid during the current tax year rather than waiting until the following year when the tax is due. Taxpayers can

also make additional contributions to charity before the close of the tax year, resulting in an income tax deduction in the current year.

DEFERRAL OF TAX GAINS

When a taxpayer disposes of property, any resulting gain is usually reported, or recognized, on the individual's income tax return in the year of disposition. However, there are several situations where a taxpayer can dispose of property and defer recognition of the gain until a later date.

Section 1031 of the IRC allows a taxpayer to exchange certain types of property without recognizing a gain. These "like-kind" exchanges are afforded beneficial tax treatment if the property exchanged is qualifying like-kind property. If property other than like-kind property, commonly called **boot**, is received in the exchange, gain may be recognized.

Like-kind property is generally any property <u>other than</u> the following:

▲ Personal use assets, such as a personal automobile.
▲ Ordinary assets, including inventory.
▲ Stocks, bonds, and other securities.
▲ Personal property exchanged for real property.
▲ Domestic property exchanged for foreign property.
▲ Different-sex livestock.

If a taxpayer is not required to recognize gain from a like-kind exchange, the basis of the property received by the taxpayer must be reduced by the unrecognized (deferred) gain, resulting in recognition of the deferred gain when the acquired property is subsequently sold.

EXAMPLE Assume Jack received business equipment worth $60,000 in exchange for business equipment with a tax basis to Jack of $35,000. Assuming the equipment qualifies as like-kind property, Jack's realized gain of $25,000 ($60,000 - $35,000) will not be reported on his income tax return. Jack's basis in the equipment received will be $35,000 ($60,000 - $25,000 deferred gain).

Taxpayers do not always dispose of their property intentionally. Occasionally, property is lost due to theft or to a casualty such as a fire or storm. When this occurs, the taxpayer may receive some sort of compensation such as insurance proceeds. The proceeds received may even exceed the taxpayer's basis in the property, resulting in a gain. Absent special provisions, the gain would be fully taxable in the year of the conversion, resulting in a potential financial hardship for the taxpayer.

Section 1033 of the IRC allows taxpayers to defer gains resulting from involuntary conversions if the taxpayer invests in qualifying replacement property within a specified period. Qualifying replacement property is any property that is similar or related in service or use to the property that is converted. The replacement period is generally two years from the end of the tax year in which the property is converted. Condemned real property receives a three-year replacement period.

boot - property (other than like-kind property) that qualifies as a tax gain when received in a property exchange

EXEMPTION OPPORTUNITIES

The IRC has traditionally provided tax breaks for homeowners, including the allowance of deductions for mortgage interest and property taxes. Recent changes in the tax law have provided for exclusion of some or all of the gain on the sale of a residence. The provision applies to residence sales as frequently as every two years, to gains in amounts up to $250,000 for single taxpayers and $500,000 for married taxpayers.

The exclusion is applicable to the sale of a residence owned by the taxpayer and used as a principle residence for two of the five years preceding the sale. If the taxpayer fails the use and/or ownership test, a partial exclusion may be available if the home is sold due to a change in employment, health, or other unforeseen circumstances. The allowed exclusion is based on a ratio of the number of qualifying months to 24 months.

Assume Mary, a single taxpayer, owned and used her home as a principle residence for 18 months. She then sold her home because of a new job in another city, realizing a gain on the sale of $300,000. Mary would be entitled to an exclusion of $187,500 ($250,000 x 18/24), resulting in a reportable capital gain of $112,500 ($300,000 - $187,500).

If a married couple filing jointly does not meet the conditions for claiming the full $500,000 exclusion, the excludible gain will be the sum of the exclusion that each spouse would be entitled to if both were single. For this purpose, each spouse is treated as owning the home for the period that either spouse owned the home.

The rules for married couples can be clarified with an example. When Al and Susan were married, Susan moved into the home Al had owned and had been using as his principle residence for over 20 years. They used the home as their principle residence for six months, then sold the home (gain of $600,000) because of a new job. The couple can exclude $312,500 of the gain, since Al will receive the full $250,000 exclusion and Susan will be entitled to a partial exclusion of $62,500 ($250,000 x 6/24).

Another exemption opportunity exists for taxpayers owning vacation homes. If the home is rented to others for 14 days or less during the year, any rental income from the home is excludible from the taxpayer's gross income, no matter how much rent is charged.

IN CONCLUSION

The federal tax system in the United States is among the most complex tax systems in the world. A financial planner must realize the importance of gaining a comprehensive understanding of the tax law, since income taxes are often the largest single expenditure of a client in a given year.

While changes to the law have made income tax avoidance much more difficult over the last few years, many tax planning opportunities still exist. It is the financial planner's duty to a client to be aware of these opportunities to prevent the client from paying more tax than he or she is obligated to pay.

PROFESSIONAL FOCUS

Do your self-employed clients make optimal use of statutory fringe benefits, such as, daycare and athletic facilities, as a form of non-taxable compensation?

After evaluating the costs of covering employee(s) through a business deductible (pre-tax) benefit plan versus purchasing (after-tax) a benefit without covering employee(s), most self-employed will in fact choose the optimum fringe benefit strategy. Optimization in this sense includes consideration of attracting and retaining employees, if applicable. When the client learns that they have to earn $1.67 to "buy" $1.00 of benefit after-tax in the 39.6 % bracket, it usually piques their interest.

With the change in capital gains rate versus ordinary income rates, has that caused you to change your asset allocation towards mutual funds with less turnover of funds?

Never let the tax tail wag the investment dog - review investments for their utility in your portfolio then compare/contrast on tax efficiencies. That being said, however, taxes do have a decimating impact on wealth accumulation. Studies have shown that taxes gobble up around 2.5 to 3.3 percentage points of return. Some tax efficient funds have "*significant built-in gains*" that could be realized in a market downturn so I have to defer to my first comment - never let the tax tail wag the investment dog.

What tips do you give to clients who have been notified that the IRS is auditing them?

If they are my clients, I remind them that this is why we substantiate and document all of our tax activities before, or at least, at the time of filing. For records, I recommend keeping them three years for personal deductible items, seven years for trade, business, or production of income activities, and, yes still, all home capital improvements (in case we exceed the exemption threshold or we convert to rental). When a return is being prepared and an aggressive tax position is being taken, I always make sure the client understands and agrees to the aggressive tax position and the added *potential* for examination or audit.

What tips would you give to a new professional who is handling a client's audit for a client?

Be a Boy Scout - BE PREPARED. Bring your documentation and have your arguments prepared with relevant statutory authority or case law cites. Be professional. The auditor or examiner is a professional as you are - give them the same due respect.

How do you encourage your clients to come to you prior to completing a transaction, so tax planning can be done before rather than after the fact?

I have a standing policy with all tax clients - anytime you have a tax or financial question or decision call me. I make this clear to them each and every time I do their returns. As their tax professional, I can fairly easily answer most questions without research and with a few minutes of conversation. I do not charge for these "non-research" queries so that it might encourage them to keep me in the loop before the fact.

Do you find clients are aware of simple things they can do to save taxes (i.e. hold an asset just a little longer to have a long-term gain, rather than short term gain)?

Clients are becoming more sophisticated and savvy but, as the old adage goes, "having enough knowledge to be dangerous" can be so painfully true in this case. If they have been educated to make the quick call before making a transaction, they can usually articulate their "situation" and "formulate" their thought on the outcome fairly well. This makes our "non-research" discussion quick and concise, and, more importantly, specific to the client's circumstance and the impact that the "action" may have on the return in its entirety.

DAVID R. BERGMAN, CLU, ChFC, CFP™

DISCUSSION QUESTIONS

1. What are the objectives of the Federal Income Tax Law?
2. What is the Alternative Minimum Tax?
3. What is a capital asset?
4. What is the formula for determining a client's income tax liability?
5. How does tax avoidance differ from tax evasion?
6. What are some of the types of government rulings issued as guidance to taxpayers?
7. What methods and procedures does the IRS use in its audit selection and screening process?
8. When taxpayers violate the tax laws, what civil penalties might they expect to incur?
9. What payroll taxes did the Federal Insurance Contributions Act and the Federal Unemployment Tax Act create?
10. Which tax-advantaged investment options are available to taxpayers?

EXERCISES

1. Dee made the following payments during 2001:

Interest on credit card accounts	$400
Interest on home mortgage	$7,500
Interest on bank loan (proceeds of loan were used to purchase tax-exempt bonds)	$3,100
Interest on credit union loan (proceeds of loan were used for a family vacation)	$1,600

   How much of the above amounts may Dee deduct as an itemized deduction for interest expense on her federal income tax return?

2. Joe, a self-employed individual, earns $100,000 in self-employment income. How much self-employment tax will Joe owe for the year 2001?

3. Kay sold the following investments during the current year:

Property	Date Sold	Date Acquired	Sales Price	Adjusted Basis
ABC stock	2/3/01	1/2/00	$3,300	$1,300
Bond	2/5/01	2/5/00	$1,200	$1,400
Land	4/5/01	5/4/00	$4,300	$3,400

   What is the amount of net long-term gain and net short-term gain on the sale of the investments?

4. Cindy sold 300 shares of XYZ stock for $5,200. She had paid $3,000 for the stock. Commissions of $300 on the sale and $180 on the purchase were paid.

   What is Cindy's amount realized and her gain realized, respectively, on this sale?

5. Don incurred $28,000 of medical expenses in the current year. His insurance company reimbursed him in the amount of $6,000. Assuming his AGI is $100,000, what is the amount of medical expense deduction Don can claim for the year?

6. The Durrs are a married couple with two school-age children they fully support. Use the following information about their year 2001 finances to answer the following question.

Gross income	$91,350
Deductions for AGI	$6,000
Itemized deductions	$4,800

Assuming the Durrs file a joint income tax return, what is their taxable income for 2001?

7. Assuming the same facts as the previous question, how much income tax will the Durrs owe on their 2001 income tax return (ignoring any credits)?

8. Susan, a single taxpayer, sold her home because she has a new job in another city. On the sale date, she had owned the home and used it as a personal residence for 18 months. What is the maximum gain that Susan can exclude on the sale of the residence?

9. During the current year, Scott had long-term capital losses of $2,000 and short-term capital losses of $1,500. If this is the first year he has experienced capital gains or losses, what amount of these losses may Scott deduct this year?

10. Pablo, a single individual, purchased a new personal residence for $375,000. Pablo sold the property 12 months later for $550,000, so he could take a new job that involved a promotion. How much gain must Pablo recognize?

11. David exchanged an apartment complex that he had owned for 8 years for farmland. The farmland was worth $1,050,000 and David's basis in the apartment complex was $475,000. David received $100,000 cash in the transaction. How much is David's gain realized and gain recognized because of this exchange?

12. Barbara exchanges investment land with an adjusted basis of $70,000 for another parcel of investment land with a fair market value of $50,000 plus $12,000 in cash. What is Barbara's realized and recognized loss on this exchange?

13. Doug and Susan, ages 45 and 40, are married, and file a joint return for 2001. The following pertains to their return for the year:

Adjusted Gross Income	$29,600
Itemized deductions	$9,000
Personal exemptions	2 (no children)

The standard deduction for married persons filing a joint return is $7,600. What is their taxable income and tax liability for 2001?

14. Joe is a single taxpayer in the 39.1 percent tax bracket. During the current year, he sold the following assets:

Investment	Gain
ABC company stock	$4,500
XYZ company stock	$1,000
Baseball card collection	$2,000
Corporate bonds	$6,000
Antiques	$8,000

All of the assets were held longer than one year. How much capital gains tax will Joe have to pay because of the sales?

15. Susan filed her tax return 70 days after the due date. She remitted a check for $8,000 that represented the balance of the tax due. Calculate her failure-to-file and failure-to-pay penalties.

16. Jim is in the 30.5 percent marginal income tax rate, and he would like to invest in state of Louisiana bonds. If similar taxable investments yield 12 percent, how much must Jim earn to make this a worthwhile investment?

17. J.J. actively participates in a rental real estate activity. During the year, he received rental income of $85,000, and incurred rental expenses of $120,000. Assuming his AGI is $120,000, how much of the rental real estate loss can he deduct in the current year?

18. Allison is age 12 and has the following income:

Investment Income	$1,800
Income from a Summer Job	$2,200

Assuming her parents claim Allison as a dependent, what is her taxable income for 2001?

19. John is age 15 and has the following income:

Investment Income	$3,550
Income from a Summer Job	$400

Assuming his parents claim John as a dependent, what is his taxable income and tax due for 2001?

20. Billy sold the following investments during the year:

Description	Holding Period	Gain/(Loss)
ABC Stock	Short-Term	$30,000
XYZ Stock	Long-Term	$45,000
Bonds	Short-Term	($20,000)
Real Estate	Long-Term	($60,000)

What is the net short-term or long-term gain or loss, and how much must Billy include or deduct in the current year?

PROBLEMS

1. David and Sue Dell are married and file a joint return. They have two children, Billy and Suzy, ages 8 and 6, respectively.

David is a self-employed real estate appraiser, and the results for his business for the current year are as follows (he paid self-employment tax of $4,700):

Gross Receipts	$50,000
Expenses:	
Advertising	$900
Insurance	$1,000
Interest	$500
Dues	$700
Depreciation	$1,200
Office Rent	$12,000
Meals and Entertainment	$800

Sue, who is employed by a marketing company, earned a salary of $40,000 for the current year. She participates in the company 401(k) plan, and made contributions to the plan of $6,000 for the current year (the company does not provide any matching contributions).

David and Sue also received the following income during the year:

Interest:

Second National Bank, Dallas	$1,100
State of Louisiana Municipal Bonds	$500

Dividends:

ABC Company Cash Dividend	$350
XYZ Company Cash Dividend	$400

They sold their principle residence after owning and living in the home for five years. The following information relates to the sale of the residence:

Sales Price	$700,000
Original Cost	$150,000

David and Sue incurred the following expenses during the current year:

Real Estate Taxes	$10,000
Mortgage Interest	$4,500
Sales Taxes	$800

Assuming David paid $5,000 in alimony to his ex-wife, calculate the Dells' taxable income for the current year.

2. Scott and Laura Davis are married and file a joint income tax return. They have taxable income for the current year of $65,000. In arriving at taxable income, they took the following deductions:

Mortgage Interest	$8,000
Real Estate Taxes	$10,000
State Income Taxes	$8,000
Charitable Deductions	$300
Accelerated Depreciation	$2,000

In addition, Scott and Laura received the following tax-exempt interest:

Municipal Bonds	$600
Private Activity Bonds	$1,000

Laura also exercised incentive stock options during the year. The option entitled her to purchase 500 shares at $50 per share. The stock was worth $110 per share at the time of exercise.

Calculate the Davis' Alternative Minimum Tax liability.

3. Steve and Elaine exchange real estate investments. Steve gives up property with an adjusted basis of $250,000 (FMV $400,000). In return for this property, Steve receives property with a FMV of $300,000 (adjusted basis $200,000) and cash of $100,000.

What are Steve and Elaine's realized, recognized, and deferred gains because of the exchange?

4. Anne Love, a CPA employed by CPAsRUs.com, is an unmarried taxpayer. She earned a salary of $100,000 for the current year, and did not participate in the firm's 401(k) plan.

Anne also received the following income and incurred the following expenses during the year:

Income:

Interest	$2,000
Dividends	$900

Expenses:

Medical (Unreimbursed)	$1,500
Real Estate Taxes	$7,000
Mortgage Interest	$5,000
Interest on Auto Loan	$2,500

Ignoring any credits, how much lower would Anne's tax liability been had she made the maximum deductible employee contribution ($10,500) to the 401(k) plan?

5. Jim and Trish are married and file a joint income tax return. The couple has no children, and do not itemize deductions. Calculate the marriage penalty if Jim and Trish each earn $90,000 from their respective jobs.

CHAPTER 17

Business Entities

LEARNING OBJECTIVES:

After learning the material in this chapter, you will be able to:

1. Identify the several different types of business entities that a business owner may choose as a legal form of business.

2. Characterize each type of business entity below with regard to formation requirements, operation, ownership restrictions, tax treatment, legal liability risk, and management operations:

   ▲ Sole Proprietorship

   ▲ Partnership

   ▲ Limited Liability Partnership

   ▲ Family Limited Partnership

   ▲ Corporation

   ▲ S Corporation

   ▲ Limited Liability Company

3. List the basic factors that a business owner should consider when selecting a legal form of business.

4. Explain how each type of business entity differs with regard to simplicity of formation and operation, ownership restrictions, limited liability, management operations, and tax characteristics.

BUSINESS ENTITIES

One of the major decisions confronting a business owner from a tax and legal perspective concerns selecting the form in which the business will operate. The business owner can choose from several different business forms, each with its own advantages and disadvantages.

Business owners may choose to run their business as a sole proprietorship, a partnership, a limited liability partnership (LLP), a corporation, or a limited liability company (LLC). Each one of these business forms has different formation requirements, tax treatment, legal liability risk, and management operation.

Once a business entity has been created, the next step is operating the business. The type of entity chosen will help determine which individuals will be responsible for making the day-to-day business decisions.

Another major consideration in the selection of a legal form of business entity is the legal liability of the owners. A major concern of business owners is the preservation and growth of personal assets, especially in today's litigious society. Therefore, it is critical to select a form of business entity that provides the desired asset protection, while allowing the appropriate level of freedom to run the company.

Income tax considerations play a major role in the selection of a business entity. Although many of the entities are taxed in a similar fashion, each entity has its own set of rules that may provide the business owner with tax consequences that are either advantageous or detrimental. The following sections detail the different tax consequences of the formation and operation of sole proprietorships, partnerships, limited liability partnerships (LLPs), corporations, and limited liability companies (LLCs).

The creator of a new business has many legal business forms to choose from. The owner must carefully analyze the available options to determine which type of business entity is most appropriate. As a personal financial planner, it is important to understand the different types of business forms available. The most common forms and their basic characteristics are discussed in this chapter.

SOLE PROPRIETORSHIP

sole proprietorship - a business owned and controlled by one person who is personally liable for all debts and claims against the business

A **sole proprietorship** is a business owned and controlled by one person who is personally liable for all debts and claims against the business. Separate accounting books and records are regularly maintained. However, for tax purposes, the sole proprietorship is not treated as a separate taxable entity. Rather, the income and deductions of the business are reported directly on the individual owner's federal income tax return (specifically, Schedule C of Form 1040).

Advantages of a sole proprietorship include its ease of formation and its simplicity of operation and taxation. **Proprietors** own all business property and need not consult partners or other managers before making business decisions. In addition, this form of business entity may provide some state and federal tax advantages over other entities. For example, if the proprietorship incurs a loss for the year, the loss will be reported on the individual's income tax return where it

proprietor - the owner of a sole proprietorship

may provide an immediate tax break because the loss may be deductible against other taxable income.

Management Operation & Decision Making Of A Proprietorship

The management structure of a sole proprietorship is very straightforward. The proprietor is responsible for the day-to-day operation of the business, and is responsible for making all of the business decisions. This allows for great flexibility in the operation of the business. For example, the owner may choose to add a new line of business or discontinue an existing line of business without any approval of others.

Legal Liability Of A Proprietorship

The major disadvantage of the sole proprietorship is that the proprietor has unlimited personal liability for the indebtedness of the sole proprietorship. Therefore, any business liabilities may be satisfied from the owner's personal assets, and any personal liabilities may be satisfied from the business assets.

The owner may purchase business liability insurance. While this insurance does not exempt the owner from creditor's claims, it provides protection against lawsuits.

Taxation Of A Proprietorship

Although separate accounting books and records are maintained for tax purposes, the sole proprietorship is not treated as a separate taxable entity.

Most small businesses are run as sole proprietorships. Sole proprietors are individuals engaged in a business without the organization of a separate legal entity. The proprietor uses a certain portion of his or her directly owned assets for business purposes.

Tax Ramifications of Formation of a Proprietorship

The formation of a sole proprietorship is very straightforward. No formal transfer of assets to the business is required to enable a proprietorship to engage in activities. Also, the owner generally is not required to file documents with local authorities (except, perhaps, a business license), unless the owner is planning to operate the business under an assumed name. When a sole proprietorship is established, there are no federal income tax ramifications.

Tax Ramifications of Business Operation of a Proprietorship

When the proprietorship generates income and incurs losses, it is not required to file a separate federal income tax return. Instead, the income or loss from the business is reported directly on Schedule C of the proprietor's individual income tax return Form 1040. When reported, the income or loss is combined with the proprietor's other income to determine the taxpayer's adjusted gross income (AGI). The income from the business is taxed at ordinary income tax rates applicable to individual taxpayers and is generally subject to self-employment taxes.

Schedule C of Form 1040 is used to report the name of the proprietor, as well as the name, address, and accounting method of the proprietorship. This form also contains separate sections to report income earned by the business, such as gross receipts, and expenses incurred by the business, such as advertising, supplies, and wages paid. A sole proprietorship generally may deduct ordinary and necessary business expenses as incurred. In addition, a self-employed business owner is allowed an above-the-line (above AGI) deduction for a portion of health insurance premiums paid. Exhibit 17.1 details the percentage of premiums that may be allowed as an above-the-line deduction.

EXHIBIT 17.1: PERCENTAGE OF HEALTH INSURANCE PREMIUMS ALLOWED AS AN ABOVE-THE-LINE DEDUCTION

Tax Year	% Eligible Costs
2001	60%
2002	70%
2003 and thereafter	100%

EXHIBIT 17.2: SCHEDULE C OF FORM 1040

SCHEDULE C (Form 1040) Department of the Treasury Internal Revenue Service (99)	**Profit or Loss From Business** (Sole Proprietorship) ▶ Partnerships, joint ventures, etc., must file Form 1065 or Form 1065-B. ▶ Attach to Form 1040 or Form 1041. ▶ See Instructions for Schedule C (Form 1040).	OMB No. 1545-0074 **2000** Attachment Sequence No. 09

Name of proprietor | Social security number (SSN)

A Principal business or profession, including product or service (see page C-1 of the instructions) | B Enter code from pages C-7 & 8 ▶

C Business name. If no separate business name, leave blank. | D Employer ID number (EIN), if any

E Business address (including suite or room no.) ▶ ....
   City, town or post office, state, and ZIP code

F Accounting method: (1) ☐ Cash (2) ☐ Accrual (3) ☐ Other (specify) ▶ ....

G Did you "materially participate" in the operation of this business during 2000? If "No," see page C-2 for limit on losses ☐ Yes ☐ No

H If you started or acquired this business during 2000, check here . . . . ▶ ☐

Part I Income

1	Gross receipts or sales. Caution. If this income was reported to you on Form W-2 and the "Statutory employee" box on that form was checked, see page C-2 and check here ▶ ☐	1
2	Returns and allowances	2
3	Subtract line 2 from line 1	3
4	Cost of goods sold (from line 42 on page 2)	4
5	Gross profit. Subtract line 4 from line 3	5
6	Other income, including Federal and state gasoline or fuel tax credit or refund (see page C-2) . . .	6
7	Gross income. Add lines 5 and 6 . . . . ▶	7

Part II Expenses. Enter expenses for business use of your home only on line 30.

8	Advertising	8	19	Pension and profit-sharing plans	19
9	Bad debts from sales or services (see page C-3) . .	9	20	Rent or lease (see page C-4):	
			a	Vehicles, machinery, and equipment .	20a
10	Car and truck expenses (see page C-3) . . .	10	b	Other business property . .	20b
11	Commissions and fees . .	11	21	Repairs and maintenance . .	21
12	Depletion	12	22	Supplies (not included in Part III) .	22
13	Depreciation and section 179 expense deduction (not included in Part III) (see page C-3) . .	13	23	Taxes and licenses	23
			24	Travel, meals, and entertainment:	
			a	Travel	24a
14	Employee benefit programs (other than on line 19) . . .	14	b	Meals and entertainment	
15	Insurance (other than health) .	15	c	Enter nondeductible amount included on line 24b (see page C-5) .	
16	Interest:				
a	Mortgage (paid to banks, etc.) .	16a	d	Subtract line 24c from line 24b .	24d
b	Other	16b	25	Utilities	25
17	Legal and professional services	17	26	Wages (less employment credits) .	26
			27	Other expenses (from line 48 on page 2) . . .	27
18	Office expense	18			

28	Total expenses before expenses for business use of home. Add lines 8 through 27 in columns . ▶	28
29	Tentative profit (loss). Subtract line 28 from line 7	29
30	Expenses for business use of your home. Attach Form 8829	30
31	Net profit or (loss). Subtract line 30 from line 29. • If a profit, enter on Form 1040, line 12, and also on Schedule SE, line 2 (statutory employees, see page C-5). Estates and trusts, enter on Form 1041, line 3. • If a loss, you must go to line 32.	31
32	If you have a loss, check the box that describes your investment in this activity (see page C-5). • If you checked 32a, enter the loss on Form 1040, line 12, and also on Schedule SE, line 2 (statutory employees, see page C-5). Estates and trusts, enter on Form 1041, line 3. • If you checked 32b, you must attach Form 6198.	32a ☐ All investment is at risk. 32b ☐ Some investment is not at risk.

For Paperwork Reduction Act Notice, see Form 1040 instructions. Cat. No. 11334P Schedule C (Form 1040) 2000

The net profit or loss from Schedule C is reflected on page 1 of the individual income tax return Form 1040. If Schedule C reflects a net profit for the year, this profit is subject to self-employment tax. Self-employment tax is calculated in the same fashion as FICA tax; however, the tax will be based on net earnings from the sole proprietorship instead of wages. Before applying the tax rates, net earnings may be reduced by 7.65 percent, which is one-half of the self-employment tax rate.

EXHIBIT 17.3: NET PROFIT/LOSS LINE FROM SCHEDULE C (ON PAGE ONE OF FORM 1040)

Income	7	Wages, salaries, tips, etc. Attach Form(s) W-2	7		
	8a	Taxable interest. Attach Schedule B if required	8a		
Attach Forms W-2 and W-2G here. Also attach Form(s) 1099-R if tax was withheld.	b	Tax-exempt interest. Do not include on line 8a . . . 8b			
	9	Ordinary dividends. Attach Schedule B if required	9		
	10	Taxable refunds, credits, or offsets of state and local income taxes (see page 22) . .	10		
	11	Alimony received	11		
	12	Business income or (loss). Attach Schedule C or C-EZ	12		
	13	Capital gain or (loss). Attach Schedule D if required. If not required, check here ▶ ☐	13		
	14	Other gains or (losses). Attach Form 4797	14		
If you did not get a W-2, see page 21.	15a	Total IRA distributions . 15a _____ b Taxable amount (see page 23)	15b		
	16a	Total pensions and annuities 16a _____ b Taxable amount (see page 23)	16b		
	17	Rental real estate, royalties, partnerships, S corporations, trusts, etc. Attach Schedule E	17		

EXAMPLE   If Stan owns his own proprietorship business, and during the year his business income after allowed deductions is $200,000, he would incur $15,325.90 in self-employment tax, calculated as follows:

Net earnings from Sole Proprietorship	$200,000
Less: 7.65% of Net Earnings	($15,300)
Amount Subject to Self-Employment Tax	$184,700
Social Security Portion (12.4% x $80,400)	$9,969.60
Medicare Portion (2.9% x $184,700)	$5,356.30
Total Self-Employment Taxes	$15,325.90

The self-employment tax is calculated on Schedule SE, which is attached to the proprietor's Form 1040. The proprietor is allowed a deduction for one-half of the self-employment tax paid, or $7,662.95, in the above example. This amount will be deducted in arriving at Adjusted Gross Income (above-the-line deduction).

EXHIBIT 17.4: SCHEDULE SE

Name of person with self-employment income (as shown on Form 1040)	Social security number of person with self-employment income ▶	

Section B —Long Schedule SE

Part I   Self-Employment Tax

Note. If your only income subject to self-employment tax is church employee income, skip lines 1 through 4b. Enter -0- on line 4c and go to line 5a. Income from services you performed as a minister or a member of a religious order is not church employee income. See page SE-1.

A   If you are a minister, member of a religious order, or Christian Science practitioner and you filed Form 4361, but you had $400 or more of other net earnings from self-employment, check here and continue with Part I . . . . . . ▶ ☐

1	Net farm profit or (loss) from Schedule F, line 36, and farm partnerships, Schedule K-1 (Form 1065), line 15a. Note. Skip this line if you use the farm optional method. See page SE-3 . .	**1**	
2	Net profit or (loss) from Schedule C, line 31; Schedule C-EZ, line 3; Schedule K-1 (Form 1065), line 15a (other than farming); and Schedule K-1 (Form 1065-B), box 9. Ministers and members of religious orders, see page SE-1 for amounts to report on this line. See page SE-2 for other income to report. Note. Skip this line if you use the nonfarm optional method. See page SE-3 .	**2**	
3	Combine lines 1 and 2	**3**	
4a	If line 3 is more than zero, multiply line 3 by 92.35% (.9235). Otherwise, enter amount from line 3	**4a**	
b	If you elect one or both of the optional methods, enter the total of lines 15 and 17 here . . .	**4b**	
c	Combine lines 4a and 4b. If less than $400, do not file this schedule; you do not owe self-employment tax. Exception. If less than $400 and you had church employee income, enter -0- and continue ▶	**4c**	

5a   Enter your church employee income from Form W-2. Caution: See page SE-1 for definition of church employee income . . . . . . | **5a** |

b	Multiply line 5a by 92.35% (.9235). If less than $100, enter -0-	**5b**	
6	Net earnings from self-employment. Add lines 4c and 5b	**6**	
7	Maximum amount of combined wages and self-employment earnings subject to social security tax or the 6.2% portion of the 7.65% railroad retirement (tier 1) tax for 2000	**7**	76,200 00

8a   Total social security wages and tips (total of boxes 3 and 7 on Form(s) W-2) and railroad retirement (tier 1) compensation . . . . . . | **8a** |

b   Unreported tips subject to social security tax (from Form 4137, line 9) | **8b** |

c	Add lines 8a and 8b	**8c**	
9	Subtract line 8c from line 7. If zero or less, enter -0- here and on line 10 and go to line 11 . ▶	**9**	
10	Multiply the smaller of line 6 or line 9 by 12.4% (.124)	**10**	
11	Multiply line 6 by 2.9% (.029)	**11**	
12	Self-employment tax. Add lines 10 and 11. Enter here and on Form 1040, line 52	**12**	

13   Deduction for one-half of self-employment tax. Multiply line 12 by 50% (.5). Enter the result here and on Form 1040, line 27 . . . . | **13** |

Part II   Optional Methods To Figure Net Earnings   (See page SE-3.)

Farm Optional Method. You may use this method only if:
- Your gross farm income[1] was not more than $2,400 or
- Your net farm profits[2] were less than $1,733.

14	Maximum income for optional methods	**14**	1,600 00
15	Enter the smaller of: two-thirds (⅔) of gross farm income[1] (not less than zero) or $1,600. Also include this amount on line 4b above	**15**	

Nonfarm Optional Method. You may use this method only if:
- Your net nonfarm profits[3] were less than $1,733 and also less than 72.189% of your gross nonfarm income[4] and
- You had net earnings from self-employment of at least $400 in 2 of the prior 3 years.

Caution: You may use this method no more than five times.

16	Subtract line 15 from line 14	**16**	
17	Enter the smaller of: two-thirds (⅔) of gross nonfarm income[4] (not less than zero) or the amount on line 16. Also include this amount on line 4b above	**17**	

[1]From Sch. F, line 11, and Sch. K-1 (Form 1065), line   [3]15b. From Sch. C, line 31; Sch. C-EZ, line 3; Sch. K-1 (Form 1065), line 15a; and Sch. K-1 (Form 1065-B), box 9.
[2]From Sch. F, line 36, and Sch. K-1 (Form 1065), line   [4]15a. From Sch. C, line 7; Sch. C-EZ, line 1; Sch. K-1 (Form 1065), line 15c; and Sch. K-1 (Form 1065-B), box 9.

✳   Schedule SE (Form 1040) 2000

PARTNERSHIP

partnership - an association of two or more entities or individuals that carry on as co-owners of a business for the purpose of making a profit

partner - two or more individuals, corporations, trusts, estates, or other partnerships that join to form a business entity known as a partnership

general partnership - a type of business entity owned entirely by general partners, each of whom can act on behalf of the partnership

limited partnership - a type of business entity formed under the limited partnership laws of a state. In a limited partnership, partners are not allowed to participate in the management of the partnership affairs, but generally are allowed to vote on major changes affecting the structure of the partnership

A **partnership** is an association of two or more entities or individuals that carry on as co-owners of a business for the purpose of making a profit. It is generally very easy to form a partnership, since formality is ordinarily unnecessary. The partnership form of business is very flexible, as there are no limitations on the number of **partners**, and partners can be individuals, corporations, trusts, estates, and even other partnerships. There are two types of partnerships, general and limited. These differ primarily in the nature of the rights and obligations of the partners. General partnerships are owned entirely by general partners. Each partner can act on behalf of the partnership. A limited partnership is a partnership formed under the limited partnership laws of a state. This partnership must have at least one general partner and at least one limited partner.

MANAGEMENT OPERATION AND DECISION MAKING OF A PARTNERSHIP

Ordinarily, when a partnership is formed, a partnership agreement is drafted outlining the identity of the partners, the division of profits and losses, and the duties of each partner in the management of the partnership business.

General Partnership

In a **general partnership**, the general partners participate in the management of the partnership and are directly responsible for the day-to-day operation of the business. With management and ownership consolidated among the same individuals, partners are relatively free to change operating policy. Thus, the partnership can change its operational direction at any time and relatively quickly.

Limited Partnership

In a **limited partnership**, limited partners are not allowed to participate in the management of the partnership affairs. If the limited partners do participate in management, they will become general partners and lose their limited liability status. It should be noted that even though limited partners are not allowed to participate in management, they generally are entitled to vote on major changes affecting the structure of the partnership, such as a change in the type of investments purchased.

LEGAL LIABILITY OF A PARTNERSHIP

General Partnership

General partnerships are owned entirely by general partners. While the partnership form of business has many advantages, it also has several disadvantages. The most significant disadvantage is the unlimited personal liability of the partners.

A general partner has unlimited liability for the acts of the partnership, the other partners, and obligations made by any partner or the partnership in the performance of partnership duties. If the partnership assets are insufficient to satisfy the liabilities of the partnership, the partnership's creditors can collect against the personal assets of the general partners. The creditors have the right to make any one partner, or several partners, satisfy the entire amount of the partnership's obligations. As a result, one partner may have to make good on the partnership's obligations and then may not be able to recover these amounts from the other partners.

In addition, a creditor of one of the partners may seek to recover unsatisfied partner debt by seizing the partner's share of partnership assets. Such a seizure of partnership assets could impede the ability of the partnership to operate.

It should be noted that a person admitted as a general partner into an existing partnership is not personally liable for partnership debts existing prior to the partner's entry into the partnership.

Limited Partnership

A limited partner is liable for partnership indebtedness only to the extent of the capital the partner has contributed or agreed to contribute. In this respect, the limited partner is treated as an investor, liable only for the amount of his or her investment.

Although the status of a limited partner generally provides the individual with limited liability, the limited liability status may disappear and the partner will be liable as a general partner under any of the following circumstances:

The surname of the limited partner is included in the partnership name. This does not apply if there is a general partner with the same surname.

The limited partner acts as a general partner by participating in the management of the partnership.

The limited partner learns that the firm is defectively formed and fails to withdraw from the partnership.

TAXATION OF A PARTNERSHIP

For federal income tax purposes, each general partner's share of partnership trade or business income is considered self-employment income, subject to self-employment taxes. A limited partner, however, is not allowed to participate in the management and control of the partnership business and, therefore, is not subject to self-employment taxes on partnership earnings.

A partnership is similar to a sole proprietorship in that both entities are **flow-through entities** for federal income tax purposes. In other words, the results of business operations for both entities are reported directly on the owner's income tax return. For federal income tax purposes, partners must take into account their distributive share of partnership taxable income and any additional items the partnership is required to report separately, such as interest and dividend income. Consequently, the partnership is not, as an entity, subject to federal income tax. The partnership items of income and expense are completely taxable to the partners at their own personal income tax rates, but are reported initially on the partnership tax return (Form 1065) and then reported to each partner (Form K-1).

flow-through entity - the results of business operations are reported directly on the owner's income tax return

Tax Ramifications of Formation of a Partnership

Partners may form a partnership by contributing cash, property, or services to the partnership in exchange for an ownership interest. When a partner contributes cash or property to the partnership, no gain or loss is recognized and the partner's basis in the partnership interest is equal to the value of the cash contributed or the value of the property contributed. If a partner contributes personal or professional services to the partnership, the partner must recognize ordinary compensation income for the value of the services. The amount of income recognized becomes the partner's basis in his or her partnership interest.

EXAMPLE   Assume Tom contributes the following to the ABC partnership in exchange for a 50 percent general partnership interest in the partnership:

Contribution	Fair Market Value
Cash	$10,000
Land (Tom's basis is $40,000)	$50,000
Services	$5,000

Tom would recognize ordinary income of $5,000, the value of the services he contributed to the partnership. His basis in the partnership interest would be $55,000 ($10,000 + 40,000 + 5,000).

Tax Ramifications of Business Operation of a Partnership

Once the partnership has been created, it is treated for federal income tax purposes as an aggregate of the separate partners, rather than as a separate taxable entity. The partnership itself is not required to pay any income tax, but must file an information return, Form 1065, detailing the items of income and expense that will be reported on the partner's individual income tax return.

Partners must take into account their distributive share of partnership taxable income and any separately stated items in computing their individual taxable incomes. Generally, a partner's interest in the partnership's capital and profits determines the partner's share of income, gain, loss, deduction, or credit. The partners may change the traditional allocation of tax items through the partnership agreement. This "special allocation" of an item or items must have substantial economic effect to be valid. In many cases, special allocations allow the benefits of deductions to pass to those partners who have a greater use for such deductions.

Each partner's distributive share of items is reported on Form 1065 Schedule K-1, which is furnished by the partnership to both the Internal Revenue Service (IRS) and to each partner. Schedule K-1 details the partner's share of partnership ordinary income, which is the net profit or loss resulting from the partnership's trade or business. If the partner is a general partner, this allocation of ordinary income will be subject not only to ordinary income tax, but also to self-employment tax, similar to the proprietorship.

The Form 1065 Schedule K-1 also reflects various items that must be reported separately from ordinary income. These separately stated items, which include dividend income, interest income, and capital gains, are afforded special treatment on the partner's individual income tax return.

SCHEDULE K-1 (Form 1065) Department of the Treasury Internal Revenue Service	**Partner's Share of Income, Credits, Deductions, etc.** ▶ See separate instructions. For calendar year 2000 or tax year beginning , 2000, and ending , 20	OMB No. 1545-0099 **2000**

Partner's identifying number ▶	Partnership's identifying number ▶
Partner's name, address, and ZIP code	Partnership's name, address, and ZIP code

A This partner is a ☐ general partner ☐ limited partner
☐ limited liability company member
B What type of entity is this partner? ▶ ....
C Is this partner a ☐ domestic or a ☐ foreign partner?
D Enter partner's percentage of:

	(i) Before change or termination	(ii) End of year
Profit sharing	.... %	.... %
Loss sharing	.... %	.... %
Ownership of capital	.... %	.... %

E IRS Center where partnership filed return:

F Partner's share of liabilities (see instructions):
Nonrecourse . . . . $ ....
Qualified nonrecourse financing . $ ....
Other . . . . $ ....
G Tax shelter registration number . ▶ ....
H Check here if this partnership is a publicly traded partnership as defined in section 469(k)(2) . . . . . ☐
I Check applicable boxes: (1) ☐ Final K-1 (2) ☐ Amended K-1

J Analysis of partner's capital account:

(a) Capital account at beginning of year	(b) Capital contributed during year	(c) Partner's share of lines 3, 4, and 7, Form 1065, Schedule M-2	(d) Withdrawals and distributions	(e) Capital account at end of year (combine columns (a) through (d))
			( )	

	(a) Distributive share item		(b) Amount	(c) 1040 filers enter the amount in column (b) on:
Income (Loss)	1 Ordinary income (loss) from trade or business activities . . .	1		See page 6 of Partner's Instructions for Schedule K-1 (Form 1065).
	2 Net income (loss) from rental real estate activities	2		
	3 Net income (loss) from other rental activities	3		
	4 Portfolio income (loss):			
	a Interest	4a		Sch. B, Part I, line 1
	b Ordinary dividends	4b		Sch. B, Part II, line 5
	c Royalties	4c		Sch. E, Part I, line 4
	d Net short-term capital gain (loss)	4d		Sch. D, line 5, col. (f)
	e Net long-term capital gain (loss):			
	(1) 28% rate gain (loss)	4e(1)		Sch. D, line 12, col. (g)
	(2) Total for year	4e(2)		Sch. D, line 12, col. (f)
	f Other portfolio income (loss) (attach schedule)	4f		Enter on applicable line of your return.
	5 Guaranteed payments to partner	5		See page 6 of Partner's Instructions for Schedule K-1 (Form 1065).
	6 Net section 1231 gain (loss) (other than due to casualty or theft)	6		
	7 Other income (loss) (attach schedule)	7		Enter on applicable line of your return.
Deductions	8 Charitable contributions (see instructions) (attach schedule) . .	8		Sch. A, line 15 or 16
	9 Section 179 expense deduction	9		See pages 7 and 8 of Partner's Instructions for Schedule K-1 (Form 1065).
	10 Deductions related to portfolio income (attach schedule) . . .	10		
	11 Other deductions (attach schedule)	11		
Credits	12a Low-income housing credit:			
	(1) From section 42(j)(5) partnerships for property placed in service before 1990	12a(1)		Form 8586, line 5
	(2) Other than on line 12a(1) for property placed in service before 1990	12a(2)		
	(3) From section 42(j)(5) partnerships for property placed in service after 1989	12a(3)		
	(4) Other than on line 12a(3) for property placed in service after 1989	12a(4)		
	b Qualified rehabilitation expenditures related to rental real estate activities	12b		See page 8 of Partner's Instructions for Schedule K-1 (Form 1065).
	c Credits (other than credits shown on lines 12a and 12b) related to rental real estate activities	12c		
	d Credits related to other rental activities	12d		
	13 Other credits	13		

For Paperwork Reduction Act Notice, see Instructions for Form 1065. Cat. No. 11394R Schedule K-1 (Form 1065) 2000

619

The partner's adjusted taxable basis in the partnership interest must be adjusted each year to reflect the allocated items of income and expense. Adjusted taxable basis is increased by a partner's distributive share of both taxable and nontaxable partnership income, and is decreased by the partner's share of partnership losses and nondeductible expenses.

Continuing with the example above, if the ABC partnership reported earnings of $40,000 for the first year, Tom, a 50 percent partner, would report $20,000 of ordinary income on his federal income tax return. His basis in the partnership after the first year would be adjusted to $75,000 ($55,000 original basis + $20,000 of allocated income). Since Tom is a general partner, the $20,000 distributable share of partnership earnings would also be subject to self-employment tax.

Tax Ramifications of Withdrawals or Distributions from a Partnership

Partners may withdraw cash or property from the partnership to meet their needs or as advance payments of their share of partnership income. Regardless of the reason for the withdrawal, the recipient partner generally recognizes no gain on the distribution. Instead, the withdrawal is treated as a return of capital that reduces the partner's adjusted taxable basis in the partnership. For example, if Tom, the ABC partner, withdrew the $20,000 earned, his adjusted taxable basis would return to $55,000. Once the partner's basis has been reduced to zero, any additional withdrawals taken from the partnership will result in a capital gain to the partner.

LIMITED LIABILITY PARTNERSHIP

A **limited liability partnership (LLP)** is similar to a general partnership, except an LLP provides additional liability protection to the partners.

MANAGEMENT OPERATION & DECISION MAKING OF A LIMITED LIABILITY PARTNERSHIP

The management of an LLP is the same as that of a general partnership. The partners participate in the management of the partnership and are directly responsible for the day-to-day operation of the business. With management and ownership consolidated among the same individuals, partners are relatively free to change operating policy. Thus, the partnership can change its operational direction at any time and relatively quickly.

LEGAL LIABILITY OF A LIMITED LIABILITY PARTNERSHIP

In an LLP, partners are personally liable for their own acts of wrongdoing, but their personal assets (those outside the partnership entity) are protected from claims arising from the wrongful acts of other partners. This liability protection in many states extends only to tort law, not contract law.

TAXATION OF LIMITED LIABILITY PARTNERSHIPS

For federal income tax purposes, an LLP is treated in the same fashion as a partnership. The LLP is considered a conduit, or flow-through entity, that is not subject to federal income tax. Part-

limited liability partnership (LLP) - a form of business entity similar to a general partnership, except an LLP provides additional liability protection to the partners

ners must take into account their distributive share of partnership taxable income and any additional items the partnership is required to report separately.

FAMILY LIMITED PARTNERSHIP

A **family limited partnership** is an estate planning technique utilizing a limited partnership between family members. The arrangement is generally structured so that a senior family member transfers appreciating property, such as real estate, to a limited partnership in return for a minimal general partnership interest (typically 1 percent) and a significant limited partnership interest (typically 99 percent). Over the senior family member's lifetime, the limited partnership interests are transferred to junior family members by gift or sale.

One of the primary objectives of the family limited partnership arrangement is to generate valuation discounts for estate and gift tax purposes on the transfer of the limited interest in the partnership. The estate and gift tax value of a limited partnership interest in a properly structured family limited partnership typically is determined by applying minority interest and lack of marketability discounts.

Minority Interest Discount - a reduction in value of an asset transferred is often allowed if the asset transferred represents a minority interest in a business. A minority interest is any interest that, in terms of voting, is not a controlling interest. Since minority owners cannot control the business or compel its sale or liquidation, outside buyers would not be willing to pay the same amount for a minority interest as they would for a majority or controlling interest.

Lack of Marketability Discount - a reduction in value of an asset transferred is often allowed if the asset transferred has an inherent lack of marketability. Limited partnership interests in a family limited partnership are more difficult to sell than interests in other assets such as publicly traded stock. Therefore, a discount is often allowed for the lack of marketability.

The family limited partnership has many advantages. One of the major advantages is that the senior family member can retain control of the business, since the senior family member is the only family member with a general partnership interest (limited partners are not allowed to participate in management of the business). Additional advantages of this technique include creditor protection, and the ability to place restrictions on transfers of limited partnership interests by junior family members.

MANAGEMENT OPERATION & DECISION MAKING OF A FAMILY LIMITED PARTNERSHIP

The management of a family limited partnership is the same as that of a limited partnership. The general partner manages the partnership and is directly responsible for the day-to-day operation of the business. Thus, the partnership can change its operational direction at any time and relatively quickly.

family limited partnership - an estate planning technique utilizing a limited partnership between family members that is used to generate valuation discounts for estate and gift tax purposes on the transfer of the limited interest in the partnership

LEGAL LIABILITY OF A FAMILY LIMITED PARTNERSHIP

The general partner (senior family member) has unlimited liability for the acts of the partnership, the other partners, and obligations made by any partner or the partnership in the performance of partnership duties.

The limited partners (junior family members) are treated as investors, liable only for the amount of his or her investment.

TAXATION OF A FAMILY LIMITED PARTNERSHIP

The partnership agreement will govern how partnership income is divided among the partners. Generally, both general and limited partners share income and cash flow based on their percentage interest in the partnership. The taxable income of the FLP is reported annually and allocated to each partner on the basis of that partner's percentage interest. The allocation is noted on the Form K-1 issued to each partner. Usually, the general partner annually distributes at least enough cash to pay the income tax liability attributable to each partner. Distributions from the partnership are not taxable to the extent the partner has basis in the partnership interest. The partnership itself (unlike a corporation) is not subject to tax, because it passes through all items of income and deduction to the partners.

CORPORATION

A corporation (regular **C corporation**) is an entity created by state law that is separate and distinct from its owners, who are called **shareholders**. A corporation can be closely held if owned by a few shareholders, or publicly held if owned by many shareholders.

The shareholders enjoy limited liability, as they can only lose the amount they have invested in the corporation. They do not represent the corporation, but instead vote for a board of directors, which determines corporate policy and appoints officers. The officers manage the corporation.

For federal income tax purposes, the corporation is treated as a separate taxable entity. The profits of a corporation are taxed to the corporation at special corporate rates. These rates are generally lower than individual income tax rates. However, there is a major tax disadvantage of a corporation. When a corporation distributes a dividend to its shareholders, the corporation does not receive an income tax deduction for the dividend payment, but rather, the shareholder is required to include the amount of dividend received as ordinary taxable income. As a result, the corporate form of business will result in the double taxation of income--once at the corporate level and once at the shareholder level.

MANAGEMENT OPERATIONS OF A CORPORATION

Corporations have management advantages over other business forms. With a corporation, there is a separation of management from ownership so that the mere ownership of corporate stock does not give the owner the right to participate in the management. The management is centralized, with the directors and officers handling management of corporate affairs.

Directors are individuals who, acting as a group known as the board of directors, manage the business and affairs of a corporation. The **board of directors** is the governing body of a corporation. Shareholders elect its members. Directors may be shareholders or individuals with no financial interest in the corporation. The directors are responsible for selecting the officers and for the supervision and general control of the corporation.

Officers of a corporation are individuals appointed by the board of directors. Like directors, officers may be shareholders or individuals with no financial interest in the corporation. The officers are responsible for carrying out the board's policies and for making day-to-day operating decisions.

The decisions made by the officers and directors are based in part on the corporation's bylaws. Bylaws are the regulations of a corporation that, subject to statutory law and the articles of incorporation, provide the basic rules for the conduct of the corporation's business and affairs.

LEGAL LIABILITY OF A CORPORATION

Because a corporation is an entity created by state law that is separate and distinct from its shareholder/owners, one of the major advantages of the corporate form of ownership is the limited liability they enjoy.

C corporation - a business entity created by state law that is separate and distinct from its shareholder/owners

shareholders - the owners of a corporation who elect the corporation's board of directors

directors - individuals who, acting as a group known as the board of directors, manage the business affairs of a corporation

board of directors - the governing body of a corporation whose members are elected by shareholders

officer - individuals appointed by a corporation's board of directors to carry out the board's policies and make day-to-day operating decisions

The shareholders' liability for the acts, omissions, debts, and other obligations of the corporation generally is limited to the shareholders' capital contributions. There are several situations, however, in which the shareholders will be held personally liable for the debts of the corporation:

A lender to a closely held corporation requires that the primary shareholders guarantee the loan to the corporation. If this is the case, the shareholders are liable to the extent of their guarantees, in addition to their capital contribution.

A court may ignore the legal fiction of the corporation as an entity (pierce the corporate veil) when the corporation has been used to perpetuate fraud, circumvent law, accomplish an illegal purpose, or otherwise evade law.

The courts may disregard the corporate form of entity if the corporation is not maintained as a separate entity from its shareholders. This arises occasionally in the case of closely held corporations.

TAXATION OF A CORPORATION

A corporation is an entity created under state law that is separate and distinct from its owners. It may be formed only through compliance with state incorporation statutes. For federal income tax purposes, the corporation is treated as a separate taxable entity, not as a flow-through entity.

Tax Ramifications of Formation of a Corporation

When a corporation is formed, cash or property is generally transferred to the corporation in exchange for shares of stock. When cash is transferred to the corporation, the transferor will recognize no gain or loss for federal income tax purposes. He or she will have a basis in the shares received equal to the cash transferred.

In the case of property transfers, no gain or loss will be recognized only if the transfer meets the requirements of IRC Section 351. Section 351 provides that gain or loss will not be recognized if property is transferred to a corporation in exchange for stock in the corporation, and immediately after the transfer, the transferors are in control of the corporation.

For purposes of Section 351, property generally includes any real or personal property, but not services. A person receiving stock in exchange for services is required to recognize ordinary income equal to the fair market value of the services provided. If the shareholder transfers both property and services to the corporation in exchange for stock, the transferor is required to allocate the stock received between the property and the services, reporting the value of the services rendered as income.

Section 351 also requires the transferors to "control" the corporation after transfer. Control of the corporation exists if, after the property transfer, the transferors own at least 80 percent of the total number of shares of stock and voting power of the corporation.

Tax Ramifications of Business Operation of a Corporation

A corporation is treated as a separate entity for federal income tax purposes. Computing a corporation's income tax liability can be complicated. The tax liability itself is a product of the corporation's taxable income, which is summarized in the formula shown in Exhibit 17.6:

EXHIBIT 17.6: CORPORATE TAXABLE INCOME FORMULA

Total Income (From Whatever Source Derived)	$xx,xxx
Less: Exclusions From Gross Income	(x,xxx)
Gross Income	$xx,xxx
Less: Deductions	(x,xxx)
Taxable Income	$xx,xxx

Total Income and Gross Income: The tax computation begins with the determination of the corporation's total income, from whatever source derived. In general, all income is taxable unless Congress has specifically exempted the income from taxation. In tax terminology, income exempt from tax and not included in a taxpayer's gross income is referred to as an exclusion. The amount of income remaining after removing the exclusions is the corporation's gross income, which is generally the starting point for the corporate income tax return (Form 1120).

Deductions: Several deductions are allowed to reduce gross income in arriving at corporate taxable income. Fewer restrictions are placed on corporate deductions than are placed on individual deductions due to the fact that all activities of a corporation are considered to be business activities. For example, casualty losses incurred are fully deductible by a corporation, but are subject to a $100 floor and 10 percent of AGI limitation for individuals.

Some deductions are allowed only for corporations. For example, corporations are allowed a deduction for dividends received from other corporations. The amount of the **dividends-received deduction (DRD)** is based on the percentage ownership of the corporation paying the dividend. If the dividend-receiving corporation owns less than 20 percent of the dividend-paying corporation, the dividends-received deduction will be 70 percent of the dividend actually received. Exhibit 17.7 summarizes the dividend-received deduction based on different ownership levels.

dividends-received deduction (DRD) - a deduction for dividends received by one corporation from another corporation. The amount of the DRD is based on the percentage ownership of the corporation paying the dividend

EXHIBIT 17.7: DIVIDEND-RECEIVED DEDUCTION BASED ON CORPORATE OWNERSHIP LEVEL

OWNERSHIP %	DRD
Less than 20%	70%
At least 20% and less than 80%	80%
At least 80% (Affiliated corporations)	100%

CHAPTER 17: BUSINESS ENTITIES

For example, if ABC Company owns 15 percent of XYZ Company, and XYZ pays a $10,000 dividend during the year to ABC Company, ABC will include the $10,000 of dividend income in its gross income, but will be entitled to a dividends-received deduction of $7,000 ($10,000 x 70%).

Taxable Income and Tax: The corporate taxable income is calculated by subtracting allowed deductions from the corporation's gross income. The tax on this income is calculated based upon the rate tables shown in Exhibit 17.8.

EXHIBIT 17.8: CORPORATION INCOME TAX RATES

Taxable Income		Pay	% on Excess	of the Amount Over
Over	But Not Over			
$ 0-	$ 50,000	$ 0	15	$ 0
50,000-	75,000	7,500	25	50,000
75,000-	100,000	13,750	34	75,000
100,000-	335,000	22,250	39	100,000
335,000-	10,000,000	113,900	34	335,000
10,000,000-	15,000,000	3,400,000	35	10,000,000
15,000,000-	18,333,333	5,150,000	38	15,000,000
18,333,333-	....	6,416,667	35	18,333,333

Taxable income of certain personal service corporations is taxed at a flat rate of 35%.

personal service corporation (PSC) - a C corporation in which substantially all of the activities involve the performance of services in the fields of health, law, engineering, architecture, accounting, actuarial science, or consulting

If a corporation incurs a net operating loss for the year, the loss may be carried back two years where it can be used to offset any corporate taxable income. If the loss is not fully utilized by the carryback, it can then be carried forward for up to 20 years.

Personal Service Corporation: A **personal service corporation** (PSC) is defined as a C corporation in which substantially all of the activities involve the performance of services in the fields of health, law, engineering, architecture, accounting, actuarial science, or consulting, and if substantially all of the stock is owned by employees. The taxable income of a personal service corporation is taxed at a flat rate of 35 percent, not at the regular corporate income tax rates. This provision encourages employee-owners of PSCs to take more salary out of the corporation.

Tax Ramifications of Withdrawals or Distributions from a Corporation

double taxation of dividends - the taxation of income at the corporate level and the subsequent taxation of dividend distributions at the individual shareholder's level

One of the major tax disadvantages of the corporate legal form of business entity is the **double taxation of dividends** paid by the corporation to its shareholders. Double taxation refers to the taxation of income at the corporate level and the subsequent taxation of dividend distributions at the individual shareholder's level. There is no deduction from the taxable income of a corporation for dividends distributed to shareholders.

For example, if a corporation has taxable income of $1,000 that is taxed at the 34 percent rate, there will only be $660 remaining to distribute to shareholders. If the shareholders are in the 36 percent tax bracket, the $660 dividend received will result in an additional tax of $238, leaving the shareholder with only $422 in cash. This double taxation may be enough incentive to discourage incorporation.

S CORPORATION

An **S corporation** is a special type of corporation for federal income tax purposes. The corporation is formed like a regular corporation (with limited liability as a separate entity) under state law; however, it is treated similar to a partnership for income tax purposes. Therefore, all items of corporation income and deduction are passed through to the shareholders and reported on their personal income tax returns. The entity itself files an informational tax return (Form 1120S).

These corporations are called "S corporations" because they must satisfy the requirements of Subchapter S of the Internal Revenue Code to receive this special tax treatment. The essential elements of an S corporation include that the corporation must be a domestic corporation and may not have more than 75 shareholders. In addition, nonresident aliens, C corporations, partnerships, and certain trusts are not allowed to hold stock in an S corporation.

MANAGEMENT OPERATION AND DECISION MAKING OF AN S CORPORATION

S corporations are identical to regular corporations in terms of their management characteristics. However, closely held S corporations are often managed in a similar fashion to partnerships.

LEGAL LIABILITY OF AN S CORPORATION

As with regular corporations, one of the major advantages of the S corporation is the limited liability enjoyed by shareholders.

The shareholders' liability for the acts, omissions, debts, and other obligations of the corporation generally is limited to the shareholders' capital contributions. There are several situations, however, in which the S corporation's shareholders will be personally liable for the debts of the corporation.

A lender to a closely held corporation requires that the primary shareholders guarantee the loan to the corporation. If this is the case, the shareholders are liable to the extent of their guarantees, in addition to their capital contribution.

A court may ignore the legal fiction of the corporation as an entity (pierce the corporate veil) when the corporation has been used to perpetuate fraud, circumvent law, accomplish an illegal purpose, or otherwise evade law.

The courts may disregard the corporate form of entity if the corporation is not maintained as a separate entity from its shareholders. This arises occasionally in the case of closely held corporations.

S corporation - a special type of corporation formed under state law like a regular corporation; however, for income tax purposes, is treated similar to a partnership

TAXATION OF AN S CORPORATION

The term "S corporation" is used to describe a corporation that is taxed under the provisions of Subchapter S of the Internal Revenue Code. Even though an S corporation is similar to a regular, or "C" corporation in that it is an entity created under state law that is separate and distinct from its owners, the federal income tax treatment of an S corporation is similar to the treatment of a partnership.

In order for a corporation to be taxed according to the rules of Subchapter S, an election must be filed on Form 2553 within 2 months and 15 days after the corporation's taxable year begins. A corporation must meet all of the following requirements at all times for the "S" election to be initially and continually valid:

Maximum of 75 Shareholders: An S corporation cannot have more than 75 eligible shareholders. Stock owned by a husband and wife is treated as owned by one shareholder.

Eligible Shareholders: Ownership of S corporation stock is restricted to individuals who are U.S. citizens or residents, estates, certain trusts, and charitable organizations. Nonresident aliens, C corporations, and partnerships are prohibited from holding stock in an S corporation.

Domestic Corporation: The corporation must be an eligible corporation created under the laws of the United States or of any state.

Eligible Corporation: Insurance companies, domestic international sales corporation (DISCs), and certain financial institutions are not eligible to be an S corporation.

One Class of Stock: The corporation is allowed only one class of stock outstanding. The shares generally must provide identical rights to all shareholders. However, an S corporation may have two classes of stock if the only difference is that one class has voting rights and the other class does not.

Tax Ramifications of Formation of an S Corporation

An S corporation is formed in the same manner as a C corporation, with the rules of Section 351 (see above) applying to transfers of property to the corporation. Therefore, under qualifying circumstances, property can be transferred to the corporation without gain or loss recognition by the transferors receiving stock.

Conceptually, the computation of a shareholder's basis in S corporation stock is similar to that for partners in a partnership. Both calculations are designed to ensure that there is neither a double taxation of income nor double deduction of expenses.

Tax Ramifications of Business Operation of an S Corporation

Once the S corporation election has been made, the corporation is treated for federal income tax purposes in a similar fashion to a partnership. The S corporation itself is generally not required to pay any income tax, but must file an information return, Form 1120S, detailing the items of income and expense that will be reported on the shareholder's individual income tax return.

Shareholders must take into account their distributive share of corporate taxable income and any separately stated items in computing their taxable incomes. A shareholder's weighted average ownership in the stock of the company determines his or her share of income, gain, loss, deduction, or credit. "Special allocations" are not allowed with S corporations. All items of income must be allocated based on pro rata ownership.

Each shareholder's distributive share of items is reported on Schedule K-1, which is furnished by the S corporation to both the IRS and the shareholder. The K-1 for an S corporation is quite similar to that of a partnership, except the K-1 for an S corporation does not include a reconciliation of capital accounts or a line for guaranteed payments. Exhibit 17.9 shows an S corporation Schedule K-1.

EXHIBIT 17.9: S CORPORATION SCHEDULE K-1

SCHEDULE K-1 (Form 1120S) Department of the Treasury Internal Revenue Service	Shareholder's Share of Income, Credits, Deductions, etc. ▶ See separate instructions. For calendar year 2000 or tax year beginning _____ , 2000, and ending _____ , 20 ___	OMB No. 1545-0130 2000

Shareholder's identifying number ▶ _____

Corporation's identifying number ▶ _____

Shareholder's name, address, and ZIP code

Corporation's name, address, and ZIP code

A Shareholder's percentage of stock ownership for tax year (see instructions for Schedule K-1) . . . . ▶ _____ %
B Internal Revenue Service Center where corporation filed its return ▶ --
C Tax shelter registration number (see instructions for Schedule K-1) . . . . ▶ --
D Check applicable boxes: (1) ☐ Final K-1   (2) ☐ Amended K-1

	(a) Pro rata share items		(b) Amount	(c) Form 1040 filers enter the amount in column (b) on:
Income (Loss)	1 Ordinary income (loss) from trade or business activities . . .	1		See pages 4 and 5 of the Shareholder's Instructions for Schedule K-1 (Form 1120S).
	2 Net income (loss) from rental real estate activities	2		
	3 Net income (loss) from other rental activities	3		
	4 Portfolio income (loss):			
	a Interest	4a		Sch. B, Part I, line 1
	b Ordinary dividends	4b		Sch. B, Part II, line 5
	c Royalties	4c		Sch. E, Part I, line 4
	d Net short-term capital gain (loss)	4d		Sch. D, line 5, col. (f)
	e Net long-term capital gain (loss):			
	(1) 28% rate gain (loss)	4e(1)		Sch. D, line 12, col. (g)
	(2) Total for year	4e(2)		Sch. D, line 12, col. (f)
	f Other portfolio income (loss) (attach schedule)	4f		(Enter on applicable line of your return.)
	5 Net section 1231 gain (loss) (other than due to casualty or theft)	5		See Shareholder's Instructions for Schedule K-1 (Form 1120S).
	6 Other income (loss) (attach schedule)	6		(Enter on applicable line of your return.)
Deductions	7 Charitable contributions (attach schedule)	7		Sch. A, line 15 or 16
	8 Section 179 expense deduction	8		See page 6 of the Shareholder's Instructions for Schedule K-1 (Form 1120S).
	9 Deductions related to portfolio income (loss) (attach schedule) .	9		
	10 Other deductions (attach schedule)	10		
Investment Interest	11a Interest expense on investment debts	11a		Form 4952, line 1
	b (1) Investment income included on lines 4a, 4b, 4c, and 4f above	11b(1)		See Shareholder's Instructions for Schedule K-1 (Form 1120S).
	(2) Investment expenses included on line 9 above	11b(2)		
Credits	12a Credit for alcohol used as fuel	12a		Form 6478, line 10
	b Low-income housing credit:			
	(1) From section 42(j)(5) partnerships for property placed in service before 1990	12b(1)		Form 8586, line 5
	(2) Other than on line 12b(1) for property placed in service before 1990	12b(2)		
	(3) From section 42(j)(5) partnerships for property placed in service after 1989	12b(3)		
	(4) Other than on line 12b(3) for property placed in service after 1989	12b(4)		
	c Qualified rehabilitation expenditures related to rental real estate activities	12c		See page 7 of the Shareholder's Instructions for Schedule K-1 (Form 1120S).
	d Credits (other than credits shown on lines 12b and 12c) related to rental real estate activities	12d		
	e Credits related to other rental activities	12e		
	13 Other credits	13		

For Paperwork Reduction Act Notice, see the Instructions for Form 1120S.   Cat. No. 11520D   Schedule K-1 (Form 1120S) 2000

The S corporation K-1 details the shareholder's share of partnership ordinary income, which is the net profit or loss resulting from the corporation's trade or business. Ordinary income allocated to a shareholder from an S corporation is not subject to self-employment tax. The Schedule K-1 also reflects various items that must be reported separately from ordinary income. These separately stated items, which include dividend income, interest income, and capital gains, are afforded special treatment on the shareholder's individual income tax return.

The shareholder's adjusted taxable basis in the stock must be adjusted each year to reflect the allocated items of income and expense. Adjusted taxable basis is increased by a shareholder's distributive share of both taxable and nontaxable S corporation income, and is decreased by the shareholder's share of S corporation losses and nondeductible expenses.

Tax Ramifications of Withdrawals or Distributions from an S Corporation

The rules regarding distributions from an S corporation to a shareholder generally follow the rules applying to distributions from partnerships. Generally, distributions represent accumulated income that has been previously taxed to its owners and, therefore, should not be taxed again. As a result, most distributions from S corporations are considered nontaxable to the extent of the shareholder's basis in the stock. Any distribution in excess of the stock adjusted taxable basis is treated as capital gain.

LIMITED LIABILITY COMPANY

A **limited liability company (LLC)** is a relatively new type of business entity, and is one of the most versatile. An LLC is created under state law by filing articles of organization. Its owners, referred to as **members**, can be individuals, partnerships, trusts, corporations, or other LLCs. A limited liability company is an entity that is generally able to provide the limited personal liability of corporations and the flow-through taxation of partnerships or S corporations.

One reason for their versatility is that they can be taxed as a sole proprietorship, partnership, C corporation, or S corporation. Generally, however, LLCs are usually treated as general partnerships for federal income tax purposes. If the LLC is taxed as a partnership or sole proprietorship, then all items of LLC income and expense are reported on the individual member's income tax return. Unlike a general partnership or sole proprietorship, however, members are not personally liable for the obligations of the LLC. This protection from personal liability for members, coupled with the favorable flow-through federal income tax treatment, has made the LLC a popular choice as a business entity.

MANAGEMENT OPERATION AND DECISION MAKING OF A LIMITED LIABILITY COMPANY

When an LLC is formed through the filing of **articles of organization**, the LLC is registered with the state. When drafting the articles of organization, the members of the LLC must determine whether the LLC will be managed directly by all of its members, or whether the administration of the LLC will be delegated to one or more managers.

limited liability company (LLC) - a relatively new and versatile form of business entity created under state law by filing articles of organization-- versatile because it can be taxed as a sole proprietorship, partnership, C corporation, or S corporation

members - the owners of a limited liability company (LLC) who can be individuals, partnerships, trusts, corporations, or other LLCs

articles of organization - document filed in compliance with state law to create a limited liability company (LLC)

managers - individuals who are responsible for the maintenance, administration, and management of the affairs of a limited liability company

Managers are individuals who are responsible for the maintenance, administration, and management of the affairs of the LLC. In most states, the managers serve a particular term and report to and serve at the discretion of the members. Specific duties of the managers may be detailed in the articles of organization or the operating agreement of the LLC. In some states, the members of an LLC may also serve as the managers.

LEGAL LIABILITY OF A LIMITED LIABILITY COMPANY

A member of an LLC has no personal liability for the debts or obligations of the LLC. This limited liability applies to both members who participate in management and those who do not. The ability to participate in management and still have limited liability is one of the most attractive features of LLCs. A member that participates in management is similar to a general partner in a partnership, except the member of the LLC has limited liability.

TAXATION OF A LIMITED LIABILITY COMPANY

An LLC with two or more owners is generally treated as a partnership for federal income tax purposes, unless it elects to be treated as a corporation. The election to be treated as a corporation is made by checking a box on Form 8832 shown below in Exhibit 17.10. If the LLC has only one member, it is treated as a sole proprietorship. LLCs that elect to be treated as a corporation for federal income tax purposes are also permitted to elect small business treatment causing the LLC to be taxed as an S corporation. The election of S corporation treatment for an LLC is accomplished in the same manner as a regular C corporation, by the filing of Form 2553.

Form **8832** (December 1996) Department of the Treasury Internal Revenue Service	Entity Classification Election	OMB No. 1545-1516

Please Type or Print

Name of entity

Employer identification number (EIN)

Number, street, and room or suite no. If a P.O. box, see instructions.

City or town, state, and ZIP code. If a foreign address, enter city, province or state, postal code and country.

1 Type of election (see instructions):

a ☐ Initial classification by a newly-formed entity (or change in current classification of an existing entity to take effect on January 1, 1997)

b ☐ Change in current classification (to take effect later than January 1, 1997)

2 Form of entity (see instructions):

a ☐ A domestic eligible entity electing to be classified as an association taxable as a corporation.

b ☐ A domestic eligible entity electing to be classified as a partnership.

c ☐ A domestic eligible entity with a single owner electing to be disregarded as a separate entity

d ☐ A foreign eligible entity electing to be classified as an association taxable as a corporation.

e ☐ A foreign eligible entity electing to be classified as a partnership.

f ☐ A foreign eligible entity with a single owner electing to be disregarded as a separate entity.

3 Election is to be effective beginning (month, day, year) (see instructions) . . . . ▶ ___ / ___ / ___

4 Name and title of person whom the IRS may call for more information

5 That person's telephone number

Consent Statement and Signature(s) (see instructions)

Under penalties of perjury, I (we) declare that I (we) consent to the election of the above-named entity to be classified as indicated above, and that I (we) have examined this consent statement, and to the best of my (our) knowledge and belief, it is true, correct, and complete. If I am an officer, manager, or member signing for all members of the entity, I further declare that I am authorized to execute this consent statement on their behalf.

Signature(s)	Date	Title

For Paperwork Reduction Act Notice, see page 2.   Cat. No. 22598R   Form **8832** (12-96)

633

A major advantage of an LLC is the limited liability of its members. The protection of owners from personal liability for obligations of the entity, coupled with the flow-through federal income tax treatment, has spurred the enactment of LLC legislation in most states.

Tax Ramifications of Formation of a Limited Liability Company

Generally, limited liability companies are classified as partnerships for federal income tax purposes. As such, the income tax consequences applicable to the formation of an LLC are identical to those applicable to a partnership.

When a member contributes cash or property to the LLC, no gain or loss is recognized and the member's basis in the LLC interest is equal to the value of the cash contributed or the basis of the property contributed. If a member instead contributes services to the LLC, the member must recognize ordinary income for the value of the services contributed.

Tax Ramifications of Business Operation of a Limited Liability Company

An LLC with two or more members can be taxed as a partnership or a corporation. If the LLC is classified as a partnership for income tax purposes, the LLC must file an information return, Form 1065, detailing the items of income and expense that will be reported on the member's individual income tax return. The members will each receive a Schedule K-1 detailing their allocable amounts of income, loss, deduction, and credit. If the LLC is classified as a corporation, the LLC will be responsible for any tax on business income.

If the LLC is comprised of only one member, all results from the business will be reported directly on Schedule C of the member's individual income tax return. Therefore, the income from the business will be taxed at the member's individual income tax rates.

SELECTING THE PROPER BUSINESS LEGAL FORM

The selection of an appropriate business legal form has probably never been as challenging as it is today. Each business entity has its own characteristics that make it more or less suitable and attractive for a particular situation. The basic factors that should be considered in selecting a business entity include simplicity of formation and operation, ownership restrictions, limited liability, management operations, and tax characteristics. Exhibit 17.11 below summarizes some of the more critical legal liability and tax considerations for various business entities.

EXHIBIT 17.11: SUMMARY OF LEGAL LIABILITY AND TAX CONSIDERATIONS

FOR VARIOUS BUSINESS ENTITIES

	Sole Proprietor	Partnership[*]	LLP	LLC[**]	S Corp	Corporation
What type of liability do the owner's have?	Unlimited	General Partnership - Unlimited; Limited Partnership - Limited	Limited	Limited	Limited	Limited
What federal tax form is required to be filed for the organization?	Form 1040, Schedule C	Form 1065	Form 1065	Form 1040, Schedule C or Form 1065 or Form 1120 or Form 1120S	Form 1120S	Form 1120
Under what concept is the organization taxed?	Individual Level	Flow-through	Flow-through	LLCs can be taxed as sole proprietorships, partnerships, corporations, or S corporations	Flow-through	Entity Level
On what tax form is the owner's compensation reported?	Form 1040, Schedule C	Schedule K-1	Schedule K-1	Form 1040, Schedule C, or Schedule K-1, or Form W-2 and Schedule K-1, or W-2	W-2 and Schedule K-1	W-2 (dividends are reported on Form 1099-div)
What is the nature of the owner's income from the organization?	Self-employment income	Self-employment income	Self-employment income	Self-employment income, or W-2 income and ordinary income, W-2 income	W-2 income and ordinary income	W-2 income and dividend income
What is the basis for determining tax-advantaged retirement plan contributions?	Net Schedule C income	Self-employment income	Self-employment income	Self-employment income or W-2 income	W-2 income	W-2 income

Flow-through: all items of income will flow from the entity to the individual partner's/owner's/member's return while retaining the character of the income at the entity level.

[*]   Limited Partners will generally not have self-employment income.

[**]   The LLC will have the same tax characteristics and attributes as the type of entity it has elected to be taxed as.

Note: Family Limited Partnerships (FLPs) have the same treatment for general partners as general partnerships and for limited partners the same treatment as limited partnerships.

SIMPLICITY OF FORMATION AND OPERATION

If the main factor in the determination of business legal form is simplicity of formation, either the sole proprietorship or the general partnership may be the business form of choice. No special documents need to be prepared for a sole proprietorship or general partnership to begin activities. However, it is customary for a general partnership to draft a written partnership agreement, and the partnership must file a separate income (informational) tax return each year.

The formation of a limited partnership requires the filing of a certificate of limited partnership with the Secretary of State in the state where the partnership is being organized. Otherwise, the operation of the limited partnership is similar to the general partnership, in that income and losses are allocated to the partners, and the limited partnership is required to file a separate tax return each year.

A corporation is often the most expensive form of entity to organize and operate. If the corporate form is selected, the business owners must prepare a certificate of incorporation, articles of incorporation, and bylaws, and must pay filing fees. Corporations must file annual reports with the state, and must file annual federal income tax returns and state franchise tax returns. An S corporation also must make an initial election to be treated as an S corporation for tax purposes.

A limited liability company is formed by filing articles of organization with the state in which the entity is to be registered. This process is similar to filing articles of incorporation for a corporation. Limited liability companies are generally classified as partnerships for federal income tax purposes. As such, the income tax consequences applicable to an LLC are almost identical to those applicable to a partnership.

OWNERSHIP RESTRICTIONS

Some business forms place restrictions on the number and types of owners. The ownership structure of the business must be considered before selecting a type of business entity.

C corporations are extremely flexible in the number and types of owners allowed. A regular C corporation can have an unlimited number of shareholders, and the shareholders are not limited to individuals. However, ownership of an S corporation is limited to 75 eligible shareholders. Eligible shareholders are individuals who are U.S. citizens or residents, estates, certain trusts, and charitable organizations. Nonresident aliens, C corporations, and partnerships are prohibited from holding stock in an S corporation.

No limit is placed on the number of members of an LLC. In addition, almost any type of entity may be a member. This flexibility in the number and types of owners makes an LLC more attractive than an S corporation in many situations.

A sole proprietorship can have only one owner. Therefore, this type of business form is unacceptable for joint owners of a business. No limit is placed on the number of partners in a general or limited partnership; however, a limited partnership must have at least one general partner.

LIMITED LIABILITY

A major concern of most business owners is the risk of personal liability. As a result, the limited liability company, although relatively new, has become a very popular business form.

Members of an LLC have no personal liability for the debts or obligations of the LLC. The ability to participate in management without assuming personal liability for debt is one of the most attractive features of an LLC. Limited liability status also applies to C corporations and S corporations.

A general partner has unlimited liability for the acts of the partnership, the other partners, and obligations made by any partner or the partnership in the performance of partnership duties. If the partnership assets are insufficient to satisfy the liabilities of the partnership, the partnership's creditors can collect against the personal assets of the general partners. Therefore, if legal liability is a major concern for the business, a general partnership is not a good choice of business form.

MANAGEMENT OPERATIONS

Another consideration in the selection of a business legal form is the structure and flexibility of management.

The management of sole proprietorships and partnerships is very straightforward. With a sole proprietorship, the proprietor is responsible for the day-to-day operation of the business and for making all of the business decisions. This allows for great flexibility in the operation of the business. With partnerships, the general partners participate directly in the management of the partnership and are directly responsible for the day-to-day operation of the business. Limited partners are not allowed to participate in management.

Corporations have management advantages and disadvantages over other business forms. One advantage is that there is a separation of management from ownership so that the mere ownership of corporate stock does not give the owner the right to participate in the management. The management is centralized, with the directors and officers handling management of corporate affairs. A disadvantage, however, is that the decision process may become time consuming and expensive due to the formalities involved.

In the case of an LLC, the members of the LLC must determine initially whether the LLC will be managed directly by all of its members, similar to a partnership, or whether the administration of the LLC will be delegated to one or more managers, similar to a corporation.

TAX CHARACTERISTICS

Startup Losses

A business that expects losses in the first few years of operation will typically opt for a different type of business legal form than that of a business expecting immediate profits. If the business expects losses, a flow-through entity such as a partnership, S corporation, or limited liability corporation, is generally the entity of choice. Losses will flow through to the owners of the entity and can generally be used immediately to offset other income at the individual level.

In contrast, losses incurred by a C corporation can only benefit the corporation. Therefore, several years may pass before the loss can be utilized against corporate profits.

Profitable Business

A business that will be highly profitable from the outset must choose a business entity that will not place the business in a tax burden. If the taxpayer conducts the business as a sole proprietorship, partnership, LLC, or S corporation, the federal tax rate applied to the business income may be as high as 39.1 percent. In contrast, if a C corporation is used to operate the business, the highest federal tax rate is only 35 percent.

Double Taxation of Dividends

As discussed earlier in this chapter, one of the major tax disadvantages of the corporate form is the double taxation of dividends paid by the corporation to its shareholders. Double taxation refers to the taxation of income at the corporate level and the subsequent taxation of dividend distributions at the individual shareholder's level. There is no deduction from the taxable income of a corporation for dividends distributed to shareholders. This double taxation may be enough incentive to discourage the use of the regular C corporation form.

PROFESSIONAL FOCUS

What criteria do you use to help clients choose their form of business entity?

I generally use three criteria in helping clients choose a business entity. The first and most important is income tax considerations. The choice of business entity can have a significant impact on both federal and state taxes. Generally, for organizations involved in real estate activities or personal services, a partnership can provide creative tax planning opportunities with provisions such as the "Optional Adjustment to Basis" election and flexibility in distribution of flow-through items, such as income/loss, credits, and so on. An S Corporation offers significant tax savings opportunities over a C Corporation for closely held business by avoiding the "Built-in Gains Tax," "Personal Holding Company Penalty Tax," and additional taxes levied against "Personal Service Corporations."

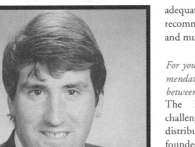

The second consideration that I evaluate is liability. I often establish a meeting between myself, my client, and my client's attorney to evaluate the liability and related exposure between the various choices of business entities. Generally, where partnerships offer tax advantages, the potential liability exposure can outweigh these benefits. Often, clients choose either a corporation or limited liability company, based upon the attorney's recommendation, to avoid undesirable personal liability.

The final consideration is the client's personality and business practices. I often explain to clients that if you want to be a "Duck" you must "Walk and Quack like a Duck." A client who wants to be a corporation must be willing to play by the rules by clearly separating personal items from business, maintaining corporate minutes, and other legal requirements. Many clients are better suited for the simplicity of a sole proprietorship. If a client forms a corporation and doesn't act like a corporation, related tax problems are bound to appear, and the legal protection of a corporation is often in jeopardy.

Each client is unique and all of the relevant criteria must be adequately considered before making a recommendation. The final decision is and must always be up to the client.

For your S Corporation clients, what recommendations do you make regarding splits between compensation and dividends?

The IRS continues to aggressively challenge S Corporation dividend distributions under the belief, often well founded, that they represent a technique to avoid Social Security taxes. I have been involved in several IRS audits where the agent challenged distributions under the provision of unreasonable compensation. One situation that occurred about ten years ago involved a restaurant client, whose restaurant (a C Corporation) was professionally managed, and the owner worked less than twenty hours per week. The IRS agent challenged the owner's compensation level as excessively high relative to time-spent working. They successfully reclassified part of the compensation as a C Corporation dividend. We then advised the client to become an S Corporation to avoid this problem. In a subsequent audit, (the owner continued to work less than twenty hours per week) the IRS Agent challenged the owner's compensation as excessively low. They unsuccessfully attempted to have part of the distribution reclassified as wages subject to Social Security and other payroll taxes. The agent's justification for the change in attitude was very simple, "My job is to support the position which will benefit the government not the taxpayer."

Another issue that must be considered is that distributions reduce the taxpayer's basis in the corporation and can have an effect on the shareholder's ability to deduct losses on the personal income tax return.

JOHN ROSSI III, MBA, CPA/PFS, CMA, CFM, CFP™, CVA

DISCUSSION QUESTIONS

1. What are the several different types of business entities that a business owner may choose as a legal form of business?
2. How is a Limited Liability Partnership taxed?
3. What are the differences between General and Limited partnerships?
4. How does each type of business entity differ from other forms of business with regard to personal liability of owners?
5. What are the tax ramifications of withdrawals or distributions from a C corporation?
6. What type of business entity should owners choose if they expect the business to produce losses the first few years?
7. What is the tax treatment of a limited liability corporation?
8. What type of business entity should an owner choose if simplicity of formation and operation is a major priority?

EXERCISES

1. A CPA performed services for ABC Partnership and, in lieu of her normal fee, accepted a 20 percent unrestricted capital interest in the partnership with a fair market value of $7,500. How much income from this arrangement should the accountant report on her tax return?

2. An S corporation has the following information for its taxable year:

Net income *before* the items below	$60,000
Salary to Z	(18,000)
Rental income	22,000
Rental expenses	(29,000)
Net income	$35,000

John is a 40 percent owner of the S corporation, and he performs services for the business. What is John's self-employment income from the corporation, which is subject to self-employment tax?

3. During the year, Susan purchased 5 shares of an S corporation's 100 shares of common stock outstanding. She held the shares for 146 days during the taxable year. If the S corporation reported taxable income of $200,000, what must Susan include on her personal income tax return?

4.	At the beginning of the current year, Kara's basis in her partnership interest was $50,000. At the end of the year, Kara received a K-1 from the partnership that showed the following:

Cash withdrawal	$30,000
Partnership taxable income	17,500
Dividend income	5,000
Short-term capital loss	1,400
Charitable contribution	2,900

What is Kara's basis in her partnership interest at the beginning of the next year?

5.	Alpha Company (a C corporation) owns 25 percent of Zeta Company. During the year, Zeta Company paid a $30,000 dividend to Alpha Company. For tax purposes, how will Alpha Company treat the dividend received?

6.	Brisco Company, a calendar year S corporation, incorporated in 1997. The company showed the following taxable income and distributions each year:

	Taxable Income	Distributions
1997	$55,000	$35,000
1998	60,000	25,000
1999	50,000	35,000
2000	40,000	50,000

The company has had a single shareholder since January 1, 1997, and his basis in the stock on that date was $10,000. Based on the figures above, what was the shareholder's basis at the end of 2000?

7.	Nelson Van Houten received a 70 percent capital interest in a general partnership by contributing the following:

Item Transferred	Nelson's Basis	FMV
Land	$60,000	$100,000
Debt (on Land)	N/A	(50,000)
Inventory	$10,000	$8,000
Services	N/A	$2,500

What is Nelson's basis in the partnership after the contribution?

8. Brooke Industries, Inc. (a C corporation) had the following income and loss items during the year:

Gross Receipts	$200,000
Cost of Goods Sold	(50,000)
Dividend income from ABC Corp	$20,000
(Brooke owns 15% of ABC)	
Operating Expenses	(40,000)
Net Operating Loss Carryforward	(12,000)

What is Brooke Industries' taxable income and tax due for the year?

9. In its first year of business, Sanifone Corp (a C corporation) had gross income of $160,000 and deductions of $40,000. The company also paid a dividend of $20,000 to its only shareholder, Joe Taylor, who is in the 35.5 percent individual income tax bracket. What are the tax implications to Sanifone and Joe?

10. Tommy is a general partner in RichTech, a general partnership. Tommy received a K-1 from the partnership, which contained the following items:

Partnership Taxable Income	$200,000
Dividend Income	$2,500
Long-Term Capital Gain (on investments)	$6,000

How much self-employment tax will Tommy have to pay?

11. Discuss the management structure of a C corporation.

12. What are the requirements for an S Corporation?

PROBLEMS

1. Hugh Elliott is a single taxpayer with no children. He is a self-employed real estate appraiser, and the results for his business for the current year are as follows:

Gross Receipts	$150,000

Expenses:

Advertising	$2,000
Insurance	$1,000
Dues	$1,500
Office Rent	$12,000
Meals and Entertainment	$800

Hugh also received the following income during the year:

Interest	$1,100
Dividends	$1,400

Hugh incurred the following expenses during the current year:

Real Estate Taxes	$9,000
Mortgage Interest	$5,000

Assuming Hugh paid $10,000 in alimony to his ex-wife, calculate his taxable income and self-employment tax for the current year.

2. Pete Johnson is a single taxpayer with no dependents. During the year, he invested $40,000 in an S corporation. He received the following information on the K-1 from the S Corporation:

Net income *before* salary	$60,000
Salary to Pete (S Corporation)	18,000
Interest Income	2,000
Dividend Income	1,000
Long-Term Capital Gain	4,500
Charitable Contributions	2,000

Pete also received a distribution of $5,500 from the S corporation, and earned a salary of $50,000 at his full time job. Calculate Pete's taxable income, as well as his adjusted taxable basis in the S corporation stock at the end of the year.

3. Doug Tanner (a single taxpayer) will be starting a new business in the year 2001. He is not sure whether to operate the business as a C corporation or as a S corporation. Given the following estimates of income and expenses, determine the total tax that would be due under either scenario.

Gross Profit	$150,000
Operating Expenses (excluding salary)	(70,000)
Salary paid to Doug	40,000
Cash distribution to Doug	10,000

- Work life expectancy

- Retirement life expectancy

- Current savings rate

- Current and projected inflation rate

- Investment analysis

- Risk analysis

- The wage replacement ratio

- Sources of retirement income

- Social Security benefits

- Evaluation of qualified plans

- Other tax-advantaged savings plans

- Capital needs analysis

- Distributions from qualified plans

- Annuity approach to capital needs approach

- Capital preservation model

- Purchasing power preservation model

- Non-qualified plans and deferred compensation

Retirement Planning

Risks

- Inadequate savings rate/amount
- Inappropriate investments
- Underestimation of life expectancy
- Starting saving program too late
- Failure to use tax advantaged accounts
- Untimely death
- Disability
- Catastrophic illness
- Tort liability
- Changes in Social Security

Data Collection

- Family history
- Current financial statements
- Savings rate
- Current asset allocation
- Investment returns
- Description of qualified plan benefits
- Current inflation rate

Goals

- Adequate retirement income
- Inflation protected retirement income
- Appropriate age to retire

Data Analysis

- Capital needs analysis
- Savings program
- Asset allocation
- Social Security benefits
- Insurance programs
- Qualified plans
- Other tax-advantaged plans
- Inflation expectations

CHAPTER 18

Introduction to Retirement Planning

LEARNING OBJECTIVES:

After learning the material in this chapter, you will be able to:

1. Define financial security.

2. Identify and understand the major factors that affect retirement planning.

3. Understand the work life expectancy/retirement life expectancy dilemma.

4. Explain the impact that timeliness of savings has on savings accumulation.

5. Discuss the balance that must be achieved between increasing and decreasing retirement income needs.

6. Define the Wage Replacement Ratio (WRR) and explain how it is used to estimate retirement income needs.

7. Differentiate between the top-down approach and the budgeting approach to calculating the Wage Replacement Ratio.

8. Discuss the qualitative factors that affect retirement planning.

9. Differentiate among the three capital needs analysis calculations: the basic, pure annuity model, the capital preservation model (CP), and the purchasing power preservation model (PPP).

10. Determine capital needs for various clients.

11. Make projections to prepare a capital needs analysis presentation.

INTRODUCTION

One of the central missions for individuals is long-term financial security and independence. This goal is realized at the point where a person is financially secure enough to live at their desired comfort level without the need for employment income. This glorious time is called retirement. To be financially secure at retirement requires that individuals carefully plan. According to a 1998 study by the SEC's Office of Investor Education and Assistance, more than 85 percent of American workers have no idea how much money they will need to fund their retirement. When coupled with changes in Social Security, tax laws, the economy, and the value structure of our society, retirement planning becomes a necessary, but difficult and time-consuming process for the individual. Due to the complex nature of retirement planning, financial planners are often enlisted to provide direction and guidance. This chapter discusses the fundamental concepts that financial planners need to know to effectively plan for clients' retirement. Chapter 19 discusses the characteristics of actual retirement plans.

BASIC FACTORS AFFECTING RETIREMENT PLANNING

Adequate retirement planning requires understanding the basic factors that affect retirement planning and the proper interrelationship of these factors. These factors must simultaneously produce sufficient capital at retirement to ensure that the retirement period is characterized by comfortably maintaining the preretirement lifestyle. A discussion of each factor and the risks to each is presented below. Later in the chapter, we will introduce a calculation essential to retirement planning--capital needs analysis.

There are several basic factors that affect retirement planning. While this text discusses the major factors, it is not inclusive of all the factors that affect retirement planning. The major factors include the remaining work life expectancy (WLE), the retirement life expectancy (RLE), basic savings concepts, the annual income needed (needs), the wage replacement ratio (WRR), the sources of retirement income, inflation, investment returns, and other qualitative factors.

REMAINING WORK LIFE EXPECTANCY (RWLE)

work life expectancy (WLE) - the years that a person spends in the work force, generally about 30-40 years

remaining work life expectancy (RWLE) - work period remaining at a certain point in time prior to retirement

The **work life expectancy (WLE)** is the period of time a person is in the work force, generally about 30-40 years. There has been a substantial decline in the overall work life expectancy (WLE) due to later entry into the workforce because of more years of education and early retirement.

The **remaining work life expectancy (RWLE)** is the work period that remains at a certain point in time before retirement. For example, a 50-year-old client who expects to retire at age 62 has a RWLE of 12 years. Determining the remaining work life expectancy is important for the financial planner because it tells the planner the number of years the client has left to save for retirement. When we speak of retirement, we think of normal retirement age as being 65. This is generally due to the retirement age requirement set forth by the Social Security Administration. In reality, the normal retirement age is several years less than 65, with 62 being a common retirement age. Early retirement has come about due to a heightened awareness of retirement planning, as well as the substantial economic growth that many individuals have been able to attain through wise investment decisions. This early retirement trend can be seen in Exhibit 18.1.

650

EXHIBIT 18.1: MEDIAN RETIREMENT AGE FROM 1965-1995

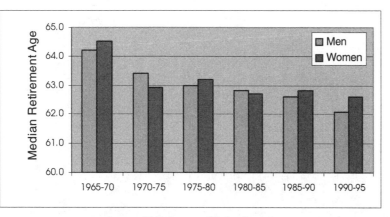

Source: U.S. Bureau of Labor Statistics

As the chart illustrates, both men and women are retiring earlier. Exhibit 18.2 presents a skewed distribution of all retirees' retirement ages. Notice that the area identified as A represents 93 percent of the area of the curve, meaning that approximately 93 percent of all individuals retire between ages 62 and 65 (inclusive). Exhibit 18.2 is significant to financial planners because, as the exhibit demonstrates, most clients will retire between 62 and 65 years of age.

EXHIBIT 18.2: AVERAGE RETIREMENT AGE (U.S.)

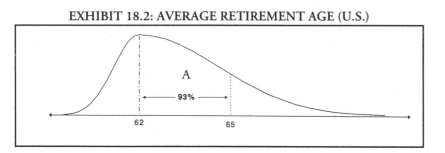

RETIREMENT LIFE EXPECTANCY (RLE)

The **retirement life expectancy (RLE)** is that time period beginning at retirement and extending until death. The RLE is the period of retirement that must be funded. While the average RLE for a group of 65-year-olds is approximately 20 years, it is common that clients live beyond the statistical average. In 1900, the average life expectancy for a newborn was 47 years. The average life expectancy had risen to 76.3 years for those born in 1997. This increase in life expectancy, and the corresponding increase in RLE, is a direct result of a decline in the death rate, especially the birth mortality rate. The overall death rate has declined due to medical and technological advances in disease diagnoses, cures, and prevention. With each new medical advancement, life expectancy will, no doubt, increase. Exhibit 18.3 presents the data depicting the increase in life expectancy from 1910 to 1998.

retirement life expectancy (RLE) - that time period beginning at retirement and extending until death; the RLE is the period of retirement that must be funded

EXHIBIT 18.3: LIFE EXPECTANCY AT BIRTH (U.S. 1940 – 1998)

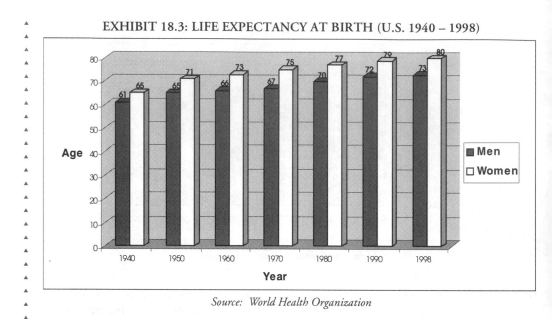

Source: World Health Organization

THE WLE AND THE RLE RELATIONSHIP

It is important that the financial planner understand the WLE and the RLE relationship. If either of the periods change then the remaining period is affected. The planner must appropriately estimate each period to avoid plan failure. Exhibit 18.4 presents the work life expectancy/ retirement life expectancy dilemma.

EXHIBIT 18.4: THE WLE/RLE DILEMMA

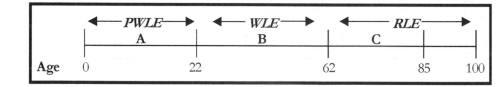

Area A represents the pre-work life expectancy (PWLE) and lasts until the person enters the work force on a full time basis. Generally, the PWLE ends between ages 18 - 26, with the average age at 22. Area B, the work life expectancy (WLE), represents the period of working years before retirement. This period begins at the end of the PWLE and ends at the beginning of C, the retirement life expectancy (RLE), usually around age 62. The RLE (Area C) generally lasts to age 85, but may continue beyond age 100. With a longer RLE period to finance and a shortened WLE in which to save and accumulate assets, careful planning is needed to meet the funding requirements for a financially secure retirement.

SAVINGS CONCEPTS

The savings amount, the savings rate, the timing of savings, and investment decisions are important concepts in retirement planning. If our society were adequately saving for retirement beginning at an early age, people would be saving about 10 percent of their gross annual income and investing in a broad portfolio of growth investments over their entire work life. They would be ever mindful of investment returns and inflation to ensure sufficient savings. Unfortunately, our society saves at a much lower rate than is needed (less than 5 percent), is not educated as to investments, and is, generally, insensitive to the impact and implications of inflation.

SAVINGS AMOUNT

In general, persons who begin the financial security planning process at an early age (25-30) should save 10-15 percent of their gross annual pay. If individuals do not begin at an early age, then they must save a greater amount of their gross pay to compensate for the missed years of contributions and compounding. Exhibit 18.5 shows how much individuals must save if they choose to wait until later years to begin saving for retirement.

EXHIBIT 18.5: REQUIRED SAVINGS RATE FOR RETIREMENT

Age beginning regular and recurring savings*	Savings (as percent of gross pay) rate required to create appropriate capital*
25-35	10-13%
35-45	15-18%
45-55	20-25%
55-65	30-35%

*Assumes appropriate asset allocation for reasonable-risk investor through accumulation year; also assumes normal raises and an 80 percent wage replacement ratio at Social Security normal age retirement (currently age 65)

Exhibit 18.5 illustrates a major problem with delaying retirement savings. Namely, many individuals find it difficult to begin saving such a large amount even if they are accustomed to saving at all. Saving requires foregoing current consumption, and most individuals find it difficult to decrease consumption by 20-30 percent, especially when they have been accustomed to maintaining a certain standard of living for long periods of time.

SAVINGS RATE

The problem identified in Exhibit 18.5 is a major concern for any planner because the average personal savings rate in the U.S. has plummeted to less than 3 percent in the year 1999 and to a negative 0.1 percent in the year 2000. Exhibit 18.6 illustrates this sharp decline.

EXHIBIT 18.6: U.S. PERSONAL SAVINGS RATE (1991-2000)

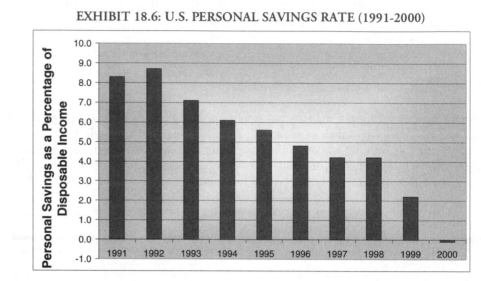

TIMING OF SAVINGS

The earlier a person saves, the greater the number of future compounding periods available before retirement. The greater number of compounding periods leads to a lower required savings rate and a larger accumulation of capital at retirement. When savings is delayed, the power of compounding is lost and individuals must compensate by saving a greater percentage of their disposable income.

EXAMPLE

Ann saves $2,000 a year from age 25-34 inclusively and invests in an account earning 8 percent annually. Ann stops investing at age 34, but does not withdraw the accumulation until age 65. Ann's accumulation at age 65 is $314,870 even though she only deposited $20,000. In contrast, Bob saves $2,000 a year from age 35-65 inclusively and invests in a similar account to Ann, earning 8 percent annually. Even though Bob saved $42,000 more than Ann, he will have accumulated $68,178 less than Ann at age 65. The deposits and balance at age 65 for Ann and Bob are presented in Exhibit 18.7.

EXHIBIT 18.7: TIME/SAVINGS EXAMPLE (ACCUMULATION AT AGE 65)

	Ann	Bob
Total Invested (OA)	$20,000	$62,000
Balance at 65	$314,870	$246,692
Earnings Rate	8%	8%

It may seem strange that while Bob invested more than three times as much as Ann, Ann has 28 percent more than Bob at age 65. This result demonstrates the power of compound earnings over the longer period of 41 years versus 31 years. Exhibit 18.8 shows this phenomenon graphically.

EXHIBIT 18.8: EXAMPLE ACCUMULATION

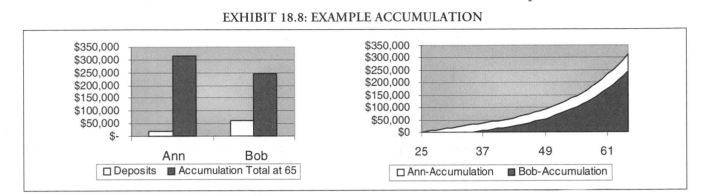

INVESTMENT DECISIONS

A fundamental understanding of investment decisions and their consequences is essential to retirement planning. In this chapter, we will briefly identify some of the relationships between investments and retirement planning. More in-depth investment information is provided in this textbook's investment chapters.

All assets do not have the same historical investment returns. When planning for retirement, it is important to have a historical perspective of investment returns for various investment alternatives. Exhibit 18.9 provides such a perspective on historical investment returns, inflation adjusted returns, and risk as measured by standard deviation.

EXHIBIT 18.9: HISTORICAL RETURNS, INFLATION ADJUSTED RETURNS, AND STANDARD DEVIATION OF ASSET CLASSES

ASSET CLASS	HISTORICAL RETURNS	INFLATION ADJUSTED RETURNS	STANDARD DEVIATION
Small Capitalization Stocks	13	10	30
Large Capitalization Stocks	11	8	20
Fixed Income Securities	6	3	8
Consumer Price Index (CPI)	3	N/A	4

Exhibit 18.9 illustrates the need to wisely choose investments for inclusion within a portfolio based on the risk and return of the asset class. You should notice that after inflation, real economic returns are extremely low for fixed income securities, and these returns are further reduced after considering the effects of taxation. This suggests that the only way to have real investment growth in an investment portfolio over a long term is to invest at least some portion of the port-

folio in common stocks. Common stocks also provide the best hedge against inflation and loss of purchasing power.

We would expect that when investors are young, their investment portfolio would be dominated by common stocks because they can generally afford the risk. As persons near retirement, their asset allocation generally shifts so that it becomes less risky while still maintaining some growth component to mitigate against the risk of inflation.

INFLATION

Inflation causes a loss of purchasing power. If a retiree has a fixed retirement income of $30,000 annually at age 65 and inflation is 4 percent, the retiree has a loss in purchasing power of 33 percent in 10 years, 54 percent in 20 years, and 69 percent in 30 years. While Social Security retirement benefits are inflation adjusted, many private pension plans are not. Thus, the financial planner will have to accommodate inflation into any projected retirement needs and advise clients to save accordingly. Exhibit 18.10 illustrates the decline in purchasing power that a 4% inflation rate can cause over a 50 year span.

EXHIBIT 18.10: IMPACT OF INFLATION

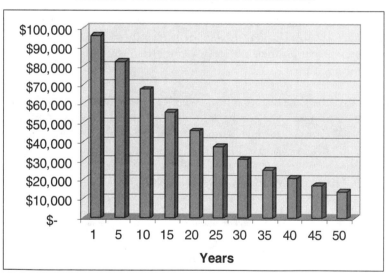

DEFINING THE RETIREMENT GOAL (NEEDS)

How much money and/or income does a person need to be financially independent? Most persons entering retirement intend to maintain the same lifestyle they had just prior to retirement. Clients generally do not radically reduce their expenses downward unless it is necessary. If we were to prepare a retirement budget, it would have similar amounts to the preretirement budget with a few adjustments. Some costs in retirement will decrease and others will increase. The reduced costs in retirement may include: (1) the elimination of costs associated with employment (certain clothing costs, parking, some meal costs); (2) the elimination of mortgage costs if the mortgage debt is scheduled to be repaid by the time of retirement; (3) the elimination of costs of children (tuition, clothes); (4) payroll costs—FICA; and (5) the elimination of savings since this is the time to use the accumulated savings. For some persons, retirement can bring increased spending on travel and other lifestyle changes. Some retirees are at risk for increases in health care costs. Exhibit 18.11 presents lists of potential decreasing and increasing costs when entering retirement.

EXHIBIT 18.11: BALANCING INCREASING AND DECREASING RETIREMENT INCOME NEEDS

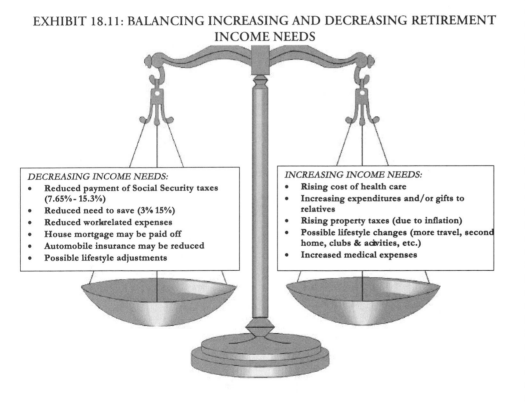

DECREASING INCOME NEEDS:
- Reduced payment of Social Security taxes (7.65% - 15.3%)
- Reduced need to save (3% 15%)
- Reduced work-related expenses
- House mortgage may be paid off
- Automobile insurance may be reduced
- Possible lifestyle adjustments

INCREASING INCOME NEEDS:
- Rising cost of health care
- Increasing expenditures and/or gifts to relatives
- Rising property taxes (due to inflation)
- Possible lifestyle changes (more travel, second home, clubs & activities, etc.)
- Increased medical expenses

PLANNING FOR RETIREMENT - PRE-TAX OR AFTER-TAX

It is possible to plan retirement needs either pre-tax or after-tax. Most financial planners who are not certified public accountants (CPAs) plan in pre-tax dollars believing that pre-tax is what their clients best understand. The pre-tax assumption is that clients are more likely to know their gross income than to know their net after-tax cash flow. Therefore, planners create retirement plans pre-tax and the clients simply pay whatever income taxes they are liable for out of their gross retirement income, similar to what clients do during preretirement years. Many CPAs think in terms of after-tax dollars and, therefore, plan for retirement after-tax. After-tax planning assumes that income taxes are paid before other retirement needs. Planning can be effective either way as long as the client understands the pre-tax or after-tax planning choice.

WAGE REPLACEMENT RATIO (WRR)

wage replacement ratio (WRR) - an estimate of the percent of income needed at retirement compared to earnings prior to retirement

The **wage replacement ratio (WRR)** is an estimate of the percent of annual income needed during retirement compared to income earned prior to retirement. The wage replacement ratio or percent is calculated by dividing the amount of money needed on an annual basis in retirement by the preretirement income. For example, if a client in the last year of work (prior to retirement) makes $100,000 and that client needs $80,000 in the first retirement year to maintain the same preretirement lifestyle, the wage replacement ratio (WRR) is 80 percent (80,000 ÷ 100,000).

CALCULATING THE WAGE REPLACEMENT RATIO

There are two alternative methods to calculate the wage replacement ratio—the top-down approach and the budgeting approach (or bottom up approach).

Top-Down Approach

The top-down approach method is commonly used with younger clients where expenditure patterns are likely to change dramatically over time. As clients approach retirement age, a more precise wage replacement ratio should be calculated using a budgeting approach. The top-down approach estimates the wage replacement ratio using common sense and percentages.

EXAMPLE

To illustrate, assume a 40-year-old client earns $50,000 a year, pays 7.65 percent of his gross pay in Social Security payroll taxes, and saves 10 percent of his gross income annually. If we assume that any work related savings resulting from retirement are expected to be completely offset by additional spending adjustments during retirement, and that the client wants to maintain his exact preretirement lifestyle, we would expect that the client would need a wage replacement ratio of 82.35% (100% - 7.65% - 10%).

$50,000	=	100.00%	of salary
(5,000)	=	(10.00%)	current savings
(3,825)	=	(7.65%)	payroll taxes
$41,175	=	82.35%	wage replacement ratio

Notice that the client is currently living on 82.35 percent of his gross pay. Therefore, the 82.35 percent is a reasonable estimate or proxy of what will be necessary as a percentage of current income to maintain the preretirement lifestyle.

Budgeting Approach

The second method used to calculate the wage replacement ratio is called the budgeting approach. It is used with older clients because as a person nears retirement, it is possible to examine the actual expenditure patterns of the person. In cooperation with the client, the planner can determine which costs in the current (preretirement) budget will change (plus or minus) in the retirement budget, and thus determine with greater precision than the top-down approach an estimate of actual retirement needs.

A and *B* each make $100,000 in preretirement income. *A* has arranged his financial affairs such that he will have no mortgage payment or car payment while in retirement. *B*, on the other hand, expects to continue to have both a mortgage payment and a car payment throughout the majority of his retirement years. Exhibit 18.12 illustrates that while *A* will need a 59.1 percent WRR, *B* will need a 77.1 percent WRR. The difference is due to *B's* $15,000 mortgage payment and $3,000 car payment.

EXAMPLE

EXHIBIT 18.12: BUDGETING APPROACH TO WAGE REPLACEMENT RATIO

	Client A & B Budget	Client A Retirement Budget	Client B Retirement Budget
Income (Current) Budget	$100,000	$100,000	$100,000
Expenses:	Current	Retirement	Retirement
Taxes	$27,650	$20,000*	$20,000*
Food	4,800	4,800	4,800
Utilities/Phone	2,400	2,400	2,400
Mortgage	15,000	0	15,000
Payroll Taxes	2,500	0	0
Health Insurance	1,000	1,000	1,000
Auto Insurance	1,000	1,000	1,000
Entertainment	5,000	5,000	5,000
Clothing	2,000	1,500	1,500
Auto Maintenance/Operation	1,000	750	750
Auto Payment	3,000	0	3,000
Church	4,800	4,800	4,800
Savings	12,000	0	0
Miscellaneous	17,850	17,850	17,850
Total Expenses	$100,000	$59,100	$77,100
*excludes payroll taxes			
Wage Replacement Percent Needed		59.1%	77.1%

659

Does a person really need the same wage replacement percentage throughout the entire retirement period? There are clear indications that consumption slows dramatically as people age. The 70-80 percent wage replacement ratio is probably most appropriate from the beginning of retirement regardless of age, to the late 70s. It appears that consumption for persons past the age of 80 declines primarily due to limited mobility. While this may be correct for society at large, there are certain individuals who will incur dramatic medical costs during the latter part of the retirement period. Therefore, while most who study retirement expenditures would suggest a consumption function similar to the one provided in Exhibit 18.13 below, such a model may not apply to a particular individual.

EXHIBIT 18.13: REAL CONSUMPTION BY AGE

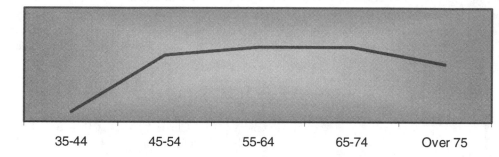

| 35-44 | 45-54 | 55-64 | 65-74 | Over 75 |

Exhibit 18.14 presents the adjustments from preretirement to retirement in terms of estimated percentages. Notice that many of the adjustments in Exhibit 18.14 will be specifically client dependent.

EXHIBIT 18.14: ADJUSTMENTS FROM PRERETIREMENT TO RETIREMENT

From Preretirement Income to Retirement Income Needs Adjustments to Expenditures	
Adjustments which decrease income needs:	Amount or Percent Saved
▲ No longer pay Social Security taxes	7.65% to 15.3%
▲ No longer need to save	3% to 15%
▲ No longer pay house mortgage	Maybe
▲ No longer pay work-related expenses	*
▲ Auto insurance may be reduced	*
▲ Possible lifestyle adjustments	*
Adjustments which may increase income needs:	
▲ Increasing cost of health care	*
▲ Lifestyle changes	*
▲ Increase in travel	*
▲ Second home	*
▲ Clubs and activities	*
▲ Expenditures on family/gifts/grandchildren	*
▲ Increased property taxes	*
* Amounts must be estimated for each individual	

Many expert financial planners conclude that most clients need approximately 70-80 percent of their preretirement current income to retire and maintain their preretirement lifestyle. While many clients would fall into this range, there are also those particularly frugal clients who may need as little as 40 percent of preretirement income, and others who need substantially more than the 80 percent wage replacement ratio (usually due to corporate perks which are discontinued in retirement).

THE SOURCES OF RETIREMENT INCOME

Retirees generally rely on three sources of income for retirement. These sources include: Social Security, private pension plans, and personal savings. All three sources compliment each other to provide adequate retirement income. Exhibit 18.15 shows the average amount of income for the average retiree from each of these three sources.

EXHIBIT 18.15: RETIREMENT INCOME SOURCES

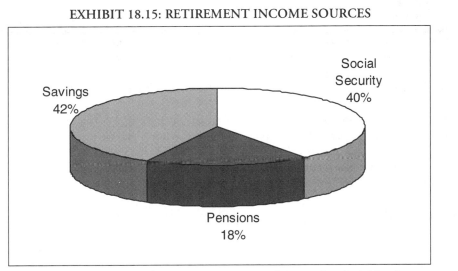

Source: Social Security Administration, Fast Facts and Figures about Social Security

SOCIAL SECURITY

Social Security provides the foundation of retirement earnings. Social Security covers almost all occupational groups (except 25 percent of state and local government employees) with retirement benefits adjusting for inflation. It is considered the safety net of a secure income, but for most income levels will not be a sufficient source of income replacement during retirement. Social Security retirement benefits provide a wage replacement ratio ranging from less than 15 percent (for high income earners) to approximately 67 percent (for low income earners who have a same age, non-working spouse). As demonstrated in Exhibit 18.16, Social Security is an adequate wage replacement for lower waged workers to maintain their lifestyle, but is clearly inadequate to provide sufficient replacement income for middle-to-upper-wage earners. (Social Security and Social Security benefits are covered in detail in Chapter 11).

EXHIBIT 18.16: SOCIAL SECURITY AS A WAGE REPLACEMENT PERCENTAGE (FOR INDIVIDUALS OF VARIOUS EARNINGS)

Current Earnings	Wage Replacement Ratio Provided by Social Security*	With Same Age, Non-Working Spouse
$13,100	53%	70%
$20,000	45%	67%
$25,000	42%	63%
$28,924	40%	60%
$35,000	38%	57%
$46,663	32%	48%
$72,100	24%	36%
$100,000	14%	21%
$200,000	7%	10%

Estimated based on single person at normal retirement age 2001. Average wages were $30,685 in 2001. A same age, non-working spouse would receive 50 percent of the benefits of the covered worker.

PRIVATE PENSION AND COMPANY SPONSORED RETIREMENT PLANS

Private pension plans are the second source of retirement income. Private pension plans provided by employers are covered in Chapter 19. As you will see, private pension plans have dramatically changed over the last few years from employer sponsored and funded plans to employee self-reliance plans, putting more and more emphasis on personal savings as the primary source of retirement income for middle-to-upper-wage workers.

PERSONAL SAVINGS

Personal savings is the third source of retirement income and is the one that is most influenced by the individual. The more personal savings put aside for retirement, the larger the accumulation at retirement and the larger the retirement income for the individual.

Exhibit 18.17 shows the significant decrease in personal savings since World War II. As shown, the savings rate has fallen from 7.6 percent of disposable income in 1959 to -0.1 percent in 2000.

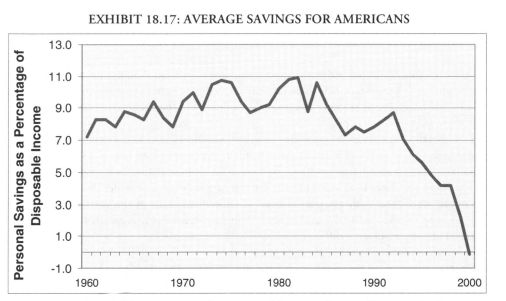

Source: Survey of Current Business, Department of Commerce, Bureau of Economic Analysis

Whenever a retiree has income from invested assets, it can mean a substantially higher overall retirement income. The median income of those retirees with asset income is more than twice as large as the income of retirees with no asset income. As the two pie charts in Exhibit 18.18 illustrate, retirees without asset income are concentrated in the lowest income categories.

EXHIBIT 18.18: RETIREES WITH INCOME FROM PERSONAL ASSETS

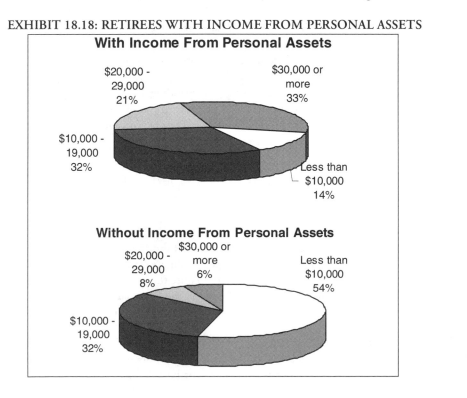

QUALITATIVE FACTORS IN RETIREMENT – ADVISING CLIENTS

Qualitative factors associated with retirement are no less important than the financial or quantitative factors. Qualitative factors include involuntary versus voluntary retirement; emotional and psychological factors, such as loss of esteem and boredom; and the decision to relocate.

The best overall advice financial planners can give their clients is to know themselves and their support system; have a well-planned qualitative side to retirement; and have a system in place to maintain their ego and self-esteem. Many persons in our culture define themselves by what they do. The mere act of going to work may be a ritual or a habit that provides that person with a sense of self worth and with a reason to live. A trusted colleague at the workplace may be a source of support and personal gratification. Voluntary retirement, even when well planned, means change—and change is difficult.

Involuntary retirement, if perceived as undesirable, can be as devastating an impact on an individual as the death of a loved one or a bitter divorce. The client may follow the same psychological pattern of grief--shock, anger, denial, and acceptance. Financial planning professionals need to recognize the emotional state of clients and realize that when someone is emotionally troubled, major decisions, financial or otherwise, are sometimes best delayed. Rather than abruptly making important financial decisions, it may be better to do the minimum financial maneuvering during a grieving period. Such grieving may last for a period of a year or longer. Trying to optimize the financial situation when the client is emotionally unable to determine his or her goals or priorities is probably counterproductive and may add stress to the situation.

A client's decision to change physical locations after retirement (that is, move to another state) should be carefully considered over a long period of planning. Some retirees do not realize that when they move, they have a completely new environment to adjust to, as well as a substantial loss of their former support system of friends and family. Someone considering moving should conduct a trial transition over a number of years, spending longer and longer periods at the desired location. This gradual adjustment will help determine if what the retiree believes will actually enhance retirement will, in fact, be true. Persons considering retiring abroad will encounter even more change, thereby necessitating even more detailed planning.

SUMMARY OF FACTORS AFFECTING RETIREMENT PLANNING

Financial planners may encounter clients who subjectively "feel" they are financially secure because they have a good job and/or a good net worth. If the good job is lost through premature death, disability, lay offs, job termination, unexpected illness, or if the net worth decreases dramatically, the financial security is suddenly lost. Thus, the actual determination of financial security is objective rather than subjective. Therefore, the financial planner is the intermediary between the client's subjective feelings and the overall objective of financial security.

Other factors that complicate the retirement planning process include at least two societal issues. Our society has become more mobile with the traditional family unit deteriorating. Having lost the close connection to family, older persons may not be able to depend on family to provide retirement assistance. Thus, there is a greater need for financial independence for each individual. Additionally, because our society seems to place more value on youth than on age and wisdom in the workplace, retirees have less chance of being hired for part-time employment with which to supplement retirement income.

Many people begin planning for retirement too late in life and save too little to effectively meet retirement capital accumulation needs. Some people do not give retirement funding a thought until they are in their 40s. Even when people do save, many of them make poor investment choices and, therefore, have poor investment returns.

Inflation reduces purchasing power. To recipients of fixed incomes, inflation is like a progressive tax causing declining purchasing power. Exhibit 18.19 lists the factors that frustrate effective retirement planning and the negative impact associated with each factor.

EXHIBIT 18.19: FACTORS THAT NEGATIVELY EFFECT RETIREMENT PLANNING AND THEIR IMPACT ON THE PLANNING PROCESS

FACTORS	IMPACT
Reduced WLE	Insufficient savings period
Increased RLE	Increase capital needs
Reduced family reliance	Less alternatives in retirement
Reduced ability to work	Less alternatives in retirement
Planned too late	Less compounding periods
Low savings rate	Unable to meet capital requirements
Inflation	Reduces purchasing power
Poor earnings rate and asset allocation	Unable to meet capital requirements

Long-term financial security does not automatically happen. It requires careful planning, a clear understanding of the quantification of the goal, and identification and management of the risks that are present. Retirement planning requires the collection and projection of data and must be conducted meticulously and conservatively.

RISKS TO FINANCIAL INDEPENDENCE

There are many risks to achieving financial independence. Selected risks are identified in Exhibit 18.20. It is a wise idea to start saving early, save a sufficient amount, invest wisely, and not underestimate retirement needs or the impact of inflation. The risks identified in Part B of Exhibit 18.20 are more thoroughly discussed in the chapters on risk management and insurance.

665

EXHIBIT 18.20: SUMMARY OF FACTORS AFFECTING RETIREMENT PLANNING

FACTOR	RISK	MITIGATOR
PART A: Risks Discussed in this Chapter		
Work Life Expectancy (WLE)	Shortened due to untimely death, disability, health, unemployment	Life insurance, disability insurance, health insurance, education, training, experience
Retirement Life Expectancy (RLE)	Lengthened	Adequate capital accumulation
Savings rate, amount, and timing	Too low and too late	Save enough; start early
Inflation	Greater than expected	Conservatively estimate inflation and needs
Retirement needs	Underestimated	Use wage replacement estimators
Investment returns	Inadequate to create necessary retirement capital	Knowledge of and investments in broad portfolio of diversified investments and proper asset allocation
Sources of retirement income	Overestimation of Social Security benefits, private pension plans, or personal income (or adverse changes in taxation of such income)	Conservatively estimate and plan for such income Monitor income projections and tax policy
PART B: Risks Discussed in Insurance Chapters		
Qualitative factors including changes in lifestyle, employment, and major assets	Unexpected cost increases due to changes in personal situation; losses due to perils	Plan conservatively to provide for the unexpected; property and liability insurance

666

CAPITAL NEEDS ANALYSIS

Capital needs analysis is the process of calculating the amount of investment capital needed at retirement to maintain the preretirement lifestyle and mitigate the impact of inflation during the retirement years. There are three methods for analyzing capital needs: the basic annuity method and the more advanced methods using the capital preservation model and the purchasing power preservation model.

BASIC PLANNING – ANNUITY METHOD

The following steps are used to determine the capital necessary at the beginning of retirement to fund the retirement period:

Step 1 - Calculate WRR. Determine the wage replacement ratio (WRR) today using one of the two methods identified earlier (top-down or budgeting).
Step 2 – Determine gross dollar needs. Determine the wage replacement amount in today's dollars from Step 1.
Step 3 – Determine net dollar needs. Reduce Step 2 by any expected Social Security benefits in today's dollars or other benefits that are indexed to inflation.
Step 4 – Calculate preretirement dollar needs inflated. Inflate Step 3 to the retirement age at the CPI rate to determine the first annual retirement payment.
Step 5 – Calculate capital needed at retirement age. Calculate the present value at retirement of an annuity due for an annual payment equal to Step 4 over the full retirement life expectancy (estimate life expectancy conservatively at 90-93) and use the inflation-adjusted earnings rate.

To determine the amount to save during the work life expectancy, discount the capital needed at retirement using the savings rate, being mindful as to whether the client is expected to save annually or more frequently, and whether the client is expected to save under an annuity due or an ordinary annuity scheme.

Mary Jones, age 41, currently makes $80,000. Her wage replacement ratio is determined to be 80 percent. She expects that inflation will average 3 percent for her entire life expectancy. She expects to earn 10 percent on her investments and retire at age 62, living possibly to age 90. She has sent for and received her Social Security benefit statement, which indicated that her Social Security retirement benefit in today's dollars adjusted for early retirement is $12,000 per year.

EXAMPLE

1.   Calculate Mary's capital needed at retirement at age 62.
2.   Calculate the amount she must save monthly, at month end, assuming she has no current savings to accumulate the capital needed for retirement at age 62.
3.   Calculate the amount she must save monthly, at month end, assuming that she has $50,000 in current retirement savings.
4.   Calculate her capital needed at retirement at age 62.

Step 1	80% WRR			
Step 2	($80,000 x 0.80)	=	$64,000	Total needs in today's dollars
Step 3			- 12,000	Less Social Security in today's dollars
			$52,000	Annual amount needed in today's dollars
Step 4	n	=	21 (62 - 41)	
	i	=	3 (inflation)	
	PV	=	$52,000 (Step 3)	
	PMT	=	0	
	FV	=	$96,735.32 (Step 4)	First year needs for retirement
Step 5	n	=	28 (90 − 62)	
	i	=	6.7961 [(1 + earnings rate/1 + inflation rate) − 1] x 100	
			[(1.10 ÷ 1.03) − 1] x 100	
	FV	=	0	
	PMT_{AD}	=	$96,735.32 (from Step 4) this is also an annuity due	
	$PV_{AD@62}$	=	$1,278,954.46 (Step 5 - amount needed at age 62)	

5. Calculate the amount she must save monthly, at month end, assuming she has no current savings to accumulate the capital needed for retirement at age 62.

$FV_{@62}$	=	$1,278,954.46 (from Step 5)
n	=	252 (21 years x 12 months)
i	=	0.83333 (10% ÷ 12)
PV	=	0
PMT_{OA}	=	$1,502.09 (monthly savings necessary)

6. Calculate the amount she must save monthly, at month end, assuming she has $50,000 in current retirement savings.

$FV_{@62}$	=	$1,278,954.46
n	=	252
i	=	0.83333
PV	=	$50,000
PMT_{OA}	=	$1,026.70 (monthly savings necessary)

ACCURATE ASSUMPTIONS ARE ESSENTIAL

Assumptions are made for the wage replacement ratio, the work life expectancy, the retirement life expectancy, inflation, earnings, and Social Security or other benefits. If these assumptions are inaccurate, any projection using those assumptions will likely be flawed. The wage replacement ratio should be carefully calculated, especially for a client near retirement. Estimating life expectancy usually begins with the IRS tables and is conservatively estimated at 90-93, due to the risk of outliving retirement money. Where family history indicates a particularly long life expectancy, that age could be increased. The estimate of the work life expectancy is critical, as one less year of work means one less year of saving and one more year of retirement funding. Conversely, working one additional year may make an otherwise unworkable retirement plan work quite nicely due to the additional year of savings, earnings accumulation, and one less year of consumption.

The assumptions regarding inflation and earnings rates are obviously essential ingredients in capital needs analysis. Historical data is available for inflation; however, inflation is hard to predict. Perhaps the best estimate is the inflation rate for the most recent few years. Earnings rates are dependent on the client's asset allocation and the markets, but can be estimated for a well-diversified portfolio over a long period. It is wise to conservatively estimate inflation (up a little) and conservatively estimate earnings (down a little). Such estimation provides a little conservatism in case one or more of the assumptions are not realized. Social Security benefits and pension benefits that are inflation protected should be carefully determined and documented. The retirement plan and capital needs analysis can be adjusted on an annual basis as information becomes more certain.

As one might expect, small changes in earnings, life expectancy, and needs may have a dramatic impact on retirement plan. The uncertainty of these assumptions can be accommodated in some of the latest retirement planning software packages that incorporate Monte Carlo analysis (MCA). MCA uses a random number generator for inputs into a software package that will provide an output with specific probabilities of outcomes. MCA provides insight into the most likely outcome, but with other possible outcomes. Provided with this analysis, the financial planner also gets a best-case scenario and a worst-case scenario with which to make decisions.

ADVANCED PLANNING – CAPITAL PRESERVATION MODEL (CP)

The basic capital needs analysis is a **pure annuity concept** generally prepared on a pre-tax basis. The annuity concept means that if all of the assumptions happen exactly as expected, the person will die exactly at the assumed life expectancy with a retirement account balance of zero. There is a substantial risk that many clients could outlive their assets using an annuity approach. Therefore, they will actually need more money at retirement. Two models used to mitigate the risk of outliving money are the capital preservation model and the purchasing power preservation model. The **capital preservation model** assumes that at life expectancy, as estimated in the annuity model, the client has exactly the same account balance as he did at retirement. The purchasing power preservation model assumes that the client will have a capital balance of equal purchasing power at life expectancy as he did at retirement. In spite of any conservatism that we may have built into the annuity model with our assumptions, it is always possible that one or more of our assumptions will be unrealized. To mitigate against the risk of the assumptions being overly optimistic, we can make use of a capital preservation model or a purchasing power preservation model rather than a simple annuity model to determine capital needs. These two additional models help to overcome the risks of the pure annuity model (primarily the risk of running out of money).

The capital preservation model maintains the original capital balance needed at retirement for the entire retirement life expectancy. Recall that the amount needed for Mary Jones at age 62 calculated from our previous example was $1,278,954.46. If we put that into Step 5 as a future value leaving the payment as it was, we can determine the amount of total capital necessary to achieve the capital preservation model.

pure annuity concept - the basic capital needs analysis approach that is generally prepared on a pre-tax basis

capital preservation model (CP) - a capital needs analysis method that assumes that at life expectancy, the client has exactly the same account balance as he did at retirement

n = 28

i = 6.7961

$FV_{@90}$ = $1,278,954.46 (amount at life expectancy)

PMT_{AD} = $96,735.32

$PV_{AD@62}$ = $1,481,863.90 (amount needed for capital preservation model)

Thus, the capital preservation model will require an additional $202,909.44 at retirement than the pure annuity model, but will reduce the risk of running out of money. Such an increase in capital will also require that savings be increased in the Mary Jones example Parts B and C.

EXHIBIT 18.21: COMPARISON OF THE CAPITAL PRESERVATION MODEL WITH THE ANNUITY METHOD (MARY JONES)

	CAPITAL PRESERVATION MODEL		ANNUITY MODEL	
	No Savings	Savings	No Savings	Savings
	B	C	B	C
$FV_{@62}$	$1,481,863.90	$1,481,863.90	$1,278,954.46	$1,278,954.46
n	252	252	252	252
i	0.83333	0.83333	0.8333	0.8333
PV	0	$50,000	0	$50,000
PMT_{OA}	$1,740.40	$1,265.01	$1,502.09	$1,026.70

Even though the capital preservation model would increase the savings need of Mary Jones by about $200 per month, it would mitigate against many of the risks in the traditional capital needs annuity approach.

ADVANCED PLANNING – PURCHASING POWER PRESERVATION MODEL (PPP)

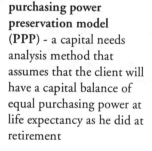

purchasing power preservation model (PPP) - a capital needs analysis method that assumes that the client will have a capital balance of equal purchasing power at life expectancy as he did at retirement

An even more conservative approach to capital needs analysis is the **purchasing power preservation model**. This model essentially maintains the purchasing power of the original capital balance at retirement.

The capital balance is inflated at the inflation rate to life expectancy, and then the entire calculation made in the original capital preservation model is repeated.

Step 1:

n = 28

i = 3

PV = $1,278,954.46 (FV from capital preservation model)

PMT = $0

FV = $2,926,155.31

Step 2:

n = 28

i = 6.7961

FV = $2,926,155.31

PMT_{AD} = $96,735.32

$PV_{AD@62}$ = $1,743,196.55 (capital needed for PPP model)

The additional accumulation at retirement using a purchasing power model is $464,242.09 greater than the pure annuity approach.

The answers to B and C in the example would change.

EXHIBIT 18.22: COMPARISON OF THE PURCHASING POWER MODEL WITH THE ANNUITY METHOD (MARY JONES)

	PURCHASING POWER MODEL		ANNUITY MODEL	
	No Savings	Savings	No Savings	Savings
	B	C	B	C
$FV_{@62}$	$1,743,196.55	$1,743,196.55	$1,278,954.46	$1,278,954.46
n	252	252	252	252
I	0.83333	0.83333	0.8333	0.8333
PV	0	$50,000	0	50,000
PMT_{OA}	$2,047.33	$1,571.94	$1,502.09	$1,026.70

EXHIBIT 18.23: CAPITAL NEEDS ANALYSIS SUMMARY FOR MARY JONES

	ANNUITY MODEL	CAPITAL PRESERVATION MODEL	PURCHASING POWER PRESERVATION MODEL
Capital needed at retirement (A)	$1,278,954.46	$1,481,863.90	$1,743,196.55
Monthly savings with no initial balance (B)	$1,502.09	$1,740.40	$2,047.33
Monthly savings with $50,000 initial balance (C)	$1,026.70	$1,265.01	$1,571.94

There are other methods of mitigating risk in projections, including sensitivity analysis, that are beyond the scope of this text, most of which would be covered in a full semester course on retirement planning.

What method do you use when determining retirement needs – capital needs, wage replacement, or another method?

I generally use the wage replacement method with clients. This approach helps to estimate the level of income needed by a retiree to sustain a standard of living they previously enjoyed. The percentage I use is roughly 70 to 80 percent of a person's final salary. The target amount set should be tempered with common sense and realistic expectations. I want to motivate the client to action, not scare a client into action.

The support for a replacement ratio of less than 100 percent of final salary rests upon the elimination of employment related taxes and expected change in spending patterns that reduce the retiree's need for income. Some of the expenditures that will probably decrease during retirement include: Social Security taxes, work related expenses, home ownership expenses, the expense of supporting children, and saving for retirement.

While some spending patterns will be reduced or eliminated, other living expenses will probably increase. These include: medical expenses, travel expense, and long term care.

It should be pointed out that as people get older, some are forced to give up their automobiles and cut back on travel and recreation because of limited mobility. Thus, there may be a downward reduction in annual income needed for retirement as one passes the age of 75 and older.

In conclusion, retirement planning is usually the most crucial aspect of a comprehensive financial plan. While each client has a unique set of individual needs, it is up to the financial services professional to understand a client's attitudes toward retirement and help the client to achieve their retirement goals.property (other than like-kind property) that qualifies as a tax gain when received in a property exchange

Do you help your client determine their appropriate age for retirement, if so how?

Probably the most important question that had to be addressed regarding retirement is at what age can the client retire. If my client wants to retire at 55, it is my responsibility to help determine whether that is a financially viable goal. I advise clients of any negative aspects of the chosen retirement age. On occasion I may even provide information that causes the client to postpone retirement. If the client will not have medical coverage at affordable rates to bridge the gap until eligibility for Medicare, I may recommend deferral of retirement. Other factors that might have to be considered in determining the appropriate age for retirement include:

▲ Have financial goals been met and can the client maintain his standard of living throughout retirement
▲ Is the client willing to accept a lower standard of living in order to leave work now
▲ Are health problems requiring the client to retire early
▲ Is the company forcing the client into early retirement because of downsizing
▲ Has the client reached the age where his pension will not be increased because of previously years worked
▲ Are incentives being offered for early retirement that the client finds hard to pass up
▲ Will full benefits from Social Security begin at age 65 or higher age
▲ Because of a longer retirement period, the client will have an increased exposure to inflation.

Although it is ultimately the client's decision to retire, explaining these factors may help to influence his decision as to the appropriate age for retirement.

DISCUSSION QUESTIONS

1. What is the U.S. savings rate?
2. List the steps necessary to calculate capital needs analysis.
3. What is the difference between capital needs analysis prepared on an annuity basis and capital needs analysis prepared using a capital preservation model? A purchasing power presentation model?
4. What are the three sources of retirement income?
5. What are the two methods for determining the wage replacement ratio?
6. Which method for determining the wage replacement ratio is appropriate for a client who is 50 years old? Why?
7. How is financial security defined?
8. List the financial factors that affect retirement planning.
9. Should retirement planning (capital needs analysis) be prepared on a pre-income tax basis or a post-income tax basis? Why?
10. What percent of retirement income is provided by Social Security for the average retiree?
11. Does Social Security favor lower or higher wage individuals in terms of retirement benefits and wage replacement? How and why?
12. What is the central mission for individuals regarding personal financial planning?
13. When is financial security realized?
14. What is the WLE?
15. What is the RWLE?
16. How has life expectancy increased from 1900 to 1997?
17. How and why does the timing of savings affect the ultimate amount of accumulation?
18. How does inflation affect retirement planning?
19. What adjustments are normally made to the preretirement budget to arrive at the retirement budget?
20. What is the wage replacement ratio?
21. Does the wage replacement ratio remain constant over the retirement life expectancy?
22. What wage replacement ratio does Social Security provide for a worker with $20,000 income and a same age spouse?
23. What is capital needs analysis?
24. What advanced methods are used to perform capital needs analysis?

EXERCISES

1. Donna, age 45, is self-employed and makes $70,000 today. She is fairly settled in her lifestyle. She currently saves 15 percent of her gross income. Her mortgage payment (P&I) is fixed at $1,166.67 per month. She has scheduled her mortgage payments to cease at retirement. What do you expect Donna's wage replacement ratio to be based on the above information?
2. Kim, age 30, begins saving $2,500 per year at year-end, continues for 8 years, then she quits saving. Joy, age 40, begins saving $2,500 per year at year-end and saves continuously until age 65. Assume that both Kim and Joy earn 12 percent compounded annually. Calculate the total amount of savings and the accumulated balance for Kim and Joy, respectively, at year-end. Explain the difference.

Use the following information for Exercises 3 - 10:

Mike, age 48, currently has $60,000 saved for retirement. He is currently saving $5,000 of his annual income of $50,000 on a monthly basis. His employer matches his savings contributions with $1,500 annually, paid on a monthly basis. Mike projects that inflation will be 3.5 percent and he can earn 9.5 percent before and during retirement. Mike needs a wage replacement ratio of 75 percent of his preretirement income. He plans to retire at age 62 with Social Security benefits of $10,000 in today's dollars. His life expectancy is to age 90.

3. How much will Mike's salary be at age 62 if he receives raises equal to inflation?
4. How much are the Social Security benefits expected to be at age 62?
5. What will be Mike's retirement needs in the 1st year of retirement, excluding Social Security?
6. How much capital will Mike need at age 62 to fund his retirement?
7. How much will Mike have at 62, assuming he continues his current savings and investment program?
8. How much additional monthly savings would be required for Mike to retire at age 62?
9. After reflection, Mike wants to know at what age he can retire, assuming he continues to follow his current savings plan. Make a schedule for years 62, 64, and 66 so Mike can make some choices.
10. You remind Mike that if he waits to age 66 to retire, he will receive $14,344 in Social Security benefits in today's dollars rather than the reduced benefit of $10,000 he was to receive at age 62. Would this additional cash flow suggest that he could retire at age 66? Perhaps earlier?
11. Mary Blue, age 65, is a pensioner who receives a fixed pension of $17,500 for life from her private pension plan where she retired. Mary also receives $12,000 currently from Social Security. Mary is concerned about how inflation will affect her rent, food, and other expenses. She estimates that inflation will be 3 percent per year for the next 10 years. What loss of purchasing power will she have in today's dollars in 10 years?
12. George Michael, a financial planner, has determined that Dennis Zabloski, his client, needs $2,000,000 at age 66 to retire using an annuity method based on a retirement income of $150,337.75 per year for 24 years to age 90. If the earnings rate was 10 percent and the inflation rate was 3 percent, what additional amount would be needed at age 66 to provide a capital presentation model solution?
13. Referring to Exercise 12, how much would Dennis need at age 66 to fund a purchasing power presentation model?

PROBLEMS

Bill, age 45, wants to retire at age 60. He currently makes $60,000 per year. He has an objective to replace 80 percent of his preretirement income. He wants the retirement income to be inflation adjusted. Bill has an investment portfolio valued at $150,000, which is currently earning 10 percent average annual returns. Bill expects inflation to average 3 percent and based on his family health he predicts he will live to age 90. Bill is currently saving 7 percent of his gross income at each year-end and expects to continue this level savings amount. Bill wants to ignore any Social Security benefits for purposes of planning.

1. What will Bill's annual needs be at age 60?
2. Will the need be for an ordinary annuity or an annuity due?
3. What total capital will Bill need at age 60?
4. How much will Bill have at age 60?
5. Will Bill have enough?
6. What is the earliest age that Bill could retire utilizing the current savings and investment plan?
7. How much would Bill need to increase his savings on an annual basis to meet his goal of retiring at age 60?
8. Even assuming that Bill increases his savings to an appropriate amount, what are the risks that may affect the success of the plan?
9. How would you modify the capital needs analysis to reduce the risks identified above?

CHAPTER 19

Basic Retirement Plans

LEARNING OBJECTIVES:

After learning the material in this chapter, you will be able to:

1. Describe a qualified retirement plan.

2. Identify and articulate the characteristics of qualified retirement plans.

3. Describe some disadvantages of qualified retirement plans.

4. Define vesting and list two accepted vesting schedules.

5. Identify the reasons for the creation of qualified retirement plans.

6. Calculate and determine the benefits of tax deferral in a qualified retirement plan.

7. Identify the various types of qualified retirement plans.

8. Distinguish between pension and profit-sharing plans.

9. Distinguish between defined-benefit plans and defined-contribution plans.

10. Distinguish between noncontributory and contributory plans.

11. Describe the operations and benefits of a 401(k) plan.

12. Distinguish between Keogh and corporate plans.

13. Identify other tax-advantaged, but nonqualified, retirement plans.

14. Describe IRAs, SEPs, SIMPLEs, and 403(b) plans.

15. Describe distributions from qualified retirement plans and other tax-advantaged retirement plans.

16. Describe and identify nonqualified plans.

17. Clarify why nonqualified plans are useful to employers.

RETIREMENT PLANS

In the previous retirement chapter, we discussed the three general sources of funding used to provide retirement income--Social Security, private retirement plans, and personal savings. It was determined that the retirement benefits from Social Security alone provided a poor wage replacement ratio during retirement except for those beneficiaries who are the lowest-waged workers. This chapter provides an introduction to private retirement plans, including qualified retirement plans, other tax-advantaged retirement plans, and nonqualified plans. Exhibit 19.1 illustrates the various types of retirement plans.

EXHIBIT 19.1: RETIREMENT PLANS

QUALIFIED PLANS		OTHER TAX ADVANTAGED PLANS	NON-QUALIFIED PLANS
Pension Plans	Profit-Sharing Plans		
Defined Benefit Plans	Profit-Sharing Plans	SEPs	Deferred Compensation Plans
Cash Balance Plans	Stock Bonus Plans	IRAs (including Roth)	Non-Qualified Stock Option Plans
Money Purchase Pension Plans	ESOPs	403(b) Plans	Incentive Stock Option Plans
Target Benefit Plans	401(k) Plans	SIMPLE (IRA)	Phantom Stock Plans
(Money Purchase Pension Plans)	Thrift Plans		Split $ Insurance
	Simple (401k)		457 Plans
	Age-Based, Profit-Sharing Plans		
	New Comparability Plans		

RETIREMENT PLAN REFORM

TRA 2001was signed by President George W. Bush in June of 2001 providing a $1.35 trillion tax cut. TRA 2001 includes significant changes to the area of qualified plans, other tax advantaged plans, and retirement planning in general. While most changes are effective for years beginning after December 31, 2001, many changes are phased in over the next several years. This chapter presents the applicable provisions prior to the TRA 2001 as well as after.

QUALIFIED RETIREMENT PLANS

Qualified retirement plans are either employer or self-employed sponsored plans. The word "qualified" means that the plan meets Internal Revenue Service, Department of Labor, and Employee Retirement Income Security Act requirements. To encourage retirement savings, Congress has created or approved various savings schemes that are somewhat tax advantaged. As a result of being qualified, there are tax advantages that accrue to the employer who sponsors the plan and to the employees who participate in the plan.

Exhibit 19.2 summarizes the advantages and disadvantages of qualified plans.

EXHIBIT 19.2: ADVANTAGES AND DISADVANTAGES OF QUALIFIED RETIREMENT PLANS

Advantages/Rules	Disadvantages	Limits (2001 and 2002)
	Costs	**Covered Compensation**
1. Employer contributions are deductible	2001 & 2002 Limits →	$170,000 (2001)
2. Employer contributions are not subject to payroll taxes	Participation	$200,000 (2002)
3. Employee contributions are deductible (except Thrift)	Vesting	**Defined Benefit**
4. Employee contributions are subject to payroll taxes	Top Heaviness	$140,000 (2001)
(Exempt FSA)	Minimum Contribution	$160,000 (2002)
5. Earnings Taxed Deferred	Reporting	**Defined Contribution**
6. 10-Year Averaging*	Disclosure	25% - $35,000 Employee (2001)
7. ERISA Protection (except QDRO)	Non Discrimination	100% - $40,000 Employee (2002)
8. Net Unrealized Appreciation	Highly Compensated	**Salary Deferral***
	Fairness Coverage	$10,500 (2001)
*5-year averaging was repealed for years after 1999	Testing	$11,000 (2002)
	Key Employees	* 401(k), 403(b), 457, SARSEP

Testing

50/40 Coverage Test – DB Plans
Ratio % Test
Average Benefit % Test
401(k) ACP
401(k) ADP

CHARACTERISTICS OF QUALIFIED RETIREMENT PLANS

Employer Contributions are Not Subject to Federal Income Tax

Unlike most business transactions that result in an income tax deduction for one party and taxable income for another party, contributions made to qualified retirement plans result in a mismatch of income and deduction. Employer contributions to a qualified plan are deductible for income tax purposes for the year in which they were made, but are not included in current employee taxable income. This favorable tax treatment is a major advantage for both employers and employees. Employers receive a current deduction while employees receive deferral of income. Because of this favorable tax treatment, however, qualified retirement plans have numerous testing requirements that must be satisfied to ensure that the majority of employees (specifically, non-highly compensated employees) are benefiting from the plan.

Employer Contributions are Not Subject to Payroll Tax

Another major advantage of contributions to qualified retirement plans is that employer contributions are not subject to payroll tax. This means that compensation in the form of qualified retirement plan contributions will avoid the 7.65 percent expense for Federal Insurance Contributions Act (FICA). Such avoidance benefits both the employer and the employee since both parties are required to pay this tax. If the same amount of money that is contributed to a qualified retirement plan is paid as employment compensation, then both the employer and the employee would be required to pay FICA taxes.

Employee Contributions are Not Subject to Federal Income Tax

Similar to employer contributions, employee contributions to qualified retirement plans are generally not includible in the taxable income of the employee. Therefore, employees can save portions of their income on a pre-tax basis. Thus, income contributed to a qualified retirement plan will avoid both federal and state income tax. An example of a qualified retirement plan that allows these pre-tax employee contributions is the 401(k) plan. There are certain older qualified retirement plans that provide for employee after-tax contributions, such as Thrift plans and certain defined-benefit plans. Obviously, these post-tax contributions are not as advantageous to the employee as the pre-tax type of contributions to the 401(k) and other plans.

Employee Contributions are Subject to Payroll Tax

Unlike the payroll tax treatment of employer contributions, employee contributions to qualified retirement plans are generally subject to payroll tax. Therefore, contributions made by employees will be subject to FICA taxes, for both the employer and the employee. This is why an employee's W-2 form may have different income amounts for federal tax and Social Security purposes. One exception to this rule is flexible spending accounts (FSAs). Employees can make contributions to FSAs on a pre-tax basis and without being subject to FICA.

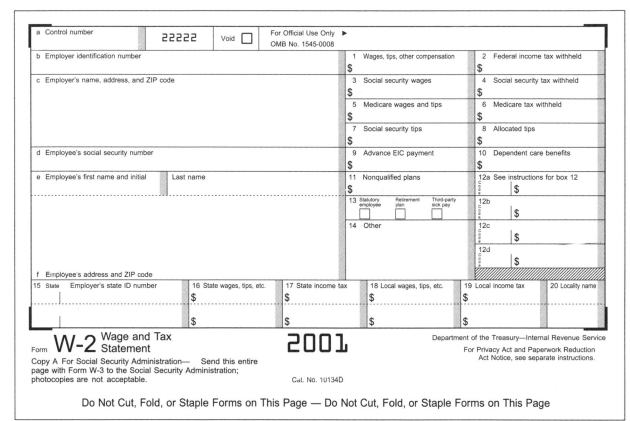

Form W-2 Wage and Tax Statement 2001 — Department of the Treasury—Internal Revenue Service. Copy A For Social Security Administration—Send this entire page with Form W-3 to the Social Security Administration; photocopies are not acceptable. Cat. No. 10134D. For Privacy Act and Paperwork Reduction Act Notice, see separate instructions. Do Not Cut, Fold, or Staple Forms on This Page — Do Not Cut, Fold, or Staple Forms on This Page

Tax-Deferred Growth

Assets that are contributed to a qualified retirement plan are held in a trust for the benefit of the employees/participants or their beneficiaries. Qualified retirement plan trusts are tax-exempt entities; therefore, the earnings accruing from contributions from both employers and employees grow income tax deferred until distributed. The tax-deferred growth of both contributions and earnings is a major benefit that qualified retirement plans provide.

Special Income Tax Averaging

There is a provision for special ten-year-forward income tax averaging on lump-sum distributions made from qualified retirement plans. This provision may reduce the income tax liability for taxpayers taking a full and complete distribution from a qualified retirement plan. Only those taxpayers who were born prior to January 1, 1936, however, are eligible for this provision.

In addition to receiving special income tax averaging, taxpayers born prior to January 1, 1936, may also be eligible to receive capital gain treatment on a portion of their lump-sum distribution.

The portion of a distribution that may receive capital gain treatment is attributable to the percentage of participation in the qualified plan prior to 1974.

Net Unrealized Appreciation

In general, distributions from qualified retirement plans are made in the form of cash and are taxable as ordinary income. There is an exception, however, for lump-sum distributions of employer securities (generally stock) that have appreciated while being held in a qualified retirement plan. When such securities are distributed (typically in the form of a lump-sum distribution) from a qualified retirement plan, the appreciation above the cost basis, called net unrealized appreciation (NUA), is not subject to income tax upon distribution. In addition, the net unrealized appreciation will be taxed as a capital gain (not as ordinary income), when the securities are sold. With the large disparity between ordinary income tax rates (39.6% prior to July 1, 2001, reduced to 35% over the next five years) and capital gains tax rates (20%), this exception provides significant benefits to taxpayers who receive qualifying distributions of employer securities. It should be noted that this special treatment is not available for distributions from Individual Retirement Accounts (IRAs). Therefore, a rollover of otherwise qualifying securities from a qualified retirement plan to an IRA will eliminate this potential benefit.

ERISA Protection

Assets held in a qualified retirement plan are protected from creditors by the Employee Retirement Income Security Act (ERISA). ERISA provides for non-alienation of benefits, which means that the benefits of the qualified retirement plan are to be used only by the participant or by the participant's family members. Therefore, even those unfortunate individuals who are forced into bankruptcy have protection for their assets held in qualified retirement plans. IRAs do not have this same federal level of protection, and planners must evaluate both federal and state law for applicability.

Timing of Income Tax Deduction

Under the U.S. federal income tax system, when an individual or entity (payer) receives an income tax deduction for a payment, generally the recipient (payee) must simultaneously recognize the receipt as taxable income. Such is not the case with qualified retirement and other tax-advantaged retirement plans. Rather, the employer receives a current income tax deduction and the employee is allowed to defer the income for current income tax purposes until distribution, usually at age 59½ or older.

Qualified retirement plans were congressionally created to provide incentives to employers to sponsor and promote retirement savings. Congress has known for some time that Social Security would not provide an adequate wage replacement for many workers. However, whenever Congress creates a plan that provides for income tax relief or tax advantage, there are usually costs, limitations, or disadvantages to the successful implementation of such a plan. Some of these disadvantages are discussed below.

DISADVANTAGES OF QUALIFIED RETIREMENT PLANS

Costs to Qualify the Plan

To establish a qualified retirement plan, employers must have a legal document, known as a plan document, drafted by a pension attorney. The plan document sets forth the rules for administration of the plan, provides for how benefits are earned and allocated to employees, and names which classes of employees will benefit under the plan. Generally, there are attorney costs to having a plan document drafted. A determination letter is generally obtained from the Internal Revenue Service (IRS) to be certain that the plan meets the requirements of the Internal Revenue Code (IRC) Section 401(a). The determination letter assures the sponsor of the plan that the plan meets the requirements to be a qualified retirement plan. With TRA 2001, some small employers may qualify to receive determination letters without paying a fee.

It should be noted that many financial institutions have prototype plans available to their clients. Prototype plans are qualified retirement plan documents that have already been approved by the IRS as meeting the requirements of IRC Section 401(a). These prototype plans usually have only a few options for the client to select regarding the plan's operation. These options are selected by the client on what is referred to as an adoption agreement. The remainder of the document is a standard form. The benefits of a prototype plan are that it is inexpensive to establish and is preapproved by the IRS.

Costs to Fund the Plan

Qualified retirement plans must be funded on a regular basis, pension plans on a yearly basis, while contributions to profit-sharing plans must be substantial and recurring. These contributions may range from 1 to 2 percent of payroll to over 25 percent of payroll, and in years of poor earnings, can be a substantial drain on a company's cash flow.

Costs of Administering the Plan

Qualified retirement plans require ongoing administration and maintenance. Information compliance tax returns (such as IRS Form 5500) need to be filed with the IRS annually. Allocation of contributions to employees' accounts, or determination of accrued benefits, must also be completed each year. Other administrative duties include annual testing to comply with IRS regulations and amending the plan document for changes in the tax law. Besides performing administrative duties, the plan sponsor must retain and monitor an investment advisor to assure themselves that plan assets are managed for the sole benefit of participants and their beneficiaries. Each of these tasks may be outsourced to a third party administrator or other provider for a specific fee.

Small Business Tax Credit

TRA 2001 provides a nonrefundable income tax credit for 50 percent of the administrative and retirement-education expenses paid or incurred after December 31, 2001 for any small business that adopts a new qualified defined benefit or defined contribution plan (including a Section 401(k) plan), SIMPLE plan, or Simplified Employee Pension (SEP). The credit applies to 50 percent of the first $1,000 in administrative and retirement-education expenses for the plan for each of the first three years of the plan. The credit is available to an employer that did not employ, in the preceding year, more than 100 employees with compensation in excess of $5,000. To be eligible for the credit, the plan must cover at least one nonhighly compensated employee. In addition, if the credit is for the cost of a payroll deduction IRA arrangement, the arrangement must be made available to all employees of the employer who have worked with the employer for at least three months.

Annual Compensation Limit

The Internal Revenue Code sets a limit on the amount of compensation that can be considered for purposes of funding qualified retirement plans. This compensation limit, although indexed, was decreased in the 1993 law change in an attempt to limit the contribution to highly compensated employees and increase the contributions to non-highly compensated employees. Exhibit 19.4 illustrates the annual compensation limits for the years from 1990 to 2001. TRA 2001 increased the limit for years beginning after 2001.

EXHIBIT 19.4: ANNUAL COMPENSATION LIMIT (1990 – 2001)

Year	Compensation Limit	Year	Compensation Limit
1990	$209,200	1996	$150,000
1991	$222,220	1997	$160,000
1992	$228,860	1998	$160,000
1993	$235,850	1999	$160,000
1994	$150,000	2000	$170,000
1995	$150,000	2001	$170,000

When the compensation limit was reduced from 1993 to 1994 ($235,850 to $150,000), it caused employers to increase percentage contributions to rank and file employees to simply maintain their current contribution amounts of previous years.

For 2001, only $170,000 of compensation can be considered for purposes of funding a qualified plan. Any income earned above this limit is disregarded. When an employer wants to provide benefits on earnings above the annual limit, it is generally done in the form of deferral compensation, which does not have the same tax benefits as qualified plans.

TRA 2001 had a significant change on the compensation limit. It increased the limit from $170,000 to $200,000 for year 2002. This increase will allow for higher contributions for owners of small businesses and for highly compensated employees. Until 2001, the compensation limit was indexed to the CPI in $10,000 increments. After 2002, the limit will be indexed in $5,000 increments. This change decreases the time that taxpayers must wait for an increase in the covered compensation limit.

Eligibility Requirements

There are minimal standards that need to be met by an employee in order to be eligible to participate in a qualified retirement plan provided by an employer. Generally, all employees who are at least age 21 and have one year of service (defined as 1,000 hours within a twelve-month period) are considered eligible for the plan. As the number of eligible employees for the plan increases, so does the number that have to benefit under the plan for the plan to remain qualified. Obviously, an increase in the number of employees under the plan increases the cost of the plan. Union employees, who are covered by a separate collective bargaining agreement, are not required to be covered by their employer's qualified retirement plan. The reason for the exception of union employees is that these individuals generally have retirement benefits provided from the union, and employers are generally required to contribute to these union plans.

Coverage of Employees

A qualified retirement plan must benefit a broad range of employees, not just the highly compensated. Although there are exceptions, in general, employers are required to cover 70 percent of the eligible non-highly compensated employees. For defined-benefit plans only, the employer must also cover 50 employees or 40 percent of those eligible, whichever is less. Coverage under the plan means that the employee is somehow benefiting, either from employer contributions or from the ability to defer employee taxable income in the plan (such as a 401(k) plan). Highly compensated employees are defined as those employees who owned more than 5 percent of the company stock or had income above a certain limit in the previous year ($85,000 in 2001). Non-highly compensated employees are simply those employees who are not classified as highly compensated.

As long as the qualified retirement plan meets the coverage requirement, it is permitted to exclude certain groups of eligible employees from participating in the plan. For example, salaried employees or commissioned employees might be excluded from the plan as a class. These types of class exclusions may reduce the employer's contribution to the plan and thus, reduce the overall cost of the plan. The plan must meet the basic coverage rules, however, and the class exclusions should be considered in the overall context of employee compensation and as a business decision.

Vesting Requirements

Vesting is the process by which employees accrue benefits in the form of ownership provided by an employer's contribution. In the context of qualified retirement plans, an employee is vested when he has ownership rights to the contributions (or benefits) provided by the employer. In general, employees vest over a specific period.

vesting - the acquisition by an employee of his or her right to receive a present or future pension benefit

The two standard vesting schedules preapproved by the IRS are referred to as "five-year-cliff" and "three-to-seven-graduated" vesting. The five-year-cliff-vesting schedule requires an employee to complete five years of service. After five years of service (a year of service is generally defined as 1,000 hours within a twelve-month period), the employee is fully or 100 percent vested, meaning that the employee has ownership rights to all previous employer contributions and any contributions made on his behalf in the future. Graduated vesting allows employees to become partially vested over a period of years. In the case of three-to-seven-year graduated vesting, employees accrue ownership rights as follows:

EXHIBIT 19.5: GRADUATED VESTING (STANDARD AND TOP HEAVY)

VESTING SCHEDULE (3-7 GRADUATED)		TOP HEAVY (2-6 GRADUATED)	
Years of Service	Portion Vested	Years of Service	Portion Vested
1	0%	1	0%
2	0%	2	20%
3	20%	3	40%
4	40%	4	60%
5	60%	5	80%
6	80%	6	100%
7	100%	7	100%

Graduated vesting allows those employees who worked for 4 years, for example, to leave the company with some benefit; whereas, under the five-year-cliff vesting schedule, such employees would receive nothing from the contributions made by the employer, nor from the earnings on employer contributions. Contributions made by the employee (such as with a 401(k) plan), however, are always 100 percent vested and remain the property of the employee.

It should be noted that the vesting schedule an employer selects could be more liberal than the prescribed vesting schedules under the Internal Revenue Code. For instance, instead of choosing a five-year-cliff vesting schedule, an employer may elect to have employees' accounts vest over four years at 25 percent each year. However, the employer may not select a vesting schedule that is more restrictive than the five-year-cliff or three-to-seven-year graduated methods.

TRA 2001 changes the vesting schedules for employer matching contributions, for years after 2001, to a three-year cliff and a two-to-six-year graduated vesting.

EXHIBIT 19.6: VESTING FOR MATCHING CONTRIBUTIONS AFTER 2001

VESTING SCHEDULE (3 YEAR CLIFF)		VESTING SCHEDULE (2-6 GRADUATED)	
Years of Service	Portion Vested	Years of Service	Portion Vested
1	0%	1	0%
2	0%	2	20%
3	100%	3	40%
4		4	60%
5		5	80%
6		6	100%

These vesting schedules for matching contributions after December 31, 2001 are the same vesting schedules that apply to plans that are considered top-heavy.

Top Heavy Plans

Under IRC Section 416(g), qualified retirement plans are considered top heavy if more than 60 percent of the benefits are attributable to a group of owners and officers called key employees. If a plan is top heavy, then there are two consequences. First, the standard vesting schedules are required to be shortened (cliff vesting to 3 years and graduated using a 2-6 year graduated schedule) such that benefits accrue faster to the non-key employee group. Second, there are certain minimum contributions that must be provided to the non-key employees. The top-heavy rules ensure that a qualified retirement plan actually benefits the rank and file employees of the company, not just owners and officers.

Disclosure Requirements

The employer is required to provide a copy of the summary plan description (a document that summarizes the details of the qualified retirement plan) to employees and participants of the plan. In addition, the employer is also required to provide to the plan participants notices of any plan amendments or changes. These documents help to inform the employee of his rights under ERISA and of the rights of the qualified retirement plan.

Annual Testing of Qualified Retirement Plans

As described previously, there are many recurring requirements that must be met to maintain a qualified retirement plan. Therefore, annual testing is necessary to ensure that the plan continues to meet each of these requirements.

Retirement Plans as Part of a Compensation Package

From the perspective of the employees in the labor market, many qualified retirement plans have essentially become part of their overall compensation package. The employee recognizes the need for retirement savings and accepts an overall compensation package as salary, retirement plan, and other employee fringe benefits, rather than just salary, such that the employee's compensation utility curves are maximized to the greatest extent possible.

This does not suggest that the employee chooses the qualified retirement plan. The employer chooses the type of qualified retirement plan, and it usually becomes part of an overall compensation package offered to current and future employees. The employees then evaluate the complete compensation package, given their personal goals and opportunity costs, to make appropriate employment decisions. Today's employees are aware of the benefits of using a qualified retirement plan's deferral of taxable income as an alternative to receiving additional current compensation, which would be currently subject to income tax.

In the last few years, many employees have chosen to work for companies that provided minimal salaries, but offered employee stock options. Employees recognized them as hi-tech companies with tremendous growth potential. Employees were willing to sacrifice current income in hopes that their employer's stock would appreciate significantly enough to compensate them for their current sacrifice of higher salaries elsewhere.

Microsoft is a good example of this phenomenon. Base salaries were small, but the right to participate in the ownership of the company was tremendously enticing to potential employees. As it turns out, many of these employees became quite wealthy because of their stock options and other fringe benefits.

BENEFITS OF TAX DEFERRAL

For an employee who participates in a qualified retirement plan, tax deferral is perhaps the biggest benefit. Neither the contributions to the plan nor the earnings on these contributions are currently subject to income tax. The expectation is that in retirement, when distributions begin, the plan participant will be in a lower income tax bracket than during the working years.

EXAMPLE   Your client's employer will either pay your client $1,000 that is (**A**) subject to payroll and income tax, or alternatively, (**B**) his employer will contribute $1,000 to a qualified retirement plan. Your client will save the net received from (**A**) and earn 12 percent per year for 40 years. The contribution made to the qualified retirement plan, (**B**), is made by the employer.

	A Not Tax Advantaged		B Qualified Plan	
Deposit	$1,000.00		$1,000.00	
Less	76.50	Payroll tax	0.00	Payroll tax
Less	280.00	28% assumed income tax rate	0.00	Tax rate
Net Deposited	$ 643.50		$1,000.00	
PV	$ 643.50		$1,000.00	
i	8.64%	(12% x 0.72) (28% tax rate)	12%	
n	40 years		40	
FV	$17,706.75		$93,050.97	
Net of tax	$17,706.75		$66,996.70	(28% tax bracket)

The assumption made in the above example (**A**) was that the 12 percent earnings was fully subject to income tax each year, thus the use of the 8.64 earnings rate (1 - tax rate)(ER) = (1 - 0.28)(12) = 8.64. However, even if we assumed a portfolio of non-dividend paying stocks that were only subject to capital gains rates of 20 percent at the end of 40 years, the advantage would still be to the qualified retirement plan.

	A	B
	Not Tax Advantaged	Qualified Plan
Deposit	$643.50	$1,000.00
PV	$643.50	$1,000.00
n	40	40
i	12%	12%
FV	$59,878.30	$93,050.97
Tax rate	20% on capital gains ($59,878.30 - $643.50)	28% on ordinary income
Net after tax	$48,031.34 [(FV - basis) x .80]	$66,996.70 (FV x (1 – 0.28))

The difference between *A* and *B* in both examples above is partially due to the payroll tax, which was not applicable to the qualified retirement plan, and partially due to the current income tax on the non-tax-advantaged fund (**A**).

TYPES OF QUALIFIED RETIREMENT PLANS

To help the reader understand the differences between types of qualified retirement plans, four different perspectives of these plans will be examined. Qualified retirement plans are classified as pension or profit-sharing plans, defined-benefit or defined-contribution plans, contributory or noncontributory plans, and corporate or Keogh plans. Exhibit 19.7 identifies eleven different types of common qualified retirement plans. An in-depth examination of each of the eleven plans is beyond the scope of this text but would be covered in a full course on retirement plans and planning.

EXHIBIT 19.7: QUALIFIED RETIREMENT PLANS

TYPES	PENSION PLANS	PROFIT-SHARING PLANS
Defined-Benefit Plans	1. Defined-Benefit Pension Plan 2. Cash-Balance Pension Plan	NONE
Defined-Contribution Plans	1. Target-Benefit Money-Purchase Pension Plan 2. Money-Purchase Pension Plan	1. Profit-Sharing Plans 2. 401(k) Plans 3. Thrift Plans 4. Stock Bonus Plans 5. Employee Stock Ownership Plans 6. Age-Based Profit-Sharing Plans 7. New Comparability Plans

PENSION PLANS

The legal requirement or "promise" of a **pension plan** is to regularly pay a fixed sum of money at retirement. Because of this promise, pension plans have certain requirements and characteristics. The first requirement is that pension plans have mandatory funding. This means that, in general, pension plans must be funded on an annual basis, regardless of whether the company has sufficient cash flow. The reason for annual funding is to insure that sufficient assets will be available to fulfill the promise of a pension during retirement.

The second requirement is that pension plans are not permitted to allow in-service withdrawals. An in-service withdrawal is an employee distribution, other than because of hardship, while the employee is still in the active service of the employer. It is worth noting that loans are not considered in-service withdrawals.

The third requirement is that pension plans are limited to investing no more than 10 percent of the assets in the qualified retirement plan in employer securities. To be consistent with the underlying promise of the pension plan, the investments of the qualified retirement plan should be reasonably diversified to limit the amount of risk undertaken by the portfolio. Investing more than 10 percent in the employer's securities would not be a prudent investment decision and would be inconsistent with the notion of paying pension benefits.

The fourth characteristic of pension plans is the generous limit on contributions. A pension plan can contribute up to, and in some cases exceed, 25 percent of covered compensation. The term, "covered compensation," describes the portion of payroll that may be considered for qualified retirement plan purposes. These high contribution limits provide ample opportunity for the employer to fulfill the promise of pension benefits.

There are four pension plans as indicated in Exhibit 19.7. These four pension plans differ from each other in complexity and costs. The defined-benefit plan is the most complex and costly, requiring the annual services of an actuary. The money-purchase pension plan is the least complex and least costly. A prototype plan for a money-purchase pension plan can be obtained from almost any financial institution. Each pension plan has particular applications that make it a better choice than the others depending on the employer-sponsor's goals, the number of participants, and the census of participants, including length of service, age, and compensation levels. Cash balance plans are beyond the scope of this text.

Small businesses, with the exception of self-employed professional persons, tend to avoid pension plans due to the strict requirement of mandatory funding. Small businesses would rather choose profit-sharing plans or other tax-advantaged retirement plans that have more discretion as to the funding of contributions.

PROFIT-SHARING PLANS

A **profit-sharing plan** is a qualified defined-contribution plan featuring a flexible (discretionary) employer-contribution provision. The funding discretion is regardless of cash flows or profits. An employer is permitted to fund a profit-sharing plan (including stock bonus plans) in any amount up to 15 percent of covered employee compensation for years prior to 2002, and 25% for years after 2001.

---

pension plan - a qualified plan structured to provide a regularly paid fixed sum at retirement

profit-sharing plan - a qualified defined-contribution plan featuring a flexible (discretionary) employer-contribution provision. Profit-sharing plans are structured to offer employees participation in company profits that they may use for retirement purposes

The legal promise of a profit-sharing plan is to defer taxes rather than provide retirement benefits. There is no particular time requirement for the deferral of taxes. The deferral period could be until retirement, in which case in-service withdrawals would not be permitted. Alternatively, a profit-sharing plan may be designed to allow in-service withdrawals as early as after two years of participation. The plan document (the plan legal description) will dictate what is, or is not, permitted.

Unlike the restriction of pension plans, profit-sharing plans do not have restrictions on the amount of employer securities that can be purchased within the plan. Profit-sharing plans are permitted to invest 100 percent of the qualified retirement plan assets in employer securities. **Stock bonus plans** and employee stock ownership plans (ESOPs) are examples of profit-sharing type plans that often invest entirely in employer securities.

There are seven different profit-sharing plans as shown in Exhibit 19.7. Each one has a particular application depending on costs, complexity, sponsor goals, and the census of employees, including age, length of service and compensation levels.

The one type of profit-sharing plan so common and important that it deserves mentioning is the **401(k) plan**. It is clearly the most popular self-reliant qualified retirement plan. The 401(k) permits an employee to save, pre-tax, up to $10,500 (for the year 2001) or a certain percentage of income per year (indexed to inflation); and in some cases, that savings is matched, or partially matched, by the employer. TRA 2001 increased the annual elective deferral limit for 401(k) plans to $11,000 in 2002. In addition, the limit is increased in increments of $1,000 until it reaches $15,000 in 2006. After 2006, the limit will be indexed in increments of $500.

Common matching schemes call for the employee to contribute up to 6 percent of salary with the employer matching $0.50 on the dollar contributed by the employee up to 3 percent per

stock bonus plan - a defined-contribution profit-sharing plan in which all employer contributions are in the form of employer stock and distributions to participants can be made in the form of employer stock

401(k) plan - a defined-contribution profit-sharing plan that gives participants the option of reducing their taxable salary and contributing the salary reduction on a tax-deferred basis to an individual account for retirement purposes

year. The employee may contribute more than the 6 percent if the plan permits, but the employer match usually is maximized at 3 percent. The advantage of this kind of plan to the employer is that the funding is heavily employee dependent and self-reliant. Advantages to the employee are the size of the pre-tax savings, any employer match, and the prospects for a substantial accumulation over the work life expectancy.

EXAMPLE

Assume Joe G, age 25, participates in a 401(k) plan and his salary is $50,000. Joe annually contributes 6 percent to his 401(k) plan and the contribution is matched with 3 percent from his employer. Joe intends to contribute the same amount each month for the next 40 years. Assume that Joe can earn 10 percent annually, compounded monthly, on his and his employer's contributions and balances. How much will Joe accumulate at age 65 assuming no increase in salary or in the amount of the monthly contribution?

PV	=	0
n	=	480 (40 x 12) months
i	=	0.83333 (10 ÷ 12)
PMT_{OA}	=	$375.00 [(50,000 x 6%) + (50,000 x 3%)] ÷ 12
$FV_{@65}$	=	$2,371,529.84

The accumulation is remarkable! Joe and his employer deposited only $180,000 ($375 x 12 x 40), and at age 65, has $2,371,530. The rate of return on earnings was reasonable at 10 percent, but Joe started early and reaped the benefits of a long period of compounding. In actual practice, we would hope and expect that as Joe's salary increased, he would maintain at least the 6 percent savings rate as opposed to the $375 per month, thus increasing his contributions with each raise. Joe's contribution, as well as the employer match, would increase with each raise in salary, thus increasing the deposits and the accumulation at age 65.

The 401(k) plan has become one of the most popular and widely used qualified retirement plans. It is self-reliant and easily understood by employees. It is popular with employers because it is relatively inexpensive since employees provide most of the funding.

TRA 2001 has made a significant change to 401(k) plans for years beginning after December 31, 2005. This change allows 401(k) plans (and 403(b) plans) to include a "qualified plus contribution program" that permits a participant to elect to have all or a portion of the participant's elective deferrals under the plan treated as Roth contributions. As with contributions to Roth IRAs, these participant elective deferrals would be subject to current taxation (not tax deferred), but would be exempt from taxation when distributed if certain requirements were met. These after-tax contributions can accumulate in the Roth account on a tax deferred basis. This addition to 401(k) plans may be one of the most beneficial aspects of qualified plans that have been seen in many years.

TRA 2001 has also excluded elective deferrals from being considered in the contribution limitations of qualified plans. This change is effective for years after 2001 and will allow employers to have higher total contributions to qualified plans.

In addition, TRA 2001 has provided for additional contributions to be made to 401(k) plans, 403(b) plans, SARSEPs, SEPs, and 457 plans for employees who are over the age of 50. These catch up contributions allow employees who are over the age of 50 to make the following additional contributions:

Year	Over 50 Years of Age Additional Catch Up Contributions
2002	$1,000
2003	$2,000
2004	$3,000
2005	$4,000
2006	$5,000
2007	The $5,000 amount is increased in $500 increments

Exhibit 19.8 summarizes the major differences between pension plans and profit-sharing plans.

EXHIBIT 19.8: MAJOR DIFFERENCES BETWEEN PENSION AND PROFIT-SHARING PLANS

PLAN FEATURES	PENSION PLANS	PROFIT-SHARING PLANS
In-Service Withdrawals	Not permitted	Permitted after 2 years
Mandatory Funding	Yes	No
Percentage of Employer Stock Permitted in the Plan	10%	100%
Employer Contribution Limit	25% of covered compensation	15%*

The 15% limit is increased to 25% for years after 2001.

DEFINED-BENEFIT VERSUS DEFINED-CONTRIBUTION PLANS

Qualified retirement plans are characterized as either defined-benefit or defined-contribution plans. In a defined-benefit plan, the contributions are actuarially determined to produce a certain future benefit under a formula at retirement. The annual funding for a defined-benefit plan depends on six factors: (1) the life expectancies of the participants, (2) the mortality experience in the employee group, (3) the earnings rate and expected earnings rate on plan assets, (4) the expected wage increases of employees, (5) the expected inflation rate associated with plan costs, and (6) the expected turnover rate of employees. An actuary makes an annual analysis of the above six variables to determine the annual funding. Obviously, defined-benefit plans are both costly and complex. There are only two defined-benefit plans, the traditional **defined-benefit pension plan**, and the cash-balance pension plan. Generally, large corporations use these where the costs of administration, including actuarial costs, can be spread over a large number of employee participants.

defined-benefit plan - a retirement plan that specifies the benefits that each employee receives at retirement. Defined-benefit plans actuarially determine the benefit to be paid at normal age retirement

Defined-benefit plan assets are invested and managed by the employer or by the plan. Defined-benefit plans actuarially determine the benefit to be paid at normal age retirement (currently age

65). Contributions to defined-benefit plans are generally provided by the employer only. Since the employer is responsible for meeting the benefit obligations, it bears the investment risk for the funding. If the performance of the fund assets is better than expected, then contributions can be reduced. If investment returns are less than expected, however, the employer is required to make higher contributions than anticipated.

The benefits of a defined-benefit plan are commonly paid for life as an annuity, although some plans provide a cash-out option at retirement. Since funding requirements are greater the older a person enters the plan, defined-benefit plans are said to favor older-age entrants.

Since there is some risk that the employer will be unable to sustain the payment of retirement benefits from a defined-benefit plan, sponsors of these plans are generally required to participate in the Pension Benefit Guarantee Corporation (PBGC). The PBGC is a federal agency that guarantees benefits to participants of defined-benefit plans. It is a type of government insurance company, similar to the FDIC, where plan sponsors make premium payments to the PBGC based on the number of plan participants and based on the level of plan funding. The PBGC does not guarantee the full amount of benefits, but only a set amount as limited by law (currently about $41,000 per year). The PBGC does not guarantee benefits of defined-contribution plans.

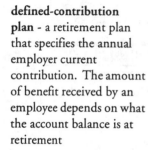

defined-contribution plan - a retirement plan that specifies the annual employer current contribution. The amount of benefit received by an employee depends on what the account balance is at retirement

Defined-contribution plans specify the annual employer current contribution (as opposed to an ultimate future benefit). The amount of benefit that an employee receives depends on whatever the account balance is at retirement. Therefore, the investment risk of a defined-contribution plan is borne by the employee.

There are two defined-contribution pension plans and seven defined-contribution profit-sharing plans. Usually, defined-contribution plan funding is borne solely by the employer (except for the 401(k) and thrift plan), but the assets are maintained in each participant's individual account. The investment risk is borne by the employee/participants with the assets in the plan often self-directed. Defined-contribution plans favor younger participants who have a longer compounding and accumulation period. Unlike defined-benefit plans, with defined-contribution profit-sharing plans there is no annual mandatory funding. Thus, accumulations in these accounts are dependent on the contributions made and the earnings performance that may or may not be realized.

Exhibit 19.9 summarizes the characteristics and differences between defined-benefit and defined-contribution plans.

EXHIBIT 19.9: CHARACTERISTICS OF SELECTED RETIREMENT PLAN

	DEFINED BENEFIT	DEFINED CONTRIBUTION
Adequate level of retirement income regardless of age	Yes	No
Plan typically benefits older employees	Yes	No
Requires PBGC insurance	Yes	No
Benefits insured by PBGC	Yes	No
Actuarial costs	Yes	No
Can encourage early retirement	Yes	No
Can provide benefits based on prior service	Yes	No
Benefit up to $90,000 indexed ($140,000 for 2001, $160,000 for 2002)	Yes	No
Higher plan costs and complexity	Yes	No
Individual accounts	No	Yes
Contribution is % of compensation	No	Yes
Investment risk	Employer	Employee
Contributions limited to lesser of 25% or $35,000 for 2001 (lesser of 100% or $40,000 for 2002)	No	Yes
Forfeitures reduce plan costs	Yes	Maybe
Assets in plan	Commingled Funds	Separate Accounts

CONTRIBUTORY VERSUS NONCONTRIBUTORY PLANS

Qualified retirement plans may be distinguished as either contributory (employee makes some contribution) or noncontributory (employer pays all). Most pension and profit-sharing plans are noncontributory. The common exceptions are the 401(k) plan and the thrift plan (an after-tax savings plan). The reason that most qualified retirement plans are noncontributory is that both employers and employees view them as a part of an overall compensation package paid for by the employer. Because noncontributory plans are so prevalent, vesting is an important issue. Vesting occurs when the employee has a federal property right in the employer contributions and earnings on those contributions.

When an employer qualifies a plan, they must indicate a vesting schedule. While faster vesting schedules are acceptable to the Internal Revenue Service, the common vesting schedules are: (a) the five-year cliff, and (b) the three-to-seven graduated vesting. Cliff vesting requires that after a certain number of years of employment an employee is 100 percent vested in contributions of the employer and earnings on their contributions. Prior to the completion of the cliff year (year 5 for 2001 and year 3 for 2002), the employee is unvested. This type of vesting schedule usually is chosen when there is fairly substantial turnover during the first few years of employment.

Graduated vesting provides for partial vesting over several years and is designed to encourage employees to continue employment. Graduated vesting is usually chosen to reduce turnover by creating an increasing vesting commitment until such time when the employee is fully vested. While vesting does not guarantee portability, it does create a permanent federal property right, which the employee will always have even if employment is terminated.

CORPORATE VERSUS KEOGH PLANS

Qualified retirement plans are either corporate-sponsored (regular C corporations and S corporations) or Keogh (self-employed, Schedule C, partnerships, LLCs filing as partnerships) plans. Corporations can adopt any of the qualified retirement plans, pension plans, or profit-sharing plans discussed above, as well as other tax-advantaged plans that are not qualified. Self-employed persons can adopt the majority of qualified retirement plans (except stock bonus and ESOP plans) and can adopt other tax-advantaged but nonqualified plans called SEPs and SIMPLEs. These will be covered in the next section of this chapter.

Keogh plan - a qualified plan for unincorporated businesses

The intent of congressional legislation regarding self-employed individuals was to put **Keogh plans** in parity with corporate plans. There are two important differences, however, between corporate plans and Keogh plans. The first is the calculation of the maximum contribution allowed by the self-employed person; and the second is the availability of loans from the Keogh plan to these self-employed individuals. Both of these differences were changed by TRA 2001.

Self-Employed Maximum Contribution Calculation

forfeitures - employer contributions that are not fully vested and thus forfeited in the event that an employee terminates service

Traditional employees receive a Form W-2 that reflects their earnings for the current year. There is a limit that no more than the lesser of 25 percent of an employee's compensation or $35,000 (year 2001) can be contributed to the defined-contribution plans sponsored by the employer within a given year. For years after 2001, TRA 2001 increases this limit to the lesser of 100% of compensation or $40,000 (the $40,000 is indexed in increments of $1,000 after 2002). Contributions include employer contributions, employee contributions, and **forfeitures**. For example, an employee who had compensation of $100,000 would be limited to $25,000 in contributions for a single year for years prior to 2002, but for years after 2001 they would be limited to $40,000.

Unfortunately for self-employed individuals, their maximum contribution calculation is more complicated. These individuals are limited in their contributions to the lesser of 25 percent of earned income or $35,000 for 2001. Earned income is different than compensation and is defined as self-employment income reduced by ½ self-employment tax (net self-employment income) and reduced by the retirement plan contribution. Reducing the income that can be used as the base for the retirement plan contribution by the retirement plan contribution creates what is known as a circular equation. To resolve this circular equation, the retirement plan contribution percentage is divided by the sum of 1 plus the retirement plan contribution percentage. This factor is then multiplied by the difference between self-employment income and ½ self-employment tax.

If Bob has self-employment income of $105,000 and self-employment tax of $10,000 in 2001, his contribution is limited to a maximum of $20,000, as follows:

KEOGH PLAN CONTRIBUTION CALCULATION

1.	Self-employment income	$105,000	
2.	Less ½ self-employment tax	$5,000	½ x $10,000
3.	Equals net self-employment income	$100,000	
4.	Less Keogh plan contribution	($20,000)	$100,000 x (0.25/1.25)
5.	Equals Earned Income	$80,000	
6.	Times Keogh contribution percentage	x 25%	
7.	Equals Keogh plan contribution	$20,000	

Notice that the contribution of $20,000 is calculated by multiplying $100,000 by 20 percent, which equals earned income (line 5 above) multiplied by 25 percent. Therefore, it is not necessary to extend the analysis through steps 5 to 7. Determining the contribution is usually calculated by dividing the plan percentage by the sum of 1 plus the plan percentage and multiplying the result by the difference between self-employment earnings and ½ self-employment tax. The following table depicts the percentage that is often used for Keogh calculations depending on the plan contribution percentage limit.

PLAN PERCENTAGE	KEOGH LIMIT	PLAN PERCENTAGE	KEOGH LIMIT
1%	0.9901%	14%	12.2807%
2%	1.9608%	15%	13.0435%
3%	2.9126%	16%	13.7931%
4%	3.8462%	17%	14.5299%
5%	4.7619%	18%	15.2542%
6%	5.6604%	19%	15.9664%
7%	6.5421%	20%	16.6667%
8%	7.4074%	21%	17.3554%
9%	8.2569%	22%	18.0328%
10%	9.0909%	23%	18.6992%
11%	9.9099%	24%	19.3548%
12%	10.7143%	25%	20.0000%
13%	11.5044%		

(15% was the profit sharing limit prior to 2002; 25% is the money purchase limit and the profit sharing limit after 2001)

Availability of Loans From Keogh Plans

The second primary difference between corporate plans and Keogh plans deals with the availability of plan loans to self-employed participants. Most qualified retirement plans are permitted to allow loans to employees. However, loans to self-employed individuals have generally been considered prohibited transactions and were not permitted. Although S corporations have corporate plans, they had similar rules relating to loans to any owner-employee.

TRA 2001 has eliminated the rules regarding loans as prohibited transactions for years after 2001. Therefore, for years after 2001, owner-employers have the same access to loans as other employees.

OTHER TAX-ADVANTAGED PLANS

Other than qualified retirement plans, there are individually sponsored and employer-sponsored retirement plans that are tax advantaged, but are not technically qualified. Generally, these plans appeal to individuals or small employers, have lower contribution limits, function about the same as qualified retirement plans as to earnings deferral and contribution deductions, but are less costly (except for 403(b) plans) and do not receive ERISA creditor protection (although some states have legislated creditor alienation protection for these plans). They might be thought of as the poor man's substitute for a qualified retirement plan. Exhibit 19.10 lists these plans.

EXHIBIT 19.10: OTHER TAX-ADVANTAGED PLANS

Individual Retirement Account or Annuity (IRA)
- Deductible
- Nondeductible
- Roth IRA

Simplified Employee Plan (SEP)

Savings Incentive Match Plan for Employees (SIMPLE)

403(b) Plans (Tax-Sheltered Annuities)

INDIVIDUAL RETIREMENT ACCOUNT (IRA) OR IRA ANNUITY

In general, the IRA is a tax-deferred investment and savings account that acts as a personal retirement fund for persons with earned income.

An individual worker with earned income who is under age 70½ can establish an IRA. Annual IRA contributions are limited to the lesser of $2,000 or earned income for 2001. If a married person has a nonworking spouse, the annual contribution limit is increased to $4,000 for 2001 ($2,000 per individual account).

TRA 2001 increased the contribution limit for IRAs using the following schedule:

2002	$3,000
2003	$3,000
2004	$3,000
2005	$4,000
2006	$4,000
2007	$4,000
2008	$5,000
2009 and later	Increased for inflation in $500 increments

The IRA contribution may be tax deductible, depending on whether the worker is covered by a qualified retirement plan or SEP and depending on the amount of his or her adjusted gross income.

TRA 2001 also provides for catch up contributions for individuals over 50 years old. Any individual who attains 50 by the end of the taxable year can make the following additional contributions:

2002	$500
2003	$500
2004	$500
2005	$500
2006 and later	$1,000

Thus, a taxpayer in year 2006 could contribute a total of $5,000 to his IRA. This contribution consists of the annual limit plus the catch up contribution.

The Roth IRA

The **Roth IRA** is a special type of nondeductible IRA. Like the traditional IRA, the Roth IRA accumulates contributions (nondeductible or after-tax) and earnings. Unlike the traditional IRA, the distributions from a Roth IRA are generally tax-exempt. Taxpayers can contribute to Roth IRAs after the age of 70½, and are not forced to receive minimum distributions at age 70½, as with traditional IRAs. Only taxpayers with incomes less than those listed below qualify to make a contribution to a Roth IRA.

Roth IRA - an individual retirement account in which contributions are made on an after-tax basis and qualifying distributions are made tax free

Taxpayer	Phase-out AGI (modified)
Single	$ 95,000 – $110,000
Married filing jointly	$150,000 – $160,000
Married filing separately	$0 – $ 10,000

Another big advantage of the Roth IRA is that owners always have the ability to distribute without tax or penalty an amount up to the total contributions to the Roth IRA without being subjected to income tax or penalties. For instance, Bob contributes $2,000 to his Roth IRA each year for five years. The account has grown to $18,000. Bob is able to distribute up to $10,000 (his total contributions) from the Roth IRA without tax or penalties. In a traditional IRA, distributions are generally taxable as ordinary income and distributions prior to age 59½ are generally subject to a 10 percent penalty.

SIMPLIFIED EMPLOYEE PENSIONS (SEP)

simplified employee pension (SEP) - a tax-deferred, noncontributory retirement plan that uses an individual retirement account (IRA) as the receptacle for contributions

A **Simplified Employee Pension (SEP)** is tax-deferred noncontributory retirement plan that is employer sponsored and is similar to a qualified profit-sharing plan with regard to funding requirements and contribution limits. In contrast to qualified profit-sharing plans, SEPs require almost none of the same filing requirements. SEPs use individual retirement accounts (IRAs) to hold the retirement benefits, making the benefits of the employees portable. Individual retirement accounts are established for each eligible employee. The funding is discretionary on the part of the employer up to 15 percent of covered employee compensation to a maximum of $170,000 (as indexed for year 2000) not to exceed $35,000. SEPs do not have vesting requirements as with most qualified retirement plans. The advantage of a SEP versus an IRA is the possible amount of funding $25,500 ($170,000 x 0.15) versus the $2,000 for the traditional or Roth IRA. The plan is uncomplicated and low cost compared to qualified retirement plans. Generally, the individual participant has the responsibility and risk for investment returns. SEPs may not be appropriate for small businesses with permanent part-time employees because part-time employees must be covered under the plan. A major advantage of a SEP is that it can be established as late as the due date of the income tax return, including extensions. IRAs, on the other hand, must be established by April 15th following the tax year.

TRA 2001 increased the compensation limit to $200,000, which should increase the maximum contribution to $30,000 ($200,000 x 0.15).

SIMPLE (IRA) PLANS

A SIMPLE (IRA) plan (Savings Incentive Match Plan for Employees) is a tax-deferred, employer-sponsored retirement plan that is mostly a self-reliant plan. Like the SEP, it has minimal filing requirements. The SIMPLE plan allows employees to make elective contributions to an individual retirement account (IRA) up to $6,500 for 2001. TRA 2001 provides that for years after 2001 the limit will be as follows:

2002	$7,000
2003	$8,000
2004	$9,000
2005	$10,000
2006 and later	Increased in $500 increments

700

TRA 2001 also provides for catch up provisions for individuals over 50 years old. Any individual who attains 50 by the end of the taxable year may be eligible to make the following additional contributions:

Year	Over 50 Years of Age Additional Catch Up Contributions
2002	$500
2003	$1,000
2004	$1,500
2005	$2,000
2006	$2,500
2007 and later	The $2,500 is indexed for inflation in $500 increments

Unlike most qualified retirement plans, there is no percentage limitation on the deferral amount. In other words, an employee who earned $6,500 (2001) could defer the entire amount. The employer is required to provide one of the following two types of benefits to the employees in the plan: 1) provide a dollar-for-dollar match up to 3 percent of the employee's compensation, or 2) make a 2 percent-of-compensation contribution for each eligible employee without regard to the employee's contribution. The total combined contribution is limited to $13,000 annually (year 2001) and there are no vesting provisions, which means that once contributed, the funds cannot be forfeited or revert back to the employer. The benefits are portable; however, withdrawals made within two years of participation are subject to a 25 percent premature-distribution penalty tax.

The advantage of the SIMPLE over the traditional IRA is the larger amount of contribution allowed. The advantage of the SIMPLE over the SEP is that the SIMPLE plan is mostly funded through employee contributions and there is no percentage limit for contributions to a SIMPLE plan.

To sponsor a SIMPLE plan, the employer must have fewer than 100 employees. SIMPLE plans are essentially governed by the same rules as IRAs. Individual accounts are created, and employees choose the investments from those offered by the plan.

One big disadvantage of a SIMPLE is that no other types of qualified retirement plans are permitted to be simultaneously maintained by the employer. Therefore, if the employer wanted to sponsor a pension or profit-sharing plan, the SIMPLE would have to be terminated.

403(b) PLANS

Congress established 403(b) plans to encourage workers in certain tax-exempt organizations to establish retirement savings programs. The name, like that of 401(k) plans, refers to the relevant code section of the Internal Revenue Code. A **403(b) plan** is a tax-deferred savings and retirement plan, and while not generally qualified, provides many of the same benefits and is governed by many of the same rules as qualified retirement plans. It is essentially the 401(k) of the not-

403(b) plan - a retirement plan similar to a 401(k) plan that is available to certain tax-exempt organizations and to public schools

for-profit industry. Participants contractually reduce their salaries with their employer for equivalent pre-tax contributions made either in mutual funds or tax-sheltered annuities. The contributions and earnings grow tax deferred until distribution, and the benefit received is equal to the account balance at the accumulation date (usually retirement). Unlike the 401(k) plan, there are usually no employer matching funds contributed to the 403(b) individual accounts. Similar to 401(k) and other defined-contribution plans, the responsibility and risk of investment returns is on the individual participant.

TRA 2001 made certain changes to 403(b) plans for years after 2001. These changes eliminated certain rules and increased the annual deferral limit to match that of 401(k) plans.

Non-Refundable Credit for Elective Deferrals

For years 2002 through 2006, a special non-refundable tax credit will be available for low and moderate income savers who make elective deferrals to a 401(k) plan, section 403(b) annuity, or eligible deferred compensation arrangement of a State or local government (a "sec. 457 plan"), SIMPLE, or SEP, contributions to a traditional or Roth IRA, and voluntary after-tax employee contributions to a qualified retirement plan.

The maximum annual contribution eligible for the credit is $2,000. The credit rates based on AGI are as follows:

Joint Filers	Head of Households	All Other Filers	Credit Rate	Max. Amount of Credit
$0 - $30,000	$0 - $22,500	$0 - $15,000	50 percent	$1,000
$30,000 - $32,500	$22,500 - $24,375	$15,000 - $16,250	20 percent	$400
$32,500 - $50,000	$24,375 - $37,500	$16,250 - $25,000	10 percent	$200
Over $50,000	Over $37,500	Over $25,000	0 percent	$0

The credit is in addition to any deduction or exclusion that would otherwise apply with respect to the contribution. The credit offsets minimum tax liability as well as regular tax liability. The credit is available to individuals who are 18 or over, other than individuals who are full-time students or claimed as a dependent on another taxpayer's return.

The amount of any contribution eligible for the credit is reduced by taxable distributions received by the taxpayer and his or her spouse from any savings arrangement described above or any other qualified retirement plan during the taxable year for which the credit is claimed, the two taxable years prior to the year the credit is claimed, and during the period after the end of the taxable year and prior to the due date for filing the taxpayer's return for the year. In the case of a distribution from a Roth IRA, this rule applies to any such distributions, whether or not taxable.

DISTRIBUTIONS FROM QUALIFIED AND OTHER TAX-ADVANTAGED PLANS

Distributions from qualified retirement plans and other tax-advantaged retirement plans generally have the same income tax consequences. In general, distributions made prior to age 59½, or prior to death, disability, or some retirements, will be penalized with a premature penalty tax of 10 percent. Annual distributions from qualified retirement plans must begin for years no later than the year in which the participant attains the age of 70½, although the first distribution may be delayed until April 1st of the following year. There is an exception if the employee/participant has not yet retired from the sponsor of that plan. This exception does not apply to other tax-advantaged accounts (IRAs, SEPs, SIMPLEs), nor does it apply to a greater-than-5% owner. Therefore, distributions from other tax-advantaged accounts must begin by age 70½.

Distributions from qualified retirement plans and other tax-advantaged plans are generally subject to the following income tax treatment: If the contributions were pre-tax, then both contributions and earnings are treated as ordinary income equal to the distribution, and thus receive ordinary income tax treatment. If the contributions were after-tax (thrift plan and nondeductible IRA), the contributions are treated as a return of capital and the earnings are treated as ordinary income. Each distribution is prorated as to return of taxable basis and ordinary income subject to income tax. This information is summarized in Exhibit 19.11.

EXHIBIT 19.11: TAXATION OF DISTRIBUTIONS

CONTRIBUTIONS	DISTRIBUTION	EARNINGS ON CONTRIBUTIONS
Pre-tax	Taxable as ordinary income	Ordinary income
After-tax	A return of capital	Ordinary income

The two common exceptions to the general income tax treatment of distributions from tax-advantaged retirement accounts include Roth IRAs and lump-sum distributions consisting of employer securities. The Roth IRA has nondeductible contributions, but generally provides for tax-exempt distributions and is not subject to minimum distributions that begin at age 70½.

As previously discussed, distributions that consist of employer securities receive deferred recognition treatment of the net unrealized appreciation in the securities, and the gains are taxable at capital gains rates instead of ordinary income tax rates.

NONQUALIFIED PLANS

A **nonqualified plan** is any retirement plan, savings plan, or deferred-compensation plan or agreement that does not meet the tax and legal requirements of ERISA and the Internal Revenue Code. All qualified retirement plans and other tax-advantaged plans are in some way a form of deferred compensation, but with some form of current income tax deduction and/or deferral of taxation on earnings. For the nonqualified plans, no such favorable tax treatment occurs. The employer receives a deduction for contributions only when the participant recognizes the distribution as income for income tax purposes. If the nonqualified plan agreement delays when the participant receives taxable income, then the employer/sponsor's income tax deduction is also delayed.

nonqualified plan - a retirement plan that can discriminate in favor of executives but which is not eligible for the special tax benefits available for qualified or other tax-advantaged retirement plans

Employers use nonqualified plans to provide additional financial benefits that are not, or cannot be, provided in qualified retirement plans. Nonqualified plans can reward employees (usually key executives) on a more selective basis than qualified retirement plans that require broad participation, coverage, and nondiscrimination. An example of one benefit that can be provided by a nonqualified plan is a deferred-compensation plan to provide retirement benefits to a key employee in excess of the limits that may be provided for in a qualified retirement plan. Recall that the limit for covered compensation that can be considered for purposes of qualified retirement plans is $170,000 for year 2001 and $200,000 for 2002. Employees who earn exactly $170,000 in 2001 have a much higher wage replacement ratio than those who make $1,000,000 under the same qualified retirement plan, because even though the person is earning $1,000,000, their qualified retirement plan acts as if they are only making $170,000 in 2001. The deferred-compensation, nonqualified plan is used to mitigate this perceived wage replacement ratio inequity.

Nonqualified plans do not receive 10-year-forward-averaging income tax treatment, as do qualified retirement plans. Nonqualified plans have some risk as to whether the employee/participant will receive the benefits (a substantial risk of forfeiture is essential for the plan to work). If there is no substantial risk of forfeiture, the Internal Revenue Service will argue that there is constructive receipt of the funds, and, therefore, the benefits are currently taxable rather than being deferred. In addition, nonqualified plans are not protected from creditors under ERISA's non alienation of benefits rules.

There are a number of nonqualified plans that may be used to attract, compensate, and retain key personnel on a discriminatory or selective basis. These include deferred-compensation plans, split-dollar life insurance plans, and employee stock option plans.

DEFERRED-COMPENSATION PLANS

Nonqualified, deferred-compensation agreements are contractual arrangements between the employer and selected employees. **Deferred-compensation plans** take the form of either salary reduction, or more commonly, salary continuation. Either way, compensation is deferred generally until retirement, disability, death, or termination of employment, but usually only at normal age retirement. In effect, no retirement, no benefits.

The employer does not receive any tax deduction unless and until the employee recognizes taxable income. The presumption is that the executive employee may be in a lower income tax bracket in retirement than in the maximum earnings years of employment. Another reason for using nonqualified plans is to delay the receipt of taxable cash flow to the executive until it is actually needed.

SPLIT-DOLLAR LIFE INSURANCE

Split-dollar life insurance is an arrangement using permanent life insurance where there is a split between the employer and employee of premiums, ownership, and benefits. There is complete flexibility to arrange such splits any way agreed to by employer and employee. A common split-dollar plan, however, has the employer paying 100 percent of the premium and owning the policy. The employer names itself as beneficiary for an amount equal to the premiums paid to the date of death, and the employee names the beneficiary for the balance of the proceeds. The

deferred-compensation plan - a nonqualified plan that is a contractual agreement between the employer and selected employees that takes the form of either salary reduction, or salary continuation. Compensation is deferred until retirement, disability, death, or termination of employment, but usually only at normal retirement age

arrangement is essentially an interest-free loan to the employee. The employer receives no income tax deduction for the payment of the premiums. The employee must recognize taxable income annually to the extent of the true mortality costs using Table 2001 costs (a schedule of mortality costs) as determined by the Internal Revenue Service. Ownership and split arrangements can take many different forms.

Essentially, the benefit to the employee of split-dollar life insurance is free, permanent insurance to the extent there is value in excess of the true mortality costs. The interest-free loans do not constitute taxable compensation to the employee.

EMPLOYEE STOCK OPTION PLAN

In employee stock option plans, the employer grants to the employee a right (option) to purchase a fixed number of shares of the employer's stock for a set price (exercise price) during a specified period of time. The purpose of granting such stock options to employees is to align executive compensation to stock performance more closely. The form of such options is either nonqualified stock options (NQSOs) or incentive stock options (ISOs). The NQSO is taxable to the recipient at the time of exercise to the extent of the difference between the fair market value of the stock and the exercise price as ordinary W-2 income. The exercise of ISOs does not create taxable income, as with NQSOs. There is income, however, for alternative minimum tax purposes created upon the exercise of the ISO. When employees exercise numerous ISOs, it may cause them to pay an alternative minimum tax. In addition, the shares that are acquired through the ISO exercise cannot be sold before one year from the date of exercise or two years from the date of grant. If this holding period is satisfied, the gain upon the sale of the ISO shares will be long-term capital gains; otherwise, the income will be ordinary. Therefore, ISOs provide some important advantages to the employees, but also have certain restrictions on the number that can be granted and when the shares can be sold.

THE FINANCIAL PLANNER'S ROLE IN RETIREMENT PLANNING

The financial planner's role in retirement planning is to assist clients in the accomplishment of their retirement goals. Retirement plans have many tax advantages, business benefits, and other advantages. Financial planners must be able to identify the objectives of the client and assist the client in choosing a retirement plan that meets those objectives. Some examples of common goals and possible choices in retirement plans are detailed in Exhibit 19.12.

EXHIBIT 19.12: COMMON GOALS AND POSSIBLE CHOICES IN RETIREMENT PLANS

COMMON GOALS	POSSIBLE RETIREMENT PLANS
To implement a simple, inexpensive plan that allows for flexible employer contributions.	Profit-sharing plan or SEP *Best Choice* - SEP
To allow employees to defer income.	401(k) Plan, SIMPLE, 403(b), or Thrift Plan *Best Choice* - 401(k) or 403(b)
To reduce turnover.	*Best Choice* - Plan with graduated vesting
To minimize employer contribution.	*Best Choice* - 401(k) or 403(b)
To guarantee employee pension.	Defined-benefit plan

A full discussion of goals and objectives and the matching of plans to those goals are beyond the scope of a fundamentals textbook. However, such plan selection is usually covered extensively in a retirement planning course.

When do you recommend a qualified plan over a non-qualified plan and vice versa?

Prior to proposing a qualified or a non-qualified plan to a client we use a very detailed process for gathering client information. Our concerns are numerous, but we focus in three primary areas of concerns: does the client have a will? does the client have an emergency fund? has the client resolved their risk exposure? After making these determinations we advise and review the tax laws with our clients to determine the need for pre-tax and tax deferred vehicles, such as retirement plans. We then move our clients on to tax deferred investments (non-qualified plans; no load annuities) and then to the mainstream of investing.

What characteristics of a qualified plan do you find most appealing?

By far the most interesting of all plans are the profit sharing/401(k) plans. From a planning standpoint, it allows the planner to offer the business owner a great deal of flexibility. The discretionary aspect of the plans provides the owner the flexibility to deal with the uncertainty of the business environment. However, its design permits the business owner the opportunity to take advantage of the plan's intrinsic benefits provided in the tax code.

Do you find that corporate clients are hesitant to fund a retirement plan for employees because they would rather direct all the funds to themselves, or do many of your corporate clients seem concerned about their employees' retirement future?

The majority of our clients have a concern for their employees. The concern is based more on the retention aspect rather than from a retirement point of view. As far as directing all the funds to themselves; if the plan is designed correctly the business owner will benefit. The tax savings alone is easily demonstrated and when combined with the long term savings on a pre-tax and a tax deferred basis, the benefits become obvious to the business owner.

What types of non-qualified plans do you recommend, and when are they useful?

The type of non-qualified plan/top-heavy plans depend on what we are trying to accomplish. Since all of these plans are designed to carve out a certain group of executives from the overall population of the corporation there are specific questions to ask. Is the employer tying to attract and retain qualified executives? Does the key executive want to maximize income tax deferral and tax-deferred savings? Is the employer attempting to provide key people parity with regard to the percentages of allowed deferred compensation? Does the employer want to prevent competition by key people after their departure from the company? In any case, whether it is a salary reduction or an employee bonus contribution the prevention of constructive receipt by design must be a vital party of the plan in order for it to be considered a non-qualified plan. The complexity of tax-deferred retirement plan rules under the code and ERISA do not apply to non-qualified plans, thus making them less burdensome and greatly simplified.

How do you recommend individuals receive distributions from 401(k) plans and other tax-deferred distributions?

One of our biggest complaints is that the government has provided retirement incentives for employers to provide to their employees without providing any counseling prior to their retirement. With the risk of employees outliving their money there must be in place alternatives in order to avoid these consequences.

Much of the problem could be resolved by having easier access to annuity type services to insure that these funds will provide a guarantee payment for life. It is basically up to the government and the insurance companies to step up to the plate and recognize that this problem exists.

A. PERRY HUBBS II, MBA, CFP™

DISCUSSION QUESTIONS

1. What is a qualified retirement plan?
2. What are the advantages of a qualified retirement plan and what are its disadvantages?
3. What is vesting?
4. What are the two accepted vesting schedules?
5. Why were qualified retirement plans created?
6. What are the benefits of tax deferral in a qualified retirement plan and how can they be calculated?
7. What are the different types of qualified retirement plans?
8. How do pension plans and profit-sharing plans differ?
9. How do defined-benefit plans and defined-contribution plans differ?
10. How do noncontributory plans and contributory plans differ?
11. What is a 401(k) plan and how does it operate?
12. How do Keogh plans and corporate plans differ?
13. What are some examples of tax-advantaged, but nonqualified, retirement plans?
14. What are IRAs, SEPs, SIMPLEs, and 403(b) plans?
15. How are distributions from qualified retirement plans and other tax-advantaged retirement plans the same and how do they differ?
16. What is a nonqualified plan and what are some examples of this type of plan?
17. Why are nonqualified plans useful to employers?
18. Which qualified retirement plans can be integrated with Social Security?
19. Which qualified retirement plans permit in-service withdrawals?
20. Which qualified retirement plans generally have loan provisions?
21. Which qualified retirement plans require immediate vesting of employer contributions?

EXERCISES

1. Shawna, a 73-year-old single taxpayer, retired two years ago and is receiving a pension of $700 per month from her previous employer's qualified pension plan. She recently started a new job with a discount retail outlet that has no pension plan. She will receive $12,000 in compensation from her current job, as well as the $8,400 from her pension. How much can she contribute to a deductible IRA this year?

2. Which of the following individuals can contribute to a deductible IRA in the current year?

Person	Marital Status	AGI	Covered by Pension Plan?
Larry	Single	$ 32,000	Yes
Mark	Married	$ 87,000	No
Lee Anne	Single	$ 56,000	No
Dennis	Married	$120,000	Yes

3. Tom and Denise are married and filed a joint income tax return for the tax year 2001. Tom earned a salary of $70,000 that year and was covered by his employer's pension plan. Tom and Denise earned interest of $5,000 in 2001 on their joint savings account. Denise is not employed, and the couple had no other income. What amount could Tom and Den-

ise contribute to IRAs for the year 2001 to take advantage of their maximum allowable IRA deduction on their 2001 tax return?

4. Evan and Jody, both age 52, are married and filed a joint income tax return for the year 2001. Their 2001 adjusted gross income was $100,000. The couple had no other income and neither spouse was covered by an employer-sponsored pension plan. What amount could Evan and Jody contribute to IRAs for 2001 to take advantage of their maximum allowable IRA deduction on their 2001 tax return?

5. Darlene and Rick are married and file a joint income tax return. They are both covered by a qualified retirement plan. Their 2001 adjusted gross income was $85,000. The couple had no other income. What amount could Darlene and Rick contribute to a Roth IRA this year?

6. In January of the current year, Phil Black (age 47) took a premature distribution from a rollover IRA in the amount of $500,000, leaving him a balance in his IRA of $1,000,000. On October 31 of the current year, Phil died with the IRA account balance of $1,200,000. Which penalty or penalties will apply to Phil as a result of these facts?

7. Which of the following persons could be classified as highly compensated for the current year?
   ▲ David, a 1 percent owner who made $150,000 in the previous year.
   ▲ Jimmy, a 6 percent owner who made $28,000 in the previous year.
   ▲ Mariette, an officer who made $84,000 in the previous year who is the 25th highest paid employee of 100 employees.
   ▲ Cassie, who made $70,000 in the previous year and is in the top 20 percent of paid employees.

8. The deductible contribution to a defined contribution qualified pension plan on behalf of Ann, a self-employed individual whose income from self-employment is $25,000 and whose social security taxes are $3,825 is limited to what dollar amount?

9. Refer back to the above exercise concerning Ann, the self-employed person. What is the maximum Ann could contribute to a profit-sharing plan?

10. Robbins, Inc., a regular C Corporation, is considering the adoption of a qualified retirement plan. The company has had fluctuating cash flows in the recent past and such fluctuations are expected to continue. The average age of non-owner employees is 24 and the average number of years of service is 3 with the high being 4 and the low 1. Approximately 25 percent of the 12 person labor force turns over each year. The 2 owners receive about 2/3 of the total covered compensation. Which is the most appropriate vesting schedule for Robbins, Inc.?

11. What is the minimum number of employees that must be covered in a defined benefit plan to conform to ERISA requirements for a company having 100 eligible employees?

PROBLEMS

1. The XYZ Company has 2 employees - John, who earns $300,000 annually and his assistant, Kim, age 26 who has worked for John for 4 years. Kim makes $20,000. XYZ has a contributing pension plan using graded vesting. Kim's account balance reflects the following:

Contributions		Earnings from Contributions		Kim's Total Balance
Employee	Employer	Employee	Employer	
$1,500	$2,000	$800	$1,200	$5,500

Reviewing the account and assuming that Kim terminated employment when the account balance was as above after 4 years of employment, how much could she take with her, plan permitting?

2. Yarbrough, Inc. has only the following employees, compensation, and other employer characteristics for years 2000 and 2001. Yarbrough, Inc. has an employer contributing plan with no employee contributions and uses cliff vesting.

	Compensation	Ownership Interest	Years of Service	Plan Account Balance*
A	$250,000	5%	2	$20,000
B	$180,000	8%	10	$300,000
C	$100,000	6%	8	$180,000
D	$60,000	1%	3	$27,000
E	$40,000	0%	2	$7,500
				*12/31/01

Please answer all of the following questions:

▲   What is the total covered compensation for 2001 and 2002 (if same compensation as 2001)?

▲   What would be the maximum profit-sharing contribution Yarbrough could make in 2001 and 2002?

▲   Which of the employees is highly compensated?

▲   Is the plan top heavy?

▲   If D and E quit in January 2002, how much do they take with them, plan permitting?

Estate Planning
in**BRIEF**→

- Estate planning process
- Estate planning objectives
- Wills
- Durable powers of attorney
- Advanced medical directives
- Annual exclusion
- Credit equivalency

- Lifetime taxable gifts
- Qualified transfers
- Use of credit equivalency
- Probate

- Gross estate
- Adjusted gross estate
- Marital deduction
- Charitable deduction
- Taxable estate
- Use of trusts

Estate Planning

Risks

- Inadequate documents
- Improper or inadequate life insurance
- Property transfers do not meet goals
- Property transfers are not cost effective
- Improper trustee/executor selection
- Excessive tax burden

Data Collection

- Wills
- Durable powers
- Advanced medical directives
- Balance sheet
- Life insurance policies
- Trusts
- Gift tax returns
- Property and titling
- Transfer goals

Goals

- Efficient and effective transfer of assets during life or at death

Data Analysis

- Wills
- Powers of attorney
- Advanced medical directives
- Gross estate - current and projected
- Current property titling
- Prior gift tax returns
- Current/projected estate tax liability
- Probate estate
- Trusts
- Liquidity needs

CHAPTER 20

Introduction to Estates

LEARNING OBJECTIVES:

After learning the material in this chapter, you will be able to:

1. Define estate planning and describe the estate planning process.

2. Discuss the objectives of and the benefits derived from planning an estate.

3. Explain the risks of failing to plan for estate transfer.

4. Identify the steps in the estate planning process.

5. List the types of client information necessary to begin and complete the estate planning process.

6. Identify the most common estate transfer objectives.

7. Discuss the types of property ownership interests and how each interest is transferred at death.

8. Identify and describe the basic essential estate planning documents.

9. Describe the probate process and list its advantages and disadvantages.

BASICS OF ESTATE PLANNING

This chapter and the next present the goals of efficient and effective wealth transfer, during life or at death, and the risks that are associated with such transfers. When a personal financial planner begins the estate planning process for a client, certain personal and financial data are collected from the client and analyses of that data are performed. Client interest in the estate planning process generally begins at or near the beginning of the distribution/gifting phase of the client's personal lifecycle. However, all clients need to have at least basic documents (e.g., will, durable power of health care, and advanced medical directives) and provisions in the will for the care of minor children.

ESTATE PLANNING REFORM

The Economic Growth and Tax Relief Reconciliation Act of 2001 (herein referred to as TRA 2001) was signed by President George W. Bush in June of 2001 providing a $1.35 trillion tax cut. While the estate and generation skipping transfer tax are repealed in 2010, the repeal is phased in over a nine year period (2001 - 2009). The new law also allows the current (2001) estate tax rules, rates, and exemptions to come back in force in 2011. Therefore, it is essential that the financial planner be familiar with the changing laws. This chapter presents the applicable provisions prior to TRA 2001 as well as after.

ESTATE PLANNING DEFINED

Estate planning may be broadly defined as the process of accumulation, management, conservation, and transfer of wealth considering legal, tax, and personal objectives. It is financial planning for our inevitable death. The goal of estate planning is the effective and efficient transfer of assets. An effective transfer occurs when the client's assets are transferred to the person or institution intended by the client. An efficient transfer occurs when wealth transfer costs are minimized consistent with the greatest assurance of effectiveness. Some estate planning experts define the process more narrowly to include only conservation and transfer, ignoring the accumulation factor in the broad definition above.

THE OBJECTIVES OF ESTATE PLANNING

Common objectives of estate planning include transferring (distributing) property to particular persons or entities consistent with client wishes; minimizing all taxes (income, gift, estate, state inheritance, and generation-skipping taxes); minimizing the transaction costs associated with the transfer (costs of documents, lawyers, and the legal probate process); and providing liquidity to the estate of the decedent at the time of death to pay for costs which commonly arise, such as taxes, funeral expenses, and final medical costs.

EXHIBIT 20.1: ESTATE PLANNING OBJECTIVES

- ▲ Fulfill client's property transfer wishes.
- ▲ Minimize taxes.
- ▲ Minimize costs.
- ▲ Provide needed liquidity.

Everyone needs a basic estate plan to provide for health care and property decisions and for transferring their property according to their wishes. An important estate planning objective is to assure that the decedent's property is received by the person, persons, or entities that the client desires.

The process of estate planning causes us to face the reality of our inherent mortality. Clients tend to delay making estate-planning decisions for both emotional and practical reasons. Some find contemplating their own mortality too morbid a task. Others are simply unaware of the total fair market value of their assets and may lack sufficient knowledge about the associated costs of transfer taxes. Still others may not realize that alternative transfer devices exist, and that each alternative carries its own cost. Whatever the reason, failing to plan for estate transfer presents clients with various risks.

Risks associated with failing to plan for estate transfer include the transfer of property contrary to the client's wishes; insufficient financial provision for the client's family; and liquidity problems at the time of death. Any of these risks could be catastrophic to the decedent's **heirs** and family. For example, a decedent's assets could be tied up in probate court for an indefinite period of time if that person has no will or has competing and conflicting heirs. Another consideration in estate planning is the excessively high transfer tax rates. The unified gift and estate taxation scheme is a progressive tax scheme and rises to 55 percent of the taxable estate transferred for estates exceeding three million dollars (50 percent or less after 2001).

heir - one who inherits; beneficiary

EXHIBIT 20.2: RISKS IN FAILING TO PLAN AN ESTATE

▲ Client's property transfer wishes go unfulfilled.
▲ Taxes are excessive.
▲ Transfer costs are excessive.
▲ Client's family not properly provided for.
▲ Insufficient liquidity to cover client's debts.

THE ESTATE PLANNING TEAM

The estate planning team consists of the attorney, accountant, life insurance consultant, trust officer, and financial planner. The role of the professional financial planner is to help integrate the work of the estate planning team in developing the overall estate plan.

The estate planning process is complex and somewhat confusing. A CPA is usually involved as a member of the estate planning team because the process requires the identification of assets, the calculation of the related adjusted tax basis, and other tax issues. An insurance specialist, such as a CLU or ChFC, is usually involved to help assure liquidity at death and protection for the client from the risks of untimely death. A licensed attorney is almost always a part of the team, as the process requires drafting numerous legal documents. The financial planner may serve as the team captain and assist in data collection, analysis, and investment decisions. While each member of the planning team may individually be an estate expert, each specialty brings with it a particular and unique perspective, the combination of which is more likely to produce a better result for the client. The financial planner, unless a licensed attorney, should be careful not to engage in any act that could be found to be the unauthorized practice of law.

THE ESTATE PLANNING PROCESS

There are eight basic steps to the estate planning process:

1. Gather client information, including the client's current financial statements.
2. Establish the client's transfer objectives, including family and charitable objectives.
3. Define any problem areas, such as the disposition of assets, liquidity issues, excessive taxes or costs, and other situational needs, such as disability of an identified heir.
4. Determine the estate liquidity needs now and at five-year intervals for the life expectancy of the transferor, including estate transfer costs.
5. Establish priorities for all client objectives.
6. Develop a comprehensive plan of transfer consistent with all information and objectives.
7. Implement the estate plan.
8. Review the estate plan periodically, and update the plan when necessary (especially for changes in family situations).

Steps 1 and 2 are briefly discussed below. An estate-planning course would cover Steps 3 through 8.

COLLECTING CLIENT INFORMATION AND DEFINING TRANSFER OBJECTIVES

The collection of information is essential to gain a complete financial and family picture of the client and to assist the client in identifying financial risks. Information about prospective heirs and legatees needs to be collected to properly arrange for any transfer that the client wants to make.

To begin the estate planning process, the planner should collect:

▲ Current financial statements.
▲ Family information (that is, parents, children, ages, health).
▲ A detailed list of assets and liabilities, including the fair market value, adjusted taxable basis, and expected growth rate for all assets, how title is held, and the date acquired.
▲ Copies of medical and disability insurance policies.
▲ Copies of all life insurance policies in force identifying the ownership of each policy, the named insured, and the designated beneficiaries.
▲ Copies of annuity contracts.
▲ Copies of wills and trusts.
▲ Identification of **powers of attorney** and **general powers of appointment**.
▲ Copies of all previously filed income tax and gift tax returns (as available).
▲ Identification of assets previously gifted.
▲ Other pertinent information.

Once client and family information is collected, the process of determining the transfer objectives can be completed. Usually the most important objective of the client is to transfer assets as the client wishes. Secondly, the client generally wishes to avoid the shrinkage of the estate resulting from costs associated with the transfer. Exhibit 20.3 provides a list of common transfer objectives.

power of attorney - the right given to another (agent) to act in the place of the giver (principal). Such right may be limited or general and may be durable or nondurable

general power of appointment - allows a terminable interest to be passed to a surviving spouse and the property to still qualify for the marital deduction

EXHIBIT 20.3: COMMON TRANSFER OBJECTIVES

- ▲ Minimizing estate and transfer taxes to maximize the assets received by heirs.

- ▲ Avoiding the probate process.

- ▲ Using lifetime transfers – gifts.

- ▲ Meeting liquidity needs at death.

- ▲ Planning for children.

- ▲ Planning for the incapacity of the transferor.

- ▲ Providing for the needs of the surviving spouse of the transferor.

- ▲ Fulfilling charitable intentions of the transferor.

BASIC DOCUMENTS INCLUDED IN AN ESTATE PLAN

The basic documents used in estate planning include wills, living wills or medical directives, durable powers of attorney for health care or property, and side letters.

WILLS

A **will** is a legal document that provides the testator, or will maker, the opportunity to control the distribution of property and avoid the state's intestacy law distribution scheme. In general, a will is valid when the will maker is at least 18 years old or an emancipated minor, and when the will maker is "of sound mind," that is, of **testamentary capacity**. The "sound mind" rules are not as rigorous as those rules that are required to form contracts. In other words, a person who may not have the legal capacity to form a contract may have sufficient legal capacity to make a will to transfer his/her assets.

Intestacy

To die "**intestate**" is to die without a valid will. In such a case, the state directs how the decedent's property will be distributed by creating a hypothetical will according to the state's **intestacy laws**. Just as "one size does <u>not</u> fit all," the intestacy laws are not likely to distribute property the way every person would wish, had they written their own will. There are possible adverse consequences of intestacy. In certain states, a spouse's share of the decedent's estate will be equal to a child's. For example, the surviving spouse's share with one child might be one-half, but with nine children it will be one-tenth. Certain states provide that a spouse's share is only a life estate with the true owner being the children. When there are no children, the surviving spouse may be forced to share with the deceased spouse's parents or brothers and sisters. Although each child's needs may be quite different, children may be treated equally, and, therefore, not necessarily equitably. Intestacy may require the appointment of an **administrator** who will usually have to furnish a surety bond, thereby raising the costs of administration. The court, not the decedent, will select any administrator of the estate.

will - a legal document used in estate planning that provides the testator, or will maker, the opportunity to control the distribution of property and avoid the state's intestacy law distribution scheme

testamentary capacity - having the mental capability to make a will to transfer assets; being of sound mind

intestate - to die without a valid will

intestacy laws - state laws that direct how a decedent's property will be distributed when the decedent dies without a will

administrator - in the event a decedent dies intestate, (without a valid will) or where an executor cannot be appointed by the probate court, the court appoints an administrator with powers called letters of administration which enable the administrator to carry out duties set down in the laws of intestacy

Types of Wills

holographic wills -
handwritten will dated
and signed by the testator

There are three types of wills: holographic, oral/noncupative, and statutory.

- ▲ **Holographic wills** are handwritten. The material provisions of the will are in the testator's handwriting. The will is dated and signed by the testator, and does not need to be witnessed. Holographic wills are valid in most states.

oral/noncupative will -
dying declarations made
before sufficient witnesses

- ▲ **Oral (Noncupative)** wills are dying declarations made before sufficient witnesses. In some states, oral/noncupative wills may only be able to pass personal property, not real property. The use of oral/noncupative wills is fairly restricted and is illegal in some states.

statutory will - generally
drawn by an attorney,
signed in the presence of
witnesses, complying with
the statutes for wills of the
domiciliary state

- ▲ **Statutory wills** are generally drawn by an attorney, complying with the statutes for wills of the domiciliary state. They are usually signed in the presence of two witnesses. An heir who is a legatee (a person who inherits by will) usually cannot be a valid witness.

Common Clauses

While all wills are different, there are certain clauses that appear in almost all wills. Common clauses that are generally found in even the simplest will include:

- ▲ An introductory clause to identify the testator.
- ▲ The establishment of the testator's domicile and residence.
- ▲ A declaration that this is the last will and testament of the testator.
- ▲ A revocation of all prior wills and codicils by the testator.
- ▲ The identification and selection of the executor/executrix and successor executor/executrix by the testator.

residuary clause - a general
provision in a will that
provides for the transfer of
the balance of any assets
not specifically mentioned
in the will to someone or
to some institution named
by the testator

- ▲ A directive for the payment of debts clause.
- ▲ A directive for the payment of taxes clause.
- ▲ A disposition of tangible personal property clause.
- ▲ A disposition of real estate clause (that is, residence).
- ▲ Clauses regarding specific bequests of intangibles and cash.
- ▲ A **residuary clause** (the transfer of the balance of any other assets to someone or to some institution). (Note that the failure to have a residuary clause will result in the risk of having intestate assets [that is, assets accumulated after the will was prepared] which pass through probate. Also, taxes will be paid from the residuary unless specifically directed otherwise.)

**simultaneous death
clause -** in the event that
both spouses die
simultaneously, this clause
provides an assumption
that one spouse
(predetermined)
predeceased the other
spouse

- ▲ An appointment and powers clause, naming fiduciaries, guardians, tutors, trustees, etc.
- ▲ A testator's signature clause.
- ▲ An attestation clause, or witness clause.
- ▲ A self-proving clause.

Other Clauses

survivorship clause -
provides that the
beneficiary must survive
the decedent for a specified
period in order to receive
the inheritance or bequest

More sophisticated wills often have additional clauses that dictate specific wishes regarding the handling of the estate. Additional clauses may include:

- ▲ A **simultaneous death clause** - In the event that both spouses die simultaneously, this clause provides an assumption of which spouse dies first.
- ▲ A **survivorship clause** - This clause provides that the beneficiary must survive the decedent for a specified period in order to receive the inheritance or bequest. This clause prevents

720

property from being included in two different estates in rapid succession. In order for transfers to qualify for the unlimited marital deduction, the survival period included in a survivorship clause for a spouse can be no longer than six months.

▲ A **disclaimer clause** - A disclaimer clause simply reminds the heir that disclaiming inheritances may be an effective tool in estate planning. A disclaimer allows property to pass from one party to another without gift tax consequences.

▲ A no-contest clause – This clause discourages heirs from contesting the will by substantially decreasing or eliminating their bequest if they file a formal contest to the will.

▲ A codicil - This document, which is separate from the will, amends a will (that is, where additional children are born after the original will is made).

disclaimer clause - a common clause in a decedent's will that allows property to pass from one party to another without gift tax consequences. It reminds the heir that disclaiming an inheritance may be an effective tool in estate planning

EXHIBIT 20.4: LAST WILL AND TESTAMENT OF JOHN F. KENNEDY, JR.

THE LAST WILL AND TESTAMENT OF JOHN F. KENNEDY, JR.

John F. Kennedy, Jr. planned to leave the bulk of his holdings to his wife, Caroline Bessette-Kennedy, or their children. But John and Caroline died together in a plane crash in July of 1999 without leaving any issue (children). Therefore, his property will go to the children of his sister, Caroline Kennedy Schlossberg. The bulk of his estate is left to the beneficiaries of a trust he established in 1983. Kennedy also left the scrimshaw set, or carved whale ivory set, once owned by his father to nephew John B.K. Schlossberg. Kennedy's cousin, Timothy P. Shriver was named executor of the will. Kennedy's estate is reportedly worth $100 million.

I, JOHN F. KENNEDY, JR., of New York, New York, make this my last will, hereby revoking all earlier wills and codicils. I do not by this will exercise any power of appointment.

FIRST: I give all my tangible property (as distinguished from money, securities and the like), wherever located, other than my scrimshaw set previously owned by my father, to my wife, Carolyn Bessette-Kennedy, if she is living on the thirtieth day after my death, or if not, by right of representation to my then living issue, or if none, by right of representation to the then living issue of my sister, Caroline Kennedy Schlossberg, or if none, to my said sister, Caroline, if she is then living. If I am survived by issue, I leave this scrimshaw set to said wife, Carolyn, if she is then living, or if not, by right of representation, to my then living issue. If I am not survived by issue, I give said scrimshaw set to my nephew John B.K. Schlossberg, if he is then living, or if not, by right of representation to the then living issue of my said sister, Caroline, or if none, to my said sister Caroline, if she is then living. I hope that whoever receives my tangible personal property will dispose of certain items of it in accordance with my wishes, however made unknown, but I impose no trust, condition or enforceable obligation of any kind in this regard. **SECOND**: I give and devise all my interest in my cooperative apartment located at 20-26 Moore Street, Apartment 9E, in said New York, including all my shares therein and any proprietary leases with respect thereto, to my said wife, Carolyn, if she is living on the thirtieth day after my death.

THIRD: If no issue of mine survive me, I give and devise all my interests in real estate, wherever located, that I own as tenants in common with my said sister, Caroline, or as tenants in common with any of her issue, by right of representation to Caroline's issue who are living on the thirtieth day after my death, or if none, to my said sister Caroline, if she is then living. References in this Article THIRD to "real estate" include shares in cooperative apartments and proprietary leases with respect thereto.

FOURTH: I give and devise the residue of all the property, of whatever kind and wherever located, that I own at my death to the then trustees of the John F. Kennedy Jr. 1983 Trust established October 13, 1983 by me, as Donor, of which John T. Fallon, of Weston, Massachusetts, and I are currently the trustees (the "1983 Trust"), to be added to the principal of the 1983 Trust and administered in accordance with the provisions thereof, as amended by a First Amendment dated April 9, 1987 and by a Second Amendment and Complete Restatement dated earlier this day, and as from time to hereafter further amended whether before or after my death. I have provided in the 1983 Trust for my children and more remote issue and for the method of paying all federal and state taxes in the nature of estate, inheritance, succession and like taxes occasioned by my death.

FIFTH: I appoint my wife, Carolyn Bessette-Kennedy, as guardian of each child of our marriage during minority. No guardian appointed in this will or a codicil need furnish any surety on any official bond.

SIXTH: I name my cousin Anthony Stanislaus Radziwill as my executor; and if for any reason, he fails to qualify or ceases to serve in that capacity, I name my cousin Timothy P. Shriver as my executor in his place. References in this will or a codicil to my "executor" mean the one or more executors (or administrators with this will annexed) for the time being in office. No executor or a codicil need furnish any surety on any official bond. In any proceeding for the allowance of an account of my executor, I request the Court to dispense with the appointment of a guardian ad litem to represent any person or interest. I direct that in any proceeding relating to my estate, service of process upon any person under a disability shall not made when another person not under a disability is a party to the proceeding and has the same interest as the person under the disability.

SEVENTH: In addition to other powers, my executor shall have power from time to time at discretion and without license of court: To retain, and to invest and reinvest in, any kind or amount of property; to vote and exercise other rights of security holders; to make such elections for federal and state estate, gift, income and generation-skipping transfer tax purposes as my executor may deem advisable; to compromise or admit to arbitration any matters in dispute; to borrow money, and to sell, mortgage, pledge, exchange, lease and contract with respect to any real or personal property, all without notice to any beneficiary and in such manner, for such consideration and on such terms as to credit or otherwise as my executor may deem advisable, whether or not the effect thereof extends beyond the period settling my estate; and in distributing my estate, to allot property, whether real or personal, at then current values, in lieu of cash.

Source: Courtroom Television Network, LLC

EXHIBIT 20.5: LAST WILL AND TESTAMENT OF MARILYN MONROE

THE WILL OF MARILYN MONROE

The legendary sex symbol, who tragically committed suicide in 1962, left most of her fortune to her friends and family.

I, MARILYN MONROE, do make, publish and declare this to be my Last Will and Testament.

FIRST: I hereby revoke all former Wills and Codicils by me made.

SECOND: I direct my Executor, hereinafter named, to pay all of my just debts, funeral expenses and testamentary charges as soon after my death as can conveniently be done.

THIRD: I direct that all succession, estate or inheritance taxes which may be levied against my estate and/or against any legacies and/or devises hereinafter set forth shall be paid out of my residuary estate.

FOURTH: (a) I give and bequeath to BERNICE MIRACLE, should she survive me, the sum of $10,000.00.

(b) I give and bequeath to MAY REIS, should she survive me, the sum of $10,000.00.

(c) I give and bequeath to NORMAN and HEDDA ROSTEN, or to the survivor of them, or if they should both predecease me, then to their daughter, PATRICIA ROSTEN, the sum of $5,000.00, it being my wish that such sum be used for the education of PATRICIA ROSTEN.

(d) I give and bequeath all of my personal effects and clothing to LEE STRASBERG, or if he should predecease me, then to my Executor hereinafter named, it being my desire that he distribute these, in his sole discretion, among my friends, colleagues and those to whom I am devoted.

FIFTH: I give and bequeath to my Trustee, hereinafter named, the sum of $100,000.00, in Trust, for the following uses and purposes:

(a) To hold, manage, invest and reinvest the said property and to receive and collect the income therefrom.

(b) To pay the net income therefrom, together with such amounts of principal as shall be necessary to provide $5,000.00 per annum, in equal quarterly installments, for the maintenance and support of my mother, GLADYS BAKER, during her lifetime.

(c) To pay the net income therefrom, together with such amounts of principal as shall be necessary to provide $2,500.00 per annum, in equal quarterly installments, for the maintenance and support of MRS. MICHAEL CHEKHOV during her lifetime.

(d) Upon the death of the survivor between my mother, GLADYS BAKER, and MRS. MICHAEL CHEKHOV to pay over the principal remaining in the Trust, together with any accumulated income, to DR. MARIANNE KRIS to be used by her for the furtherance of the work of such psychiatric institutions or groups as she shall elect.

SIXTH: All the rest, residue and remainder of my estate, both real and personal, of whatsoever nature and wheresoever situate, of which I shall die seized or possessed or to which I shall be in any way entitled, or over which I shall possess any power of appointment by Will at the time of my death, including any lapsed legacies, I give, devise and bequeath as follows:

(a) to MAY REIS the sum of $40,000.00 or 25% of the total remainder of my estate, whichever shall be the lesser,

(b) To DR. MARIANNE KRIS 25% of the balance thereof, to be used by her as set forth in ARTICLE FIFTH (d) of this my Last Will and Testament.

(c) To LEE STRASBERG the entire remaining balance.

SEVENTH: I nominate, constitute and appoint AARON R. FROSCH Executor of this my Last Will and Testament. In the event that he should die or fail to qualify, or resign or for any other reason be unable to act, I nominate, constitute and appoint L. ARNOLD WEISSBERGER in his place and stead.

EIGHTH: I nominate, constitute and appoint AARON R. FROSCH Trustee under this my Last Will and Testament. In the event he should die or fail to qualify, or resign or for any other reason be unable to act, I nominate, constitute and appoint L. Arnold Weissberger in his place and stead.

Marilyn Monroe (L.S.)

SIGNED, SEALED, PUBLISHED and DECLARED by MARILYN MONROE, the Testatrix above named, as and for her Last Will and Testament, in our presence and we, at her request and in her presence and in the presence of each other, have hereunto subscribed our names as witnesses this 14th day of January, One Thousand Nine Hundred Sixty-One

Source: Courtroom Television Network, LLC

attorney-in-fact - the person designated by the principal in a power of attorney to act in place of the principal on the principal's behalf

principal - in a power of attorney document, the person (power giver) who designates another person or persons to act as his attorney-in-fact

POWER OF ATTORNEY

People frequently need another trusted person to make decisions for them regarding property or to make health care decisions for them under certain circumstances. A power of attorney is the legal document that allows the trusted person to act in one's place. It gives the right to one person, the **attorney-in-fact** (the power holder), to act in the place of the other person, the **principal** (power giver). A power of attorney may be very broad or very specific. The broadest power a person can give another is a general power of attorney or appointment. Such a power grants to the holder the power to do anything the giver could have done, including the power to make gifts to the holder or pay the holder's creditors. A special or limited power of attorney or appointment may be extremely narrow (that is, I give you the power to pay my bills) or very broad (that is, You can do anything I can do, except appoint my assets to yourself, your creditors, your heirs, or their creditors). All powers are revocable by the giver and all powers cease at the death of giver. A durability feature should be included if the giver intends that the power survive the incapacity or disability of the giver. The principal (the power giver) must be 18 years old and legally competent. An unlimited power-to-appoint-to-oneself may result in inclusion in the gross estate the assets over which one has power, were the power holder to die before the principal.

724

EXHIBIT 20.6: POWER OF ATTORNEY

UNITED STATES OF AMERICA
STATE OF LOUISIANA
PARISH OF JEFFERSON

Be it known, that on this _____day of _____, in the year _____:

1. Before me, the undersigned authority, a Notary Public duly commissioned and qualified in and for the State and Parish set forth above, therein residing, and in the presence of the undersigned competent witnesses, personally came and appeared: _____ a person of the full age of majority and domiciled in St. Rose, Louisiana (the "Principal"), who declared that the Principal appoints his children,_____(the "Agent," whether one or more, with either authorized to act alone), as the Principal's true and lawful agent and attorney-in-fact, general and special, granting unto the Agent full power and authority for the Principal and in the Principal's name and behalf, and to the Principal's use, to conduct, manage and transact all of the Principal's affairs, business, concerns and matters of whatever nature or kind, without any reservation whatsoever, except as hereinafter specifically set forth and subject to the following effective date. The Power of Attorney shall not become effective unless and until a personal physician of the Principal certifies in writing that the Principal is mentally or physically incapable of administering her affairs. In furtherance of this general grant of authority to the Agent, but not in limitation thereof, the Principal specifically authorizes the Agent to perform all of the following acts and exercise all of the following powers for the Principal and in the Principal's name.

2. To open all letters or correspondence addressed to the Principal and answer them.

3. To open accounts with any bank, brokerage or other entity; to deposit funds (whether represented by cash, checks or otherwise) in any account maintained by or for the Principal with any bank or other entity; to endorse all checks, bills of exchange and other instruments; to withdraw funds from any account maintained by the Principal with any bank or other person; to sign checks, bills or exchange and other instruments; to deposit any obligation with any bank or other entity for collection.

4. To represent the Principal in the Principal's capacity as a creditor or obligee of any person; to collect any funds or things owed the Principal by any person; and to attend any meeting of creditors in which the Principal may be interested and to vote in the Principal's name on all matters that may be submitted to the meeting.

5. To represent the Principal in the Principal's capacity as a stockholder of any corporation, partner in any partnership, beneficiary of any trust or member of any association or entity or as a security holder thereof. This authority shall include (but is not limited to) the authority to execute consent agreements and to attend any meetings of stockholders, partners, members, or beneficiaries or security holders of any corporation, partnership, association, trust or entity and to agree or vote (or execute proxies in favor of others to agree or vote) in the name of the Principal on all questions, including merger, sale, consolidation, any type of reorganization or matters.

6. To borrow any amounts of money for the Principal and in the Principal's name upon such terms and conditions as the Agent may in the Agent's sole discretion deem appropriate.

7. To sell, exchange, donate, transfer, or convey any property, whether immovable (real), movable (personal), tangible or intangible or corporeal or incorporeal, including stocks, bonds, notes, bills or any other security, belonging to the Principal or any interest therein and to receive the price or other consideration thereof.

8. To make gifts or other gratuitous transfers of any property belonging to the Principal either outright or in trust (including the forgiveness of debt), to any of the Principal's descendants or to the agent.

9. To purchase, acquire by exchange or otherwise acquire any property for and in the name of the Principal and to make payment therefore out of the Principal's funds or assets.

10. To create servitudes, building restrictions, other real rights, easements and covenants of any kind that burden, benefit or otherwise affect any property of the Principal.

11. To accept donations.

12. To lease, rent, let or hire (as lessor) any property belonging to the Principal.

13. To lease, rent, hire or let (as lessee) any property.

14. To encumber, mortgage, pledge, pawn or otherwise grant any security interest in any property of the Principal, whether to secure obligations of the Principal or any other person or entity.

15. To grant or convey oil, gas, and other mineral leases, net profits interests, production payments, royalty interests, mineral servitudes and other interests in oil, gas and any other minerals on or under any property of the Principal; to sign division orders and transfer orders; to grant rights-of-way and easements; and otherwise to execute documents incident to the exploration for oil, gas or other minerals on or underlying property of the Principal.

16. To enter into transactions pursuant to which the Principal is lessee, grantee or vendee under or of any oil, gas or mineral lease, net profits interest, production payment, royalty deed, mineral servitude or any other interest in oil, gas or other minerals.

17. To undertake any obligations for the Principal, to act for the Principal in agreeing to guarantee any obligations of others or agreeing to defend and indemnify any person or entity against any claims, obligations or liabilities.

18. To act for the Principal and be the Principal's substitute in all cases in which the Principal may be appointed the agent or attorney of others.

19. To refer matters to arbitration and to initiate, prosecute, defend and otherwise represent the Principal in any judicial or arbitration proceeding (whether as plaintiff or defendant) and to settle and compromise any claim, dispute or proceeding; to apply for and obtain any attachments, sequestrations, injunctions, and appeals, give the requisite security, and sign the necessary bonds.

20. To represent the Principal in connection with any succession or estate in which the Principal may be or become interested (whether as heir, legatee, creditor, executor, administrator or otherwise), including the execution of any acceptance or renunciation thereof on the Principal's behalf; to apply for the administration thereof, and to demand, obtain and execute all orders and decrees as the Agent may deem proper; to settle, compromise, and liquidate the Principal's interest therein; and to receive and receipt for all property to which Principal may be entitled in respect of successions or estates.

21. To acknowledge any debt of the Principal.

22. To settle and compromise any dispute or matter involving the Principal.

23. To file any United States, State or other tax returns (including but not limited to income tax returns); to apply for extensions of time to file tax returns; and to represent the Principal in connection with any matter or dispute relating to United States, State or other taxes.

24. The Principal further authorizes and empowers the Agent to take any other action concerning the affairs, business or assets of the Principal as fully, completely and effectively and for all intents and purposes with the same validity as though the action had been expressly provided for herein and as though the Principal had taken the action in person.

25. The transactions entered into by the Agent for the Principal shall be on such terms and conditions as to payment and otherwise as the Agent may in the Agent's sole discretion determine.

26. The Agent is authorized to make, sign and execute in the name of the Principal all agreements, contracts, and instruments that may be necessary or convenient in the Agent's sole discretion to carry out transactions entered into by the Agent for the Principal or to enable the Agent fully to exercise the powers granted herein and to include therein any terms, conditions and provisions that the Agent shall deem appropriate and to bind the Principal thereby as fully as though each instrument had been signed by the Principal in person.

27. The agency created by this Power of Attorney shall be "durable" as provided by Louisiana Civil Code article 3027(B) and shall not be deemed revoked by the Principal's disability or incapacity.

28. The Principal agrees to ratify and confirm all actions that the Agent shall take pursuant to this Power of Attorney.

29. References herein to one gender shall be deemed to include the other whenever appropriate.

30. The term "property" means all kinds of property, whether movable, immovable, real, personal, mixed, corporeal, incorporeal, tangible or intangible. The term "entity" includes natural persons, corporations, partnerships, trusts, associations and any other form of legal entity and governmental and political organizations.

31. THUS DONE AND PASSED in multiple originals on the date first above written in the presence of the undersigned competent witnesses, who sign their names with the Principal and me, Notary, after reading of the whole.

WITNESSES:

_____   _____

Print Name:_____   Principal

_____

Print Name:_____

_____

Notary Public

DURABLE POWER OF ATTORNEY FOR HEALTH CARE OR PROPERTY

A specific form of power of attorney is a **durable power of attorney issued either for health care or for property**. These powers are frequently issued to separate persons or, in the case of property, a financial institution. The power of attorney for health care or property eliminates the necessity to petition a local court to appoint a guardian ad litem or conservator to make health care or property decisions for a person who is incapacitated. It provides for continuity in the management of affairs in the event of disability and/or incapacity. The power may be springing or immediately effective (non-springing). Generally, if the power is springing, the device must indicate that the power springs upon disability or incapacity and is not affected by subsequent disability or incapacity. The power is revocable by the principal. Durable powers of attorney are generally less expensive to set up and administer than a living trust or conservatorship. Durable powers of attorney can be abused, so the principal should give serious consideration to choosing the person to hold such power. The **durable feature** means the power survives incapacity and disability.

Note: A person possessing a durable power of attorney, in most cases, is not permitted to make gifts to himself or other family members (usually in conjunction with estate planning). If the power to gift to charitable or noncharitable donees is a desirable feature of the power of attorney, it should be separately and explicitly stated.

durable power of attorney issued either for health care or for property - a written document enabling one individual, the principal, to designate another person or persons to act as his or her "attorney-in-fact"

durable feature - the power survives incapacity and disability

EXHIBIT 20.7: MEDICAL POWER OF ATTORNEY

MEDICAL POWER OF ATTORNEY

1. BE IT KNOWN, that on this _____ day of _____, in the year Two Thousand:

2. BEFORE ME, the undersigned authority, a Notary Public duly commissioned and qualified in and for the State and Parish set forth above, therein residing, and in the presence of the undersigned competent witnesses, personally came and appeared:

   (The "Principal"), who after being duly sworn, declared that the Principal appoints his children, _____ (the "Agent", whether one or more, with either authorized to act alone), as the Principal's true and lawful agent and attorney-in-fact, granting unto the Agent full power and authority regarding the matters set forth below.

3. <u>Durability</u>. This agency is "durable" and shall not be deemed revoked by the Principal's disability or incapacity.

HEALTH CARE

4. The Principal grants unto the Agent full power and authority regarding the following health care matters that the Principal could exercise on the Principal's own behalf, if capable of doing so. The Principal specifically authorizes the Agent to:

   4.1 <u>Medical Records.</u> Have access to any medical information in any form regarding the Principal's physical condition, and to execute such consents as may be necessary to obtain such medical information.

   4.2 <u>Professionals.</u> Retain, compensate and discharge any health care professionals the Agent deems necessary to examine, evaluate or treat the Principal, whether for emergency, elective, recuperative, convalescent or other care.

   4.3 <u>Institutionalization.</u> Admit the Principal to any health care facility recommended by a qualified health care professional, whether for physical or mental care or treatment, and remove the Principal from such institution at any time, even if contrary to medical advice.

   4.4 <u>Treatment.</u> Consent on the Principal's behalf to tests, treatment, medication, surgery, organ transplant or other procedures, and to revoke that consent, even if contrary to medical advice.

   4.5 <u>Chemical Dependency.</u> Consent on the Principal's behalf to a course of treatment for chemical dependency, whether suspected or diagnosed, and to revoke such consent.

   4.6 <u>Pain Relief.</u> Consent on the Principal's behalf to pain relief procedures, even if they are unconventional or experimental, even if they risk addiction, injury or foreshortening the Principal's life.

   4.7 <u>Releases.</u> Release from liability any health care professional or institution that acts on the Principal's behalf in reliance on the Agent.

PERSONAL CARE

5. The Principal grants unto the Agent full power and authority regarding the following personal care matters that the Principal could act on the Principal's own behalf, if capable of doing so. The Principal specifically authorizes the Agent to:

   5.1 <u>Home Care.</u> Provide for the Principal's continued maintenance and support. As nearly as possible, the Principal expressly authorizes the Agent to maintain the Principal's accustomed standard of living. The Agent shall provide the Principal with a suitable place to live by maintaining the Principal in the Principal's family residence or apartment (home), paying principal, interest, taxes, insurance and repairs as necessary. The Agent may retain or discharge domestic servants, attendants, companions, nurses, sitters or other persons who provide care to the Principal and the Principal's home. The Agent may authorize purchases of food, clothing, medical care and customary luxuries on the Principal's behalf.

   5.2 <u>Institutional Care.</u> Arrange and contract for institutional health care (hospital, retirement facility, nursing home, hospice or other) on the Principal's behalf if recommended by the Principal's physician. If reasonably advised that the Principal's return home is unlikely because of the Principal's condition, the Agent may sell, exchange, lease, sublease or dispose of the Principal's home and such of its contents as are no longer useful to the Principal and are not specifically bequeathed in the Principal's will, all on such terms as to price, payment and security as the Agent deems reasonable.

   5.3 <u>Religious Needs.</u> Continue the Principal's affiliation with the Principal's church, keeping the Principal accessible to the Principal's clergy, members and other representatives, continuing and renewing any pledge made by the Principal whether for capital, operations or other purposes, and generally to assist the Principal in maintaining the Principal's church relationships to the extent the Principal's health permits.

   5.4 <u>Companions and Recreation.</u> Hire, discharge, direct and compensate such companions as may be necessary for the Principal's health, recreation, travel, and general well-being.

   5.5 <u>Funeral Arrangements.</u> Arrange and contract for the Principal's funeral including appropriate arrangements and instruction for the Principal's funeral service or memorial service, including purchase of a burial plot or other appropriate disposition of the Principal's body. The Agent shall comply with any known written instructions as the Principal may have or leave.

   5.6 <u>Curator or Guardian.</u> Nominate on the Principal's behalf any person the Agent deems qualified, including the Agent, as the Principal's curator, undercurator, curator ad hoc, guardian, or conservator or any other fiduciary office the Principal has a right to nominate or designate, to waive any bond on the Principal's behalf and to grant to that fiduciary or representative any powers that the Principal might extend on the Principal's own behalf.

<u>REFUSAL OF MEDICAL TREATMENT</u>

6. The Principal declares that the Principal does not wish the Principal's dying to be prolonged artificially through extraordinary or heroic means if the Principal's condition is terminal. Even over the objection of members of the Principal's family, the Principal authorizes the Agent to:

    6.1 <u>Withdraw or Withhold Life Support.</u> Sign on behalf of the Principal any documents, waivers or releases necessary to withdraw, withhold or cease any procedure calculated only to prolong the Principal's life, including the use of a respirator, cardiopulmonary resuscitation, surgery, dialysis, blood transfusion, antibiotics, antiarrhythmic and pressor drugs or transplants if two licensed physicians, one of whom is the Principal's attending physician, have personally examined the Principal and the Principal's attending physician has noted in the Principal's medical records that the Principal's condition is terminal and irreversible.

    6.2 <u>Nourishment.</u> Refuse or discontinue intravenous or parenteral feeding, hydration, misting and endotracheal or nasogastric tubes, if advised that no undue pain will be caused to the Principal.

<u>DECLARATION</u>

7. Contemplating that the Principal's medical care may be rendered in Louisiana, or that state law might apply, the Principal has executed a Declaration Concerning Life-Sustaining Procedures ("Declaration") pursuant to State Revised Statues 40:1299.58.1 and following as amended, a copy of which is attached. The Principal declares that by executing that Declaration the Principal does not intend to limit or reduce the powers over the Principal's person elsewhere granted to the Agent in this agency, but rather to convey to the Agent any additional powers as are necessary to make or carry out the terms of that Declaration.

8. THUS DONE AND PASSED in multiple originals on the date first above written in the presence of the undersigned competent witnesses, who signed their names with the Principal and me Notary, after reading of the whole.

WITNESSES:

_____   _____

Print Name:_____   Principal

_____

Print Name:_____

_____

Notary Public

Where on the Web

American Bar Assn's Publishing Subject Index *www.abanet.org/abapubs/estates.html*

American Bar Assn's Probate and Trust Law Section *www.abanet.org/rppt/home.html*

American College of Trust and Estate Counsel *www.actec.org*

Estate Planning Links *www.estateplanninglinks.com* & *www.ca-probate.com/links.htm*

FindLaw Internet Legal Resources *www.findlaw.com*

LifeNet *www.lifenet.com*

National Association of Financial and Estate Planning Website *www.nafep.com*

Nolo Press Self-Help Law Center *www.nolo.com*

U.S. Estate Planning Law (Cornell University) *www.law.cornell.edu/topics/estate_planning.html*

U.S. House Law Library: Trusts and Estates *law.house.gov/112.htm*

WebTrust *www.webtrust.com*

Wills on the Web *www.courttv.com/legaldocs/newsmakers/wills*

LIVING WILLS AND ADVANCED MEDICAL DIRECTIVES

A living will (also known as an advanced medical directive) is not a will at all, but rather the maker's last wishes regarding sustainment of life. It establishes the medical situations and circumstances in which the maker of the document no longer wants life-sustaining treatment. Such a document, though authorized in all states, must generally meet the requirements of a formally drafted state statute. A living will, or advanced medical directive, only covers a narrow range of situations, and usually applies only to terminal patients. It may create problems that arise from vagueness or ambiguities in its drafting if it is not drafted by a competent attorney. Some states have a registry of those who have filed such documents so that if a person is terminally ill, the caring institution can determine if such a document exists, and thus avail itself of the wishes of the registrants. Generally, a durable power of attorney issued for health care is insufficient to make decisions regarding the termination of life sustaining procedures.

EXHIBIT 20.8: LIVING WILL

LIVING WILL DECLARATION

This Declaration is made on the _____ day of _____, 2000, pursuant to the Louisiana Natural Death Act, La. R.S. 40:1299.58.1 *et seq.*

I,_____, being of sound mind, willfully and voluntarily make known my desire that my dying shall not be artificially prolonged under the circumstances set forth below and do hereby declare:

If at any time I should have an incurable injury, disease or illness certified to be a terminal and irreversible condition or a continual profound comatose state with no reasonable chance of recovery by two physicians who have personally examined me, one of whom shall be my attending physician, and the physicians have determined that my death will occur whether or not life-sustaining procedures are utilized and where the application of life-sustaining procedures would only serve to prolong artificially the dying process, I direct that such procedures (including but not limited to artificial means of respiration, hydration and/or nutrition) be withheld or withdrawn and that I be permitted to die naturally with only the administration of medication or the performance of any medical procedure deemed necessary to provide me with comfort care.

In the absence of my ability to give direction regarding the use of such life-sustaining procedures, it is my intention that this Declaration shall be honored by my family and physician(s) as the final expression of my legal right to refuse medical or surgical treatment and accept the consequences from such refusal.

I understand the full import of this Declaration, and I am emotionally and mentally competent to make this Declaration. Terms used in this Declaration shall have the meanings prescribed in the Louisiana Natural Death Act, La. R.S. 40:1299.58 *et seq.*, as amended now or hereafter.

_____
Declarant

Metairie, Jefferson Parish, Louisiana

The declarant has been personally known to me, and I believe the declarant to be of sound mind. Both witnesses are competent adults who are not entitled to any portion of the estate of the declarant upon declarant's decease. The declarant signed this Declaration in our presence on the date set forth above.

_____
Witnesses

_____
Witnesses

A SIDE INSTRUCTION LETTER OR PERSONAL INSTRUCTION LETTER

A **side instruction letter**, or personal instruction letter, details the testator's wishes regarding the disposition of tangible possessions (household goods), the disposition of the decedent's body, and funeral arrangements. Because the side instruction letter exists separately from the will itself, it avoids cluttering the will with small details that may cause conflict among heirs. The letter is given to the executor or executrix. Such a letter may contain information regarding the location of important personal documents, safe deposit boxes, outstanding loans, and other personal and financial information that is invaluable to the executor. While the letter has no legal standing, the executor will generally carry out the wishes of the decedent.

side instruction letter - also known as a personal instruction letter, exists separate from a will and details the testator's wishes regarding the disposition of tangible possessions (household goods), the disposition of the decedent's body, and funeral arrangements

THE PROBATE PROCESS DEFINED

probate process - serves to prove the validity of any will, supervise the orderly distribution of assets to the heirs, and protect creditors by insuring that valid debts of the estate are paid. Probate is also the legal process that performs the function of changing property title from a decedent's name to an heir's name

The **probate process** serves to prove the validity of any will, supervise the orderly distribution of assets to the heirs, and protect creditors by insuring that valid debts of the estate are paid. In addition, when a person dies, there must be some legal way for the surviving heir to obtain legal title to the property inherited by that heir. Probate is the legal process that performs the function of changing title to those properties that do not change title any other way.

Exhibit 20.9 identifies the primary duties of an executor or administrator in the probate process. In the case of a valid will in which an executor is named, the probate court usually accepts such person and provides the executor with powers called letters testamentary. In the event of intestacy, or where an executor cannot be appointed by the probate court, the court will appoint an administrator (generally, a family member of the decedent). The court provides any appointed administrator with powers called letters of administration. The main differences between an executor and an administrator are that the decedent chooses the executor, the probate court names the administrator, and the administrator (but not the executor) must post a bond.

732

EXHIBIT 20.9: DUTIES OF EXECUTOR AND/OR ADMINISTRATOR

When the Decedent Dies Testate (with a will)	When the Decedent Dies Intestate (without a will)
The Executor:	**The Administrator:**
▲ Locates and proves the will.	▲ Petitions court for his or her own appointment.
▲ Locates witnesses to the will.	▲ Receives letters of administration.
▲ Receives letters testamentary from court.	▲ Posts the required bond.

Duties of the Executor or Administrator

▲ Locates and assembles property.

▲ Safeguards, manages, and invests property.

▲ Advertises in legal newspapers that person has died and creditors and other interested parties are on notice.

▲ Locates and communicates with potential beneficiaries.

▲ Pays the expenses of the decedent.

▲ Pays the debts of the decedent.

▲ Files tax returns, such as Forms 1040, 1041, and 706, and makes tax payments.

▲ Distributes assets to beneficiaries according to the will or the laws of intestacy.

PROPERTY PASSING THROUGH PROBATE

Property passing through probate includes property disposed of by a will, such as the fee simple (title), tenancy in common, and all other willed property. The next major section will discuss the different ways to title property. Also included in probate is property owned but not covered by a will, such as intestate property resulting from the failure to provide a residuary clause. Exhibit 20.10 illustrates various assets that pass through and around probate.

EXHIBIT 20.10: ASSETS PASSING THROUGH AND AROUND THE PROBATE PROCESS

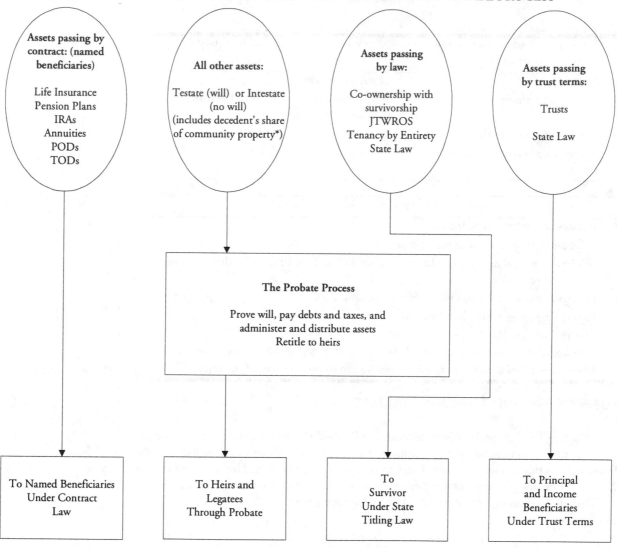

*Note that community property states vary on their probate treatment of community property passed to spouses

PROPERTY PASSING OUTSIDE OF THE PROBATE PROCESS

Property that passes outside of the probate process includes contractual properties and those that are retitled by law. Contractual properties include life insurance proceeds with a named beneficiary, all pension plans and IRAs with named beneficiaries, all annuities with named joint annuitants, and pay-on-death/transfer-on-death accounts. Examples of other types of property that legally pass outside probate include property held by joint tenants with survivorship rights (JTWROS or Tenants by Entirety), and all trust property according to trust terms under state trust laws.

ADVANTAGES OF THE PROBATE PROCESS

The probate process has many advantages. It protects creditors by insuring that the debts of the estate are paid prior to distribution to heirs. It implements the disposition objectives of the testator of the valid will. It provides clean title to heirs or legatees. It increases the chances that all parties in interest have notice of the proceedings and, therefore, a right to be heard. Finally, it provides for an orderly administration of the decedent's assets. The probate process requires the executor or administrator to advertise the upcoming probate for a period of time in legal newspapers to give interested parties notice to enter into the process.

DISADVANTAGES OF THE PROBATE PROCESS

The probate process also has disadvantages. Probate can be both costly and complex. The legal notice requirement, attorney fees, and court costs create some of the costs. Delays are frequently caused by identification of property, valuation, identification of creditors and heirs, court delays, conflicts, and filing of taxes, to name a few. Real property located in a state outside the testator's domicile will require a separate ancillary probate in that state. One of the biggest disadvantages is loss of privacy since probate is open to public scrutiny.

OWNERSHIP AND TRANSFER OF PROPERTY

At any point in time, all property is owned by someone. Property may be described as real (that is, land and buildings), tangible personalty (that is, that property may be touched and is not realty – not affixed to the land, generally moveable), or intangible (that is, stocks, bonds, patents, copyrights). Some property is specifically titled to a named person. Examples include real estate, automobiles (assuming the state has a motor vehicle title law), stocks, bonds, bank accounts, and retirement accounts. Other property may not have a specific title, for example, household goods. The state law in which a person is domiciled, or situs (location) of the property, determines the various types of ownership interests and the ways in which these interests can be transferred from one person to another, either during life or at death. Not all states have every alternative type or form of property interest. The forms have developed over time for the convenience of the citizens of the states that have adopted such forms.

The financial planning professional needs a working knowledge of the various forms of property interest and how each is transferred. Clients will need to be advised as to the initial ownership form depending on the client's objectives and the process the client will have to go through to transfer the property during life or at death.

PROPERTY INTERESTS (TITLE AND OWNERSHIP)

Property interests take several different legal forms and include fee simple, tenancy in common, joint tenancy, tenancy by the entirety, community property, pay-on-death accounts, and transfer-on-death accounts. In addition, there are property ownerships that are less than complete, including life estates, usufructs, and interests for term.

Fee Simple

fee simple - the complete individual ownership of property with all rights associated with outright ownership, such as the right to use, sell, gift, alienate, or convey

Fee simple is the complete individual ownership of property with all rights associated with outright ownership, such as the right to use, sell, gift, alienate, or convey. When the property passes through the probate process, this type of property ownership interest is known as fee simple absolute.

Tenancy in Common

tenancy in common - two or more persons hold an undivided interest in a whole property

Tenancy in common is where two or more persons hold an undivided interest in the whole property. The percent owned by each party may differ. The property interest is treated as if it were owned outright and the owner's interest can be used, sold, donated, willed, or passed with or without a will. When one of the owners dies, the other owner does not necessarily receive the decedent's interest. The property passes through the probate process for retitling purposes. There is a right of partition, called the right to sever, in the event the owning parties cannot agree.

Joint Tenancy With Right of Survivorship (JTWROS)

joint tenancy - a form of property interest where two or more persons, called equal owners, hold the same fractional interest in a property

Joint tenancy is where two or more persons called equal owners hold the same fractional interest in a property. The right of survivorship (JTWROS) is normally implied. Joint tenants have the right to sever their interest in property without the consent of the other joint tenant, thereby destroying the survivorship right. Property held JTWROS at the time of death of a tenant passes to the surviving tenant outside of the probate process according to state law regarding survivorship rights.

Tenancy by the Entirety

tenancy by the entirety - a joint tenancy with right of survivorship (JTWROS) that can only occur between a husband and wife

Tenancy by the entirety is a JTWROS that can only occur between a husband and wife. Generally, neither tenant is able to sever their interest without the consent of the other tenant spouse. At the death of the first tenant, the property is passed to the surviving spouse according to the state law regarding tenancy by the entirety. Because the state law provides for retitling upon presentation of a legal death certificate, there is no need for this property to go through the probate process.

Community Property

Community property is a regime where married individuals own an equal undivided interest in all wealth accumulated during the marriage. Spouses may also own separate property that was acquired before marriage, inherited, or received by gift. It is possible to create separate property out of a community property by donating a spouse's interest to the other spouse. The community property states include: Arizona, California, Idaho, Louisiana, Nevada, New Mexico, Texas, Washington, and Wisconsin. Community property does not have a survivorship feature, and thus, the decedent's half will generally require the probate process for retitling (California does not require probate for property passing to a spouse). Community property may be dissolved by death, divorce, or by agreement between the spouses.

EXHIBIT 20.11: COMMUNITY PROPERTY STATES

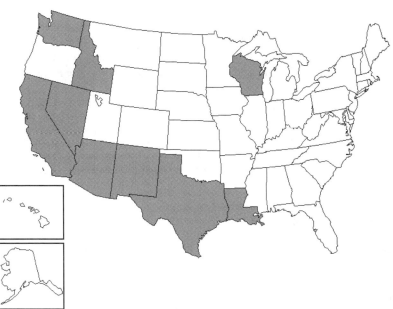

Pay-on-Death (POD), Transfer-on-Death (TOD) Accounts

Pay-on-death bank accounts are fairly new devices. At this writing, 47 states have adopted these devices for bank accounts (PODs) and/or for investment accounts (TODs). Essentially they provide that if the owner of the account has a named beneficiary for such account, that account will legally transfer to the named beneficiary without going through the probate process. Such transfers reduce transfer transaction costs and may improve liquidity for the named heirs, thereby providing estate liquidity. A similar transfer mechanism has existed for a long time with regard to IRAs and other retirement accounts, annuities, and life insurance where a named person is the beneficiary of the accounts or policy. These beneficiary transfer mechanisms are easy and efficient and avoid the probate process, as they have no need to retitle.

LESS THAN COMPLETE OWNERSHIP INTERESTS

There are instances that provide for the creation of, or transfer of, less than the full and complete ownership of property under state law. Three of the most common types of less than full ownership are the life estate, the usufruct, and the interest for term.

Life Estate

life estate - an interest in property that ceases upon the death of the owner of the life interest or estate

A **life estate** is an interest in property that ceases upon the death of the owner of the life interest or estate. A life estate provides a right to income or a right to use, or both. It may be thought of as a right for a life term. Generally at the date of death of the party having the life estate, the property is transferred to the person who has the remainder interest. An example of a life estate is where one person leaves another the use of their beach property for the life of the other.

Usufruct

usufruct - a Louisiana legal device similar to a life estate that provides the holder with the right to use and/or the right to income from a particular property

A **usufruct** is a Louisiana device similar to a life estate. A usufruct provides the holder with the right to use property and/or the right to income from a particular property. At the death of the usufructuary (the person with the usufruct), the property passes to the named owners (remaindermen).

Interest for Term

An interest for term is another version of the life estate or usufruct, but instead of a life interest, the interest is for a definite term. An interest for term could involve an income or a use interest, or both. At the end of the interest for term, the property is transferred to the remainderman.

METHODS OF TRANSFER

In general, property ownership can be transferred during life or at death using one of the following three methods: outright, legal, or beneficial. In an outright transfer, the transferee receives both the legal title and beneficial or economic ownership. In a legal transfer, the transferee, such as a trust officer, receives only the legal title but not the beneficial or economic ownership. In a beneficial transfer, the transferee receives beneficial or economic ownership, as in a trust, but not the legal title.

Transfers During Life

Property ownership transfers during life include transfer by sale, by gift, and by partial gift or sale. Transfer by sale is a transfer for the full value and full consideration (that is, straight sale or installment sale). Transfer by completed gift is a transfer for less than full fair market value. The concept of a completed gift is where the donor cannot recall and no longer has any control over the property that constituted the gift. Transfer by partial gift or sale is when the value received by the transferor is less than the fair market value of the property, the balance of which is treated as a gift referred to as a bargain sale. This type of transaction may be treated as a completed sale for state property law, but will be treated by the IRS as a transfer without full and adequate consideration.

Transfers at Death

Transfers at death include transfers by will, by laws of intestacy, by other laws such as jointly held property with a survivorship feature (that is, JTWROS, or tenants by the entirety), by contract, and by trust. Transfers at death by contract with a named beneficiary other than the estate of the decedent include insurance policies, IRAs, retirement plan assets such as 401(k) plans, marriage contracts, and annuities. Transfers at death by trust instrument include revocable trusts and irrevocable trusts. All revocable trusts become irrevocable at death.

Transfers at death require retitling of the property from the decedent to the new owner. There are various retitling mechanisms, including state laws, which automatically retitle jointly held property where a survivorship feature exists. There are also legal contracts, which call for immediate retitling, such as life insurance and annuities, retirement accounts, and PODs/TODs with named beneficiaries. Where property is not automatically retitled under one of these other mechanisms, it will go through the probate process either provided by the decedent's will (testate) or following the state laws of intestacy for retitling to the heirs.

CONSEQUENCES OF PROPERTY TRANSFERS

The consequences of transfers of property ownership depend on the method of transfer. If there is a loss of control by the transferor, the transfer is by gift. Gift taxes may be due for *inter vivos* (during life) transfers and are usually paid by the donor/transferor. If the transfer is by sale, there is a loss of the sold asset and the possibility of capital gain taxes; however, the consideration received replaces the asset sold. If the transfer is at death through probate, either testate or intestate, there are the issues of costs, federal and state estate taxes, delays, and publicity.

INTRODUCTION TO TRUSTS

A **trust** is a legal arrangement (usually provided for under state law) in which property is transferred by a grantor to a trustee for the management and conservation of the property for the benefit of the named beneficiaries. The trustee could be either an individual or a financial institution (that is, bank). There are usually three parties to a trust: the grantor, the trustee, and the beneficiary. The grantor or creator transfers property to a trustee who takes legal title to those assets for the benefit of all trust beneficiaries. The trustee must adhere to the trust provisions regarding investments, distributions of income and corpus, and eventual termination of the trust. The trust earns income on the trust assets and may distribute such income to those entitled to it called income beneficiaries. Usually, the grantor has created two types of beneficiaries, the income beneficiary and the remainder beneficiary. The remainder beneficiary receives the trust corpus upon termination of the trust. The income beneficiary and remainder beneficiary may in some cases be the same person, in which case we refer to such a trust as a single beneficiary trust. Exhibit 20.12 illustrates the basic structure of a trust.

trust - a legal arrangement, usually provided for under state law, in which property is transferred by a grantor to a trustee for the management and conservation of the property for the benefit of the named beneficiaries

EXHIBIT 20.12: STRUCTURE OF A TRUST

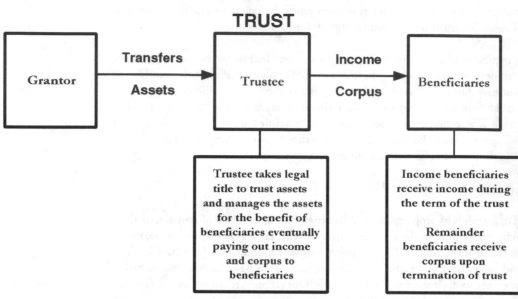

Trusts are created for a variety of purposes, including the avoidance of probate, transfer tax reduction, and the management of the trust assets. Exhibit 20.13 lists some types of trusts and their uses.

EXHIBIT 20.13: TYPES AND USES OF TRUSTS

TYPE OF TRUST	USE OF TRUST
Living Trust (Revocable)	Used to manage assets. Protects in emergencies, such as medical. Avoids publicity and costs of probate. Property is included in the gross estate of the grantor (a type of grantor trust).
Irrevocable Trusts (Inter Vivos)	Used to make gifts. Grantor has loss of control. Assets not included in gross estate of grantor.
Testamentary Trusts	Created by the will. Property is included in the gross estate and does not avoid probate. Generally used to manage assets of heirs.
Trust for Minors	Manages assets for minors. May shift income tax burden to lower bracket taxpayer.
Irrevocable Life Insurance Trust (ILIT)	An irrevocable trust, usually created during life, used to hold an insurance policy, and thus remove the proceeds from the insured's gross estate. The ILIT usually provides income to the spouse and the remainder interest to children or grandchildren.

Whether a trust is selected depends somewhat on the transfer goals of the grantor; the size of the estate; the nature of the relationship with and the financial competence of the spouse; any income needs of the spouse; the nature of the relationship with and financial security and competence of any adult children; any minor children; and any charitable intentions of the grantor. Where there is a split interest in assets (an income interest to one party, and the remainder interest to a different party) a trust is called for to reduce the risk that the income party will utilize all of the assets leaving nothing for the remaindermen. Common split interest trusts include the irrevocable life insurance trust, the credit equivalency trust, and QTIP trust, all of which may call for income to the decedent's spouse and the remainder to children or grandchildren. Trusts are also created to provide income to a non-charitable beneficiary (grantor/grantor spouse) with the remainder to a charity.

A trust with the goal of asset management and conservation is called for when the beneficiary is a single beneficiary. Such is always the case for minor children, and may be the case for adult children who are thought to be insufficiently mature to receive a direct bequest or gift of the size the grantor is contemplating. Sometimes, even amounts given or bequeathed to spouses are put in trust due to financial naïveté or indifference to the management or conservation of assets on the spouse's part.

In this age of multiple marriages and divorces, trusts are used to protect the interest of parties who may have little or no relationship or even a hostile relationship between them. For example, a marriage where the grantor has a spouse of similar age to the adult children of the grantor from a former marriage. Such possible conflicts and complications where the grantor wishes to provide for both the current spouse and to preserve assets for the adult children creates complexities that are usually solved using trusts.

Trusts are either revocable or irrevocable and are either created during life (inter vivos) or at death (testamentary or mortis causa). If the trust is revocable, the property will be included in the gross estate of the grantor. If irrevocable, the property will generally <u>not</u> be included in the gross estate of the grantor. Irrevocable lifetime trusts are used to reduce estate taxes and to avoid probate. One example is the irrevocable life insurance trust (ILIT). If revocable, it will avoid the costs and process of probate, but will not reduce federal estate taxes since the grantor will still have ownership rights. The inter vivos trust is created during the life of the grantor and may be revocable or irrevocable by the grantor. The property in an inter vivos trust avoids the probate process because it does not require the probate process to change title, as it is titled to the trust and not to the decedent. Alternatively, the property used to fund trusts created testamentary (by the will) first goes through the probate process prior to being retitled to the trust.

Although testamentary trusts neither reduce the estate tax nor avoid the costs and process of probate, they are useful in estate planning to protect the interests of minors, incompetents, or spendthrifts. Testamentary trusts are also useful when there is a split interest (income to one person and the remainder to someone else) such that the grantor did not want either party to be dependent on the other party for their interest.

Established During Life	Probate	Gross Estate	Income Tax	Gift Tax
Revocable	Avoid	Included	To grantor	None at creation
Irrevocable	Avoid	Excluded	To trust or beneficiary	May be subject to
Established by Will				
Testamentary	Do not avoid	Included	To trust or beneficiary	Not applicable

LIVING TRUSTS

A living trust is one in which the grantor creates an inter vivos trust that is funded with part or all of the grantor's property. The advantage of a living trust is that the property does <u>not</u> pass through probate at death, but rather transfer at death is accomplished according to the trust provisions and with a minimum of publicity, expense, and delays. A revocable living trust is revocable during the grantor's life, and becomes irrevocable at the grantor's death. The fair market value of the assets in a revocable trust is included in the gross estate of the grantor. The transferor incurs no gift tax at the time of creation of a revocable trust, because there is no completed gift. For an irrevocable trust created during life, the grantor places property into a trust that he cannot rescind or amend. Transfers of property to an irrevocable trust constitute completed gifts and any gift tax applies at the time the trust is created and funded. Assuming the grantor of such trust has no retained ownership interest in the irrevocable trust assets at the time of his death, such assets are generally not included in the gross estate of the transferor (grantor), thereby providing both income tax and estate tax benefits to the grantor. The grantor is not taxed on the income from an irrevocable trust where he has no beneficial interests, and the trust assets are not included in the grantor's gross estate at his death.

GRANTOR TRUSTS

A grantor trust is a trust in which the grantor transfers property into a trust but retains some right of enjoyment of the property, usually an income right. The Internal Revenue Code provides that if a grantor has control over the trust then a completed gift has not been made. The grantor still has ownership of the assets, and the trust is not a separate taxable entity. Consequently, all the income, deductions, and credits of the trust are attributable to the grantor for income tax purposes and possibly estate tax purposes.

In Chapter 21, we identify some other trusts that are useful in certain situations and are used to reduce transfer taxes. These application trusts listed in Exhibit 20.15 include:

EXHIBIT 20.15: APPLICATION TRUSTS AND THEIR USES

APPLICATION TRUSTS	TRUST USES
Credit Equivalency Trust (B Trust - B stands for "bypassing the spouses estate")	A trust usually created by the will (testamentary) that provides an amount equal to any credit equivalency ($675,000 for 2001) to be placed in trust with the spouse, the usual income beneficiary, and the children or grandchildren, the remaindermen. The principal of the trust is not included in the estate of the surviving spouse.
Power of Appointment Trust (POA)	A power of appointment trust is usually created by will (testamentary) providing all income annually to the spouse and with the spouse having a power to invade the principal. The assets in this trust qualify for the unlimited marital deduction at the death of the first spouse. The assets will be included in the estate of the surviving spouse.
Qualified Terminable Interest Trust (QTIP)	A trust created testamentary whereby the executor elects QTIP status. The assets selected for this trust qualify for the unlimited marital deduction. The income beneficiary is always the spouse for all the income, at least annually. The remaindermen are chosen by the decedent. The assets remaining at the death of the surviving spouse are included in the estate of the surviving spouse.
Charitable Remainder Trusts (CRTs)	Charitable remainder trusts are irrevocable and may be created during life or testamentary. They are created to provide income to non-charitable beneficiaries (sometimes the grantor and/or spouse) with the remainder interest going to a charity at the end of the trust term.

REDUCING THE GROSS ESTATE

Generally, the smaller the gross estate, the smaller the estate tax liability. Appropriate use of qualified transfers (qualifying transfers directly to medical or educational institutions), gifts under the annual exclusion, and the lifetime use of the exemption equivalency, will all serve to reduce the size of the gross estate at death. Obviously, personal consumption and lifetime transfers to charities will also reduce the gross estate. Removing the proceeds value of life insurance from the gross estate can have a dramatic effect on reducing the size of the gross estate. There is generally little value in a decedent having an ownership interest in a life insurance policy where the decedent is the insured. The insured has no way to benefit from the proceeds during life and is usually attempting to benefit heirs at the time of the decedent's death. Why not then let heirs (beneficiaries) or an ILIT trust own the insurance policy on the life of the insured? These are the two preferred financial and estate planning methods of owning life insurance. However, like everything else in financial planning, there are no absolutes and therefore careful consideration should be given as to whom should own any insurance policy for a particular insured.

It is relatively easy to have a zero estate tax liability – either leave the entire taxable estate to a charity or leave the estate in a qualifying way to the decedent's spouse. However, the decedent may not have any charitable intentions and/or may not have a spouse, or not a spouse to whom the decedent wants to leave the balance of the estate.

If a first spouse decedent leaves everything in a qualifying way to the surviving spouse, that will cause the deferral of estate tax until the death of the second spouse, which may (and many times does) occur shortly after the first death. In addition, since qualified transfers to a surviving spouse are added to the surviving spouse's personally owned assets to determine the gross estate of the surviving spouse, such transfers could increase the combined federal estate tax rate and amount of tax for the surviving spouse.

There are a wide variety of estate planning techniques for reducing the estate tax which will all be thoroughly covered in an estate planning course and are thus beyond the scope of this text. However, consider that only "qualified" transfers to a spouse are deductible. Is it possible to have a spouse benefit from assets without those assets qualifying for the unlimited marital deduction? The answer is yes, and as a result the first decedent can transfer an amount equal to the lifetime exemption to non-spouse beneficiaries simultaneously providing the spouse with a life income interest from that same transfer. Because this type of transfer is a so-called split interest (an income interest to the spouse and a remainder interest to someone else) the arrangement calls for a trust to insure that neither party is dependent on the other for their interest.

THE USE OF LIFE INSURANCE IN ESTATE PLANNING

The federal estate tax return (Form 706) and the tax liability are due within nine months of the decedent's death. Thus, estate liquidity planning is essential and may require the purchase of life insurance since the life insurance proceeds are quickly available from the insurer upon presentation of a proper death certificate to the insurer.

There is usually a need for liquid assets at the time of someone's death. The hospital wants to be paid, the funeral home and cemetery must be paid, and creditors want to be paid. Even the costs associated with getting a death certificate from the coroner must be paid. Often the need for liquidity at death is satisfied with life insurance proceeds because life insurance is one of the quickest sources of liquidity. The beneficiary only needs to send a certified copy of the death certificate to the insurer and the proceeds are generally paid immediately. While insurance is an effective tool to provide liquidity at death, the proceeds of such insurance will be included in the decedent's gross estate if the insured (decedent) has any incidence of ownership in the life insurance policy at death or if the decedent assigned or transferred gratuitously the policy within three years prior to death. Therefore, it is commonly thought wise that life insurance on one's life should be owned by either the beneficiary of such insurance or alternatively owned by an irrevocable life insurance trust. Either of these arrangements will avoid the proceeds of the life insurance policy being included in the insured's (decedent's) gross estate.

COMMON ESTATE PLANNING MISTAKES

INVALID, OUT-OF-DATE, OR POORLY DRAFTED WILLS

Having an invalid, out-of-date, or poorly drafted will can be detrimental to estate planning. There is nothing worse than spending time developing an estate plan only to have it fall apart due to an inadequate will. An invalid will subjects the estate to intestacy laws that may distribute property according to the decedent's wishes. The will is often deemed invalid because it does not meet statutory requirements, or because the decedent has moved to another state or domicile and has not reflected the new state's laws in the will. An outdated will often fails to minimize estate taxes because it does not contemplate changes in the tax law. Poorly drafted wills generally lack residuary clauses or other common drafting specificities, which can leave estate issues unresolved.

SIMPLE WILLS ("SWEETHEART" OR "I LOVE YOU" WILLS)

A simple will leaves everything to the decedent's spouse. Leaving everything to a spouse can cause an over-qualification of the estate because it fails to take advantage of the credit equivalency for the first spouse who dies. The second spouse to die may pay estate taxes that could have been avoided with a credit equivalency trust or bequest. There is also the risk of a mismanagement of assets. Assets may be put in the hands of a spouse who does not have the education, experience, training, or desire to manage them efficiently and effectively,

IMPROPERLY ARRANGED OR INADEQUATE LIFE INSURANCE

Improperly arranged or inadequate life insurance can defeat successful estate planning. One common way an insurance policy is improperly arranged is when the proceeds are included in the decedent's gross estate. Inclusion will occur when the policy is owned by the decedent, the proceeds are made payable to the estate, or if the decedent has any incidents of ownership. Inclusion will also occur if the insurance was transferred within the last three years of the decedent's life.

A second, common way an insurance policy can be improperly arranged is when the beneficiary is ill equipped (emotionally, in legal capacity, or is a minor) to receive and manage those assets. A trust may provide the needed management of the insurance needs.

Another way an insurance policy can be improperly arranged is when the decedent fails to name a contingent beneficiary. If the original beneficiary predeceases the decedent, then the proceeds may be placed back in the estate where it may be subject to creditor claims, state inheritance laws, federal estate taxes, or all three.

Another improper arrangement of life insurance that should be avoided is the so-called "unholy trinity." The policy is owned by the spouse in the insured's life, and the spouse then names a child the beneficiary. At the death of the insured, the spouse has made a gift to the child.

An insurance policy is generally inadequate when it does not cover the needs of the insured including survivor needs and estate liquidity needs. Survivor needs are generally calculated as the present value of the lost income (net of taxes and the decedent's consumption) over the remaining work life expectancy. An industry heuristic is to use 10 times salary to offset inflation. However, either or both of these may be inadequate with regard to providing sufficient estate liquidity where the majority of the other assets in the estate are both large in value and illiquid (real estate or a closely held business).

POSSIBLE ADVERSE CONSEQUENCES OF JOINTLY HELD PROPERTY

While having jointly held property with survivorship rights (JTWROS) offers some benefits, it can also pose several problems. One problem that may be encountered is that the decedent will not be able to direct the property to the person or entity to whom he or she wishes because the survivor will have the ultimate opportunity to name the remainderman. Another problem is that some jointly held property might result in a completed gift. The consequence of this may be a federal and state gift tax liability as well as an estate tax liability.

ESTATE LIQUIDITY PROBLEMS

Insufficient cash assets and inadequate planning are two estate liquidity problems that should be avoided. When there are insufficient cash assets and estate planning has been inadequate, the estate may be forced to liquidate assets at a time when they are not fully valued or have not reached their potential value. The result is that assets may have to be sold at less than full value.

WRONG EXECUTOR/TRUSTEE/MANAGER

Having the wrong executor/trustee/manager can cause several problems in the estate plan. When the named executor/trustee is incapable of administering the estate efficiently and effectively, it can make costs increase due to poor estate management. It can also cause potential conflict of interest when there are proximity problems or family conflicts.

PROFESSIONAL

FOCUS

Do many of your clients believe they do not need estate planning, and if so, how do you convince them of its importance?

As an attorney specializing in estate planning, clients are referred to me because they have recognized a need for estate planning. However, this recognition often occurs because some other professional -- a financial planner, accountant, stock broker, or insurance agent -- has reviewed some aspect of the client's assets and identified one or more estate planning issues which need to be resolved. Absent this threshold contact with another professional, few clients would recognize the complex issues involved in planning for their death or incompetence.

What do you believe are the biggest risks in failing to plan an estate?

▲ The decedent's property may not be distributed to the people or organizations he would have chosen or it may be distributed too soon (e.g., at what age(s) should children receive assets?).

▲ The decedent's estate may be subject to probate. A common scenario involves a married couple who own property together with a right of survivorship and name each other as beneficiaries of life insurance, IRAs, and qualified plan (e.g., 401k) assets. If both spouses are killed in a common accident, all those assets are subject to probate.

▲ The decedent's estate may owe estate taxes. Few people recognize that they own assets of sufficient value to incur estate taxes at their death. While the use of a Credit Equivalency Trust is a relatively simple estate planning technique to achieve estate tax savings for a married couple, without professional assistance the couple would most likely not understand the problem, or comprehend the solution.

▲ Guardianship of minor children. A decedent may nominate in advance a guardian for his minor children. If no guardianship preferences have been expressed by the decedent, the appointed guardian may not be the person the decedent would have chosen.

What advantages and disadvantages do you give your clients for having their assets pass through probate versus through the operation of law, contract or lifetime giving?

The probate process is both costly (7 - 10% of the estate's value) and lengthy (averaging 18 - 24 months). The advantages of probate are primarily to creditors and disappointed heirs who are given the opportunity to litigate their claims against the decedent's estate. One way to avoid probate is to pass property at death by operation of law (e.g., JTWROS). However, this solution raises other problems -- adding a joint owner to the title of property can create issues regarding asset protection, income taxes, and gift taxes. Passing property by contract (e.g., a life insurance beneficiary) also is preferable to probate, but a client must plan for the contingency that the beneficiary will predecease him. My preference is to have assets owned by a Revocable Living Trust and/or to have that trust named as primary or contingent beneficiary of property passing by contract. This avoids all of the problems discussed above. Lifetime giving is usually desirable if the donor can afford to give the asset away, but the recipient is denied a "stepped-up" basis in the asset for income tax purposes.

Do you recommend the use of trusts to your clients? If so, which ones?

I strongly favor the use of a revocable living trust in conjunction with a will and with property passing by contract . I often structure such a trust to activate sub-trusts upon the occurrence of a certain condition (e.g., death). Depending on the needs of the client, these sub-trusts may include a Power of Appointment Trust, Credit Equivalency Trust, Disclaimer Trust, Qualified Terminable Interest Property Trust / QTIP and Qualified Domestic Trust /QDOT. In addition to the above, to meet the needs of high net worth clients, I use Irrevocable Life Insurance Trusts and Charitable Remainder Trusts.

ROBERT KIRBY, JD, CFP™

DISCUSSION QUESTIONS

1. What is estate planning and what are its objectives?
2. What risks are associated with failing to plan for an estate transfer?
3. Which professionals make up the estate planning team?
4. What steps make up the estate planning process?
5. What client information needs to be gathered to begin a successful estate transfer?
6. What are some common estate transfer objectives?
7. What are the basic documents used in estate planning?
8. What is the probate process and what are its advantages and disadvantages?
9. Why is having a will important?
10. What are the three types of wills and how do they differ?
11. What are the characteristics of a valid will?
12. What is a power of attorney?
13. What is a durable power of attorney for health care?
14. What are the definitions of the terms community property, separate property, and tenancy-by-the-entirety?
15. What are the types of property ownership interests and how are they transferred?
16. What are the duties of the executor/administrator of a will?
17. What is a living trust?
18. What is a grantor trust?
19. How can the gross estate be reduced?
20. What are the common estate planning mistakes?

EXERCISES

1. Which of the following persons need estate planning?
   - ▲ Steve, who has a wife and one small child, and a net worth of $350,000.
   - ▲ Earl, married with nine children, six grandchildren, and a net worth of $4,000,000.
   - ▲ Ellen, divorced, whose only son is severely challenged intellectually.
   - ▲ Mary, who is single, has a net worth of $150,000, and has two cats who she considers as "her children."
2. Place the following estate-planning steps in their proper order.
   - ▲ Establish priorities for estate objectives.
   - ▲ Prepare a written plan.
   - ▲ Define problem areas including liquidity, taxes, etc.
   - ▲ Gather client information and establish objectives.
3. List and describe the arrangements that are plausible when dealing with unanticipated incapacity.
4. Describe why each of the following would be considered potential problems of an estate plan.
   - ▲ Ancillary probate.
   - ▲ A will that includes funeral instructions.
   - ▲ A will that attempts to disinherit a spouse and/or minor children.

5. Describe each of the following common provisions in a well-drafted will.
   - ▲ Establishment of the domicile of testator.
   - ▲ An appointment and powers clause.
   - ▲ A survivorship clause.
   - ▲ A residuary clause.
6. Which of the following statements is/are incorrect?
   - ▲ A durable power of attorney for health care is always a direct substitute for a living will.
   - ▲ A living will only covers a narrow range of situations.
   - ▲ A living will must generally meet the requirements of a formally drafted state statute.
   - ▲ Many well-intentioned living wills have failed due to vagueness and/or ambiguities.
7. Marleen has a general power of appointment over her mother's assets. Which of the following is/are true regarding the power?
   - ▲ Marleen can appoint her mother's money to pay for the needs of her mother.
   - ▲ Marleen can appoint money to Marleen's creditors.
   - ▲ Marleen must only appoint money using an ascertainable standard (health, education, maintenance, and support).
   - ▲ If Marleen were to die before her mother, Marleen's gross estate would include her mother's assets although they were not previously appointed to Marleen.
8. Describe each of the following property ownership arrangements.
   - ▲ Tenancy in common.
   - ▲ Joint tenancy with right of survivorship.
   - ▲ Tenancy by the entirety.
   - ▲ Community property.
9. Which of the following statements regarding joint tenancy is/are correct?
   - ▲ Under a joint tenancy, each tenant has an undivided interest in the property.
   - ▲ Joint tenancies may only be established between spouses.
   - ▲ Community property is the same as joint tenancy and has been adopted in many states.
   - ▲ Assuming a spousal joint tenancy, the full value of the property will be included in the probate estate of the first spouse to die without regard to the contribution of each spouse.
10. Generally speaking, which of the following property is included in the probate estate?
    - ▲ Property owned outright in one's own name at the time of death.
    - ▲ An interest in property held as a tenant in common with others.
    - ▲ Life insurance, and other death proceeds, payable to one's estate at death.
    - ▲ The decedent's half of any community property.
11. Describe at least 3 advantages and 3 disadvantages of the probate process.
12. Identify alternatives to probate regarding disposition of property.
13. John and Mary Hurley are both 36 years old with one child, Patrick, age 6. What documents do the Hurley's need for estate planning?
14. Given Mark's assets below, which will go through the probate process if Mark dies?

Life Insurance	Face	$100,000	Beneficiary is Mary
IRA	Balance	$200,000	Beneficiary is Mary
Personal Residence	Value	$280,000	Titled JTWROS with Mary
Automobile	Value	$4,000	Owned by Mark

15. Ann is married to Roy. They have no children. Given that Ann has the following assets, what could she do to reduce her gross estate?

| Life Insurance | Face | $100,000,000 | Owner is Ann |
| Cash | Amount | $200,000,000 | Owner is Ann |

PROBLEMS

1. Kristi and Patrick Moore are 35 years old with two children, Christopher (4 years old) and Andrew (2 years old). The Moore's have simple wills that leave everything to each other. They have asked you to help them update their will. What would you recommend?
2. Tiger Tree is a wealthy golfer who would prefer that his assets not be subject to public scrutiny when he dies. What tools can he use to accomplish his goal?
3. George owns the following property:

    ▲ Boat (fee simple).
    ▲ Condominium on the beach (tenancy in common with his brother and sister).
    ▲ House and two cars with his wife, Ann (tenancy by the entirety).
    ▲ Checking account with his son, Bill (POD).
    ▲ Karate business (joint tenancy with his partner, Eric).

Which items will go through probate? Which property ownership could he sell?

4. List 8 provisions that John F. Kennedy, Jr. used in his will.
5. List 10 provisions that Marilyn Monroe used in her will.
6. Aaron, a Florida resident, owns the following items of property:

    ▲ 100 percent of a securities brokerage account. The account has a named beneficiary.
    ▲ 45 percent of a business. His brother owns the other 55 percent. Aaron's will names his wife, Paige, the beneficiary of his share.
    ▲ 50 percent of a condo in Colorado. Paige owns the other 50 percent and the interest cannot be severed without the other's consent.
    ▲ 50 percent of a stamp collection. His son, Jacob, owns the other 50 percent. Upon Aaron's death, Jacob would receive Aaron's share.
    ▲ 100 percent of his deceased parents' house.

Identify the type of property ownership of each property described above.

CHAPTER 21

Taxation of Gifts and Estates

LEARNING OBJECTIVES:

After learning the material in this chapter, you will be able to:

1. Understand why a unified gift and estate tax system exists.

2. Define the annual exclusion and explain its tax ramifications.

3. Explain the concept of gift splitting.

4. Identify the basic strategies for transferring wealth through the process of making gifts.

5. Define and explain the purpose of the federal estate tax.

6. Describe the gross estate, what assets are included in the gross estate, and the expenses and deductions that reduce the gross estate.

7. Describe how charitable planning impacts estate planning.

8. Define the marital deduction and explain how it affects estate planning.

9. Define the generation skipping transfer tax and explain how it affects estate planning.

10. List the various estate planning techniques available to reduce the estate tax.

THE UNIFIED GIFT AND ESTATE TRANSFER TAX SYSTEM

The federal estate tax exists as a method of raising revenue for the federal government. It also functions as a method of social reallocation of wealth. The estate tax system prevents large masses of wealth from being transferred from one generation to subsequent generations. When a taxpayer with a large estate dies, a large portion of the estate will be paid to the federal government in the form of estate tax and thus, will be reallocated to other members of society.

The unified estate and gift transfer tax system exists for the purpose of preventing individuals (donors) from freely transferring property to family members (donees) in an attempt to minimize income and estate tax. Congress, being ever mindful of the resolve and ingenuity with which some taxpayers try to avoid federal taxes, established an excise tax for gifts during life. The excise tax is applied to the transfer of property gratuitously during life. In 1976, Congress unified the gift and estate tax schedules (Exhibit 21.1) to prevent taxpayers from manipulating transfers during life and death.

unified gift and estate transfer tax system - unified tax transfer system created by Congress to ensure that at the time of transfer of property, either during life (gifts) or at death (bequests), the transferor will pay the same tax rate or amount for the transfer, regardless of when the transfer is made

The general theory behind the **unified gift and estate transfer tax system** is that at the time of transfer of property, either during life (gifts) or at death (bequests), the transferor will pay the same tax rate or amount for the transfer, regardless of when the transfer is made. Later in the chapter, we will point out major differences between transfers made during life and those made at death. Observe in Exhibit 21.1 that the unified gift and estate transfer tax rates begin at 18 percent and progress to 55 percent. For taxable estates of over three million dollars the transfer tax rate may well be 55 percent (2001 only). As with many other types of taxes, there are ways to arrange one's financial affairs to reduce or eliminate the transfer tax, thus preserving a greater portion of the estate for heirs.

ESTATE PLANNING REFORM

The Economic Growth and Tax Relief Reconciliation Act of 2001 (herein referred to as TRA 2001) was signed by President George W. Bush in June of 2001 providing a $1.35 trillion tax cut. While the estate and generation skipping transfer tax are repealed in 2010, the repeal is phased in over a nine year period (2001 - 2009). The new law also allows the current (2001) estate tax rules, rates, and exemptions to come back in force in 2011. Therefore, it is essential that the financial planner be familiar with the changing laws. This chapter presents the applicable provisions prior to TRA 2001 as well as after.

EXHIBIT 21.1: UNIFIED TAX RATE SCHEDULE FOR GIFTS AND ESTATES (UNTIL 12/31/01)

Over $0 but not over $10,000	18% of such amount.
Over $10,000 but not over $20,000	$1,800 plus **20%** of the excess of such amount over $10,000
Over $20,000 but not over $40,000	$3,800 plus **22%** of the excess of such amount over $20,000
Over $40,000 but not over $60,000	$8,200 plus **24%** of the excess of such amount over $40,000
Over $60,000 but not over $80,000	$13,000 plus **26%** of the excess of such amount over $60,000
Over $80,000 but not over $100,000	$18,200 plus **28%** of the excess of such amount over $80,000
Over $100,000 but not over $150,000	$23,800 plus **30%** of the excess of such amount over $100,000
Over $150,000 but not over $250,000	$38,800 plus **32%** of the excess of such amount over $150,000
Over $250,000 but not over $500,000	$70,800 plus **34%** of the excess of such amount over $250,000
Over $500,000 but not over $750,000	$155,800 plus **37%** of the excess of such amount over $500,000
Over $750,000 but not over $1,000,000	$248,300 plus **39%** of the excess of such amount over $750,000
Over $1,000,000 but not over $1,250,000	$345,800 plus **41%** of the excess of such amount over $1,000,000
Over $1,250,000 but not over $1,500,000	$448,300 plus **43%** of the excess of such amount over $1,250,000
Over $1,500,000 but not over $2,000,000	$555,800 plus **45%** of the excess of such amount over $1,500,000
Over $2,000,000 but not over $2,500,000	$780,800 plus **49%** of the excess of such amount over $2,000,000
Over $2,500,000 but not over $3,000,000	$1,025,800 plus **53%** of the excess of such amount over $2,500,000
Over $3,000,000	$1,290,800 plus **55%** of the excess of such amount over $3,000,000

Note: The benefits of the graduated rates are phased out for taxable estates over $10 million.

From 2002 through 2009, the estate and gift tax rates and unified credit effective exemption amount for estate tax purposes are as shown in Exhibit 21.2.

EXHIBIT 21.2: ESTATE AND GIFT TAX RATES AND UNIFIED CREDIT EXEMPTION AMOUNT AND 2001 LEGISLATION

Calendar Year	Estate and GST Tax Deathtime Transfer Exemption	Highest Estate and Gift Tax Rates	Other
2002	$1 million	50%	
2003	$1 million	49%	
2004	$1.5 million	48%	Family-owned business deduction repealed*
2005	$1.5 million	47%	
2006	$2 million	46%	
2007	$2 million	45%	
2008	$2 million	45%	
2009	$3.5 million	45%	
2010	N/A (taxes repealed)	Top individual rate under the bill (gift tax only)	

The family-owned business deduction is allowed for closely-held businesses and applies to certain estates of decedents dying after December 31, 1997. The allowable deduction is up to $675,000 of a qualified family-owned business interest from the decedent's gross estate.

In 2010, the estate and generation-skipping transfer taxes are repealed (TRA 2001). Also beginning in 2010, the top gift tax rate will be the top individual income tax rate as provided under the bill, and except as provided in regulations, a transfer to trust will be treated as a taxable gift, unless the trust is treated as wholly owned by the donor or the donor's spouse under the grantor trust provisions of the Code.

After repeal of the estate and generation-skipping transfer taxes, the present-law rules providing for a fair market value (i.e., stepped-up) basis for property acquired from a decedent are repealed. A modified carryover basis regime generally takes effect, which provides that recipients of property transferred at the decedent's death will receive a basis equal to the lesser of the adjusted basis of the decedent or the fair market value of the property on the date of the decedent's death.

THE FEDERAL GIFT TAX SYSTEM

PURPOSE AND DEFINITION

gift - in estate planning, a direct transfer of property or cash made during life

Recall that one of the estate planning objectives mentioned in the last chapter was the effective and efficient transfer of property. What could be more effective or efficient than a direct **gift** from the client during life to a loved one? First, since the client is still living, the transferor can assure the completion of the gift. Second, the direct gift generally has little transaction cost except for perhaps the cost to change the title to the asset (such as in the case of retitling a car in the name of the donee). Third, the client (transferor) is able to see the beneficial effect of his transfer and the joy the gift brings to the donee while also enjoying the pleasure of making the gift. Unfortunately, whenever a gift is made, the client loses control of the asset given and loses income from the asset, which may be needed currently or at some point in the future. The creation of a joint bank account is not a gift until the joint tenant removes the money for his/her own benefit. Also, the client has financially empowered the donee (transferee), which may turn out to be ill advised. The transferee may not use the property wisely, as the transferor intended, or may no longer behave in a way in which the transferor desired. Even with these noted disadvantages, lifetime gifts remain a cornerstone of estate planning for the reasons stated above, and for reasons discussed below.

If the overall objective of the client is estate reduction, it may be wise to transfer that property belonging to the transferor that has the greatest potential for future appreciation, rather than to transfer cash or property that has already appreciated. A gift of property will be valued for gift tax purposes at the fair market value as of the date of the gift or transfer. Therefore, any future appreciation on the transferred property will be to the transferee (donee) and, thus, out of the transferor's gross estate. Property, which commonly has substantial future appreciation includes, but is not limited to (1) business interests, (2) real estate, (3) art or other collections, (4) investment securities (stocks and bonds), and (5) other intangible rights (patents, copyrights, royalties). Thus, the selection of property for gifting requires careful financial and estate planning consideration.

ANNUAL EXCLUSION

All individuals are allowed to gift, tax free, up to $10,000 per donee per year. This **annual exclusion** is a result of a de minimus rule by Congress to help reduce reporting requirements of taxpayers for small gifts. However, to qualify for the annual exclusion, the gift must be of a present interest, which means that the donee can currently benefit from the gift. If the gift is of a future interest, such as a gift of a remainder interest in a trust, then the gift does not qualify for the annual exclusion and must be reported. The $10,000 annual exclusion is indexed to the CPI.

If a person (transferor) is married and joins with his spouse to use both annual exclusions for a particular donee, the exclusion is effectively increased to $20,000 per donee per year. Since the exclusion per donee perishes annually, the spouse donor is essentially using the exclusion right for this particular donee, this particular year, because the non-donor spouse would not have used it. When one donor makes the gift, but the donor's spouse consents and agrees to use their annual exclusion for that donee then the joint gift is called a split gift. A gift tax return (Form 709) is required for all split gifts, and both spouses are required to sign the gift tax return. In addition, if an election to split gifts is made, it applies to all gifts made from both spouses during the year while the spouses were married. Only gifts made while the donors are married qualify for split-gift treatment.

Not all joint gifts are subject to gift splitting. Gifts of community property, for example, do not require gift splitting, since each spouse is deemed to own one-half of any community property. Therefore, any gift of community property is a joint gift not subject to gift splitting. Gift splitting was enacted as a way to equalize community and non-community property states. Since gifts of community property are not considered gift splits, a return is not required unless the gifts constitute taxable gifts.

annual exclusion - a result of a de minimus rule by Congress to help reduce income tax reporting by eliminating the need for taxpayers to keep an account of, or report, small gifts. All individuals are allowed to gift, tax free, up to $10,000 per donee per year

Gift Splitting

Kelly made the following gifts in the current year:

Gift	Donee	Value
Cash	Nephew	$12,000
6-month CD	Niece	8,000
Antique rifle	Friend	20,000
Bonds in trust: Life estate to:	Father	60,000
Remainder to:	Niece	18,000
Total		$118,000

Kelly's total taxable gifts for the current year equal $80,000 as described below:

Donee	FMV	Less Annual Exclusion	Total Taxable Gifts
Nephew	$12,000	$10,000	$2,000
Niece	8,000	8,000	0
Friend	20,000	10,000	10,000
Father	60,000	10,000	50,000
Niece	18,000	- -	18,000
Total Gifts	$118,000	$38,000	$80,000

All of Kelly's gifts qualified for the annual exclusion except the gift to her niece consisting of the remainder interest in a trust. Because her niece is unable to currently use the gift, it is not a gift of a present interest and therefore does not qualify for the annual exclusion. All of the other gifts qualify since they are of a present interest.

Gift Splitting Comparison

John and Mary made the following gifts during the current year:

	From John	From Mary	Total
To son, Paul	$40,000	$16,000	$56,000
To daughter, Virginia	40,000	6,000	46,000
To granddaughter, Terry	20,000	4,000	24,000
	$100,000	$26,000	$126,000

A comparison of gift splitting and not using gift splitting is provided for John and Mary's taxable gifts below.

If Gift Splitting is Elected (The parties must split all gifts made during year)

	From John	From Mary	Total
To Paul	$28,000	$28,000	$56,000
To Virginia	23,000	23,000	46,000
To Terry	12,000	12,000	24,000
Total Gross Gifts	$63,000	$63,000	$126,000
Less Annual Exclusions			
For Paul	$10,000	$10,000	$20,000
For Virginia	$10,000	$10,000	$20,000
For Terry	$10,000	$10,000	$20,000
Total Exclusions	$30,000	$30,000	$60,000
Equals Current Taxable Gifts	$33,000	$33,000	$66,000

If Gift Splitting is Not Elected

	From John	From Mary	Total
To Paul	$40,000	$16,000	$56,000
To Virginia	40,000	6,000	46,000
To Terry	20,000	4,000	24,000
Total Gross Gifts	$100,000	$26,000	$126,000
Less Annual Exclusions			
For Paul	$10,000	$10,000	$20,000
For Virginia	$10,000	$6,000	$16,000
For Terry	$10,000	$4,000	$14,000
Total Exclusions	$30,000	$20,000	$50,000
Equals Current Taxable Gifts	$70,000	$6,000	$76,000

Electing to split gifts in the above example results in a decrease in the total taxable gifts from $76,000 to $66,000. The $10,000 difference is a result of Mary not making full use of her annual exclusion for gifts to Virginia ($10,000 - $6,000 = $4,000) and gifts to Terry ($10,000 - $4,000 = $6,000).

UNIFIED CREDIT

In addition to the annual exclusion, there is a lifetime gift and estate tax credit that is used to off-set the gift and estate tax on inter vivos and testamentary transfers. This credit allows taxpayers to transfer, either during life or at death, assets totaling $675,000 (for year 2001) without incurring any transfer tax. Any cumulative amount of taxable gifts that exceeds the annual exclusion first goes to reduce the unified credit with any remaining credit being available to exclude transfers at death. The so-called unified credit (tax credit) has a dollar equivalency amount (lifetime exemption) as indicated in Exhibit 21.3. In addition, the system provides for a lifetime unified tax credit for transfer equal to the following schedule:

EXHIBIT 21.3: UNIFIED CREDIT (1997 - 2010)

Year of Death	Unified Tax Credit	Exemption Equivalent in Dollars
1997	$192,800	$600,000
1998	$202,050	$625,000
1999	$211,300	$650,000
2000	$220,550	$675,000
2001	$220,550	$675,000
2002	$345,800	$1,000,000
2003	$345,800	$1,000,000
2004	$555,800	$1,500,000
2005	$555,800	$1,500,000
2006 - 2008	$780,800	$2,000,000
2009	$1,455,800	$3,500,000
2010	Repealed	Repealed

QUALIFIED TRANSFERS

qualified transfer - a payment made directly to an educational institution for tuition and fees or to a medical institution for medical expenses for the benefit of someone else

Certain transfers, called qualified transfers, are not subject to transfer tax. A **qualified transfer** is a payment made directly to an educational institution for tuition and fees or a payment made directly to a medical institution for medical expenses for the benefit of someone else. These qualified transfers allow taxpayers to effectively transfer wealth to others without being subject to transfer tax. However, to qualify for this treatment, the payments must be paid directly to the specific institution.

EXAMPLE

Jennifer, who is single, gave an outright gift of $60,000 to a friend, Tiffany, who needed the money to pay her medical expenses. Because the gift was made to Tiffany, instead of being paid directly to the medical institution, it cannot be considered a qualified transfer. However, the gift is of a present interest and therefore qualifies for the $10,000 annual exclusion. Therefore, Jennifer has made taxable gifts of $50,000 and must file a gift tax return to report the gift. If Jennifer had paid the medical expenses directly to the medical institution for Tiffany, the entire $60,000 received for Tiffany would have escaped gift taxes. In addition, Jennifer would have been able to give Tiffany another $10,000 that would qualify for the annual exclusion.

Because qualified transfers are not subject to gift tax and there is no limitation on the amount of the qualified transfer, it allows family members to provide assistance to other family members without worrying about transfer taxes. In addition, families can make use of the rules to minimize gift tax within the family by allowing, for example, grandparents to pay for college education for their grandchildren instead of making taxable gifts to the parents, who would in turn pay for the college expenses.

GIFTS TO SPOUSES

The law allows for unlimited transfers to be made between spouses during life or at death. However, to be eligible for the unlimited marital deduction, the donee spouse must be a citizen of the United States. The unlimited marital deduction allows for one spouse to leave their entire estate to the surviving spouse without encumbering it with transfer taxes. Therefore, the surviving spouse will have full use of all property that was held by the deceased spouse.

PAYMENTS FOR SUPPORT

Payments for legal support are transfers to children that are essentially legal support obligations. Payments of support are exempt from the gift tax rules.

payments for legal support - transfers to children that are essentially legal support obligations that are exempt from gift tax rules

EXHIBIT 21.4: BASIC STRATEGIES FOR TRANSFERRING WEALTH THROUGH GIFTING

Generally, if the objective of the transferor is to reduce the size of the transferor's gross estate, the transferor can use the following lifetime gifting techniques to achieve a lower gross estate at death:

▲ Make optimal use of qualified educational transfers (pay tuition for children and grand-children from private school through professional education).

▲ Pay medical costs for children, grandchildren, and heirs directly to provider institutions.

▲ Make optimal use of the $10,000 annual gift exclusion ($20,000 if the gift is made jointly with the spouse). Example: John is married to Joan and has 3 adult children who all have stable marriages and there are 7 grandchildren. John and Joan can gift $260,000 per year without coming into the gift tax system. ($20,000 x 13 transferees – 3 children, 3 spouses, 7 grandchildren)

▲ A spouse may make unlimited lifetime gifts to their spouse who is a U.S. citizen.

▲ If the above four (1-4) are completely exhausted, the transferor can begin using his/her lifetime credit equivalency ($675,000 in year 2000) while still paying no gift tax until the summation of lifetime taxable gifts exceeds the lifetime credit equivalency amount.

▲ Any gift tax paid on gifts prior to three years of death will also reduce the estate of the transferor. This is discussed later in this chapter.

REPORTING AND PAYING TAXES

Taxable gifts are reported on the Federal Gift Tax Return, which is Form 709. The gift tax return is due April 15th, but may be extended until October 15th, as with individual income tax returns. However, the gift tax is not extended as a result of the extension of time to file, and is therefore due on April 15th, similar to individual income tax. The donor is liable for any gift tax due. The gift tax return is also used to report transfers that are subject to generation skipping transfer tax, which is discussed later in the chapter.

EXHIBIT 21.5: ABBREVIATED FORM 709

Form **709**	United States Gift (and Generation-Skipping Transfer) Tax Return	OMB No. 1545-0020
Department of the Treasury Internal Revenue Service	(Section 6019 of the Internal Revenue Code) (For gifts made during calendar year 2000) ▶ See separate instructions.	**2000**

1 Donor's first name and middle initial	2 Donor's last name	3 Donor's social security number
4 Address (number, street, and apartment number)		5 Legal residence (domicile) (county and state)
6 City, state, and ZIP code		7 Citizenship

Part 1—General Information

		Yes	No
8	If the donor died during the year, check here ▶ ☐ and enter date of death . . . . , ...		
9	If you received an extension of time to file this Form 709, check here ▶ ☐ and attach the Form 4868, 2688, 2350, or extension letter .		
10	Enter the total number of separate donees listed on Schedule A—count each person only once. ▶		
11a	Have you (the donor) previously filed a Form 709 (or 709-A) for any other year? If the answer is "No," do not complete line 11b .		
11b	If the answer to line 11a is "Yes," has your address changed since you last filed Form 709 (or 709-A)?		
12	Gifts by husband or wife to third parties.—Do you consent to have the gifts (including generation-skipping transfers) made by you and by your spouse to third parties during the calendar year considered as made one-half by each of you? (See instructions.) (If the answer is "Yes," the following information must be furnished and your spouse must sign the consent shown below. If the answer is "No," skip lines 13–18 and go to Schedule A.)		
13	Name of consenting spouse 14 SSN		
15	Were you married to one another during the entire calendar year? (see instructions)		
16	If the answer to 15 is "No," check whether ☐ married ☐ divorced or ☐ widowed, and give date (see instructions) ▶		
17	Will a gift tax return for this calendar year be filed by your spouse?		
18	Consent of Spouse— I consent to have the gifts (and generation-skipping transfers) made by me and by my spouse to third parties during the calendar year considered as made one-half by each of us. We are both aware of the joint and several liability for tax created by the execution of this consent.		

Consenting spouse's signature ▶   Date ▶

Part 2—Tax Computation

1	Enter the amount from Schedule A, Part 3, line 15	1	
2	Enter the amount from Schedule B, line 3	2	
3	Total taxable gifts (add lines 1 and 2)	3	
4	Tax computed on amount on line 3 (see Table for Computing Tax in separate instructions) . . .	4	
5	Tax computed on amount on line 2 (see Table for Computing Tax in separate instructions) . . .	5	
6	Balance (subtract line 5 from line 4)	6	
7	Maximum unified credit (nonresident aliens, see instructions)	7	220,550	00
8	Enter the unified credit against tax allowable for all prior periods (from Sch. B, line 1, col. C) . .	8	
9	Balance (subtract line 8 from line 7)	9	
10	Enter 20% (.20) of the amount allowed as a specific exemption for gifts made after September 8, 1976, and before January 1, 1977 (see instructions)	10	
11	Balance (subtract line 10 from line 9)	11	
12	Unified credit (enter the smaller of line 6 or line 11)	12	
13	Credit for foreign gift taxes (see instructions)	13	
14	Total credits (add lines 12 and 13)	14	
15	Balance (subtract line 14 from line 6) (do not enter less than zero)	15	
16	Generation-skipping transfer taxes (from Schedule C, Part 3, col. H, Total)	16	
17	Total tax (add lines 15 and 16)	17	
18	Gift and generation-skipping transfer taxes prepaid with extension of time to file	18	
19	If line 18 is less than line 17, enter balance due (see instructions)	19	
20	If line 18 is greater than line 17, enter amount to be refunded	20	

Sign Here

Under penalties of perjury, I declare that I have examined this return, including any accompanying schedules and statements, and to the best of my knowledge and belief, it is true, correct, and complete. Declaration of preparer (other than donor) is based on all information of which preparer has any knowledge.

▶ Signature of donor	Date

Paid Preparer's Use Only

Preparer's signature ▶	Date	Check if self-employed ▶ ☐
Firm's name (or yours if self-employed), address, and ZIP code ▶		Phone no. ▶ ( )

Attach check or money order here.

For Disclosure, Privacy Act, and Paperwork Reduction Act Notice, see page 11 of the separate instructions for this form. Cat. No. 16783M   Form **709** (2000)

THE FEDERAL ESTATE TAX SYSTEM

PURPOSE AND DEFINITION

federal estate tax - an excise tax on the right to transfer assets by a decedent

The **federal estate tax** is an excise tax on the right to transfer assets by a decedent. In order to properly determine the estate tax liability, the executor must first determine what assets are included in the gross estate. Generally, the gross estate includes all property that the decedent owned at the time of death at the fair market value of the decedent's interest.

The gross estate (Exhibit 21.6, line 1) less the enumerated deductible expenses (lines 2-6) equals the adjusted gross estate (line 7). From the adjusted gross estate (line 7) are two deductions: (1) the value of property left to a qualified charity, and (2) the value of qualified property left to the decedent's spouse. The net result of the adjusted gross estate (line 7) less any marital deduction (line 8) and any charitable deduction (line 9) equals the taxable estate (line 10).

Following the determination of the taxable estate, any taxable gifts (those transfers that did not qualify for the annual exclusion) made after 1976 are added to determine the tentative tax base (line 10 + line 11 = line 12). The tentative tax (line 13) is calculated using the Unified Estate and Gift Tax Schedule as shown in Exhibit 21.1. From the tentative tax are subtracted any credits, such as previous gift tax paid (line 14), the unified credit (line 15) obtained from Exhibit 21.3, and any state death taxes paid (line 16) to determine the federal estate tax liability (line 17).

EXHIBIT 21.6: THE ESTATE TAX FORMULA

(1)	Gross Estate (GE)		$ _____	Gross Estate
	Less Deductions:			
(2)	Last Medical	$ _____		
(3)	Administrative Costs	$ _____		
(4)	Funeral	$ _____		
(5)	Debts	$ _____		
(6)	Losses During Estate Administration	$ _____	$ _____	Deductions
(7)	Equals: Adjusted Gross Estate (AGE)		$ _____	Adjusted Gross Estate
(8)	Less: Charitable Deduction	$ _____		
(9)	Less: Marital Deduction	$ _____	$ _____	
(10)	Equals: Taxable Estate (TE)		$ _____	Taxable Estate
(11)	Add: Previous Taxable Gifts (post 1976)		$ _____	Post-1976 Gifts
(12)	Equals: Tentative Tax Base (TTB)		$ _____	Tentative Tax Base
(13)	Tentative Tax (TT) (Exhibit 21.1)		$ _____	Tentative Tax
	Less: Credits			
(14)	Previous Gift Tax Paid	$ _____		
(15)	Unified Credit (Exhibit 21.3)	$ _____		
(16)	State Death Tax Paid	$ _____	$ _____	
(17)	Equals: Federal Estate Tax Liability (FETL)		$ _____	Federal Estate Tax Liability

REPORTING AND PAYING TAXES

Federal estate tax is reported on the federal estate tax return (Form 706). The federal estate tax return is due nine months from the date of death, but may be extended six months. However, an extension of time for filing does not extend the time for paying the estate tax. Therefore, unless permitted by one of the statutory exceptions, estate tax is payable nine months after the date of death.

THE GROSS ESTATE

The financial planner must have a clear understanding of the size of the client's **gross estate** in order to develop a meaningful estate plan. The size and types of assets included in the gross estate will directly determine which planning techniques should be implemented. Exhibit 21.7 illustrates most of the asset types that are included in the gross estate as covered in Section 2033 (the relevant code section) of the Internal Revenue Code:

gross estate - all assets included in a decedent's estate including, but not limited to, cash, stocks, bonds, annuities, retirement accounts, notes receivable, personal residences, automobiles, art collections, life insurance proceeds, and income tax refunds due

EXHIBIT 21.7: THE GROSS ESTATE

	Fair Market Value
Cash	$XXX
Stocks and bonds	XXX
Annuities	XXX
Retirement accounts	XXX
Notes receivable	XXX
Personal residence	XXX
Other real estate	XXX
Household goods	XXX
Automobiles	XXX
Business interests	XXX
Proceeds of life insurance	XXX
Collections (art, wine, jewelry)	XXX
Vested future rights	XXX
Outstanding loans by decedent to others	XXX
Income tax refunds due	XXX
Patents/copyrights	XXX
Damages owed decedent	XXX
Dividends declared and payable	XXX
Income in respect of decedent	XXX
Decedent's share of property held with others	XXX
Other tangible personal property	XXX
The Gross Estate	$XXX

Note that the gross estate includes the decedent's interest in any jointly held property and the proceeds of life insurance on the decedents life where (1) the decedent had any incidents of ownership in the policy at the time of death or (2) where the decedent had assigned (gifted) the insurance to someone else within three years of the decedent's death. The valuation of property included in the gross estate is either the fair market value at the date of death, or if properly elected, the value for the alternate valuation date (six months from the date of death). Because death is presumed to be involuntary, the alternate valuation date is provided so as to give relief to a decedent who just happened to die on a date where the gross estate was valued at a very high value due to the temporary market conditions.

DEDUCTIONS FROM THE GROSS ESTATE

adjusted gross estate - gross estate less deductions provided for by law in recognition that the entire value of the gross estate will not be transferred to the heirs due to costs, debts, and certain other deductions

Once the assets are identified and the value of the gross estate is determined, the next step is to determine the allowed deductions to arrive at the **adjusted gross estate** (see Exhibit 21.6). The deductions are provided for by law in recognition that the entire value of the gross estate will not be transferred to the heirs due to costs, debts, and certain other deductions. Rather, a smaller amount than the full gross estate will be transferred to heirs.

The adjusted gross estate is determined by deducting the following:

- ▲ Funeral expenses.
- ▲ Last medical costs.
- ▲ Administration expenses.
- ▲ Debts.
- ▲ Losses during estate administration.

Funeral Costs

Reasonable expenditures related to the funeral, such as interment costs, burial plot, grave marker, and transportation of the body to the place of burial, are deductible for estate tax purposes.

Last Medical Costs

Medical costs related to the decedent's last illness are deductible from the gross estate as long as they are not deducted on the decedent's final federal income tax return.

Administrative Expenses

Any expenses related to the administration of the estate are deductible from either the estate tax return (Form 706) or the estate's income tax return (Form 1041). These expenses generally include attorney and accountant fees for preparing the estate tax return, the final Form 1040, and the estate income tax return; and expenses related to the retitling of assets through the probate process. These costs may also include appraisal and valuation fees necessary to determine values of assets included in the gross estate for estate tax purposes.

Debts

All debts of the decedent are deductible from the gross estate. These debts include any amounts the decedent was obligated to pay while alive, plus interest accrued to the date of death. Debts generally include such items as outstanding mortgages, income tax due, credit card balances, and other miscellaneous outstanding debts.

Losses During Estate Administration

Any losses to the estate during the period of administration, including casualty and theft losses, are deductible expenses.

THE CHARITABLE DEDUCTION

DEFINITION

Internal Revenue Code 170(c) defines a charitable contribution as a gift made to a qualified organization. To be a **charitable deduction**, a contribution must be made to one of the following organizations:

▲ A state or possession of the United States or any subdivision thereof.
▲ A corporation, trust, or community chest, fund, or foundation that is situated in the United States and is organized exclusively for religious, charitable, scientific, literary, or educational purposes, or for the prevention of cruelty to children or animals.
▲ A veteran's organization.
▲ A fraternal organization operating under the lodge system.
▲ A cemetery company.

The IRS publishes a list (Publication 78) of organizations that have applied for and received tax-exempt status under section 501 of the Internal Revenue Code.

TYPES OF CHARITABLE BEQUESTS

Direct Charitable Bequests

A direct charitable bequest of any property to a qualifying organization is fully deductible from the gross estate in arriving at the taxable estate.

Charitable Trusts

A **charitable remainder trust (CRT)** is an estate planning vehicle used to reduce the impact of estate taxes. A CRT is created by transferring property to a charitable trust. Although the property transferred to the trust may be cash, it generally consists of appreciated property. Because it is a non-taxable entity, the CRT can dispose of property without incurring taxable income upon the disposition. The trust is established so that an income interest, which may be in the form of an annuity or a unitrust payment, is paid to either the donor or a family member of the donor. At the termination of the income interest, which generally occurs at the death of the income ben-

charitable deduction - a charitable contribution made as a gift to a qualified organization

charitable remainder trust (CRT) - a split interest trust. If created during life, the income goes to one or more parties, usually the grantor or grantor and spouse for life, and upon the income beneficiary's death, the principal (remainder) is transferred to a charity. If the CRT is created testamentary, the usual income beneficiary is the spouse for life

eficiary, the remaining assets in the CRT are transferred to the charity named in the trust document. Because there are two beneficiaries, the income beneficiary or annuitant and the named charity of a CRT, the CRT is considered a split interest trust.

Charitable remainder trusts can be established for any term during life or at the death of the donor. CRTs that are established during life provide several benefits. First, the donor will receive an income tax deduction equal to the value of the property transferred to the trust less the value of the income stream that is expected to be received by the income beneficiary. Second, the asset that was transferred to the trust is no longer included in the gross estate, thereby reducing the estate tax of the donor. Third, the CRT provides an income stream to the donor or the donor's family member. Finally, if the property transferred to the trust was highly appreciated, the trust is able to dispose of the property without current income taxation. CRTs that are established at death are primarily used to reduce the estate tax and to provide an income stream to one of the donor's heirs. This amounts to social reallocation of wealth by the donor's choice.

In some cases, the income beneficiary is the charity with the remaining property being passed to one of the donor's heirs. This type of arrangement is called a **charitable lead trust (CLT)**. A CLT is generally used as a method of transferring property to heirs in the future while paying gift tax at the current valuation of the property. Any appreciation in the value of the property will escape transfer tax.

THE MARITAL DEDUCTION

DEFINITION

A **marital deduction** occurs when the decedent's estate claims as a deduction from the adjusted gross estate an unlimited qualifying bequest or transfer of property to a surviving spouse. This treatment parallels the unlimited marital deduction for gifts and for gift tax purposes. As discussed above, the donee spouse must be a U.S. citizen for the transfer to qualify for the unlimited marital deduction.

QUALIFICATIONS FOR THE MARITAL DEDUCTION

To qualify for the marital deduction, the property must be included in the decedent's gross estate and must be passed to the decedent's spouse. The interest in the property must not be one that is a terminable interest. A terminable interest is defined as an interest that ends upon an event or contingency. In other words, if the spouse initially gets the interest in the property and then later this interest terminates upon some event (usually death), then the interest passes to someone else, it is a terminable interest. Terminal interests do not qualify for the unlimited marital deduction unless they meet one of the exceptions to the "terminal interest rule."

---

charitable lead trust (CLT) - a split interest trust where a charity is the income beneficiary and there is a non-charitable remainderman

marital deduction - a deduction of an unlimited qualifying bequest or transfer of property to a surviving spouse claimed from the adjusted gross estate of the decedent's estate

The following are some exceptions to the terminable interest rule:

▲ When the only condition of a bequest is that the survivor spouse lives for a period not exceeding six months, the marital deduction is allowed if the surviving spouse actually lives for the period specified.

▲ When there is a right to a life annuity coupled with a power of appointment.

▲ When there is a bequest to a spouse of income from a Charitable Remainder Annuity Trust or a Charitable Remainder Unitrust and the spouse is the only non-charitable beneficiary.

▲ Certain marital trusts are exceptions to the terminable interest rule (that is, Qualified Terminal Interest Property, or QTIP).

DIRECT BEQUESTS TO A SPOUSE

In a **direct bequest**, the first spouse who dies leaves everything outright to the surviving spouse. The estate of the decedent spouse gets a 100 percent marital deduction equal to the adjusted gross estate. The property will ultimately be consumed by the surviving spouse or will be included in the gross estate of the surviving spouse. The advantages of direct bequests are that they are simple and inexpensive. The surviving spouse gets unfettered control over all of the assets of the decedent. One disadvantage of this approach is that a direct bequest may overqualify the estate since the first spouse to die does not take advantage of the decedent's available unified credit or its equivalency. Overqualification means that the decedent failed to make use of his credit equivalency opportunity to pass his exemption equivalency amount (currently $675,000 for the year 2001) to someone other than the spouse and still pay no estate tax. If an estate is overqualified, the total estate tax on the death of the second spouse may be greater than it would have been had they arranged their affairs differently. Another disadvantage is that the first spouse is unable to retain control over the ultimate disposition of the assets.

QUALIFIED TERMINABLE INTEREST PROPERTY TRUST (QTIP)

If a direct bequest to a spouse is determined to be inappropriate and the decedent wishes no transfer tax at the first death, the alternatives are a QTIP or a Power of Appointment trust. A **qualified terminable interest property trust**, sometimes called a "C" Trust or a "Q" Trust, allows a terminable interest to be passed to a surviving spouse and the property to still qualify for the unlimited marital deduction. The election is made by the executor on IRS Form 706. There are certain rules associated with QTIPs that must be followed to qualify the transfer for the unlimited marital deduction.

Any income from the trust must be payable to the surviving spouse at least annually and for life. The trust income cannot be payable to anyone other than the surviving spouse. The trust assets will be included in the gross estate of the surviving spouse at death. The first spouse to die determines the ultimate disposition of the property from the trust (names the remainder beneficiaries). This is an especially useful device when the surviving spouse is not the parent of the children of the decedent spouse.

direct bequest - (to a spouse) the first spouse who dies, leaves everything outright to the surviving spouse

qualified terminable interest property trust (QTIP) - allows a terminable interest to be passed to a surviving spouse and the property to still qualify for the unlimited marital deduction. The election is made by the executor on IRS Form 706

C trust

power of appointment trust - allows a terminable interest to be passed to a surviving spouse and the property to still qualify for the marital deduction. Unlike a QTIP Trust, no election is required

POWER OF APPOINTMENT TRUST

A **Power of Appointment Trust**, sometimes called an "A" Trust, allows a terminable interest to be passed to a surviving spouse and the property to still qualify for the marital deduction. Unlike a QTIP Trust, no election is required. The rules require that income from the trust must be payable to the surviving spouse at least annually for life. Any assets in the trust will be included in the gross estate of the surviving spouse at death. The surviving spouse is given a general power of appointment (the power to appoint the assets to anyone, including herself) over the property during life or at death. The first spouse to die may not control the ultimate disposition of the property because the surviving spouse has a general power of appointment over the trust assets.

OPTIMIZING THE MARITAL DEDUCTION

If the objective of the married decedent is to have a zero-tax-liability estate, he can simply leave all assets in a qualifying way to the surviving spouse. The problem with such a strategy is that it fails to utilize the decedent's right to leave a credit equivalency amount (currently $675,000 for year 2001) to someone other than the spouse. Therefore, all assets, less the credit equivalency ($675,000), can be left to the spouse in a qualifying way and still have a zero estate tax liability for the first spouse. Although the $675,000 is left to another heir, the decedent spouse may provide that income from the property is to be paid exclusively to the surviving spouse while the spouse is alive. The common method of leaving the credit equivalency amount where the spouse has a need for the income from such assets is called a credit equivalency, or bypass, trust. In the event a spouse has no need for the income or assets from the credit equivalency amount, such spouse can disclaim, as discussed below. Keep in mind, however, that only citizen spouses can qualify for the unlimited marital deduction. Alien surviving spouses have special rules described later in this section.

The Credit Equivalency (Bypass) Trust

A **bypass trust** avoids inclusion in, or bypasses, the surviving spouse's gross estate. The assets transfer to a future generation free of estate taxes. The purpose of a bypass trust (known as a "B" trust) is to take advantage of the unified credit or credit equivalency. The property does not qualify for the unlimited marital deduction and is therefore taxed in the estate of the first spouse to die. A common scenario is for the first spouse to leave everything to the surviving spouse except for the credit equivalent amount, which goes into a bypass trust. The surviving spouse may be the income beneficiary of the bypass trust and may also be able to invade the trust for health, education, maintenance or support. When the surviving spouse dies, the bypass trust assets are not included in that spouse's gross estate, but rather pass to children or other heirs.

A bypass trust can be used instead of an outright bypass bequest to heirs who are not sufficiently sophisticated or mature enough to handle property. In addition, the bypass trust is used where the surviving spouse needs the income from the trust but wants to avoid inclusion of the assets in the surviving spouse's gross estate. In this case, the choice of the trust over the simple bequest does not save any estate tax dollars, but may give the transferor some peace of mind. Often, highly appreciating assets are placed into the bypass trust. This freezes the value for estate tax purposes for the spouses at the death of the first spouse. A bypass trust may also be called a credit equivalency trust, a credit shelter trust, a family trust, or a "B" Trust.

The Mechanics of the Credit Equivalency (Bypass) Trust

Recall that property which qualified for the marital deduction reduced the taxable estate of the decedent and that the amount of such transfer is unlimited. Recall that each individual has a lifetime exemption (Exhibit 21.2) and that such exemption would be lost to the first spouse were they to transfer to the surviving spouse all of their property in a qualifying way. A credit equivalency (bypass) trust can be used to avoid this problem. Usually testamentary, a credit equivalency trust is provided for in the will with a provision to fund such trust with an amount of money equal to the current (at the time of death) credit equivalency amount with the spouse having a lifetime interest in the income and the remaindermen being someone else, usually children. Such a transfer does not qualify for the qualified marital deduction, and therefore those assets will not be included in the gross estate of the surviving spouse when such surviving spouse dies. However, the assets are included in the taxable estate of the grantor, but will not result in any federal estate tax liability as demonstrated in the following example.

bypass trust - avoids inclusion in, or bypasses, the surviving spouse's gross estate--the assets transfer to a future generation free of estate taxes. The purpose of a bypass trust (known as a "B" trust) is to take advantage of the unified credit or equivalency

EXAMPLE Sherri and Gary are married with two children. They have community property of $5,000,000. Each spouse has a will bequeathing all property to the surviving spouse.

Calculation of the total estate tax paid, assuming Gary dies first on January 1, 2001.

	Gary	Sherri
Assets	$2,500,000	$2,500,000
Inheritance		2,500,000
Gross Estate	$2,500,000	$5,000,000
Marital Deductions	(2,500,000)	-0-
Taxable Estate	-0-	$5,000,000
Tentative Tax	-0-	2,390,800
Unified Credit	-0-	(220,550) (2001)
Estate Tax	$ -0-	$2,170,250

Total estate tax paid by family $2,170,250

Calculation of the total estate tax paid assuming Gary dies on January 1, 2001, using a maximized credit equivalency trust with the children as beneficiaries.

	Gary	Sherri
Assets	$2,500,000	$2,500,000
Inheritance	-0-	1,825,000
Gross Estate	$2,500,000	$4,325,000
Marital Deductions	(1,825,000)	-0-
Taxable Estate	$675,000	$4,325,000
Tentative Tax	$220,550	$2,019,550
Unified Credit	(220,550)	(220,550) (2001)
Estate Tax	$ -0-	$1,799,000

Total estate tax paid by family $1,799,000

Conclusion: By using the credit equivalency trust the family saved $371,250 [$2,170,250 (without shelter) - $1,799,000 (with shelter) = $371,250 savings] in estate tax. This savings is a result of the couple taking full advantage of the unified credit by placing the credit equivalency amount of funds at the first death in a credit equivalency trust for the children. Sherri can receive income from the trust for the remainder of her life and have the right to withdraw limited amounts of principal. The credit equivalency trust assets will pass untaxed to the children at Sherri's death.

Understanding the savings:

$2,170,250	Example 1
-1,799,000	Example 2
$ 371,250	Savings

The credit equivalency amount of $675,000 was not taxed in Example 2. The savings that resulted was equal to the marginal tax bracket (55 percent) times the credit equivalency amount.

$675,000
x 55%
$ 371,250

Note that for smaller estates, the savings amount will vary with the size of the estate and the marginal estate tax rate.

If we assume instead that Gary and Sherri's community property was only worth $2,000,000, then the savings would fall to $300,250, because the size of the estate falls in a lower progressive tax bracket. However, if the community property is worth $10,000,000, then the savings is, again, $371,250 (like the original example $675,000 x 55 percent) because the tax rates have caused the savings to stabilize. The conclusion here is that the use of a credit equivalency trust will save estate taxes to varying degrees, with increasing savings as the assets increase, but there will be a stabilizing effect that will occur due to the leveling of the 55 percent tax bracket.

	Net Community Property = $2,000,000		Net Community Property = $10,000,000	
	No Credit Equivalency	Credit Equivalency	No Credit Equivalency	Credit Equivalency
Taxable Estate	$ 2,000,000	$ 1,325,000	$10,000,000	$ 9,325,000
Tentative Tax	$ 780,800	$ 480,550	$ 5,140,800	$ 4,769,550
Unified Credit	(220,550)	(220,550)	(220,550)	(220,550)
Tax Liability	$ 560,250	$ 260,000	$ 4,920,250	$ 4,549,000
Total Savings	$300,250		$371,250	

USE OF DISCLAIMERS

disclaimer - the refusal of the receipt of an estate. The use of disclaimers allows a spouse or anyone else to disclaim or renounce receiving any part of an estate

A **disclaimer** allows a spouse or anyone else to disclaim or renounce receiving any part of a bequest. A specific direction to disclaim is not necessary in the will or trust device. If the spouse disclaims property, their interest in and control over the property is extinguished. Since disclaimers must be made within nine months of the first spouse's death, the surviving spouse may find it difficult to give up property at a time when he or she may not be feeling emotionally or financially secure. When a person disclaims they are not making a gift, but rather the person is simply bypassed.

ALIEN SURVIVING SPOUSES

qualified domestic trust (QDOT) - for a non-citizen spouse who was a U.S. resident at the time of the decedent's death, the marital deduction is allowed if the property is placed in a QDOT that passes to a non-citizen surviving spouse

Section 2056(d) disallows the unlimited marital deduction if the surviving spouse is not a U.S. citizen. If a non-citizen spouse becomes a citizen before the federal estate tax return is filed (Form 706 within nine months), Section 2056(d) does not apply. For a non-citizen spouse who was a U.S. resident at the time of the decedent's death, the marital deduction is allowed if the property is placed in a **Qualified Domestic Trust (QDOT)** that passes to a non-citizen surviving spouse. The trust document for a QDOT requires at least one trustee to be U.S. citizen or U.S. corporation. The trustee must have a right to withhold estate tax on distribution of assets or income and must meet requirements of the U.S. Treasury. The executor must make an irrevocable election to establish a QDOT.

GENERATION SKIPPING TRANSFER TAX (GSTT)

generation skipping transfer tax (GSTT) - a tax that is in addition to the unified gift and estate tax and is designed to tax large transfers that skip a generation (that is, from grandparent to grandchild)

The **generation skipping transfer tax (GSTT)** is in addition to the unified gift and estate tax and is designed to tax large transfers that skip a generation (that is, from grandparent to grandchild). The purpose of the tax is to collect potentially lost tax dollars from the skipped generation. But for the generation skipping tax, one could leave all of one's assets to a grandchild and avoid the unified gift and estate tax on the middle generation. The current unified tax scheme would tax from the first to the second generation and from the second to the third generation. For a transfer made from the first generation directly to the third generation, some unified gift and estate tax is avoided. The generation skipping transfer tax attempts to make up for that loss of tax.

The GSTT rate is the highest marginal rate for the unified gift and estate tax rates (currently 55 percent). There are several exceptions to this tax. First, the annual exclusion also applies to a generation skipping transfer ($10,000 in 2001). Second, there is a lifetime exemption per donor ($1,060,000 in 2001). There is also an exception for transfers to a person of a skipped generation where a parent has predeceased the transferee prior to the transfer. For example, if a parent died, the grandparent may donate or bequest to the grandchild without the grandchild being considered a skip person. In effect, the grandchild steps into the shoes of the deceased parent. Finally, qualified transfers, such as medical costs and tuition are also excluded from GSTT. Gift splitting is available for the annual exclusion exceptions as long as both spouses elect to split gifts. The generation skipping transfer tax is repealed after 2009.

THE ROLE OF THE FINANCIAL PLANNER IN ESTATE PLANNING

Estate planning is very personal in nature and requires the financial planner to seek out the particulars that characterize each client's individual situation and goals. Financial planners must be able to ascertain the objectives of the client, while forecasting the long-range ramifications of the plan.

Reducing the estate tax is a matter of taking full advantage of various planning opportunities (summarized in Exhibit 21.8). Initially, getting the life insurance out of the gross estate is generally a wise idea. The next step for most clients is to make full use of the qualified transfers to educational and medical institutions. Then, the client should be encouraged to make optimal use of the annual exclusion ($10,000, $20,000 if split) on a yearly basis. At some time, either during life or at death, the client should make effective use of the credit equivalency ($675,000 for year 2001) by transferring these assets so as to avoid inclusion in the surviving spouse's gross estate. Then the spouse who has accomplished all of the above can leave the balance of the gross estate to his spouse in a qualifying way and, thus, have an estate tax liability of zero. Charitable contributions during life will reduce his gross estate, and the income on those transferred assets will not be taxed to the transferor. Charitable transfers at death are deductible from the adjusted gross estate, and, thus are not taxable.

EXHIBIT 21.8: ESTATE TAX REDUCTION TECHNIQUES

There are several techniques to reduce estate tax:
- ▲ Do not over-qualify the estate. Use the credit equivalency.
- ▲ Do not under-qualify the estate. Use an appropriate amount for the marital deduction, generally to reduce estate tax to zero.
- ▲ Generally, remove life insurance from the estate of the client.
- ▲ Change the ownership of life insurance or use irrevocable life insurance trust (must remove all incidents of ownership).
- ▲ Use lifetime gifts. Make use of annual exclusions with gift splitting.
- ▲ Use basic trusts.
- ▲ Use charitable contributions, transfers, and trusts.

Estate planning calls for a broad range of sophisticated talents. An attorney and CPA may need to be called into the estate team at this point, if not before, to cover the legal and tax aspects.

CONCLUDING COMMENTS ON THE UNIFICATION SCHEME OF GIFTS AND ESTATES

While it may appear that the unification scheme (the unified tax table) for gifts and estates provides equality or parity for transfers during life or at death, there are at least four important distinctions.

First, the annual exclusion of $10,000 per donee per year that is provided for gifts is essentially lost if the transfer does not occur until death. Thus, the annual exclusion is a perishable right, the total value of which declines with each passing year. A married couple with four children and two grandchildren can transfer $120,000 ($20,000 each) per year total during life to the six donees without any gift tax consequences. If this money is not transferred by gift or consumed by the decedent, it will be included in the gross estate at the decedent's death and may be subject to estate tax.

The second, and perhaps the most important advantage of making lifetime gifts is that any future appreciation of any asset transferred is not included in the gross estate of the transferor at death. For example, suppose Mr. William Brown gave his son, James, some XYZ.com stock, having a fair market value of $10,000. Mr. Brown (donor) pays no gift tax on the transfer because it is equal to the annual exclusion amount of $10,000. Now assume that James Brown holds the stock for ten years and that at the end of the ten-year period the stock is worth $300,000, and William Brown dies. No part of the value of the stock is included in William Brown's gross estate. If William Brown had retained the stock, he would have had to include the entire $300,000 in his gross estate. Thus, for assets that appreciate, transfers during life are more advantageous than transfers at death in reducing the gross estate.

Third, if any gift tax is paid on gifts made, that gift tax is also not included in the gross estate of the donor, unless such gift tax is paid on gifts made within three years of death.

For example, suppose John Hurly gave $10,000 cash under the annual exclusion and a taxable gift of $1,000,000 of stock in Finplan.com to his son, Patrick, in 1996. He would have paid $153,000 in gift tax. That $153,000 would have been excluded from John's gross estate as long as he died after 1999 (three years after the gift).

Fourth, the transfer of property during life subjects the transferee (donee) to the income tax consequences associated with the property, as opposed to subjecting the transferor (donor) to such income tax consequences. Thus, not only does future appreciation of assets get transferred, so does the future income, and, therefore, the income tax associated with the income earned from the transferred asset.

PROFESSIONAL

FOCUS

How do you approach the subject of lifetime gifting for older clients, who have lived through the Depression Era and are unwilling to relinquish assets?

Not only Depression Era but other clients as well are reluctant to give up assets. The question then becomes one of education-- would you rather give it to your kids and grandchildren or Uncle Sam? The quantification of estate erosion from estate taxes usually gets their attention. An aggressive gifting program can save hundreds of thousands of dollars in estate taxes and pass the money to their beneficiaries rather than go to Washington.

Additionally, gifting has some non-tax advantages:

▲ The donees show their appreciation while the donors are alive, and
▲ The donors can see how the donees manage the gifts, thereby assisting in the decision process of testamentary bequests in cash or in trust.

Do you recommend that clients participate in gifting of the yearly annual exclusion? If so, do you focus on clients of a particular wealth status?

Gifting and use of the annual exclusions can be beneficial to clients of various net worth levels. Those with a taxable estate in excess of the exemption equivalent level should seriously consider gifting to reduce or eliminate estate taxes.

Gifting of assets not needed for the donors' long term well-being has the additional potential advantages of possibly shifting income to a lower income tax bracket, getting potentially appreciating assets out of one's estate and providing financial assistance for beneficiaries who have current needs.

Care needs to be taken that gifted assets may not be needed by the donor in an era of expanding longevity. Also, clients need to be willing to give up control, something that some clients have difficulty doing.

What techniques do you use to reduce your clients' estate and gift taxes?

One of the exciting aspects of estate planning is that there is no patented or textbook answer. The answer(s) depend on the clients' financial situation, their wishes and their mentalities.

▲ Do they have charitable desires? If so, a Charitable Remainder Trust might be advised.
▲ Do they wish to pass on a closely held business interest? If so, a Family Limited Partnership might be a possible solution.
▲ Is this a second marriage? If so, a Q-TIP trust could be used to protect the interests of the respective off spring.

Even though a decedent cannot continue to control from the grave, as much post-mortem flexibility as possible is desirable. The use of Qualified Disclaimers is a very potent post-mortem tool. However, the decedent's will needs to direct where disclaimed property would go to best use this tool. In special cases and selected circumstances, more sophisticated approaches may be warranted, such as Grantor Retained Annuity Trusts, Qualified Personal Residence Trusts and installment sales to Intentionally Defective Trusts.

Estate planning is an area in which proper planning can significantly serve the client and the recommended solutions can be as varied as the unique client circumstances.

PETER BLACKWELL, MBA, CFP™

DISCUSSION QUESTIONS

1. What is the unified credit and how does it affect an individual's federal estate tax liability?
2. How can the annual gift tax exclusion be used as an estate planning tool?
3. What is gift splitting?
4. What are qualified transfers?
5. When is the gift tax return due?
6. What are the advantages and disadvantages of the unlimited marital deduction?
7. What are the steps in calculating the estate tax?
8. What are at least three estate planning techniques available to reduce gift and estate taxes?
9. When is the estate tax return due?
10. What is the unified credit against federal gift and estate tax for year 2001?
11. On which IRS form do you file funeral expenses?
12. What is a trust and what are the benefits of creating one?
13. What are different types of trusts that can be created?
14. What is the generation-skipping tax?

EXERCISES

1. During this year, Bob gave $100,000 to his son and $100,000 to his daughter. Bob's wife, Lori, also gave $5,000 to their son. No other gifts were made during the year. Bob and Lori elected to split the gifts on their gift tax returns. What is the amount of taxable gifts made by Bob and Lori?

2. Which of the following situations would not constitute a taxable transfer under the gift tax statutes?
    ▲ Father creates an irrevocable trust under the terms of which his son is to receive income for life and his grandson the remainder at his son's death.
    ▲ Father, with personal funds, purchases real property and has title conveyed to himself and his brother as joint tenants with right of survivorship.
    ▲ Father creates a trust giving income for life to wife and providing that, at her death, the corpus is to be distributed to their daughter. Father reserves the right to revoke the transfer at any time.

3. Stephen created a joint bank account for himself and his friend, Anna. When is there a gift to Anna?

4. During this year, Mr. and Mrs. Buzzetta made joint gifts of the following items to their son:
    ▲ A bond with an adjusted basis of $12,000 and a fair market value of $40,000.
    ▲ Stock with an adjusted basis of $22,000 and a fair market value of $33,000.
    ▲ An auto with an adjusted basis of $12,000 and a fair market value of $14,000.
    ▲ An interest-free loan of $6,000 for a computer (for the son's personal use) on January 1st, which was paid by their son on December 31st. Assume the applicable federal rate was 8 percent per annum.

    What is the gross amount of gifts includible in Mr. and Mrs. Buzzetta's gift tax returns for this year?

5. Tamara, who is single, gave an outright gift of $50,000 to a friend, Heather, who needed the money to pay her medical expenses. In filing the gift tax return, how much is Tamara entitled to exclude?

6. Which of the following situations constitutes a transfer that comes within the gift tax statutes?

5. Tamara, who is single, gave an outright gift of $50,000 to a friend, Heather, who needed the money to pay her medical expenses. In filing the gift tax return, how much is Tamara entitled to exclude?

6. Which of the following situations constitutes a transfer that comes within the gift tax statutes?
   ▲ Mark creates a trust under the terms of which his son is to get income for life and his grandson the remainder at his son's death.
   ▲ Mark purchases real property and has the title conveyed to himself and to his brother as joint tenants.
   ▲ Mark creates an irrevocable trust giving income for life to his wife and providing that upon her death the corpus is to be distributed to his daughter.
   ▲ Mark purchases a U.S. Savings Bond made payable to himself and his wife. The wife surrenders the bond for cash to be used for her benefit.

7. Which of the following situations would not constitute a transfer that comes within the gift tax statutes?
   ▲ Robin creates a trust under the terms of which her daughter is to get income for life and her granddaughter the remainder at the daughter's death.
   ▲ Robbie purchases real property and has title conveyed to himself and to his brother, Ritchie, as joint tenants.
   ▲ Randal creates an irrevocable trust giving income for life to his wife and providing that at her death the corpus is to be distributed to his son.
   ▲ Ray purchases a U.S. Savings Bond made payable to himself and his wife, Raquel. Raquel cashes the bond to be used for her own benefit.
   ▲ Rose creates a joint bank account for herself and her daughter, Daisy. There have been no withdrawals from the account.

8. Which of the following represent taxable gifts?
   ▲ The transfer of wealth by a parent to a dependent child that represents legal support.
   ▲ Payment of a child's tuition to Loyola's Law School by a parent.
   ▲ Payment of $20,000 from a grandparent to a grandchild for educational purposes.
   ▲ Payment of $11,000 of medical bills for a friend paid directly to the medical institution.

9. Victor wants to begin a program of lifetime giving to his 3 grandchildren and 5 great-grandchildren. He wants to control the amount of annual gifts to avoid the imposition of federal gift tax, and he does not desire to use any of his or his wife's (Veronica) unified tax credit. Veronica is willing to split each gift over a period of 10 years. What is the total amount of gifts, including gift splitting, that Victor can give over the 10-year period?

10. Rodney and his wife, Lois, have 4 children, each over the age of majority, 2 grandchildren over age 21, and 6 minor grandchildren. Rodney and Lois want to make gifts to their children and grandchildren sufficient to make maximum use of the tax provisions providing for annual exclusions from federal gift tax. Considering that desire only, what is the total amount of gifting that Rodney and Lois can make during the year?

11. Kurt died on July 31st. His assets and their fair market value at the time of his death were:

Cash	$15,000
Personal Residence	$250,000
Life insurance on Kurt's life	$150,000
Series EE bonds	$20,000

Kurt had a balance on his residence mortgage of $15,000. What is the total of Kurt's gross estate?

12. Evelyn died on August 1st this year. What is her gross estate?
  ▲ In 1998, Evelyn gave cash of $30,000 to her friend. No gift tax was paid on the gift.
  ▲ Evelyn held property jointly with her brother. Each paid $45,000 of the total purchase price of $90,000. Fair market value of the property at date of death was $200,000.
  ▲ In 1998, Evelyn purchased a life insurance policy on her own life and gave it as a gift to her sister. Evelyn retained the right to change the beneficiary. Upon Evelyn's death, her sister received $200,000 under the policy.
  ▲ In 1983, Evelyn gave her son a summer home (fair market value in 1982, $100,000). Evelyn continued to use it until her death pursuant to an understanding with her son. The fair market value at date of death was $190,000.

13. Jane died on May 2nd, of the current year, leaving an adjusted gross estate of $1,200,000 at the date of death. Under the terms of the will, $375,000 was bequeathed outright to her husband. The remainder of the estate was left to her mother. No taxable gifts were made during her lifetime. In computing the taxable estate, how much should the executor claim as a marital deduction?

14. Joshua died in 2001 with a taxable estate of $2,000,000. He had made no previous taxable gifts during his lifetime. His estate will receive a credit for state death tax of $100,000. How much is his federal estate tax?

15. Joseph died in 2001 with a taxable estate of $1,600,000 and had previously given adjusted taxable gifts of $700,000. During his life he used unified credits of $64,800. What amount will Joseph subtract on his estate tax return for his unified credit?

16. Identify at least 3 alternative methods of limiting, reducing, or avoiding federal estate taxes.

17. Which of the following transfers qualify for the unlimited marital deduction?
  ▲ Outright bequest to resident alien spouse.
  ▲ Property passing to citizen spouse in QTIP.
  ▲ Income beneficiary of CRT is a non-resident alien spouse (Trust is not a QDOT).
  ▲ Outright bequest to resident spouse who, prior to the decedent's death was a non-citizen, but who after the decedent's death and before the estate return was filed became an U.S. citizen.

18. Who among the following would be skip persons for purposes of the GSTT? Matt is the transferor and is 82 years old.

 ▲ Tim, the grandson of Matt whose mother, Bonnie, is living but whose father, Ben, is deceased.

 ▲ Mindy is the great-grandchild of Matt. Both Mindy's parents and grandparents are living.

 ▲ Sharon is the 21-year-old wife of Matt's second son, Alan, age 65.

19. Rosalie, who is single, is diagnosed with a serious disease and expects to be completely incapacitated in three years. Rosalie has two daughters and two grandchildren. She has $500,000 in net worth including her principal residence. Which of the following estate planning tools would you recommend for Rosalie?

 ▲ Set up a durable power of attorney.

 ▲ Immediately gift annual exclusion amounts to children and grandchildren.

 ▲ Set up a revocable living trust.

 ▲ Set up an irrevocable living trust.

 ▲ Set up a QTIP trust.

20. On April 30th, Dennis transfers property to a trust over which he retains a right to revoke one-fourth of the trust. The trust is to pay Kim 5 percent of the trust assets valued annually for her life with the remainder to be paid to a qualified charity. On August 31st, Dennis dies and the trust becomes irrevocable. Identify the type of trust.

PROBLEMS

1. Neal is a widower with a taxable estate of $1,400,000. He had made no taxable lifetime gifts. What is his federal estate tax due before the unified credit if Neal dies in 2001? What is the amount of the unified credit?

2. Denise and Barry are married and have a taxable estate of $2 million. What is the gross tax on the estate? What is the net tax due?

3. In 2001, Georgia gave a $10,000 cash gift to her friend, Mary. How much is the taxable gift?

4. For each of the past 10 years, Jessica has given $12,000 to each of her six grandchildren and $25,000 each to her son and daughter. What is the total amount of gifts and how much gift tax is due?

5. Ken and Libby have the following assets:

 ▲ $300,000 house in Ken's name.

 ▲ $500,000 investment account in Libby's name.

 ▲ $500,000 in rental property jointly owned with JTWROS.

 ▲ $200,000 beach condo that Libby co-owns with her sister as tenants in common.

They have two adult children and have made no previous taxable gifts. How much can they transfer to the children free of all transfer tax?

6. Chance is an 85-year-old widower with two sons and a daughter, three grandchildren, and a 27-year old girlfriend. He has an estate currently worth $650,000, including a house worth $300,000. His estate also includes a life insurance policy on his life with a face value of $120,000, and the primary beneficiaries are his children. Chance was recently diagnosed with Alzheimers. The doctors predict a rapid progression and recommend that Chance go into a nursing home soon. He currently has a will that leaves all of his assets equally to his children. He has not taken advantage of any other estate planning techniques. Which of the following would you recommend to Chance while he still has all his mental faculties, and why?

   ▲ Create a living will, a general power of attorney, and a power of attorney for health care.

   ▲ Transfer ownership of his residence to his children so that it will not be counted as a resource when he goes into the nursing home.

   ▲ Create an irrevocable trust containing all of his assets and naming his children as beneficiaries.

   ▲ Create a revocable trust containing all of his assets and naming his children as beneficiaries.

   ▲ Create a QTIP trust naming his girlfriend as the income beneficiary and his children as the remaindermen beneficiaries.

7. Harrison Cross had the following assets* at his death in 2001:

Boat	$50,000	Owned in his name only.
Note Receivable (present value)	$250,000	Owned in his name only.
Insurance (policy on Harrison at face value)	$125,000	Owned in his name only/spouse beneficiary.
Ranch	$400,000	Owned in his name only.
House	$120,000	Owned jointly with his spouse (JTWROS) FMV = $120,000 (50 percent = $60,000).
Annuity	$80,000	Payable to his spouse.

All assets (except the life insurance) are stated at fair market value.

At death, Harrison also had $60,000 in debts and a $100,000 mortgage on his ranch. His insurance was payable to his spouse. His will gave everything to his daughter and son equally and provided that all debts, expenses and taxes were to be paid out of his probate residue. The expenses of administering his estate were $40,000. He made no taxable gifts during his life. His estate has no credits against the tax except the unified credit and the state death tax credit. Calculate the net federal estate tax, if any, due on Harrison's estate.

8. If, alternatively, Harrison Cross had left his entire estate to his spouse and he had the following assets* at his death in 2001:

Boat	$50,000	Owned in his name only.
Note Receivable (present value)	$250,000	Owned in his name only.
Insurance (policy on Harrison at face value)	$125,000	Owned in his name only/spouse beneficiary.
Ranch	$400,000	Owned in his name only.
House	$120,000	Owned jointly with his spouse (JTWROS) FMV = $120,000 (50 percent = $60,000).
Annuity	$80,000	Payable to his spouse.

All assets (except the life insurance) are stated at fair market value.

At his death, he also had $60,000 in debts and a $100,000 mortgage on his ranch. His insurance was payable to his spouse. His will gave everything to his spouse and provided that all debts, expenses, and taxes were to be paid out of his probate residue. The expenses of administering his estate were $40,000. He made no taxable gifts during his life. His estate has no credits against the tax except the unified credit and the state death tax credit. Calculate the net federal estate tax, if any, due on Harrison's estate.

9. Harrison Cross had the following assets at his death in 2001:

Boat	$50,000	Owned in his name only.
Note Receivable (present value)	$250,000	Owned in his name only.
Insurance (policy on Harrison at face value)	$125,000	Owned in his name only/children beneficiaries.
Ranch	$400,000	Owned in his name only.
House	$120,000	Owned jointly with his spouse FMV = $120,000 (50 percent = $60,000).
Annuity	$80,000	Payable to his children.

All assets (except the life insurance) are stated at fair market value.

At his death, he also had $60,000 in debts and a $100,000 mortgage on his ranch. His insurance was payable to his children. His will gave everything to his son and daughter and provided that all debts, expenses, and taxes were to be paid out of his probate residue. The expenses of administering his estate were $40,000. He made no taxable gifts during his life. His estate has no credits against the tax except the unified credit. Calculate the net federal estate tax, if any, due on Harrison's estate.

Financial Planning Profession

in BRIEF

- Financial planning institutions
- Financial planning professionals
- The Code of Ethics
- Disciplinary Rules and Procedures
- The Practice Standards
- State laws
- Civil liability

- Developing a financial planning practice
- Maintaining competence
- Developing clients

- Practice competently, ethically, and legally
- Procedures regarding discipline
- Civil liability

The Financial Planning Profession

Risks

- Incompentence of planner
- Improper practice
- Unethical practice
- Illegal practice
- Professional discipline
- Civil liabilty

Data Collection

- Financial planning institutions
- Financial planning professionals
- The Code of Ethics
- Practice Standards
- Laws regarding malpractice
- Disciplinary rules
- Civil liability

Goals

- The competent, legal, and ethical practice of financial planning

Data Analysis

- Maintaining professional competence
- Continuing education
- Practicing lawfully and ethically
- How to build a practice

CHAPTER 22

The Practice of Financial Planning

LEARNING OBJECTIVES:

After learning the material in this chapter, you will be able to:

1. Describe various types of financial planning institutions.

2. Identify the types of services that are provided by the various types of financial planning institutions.

3. List some of the common credentials associated with the financial planning industry.

4. Discuss common compensation methods for professional financial planners.

5. Identify some important aspects of building a financial planning practice and maintaining clients.

6. Discuss why continued education is important for financial planners.

INTRODUCTION

The professional financial planner understands that the overall purpose of personal financial planning is to assist the client in achieving goals and objectives. While most of those goals are financially related, many are more qualitative than quantitative. The planner realizes that personal financial planning is about the adaptation of the individual client's strengths and weaknesses in an environment characterized by opportunities and threats. Generally throughout the text, we have referred to these threats as risks.

The planner must possess a wide variety of skills and knowledge and must be able to apply those skills in any given client situation to assess the client's current financial situation, to help the client establish realistic financial goals, and to develop a plan or strategy for accomplishing those goals.

To be successful as a financial planner, the professional should have a working knowledge of the concepts within the financial planning pyramid.

EXHIBIT 22.1: FINANCIAL PLANNER'S PYRAMID OF KNOWLEDGE

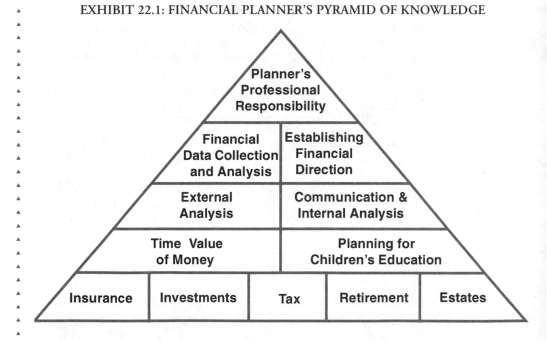

THE FINANCIAL PLANNING PROFESSION

The financial planning profession is practiced by a diverse group of individuals and institutions. Many practitioners have individual private practices. However, most financial planners work for accounting firms, law firms, insurance companies, personal financial planning firms, brokerage houses, and other financial institutions that provide financial planning-related services.

FINANCIAL PLANNING INSTITUTIONS

Accounting Firms

Accounting firms have traditionally provided accounting, tax, and auditing-related services. From an individual's perspective, these services were limited to preparing tax returns, preparing financial statements, business consulting, and business and individual tax planning. However, accounting firms today are providing more services related to financial planning. These services include assistance in investment planning, retirement planning, and estate planning.

The American Institute of Certified Public Accountants (AICPA) has been actively assisting CPAs in the development of financial planning practices in recent years. They provide training for members at national conferences and have instituted a designation devoted solely to financial planning. The AICPA has also been able to establish relationships with other financial services firms that are allowing CPAs to deliver more financial planning services to their new and existing clients.

Law Firms

Attorneys have always been an integral part of developing and implementing financial and estate plans. Since attorneys are the ones who draft legal documents, they are in a perfect position to provide additional services to their clients. Law firms have always drafted such documents as wills, powers of attorney, trusts, qualified plan documents, partnership agreements and other similar documents. Their traditional services include tax planning, estate planning, and retirement and benefit planning.

Insurance Companies

Insurance companies primarily sell life, health and/or property and casualty insurance products. Many insurance companies are expanding their services to include other areas of financial planning, particularly estate planning and retirement planning. Some have their own proprietary mutual funds.

Personal Financial Planning Firms (PFP Firms)

These firms are generally small and specialize in a particular market niche. Some PFP Firms manage assets, while others provide comprehensive financial planning or sell products.

Brokerage Houses

Many brokerage houses provide global financial management and advisory services, including financial planning, securities underwriting, and trading and brokering. Some brokerage firms provide research, banking and insurance services, and investment banking. Brokerage houses are currently in the process of changing the nature of their business from transaction oriented to more service-and-planning related. These new services include basic retirement and estate planning.

Mutual Funds

Many mutual fund companies now provide financial planning assistance to their customers as a method of better servicing their clients and as a method of differentiating themselves from their competition. Some have established personal counselors for some of their large customers while providing generic planning on the Internet for all customers.

Banks

Banks offer a wide range of financial planning services. Banks generally offer checking and savings, mortgages, loans, and other credit products. Some banks also offer comprehensive brokerage services, including stocks, bonds, and mutual funds. Banks are also in the process of developing financial planning practices as a method of better servicing their clients.

EXHIBIT 22.2: SUMMARY OF FINANCIAL PLANNING INSTITUTIONS

Common Practice Areas	Accounting Firms	Law Firms	Insurance Companies	PFP Firms	Brokerage Houses	Mutual Funds	Banks
Insurance			✔	✔	✔		✔
Investments	✔		✔	✔	✔	✔	✔
Tax	✔	✔		✔			
Retirement	✔	✔	✔	✔	✔		
Estate Planning	✔	✔	✔	✔	✔		

As competition for clients increases, and as more firms and individual practices attempt to attract more clients in an effort to increase the assets under management, many firms are expanding their services to include all aspects of financial planning. Such diversification allows the client the opportunity for one-stop shopping. Firms have accomplished this change and expansion by keeping their traditional expertise, such as tax planning for accounting firms and investment advice for brokerage houses, and hiring "office specialists" in the other areas. Thus, the institutions appear to continue to have a dominance of service and training in one specific area, but have the capacity through company experts to cover all aspects of financial planning. In addition, the institutions themselves continue to expand as the competition increases, in order to spread the costs of experts and additional services over the greatest number of clients and the amount of assets under management.

The consolidation of the various practice areas will likely provide an opportunity for lower to middle-income clients to receive better financial planning services. Those services may become less personal, however, with computerized planning being offered over the Internet. Meanwhile, the wealthiest clients will likely continue to seek the service of a team of professionals, generally from more than one institution. Individuals with a large amount of investments generally seek independence of thought and appreciate reasonable differences of opinion, which may be unlikely from a single institution.

FINANCIAL PLANNING PROFESSIONALS

The public perceives, and has a reasonable expectation, that those who "practice" financial planning are competent and ethical. Many financial professionals are licensed at the state and federal levels in specific areas such as insurance or securities. They are not specifically regulated, however, for their financial planning activities, with the exception of the CERTIFIED FINANCIAL PLANNER™ practitioner, who is certified by the CFP Board of Standards. Persons who have only an elementary understanding of one or two functional areas are not prepared to assist clients faced with complex choices in a changing environment. While there are many competent, highly trained, and highly credentialed persons practicing financial planning, there are many more persons holding themselves out as financial planners who are not trained, competent, or credentialed. Unfortunately, therefore, the practice of financial planning is currently characterized by a lack of uniform educational standards, a lack of professional competence standards, and a lack of commitment to one profession with a self-regulating set of ethical standards.

There is, of course, hope. The professionalism in personal financial planning is changing, albeit slowly. As the planners themselves recognize that they need to become competent to distinguish themselves, the consuming public is shedding its unrealistic expectations and becoming more sophisticated when choosing financial planning professionals.

As the practice of personal financial planning is conducted by a wide variety of individuals calling themselves financial planners, consumer confusion is common. Many financial planning professionals attempt to distinguish themselves by earning financial planning designations. The following three sections briefly describe some of the more common credentials for individuals who work in the financial planning areas.

Financial Planning Designations

Certified Financial Planner (CFP™)

The CFP™ credential is perhaps the most recognized and respected financial planning designation and is awarded by the CFP Board of Standards. CFP™ certificants are individuals who have met the CFP Board's education, examination, and experience requirements. These individuals are committed to high standards of ethical conduct and must complete biennial certification requirements. Additional information about the CFP Board and the ethics code is provided in the next chapter.

Chartered Financial Consultant (ChFC)

The ChFC credential is a financial planning designation awarded by The American College to those individuals who complete the required education program, meet the experience requirements, and agree to adhere to the code of ethics.

Personal Financial Specialist (PFS)

The PFS designation is granted exclusively to CPAs who wish to specialize in personal financial planning. The PFS credential is a financial planning designation awarded by the AICPA to those candidates who have met the CPA educational requirements exam, have the minimum hours of financial planning experience, and successfully complete a six-hour exam.

EXHIBIT 22.3: SUMMARY OF FINANCIAL PLANNING DESIGNATIONS

	Education/ Experience	Exam	Ethics	Continuing Education	Designating Organization	Number Licensed
CFP™	Three years (with bachelors degree) of financial planning-related experience; five years without degree	10 hrs over two days.	Yes	30 hrs every 2 years	CFP Board	35,787 (as of 5/00)
ChFC	10-course financial planning curriculum from The American College	Two-hour exam for each of the 10 courses	Adherence to The American College's Code of Ethics	30 hours every two years (mandatory for certain designees who matriculated after 6/30/89; voluntary for others)	The American College	33,478 (as of 5/00)
PFS	Candidates must have be a CPA and practice in the area of financial planning for a minimum number of hours per year.	Comprehensive six-hour exam covering six financial planning topic areas	Adherence to the AICPA's Code of Professional Conduct	72 hours every three years	AICPA only to members who meet its requirements	2,525 (as of 6/00)

Other Designations Held by Financial Services Professionals

Chartered Life Underwriter (CLU)

The CLU designation is awarded by The American College to insurance and financial services professionals who have met the College's three-year business experience requirement, passed its 10 college-level education courses, and agreed to abide by its code of ethics.

Chartered Financial Analyst (CFA)

This designation is awarded by the Association for Investment Management and Research (AIMR) to experienced financial analysts who successfully complete a CFA study course and pass three annual examinations covering economics, financial accounting, portfolio management, securities analysis, and ethics.

Certified Public Accountant (CPA)

The CPA designation is awarded by the American Institute of Certified Public Accountants (AICPA) to accountants who pass the AICPA's Uniform CPA Examination and satisfy the work experience and statutory and licensing requirements of the state(s) in which they practice.

Other Licenses Held by Financial Services Professionals

Attorney (JD)

As mentioned in the previous section, a small percentage of attorneys provide financial planning services. Generally, those that do provide such services, specialize in estate and/or tax planning. The attorney is typically part of a financial planning team and may provide specific legal advice to a client, prepare legal documents, and consult on estate and tax planning issues.

Insurance Agent

Insurance agents are individuals licensed by a state or states to sell or give advice on insurance products, including life, health, property, and casualty insurance. Financial planning services will vary based on the type of agent. Independent insurance agents sell products for more than one insurance company, where exclusive insurance agents represent only one company.

Securities Analyst

These professionals are usually employed by investment brokers, banks, mutual fund managers, or other investment institutions to conduct investment research and analyze the value of securities and financial condition of a company, group of companies, or industry sector. Based on their analysis, securities analysts will make investment recommendations.

Registered Investment Adviser (RIA)

Registered Investment Advisors are individuals (or firms) providing securities advice for compensation. They must be registered with the Securities and Exchange Commission (SEC) and/or appropriate state securities agencies. Financial planning services provided by RIAs include recommendations of stocks, bonds, mutual funds, and other investments.

Real Estate Broker

Real estate brokers are licensed by a state or states in which they practice. These individuals arrange the purchase or sale of property in return for a commission. Financial planning services provided by real estate brokers are limited and may include helping customers finance a real estate purchase through their contacts with banks, savings and loans, and mortgage bankers.

COMPENSATION METHODS

The methods of compensation for professional financial planners are as diverse as the planners themselves, and include fee-only planners, fee-based planners, commission-based, and those receiving fees for assets under management. In recent years, there has been a move toward fee-only and fee-based planners due to the perception on the part of the public of a conflict of interest for commission-based planners.

Fee-Only Planners

Fee-only planners typically charge an hourly rate for advice or a fixed fee for a defined engagement. These planners do not receive commissions and, therefore, their compensation is not contingent on the purchase or sale of a product. Many attorneys, CPAs, and CFP practitioners are compensated as fee-only financial planners.

Fee-Based Planners

Fee-based planners are compensated by both fees and commissions that are contingent on the purchase or sale of financial products.

Commission-Based Planners

Commission-based planners are compensated solely by commissions that are contingent on the purchase or sale of financial products. These products are used in the implementation of the financial plan.

Fees for Assets under Management

Some planners are fee-only for advice, and then, if they take investment assets under management will charge a monthly, quarterly, or annual fee of some percent of the overall portfolio value. Fees charged for the management of assets are predominately based on a percentage of assets. The percentage charged will generally be lower as the size of the asset pool increases.

COMPLIANCE ISSUES

The financial planning profession has few standards set by state and federal agencies regarding the regulation of financial planners as a group. However, most financial planners render some sort of advice in specific areas that does require either state or federal regulations. Planners selling stocks and bonds, insurance products, real estate, or providing legal or tax advice are all required to have licenses for the specific services they provide. In addition, most planners providing investment advice must register with their state as well as with the Securities and Exchange Commission in accordance with the Investment Advisors Act of 1940. In the absence of government regulation of financial planners, those planners who are CFP[TM] certificants have voluntarily chosen to be regulated by a professional regulatory organization, the CFP Board.

DEVELOPING A PROFESSIONAL PRACTICE

BUILDING A PRACTICE

Like any other service-oriented professional practice, the growth and development of a personal financial planning practice will occur slowly. The professional developing a practice generally begins by writing a business or strategic plan that identifies the exact market niche of clients to be targeted as well as establishes goals and objectives for the practice. The planner assesses the competition for that market niche, the external environment, and his/her internal strengths and weaknesses. The planner then selects from alternative strategies and begins to implement the strategies to begin the development of the practice. Finally, the planner must monitor and adjust the practice on a continuing basis.

Choosing a market niche is perhaps the most important strategic decision a professional can make regarding the development of a long lasting, viable practice. An individual planner cannot be all things to all clients. Therefore, a professional must direct attention to the niches that he can penetrate and that will allow him to prosper. An appropriate approach to developing a practice is to scan the environment for a market niche that is currently not being well served or for a newly developing market need that is underserved or will soon be underserved.

Once a market niche is selected, the planner must promote the professional services that are relevant to that particular niche in such a way as to be effective. Finding the best form of promotion depends on the market niche, the external environment, and the professional's strengths and weaknesses.

Clients typically feel insecure, skeptical, and somewhat threatened when buying professional services. Therefore, the client must not only have confidence in the planner's technical abilities, but must also feel that they can trust the planner. After all, the client is not just buying a product, but entering into a relationship. With that in mind, a successful marketing plan generally begins with promoting to an already existing client base. Such client-centered marketing is a good start because the planner and client have already developed a relationship. In addition, the planner is already familiar with the client's concerns and needs. If the planner is developing a new practice, an alternative option may be to partner with other professionals who do not provide the same services that the planner expects to provide.

The pursuit of new clients is more of a challenge, as the ability to win the client's trust and confidence is a substantial obstacle in the sale of professional services. Clients of "less than competent" practitioners do not leave those practitioners just because a more competent professional becomes available. Many clients lack the ability to assess a practitioner's competence and, even if they can assess competence, they fear and resist changing practitioners. Thus, many clients stay with poor practitioners because the relationship is "comfortable." An understanding of this phenomenon should lead the developing professional to understand that they must be creative, aggressive, and patient in developing a practice. Marketing to new clients may take the form of referrals, networking, educational and professional seminars, teaching courses, and direct advertising. The development of a successful practice will require a variety of promotional tools used in combination, consistent with an overall marketing and development plan.

MAINTAINING CLIENTS

As mentioned, a high level of interpersonal trust is the key to long-term planner-client relationships. Regular contact and effective communication help to develop the personal relationships that are essential in maintaining clients. Regular contact with clients, such as written communications, telephone conversations, lunch meetings, and other social activities help to develop the personal relationships.

Although regular contact is important, perhaps the most essential key to good planner-client relationships is the ability of the planner to listen. Clients should feel like the planner is listening to their concerns and respects them. According to researchers at the University of Minnesota, on the average, people spend nearly half of their communication time listening. Good listening is an active and complex process that takes knowledge of a few basic skills and lots of practice. Many professionals are so used to selling that they do not stop to listen. Some tips to demonstrate that the planner is listening to the client include taking notes during client meetings; restating what the client has just said and getting acknowledgement from the client; and speaking up when an issue is unclear. Such active listening improves interpersonal skills, human relations, and personal selling capabilities.

Nurturing client relationships takes time, but will greatly benefit the planner in the long run and may result in additional business.

Where on the Web

American Bar Association *www.abanet.org*

American Institute of Certified Public Accountants (CPA/PFS) *www.aicpa.org*

Association for Investment Management and Research (CFA designation) *www.aimr.org*

Certified Financial Planner Board of Standards *www.CFP-Board.org*

Financial Planning Association *www.fpanet.org*

Financial Planning Magazine Online *www.financial-planning.com*

National Association of Insurance Commissioners *www.naic.org*

National Association of Personal Financial Advisors *www.napfa.org*

National Association of Securities Dealers, Inc. *www.nasd.com*

National Association of State Boards of Accountancy *www.nasba.org*

North American Securities Administrators Association *www.nasaa.org*

Securities and Exchange Commission *www.sec.gov*

Small Business Association *www.sba.gov*

Society of Financial Service Professionals (formerly the American Society of CLU & ChFC) *www.asclu.org*

U.S. Chamber of Commerce *www.uschamber.org*

EDUCATION AND CONTINUING EDUCATION

Although a financial planner does not have to be an expert in all areas, it is critical for the planner to be familiar with the various life stages and the kinds of planning issues with which their clients are faced. The professional financial planner must obtain an initial education, followed by a life-time of continuing professional monitoring and education.

The external environment is complex and constantly changing, as are some of the functional areas of financial planning. The risks to life, health, disability, property, and liability change. The tax laws are complex and change so frequently that the average client has no understanding of them. While investment information is more readily available today, discerning what is relevant and useful requires more than a primer education and knowledge of investments. Competent financial planning professionals will make staying abreast of these changes a major priority throughout their professional careers.

EXHIBIT 22.4: SAMPLE ENGAGEMENT LETTER

(Date)

(Name of Client)
(Address of Client)

Dear (Name of Client):

This letter sets forth our understanding of the terms and objectives of our engagement to provide personal financial planning services to you. The scope and nature of the services to be provided are as follows:

1. **Review and Evaluation**
    We will review and analyze all information furnished to us including:
    (list items)

2. **Written Plan**
    Based on our review and analysis, we will prepare a written analysis of your:
    (list items)

    We will also prepare, in writing, specific initial recommendations to address your concerns and issues, including goals, objectives, and risks with respect to:
    (list items)

    Our recommendations will include strategies based on our analysis of your circumstances. Where appropriate, we will include financial illustrations and financial projections to enhance your understanding of the potential outcomes of the alternatives.

    We will meet with you to discuss our analysis and will provide you with a preliminary draft copy of our recommended strategies. You will be given an opportunity to concur with the preliminary recommendations or suggest modifications. Following agreement on your personal financial goals and the strategies to be used to achieve them, we will provide you with a finalized version of the plan.

3. **Fees**
    Our fee for these services is based on our standard hourly rates and the number of hours required. We expect our fees to be no less than $_____ but not to exceed $_____. We will bill you beginning with our next regular billing cycle. The final payment will be adjusted to reflect actual time expended, not to exceed the maximum total amount quoted for the year, and will be due upon completion of the engagement.

4. **Implementation**
    We will assist you in implementing the strategies that have been agreed upon. Accordingly, we will be available on an ongoing basis, by telephone or in person, to answer questions, to assist you or your other advisors to take necessary actions, and to make recommendations regarding these matters. We will bill you for these additional services based on time expended at our standard hourly rate.

5. **Limitation on Scope of Services**

    These services are not intended to include:
    (list items)

We will bill separately for any such additional services provided, based on time expended at our standard hourly rates.

If this letter correctly sets forth your understanding of the terms and objectives of the engagement, please so indicate by signing in the space provided below.

Respectfully yours,

(Name of Planner)
(Name of Firm)

The above letter sets forth my understanding of the terms and objectives of the engagement to provide personal financial planning services.

Signed: _____   Date: _____

DISCUSSION QUESTIONS

1. What are the primary differences in services provided by accounting firms and law firms?
2. Generally, which types of financial planning firms specialize in investment planning?
3. Generally, which types of financial planning firms specialize in estate planning?
4. How is the Internet changing the financial planning industry?
5. Which is the most recognized and respected financial planning designation?
6. What are the differences between the CFP^{TM} designation and the CFA designation?
7. Describe the fee-only compensation method.
8. What is one of the most important strategic decisions that must be made when developing a financial planning practice?
9. What can the planner do to improve the planner-client relationship?

CHAPTER 23

Ethical Responsibilities

LEARNING OBJECTIVES:

After learning the material in this chapter, you will be able to:

1. Differentiate among ethics, law, and an ethics code giving similarities and differences.

2. Define the Certified Financial Planner Board of Standards, Inc. (the CFP Board).

3. Define the Code of Ethics and Professional Responsibility (the Code).

4. Explain the role of the CFP Board's Practice Standards in relation to the Code.

5. Explain the role of the Board of Professional Review (BOPR), the Board of Practice Standards, and the Board of Governors in relation to the Code.

6. Explain the role of the Disciplinary Rules and Procedures (the Procedures) and the Financial Planning Practice Standards (the Standards) in relation to the Code.

7. Describe the structure of the Code and give the role of each of its parts.

8. List the seven Principles of the Code and give a rule that relates to each Principle.

9. Explain how the "commingling of funds" and the "fiduciary relationship" relate to the Code's Principle of Integrity.

10. Compare the three distinct standards or "burdens" of proof to illustrate different treatment of the CFP Board designee at various stages of disciplinary proceedings.

11. Differentiate among the four forms of discipline that can be applied by the BOPR to a CFP Board designee.

12. State the primary purpose or aim of the CFP Board's Practice Standards.

ETHICS, LAW, AND CODES OF ETHICS

CFP Code of Ethics and Professional Responsibility - the set of principles of conduct that seeks to regulate behavior of CFP™ certificants

This chapter identifies, describes, and explains ethical rules for those involved in the financial planning industry through an analysis of the **Code of Ethics and Professional Responsibility (the "Code")** established by the **Certified Financial Planner Board of Standards, Inc. (the "CFP Board")** for CFP Board designees. Analyzing the Code as it pertains to CFP™ certificants an independent professional regulatory organization that regulates financial planners through trademark law by certifying individuals who meet the CFP Board's certification requirements to use the federally registered marks, CERTIFIED FINANCIAL PLANNER™ and CFP™, including its rules, principles, and procedures of professional ethics and responsibility, in turn proves to be an excellent guide for all of those involved in the financial planning field. Before delving into the Code, however, it is important to distinguish between ethics, law, and ethics codes.

Certified Financial Planner Board of Standards, Inc. - an independent professional regulatory organization that regulates financial planners

Ethics is the discipline of dealing with the moral principles or values that guide one's self. In situations where a decision must be made about a certain act, ethics aids us in dealing with what is good and bad. In other words, ethics is doing or not doing what one feels is right. This feeling comes from within ourselves. Morals relate to one's conscience, character, and social relations. Morals form one's behavior and basically dictate whether one engages in conduct that is considered to be right or wrong. Thus, each individual's set of morals and values forms the ethics or ethical behavior of that individual.

ethics - the discipline of dealing with the moral principles or values that guide one's self

Law is defined as rules of conduct that are established by a government or other authority that command and encourage behavior considered right and prohibit behavior considered wrong. Law and ethics differ in that laws apply to everyone, under certain authority, and compliance with laws is mandatory for those individuals. If the law is broken, that person is subject to punishment by governmental authorities. A violation of or deviation from one's own ethics, on the other hand, does not necessarily subject that person to punishment.

law - rules of conduct that are established by a government or other authority that command and encourage behavior considered right and prohibit behavior considered wrong

A **code of ethics** is a set of principles of conduct that governs a group of individuals and usually requires conformity to professional standards of conduct. Although the Code provides rules for ethical behavior, the Code itself is more closely aligned with law. The same goes for attorneys concerning State Bar Ethics Codes, for example. The Code is considered to be a set of laws or rules for CFP Board designees because compliance is mandatory, and failure to abide by these ethics rules may result in discipline, such as revocation or suspension of one's CFP™ certification. These ethics rules must be followed. The ethics rules are, therefore, law as far as the CFP™ certificant is concerned.

code of ethics - a set of principles of conduct that governs a group of individuals and usually requires conformity to professional standards of conduct

Many professions have codes of ethics or sets of laws of conduct for that particular profession designed to promote ethical behavior on the part of all such professionals. However, no finite set of ethical rules can anticipate all situations or future developments in the industry. To truly satisfy the goal of ethics codes, the applicable professional must do more than merely fulfill ethics codes' minimum requirements. To reach the ideals of these codes, there must be a conscientious, good faith commitment by the professional to the spirit of the standards of the code under any circumstance.

Ethical behavior, which conforms to moral principles, is the aim of the CFP Board's Code. If financial planners abide by the highest standards of ethical behavior, the financial services industry will maintain or gain public trust There is a need for a common, accepted set of ethical principles to ensure fair representation and full disclosure in financial planning services. The Code basically seeks to regulate behavior of CFP Board designees with the intent to provide fairness to clients, maintain and increase public trust, and foster accountability on the CFP Board designee's behalf. Public trust in the profession is crucial because numerous opportunities for unethical behavior arise frequently in the financial planning services industry. It is imperative for the profession to maintain and increase the public trust because people place their money, trust, and financial well-being into the hands of the CFP Board designee. Without that trust, people will not seek the advice of CFP Board designees, but will instead consult other professionals, or simply not seek services in financial planning. Hence, the importance of an ethics code, and of compliance with it, is clear.

In short, although an ethics code is a set of laws or rules for the professional that must be followed, the Board or governing authority, through the adoption of its ethics code, attempts to instill in the professional a set of internal morals and values that will hopefully guide the professional in all situations.

Aside from the mandatory nature of the Code, the principles and rules embodied in the Code comprise a framework for ethical practices that will serve clients and CFP Board designees well in the long run. The CFP Board's Practice Standards further seek to add to the quality of those ethical practices by requiring excellence, not minimum effort, from CFP Board designees. In a time when the public is yearning for quality services from financial planners, virtually every member of the public can benefit from ethical and competent advice from those who follow the rules and principles found in the Code. For these reasons, a closer look at the Code and the standards and principles it discusses is appropriate.

THE CFP BOARD AND THE ETHICS CODE

The CFP Board is an independent professional regulatory organization that owns the federally registered "CFP" and "Certified Financial Planner" marks (the "marks"). The CFP Board regulates financial planners through trademark law by licensing individuals who meet the CFP Board's certification requirements to use these federally registered marks. The CFP Board has four subsidiary boards, one of which is the **Board of Professional Review** ("BOPR") which interprets and applies the Code, and further investigates, reviews, and takes appropriate action in connection with alleged violations of the Code by CFP Board designees. The Board of Practice Standards (another subsidiary board) develops and promulgates standards for the practice of personal financial planning for CFP Board designees.

The **CFP Board of Governors** requires compliance with this Code by all those who have been recognized and certified to use the CFP mark, as well as those who seek certification. The Code represents the minimum standards of acceptable professional conduct for the CFP Board designees. Violations of the Code may result in a letter of admonition, private censure, suspension, or revocation of the right to use the CFP Board designation. These forms of discipline are established in the Disciplinary Rules and Procedures (the "Procedures") to enforce the Code. The

Certified Financial Planner Board of Professional Review ("BOPR") - a subsidiary board of the CFP Board of Standards that interprets and applies the CFP Code

Certified Financial Planner Board of Governors - the governing board for the certified financial planning profession

Procedures also explain the disciplinary process. The final area of rules established by the CFP Board are the Financial Planning Practice Standards (the "Practice Standards"). The final authority for CFP Board designees in all disciplinary matters rests solely with the CFP Board and BOPR under the limitations of the Code.

The CFP Board requires adherence to the Code by all those recognized and certified to use the marks, as well as those candidates who seek to obtain the marks. Compliance with the Code on an individual basis and by the profession as a whole depends upon each CFP Board designee's knowledge and voluntary compliance with the applicable Rules and Principles. Compliance also depends on the influence of fellow professionals and public opinion. The effectiveness of the Code and the success of the profession depend on the appropriate application of disciplinary proceedings involving CFP Board designees who fail to comply with the Code.

The Code is divided into two main parts, Principles and Rules. The **Principles** of the Code address the profession's recognition of the responsibilities of its members to the public, clients, colleagues, and employers, and provide guidance to members during the performance of their professional duties. The Principles apply to all those who have been recognized and allowed to use the CFP Board designation or those seeking certification. Throughout this chapter, reference will be made to one who uses the CFP Board designation as a *"CFP Board designee."* For purposes of the Code, the term **CFP Board designee** is deemed to include candidates for the marks.

The Principles apply to all CFP Board designees and provide guidance to CFP Board designees in the performance of their duties. The seven separate Principles are: Integrity, Objectivity, Competence, Fairness, Confidentiality, Professionalism, and Diligence. These seven Principles form the framework of the Code. Each Principle has a set of corresponding Rules that are examined below. Although the Principles apply to all CFP Board designees, certain Rules may not apply to a particular CFP Board designee's activities because of the nature of the CFP Board designee's particular field. CFP Board designees have diverse activities, and as a result, a CFP Board designee must recognize what specific services he or she is rendering and determine whether a given Rule applies to those services. The following is an evaluation of each Principle and the accompanying Rules relating to that Principle. All text below within quotation marks in *italicized type* is a direct quote from the Code.

The **Rules** are derived from the doctrine expressed in the Principles and help to establish a foundation for complying with the Principles of the Code. The Rules apply only in certain specific professional instances. The Rules tend to be somewhat situation-specific to a particular service being offered.

NOTE ON CIVIL LIABILITY

The Code does not define standards of professional conduct of CFP Board designees for purposes of civil liability. Nonetheless, there are various areas where a violation of the Code could likely result in civil liability for malpractice or professional negligence on the part of the CFP Board designee if the client sustains "damages" resulting from the CFP Board designee's action or inaction. For instance, if a CFP Board designee violates the Rules regarding Competence, the

---

principles - one of two main parts of the CFP Code that addresses the profession's recognition of the responsibilities of its members to the public, clients, colleagues, and employers, and provides guidance to members during the performance of their professional duties

CFP Board designee - throughout this textbook, "CFP Board designee" refers to an individual who uses the CFP Board designation

rules - one of two main parts of the CFP Code that is derived from the doctrine expressed in the Principles and helps to establish a foundation for complying with the Principles of the Code

CFP Board designee is probably susceptible to a lawsuit for professional negligence or malpractice if the client sustained losses or damages because of the CFP Board designee's incompetence. The CFP Board designee can avoid such a situation if he or she seeks the advice of, or refers his or her client to, another CFP Board designee or qualified individual who is competent in the areas where the CFP Board designee was not professionally competent, as stated by Rule 302 of the Code.

PRINCIPLE 1: INTEGRITY

The Code provides that *"[a] CFP Board designee shall offer and provide professional services with integrity." See Code of Ethics and Prof. Resp., Part I, Principle I, p. 9.* Clients often place CFP Board designees in positions of trust and confidence. A client denotes a person, persons, or entity for whom professional services are rendered. A practitioner is engaged when an individual, based on the relevant facts and circumstances, reasonably relies upon information or service provided by that practitioner. For the field of financial planning to prosper, there must be a foundation of trust in the CFP Board designee. The ultimate source of such public trust is personal integrity. In determining what is right and just, a CFP Board designee should rely on his or her integrity as the appropriate touchstone. Integrity demands honesty and candor that must not be subordinated to personal gain and advantage. The CFP Board designee must be incorruptible.

Although there is some room for innocent error and legitimate difference of opinion, integrity cannot coexist with deceit or subordination of one's principles. Indeed, the interests of the client must come before the interests of the CFP Board designee. Integrity requires a CFP Board designee to observe not simply the letter of the Code, but also the spirit of the Code. In other words, the CFP Board designee must not merely follow the specific rules outlined in the Code. Instead, the CFP Board designee must strive to conduct himself or herself in a manner that the CFP Board designee believes is consistent with the Principles and Rules when situations arise that are not specified or outlined in the Code. This is the essence of integrity.

RULES THAT RELATE TO THE PRINCIPLE OF INTEGRITY

Rule 101 of the Code prohibits the solicitation of clients through *"false or misleading communications or advertisements." See Code of Ethics and Prof. Resp., Part II, Rule 101, p. 11.* Rule 101 emphasizes (a) misleading advertising, (b) promotional activities, and (c) representation of authority.

Rule 101(a) prohibits a CFP Board designee from making false or misleading communications about the size, scope, or areas of competence of the CFP™ certificant's practice. In other words, a CFP Board designee cannot try to lure in clients by stating that the CFP™ certificant's practice is larger than it really is or that the CFP Board designee specializes in a certain area when he or she in fact does not.

Under Rule 101(b), a CFP Board designee shall not *"create unjustified expectations"* in promotional activities regarding financial planning or the CFP Board designee's professional activities and competence. *See Code of Ethics and Prof. Resp., Part II, Rule 101(b), p. 11.* Promotional activities include, but are not limited to, speeches, interviews, books, printed publications, seminars, radio shows, television shows, and videocassettes. For example, Fred, a CFP Board designee, promotes his services in an ad in a trade magazine. One of Fred's clients, Julia, states in the ad: "I was almost bankrupt when I consulted Fred. Six months after our consultation, I had a net worth of half a million dollars." The ad also stated: "If I can achieve these results for Julia, just imagine the results I can achieve for you." Fred is subject to discipline for this promotional activity because Julia's statement concerning her financial resurrection would likely be construed as creating unjustified expectations regarding Fred's services.

Rule 101(c) prohibits a CFP Board designee from giving the impression that he or she represents the views of the CFP Board or any other group without authorization. Personal opinions must be clearly identified as such.

Under Rule 102, a CFP Board designee must not, in the course of professional activities, "*engage in conduct involving dishonesty, fraud, deceit or misrepresentation, or knowingly make a false or misleading statement to a client, employer, employee, professional colleague, governmental or other regulatory body or official, or any other person or entity.*" *See Code of Ethics and Prof. Resp., Part II, Rule 102, p. 11.* Rule 102 is very clear and self-explanatory. Even though several rules deal with integrity, none are more important than Rule 102's simple prohibition of "*conduct involving dishonesty, fraud, deceit or misrepresentation, or knowingly making a false or misleading statement.*" Although Rule 102 only prohibits dishonesty or deceit in the course of professional activities, integrity would require the CFP Board designee to refrain from dishonesty or deceit in the course of all activities, whether the CFP Board designee has clients or only carries the CFP mark. This furthers the spirit of the Code and will increase the public's trust in the profession.

Nonetheless, fraudulent or deceitful conduct on the part of the CFP Board designee outside the course of the CFP Board designee's professional activities would likely have an adverse effect on the CFP Board designee's fitness as a CFP Board designee or upon the profession as a whole. Accordingly, fraudulent or deceitful conduct outside the course of professional activities would be a direct violation of Rule 607, which relates to the principle of Professionalism.

Rule 103 establishes responsibilities for a CFP Board designee regarding funds and property of clients. First, a CFP Board designee must act only according to the authority set forth in the legal instrument governing the relationship between the CFP Board designee and client when the CFP Board designee exercises custody or discretionary authority over client funds or property. *See Code of Ethics and Prof. Resp., Part II, Rule 103(a), p. 11.* For instance, if the CFP Board designee is acting as trustee for a client who is the beneficiary of a trust, the CFP Board designee must not exceed his or her authority as delineated within the trust documents. Other such legal instruments include special powers of attorney.

Second, a CFP Board designee must keep complete records of all property or funds of a client which are under the custody of the CFP Board designee. *See Code of Ethics and Prof. Resp., Part II, Rule 103(b), p. 11.* If a client or third party is entitled to receive funds or property of a client, the CFP Board designee must deliver the funds or property promptly to the client or third party. Also, upon the client's request, the CFP Board designee must "*render a full accounting*" of such property and funds while in the custody of the CFP Board designee. *Rule 103(c), p. 11.*

Commingling of Funds

Under Rule 103(d), a "*CFP Board designee shall not commingle client funds or other property with a CFP Board designee's personal funds and/or other property or the funds and/or other property of a CFP Board designee's firm. Commingling one or more clients' funds or other property together is permitted, subject to compliance with applicable legal requirements and provided accurate records are maintained for each client's funds or other property.*" *See Code of Ethics and Prof. Resp., Part II, Rule 103(d), p. 11.* In other words, under Rule 103(d) a CFP Board designee shall not **commingle client funds** with the CFP Board designee's funds, whereas commingling one or more clients' funds is permissible if accurate records are maintained.

Even if a CFP Board designee deposits a nominal amount of money of his own funds into a holding account for a client's funds just to ensure that the account is never overdrawn and to avoid unnecessary account charges for minimum balances, such action is improper because a CFP Board designee may commingle one or more clients' funds if accurate records are maintained, but is prohibited from commingling the CFP Board designee's funds with the client's funds. Thus, even if the CFP Board designee has no "negative" intent, the Code simply restricts such behavior that gives the appearance of impropriety.

Fiduciary Relationship

Rule 103(e) of the Code provides that CFP Board designees who take custody of clients' assets for investment purposes must "*do so with the care required of a fiduciary.*" *Code of Ethics and Prof. Resp., Part II, Rule 103(e), p. 11.* The Code uses the word "*fiduciary*" in Rule 103(e), but does not provide a definition of the word fiduciary. Although its definition is subject to various interpretations and standards in different state jurisdictions, the term, fiduciary, generally describes a person that holds the character similar in nature to that of a trustee who is placed in a position of trust and confidence based on that character and the scrupulous good faith and candor it requires. By virtue of his or her engagement or undertaking, the fiduciary has a duty to act primarily for another's benefit in matters concerning the undertaking.

More particularly, a fiduciary is a person who manages money or property for another and who must exercise a standard of care in such management activity imposed by law or by contract, such as an executor of an estate, a receiver in bankruptcy, or a trustee of a trust. A trustee, for example, possesses a fiduciary responsibility to the beneficiary of the trust to follow the terms of the trust and the requirements of applicable state law. Out of this fiduciary relationship where one places special confidence in another, the law recognizes the rule that neither party may exert influence or pressure upon the other, take selfish advantage of his or her trust, or deal with the subject matter of the undertaking in such a way as to benefit himself or herself. Accordingly, the status of being a fiduciary for another gives rise to certain legal obligations, including the prohibition against investing money or property in investments that are imprudent or inappropriately speculative. See Rule 103(e) of the Code which requires the CFP Board designee who takes custody of a client's assets for investment purposes to do so with the care required of a fiduciary.

A **fiduciary relationship** is thus a relationship where a person places special trust and confidence in another. The fiduciary must abide by a heightened standard of care during the engagement. In the circumstance described in Rule 103(e), the CFP Board designee is charged with the obligation to act with the same care required of a fiduciary. This places a higher burden on the CFP

commingle client funds - Rules specifically prohibit the combining (or commingling) of client funds or other property with a CFP Board designee's personal funds and/or other property or the funds and/or other property of a CFP Board designee's firm

fiduciary relationship - relationship between a CFP™ practitioner and a client where the client places special trust and confidence in the CFP™ practitioner. This relationship places a higher burden on the CFP Board designee, which is warranted, because the CFP Board designee is dealing with the client's funds or property for investment purposes

Board designee, which is warranted because the CFP Board designee is dealing with the clients' funds or property for investment purposes.

PRINCIPLE 2: OBJECTIVITY

The Code provides that a "*CFP Board designee shall be objective in providing professional services to clients.*" *Code of Ethics and Prof. Resp., Part I, Principle 2, p. 9.* Objectivity requires intellectual honesty and impartiality. Irrespective of the CFP Board designee's capacity or function, a CFP Board designee should protect the integrity of his or her work, maintain objectivity, and avoid subordination of his or her judgment that would be a violation of this Code.

There is obviously some overlap between Integrity and Objectivity. However, Objectivity focuses on the interests of the client, while Integrity focuses on the actions of the CFP Board designee. With regard to Objectivity, a CFP Board designee must not let the enticement of profit sway his or her professional judgment. The decision made by the CFP Board designee and accompanying advice given should instead be driven by what is best for the client. Objectivity also focuses on Certified Financial Planner practitioners because they provide professional services to clients, whereas some CFP Board designees may not necessarily be Certified Financial Planner practitioners.

RULES THAT RELATE TO THE PRINCIPLE OF OBJECTIVITY

Rule 201 states as follows: "*A CFP Board designee shall exercise reasonable and prudent professional judgment in providing professional services.*" *Code of Ethics and Prof. Resp., Part II, Rule 201, p. 12.* Here, the CFP Board designee is held to a standard of a reasonable, prudent person. In other words, the CFP Board designee must act as an ordinary, reasonably prudent CFP Board designee would act when faced with similar facts and circumstances.

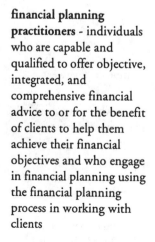

financial planning practitioners - individuals who are capable and qualified to offer objective, integrated, and comprehensive financial advice to or for the benefit of clients to help them achieve their financial objectives and who engage in financial planning using the financial planning process in working with clients

Rule 202 provides as follows: "*A financial planning practitioner shall act in the interest of the client.*" *Code of Ethics and Prof. Resp., Part II, Rule 202, p. 12.* Rule 202 does not speak to CFP Board designees in general, but to the "*financial planning practitioner*" because **financial planning practitioners** are those CFP Board designees who have clients. A financial planning practitioner denotes a person who is capable and qualified to offer objective, integrated, and comprehensive financial advice to or for the benefit of clients to help them achieve their financial objectives and who engage in financial planning using the financial planning process in working with clients. The financial planning process denotes the process which typically includes, but is not limited to, the six elements of establishing and defining the client-planner relationship, gathering data including goals, analyzing and evaluating the client's financial status, developing and presenting financial planning recommendations and/or alternatives, implementing the financial planning recommendations and monitoring the financial planning recommendations.

In an actual disciplinary case before the CFP Board, a CFP Board designee reported on his Annual CFP License Renewal form that a former client filed a civil lawsuit against him, alleging fraud, breach of fiduciary duty, negligent misrepresentation and "churning" in connection with investments he recommended. Of the $394,765 the client invested through the CFP Board designee, the client lost $382,240. The CFP Board designee settled the case for $26,500. The CFP Board designee was disciplined through private censure. One mitigating factor in the CFP

Board designee's favor was that the CFP Board designee disclosed the matter to the CFP Board and cooperated with the CFP Board's investigation.

PRINCIPLE 3: COMPETENCE

The Code provides that CFP Board designees *"shall provide services to clients competently and maintain the necessary knowledge and skill to continue to do so in those areas in which the designee is engaged." Code of Ethics and Prof. Resp., Part I, Principle 3, p. 9.* Competence can be described as that point where a CFP Board designee has acquired and maintained an adequate level of knowledge and skill, and the CFP Board designee applies that knowledge effectively in providing services to clients. Along these same lines, competence also includes the wisdom and insight to recognize the limitations of one's knowledge. In those instances where the CFP Board designee realizes his or her knowledge is limited, consultation by the CFP Board designee with another CFP Board designee or other professional for guidance in those areas where the CFP Board designee's knowledge is limited is appropriate. Referral of the client to another CFP Board designee or other professional may also be appropriate.

By virtue of having earned the CFP Board designation, a CFP Board designee is deemed to be qualified to practice in the field of financial planning and is deemed to be knowledgeable in the field of financial planning. However, it is not sufficient to simply assimilate and absorb the common body of knowledge required to obtain the CFP certification, nor is it sufficient to simply acquire the necessary experience for the license. Rather, a CFP Board designee must make a continuing commitment to learn and improve professionally. The CFP Board thus requires that the CFP Board designee satisfy minimum continuing education requirements. Nonetheless, the CFP Board designee's commitment to continue to learn and to improve professionally should not stop there.

The two areas of competence are knowledge and the application of that knowledge. One can avoid incompetence pertaining to lack of knowledge by consulting or associating with, or by referring a client to, qualified individuals with the appropriate knowledge. Indeed, this is a situation where the CFP Board designee recognizes that he or she is not competent or is inexperienced in a certain area of financial planning. However, issues of competence regarding one's application of knowledge normally arise after the application has been undertaken. Therefore, it is this area, the misapplication of one's knowledge, where most violations of the rules of Competence occur because the CFP Board designee unwittingly fails in applying knowledge and cannot necessarily recognize such incompetence.

On a related note, the principle of Competence is closely aligned with the standard for malpractice or professional negligence in the field of financial planning. Although malpractice or professional negligence is determined by the standards and rules of each individual state, generally a CFP Board designee can be held liable for malpractice or professional negligence if the plaintiff demonstrates the ordinary standard of knowledge or skills for CFP Board designees, that the CFP Board designee did not possess that standard of knowledge or failed in applying that knowledge, and that the CFP Board designee's breach of that standard caused injury or loss to the plaintiff. All three items must be present.

It is important to note that the principle of Competence generally involves CFP Board designee-client relationships. The Code specifically refers to clients in defining the principle of Competence and the rules relating to Competence. The driving force behind this is that the financial planning "client" or consumer must be protected from incompetence. In CFP Board designee-client relationships, a CFP Board designee's incompetence can result in damage or loss to the client, not simply a disappointment or disciplinary action for the individual CFP Board designee. Thus, Competence requires the CFP Board designee to continue to educate himself or herself and maintain a high level of standards. Competence also prohibits a CFP Board designee from failing to acquire or properly apply knowledge, as such failure on the CFP Board designee's behalf may reflect poorly upon the profession and/or result in loss or damage to the client. Still, a CFP Board designee who is purely an educator and does not have clients can violate the principle of Competence, for example, by failing to satisfy minimum continuing education requirements established for CFP Board designees by the CFP Board.

RULES THAT RELATE TO THE PRINCIPLE OF COMPETENCE

Rule 301 states as follows: "*A CFP Board designee shall keep informed of developments in the field of financial planning and participate in continuing education throughout the CFP Board designee's professional career in order to improve professional competence in all areas in which the CFP Board designee is engaged. As a distinct part of this requirement, a CFP Board designee shall satisfy all minimum continuing education requirements established for CFP Board designees by the CFP Board.*" *Code of Ethics and Prof. Resp., Part II, Rule 301, p. 12.* Under Rule 301, CFP Board designees must keep informed of developments in financial planning and must participate in minimum continuing education requirements established for CFP Board designees by the CFP Board. The aim of Rule 301 is to improve the CFP Board designee's professional competence in all areas in which the CFP Board designee is engaged. The CFP Board requires thirty (30) hours of continuing education bi-annually; of these 30 hours, at least 2 hours must cover ethics.

Under Rule 302, a CFP Board designee must offer advice "*only in those areas in which the CFP Board designee has competence. In areas where the CFP Board designee is not professionally competent, the CFP Board designee shall seek the counsel of qualified individuals and/or refer clients to such parties.*" *Code of Ethics and Prof. Resp., Part II, Rule 302, p. 12.* Rule 302 is very clear in dealing with areas of financial planning not thoroughly understood by the CFP Board designee. The first sentence provides that CFP Board designees must offer advice only in those areas in which the CFP Board designee has competence. This permits CFP Board designees to offer advice only in those areas where the CFP Board designee is competent. Conversely, this means that a CFP Board designee is prohibited from extending any advice to a client in an area where the CFP Board designee does not have an adequate level of knowledge. Keep in mind that financial planning is very broad, and a CFP Board designee may be knowledgeable in many areas but deficient in others. This is particularly true today because financial services are quite complicated, and few people can be experts in all areas due to the vast diversity and scope of financial services.

The second sentence of Rule 302 requires CFP Board designees to seek advice of qualified individuals or to refer clients to qualified individuals in those areas in which the CFP Board designee is not professionally competent. Here, the CFP Board designee must be able to recognize his or her deficiencies in areas of financial planning and seek advice of others or client referral when necessary.

PRINCIPLE 4: FAIRNESS

The Code provides that a CFP Board designee *"shall perform professional services in a manner that is fair and reasonable to clients, principals, partners, and employers and shall disclose conflict(s) of interest(s) in providing such services." Code of Ethics and Prof. Resp., Part I, Principle 4, p. 9.* Fairness is an essential trait for any professional in any profession. The principle of Fairness is basically a culmination or combination of the first three principles of the Code: Integrity, Objectivity, and Competence.

Like Objectivity, Fairness requires impartiality and intellectual honesty. The CFP Board's reason for including Fairness as one of the principles in the Code is to guide the CFP Board designee in achieving a proper balance of conflicting interests. Similar to Integrity, Fairness demands that CFP Board designees put the interests of the client first. Fairness also involves a subordination of a CFP Board designee's own feelings, prejudices, desires, and personal gain. Like Competence, CFP Board designees must under the principle of Fairness provide fair and reasonable professional services.

Further, a major obligation on the part of CFP Board designees with respect to Fairness is disclosure of conflicts of interests. A **conflict of interest** denotes circumstances, relationships or other facts about the CFP Board designee's own financial, business, property, and/or personal interests which will, or reasonably may, impair the CFP Board designee's rendering of disinterested advice, recommendations, or services. Fairness is also treating others in the same fashion that you would want to be treated.

Under the principle of Fairness, CFP Board designees are required to disclose conflicts of interests and sources of compensation. Because of the disclosure requirements of the Code, it is necessary to call attention to the inherent conflicts of interests that frequently arise in CFP Board designee-client relationships. The very nature of providing financial services as a financial planning practitioner is to provide the client with the best possible financial advice for the specific needs of the client that will maximize the financial well-being of the client. On the other hand, the CFP Board designee is engaged in the provision of financial planning services to earn money -- it is an occupation. In order for the CFP Board designee to earn money, the CFP Board designee must be compensated for his or her services. This compensation comes from the client, the same client that has engaged the CFP Board designee to improve the client's financial status. Theoretically speaking, this is a conflict of interest in and of itself.

Compare the CFP Board designee-client relationship with a physician-patient relationship. When an individual seeks the advice of a physician regarding his or her physical health, the patient seeks to improve his or her health or to solve a physical problem. When the patient compensates the physician, there is no conflict of interest. However, when an individual seeks the advice of a CFP Board designee to improve his or her financial status, the client compensates the CFP Board designee with money, the same object that the client seeks to keep or maximize. Although this analysis may seem somewhat absurd, it becomes more apparent when identifying certain situations that all too often arise during the normal course of activities of the CFP Board designee.

conflict of interest - denotes circumstances, relationships or other facts about a CFP Board designee's own financial, business, property, and/or personal interests which will, or reasonably may, impair the CFP Board designee's rendering of disinterested advice, recommendations, or services

For example, many CFP Board designees sell stocks, bonds, mutual funds, life insurance, or annuities and earn commissions from the sale of these products to their clients. A commission is the compensation received by an agent or broker when the compensation is calculated as a percentage on the amount of his or her sales or purchase transactions. If this is the only source of compensation for the CFP Board designee, then the CFP Board designee is considered a "commission-only" financial planner. The commission-only financial planner thus receives a commission for the products that he or she sells to the client. This arguably creates an incentive for the CFP Board designee to recommend products that provide the CFP Board designee with higher commissions, like annuities or life insurance, instead of products with lower or no commissions, such as bonds. This "incentive" is the foundation for the conflict of interest. There may also exist an incentive to sway the CFP Board designee from recommending another course of action for the client that may be in the client's best interest, but would not provide the CFP Board designee with any compensation through commissions. Even though the CFP Board designee may not in fact be swayed in this scenario, there is simply an appearance that the CFP Board designee would be swayed or that the interests of the CFP Board designee and the client are in conflict. Indeed, when a conflict of interest exists, unfortunately there is an assumption that the CFP Board designee will act in his or her interest, instead of in the client's interests.

In such a situation where a conflict exists, it would be impractical for the CFP Board designee to disqualify or disengage himself or herself from the relationship with the client because there would basically be no circumstance in which a CFP Board designee could earn a commission from a client for the sale of a product. Instead of disqualification or disengagement, the Code requires that the financial planning practitioner disclose all conflicts of interests to the client in writing. See Rule 402, for example. Also, the CFP Board designee must disclose in writing to the client sources of compensation and a statement of compensation "*which in reasonable detail discloses the source(s) and any contingencies or other aspects material to the fee and/or commission arrangement.*" *Code of Ethics and Prof. Resp., Part II, Rule 402(c), p. 12.* Such disclosure in situations where there may be a conflict helps to diffuse or negate public distrust or suspicion.

In short, although conflicts of interests may arise in the CFP Board designee-client relationship, these conflicts can be minimized or dealt with through disclosure by the CFP Board designee to the client. The assumption is that, if the CFP Board designee discloses the information to the client, the client will feel as if the CFP Board designee has nothing to hide, while at the same time, the CFP Board designee is reminding himself or herself to be objective. Nonetheless, even though the CFP Board designee has disclosed the "conflict" and arguably set aside the appearance of impropriety, it is conceivable that the credibility of the financial planner is tainted when the compensation of the financial planner is directly related to the purchase of recommended investments. However, some if not all credibility can be restored through disclosure. Moreover, the appearance of impropriety is diminished because the CFP Board designee and the client at the inception of the relationship choose the compensation structure on an individual basis according to their comfort level.

RULES THAT RELATE TO THE PRINCIPLE OF FAIRNESS

Under Rule 401, when rendering professional services, a CFP Board designee must "*disclose to the client:*

> Material information relevant to the professional relationship, including but not limited

to conflict(s) of interest(s), changes in the CFP Board designee's business affiliation, address, telephone number, credentials, qualifications, licenses, compensation structure, and any agency relationships, and the scope of the CFP Board designee's authority in that capacity; and the information required by all laws applicable to the relationship in a manner complying with such laws." Code of Ethics and Prof. Resp., Part II, Rule 401, p. 12.

As seen, Rule 401 applies to all CFP Board designees who render "*professional services.*" Rule 401 states the general rule that CFP Board designees must disclose conflicts of interest and any other material information relevant to the relationship. Rule 401 does not, however, provide for the method (that is, written or otherwise) that the CFP Board designee should use to satisfy the disclosure requirements of Rule 401.

Rule 402 requires the financial planning practitioner to make "*timely written disclosure of all material information relative to the professional relationship.*" Code of Ethics and Prof. Resp., Part II, Rule 402, p. 12. This written disclosure must "*include conflict(s) of interest(s) and sources of compensation.*" *See Rule 402.* Such disclosure regarding sources of compensation must be made annually for ongoing clients according to Rule 405. Rule 405 permits, but does not require, this annual disclosure to be satisfied by offering to provide clients with the current copy of SEC Form ADV, part 2 or the disclosure called for by Rule 402.

The following information is permitted and encouraged with respect to the written disclosure under Rule 402:

A statement disclosing the CFP Board designee's basic philosophy, theory, and principles of financial planning. *See Rule 402(a).*

Resumes' of employees who are expected to provide financial planning services to the client. *See Rule 402(b).* These resumes' must include educational background, professional history, employment history, professional designations or licenses, and areas of competence and specialization (if applicable).

A statement of compensation disclosing in reasonable detail aspects material to the fee. *See Rule 402(c).*

A statement clarifying the CFP Board designee's compensation as fee-only, commission-only, or fee and commission. *See Rule 402(d).* Although the CFP Board designee may only directly charge a client a flat fee for a financial plan, the CFP Board designee cannot hold himself or herself out as a "fee-only" financial planning practitioner if the CFP Board designee receives commissions or other forms of economic benefit from related parties, such as receiving a commission from the sale of a mutual fund. "Fee-only" is defined as a method of compensation in which compensation is received solely from a client with neither the personal financial planning practitioner nor any related party receiving compensation which is contingent upon the purchase or sale of any financial product.

A statement describing material agency or employment relationships between the CFP Board designee and third parties and any fees or commissions resulting from those relationships. *See Rule 402(e).*

A statement identifying conflicts of interests. *See Rule 402(f).* Rule 402(f) is the fourth instance in which the Code requires disclosure of conflicts of interests. However, written disclosure of conflicts of interests is only required of the financial planning practitioner. Meanwhile, a CFP Board designee who is *"engaged solely in the sale of securities as a registered representative"* is not subject to the written disclosure requirements of Rule 402. *See Code of Ethics and Prof. Resp, p. 7.* Rule 402 as stated is only applicable to CFP Board designees engaged in personal financial planning, although the CFP Board designee may have disclosure responsibilities under Rule 401. A CFP Board designee is thus obligated to determine what responsibilities the CFP Board designee has in each professional relationship including, for instance, duties that arise in particular circumstances from a position of trust or confidence that a CFP Board designee may have. A CFP Board designee is obligated to meet those responsibilities in accordance with the rules of Fairness.

Rule 403 requires a CFP Board designee providing financial planning services to disclose in writing relationships which reasonably may compromise the CFP Board designee's objectivity or independence. The written disclosure requirement of Rule 403 must be done prior to establishing a client relationship. *Code of Ethics and Prof. Resp., Part II, Rule 403, p. 13.* Rule 403 lets the client know from the outset that the CFP Board designee may have conflicts of interests. The key for the CFP Board designee is to put the client on written notice from the inception of the relationship. Note, however, that the CFP Board designee is not absolved from having to comply with the principle of, and rules relating to, Objectivity by providing written disclosure under Rule 403. Instead, the CFP Board designee reduces the appearance of impropriety by disclosing in writing appropriate information from the beginning, which is a good practice that furthers the letter and spirit of the Code.

Rule 404 mandates CFP Board designees to promptly disclose conflicts of interests to the client or other necessary parties if conflicts arise after commencement of the relationship but before services are completed. *Code of Ethics and Prof. Resp., Part II, Rule 404, p. 13.* Rule 404 is thus an extension of Rule 403. Rule 404 does not require the disclosure to be in writing. Nonetheless, it would be wise to do so in writing because, in disciplinary procedures and even litigation dealing with malpractice or professional negligence, the CFP Board designee can more easily prove that disclosure was made if it was done in writing.

Rule 406 provides as follows: *"A CFP Board designee's compensation shall be fair and reasonable."* *See Code of Ethics and Prof. Resp., Part II, Rule 406, p. 13.* The "reasonableness" test of Rule 406 is both objective and subjective.

An objective test means that the disciplinary board, or a court, would ask whether the compensation received was reasonable under similar or like circumstances based on the industry and generally accepted norms. A subjective test, as opposed to an objective test, seeks to determine that the compensation was reasonable considering various factors such as the CFP Board designee's experience and knowledge, the time and labor required by the CFP Board designee, the compensation normally charged in the locality for similar financial planning services, the nature and length of the professional relationship with the client, whether the compensation is fee-based or commission-based or both, and the client's financial position. Obviously, there is no clear test as to what is fair and reasonable. However, the CFP Board designee must be careful not to charge an excessive fee because the CFP Board designee may subject himself or herself to disciplinary proceedings.

Under Rule 407, a CFP Board designee "*may provide references*" from present or former clients before establishing a client relationship. *See Code of Ethics and Prof. Resp., Part II, Rule 407, p. 13.* As you can see, Rule 407 is not mandatory, but is permissive by use of the word "may." Therefore, the CFP Board designee's failure to provide references from present or former clients before establishment of a client relationship will not subject the CFP Board designee to discipline. Nonetheless, as the Code should, Rule 407 encourages CFP Board designees to provide references, which is a sound, professional practice to follow.

When the CFP Board designee is acting as an agent for a principal, the CFP Board designee "*shall assure that the scope of his or her authority is clearly defined and properly documented.*" *See Code of Prof. Resp., Part II, Rule 408, p. 13.* Rule 408 places a significant obligation on the part of the CFP Board designee because Rule 408 applies to any situation where the CFP Board designee is acting as an agent for a "principal," not only a client. A principal can be any legal entity such as an individual, a client, a corporation, or a partnership. Thus, in any setting and even beyond CFP Board designee-client relationships, the CFP Board designee must clearly define and properly document the scope of the agency relationship.

Rule 409 requires all CFP Board designees to adhere to "*the same standards of disclosure and service*" whether the CFP Board designee is employed by a financial planning firm, an investment institution, or serves as an agent for such an organization. *See Code of Ethics and Prof. Resp., Part II, Rule 409, p. 13.* Whereas, Rule 410 provides a "catch-all" provision for all CFP Board designees who are employees. The test of Rule 410 provides: "*A CFP Board designee who is an employee shall perform professional services with dedication to the lawful objectives of the employer and in accordance with this Code.*" *See Code of Ethics and Prof. Resp., Part II, Rule 410, p. 13.* Rule 410 was drafted to address the problem of violations of the Code by employees who are CFP Board designees. There are some unfortunate situations where a CFP Board designee is forced to act in violation of the Code or other laws by an employer or superior. Rule 410 basically prevents CFP Board designees from asserting a defense or justification for unethical conduct by stating that they were ordered to do so by their superiors or employers. Rule 410 hence expressly requires employees to perform services in accordance with the Code and in compliance with lawful objectives of employers.

Rule 411 deals with CFP Board designees' obligations to their employers. Under Rule 411, a CFP Board designee must "*advise the CFP Board designee's employer of outside affiliations which reasonably may compromise service to an employer and provide timely notice to the employer and clients, unless precluded by contractual obligation, in the event of change of employment or CFP Board licensing status.*" *See Code of Ethics and Prof. Resp., Part II, Rule 411, p. 13.* Rule 411 requires a CFP Board designee to advise his or her employer of outside affiliations of the CFP Board designee that may compromise the CFP Board designee's service to an employer. Rule 411 also requires timely notice to employers and to clients of any change of employment or CFP Board licensing status. Rule 411 places responsibilities on CFP Board designees to give pertinent information to their employers, thus providing added safeguards to employers. Of course, this ultimately benefits clients and the public because the CFP Board designee is required to advise employers of affiliations that would compromise the CFP Board designee's service to an employer, that very service which is normally provided to clients.

According to Rule 412, CFP Board designees who are partners or principals of a financial services firm owe the other partners or principals (co-owners) a responsibility to act in good faith.

This duty of good faith specifically includes disclosure of relevant and material financial information. *See Code of Ethics and Prof. Resp., Part II, Rule 412, p. 14.* Now, the Code is governing the actions of CFP Board designees among themselves. It places a duty of good faith upon partners in a financial services firm.

"Good faith" is not defined in the Code. "Good faith" generally encompasses, among other things, an honest belief, the absence of malice, and the absence of an intention to mislead or obtain an unfair advantage. Good faith is also an honest intention to abstain from taking conscious advantage of another. This term is ordinarily used to describe an intention indicating faithfulness, duty, or obligation to another. As utilized in Rule 412, good faith entails being honest and faithful to other co-owners or partners in a financial planning services firm. Rule 412 requires disclosure of relevant information among partners, but does not require written disclosure.

Rule 413 is basically an extension or clarification of Rule 412. Rule 413 provides: *"A CFP Board designee shall join a financial planning firm as a partner or principal only on the basis of mutual disclosure of relevant and material information regarding credentials, competence, experience, licensing and/or legal status, and financial stability of the parties involved." See Code of Ethics and Prof. Resp., Part II, Rule 413, p. 14.* Rule 413 requires mutual disclosure of relevant material information when a CFP Board designee joins a firm as a partner or principal. Rule 413 hence requires disclosure of all relevant information at the inception of a partnership, while Rule 412 requires, among other things, disclosure throughout the partnership, as new circumstances may arise after the partnership is commenced. Relevant material information under Rule 413 includes credentials, competence, experience, licensing status, and financial stability of the parties involved.

If a CFP Board designee withdraws from a firm or partnership, the CFP Board designee must deal with his or her business interest *"in a fair and equitable manner"* and in accordance with any applicable agreements. *See Code of Prof. Resp., Part II, Rule 414, p. 14.* Rule 414 embodies the concept of fair dealing. In short, the Code requires CFP Board designees to maintain responsibility and act equitably with respect to other partners even though the partnership has come, or is coming, to an end.

Rule 415 requires CFP Board designees to "*inform*" employers or partners of compensation in connection with their services to clients that are in addition to compensation from the employers or partners from such services. Although the CFP Board designee's duty to inform employers or partners of other compensation is broad, Rule 415 has a limitation. This duty to inform applies only when the services performed by the CFP Board designee for the client will be compensated by the employer or partner. If the CFP Board designee advises individual clients (not clients of the CFP Board designee's employer) in his spare time, then Rule 415 does not require the CFP Board designees to inform his or her employer of the hourly fee received.

The final rule pertaining to the principal of Fairness is Rule 416, which mandates CFP Board designees entering into business transactions with clients to be *"fair and reasonable"* and to disclose risks, conflicts of interest, and other relevant information.

PRINCIPLE 5: CONFIDENTIALITY

A CFP Board designee "*shall not disclose any confidential client information without the specific consent of the client unless in response to proper legal process, to defend against charges of wrongdoing by the CFP Board designee or in connection with a civil dispute between the CFP Board designee and client.*" *See Code of Ethics and Prof. Resp., Principle 5, p. 10.* When a client consults or seeks the services of a CFP Board designee, the client is typically interested in creating a relationship of personal trust and confidence with the CFP Board designee. Indeed, the client is placing his or her financial well-being into the hands of the CFP Board designee. The CFP Board designee-client relationship can only be built upon the client's understanding that the information supplied to the CFP Board designee will be held in confidence by the CFP Board designee. This understanding will promote candor and productive consultation with the CFP Board designee, which will benefit the client.

As in any profession where a client seeks advice of a professional, the CFP Board designee must safeguard the confidentiality of all information gained from the relationship in order to provide the contemplated services effectively. This will also help the CFP Board designee protect the client's privacy.

RULES THAT RELATE TO THE PRINCIPLE OF CONFIDENTIALITY

Rule 501 of the Code provides that a CFP Board designee is prohibited from revealing "*or use for his or her own benefit -- without the client's consent, any personally identifiable information relating to the client relationship or the affairs of the client, except and to the extent disclosure or use is reasonably necessary:*

To establish an advisory or brokerage account, to effect a transaction for the client, or as otherwise impliedly authorized in order to carry out the client engagement; or

To comply with legal requirements or legal process; or

To defend the CFP Board designee against charges of wrongdoing; or

In connection with a civil dispute between the CFP Board designee and the client."

Code of Ethics and Prof. Resp., Rule 501, p. 14. The use of client information is improper whether or not it actually causes harm to the client.

Rule 501 characterizes confidential information as any personally identifiable information relating to the client relationship or the affairs of the client. This means that a CFP Board designee could probably describe the basic facts of a client's affairs to another but in no way reveal information that would identify that client either by name or by other detectable means.

There are a few narrow exceptions to the rule of confidentiality.

1. <u>Consent</u>. A CFP Board designee can reveal confidential information if the client consents to the revelation. In cases where the client expressly consents, the CFP Board designee's

authorization is clear. It would be wise for the CFP Board designee to reduce the express consent to writing, but there are situations where consent is implied although not expressly given by the client.

2. Implied authorization. There are situations where consent, although not expressly given by the client, is implied or tacitly given. Rule 501(a) lists those situations. The basic question to ask is whether the CFP Board designee was impliedly authorized to divulge the information in order to carry out the client engagement. For instance, Mike, a client, consults Patty, a CFP Board designee, about a trust and ultimately asks Patty to draft a trust. Patty indicates that she uses an attorney to help her draft the necessary documents that she will revise accordingly. Here, although Mike did not expressly authorize Patty to divulge confidential information, Mike implicitly authorized Patty to consult with the attorney. Patty will need to tell the attorney certain confidential information. Also, there will be others at the attorney's office who will need to hear the information as well like a paralegal or secretary. Such situations are not violations of the Principle of Confidentiality.

3. Compliance with legal requirements. Under Rule 501(b), a CFP Board designee may reveal confidential information to comply with legal requirements or legal process (that is, a subpoena or court order).

4. CFP Board designee's defense. Under Rule 501(c), a CFP Board designee may reveal confidential information to defend the CFP Board designee against charges of wrongdoing.

5. CFP Board/Client disputes. Rule 501(d) allows a CFP Board designee to divulge confidential information in connection with a civil dispute between the CFP Board designee and the client. It would be absurd to allow a client to divulge information pertaining to the CFP Board designee-client relationship against a CFP Board designee while prohibiting the CFP Board designee from defending against those claims. In situations where the client claims wrongdoing on the part of the CFP Board designee, the client is said to have "opened the door" to rebuttal by the CFP Board designee.

Except for those instances where the client expressly consents to the CFP Board designee's unbridled use of confidential information, the CFP Board designee is not free to disclose all confidential information even though one of the previous exceptions apply. Instead, it is important to note that Rule 501 allows disclosure by the CFP Board designee of confidential information only to the extent "*reasonably necessary*" to comply with the exception. In other words, when an exception to the rule of Confidentiality applies, the CFP Board designee's right to divulge confidential information is not absolute; rather, the CFP Board designee is limited to remain within the scope of the exception and can go no further.

Finally, the CFP Board designee is subject to discipline for violation of Rule 501 whether or not the CFP Board designee's breach of confidentiality causes harm to the client. Thus, the old adage of "no harm - no foul" is not an available defense to the CFP Board designee. In a professional negligence or malpractice case against the CFP Board designee, the client must prove (1) that the CFP Board designee was somehow negligent or acted below the standard of care for ordinary CFP Board designees, (2) that the client sustained damage (this is referred to as "proof of damages"), and (3) that the CFP Board designee's misconduct caused damage to the client (this is referred to as proof of "causation"). However, Rule 501 prohibits improper disclosure of confidential information without regard for causation or damages. Accordingly, Rule 501 goes far beyond professional negligence standards, as it should, and goes to the heart of ethics. Even though the client may not have been damaged or harmed financially due to the CFP Board designee's improper disclosure of confidential information, the client's trust in the CFP Board designee and the profession as a whole are damaged. Thus, the CFP Board designee should be subjected to discipline.

Rule 502 requires a CFP Board designee to "*maintain the same standards of confidentiality to employers as to clients*." *See Code of Ethics and Prof. Resp., Part II, Rule 502, p. 14*. These are the same standards discussed above regarding Rule 501. Accordingly, those standards should apply to employers as well.

Rule 503 states that a CFP Board designee doing business as a partner of a financial services firm "*owes to the CFP Board designee's partners or co-owners a responsibility to act in good faith. This includes, but is not limited to, adherence to reasonable expectations of confidentiality both while in business together and thereafter*." *See Code of Ethics and Prof. Resp., Part II, Rule 503, p. 14*. Rule 503 reiterates Rule 412's requirement concerning the responsibility of CFP Board designees who are partners to act in good faith. Within this responsibility of good faith, Rule 503 expressly requires CFP Board designees as partners to adhere to reasonable expectations of confidentiality during and after the partnership.

For example, two CFP Board designees are partners in a financial services firm, and during the partnership, one learns of the other's debt problems. Even if the partnership later dissolves, the partner should be able to reasonably rely on the other to keep that information confidential despite dissolution of the partnership because CFP Board designees who are partners must adhere to reasonable expectations of confidentiality during the partnership and after its dissolution.

PRINCIPLE 6: PROFESSIONALISM

"*A CFP Board designee's conduct in all matters shall reflect credit upon the profession*." *See Code of Ethics and Prof. Resp., Part I, Principle 6, p. 10*. In order to better the CFP™ profession and foster significant growth, the profession and its individuals must be held to a standard of professionalism and accountability. Because of the importance and magnitude of the professional services rendered by CFP Board designees, CFP Board designees must have attendant responsibilities to behave with dignity and courtesy to all of those who seek or use those services. CFP Board designees also have responsibilities to behave with dignity and courtesy to fellow professionals and to those in related professions (that is, CPAs and attorneys).

A CFP Board designee is further obligated to cooperate with fellow CFP Board designees to maintain and enhance the public image of the profession. The CFP Board designee also has an obligation to cooperate and work jointly with other CFP Board designees to improve the quality of services. The vision of maintaining and enhancing the public image of the profession can only be realized through the combined efforts of all CFP Board designees in cooperation with other professionals.

RULES THAT RELATE TO THE PRINCIPLE OF PROFESSIONALISM

CFP Board designees must "*use the marks in compliance with the rules and regulations of the CFP Board*." *See Code of Ethics and Prof. Resp., Part II, Rule 601, p. 15*. Under Rule 602, CFP Board designees must show respect for, and engage in fair and honorable competitive practices with, other financial planning professionals and related occupational groups. "Financial planning professional" denotes a person who is capable and qualified to offer objective, integrated, and comprehensive financial advice to, or for the benefit of, individuals to help them achieve their financial objectives. A financial planning professional must have the ability to provide financial planning services to clients, using the financial planning process covering the basic financial planning subjects. Of course, Rule 602 should not prevent CFP Board designees from engaging in competition with each other as long as the competition is fair and honorable.

The text of Rule 603 requires a CFP Board designee who has knowledge that is not confidential that another CFP Board designee violated the Code which *"raises substantial questions as to the designee's honesty, trustworthiness or fitness as a CFP Board designee in other respects, shall promptly inform the CFP Board . . ."* See *Code of Ethics and Prof. Resp., Part II, Rule 603, p. 15.* Under Rule 603, a CFP Board designee who has knowledge (that is, no substantial doubt) that another CFP Board designee has violated the Code raising substantial questions as to the CFP Board designee's honesty or fitness as a CFP Board designee, must promptly inform the CFP Board. Rule 603 thus requires a CFP Board designee to inform the CFP Board of violations of the Code by another CFP Board designee. There are two (2) stated exceptions to this rule. First, a CFP Board designee does not have to inform the CFP Board if the CFP Board designee is required to keep the information confidential under the Code. Second, Rule 603 does not require disclosure based on knowledge gained as a consultant or expert witness in anticipation of, or relating to, litigation.

Under Rule 604, a CFP Board designee with knowledge that raises a substantial question of unprofessional, fraudulent, or illegal conduct by a CFP Board designee or other financial professional must promptly inform the appropriate regulatory body. *Code of Ethics and Prof. Resp., Part II, Rule 604, p. 15.* Rule 604 is similar to Rule 603, except that Rule 604 requires the CFP Board designee to report improper conduct by other CFP Board designees or by other financial professionals. The same two (2) exceptions to Rule 603 apply to Rule 604.

If a CFP Board designee has reason to suspect illegal conduct within a CFP Board designee's organization, the CFP Board designee must timely inform his or her immediate supervisor or partner. If appropriate measures are not taken to remedy the situation and the CFP Board designee is convinced that the illegal conduct exists, the CFP Board designee is required by Rule 605 to alert the appropriate authorities including the CFP Board.

Rule 605 requires a CFP Board designee to inform his or her organization if the CFP Board designee has *"reason to suspect"* illegal conduct. However, a CFP Board designee is not required to report to the authorities or CFP Board unless no remedial measures were taken and the CFP Board designee is *"convinced"* illegal conduct still exists. *"Convinced"* is much stronger than *"reason to suspect."* Rule 605 is drafted this way to promote internal investigation when one becomes suspicious of illegal conduct, but to require something more than suspicion when contacting third party regulatory bodies.

When rendering professional activities, a CFP Board designee must perform services according to applicable laws, rules, and regulations of governmental agencies or authorities or rules or policies of the CFP Board. *Code of Ethics and Prof. Resp., Part II, Rule 606, p. 15.* A CFP Board designee must provide services in compliance with applicable laws, rules, regulations, and policies of governmental agencies and of the CFP Board. Failure to do so would damage the public image of the profession.

Rule 607 of the Code prohibits CFP Board designees from engaging in any conduct that reflects adversely (1) on his or her integrity or fitness as a CFP Board designee, (2) upon the CFP mark, or (3) upon the profession. The scope of Rule 607 is broader than the other rules pertaining to Professionalism. Rule 607 applies to any conduct that has an adverse effect on the CFP Board designee or the profession. In short, the principle of Professionalism is essentially embodied into Rule 607. Also, as is done on several occasions throughout the Code, there is some overlap between Rule 607 and the principle of Integrity.

Actions Reflecting Upon the Profession

In the case of *Ibanez v. Florida Department of Business and Professional Regulation, Board of Accountancy*, 512 U.S. 136, 114 S. Ct. 2084, 129 L. Ed. 2d 118 (1994), Ibanez, an attorney, licensed CPA, and CFP™ certificant, was reprimanded by the Florida Board of Accountancy for engaging in "false, deceptive, and misleading" advertising. Ibanez referred to her credentials as an attorney, a CPA, and CFP Board designee in her advertising and other communications with the public concerning her law practice, placing CPA and CFP Board designee next to her name in her yellow pages listing and in her business cards and law office stationery.

The Florida Board of Accountancy argued that the term "certified" in the phrase "*Certified Financial Planner*" was inherently misleading by causing the public to infer state approval and recognition, when in fact the CFP Board designation is not given by the state. The United States Supreme Court rejected this argument and instead ruled that Ibanez had a constitutional right to promote herself as an attorney/CPA that was also a CFP Board designee. The Court then approvingly stated: "Noteworthy in this connection, 'Certified Financial Planner' and 'CFP' are well-established, protected federal trademarks that have been described as the most recognized designation(s) in the planning field. Approximately 27,000 persons have qualified for the designation nationwide. Over 50 accredited universities and colleges have established courses of study in financial planning approved by the Certified Financial Planner Board of Standards, and standards for licensure include satisfaction of certain core educational requirements, a passing score on a certification examination similar in concept to the Bar or CPA examinations, completion of a planning-related work experience requirement, agreement to abide by the CFP Code of Ethics and Professional Responsibility, and an annual continuing education requirement." The Court concluded that Ibanez could use all three credentials in her advertising because it was not misleading or false and because she had a constitutional right to commercial speech.

The *Ibanez* case shows that CFP Board designees who have other credentials can promote those credentials without engaging in misleading, deceptive, or false communications with the public. The case also casts the CFP mark in a favorable light, recognizing the credibility that accompanies the CFP mark. Thus, Ibanez's actions did not mislead the public with respect to Rule 101(b) and did not adversely affect the profession with respect to Rule 607.

Meanwhile, Rule 608 of the Code deals with **registered investment advisors,** or RIAs. A registered investment advisor is a person or company that offers ongoing portfolio management or investment advice and charges money for it. Rule 608 requires CFP Board designees to disclose

Registered Investment Advisor (RIA) - a person or company that offers ongoing portfolio management or advice and charges money for it

to clients their firm's status as Registered Investment Advisors. Use of the letters RIA or R.I.A. following a CFP Board designee's name in advertising, letterhead, stationery, and business cards can be misleading and is prohibited by Rule 608 and by SEC regulations because this tends to indicate that the CFP Board designee has a higher level of competency or skill, which may create unjustified expectations on the part of the client.

Rule 609 forbids CFP Board designees from practicing any other profession unless the CFP Board designee is qualified and licensed (if applicable) to practice in that field: "*A CFP Board designee shall not practice any other profession or offer to provide such services unless the CFP Board designee is qualified to practice in those fields and is licensed as required by state law.*" *Code of Ethics and Prof. Resp., Part II, Rule 609, p. 16.* Rule 609 was implemented because a CFP Board designee's failure to service others competently in another profession would adversely affect the public image of CFP Board designees.

Rule 610 mandates that CFP Board designees return clients' original records timely upon request. "*A CFP Board designee shall return the client's original records in a timely manner after their return has been requested by a client.*" *Code of Ethics and Prof. Resp., Part II, Rule 610, p. 16.* Procrastination or outright refusal to return the client's original records is unprofessional and totally inappropriate. A CFP Board designee is thus bound by Rule 610 to return the client's original records promptly upon request even though he or she has not been paid. For instance, a financial plan developed and drafted by a CFP Board designee is not considered the client's original records, but the proformas, budgets and bank statements of the client provided to the CFP Board designee to draft a plan are original records.

A CFP Board designee is required to report information to the CFP Board under Rule 603 and 604. However, under Rule 611, a CFP Board designee is prohibited from bringing or threatening to bring disciplinary proceedings "*for no substantial purpose other than to harass, maliciously injure, embarrass, and/or unfairly burden another CFP Board designee.*" *Code of Ethics and Prof. Resp., Part II, Rule 611, p. 16.*

Rule 612 commands CFP Board designees to comply with the CFP Board's post-certification requirements which include 30 hours of continuing education every two years, annual licensing fees, license renewal requirements, and compliance with the Code.

PRINCIPLE 7: DILIGENCE

"*A CFP Board designee shall act diligently in providing professional services.*" *Code of Ethics and Prof. Resp., Part I, Principle 7, p. 10.* Diligence means the CFP Board designee provides services in a reasonably prompt and thorough manner. Diligence also includes proper planning for the provision of professional services, as well as proper supervision of the provision of professional services.

RULES THAT RELATE TO THE PRINCIPLE OF DILIGENCE

Under Rule 701, a CFP Board designee "*shall provide services diligently.*" CFP Board designees are bound to insure that the services are diligently provided to the client under the circumstances. Failure to properly supervise other CFP Board designees working for others could potentially result in disciplinary action under Rule 701.

A financial planning practitioner shall enter into an engagement by a client only after determining that the relationship is warranted by the client's needs and objectives and that the CFP Board designee can provide competent services or involve other professionals who can provide competent services. *Code of Ethics and Prof. Resp., Part II, Rule 702, p. 16.* There is some common ground between Rule 702 and Rule 302, which relates to the principle of Competence. However, if the CFP Board designee complies with Rule 702 and determines that he or she is not competent regarding the individual's objectives, the CFP Board designee will not enter into the engagement and will ultimately avoid a potential situation where the CFP Board designee would violate the rules of Competence. This could also prevent a professional negligence case against the CFP Board designee.

Rule 703 directs a CFP Board designee to "*make and/or implement only recommendations which are suitable for the client.*" *Code of Ethics and Prof. Resp., Part II, Rule 703, p. 16.* The key word in Rule 703 is "suitable." What is suitable for the client obviously depends upon the facts and circumstances of the client's situation. Again, one can detect some common ground between the Diligence requirement of Rule 703 and Competence in Rule 302.

For instance, if the CFP Board designee recommends a course of action that is not suitable for the client, the question then becomes, for purposes of this Code, whether the CFP Board designee attempted to determine if the recommendation was suitable for the client. If there is evidence that the CFP Board designee determined that the recommended course of action was suitable for the client, when in fact it clearly was not, then the CFP Board designee is probably subject to discipline under Rule 302 for incompetence. However, if there is evidence that the CFP Board designee failed to even attempt to determine if the recommended course of action was suitable for the client, the CFP Board designee is probably subject to discipline under Rule 703 for lack of Diligence.

Under Rule 704, the CFP Board designee is required to "*make a reasonable investigation regarding the financial products recommended to clients.*" *Code of Ethics and Prof. Resp., Part II, Rule 704, p. 16.* This does not mean, however, that the CFP Board designee must make the investigation. Although the Code permits the CFP Board designee to do the actual investigation, Rule 704 adds the provision that the investigation "may" be done by others if the CFP Board designee acts reasonably in relying upon such investigation. For example, a CFP Board designee who recommends a small cap stock to a client may rely on a report about that stock from <u>Barron's</u> financial newspaper that the stock was recommended by several mutual fund managers and had good ratings from ratings companies. The CFP Board designee need not necessarily investigate the stock on his own. It is reasonable for the CFP Board designee to rely on the investigation of <u>Barron's</u>, mutual fund managers, and ratings companies.

A CFP Board designee must properly "*supervise subordinates with regard to their delivery of financial planning services, and shall not accept or condone conduct in violation of this Code.*" *Code of Ethics and Prof. Resp., Part II, Rule 705, p. 16.* Rule 705 requires CFP Board designees to properly supervise subordinates regarding their delivery of financial planning services. Rule 705 also prohibits CFP Board designees from accepting or condoning conduct in violation of the Code. Thus, Rule 705 adds the requirement of diligence to CFP Board designees who supervise subordinates. This is yet another safeguard that ultimately benefits the client and should strengthen the public's trust in the profession. Also, Rule 705 is the converse of Rule 410. You will recall that Rule 410 prohibits employees from violating the Code, which includes situations where a superior orders a CFP Board designee to engage in unethical conduct. Rule 705 forbids CFP Board designees from accepting or condoning unethical conduct which could occur when an employer or superior discovers unethical conduct by an employee and either conceals the conduct or fails to report the conduct to the proper parties.

DISCIPLINARY RULES AND PROCEDURES

The Code also provides the rules and regulations for disciplinary proceedings against CFP Board designees. The enforcement of the Code is accomplished through the CFP Board's **Disciplinary Rules and Procedures** (the "Procedures"). Adherence to the Code is mandatory for all CFP Board designees. The CFP Board strictly enforces the provisions of the Code through the Procedures.

NOTES ON BURDENS OF PROOF

It is important to understand the various standards of proof that are involved with litigation in general and in disciplinary procedures (including subjecting a CFP Board designee to discipline). A standard of proof, or "**burden of proof**," is the requirement of proving facts to a certain degree of probability. Basically, there are three distinct burdens of proof: (1) preponderance of the evidence; (2) clear and convincing evidence; and (3) evidence beyond a reasonable doubt. A comparison of these burdens of proof illustrates different treatment of the CFP Board designee at various stages of disciplinary proceedings. Note that burden of proof in disciplinary proceedings is upon the CFP Board. The CFP Board designee is presumed to be free from ethical violations until proven otherwise.

The "Preponderance of the Evidence" Standard

"**Preponderance of the evidence**" means that the evidence as a whole shows what it was intended to prove with a probability of 51 percent or better. To say it another way, the evidence tends to prove that the existence of a fact is more likely than not. For example, proof of misconduct by a CFP Board designee must be "*established by a preponderance of the evidence.*" In other words, it must be shown that a CFP Board designee more likely than not violated the Code. In professional negligence or malpractice cases, the standard of proof is generally by a preponderance of the evidence.

The "Clear and Convincing Evidence" Standard

"*Clear and convincing evidence*" requires more proof or more certainty in the eyes of the fact finder than a preponderance of the evidence. **Clear and convincing evidence** is the measure or degree of proof that will produce in the mind of the finder of fact a firm belief or conviction as to allegations sought to be established. It is loosely described as a 75 percent certainty that a fact has been proven. Under the Procedures, a CFP Board designee who has been suspended for over a year must petition the Board of Professional Review (BOPR) for reinstatement and prove by clear and convincing evidence that he or she has been rehabilitated, has met continuing education requirements, and is fit to use the marks. In other words, the CFP Board designee must clearly and convincingly prove that he or she is worthy of reinstatement, which is more certainty

---

Disciplinary Rules and Procedures - the rules and regulations for disciplinary proceedings against CFP Board designees

burden of proof - the requirement of proving facts to a certain degree of probability. With regard to CFP disciplinary rules and procedures, there are three distinct burdens of proof: (1) preponderance of the evidence; (2) clear and convincing evidence; and (3) evidence beyond a reasonable doubt

preponderance of the evidence standard - a measure or degree of proof – with regard to CFP disciplinary rules and procedures, "preponderance of the evidence" means the evidence as a whole shows what it was intended to prove with a probability of 51 percent or better

clear and convincing evidence - a measure or degree of proof – with regard to CFP disciplinary rules and procedures, "clear and convincing evidence" means the evidence as a whole shows what it was intended to prove with a probability of 75 percent or better

than by a preponderance of the evidence, but less than that **beyond a reasonable doubt**. In litigation involving fraud, usually the party alleging fraud must prove fraud by clear and convincing evidence.

The "Beyond a Reasonable Doubt" Standard

"*Beyond a reasonable doubt*" in evidence means that the finder of fact is fully satisfied, entirely convinced, and satisfied to a moral certainty that a fact has been established. The fact finder can have no doubt as to the existence of a fact unless that doubt is unreasonable or irrational. Some define the term as a 99 percent certainty that the evidence shows as a whole the fact sought to be proved. For example, this standard of proof comes into play in the Procedures under Article 11.1 where a CFP Board designee who has been convicted of a crime is subject to discipline, and the conviction is conclusive proof of the commission of the crime. In criminal proceedings, the burden of proof is beyond a reasonable doubt.

GROUNDS AND FORMS OF DISCIPLINE

The grounds for discipline of a CFP Board designee under the Procedures are:

- ▲ Any act which violates the Code.
- ▲ Any act which fails to comply with the Practice Standards.
- ▲ Any act which violates any criminal laws, whether the CFP Board designee is convicted or acquitted.
- ▲ Any act which is the proper basis for professional suspension.
- ▲ Any act which violates these Procedures or an order of discipline.
- ▲ Failure to respond to a request of the CFP Board without good cause, or obstruction of the CFP Board or staff in the performance of their duties.
- ▲ Any false or misleading statement made to the CFP Board.
- ▲ Other acts amounting to unprofessional conduct.

If grounds for discipline are established, the BOPR has discretion to use any of the following forms of discipline:

- ▲ **Private Censure** - an unpublished written reproach that is mailed to the censured CFP Board designee by the BOPR.
- ▲ **Public Letter of Admonition** - a publishable written reproach of the CFP Board designee's behavior that will normally be published in a press release or other form of publicity selected by the BOPR, unless mitigating circumstances exist and the BOPR in its discretion decides to withhold public notification.
- ▲ **Suspension** - may be ordered by the BOPR for a specified period of time, not to exceed five (5) years, for individuals it deems can be rehabilitated. The suspension will normally be published in a press release or other form of publicity, unless extreme mitigating circumstances exist. CFP Board designees who are suspended may qualify for reinstatement.
- ▲ **Revocation** - The BOPR may order permanent revocation of a CFP Board designee's right to use the mark. All revocations are "*permanent*." It is standard procedure to publish the revocation in a press release or other form of publicity, unless extreme mitigating circumstances persuade the BOPR to withhold public notification.

revocation - the CFP BOPR may order permanent revocation of a CFP Board designee's right to use the mark, and publish the revocation in a press release or other form of publicity, unless extreme mitigating circumstances persuade the BOPR to withhold public notification

Disciplinary proceedings under the Procedures are commenced upon a written request by any person. After commencement, the matter is referred to the BOPR. If the BOPR in its discretion determines to proceed with the investigation, the CFP Board provides written notice to the CFP Board designee of the investigation and of the allegations made, and the CFP Board designee has twenty (20) calendar days from the date of notice of the investigation to file a written response to the allegations. If a timely response is received, a report of all documents and materials is given to an Inquiry Panel.

Based on the report of Staff Counsel, the Inquiry Panel determines if there is "probable cause" for disciplinary action and then does one of the following: dismiss the allegations as being without merit; dismiss the allegations with a letter of caution; or refer the matter to the CFP Board in continuation of disciplinary proceedings. If the Inquiry Panel finds probable cause, it issues a formal Complaint, stating the grounds for discipline and the alleged wrongful conduct of the CFP Board designee. Within 20 days, the CFP Board designee must admit or deny all allegations and set forth any affirmative defenses. If the CFP Board designee fails to file an answer within 20 days of service, the CFP Board designee will be in default and the allegations of the Complaints will be deemed admitted. Staff Counsel must serve the CFP Board designee with an Order of Revocation, stating clearly and with reasonable particularity the grounds for revocation of the CFP Board designee's right to use the CFP marks.

hearing panel - panel that establishes the rules of procedures and evidence to be observed at a complaint hearing seeking disciplinary action against a CFP Board designee

All hearings on Complaints seeking disciplinary action against a CFP Board designee are required to be conducted by a **Hearing Panel**. The Hearing Panel must establish the rules of procedures and evidence to be observed at the hearing. Proof of misconduct is established by a "preponderance of the evidence." A CFP Board designee may not be required to testify or to produce records over the objection of the CFP Board designee if it would violate the CFP Board designee's constitutional privilege against self-incrimination in a court of law. Staff Counsel or the CFP Board designee may request written discovery or depositions. A deposition is an examination of a person whereby that person answers questions while under oath or affirmation with a court reporter present. The Hearing Panel must rule on such requests and may order the party to comply with the request. All testimony at hearings before the Hearing Panel must be transcribed.

Self-incrimination

Self-incrimination is the process whereby acts or declarations either as testimony at trial or prior to trial implicate oneself in a crime. The Fifth Amendment to the United States Constitution, as well as provisions in many state constitutions, prohibits the government from requiring a person to be a witness or furnish evidence against himself or herself involuntarily. This privilege against self-incrimination requires the government to prove a criminal case against defendants without the aid of defendants as witnesses against themselves. However, this privilege against self-incrimination is waived when the witness voluntarily testifies. Interestingly, the Fifth Amendment privilege against self-incrimination protects a witness not only from the requirement of answering questions which might call for directly incriminating answers, but also from answers which might tie or link oneself to criminal activity in the chain of evidence.

Rather than coerce the CFP Board designee into a confession or admission or require the CFP Board designee to provide a link in the chain of evidence of criminal activity, the BOPR must turn to other evidence to prove that a CFP Board designee violated the Code in the event that the CFP Board designee objects to testifying or to producing records.

REPORT, FINDINGS OF FACT, AND RECOMMENDATION

After the hearing, the Hearing Panel records its findings of fact and recommendations and submits them to the BOPR for consideration. The report must dismiss the Complaint as not proven or refer the matter to the BOPR with the recommendation of discipline, stating which form of discipline the Hearing Panel deems appropriate. The Hearing Panel may also recommend that the BOPR enter other appropriate orders.

The BOPR has the power to review any determination made during disciplinary proceedings or practice standards proceedings. The BOPR may, in its discretion, approve or modify the report. However, the BOPR must accept the Hearing Panel's findings of fact unless it determines that such findings are "clearly erroneous" based on a review of the record. The BOPR may modify the Hearing Panel's recommendation without reviewing the record, whether or not the recommendation is clearly erroneous.

The "Clearly Erroneous" Standard – Explanation

When the Hearing Panel makes findings of fact, these findings are based on the broad discretion and judgment of those serving on the panel. Their findings should not be taken lightly because the panel members were present during the hearing and were able to see firsthand the evidence, to hear the live witnesses, if any, and to evaluate the CFP Board designee and the CFP Board designee's demeanor. Under these circumstances, the Hearing Panel should be given vast discretion as to factual findings. Accordingly, these findings should only be set aside or altered by the BOPR if the findings are clearly erroneous or clearly wrong. Many appellate courts of law utilize this clearly erroneous standard. The **clearly erroneous standard** boils down to this basic question: Could a reasonable finder of fact have possibly ruled this way, based on the entire record? Only when review of the entire record reveals that a reasonable person could <u>not</u> have ruled that way will the findings be considered clearly erroneous.

The factual findings of the Hearing Panel are given much discretion and deference by the BOPR. If the Hearing Panel makes unfavorable factual findings for the CFP Board designee, these factual findings will be binding upon the CFP Board designee and are not taken lightly. The Hearing Panel's factual findings normally will not be overturned or disturbed by the BOPR or the Board of Appeals, much like litigation during the appellate process.

In contrast to findings of fact, however, the recommendations of the Hearing Panel are subject to modification as the BOPR deems appropriate. The BOPR must, however, state the reasons for modification. All appeals from orders of the BOPR shall be submitted to the Board of Appeals within thirty (30) calendar days after notice of the order is sent to the CFP Board designee. If no appeal is lodged with the Board of Appeals within that time frame, the order shall become final and binding.

clearly erroneous standard - standard applied by a CFP Hearing Panel at a CFP complaint hearing that states that only when review of the entire record reveals that a reasonable person could <u>not</u> have ruled that way will the findings be considered clearly erroneous

CONVICTION OF A CRIME OR PROFESSIONAL SUSPENSION

Conviction of a crime or an order of professional suspension is conclusive evidence and proof of the commission of the act for purposes of disciplinary proceedings. The CFP Board designee has a duty to report convictions or professional suspension to the CFP Board within ten (10) days after the date on which the CFP Board designee is notified of the conviction or suspension. After receiving notice that a CFP Board designee has been convicted of a crime other than a serious crime, the CFP Board shall refer the matter to an Inquiry Panel. If a CFP Board designee is convicted of a serious crime or is the subject of a professional suspension, the CFP Board shall obtain the record of the conviction or suspension and file a Complaint against the CFP Board designee. The CFP Board may report the name of any CFP Board designee who is convicted of a serious crime or is the subject of a professional suspension to the BOPR and may issue a notice to the convicted CFP Board designee to show cause why the CFP Board designee's right to use the marks should not be immediately suspended.

SETTLEMENT PROCEDURE

A CFP Board designee may tender an **Offer of Settlement** in exchange for a stipulated form of action by the BOPR. The Offer of Settlement may be made where the public interests and CFP Board permit. A CFP Board designee is allowed only one Offer of Settlement during the course of a disciplinary proceeding. If an Offer of Settlement is accepted by the Hearing Panel, it must propose an **Order of Acceptance** containing findings of fact. The Order of Acceptance must be reviewed by the BOPR. If the Offer of Settlement is rejected by the Hearing Panel, the Offer is deemed withdrawn. The CFP Board designee shall not be prejudiced in any way by a rejection.

REQUIRED ACTION AFTER REVOCATION OR SUSPENSION

When an order of revocation or suspension becomes final, the CFP Board designee "*shall promptly terminate*" any use of the CFP mark. If one's right to use the CFP mark is revoked, there is no opportunity for reinstatement. Revocation is "*permanent.*" A CFP Board designee who has been suspended for less than one year shall be automatically reinstated after expiration of the suspension, provided that the CFP Board designee complies with the order of suspension and files an affidavit verifying such compliance. A CFP Board designee who has been suspended over one year must petition the BOPR for reinstatement within six months of the end of the suspension, or else reinstatement is relinquished or waived. If the CFP Board designee petitions the BOPR within six months of reinstatement, the CFP Board designee has the burden of proving by "*clear and convincing evidence*" that the CFP Board designee has been rehabilitated; has complied with all applicable disciplinary Procedures; has met all CFP Board designee continuing education requirements; and is fit to use the marks.

If the CFP Board designee petitions for reinstatement, Staff Counsel will initiate an investigation. The CFP Board designee must cooperate with the investigation, and Staff Counsel shall submit a report of the investigation that shall report on the CFP Board designee's past disciplinary record and any recommendation regarding reinstatement. If the CFP Board designee is denied reinstatement, the CFP Board designee must wait two years to petition again for reinstatement. If the second petition is denied, the CFP Board designee's right to use the marks is relinquished.

offer of settlement - a CFP Board designee may tender an Offer of Settlement in exchange for a stipulated form of disciplinary action by the CFP BOPR

order of acceptance - if an Offer of Settlement is accepted by the Hearing Panel during a disciplinary review, it must propose an Order of Acceptance containing findings of fact to be reviewed by the CFP Board of Professional Review

All proceedings and records conducted in accordance with the Procedures are confidential. They will not be made public, unless otherwise provided in the Procedures. The Procedures allow disclosure of disciplinary proceedings if the proceeding is based on criminal conviction or professional suspension; the CFP Board designee has waived confidentiality; or disclosure is required by legal process.

THE PRACTICE STANDARDS

The CFP Board established the Board of Practice Standards to draft **Practice Standards** to assure that the financial planning practice by CFP Board designees is based on agreed-upon norms of practice. The Practice Standards are also in place to advance professionalism in the practice of financial planning and to enhance the value of the personal financial planning process. A Practice Standard establishes the level of professional practice that is expected of CFP Board designees engaged in personal financial planning. The facts and circumstances of each particular situation determine the services to be provided.

Currently, there are four sections of Practice Standards in effect, the "100 Series", the "200 Series", the "300 Series" and the "400 Series." There are two other sections planned that are being reviewed, exposed for comment or drafted by the Board of Practice Standards.

THE 100 SERIES

Practice Standard 100-1

<u>Establishing and defining the relationship with the client</u> -- Defining the scope of the engagement. The scope of the engagement shall be mutually defined by the financial planning practitioner and the client prior to providing any financial planning service.

THE 200 SERIES

Practice Standard 200-1

<u>Gathering client data</u> -- Determining a client's personal and financial goals, needs and priorities. A client's personal financial goals, needs, and priorities that are relevant to the scope of the engagement and the service(s) being provided shall be mutually defined by the financial planning practitioner and the client prior to making and/or implementing any recommendation.

Practice Standards 200-2

<u>Gathering client data</u> -- Obtaining quantitative information and documents. A financial planning practitioner shall obtain sufficient and relevant quantitative information and documents about a client applicable to the scope of the engagement and the services being provided prior to making and/or implementing any recommendation.

practice standards - the set of standards that establish: (1) the level of professional practice that is expected of CFP Board designees engaged in personal financial planning, (2) advance professionalism in the practice of financial planning, and (3) enhance the value of the personal financial planning process

THE 300 SERIES

Practice Standard 300-1

<u>Analyzing and evaluating the client's financial status</u> -- Analyzing and evaluating the client's information. A financial planning practitioner must analyze the client's information in order to gain a full understanding of the client's financial situation; then evaluate and assess to what extent the client's goals, needs and priorities can be met by the client's resources and current course of action. Analysis and evaluation are critical to the process of financial planning. After this analysis and evaluation, it may even be appropriate to amend the scope of the engagement and/or to obtain additional information.

THE 400 SERIES

Practice Standard 400-1

<u>Developing and presenting the financial planning recommendation(s)</u> -- Identifying and evaluating financial planning alternatives. A financial planning practitioner shall consider sufficient and relevant alternatives to the client's current course of action in an effort to reasonably meet the client's goals, needs and priorities. This evaluation, which is done prior to any recommendations, may involve multiple reasonable assumptions, research or consultation with other competent professionals. This process may result in one alternative, no alternatives, multiple alternatives or various combinations in relation to the client's current course of action.

Practice Standard 400-2

<u>Developing and presenting the financial planning recommendation(s)</u> -- Developing the financial planning recommendation(s). A financial planning practitioner must develop recommendations based on the selected alternatives and the current course of action in order to reasonably achieve the client's goals, needs and priorities. A recommendation may be an independent action, continuation of the current course of action, inaction or a combination of actions that may need to be implemented collectively.

Practice Standard 400-3

<u>Developing and presenting the financial planning recommendation(s)</u> -- Presenting the financial planning recommendation(s). A financial planning practitioner shall communicate the recommendations to the client in a manner and to an extent reasonable necessary to assist the client in making an informed decision. The practitioner is henced charged with the responsibility of assisting the client in understanding (i) the client's current situation, (ii) the recommendation itself, and (iii) the impact of the recommendation on the ability to achieve the client's goals, needs and priorities. If the client possesses an understanding of these items, the client can make the truly informed decision. Presenting recommendations also provides the practitioner an opportunity to further assess whether the recommendations meet the client's expectations, the client's willingness to act on the recommendations and whether modifications are in order.

These Practice Standards are excellent ways to promote sound practices and basically good business for CFP Board designees when rendering financial planning services. Similar to an ethics code, such standards can only add to the value of services of the financial planning industry as a whole. Even though these standards are applicable only to CFP Board designees, these standards (and the ensuing Practice Standards) are admirable guides for those in the financial world in general.

THE IMPORTANCE OF ETHICS

While learning the fundamentals of financial planning is vital to those who aspire to work and interact in the world of business and finance, equally important is understanding and being able to handle ethical issues that accompany interaction in the finance industry and that accompany the provision of financial services. The negative effects of unethical practices and actions of a few not only damage the individual engaging in unethical behavior and the victim of such behavior, but damage the image and the productivity of the entire industry. Ethics codes and practice standards can help significantly in reducing the incidence of unethical and damaging conduct, while providing much needed counsel, tutelage, guidance, and direction to the individual professional.

DISCUSSION QUESTIONS

1. How do ethics, law, and an ethics code differ and how are they similar?
2. What is the Certified Financial Planner Board of Standards, Inc.?
3. What is the Code of Ethics and Professional Responsibility (the Code)?
4. What is the role of the CFP Board's Practice Standards in relation to the Code?
5. What is the role of the Board of Professional Review (BOPR), the Board of Practice Standards, and the Board of Governors in relation to the Code?
6. What is the role of the Disciplinary Rules and Procedures (the Procedures) and the Financial Planning Practice Standards (the Standards) in relation to the Code?
7. How is the Code structured and what is the role of each of its parts?
8. What are the seven Principles of the Code? Give a rule that relates to each Principle?
9. How does the "commingling of funds" and the "fiduciary relationship" relate to the Code's Principle of Integrity?
10. How do the three distinct standards or "burdens" of proof affect the treatment of the CFP Board designee at various stages of disciplinary proceedings?
11. What four forms of discipline can be applied by the BOPR to a CFP Board designee?
12. What is the primary purpose or aim of the CFP Board's Practice Standards?

Appendices

Appendix A

Comprehensive Case

Today is January 1, 2002. Mark and Ava Lane have come to you, a financial planner, for help in developing a plan to accomplish their financial goals. From your initial meeting together, you have gathered the following information:

PERSONAL BACKGROUND AND INFORMATION

MARK LANE (AGE 30)

Mark is an assistant in the marketing department for Gas & Electric, Inc. His annual salary is $26,000.

AVA LANE (AGE 30)

Ava is a legal research assistant with the law firm of Sabrio, Johnson & Williams, L.L.C. Her annual salary is $20,000.

THE CHILDREN

Mark and Ava have no children from this marriage. Mark has two children, Shawn (Age 4) and Ronald (Age 3), from a former marriage. Shawn and Ronald live with their mother, Kimberly.

THE LANES

Mark and Ava have been married for two years.

Mark must pay $325 per month in child support until both Shawn and Ronald reach age 18. The divorce decree also requires Mark to create an insurance trust for the benefit of the children and contribute $175 per month to the trustee. The trustee is Kimberly's father. There are no withdrawal powers on the part of the beneficiaries. The trust is to be used for the education and/or maintenance of the children in the event of Mark's death. The trustee has the power to invade any trust principal for the beneficiaries at the earlier of the death of Mark or when Ronald reaches age 18.

ECONOMIC INFORMATION

▲ Inflation is expected to be 4.0% annually.
▲ Their salaries should increase 5.0% for the next five to ten years.
▲ No state income tax.
▲ Slow growth economy; stocks are expected to grow at 9.5%.

BANK LENDING RATES ARE AS FOLLOWS:

▲ 15-year mortgage 7.5%.
▲ 30-year mortgage 8.0%.
▲ Secured personal loan 10.0%.

INSURANCE INFORMATION

LIFE INSURANCE

	Policy A	Policy B	Policy C
Insured	Mark	Mark	Ava
Face Amount	$300,000	$78,000[2]	$20,000
Type	Whole Life	Group Term	Group Term
Cash Value	$2,000	$0	$0
Annual Premium	$2,100	$178	$50
Who pays premium	Trustee	Employer	Employer
Beneficiary	Trustee[1]	Kimberly	Mark
Policy Owner	Trust	Mark	Ava
Settlement options clause selected	None	None	None

[1] Shawn and Ronald are beneficiaries of the trust.
[2] This was increased from $50,000 to $78,000 January 1, 2002.

HEALTH INSURANCE

▲ Mark and Ava are covered under Mark's employer plan which is an indemnity plan with a $200 deductible per person per year and an 80/20 major medical co-insurance clause with a family annual stop loss of $1,500.

LONG-TERM DISABILITY INSURANCE

▲ Mark is covered by an "own occupation" policy with premiums paid by his employer. The benefits equal 60% of his gross pay after an elimination period of 180 days. The policy covers both sickness and accidents and is guaranteed renewable.

▲ Ava is not covered by disability insurance.

RENTERS INSURANCE

▲ The Lanes have a HO4 renters policy without endorsements.

▲ Content Coverage $25,000; Liability $100,000.

AUTOMOBILE INSURANCE

▲ Both Car and Truck

▲ They do not have any additional insurance on Mark's motorcycle.

Type	PAP
Bodily Injury	$25,000/$50,000
Property Damage	$10,000
Medical Payments	$5,000 per person
Physical Damage	Actual Cash Value
Uninsured Motorist	$25,000/$50,000
Comprehensive Deductible	$200
Collision Deductible	$500
Premium (annual)	$3,300

INVESTMENT INFORMATION

The Lanes think that they need six months of cash flow net of all taxes, savings, vacation, and discretionary cash flow in an emergency fund. They are willing to include in the emergency fund the savings account and Mark's 401(k) balance because it has borrowing provisions.

The Amazon.com stock was a gift to Mark from his Uncle Bill. At the date of the gift (July 1, 1999), the fair market value of the stock was $3,500. Uncle Bill's tax basis was $2,500, and Uncle Bill paid gift tax of $1,400 on the gift. Uncle Bill had already used up both his unified credit and annual exclusion to Mark.

The K&B stock was a gift to Ava of 100 shares from her Uncle Mike. At the date of the gift (December 25, 1999) the fair market value was $8,000 and Mike had paid $10,000 for the stock in 1992 (his tax basis).

The Growth Mutual Fund (currently valued at $13,900) had been acquired by Mark over the years 1996, 1997, 1998, 1999, 2000, and 2001 with deposits of $1,000, $1,000, $2,000, $2,000, $2,500 and $3,000. The earnings were all reinvested and Mark received 1099s for the income and capital gains during the years of earnings ($0/1996, $200/1997, $400/1998, $400/1999, $650/2000, $750/2001).

INCOME TAX INFORMATION

The filing status of the Lanes for Federal income tax is married filing jointly. Both the children (Shawn and Ronald) are claimed as dependents on the Lane's tax return as part of the divorce agreement. The Lanes live in a state that does not have state income tax.

Section 79 Limit on Premium Schedule
Age 29 and under $0.08 per month/per $1,000.

RETIREMENT INFORMATION

Mark currently contributes 3% of his salary to his 401(k). The employer matches each $1 contributed with $0.50 up to a total employer contribution of 3% of salary.

GIFTS, ESTATES, TRUSTS, AND WILL INFORMATION

▲ Mark has a will leaving all of his probate estate to his children.
▲ Ava does not have a will.
▲ The Lanes live in a common law state that has adopted the Uniform Probate Code.

STATEMENT OF CASH FLOWS

Mark and Ava Lane
Statement of Cash Flows (Expected to be similar in 2002)
January 1, 2001 - December 31, 2001

CASH INFLOWS

Salaries		
Mark-Salary	$26,000	
Ava-Salary	20,000	
Investment Income*	1,090	
Total Inflows		$47,090

CASH OUTFLOWS

Savings-House down payment	$ 1,200	
Reinvestment of Investment Income	1,090	
401(k) Contribution	780	
Total Savings		$ 3,070

FIXED OUTFLOWS

Child Support	$ 3,900	
Life Insurance Payment (To Trustee)	2,100	
Rent	6,600	
Renters Insurance	480	
Utilities	720	
Telephone	360	
Auto payment P&I as of 1/1/2001	3,600	
Auto Insurance	3,300	
Gas, Oil, Maintenance	2,400	
Student loans	3,600	
Credit Card Debt	1,800	
Furniture payments	1,302	
Total Fixed Outflows		$30,162

VARIABLE OUTFLOWS

Taxes-Mark FICA	$ 1,989	
Taxes-Ava FICA	1,530	
Taxes-Federal Tax Withheld	4,316	
Food	3,600	
Clothing	1,000	
Entertainment/Vacation	1,500	
Total Variable Outflows		$13,935
Total Cash Outflows		$47,167
Discretionary Cash Flows (negative)		$ (77)
TOTAL CASH OUTFLOWS		$47,090

$340 from dividends and $750 from other investment sources.

834

STATEMENT OF FINANCIAL POSITION

Mark and Ava Lane
Balance Sheet
As of January 1, 2002

ASSETS[1]		LIABILITIES & NET WORTH	
Cash and Equivalents		Liabilities[2]	
Cash	$ 500	Credit Card balance VISA	$ 9,000
Savings Account	1,000	Credit Card balance M/C	0
Total Cash and Equivalents	$1,500	Student Loan-Mark[4]	45,061
		Auto Loan-Ava	14,796
Invested Assets		Furniture Loan	1,533
Amazon.com Stock (100 Shares)[3]	$ 5,000	Total Liabilities	$70,390
K&B Stock (100 shares)	7,200		
Growth Mutual Fund	13,900		
401(k) Account	1,500	Net Worth	(46)
Total Invested Assets	$27,600		
Use Assets			
Auto-Ava	$18,494		
Truck-Mark	4,000		
Motorcycle – Mark	1,000		
Personal Property & Furniture	17,750		
Total Use Of Assets	$41,244		
Total Assets	$70,344	Total Liabilities & Net Worth	$70,344

Notes to Financial Statements:
1. Assets are stated at fair market value.
2. Liabilities are stated at principal only as of January 1, 2002 before January payments.
3. Amazon.com's current dividend is $3.40.
4. Mark's parents took out the student loans, but he is repaying them.

INFORMATION REGARDING ASSETS AND LIABILITIES

HOME FURNISHINGS

The furniture was purchased with 20% down and 18% interest over 36 months. The monthly payment is $108.46.

AUTOMOBILE

The automobile was purchased January 1, 2001 for $18,494 with 20% down and 80% financed over 60 months with payments of $300 per month.

STEREO SYSTEM

The Lanes have a fabulous stereo system (FMV $10,000). They asked and received permission to alter the apartment to build speakers into every room. The agreement with the landlord requires the Lanes to leave the speakers if they move because the speakers are permanently installed and affixed to the property. The replacement value of the installed speakers is $4,500, and the non-installed components are valued at $5,500. The cost of the system was $10,000, and it was purchased in late 2000.

REQUIREMENTS:

▲ Complete an Engagement Letter to the Lanes to advise them on financial planning.
▲ Complete a Client Planner Worksheet.
▲ Calculate financial ratios for the Lanes.
▲ Identify the financial strengths and weaknesses of the Lanes.
▲ Identify the likely appropriate mission, goals, and objectives of the Lanes.
▲ Make recommendations based on the goals and risks of the Lanes in all areas of their financial situation.

Appendix B-1

Present Value of a Dollar

Present Value of $1

$$\left[\dfrac{1}{(1+i)^n}\right]$$

Period	1%	2%	3%	4%	5%	6%	7%	8%	9%	10%	11%	12%	13%
1	0.9901	0.9804	0.9709	0.9615	0.9524	0.9434	0.9346	0.9259	0.9174	0.9091	0.9009	0.8929	0.8850
2	0.9803	0.9612	0.9426	0.9246	0.9070	0.8900	0.8734	0.8573	0.8417	0.8264	0.8116	0.7972	0.7831
3	0.9706	0.9423	0.9151	0.8890	0.8638	0.8396	0.8163	0.7938	0.7722	0.7513	0.7312	0.7118	0.6931
4	0.9610	0.9238	0.8885	0.8548	0.8227	0.7921	0.7629	0.7350	0.7084	0.6830	0.6587	0.6355	0.6133
5	0.9515	0.9057	0.8626	0.8219	0.7835	0.7473	0.7130	0.6806	0.6499	0.6209	0.5935	0.5674	0.5428
6	0.9420	0.8880	0.8375	0.7903	0.7462	0.7050	0.6663	0.6302	0.5963	0.5645	0.5346	0.5066	0.4803
7	0.9327	0.8706	0.8131	0.7599	0.7107	0.6651	0.6227	0.5835	0.5470	0.5132	0.4817	0.4523	0.4251
8	0.9235	0.8535	0.7894	0.7307	0.6768	0.6274	0.5820	0.5403	0.5019	0.4665	0.4339	0.4039	0.3762
9	0.9143	0.8368	0.7664	0.7026	0.6446	0.5919	0.5439	0.5002	0.4604	0.4241	0.3909	0.3606	0.3329
10	0.9053	0.8203	0.7441	0.6756	0.6139	0.5584	0.5083	0.4632	0.4224	0.3855	0.3522	0.3220	0.2946
11	0.8963	0.8043	0.7224	0.6496	0.5847	0.5268	0.4751	0.4289	0.3875	0.3505	0.3173	0.2875	0.2607
12	0.8874	0.7885	0.7014	0.6246	0.5568	0.4970	0.4440	0.3971	0.3555	0.3186	0.2858	0.2567	0.2307
13	0.8787	0.7730	0.6810	0.6006	0.5303	0.4688	0.4150	0.3677	0.3262	0.2897	0.2575	0.2292	0.2042
14	0.8700	0.7579	0.6611	0.5775	0.5051	0.4423	0.3878	0.3405	0.2992	0.2633	0.2320	0.2046	0.1807
15	0.8613	0.7430	0.6419	0.5553	0.4810	0.4173	0.3624	0.3152	0.2745	0.2394	0.2090	0.1827	0.1599
16	0.8528	0.7284	0.6232	0.5339	0.4581	0.3936	0.3387	0.2919	0.2519	0.2176	0.1883	0.1631	0.1415
17	0.8444	0.7142	0.6050	0.5134	0.4363	0.3714	0.3166	0.2703	0.2311	0.1978	0.1696	0.1456	0.1252
18	0.8360	0.7002	0.5874	0.4936	0.4155	0.3503	0.2959	0.2502	0.2120	0.1799	0.1528	0.1300	0.1108
19	0.8277	0.6864	0.5703	0.4746	0.3957	0.3305	0.2765	0.2317	0.1945	0.1635	0.1377	0.1161	0.0981
20	0.8195	0.6730	0.5537	0.4564	0.3769	0.3118	0.2584	0.2145	0.1784	0.1486	0.1240	0.1037	0.0868
25	0.7798	0.6095	0.4776	0.3751	0.2953	0.2330	0.1842	0.1460	0.1160	0.0923	0.0736	0.0588	0.0471
30	0.7419	0.5521	0.4120	0.3083	0.2314	0.1741	0.1314	0.0994	0.0754	0.0573	0.0437	0.0334	0.0256
35	0.7059	0.5000	0.3554	0.2534	0.1813	0.1301	0.0937	0.0676	0.0490	0.0356	0.0259	0.0189	0.0139
40	0.6717	0.4529	0.3066	0.2083	0.1420	0.0972	0.0668	0.0460	0.0318	0.0221	0.0154	0.0107	0.0075
45	0.6391	0.4102	0.2644	0.1712	0.1113	0.0727	0.0476	0.0313	0.0207	0.0137	0.0091	0.0061	0.0041
50	0.6080	0.3715	0.2281	0.1407	0.0872	0.0543	0.0339	0.0213	0.0134	0.0085	0.0054	0.0035	0.0022

Appendix B-1

Present Value of a Dollar (continued)

Present Value of $1

$$\left[\frac{1}{(1+i)^n}\right]$$

Period	14%	15%	16%	17%	18%	19%	20%	25%	30%	35%	40%	45%	50%
1	0.8772	0.8696	0.8621	0.8547	0.8475	0.8403	0.8333	0.8000	0.7692	0.7407	0.7143	0.6897	0.6667
2	0.7695	0.7561	0.7432	0.7305	0.7182	0.7062	0.6944	0.6400	0.5917	0.5487	0.5102	0.4756	0.4444
3	0.6750	0.6575	0.6407	0.6244	0.6086	0.5934	0.5787	0.5120	0.4552	0.4064	0.3644	0.3280	0.2963
4	0.5921	0.5718	0.5523	0.5337	0.5158	0.4987	0.4823	0.4096	0.3501	0.3011	0.2603	0.2262	0.1975
5	0.5194	0.4972	0.4761	0.4561	0.4371	0.4190	0.4019	0.3277	0.2693	0.2230	0.1859	0.1560	0.1317
6	0.4556	0.4323	0.4104	0.3898	0.3704	0.3521	0.3349	0.2621	0.2072	0.1652	0.1328	0.1076	0.0878
7	0.3996	0.3759	0.3538	0.3332	0.3139	0.2959	0.2791	0.2097	0.1594	0.1224	0.0949	0.0742	0.0585
8	0.3506	0.3269	0.3050	0.2848	0.2660	0.2487	0.2326	0.1678	0.1226	0.0906	0.0678	0.0512	0.0390
9	0.3075	0.2843	0.2630	0.2434	0.2255	0.2090	0.1938	0.1342	0.0943	0.0671	0.0484	0.0353	0.0260
10	0.2697	0.2472	0.2267	0.2080	0.1911	0.1756	0.1615	0.1074	0.0725	0.0497	0.0346	0.0243	0.0173
11	0.2366	0.2149	0.1954	0.1778	0.1619	0.1476	0.1346	0.0859	0.0558	0.0368	0.0247	0.0168	0.0116
12	0.2076	0.1869	0.1685	0.1520	0.1372	0.1240	0.1122	0.0687	0.0429	0.0273	0.0176	0.0116	0.0077
13	0.1821	0.1625	0.1452	0.1299	0.1163	0.1042	0.0935	0.0550	0.0330	0.0202	0.0126	0.0080	0.0051
14	0.1597	0.1413	0.1252	0.1110	0.0985	0.0876	0.0779	0.0440	0.0254	0.0150	0.0090	0.0055	0.0034
15	0.1401	0.1229	0.1079	0.0949	0.0835	0.0736	0.0649	0.0352	0.0195	0.0111	0.0064	0.0038	0.0023
16	0.1229	0.1069	0.0930	0.0811	0.0708	0.0618	0.0541	0.0281	0.0150	0.0082	0.0046	0.0026	0.0015
17	0.1078	0.0929	0.0802	0.0693	0.0600	0.0520	0.0451	0.0225	0.0116	0.0061	0.0033	0.0018	0.0010
18	0.0946	0.0808	0.0691	0.0592	0.0508	0.0437	0.0376	0.0180	0.0089	0.0045	0.0023	0.0012	0.0007
19	0.0829	0.0703	0.0596	0.0506	0.0431	0.0367	0.0313	0.0144	0.0068	0.0033	0.0017	0.0009	0.0005
20	0.0728	0.0611	0.0514	0.0433	0.0365	0.0308	0.0261	0.0115	0.0053	0.0025	0.0012	0.0006	0.0003
25	0.0378	0.0304	0.0245	0.0197	0.0160	0.0129	0.0105	0.0038	0.0014	0.0006	0.0002	0.0001	0.0000
30	0.0196	0.0151	0.0116	0.0090	0.0070	0.0054	0.0042	0.0012	0.0004	0.0001	0.0000	0.0000	0.0000
35	0.0102	0.0075	0.0055	0.0041	0.0030	0.0023	0.0017	0.0004	0.0001	0.0000	0.0000	0.0000	0.0000
40	0.0053	0.0037	0.0026	0.0019	0.0013	0.0010	0.0007	0.0001	0.0000	0.0000	0.0000	0.0000	0.0000
45	0.0027	0.0019	0.0013	0.0009	0.0006	0.0004	0.0003	0.0000	0.0000	0.0000	0.0000	0.0000	0.0000
50	0.0014	0.0009	0.0006	0.0004	0.0003	0.0002	0.0001	0.0000	0.0000	0.0000	0.0000	0.0000	0.0000

Appendix B-2

Future Value of a Dollar

Future Value of $1

$$\left[\, (1+i)^n \,\right]$$

Period	1%	2%	3%	4%	5%	6%	7%	8%	9%	10%	11%	12%	13%
1	1.0100	1.0200	1.0300	1.0400	1.0500	1.0600	1.0700	1.0800	1.0900	1.1000	1.1100	1.1200	1.1300
2	1.0201	1.0404	1.0609	1.0816	1.1025	1.1236	1.1449	1.1664	1.1881	1.2100	1.2321	1.2544	1.2769
3	1.0303	1.0612	1.0927	1.1249	1.1576	1.1910	1.2250	1.2597	1.2950	1.3310	1.3676	1.4049	1.4429
4	1.0406	1.0824	1.1255	1.1699	1.2155	1.2625	1.3108	1.3605	1.4116	1.4641	1.5181	1.5735	1.6305
5	1.0510	1.1041	1.1593	1.2167	1.2763	1.3382	1.4026	1.4693	1.5386	1.6105	1.6851	1.7623	1.8424
6	1.0615	1.1262	1.1941	1.2653	1.3401	1.4185	1.5007	1.5869	1.6771	1.7716	1.8704	1.9738	2.0820
7	1.0721	1.1487	1.2299	1.3159	1.4071	1.5036	1.6058	1.7138	1.8280	1.9487	2.0762	2.2107	2.3526
8	1.0829	1.1717	1.2668	1.3686	1.4775	1.5938	1.7182	1.8509	1.9926	2.1436	2.3045	2.4760	2.6584
9	1.0937	1.1951	1.3048	1.4233	1.5513	1.6895	1.8385	1.9990	2.1719	2.3579	2.5580	2.7731	3.0040
10	1.1046	1.2190	1.3439	1.4802	1.6289	1.7908	1.9672	2.1589	2.3674	2.5937	2.8394	3.1058	3.3946
11	1.1157	1.2434	1.3842	1.5395	1.7103	1.8983	2.1049	2.3316	2.5804	2.8531	3.1518	3.4785	3.8359
12	1.1268	1.2682	1.4258	1.6010	1.7959	2.0122	2.2522	2.5182	2.8127	3.1384	3.4985	3.8960	4.3345
13	1.1381	1.2936	1.4685	1.6651	1.8856	2.1329	2.4098	2.7196	3.0658	3.4523	3.8833	4.3635	4.8980
14	1.1495	1.3195	1.5126	1.7317	1.9799	2.2609	2.5785	2.9372	3.3417	3.7975	4.3104	4.8871	5.5348
15	1.1610	1.3459	1.5580	1.8009	2.0789	2.3966	2.7590	3.1722	3.6425	4.1772	4.7846	5.4736	6.2543
16	1.1726	1.3728	1.6047	1.8730	2.1829	2.5404	2.9522	3.4259	3.9703	4.5950	5.3109	6.1304	7.0673
17	1.1843	1.4002	1.6528	1.9479	2.2920	2.6928	3.1588	3.7000	4.3276	5.0545	5.8951	6.8660	7.9861
18	1.1961	1.4282	1.7024	2.0258	2.4066	2.8543	3.3799	3.9960	4.7171	5.5599	6.5436	7.6900	9.0243
19	1.2081	1.4568	1.7535	2.1068	2.5270	3.0256	3.6165	4.3157	5.1417	6.1159	7.2633	8.6128	10.1974
20	1.2202	1.4859	1.8061	2.1911	2.6533	3.2071	3.8697	4.6610	5.6044	6.7275	8.0623	9.6463	11.5231
25	1.2824	1.6406	2.0938	2.6658	3.3864	4.2919	5.4274	6.8485	8.6231	10.8347	13.5855	17.0001	21.2305
30	1.3478	1.8114	2.4273	3.2434	4.3219	5.7435	7.6123	10.0627	13.2677	17.4494	22.8923	29.9599	39.1159
35	1.4166	1.9999	2.8139	3.9461	5.5160	7.6861	10.6766	14.7853	20.4140	28.1024	38.5749	52.7996	72.0685
40	1.4889	2.2080	3.2620	4.8010	7.0400	10.2857	14.9745	21.7245	31.4094	45.2593	65.0009	93.0510	132.7816
45	1.5648	2.4379	3.7816	5.8412	8.9850	13.7646	21.0025	31.9204	48.3273	72.8905	109.5302	163.9876	244.6414
50	1.6446	2.6916	4.3839	7.1067	11.4674	18.4202	29.4570	46.9016	74.3575	117.3909	184.5648	289.0022	450.7359

Appendix B-2

Future Value of a Dollar (continued)

Future Value of $1

$$[(1+i)^n]$$

Period	14%	15%	16%	17%	18%	19%	20%	25%	30%	35%	40%	45%	50%
1	1.1400	1.1500	1.1600	1.1700	1.1800	1.1900	1.2000	1.2500	1.3000	1.3500	1.4000	1.4500	1.5000
2	1.2996	1.3225	1.3456	1.3689	1.3924	1.4161	1.4400	1.5625	1.6900	1.8225	1.9600	2.1025	2.2500
3	1.4815	1.5209	1.5609	1.6016	1.6430	1.6852	1.7280	1.9531	2.1970	2.4604	2.7440	3.0486	3.3750
4	1.6890	1.7490	1.8106	1.8739	1.9388	2.0053	2.0736	2.4414	2.8561	3.3215	3.8416	4.4205	5.0625
5	1.9254	2.0114	2.1003	2.1924	2.2878	2.3864	2.4883	3.0518	3.7129	4.4840	5.3782	6.4097	7.5938
6	2.1950	2.3131	2.4364	2.5652	2.6996	2.8398	2.9860	3.8147	4.8268	6.0534	7.5295	9.2941	11.3906
7	2.5023	2.6600	2.8262	3.0012	3.1855	3.3793	3.5832	4.7684	6.2749	8.1722	10.5414	13.4765	17.0859
8	2.8526	3.0590	3.2784	3.5115	3.7589	4.0214	4.2998	5.9605	8.1573	11.0324	14.7579	19.5409	25.6289
9	3.2519	3.5179	3.8030	4.1084	4.4355	4.7854	5.1598	7.4506	10.6045	14.8937	20.6610	28.3343	38.4434
10	3.7072	4.0456	4.4114	4.8068	5.2338	5.6947	6.1917	9.3132	13.7858	20.1066	28.9255	41.0847	57.6650
11	4.2262	4.6524	5.1173	5.6240	6.1759	6.7767	7.4301	11.6415	17.9216	27.1439	40.4957	59.5728	86.4976
12	4.8179	5.3503	5.9360	6.5801	7.2876	8.0642	8.9161	14.5519	23.2981	36.6442	56.6939	86.3806	129.7463
13	5.4924	6.1528	6.8858	7.6987	8.5994	9.5964	10.6993	18.1899	30.2875	49.4697	79.3715	125.2518	194.6195
14	6.2613	7.0757	7.9875	9.0075	10.1472	11.4198	12.8392	22.7374	39.3738	66.7841	111.1201	181.6151	291.9293
15	7.1379	8.1371	9.2655	10.5387	11.9737	13.5895	15.4070	28.4217	51.1859	90.1585	155.5681	263.3419	437.8939
16	8.1372	9.3576	10.7480	12.3303	14.1290	16.1715	18.4884	35.5271	66.5417	121.7139	217.7953	381.8458	656.8408
17	9.2765	10.7613	12.4677	14.4265	16.6722	19.2441	22.1861	44.4089	86.5042	164.3138	304.9135	553.6764	985.2613
18	10.5752	12.3755	14.4625	16.8790	19.6733	22.9005	26.6233	55.5112	112.4554	221.8236	426.8789	802.8308	1477.892
19	12.0557	14.2318	16.7765	19.7484	23.2144	27.2516	31.9480	69.3889	146.1920	299.4619	597.6304	1164.105	2216.838
20	13.7435	16.3665	19.4608	23.1056	27.3930	32.4294	38.3376	86.7362	190.0496	404.2736	836.6826	1687.952	3325.257
25	26.4619	32.9190	40.8742	50.6578	62.6686	77.3881	95.3962	264.6978	705.6410	1812.776	4499.880	10819.32	25251.17
30	50.9502	66.2118	85.8499	111.0647	143.3706	184.6753	237.3763	807.7936	2619.996	8128.550	24201.43	69348.98	191751.1
35	98.1002	133.1755	180.3141	243.5035	327.9973	440.7006	590.6682	2465.190	9727.860	36448.69	130161.1	444509	1456110
40	188.8835	267.8635	378.7212	533.8687	750.3783	1051.668	1469.772	7523.164	36118.86	163437.1	700037.7	2849181	11057332
45	363.6791	538.7693	795.4438	1170.479	1716.684	2509.651	3657.262	22958.87	134106.8	732857.6	3764971	18262495	83966617
50	700.2330	1083.657	1670.704	2566.215	3927.357	5988.914	9100.438	70064.92	497929.2	3286158	20248916	117057734	637621500

Appendix B-3

Present Value of an Ordinary Annuity

Present Value of Ordinary Annuity

$$\left[\dfrac{1-\dfrac{1}{(1+i)^n}}{i}\right]$$

Period	1%	2%	3%	4%	5%	6%	7%	8%	9%	10%	11%	12%	13%
1	0.9901	0.9804	0.9709	0.9615	0.9524	0.9434	0.9346	0.9259	0.9174	0.9091	0.9009	0.8929	0.8850
2	1.9704	1.9416	1.9135	1.8861	1.8594	1.8334	1.8080	1.7833	1.7591	1.7355	1.7125	1.6901	1.6681
3	2.9410	2.8839	2.8286	2.7751	2.7232	2.6730	2.6243	2.5771	2.5313	2.4869	2.4437	2.4018	2.3612
4	3.9020	3.8077	3.7171	3.6299	3.5460	3.4651	3.3872	3.3121	3.2397	3.1699	3.1024	3.0373	2.9745
5	4.8534	4.7135	4.5797	4.4518	4.3295	4.2124	4.1002	3.9927	3.8897	3.7908	3.6959	3.6048	3.5172
6	5.7955	5.6014	5.4172	5.2421	5.0757	4.9173	4.7665	4.6229	4.4859	4.3553	4.2305	4.1114	3.9975
7	6.7282	6.4720	6.2303	6.0021	5.7864	5.5824	5.3893	5.2064	5.0330	4.8684	4.7122	4.5638	4.4226
8	7.6517	7.3255	7.0197	6.7327	6.4632	6.2098	5.9713	5.7466	5.5348	5.3349	5.1461	4.9676	4.7988
9	8.5660	8.1622	7.7861	7.4353	7.1078	6.8017	6.5152	6.2469	5.9952	5.7590	5.5370	5.3282	5.1317
10	9.4713	8.9826	8.5302	8.1109	7.7217	7.3601	7.0236	6.7101	6.4177	6.1446	5.8892	5.6502	5.4262
11	10.3676	9.7868	9.2526	8.7605	8.3064	7.8869	7.4987	7.1390	6.8052	6.4951	6.2065	5.9377	5.6869
12	11.2551	10.5753	9.9540	9.3851	8.8633	8.3838	7.9427	7.5361	7.1607	6.8137	6.4924	6.1944	5.9176
13	12.1337	11.3484	10.6350	9.9856	9.3936	8.8527	8.3577	7.9038	7.4869	7.1034	6.7499	6.4235	6.1218
14	13.0037	12.1062	10.9961	10.5631	9.8986	9.2950	8.7455	8.2442	7.7862	7.3667	6.9819	6.6282	6.3025
15	13.8651	12.8493	11.9379	11.1184	10.3797	9.7122	9.1079	8.5595	8.0607	7.6061	7.1909	6.8109	6.4624
16	14.7179	13.5777	12.5611	11.6523	10.8378	10.1059	9.4466	8.8514	8.3126	7.8237	7.3792	6.9740	6.6039
17	15.5623	14.2919	13.1661	12.1657	11.2741	10.4773	9.7632	9.1216	8.5436	8.0216	7.5488	7.1196	6.7291
18	16.3983	14.9920	13.7535	12.6593	11.6896	10.8276	10.0591	9.3719	8.7556	8.2014	7.7016	7.2497	6.8399
19	17.2260	15.6785	14.3238	13.1339	12.0853	11.1581	10.3356	9.6036	8.9501	8.3649	7.8393	7.3658	6.9380
20	18.0456	16.3514	14.8775	13.5903	12.4622	11.4699	10.5940	9.8181	9.1285	8.5136	7.9633	7.4694	7.0248
25	22.0232	19.5235	17.4131	15.6221	14.0939	12.7834	11.6536	10.6748	9.8226	9.0770	8.4217	7.8431	7.3300
30	25.8077	22.3965	19.6004	17.2920	15.3725	13.7648	12.4090	11.2578	10.2737	9.4269	8.6938	8.0552	7.4957
35	29.4086	24.9986	21.4872	18.6646	16.3742	14.4982	12.9477	11.6546	10.5668	9.6442	8.8552	8.1755	7.5856
40	32.8347	27.3555	23.1148	19.7928	17.1591	15.0463	13.3317	11.9246	10.7574	9.7791	8.9511	8.2438	7.6344
45	36.0945	29.4902	24.5187	20.7200	17.7741	15.4558	13.6055	12.1084	10.8812	9.8628	9.0079	8.2825	7.6609
50	39.1961	31.4236	25.7298	21.4822	18.2559	15.7619	13.8007	12.2335	10.9617	9.9148	9.0417	8.3045	7.6752

Appendix B-3

Present Value of an Ordinary Annuity (continued)

Present Value of Ordinary Annuity

$$\left[\dfrac{1-\dfrac{1}{(1+i)^n}}{i}\right]$$

Period	14%	15%	16%	17%	18%	19%	20%	25%	30%	35%	40%	45%	50%
1	0.8772	0.8696	0.8621	0.8547	0.8475	0.8403	0.8333	0.8000	0.7692	0.7407	0.7143	0.6897	0.6667
2	1.6467	1.6257	1.6052	1.5852	1.5656	1.5465	1.5278	1.4400	1.3609	1.2894	1.2245	1.1653	1.1111
3	2.3216	2.2832	2.2459	2.2096	2.1743	2.1399	2.1065	1.9520	1.8161	1.6959	1.5889	1.4933	1.4074
4	2.9137	2.8550	2.7982	2.7432	2.6901	2.6386	2.5887	2.3616	2.1662	1.9969	1.8492	1.7195	1.6049
5	3.4331	3.3522	3.2743	3.1993	3.1272	3.0576	2.9906	2.6893	2.4356	2.2200	2.0352	1.8755	1.7366
6	3.8887	3.7845	3.6847	3.5892	3.4976	3.4098	3.3255	2.9514	2.6427	2.3852	2.1680	1.9831	1.8244
7	4.2883	4.1604	4.0386	3.9224	3.8115	3.7057	3.6046	3.1611	2.8021	2.5075	2.2628	2.0573	1.8829
8	4.6389	4.4873	4.3436	4.2072	4.0776	3.9544	3.8372	3.3289	2.9247	2.5982	2.3306	2.1085	1.9220
9	4.9464	4.7716	4.6065	4.4506	4.3030	4.1633	4.0310	3.4631	3.0190	2.6653	2.3790	2.1438	1.9480
10	5.2161	5.0188	4.8332	4.6586	4.4941	4.3389	4.1925	3.5705	3.0915	2.7150	2.4136	2.1681	1.9653
11	5.4527	5.2337	5.0286	4.8364	4.6560	4.4865	4.3271	3.6564	3.1473	2.7519	2.4383	2.1849	1.9769
12	5.6603	5.4206	5.1971	4.9884	4.7932	4.6105	4.4392	3.7251	3.1903	2.7792	2.4559	2.1965	1.9846
13	5.8424	5.5831	5.3423	5.1183	4.9095	4.7147	4.5327	3.7801	3.2233	2.7994	2.4685	2.2045	1.9897
14	6.0021	5.7245	5.4675	5.2293	5.0081	4.8023	4.6106	3.8241	3.2487	2.8144	2.4775	2.2100	1.9931
15	6.1422	5.8474	5.5755	5.3242	5.0916	4.8759	4.6755	3.8593	3.2682	2.8255	2.4839	2.2138	1.9954
16	6.2651	5.9542	5.6685	5.4053	5.1624	4.9377	4.7296	3.8874	3.2832	2.8337	2.4885	2.2164	1.9970
17	6.3729	6.0472	5.7487	5.4746	5.2223	4.9897	4.7746	3.9099	3.2948	2.8398	2.4918	2.2182	1.9980
18	6.4674	6.1280	5.8178	5.5339	5.2732	5.0333	4.8122	3.9279	3.3037	2.8443	2.4941	2.2195	1.9986
19	6.5504	6.1982	5.8775	5.5845	5.3162	5.0700	4.8435	3.9424	3.3105	2.8476	2.4958	2.2203	1.9991
20	6.6231	6.2593	5.9288	5.6278	5.3527	5.1009	4.8696	3.9539	3.3158	2.8501	2.4970	2.2209	1.9994
25	6.8729	6.4641	6.0971	5.7662	5.4669	5.1951	4.9476	3.9849	3.3286	2.8556	2.4994	2.2220	1.9999
30	7.0027	6.5660	6.1772	5.8294	5.5168	5.2347	4.9789	3.9950	3.3321	2.8568	2.4999	2.2222	2.0000
35	7.0700	6.6166	6.2153	5.8582	5.5386	5.2512	4.9915	3.9984	3.3330	2.8571	2.5000	2.2222	2.0000
40	7.1050	6.6418	6.2335	5.8713	5.5482	5.2582	4.9966	3.9995	3.3332	2.8571	2.5000	2.2222	2.0000
45	7.1232	6.6543	6.2421	5.8773	5.5523	5.2611	4.9986	3.9998	3.3333	2.8571	2.5000	2.2222	2.0000
50	7.1327	6.6605	6.2463	5.8801	5.5541	5.2623	4.9995	3.9999	3.3333	2.8571	2.5000	2.2222	2.0000

Appendix B-4

Future Value of an Ordinary Annuity

Future Value of an Ordinary Annuity

$$\left[\frac{(1+i)^n - 1}{i}\right]$$

Period	1%	2%	3%	4%	5%	6%	7%	8%	9%	10%	11%	12%	13%
1	1.0000	1.0000	1.0000	1.0000	1.0000	1.0000	1.0000	1.0000	1.0000	1.0000	1.0000	1.0000	1.0000
2	2.0100	2.0200	2.0300	2.0400	2.0500	2.0600	2.0700	2.0800	2.0900	2.1000	2.1100	2.1200	2.1300
3	3.0301	3.0604	3.0909	3.1216	3.1525	3.1836	3.2149	3.2464	3.2781	3.3100	3.3421	3.3744	3.4069
4	4.0604	4.1216	4.1836	4.2465	4.3101	4.3746	4.4399	4.5061	4.5731	4.6410	4.7097	4.7793	4.8498
5	5.1010	5.2040	5.3091	5.4163	5.5256	5.6371	5.7507	5.8666	5.9847	6.1051	6.2278	6.3528	6.4803
6	6.1520	6.3081	6.4684	6.6330	6.8019	6.9753	7.1533	7.3359	7.5233	7.7156	7.9129	8.1152	8.3227
7	7.2135	7.4343	7.6625	7.8983	8.1420	8.3938	8.6540	8.9228	9.2004	9.4872	9.7833	10.0890	10.4047
8	8.2857	8.5830	8.8923	9.2142	9.5491	9.8975	10.2598	10.6366	11.0285	11.4359	11.8594	12.2997	12.7573
9	9.3685	9.7546	10.1591	10.5828	11.0266	11.4913	11.9780	12.4876	13.0210	13.5795	14.1640	14.7757	15.4157
10	10.4622	10.9497	11.4639	12.0061	12.5779	13.1808	13.8164	14.4866	15.1929	15.9374	16.7220	17.5487	18.4197
11	11.5668	12.1687	12.8078	13.4864	14.2068	14.9716	15.7836	16.6455	17.5603	18.5312	19.5614	20.6546	21.8143
12	12.6825	13.4121	14.1920	15.0258	15.9171	16.8699	17.8885	18.9771	20.1407	21.3843	22.7132	24.1331	25.6502
13	13.8093	14.6803	15.6178	16.6268	17.7130	18.8821	20.1406	21.4953	22.9534	24.5227	26.2116	28.0291	29.9847
14	14.9474	15.9739	17.0863	18.2919	19.5986	21.0151	22.5505	24.2149	26.0192	27.9750	30.0949	32.3926	34.8827
15	16.0969	17.2934	18.5989	20.0236	21.5786	23.2760	25.1290	27.1521	29.3609	31.7725	34.4054	37.2797	40.4175
16	17.2579	18.6393	20.1569	21.8245	23.6575	25.6725	27.8881	30.3243	33.0034	35.9497	39.1899	42.7533	46.6717
17	18.4304	20.0121	21.7616	23.6975	25.8404	28.2129	30.8402	33.7502	36.9737	40.5447	44.5008	48.8837	53.7391
18	19.6147	21.4123	23.4144	25.6454	28.1324	30.9057	33.9990	37.4502	41.3013	45.5992	50.3959	55.7497	61.7251
19	20.8109	22.8406	25.1169	27.6712	30.5390	33.7600	37.3790	41.4463	46.0185	51.1591	56.9395	63.4397	70.7494
20	22.0190	24.2974	26.8704	29.7781	33.0660	36.7856	40.9955	45.7620	51.1601	57.2750	64.2028	72.0524	80.9468
25	28.2432	32.0303	36.4593	41.6459	47.7271	54.8645	63.2490	73.1059	84.7009	98.3471	114.4133	133.3339	155.6196
30	34.7849	40.5681	47.5754	56.0849	66.4388	79.0582	94.4608	113.2832	136.3075	164.4940	199.0209	241.3327	293.1992
35	41.6603	49.9945	60.4621	73.6522	90.3203	111.4348	138.2369	172.3168	215.7108	271.0244	341.5896	431.6635	546.6808
40	48.8864	60.4020	75.4013	95.0255	120.7998	154.7620	199.6351	259.0565	337.8824	442.5926	581.8261	767.0914	1013.704
45	56.4811	71.8927	92.7199	121.0294	159.7002	212.7435	285.7493	386.5056	525.8587	718.9048	986.6386	1358.230	1874.165
50	64.4632	84.5794	112.7969	152.6671	209.3480	290.3359	406.5289	573.7702	815.0836	1163.909	1668.771	2400.018	3459.507

Appendix B-4

Future Value of an Ordinary Annuity (continued)

Future Value of Ordinary Annuity

$$\left[\frac{(1+i)^n - 1}{i}\right]$$

Period	14%	15%	16%	17%	18%	19%	20%	25%	30%	35%	40%	45%	50%
1	1.0000	1.0000	1.0000	1.0000	1.0000	1.0000	1.0000	1.0000	1.0000	1.0000	1.0000	1.0000	1.0000
2	2.1400	2.1500	2.1600	2.1700	2.1800	2.1900	2.2000	2.2500	2.3000	2.3500	2.4000	2.4500	2.5000
3	3.4396	3.4725	3.5056	3.5389	3.5724	3.6061	3.6400	3.8125	3.9900	4.1725	4.3600	4.5525	4.7500
4	4.9211	4.9934	5.0665	5.1405	5.2154	5.2913	5.3680	5.7656	6.1870	6.6329	7.1040	7.6011	8.1250
5	6.6101	6.7424	6.8771	7.0144	7.1542	7.2966	7.4416	8.2070	9.0431	9.9544	10.9456	12.0216	13.1875
6	8.5355	8.7537	8.9775	9.2068	9.4420	9.6830	9.9299	11.2588	12.7560	14.4384	16.3238	18.4314	20.7813
7	10.7305	11.0668	11.4139	11.7720	12.1415	12.5227	12.9159	15.0735	17.5828	20.4919	23.8534	27.7255	32.1719
8	13.2328	13.7268	14.2401	14.7733	15.3270	15.9020	16.4991	19.8419	23.8577	28.6640	34.3947	41.2019	49.2578
9	16.0853	16.7858	17.5185	18.2847	19.0859	19.9234	20.7989	25.8023	32.0150	39.6964	49.1526	60.7428	74.8867
10	19.3373	20.3037	21.3215	22.3931	23.5213	24.7089	25.9587	33.2529	42.6195	54.5902	69.8137	89.0771	113.3301
11	23.0445	24.3493	25.7329	27.1999	28.7551	30.4035	32.1504	42.5661	56.4053	74.6967	98.7391	130.1618	170.9951
12	27.2707	29.0017	30.8502	32.8239	34.9311	37.1802	39.5805	54.2077	74.3270	101.8406	139.2348	189.7346	257.4927
13	32.0887	34.3519	36.7862	39.4040	42.2187	45.2445	48.4966	68.7596	97.6250	138.4848	195.9287	276.1151	387.2390
14	37.5811	40.5047	43.6720	47.1027	50.8180	54.8409	59.1959	86.9495	127.9125	187.9544	275.3002	401.3670	581.8585
15	43.8424	47.5804	51.6595	56.1101	60.9653	66.2607	72.0351	109.6868	167.2863	254.7385	386.4202	582.9821	873.7878
16	50.9804	55.7175	60.9250	66.6488	72.9390	79.8502	87.4421	138.1085	218.4722	344.8970	541.9883	846.3240	1311.682
17	59.1176	65.0751	71.6730	78.9792	87.0680	96.0218	105.9306	173.6357	285.0139	466.6109	759.7837	1228.170	1968.523
18	68.3941	75.8364	84.1407	93.4056	103.7403	115.2659	128.1167	218.0446	371.5180	630.9247	1064.697	1781.846	2953.784
19	78.9692	88.2118	98.6032	110.2846	123.4135	138.1664	154.7400	273.5558	483.9734	852.7483	1491.576	2584.677	4431.676
20	91.0249	102.4436	115.3797	130.0329	146.6280	165.4180	186.6880	342.9447	630.1655	1152.210	2089.206	3748.782	6648.513
25	181.8708	212.7930	249.2140	292.1049	342.6035	402.0425	471.9811	1054.791	2348.803	5176.504	11247.20	24040.72	50500.34
30	356.7868	434.7451	530.3117	647.4391	790.9480	966.7122	1181.882	3227.174	8729.985	23221.57	60501.08	154106.6	383500.1
35	693.5727	881.1702	1120.713	1426.491	1816.652	2314.214	2948.341	9856.761	32422.87	104136.3	325400.3	987794.5	2912217
40	1342.025	1779.090	2360.757	3134.522	4163.213	5529.829	7343.858	30088.66	120392.9	466960.4	1750092	6331512	22114663
45	2590.565	3585.128	4965.274	6879.291	9531.577	13203.42	18281.31	91831.50	447019.4	2093876	9412424	40583319	167933233
50	4994.521	7217.716	10435.65	15089.50	21813.09	31515.34	45497.19	280255.7	1659761	9389020	50622288	260128295	1275242998

Appendix B-5

Present Value of an Annuity Due

Present Value of Annuity Due

$$\left[\; \frac{1-\dfrac{1}{(1+i)^{n-1}}}{i} + 1 \;\right]$$

Period	1%	2%	3%	4%	5%	6%	7%	8%	9%	10%	11%	12%	13%
1	1.0000	1.0000	1.0000	1.0000	1.0000	1.0000	1.0000	1.0000	1.0000	1.0000	1.0000	1.0000	1.0000
2	1.9901	1.9804	1.9709	1.9615	1.9524	1.9434	1.9346	1.9259	1.9174	1.9091	1.9009	1.8929	1.8850
3	2.9704	2.9416	2.9135	2.8861	2.8594	2.8334	2.8080	2.7833	2.7591	2.7355	2.7125	2.6901	2.6681
4	3.9410	3.8839	3.8286	3.7751	3.7232	3.6730	3.6243	3.5771	3.5313	3.4869	3.4437	3.4018	3.3612
5	4.9020	4.8077	4.7171	4.6299	4.5460	4.4651	4.3872	4.3121	4.2397	4.1699	4.1024	4.0373	3.9745
6	5.8534	5.7135	5.5797	5.4518	5.3295	5.2124	5.1002	4.9927	4.8897	4.7908	4.6959	4.6048	4.5172
7	6.7955	6.6014	6.4172	6.2421	6.0757	5.9173	5.7665	5.6229	5.4859	5.3553	5.2305	5.1114	4.9975
8	7.7282	7.4720	7.2303	7.0021	6.7864	6.5824	6.3893	6.2064	6.0330	5.8684	5.7122	5.5638	5.4226
9	8.6517	8.3255	8.0197	7.7327	7.4632	7.2098	6.9713	6.7466	6.5348	6.3349	6.1461	5.9676	5.7988
10	9.5660	9.1622	8.7861	8.4353	8.1078	7.8017	7.5152	7.2469	6.9952	6.7590	6.5370	6.3282	6.1317
11	10.4713	9.9826	9.5302	9.1109	8.7217	8.3601	8.0236	7.7101	7.4177	7.1446	6.8892	6.6502	6.4262
12	11.3676	10.7868	10.2526	9.7605	9.3064	8.8869	8.4987	8.1390	7.8052	7.4951	7.2065	6.9377	6.6869
13	12.2551	11.5753	10.9540	10.3851	9.8633	9.3838	8.9427	8.5361	8.1607	7.8137	7.4924	7.1944	6.9176
14	13.1337	12.3484	11.6350	10.9856	10.3936	9.8527	9.3577	8.9038	8.4869	8.1034	7.7499	7.4235	7.1218
15	14.0037	13.1062	12.2961	11.5631	10.8986	10.2950	9.7455	9.2442	8.7862	8.3667	7.9819	7.6282	7.3025
16	14.8651	13.8493	12.9379	12.1184	11.3797	10.7122	10.1079	9.5595	9.0607	8.6061	8.1909	7.8109	7.4624
17	15.7179	14.5777	13.5611	12.6523	11.8378	11.1059	10.4466	9.8514	9.3126	8.8237	8.3792	7.9740	7.6039
18	16.5623	15.2919	14.1661	13.1657	12.2741	11.4773	10.7632	10.1216	9.5436	9.0216	8.5488	8.1196	7.7291
19	17.3983	15.9920	14.7535	13.6593	12.6896	11.8276	11.0591	10.3719	9.7556	9.2014	8.7016	8.2497	7.8399
20	18.2260	16.6785	15.3238	14.1339	13.0853	12.1581	11.3356	10.6036	9.9501	9.3649	8.8393	8.3658	7.9380
25	22.2434	19.9139	17.9355	16.2470	14.7986	13.5504	12.4693	11.5288	10.7066	9.9847	9.3481	8.7843	8.2829
30	26.0658	22.8444	20.1885	17.9837	16.1411	14.5904	13.2777	12.1584	11.1983	10.3696	9.6501	9.0218	8.4701
35	29.7027	25.4986	22.1318	19.4112	17.1929	15.3681	13.8540	12.5869	11.5178	10.6086	9.8293	9.1566	8.5717
40	33.1630	27.9026	23.8082	20.5845	18.0170	15.9491	14.2649	12.8786	11.7255	10.7570	9.9357	9.2330	8.6268
45	36.4555	30.0800	25.2543	21.5488	18.6628	16.3832	14.5579	13.0771	11.8605	10.8491	9.9988	9.2764	8.6568
50	39.5881	32.0521	26.5017	22.3415	19.1687	16.7076	14.7668	13.2122	11.9482	10.9063	10.0362	9.3010	8.6730

Appendix B-5

Present Value of an Annuity Due (continued)

Present Value of Annuity Due

$$\left[1 - \dfrac{1}{\dfrac{(1+i)^{n-1}}{i}} + 1 \right]$$

Period	14%	15%	16%	17%	18%	19%	20%	25%	30%	35%	40%	45%	50%
1	1.0000	1.0000	1.0000	1.0000	1.0000	1.0000	1.0000	1.0000	1.0000	1.0000	1.0000	1.0000	1.0000
2	1.8772	1.8696	1.8621	1.8547	1.8475	1.8403	1.8333	1.8000	1.7692	1.7407	1.7143	1.6897	1.6667
3	2.6467	2.6257	2.6052	2.5852	2.5656	2.5465	2.5278	2.4400	2.3609	2.2894	2.2245	2.1653	2.1111
4	3.3216	3.2832	3.2459	3.2096	3.1743	3.1399	3.1065	2.9520	2.8161	2.6959	2.5889	2.4933	2.4074
5	3.9137	3.8550	3.7982	3.7432	3.6901	3.6386	3.5887	3.3616	3.1662	2.9969	2.8492	2.7195	2.6049
6	4.4331	4.3522	4.2743	4.1993	4.1272	4.0576	3.9906	3.6893	3.4356	3.2200	3.0352	2.8755	2.7366
7	4.8887	4.7845	4.6847	4.5892	4.4976	4.4098	4.3255	3.9514	3.6427	3.3852	3.1680	2.9831	2.8244
8	5.2883	5.1604	5.0386	4.9224	4.8115	4.7057	4.6046	4.1611	3.8021	3.5075	3.2628	3.0573	2.8829
9	5.6389	5.4873	5.3436	5.2072	5.0776	4.9544	4.8372	4.3289	3.9247	3.5982	3.3306	3.1085	2.9220
10	5.9464	5.7716	5.6065	5.4506	5.3030	5.1633	5.0310	4.4631	4.0190	3.6653	3.3790	3.1438	2.9480
11	6.2161	6.0188	5.8332	5.6586	5.4941	5.3389	5.1925	4.5705	4.0915	3.7150	3.4136	3.1681	2.9653
12	6.4527	6.2337	6.0286	5.8364	5.6560	5.4865	5.3271	4.6564	4.1473	3.7519	3.4383	3.1849	2.9769
13	6.6603	6.4206	6.1971	5.9884	5.7932	5.6105	5.4392	4.7251	4.1903	3.7792	3.4559	3.1965	2.9846
14	6.8424	6.5831	6.3423	6.1183	5.9095	5.7147	5.5327	4.7801	4.2233	3.7994	3.4685	3.2045	2.9897
15	7.0021	6.7245	6.4675	6.2293	6.0081	5.8023	5.6106	4.8241	4.2487	3.8144	3.4775	3.2100	2.9931
16	7.1422	6.8474	6.5755	6.3242	6.0916	5.8759	5.6755	4.8593	4.2682	3.8255	3.4839	3.2138	2.9954
17	7.2651	6.9542	6.6685	6.4053	6.1624	5.9377	5.7296	4.8874	4.2832	3.8337	3.4885	3.2164	2.9970
18	7.3729	7.0472	6.7487	6.4746	6.2223	5.9897	5.7746	4.9099	4.2948	3.8398	3.4918	3.2182	2.9980
19	7.4674	7.1280	6.8178	6.5339	6.2732	6.0333	5.8122	4.9279	4.3037	3.8443	3.4941	3.2195	2.9986
20	7.5504	7.1982	6.8775	6.5845	6.3162	6.0700	5.8435	4.9424	4.3105	3.8476	3.4958	3.2203	2.9991
25	7.8351	7.4338	7.0726	6.7465	6.4509	6.1822	5.9371	4.9811	4.3272	3.8550	3.4992	3.2219	2.9999
30	7.9830	7.5509	7.1656	6.8204	6.5098	6.2292	5.9747	4.9938	4.3317	3.8567	3.4999	3.2222	3.0000
35	8.0599	7.6091	7.2098	6.8541	6.5356	6.2489	5.9898	4.9980	4.3329	3.8570	3.5000	3.2222	3.0000
40	8.0997	7.6380	7.2309	6.8695	6.5468	6.2572	5.9959	4.9993	4.3333	3.8571	3.5000	3.2222	3.0000
45	8.1205	7.6524	7.2409	6.8765	6.5517	6.2607	5.9984	4.9998	4.3333	3.8571	3.5000	3.2222	3.0000
50	8.1312	7.6596	7.2457	6.8797	6.5539	6.2621	5.9993	4.9999	4.3333	3.8571	3.5000	3.2222	3.0000

Appendix B-6

Future Value of an Annuity Due

Future Value of Annuity Due

$$\left[\frac{(1+i)^n - 1}{i}\right] \times \left[\,1+i\,\right]$$

Period	1%	2%	3%	4%	5%	6%	7%	8%	9%	10%	11%	12%	13%
1	1.0100	1.0200	1.0300	1.0400	1.0500	1.0600	1.0700	1.0800	1.0900	1.1000	1.1100	1.1200	1.1300
2	2.0301	2.0604	2.0909	2.1216	2.1525	2.1836	2.2149	2.2464	2.2781	2.3100	2.3421	2.3744	2.4069
3	3.0604	3.1216	3.1836	3.2465	3.3101	3.3746	3.4399	3.5061	3.5731	3.6410	3.7097	3.7793	3.8498
4	4.1010	4.2040	4.3091	4.4163	4.5256	4.6371	4.7507	4.8666	4.9847	5.1051	5.2278	5.3528	5.4803
5	5.1520	5.3081	5.4684	5.6330	5.8019	5.9753	6.1533	6.3359	6.5233	6.7156	6.9129	7.1152	7.3227
6	6.2135	6.4343	6.6625	6.8983	7.1420	7.3938	7.6540	7.9228	8.2004	8.4872	8.7833	9.0890	9.4047
7	7.2857	7.5830	7.8923	8.2142	8.5491	8.8975	9.2598	9.6366	10.0285	10.4359	10.8594	11.2997	11.7573
8	8.3685	8.7546	9.1591	9.5828	10.0266	10.4913	10.9780	11.4876	12.0210	12.5795	13.1640	13.7757	14.4157
9	9.4622	9.9497	10.4639	11.0061	11.5779	12.1808	12.8164	13.4866	14.1929	14.9374	15.7220	16.5487	17.4197
10	10.5668	11.1687	11.8078	12.4864	13.2068	13.9716	14.7836	15.6455	16.5603	17.5312	18.5614	19.6546	20.8143
11	11.6825	12.4121	13.1920	14.0258	14.9171	15.8699	16.8885	17.9771	19.1407	20.3843	21.7132	23.1331	24.6502
12	12.8093	13.6803	14.6178	15.6268	16.7130	17.8821	19.1406	20.4953	21.9534	23.5227	25.2116	27.0291	28.9847
13	13.9474	14.9739	16.0863	17.2919	18.5986	20.0151	21.5505	23.2149	25.0192	26.9750	29.0949	31.3926	33.8827
14	15.0969	16.2934	17.5989	19.0236	20.5786	22.2760	24.1290	26.1521	28.3609	30.7725	33.4054	36.2797	39.4175
15	16.2579	17.6393	19.1569	20.8245	22.6575	24.6725	26.8881	29.3243	32.0034	34.9497	38.1899	41.7533	45.6717
16	17.4304	19.0121	20.7616	22.6975	24.8404	27.2129	29.8402	32.7502	35.9737	39.5447	43.5008	47.8837	52.7391
17	18.6147	20.4123	22.4144	24.6454	27.1324	29.9057	32.9990	36.4502	40.3013	44.5992	49.3959	54.7497	60.7251
18	19.8109	21.8406	24.1169	26.6712	29.5390	32.7600	36.3790	40.4463	45.0185	50.1591	55.9395	62.4397	69.7494
19	21.0190	23.2974	25.8704	28.7781	32.0660	35.7856	39.9955	44.7620	50.1601	56.2750	63.2028	71.0524	79.9468
20	22.2392	24.7833	27.6765	30.9692	34.7193	38.9927	43.8652	49.4229	55.7645	63.0025	71.2651	80.6987	91.4699
25	28.5256	32.6709	37.5530	43.3117	50.1135	58.1564	67.6765	73.9544	92.3240	108.1818	126.9988	149.3339	175.8501
30	35.1327	41.3794	49.0027	58.3283	69.7608	83.8017	101.0730	122.3459	148.5752	180.9434	220.9132	270.2926	331.3151
35	42.0769	50.9944	62.2759	76.5983	94.8363	118.1209	147.9135	185.1021	235.1247	298.1268	379.1644	483.4631	617.7493
40	49.3752	61.6100	77.6633	98.8265	126.8398	164.0477	213.6096	273.7810	368.2919	486.8518	645.8269	859.1424	1145.486
45	57.0459	73.3306	95.5015	125.8706	167.6852	225.5081	305.7518	417.4261	573.1860	790.7953	1095.169	1521.218	2117.806
50	65.1078	86.2710	116.1808	158.7738	219.8154	307.7561	434.9860	613.6718	888.4411	1280.299	1852.336	2688.020	3909.243

Appendix B-6
Future Value of an Annuity Due (Continued)

Future Value of Annuity Due

$$\left[\frac{(1+i)^n - 1}{i}\right] \times \left[1+i\right]$$

Period	14%	15%	16%	17%	18%	19%	20%	25%	30%	35%	40%	45%	50%
1	1.1400	1.1500	1.1600	1.1700	1.1800	1.1900	1.2000	1.2500	1.3000	1.3500	1.4000	1.4500	1.5000
2	2.4396	2.4725	2.5056	2.5389	2.5724	2.6061	2.6400	2.8125	2.9900	3.1725	3.3600	3.5525	3.7500
3	3.9211	3.9934	4.0665	4.1405	4.2154	4.2913	4.3680	4.7656	5.1870	5.6329	6.1040	6.6011	7.1250
4	5.6101	5.7424	5.8771	6.0144	6.1542	6.2966	6.4416	7.2070	8.0431	8.9544	9.9456	11.0216	12.1875
5	7.5355	7.7537	7.9775	8.2068	8.4420	8.6830	8.9299	10.2588	11.7560	13.4384	15.3238	17.4314	19.7813
6	9.7305	10.0668	10.4139	10.7720	11.1415	11.5227	11.9159	14.0735	16.5828	19.4919	22.8534	26.7255	31.1719
7	12.2328	12.7268	13.2401	13.7733	14.3270	14.9020	15.4991	18.8419	22.8577	27.6640	33.3947	40.2019	48.2578
8	15.0853	15.7858	16.5185	17.2847	18.0859	18.9234	19.7989	24.8023	31.0150	38.6964	48.1526	59.7428	73.8867
9	18.3373	19.3037	20.3215	21.3931	22.5213	23.7089	24.9587	32.2529	41.6195	53.5902	68.8137	88.0771	112.3301
10	22.0445	23.3493	24.7329	26.1999	27.7551	29.4035	31.1504	41.5661	55.4053	73.6967	97.7391	129.1618	169.9951
11	26.2707	28.0017	29.8502	31.8239	33.9311	36.1802	38.5805	53.2077	73.3270	100.8406	138.2348	188.7346	256.4927
12	31.0887	33.3519	35.7862	38.4040	41.2187	44.2445	47.4966	67.7596	96.6250	137.4848	194.9287	275.1151	386.2390
13	36.5811	39.5047	42.6720	46.1027	49.8180	53.8409	58.1959	85.9495	126.9125	186.9544	274.3002	400.3670	580.8585
14	42.8424	46.5804	50.6595	55.1101	59.9653	65.2607	71.0351	108.6868	166.2863	253.7385	385.4202	581.9821	872.7878
15	49.9804	54.7175	59.9250	65.6488	71.9390	78.8502	86.4421	137.1085	217.4722	343.8970	540.9883	845.3240	1310.6817
16	58.1176	64.0751	70.6730	77.9792	86.0680	95.0218	104.9306	172.6357	284.0139	465.6109	758.7837	1227.1699	1967.5225
17	67.3941	74.8364	83.1407	92.4056	102.7403	114.2659	127.1167	217.0446	370.5180	629.9247	1063.697	1780.8463	2952.7838
18	77.9692	87.2118	97.6032	109.2846	122.4135	137.1664	153.7400	272.5558	482.9734	851.7483	1490.576	2583.6771	4430.6756
19	90.0249	101.4436	114.3797	129.0329	145.6280	164.4180	185.6880	341.9447	629.1655	1151.210	2088.206	3747.7818	6647.5135
20	103.7684	117.8101	133.8405	152.1385	173.0210	196.8474	224.0256	428.6809	819.2151	1555.484	2924.889	5435.7336	9972.7702
25	207.3327	244.7120	289.0883	341.7627	404.2721	478.4306	566.3773	1318.489	3053.444	6988.280	15746.08	34859.038	75750.5049
30	406.7370	499.9569	615.1616	757.5038	933.3186	1150.387	1418.258	4033.968	11348.98	31349.12	84701.51	223454.60	575250.178
35	790.6729	1013.346	1300.027	1668.994	2143.649	2753.914	3538.009	12320.95	42149.73	140583.9	455560.4	1432302.0	4368325.82
40	1529.909	2045.954	2738.478	3667.391	4912.591	6580.496	8812.629	37610.82	156510.7	630396.5	2450128	9180692.2	33171994.0
45	2953.244	4122.898	5759.718	8048.770	11247.26	15712.07	21937.57	114789.4	581125.2	2826733	13177394	58845813	251899849
50	5693.75	8300.37	12105.35	17654.72	25739.45	37503.25	54596.63	350319.6	2157689	12675177	70871203	377186028	1912864498

Appendix C
Regulatory Requirements

REGULATORY REQUIREMENTS—FEDERAL SECURITIES REGULATION

INTRODUCTION

The issuance and sale of corporate securities are extensively regulated by the Securities and Exchange Commission (SEC), a Federal agency that administers the Securities Act of 1933, the Securities Exchange Act of 1934, and other Federal statutes. A major objective of securities regulation is to protect the investing public by requiring full and correct disclosure of relevant information. Both the federal and state governments require a substantial amount of regulation; however, most is from the federal government because the majority of trading is across state boarders.

THE SECURITIES ACT OF 1933

This securities act is primarily concerned with new issues of securities or issues in the primary market. The term investment security is broadly defined:

"Any note, stock, treasury stock, bond, debenture, evidence of indebtedness, certificate of interest or participation in any profit-sharing agreement ... investment contract... or, in general, any interest or instrument commonly known as a 'security' or any certificate of interest or participation in ... receipt for ... or right to subscribe to or purchase, any of the foregoing".

Any transaction in which a person invests money or property in a common enterprise or venture or an investor who reasonably expects to make a profit primarily or substantially as a result of the managerial efforts of others is regulated by this act.

The 1933 Act requires full disclosure of material information that is relevant to investment decisions, and prohibits fraud and misstatements when securities are offered to the public through the mail and/or interstate commerce. Registration statements, including financial statements, must be filed with the Securities and Exchange Commission (SEC) before investment securities can be offered for sale by issuer. A registration statement contains a thorough description of the securities, the financial structure, condition and management personnel of the issuing corporation, and a description of material pending litigation against the issuing corporation. This statement is filed with the SEC. The 1933 Act also requires that a prospectus, based upon the information in the registration statement, be given to any prospective investor or purchaser.

Securities that are exempt from registration requirements include:

- ▲ Intrastate offerings where all offerees and issuers are residents of the state in which issuer performs substantially all of its operations.
- ▲ The issuer is a governmental body or nonprofit organization.
- ▲ The issuer is a bank, savings institution, common carrier, or farmers' cooperative and is subject to other regulatory legislation.
- ▲ Commercial paper having a maturity date of less than 9 months (270 days).
- ▲ Stock dividends, stock splits, and securities issued in connection with corporate reorganizations.
- ▲ Insurance, endowment, and annuity contracts.

Regulation A requires less demanding disclosures and registration for small issues of less than $1,500,000. Regulation D lists those transactions that are exempt from registration requirement:

▲ Private, non-investment company sales of less than $500,000 worth of securities in a twelve-month period to investors who will not resell the securities within two years.
▲ Private, non-investment company sales of less than $5,000,000 worth of securities in a twelve-month period to:
  ▲ Accredited investors - Natural persons with annual income of more than $200,000 or whose net worth exceeds $1,000,000; or
  ▲ Investors who are furnished with purchaser representatives who are knowledgeable and experienced regarding finance and business; or
  ▲ Up to 35 unaccredited investors that have financial and business knowledge and experience, who are furnished with the same information as would be contained in a full registration statement prospectus.
  ▲ Sales of any amount of securities to accredited investors or those furnished with independent purchaser representatives (private placement).

THE SECURITIES EXCHANGE ACT OF 1934 (SEA)

While the Securities Act of 1933 was limited to new issues, the 1934 Securities Act extended the regulation to securities sold in the secondary markets. The Act provided the following provisions:

▲ Establishment of the SEC - The SEC's primary function is to regulate the securities markets.
▲ Disclosure requirements for Secondary Market - Annual reports and other financial reports are required to be filed with the SEC prior to listing on the organized exchanges. These reports include the annual 10K Report, which must be audited, and the quarterly 10Q Report, which is not required to be audited.
▲ Registration of organized exchanges - All organized exchanges must register with the SEC and provide copies of their rules and bylaws.
▲ Credit regulation - Congress gave the Federal Reserve Board the power to set margin requirements for credit purchases of securities. Securities dealers' indebtedness was also limited to 20 times their owners' equity capital by this act.
▲ Proxy solicitation - Specific rules governing solicitation of proxies were established.
▲ Exemptions - Securities of federal, state, and local governments, securities that are not traded across state lines, and any other securities specified by the SEC are exempt from registering with the SEC. This includes Treasury bonds and municipal bonds.
▲ Insider activities - A public report, called an insider report, must be filed with the SEC in every month that a change in the holding of a firm's securities occurs for an officer, director, or 10% or more shareholder. The 1934 SEA forbids insiders profiting from securities held less than 6 months and requires these profits be returned to the organization. In addition, short sales are not permitted by individuals considered to be insiders.
▲ Price manipulation - The SEA of 1934 forbids price manipulation schemes such as wash sales, pools, circulation of manipulative information, and false and misleading statements about securities.

Liability under the Securities Exchange Act of 1934

The Securities Exchange Act of 1934 relates to the purchase and sale of investment securities in the market (i.e., being public). Section 18 states that a financial planner is liable for false and/or misleading statements of material facts that are made in applications, reports, documents, and registration statements, which are prepared by the financial planner and filed with the SEC. Liability is imposed upon those (including financial planners) who, because of their inside positions, have access to material information (which is not available to the public and which may affect the value of securities) and trade in the securities without making a disclosure.

A financial planner may be liable to a person who purchased or sold securities when it can be established that:

▲ The statement or omission was material.
▲ The financial planner intended to deceive or defraud others.
▲ As a result of his or her reasonable reliance upon the misrepresentation, the purchaser or seller incurred a loss.

Criminal liability for willful conduct is imposed by the Securities Act of 1933, the Securities Exchange Act of 1934, the Internal Revenue Act, and other Federal statutes as well as state criminal codes.

NASD

Note: The following excerpts from "An Explanation of the NASD Regulations and Qualification Requirements – February 1998" have been reprinted with the permission of the NASD.

The National Association of Securities Dealers, Inc. (NASD) is a self-regulatory organization of the securities industry that was established under the 1938 Maloney Act Amendments and is subject to oversight by the Securities and Exchange Commission. The NASD is responsible for the regulation of the NASDAQ Stock Market as well as the over-the-counter securities market. Through its subsidiaries, NASD Regulation Inc. and the NASDAQ Stock Market, Inc., the NASD develops rules and regulations, conducts regulatory reviews of members' business activities, and designs and operates marketplace services and facilities. The NASD helps establish and coordinate the policies for its two subsidiaries and oversees their effectiveness.

NASD Regulation, Inc. (NASDR) was established in 1996 as a separate, independent subsidiary of the National Association of Securities Dealers, Inc. to separate the regulation of the broker/dealer professional from the operation of the NASDAQ Stock Market. The purpose of NASDR is to regulate the securities markets for the benefit and protection of investors.

Membership in the NASD entitles a firm to participate in the investment banking and over-the-counter securities business, to distribute new issues underwritten by NASD members and to distribute shares of investment companies sponsored by NASD members.

THE INVESTMENT ADVISORS ACT OF 1940

Any individual who provides investment advice to 15 or more interstate clients during a twelve-month period is required to register with the SEC and file educational and background information for all Registered Investment Advisors (RIAs). This act also forbids RIAs from assigning investment advisory contracts to other advisors without permission from the client, entering into profit-sharing agreements with clients, and prohibits advertising with selected testimonials. An investment adviser is a person who meets the following three tests:

▲ Provides advice, or issues reports or analyses, regarding securities;
▲ Is in the business of providing such services; and
▲ Provides such services for compensation (compensation is "the receipt of any economic benefit" including commissions on the sale of products).

Certain organizations and individuals are excluded, including:

- ▲ Banks and bank holding companies (except as amended by the Gramm-Leach-Bliley Act of 1999).
- ▲ Lawyers, accountants, engineers, or teachers, if their performance of advisory services is solely incidental to their professions.
- ▲ Brokers or dealers, if their performance of advisory services is solely incidental to the conduct of their business as brokers or dealers, and they do not receive any special compensation for their advisory services.
- ▲ Publishers of bona fide newspapers, newsmagazines, or business or financial publications of general and regular circulation.
- ▲ Those persons whose advice is related only to securities, which are, direct obligations of, or guaranteed by, the United States.
- ▲ Incidental practice exception is not available to individuals who hold themselves out to the public as providing financial planning, pension consulting, or other financial advisory services.

The Act provides limited exemptions. Investment advisers who, during the course of the preceding 12 months, had fewer than 15 clients and do not hold themselves out generally to the public as investment advisers. The Act generally requires investment advisers entering into an advisory contract with a client to deliver a written disclosure statement on their background and business practices. Form ADV Part II must be given to a client under Rule 204-3, known as the "brochure" rule. The 1940 Adviser's Act and the SEC's rules require that advisers maintain and preserve specified books and records and are made available for inspection.

In accordance with the Investment Adviser Brochure Rule, an investment adviser shall furnish each advisory client and prospective client with a written disclosure statement which may be a copy of Part II of Form ADV, or written documents containing at least the information then so required by Part II of Form ADV, or such other information as the administrator may require.

Disclosure should be delivered not less than 48 hours prior to entering into any investment advisory contract with such client or prospective client, or at the time of entering into any contract, if the advisory client has a right to terminate the contract without penalty within five business days after entering into the contract.

If an investment adviser renders substantially different types of investment advisory services to different advisory clients, any information required by Part II of Form ADV may be omitted from the statement furnished to an advisory client or prospective advisory client if such information is applicable only to a type of investment advisory service or fee which is not rendered or charged, or proposed to be rendered or charged, to that client or prospective client.

Inspections - The 1940 Investment Advisors Act and the SEC's rules require that advisers maintain and preserve specified books and records and are made available for inspection.

Restriction on the use of the term Investment Counsel - A registered investment adviser may not use the term investment counsel unless its principal business is acting as an investment adviser and a substantial portion of its business is providing "investment supervisory services."

Anti-Fraud Provisions - Section 206 of the Act, Section 17 of the Securities Act of 1933, Section 10(b) of the Securities Exchange Act of 1934, and Rule 10b-5 prohibit misstatements or misleading omissions of material facts, fraudulent acts, and practices in connection with the purchase or sale of securities or the conduct of an investment advisory business. An investment adviser owes his or her clients undivided loyalty and may not engage in activity that conflicts with a client's interest.

- ▲ Registration - Form ADV is kept current by filing periodic amendments. Form ADV-W is used to withdraw as an investment adviser.
- ▲ Filing Requirements.
- ▲ Forms - ADV and ADV-W can be obtained from the SEC's Office of Consumer Affairs and Information Services in Washington, DC, or from the Commission office in your area (www.sec.gov/offices/invmgmt/advinst.htm).
- ▲ Copies - All advisers' filings must be submitted in triplicate and typewritten. Copies can be filed, but each must be signed manually.
- ▲ Fees - Must include a registration fee of $150, by check or money order payable to the Securities and Exchange Commission, with your initial application of Form ADV. No part of this fee can be refunded.
- ▲ Name and Signatures - Full names are required. Each copy of an execution page must contain an original manual signature.

REGISTRATION

In the Fall of 1996, Congress amended the Advisors Act to reallocate regulatory responsibility for investment advisers between the Commission and state authorities. Congress did this by prohibiting certain advisers from registering with the Commission. As a result, for the most part, larger advisers will be regulated by the Commission, and smaller advisers will be regulated by state securities authorities. Only certain types of advisers are permitted to register with the Commission (and therefore must register with the Commission, unless exempt under a specific rule). Following is a list of advisers who are permitted to register with the Commission:

- ▲ Advisers having "assets under management" of $25 million or more. The $25 million threshold has been increased to $30 million. However, advisers with assets under management between $25 million and $30 million may still register with the Commission. Advisers with assets under management less than $25 million are generally required to register at the state level.
- ▲ Advisers to registered investment companies.
- ▲ Advisers who have their principal office and place of business in a state that has not enacted an investment adviser statute or that have their principal office and place of business outside the United States.
- ▲ Advisers are required to report their eligibility for Commission registration on Schedule I to Form ADV upon initial registration. Schedule I must be filed every year to establish and report their continuing eligibility for Commission registrations.

Investment Adviser Registration Depository

Note: The following excerpts from "What is IARD?" have been reprinted with the permission of the NASD.

The Investment Adviser Registration Depository (IARD) is an electronic filing system for Investment Advisers sponsored by the Securities and Exchange Commission (SEC) and North American Securities Administrators Association (NASAA), with NASD Regulation, Inc. serving as the developer and operator of the system. The IARD system collects and maintains the registration and disclosure information for Investment Advisers and their associated persons. The new IARD system supports electronic filing of the revised Forms ADV and ADV-W, centralized fee and form processing, regulatory review, the annual registration renewal process, and public disclosure of Investment Adviser information (www.iard.com).

NASD Regulation does not have regulatory authority over Investment Advisers; however, it was chosen to develop, operate, and maintain the system because of its regulatory business and technical expertise and the success of its Web-based licensing and regulation system, Web CRD^{SM}, deployed in 1999. Web CRD is a state-of-the-art Web application for the registration of broker/dealers and their representatives. IARD provides regulators with the ability to monitor and process Investment Adviser information via a single, centralized system.

The SEC has mandated its Investment Adviser registrants use the system to make all filings with the Commission beginning January 1, 2001. The IARD system satisfies the requirements of the National Securities Markets Improvement Act (NSMIA,1996), which authorized electronic system registration of Investment Advisers.

IARD provides a mechanism that allows federal Investment Advisers to satisfy the SEC mandate for electronic filing and related public disclosure. The system also offers states similar benefits by facilitating "Notice Filing" requirements for federal filers and registration requirements of state-regulated Investment Advisers. In the near future, IARD will provide for the registration of Investment Adviser Representatives (IARs).

IARD is composed of four critical components: IA Firm Registration, IA Firm Public Disclosure, IAR Registration, which is registration of individual investment advisers, and IAR Public Disclosure. The Firm Registration component was released into production on January 1, 2001. This allows Investment Adviser firms to file a Form ADV and/or Form ADV-W electronically with the SEC and states. This release also provides the ability to view the information contained on the filings, collect and disburse fees associated with these filings, request reports, and allow firms that are both broker/dealers and Investment Advisers to share filing information between Web CRD and IARD.

Due Diligence

Due diligence requires that investment advisers investigate any security prior to offering it for sale to a client. Additionally, the security must be "suited" to the client's needs and objectives.

Due diligence is addressed in the Securities Act of 1933.

REFORM OF PREVIOUS ACTS

The Glass-Steagall Act (1933) prohibited commercial banks from acting as investment bankers, established the Federal Deposit Insurance Corporation (FDIC), and prohibited commercial banks from paying interest on demand deposits. This was one of the first of many securities regulation laws that has impacted the investment markets. However, the Gramm-Leach-Bliley Act, passed by Congress in November 1999, eliminates many of the restrictions against affiliations among banks, securities firms, and insurance companies:

The Act repeals the affiliation sections of the Glass-Steagall Act that prohibit a bank holding company and a securities firm that underwrites and deals in ineligible securities from owning and controlling each other.

It also amends the Bank Holding Company Act (1956) to permit cross-ownership and control among bank holding companies, securities firms and insurance companies, provided that such cross-ownership and control is effected through a financial holding company that engages in activities that conform to the Act.

A bank must register as an investment adviser if it provides investment advice to a registered investment company, provided that, if the bank provides such advice through a "separately identified department or division," that department or division shall be deemed to be the investment adviser.

INVESTMENT COMPANY ACT OF 1940

Investment Company Act of 1940 requires registration with the SEC and restricts activities of investment companies (including mutual funds). The Investment Company Act of 1940 governs the management of investment companies. This act requires that investment companies register with the SEC, provide prospectuses to investors prior to the sale of shares, disclose the investment goals of the company, have outside members on the board of directors, use uniform accounting practices, and gain approval by shareholders for changes in management.

Appendix D

Topic List for the CFP™ Certification Examination

General Principles of Financial Planning	**Investment Planning**	**Retirement Planning**
1. Financial planning process 2. CFP Board's Code of Ethics and Professional Responsibility and Disciplinary Rules and Procedures 3. CFP Board's Financial Planning Practice Standards 4. Personal financial statements 5. Budgeting 6. Emergency fund planning 7. Credit and debt management 8. Buying vs. leasing 9. Function, purpose, and regulation of financial institutions 10. Client attitudes and behavioral characteristics 11. Educational funding 12. Financial planning for special circumstances 13. Economic concepts 14. Time value of money concepts and calculations 15. Characteristics and consequences of types of entities 16. Characteristics and consequences of property titling 17. Financial services industry regulation requirements 18. Business Law 19. Quantitative analysis 20. Monetary settlement planning	1. Types and use of investment vehicles 2. Types of investment risk 3. Measures of investment risk 4. Measures of investment returns 5. Time-influenced security valuation concepts 6. Bond and stock valuation methods 7. Portfolio management and measurement concepts 8. Formula investing 9. Investment strategies 10. Asset allocation and portfolio diversification 11. Efficient Market Theory (EMT) 12. Asset pricing models 13. Leverage of investment assets 14. Hedging and option strategies 15. Tax efficient investing 16. Investment strategies in tax-advantaged accounts 17. Taxation of investment vehicles	1. Retirement needs analysis 2. Social Security [Old Age, Survivor, and Disability Insurance (OASDI)] 3. Medicare 4. Types of retirement plans 5. Qualified plan rules and options 6. Other tax-advantaged retirement plans 7. Regulatory considerations 8. Plan selection for businesses (key factors affecting selection) 9. Investment considerations for retirement plans 10. Distribution rules, alternatives, and taxation
Insurance Planning and Risk Management	**Income Tax Planning**	**Estate Planning**
1. Principles of insurance 2. Analysis and evaluation of risk exposures 3. Legal aspects of insurance 4. Property and casualty insurance (individual and business) 5. General business liability 6. Health insurance (individual) 7. Disability income insurance (individual) 8. Long-term care insurance (individual and joint) 9. Life insurance 10. Viatical settlements 11. Insurance needs analysis and rationale 12. Taxation of life, disability, and long-term care insurance 13. Insurance policy selection 14. Insurance company selection and due diligence **Employee Benefits Planning** 1. Employee benefit plans 2. Employee stock options 3. Stock plans 4. Non-qualified deferred compensation 5. Employer/employee insurance arrangements	1. Income tax law fundamentals 2. Tax compliance 3. Income tax fundamentals and calculations 4. Tax accounting methods 5. Tax characteristics of entities 6. Income taxation of trusts and estates 7. Basis 8. Cost-recovery concepts 9. Tax consequences of like-kind exchanges 10. Tax consequences of gain or loss on sale of assets 11. Alternative Minimum Tax (AMT) 12. Tax management techniques 13. Passive activity and at-risk rules 14. Tax implications of changing circumstances 15. Charitable contributions and deductions	1. Methods of property transfer at death 2. Estate planning documents 3. Gifting strategies 4. Gift taxation and compliance 5. Incapacity planning 6. Estate tax calculation and compliance 7. Satisfying liquidity needs 8. Powers of appointment 9. Types, features, and taxation of trusts 10. Qualified interest trusts 11. Charitable giving 12. Use of life insurance in estate planning 13. Valuation issues 14. Marital deduction 15. Deferral and minimization of estate taxes 16. Intra-family and other business transfer techniques 17. Disposition of estate 18. Generation-Skipping Transfer Tax (GSTT) 19. Fiduciary responsibilities 20. Income in Respect of Decedent (IRD)

Glossary

"above-the-line" deductions - an above the line deduction (also known as a deduction for AGI) is one that reduces gross income directly.

accuracy-related penalty - a penalty of 20% of the portion of the tax underpayment attributable to negligence, substantial understatement of tax, or substantial valuation misstatement without intent to defraud.

actual cash value - one of three ways in which losses are valued in most insurance policies. Actual cash value (ACV) is calculated as replacement cost minus functional depreciation.

adhesion - a characteristic of insurance meaning that insurance is "a take it or leave it contract." The insured must accept (or adhere to) the contract as written, without any bargaining over its terms and conditions.

adjusted gross estate - gross estate *less* deductions provided for by law in recognition that the entire value of the gross estate will not be transferred to the heirs due to costs, debts, and certain other deductions.

adjusted gross income (AGI) - a determination peculiar to individual taxpayers that represents gross income less business expenses, expenses attributable to the production of rent or royalty income, the allowed capital loss deduction, and certain personal expenses (deductions for AGI).

administrator - in the event a decedent dies intestate (without a valid will), or where an executor cannot be appointed by the probate court, the court appoints an administrator with powers called letters of administration which enable the administrator to carry out duties set down in the laws of intestacy

audits - correspondence; office; field inspection and verification of a taxpayer's return or other transactions possessing tax consequences. Correspondence audits are conducted by mail; office audits are conducted in the tax agents office; field audits are conducted on the business premises of the taxpayer or in the office of the tax practitioner representing the taxpayer.

adverse selection - the tendency of higher-than-average risks (people who need insurance the most) to purchase or renew insurance policies.

aleatory - a characteristic of insurance meaning that monetary values exchanged by each party in an insurance agreement are unequal.

American Depositary Receipts (ADRs) - certificates of ownership issued by U.S. banks representing ownership in shares of stock of a foreign company that are held on deposit in a bank in the firm's home country.

amortization table - a TVM tool used primarily to illustrate the amortization, or extinguishments, of debt. The table presents the number of years of indebtedness, the beginning balance, level payments, interest amount, principal reduction, and ending balance of indebtedness.

annual exclusion - a result of a de minimus rule by Congress to help reduce income tax reporting by eliminating the need for taxpayers to keep an account of, or report, small gifts. All individuals are allowed to gift, tax free, up to $10,000 per donee per year.

annuity - periodic payment to an individual that continues for a fixed period or for the duration of a designated life or lives.

anomalies - occurrences in the stock market that are not supported by the concept of the Efficient Market Hypothesis.

antitrust legislation - laws passed to protect consumers from monopolistic price practices and to protect investors by promoting fair competition.

any occupation - a disability definition that states a person insured under the "any occupation" clause is considered totally disabled if he or she cannot perform the duties of *any* occupation.

articles of organization - document filed in compliance with state law to create a limited liability company (LLC).

arithmetic mean - also called the arithmetic average rate of return, a measure of investment return that is the result of averaging period returns.

asset accumulation phase - lifecycle phase through which clients pass usually beginning somewhere between the ages of 20 and 25 and lasting until somewhere around age 50 for many persons, characterized by limited excess funds for investing, high degree of debt-to-net worth, and low net worth.

asset allocation - provides an investor with a guide to how much of his portfolio should be invested in each asset class.

asset-backed securities - securities issued against some type of asset-linked debts bundled together, such as credit card receivables or mortgages.

assets - property owned completely or partially by the client.

attorney-in-fact- the person designated by the principal in a power of attorney to act in place of the principal on the principal's behalf.

audit - correspondence; office; field - inspection and verification of a taxpayer's return or other transactions possessing tax consequences. Correspondence audits are conducted by mail; office audits are conducted in the tax agent's office; field audits are conducted on the business premises of the taxpayer or in the office of the tax practitioner representing the taxpayer.

average indexed monthly earnings (AIME) - calculation that adjusts, or indexes, a worker's actual earnings to current dollars to account for changes in average wages since the year the earnings were received during the 35 years in which the worker earned the most.

back-end load - a sales charge incurred upon the ultimate sale or redemption of mutual fund shares rather than at the time of purchase.

balance sheet - a listing of assets, liabilities, and net worth.

bankruptcy- the financial condition when a debtor is determined by the court to be unable to pay creditors.

basic standard deduction - the amount allowed all taxpayers who do not itemize deductions.

"below-the-line" deductions - (also known as a deduction from AGI) is one that is subtracted from AGI in arriving at taxable income.

bend points- the three separate percentages of portions of the AIME that are summed to arrive at the PIA.

benefit period- the number of days that Medicare covers care in hospitals and skilled nursing facilities.

benefits of personal financial planning - goals identified are more likely to be achieved; helps to clearly identify risk exposures; is proactive rather than reactive; creates a framework for feedback, evaluation, and control; establishes measurable goals and expectations; develops an improved awareness of financial choices; provides an opportunity for an increased commitment to financial goals.

beta - a commonly used measure of systematic risk that provides an indication of the volatility of a portfolio compared to the market.

beyond a reasonable doubt standard - a measure or degree of proof – with regard to CFP disciplinary rules and procedures, "beyond a reasonable doubt" means the evidence as a whole shows what it was intended to prove with a probability of 99 percent or better.

blue chip stocks - a type of stock issued by older, well-established companies that maintain the ability to pay dividends both in years the company has income and in years the company has losses.

board of directors - the governing body of a corporation whose members are elected by shareholders.

bond indenture agreement - the legal document that sets forth the repayment schedules, restrictions, and promises between the issuer of a corporate bond and the borrower.

boot - property (other than like-kind property) that qualifies as a tax gain when received in a property exchange.

burden of proof -the requirement of proving facts to a certain degree of probability. With regard to CFP disciplinary rules and procedures, there are three distinct burdens of proof: (1) preponderance of the evidence; (2) clear and convincing evidence; and (3) evidence beyond a reasonable doubt.

business cycles - swings in total national output, income, and employment marked by widespread expansion or contraction in many sectors of the economy.

business risk - an unsystematic risk based on the riskiness of the specific business with regard to its speculative nature, its management, and philosophy.

bypass trust - avoids inclusion in, or bypasses, the surviving spouse's gross estate--the assets transfer to a future generation free of estate taxes. The purpose of a bypass trust (known as a "B" trust) is to take advantage of the unified credit or equivalency.

C corporation - a business entity created by state law that is separate and distinct from its shareholder/owners.

call options - a derivative that gives the holder the right to purchase the underlying security, generally stock, at a specified price within a specified period.

capital appreciation - when a company chooses to retain the earnings to invest in additional projects, the investor receives his return in the form of appreciation of the stock.

capital asset - broadly speaking, all assets are capital except those specifically excluded by the Internal Revenue Code, including property held for resale in the normal course of business (inventory), trade accounts and notes receivable, and depreciable property and real estate used in a trade or business.

Capital Asset Pricing Model (CAPM) - an asset-pricing model that developed from the Markowitz efficient frontier and the introduction of a risk-free asset.

capital formation - production of buildings, machinery, tools, and other equipment that will assist in the ability of economic participants to produce in the future.

capital gains - long-term; short-term - a long-term capital gain is the gain from a sale or exchange of a capital asset that has been held for more than one year (that is, at least a year and one day). A short-term capital gain is the gain from a sale or exchange of a capital asset that has been held for less than one year.

capital loss - the loss from the sale or exchange of a capital asset.

capital needs analysis - the process of calculating the amount of investment capital needed at retirement to maintain the preretirement lifestyle and mitigate the impact of inflation during the retirement years.

capital preservation model (CP) - a capital needs analysis method that assumes that at life expectancy, the client has exactly the same account balance as he did at retirement.

capital retention approach - one of three recognized methods used to determine the amount of life insurance one should purchase. The capital retention approach first determines what level of annual income the insured wishes to provide for the family. The insured then determines what amount of life insurance is needed *in addition to existing income-producing assets* to provide the desired level of income

cash accounts - a type of brokerage account that requires that all securities purchased by the investor be paid for in full without any indebtedness.

cash flow timeline - a time value of money analysis tool that graphically depicts cash inflows (future value of the investment) and cash outflows (the initial dollar investment) over a certain period (the term).

cash flows from financing - cash inflows from the issuance of additional debt and cash outflows for the repayment of debt.

cash flows from investing - cash receipts or expenditures for the sale or purchase of assets.

cash flows from operations - net cash generated or used due to normal work and living.

cash value - amount payable to the owner of a life insurance policy should he or she decide it is no longer wanted.

Certified Financial Planner Board of Governors - the governing board for the certified financial planning profession.

Certified Financial Planner Board of Professional Review ("BOPR") - a subsidiary board of the CFP Board of Standards that interprets and applies the CFP Code.

Certified Financial Planner Board of Standards, Inc. - an independent professional regulatory organization that regulates financial planners.

Certified Financial Planner (CFP) Code of Ethics and Professional Responsibility - the set of principles of conduct that seeks to regulate behavior of CFP designees.

CFA - Chartered Financial Analyst.

CFP™ - Certified Financial Planner designation.

CFP Board designee - throughout this textbook, "CFP Board designee" refers to an individual who uses the CFP Board designation.

charitable deduction- a charitable contribution made as a gift to a qualified organization.

charitable lead trust (CLT) - a split interest trust where a charity is the income beneficiary and there is a non-charitable remainderman.

charitable remainder trust (CRT) - a split interest trust. If created during life, the income goes to one or more parties, usually the grantor or grantor and spouse for life, and upon the income beneficiary's death, the principal (remainder) is transferred to a charity. If the CRT is created testamentary, the usual income beneficiary is the spouse for life.

ChFC - Chartered Financial Consultant.

clear and convincing evidence standard - a measure or degree of proof – with regard to CFP disciplinary rules and procedures, "clear and convincing evidence" means the evidence as a whole shows what it was intended to prove with a probability of 75 percent or better.

clearly erroneous standard - standard applied by a CFP Hearing Panel at a CFP complaint hearing that states that only when review of the entire record reveals that a reasonable person could not have ruled a certain way will the findings be considered clearly erroneous.

client data collection questionnaire - a survey used by financial planners to gather internal data from clients, such as their tolerance for risk and their personal perception of their financial situation, as well as tax-related data, such as Social Security numbers, information relating to their dependents, and so on.

closed-end fund - a type of investment company whose shares trade in the same manner that other publicly traded stocks trade in the secondary market.

CLU - Chartered Life Underwriter.

code of ethics - a set of principles of conduct that governs a group of individuals and usually requires conformity to professional standards of conduct.

coefficient of determination (R^2) - a modern portfolio theory statistic that indicates the percent change in a portfolio or mutual fund that can be explained by changes in the market (generally defined by an index).

coinsurance - the percentage of financial responsibility that the insured and the insurer must uphold in order to achieve equity in rating.

collision - auto insurance coverage that protects the insured against upset and collision damages, such as those sustained in an accident involving other vehicles, or those sustained when an auto runs off the road and into a lake.

combined income - on the 1040 federal tax return, combined income is the sum of adjusted gross income, plus nontaxable interest, plus one-half of Social Security benefits.

commingle client's funds - CFP Board Rules specifically prohibit the combining (or commingling) of client funds or other property with a CFP Board designee's personal funds and/or other property or the funds and/or other property of a CFP Board designee's firm.

common stock - ownership interest in a company.

compound interest - interest earned on interest.

concealment - occurs when the insured is silent about a fact that is material to the risk.

conflict of interest - denotes circumstances, relationships or other facts about a CFP Board designee's own financial, business, property, and/or personal interests which will, or reasonably may, impair the CFP Board designee's rendering of disinterested advice, recommendations, or services.

conservation/protection phase - lifecycle phase through which clients pass characterized by an increase in cash flow, assets, and net worth with some decrease in the proportional use of debt.

Consolidated Omnibus Budget Reconciliation Act (COBRA) - a federal law that requires certain employers to provide the previously covered persons (including dependents and spouses) with the same insurance coverage he or she received prior to unemployment.

consolidation loan - a loan that provides borrowers with a way to consolidate various types of federal student loans that have separate repayment schedules into one loan.

COLA - cost-of-living adjustments provided for Social Security benefits.

Consumer Price Index (CPI) - a price index that measures the cost of a "market basket" of consumer goods and services purchased for day-to-day living.

consumption movements - an economic variable that fluctuates during the business cycle, usually lags behind trends, and seems to be the effect of a business cycle phase rather than its cause.

contraction phase - one of the two general business cycle phases characterized by a fall in business sales, decreased growth of Gross Domestic Product, and increased unemployment.

convertible securities - hybrid securities that permit the holder to acquire shares of common stock from the issuing company by exchanging the currently held debt security under a specific formula.

co-payment - a loss-sharing arrangement whereby the insured pays a percentage of the loss in excess of the deductible.

country (or regulation) risk - an unsystematic risk where changes in a country's laws or political situation will have an adverse effect on an investment.

coupon payments - interest payments paid to the bondholder on a semiannual basis and based on a percentage of the face value or par value of the bond.

CPA - Certified Public Accountant.

current assets - assets expected to be converted to cash within one year.

current liability - debt owed by the client that is expected to be paid off within the year.

current yield - a bond's annual coupon divided by the current market price.

cyclical stocks - a type of stock that tends to prosper in expanding economies and do poorly during down business cycles.

date of declaration - date a corporation's board of directors declares a dividend payment which creates an obligation on the company to make a dividend payment to shareholders.

date of payment - the date that the dividend will actually be paid.

date of record - the date at which an owner of the common stock of a corporation is entitled to receive the dividend payment.

date of x-dividend - the date at which the market reflects the dividend payment

debentures - unsecured corporate bonds whose holders have no claim to specific assets of the issuing corporation.

deductible - a stated amount of money the insured is required to pay on a loss before the insurer will make any payments under the policy conditions.

deductions - above-the-line; below-the-line; standard; itemized - an above-the-line deduction (also known as a deduction *for* AGI) is one that reduces gross income directly; a below-the-line deduction (also known as a deduction *from* AGI) is one that reduces AGI; the basic standard deduction is the amount allowed all taxpayers who do not itemize their deductions; itemized deductions are ones that are in excess of the standard deduction and are used in lieu of the standard deduction.

default risk - an unsystematic risk where a business will be unable to service its debt to creditors.

defensive stocks - a type of stock that is relatively unaffected by general fluctuations in the economy.

deferred-compensation plan - a nonqualified plan that is a contractual agreement between the employer and selected employees that takes the form of either salary reduction, or salary continuation. Compensation is deferred until retirement, disability, death, or termination of employment, but usually only at normal retirement age.

deficit spending - occurs when governmental expenditures exceed the government's tax collections.

defined-benefit plan - a retirement plan that specifies the benefits that each employee receives at retirement. Defined-benefit plans actuarially determine the benefit to be paid at normal age retirement.

defined-contribution plan - a retirement plan that specifies the annual employer current contribution. The amount of benefit received by an employee depends on what the account balance is at retirement.

deflation - the opposite of inflation, deflation occurs when the general level of prices is falling.

demand - the quantity of a particular good that people are willing to buy. Demand is heavily dependent on price.

demand curve - the graphic depiction that illustrates the relationship between a particular good's price and the quantity demanded.

dependent - an individual who can be claimed by a taxpayer for an exemption on an income tax return.

depression - a persistent recession that brings a severe decline in economic activity.

derivatives - securities whose value is based on, or derived from, the value of some other security or proxy.

determination letter - a written statement issued by an IRS district director that applies the principles and precedents announced by the National Office to a given set of facts.

direct bequest - (to a spouse) the first spouse who dies, leaves everything outright to the surviving spouse.

direct investing - a process of investing where investors purchase actual securities.

directors - individuals who, acting as a group known as the board of directors, manage the business affairs of a corporation.

disclaimer - the refusal of the receipt of an estate. The use of disclaimers allows a spouse or anyone else to disclaim or renounce receiving any part of an estate.

disability benefit - Social Security benefit available to recipients who have a severe physical or mental impairment that is expected to either prevent them from performing substantial work for at least a year, or result in death and who have the sufficient amount of Social Security credits.

disability income insurance - a type of insurance that provides a regular income while the insured is unable to work because of illness or injury.

Disciplinary Rules and Procedures (the "Procedures") - rules and procedures that enforce the CFP Code and regulate disciplinary proceedings against CFP Board designees.

disclaimer clause - a common clause in a decedent's will that allows property to pass from one party to another without gift tax consequences. It reminds the heir that disclaiming an inheritance may be an effective tool in estate planning.

discretionary cash flow - money available after all expenses are accounted for.

discretionary expenses - luxuries or expenses over which the client has complete control.

Discriminant Function System (DIF) - a mathematical technique used to classify tax returns as to their examination potential.

disinflation - the term used to denote a decline in the rate of inflation.

distribution/gifting phase - lifecycle phase through which clients pass characterized by excess relative cash flows, low debt, and high relative net worth.

dividend yield - the measure of a securities dividend payment as a percent of the current market price.

dividends - positive net income that is paid to the shareholders of a corporation.

dividends-received deduction (DRD) - a deduction for dividends received by one corporation from another corporation. The amount of the DRD is based on the percentage ownership of the corporation paying the dividend.

dollar weighted returns - a method of determining an internal rate of return an individual investor earned based on the investor's particular cash flow into and out of the portfolio.

double taxation of dividends - the taxation of income at the corporate level and the subsequent taxation of dividend distributions at the individual shareholder's level.

Dow Jones Industrial Average (DJIA) - a financial index that is a price weighted average of thirty leading industrial stocks used to measure the status of the equity market.

durable goods - products that are not consumed or quickly disposed of, and can be used for several years.

durable power of attorney for health care or property - a written document enabling one individual, the principal, to designate another person or persons to act as his or her "attorney-in-fact."

duration - a concept developed by Fred Macaulay in 1938, that provides a time-weighted measure of a security's cash flows in terms of payback.

dwelling - residential structure covered under a homeowners insurance policy.

EAFE Index - the Europe, Australia, and Far East (EAFE) index created as a measure of the international securities markets.

earned income - income from personal services as distinguished from income generated by property.

Educational IRA - an investment account established with cash that whose contributions are allowed to grow tax free within the account. Money withdrawn from the account remains free from tax or penalty if the funds are used for higher education expenses. If not, the earnings are subject to income tax and a 10% penalty.

efficient frontier - consists of investment portfolios with the highest expected return for a given level of risk.

Efficient Market Hypothesis - a theory that suggests that securities are priced fairly and efficiently by the market and that investors are unable to outperform the market on a consistent basis without accepting additional risk.

elimination period - a waiting period of one month to one year from the date of disability included in a disability income policy to reduce unnecessary small claims and moral hazards. During this waiting period, disability income benefits are not being paid.

Employer's Educational Assistance Program - under this program, an employer can pay for an employee's undergraduate tuition, enrollment fees, books, supplies, and equipment while these employer benefits are excluded from the employee's income up to $5,250.

engagement letter - a tool of communication between client and financial planner that sets down in writing information about any agreements or understandings obtained at client/planner meetings including the plan of action for developing a financial plan, the expected outcome of the engagement, and the method of compensation.

equity mutual funds - a mutual fund that invests primarily in equity securities, such as preferred stock and common stock.

ethics - the discipline of dealing with the moral principles or values that guide one's self.

exchange rate risk - a systematic risk where a change in the relationship between the value of the dollar (or investor's currency) and the value of the foreign currency will occur where the investment is made.

exchange traded funds (ETFs) - a type of investment company whose investment objective is to achieve the same return as a particular market index.

exclusion - income exempt from tax and not included in a taxpayer's gross income.

exemptions - personal; dependency - a basic deduction to which a taxpayer is entitled for self support (personal exemption) or for the support of a spouse and/or dependent (dependency exemption).

exercise price - the price at which an underlying stock will either be sold (put) or purchased (call) by the holder of an option.

expected family contribution (EFC) - a formula that indicates how much of a student's family resources ought to be available to assist in paying for the student's college education. Some of the factors used in this calculation include taxable and nontaxable income, assets, retirement funds, and benefits, such as unemployment and Social Security.

expansion phase - one of the two general business cycle phases characterized by a rise in business sales, growth of Gross Domestic Product, and a decline in unemployment.

expense ratio - disclosed by all mutual funds in their fund prospectuses as an indication of the annual fund expenses that are stated as a percentage of total assets.

expenses - recurring obligations.

external business cycle theory - a business cycle theory that finds the root of the business cycle in the fluctuations of something outside the economic system, such as wars, revolutions, political events, rates of population growth and migration, discoveries of new lands and resources, scientific and technological discoveries, and innovation.

external environment - the whole complex of factors that influence the financial planning process, including economic, legal, social, technological, political, and taxation factors.

failure-to-file penalty - a civil penalty imposed on taxpayers and tax return preparers who fail to file tax returns according to the requirements of tax law.

failure-to-pay-tax penalty - a civil penalty imposed on taxpayers who, without reasonable cause, fail to pay the tax shown on their return.

fair market value - the price at which an exchange will take place between a willing buyer and a willing seller.

family benefit - Social Security benefit available to certain family members of workers eligible for retirement or disability benefits.

family limited partnership - an estate planning technique utilizing a limited partnership between family members used to generate valuation discounts for estate and gift tax purposes on the transfer of the limited interest in the partnership.

Fed Funds Rate - the overnight lending rate between Federal Reserve member banks.

federal agency securities - public debt issued by agencies of the U.S. government as a means of raising funds for operations of the respective agency.

federal estate tax - an excise tax on the right to transfer assets by a decedent.

Federal Insurance Contributions Act (FICA) - the law allowing Social Security taxes, including Medicare, to be deducted from paychecks.

Federal Perkins Loan Program - federally funded, campus-based, low-interest student loan that is provided to undergraduate and graduate students that have exceptional financial need, that is, very low EFCs.

Federal Reserve (the Fed) - the banking and financial system developed under the Federal Reserve Act of 1913 that makes the basic policy decisions that regulate our money and banking systems.

Federal Reserve discount rate - the rate at which Federal Reserve member banks can borrow funds to meet reserve requirements. The Fed will lower the discount rate when it wants to increase the money supply.

Federal Supplemental Education Opportunity Grant (FSEOG) - campus-based student financial aid grant awarded to undergraduate students with low EFCs that gives priority to students who receive Federal Pell Grants.

Federal Trade Commission (FTC) - the federal organization created in 1914 to keep competition free and fair and to protect U. S. consumers.

Federal Work-Study Program - campus-based student financial aid program that enables undergraduate and graduate students to earn money for education expenses through jobs that pay at least current minimum wages but do not exceed the award received through the program.

fee simple - the complete individual ownership of property with all rights associated with outright ownership, such as the right to use, sell, gift, alienate, or convey.

fiduciary relationship - relationship between a CFP^{TM} practitioner and a client where the client places special trust and confidence in the CFP^{TM} practitioner. This relationship places a higher burden on the CFP Board designee, which is warranted, because the CFP Board designee is dealing with the client's funds or property for investment purposes.

Financial Accounting Standards Board (FASB) - non-governmental board that sets standards for financial statements and generally accepted accounting principals (GAAP).

financial goals - high-level statements of financial desire that may be for the short run or the long run.

financial mission - a broad and enduring statement that identifies the client's long-term purpose for wanting a financial plan.

financial objectives - statements of financial desire that contain time and measurement attributes making them more specific than financial goals.

financial planning practitioners - individuals who are capable and qualified to offer objective, integrated, and comprehensive financial advice to or for the benefit of clients to help them achieve their financial objectives and who engage in financial planning using the financial planning process in working with clients.

financial risk - an unsystematic risk based on the capital structure of a firm which affects the return on equity (ROE) for a company.

financial success - for most individuals, financial success means accomplishing one's financial goals.

fiscal policy - taxation, expenditures, and debt management of the federal government.

fixed expenses - expenses that remain constant over a period of time over which the client has little control.

fixed income (or bond) mutual funds - a mutual fund that invests in fixed income securities ranging in maturity of several months to thirty years or longer. Bond funds invest in numerous bond issues to diversify the investment portfolio from default risk.

fixed income securities - securities with specified payment dates and amounts, primarily bonds.

flow-through entity - the results of business operations are reported directly on the owner's income tax return.

foreign currency risk - a systematic risk where a change in the relationship between the value of the dollar (or investor's currency) and the value of the foreign currency will occur where the investment is made.

foreign closed-end funds - securities that provide the same basic benefits as foreign mutual funds, except that since closed-end funds trade on exchanges, they do not have the cash inflow and outflow that mutual funds frequently experience.

foreign mutual funds - securities that provide investors with the easiest method of investing in foreign markets in the context of a diversified portfolio.

foreign securities - securities from developed countries or emerging markets.

forfeitures - employer contributions that are not fully vested and thus forfeited in the event that an employee terminates service

401(k) plan - a defined-contribution profit-sharing plan that gives participants the option of reducing their taxable salary and contributing the salary reduction on a tax-deferred basis to an individual account for retirement purposes.

403(b) plan - a retirement plan similar to a 401(k) plan that is available to certain tax-exempt organizations and to public schools.

fourth market - comprised of institutional traders that trade without the help of brokers.

fraud penalty - a penalty levied against a taxpayer by the IRS after it has proven an underpayment of tax by the taxpayer and proven that the underpayment was attributable to a willful attempt to evade tax.

Free Application for Federal Student Aid (FAFSA) - an application form that must be submitted by a college student to become eligible for federal financial aid.

"free cash flow" to equity - term that describes the available cash after meeting all of a firm's operating and financial needs. Used to calculate the value a company.

front-end load - a sales charge based on the initial investment into a mutual fund.

fundamental analysis - the analysis of a stock's value using basic, publicly available data such as the stock's earnings, sales, risk, and industry analysis.

future value - the future amount to which $1 today will increase based on a defined interest rate and a period of time.

future value of an annuity due - the future amount to which a series of deposits of equal size will increase when deposited over a definite number of equal interval time periods, at the *beginning* of those time periods, based on a defined interest rate.

future value of an ordinary annuity - the future amount to which a series of deposits of equal size will increase when deposited over a definite number of equal interval time periods, at the *end* of those time periods, based on a defined interest rate.

futures contract - an agreement to do something in the future--generally, purchasing (selling) a futures contract obligates the buyer to take delivery (make delivery) of a specific commodity at a specific time in the future.

galloping inflation - inflation that occurs when money loses its value very quickly and when real interest rates can be minus 50 or 100 percent per year.

general partnership - a type of business entity owned entirely by general partners, each of whom can act on behalf of the partnership.

general power of appointment - allows a terminable interest to be passed to a surviving spouse and the property to still qualify for the marital deduction

generation skipping transfer tax (GSTT) - a tax that is in addition to the unified gift and estate tax and is designed to tax large transfers that skip a generation (that is, from grandparent to grandchild).

geometric mean - also known as geometric average return, a method of calculating the internal rate of return based on periodic rates of return.

gift - in estate planning, a direct transfer of property or cash made during life.

grace period - period of time during which a policyowner may convert a group term policy, upon termination from a company, to a regular cash value policy at a rate that is commensurate with his or her attained age without losing coverage.

Gross Domestic Product (GDP) - the value of all goods and services produced in the country, GDP is the broadest measure of the general state of the economy.

gross estate - all assets included in a decedent's estate including, but not limited to, cash, stocks, bonds, annuities, retirement accounts, notes receivable, personal residences, automobiles, art collections, life insurance proceeds, and income tax refunds due.

gross income - income subject to the federal income tax. Gross income does not include income for which the IRC permits exclusion treatment.

growth stocks - a type of stock issued by companies whose sales, earnings, and market share are growing at higher rates than average companies or the general economy.

guaranteed insurability option - if the insured has purchased this relatively inexpensive option, term policies can be renewed without proof of insurability.

hazard (moral, morale, and physical) - a condition that creates or increases the likelihood of a loss occurring. A moral hazard is a character flaw or level of dishonesty an individual possesses that causes or increases the chance for loss. A morale hazard is indifference to a loss based on the existence of insurance. A physical hazard is a tangible condition or circumstance that increases the probability of a peril occurring and/or the severity of damages that result from a peril.

head of household - the filing status that identifies a taxpayer as an unmarried individual who maintains a household for another and satisfies certain conditions set forth in the Internal Revenue Code.

Health Insurance Portability and Accountability Act (HIPAA) - this law eliminates the previously detrimental effects of changing jobs, and starting a new health plan with a new preexisting exclusions clause.

health maintenance organization (HMO) - organized system of health care that provides comprehensive health services to its members for a fixed prepaid fee.

hearing panel - panel that establishes the rules of procedures and evidence to be observed at a complaint hearing seeking disciplinary action against a CFP Board designee.

heir - one who inherits; beneficiary.

holding period return - measures the total return an investor receives over the life of an investment.

holographic will - handwritten will dated and signed by the testator.

homeowners insurance - a package insurance policy that provides both property and liability coverage for the insured's dwelling, other structures, personal property, and loss of use.

Hope Scholarship Credit - a tax credit available for qualified tuition and enrollment fees incurred and paid after 1997 in the first two years of post-secondary education for the taxpayer, spouse, or dependent.

hospital expense insurance - provides payment for expenses incurred by the insured while in the hospital.

housing costs - principal and interest to pay the mortgage loan, real estate taxes, and homeowners insurance.

human life value approach - one of three recognized methods used to determine the amount of insurance one should purchase. The human life value approach determines the value of a human life as his or her monetary contribution to dependents.

hybrid (or balanced) mutual funds - a mutual fund that invests in a combination of cash, fixed income securities, and/or equity securities, such as an asset allocation fund.

immunization - the concept of minimizing the impact of changes in interest rates on the value of investments.

income - all monies received from employment, investments, or other sources.

income and expense statement - summary of the client's income and expenses during an interval of time, usually one year.

income stock - a type of stock issued by companies in the maturity phase of the industry life cycle and payout the majority of their earnings in the form of dividends.

indirect investing - a process of investing where investors invest in companies that invest directly.

industry life cycle - phases through which an industry moves—start up, rapid growth, growth, maturity, and decline.

inflation - an increase in price without a simultaneous increase in productivity.

information returns - a written statement provided to the taxpayer after the end of each tax year detailing the amount of income (as well as unearned income such as interest or dividends) earned by the taxpayer. The most common information return is the Form W-2.

insurance - pooling of fortuitous losses by transfer of risks to insurers who agree to indemnify insureds for such losses, to provide other pecuniary benefits on their occurrence, or to render services connected with the risk.

interest - the payment made for the use of money.

interest sensitive stock - a type of stock issued by companies whose performance is largely affected by changes in interest rates.

interest rate risk - a systematic risk where changes in interest rates will affect the value of securities.

internal business cycle theory - a business cycle theory that looks for mechanisms within the economic system that give rise to self-generating business cycles.

internal environment - the whole complex of factors that influence clients from within, such as their lifecycle positioning, attitudes and beliefs, special needs, financial position, and their perception of their financial situation.

internal rate of return (IRR) - a method of determining the exact discount rate to equalize cash inflows and outflows, thus allowing comparison of rates of return on alternative investments of unequal size and investment amounts.

intestacy laws - state laws that direct how a decedent's property will be distributed when the decedent dies without a valid will.

intestate - to die without a valid will.

investment companies - financial services companies that sell shares of stock to the public and use the proceeds to invest in a portfolio of securities.

Investment Adviser Registration Depository (IARD) - an electronic filing system that collects and maintains the registration and disclosure information for Investment Advisers and their associated persons.

iShares - passively managed index funds.

itemized deductions - itemized deductions are ones that are in excess of the standard deduction and are used in lieu of the standard deduction.

JD - Attorney.

Jensen's Alpha - an absolute measure of performance that indicates how the actual performance of an investment compares with the expected performance.

joint and survivor annuity - an annuity based on the lives of two or more annuitants, usually husband and wife. Annuity payments are made until the last annuitant dies.

joint tenancy - a form of property interest where two or more persons, called equal owners, hold the same fractional interest in a property.

Keogh plan - a qualified plan for unincorporated businesses.

law - rules of conduct that are established by a government or other authority that command and encourage behavior considered right and prohibit behavior considered wrong.

law of large numbers- concept that the greater the number of exposures, the more closely will actual results approach the probable results expected from an indefinite number of exposures.

learning styles (auditory, visual, kinetic or tactile) - the conditions under which people learn best—clients whose preferred learning style is auditory, learn best by hearing information; clients who prefer a visual learning style, learn best by reading and viewing; those who prefer a kinetic or tactile style, learn best through manipulation and testing information.

lending securities - securities where an investor of bonds lends funds to the issuer in exchange for a promise to a stream of periodic interest payments and a repayment of the loaned principal at the maturity of the bond.

letter ruling - a written statement issued by the National Office of the IRS that giving guidance on the way the IRS will treat a prospective or contemplated transaction for tax purposes.

liability - money owed by the client.

lifecycle phase - an interval in a client's lifecycle that tends to give a planner insight into the client's financial objectives and concerns—the Asset Accumulation phase, the Conservation/Protection phase, the Distribution/Gifting phase.

lifecycle positioning - information about a client's age, marital status, dependents, income level, and net worth.

life estate - an interest in property that ceases upon the death of the owner of the life interest or estate.

lifetime learning credit - a tax credit available to pay for tuition and enrollment fees for undergraduate, graduate, or professional degree programs paid after June 30, 1998.

like-kind exchange - an exchange of property held for productive use in a trade or business or for investment (except inventory, stocks and bonds, and partnership interests) for other investment or trade or business property.

limited liability company (LLC) - a relatively new and versatile form of business entity created under state law by filing articles of organization--versatile because it can be taxed as a sole proprietorship, partnership, C corporation, or S corporation.

limited liability partnership (LLP) - a form of business entity similar to a general partnership, except an LLP provides additional liability protection to the partners.

limited partnership - a type of business entity formed under the limited partnership laws of a state. In a limited partnership, partners are not allowed to participate in the management of the partnership affairs, but generally are allowed to vote on major changes affecting the structure of the partnership.

liquidity - the ability to sell an investment quickly and at a competitive price, with no loss of principal and little price concession. The length of time expected for the asset to be converted back to cash.

load funds - mutual funds that charge either a front-end load or back-end load.

long position - the most prevalent type of position investors take when purchasing equity securities where an investor will purchase a stock in hopes that it will appreciate over time.

long-term capital gains - A long term capital gain is the gain from a sale or exchange of a capital asset that has been held for more than one year (that is a year and one day).

long-term care insurance - provides coverage for nursing home stays and other types of routine care that are not covered by health insurance. There are five levels of coverage: skilled nursing care, intermediate nursing care, custodial care, home health care, and adult day care.

long-term liability - debt extending beyond one year.

loss control - activities that reduce the frequency or severity of losses.

loss of use - under homeowners insurance coverage, loss of use is a combination of additional living expenses and loss of rental income.

major medical insurance - health insurance that provides broad coverage of all reasonable and necessary expenses associated with an illness or injury, whether incurred at a doctor's office, a hospital, or the insured's home.

managed care - health plans that arrange for the delivery of medical and health services, review the quality and appropriateness of services rendered, and reimburse the providers who deliver services to plan participants.

management fee - a fee charged by an investment advisor for the management of a mutual fund's assets.

managers - individuals who are responsible for the maintenance, administration and management of the affairs of a limited liability company.

margin accounts - a type of brokerage account that allows the investor to borrow funds from the broker to purchase additional securities without adding additional cash to the account.

marital deduction - a deduction of an unlimited qualifying bequest or transfer of property to a surviving spouse claimed from the adjusted gross estate of the decedent's estate.

market risk - a systematic risk where stocks tend to move with the market.

marketability - the ability of an investor to find a ready market where the investor may sell his or her investment.

maturity - the period of time through which the issuer has control over the bond proceeds and the period of time it must continue to pay coupon payments.

maximum family benefit - the limit on the amount of monthly Social Security benefits that may be paid to a family.

mean-variance optimization model - used to determine the highest level of return (based on combinations of asset classes and different weightings of asset classes) for a specified level of risk tolerance.

Medicaid - provides medical assistance for persons with low incomes and resources.

Medicare- a federal health insurance plan for people who are 65 and older, whether retired or still working.

medical payments - a no-fault, first-party insurance coverage designed to pay for bodily injuries sustained in an auto accident.

members - the owners of a limited liability company (LLC) who can be individuals, partnerships, trusts, corporations, or other LLCs.

moderate inflation - inflation characterized by slowly rising prices.

money market - consists of securities that have the following characteristics: short-term maturity, low credit risk, and high liquidity.

money market mutual funds - a mutual fund that invests in money market instruments, such as Treasury bills and negotiable CDs.

mortality charge - the cost of paying death claims for those persons who die during the year.

mortgage-backed securities (MBSs) - ownership claims on a pool of mortgages.

municipal bonds - debt instruments issued by municipalities (states, counties, parishes, cities, towns) as general obligation bonds or revenue bonds.

mutual funds - an open-end investment company that sells shares of stock to the public and uses the proceeds to invest in a portfolio of securities on behalf of their shareholders.

named perils - perils specifically listed in an insurance policy.

NASD - (National Association of Securities Dealers, Inc.) a self-regulatory organization of the securities industry established under the 1938 Maloney Act Amendments subject to oversight by the SEC.

NASDAQ - the first electronic trading system made up of leading technology and Internet-related companies.

needs approach - one of three recognized methods used to determine the amount of insurance one should purchase. The needs approach evaluates the basic needs of one's survivors in the event of death. Monetary values in present value terms are then placed on these needs and they are summed. After summing all the financial needs of dependents, existing assets plus the face amount of life insurance in force can be subtracted to determine the amount of money that dependents will need at death.

net asset value (NAV) - the price at which shares of an open-end investment company are sold. The NAV of a fund is determined by subtracting total liabilities from total assets of the fund and dividing the difference by the outstanding shares.

net present value (NPV) - the difference between the initial cash outflow (investment) and the present value of discounted cash inflows.

net worth - the amount of wealth or equity the client has in owned assets.

new economy stocks - a type of stock within the technology industry that is expected to benefit greatly from the popularity and mainstreaming of the Internet.

no-load funds - mutual funds purchased directly through the mutual fund family without the assistance of a broker.

nominal return - the stated return from an investment.

nonqualified plan - a retirement plan that can discriminate in favor of executives but is not eligible for the special tax benefits available for qualified or other tax-advantaged retirement plans.

objective risk - the relative variation of an actual loss from an expected loss.

offer of settlement - a CFP Board designee may tender an Offer of Settlement in exchange for a stipulated form of disciplinary action by the CFP Board of Professional Review.

officers - individuals appointed by a corporation's board of directors to carry out the board's policies and make day-to-day operating decisions.

OASDI - Old Age and Survivor Disability Insurance, commonly referred to as Social Security.

online trading - a method of buying and selling securities over the Internet without the use of a broker.

open-end investment company - an investment company whose capitalization constantly changes as new shares are sold and outstanding shares are redeemed.

open market operations - the process by which the Federal Reserve purchases and sells government securities in the open market. The Fed buys government securities to cause more money to circulate, thereby, increasing lending and lowering interest rates.

open perils - all-risk coverage for personal property that provides for a much broader and comprehensive protection program than named-perils coverage.

open-perils policy - a policy in which all perils or causes of loss are covered, unless they are specifically listed under the exclusions section.

opportunity cost - when faced with investment alternatives, it is the highest-valued alternative *not* chosen and represents what is forgone by choosing another alternative. When discounting a future sum or series of payments back to present value, it is the composite rate of return on the client's assets with similar risk to the assets being examined.

options - derivatives that give the holder or buyer the right to do something.

oral/noncupative will - dying declarations made before sufficient witnesses.

ordinary income - any income that arises from services, or from property that is not classified as a capital asset.

order of acceptance - if an Offer of Settlement is accepted by the Hearing Panel during a disciplinary review, it must propose an Order of Acceptance containing findings of fact to be reviewed by the CFP Board of Professional Review.

other structures - small detached structures on insured's property in addition to the main house, such as garages, greenhouses, or storage buildings.

other-than-collision - auto insurance coverage that protects the insured's auto against perils out of the insured's control, such as missiles or falling objects, fire, theft, earthquake, hail, flood, and vandalism.

own occupation - a definition of disability that states that the insured must be unable to perform each and every duty of his or her *own* occupation.

Parent Loans for Undergraduate Students (PLUS Loans) - loans available through the Direct Loan and FFEL programs that allow parents with good credit histories to borrow funds for a child's educational expenses.

partner - two or more individuals, corporations, trusts, estates, or other partnerships that join to form a business entity known as a partnership.

partnership - an association of two or more entities or individuals that carry on as co-owners of a business for the purpose of making a profit.

payments for support - transfers to children that are essentially legal support obligations that are exempt from gift tax rules.

P/E ratio - a measure of how much the market is willing to pay for each dollar of earnings of a company; the price per earnings ratio.

peak - the point in the business cycle that appears at the end of the expansion phase when most businesses are operating at full capacity and Gross Domestic Product is increasing rapidly.

Pell Grant - a grant from the federal government awarded to undergraduate students who have not earned bachelors or professional degrees. A student's EFC is used to determine the student's eligibility for a Pell Grant and how much is awarded to the student.

pension plan - a qualified plan structured to provide a regularly paid fixed sum at retirement.

peril - the approximate or actual cause of a loss.

personal auto policy - insurance policy that covers liability for injuries and damages to persons inside and outside the vehicle and covers the cost to repair/replace a damaged or stolen vehicle.

personal financial planning - the process, both art and science, of formulating, implementing, and monitoring multifunctional decisions that enable an individual or family to achieve financial goals.

PFS - Personal Financial Specialist.

personal property - valuable items owned by the insured that are covered under homeowners insurance.

personal service corporation (PSC) - a C corporation in which substantially all of the activities involve the performance of services in the fields of health, law, engineering, architecture, accounting, actuarial science, or consulting.

personal umbrella policy - coverage designed to provide a catastrophic layer of liability coverage on top of the individual's homeowners and automobile insurance policies.

personal utility curves - economic curves that describe the satisfaction that an individual receives from a selected thing and/or additional units of that thing.

physician's expense insurance - pays for fees charged by physicians who provide the insured with nonsurgical care.

power of appointment trust - allows a terminable interest to be passed to a surviving spouse and the property to still qualify for the marital deduction. Unlike a QTIP Trust, no election is required.

power of attorney - the right given to another (agent) to act in the place of the giver (principal). Such right may be limited or general and may be durable or nondurable.

practice standards - the set of standards that (1) establish the level of professional practice that is expected of CFP Board designees engaged in personal financial planning, (2) advance professionalism in the practice of financial planning, and (3) enhance the value of the personal financial planning process.

preferred provider organization (PPO) - a contractual arrangement between the insured, the insurer, and the health care provider that allows the insurer to receive discounted rates from service providers.

preferred stock - a type of stock that has characteristics of both fixed income investments and of common stock in that dividend payments must be paid each year before paying a dividend to the common shareholders.

premium - the cost of an option contract.

prepaid tuition plans - plans where prepayment of college tuition is allowed at current prices for enrollment in the future--in other words, a parent can "lock in" future tuition at current rates.

prepayment risk - the risk that homeowners will pay off their loans before the scheduled loan maturity date.

preponderance of the evidence standard - a measure or degree of proof – with regard to CFP disciplinary rules and procedures, "preponderance of the evidence" means the evidence as a whole shows what it was intended to prove with a probability of 51 percent or better.

present value - what a sum of money to be received in a future year is worth in today's dollars based on a specific discount rate.

present value of an annuity due - the value today of a series of equal payments made at the *beginning* of each period for a finite number of periods.

present value of an ordinary annuity - the value today of a series of equal payments made at the *end* of each period for a finite number of periods.

price elasticity - the quantity demanded of a good in response to changes in that good's price. A good is *elastic* when its quantity demanded responds greatly to price changes (luxuries). A good is *inelastic* when its quantity demanded responds little to price changes (necessities).

price index - a weighted average of the prices of numerous goods and services, for example, the consumer price index, the gross national product deflator, and the producer price index.

primary insurance amount (PIA) - calculation on which a worker's retirement benefit is based, the PIA determines the amount the applicant will receive at his or her full retirement age, but the amount of the benefit depends on the year in which the retiree turns age 62. The PIA is indexed to the consumer price index (CPI) annually.

primary market - the market where new issues of securities are first offered to the public.

principal (re: power of attorney) - in a power of attorney document, the person (power giver) who designates another person or persons to act as his attorney-in-fact.

principle of indemnity - states that a person is entitled to compensation only to the extent that financial loss has been suffered.

principle of insurable interest - to have an insurable interest, an insured must be subject to emotional or financial hardship resulting from damage, loss, or destruction.

principle of utmost good faith - also known as the principle of fair dealing, the principle of utmost good faith requires that the insured and the insurer both be forthcoming with all relevant facts about the insured risk and the coverage provided for that risk.

Principles - one of two main parts of the CFP Code that addresses the profession's recognition of the responsibilities of its members to the public, clients, colleagues, and employers, and provides guidance to members during the performance of their professional duties.

private censure - an unpublished written reproach that is mailed to the censured CFP Board designee by the CFP Board of Professional Review.

private letter rulings - statements issued for a fee upon a taxpayer's request that describe how the IRS will treat a proposed transaction for tax purposes.

probate - the legal process that performs the function of changing property title from a decedent's name to an heir's name.

Producer Price Index (PPI) - the oldest continuous statistical series published by the Labor Department that measures the level of prices at the wholesale or producer stage.

profit-sharing plan - a qualified defined-contribution plan featuring a flexible (discretionary) employer-contribution provision. Profit-sharing plans are structured to offer employees participation in company profits that they may use for retirement purposes.

proprietor - the owner of a sole proprietorship.

public letter of admonition - a publishable written reproach of the CFP Board designee's behavior that will normally be published in a press release or other form of publicity selected by the CFP Board of Professional Review (BOPR), unless mitigating circumstances exist and the BOPR in its discretion decides to withhold public notification.

purchasing power preservation model (PPP) - a capital needs analysis method that assumes that the client will have a capital balance of equal purchasing power at life expectancy as he did at retirement.

purchasing power risk - a systematic risk where inflation will erode the real value of the investor's assets.

pure annuity concept - the basic capital needs analysis approach that is generally prepared on a pre-tax basis.

pure risk - a risk that creates a financial loss when it occurs.

put option - a derivative that gives the holder the right to sell the underlying security, generally stock, at a specified price within a specified period.

qualified domestic trust (QDOT) - for a non-citizen spouse who was a U.S. resident at the time of the decedent's death, the marital deduction is allowed if the property is placed in a QDOT that passes to a non-citizen surviving spouse.

qualified state tuition plans (QSTPs) - also known as 529 plans, QSTPs allow individuals to either participate in prepaid tuition plans whereby tuition credits are purchased for a designated beneficiary for payment or waiver of higher education expenses, or participate in savings plans whereby contributions of money are made to an account to eventually pay for higher education expenses of a designated beneficiary.

qualified terminable interest property trust (QTIP) - allows a terminable interest to be passed to a surviving spouse and the property to still qualify for the unlimited marital deduction. The executor makes the election on IRS Form 706.

qualified transfer - a payment made directly to an educational institution for tuition and fees or to a medical institution for medical expenses for the benefit of someone else.

random walk - the unpredictable pattern that security prices should follow as new information about the security becomes known. As new information that affects a security is released, the price of the security will increase if the information is positive and decrease if the information is negative.

ratio analysis - the relationship or relative value of two characteristics used to analyze the financial and operational health of an individual and to conduct comparison and trend analysis.

real interest rate adjustment - the rate of interest expressed in dollars of constant value (adjusted for inflation); and equal to the nominal interest rate less the rate of inflation.

real rate of return - the combination of the nominal earnings rate reduced mathematically by the inflation rate.

recession - a decline in real Gross Domestic Product for two or more successive quarters.

registered investment advisor (RIA) - a person or company that offers ongoing portfolio management or investment advice and charges money for it.

reinvestment risk - a systematic risk where earnings (cash flows) distributed from current investments will be unable to be reinvested to yield a rate of return equal to the yields of the current investments.

remaining work life expectancy (RWLE) - work period remaining at a certain point in time before retirement.

replacement cost - the amount necessary to purchase, repair, or replace the dwelling with materials of the same or similar quality at current prices.

representations - statements made by the insured to the insurer in the application process.

reserve requirement - for a member bank of the Federal Reserve, it is the percent of deposit liabilities that must be held in reserve. As the reserve requirement is increased, less money is available to be loaned, resulting in a restriction of the money supply.

residuary clause - a general provision in a will that provides for the transfer of the balance of any assets not specifically mentioned in the will to a person or institution named by the testator.

retirement benefit - the most familiar Social Security benefit, full retirement benefits are payable at full retirement age with reduced benefits as early as age 62, to anyone who has obtained at least a minimum amount of Social Security credits.

retirement earnings limitations test - one of the ways in which Social Security benefit recipients can have their benefits reduced based on exceeding earnings limitations.

retirement life expectancy (RLE) - that period beginning at retirement and extending until death; the RLE is the period of retirement that must be funded.

revenue procedures- statements reflecting the internal management practices of the IRS that affect the rights and duties of taxpayers.

revenue rulings- official pronouncements of the National Office of the IRS.

revocation - the CFP Board of Professional Review (BOPR) may order permanent revocation of a CFP designee's right to use the mark, and publish the revocation in a press release or other form of publicity, unless extreme mitigating circumstances persuade the BOPR to withhold public notification.

RIA - Registered Investment Advisor; any individual who provides investment advice to 15 or more interstate clients during a 12-month period.

risk tolerance - an estimate of the level of risk an investor is willing to accept in his or her portfolio. The choice of balancing lower premiums with self-reliance for smaller losses, or alternatively, higher premiums with less loss exposure.

Roth IRA - an individual retirement account in which contributions are made on an after-tax basis and qualifying distributions are made tax free.

Rule of 72 - a method of approximation that estimates the time that it takes to double the value of an investment where the earnings (interest) rate is known (by dividing 72 by the interest rate). Alternatively, it can also estimate the earnings (interest) rate necessary to double an investment value if the time is known (by dividing 72 by the period of investment).

Rules - one of two main parts of the CFP Code that is derived from the doctrine expressed in the Principles and helps to establish a foundation for complying with the Principles of the Code.

Russell Indexes - a collection of financial indexes made up of over 21 U.S. stock indexes, as well as foreign indexes in Australia, Canada, Japan, and the United Kingdom, maintained by the Frank Russell Company.

S corporation - a special type of corporation formed under state law like a regular corporation; however, for income tax purposes, is treated similar to a partnership.

savings - deferred consumption.

Savings Plan - a type of Qualified State Tuition Plan similar to an Educational IRA where the owner of the account, the parent or grandparent of the student, contributes cash to the account so that the contributions can grow tax deferred and, hopefully, realize a higher return on the investment than could be achieved outside of the plan.

secondary market - the market where investors can freely buy and sell securities with other investors.

securitization - the process of transforming mortgages into securities that can be sold to the public.

self-employment tax - tax paid by self-employed individuals that is based on net earnings, not on the individual's wages. Since the self-employed must bear the burden of both the employer and employee portion of FICA, the self-employment tax rate is 15.3%--double the employee's rate of 7.65%.

self-insured retention - a payment similar to a deductible that an insured is usually required to pay for each loss under a personal umbrella policy.

serial payment - a payment that increases at a constant rate (usually, the rate of inflation) on an annual (ordinary) basis.

Series EE United States Savings Bonds (EE Bonds) - if used to pay for qualified higher education expenses at an eligible institution or state tuition plan, EE Bonds bestow significant tax savings, that is, no federal income tax on the interest.

side letter (personal instruction letter) - also known as a personal instruction letter, it exists separate from a will and details the testator's wishes regarding the disposition of tangible possessions (household goods), the disposition of the decedent's body, and funeral arrangements.

simplified employee pension (SEP) - a tax-deferred, noncontributory retirement plan that uses an individual retirement account (IRA) as the receptacle for contributions.

simultaneous death clause - in the event that both spouses die simultaneously, this clause provides an assumption that one spouse (predetermined) predeceased the other spouse.

shareholders - the owners of a corporation who elect the corporation's board of directors.

Sharpe ratio - a measure of risk-adjusted portfolio performance that uses standard deviation as the risk measure.

short position - a type of position investors take by selling borrowed shares in hopes that the stock price will decline over time.

short - term capital gains - A short term capital gain is the gain from a sale or exchange of a capital asset that has been held for less than one year.

Social Security Statement, Form SSA-7005 - a written report mailed by the Social Security Administration to all workers age 25 and over who are not yet receiving Social Security benefits that provides an estimate of the worker's eventual Social Security benefits and instructions on how to qualify for those benefits.

sole proprietorship - a business owned and controlled by one person who is personally liable for all debts and claims against the business.

split definition - a definition of disability that combines the "any" and "own" occupation clauses.

split limits - three separate liability coverage limits covering bodily injury (per person and per occurrence) and property damage.

standard deviation - measures a portfolio's total volatility and its total risk (that is, systematic and unsystematic risk).

Stafford Loan - the primary type of financial aid provided by the United States Department of Education. There are two types of Stafford Loans: Direct Stafford Loans ("Direct Loans") provided directly to the student, and Federal Family Education Stafford Loans ("FFEL Loans") made to the student through a lender (such as a bank or other approved financial institution) that participates in the FFEL program.

Standard & Poor's 500 Index (S&P 500) - a financial index of 500 U.S. equities based on market size, liquidity, and industry group representation.

statement of cash flows - summary of the client's changes to the cash account.

statement of changes in net worth - summary of each change from one balance sheet to the next.

statutory will - generally drawn by an attorney, signed in the presence of witnesses, complying with the statutes for wills of the domiciliary state.

stock bonus plan - a defined-contribution profit-sharing plan in which all employer contributions are in the form of employer stock and distributions to participants can be made in the form of employer stock.

STRIPS - acronym for Separate Trading of Registered Interest and Principal of Securities—a program that permits investors to hold and trade the individual interest and principal components of eligible Treasury notes and bonds as separate securities.

subrogation clause - states that the insured cannot indemnify himself or herself from both the insurance company and a negligent third party for the same claim.

Supplemental Security Income (SSI) - program administered by the Social Security Administration and funded by the general Treasury that is available to those age 65 or older, or those who are disabled and have a low income and few assets.

supply - that quantity of a particular good which businesses are willing to produce or sell.

supply curve - the graphic depiction that shows the relationship between the market price of a particular good and the quantity supplied.

surgical expense insurance - insurance that may be added to a hospital expense insurance policy to provide for the payment of the surgeon's fees, even when surgery is not performed in a hospital.

survivors' benefit - Social Security benefit available to surviving family members of a deceased, eligible worker.

survivorship clause - provides that the beneficiary must survive the decedent for a specified period in order to receive the inheritance or bequest.

suspension - a form of discipline that the CFP Board of Professional Review (BOPR) may order for a specified period, not to exceed five (5) years, for individuals it deems can be rehabilitated.

SWOT analysis - an analysis that helps the financial planner understand how internal and external environmental factors affects the client's financial situation. The acronym, SWOT, stands for Strengths, Weaknesses, Opportunities, and Threats.

systematic risk - investment risk impacted by broad macroeconomic factors that influence all securities.

tax avoidance - the legal minimization of taxes, which is accomplished by applying knowledge of the IRC and the Treasury regulations to an individual's income tax situation.

tax evasion - any of the various fraudulent methods by which a taxpayer may pay less than his or her proper tax liability.

tax-exempt bond market - one of the two markets that make up the United States bond market, and that consists of municipal bonds.

taxable bond market - one of two markets that make up the United States bond market, and that consists of U.S. Treasury bonds, U.S. government agency bonds, and corporate bonds.

Technical Advice Memoranda - advice or guidance in memorandum form furnished by the National Office of the IRS to IRS agents who request such advice or guidance during an audit. Technical Advice Memoranda help to close cases and establish and maintain consistent holdings throughout the IRS.

technical analysis - the search for identifiable and recurring stock price patterns.

tenancy by the entirety - a joint tenancy with right of survivorship (JTWROS) that can only occur between a husband and wife.

tenancy in common - two or more persons hold an undivided interest in a whole property.

term - the specific period of time for which an investment is held.

term insurance - type of life insurance that provides temporary protection for a specified number of years.

testamentary capacity - having the mental capability to make a will to transfer assets; being of sound mind.

testate - having left a valid will.

testator - one who makes a will.

third market - over-the-counter trading of equity shares that are listed on an exchange.

time value of money (TVM) - the concept that money received today is worth more than the same amount of money received sometime in the future.

time weighted returns - a method of determining an internal rate of return by evaluating the performance of portfolio managers without the influence of cash inflows or outflows to or from the portfolio.

Treynor ratio - a measure of a risk adjusted portfolio performance that uses beta as the risk measure.

trough - the point in the business cycle that appears at the end of the contraction phase when most businesses are operating at their lowest capacity levels and Gross Domestic Product is at its lowest or is negative.

trust - a legal arrangement, usually provided for under state law, in which a grantor transfers property to a trustee for the management and conservation of the property for the benefit of the named beneficiaries.

12b-1 fees - a fee that pays for the services of brokers who sell mutual funds and who maintain the client relationship.

underwriting - the process by which investment bankers purchase an issue of securities from a firm and resell it to the public.

unearned income - also referred to investment income, it includes such income as interest, dividends, capital gains, rents, royalties, and pension and annuity income.

uneven cash flows - investment returns or deposits that may not be single interval deposits or equal payments.

unified gift and estate transfer tax system - unified tax transfer system created by Congress to ensure that at the time of transfer of property, either during life (gifts) or at death (bequests), the transferor will pay the same tax rate or amount for the transfer, regardless of when the transfer is made.

Uniform Gift to Minor's Act (UGMA) - allows parents the option to put assets in a custodial account for a child, for example, to pay for college tuition.

uninsured motorists coverage - that part of the personal auto policy designed to insure against bodily injury caused by an uninsured motorist, a hit-and-run driver, or a driver whose company is insolvent.

unit investment trust (UIT) - a registered investment company that is passively managed and may invest in stocks, bonds, or other securities.

universal life - insurance that allows the insured to buy death protection similar to that provided by term insurance, and then to invest an additional amount with the insurer that is similar to the savings element in whole life coverage.

unsystematic risks - types of investment risks unique to a single company, industry, or country that can be eliminated by portfolio diversification.

usufruct - a Louisiana legal device similar to a life estate that provides the holder with the right to use and/or the right to income from a particular property.

value stocks - a type of stock trading at prices that are low given the stock's historical earnings and current asset value.

variable expenses - expenses that fluctuate from time to time over which the client has some control.

variable life - a form of whole life insurance in which cash values are invested in the policyowner's choice of investments.

variable universal life - a combination of variable life and universal life whose features include increasing or decreasing death benefits and flexibility of premium payments that mirror the universal life policy options, and a guaranteed minimum death benefit and policyowner chosen investments, similar to a variable life policy.

vesting - an employee's acquisition of his or her right to receive a present or future pension benefit.

wage replacement ratio (WRR) - an estimate of the amount of capital needed at retirement to properly fund the period called the retirement life expectancy (RLE).

whole life insurance - insurance that provides protection for the insured's *entire life*, compared to term insurance that expires after a certain number of years.

will - a legal document used in estate planning that provides the testator, or will maker, the opportunity to control the distribution of property and avoid the state's intestacy law distribution scheme.

Wilshire 5000 Index - a financial index consisting of over 7,000 U.S. based companies that is often used as a measure of the overall market within the U.S.

work life expectancy (WLE) - the years that a person spends in the work force, generally about 30-40 years.

x-dividend date - the date at which the market reflects the dividend payment.

yield curves - graphical representations that reflect current market interest rates for various bond maturities.

yield to call (YTC) - the promised return on a bond from the present to the date that the bond may be called.

yield to maturity (YTM) - the promised compounded rate of return on a bond purchased at the current market price and held to maturity.

zero-coupon bond - a bond that does not pay periodic coupon or interest payments.

Index

Truth in Lending Act, 34